W9-DHH-400

The Open Society and Its Enemies

Karl

Popper

The Open Society and Its Enemies

New One-Volume Edition

With a new introduction by Alan Ryan
and an essay by E. H. Gombrich

Princeton University Press
Princeton and Oxford

Published in the United States and Canada by Princeton University Press, 41 William Street, Princeton, New Jersey 08540
press.princeton.edu

Published in two volumes in 1945 by Princeton University Press
First Princeton University Press paperback printing, in two volumes, 1971
First single-volume Princeton University Press printing, 2013

Library of Congress Control Number 2012952689
ISBN 978-0-691-15813-6

This book has been composed in Joanna

Printed on acid-free paper. ∞

Printed in the United States of America

10 9 8 7 6 5 4 3 2 1

Contents

Introduction

Alan Ryan

Karl Popper was one of the most important philosophers of science of the twentieth century, and among the most important philosophers of the century *tout court*. Unlike most philosophers of science, he was admired by practising scientists, several of whom claimed that he had influenced their work. They included the Nobel prizewinners Sir Peter Medawar and Sir John Eccles. Popper's influence was reflected in the fact that he enjoyed the rare distinction of being a Fellow of both the Royal Society and the British Academy. Although *The Open Society and Its Enemies* is commonly thought of as a work of political theory, it is just as much a work in the philosophy of history and social science, and because Popper thought there were no important methodological differences between the social and natural sciences, it bears directly on Popper's philosophy of the natural sciences, too.

Although *The Open Society*'s assault on Plato, Hegel, and Marx—its primary targets—rests on ideas formulated in Popper's philosophy of science, his political interests had underpinned the development of his philosophy of science in the first place. Popper wrote *The Open Society* and completed a companion essay on the philosophy of history, *The Poverty of Historicism*, in New Zealand during the Second World War, but their roots lie in Viennese politics, and more specifically in the catastrophes that befell Austrian socialism.

Popper was born in Vienna on July 28, 1902, into a highly cultivated upper-middle-class family; his father Simon was a lawyer, and his mother, Jenny Schiff, an accomplished pianist. His family was Jewish by origin, but his parents converted to Lutheranism before he was born. This was not out of religious conviction or embarrassment at their Jewish antecedents. Simon Popper was, in his son's words, 'a radical liberal of the school of John Stuart Mill'; his politics were secular and sceptical, but he believed that going along with one's community's religious practices was a form of politeness.

Simon Popper was highly educated and widely read, possessing a library of some 12,000 to 14,000 volumes; and Popper's background was, as he wrote in his autobiography, *Unended Quest*, 'decidedly bookish'.[1] On his father's shelves were Plato, Aristotle, Kant, and the Collected Works of John Stuart Mill in the six-volume translation by Theodore Gomperz. It was a musical household as well, with a Bosendorfer grand piano in the drawing room, and Popper himself held interesting, if unusual, views about the history of music, including a marked preference for classicism over modernism. He sometimes said that Schubert was the last great composer; Wagner he loathed as much on account of the text of the Ring Cycle as for the music; Richard Strauss was dismissed as *pastiche*.

The First World War broke out as Popper turned twelve; Austria went to war with Serbia on his birthday. He subsequently had a rather fragmented secondary education, but not because of the war; he found the teaching at his *Realschule* dull and slow-moving, and some of his teachers obnoxiously anti-semitic. He left school at the age of sixteen and began to attend classes at the University of Vienna in 1918, but did not matriculate to attend as a regular student until 1922, a couple of years later than he would have done if he had remained at school. However, it was 1919, the year after the ending of the war, that was one of the most significant of his life, both politically and intellectually. Several of his relatives were committed socialists, as were his closest friends; many of them were Marxists, and for a short time Popper himself succumbed to the charms of historical materialism. He also joined the student wing of the Austrian Social Democratic Party. He was alienated by the easy assumption of his middle-class and highly-educated friends that they were the natural leaders of the manual working class; he at least had tried—and failed—to work as a road-mender. Nonetheless, he was a committed socialist.

What he came to think of as a decisive refutation of Marx's theory of social and political change was an incident in the summer of 1919 when some young socialists tried to rescue a number of communists being held

[1] *Unended Quest* (rev. ed., Routledge, 1992) is an expanded version of the *Autobiography* that Popper contributed to Paul Arthur Schilp, *The Philosophy of Karl Popper*, Open Court, 1974; it is not wholly reliable as a guide to Popper's early life. Malachi Hacohen, *Karl Popper: The Formative Years: 1902–45* (Cambridge University Press, 2000) takes almost 600 meticulously researched pages to tell the true story. Among general accounts of Popper's life and work, Bryan Magee's *Popper* (Fontana Collins, 1997) is as good as any. Jeremy Shearmur, *The Political Thought of Karl Popper*, Routledge, 1996, is the only full-scale discussion of Popper's political ideas.

by the police. The demonstrators were unarmed, but the police opened fire and several of the demonstrators were killed. Popper was not a pacifist in the sense of thinking that a resort to violence was never justified; he had no doubt that Hitler could only be stopped by force. On this occasion, he concluded that although the police were brutal, the demonstrators were misled by Marx's views on the need to intensify the class struggle, and were likely to get both themselves and those whose lives they hoped to improve killed to no purpose. Writing about these events years later, Popper was no doubt guilty of imposing the lessons of hindsight on his reactions; but he never renounced his view that the social democratic students and the Austrian workers' movement were morally admirable, deeply and altruistically committed to building a better world. Indeed, he said as late as 1976 that he would have remained a socialist all his life if he had thought that it was possible to reconcile socialist egalitarianism with freedom.

At the time, he was working as a volunteer with Adlerian psychologists trying to help neglected children. So, before he turned seventeen, Popper had already been exposed to the two great redemptive theories of the early twentieth century, Marxism and psychoanalysis. He maintained that the encounter with Marxism made much the more important impact on his thinking, but absent that provocation, he would have been quick to reach the conclusion that psychoanalysis, whether Freudian or Adlerian, owed more to poetry and myth than to science properly speaking. The event which, in memory at least, propelled Popper towards the fundamental ideas of his philosophy of science was far removed from street battles or the struggle to help distressed children; it was hearing Einstein lecture on the theory of relativity. 'Dazed' is how Popper later described his reaction. The theory of general relativity made surprising experimental predictions which had been confirmed in May 1919. Had they not been confirmed, the theory would have been refuted, as Einstein himself insisted. The theory had not been proved true—Popper was already working towards his 'fallibilist' view that theories can never be proved, although they can be decisively disproved—but it had survived a severe test, and had emerged as a theory worth embracing.

His Adlerian and Marxist colleagues displayed none of Einstein's theoretical modesty, and none of his readiness to abandon a much-loved theory in the face of a decisive refutation. They were verificationists, pointing to evidence that was in line with their theoretical allegiances while either ignoring evidence that contradicted their beliefs or rewriting the theory to turn apparent contradictions into verifications. The most obvious example is the psychoanalytical concept of resistance, which enables the analyst to claim either that the patient's acceptance of a diagnosis confirms it, or that the patient's rejection of the diagnosis demonstrates resistance and therefore likewise confirms it. We cannot know how much of this was clear to Popper at the age of seventeen; if he had read as widely in his father's library as he appears to have done, he would have encountered Mill's claim in *On Liberty*, that the strength of our conviction should be proportionate to the ability of our beliefs to withstand the severest criticism we can direct at them. Subsequently, at least, he thought that Marxism was not so much non-science as bad science; Marx had made many predictions that had proven false. In his sixties, and responding to new work in the sociology and history of science, he dismissed much of social science as only 'dubiously' scientific.

At the University of Vienna, Popper studied mathematics and physics as well as philosophy and psychology. He later recalled that he had given no thought to how he would eventually earn his living, since the economic situation made it impossible to plan a career. Nonetheless, he was certified as an infant teacher in 1925, gained his PhD in cognitive psychology in 1928, and qualified as a secondary school teacher in 1930. Like many upper-middle-class families, the Poppers had lost almost all their savings in the inflation at the end of the war. To avoid burdening the family, Popper took a variety of jobs both before and during his time at the University of Vienna, from road-making at one end of the spectrum to giving German lessons to American students at the other. Between 1922 and 1924, he was apprenticed to a cabinetmaker; he was, however, already obsessed with the philosophy of science, and his carpentry suffered. He joked in his autobiography that it was only when he became a lecturer in philosophy in 1937 that he finally discovered how to work on a writing desk while thinking about epistemology.

To secure employment as a secondary school teacher, he had to enrol at the newly founded Pedagogic Institute, although many of the courses were given at the University of Vienna. It meant giving up his work with neglected children, but he was enthusiastic about the prospects of school reform and an eager student. The course involved a lot of educational theory, 'imported from America (John Dewey) or Germany (Georg Kerstenheimer)', about which his experience with neglected children made him decidedly sceptical. In fact, his casual remarks about education elsewhere in *Unended Quest* come very close to denying that teaching is either possible or necessary. Once children have mastered reading and writing, they can take care of the learning process for themselves, albeit with the aid of the persons who are conventionally labelled 'teachers'. *Unended Quest* is, in fact, generous to Kurt Bühler, his PhD supervisor, and to Heinrich Gomperz, son of the great Theodore Gomperz, and the key figure in his early philosophical development.

Learning, as distinct from teaching, lay at the heart both of Popper's account of science and of his defence of the open society. Science is a 'trial and error' learning process, and one of the virtues of an open society is its ability to learn from experience. Closed societies resist novelty and therefore pass up the chance to learn from experience. The years from 1925 to 1930 were happy in spite of the uncertain political and economic situation, not least because it was at the Pedagogic Institute that he met Josefina Henninger (always known as 'Hennie'), whom he married in 1930 when they both took their first teaching posts. The marriage produced no children, but it was a close, if not always a happy, one. Hennie found the move to New Zealand almost unbearable, did not much like London when she and Popper moved there in 1946, and seems to have been frequently depressed even when they moved out of London to Penn in Buckinghamshire. On the other hand, she was indispensable to Popper's career; she typed everything he wrote, dealt with publishers, and was altogether more deft in dealing with other people than he was.

Popper was not unhappy teaching science to secondary school students, but his passion was by now for philosophy, and more narrowly for the philosophy of science. How far this was a natural outgrowth of his 1928 doctoral work on issues of method in cognitive psychology, is debatable; his thesis was titled *Zur Methodenfrage der Denkpsychologie* (The Question of Method in Cognitive Psychology). Almost immediately after passing his PhD examination, which involved examinations in philosophy and the history of music as well as psychology, he wrote a further dissertation on analytical geometry to qualify to teach mathematics and science in secondary school. Between 1929 and 1932 he wrote a typescript on epistemological issues that remained unpublished until 1979; but in 1934 he published *Logik der Forschung*, an incontestable masterpiece and the moment when the essential Popper—a phrase the great enemy of essentialism would have hated—emerged. It was only with the assistance of members of the Vienna Circle, in particular Herbert Feigl, that Popper was able to publish *Logik*, but the prestige of the series of monographs by members of the Vienna Circle in which it appeared secured it a wide audience. Many years later, Popper grumbled that it had been reviewed more widely than its English translation, *The Logic of Scientific Discovery*, was when it appeared in 1959.

He was on friendly terms with several members of the Vienna Circle, the group of philosophers usually described as the Logical Positivists, but he was never invited to join.[2] One reason was that he was regarded as arrogant, obsessive, and unamenable to argument; the near-paranoia that poisoned working relationships in England after 1946 was visible long before. Doctrinally, he and the Vienna Circle were entirely at odds. The Vienna Circle embraced the so-called 'verification principle', the doctrine that the meaning of propositions and their constitutive terms lay in their method of verification. Popper espoused what became known as 'falsificationism', the doctrine that what we are interested in in the sciences is the conditions under which we should *reject* a proposed law or theory; the proposition that 'all swans are white' is decisively refuted by one black swan, no matter how often it has been 'verified' by sightings of white swans. The Vienna Circle's view of philosophical analysis was reductive: propositions about physical objects were 'reduced' or analysed into propositions about actual and possible sensations. Popper was a common sense realist about the physical world; conversely, he thought there were no unchallengeable statements about observations and sensations. All observation is 'theory-laden', and we cannot but approach the world with preconceptions. The Vienna Circle was empiricist and phenomenalist, Popper was a critical rationalist.

Popper and the Vienna Circle were at bottom interested in very different issues; both were a matter of 'demarcation', but whereas the Vienna Circle was interested in questions of meaning and looked for a principle to demarcate sense and nonsense, Popper was contemptuous of arguments about meaning, regarded a concern for definition as mostly mistaken, and sought to distinguish claims about the world that could plausibly feature in science from those that could not. The Vienna Circle's conviction that metaphysics was nonsense was very different from Popper's view. He held that many metaphysical propositions were not only meaningful but indispensable; but because they were not susceptible of refutation, they were not 'scientific'. The proposition that every event has a cause is one such; failure to find the cause of an event would not count as a disconfirmation, but only as evidence that we would have to look further to find it. Popper was not a faithful disciple of Kant, but Kant's insight into the 'regulative' function of metaphysical ideas was one he could use.

The success of *Logik* resulted in invitations to lecture in England in 1935. Popper took a year's unpaid leave from teaching, as did Hennie, and they began to think about a permanent departure from Austria. Although the political scene was increasingly ugly, Popper was in no immediate danger;

[2] A.J. Ayer popularised the Vienna Circle's views for English readers in his best-selling *Language, Truth and Logic*, Victor Gollancz, 1936.

unlike many of his philosophical contemporaries, he was not politically active during the 1920s and early 1930s. In retrospect, he said that he thought his Jewishness would prove a liability to the social democrats he supported, though it is not obvious that he was prominent enough for it to have had much effect. In any event, in July of 1927 he was present with Hennie when the police opened fire on a crowd of mostly unarmed socialists and workers protesting the acquittal of some members of the *Heimwehr*, the Catholic, nationalist, and conservative militia. A socialist and his child were killed. The event confirmed Popper's view that Austria was on a path that would lead either to civil war or to a fascist dictatorship.

Tensions between socialists and their opponents indeed got steadily worse, and were only exacerbated by the onset of the Great Depression at the end of the 1920s. In retrospect it was easy to see that the socialists had made a crucial error in arming themselves sufficiently to frighten their enemies, though without seriously intending to fight. Their opponents were all too ready to fight, and much better organised. By the time of the Nazi accession to power in Germany in 1933, the Austrian socialists were entirely on the defensive. In February 1934, the Austrian Chancellor, Engelbert Dollfuss, a Christian fascist, launched a *coup* to suppress the socialist opposition and to bolster himself against the Austrian Nazis to his right. The socialist militias fought a disorganized battle in Vienna and elsewhere, and two days of fighting saw the end of Austrian social democracy. A botched attempt at a *coup* by the Austrian Nazis a few months later resulted in the assassination of Dollfuss and his replacement as Chancellor by Kurt Schuschnigg. Schuschnigg resisted German pressure to unite Austria with Germany in Hitler's Third Reich, but the *Anschluss* of March 1938 was inevitable. Schuschnigg spent the next seven years in jail and the rest of his life teaching in the United States.

Popper left Vienna in 1937, when it became clear that anyone of Jewish origin or socialist political leanings had no future in Austria. He could have gone to England, as F. A. von Hayek and Ernst Gombrich had done, but instead he accepted the offer of a lecturership at Canterbury University College in Christchurch, New Zealand, freeing up a refugee lecturership in England for others in greater need. It is impossible to guess what he expected to find at the other end of the earth, in a country with 1.6 million human inhabitants and thirty million sheep. What he did find was a small, stuffy college which more closely resembled a teachers' training college or a vocationally oriented community college than the research university that is the University of Christchurch today.

Professors familiar with the injunction to publish or perish will be astonished that Popper had to reassure the Principal of the then Canterbury University College that any research he did would be done entirely in his own time and on his own resources. Popper was already one of the world's most distinguished philosophers of science, but the news had not yet penetrated to the Antipodes. It would have made little impact if it had. Popper's contempt for his head of department was withering and his unwillingness to disguise it was imprudent, but it was not wholly unmerited. Popper found intellectual companionship among his colleagues in the sciences, with the economist Colin Simkin, and eventually with the future Nobel Prize winner, John Eccles. His closest philosophical colleague was J. N. Findlay, the Hegel scholar, who was then teaching in Dunedin at the University of Otago.

Popper was an excellent lecturer, warmly remembered sixty years later by his former students at Christchurch. His attention, however, was focussed on events on the other side of the globe, and he was unsurprisingly frustrated at the difficulty of doing anything to assist other scholars to escape persecution. He gloomily estimated that he had at most helped twenty to escape from almost certain death at the hands of the Nazis, which seems a harsh judgment on himself. Of his own relatives, it appears that sixteen were murdered by the Nazis or died by their own hand. Once war had broken out, his isolation was even greater. *The Open Society* and its companion work, *The Poverty of Historicism*, were his contribution to the war effort. It may seem surprising that anyone should think that it was 'war work' to write two substantial volumes, the first of which demolished almost everything that Plato thought about almost everything from metaphysics to politics, and the second of which did the same for Hegel and Marx. The range of topics that *The Open Society* tackles is so much wider than anything one could plausibly describe as the intellectual hinterland of Nazism and Stalinism that even a friendly reader might wonder at whom the work was aimed. Few Nazis were likely to be moved by Popper's assault on Plato, and devout communists were long practised in dismissing their bourgeois critics. As to a presumably liberal and democratic readership, how much would their political allegiances be improved by a better understanding of Heraclitus and other pre-Socratics?

The full answer lies in the book that follows this introduction, but the short answer is simple. In 1936 Popper had given a talk to F. A. von Hayek's seminar at the London School of Economics on 'the poverty of historicism'. It was an attack on the idea that the task of the social sciences is to emulate the success of astronomy by predicting the long-term future of society.

Popper thought that Marxism in particular was both intellectually and politically disastrous, because it painted a picture of the inevitable triumph of the proletariat that misled everyone who believed it. In New Zealand, he began to expand the essay, and found it turning into another book entirely. So, setting it to one side, he wrote *The Open Society and Its Enemies*.

The connection with his philosophy of science was not hard to see, but readers who saw *The Open Society* as primarily an attack on Nazism and Stalinism often paid no attention. Popper had no doubt that science, the process of making bold conjectures about the world and subjecting them to experimental test, was deeply unnatural. The 'open society' is not wholly comfortable; its opposite, what Popper and his admirers usually referred to as 'tribal' society, is much more so.[3] We accept our beliefs uncritically on the authority of tradition or the say-so of priests and elders, and react with shock and surprise to contradiction. This is not a failing of one or a few people or societies; most of us want our beliefs not only to be true, but generally accepted as true, and we are tempted to evade or ignore whatever evidence contradicts them. The scientific community, which is Popper's model for 'openness', exists to prevent our doing so. We are to believe nothing *de fide* or on the say-so of our boss, head of department, or whomever. Plato, the target of the first volume of *The Open Society*, stands for all those who claim that they have an unchallengeable insight into the nature of things; Popper's long-held anti-essentialism is targeted at Plato and Aristotle.

The deeper Popper dug into Plato, the more he found to dislike. Plato was the originator of totalitarian political thought, and all the more dangerous because he was an undeniably great philosopher. Popper thought that Aristotle was infinitely Plato's inferior. It was not merely that Plato divided the human race into mindless sheep and philosophically enlightened shepherds; he was the originator of historicist fantasies and myths about racial destiny that fed straight into nineteenth-century authoritarianism and eventually into both Marxism and Nazism. Plato's insistence that *everything* must be altered if anything is to be altered successfully was dangerous in the same way as Marx's revolutionary utopianism. This was what Popper dismissed as 'holistic social engineering', as distinct from the reformist 'piecemeal social engineering' of which he approved.

[3] The philosopher and anthropologist Ernest Gellner argued this case at length in much of his work, perhaps most importantly in *Legitimation of Belief*; Cambridge University Press, 1975; his *Conditions of Liberty*, published posthumously in 1994, Penguin 1996, explores the nature of the open society and its rivals in ways that Popper might well have approved but never himself did.

Getting *The Open Society* published once he had finished writing it in 1943 was a nightmare. In Britain, paper was rationed, and the prospects of a substantial two-volume work were bleak. Popper tried to have it published in the United States, but after a long delay it was turned down; he thought this was because the publisher's readers were shocked by the ferocity of the assault on Plato. Finally, right at the end of the war, his friends Hayek and Gombrich came to the rescue, and the book was published by Routledge and Kegan Paul. It was much praised, sold well, and established Popper's reputation with a wider public. It was also the last time Popper wrote on political philosophy, and with the serialization of *The Poverty of Historicism* in Hayek's journal *Economica* in 1944–45, almost the last time he wrote about the philosophy of the social sciences.[4] He was less pleased than irritated that his defence of the applicability of the familiar 'hypothetico-deductive' model of explanation to history and the social sciences gave rise to an enormous subsequent literature. He was somewhat interested in economics, but in no other social science, nor in the philosophy of history. His abiding interest lay in probability, to which much of his subsequent work was devoted.

Summarising Popper's political ideas is not easy, not least because he had no great interest in the politics of Britain where he spent the last forty-nine years of life, and no desire to pronounce on issues of public policy. He had preoccupations, as anyone might who lived through the Cold War and under the threat of nuclear annihilation; he was deeply alarmed by the danger of nuclear war, unwaveringly hostile to the Soviet Union, and a passionate supporter of a more integrated Europe. . The end of the Soviet empire in Eastern Europe gave him the pleasure one would expect. It is clear enough from his own account that he was a committed socialist until his thirties, and a pragmatic social democrat in the immediately postwar years.

He says himself how much he liked the social egalitarianism of New Zealand, which he regarded as both a well-governed society and perhaps the easiest society in the world to govern well; he also found the uninhibited liberalism of the United States invigorating, and was less alarmed by the phenomenon of McCarthyism than many critics of the country. The Popper of *The Open Society* was a mildly left-of-centre reformist of a kind familiar in 1940s Britain: non-Marxist, humanitarian, pragmatic, a defender of the welfare state, a believer as he said in 'piecemeal social engineering'. That phrase was slightly unfortunate inasmuch as it led some critics to believe that Popper thought that we should be governed by a scientific elite. Nothing could be further from the truth. The analogy Popper relied on was that

[4] *Poverty* was published as a book in 1957 (by Routledge).

between the behaviour of a scientific community governed by the ideals of free inquiry and a well-ordered constitutional democracy. 'Openness' was crucial. Because he believed adamantly in the logical distinctness of facts and values, he had no doubt that the role of experts, such as it was, was to tell us how to achieve what we had a mind to; it was up to us to decide what it was we wanted to achieve. Anything more was the kind of concession to the pretensions of philosopher-kings that he would not tolerate.

With the passage of time, he became more conservative in much the way that his contemporaries such as Isaiah Berlin did. This was not a principled conservatism, nor the attachment to free-market capitalism of the disciples of Hayek, but the recognition that social reform was harder work than it had seemed in the aftermath of World War Two, and that the modest egalitarianism of the European welfare state was perhaps as much as could reasonably be hoped for. Like many others of his generation, he came to suspect that sustaining a lively and innovative economic system might place more constraints on the pursuit of equality than he had once thought. Again, he was, like Isaiah Berlin, a 'cold war liberal', whose antipathy to totalitarianism made him more friends to his political right than to his political left. He was frequently mistaken for a principled neo-conservative of a Hayekian kind, in part because he was a founding member of the Mont Pelerin Society that Hayek took the lead in setting up 1947. Many of its members were devout free-market economists, including Ludwig von Mises himself. However, the guiding principles of the society, as distinct from what its members gravitated towards over the next fifty years, were reformist rather than purist. Hayek himself deplored Popper's lack of interest in economics. Some of those who have written about Popper's social and political ideas have thought that he *should* have been more of a 'classical liberal', which is to say a Hayekian, than he was. Whatever he should have been, he was in political matters much more of a pragmatist than that. The only absolute was substantially negative: anti-totalitarianism, and its positive face the protection of an open society.

Popper was an opponent of the politicization of science represented, for instance, by the Soviet geneticist Trofim Lysenko, whose ability to silence his critics owed everything to Stalin's support, and nothing to science. But Popper understood very well that ensuring that science can be driven only by its own intellectual standards is itself a political as well as a cultural achievement. That illuminates two things of some interest. The first is that Popper was an early proponent of the thought that a liberal society has no duty to tolerate the intolerant. It is not an uncommon view; many writers whose liberalism is built on a theory of rights think that any claim of a right implies a willingness to extend that right to others. Anyone demanding toleration for the free expression of their views must allow the same toleration to the expression of views with which they disagree; conversely, the intolerant cannot expect toleration. For all its obvious good sense, this is a dangerous doctrine. Radical students campaigning on the basis of 'no platform for racists' have in the United Kingdom frequently silenced speakers at public events, usually to the benefit of the speakers' cause rather than their own. The view that only immediate self-defence or the need to prevent a breach of the peace are grounds for silencing someone allows the obnoxious more opportunity to offend their hearers, but it may prove a policy less liable to abuse. Popper's position was not grounded in any elaborate theory of rights, but in his sense that the enemies of liberal democracy had taken advantage of its freedoms to undermine it in the twenties and thirties. This was not an uncommon reaction among his contemporaries.

A second interesting aspect of Popper's views on 'openness' is his response to positions in the history and philosophy of science that challenged his own emphasis on 'conjecture and refutation'. The main example was his reaction to Thomas Kuhn's little book, *The Structure of Scientific Revolution*. Popper was more measured than some of his then *epigone*, but like them he deplored what appeared to be Kuhn's concessions to assorted forms of epistemological relativism. Kuhn argued that for long periods science is governed by a dominant 'paradigm', an overarching set of beliefs about the world, about what constitutes good science, and about how to practise it; during these periods, there is little or no debate about deep issues, as scientists practise what Kuhn calls 'normal' science. Popper denied Kuhn's account of the history of science, but added for good measure that the apparent relativism of Kuhn's position was a threat to civilisation. Popper's philosophy of science was not politically innocent, but its practical implications beyond the preservation of free speech, the rule of law, and some form of constitutional democracy are few. Social policy is eminently a matter of conjecture and refutation, piecemeal social engineering. George Soros's *Open Society Institute*, founded in 1993 but building on the Soros Foundation created a decade earlier, was aptly named, and not only because Soros had been a student of Popper. Its commitment to the rule of law, democratic governance, social reform, and a thriving civil society leaves a great deal of room for the kind of experiments in health care, education, and other forms of social provision that marked the postwar welfare state.

With his appointment to the London School of Economics in 1946, followed by his promotion to Professor of Logic and Scientific Method in 1949, Popper was secure and at the centre of postwar philosophical discussion. He remained at the London School of Economics until he retired in 1969. Although secure, he was not entirely happy. His eminence did not satisfy his craving for recognition; nor did his emphasis on the way intellectual progress proceeds by constant criticism make him any more willing to accept criticism of his own views. One by one, his disciples found themselves repudiated. Only half in jest, students at the London School of Economics renamed his great book *The Open Society by One of Its Enemies*. Popper had some grounds for thinking that he received less than his due. He was never offered a chair at Oxford or Cambridge, for instance. On the other hand, he was a very difficult colleague, and after he moved to Penn, he became something of a recluse. Matters were not helped by his phobic reaction to tobacco smoke, which made it a nightmare for anyone who invited him to lecture to find a space where he could do so. He was certainly a great man; public honours such as his 1965 knighthood and his appointment as Companion of Honour in 1982 acknowledged the fact. But he was not easy. It is hard not to wonder whether he ever felt completely at home in Britain; at all events, when he died in 1994, it was in Vienna that his ashes were buried.

Personal Recollections of the Publication of *The Open Society**

E. H. Gombrich

Karl Popper's two-volume work *The Open Society and Its Enemies* was published fifty years ago. It stands to reason that this happy event was preceded by a long period of preparation and uncertainty. In fact the publication took two-and-a-half years from the moment that he sent the manuscript from New Zealand to wartime England, and by that time, he and his wife were on the boat taking them to London to start a new life here at the LSE.

Though all this is by now very long ago, fortunately I need not rely on my memory of these events, because I was personally much involved, and hence the recipient of any number of letters which I naturally kept. During most of the war such air letters from overseas were miniaturized to save space and weight, and I have no less than ninety-five such aerogramme forms in addition to other communications relating to his job here at the LSE. They make fascinating reading, and all I can try is to give you samples of these surviving documents.

But first a few words about the background. Popper was seven years my senior, and though I had heard of him in my native Vienna, we only met very fleetingly. It so happened that my father, who was a solicitor, had spent the statutory years of his apprenticeship with Karl's father, who was also a lawyer, and they must have kept in touch, for Karl mentioned in one of his letters how helpful my father had been at the time after Karl's father had died.

* Appeared in *Popper's Open Society After Fifty Years: The Continuing Relevance of Karl Popper*, edited by Ian Jarvie and Sandra Pralong, Routledge, 1999.

In any case, our friendship only dates from the spring of 1936 when I was a junior research fellow at the Warburg Institute, and he came to this country at the invitation of Susan Stebbing. One of our joint acquaintances must have given him my address. We both lived in horrible bedsitters in the Paddington area, and we met with increasing frequency. I still remember having been incautious enough to mention that I had read a pamphlet by Rudolf Carnap on the question of other minds, and found it interesting. Karl was visibly distressed. "I am greatly disappointed that you found that interesting," he said, and from then on I remained a little selective in what I told him.

In 1936 I was twenty-seven and Popper thirty-four. My wife and I visited him and his wife Hennie during a stay in Vienna, and we also saw them during the few days they again spent in London in 1937, before sailing to New Zealand, which was then, as Hennie once wrote "halfway to the moon."

After the outbreak of the war in 1939, I joined the Listening Post, or Monitoring Service, of the BBC. I remember writing to Karl, possibly before that date, but I do not think I received an answer.

Then in May 1943, when the BBC had moved to Reading, I got a letter from him dated 16 April, the first of the ninety-five; it turned out later that Karl had had no idea where I lived, and only got my address almost fortuitously, thanks to a common acquaintance. And so begins the saga of the book, intertwined with that of his Readership here for which Hayek had asked him to apply.

"Dear Ernst" the letter began:

> I have not heard from you for a long time and I was very glad to get your cable. I very much hope that all is well with you and your family. The reason why you have not heard from us is that I have been writing a book. The manuscript is finished; its title is "A Social Philosophy for Everyman." (It has about 700 pages i.e. about 280.000 words.) I believe that the book is topical and its publication urgent – if one can say such a thing at a time when only one thing is really important, the winning of the war. The book is a new philosophy of politics and of history, and an examination of the principles of democratic reconstruction. It also tries to contribute to an understanding of the totalitarian revolt against civilization, and to show that this is as old as our democratic civilization itself.

Let me pause here for a moment to allow Popper's own description of his book to sink in: that the totalitarian revolt against civilization is as old as our democratic civilization itself.

I feel that too many readers of the book were either dazzled or irritated by its lengthy polemics and all but missed the central point of the argument. The book offers an explanatory hypothesis for the persistent hostility to the open society. Totalitarian ideologies are interpreted as reactions to what is described as the strain of civilization, or the sense of drift which is associated with the transition from the closed tribal societies of the past to the individualistic civilization that originated in Athens in the fifth century B.C.

You may call it a psychological diagnosis, though Karl might not have accepted this description without qualification. In any case, I must return to his letter:

> In view of the immense postal and other difficulties it is absolutely impossible to send the book from here to a publisher and have it sent back if it is rejected; for that would mean anything up to one year's delay in case of one rejection. This is why I need somebody in England who sends the MS to the various publishers ...

On 28 April, having received my consent, he sent me the manuscript, together with a letter and other material.

> I am ashamed that I have not written to you for such a long time ... I cannot tell you how much it means to me that you are there and will look after the manuscript. You have no idea how completely hopeless and isolated one often feels in my situation ... But I must tell you what happened so far to the book since I finished it in October [1942]. I had heard that the paper shortage was less pressing in USA; also, the distance is smaller. For these reasons I sent a copy to the USA branch of Macmillan (which, I gather, is quite independent of the English Macmillan). At the same time I wrote to the only friend I had in the USA of whose address I was sure, asking him to act on my behalf. Macmillan turned the book down without even having read it. And this is more or less all I know after 6 months! My friend unfortunately seems to have done absolutely nothing although he had very full instructions. He did not even bother to write before February 16th, acknowledging the receipt of the MS which he got in December! And in this acknowledgment he wrote *nothing* about what he had done (because he had done nothing and obviously he is not going to do anything); he only congratulates me to [sic] my effort in writing such a big book. I don't blame him much, after all, it isn't his book, but you can understand what it means to get such a completely empty letter after waiting for six months!

> The situation is really rather dreadful. I feel that if one has written a book one ought not to be forced to go begging to have it read, and printed.

From later conversations I know, of course, who that unreliable friend was, but I am not going to reveal his name. It turns out not to have been quite true that he did absolutely nothing. Feeling quite helpless with such a work which was far removed from his field, he sent it to a well-known professor of Political Science, at one of the ivy league universities. After a time the manuscript was returned to him, with a note saying that it was impossible to advocate the publication of a book which speaks so disrespectfully of Plato.

In the parcel which I received I found a carefully drafted letter which Karl wanted me to send to publishers, together with the manuscript. There were another formidable three pages with the heading: "*What I should like you to do*," giving a list of seventeen publishers with their addresses in the order of desirability. There are eighteen points of instructions, some with sub-headings a) b) c), but let me just quote item five: "I enclose two *different* title pages: 'A Social Philosophy For Everyman' and 'A Critique of Political Philosophy' … The reason why I have two different titles is that I am not quite satisfied with either. What would you say to 'A Social Philosophy For Our Time'? (Too pretentious?)"

On 4 May, Karl wrote another lengthy letter revising the order of publishers. Up to that point we had very little idea of how the Poppers were actually living in New Zealand, but on 29 July Hennie sent us a very lively three-page letter from which I want to quote a few passages:

> We live in a suburb on the hills with a very beautiful view across Christchurch and the Canterbury plains. The climate is as nearly perfect as things in this world can be, very long summers with an abundance of sunshine; ... It gets frightfully dry ... and the raising of vegetables is not quite easy. I try hard in the little time I have and from October till March we eat only "homegrown" vegetables, mainly peas, beans, potatoes, carrots, spinach, silverbeet, lettuce and tomatoes. It is really never quite sufficient, but we have to make the best of it. The rest of the year we live chiefly on a carrot and rice diet, for economy's sake. Karl's salary was never adequate and is now less so than ever ... During term-time Karl can only work at the week ends, but during the summer holidays he worked literally 24 hours a day. For the last three or four months he was in a state of almost complete exhaustion; he hardly went to bed because he could not sleep ... Karl finished just two days before

> College started again. On both days which remained from our "holiday" we went to the sea and ate as many icecreams as we could (I had planned it long ago that we would celebrate the end with eating as many icecreams as we wanted).

Poor Hennie! – What she does not say in this letter is how hard *she* had to work on the book and the correspondence, almost day and night. At a much later date [24 October 1944], she wrote to us: "This isn't a proper letter at all, I'm just rattling it off on the typewriter … of course, 'rattling it off' is terribly exaggerated – I'm the worst possible typist, and the more distance I gain from the last nightmare years of typing, the less I can understand how on earth I managed it." Let me add, by way of explanation, that Karl always wrote by hand, in the fluent, lucid script of a former schoolteacher. I could not but smile when I saw an item in Sotheby's catalogue photographed and described as "Popper's typewriter." I very much doubt that Karl ever touched its keyboard. He left it to Hennie, in what she described as the nightmare years, to type and retype countless versions and revisions. Not that Karl was not utterly devoted to her. He suffered agonies when she was ill. But he was convinced that the importance of his work had always to override his own comfort, that of Hennie, and possibly also my own, as the future was to show.

Meanwhile, on 19 August I received a long letter dealing with some critical remarks which he had encouraged me to make on reading the book, for instance: "I fully agree with your remark that the humanitarian democratic creed of the West is historically and emotionally based on Christianity. But this fact has no bearing on my theory, as far as I can see. Or has it?" I must have expostulated to him that he ridiculed Hegel, but did not say a word about Schopenhauer, and he replied:

> Although Schopenhauer was a reactionary, egoistically concerned only with the safety of his investments (he openly acknowledges this), his absolute intellectual integrity is beyond doubt. To be sure, his "Will" is not better than Hegel's "Spirit." But what Schopenhauer says, and how he says it, sufficiently proves that he was an honest thinker; he did all he could to make himself understood. Hegel did not intend to be understood; he wanted to impress, to dazzle his readers. Schopenhauer always wrote sense, and sometimes excellent sense; his Critique of Kant's philosophy is one of the most lucid and worthwhile philosophical writings ever published in the German language. A reactionary may be perfectly honest. But Hegel was dishonest.

I must not give the impression, however, that this correspondence frequently turned on philosophical issues. Perhaps there was only one other occasion, when I sent him Arthur Waley's *Three Ways of Thought in Ancient China*, because I had been struck by certain similarities between his analysis of the Greek situation and that described by Waley. Popper responded by writing that he "had always been much attracted by the Chinese, but always felt diffident concerning the possibility of a proper interpretation, considering how much Plato, for example, has been misinterpreted in spite of the fact that his thought and language has immediately influenced our own." This remained his attitude. It was never easy to interest him in the ideas of other civilizations because he felt he lacked their context.

And now for the other theme of this symphony. On 9 December 1943 he wrote: "A few days ago I got a truly overpowering airgraph from Hayek, whose indefatigable kindness to me promises no less than to change the whole course of my life." Hayek had been asked to find out whether Karl would accept a Readership at the LSE. Since the post had to be advertised, Hayek advised Karl "to instruct your friend who is acting for you over here, to apply in your name when such an advertisement is published, and to supply him for that purpose with all the usual information …". "– Now my poor dear friend who is acting for me over there," Karl continued, "you see that I have, indeed, no choice: I *must* trouble you again, much as I should like to spare you." Four days later Karl wrote:

> We are of course terribly excited, and shaken up in consequence of Hayek's airgraph concerning the LSE readership. I do not think that I shall get it, owing to the fact that I have so few publications; but if I don't get it, we shall be, of course, disappointed, much as we try to fortify ourselves against such a development. I was so nicely working along with a new paper on probability, and now: "My peace is gone, my heart is heavy." Don't think that I am ungrateful. Nobody can feel more strongly than I feel about Hayek. He must have worked for me like anything. And the moral effect of this on me is, of course, tremendous.

In consequence I received more instructions from Karl, his CV, a list of references, and texts and testimonials he had previously had. I also received, then or a little later, two and a half folio pages with comments on the notes of the book. Karl realized, of course, that the notes seemed excessively long and complex, and I had also made certain suggestions. Needless to say he tried to prove that the arrangement he had chosen was the only possible one:

> I have most carefully constructed the text in such a way that it is absolutely self-contained for a reader who simply belongs to the educated public, and who has no scientific axe to grind. There is *nothing* in the text that is hard to understand without the notes. I have spent immense labour on this point.

His comments, in fact, revealed, if that is the word, the importance Karl attached to his book:

> I am ... definitely against cuts. I believe that the book is of sufficient value to be sometimes a trifle less brief than it might be possible to make it. *I do not know any work of which one could not say the same*, often in a much higher degree. The book is written with unusual care; I know hardly anybody who is so scrupulous and conscientious in all details as I am; with the effect that, as everybody admits at once, the book achieves a rare degree of lucidity and simplicity; and this in a book which is, as you will admit, thronged with thoughts on every single page. I entirely reject the contention that there is the slightest intrinsic reason for cuts. The extrinsic reason that the book is a very long book, I admit. But since ordinary intelligent people have read through the text in one week-end, it cannot be too long. And regarding the prospect of selling a long book: the ordinary intelligent man does not like to be treated as illiterate or as an imbecile. He is ready, and even proud, to buy a thick book ... I know there is no page in the book which is not full with worthwhile thoughts. This cannot be said of so very many books.

He was surely right. And now the period began when he kept sending me revisions and changes to be made to his manuscript. He was still very uncertain about the best title, and asked, on the 22nd: "What do you think of 'The Open Society and its Enemies' or of 'A Social Philosophy for our Time'? which latter title is of course, very pretentious."

The winter and spring of 1943 and 1944 I had to report to him many disappointments, and a number of publishers who had rejected the book. I believe that is a story that can be told of many important books, but here I can document it. However, in February 1944, I got a letter from Herbert Read, then a director of Routledge, reporting that Hayek had sent him Karl's manuscript. "I am enormously impressed by it, but before presenting a case to my colleagues I should be glad if you would kindly give me a little more information about the author." This I did, and Herbert Read acknowledged it gratefully.

Karl received the contract from Routledge in April 1944, but he instantly began to worry about the US copyright. And now he began to rewrite the book, and I was charged with applying these corrections to the manuscript. It is true that I had his approval to engage somebody to help, an approval which was very necessary, because, after all, I had to do my own work. For instance, on 30 April, he announced that he was sending "by the same mail eleven other airgraphs containing the *corrections*. They look more than they are," writes Karl, but to me they seemed quite sufficient. He expressed the hope that nobody would touch his text, confirming what I have also experienced: "I have only too often found that corrections made matters worse. To be sure, any suggestion for a correction proves that *something* is not quite in order; but only too often the remedy turns out to be worse than the original mistake." On 4 September he announced in addition that he had completely rewritten chapter 17, which duly arrived. I hope I may quote a fuller sample of the type of letters which arrived so frequently:

> In my typed airgraph of today, I mentioned that, as far as *Ch. 12* is concerned, *only* the Section Number Corrections have *first priority*. I now wish to amend this: there is also a false quotation which is important to replace. It is the quotation on MS p.281, from "Hence" in line 5 to the end of paragraph in line 7. – I suggest to correct these lines in accordance with my "Corr. to Ch. 12", Airgraph 4. This however would imply that the passage on p. 281 is replaced by one that is about 2 lines longer. If this creates difficulties, then I suggest to replace the "Hence ..." passage by the following of about equal length: + + States may enter into agreements, but they are superior to agreements (i.e., they may break them). + + In this case, it would suffice to amend the corresponding Note 72 simply by replacing, in line 3 of this note, "336" by + + 330 + +. If, however, there was room enough for using my original correction to p.281, the "336" should be replaced by + + 330 + + and 333 + + . – Of course, if the full corrections of Airgraphs 1 to 11(?) can be used, then Note 72 should be corrected in accordance with Airgraph 9.

No wonder he wrote: "it will be a colossal job for everybody concerned. It was a colossal job here and I was (and am) very ill while doing it. The doctor has strictly forbidden any work, and I am, of course, now absolutely down again."

Around that time there occurred an episode which is not recorded in the correspondence, and for which I shall have to rely on my memory. It happened when Routledge decided to publish the book in two volumes, an idea which, of course, much agitated Karl; all the more as it was mooted that paper shortage might necessitate publishing the second volume after a time interval. It was during these discussions that I sent a cable to Karl from our village post office: "Routledges [sic] want division after Chapter 10." A few hours later I was summoned to the post office and asked to explain what it all meant. The word "division" had alerted a censor who thought, of course, of army divisions. Luckily I was believed.

Another complication was that Karl received a number of offers from other universities in New Zealand and Australia, and naturally did not want to give up the chance of London, but needed badly to get a decision. In October he reports on

> two important articles ... "Private and Public Values," the other "The Refutation of Determinism." A third one, under the title "The Logic of Freedom" is probably too long for being tackled during the vacations. When these three articles are finished, I intend to give up political philosophy, and to return to practical methodology, especially of the natural sciences. Last year I finished some papers on mathematical logic which I did not try to publish so far because of their length. If possible, I should like to cut them now. This is my working programme. Apart from that, I want to do some music. We have not been able to afford a piano here; I had a beautiful Boesendorfer in Vienna, and I could not bring myself to buying a very bad piano; besides, even the worst ones cost more than we could afford. So I bought a harmonium for £3–10–0; I repaired it, and it is not so bad, but I am getting hungry for a piano. I have had *very* little time for playing.

Meanwhile he was even more impatient to receive a binding promise of a publication date from Routledge. All this was mixed up with the worries about the various offers of a post. In one of his letters he wrote:

> You kindly advise me to prefer Otago to Perth, in spite of the Cangeroos [sic]. But I think you don't really know enough of Australia by far: the nicest animal there (and perhaps the loveliest animal that exists) is the Koala bear. Cangeroos may be nice, but the opportunity of seeing a Koala bear is worth putting up with anything, and it is without reservation my strongest motive in wishing to go to Australia.

In April 1945 another cloud appeared on the horizon. I had to write to him that Hayek was going to the United States for a period, and Karl wrote, characteristically, "As you say yourself, the whole affair is pretty awful; and so is the fact that 18 days after you sent your letter, the registrar of

London University has not yet answered you." He was eager to leave Canterbury, for though he had many admirers and friends among his colleagues, the head of his department had all but persecuted him. It was reported to Karl that he had once said: "We know that he is too good for this place. This we cannot help; and nobody will hold him if he goes elsewhere." "The main fact", Karl explained, in a letter of 9 April,

> is the presence of somebody who works hard and endangers certain accepted standards. I mean standards of relaxation (all chairs are easy chairs). These difficulties have much increased by the writing of a book, and still more, of course, by the delay in its publication. – I am terribly sorry to hear that you feel so exhausted. But I can well understand it. I long to hear you speak of your experiences, and of what you have learned during these years. (Will it ever be? I am nearly 43 now, and if I don't manage to see you before I am 45, I may never have the opportunity: I don't think that anybody would import to England a lecturer over the age of 45 ...).

Though I know the time is getting on, I really must quote for you the whole story of how Karl received the news of his appointment, as he told in his letter of 12 June 1945:

> During the whole of April I was ill again. I am now always getting such terrible colds – starting with a very sore throat, and developing in all directions. I was very weak. My doctor insisted that I should go to the mountains during the May vacations and we went both to the Hermitage, at the foot of Mt Cook (the highest mountain here). I was first pretty miserable there, but after two days I had a marvellous recovery; we went up to a hut (the Ball Hut – see pictures in "Mt Cook and the Glaciers") where we were very happy. On the bus journey back from the Hermitage, on May 21st, in the first village (called Fairlie), the Postmistress came with a cable to the bus. It was addressed to "Karl Popper c/o Bus from Hermitage to Fairlie" and said "Congratulations on London appointment and thanks for excellent article enquiring about permits Frederick Hayek." It was from Cambridge, May 16th. This was the first we heard about it. I had given up the idea of going to London – though subconsciously I still believed in it. – We were both somewhat frightened, mainly in view of my rather bad health, and especially the silly way in which my corpse reacts to bad weather. I am sick of being sick, you will think me a terrible hypochonder [sic]. So do I, but my doctor (a very nice and kind person and an excellent doctor) says that it is unfortunately all true. Anyway, it cannot be helped.

And Hennie added: "I am frightfully scared by the prospect of going to London: I hate meeting new people, and tea parties. I can only hope that tea is so rare and precious that parties have gone out of fashion!"

The new worry arose that Hayek had offered to write a preface to the book. "I need not tell you that I could not accept this under any circumstances (1) because I am too proud to accept such an offer (even if it came from President Truman or John Dewey or Shirley Temple), (2) because it would brand the book and myself." Our correspondence had by then switched to the prospect of their arrival in England, and they kindly inquired how much they should take with them to wartime England, and what presents they might possibly bring. We suggested that it would be lovely if they could bring a cricket bat for our son, and Karl "enlisted the help of the very nice son of a friend of ours and now he knows all about cricket and bats." Not that the complaints stopped. On 25 August he wrote:

> Our departure problems are appalling and (but don't tell that to Routledges!) we probably won't be in England before the beginning of December: we have still no permits to enter Great Britain and I begin to fear that we won't get any. I am, of course, in continuous contact about this with Hayek who says that London University administration has completely broken down.

So let me only quote the last letter of the sequence in full. It came from Auckland, and was dated 16 November:

> Dear Ernst, This time we are really off, I think, We have been allotted berths – in two different four-berths cabins, though – on the M.V. "New Zealand Star", sailing from Auckland between Nov. 28th and December 5th (according to the strike situation). It is a frighter [sic], Blue Star Line, carrying normally 12 passengers, and at present (in the same cabins) 30. We are not terribly pleased to pay £320 for the pleasure of spending 5 or 6 very rough weeks in the company of strangers. I am particularly concerned about the fact that I cannot endure the smell of cigarets [sic] at sea without getting sick – still, I shall have to get used to it. The passage will be very rough since we sail via Cape Horn – perhaps the roughest spot in all the Seven Seas. Our corpses are expected to arrive, by the New Zealand Star, on January 8th or thereabouts. Please receive them kindly. If there is important news it can, I suppose, be wirelessed to the ship. I shall let you know more precisely when they arrive, and if you *could* find them a room in a Boarding house or Hotel (where they might perhaps be brought to life again), it would be very nice

> indeed. But I know this is practically impossible: so don't waste your time, if you don't happen to hear about such a room: burry [sic] them. To be serious, I am really cheered up by the prospect of seeing you in less than two months – a very short time (at my age). Yours ever, K.

When they arrived we met them at the docks, and I was happy to be able to bring him the first copy of *The Open Society and Its Enemies*, which he eagerly scrutinized on the train and bus to our little semi-detached house in Brent. Who of us would have dared to hope on that day that despite his fragile health the new life he had just started would extend over nearly half a century, let alone predict how immensely we would all be enriched during these years by his ever active mind?

Acknowledgements

I wish to express my gratitude to all my friends who have made it possible for me to write this book. Professor C. G. F. Simkin has not only helped me with an earlier version, but has given me the opportunity of clarifying many problems in detailed discussions over a period of nearly four years. Dr. Margaret Dalziel has assisted me in the preparation of various drafts and of the final manuscript. Her untiring help has been invaluable. Dr. H. Larsen's interest in the problem of historicism was a great encouragement. Professor T. K. Ewer has read the manuscript and has made many suggestions for its improvement.

I am deeply indebted to Professor F. A. von Hayek. Without his interest and support the book would not have been published. Professor E. Gombrich has undertaken to see the book through the press, a burden to which was added the strain of an exacting correspondence between England and New Zealand. He has been so helpful that I can hardly say how much I owe to him.

Christchurch, N.Z., *April 1944.*

In preparing the revised edition, I have received great help from detailed critical annotations to the first edition kindly put at my disposal by Professor Jacob Viner and by Mr. J. D. Mabbott.

London, *August 1951.*

In the third edition an Index of Subjects and an Index of Platonic Passages have been added, both prepared by Dr. J. Agassi. He has also drawn my attention to a number of mistakes which I have corrected. I am very grateful for his help. In six places I have tried to improve and correct quotations from Plato, or references to his text, in the light of Mr. Richard Robinson's stimulating and most welcome criticism (*The Philosophical Review*, vol. 60) of the American edition of this book.

STANFORD, CALIFORNIA, *May* 1957

Most of the improvements in the fourth edition I owe to Dr. William W. Bartley and to Mr. Bryan Magee.

PENN, BUCKINGHAMSHIRE, *May* 1961

The fifth edition contains some new historical material (especially on page 312 of volume I and in the *Addenda*) and also a brief new *Addendum* in each volume. Additional material will be found in my *Conjectures and Refutations*, especially in the second edition (1965). Mr. David Miller has discovered, and corrected, many mistakes.

PENN, BUCKINGHAMSHIRE, *July* 1965

K. R. P.

Preface to the First Edition

If in this book harsh words are spoken about some of the greatest among the intellectual leaders of mankind, my motive is not, I hope, the wish to belittle them. It springs rather from my conviction that, if our civilization is to survive, we must break with the habit of deference to great men. Great men may make great mistakes; and as the book tries to show, some of the greatest leaders of the past supported the perennial attack on freedom and reason. Their influence, too rarely challenged, continues to mislead those on whose defence civilization depends, and to divide them. The responsibility for this tragic and possibly fatal division becomes ours if we hesitate to be outspoken in our criticism of what admittedly is a part of our intellectual heritage. By our reluctance to criticize some of it, we may help to destroy it all.

The book is a critical introduction to the philosophy of politics and of history, and an examination of some of the principles of social reconstruction. Its aim and the line of approach are indicated in the *Introduction*. Even where it looks back into the past, its problems are the problems of our own time; and I have tried hard to state them as simply as I could, in the hope of clarifying matters which concern us all.

Although the book presupposes nothing but open-mindedness in the reader, its object is not so much to popularize the questions treated as to solve them. In an attempt, however, to serve both of these purposes, I have confined all matters of more specialized interest to *Notes* which have been collected at the end of the book.

1943

Preface to the Second Edition

Although much of what is contained in this book took shape at an earlier date, the final decision to write it was made in March 1938, on the day I received the news of the invasion of Austria. The writing extended into 1943; and the fact that most of the book was written during the grave years when the outcome of the war was uncertain may help to explain why some of its criticism strikes me to-day as more emotional and harsher in tone than I could wish. But it was not the time to mince words—or at least, this was what I then felt. Neither the war nor any other contemporary event was explicitly mentioned in the book; but it was an attempt to understand those events and their background, and some of the issues which were likely to arise after the war was won. The expectation that Marxism would become a major problem was the reason for treating it at some length.

Seen in the darkness of the present world situation, the criticism of Marxism which it attempts is liable to stand out as the main point of the book. This view of it is not wholly wrong and perhaps unavoidable, although the aims of the book are much wider. Marxism is only an episode—one of the many mistakes we have made in the perennial and dangerous struggle for building a better and freer world.

Not unexpectedly, I have been blamed by some for being too severe in my treatment of Marx, while others contrasted my leniency towards him with the violence of my attack upon Plato. But I still feel the need for looking at Plato with highly critical eyes, just because the general adoration of the 'divine philosopher' has a real foundation in his overwhelming intellectual achievement. Marx, on the other hand, has too often been attacked on personal and moral grounds, so that here the need is, rather, for a severe rational criticism of his theories combined with a sympathetic understanding of their astonishing moral and intellectual appeal. Rightly or wrongly, I felt that my criticism was devastating, and that I could therefore afford to search for Marx's real contributions, and to give his motives the benefit of the doubt. In any case, it is obvious that we must try to appreciate the strength of an opponent if we wish to fight him successfully. (I have added in 1965 a new note on this subject as *Addendum* II to my second volume.)

No book can ever be finished. While working on it we learn just enough to find it immature the moment we turn away from it. As to my criticism of Plato and Marx, this inevitable experience was not more disturbing than usual. But most of my positive suggestions and, above all, the strong feeling of optimism which pervades the whole book struck me more and more as naïve, as the years after the war went by. My own voice began to sound to me as if it came from the distant past—like the voice of one of the hopeful social reformers of the eighteenth or even the seventeenth century.

But my mood of depression has passed, largely as the result of a visit to the United States; and I am now glad that, in revising the book, I confined myself to the addition of new material and to the correction of mistakes of matter and style, and that I resisted the temptation to subdue its tenor. For in spite of the present world situation I feel as hopeful as I ever did.

I see now more clearly than ever before that even our greatest troubles spring from something that is as admirable and sound as it is dangerous—from our impatience to better the lot of our fellows. For these troubles are the by-products of what is perhaps the greatest of all moral and spiritual revolutions of history, a movement which began three centuries ago. It is the longing of uncounted unknown men to free themselves and their minds from the tutelage of authority and prejudice. It is their attempt to build up an open society which rejects the absolute authority of the merely established and the merely traditional while trying to preserve, to develop, and to establish traditions, old or new, that measure up to their standards of freedom, of humaneness, and of rational criticism. It is their unwillingness to sit back and leave the entire responsibility for ruling the world to human or superhuman authority, and their readiness to share the burden of responsibility for avoidable suffering, and to work for its avoidance. This revolution has created powers of appalling destructiveness; but they may yet be conquered.

1950

INTRODUCTION

> I do not wish to hide the fact that I can only look with repugnance ... upon the puffed-up pretentiousness of all these volumes filled with wisdom, such as are fashionable nowadays. For I am fully satisfied that ... the accepted methods must endlessly increase these follies and blunders, and that even the complete annihilation of all these fanciful achievements could not possibly be as harmful as this fictitious science with its accursed fertility.
>
> KANT.

This book raises issues which may not be apparent from the table of contents.

It sketches some of the difficulties faced by our civilization—a civilization which might be perhaps described as aiming at humaneness and reasonableness, at equality and freedom; a civilization which is still in its infancy, as it were, and which continues to grow in spite of the fact that it has been so often betrayed by so many of the intellectual leaders of mankind. It attempts to show that this civilization has not yet fully recovered from the shock of its birth—the transition from the tribal or 'closed society', with its submission to magical forces, to the 'open society' which sets free the critical powers of man. It attempts to show that the shock of this transition is one of the factors that have made possible the rise of those reactionary movements which have tried, and still try, to overthrow civilization and to return to tribalism. And it suggests that what we call nowadays totalitarianism belongs to a tradition which is just as old or just as young as our civilization itself.

It tries thereby to contribute to our understanding of totalitarianism, and of the significance of the perennial fight against it.

It further tries to examine the application of the critical and rational methods of science to the problems of the open society. It analyses the principles of democratic social reconstruction, the principles of what I may term 'piecemeal social engineering' in opposition to 'Utopian social engineering' (as explained in Chapter 9). And it tries to clear away some of the obstacles impeding a rational approach to the problems of social reconstruction. It does so by criticizing those social philosophies which are responsible for the widespread prejudice against the possibilities of democratic reform. The most powerful of these philosophies is one which I have called *historicism*. The story of the rise and influence of some important forms of historicism is one of the main topics of the book, which might even be described as a collection of marginal notes on the development of certain historicist philosophies. A few remarks on the origin of the book will indicate what is meant by historicism and how it is connected with the other issues mentioned.

Although I am mainly interested in the methods of physics (and consequently in certain technical problems which are far removed from those treated in this book), I have also been interested for many years in the problem of the somewhat unsatisfactory state of some of the social sciences and especially of social philosophy. This, of course, raises the problem of their methods. My interest in this problem was greatly stimulated by the rise of totalitarianism, and by the failure of the various social sciences and social philosophies to make sense of it.

In this connection, one point appeared to me particularly urgent.

One hears too often the suggestion that some form or other of totalitarianism is inevitable. Many who because of their intelligence and training should be held responsible for what they say, announce that there is no escape from it. They ask us whether we are really naïve enough to believe that democracy can be permanent; whether we do not see that it is just one of the many forms of government that come and go in the course of history. They argue that democracy, in order to fight totalitarianism, is forced to copy its methods and thus to become totalitarian itself. Or they assert that our industrial system cannot continue to function without adopting the methods of collectivist planning, and they infer from the inevitability of a collectivist economic system that the adoption of totalitarian forms of social life is also inevitable.

Such arguments may sound plausible enough. But plausibility is not a reliable guide in such matters. In fact, one should not enter into a discussion of these specious arguments before having considered the following question of method: Is it within the power of any social science to make such sweeping historical prophecies? Can we expect to get more than the irresponsible reply of the soothsayer if we ask a man what the future has in store for mankind?

This is a question of the method of the social sciences. It is clearly more fundamental than any criticism of any particular argument offered in support of any historical prophecy.

A careful examination of this question has led me to the conviction that such sweeping historical prophecies are entirely beyond the scope of scientific method. The future depends on ourselves, and we do not depend on any historical necessity. There are, however, influential social philosophies which hold the opposite view. They claim that everybody tries to use his brains to predict impending events; that it is certainly legitimate for a strategist to try to foresee the outcome of a battle; and that the boundaries between such a prediction and more sweeping historical prophecies are fluid. They assert that it is the task of science in general to make predictions, or rather, to improve upon our everyday predictions, and to put them upon a more secure basis; and that it is, in particular, the task of the social sciences to furnish us with long-term historical prophecies. They also believe that they have discovered laws of history which enable them to prophesy the course of historical events. The various social philosophies which raise claims of this kind, I have grouped together under the name *historicism*. Elsewhere, in *The Poverty of Historicism*, I have tried to argue against these claims, and to show that in spite of their plausibility they are based on a gross misunderstanding of the method of science, and especially on the neglect of the distinction between *scientific prediction* and *historical prophecy*. While engaged in the systematic analysis and criticism of the claims of historicism, I also tried to collect some material to illustrate its development. The notes collected for that purpose became the basis of this book.

The systematic analysis of historicism aims at something like scientific status. This book does not. Many of the opinions expressed are personal. What it owes to scientific method is largely the awareness of its limitations: it does not offer proofs where nothing can be proved, nor does it pretend to be scientific where it cannot give more than a personal point of view. It does not try to replace the old systems of philosophy by a new system. It does not try to add to all these volumes filled with wisdom, to the metaphysics of history and destiny, such as are fashionable nowadays. It rather tries to show that this prophetic wisdom is harmful, that the metaphysics of history impede the application of the piecemeal methods of science to the problems of social reform. And it further tries to show that we may become the makers of our fate when we have ceased to pose as its prophets.

In tracing the development of historicism, I found that the dangerous habit of historical prophecy, so widespread among our intellectual leaders, has various functions. It is always flattering to belong to the inner circle of the initiated, and to possess the unusual power of predicting the course of history. Besides, there is a tradition that intellectual leaders are gifted with such powers, and not to possess them may lead to loss of caste. The danger, on the other hand, of their being unmasked as charlatans is very small, since they can always point out that it is certainly permissible to make less sweeping predictions; and the boundaries between these and augury are fluid.

But there are sometimes further and perhaps deeper motives for holding historicist beliefs. The prophets who prophesy the coming of a millennium may give expression to a deep-seated feeling of dissatisfaction; and their dreams may indeed give hope and encouragement to some who can hardly do without them. But we must also realize that their influence is liable to prevent us from facing the daily tasks of social life. And those minor prophets who announce that certain events, such as a lapse into totalitarianism (or perhaps into 'managerialism'), are bound to happen may, whether they like it or not, be instrumental in bringing these events about. Their story that democracy is not to last for ever is as true, and as little to the point, as the assertion that human reason is not to last for ever, since only democracy provides an institutional framework that permits reform without violence, and so the use of reason in political matters. But their story tends to discourage those who fight totalitarianism; its motive is to support the revolt against civilization. A further motive, it seems, can be found if we consider that historicist metaphysics are apt to relieve men from the strain of their responsibilities. If you know that things are bound to happen whatever you do, then you may feel free to give up the fight against them. You may, more especially, give up the attempt to control those things which most people agree to be social evils, such as war; or, to mention a smaller but nevertheless important thing, the tyranny of the petty official.

I do not wish to suggest that historicism must always have such effects. There are historicists—especially the Marxists—who do not wish to relieve men from the strain of their responsibilities. On the other hand, there are some social philosophies which may or may not be historicistic but which preach the impotence of reason in social life, and which, by this anti-rationalism, propagate the attitude: 'either follow the Leader, the Great Statesman, or become a Leader yourself'; an attitude which for most people must mean passive submission to the forces, personal or anonymous, that rule society.

Now it is interesting to see that some of those who denounce reason, and even blame it for the social evils of our time, do so on the one hand because they realize the fact that historical prophecy goes beyond the power of reason, and on the other hand because they cannot conceive of a social science, or of reason in society, having another function but that of historical prophecy. In other words, they are disappointed historicists; they are men who, in spite of realizing the poverty of historicism, are unaware that they retain the fundamental historicistic prejudice—the doctrine that the social sciences, if they are to be of any use at all, must be prophetic. It is clear that this attitude must lead to a rejection of the applicability of science or of reason to the problems of social life—and ultimately, to a doctrine of power, of domination and submission.

Why do all these social philosophies support the revolt against civilization? And what is the secret of their popularity? Why do they attract and seduce so many intellectuals? I am inclined to think that the reason is that they give expression to a deepfelt dissatisfaction with a world which does not, and cannot, live up to our moral ideals and to our dreams of perfection. The tendency of historicism (and of related views) to support the revolt against civilization may be due to the fact that historicism itself is, largely, a reaction against the strain of our civilization and its demand for personal responsibility.

These last allusions are somewhat vague, but they must suffice for this introduction. They will later be substantiated by historical material, especially in the chapter 'The Open Society and Its Enemies'. I was tempted to place this chapter at the beginning of the book; with its topical interest it would certainly have made a more inviting introduction. But I found that the full weight of this historical interpretation cannot be felt unless it is preceded by the material discussed earlier in the book. It seems that one has first to be disturbed by the similarity between the Platonic theory of justice and the theory and practice of modern totalitarianism before one can feel how urgent it is to interpret these matters.

Volume I

The Spell of Plato

It will be seen ... that the Erewhonians are a meek and long-suffering people, easily led by the nose, and quick to offer up common sense at the shrine of logic, when a philosopher arises among them who carries them away ... by convincing them that their existing institutions are not based on the strictest principles of morality.

SAMUEL BUTLER.

In my course I have known and, according to my measure, have co-operated with great men; and I have never yet seen any plan which has not been mended by the observations of those who were much inferior in understanding to the person who took the lead in the business.

EDMUND BURKE.

THE SPELL OF PLATO

For the Open Society (*about 430* B.C.):
Although only a few may originate a policy, we are all able to judge it.

PERICLES OF ATHENS.

Against the Open Society (*about 80 years later*):
The greatest principle of all is that nobody, whether male or female, should be without a leader. Nor should the mind of anybody be habituated to letting him do anything at all on his own initiative; neither out of zeal, nor even playfully. But in war and in the midst of peace—to his leader he shall direct his eye and follow him faithfully. And even in the smallest matter he should stand under leadership. For example, he should get up, or move, or wash, or take his meals ... only if he has been told to do so. In a word, he should teach his soul, by long habit, never to dream of acting independently, and to become utterly incapable of it.

PLATO OF ATHENS.

The Myth of Origin and Destiny

1

HISTORICISM AND THE MYTH OF DESTINY

It is widely believed that a truly scientific or philosophical attitude towards politics, and a deeper understanding of social life in general, must be based upon a contemplation and interpretation of human history. While the ordinary man takes the setting of his life and the importance of his personal experiences and petty struggles for granted, it is said that the social scientist or philosopher has to survey things from a higher plane. He sees the individual as a pawn, as a somewhat insignificant instrument in the general development of mankind. And he finds that the really important actors on the Stage of History are either the Great Nations and their Great Leaders, or perhaps the Great Classes, or the Great Ideas. However this may be, he will try to understand the meaning of the play which is performed on the Historical Stage; he will try to understand the laws of historical development. If he succeeds in this, he will, of course, be able to predict future developments. He might then put politics upon a solid basis, and give us practical advice by telling us which political actions are likely to succeed or likely to fail.

This is a brief description of an attitude which I call *historicism*. It is an old idea, or rather, a loosely connected set of ideas which have become, unfortunately, so much a part of our spiritual atmosphere that they are usually taken for granted, and hardly ever questioned.

I have tried elsewhere to show that the historicist approach to the social sciences gives poor results. I have also tried to outline a method which, I believe, would yield better results.

But if historicism is a faulty method that produces worthless results, then it may be useful to see how it originated, and how it succeeded in entrenching itself so successfully. An historical sketch undertaken with this aim can, at the same time, serve to analyse the variety of ideas which have gradually accumulated around the central historicist doctrine—the doctrine that history is controlled by specific historical or evolutionary laws whose discovery would enable us to prophesy the destiny of man.

Historicism, which I have so far characterized only in a rather abstract way, can be well illustrated by one of the simplest and oldest of its forms, the doctrine of the chosen people. This doctrine is one of the attempts to make history understandable by a theistic interpretation, i.e. by recognizing God as the author of the play performed on the Historical Stage. The theory of the chosen people, more specifically, assumes that God has chosen one people to function as the selected instrument of His will, and that this people will inherit the earth.

In this doctrine, the law of historical development is laid down by the Will of God. This is the specific difference which distinguishes the theistic form from other forms of historicism. A naturalistic historicism, for instance, might treat the developmental law as a law of nature; a spiritual historicism would treat it as a law of spiritual development; an economic historicism, again, as a law of economic development. Theistic historicism shares with these other forms the doctrine that there are specific historical laws which can be discovered, and upon which predictions regarding the future of mankind can be based.

There is no doubt that the doctrine of the chosen people grew out of the tribal form of social life. Tribalism, i.e. the emphasis on the supreme importance of the tribe without which the individual is nothing at all, is an element which we shall find in many forms of historicist theories. Other forms which are no longer tribalist may still retain an element of *collectivism*[1]; they may still emphasize the significance of some group or collective—for example, a class—without which the individual is nothing at all. Another aspect of the doctrine of the chosen people is the remoteness of what it proffers as the end of history. For although it may describe this end with some degree of definiteness, we have to go a long way before we reach it. And the way is not only long, but winding, leading up and down, right and left. Accordingly, it will be possible to bring every conceivable historical event well within the scheme of the interpretation. No conceivable experience can refute it.[2] But to those who believe in it, it gives *certainty* regarding the ultimate outcome of human history.

A criticism of the theistic interpretation of history will be attempted in the last chapter of this book, where it will also be shown that some of the greatest Christian thinkers have repudiated this theory as idolatry. An attack upon this form of historicism should therefore not be interpreted as an attack upon religion. In the present chapter, the doctrine of the chosen people serves only as an illustration. Its value as such can be seen from the fact that its chief characteristics[3] are shared by the two most important modern versions of historicism, whose analysis will form the major part of this book—the historical philosophy of racialism or fascism on the one (the right) hand and the Marxian historical philosophy on the other (the left). For the chosen people racialism substitutes the chosen race (of Gobineau's choice), selected as the instrument of destiny, ultimately to inherit the earth. Marx's historical philosophy substitutes for it the chosen class, the instrument for the creation of the classless society, and at the same time, the class destined to inherit the earth. Both theories base their historical forecasts on an interpretation of history which leads to the discovery of a law of its development. In the case of racialism, this is thought of as a kind of natural law; the biological superiority of the blood of the chosen race explains the course of history, past, present, and future; it is nothing but the struggle of races for mastery. In the case of Marx's philosophy of history, the law is economic; all history has to be interpreted as a struggle of classes for economic supremacy.

The historicist character of these two movements makes our investigation topical. We shall return to them in later parts of this book. Each of them goes back directly to the philosophy of Hegel. We must, therefore, deal with that philosophy as well. And since Hegel[4] in the main follows certain ancient philosophers, it will be necessary to discuss the theories of Heraclitus, Plato and Aristotle, before returning to the more modern forms of historicism.

2

HERACLITUS

It is not until Heraclitus that we find in Greece theories which could be compared in their historicist character with the doctrine of the chosen people. In Homer's theistic or rather polytheistic interpretation, history is the product of divine will. But the Homeric gods do not lay down general laws for its development. What Homer tries to stress and to explain is not the unity of history, but rather its lack of unity. The author of the play on the Stage of History is not one God; a whole variety of gods dabble in it. What the Homeric interpretation shares with the Jewish is a certain vague feeling of destiny, and the idea of powers behind the scenes. But ultimate destiny, according to Homer, is not disclosed; unlike its Jewish counterpart, it remains mysterious.

The first Greek to introduce a more markedly historicist doctrine was Hesiod, who was probably influenced by oriental sources. He made use of the idea of a general trend or tendency in historical development. His interpretation of history is pessimistic. He believes that mankind, in their development down from the Golden Age, are destined to *degenerate*, both physically and morally. The culmination of the various historicist ideas proffered by the early Greek philosophers came with Plato, who, in an attempt to interpret the history and social life of the Greek tribes, and especially of the Athenians, painted a grandiose philosophical picture of the world. He was strongly influenced in his historicism by various forerunners, especially by Hesiod; but the most important influence came from Heraclitus.

Heraclitus was the philosopher who discovered the idea of *change*. Down to this time, the Greek philosophers, influenced by oriental ideas, had viewed the world as a huge edifice of which the material things were the building material.[1] It was the totality of things—the *cosmos* (which originally seems to have been an oriental tent or mantle). The questions which the philosophers asked themselves were, 'What stuff is the world made of?' or 'How is it constructed, what is its true ground-plan?'. They considered philosophy, or physics (the two were indistinguishable for a long time), as the investigation of 'nature', i.e. of the original material out of which this edifice, the world, had been built. As far as any *processes* were considered, they were thought of either as going on within the edifice, or else as constructing or maintaining it, disturbing and restoring the stability or balance of a structure which was considered to be fundamentally static. They were cyclic processes (apart from the processes connected with the origin of the edifice; the question 'Who has made it?' was discussed by the orientals, by Hesiod, and by others). This very natural approach, natural even to many of us to-day, was superseded by the genius of Heraclitus. The view he introduced was that there was no such edifice, no stable structure, no cosmos. 'The cosmos, at best, is like a rubbish heap scattered at random', is one of his sayings.[2] He visualized the world not as an edifice, but rather as one colossal process; not as the sum-total of all *things*, but rather as the totality of all events, or changes, or *facts*. 'Everything is in flux and nothing is at rest', is the motto of his philosophy.

Heraclitus' discovery influenced the development of Greek philosophy for a long time. The philosophies of Parmenides, Democritus, Plato, and Aristotle can all be appropriately described as attempts to solve the problems of that changing world which Heraclitus had discovered. The greatness of this discovery can hardly be overrated. It has been described as a terrifying one, and its effect has been compared with that of 'an earthquake, in which everything ... seems to sway'[3]. And I do not doubt that this discovery was impressed upon Heraclitus by terrifying personal experiences suffered as a result of the social and political disturbances of his day. Heraclitus, the first philosopher to deal not only with 'nature' but even more with ethico-political problems, lived in an age of social revolution. It was in his time that the Greek tribal aristocracies were beginning to yield to the new force of democracy.

In order to understand the effect of this revolution, we must remember the stability and rigidity of social life in a tribal aristocracy. Social life is determined by social and religious taboos; everybody has his assigned place within the whole of the social structure; everyone feels that his place is the proper, the 'natural' place, assigned to him by the forces which rule the world; everyone 'knows his place'.

According to tradition, Heraclitus' own place was that of heir to the royal family of priest kings of Ephesus, but he resigned his claims in favour of his brother. In spite of his proud refusal to take part in the political life of his city, he supported the cause of the aristocrats who tried in vain to stem the rising tide of the new revolutionary forces. These experiences, in the social or political field are reflected in the remaining fragments of his work.[4] 'The Ephesians ought to hang themselves man by man, all the adults, and leave the city to be ruled by infants ...' is one of his outbursts, occasioned by the people's decision to banish Hermodorus, one of Heraclitus's aristocratic friends. His interpretation of the people's motives is most interesting, for it shows that the stock-in-trade of anti-democratic argument has not changed much since the earliest days of democracy. 'They said: nobody shall be the best among us; and if someone is outstanding, then let him be so elsewhere, and among others.' This hostility towards democracy breaks through everywhere in the fragments: '... the mob fill their bellies like the beasts ... They take the bards and popular belief as their guides, unaware that the many are bad and that only the few are good ... In Priene lived Bias, son of Teutames, whose word counts more than that of other men. (He said: "Most men are wicked.") ... The mob does not care, not even about the things they stumble upon; nor can they grasp a lesson—though they think they do.' In the same vein he says: 'The law can demand, too, that the will of One Man must be obeyed.' Another expression of Heraclitus' conservative and anti-democratic outlook is, incidentally, quite acceptable to democrats in its wording, though probably not in its intention: 'A people ought to fight for the laws of the city as if they were its walls.'

But Heraclitus' fight for the ancient laws of his city was in vain, and the transitoriness of all things impressed itself strongly upon him. His theory of change gives expression to this feeling[5]: 'Everything is in flux', he said; and 'You cannot step twice into the same river.' Disillusioned, he argued against the belief that the existing social order would remain for ever: 'We must not act like children reared with the narrow outlook "As it has been handed down to us".'

This emphasis on change, and especially on change in social life, is an important characteristic not only of Heraclitus' philosophy but of historicism in general. That things, and even kings, change, is a truth which needs to be impressed especially upon those who take their social environment for granted. So much is to be admitted. But in the Heraclitean philosophy one of the less commendable characteristics of historicism manifests itself, namely, an over-emphasis upon change, combined with the complementary belief in an inexorable and immutable *law of destiny*.

In this belief we are confronted with an attitude which, although at first sight contradictory to the historicist's over-emphasis upon change, is characteristic of most, if not all, historicists. We can explain this attitude, perhaps, if we interpret the historicist's over-emphasis on change as a symptom of an effort needed to overcome his unconscious resistance to the idea of change. This would also explain the emotional tension which leads so many historicists (even in our day) to stress the novelty of the unheard-of revelation which they have to make. Such considerations suggest the possibility that these historicists are afraid of change, and that they cannot accept the idea of change without serious inward struggle. It often seems as if they were trying to comfort themselves for the loss of a stable world by clinging to the view that change is ruled by an unchanging law. (In Parmenides and in Plato, we shall even find the theory that the changing world in which we live is an illusion and that there exists a more real world which does not change.)

In the case of Heraclitus, the emphasis upon change leads him to the theory that all material things, whether solid, liquid, or gaseous, are like flames—that they are processes rather than things, and that they are all transformations of fire; the apparently solid earth (which consists of ashes) is only a fire in a state of transformation, and even liquids (water, the sea) are transformed fire (and may become fuel, perhaps in the form of oil). 'The first transformation of fire is the sea; but of the sea, half is earth, and half hot air.'[6] Thus all the other 'elements'—earth, water, and air—are transformed fire: 'Everything is an exchange for fire, and fire for everything; just as gold for wares, and wares for gold.'

But having reduced all things to flames, to processes, like combustion, Heraclitus discerns in the processes a law, a measure, a reason, a wisdom; and having destroyed the cosmos as an edifice, and declared it to be a rubbish heap, he re-introduces it as the destined order of events in the world-process.

Every process in the world, and especially fire itself, develops according to a definite law, its 'measure'[7]. It is an inexorable and irresistible law, and to this extent it resembles our modern conception of natural law as well as the conception of historical or evolutionary laws of modern historicists. But it differs from these conceptions in so far as it is the decree of reason, enforced by punishment, just as is the law imposed by the state. This failure to distinguish between legal laws or norms on the one hand and natural laws or regularities on the other is characteristic of tribal tabooism: both kinds of law alike are treated as magical, which makes a rational criticism of the man-made taboos as inconceivable as an attempt to improve upon the ultimate wisdom and reason of the laws or regularities of the natural world: 'All events proceed with the necessity of fate … The sun will not outstep the measure of his path; or else the goddesses of Fate, the handmaids of Justice, will know how to find him.' But the sun does not only obey the law; the Fire, in the shape of the sun and (as we shall see) of Zeus' thunderbolt, watches over the law, and gives judgement according to it. 'The sun is the keeper and guardian of the periods, limiting and judging and heralding and manifesting the changes and seasons which bring forth all things … This cosmic order which is the same for all things has not been created, neither by gods nor by men; it always was, and is, and will be, an ever living Fire, flaring up according to measure, and dying down according to measure … In its advance, the Fire will seize, judge, and execute, everything.'

Combined with the historicist idea of a relentless destiny we frequently find an element of mysticism. A critical analysis of mysticism will be given in chapter 24. Here I wish only to show the rôle of anti-rationalism and mysticism in Heraclitus' philosophy[8]: 'Nature loves to hide', he writes, and 'The Lord whose oracle is at Delphi neither reveals nor conceals, but he indicates his meaning through hints.' Heraclitus' contempt of the more empirically minded scientists is typical of those who adopt this attitude: 'Who knows many things need not have many brains; for otherwise Hesiod and Pythagoras would have had more, and also Xenophanes … Pythagoras is the grandfather of all impostors.' Along with this scorn of scientists goes the mystical theory of an intuitive understanding. Heraclitus' theory of reason takes as its starting point the fact that, if we are awake, we live in a common world. We can communicate, control, and check one another; and herein lies the assurance that we are not victims of illusion. But this theory is given a second, a symbolic, a mystical meaning. It is the theory of a mystical intuition which is given to the chosen, to those who are awake, who have the power to see, hear, and speak: 'One must not act and talk as if asleep … Those who are awake have One common world; those who are asleep, turn to their private worlds … They are incapable both of listening and of talking … Even if they do hear they are like the deaf. The saying applies to them: They are present yet they are not present … One thing alone is wisdom: to understand the thought which steers everything through everything.' The world whose experience is common to those who are awake is the mystical unity, the oneness of all things which can be apprehended only by reason: 'One must follow what is common to all … Reason is common to all … All becomes One and One becomes All … The One which alone is wisdom wishes and does not wish to be called by the name of Zeus … It is the thunderbolt which steers all things.'

So much for the more general features of the Heraclitean philosophy of universal change and hidden destiny. From this philosophy springs a theory of the driving force behind all change; a theory which exhibits its historicist character by its emphasis upon the importance of 'social dynamics' as opposed to 'social statics'. Heraclitus' dynamics of nature in general and especially of social life confirms the view that his philosophy was inspired by the social and political disturbances he had experienced. For he declares that strife or war is the dynamic as well as the creative principle of all change, and especially of all differences between men. And being a typical historicist, he accepts the judgement of history as a moral one[9]; for he holds that the outcome of war is always just[10]: 'War is the father and the king of all things. It proves some to be gods and others to be mere men, turning these into slaves and the former into masters ... One must know that war is universal, and that justice—the lawsuit—is strife, and that all things develop through strife and by necessity.'

But if justice is strife or war; if 'the goddesses of Fate' are at the same time 'the handmaids of Justice' if history, or more precisely, if success, i.e. success in war, is the criterion of merit, then the standard of merit must itself be 'in flux'. Heraclitus meets this problem by his relativism, and by his doctrine of the identity of opposites. This springs from his theory of change (which remains the basis of Plato's and even more of Aristotle's theory). A changing thing must give up some property and acquire the opposite property. It is not so much a thing as a process of transition from one state to an opposite state, and thereby a unification of the opposite states[11]: 'Cold things become warm and warm things become cold; what is moist becomes dry and what is dry becomes moist ... Disease enables us to appreciate health ... Life and death, being awake and being asleep, youth and old age, all this is identical; for the one turns into the other and the other turns into the one ... What struggles with itself becomes committed to itself: there is a link or harmony due to recoil and tension, as in the bow or the lyre ... The opposites belong to each other, the best harmony results from discord, and everything develops by strife ... The path that leads up and the path that leads down are identical ... The straight path and the crooked path are one and the same ... For gods, all things are beautiful and good and just; men, however, have adopted some things as just, others as unjust ... The good and the bad are identical.'

But the relativism of values (it might even be described as an ethical relativism) expressed in the last fragment does not prevent Heraclitus from developing upon the background of his theory of the justice of war and the verdict of history a tribalist and romantic ethic of Fame, Fate, and the superiority of the Great Man, all strangely similar to some very modern ideas[12]: 'Who falls fighting will be glorified by gods and by men … The greater the fall the more glorious the fate … The best seek one thing above all others: eternal fame … One man is worth more than ten thousand, if he is Great.'

It is surprising to find in these early fragments, dating from about 500 B.C., so much that is characteristic of modern historicist and anti-democratic tendencies. But apart from the fact that Heraclitus was a thinker of unsurpassed power and originality, and that, in consequence, many of his ideas have (through the medium of Plato) become part of the main body of philosophic tradition, the similarity of doctrine can perhaps be explained, to some extent, by the similarity of social conditions in the relevant periods. It seems as if historicist ideas easily become prominent in times of great social change. They appeared when Greek tribal life broke up, as well as when that of the Jews was shattered by the impact of the Babylonian conquest[13]. There can be little doubt, I believe, that Heraclitus' philosophy is an expression of a feeling of drift; a feeling which seems to be a typical reaction to the dissolution of the ancient tribal forms of social life. In modern Europe, historicist ideas were revived during the industrial revolution, and especially through the impact of the political revolutions in America and France[14]. It appears to be more than a mere coincidence that Hegel, who adopted so much of Heraclitus' thought and passed it on to all modern historicist movements, was a mouthpiece of the reaction against the French Revolution.

3

PLATO'S THEORY OF FORMS OR IDEAS

I

Plato lived in a period of wars and of political strife which was, for all we know, even more unsettled than that which had troubled Heraclitus. While he grew up, the breakdown of the tribal life of the Greeks had led in Athens, his native city, to a period of tyranny, and later to the establishment of a democracy which tried jealously to guard itself against any attempts to reintroduce either a tyranny or an oligarchy, i.e. a rule of the leading aristocratic families[1]. During his youth, democratic Athens was involved in a deadly war against Sparta, the leading city-state of the Peloponnese, which had preserved many of the laws and customs of the ancient tribal aristocracy. The Peloponnesian war lasted, with an interruption, for twenty-eight years. (In chapter 10, where the historical background is reviewed in more detail, it will be shown that the war did not end with the fall of Athens in 404 B.C., as is sometimes asserted[2].) Plato was born during the war, and he was about twenty-four when it ended. It brought terrible epidemics, and, in its last year, famine, the fall of the city of Athens, civil war, and a rule of terror, usually called the rule of the Thirty Tyrants; these were led by two of Plato's uncles, who both lost their lives in the unsuccessful attempt to uphold their régime against the democrats. The re-establishment of the democracy and of peace meant no respite for Plato. His beloved teacher Socrates, whom he later made the main speaker of most of his dialogues, was tried and executed. Plato himself seems to have been in danger; together with other companions of Socrates he left Athens.

Later, on the occasion of his first visit to Sicily, Plato became entangled in the political intrigues which were spun at the court of the older Dionysius, tyrant of Syracuse, and even after his return to Athens and the foundation of the Academy, Plato continued, along with some of his pupils, to take an active and ultimately fateful part in the conspiracies and revolutions[3] that constituted Syracusan politics.

This brief outline of political events may help to explain why we find in the work of Plato, as in that of Heraclitus, indications that he suffered desperately under the political instability and insecurity of his time. Like Heraclitus, Plato was of royal blood; at least, the tradition claims that his father's family traced its descent from Codrus, the last of the tribal kings of Attica[4]. Plato was very proud of his mother's family which, as he explains in his dialogues (in the *Charmides* and the *Timaeus*), was related to that of Solon, the lawgiver of Athens. His uncles, Critias and Charmides, the leading men of the Thirty Tyrants, also belonged to his mother's family. With such a family tradition, Plato could be expected to take a deep interest in public affairs; and indeed, most of his works fulfil this expectation. He himself relates (if the *Seventh Letter* is genuine) that he was[5] 'from the beginning most anxious for political activity', but that he was deterred by the stirring experiences of his youth. 'Seeing that everything swayed and shifted aimlessly, I felt giddy and desperate.' From the feeling that society, and indeed 'everything', was in flux, arose, I believe, the fundamental impulse of his philosophy as well as of the philosophy of Heraclitus; and Plato summed up his social experience, exactly as his historicist predecessor had done, by proffering a law of historical development. According to this law, which will be more fully discussed in the next chapter, *all social change is corruption or decay or degeneration*.

This fundamental historical law forms, in Plato's view, part of a cosmic law—of a law which holds for all created or generated things. All things in flux, all generated things, are destined to decay. Plato, like Heraclitus, felt that the forces which are at work in history are cosmic forces.

It is nearly certain, however, that Plato believed that this law of degeneration was not the whole story. We have found, in Heraclitus, a tendency to visualize the laws of development as cyclic laws; they are conceived after the law which determines the cyclic succession of the seasons. Similarly we can find, in some of Plato's works, the suggestion of a Great Year (its length appears to be 36,000 ordinary years), with a period of improvement or generation, presumably corresponding to Spring and Summer, and one of degeneration and decay, corresponding to Autumn and Winter. According to one of Plato's dialogues (the *Statesman*), a Golden Age, the age of Cronos—an age in which Cronos himself rules the world, and in which men spring from the earth—is followed by our own age, the age of Zeus, an age in which the world is abandoned by the gods and left to its own resources, and which consequently is one of increasing corruption. And in the story of the *Statesman* there is also a suggestion that, after the lowest point of complete corruption has been reached, the god will again take the helm of the cosmic ship, and things will start to improve.

It is not certain how far Plato believed in the story of the *Statesman*. He made it quite clear that he did not believe that all of it was literally true. On the other hand, there can be little doubt that he visualized human history in a cosmic setting; that he believed his own age to be one of deep depravity—possibly of the deepest that can be reached—and the whole preceding historical period to be governed by an inherent tendency toward decay, a tendency shared by both the historical and the cosmic development.[6] Whether or not he also believed that this tendency must *necessarily* come to an end once the point of extreme depravity has been reached seems to me uncertain. But he certainly believed that it is *possible* for us, by a human, or rather by a superhuman effort, to break through the fatal historical trend, and to put an end to the process of decay.

II

Great as the similarities are between Plato and Heraclitus, we have struck here an important difference. Plato believed that the law of historical destiny, the law of decay, can be broken by the moral will of man, supported by the power of human reason.

It is not quite clear how Plato reconciled this view with his belief in a law of destiny. But there are some indications which may explain the matter.

Plato believed that the law of degeneration involved moral degeneration. Political degeneration at any rate depends in his view mainly upon moral degeneration (and lack of knowledge); and moral degeneration, in its turn, is due mainly to racial degeneration. This is the way in which the general cosmic law of decay manifests itself in the field of human affairs.

It is therefore understandable that the great cosmic turning-point may coincide with a turning-point in the field of human affairs—the moral and intellectual field—and that it may, therefore, appear to us to be brought about by a moral and intellectual human effort. Plato may well have believed that, just as the general law of decay did manifest itself in moral decay leading to political decay, so the advent of the cosmic turning-point would manifest itself in the coming of a great law-giver whose powers of reasoning and whose moral will are capable of bringing this period of political decay to a close. It seems likely that the prophecy, in the *Statesman*, of the return of the Golden Age, of a new millennium, is the expression of such a belief in the form of a myth. However this may be, he certainly believed in both—in a general historical tendency towards corruption, and in the possibility that we may stop further corruption in the political field by *arresting all political change*. This, accordingly, is the aim he strives for.[7] He tries to realize it by the establishment of a state which is free from the evils of all other states because it does not degenerate, because it does not change. The state which is free from the evil of change and corruption is the best, the perfect state. It is the state of the Golden Age which knew no change. It is the *arrested state*.

III

In believing in such an ideal state which does not change, Plato deviates radically from the tenets of historicism which we found in Heraclitus. But important as this difference is, it gives rise to further points of similarity between Plato and Heraclitus.

Heraclitus, despite the boldness of his reasoning, seems to have shrunk from the idea of replacing the cosmos by chaos. He seems to have comforted himself, we said, for the loss of a stable world by clinging to the view that change is ruled by an unchanging law. This tendency to shrink back from the last consequences of historicism is characteristic of many historicists.

In Plato, this tendency becomes paramount. (He was here under the influence of the philosophy of Parmenides, the great critic of Heraclitus.) Heraclitus had generalized his experience of social flux by extending it to the world of 'all things', and Plato, I have hinted, did the same. But Plato also extended his belief in a perfect state that does not change to the realm of 'all things'. He believed that to every kind of ordinary or decaying thing there corresponds also a perfect thing that does not decay. This belief in perfect and unchanging things, usually called the *Theory of Forms or Ideas*[8], became the central doctrine of his philosophy.

Plato's belief that it is possible for us to break the iron law of destiny, and to avoid decay by arresting all change, shows that his historicist tendencies had definite limitations. An uncompromising and fully developed historicism would hesitate to admit that man, by any effort, can alter the laws of historical destiny even after he has discovered them. It would hold that he cannot work against them, since all his plans and actions are means by which the inexorable laws of development realize his historical destiny; just as Oedipus met his fate *because* of the prophecy, and the measures taken by his father for avoiding it, and not in spite of them. In order to gain a better understanding of this out-and-out historicist attitude, and to analyse the opposite tendency inherent in Plato's belief that he could influence fate, I shall contrast historicism, as we find it in Plato, with a diametrically opposite approach, also to be found in Plato, which may be called the *attitude of social engineering*[9].

IV

The social engineer does not ask any questions about historical tendencies or the destiny of man. He believes that man is the master of his own destiny and that, in accordance with our aims, we can influence or change the history of man just as we have changed the face of the earth. He does not believe that these ends are imposed upon us by our historical background or by the trends of history, but rather that they are chosen, or even created, by ourselves, just as we create new thoughts or new works of art or new houses or new machinery. As opposed to the historicist who believes that intelligent political action is possible only if the future course of history is first determined, the social engineer believes that a scientific basis of politics would be a very different thing; it would consist of the factual information necessary for the construction or alteration of social institutions, in accordance with our wishes and aims. Such a science would have to tell us what steps we must take if we wish, for instance, to avoid depressions, or else to produce depressions; or if we wish to make the distribution of wealth more even, or less even. In other words, the social engineer conceives as the scientific basis of politics something like a *social technology* (Plato, as we shall see, compares it with the scientific background of medicine), as opposed to the historicist who understands it as a science of immutable historical tendencies.

From what I have said about the attitude of the social engineer, it must not be inferred that there are no important differences within the camp of the social engineers. On the contrary, the difference between what I call 'piecemeal social engineering' and 'Utopian social engineering' is one of the main themes of this book. (Cp. especially chapter 9, where I shall give my reasons for advocating the former and rejecting the latter.) But for the time being, I am concerned only with the opposition between historicism and social engineering. This opposition can perhaps be further clarified if we consider the attitudes taken up by the historicist and by the social engineer towards *social institutions*, i.e. such things as an insurance company, or a police force, or a government, or perhaps a grocer's shop.

The historicist is inclined to look upon social institutions mainly from the point of view of their history, i.e. their origin, their development, and their present and future significance. He may perhaps insist that their origin is due to a definite plan or design and to the pursuit of definite ends, either human or divine; or he may assert that they are not designed to serve any clearly conceived ends, but are rather the immediate expression of certain instincts and passions; or he may assert that they have once served as means to definite ends, but that they have lost this character. The social engineer and technologist, on the other hand, will hardly take much interest in the origin of institutions, or in the original intentions of their founders (although there is no reason why he should not recognize the fact that 'only a minority of social institutions are consciously designed, while the vast majority have just "grown", as the undesigned results of human actions'[10]). Rather, he will put his problem like this. If such and such are our aims, is this institution well designed and organized to serve them? As an example we may consider the institution of insurance. The social engineer or technologist will not worry much about the question whether insurance originated as a profit-seeking business; or whether its historical mission is to serve the common weal. But he may offer a criticism of certain institutions of insurances, showing, perhaps, how to increase their profits, or, which is a very different thing, how to increase the benefit they render to the public; and he will suggest ways in which they could be made more efficient in serving the one end or the other. As another example of a social institution, we may consider a police force. Some historicists may describe it as an instrument for the protection of freedom and security, others as an instrument of class rule and oppression. The social engineer or technologist, however, would perhaps suggest measures that would make it a suitable instrument for the protection of freedom and security, and he might also devise measures by which it could be turned into a powerful weapon of class rule. (In his function as a citizen who pursues certain ends in which he believes, he may demand that these ends, and the appropriate measures, should be adopted. But as a technologist, he would carefully distinguish between the question of the ends and their choice and questions concerning the facts, i.e. the social effects of any measure which might be taken[11].)

Speaking more generally, we can say that the engineer or the technologist approaches institutions rationally as means that serve certain ends, and that as a technologist he judges them wholly according to their appropriateness, efficiency, simplicity, etc. The historicist, on the other hand, would rather attempt to find out the origin and destiny of these institutions in order to assess the 'true rôle' played by them in the development of history—

evaluating them, for instance, as 'willed by God', or as 'willed by Fate', or as 'serving important historical trends', etc. All this does not mean that the social engineer or technologist will be committed to the assertion that institutions *are* means to ends, or instruments; he may be well aware of the fact that they are, in many important respects, very different from mechanical instruments or machines. He will not forget, for example, that they 'grow' in a way which is similar (although by no means equal) to the growth of organisms, and that this fact is of great importance for social engineering. He is not committed to an 'instrumentalist' philosophy of social institutions. (Nobody will say that an orange *is* an instrument, or a means to an end; but we often *look upon* oranges as means to ends, for example, if we wish to eat them, or, perhaps, to make our living by selling them.)

The two attitudes, historicism and social engineering, occur sometimes in typical combinations. The earliest and probably the most influential example of these is the social and political philosophy of Plato. It combines, as it were, some fairly obvious technological elements in the foreground, with a background dominated by an elaborate display of typically historicist features. The combination is representative of quite a number of social and political philosophers who produced what have been later described as Utopian systems. All these systems recommend some kind of social engineering, since they demand the adoption of certain institutional means, though not always very realistic ones, for the achievement of their ends. But when we proceed to a consideration of these ends, then we frequently find that they are determined by historicism. Plato's political ends, especially, depend to a considerable extent on his historicist doctrines. First, it is his aim to escape the Heraclitean flux, manifested in social revolution and historical decay. Secondly, he believes that this can be done by establishing a state which is so perfect that it does not participate in the general trend of historical development. Thirdly, he believes that the *model or original* of his perfect state can be found in the distant past, in a Golden Age which existed in the dawn of history; for if the world decays in time, then we must find increasing perfection the further we go back into the past. The perfect state is something like the first ancestor, the primogenitor, of the later states, which are, as it were, the degenerate offspring of this perfect, or best, or 'ideal' state[12]; an ideal state which is not a mere phantasm, nor a dream, nor an 'idea in our mind', but which is, in view of its stability, more real than all those decaying societies which are in flux, and liable to pass away at any moment.

Thus even Plato's political end, the best state, is largely dependent on his historicism; and what is true of his philosophy of the state can be extended, as already indicated, to his general philosophy of 'all things', to his *Theory of Forms or Ideas*.

V

The things in flux, the degenerate and decaying things, are (like the state) the offspring, the children, as it were, of perfect things. And like children, they are copies of their original primogenitors. The father or original of a thing in flux is what Plato calls its 'Form' or its 'Pattern' or its 'Idea'. As before, we must insist that the Form or Idea, in spite of its name, is no 'idea in our mind'; it is not a phantasm, nor a dream, but a real thing. It is, indeed, more real than all the ordinary things which are in flux, and which, in spite of their apparent solidity, are doomed to decay; for the Form or Idea is a thing that is perfect, and does not perish.

The Forms or Ideas must not be thought to dwell, like perishable things, in space and time. They are outside space, and also outside time (because they are eternal). But they are in contact with space and time; for since they are the primogenitors or models of the things which are generated, and which develop and decay in space and time, they must have been in contact with space, at the beginning of time. Since they are not with us in our space and time, they cannot be perceived by our senses, as can the ordinary changing things which interact with our senses and are therefore called 'sensible things'. Those sensible things, which are copies or children of the same model or original, resemble not only this original, their Form or Idea, but also one another, as do children of the same family; and as children are called by the name of their father, so are the sensible things, which bear the name of their Forms or Ideas; 'They are all called after them', as Aristotle says[13].

As a child may look upon his father, seeing in him an ideal, a unique model, a god-like personification of his own aspiration; the embodiment of perfection, of wisdom, of stability, glory, and virtue; the power which created him before his world began; which now preserves and sustains him; and in 'virtue' of which he exists; so Plato looks upon the Forms or Ideas. The Platonic Idea is the original and the origin of the thing; it is the rationale of the thing, the reason of its existence—the stable, sustaining principle in 'virtue' of which it exists. It is the virtue of the thing, its ideal, its perfection.

The comparison between the Form or Idea of a class of sensible things and the father of a family of children is developed by Plato in the *Timaeus*, one of his latest dialogues. It is in close agreement[14] with much of his earlier writing, on which it throws considerable light. But in the *Timaeus*, Plato goes one step beyond his earlier teaching when he represents the contact of the

Form or Idea with the world of space and time by an extension of his simile. He describes the abstract 'space' in which the sensible things move (originally the space or gap between heaven and earth) as a receptacle, and compares it with the mother of things, in which at the beginning of time the sensible things are created by the Forms which stamp or impress themselves upon pure space, and thereby give the offspring their shape. 'We must conceive', writes Plato, 'three kinds of things: first, those which undergo generation; secondly, that in which generation takes place; and thirdly, the model in whose likeness the generated things are born. And we may compare the receiving principle to a mother, and the model to a father, and their product to a child.' And he goes on to describe first more fully the models—the fathers, the unchanging Forms or Ideas: 'There is first the unchanging Form which is uncreated and indestructible, … invisible and imperceptible by any sense, and which can be contemplated only by pure thought.' To any single one of these Forms or Ideas belongs its offspring or race of sensible things, 'another kind of things, bearing the name of their Form and resembling it, but perceptible to sense, created, always in flux, generated in a place and again vanishing from that place, and apprehended by opinion based upon perception'. And the abstract space, which is likened to the mother, is described thus: 'There is a third kind, which is space, and is eternal, and cannot be destroyed, and which provides a home for all generated things …'[15]

It may contribute to the understanding of Plato's theory of Forms or Ideas if we compare it with certain Greek religious beliefs. As in many primitive religions, some at least of the Greek gods are nothing but idealized tribal primogenitors and heroes—personifications of the 'virtue' or 'perfection' of the tribe. Accordingly, certain tribes and families traced their ancestry to one or other of the gods. (Plato's own family is reported to have traced its descent from the god Poseidon[16].) We have only to consider that these gods are immortal or eternal, and perfect—or very nearly so—while ordinary men are involved in the flux of all things, and subject to decay (which indeed is the ultimate destiny of every human individual), in order to see that these gods are related to ordinary men in the same way as Plato's Forms or Ideas are related to those sensible things which are their copies[17] (or his perfect state to the various states now existing). There is, however, an important difference between Greek mythology and Plato's Theory of Forms or Ideas. While the Greeks venerated many gods as the ancestors of various tribes or families, the Theory of Ideas demands that there should be only one Form or Idea of man[18]; for it is one of the central doctrines of the Theory of Forms that there is only one Form of every 'race' or 'kind' of things. The uniqueness of the Form which corresponds to the uniqueness of the primogenitor is a necessary element of the theory if it is to perform one of its most important functions, namely, to explain the similarity of sensible things, by proposing that the similar things are copies or imprints of *one* Form. Thus if there were two equal or similar Forms, their similarity would force us to assume that both are copies of a third original which thereby would turn out to be the only true and single Form. Or, as Plato puts it in the *Timaeus*: 'The resemblance would thus be explained, more precisely, not as one between these two things, but in reference to that superior thing which is their prototype.'[19] In the *Republic*, which is earlier than the *Timaeus*, Plato had explained his point even more clearly, using as his example the 'essential bed', i.e. the Form or Idea of a bed: 'God … has made one essential bed, and only one; two or more he did not produce, and never will … For … even if God were to make two, and no more, then another would be brought to light, namely the Form exhibited by those two; this, and not those two, would then be the essential bed.'[20]

This argument shows that the Forms or Ideas provide Plato not only with an origin or starting point for all developments in space and time (and especially for human history) but also with an explanation of the similarities between sensible things of the same kind. If things are similar because of some virtue or property which they share, for instance, whiteness, or hardness, or goodness, then this virtue or property must be one and the same in all of them; otherwise it would not make them similar. According to Plato, they all participate in the one Form or Idea of whiteness, if they are white; of hardness, if they are hard. They participate in the sense in which children participate in their father's possessions and gifts; just as the many particular reproductions of an etching which are all impressions from one and the same plate, and hence similar to one another, may participate in the beauty of the original.

The fact that this theory is designed to explain the similarities in sensible things does not seem at first sight to be in any way connected with historicism. But it is; and as Aristotle tells us, it was just this connection which induced Plato to develop the Theory of Ideas. I shall attempt to give an outline of this development, using Aristotle's account together with some indications in Plato's own writings.

If all things are in continuous flux, then it is impossible to say anything definite about them. We can have no real knowledge of them, but, at the best, vague and delusive 'opinions'. This point, as we know from Plato and Aristotle[21], worried many followers of Heraclitus. Parmenides, one of Plato's predecessors who influenced him greatly, had taught that the pure knowledge of reason, as opposed to the delusive opinion of experience, could have as its object only a world which did not change, and that the pure knowledge of reason did in fact reveal such a world. But the unchanging and undivided reality which Parmenides thought he had discovered behind the world of perishable things[22] was entirely unrelated to this world in which we live and die. It was therefore incapable of explaining it.

With this, Plato could not be satisfied. Much as he disliked and despised this empirical world of flux, he was, at bottom, most deeply interested in it. He wanted to unveil the secret of its decay, of its violent changes, and of its unhappiness. He hoped to discover the means of its salvation. He was deeply impressed by Parmenides' doctrine of an unchanging, real, solid, and perfect world behind this ghostly world in which he suffered; but this conception did not solve his problems as long as it remained unrelated to the world of sensible things. What he was looking for was knowledge, not opinion; the pure rational knowledge of a world that does not change; but, at the same time, knowledge that could be used to investigate this changing world, and especially, this changing society; political change, with its strange historical laws. Plato aimed at discovering the secret of the royal knowledge of politics, of the art of ruling men.

But an exact science of politics seemed as impossible as any exact knowledge of a world in flux; there were no fixed objects in the political field. How could one discuss any political questions when the meaning of words like 'government' or 'state' or 'city' changed with every new phase in the historical development? Political theory must have seemed to Plato in his Heraclitean period to be just as elusive, fluctuating, and unfathomable as political practice.

In this situation Plato obtained, as Aristotle tells us, a most important hint from Socrates. Socrates was interested in ethical matters; he was an ethical reformer, a moralist who pestered all kinds of people, forcing them to think, to explain, and to account for the principles of their actions. He used to question them and was not easily satisfied by their answers. The typical reply which he received—that we act in a certain way because it is 'wise' to act in this way or perhaps 'efficient', or 'just', or 'pious', etc.—only incited him to continue his questions by asking *what is* wisdom; or efficiency; or justice; or piety. In other words, he was led to enquire into the 'virtue' of a thing. So he discussed, for instance, the wisdom displayed in various trades and professions, in order to find out what is common to all these various and changing 'wise' ways of behaviour, and so to find out what wisdom really is, or what 'wisdom' really means, or (using Aristotle's way of putting it) what its *essence* is. 'It was natural', says Aristotle, 'that Socrates should search for the essence'[23], i.e. for the virtue or rationale of a thing and for the real, the unchanging or essential meanings of the terms. 'In this connection he became the first to raise the problem of universal definitions.'

These attempts of Socrates to discuss ethical terms like 'justice' or 'modesty' or 'piety' have been rightly compared with modern discussions on Liberty (by Mill[24], for instance), or on Authority, or on the Individual and Society (by Catlin, for instance). There is no need to assume that Socrates, in his search for the unchanging or essential meaning of such terms, personified them, or that he treated them like things. Aristotle's report at least suggests that he did not, and that it was Plato who developed Socrates' method of searching for the meaning or essence into a method of determining the real nature, the Form or Idea of a thing. Plato retained 'the Heraclitean doctrines that all sensible things are ever in a state of flux, and that there is no knowledge about them', but he found in Socrates' method a way out of these difficulties. Though there 'could be no definition of any sensible thing, as they were always changing', there could be definitions and true knowledge of things of a different kind—of the virtues of the sensible things. 'If knowledge or thought were to have an object, there would have to be some different, some unchanging entities, apart from those which are sensible', says Aristotle[25], and he reports of Plato that 'things of this other sort, then, he called Forms or Ideas, and the sensible things, he said, were distinct from them, and all called after them. And the many things which have the same name as a certain Form or Idea exist by participating in it'.

This account of Aristotle's corresponds closely to Plato's own arguments proffered in the *Timaeus*[26], and it shows that Plato's fundamental problem was to find a scientific method of dealing with sensible things. He wanted to obtain purely rational knowledge, and not merely opinion; and since pure knowledge of sensible things could not be obtained, he insisted, as mentioned before, on obtaining at least such pure knowledge as was in some way related, and applicable, to sensible things. Knowledge of the Forms or Ideas fulfilled this demand, since the Form was related to its sensible things like a father to his children who are under age. The Form was the accountable representative of the sensible things, and could therefore be consulted in important questions concerning the world of flux.

According to our analysis, the theory of Forms or Ideas has at least three different functions in Plato's philosophy. (1) It is a most important methodological device, for it makes possible pure scientific knowledge, and even knowledge which could be applied to the world of changing things of which we cannot immediately obtain any knowledge, but only opinion. Thus it becomes possible to enquire into the problems of a changing society, and to build up a political science. (2) It provides the clue to the urgently needed *theory of change*, and of decay, to a theory of generation and degeneration, and especially, the clue to history. (3) It opens a way, in the social realm, towards some kind of social engineering; and it makes possible the forging of instruments for arresting social change, since it suggests designing a 'best state' which so closely resembles the Form or Idea of a state that it cannot decay.

Problem (2), the theory of change and of history, will be dealt with in the next two chapters, 4 and 5, where Plato's descriptive sociology is treated, i.e. his description and explanation of the changing social world in which he lived. Problem (3), the arresting of social change, will be dealt with in chapters 6 to 9, treating Plato's political programme. Problem (1), that of Plato's methodology, has with the help of Aristotle's account of the history of Plato's theory been briefly outlined in the present chapter. To this discussion, I wish to add here a few more remarks.

VI

I use the name *methodological essentialism* to characterize the view, held by Plato and many of his followers, that it is the task of pure knowledge or 'science' to discover and to describe the true nature of things, i.e. their hidden reality or essence. It was Plato's peculiar belief that the essence of sensible things can be found in other and more real things—in their primogenitors or Forms. Many of the later methodological essentialists, for instance Aristotle, did not altogether follow him in this; but they all agreed with him in determining the task of pure knowledge as the discovery of the hidden nature or Form or essence of things. All these methodological essentialists also agreed with Plato in holding that these essences may be discovered and discerned with the help of intellectual intuition; that every essence has a name proper to it, the name after which the sensible things are called; and that it may be described in words. And a description of the essence of a thing they all called a 'definition'. According to methodological essentialism, there can be three ways of knowing a thing: 'I mean that we can know its unchanging reality or essence; and that we can know the definition of the essence; and that we can know its name. Accordingly, two questions may be formulated about any real thing ...: A person may give the name and ask for the definition; or he may give the definition and ask for the name.' As an example of this method, Plato uses the essence of 'even' (as opposed to 'odd'): 'Number ... may be a thing capable of division into equal parts. If it is so divisible, number is named "even"; and the definition of the name "even" is "a number divisible into equal parts"...

And when we are given the name and asked about the definition, or when we are given the definition and asked about the name, we speak, in both cases, of one and the same essence, whether we call it now "even" or "a number divisible into equal parts".' After this example, Plato proceeds to apply this method to a 'proof' concerning the real nature of the soul, about which we shall hear more later[27].

Methodological essentialism, i.e. the theory that it is the aim of science to reveal essences and to describe them by means of definitions, can be better understood when contrasted with its opposite, *methodological nominalism*. Instead of aiming at finding out what a thing really is, and at defining its true nature, methodological nominalism aims at describing how a thing behaves in various circumstances, and especially, whether there are any regularities in its behaviour. In other words, methodological nominalism sees the aim of science in the description of the things and events of our experience, and in an 'explanation' of these events, i.e. their description with the help of universal laws[28]. And it sees in our language, and especially in those of its rules which distinguish properly constructed sentences and inferences from a mere heap of words, the great instrument of scientific description[29]; words it considers rather as subsidiary tools for this task, and not as names of essences. The methodological nominalist will never think that a question like '*What is* energy?' or '*What is* movement?' or '*What is* an atom?' is an important question for physics; but he will attach importance to a question like: 'How can the energy of the sun be made useful?' or 'How does a planet move?' or 'Under what condition does an atom radiate light?' And to those philosophers who tell him that before having answered the 'what is' question he cannot hope to give exact answers to any of the 'how' questions, he will reply, if at all, by pointing out that he much prefers that modest degree of exactness which he can achieve by his methods to the pretentious muddle which they have achieved by theirs.

As indicated by our example, methodological nominalism is nowadays fairly generally accepted in the natural sciences. The problems of the social sciences, on the other hand, are still for the most part treated by essentialist methods. This is, in my opinion, one of the main reasons for their backwardness. But many who have noticed this situation[30] judge it differently. They believe that the difference in method is necessary, and that it reflects an 'essential' difference between the 'natures' of these two fields of research.

The arguments usually offered in support of this view emphasize the importance of change in society, and exhibit other aspects of historicism. The physicist, so runs a typical argument, deals with objects like energy or atoms which, though changing, retain a certain degree of constancy. He can describe the changes encountered by these relatively unchanging entities, and does not have to construct or detect essences or Forms or similar unchanging entities in order to obtain something permanent on which he can make definite pronouncements. The social scientist, however, is in a very different position. His whole field of interest is changing. There are no permanent entities in the social realm, where everything is under the sway of historical flux. How, for instance, can we study government? How could we identify it in the diversity of governmental institutions, found in different states at different historical periods, without assuming that they have something *essentially* in common? We call an institution a government if we think that it is essentially a government, i.e. if it complies with our intuition of what a government is, an intuition which we can formulate in a definition. The same would hold good for other sociological entities, such as 'civilization'. We must grasp their essence, so the historicist argument concludes, and lay it down in the form of a definition.

These modern arguments are, I think, very similar to those reported above which, according to Aristotle, led Plato to his doctrine of Forms or Ideas. The only difference is that Plato (who did not accept the atomic theory and knew nothing about energy) applied his doctrine to the realm of physics also, and thus to the world as a whole. We have here an indication of the fact that, in the social sciences, a discussion of Plato's methods may be topical even to-day.

Before proceeding to Plato's sociology and to the use he made of his methodological essentialism in that field, I wish to make it quite clear that I am confining my treatment of Plato to his historicism, and to his 'best state'. I must therefore warn the reader not to expect a representation of the whole of Plato's philosophy, or what may be called a 'fair and just' treatment of Platonism. My attitude towards historicism is one of frank hostility, based upon the conviction that historicism is futile, and worse than that. My survey of the historicist features of Platonism is therefore strongly critical. Although I admire much in Plato's philosophy, far beyond those parts which I believe to be Socratic, I do not take it as my task to add to the countless tributes to his genius. I am, rather, bent on destroying what is in my opinion mischievous in this philosophy. It is the totalitarian tendency of Plato's political philosophy which I shall try to analyse, and to criticize.[31]

Plato's Descriptive Sociology

4

CHANGE AND REST

Plato was one of the first social scientists and undoubtedly by far the most influential. In the sense in which the term 'sociology' was understood by Comte, Mill, and Spencer, he was a sociologist; that is to say, he successfully applied his idealist method to an analysis of the social life of man, and of the laws of its development as well as the laws and conditions of its stability. In spite of Plato's great influence, this side of his teaching has been little noticed. This seems to be due to two factors. First of all, much of Plato's sociology is presented by him in such close connection with his ethical and political demands that the descriptive elements have been largely overlooked. Secondly, many of his thoughts were taken so much for granted that they were simply absorbed unconsciously and therefore uncritically. It is mainly in this way that his sociological theories became so influential.

Plato's sociology is an ingenious blend of speculation with acute observation of facts. Its speculative setting is, of course, the theory of Forms and of universal flux and decay, of generation and degeneration. But on this idealist foundation Plato constructs an astonishingly realistic theory of society, capable of explaining the main trends in the historical development of the Greek city-states as well as the social and political forces at work in his own day.

I

The speculative or metaphysical setting of Plato's theory of social change has already been sketched. It is the world of unchanging Forms or Ideas, of which the world of changing things in space and time is the offspring. The Forms or Ideas are not only unchanging, indestructible, and incorruptible, but also perfect, true, real, and good; in fact, 'good' is once, in the *Republic*[1], explained as 'everything that preserves', and 'evil' as 'everything that destroys or corrupts'. The perfect and good Forms or Ideas are prior to the copies, the sensible things, and they are something like primogenitors or starting points[2] of all the changes in the world of flux. This view is used for evaluating the general trend and main direction of all changes in the world of sensible things. For if the starting point of all change is perfect and good, then change can only be a movement that leads away from the perfect and good; it must be directed towards the imperfect and the evil, towards corruption.

This theory can be developed in detail. The more closely a sensible thing resembles its Form or Idea, the less corruptible it must be, since the Forms themselves are incorruptible. But sensible or generated things are not perfect copies; indeed, no copy can be perfect, since it is only an imitation of the true reality, only appearance and illusion, not the truth. Accordingly, no sensible things (except perhaps the most excellent ones) resemble their Forms sufficiently closely to be unchangeable. 'Absolute and eternal immutability is assigned only to the most divine of all things, and bodies do not belong to this order'[3], says Plato. A sensible or generated thing—such as a physical body, or a human soul—if it is a good copy, may change only very little at first; and the most ancient change or motion—the motion of the soul—is still 'divine' (as opposed to secondary and tertiary changes). But every change, however small, must make it different, and thus less perfect, by reducing its resemblance to its Form. In this way, the thing becomes more changeable with every change, and more corruptible, since it becomes further removed from its Form which is its 'cause of immobility and of being at rest', as Aristotle says, who paraphrases Plato's doctrine as follows: 'Things are generated by participating in the Form, and they decay by losing the Form.' This process of degeneration, slow at first and more rapid afterwards—this law of decline and fall—is dramatically described by Plato in the *Laws*, the last of his great dialogues. The passage deals primarily with the destiny of the human soul, but Plato makes it clear that it holds for all things that 'share in soul', by which he means all living things. 'All things that share in soul change', he writes, '... and while they change, they are carried along by the order and law of destiny. The smaller the change in their character, the less significant is the beginning decline in their level of rank. But when the change increases, and with it the iniquity, then they fall—down into the abyss and what is known as the infernal regions.' (In the continuation of the passage, Plato mentions the possibility that 'soul gifted with an exceptionally large share of virtue can, by force of its own will . . . , if it is in communion with the divine virtue, become supremely virtuous and move to an exalted region'. The problem of the exceptional soul which can save itself—and perhaps others—from the general law of destiny will be discussed in chapter 8.) Earlier in the *Laws*, Plato summarizes his doctrine of change: 'Any change whatever, except the change of an evil thing, is the gravest of all the treacherous dangers that can befall a thing—whether it is now a change of season, or of wind, or of the diet of the body, or of the character of the soul.' And he adds, for the sake of emphasis: 'This statement applies to everything, with the sole exception, as I said just now, of something evil.' In brief, Plato teaches *that change is evil, and that rest is divine*.

We see now that Plato's theory of Forms or Ideas implies a certain trend in the development of the world in flux. It leads to the law that the corruptibility of all things in that world must continually increase. It is not so much a rigid law of universally increasing corruption, but rather a law of increasing corruptibility; that is to say, the danger or the likelihood of corruption increases, but exceptional developments in the other direction are not excluded. Thus it is possible, as the last quotations indicate, that a very good soul may defy change and decay, and that a very evil thing, for instance a very evil city, may be improved by changing it. (In order that such an improvement should be of any value, we would have to try to make it permanent, i.e. to arrest all further change.)

In full accordance with this general theory is Plato's story, in the *Timaeus*, of the origin of species. According to this story, man, the highest of animals, is generated by the gods; the other species originate from him by a process of corruption and degeneration. First, certain men—the cowards and villains—degenerate into women. Those who are lacking wisdom degenerate step by step into the lower animals. Birds, we hear, came into being through the transformation of harmless but too easy-going people who would trust their senses too much; 'land animals came from men who had no interest in philosophy'; and fishes, including shell-fish, 'degenerated from the most foolish, stupid, and . . . unworthy' of all men[4].

It is clear that this theory can be applied to human society, and to its history. It then explains Hesiod's[5] pessimistic law of development, the law of historical decay. If we are to believe Aristotle's report (outlined in the last chapter), then the theory of Forms or Ideas was originally introduced in order to meet a methodological demand, the demand for pure or rational knowledge which is impossible in the case of sensible things in flux. We now see that the theory does more than that. Over and above meeting these methodological demands, it provides a *theory of change*. It explains the general direction of the flux of all sensible things, and thereby the historical tendency to degenerate shown by man and human society. (And it does still more; as we shall see in chapter 6, the theory of Forms determines the trend of Plato's political demands also, and even the means for their realization.) If, as I believe, the philosophies of Plato as well as Heraclitus sprang from their social experience, especially from the experience of class war and from the abject feeling that their social world was going to pieces, then we can understand why the theory of Forms came to play such an important part in Plato's philosophy when he found that it was capable of explaining the trend towards degeneration. He must have welcomed it as the solution of a most mystifying riddle. While Heraclitus had been unable to pass a direct ethical condemnation upon the trend of the political development, Plato found, in his theory of Forms, the theoretical basis for a pessimistic judgement in Hesiod's vein.

But Plato's greatness as a sociologist does not lie in his general and abstract speculations about the law of social decay. It lies rather in the wealth and detail of his observations, and in the amazing acuteness of his sociological intuition. He saw things which had not been seen before him, and which were rediscovered only in our own time. As an example I may mention his theory of the primitive beginnings of society, of tribal patriarchy, and, in general, his attempt to outline the typical periods in the development of social life. Another example is Plato's sociological and economic historicism, his emphasis upon the *economic background* of the political life and the historical development; a theory revived by Marx under the name 'historical materialism'. A third example is Plato's most interesting law of political revolutions, according to which all revolutions presuppose a disunited ruling class (or 'élite'); a law which forms the basis of his analysis of the means of arresting political change and creating a social equilibrium, and which has been recently rediscovered by the theoreticians of totalitarianism, especially by Pareto.

I shall now proceed to a more detailed discussion of these points, especially the third, the theory of revolution and of equilibrium.

II

The dialogues in which Plato discusses these questions are, in chronological order, the *Republic*, a dialogue of much later date called the *Statesman* (or the *Politicus*), and the *Laws*, the latest and longest of his works. In spite of certain minor differences, there is much agreement between these dialogues, which are in some respects parallel, in others complementary, to one another. The *Laws*[6], for instance, present the story of the decline and fall of human society as an account of Greek prehistory merging without any break into history; while the parallel passages of the *Republic* give, in a more abstract way, a systematic outline of the development of government; the *Statesman*, still more abstract, gives a logical classification of types of government, with only a few allusions to historical events. Similarly, the *Laws* formulate the historicist aspect of the investigation very clearly. 'What is the archetype or origin of a state?' asks Plato there, linking this question with the other: 'Is not the best method of looking for an answer to this question … that of contemplating the growth of states as they change either towards the good or towards the evil?' But within the sociological doctrines, the only major difference appears to be due to a purely speculative difficulty which seems to have worried Plato. Assuming as the starting point of the development a perfect and therefore incorruptible state, he found it difficult to explain the first change, the Fall of Man, as it were, which sets everything going[7]. We shall hear, in the next chapter, of Plato's attempt to solve this problem; but first I shall give a general survey of his theory of social development.

According to the *Republic*, the original or primitive form of society, and at the same time, the one that resembles the Form or Idea of a state most closely, the 'best state', is a kingship of the wisest and most godlike of men. This ideal city-state is so near perfection that it is hard to understand how it can ever change. Still, a change does take place; and with it enters Heraclitus' strife, the driving force of all movement. According to Plato, internal strife, class war, fomented by self-interest and especially material or economic self-interest, is the main force of 'social dynamics'. The Marxian formula 'The history of all hitherto existing societies is a history of class struggle'[8] fits Plato's historicism nearly as well as that of Marx. The four most conspicuous periods or 'landmarks in the history of political degeneration', and, at the same time, 'the most important … varieties of existing states'[9], are described by Plato in the following order. First after the perfect state comes 'timarchy' or 'timocracy', the rule of the noble who seek honour and fame; secondly, oligarchy, the rule of the rich families; 'next in order, democracy is born', the rule of liberty which means lawlessness; and last comes 'tyranny … the fourth and final sickness of the city'[10].

As can be seen from the last remark, Plato looks upon history, which to him is a history of social decay, as if it were the history of an illness: the patient is society; and, as we shall see later, the statesman ought to be a physician (and vice versa)—a healer, a saviour. Just as the description of the typical course of an illness is not always applicable to every individual patient, so is Plato's historical theory of social decay not intended to apply to the development of every individual city. But it is intended to describe both the original course of development by which the main forms of constitutional decay were first generated, and the typical course of social change[11]. We see that Plato aimed at setting out a system of historical periods, governed by a law of evolution; in other words, he aimed at a historicist theory of society. This attempt was revived by Rousseau, and was made fashionable by Comte and Mill, and by Hegel and Marx; but considering the historical evidence then available, Plato's system of historical periods was just as good as that of any of these modern historicists. (The main difference lies in the evaluation of the course taken by history. While the aristocrat Plato condemned the development he described, these modern authors applauded it, believing as they did in a law of historical progress.)

Before discussing Plato's perfect state in any detail, I shall give a brief sketch of his analysis of the rôle played by economic motives and the class struggle in the process of transition between the four decaying forms of the state. The first form into which the perfect state degenerates, timocracy, the rule of the ambitious noblemen, is said to be in nearly all respects similar to the perfect state itself. It is important to note that Plato explicitly identified this best and oldest among the existing states with the Dorian constitution of Sparta and Crete, and that these two tribal aristocracies did in fact represent the oldest existing forms of political life within Greece. Most of Plato's excellent description of their institutions is given in certain parts of his description of the best or perfect state, to which timocracy is so similar. (Through his doctrine of the similarity between Sparta and the perfect state, Plato became one of the most successful propagators of what I should like to call 'the Great Myth of Sparta'—the perennial and influential myth of the supremacy of the Spartan constitution and way of life.)

The main difference between the best or ideal state and timocracy is that the latter contains an element of instability; the once united patriarchal ruling class is now disunited, and it is this disunity which leads to the next step, to its degeneration into oligarchy. Disunion is brought about by ambition. 'First', says Plato, speaking of the young timocrat, 'he hears his mother complaining that her husband is not one of the rulers ...'[12] Thus he becomes ambitious and longs for distinction. But decisive in bringing about the next change are competitive and acquisitive social tendencies. 'We must describe', says Plato, 'how timocracy changes into oligarchy ... Even a blind man must see how it changes ... It is the treasure house that ruins this constitution. They' (the timocrats) 'begin by creating opportunities for showing off and spending money, and to this end they twist the laws, and they and their wives disobey them ...; and they try to outrival one another.' In this way arises the first class conflict: that between virtue and money, or between the old-established ways of feudal simplicity and the new ways of wealth. The transition to oligarchy is completed when the rich establish a law that 'disqualifies from public office all those whose means do not reach the stipulated amount. This change is imposed by force of arms, should threats and blackmail not succeed ...'

With the establishment of the oligarchy, a state of potential civil war between the oligarchs and the poorer classes is reached: 'just as a sick body ... is sometimes at strife with itself ..., so is this sick city. It falls ill and makes war on itself on the slightest pretext, whenever the one party or the other manages to obtain help from outside, the one from an oligarchic city, or the other from a democracy. And does not this sick state break out at times into civil war, even without any such help from outside?'[13] This civil war begets democracy: 'Democracy is born ... when the poor win the day, killing some ..., banishing others, and sharing with the rest the rights of citizenship and of public offices, on terms of equality ...'

Plato's description of democracy is a vivid but intensely hostile and unjust parody of the political life of Athens, and of the democratic creed which Pericles had formulated in a manner which has never been surpassed, about three years before Plato was born. (Pericles' programme is discussed in chapter 10, below[14].) Plato's description is a brilliant piece of political propaganda, and we can appreciate what harm it must have done if we consider, for instance, that a man like Adam, an excellent scholar and editor of the *Republic*, is unable to resist the rhetoric of Plato's denunciation of his native city. 'Plato's description of the genesis of the democratic man', Adam[15] writes, 'is one of the most royal and magnificent pieces of writing in the whole range of literature, whether ancient or modern.' And when the same writer continues: 'the description of the democratic man as the chameleon of the human society *paints him for all time*', then we see that Plato has succeeded at least in turning this thinker against democracy, and we may wonder how much damage his poisonous writing has done when presented, unopposed, to lesser minds.

It seems that often when Plato's style, to use a phrase of Adam's[16], becomes a 'full tide of lofty thoughts and images and words', he is in urgent need of a cloak to cover up the rags and tatters of his argumentation, or even, as in the present case, the complete absence of rational arguments. In their stead he uses invective, identifying liberty with lawlessness, freedom with licence, and equality before the law with disorder. Democrats are described as profligate and niggardly, as insolent, lawless, and shameless, as fierce and as terrible beasts of prey, as gratifying every whim, as living solely for pleasure, and for unnecessary and unclean desires. ('They fill their bellies like the beasts', was Heraclitus' way of putting it.) They are accused of calling 'reverence a folly ...; temperance they call cowardice ...; moderation and orderly expenditure they call meanness and boorishness'[17], etc. 'And there are more trifles of this kind', says Plato, when the flood of his rhetorical abuse begins to abate, 'the schoolmaster fears and flatters his pupils ..., and old men condescend to the young ... in order to avoid the appearance of being sour and despotic.' (It is Plato the Master of the Academy who puts this into the mouth of Socrates, forgetting that the latter had never been a schoolmaster, and that even as an old man he had never appeared to be sour or despotic. He had always loved, not to 'condescend' to the young, but to treat them, for instance the young Plato, as his companions and friends. Plato himself, we have reason to believe, was less ready to 'condescend', and to discuss matters with his pupils.) 'But the height of all this abundance of freedom ... is reached', Plato continues, 'when slaves, male as well as female, who have been bought on the market, are every whit as free as those whose property they are ... And what is the cumulative effect of all this? That the citizens' hearts become so very tender that they get irritated at the mere sight of anything like slavery and do not suffer anybody to submit to its presence ... so that they may have no master over them.' Here, after all, Plato pays homage to his native city, even though he does it unwittingly. It will for ever remain one of the greatest triumphs of Athenian democracy that it treated slaves humanely, and that in spite of the inhuman propaganda of philosophers like Plato himself and Aristotle it came, as he witnesses, very close to abolishing slavery.[18]

Of much greater merit, although it too is inspired by hatred, is Plato's description of tyranny and especially of the transition to it. He insists that he describes things which he has seen himself[19]; no doubt, the allusion is to his experiences at the court of the older Dionysius, tyrant of Syracuse. The transition from democracy to tyranny, Plato says, is most easily brought about by a popular leader who knows how to exploit the class antagonism between the rich and the poor within the democratic state, and who succeeds in building up a bodyguard or a private army of his own. The people who have hailed him first as the champion of freedom are soon enslaved; and then they must fight for him, in 'one war after another which he must stir up ... because he must make the people feel the need of a general'[20]. With tyranny, the most abject state is reached.

A very similar survey of the various forms of government can be found in the *Statesman*, where Plato discusses 'the origin of the tyrant and king, of oligarchies and aristocracies, and of democracies'[21]. Again we find that the various forms of existing governments are explained as debased copies of the true model or Form of the state, of the perfect state, the standard of all imitations, which is said to have existed in the ancient times of Cronos, father of Zeus. One difference is that Plato here distinguishes six types of debased states; but this difference is unimportant, especially if we remember that Plato says in the *Republic*[22] that the four types discussed are not exhaustive, and that there are some intermediate stages. The six types are arrived at, in the *Statesman*, by first distinguishing between three forms of government, the rule of one man, of a few, and of the many. Each of these is then subdivided into two types, of which one is comparatively good and the other bad, according to whether or not they imitate 'the only true original' by copying and preserving its ancient laws[23]. In this way, three conservative or lawful and three utterly depraved or lawless forms are distinguished; monarchy, aristocracy, and a conservative form of democracy are the lawful imitations, in order of merit. But democracy changes into its lawless form, and deteriorates further, through oligarchy, the lawless rule of the few, into a lawless rule of the one, tyranny, which, just as Plato has said in the *Republic*, is the worst of all.

That tyranny, the most evil state, need not be the end of the development is indicated in a passage in the *Laws* which partly repeats, and partly[24] connects with, the story of the *Statesman*. 'Give me a state governed by a young tyrant', exclaims Plato there, '… who has the good fortune to be the contemporary of a great legislator, and to meet him by some happy accident. What more could a god do for a city which he wants to make happy?' Tyranny, the most evil state, may be reformed in this way. (This agrees with the remark in the *Laws*, quoted above, that all change is evil, 'except the change of an evil thing'. There is little doubt that Plato, when speaking of the great lawgiver and the young tyrant, must have been thinking of himself and his various experiments with young tyrants, and especially of his attempts at reforming the younger Dionysius' tyranny over Syracuse. These ill-fated experiments will be discussed later.)

One of the main objects of Plato's analysis of political developments is to ascertain the driving force of all historical change. In the *Laws*, the historical survey is explicitly undertaken with this aim in view: 'Have not uncounted thousands of cities been born during this time … and has not each of them been under all kinds of government? … Let us, if we can, get hold of the cause of so much change. I hope that we may thus reveal the secret both of the birth of constitutions, and also of their changes.'[25] As the result of these investigations he discovers the sociological law that internal disunion, class war fomented by the antagonism of economic class interests, is the driving force of all political revolutions. But Plato's formulation of this fundamental law goes even further. He insists that only internal sedition within the ruling class itself can weaken it so much that its rule can be overthrown. 'Changes in any constitution originate, without exception, within the ruling class itself, and only when this class becomes the seat of disunion'[26], is his formula in the *Republic*; and in the *Laws* he says (possibly referring to this passage of the *Republic*): 'How can a kingship, or any other form of government, ever be destroyed by anybody but the rulers themselves? Have we forgotten what we said a while ago, when dealing with this subject, as we did the other day?' This sociological law, together with the observation that economic interests are the most likely causes of disunion, is Plato's clue to history. But it is more. It is also the clue to his analysis of the conditions necessary for the establishment of political equilibrium, i.e. for arresting political change. He assumes that these conditions were realized in the best or perfect state of ancient times.

III

Plato's description of the perfect or best state has usually been interpreted as the Utopian programme of a progressivist. In spite of his repeated assertions, in the *Republic*, *Timaeus*, and *Critias*, that he is describing the distant past, and in spite of the parallel passages in the *Laws* whose historical intention is manifest, it is often assumed that it was his intention to give a veiled description of the future. But I think that Plato meant what he said, and that many characteristics of his best state, especially as described in Books Two to Four of the *Republic*, are intended (like his accounts of primitive society in the *Statesman* and the *Laws*) to be historical[27], or perhaps prehistorical. This may not apply to all characteristics of the best state. Concerning, for example, the kingship of the philosophers (described in Books Five to Seven of the *Republic*), Plato indicates himself that it may be a characteristic only of the timeless world of Forms or Ideas, of the 'City in Heaven'. These intentionally unhistorical elements of his description will be discussed later, together with Plato's ethico-political demands. It must, of course, be admitted that he did not intend, in his description of the primitive or ancient constitutions, to give an exact historical account; he certainly knew that he did not possess the necessary data for achieving anything like that. I believe, however, that he made a serious attempt to reconstruct the ancient tribal forms of social life as well as he could. There is no reason to doubt this, especially since the attempt was, in a good number of its details, very successful. It could hardly be otherwise, since Plato arrived at his picture by an idealized description of the ancient tribal aristocracies of Crete and Sparta. With his acute sociological intuition he had seen that these forms were not only old, but petrified, arrested; that they were relics of a still older form. And he concluded that this still older form had been even more stable, more securely arrested. This very ancient and accordingly very good and very stable state he tried to reconstruct in such a way as to make clear how it had been kept free from disunion; how class war had been avoided, and how the influence of economic interests had been reduced to a minimum, and kept well under control. These are the main problems of Plato's reconstruction of the best state.

How does Plato solve the problem of avoiding class war? Had he been a progressivist, he might have hit on the idea of a classless, equalitarian society; for, as we can see for instance from his own parody of Athenian democracy, there were strong equalitarian tendencies at work in Athens. But he was not out to construct a state that might come, but a state that had been—the father of the Spartan state, which was certainly not a classless society. It was a slave state, and accordingly Plato's best state is based on the most rigid class distinctions. It is a caste state. The problem of avoiding class war is solved, not by abolishing classes, but by giving the ruling class a superiority which cannot be challenged. As in Sparta, the ruling class alone is permitted to carry arms, it alone has any political or other rights, and it alone receives education, i.e. a specialized training in the art of keeping down its human sheep or its human cattle. (In fact, its overwhelming superiority disturbs Plato a little; he fears that its members 'may worry the sheep', instead of merely shearing them, and 'act as wolves rather than dogs'[28]. This problem is considered later in the chapter.) As long as the ruling class is united, there can be no challenge to their authority, and consequently no class war.

Plato distinguishes three classes in his best state, the guardians, their armed auxiliaries or warriors, and the working class. But actually there are only two castes, the military caste—the armed and educated rulers—and the unarmed and uneducated ruled, the human sheep; for the guardians are no separate caste, but merely old and wise warriors who have been promoted from the ranks of the auxiliaries. That Plato divides his ruling caste into two classes, the guardians and the auxiliaries, without elaborating similar subdivisions within the working class, is largely due to the fact that he is interested only in the rulers. The workers, tradesmen, etc., do not interest him at all, they are only human cattle whose sole function is to provide for the material needs of the ruling class. Plato even goes so far as to forbid his rulers to legislate for people of this class, and for their petty problems.[29] This is why our information about the lower classes is so scanty. But Plato's silence is not wholly uninterrupted. 'Are there not drudges', he asks once, 'who do not possess a spark of intelligence and are unworthy to be admitted into the community, but who have strong bodies for hard labour?' Since this nasty remark has given rise to the soothing comment that Plato does not admit slaves into his city, I may here point out that this view is mistaken. It is true that Plato discusses nowhere explicitly the status of slaves in his best state, and it is even true that he says that the *name* 'slave' should better be avoided, and that we should *call* the workers 'supporters' or even 'employers'. But this is done for propagandist reasons. Nowhere is the slightest suggestion to be found that the institution of slavery is to be abolished, or to be mitigated. On the contrary, Plato has only scorn for those 'tenderhearted' Athenian democrats who supported the abolitionist movement. And he makes his view quite clear, for example, in his description of timocracy, the second-best state, and the one directly following the best. There he says of the timocratic man: 'He will be inclined to treat slaves cruelly, for he does not despise them as much as a well-educated man would.' But since only in the best city can education be found which is superior to that of timocracy, we are bound to conclude that there are slaves in Plato's best city, and that they are not treated with cruelty, but are properly despised. In his righteous contempt for them, Plato does not elaborate the point. This conclusion is fully corroborated by the fact that a passage in the *Republic* which criticizes the current practice of Greeks enslaving Greeks ends up with the explicit endorsement of the enslaving of barbarians, and even with a recommendation to 'our citizens'—i.e. those of the best city—to 'do unto barbarians as Greeks now do unto Greeks'. And it is further corroborated by the contents of the *Laws*, and the most inhuman attitude towards slaves adopted there.

Since the ruling class alone has political power, including the power of keeping the number of the human cattle within such limits as to prevent them from becoming a danger, the whole problem of preserving the state is reduced to that of preserving the internal unity of the master class. How is this unity of the rulers preserved? By training and other psychological influences, but otherwise mainly by the elimination of economic interests which may lead to disunion. This economic abstinence is achieved and controlled by the introduction of communism, i.e. by the abolition of private property, especially of precious metals. (The possession of precious metals was forbidden in Sparta.) This communism is confined to the ruling class, which alone must be kept free from disunion; quarrels among the ruled are not worthy of consideration. Since all property is common property, there must also be a common ownership of women and children. No member of the ruling class must be able to identify his children, or his parents. The family must be destroyed, or rather, extended to cover the whole warrior class. Family loyalties might otherwise become a possible source of disunion; therefore 'each should look upon all as if belonging to one family'[30]. (This suggestion was neither so novel nor so revolutionary as it sounds; we must remember such Spartan restrictions on the privacy of family life as the ban on private meals, constantly referred to by Plato as the institution of 'common meals'.) But even the common ownership of women and children is not quite sufficient to guard the ruling class from all economic dangers. It is important to avoid prosperity as well as poverty. Both are dangers to unity: poverty, because it drives people to adopt desperate means to satisfy their needs; prosperity, because most change arises from abundance, from an accumulation of wealth which makes dangerous experiments possible. Only a communist system which has room neither for great want nor for great wealth can reduce economic interests to a minimum, and guarantee the unity of the ruling class.

The communism of the ruling caste of his best city can thus be derived from Plato's fundamental sociological law of change; it is a necessary condition of the political stability which is its fundamental characteristic. But although an important condition, it is not a sufficient one. In order that the ruling class may feel really united, that it should feel like one tribe, i.e. like one big family, pressure from without the class is as necessary as are the ties between the members of the class. This pressure can be secured by emphasizing and widening the gulf between the rulers and the ruled. The stronger the feeling that the ruled are a different and an altogether inferior race, the stronger will be the sense of unity among the rulers. We arrive in this way at the fundamental principle, announced only after some hesitation, that there must be no mingling between the classes[31]: 'Any meddling or changing over from one class to another', says Plato, 'is a great crime against the city and may rightly be denounced as the basest wickedness.' But such a rigid division of the classes must be justified, and an attempt to justify it can only proceed from the claim that the rulers are superior to the ruled. Accordingly, Plato tries to justify his class division by the threefold claim that the rulers are vastly superior in three respects—in race, in education, and in their scale of values. Plato's moral valuations, which are, of course, identical with those of the rulers of his best state, will be discussed in chapters 6 to 8; I may therefore confine myself here to describing some of his ideas concerning the origin, the breeding, and the education of his ruling class. (Before proceeding to this description, I wish to express my belief that personal superiority, whether racial or intellectual or moral or educational, can never establish a claim to political prerogatives, even if such superiority could be ascertained. Most people in civilized countries nowadays admit racial superiority to be a myth; but even if it were an established fact, it should not create special political rights, though it might create special moral responsibilities for the superior persons. Analogous demands should be made of those who are intellectually and morally and educationally superior; and I cannot help feeling that the opposite claims of certain intellectualists and moralists only show how little successful their education has been, since it failed to make them aware of their own limitations, and of their Pharisaism.)

IV

If we want to understand Plato's views about the origin, breeding, and education of his ruling class, we must not lose sight of the two main points of our analysis. We must keep in mind, first of all, that Plato is reconstructing a city of the past, although one connected with the present in such a way that certain of its features are still discernible in existing states, for instance, in Sparta; and secondly, that he is reconstructing his city with a view to the conditions of its stability, and that he seeks the guarantees for this stability solely within the ruling class itself, and more especially, in its unity and strength.

Regarding the origin of the ruling class, it may be mentioned that Plato speaks in the *Statesman* of a time, prior even to that of his best state, when 'God himself was the shepherd of men, ruling over them exactly as man … still rules over the beasts. There was … no ownership of women and children'[32]. This is not merely the simile of the good shepherd; in the light of what Plato says in the *Laws*, it must be interpreted more literally than that. For there we are told that this primitive society, which is prior even to the first and best city, is one of nomad hill shepherds under a patriarch: 'Government originated', says Plato there of the period prior to the first settlement, '… as the rule of the eldest who inherited his authority from his father or mother; all the others followed him like a flock of birds, thus forming one single horde ruled by that patriarchal authority and kingship which of all kingships is the most just.' These nomad tribes, we hear, settled in the cities of the Peloponnese, especially in Sparta, under the name of 'Dorians'. How this happened is not very clearly explained, but we understand Plato's reluctance when we get a hint that the 'settlement' was in fact a violent subjugation. This, for all we know, is the true story of the Dorian settlement in the Peloponnese. We therefore have every reason to believe that Plato intended his story as a serious description of prehistoric events; as a description not only of the origin of the Dorian master race but also of the origin of their human cattle, i.e. the original inhabitants. In a parallel passage in the *Republic*, Plato gives us a mythological yet very pointed description of the conquest itself, when dealing with the origin of the 'earthborn', the ruling class of the best city. (The Myth of the Earthborn will be discussed from a different point of view in chapter 8.) Their victorious march into the city, previously founded by the tradesmen and workers, is described as follows: 'After having armed and trained the earthborn, let us now make them advance, under the command of the guardians, till they arrive in the city. Then let them look round to find out the best place for their camp—the spot that is most suitable for keeping down the inhabitants, should anyone show unwillingness to obey the law, and for holding back external enemies who may come down like wolves on the fold.' This short but triumphant tale of the subjugation of a sedentary population by a conquering war horde (who are identified, in the *Statesman*, with the nomad hill shepherds of the period before the settlement) must be kept in mind when we interpret Plato's reiterated insistence that good rulers, whether gods or demigods or guardians, are patriarchal shepherds of men, and that the true political art, the art of ruling, is a kind of herdsmanship, i.e. the art of managing and keeping down the human cattle. And it is in this light that we must consider his description of the breeding and training of 'the auxiliaries who are subject to the rulers like sheep-dogs to the shepherds of the state'.

The breeding and the education of the auxiliaries and thereby of the ruling class of Plato's best state is, like their carrying of arms, a class symbol and therefore a class prerogative[33]. And breeding and education are not empty symbols but, like arms, instruments of class rule, and necessary for ensuring the stability of this rule. They are treated by Plato solely from this point of view, i.e. as powerful political weapons, as means which are useful for herding the human cattle, and for unifying the ruling class.

To this end, it is important that the master class should feel as one superior master race. 'The race of the guardians must be kept pure'[34], says Plato (in defence of infanticide), when developing the racialist argument that we breed animals with great care while neglecting our own race, an argument which has been repeated ever since. (Infanticide was not an Athenian institution; Plato, seeing that it was practised at Sparta for eugenic reasons, concluded that it must be ancient and therefore good.) He demands that the same principles be applied to the breeding of the master race as are applied, by an experienced breeder, to dogs, horses, or birds. 'If you did not breed them in this way, don't you think that the race of your birds or dogs would quickly degenerate?' Plato argues; and he draws the conclusion that 'the same principles apply to the race of men'. The racial qualities demanded from a guardian or from an auxiliary are, more specifically, those of a sheep-dog. 'Our warrior-athletes ... must be vigilant like watch-dogs', demands Plato, and he asks: 'Surely, there is no difference, so far as their natural fitness for keeping guard is concerned, between a gallant youth and a well-bred dog?' In his enthusiasm and admiration for the dog, Plato goes so far as to discern in him a 'genuine philosophical nature'; for 'is not the love of learning identical with the philosophical attitude?'

The main difficulty which besets Plato is that guardians and auxiliaries must be endowed with a character that is fierce and gentle at the same time. It is clear that they must be bred to be fierce, since they must 'meet any danger in a fearless and unconquerable spirit'. Yet 'if their nature is to be like that, how are they to be kept from being violent against one another, or against the rest of the citizens?'[35] Indeed, it would be 'simply monstrous if the shepherds should keep dogs ... who would worry the sheep, behaving like wolves rather than dogs'. The problem is important from the point of view of the political equilibrium, or rather, of the stability of the state, for Plato does not rely on an equilibrium of the forces of the various classes, since that would be unstable. A control of the master class, its arbitrary powers, and its fierceness, through the opposing force of the ruled, is out of the question, for the superiority of the master class must remain unchallenged. The only admissible control of the master class is therefore self-control. Just as the ruling class must exercise economic abstinence, i.e. refrain from an excessive economic exploitation of the ruled, so it must also be able to refrain from too much fierceness in its dealings with the ruled. But this can only be achieved if the fierceness of its nature is balanced by its gentleness. Plato finds this a very serious problem, since 'the fierce nature is the exact opposite of the gentle nature'. His speaker, Socrates, reports that he is perplexed, until he remembers the dog again. 'Well-bred dogs are by nature most gentle to their friends and acquaintances, but the very opposite to strangers', he says. It is therefore proved 'that the character we try to give our guardians is not contrary to nature'. The aim of breeding the master race is thus established, and shown to be attainable. It has been derived from an analysis of the conditions which are necessary for keeping the state stable.

Plato's educational aim is exactly the same. It is the purely political aim of stabilizing the state by blending a fierce and a gentle element in the character of the rulers. The two disciplines in which children of the Greek upper class were educated, gymnastics and music (the latter, in the wider sense of the word, included all literary studies), are correlated by Plato with the two elements of character, fierceness and gentleness. 'Have you not observed', asks Plato[36], 'how the character is affected by an exclusive training in gymnastics without music, and how it is affected by the opposite training? ... Exclusive preoccupation with gymnastics produces men who are fiercer than they ought to be, while an analogous preoccupation with music makes them too soft ... But we maintain that our guardians must combine both of these natures ... This is why I say that some god must have given man these two arts, music and gymnastics; and their purpose is not so much to serve soul and body respectively, but rather to tune properly the two main strings', i.e. to bring into harmony the two elements of the soul, gentleness and fierceness. 'These are the outlines of our system of education and training', Plato concludes in his analysis.

In spite of the fact that Plato identifies the gentle element of the soul with her philosophic disposition, and in spite of the fact that philosophy is going to play such a dominant rôle in the later parts of the *Republic*, he is not at all biased in favour of the gentle element of the soul, or of musical, i.e. literary, education. The impartiality in balancing the two elements is the more remarkable as it leads him to impose the most severe restrictions on literary education, compared with what was, in his time, customary in Athens. This, of course, is only part of his general tendency to prefer Spartan customs to Athenian ones. (Crete, his other model, was even more anti-musical than Sparta[37].) Plato's political principles of literary education are based upon a simple comparison. Sparta, he saw, treated its human cattle just a little too harshly; this is a symptom or even an admission of a feeling of weakness[38], and therefore a symptom of the incipient degeneration of the master class. Athens, on the other hand, was altogether too liberal and slack in her treatment of slaves. Plato took this as proof that Sparta insisted just a little too much on gymnastics, and Athens, of course, far too much on music. This simple estimate enabled him readily to reconstruct what in his opinion must have been the true measure or the true blend of the two elements in the education of the best state, and to lay down the principles of his educational policy. Judged from the Athenian viewpoint, it is nothing less than the demand that all literary education be strangled[39] by a close adherence to the example of Sparta with its strict state control of all literary matters. Not only poetry but also music in the ordinary sense of the term are to be controlled by a rigid censorship, and both are to be devoted entirely to strengthening the stability of the state by making the young more conscious of class discipline[40], and thus more ready to serve class interests. Plato even forgets that it is the function of music to make the young more gentle, for he demands such forms of music as will make them braver, i.e. fiercer. (Considering that Plato was an Athenian, his arguments concerning music proper appear to me almost incredible in their superstitious intolerance, especially if compared with a more enlightened contemporary criticism[41]. But even now he has many musicians on his side, possibly because they are flattered by his high opinion of the importance of music, i.e. of its political power. The same is true of educationists, and even more of philosophers, since Plato demands that they should rule; a demand which will be discussed in chapter 8.)

The political principle that determines the education of the soul, namely, the preservation of the stability of the state, determines also that of the body. The aim is simply that of Sparta. While the Athenian citizen was educated to a general versatility, Plato demands that the ruling class shall be trained as a class of professional warriors, ready to strike against enemies from without or from within the state. Children of both sexes, we are told twice, 'must be taken on horseback within the sight of actual war; and provided it can be done safely, they must be brought into battle, and made to taste blood; just as one does with young hounds'[42]. The description of a modern writer, who characterizes contemporary totalitarian education as 'an intensified and continual form of mobilization', fits Plato's whole system of education very well indeed.

This is an outline of Plato's theory of the best or most ancient state, of the city which treats its human cattle exactly as a wise but hardened shepherd treats his sheep; not too cruelly, but with the proper contempt … As an analysis both of Spartan social institutions and of the conditions of their stability and instability, and as an attempt at reconstructing more rigid and primitive forms of tribal life, this description is excellent indeed. (Only the descriptive aspect is dealt with in this chapter. The ethical aspects will be discussed later.) I believe that much in Plato's writings that has been usually considered as mere mythological or Utopian speculation can in this way be interpreted as sociological description and analysis. If we look, for instance, at his myth of the triumphant war hordes subjugating a settled population, then we must admit that from the point of view of descriptive sociology it is most successful. In fact, it could even claim to be an anticipation of an interesting (though possibly too sweeping) modern theory of the origin of the state, according to which centralized and organized political power generally originates in such a conquest[43]. There may be more descriptions of this kind in Plato's writings than we can at present estimate.

V

To sum up. In an attempt to understand and to interpret the changing social world as he experienced it, Plato was led to develop a systematic historicist sociology in great detail. He thought of existing states as decaying copies of an unchanging Form or Idea. He tried to reconstruct this Form or Idea of a state, or at least to describe a society which resembled it as closely as possible. Along with ancient traditions, he used as material for his reconstruction the results of his analysis of the social institutions of Sparta and Crete—the most ancient forms of social life he could find in Greece—in which he recognized arrested forms of even older tribal societies. But in order to make a proper use of this material, he needed a principle for distinguishing between the good or original or ancient traits of the existing institutions and their symptoms of decay. This principle he found in his law of political revolutions, according to which disunion in the ruling class, and their preoccupation with economic affairs, are the origin of all social change. His best state was therefore to be reconstructed in such a way as to eliminate all the germs and elements of disunion and decay as radically as this could be done; that is to say, it was to be constructed out of the Spartan state with an eye to the conditions necessary for the unbroken unity of the master class, guaranteed by its economic abstinence, its breeding, and its training.

Interpreting existing societies as decadent copies of an ideal state, Plato furnished Hesiod's somewhat crude views of human history at once with a theoretical background and with a wealth of practical application. He developed a remarkably realistic historicist theory which found the cause of social change in Heraclitus' disunion, and in the strife of classes in which he recognized the driving as well as the corrupting forces of history. He applied these historicist principles to the story of the Decline and Fall of the Greek city-states, and especially to a criticism of democracy, which he described as effeminate and degenerate. And we may add that later, in the *Laws*[44], he applied them also to a story of the Decline and Fall of the Persian Empire, thus making the beginning of a long series of Decline-and-Fall dramatizations of the histories of empires and civilizations. (O. Spengler's notorious *Decline of the West* is perhaps the worst but not the last[45] of them.) All this, I think, can be interpreted as an attempt, and a most impressive one, to explain, and to rationalize, his experience of the breakdown of the tribal society; an experience analogous to that which had led Heraclitus to develop the first philosophy of change.

But our analysis of Plato's descriptive sociology is still incomplete. His stories of the Decline and Fall, and with it nearly all the later stories, exhibit at least two characteristics which we have not discussed so far. He conceived these declining societies as some kind of organism, and the decline as a process similar to ageing. And he believed that the decline is well deserved, in the sense that moral decay, a fall and decline of the soul, goes hand in hand with that of the social body. All this plays an important rôle in Plato's theory of the first change—in the Story of the Number and of the Fall of Man. This theory, and its connection with the doctrine of Forms or Ideas, will be discussed in the next chapter.

5

NATURE AND CONVENTION

Plato was not the first to approach social phenomena in the spirit of scientific investigation. The beginning of social science goes back at least to the generation of Protagoras, the first of the great thinkers who called themselves 'Sophists'. It is marked by the realization of the need to distinguish between two different elements in man's environment—his natural environment and his social environment. This is a distinction which is difficult to make and to grasp, as can be inferred from the fact that even now it is not clearly established in our minds. It has been questioned ever since the time of Protagoras. Most of us, it seems, have a strong inclination to accept the peculiarities of our social environment as if they were 'natural'.

It is one of the characteristics of the magical attitude of a primitive tribal or 'closed' society that it lives in a charmed circle[1] of unchanging taboos, of laws and customs which are felt to be as inevitable as the rising of the sun, or the cycle of the seasons, or similar obvious regularities of nature. And it is only after this magical 'closed society' has actually broken down that a theoretical understanding of the difference between 'nature' and 'society' can develop.

I

An analysis of this development requires, I believe, a clear grasp of an important distinction. It is the distinction between (*a*) *natural laws*, or laws of nature, such as the laws describing the movements of the sun, the moon, and the planets, the succession of the seasons, etc., or the law of gravity or, say, the laws of thermodynamics and, on the other hand, (*b*) *normative laws*, or norms, or prohibitions and commandments, i.e. such rules as forbid or demand certain modes of conduct; examples are the Ten Commandments or the legal rules regulating the procedure of the election of Members of Parliament, or the laws that constitute the Athenian Constitution.

Since the discussion of these matters is often vitiated by a tendency to blur this distinction, a few more words may be said about it. A law in sense (*a*)—a natural law—is describing a strict, unvarying regularity which either in fact holds in nature (in this case, the law is a true statement) or does not hold (in this case it is false). If we do not know whether a law of nature is true or false, and if we wish to draw attention to our uncertainty, we often call it an 'hypothesis'. A law of nature is unalterable; there are no exceptions to it. For if we are satisfied that something has happened which contradicts it, then we do not say that there is an exception, or an alteration to the law, but rather that our hypothesis has been refuted, since it has turned out that the supposed strict regularity did not hold, or in other words, that the supposed law of nature was not a true law of nature, but a false statement. Since laws of nature are unalterable, they can be neither broken nor enforced. They are beyond human control, although they may possibly be used by us for technical purposes, and although we may get into trouble by not knowing them, or by ignoring them.

All this is very different if we turn to laws of the kind (*b*), that is, to normative laws. A normative law, whether it is now a legal enactment or a moral commandment, can be enforced by men. Also, it is alterable. It may be perhaps described as good or bad, right or wrong, acceptable or unacceptable; but only in a metaphorical sense can it be called 'true' or 'false', since it does not describe a fact, but lays down directions for our behaviour. If it has any point or significance, then it can be broken; and if it cannot be broken then it is superfluous and without significance. 'Do not spend more money than you possess' is a significant normative law; it may be significant as a moral or legal rule, and the more necessary as it is so often broken. 'Do not take more money out of your purse than there was in it' may be said to be, by its wording, also a normative law; but nobody would consider seriously such a rule as a significant part of a moral or legal system, since it cannot be broken. If a significant normative law is observed, then this is always due to human control—to human actions and decisions. Usually it is due to the decision to introduce sanctions—to punish or restrain those who break the law.

I believe, in common with a great number of thinkers, and especially with many social scientists, that the distinction between laws in sense (*a*), i.e. statements describing regularities of nature, and laws in sense (*b*), i.e. norms such as prohibitions or commandments, is a fundamental one, and that these two kinds of law have hardly more in common than a name. But this view is by no means generally accepted; on the contrary, many thinkers believe that there are norms—prohibitions or commandments—which are 'natural' in the sense that they are laid down in accordance with natural laws in sense (*a*). They say, for example, that certain legal norms are in accordance with human nature, and therefore with psychological natural laws in sense (*a*), while other legal norms may be contrary to human nature; and they add that those norms which can be shown to be in accordance with human nature are really not very different from natural laws in sense (*a*). Others say that natural laws in sense (*a*) are really very similar to normative laws since they are laid down by the will or decision of the Creator of the Universe—a view which, undoubtedly, lies behind the use of the originally normative word 'law' for laws of the kind (*a*). All these views may be worthy of being discussed. But in order to discuss them, it is necessary first to distinguish between laws in the sense of (*a*) and laws in the sense of (*b*), and not to confuse the issue by a bad terminology. Thus we shall reserve the term 'natural laws' exclusively for laws of type (*a*), and we shall refuse to apply this term to any norms which are claimed to be, in some sense or other, 'natural'. The confusion is quite unnecessary since it is easy to speak of 'natural rights and obligations' or of 'natural norms' if we wish to stress the 'natural' character of laws of type (*b*).

II

I believe that it is necessary for the understanding of Plato's sociology to consider how the distinction between natural and normative laws may have developed. I shall first discuss what seem to have been the starting point and the last step of the development, and later what seem to have been three intermediate steps, which all play a part in Plato's theory. The starting point can be described as a *naïve monism*. It may be said to be characteristic of the 'closed society'. The last step, which I describe as *critical dualism* (or critical conventionalism), is characteristic of the 'open society'. The fact that there are still many who try to avoid making this step may be taken as an indication that we are still in the midst of the transition from the closed to the open society. (With all this, compare chapter 10.)

The starting point which I have called 'naïve monism' is the stage at which the distinction between natural and normative laws is not yet made. Unpleasant experiences are the means by which man learns to adjust himself to his environment. No distinction is made between sanctions imposed by other men, if a normative taboo is broken, and unpleasant experiences suffered in the natural environment. Within this stage, we may further distinguish between two possibilities. The one can be described as a *naïve naturalism*. At this stage regularities, whether natural or conventional, are felt to be beyond the possibility of any alteration whatever. But I believe that this stage is only an abstract possibility which probably was never realized. More important is a stage which we can describe as a *naïve conventionalism*—a stage at which both natural and normative regularities are experienced as expressions of, and as dependent upon, the decisions of man-like gods or demons. Thus the cycle of the seasons, or the peculiarities of the movements of the sun, the moon, and the planets, may be interpreted as obeying the 'laws' or 'decrees' or 'decisions' which 'rule heaven and earth', and which were laid down and 'pronounced by the creator-god in the beginning'[2]. It is understandable that those who think in this way may believe that even the natural laws are open to modifications, under certain exceptional circumstances; that with the help of magical practices man may sometimes influence them; and that natural regularities are upheld by sanctions, as if they were normative. This point is well illustrated by Heraclitus' saying: 'The sun will not outstep the measure of his path; or else the goddesses of Fate, the handmaids of Justice, will know how to find him.'

The breakdown of magic tribalism is closely connected with the realization that taboos are different in various tribes, that they are imposed and enforced by man, and that they may be broken without unpleasant repercussions if one can only escape the sanctions imposed by one's fellow-men. This realization is quickened when it is observed that laws are altered and made by human lawgivers. I have in mind not only such lawgivers as Solon, but also the laws which were made and enforced by the common people of democratic cities. These experiences may lead to a conscious differentiation between the man-enforced normative laws, based on decisions or conventions, and the natural regularities which are beyond his power. When this differentiation is clearly understood, then we can describe the position reached as a *critical dualism*, or critical conventionalism. In the development of Greek philosophy this dualism of facts and norms announces itself in terms of the opposition between nature and convention.[3]

In spite of the fact that this position was reached a long time ago by the Sophist Protagoras, an older contemporary of Socrates, it is still so little understood that it seems necessary to explain it in some detail. First, we must not think that critical dualism implies a theory of the historical origin of norms. It has nothing to do with the obviously untenable historical assertion that norms in the first place were *consciously* made or introduced by man, instead of having been found by him to be simply there (whenever he was first able to find anything of this kind). It therefore has nothing to do with the assertion that norms originate with man, and not with God, nor does it underrate the importance of normative laws. Least of all has it anything to do with the assertion that norms, since they are conventional, i.e. man-made, are therefore 'merely arbitrary'. Critical dualism merely asserts that norms and normative laws *can* be made and changed by man, more especially by a decision or convention to observe them or to alter them, and that it is therefore man who is morally responsible for them; not perhaps for the norms which he finds to exist in society when he first begins to reflect upon them, but for the norms which he is prepared to tolerate once he has found out that he can do something to alter them. Norms are man-made in the sense that we must blame nobody but ourselves for them; neither nature, nor God. It is our business to improve them as much as we can, if we find that they are objectionable. This last remark implies that by describing norms as conventional, I do not mean that they must be arbitrary, or that one set of normative laws will do just as well as another. By saying that some systems of laws can be improved, that some laws may be better than others, I rather imply that we can compare the existing normative laws (or social institutions) with some standard norms which we have decided are worthy of being realized. But even these standards are of our making in the sense that our decision in favour of them is our own decision, and that we alone carry the responsibility for adopting them. The standards are not to be found in nature. Nature consists of facts and of regularities, and is in itself neither moral nor immoral. It is we who impose our standards upon nature, and who in this way introduce morals into the natural world[4], in spite of the fact that we are part of this world. We are products of nature, but nature has made us together with our power of altering the world, of foreseeing and of planning for the future, and of making far-reaching decisions for which we are morally responsible. Yet responsibility, decisions, enter the world of nature only with us.

III

It is important for the understanding of this attitude to realize that these decisions can never be derived from facts (or from statements of facts), although they pertain to facts. The decision, for instance, to oppose slavery does not depend upon the fact that all men are born free and equal, and that no man is born in chains. For even if all were born free, some men might perhaps try to put others in chains, and they may even believe that they ought to put them in chains. And conversely, even if men were born in chains, many of us might demand the removal of these chains. Or to put this matter more precisely, if we consider a fact as alterable—such as the fact that many people are suffering from diseases—then we can always adopt a number of different attitudes towards this fact: more especially, we can decide to make an attempt to alter it; or we can decide to resist any such attempt; or we can decide not to take action at all.

All moral decisions pertain in this way to some fact or other, especially to some fact of social life, and all (alterable) facts of social life can give rise to many different decisions. Which shows that the decisions can never be derivable from these facts, or from a description of these facts.

But they cannot be derived from another class of facts either; I mean those natural regularities which we describe with the help of natural laws. It is perfectly true that our decisions must be compatible with the natural laws (including those of human physiology and psychology), if they are ever to be carried into effect; for if they run counter to such laws, then they simply cannot be carried out. The decision that all should work harder and eat less, for example, cannot be carried out beyond a certain point for physiological reasons, i.e. because beyond a certain point it would be incompatible with certain natural laws of physiology. Similarly, the decision that all should work less and eat more also cannot be carried out beyond a certain point, for various reasons, including the natural laws of economics. (As we shall see below, in section iv of this chapter, there are natural laws in the social sciences also; we shall call them 'sociological laws'.)

Thus certain decisions may be eliminated as incapable of being executed, because they contradict certain natural laws (or 'unalterable facts'). But this does not mean, of course, that any decision can be logically derived from such 'unalterable facts'. Rather, the situation is this. In view of any fact whatsoever, whether it is alterable or unalterable, we can adopt various decisions—such as to alter it; to protect it from those who wish to alter it; not to interfere, etc. But if the fact in question is unalterable—either because an alteration is impossible in view of the existing laws of nature, or because an alteration is for other reasons too difficult for those who wish to alter it—then any decision to alter it will be simply impracticable; in fact, any decision concerning such a fact will be pointless and without significance.

Critical dualism thus emphasizes the impossibility of reducing decisions or norms to facts; it can therefore be described as a *dualism of facts and decisions*.

But this dualism seems to be open to attack. Decisions *are* facts, it may be said. If we decide to adopt a certain norm, then the making of this decision is itself a psychological or sociological fact, and it would be absurd to say that there is nothing in common between such facts and other facts. Since it cannot be doubted that our decisions about norms, i.e. the norms we adopt, clearly depend upon certain psychological facts, such as the influence of our upbringing, it seems to be absurd to postulate a dualism of facts and decisions, or to say that decisions cannot be derived from facts. This objection can be answered by pointing out that we can speak of a 'decision' in two different senses. We may speak of a certain decision which has been submitted, or considered, or reached, or been decided upon; or alternatively, we may speak of an act of deciding and call this a 'decision'. Only in the second sense can we describe a decision as a fact. The situation is analogous with a number of other expressions. In one sense, we may speak of a certain resolution which has been submitted to some council, and in the other sense, the council's act of taking it may be spoken of as the council's resolution. Similarly, we may speak of a proposal or a suggestion before us, and on the other hand of the act of proposing or suggestion something, which may also be called 'proposal' or 'suggestion'. An analogous ambiguity is well known in the field of descriptive statements. Let us consider the statement: 'Napoleon died on St. Helena.' It will be useful to distinguish this statement from the fact which it describes, and which we may call the primary fact, viz. the fact that Napoleon died at St. Helena. Now a historian, say Mr. A, when writing the biography of Napoleon, may make the statement mentioned. In doing so, he is describing what we called the primary fact. But there is also a secondary fact, which is altogether different from the primary one, namely the fact that he made this statement; and another historian, Mr. B, when writing the biography of Mr. A, may describe this second fact by saying: 'Mr. A stated that Napoleon died on St. Helena.' The secondary fact described in this way happens to be itself a description. But it is a description in a sense of the word that must be distinguished from the sense in which we called the statement 'Napoleon died on St. Helena' a description. The making of a description, or of a statement, is a sociological or psychological fact. But *the description made is to be distinguished from the fact that it has been made*. It cannot even be derived from this fact; for that would mean that we can validly deduce 'Napoleon died on St. Helena' from 'Mr. A stated that Napoleon died on St. Helena', which obviously we cannot.

In the field of decisions, the situation is analogous. The making of a decision, the adoption of a norm or of a standard, is a fact. But the norm or standard which has been adopted, is not a fact. That most people agree with the norm 'Thou shalt not steal' is a sociological fact. But the norm 'Thou shalt not steal' is not a fact, and can never be inferred from sentences describing facts. This will be seen most clearly when we remember that there are always various and even opposite decisions possible with respect to a certain relevant fact. For instance, in face of the sociological fact that most people adopt the norm 'Thou shalt not steal', it is still possible to decide either to adopt this norm, or to oppose its adoption; it is possible to encourage those who have adopted the norm, or to discourage them, and to persuade them to adopt another norm. To sum up, *it is impossible to derive a sentence stating a norm or a decision or, say, a proposal for a policy from a sentence stating a fact*; this is only another way of saying that it is impossible to derive norms or decisions *or proposals* from facts.[5]

The statement that norms are man-made (man-made not in the sense that they were consciously designed, but in the sense that men can judge and alter them—that is to say, in the sense that the responsibility for them is entirely ours) has often been misunderstood. Nearly all misunderstandings can be traced back to one fundamental misapprehension, namely, to the belief that 'convention' implies 'arbitrariness'; that if we are free to choose any system of norms we like, then one system is just as good as any other. It must, of course, be admitted that the view that norms are conventional or artificial indicates that there will be a certain element of arbitrariness involved, i.e. that there may be different systems of norms between which there is not much to choose (a fact that has been duly emphasized by Protagoras). But artificiality by no means implies full arbitrariness. Mathematical calculi, for instance, or symphonies, or plays, are highly artificial, yet it does not follow that one calculus or symphony or play is just as good as any other. Man has created new worlds—of language, of music, of poetry, of science; and the most important of these is the world of the moral demands, for equality, for freedom, and for helping the weak[6]. When comparing the field of morals with the field of music or of mathematics, I do not wish to imply that these similarities reach very far. There is, more especially, a great difference between moral decisions and decisions in the field of art. Many moral decisions involve the life and death of other men. Decisions in the field of art are much less urgent and important. It is therefore most misleading to say that a man decides for or against slavery as he may decide for or against certain works of music and literature, or that moral decisions are purely matters of taste. Nor are they merely decisions about how to make the world more beautiful, or about other luxuries of this kind; they are decisions of much greater urgency. (With all this, cp. also chapter 9.) Our comparison is only intended to show that the view that moral decisions rest with us does not imply that they are entirely arbitrary.

The view that norms are man-made is also, strangely enough, contested by some who see in this attitude an attack on religion. It must be admitted, of course, that this view is an attack on certain forms of religion, namely, on the religion of blind authority, on magic and tabooism. But I do not think that it is in any way opposed to a religion built upon the idea of personal responsibility and freedom of conscience. I have in mind, of course, especially Christianity, at least as it is usually interpreted in democratic countries; that Christianity which, as against all tabooism, preaches, 'Ye have heard that it was said by them of old time ... But I say unto you ...'; opposing in every case the voice of conscience to mere formal obedience and the fulfilment of the law.

I would not admit that to think of ethical laws as being man-made in this sense is incompatible with the religious view that they are given to us by God. Historically, all ethics undoubtedly begin with religion; but I do not now deal with historical questions. I do not ask who was the first ethical lawgiver. I only maintain that it is we, and we alone, who are responsible for adopting or rejecting some suggested moral laws; it is we who must distinguish between the true prophets and the false prophets. All kinds of norms have been claimed to be God-given. If you accept the 'Christian' ethics of equality and toleration and freedom of conscience only because of its claim to rest upon divine authority, then you build on a weak basis; for it has been only too often claimed that inequality is willed by God, and that we must not be tolerant with unbelievers. If, however, you accept the Christian ethics not because you are commanded to do so but because of your conviction that it is the right decision to take, then it is you who have decided. My insistence that we make the decisions and carry the responsibility must not be taken to imply that we cannot, or must not, be helped by faith, and inspired by tradition or by great examples. Nor does it imply that the creation of moral decisions is merely a 'natural' process, i.e. of the order of physico-chemical processes. In fact, Protagoras, the first critical dualist, taught that nature does not know norms, and that the introduction of norms is due to man, and the most important of human achievements. He thus held that 'institutions and conventions were what raised men above the brutes', as Burnet[7] puts it. But in spite of his insistence that man creates norms, that it is man who is the measure of all things, he believed that man could achieve the creation of norms only with supernatural help. Norms, he taught, are superimposed upon the original or natural state of affairs by man, but with the help of Zeus. It is at Zeus' bidding that Hermes gives to men an understanding of justice and honour; and he distributes this gift to all men equally. The way in which the first clear statement of critical dualism makes room for a religious interpretation of our sense of responsibility shows how little critical dualism is opposed to a religious attitude. A similar approach can be discerned, I believe, in the historical Socrates (see chapter 10) who felt compelled, by his conscience as well as by his religious beliefs, to question all authority, and who searched for the norms in whose justice he could trust. The doctrine of the autonomy of ethics is independent of the problem of religion, but compatible with, or perhaps even necessary for, any religion which respects individual conscience.

IV

So much concerning the dualism of facts and decisions, or the doctrine of the autonomy of ethics, first advocated by Protagoras and Socrates[8]. It is, I believe, indispensable for a reasonable understanding of our social environment. But of course this does not mean that all 'social laws', i.e. all regularities of our social life, are normative and man-imposed. On the contrary, there are important natural laws of social life also. For these, the term *sociological laws* seems appropriate. It is just the fact that in social life we meet with both kinds of laws, natural and normative, which makes it so important to distinguish them clearly.

In speaking of sociological laws or natural laws of social life, I do not think so much of the alleged laws of evolution in which historicists such as Plato are interested, although if there are any such regularities of historical developments, their formulations would certainly fall under the category of sociological laws. Nor do I think so much of the laws of 'human nature', i.e. of psychological and socio-psychological regularities of human behaviour. I have in mind, rather, such laws as are formulated by modern economic theories, for instance, the theory of international trade, or the theory of the trade cycle. These and other important sociological laws are connected with the functioning of *social institutions*. (Cp. chapters 3 and 9.) These laws play a rôle in our social life corresponding to the rôle played in mechanical engineering by, say, the principle of the lever. For institutions, like levers, are needed if we want to achieve anything which goes beyond the power of our muscles. Like machines, institutions multiply our power for good and evil. Like machines, they need intelligent supervision by someone who understands their way of functioning and, most of all, their purpose, since we cannot build them so that they work entirely automatically. Furthermore, their construction needs some knowledge of social regularities which impose limitations upon what can be achieved by institutions[9]. (These limitations are somewhat analogous, for instance, to the law of conservation of energy, which amounts to the statement that we cannot build a perpetual motion machine.) But fundamentally, institutions are always made by establishing the observance of certain norms, designed with a certain aim in mind. This holds especially for institutions which are consciously created; but even those—the vast majority—which arise as the undesigned results of human actions (cp. chapter 14) are the indirect results of purposive actions of some kind or other; and their functioning depends, largely, on the observance of norms. (Even mechanical engines are made, as it were, not only of iron, but by combining iron and norms; i.e. by transforming physical things, but according to certain normative rules, namely their plan or design.) In institutions, normative laws and sociological, i.e. natural, laws are closely interwoven, and it is therefore impossible to understand the functioning of institutions without being able to distinguish between these two. (These remarks are intended to suggest certain problems rather than to give solutions. More especially, the analogy mentioned between institutions and machines must not be interpreted as proposing the theory that institutions *are* machines—in some essentialist sense. Of course they are not machines. And although the thesis is here proposed that we may obtain useful and interesting results if we ask ourselves whether an institution does serve any purpose, and what purposes it may serve, it is not asserted that every institution serves some definite purpose—its essential purpose, as it were.)

V

As indicated before, there are many intermediate steps in the development from a naïve or magical monism to a critical dualism which clearly realizes the distinction between norms and natural laws. Most of these intermediate positions arise from the misapprehension that if a norm is conventional or artificial, it must be wholly arbitrary. To understand Plato's position, which combines elements of them all, it is necessary to make a survey of the three most important of these intermediate positions. They are (1) biological naturalism, (2) ethical or juridical positivism, and (3) psychological or spiritual naturalism. It is interesting that every one of these positions has been used for defending ethical views which are radically opposed to each other; more especially, for defending the worship of power, and for defending the rights of the weak.

(1) Biological naturalism, or more precisely, the biological form of ethical naturalism, is the theory that in spite of the fact that moral laws and the laws of states are arbitrary, there are some eternal unchanging laws of nature from which we can derive such norms. Food habits, i.e. the number of meals, and the kind of food taken, are an example of the arbitrariness of conventions, the biological naturalist may argue; yet there are undoubtedly

certain natural laws in this field. For instance, a man will die if he takes either insufficient or too much food. Thus it seems that just as there are realities behind appearances, so behind our arbitrary conventions there are some unchanging natural laws and especially the laws of biology.

Biological naturalism has been used not only to defend equalitarianism, but also to defend the anti-equalitarian doctrine of the rule of the strong. One of the first to put forward this naturalism was the poet Pindar, who used it to support the theory that the strong should rule. He claimed[10] that it is a law, valid throughout nature, that the stronger does with the weaker whatever he likes. Thus laws which protect the weak are not merely arbitrary but artificial distortions of the true natural law that the strong should be free and the weak should be his slave. The view is discussed a good deal by Plato; it is attacked in the *Gorgias*, a dialogue which is still much influenced by Socrates; in the *Republic*, it is put in the mouth of Thrasymachus, and identified with ethical individualism (see the next chapter); in the *Laws*, Plato is less antagonistic to Pindar's view; but he still contrasts it with the rule of the wisest, which, he says, is a better principle, and just as much in accordance with nature (see also the quotation later in this chapter).

The first to put forward a humanitarian or equalitarian version of biological naturalism was the Sophist Antiphon. To him is due also the identification of nature with truth, and of convention with opinion (or 'delusive opinion'[11]). Antiphon is a radical naturalist. He believes that most norms are not merely arbitrary, but directly contrary to nature. Norms, he says, are imposed from outside, while the rules of nature are inevitable. It is disadvantageous and even dangerous to break man-imposed norms if the breach is observed by those who impose them; but there is no inner necessity attached to them, and nobody needs to be ashamed of breaking them; shame and punishment are only sanctions arbitrarily imposed from outside. On this criticism of conventional morals, Antiphon bases a utilitarian ethics. 'Of the actions here mentioned, one would find many to be contrary to nature. For they involve more suffering where there should be less, and less pleasure where there could be more, and injury where it is unnecessary.'[12] At the same time, he taught the need for self-control. His equalitarianism he formulates as follows: 'The nobly born we revere and adore; but not the lowly born. These are barbarous habits. For as to our natural gifts, we are all on an equal footing, on all points, whether we now happen to be Greeks or Barbarians … We all breathe the air through our mouths and nostrils.'

A similar equalitarianism was voiced by the Sophist Hippias, whom Plato represents as addressing his audience: 'Gentlemen, I believe that we are all kinsmen and friends and fellow-citizens; if not by conventional law, then by nature. For by nature, likeness is an expression of kinship; but conventional law, the tyrant of mankind, compels us to do much that is against nature.'[13] This spirit was bound up with the Athenian movement against slavery (mentioned in chapter 4) to which Euripides gave expression: 'The name alone brings shame upon the slave who can be excellent in every way and truly equal to the free born man.' Elsewhere, he says: 'Man's law of nature is equality.' And Alcidamas, a disciple of Gorgias and a contemporary of Plato, wrote: 'God has made all men free; no man is a slave by nature.' Similar views are also expressed by Lycophron, another member of Gorgias' school: 'The splendour of noble birth is imaginary, and its prerogatives are based upon a mere word.'

Reacting against this great humanitarian movement—the movement of the 'Great Generation', as I shall call it later (chapter 10)—Plato, and his disciple Aristotle, advanced the theory of the biological and moral inequality of man. Greeks and barbarians are unequal by nature; the opposition between them corresponds to that between natural masters and natural slaves. The natural inequality of men is one of the reasons for their living together, for their natural gifts are complementary. Social life begins with natural inequality, and it must continue upon that foundation. I shall discuss these doctrines later in more detail. At present, they may serve to show how biological naturalism can be used to support the most divergent ethical doctrines. In the light of our previous analysis of the impossibility of basing norms upon facts this result is not unexpected.

Such considerations, however, are perhaps not sufficient to defeat a theory as popular as biological naturalism; I therefore propose two more direct criticisms. First, it must be admitted that certain forms of behaviour may be described as more 'natural' than other forms; for instance, going naked or eating only raw food; and some people think that this in itself justifies the choice of these forms. But in this sense it certainly is not natural to interest oneself in art, or science, or even in arguments in favour of naturalism. The choice of conformity with 'nature' as a supreme standard leads ultimately to consequences which few will be prepared to face; it does not lead to a more natural form of civilization, but to beastliness[14]. The second criticism is more important. The biological naturalist assumes that he can derive his norms from the natural laws which determine the conditions of health, etc., if he does not naïvely believe that we need adopt no norms whatever but simply live according to the 'laws of nature'. He overlooks the fact that he makes a choice, a decision; that it is possible that some other people cherish certain things more than their health (for instance, the many who have consciously risked their lives for medical research). And he is therefore mistaken if he believes that he has not made a decision, or that he has derived his norms from biological laws.

(2) Ethical positivism shares with the biological form of ethical naturalism the belief that we must try to reduce norms to facts. But the facts are this time sociological facts, namely, the actual existing norms. Positivism maintains that there are no other norms but the laws which have actually been set up (or 'posited') and which have therefore a positive existence. Other standards are considered as unreal imaginations. The existing laws are the only possible standards of goodness: what is, is good. (Might is right.) 'According to some forms of this theory, it is a gross misunderstanding to believe that the individual can judge the norms of society; rather, it is society which provides the code by which the individual must be judged.

As a matter of historical fact, ethical (or moral, or juridical) positivism has usually been conservative, or even authoritarian; and it has often invoked the authority of God. Its arguments depend, I believe, upon the alleged arbitrariness of norms. We must believe in existing norms, it claims, because there are no better norms which we may find for ourselves. In reply to this it might be asked: What about this norm 'We must believe etc.'? If this is only an existing norm, then it does not count as an argument in favour of these norms; but if it is an appeal to our insight, then it admits that we can, after all, find norms ourselves. And if we are told to accept norms on authority because we cannot judge them, then neither can we judge whether the claims of the authority are justified, or whether we may not follow a false prophet. And if it is held that there are no false prophets because laws are arbitrary anyhow, so that the main thing is to have some laws, then we may ask ourselves why it should be so important to have laws at all; for if there are no further standards, why then should we not choose to have no laws? (These remarks may perhaps indicate the reasons for my belief that authoritarian or conservative principles are usually an expression of ethical nihilism; that is to say, of an extreme moral scepticism, of a distrust of man and of his possibilities.)

While the theory of natural rights has, in the course of history, often been proffered in support of equalitarian and humanitarian ideas, the positivist school was usually in the opposite camp. But this is not much more than an accident. As has been shown, ethical naturalism may be used with very different intentions. (It has recently been used for confusing the whole issue by advertising certain allegedly 'natural' rights and obligations as 'natural laws'.) Conversely, there are also humanitarian and progressive positivists. For if all norms are arbitrary, why not be tolerant? This is a typical attempt to justify a humanitarian attitude along positivist lines.

(3) Psychological or spiritual naturalism is in a way a combination of the two previous views, and it can best be explained by means of an argument against the one-sidedness of these views. The ethical positivist is right, this argument runs, if he emphasizes that all norms are conventional, i.e. a product of man, and of human society; but he overlooks the fact that they are therefore an expression of the psychological or spiritual nature of man, and of the nature of human society. The biological naturalist is right in assuming that there are certain natural aims or ends, from which we can derive natural norms; but he overlooks the fact that our natural aims are not necessarily such aims as health, pleasure, or food, shelter or propagation. Human nature is such that man, or at least some men, do not want to live by bread alone, that they seek higher aims, spiritual aims. We may thus derive man's true natural aims from his own true nature, which is spiritual, and social. And we may, further, derive the natural norms of life from his natural ends.

This plausible position was, I believe, first formulated by Plato, who was here under the influence of the Socratic doctrine of the soul, i.e. of Socrates' teaching that the spirit matters more than the flesh[15]. Its appeal to our sentiments is undoubtedly very much stronger than that of the other two positions. It can however be combined, like these, with any ethical decision; with a humanitarian attitude as well as with the worship of power. For we can, for instance, decide to treat all men as participating in this spiritual human nature; or we can insist like Heraclitus, that the many 'fill their bellies like the beasts', and are therefore of an inferior nature, and that only a few elect ones are worthy of the spiritual community of men. Accordingly, spiritual naturalism has been much used, and especially by Plato, to justify the natural prerogatives of the 'noble' or 'elect' or 'wise' or of the 'natural leader'. (Plato's attitude is discussed in the following chapters.) On the other hand, it has been used by Christian and other[16] humanitarian forms of ethics, for instance by Paine and by Kant, to demand the recognition of the 'natural rights' of every human individual. It is clear that spiritual naturalism can be used to defend any 'positive', i.e. existing, norm. For it can always be argued that these norms would not be in force if they did not express some traits of human nature. In this way, spiritual naturalism can, in practical problems, become one with positivism, in spite of their traditional opposition. In fact, this form of naturalism is so wide and so vague that it may be used to defend anything. There is nothing that has ever occurred to man which could not be claimed to be 'natural'; for if it were not in his nature, how could it have occurred to him?

Looking back at this brief survey, we may perhaps discern two main tendencies which stand in the way of adopting a critical dualism. The first is a general tendency towards monism[17], that is to say, towards the reduction of norms to facts. The second lies deeper, and it possibly forms the background of the first. It is based upon our fear of admitting to ourselves that the responsibility for our ethical decisions is entirely ours and cannot be shifted to anybody else; neither to God, nor to nature, nor to society, nor to history. All these ethical theories attempt to find somebody, or perhaps some argument, to take the burden from us[18]. But we cannot shirk this responsibility. Whatever authority we may accept, it is we who accept it. We only deceive ourselves if we do not realize this simple point.

VI

We now turn to a more detailed analysis of Plato's naturalism and its relation to his historicism. Plato, of course, does not always use the term 'nature' in the same sense. The most important meaning which he attaches to it is, I believe, practically identical with that which he attaches to the term 'essence'. This way of using the term 'nature' still survives among essentialists even in our day; they still speak, for instance, of the nature of mathematics, or of the nature of inductive inference, or of the 'nature of happiness and misery'[19]. When used by Plato in this way, 'nature' means nearly the same as 'Form' or 'Idea'; for the Form or Idea of a thing, as shown above, is also its essence. The main difference between natures and Forms or Ideas seems to be this. The Form or Idea of a sensible thing is, as we have seen, not in that thing, but separated from it; it is its forefather, its primogenitor; but this Form or father passes something on to the sensible things which are its offspring or race, namely, their nature. This 'nature' is thus the inborn or original quality of a thing, and in so far, its inherent essence; it is the original power or disposition of a thing, and it determines those of its properties which are the basis of its resemblance to, or of its innate participation in, its Form or Idea.

'Natural' is, accordingly, what is innate or original or divine in a thing, while 'artificial' is that which has been later changed by man or added or imposed by him, through external compulsion. Plato frequently insists that all products of human 'art' at their best are only copies of 'natural' sensible things. But since these in turn are only copies of the divine Forms or Ideas, the products of art are only copies of copies, twice removed from reality, and therefore less good, less real, and less true[20] than even the (natural) things in flux. We see from this that Plato agrees with Antiphon[21] in at least one point, namely in assuming that the opposition between nature and convention or art corresponds to that between truth and falsehood, between reality and appearance, between primary or original and secondary or man-made things, and to that between the objects of rational knowledge and those of delusive opinion. The opposition corresponds also, according to Plato, to that between 'the offspring of divine workmanship' or 'the products of divine art', and 'what man makes out of them, i.e. the products of human art'.[22] All those things whose intrinsic value Plato wishes to emphasize he therefore claims to be natural as opposed to artificial. Thus he insists in the *Laws* that the soul has to be considered prior to all material things, and that it must therefore be said to exist by nature: 'Nearly everybody ... is ignorant of the power of the soul, and especially of her origin. They do not know that she is among the first of things, and prior to all bodies ... In using the word "nature" one wants to describe the things that were created first; but if it turns out that it is the soul which is prior to other things (and not, perhaps, fire or air), ... then the soul, beyond all others, may be asserted to exist by nature, in the truest sense of the word.'[23] (Plato here re-affirms his old theory that the soul is more closely akin to the Forms or Ideas than the body; a theory which is also the basis of his doctrine of immortality.)

But Plato not only teaches that the soul is prior to other things and therefore exists 'by nature'; he uses the term 'nature', if applied to man, frequently also as a name for spiritual powers or gifts or natural talents, so that we can say that a man's 'nature' is much the same as his 'soul'; it is the divine principle by which he participates in the Form or Idea, in the divine primogenitor of his race. And the term 'race', again, is frequently used in a very similar sense. Since a 'race' is united by being the offspring of the same primogenitor, it must also be united by a common nature. Thus the terms 'nature' and 'race' are frequently used by Plato as synonyms, for instance, when he speaks of the 'race of philosophers' and of those who have 'philosophic natures'; so that both these terms are closely akin to the terms 'essence' and 'soul'.

Plato's theory of 'nature' opens another approach to his historicist methodology. Since it seems to be the task of science in general to examine the true nature of its objects, it is the task of a social or political science to examine the nature of human society, and of the state. But the nature of a thing, according to Plato, is its origin; or at least it is determined by its origin. Thus the method of any science will be the investigation of the origin of things (of their 'causes'). This principle, when applied to the science of society and of politics, leads to the demand that the origin of society and of the state must be examined. History therefore is not studied for its own sake but serves as *the* method of the social sciences. *This is the historicist methodology*.

What is the nature of human society, of the state? According to historicist methods, this fundamental question of sociology must be reformulated in this way: what is the origin of society and of the state? The reply given by Plato in the *Republic* as well as in the *Laws*[24], agrees with the position described above as spiritual naturalism. The origin of society is a convention, a *social contract*. But it is not only that; it is, rather, a natural convention, i.e. a convention which is based upon human nature, and more precisely, upon the social nature of man.

This social nature of man has its origin in the *imperfection of the human individual*. In opposition to Socrates[25], Plato teaches that the human individual cannot be self-sufficient, owing to the limitations inherent in human nature. Although Plato insists that there are very different degrees of human perfection, it turns out that even the very few comparatively perfect men still depend upon others (who are less perfect); if for nothing else, then for having the dirty work, the manual work, done by them[26]. In this way, even the 'rare and uncommon natures' who approach perfection depend upon society, upon the state. They can reach perfection only through the state and in the state; the perfect state must offer them the proper 'social habitat', without which they must grow corrupt and degenerate. The state therefore must be placed higher than the individual since only the state can be self-sufficient ('autark'), perfect, and able to make good the necessary imperfection of the individual.

Society and the individual are thus interdependent. The one owes its existence to the other. Society owes its existence to human nature, and especially to its lack of self-sufficiency; and the individual owes his existence to society, since he is not self-sufficient. But within this relationship of interdependence, the superiority of the state over the individual manifests itself in various ways; for instance, in the fact that the seed of the decay and disunion of a perfect state does not spring up in the state itself, but rather in its individuals; it is rooted in the imperfection of the human soul, of human nature; or more precisely, in the fact that the race of men is liable to degenerate. To this point, the origin of political decay, and its dependence upon the degeneration of human nature, I shall return presently; but I wish first to make a few comments on some of the characteristics of Plato's sociology, especially upon his version of the theory of the social contract, and upon his view of the state as a super-individual, i.e. his version of the biological or organic theory of the state.

Whether Protagoras first proposed a theory that laws originate with a social contract, or whether Lycophron (whose theory will be discussed in the next chapter) was the first to do so, is not certain. In any case, the idea is closely related to Protagoras' conventionalism. The fact that Plato consciously combined some conventionalist ideas, and even a version of the contract theory, with his naturalism, is in itself an indication that conventionalism in its original form did not maintain that laws are wholly arbitrary; and Plato's remarks on Protagoras confirm this[27]. How conscious Plato was of a conventionalist element in his version of naturalism can be seen from a passage in the *Laws*. Plato there gives a list of the various principles upon which political authority might be based, mentioning Pindar's biological naturalism (see above), i.e. 'the principle that the stronger shall rule and the weaker be ruled', which he describes as a principle 'according to nature, as the Theban poet Pindar once stated'. Plato contrasts this principle with another which he recommends by showing that it combines conventionalism with naturalism: 'But there is also a ... claim which is the greatest principle of all, namely, that the wise shall lead and rule, and that the ignorant shall follow; and this, O Pindar, wisest of poets, is surely not contrary to nature, but according to nature; for what it demands is not external compulsion but the truly natural sovereignty of a law which is based upon mutual consent.'[28]

In the *Republic* we find elements of the conventionalist contract theory in a similar way combined with elements of naturalism (and utilitarianism). 'The city originates', we hear there, 'because we are not self-sufficient; ... or is there another origin of settlement in cities? ... Men gather into one settlement many ... helpers, since they need many things ... And when they share their goods with one another, the one giving, the other partaking, does not every one expect in this way to further his own interest?'[29] Thus the inhabitants gather in order that each may further his own interest; which is an element of the contract theory. But behind this stands the fact that they are not self-sufficient, a fact of human nature; which is an element of naturalism. And this element is developed further. 'By nature, no two of us are exactly alike. Each has his peculiar nature, some being fit for one kind of work and some for another ... Is it better that a man should work in many crafts or that he should work in one only? ... Surely, more will be produced and better and more easily if each man works in one occupation only, according to his natural gifts.'

In this way, the economic principle of the division of labour is introduced (reminding us of the affinity between Plato's historicism and the materialist interpretation of history). But this principle is based here upon an element of biological naturalism, namely, upon the natural inequality of men. At first, this idea is introduced inconspicuously and, as it were, innocently. But we shall see in the next chapter that it has far-reaching consequences; indeed, the only really important division of labour turns out to be that between rulers and ruled, claimed to be based upon the natural inequality of masters and slaves, of wise and ignorant.

We have seen that there is a considerable element of conventionalism as well as of biological naturalism in Plato's position; an observation which is not surprising when we consider that this position is, on the whole, that of spiritual naturalism which, because of its vagueness, easily allows for all such combinations. This spiritual version of naturalism is perhaps best formulated in the *Laws*. 'Men say', says Plato, 'that the greatest and most beautiful things are natural … and the lesser things artificial.' So far he agrees; but he then attacks the materialists who say 'that fire and water, and earth and air, all exist by nature … and that all normative laws are altogether unnatural and artificial and based upon superstitions which are not true.' Against this view, he shows first, that it is not bodies nor elements, but the soul which truly 'exists by nature'[30] (I have quoted this passage above); and from this he concludes that order, and law, must also be by nature, since they spring from the soul: 'If the soul is prior to the body, then things dependent upon the soul' (i.e. spiritual matters) 'are also prior to those dependent upon body … And the soul orders and directs all things.' This supplies the theoretical background for the doctrine that 'laws and purposeful institutions exist by nature, and not by anything lower than nature, since they are born of reason and true thought.' This is a clear statement of spiritual naturalism; and it is combined as well with positivist beliefs of a conservative kind: 'Thoughtful and prudent legislation will find a most powerful help because the laws will remain unchanged once they have been laid down in writing.'

From all this it can be seen that arguments derived from Plato's spiritual naturalism are quite incapable of helping to answer any question which may arise concerning the 'just' or 'natural' character of any particular law. Spiritual naturalism is much too vague to be applied to any practical problem. It cannot do much beyond providing some general arguments in favour of conservativism. In practice, everything is left to the wisdom of the great lawgiver (a godlike philosopher, whose picture, especially in the *Laws*, is undoubtedly a self-portrait; see also chapter 8). As opposed to his spiritual naturalism, however, Plato's theory of the interdependence of society and the individual furnishes more concrete results; and so does his anti-equalitarian biological naturalism.

VII

It has been indicated above that because of its self-sufficiency, the ideal state appears to Plato as the perfect individual, and the individual citizen, accordingly, as an imperfect copy of the state. This view which makes of the state a kind of super-organism or Leviathan introduces into the occident the so-called organic or biological theory of the state. The principle of this theory will be criticized later[31]. Here I wish first to draw attention to the fact that Plato does not defend the theory, and indeed hardly formulates it explicitly. But it is clearly enough implied; in fact, the fundamental analogy between the state and the human individual is one of the standard topics of the *Republic*. It is worth mentioning, in this connection, that the analogy serves to further the analysis of the individual rather than that of the state. One could perhaps defend the view that Plato (perhaps under the influence of Alcmaeon) does not offer so much a biological theory of the state as a political theory of the human individual[32]. This view, I think, is fully in accordance with his doctrine that the individual is lower than the state, and a kind of imperfect copy of it. In the very place in which Plato introduces his fundamental analogy, it is used in this way; that is to say, as a method of explaining and elucidating the individual. The city, it is said, is greater than the individual, and therefore easier to examine. Plato gives this as his reason for suggesting that 'we should begin our inquiry' (namely, into the nature of justice) 'in the city, and continue it afterwards in the individual, always watching for points of similarity ... May we not expect in this way to discern more easily what we are looking for?'

From his way of introducing it we can see that Plato (and perhaps his readers) took his fundamental analogy for granted. This may well be a symptom of nostalgia, of a longing for a unified and harmonious, an 'organic' state: for a society of a more primitive kind. (See chapter 10.) The city state ought to remain small, he says, and should grow only as long as its increase does not endanger its unity. The whole city should, by its nature, be one, and not many.[33] Plato thus emphasizes the 'oneness' or individuality of his city. But he also emphasizes the 'manyness' of the human individual. In his analysis of the individual soul, and of its division into three parts, reason, energy, and animal instincts, corresponding to the three classes of his state, the guardians, warriors, and workers (who still continue to 'fill their bellies like the beasts', as Heraclitus had said), Plato goes so far as to oppose these parts to one another as if they were 'distinct and conflicting persons'[34]. 'We are thus told', says Grote, 'that though man is apparently One, he is in reality Many ... though the perfect Commonwealth is apparently Many, it is in reality One.' It is clear that this corresponds to the Ideal character of the state of which the individual is a kind of imperfect copy. Such an emphasis upon oneness and wholeness—especially of the state; or perhaps of the world—may be described as 'holism'. Plato's holism, I believe, is closely related to the tribal collectivism mentioned in earlier chapters. Plato was longing for the lost unity of tribal life. A life of change, in the midst of a social revolution, appeared to him unreal. Only a stable whole, the permanent collective, has reality, not the passing individuals. It is 'natural' for the individual to subserve the whole, which is no mere assembly of individuals, but a 'natural' unit of a higher order.

Plato gives many excellent sociological descriptions of this 'natural', i.e. tribal and collectivist, mode of social life: 'The law', he writes in the *Republic*, '... is designed to bring about the welfare of the state as a whole, fitting the citizens into one unit, by means of both persuasion and force. It makes them all share in whatever benefit each of them can contribute to the community. And it is actually the law which creates for the state men of the right frame of mind; not for the purpose of letting them loose, so that everybody can go his own way, but in order to utilize them all for welding the city together.'[35] That there is in this holism an emotional æstheticism, a longing for beauty, can be seen, for instance, from a remark in the *Laws*: 'Every artist ... executes the part for the sake of the whole, and not the whole for the sake of the part.' At the same place, we also find a truly classical formulation of political holism: 'You are created for the sake of the whole, and not the whole for the sake of you.' Within this whole, the different individuals, and groups of individuals, with their natural inequalities, must render their specific and very unequal services.

All this would indicate that Plato's theory was a form of the organic theory of the state, even if he had not sometimes spoken of the state as an organism. But since he did this, there can be no doubt left that he must be described as an exponent, or rather, as one of the originators, of this theory. His version of this theory may be characterized as a personalist or psychological one, since he describes the state not in a general way as similar to some organism or other, but as analogous to the human individual, and more specifically to the human soul. Especially the disease of the state, the dissolution of its unity, corresponds to the disease of the human soul, of human nature. In fact, the disease of the state is not only correlated with, but is directly produced by, the corruption of human nature, more especially of the members of the ruling class. Every single one of the typical stages in the degeneration of the state is brought about by a corresponding stage in the degeneration of the human soul, of human nature, of the human race. And since this moral degeneration is interpreted as based upon racial degeneration, we might say that the biological element in Plato's naturalism turns out, in the end, to have the most important part in the foundation of his historicism. For the history of the downfall of the first or perfect state is nothing but the history of the biological degeneration of the race of men.

VIII

It was mentioned in the last chapter that the problem of the beginning of change and decay is one of the major difficulties of Plato's historicist theory of society. The first, the natural and perfect city-state, cannot be supposed to carry within itself the germ of dissolution, 'for a city which carries within itself the germ of dissolution is for that very reason imperfect'[36]. Plato tries to get over the difficulty by laying the blame on his universally valid historical, biological, and perhaps even cosmological, evolutionary law of degeneration, rather than on the particular constitution of the first or perfect city[37]: 'Everything that has been generated must decay.' But this general theory does not provide a fully satisfactory solution, for it does not explain why even a sufficiently perfect state cannot escape the law of decay. And indeed, Plato hints that historical decay might have been avoided[38], had the rulers of the first or natural state been trained philosophers. But they were not. They were not trained (as he demands that the rulers of his heavenly city should be) in mathematics and dialectics; and in order to avoid degeneration, they would have needed to be initiated into the higher mysteries of eugenics, of the science of 'keeping pure the race of the guardians', and of avoiding the mixture of the noble metals in their veins with the base metals of the workers. But these higher mysteries are difficult to reveal. Plato distinguishes sharply, in the fields of mathematics, acoustics, and astronomy, between mere (delusive) opinion which is tainted by experience, and which cannot reach exactness, and is altogether on a low level, and pure rational knowledge, which is free from sensual experience and exact. This distinction he applies also to the field of eugenics. A merely empirical art of breeding cannot be precise, i.e. it cannot keep the race perfectly pure. This explains the downfall of the original city which is so good, i.e. so similar to its Form or Idea, that 'a city thus constituted can hardly be shaken'. 'But this', Plato continues, 'is the way it dissolves', and he proceeds to outline his theory of breeding, of the Number, and of the Fall of Man.

All plants and animals, he tells us, must be bred according to definite periods of time, if barrenness and degeneration are to be avoided. Some knowledge of these periods, which are connected with the length of the life of the race, will be available to the rulers of the best state, and they will apply it to the breeding of the master race. It will not, however, be rational, but only empirical knowledge; it will be '*calculation aided by (or based on) perception*' (cp. the next quotation). But as we have just seen, perception and experience can never be exact and reliable, since its objects are not the pure Forms or Ideas, but the world of things in flux; and since the guardians have no better kind of knowledge at their disposal, the breed cannot be kept pure, and racial degeneration must creep in. This is how Plato explains the matter: 'Concerning your own race' (i.e. the race of men, as opposed to animals), 'the rulers of the city whom you have trained may be wise enough; but since they are using calculation aided by perception, they will not hit, accidentally, upon the way of getting either good offspring, or none at all.' Lacking a purely rational method,[39] 'they will blunder, and some day they will beget children in the wrong way'. In what follows next, Plato hints, rather mysteriously, that there is now a way to avoid this through the discovery of a purely rational and mathematical science which possesses in the 'Platonic Number' (a number determining the True Period of the human race) the key to the master law of higher eugenics. But since the guardians of old times were ignorant of Pythagorean number-mysticism, and with it, of this key to the higher knowledge of breeding, the otherwise perfect natural state could not escape decay. After partially revealing the secret of his mysterious Number, Plato continues: 'This … number is master over better or worse births; and whenever these guardians of yours—who are ignorant of these matters—unite bride and bridegroom in the wrong manner[40], the children will have neither good natures nor good luck. Even the best of them … will prove unworthy when succeeding to the power of their fathers; and as soon as they are guardians, they will not listen to us any more'—that is, in matters of musical and gymnastic education, and, as Plato especially emphasizes, in the supervision of breeding. 'Hence rulers will be appointed who are not altogether fit for their task as guardians; namely to watch, and to test, the metals in the races (which are Hesiod's races as well as yours), gold and silver and bronze and iron. So iron will mingle with silver and bronze with gold and from this mixture, Variation will be born and absurd Irregularity; and whenever these are born they will beget Strife and Hostility. And this is how we must describe the ancestry and birth of Dissension, wherever she arises.'

This is Plato's story of the Number and of the Fall of Man. It is the basis of his historicist sociology, especially of his fundamental law of social revolutions discussed in the last chapter[41]. For racial degeneration explains the origin of disunion in the ruling class, and with it, the origin of all historical development. The internal disunion of human nature, the schism of the soul, leads to the schism of the ruling class. And as with Heraclitus, war, class war, is the father and promoter of all change, and of the history of man, which is nothing but the history of the breakdown of society. We see that Plato's idealist historicism ultimately rests not upon a spiritual, but upon a biological basis; it rests upon a kind of meta-biology[42] of the race of men. Plato was not only a naturalist who proffered a biological theory of the state, he was also the first to proffer a biological and racial theory of social dynamics, of political history. 'The Platonic Number', says Adam[43], 'is thus the setting in which Plato's "Philosophy of History" is framed.'

It is, I think, appropriate to conclude this sketch of Plato's descriptive sociology with a summary and an evaluation.

Plato succeeded in giving an astonishingly true, though of course somewhat idealized, reconstruction of an early Greek tribal and collectivist society similar to that of Sparta. An analysis of the forces, especially the economic forces, which threaten the stability of such a society, enables him to describe the general policy as well as the social institutions which are necessary for arresting it. And he gives, furthermore, a rational reconstruction of the economic and historical development of the Greek city-states.

These achievements are impaired by his hatred of the society in which he was living, and by his romantic love for the old tribal form of social life. It is this attitude which led him to formulate an untenable law of historical development, namely, the law of universal degeneration or decay. And the same attitude is also responsible for the irrational, fantastic, and romantic elements of his otherwise excellent analysis. On the other hand, it was just his personal interest and his partiality which sharpened his eye and so made his achievements possible. He derived his historicist theory from the fantastic philosophical doctrine that the changing visible world is only a decaying copy of an unchanging invisible world. But this ingenious attempt to combine a historicist pessimism with an ontological optimism leads, when elaborated, to difficulties. These difficulties forced upon him the adoption of a biological naturalism, leading (together with 'psychologism'[44], i.e. the theory that society depends on the 'human nature' of its members) to mysticism and superstition, culminating in a pseudo-rational mathematical theory of breeding. They even endangered the impressive unity of his theoretical edifice.

IX

Looking back at this edifice, we may briefly consider its ground-plan[45]. This ground-plan, conceived by a great architect, exhibits a fundamental metaphysical dualism in Plato's thought. In the field of logic, this dualism presents itself as the opposition between the universal and the particular. In the field of mathematical speculation, it presents itself as the opposition between the One and the Many. In the field of epistemology, it is the opposition between rational knowledge based on pure thought, and opinion based on particular experiences. In the field of ontology, it is the opposition between the one, original, invariable, and true, reality, and the many, varying, and delusive, appearances; between pure being and becoming, or more precisely, changing. In the field of cosmology, it is the opposition between that which generates and that which is generated, and which must decay. In ethics, it is the opposition between the good, i.e. that which preserves, and the evil, i.e. that which corrupts. In politics, it is the opposition between the one collective, the state, which may attain perfection and autarchy, and the great mass of the people—the many individuals, the particular men who must remain imperfect and dependent, and whose particularity is to be suppressed for the sake of the unity of the state (see the next chapter). And this whole dualist philosophy, I believe, originated from the urgent wish to explain the contrast between the vision of an ideal society, and the hateful actual state of affairs in the social field—the contrast between a stable society, and a society in the process of revolution.

Plato's Political Programme

6

TOTALITARIAN JUSTICE

The analysis of Plato's sociology makes it easy to present his political programme. His fundamental demands can be expressed in either of two formulæ, the first corresponding to his idealist theory of change and rest, the second to his naturalism. The idealist formula is: *Arrest all political change!* Change is evil, rest divine[1]. All change can be arrested if the state is made an exact copy of its original, i.e. of the Form or Idea of the city. Should it be asked how this is practicable, we can reply with the naturalistic formula: *Back to nature!* Back to the original state of our forefathers, the primitive state founded in accordance with human nature, and therefore stable; back to the tribal patriarchy of the time before the Fall, to the natural class rule of the wise few over the ignorant many.

I believe that practically all the elements of Plato's political programme can be derived from these demands. They are, in turn, based upon his historicism; and they have to be combined with his sociological doctrines concerning the conditions for the stability of class rule. The principal elements I have in mind are:

(a) The strict division of the classes; i.e. the ruling class consisting of herdsmen and watch-dogs must be strictly separated from the human cattle.

(b) The identification of the fate of the state with that of the ruling class; the exclusive interest in this class, and in its unity; and subservient to this unity, the rigid rules for breeding and educating this class, and the strict supervision and collectivization of the interests of its members.

From these principal elements, others can be derived, for instance the following:

(c) The ruling class has a monopoly of things like military virtues and training, and of the right to carry arms and to receive education of any kind; but it is excluded from any participation in economic activities, and especially from earning money.
(d) There must be a censorship of all intellectual activities of the ruling class, and a continual propaganda aiming at moulding and unifying their minds. All innovation in education, legislation, and religion must be prevented or suppressed.
(e) The state must be self-sufficient. It must aim at economic autarchy; for otherwise the rulers would either be dependent upon traders, or become traders themselves. The first of these alternatives would undermine their power, the second their unity and the stability of the state.

This programme can, I think, be fairly described as totalitarian. And it is certainly founded upon a historicist sociology.

But is that all? Are there no other features of Plato's programme, elements which are neither totalitarian nor founded upon historicism? What about Plato's ardent desire for Goodness and Beauty, or his love of Wisdom and of Truth? What about his demand that the wise, the philosophers, should rule? What about his hopes of making the citizens of his state virtuous as well as happy? And what about his demand that the state should be founded upon Justice? Even writers who criticize Plato believe that his political doctrine, in spite of certain similarities, is clearly distinguished from modern totalitarianism by these aims of his, the happiness of the citizens, and the rule of justice. Crossman, for instance, whose critical attitude can be gauged from his remark that 'Plato's philosophy is the most savage and most profound attack upon liberal ideas which history can show'[2], seems still to believe that Plato's plan is 'the building of a perfect state in which every citizen is really happy'. Another example is Joad who discusses the similarities between Plato's programme and that of fascism at some length, but who asserts that there are fundamental differences, since in Plato's best state 'the ordinary man … achieves such happiness as appertains to his nature', and since this state is built upon the ideas of 'an absolute good and an absolute justice'.

In spite of such arguments I believe that Plato's political programme, far from being morally superior to totalitarianism, is fundamentally identical with it. I believe that the objections against this view are based upon an ancient and deep-rooted prejudice in favour of idealizing Plato. That

Crossman has done much to point out and to destroy this inclination may be seen from this statement: 'Before the Great War ... Plato ... was rarely condemned outright as a reactionary, resolutely opposed to every principle of the liberal creed. Instead he was elevated to a higher rank, ... removed from practical life, dreaming of a transcendent City of God.'[3] Crossman himself, however, is not free from that tendency which he so clearly exposes. It is interesting that this tendency could persist for such a long time in spite of the fact that Grote and Gomperz had pointed out the reactionary character of some doctrines of the *Republic* and the *Laws*. But even they did not see all the implications of these doctrines; they never doubted that Plato was, fundamentally, a humanitarian. And their adverse criticism was ignored, or interpreted as a failure to understand and to appreciate Plato who was by Christians considered a 'Christian before Christ', and by revolutionaries a revolutionary. This kind of complete faith in Plato is undoubtedly still dominant, and Field, for instance, finds it necessary to warn his readers that 'we shall misunderstand Plato entirely if we think of him as a revolutionary thinker'. This is, of course, very true; and it would clearly be pointless if the tendency to make of Plato a revolutionary thinker, or at least a progressivist, were not fairly widespread. But Field himself has the same kind of faith in Plato; for when he goes on to say that Plato was 'in strong opposition to the new and subversive tendencies' of his time, then surely he accepts too readily Plato's testimony for the subversiveness of these new tendencies. The enemies of freedom have always charged its defenders with subversion. And nearly always they have succeeded in persuading the guileless and well-meaning.

The idealization of the great idealist permeates not only the interpretations of Plato's writings, but also the translations. Drastic remarks of Plato's which do not fit the translator's views of what a humanitarian should say are frequently either toned down or misunderstood. This tendency begins with the translation of the very title of Plato's so-called 'Republic'. What comes first to our mind when hearing this title is that the author must be a liberal, if not a revolutionary. But the title 'Republic' is, quite simply, the English form of the Latin rendering of a Greek word that had no associations of this kind, and whose proper English translation would be 'The Constitution' or 'The City State' or 'The State'. The traditional translation 'The Republic' has undoubtedly contributed to the general conviction that Plato could not have been a reactionary.

In view of all that Plato says about Goodness and Justice and the other Ideas mentioned, my thesis that his political demands are purely totalitarian and anti-humanitarian needs to be defended. In order to undertake this defence, I shall, for the next four chapters, break off the analysis of historicism, and concentrate upon a critical examination of the ethical Ideas mentioned, and of their part in Plato's political demands. In the present chapter, I shall examine the Idea of Justice; in the three following chapters, the doctrine that the wisest and best should rule, and the Ideas of Truth, Wisdom, Goodness, and Beauty.

I

What do we really mean when we speak of 'Justice'? I do not think that verbal questions of this kind are particularly important, or that it is possible to make a definite answer to them, since such terms are always used in various senses. However, I think that most of us, especially those whose general outlook is humanitarian, mean something like this: (*a*) an equal distribution of the burden of citizenship, i.e. of those limitations of freedom which are necessary in social life[4]; (*b*) equal treatment of the citizens before the law, provided, of course, that (*c*) the laws show neither favour nor disfavour towards individual citizens or groups or classes; (*d*) impartiality of the courts of justice; and (*e*) an equal share in the advantages (and not only in the burden) which membership of the state may offer to its citizens. If Plato had meant by 'justice' anything of this kind, then my claim that his programme is purely totalitarian would certainly be wrong and all those would be right who believe that Plato's politics rested upon an acceptable humanitarian basis. But the fact is that he meant by 'justice' something entirely different.

What did Plato mean by 'justice'? I assert that in the *Republic* he used the term 'just' as a synonym for 'that which is in the interest of the best state'. And what is in the interest of this best state? To arrest all change, by the maintenance of a rigid class division and class rule. If I am right in this interpretation, then we should have to say that Plato's demand for justice leaves his political programme at the level of totalitarianism; and we should have to conclude that we must guard against the danger of being impressed by mere words.

Justice is the central topic of the *Republic*; in fact, 'On Justice' is its traditional sub-title. In his enquiry into the nature of justice, Plato makes use of the method mentioned[5] in the last chapter; he first tries to search for this Idea in the state, and then attempts to apply the result to the individual. One cannot say that Plato's question 'What is justice?' quickly finds an answer, for it is only given in the Fourth Book. The considerations which lead up to it will be analysed more fully later in this chapter. Briefly, they are these.

The city is founded upon human nature, its needs, and its limitations[6]. 'We have stated, and, you will remember, repeated over and over again that each man in our city should do one work only; namely, that work for which his nature is naturally best fitted.' From this Plato concludes that everyone should mind his own business; that the carpenter should confine himself to carpentering, the shoemaker to making shoes. Not much harm is done, however, if two workers change their natural places. 'But should anyone who is by nature a worker (or else a member of the money-earning class) ... manage to get into the warrior class; or should a warrior get into the class of the guardians, without being worthy of it; ... then this kind of change and of underhand plotting would mean the downfall of the city.' From this argument which is closely related to the principle that the carrying of arms should be a class prerogative, Plato draws his final conclusion that any changing or intermingling within the three classes must be injustice, and that the opposite, therefore, is justice: 'When each class in the city minds its own business, the money-earning class as well as the auxiliaries and the guardians, then this will be justice.' This conclusion is reaffirmed and summed up a little later: 'The city is just ... if each of its three classes attends to its own work.' But this statement means that Plato identifies justice with the principle of class rule and of class privilege. For the principle that every class should attend to its own business means, briefly and bluntly, that *the state is just if the ruler rules, if the worker works, and*[7] *if the slave slaves*.

It will be seen that Plato's concept of justice is fundamentally different from our ordinary view as analysed above. Plato calls class privilege 'just', while we usually mean by justice rather the absence of such privilege. But the difference goes further than that. We mean by justice some kind of equality in the treatment of *individuals*, while Plato considers justice not as a relationship between individuals, but as a property of the *whole state*, based upon a relationship between its classes. The state is just if it is healthy, strong, united—stable.

II

But was Plato perhaps right? Does 'justice' perhaps mean what he says? I do not intend to discuss such a question. If anyone should hold that 'justice' means the unchallenged rule of one class, then I should simply reply that I am all for injustice. In other words, I believe that nothing depends upon words, and everything upon our practical demands or upon the proposals for framing our policy which we decide to adopt. Behind Plato's definition of justice stands, fundamentally, his demand for a totalitarian class rule, and his decision to bring it about.

But was he not right in a different sense? Did his idea of justice perhaps correspond to the Greek way of using this word? Did the Greeks perhaps mean by 'justice', something holistic, like the 'health of the state', and is it not utterly unfair and unhistorical to expect from Plato an anticipation of our modern idea of justice as equality of the citizens before the law? This question, indeed, has been answered in the affirmative, and the claim has been made that Plato's holistic idea of 'social justice' is characteristic of the traditional Greek outlook, of the 'Greek genius' which 'was not, like the Roman, specifically legal', but rather 'specifically metaphysical'[8]. But this claim is untenable. As a matter of fact, the Greek way of using the word 'justice' was indeed surprisingly similar to our own individualistic and equalitarian usage.

In order to show this, I may first refer to Plato himself who, in the dialogue *Gorgias* (which is earlier than the *Republic*), speaks of the view that 'justice is equality' as one held by the great mass of the people, and as one which agrees not only with 'convention', but with 'nature itself'. I may further quote Aristotle, another opponent of equalitarianism, who, under the influence of Plato's naturalism, elaborated among other things the theory that some men are by nature born to slave[9]. Nobody could be less interested in spreading an equalitarian and individualistic interpretation of the term 'justice'. But when speaking of the judge, whom he describes as 'a personification of that which is just', Aristotle says that it is the task of the judge to 'restore equality'. He tells us that 'all men think justice to be a kind of equality', an equality, namely, which 'pertains to persons'. He even thinks (but here he is wrong) that the Greek word for 'justice' is to be derived from a root that means 'equal division'. (The view that 'justice' means a kind of 'equality in the division of spoils and honours to the citizens' agrees with Plato's views in the *Laws*, where two kinds of equality in the distribution of spoils and honours are distinguished—'numerical' or 'arithmetical' equality and 'proportionate' equality; the second of which takes account of the degree in which the persons in question possess virtue, breeding, and wealth—and where this proportionate equality is said to constitute 'political justice'.) And when Aristotle discusses the principles of democracy, he says that 'democratic justice is the application of the principle of arithmetical equality (as distinct from proportionate equality).' All this is certainly not merely his personal impression of the meaning of justice, nor is it perhaps only a description of the way in which the word was used, after Plato, under the influence of the *Gorgias* and the *Laws*; it is, rather, the expression of a universal and ancient as well as popular use of the word 'justice'.[10]

In view of this evidence, we must say, I think, that the holistic and anti-equalitarian interpretation of justice in the *Republic* was an innovation, and that Plato attempted to present his totalitarian class rule as 'just' while people generally meant by 'justice' the exact opposite.

This result is startling, and opens up a number of questions. Why did Plato claim, in the *Republic*, that justice meant inequality if in general usage, it meant equality? To me the only likely reply seems to be that he wanted to make propaganda for his totalitarian state by persuading the people that it was the 'just' state. But was such an attempt worth his while, considering that it is not words but what we mean by them that matters? Of course it was worth while; this can be seen from the fact that he fully succeeded in persuading his readers, down to our own day, that he was candidly advocating justice, i.e. that justice they were striving for. And it is a fact that he thereby spread doubt and confusion among equalitarians and individualists who, under the influence of his authority, began to ask themselves whether his idea of justice was not truer and better than theirs. Since the word 'justice' symbolizes to us an aim of such importance, and since so many are prepared to endure anything for it, and to do all in their power for its realization, the enlistment of these humanitarian forces, or at least, the paralysing of equalitarianism, was certainly an aim worthy of being pursued by a believer in totalitarianism. But was Plato aware that justice meant so much to men? He was; for he writes in the *Republic*: 'When a man has committed an injustice, … is it not true that his courage refuses to be stirred? … But when he believes that he has suffered injustice, does not his vigour and his wrath flare up at once? And is it not equally true that when fighting on the side of what he believes to be just, he can endure hunger and cold, and any kind of hardship? And does he not hold on until he conquers, persisting in his exalted state until he has either achieved his aim, or perished?'[11]

Reading this, we cannot doubt that Plato knew the power of faith, and, above all, of a faith in justice. Nor can we doubt that the *Republic* must tend to pervert this faith, and to replace it by a directly opposite faith. And in the light of the available evidence, it seems to me most probable that Plato knew very well what he was doing. Equalitarianism was his arch-enemy, and he was out to destroy it; no doubt in the sincere belief that it was a great evil and a great danger. But his attack upon equalitarianism was not an honest attack. Plato did not dare to face the enemy openly.

I proceed to present the evidence in support of this contention.

III

The *Republic* is probably the most elaborate monograph on justice ever written. It examines a variety of views about justice, and it does this in a way which leads us to believe that Plato omitted none of the more important theories known to him. In fact, Plato clearly implies[12] that because of his vain attempts to track it down among the current views, a new search for justice is necessary. Yet in his survey and discussion of the current theories, the view that justice is equality before the law ('*isonomy*') is never mentioned. This omission can be explained only in two ways. Either he overlooked the equalitarian theory[13], or he purposely avoided it. The first possibility seems very unlikely if we consider the care with which the *Republic* is composed, and the necessity for Plato to analyse the theories of his opponents if he was to make a forceful presentation of his own. But this possibility appears even more improbable if we consider the wide popularity of the equalitarian theory. We need not, however, rely upon merely probable arguments since it can be easily shown that Plato was not only acquainted with the equalitarian theory but well aware of its importance when he wrote the *Republic*. As already mentioned in this chapter (in section II), and as will be shown in detail later (in section VIII), equalitarianism played a considerable rôle in the earlier *Gorgias* where it is even defended; and in spite of the fact that the merits or demerits of equalitarianism are nowhere seriously discussed in the *Republic*, Plato did not change his mind regarding its influence, for the *Republic* itself testifies to its popularity. It is there alluded to as a very popular democratic belief; but it is treated only with scorn, and all we hear about it consists of a few sneers and pin-pricks[14], well matched with the abusive attack upon Athenian democracy, and made at a place where justice is not the topic of the discussion. The possibility that the equalitarian theory of justice was overlooked by Plato is therefore ruled out, and so is the possibility that he did not see that a discussion of an influential theory diametrically opposed to his own was requisite. The fact that his silence in the *Republic* is broken only by a few jocular remarks (apparently he thought them too good to be suppressed[15]) can be explained only as a conscious refusal to discuss it. In view of all that, I do not see how Plato's method of impressing upon his readers the belief that all important theories have been examined can be reconciled with the standards of intellectual honesty; though we must add that his failure is undoubtedly due to his complete devotion to a cause in whose goodness he firmly believed.

In order to appreciate fully the implications of Plato's practically unbroken silence on this issue, we must first see clearly that the equalitarian movement as Plato knew it represented all he hated, and that his own theory, in the *Republic* and in all later works, was largely a reply to the powerful challenge of the new equalitarianism and humanitarianism. To show this, I shall discuss the main principles of the humanitarian movement, and contrast them with the corresponding principles of Platonic totalitarianism.

The humanitarian theory of justice makes three main demands or proposals, namely (*a*) the equalitarian principle proper, i.e. the proposal to eliminate 'natural' privileges, (*b*) the general principle of individualism, and (*c*) the principle that it should be the task and the purpose of the state to protect the freedom of its citizens. To each of these political demands or proposals there corresponds a directly opposite principle of Platonism, namely (a^1) the principle of natural privilege, (b^1) the general principle of holism or collectivism, and (c^1) the principle that it should be the task and the purpose of the individual to maintain, and to strengthen, the stability of the state.—I shall discuss these three points in order, devoting to each of them one of the sections IV, V, and VI of this chapter.

IV

Equalitarianism proper is the demand that the citizens of the state should be treated impartially. It is the demand that birth, family connection, or wealth must not influence those who administer the law to the citizens. In other words, it does not recognize any 'natural' privileges, although certain privileges may be conferred by the citizens upon those they trust.

This equalitarian principle had been admirably formulated by Pericles a few years before Plato's birth, in an oration which has been preserved by Thucydides[16]. It will be quoted more fully in chapter 10, but two of its sentences may be given here: 'Our laws', said Pericles, 'afford equal justice to all alike in their private disputes, but we do not ignore the claims of excellence. When a citizen distinguishes himself, then he is preferred to the public service, not as a matter of privilege, but as a reward for merit; and poverty is not a bar ...' These sentences express some of the fundamental aims of the great equalitarian movement which, as we have seen, did not even shrink from attacking slavery. In Pericles' own generation, this movement was represented by Euripides, Antiphon, and Hippias, who have all been quoted in the last chapter, and also by Herodotus[17]. In Plato's generation, it was represented by Alcidamas and Lycophron, both quoted above; another supporter was Antisthenes, who had been one of Socrates' closest friends.

Plato's principle of justice was, of course, diametrically opposed to all this. He demanded natural privileges for the natural leaders. But how did he contest the equalitarian principle? And how did he establish his own demands?

It will be remembered from the last chapter that some of the best-known formulations of the equalitarian demands were couched in the impressive but questionable language of 'natural rights', and that some of their representatives argued in favour of these demands by pointing out the 'natural', i.e. biological, equality of men. We have seen that the argument is irrelevant; that men are equal in some important respects, and unequal in others; and that normative demands cannot be derived from this fact, or from any other fact. It is therefore interesting to note that the naturalist argument was not used by all equalitarians, and that Pericles, for one, did not even allude to it[18].

Plato quickly found that naturalism was a weak spot within the equalitarian doctrine, and he took the fullest advantage of this weakness. To tell men that they are equal has a certain sentimental appeal. But this appeal is small compared with that made by a propaganda that tells them that they are superior to others, and that others are inferior to them. Are you naturally equal to your servants, to your slaves, to the manual worker who is no better than an animal? The very question is ridiculous! Plato seems to have been the first to appreciate the possibilities of this reaction, and to oppose contempt, scorn, and ridicule to the claim to natural equality. This explains why he was anxious to impute the naturalistic argument even to those of his opponents who did not use it; in the *Menexenus*, a parody of Pericles' oration, he therefore insists on linking together the claims to equal laws and to natural equality: 'The basis of our constitution is equality of birth', he says ironically. 'We are all brethren, and are all children of one mother; ... and the natural equality of birth induces us to strive for equality before the law.'[19]

Later, in the *Laws*, Plato summarizes his reply to equalitarianism in the formula: 'Equal treatment of unequals must beget inequity'[20]; and this was developed by Aristotle into the formula 'Equality for equals, inequality for unequals'. This formula indicates what may be termed the standard objection to equalitarianism; the objection that equality would be excellent if only men were equal, but that it is manifestly impossible since they are not equal, and since they cannot be made equal. This apparently very realistic objection is, in fact, most unrealistic, for political privileges have never been founded upon natural differences of character. And, indeed, Plato does not seem to have had much confidence in this objection when writing the *Republic*, for it is used there only in one of his sneers at democracy when he says that it 'distributes equality to equals and unequals alike.'[21] Apart from this remark, he prefers not to argue against equalitarianism, but to forget it.

Summing up, it can be said that Plato never underrated the significance of the equalitarian theory, supported as it was by a man like Pericles, but that, in the *Republic*, he did not treat it at all; he attacked it, but not squarely and openly.

But how did he try to establish his own anti-equalitarianism, his principle of natural privilege? In the *Republic*, he proffered three different arguments, though two of them hardly deserve the name. The first[22] is the surprising remark that, since all the other three virtues of the state have been examined, the remaining fourth, that of 'minding one's own business', must be 'justice'. I am reluctant to believe that this was meant as an argument; but it must be, for Plato's leading speaker, 'Socrates', introduces it by asking: 'Do you know how I arrive at this conclusion?' The second argument is more interesting, for it is an attempt to show that his anti-equalitarianism can be derived from the ordinary (i.e. equalitarian) view that justice is impartiality. I quote the passage in full. Remarking that the rulers of the city will also be its judges, 'Socrates' says[23]: 'And will it not be the aim of their jurisdiction that no man shall take what belongs to another, and shall be deprived of what is his own?'—'Yes', is the reply of 'Glaucon', the interlocutor, 'that will be their intention.'—'Because that would be just?'—'Yes.'—'Accordingly, to keep and to practise what belongs to us and is our own will be generally agreed upon to be justice.' Thus it is established that 'to keep and to practise what is one's own' is the principle of just jurisdiction, according to our ordinary ideas of justice. Here the second argument ends, giving way to the third (to be analysed below) which leads to the conclusion that it is justice to keep one's own station (or to do one's own business), which is the station (or the business) *of one's own class or caste*.

The sole purpose of this second argument is to impress upon the reader that 'justice', in the ordinary sense of the word, requires us to keep our own station, since we should always keep what belongs to us. That is to say, Plato wishes his readers to draw the inference: 'It is just to keep and to practise what is one's own. My place (or my business) is my own. Thus it is just for me to keep to my place (or to practise my business).' This is about as sound as the argument: 'It is just to keep and to practise what is one's own. This plan of stealing your money is my own. Thus it is just for me to keep to my plan, and to put it into practice, i.e. to steal your money.' It is clear that the inference which Plato wishes us to draw is nothing but a crude juggle with the meaning of the term 'one's own'. (For the problem is whether justice demands that everything which is in some sense 'our own', e.g. 'our own' class, should therefore be treated, not only as our possession, but as our inalienable possession. But in such a principle Plato himself does not believe;

for it would clearly make a transition to communism impossible. And what about keeping our own children?) This crude juggle is Plato's way of establishing what Adam calls 'a point of contact between his own view of Justice and the popular ... meaning of the word'. This is how the greatest philosopher of all time tries to convince us that he has discovered the true nature of justice.

The third and last argument which Plato offers is much more serious. It is an appeal to the principle of holism or collectivism, and is connected with the principle that it is the purpose of the individual to maintain the stability of the state. It will therefore be discussed, in this analysis, below, in sections V and VI.

But before proceeding to these points, I wish to draw attention to the 'preface' which Plato places before his description of the 'discovery' which we are here examining. It must be considered in the light of the observations we have made so far. Viewed in this light, the 'lengthy preface'—this is how Plato himself describes it—appears as an ingenious attempt to prepare the reader for the 'discovery of justice' by making him believe that there is an argument going on when in reality he is only faced with a display of dramatic devices, designed to soothe his critical faculties.

Having discovered wisdom as the virtue proper to the guardians and courage as that proper to the auxiliaries, 'Socrates' announces his intention of making a final effort to discover justice. 'Two things are left'[24], he says, 'which we shall have to discover in the city: temperance, and finally that other thing which is the main object of all our investigations, namely justice.' — 'Exactly', says Glaucon. Socrates now suggests that temperance shall be dropped. But Glaucon protests and Socrates gives in, saying that 'it would be wrong' (or 'crooked') to refuse. This little dispute prepares the reader for the re-introduction of justice, suggests to him that Socrates possesses the means for its 'discovery', and reassures him that Glaucon is carefully watching Plato's intellectual honesty in conducting the argument which he, the reader himself, need not therefore watch at all[25].

Socrates next proceeds to discuss temperance which he discovers to be the only virtue proper to the workers. (By the way, the much debated question whether Plato's 'justice' is distinguishable from his 'temperance' can be easily answered. Justice means *to keep one's place*; temperance means *to know one's place*—that is to say, more precisely, to be satisfied with it. What other virtue could be proper to the workers who fill their bellies like the beasts?) When temperance has been discovered, Socrates asks: 'And what about the last principle? Obviously it will be justice.'—'Obviously', replies Glaucon.

'Now, my dear Glaucon', says Socrates, 'we must, like hunters, surround her cover and keep a close watch, and we must not allow her to escape, and to get away; for surely, justice must be somewhere near this spot. You had better look out and search the place. And if you are the first to see her, then give me a shout!' Glaucon, like the reader, is of course unable to do anything of the sort, and implores Socrates to take the lead. 'Then offer your prayers with me', says Socrates, 'and follow me.' But even Socrates finds the ground 'hard to traverse, since it is covered with underwood; it is dark, and difficult to explore ... But', he says, 'we must go on with it'. And instead of protesting 'Go on with what? With our exploration, i.e. with our argument? But we have not even started. There has not been a glimmer of sense in what you have said so far', Glaucon, and the naïve reader with him replies meekly: 'Yes, we must go on.' Now Socrates reports that he has 'got a glimpse' (we have not), and gets excited. 'Hurray! Hurray!' he cries, 'Glaucon! There seems to be a track! I think now that the quarry will not escape us!'—'That is good news', replies Glaucon. 'Upon my word', says Socrates, 'we have made utter fools of ourselves. What we were looking for at a distance, has been lying at our very feet all the time! And we never saw it!' With exclamations and repeated assertions of this kind, Socrates continues for a good while, interrupted by Glaucon, who gives expression to the reader's feelings and asks Socrates what he has found. But when Socrates says only 'We have been talking of it all the time, without realizing that we were actually describing it', Glaucon expresses the reader's impatience and says: 'This preface gets a bit lengthy; remember that I want to hear what it is all about.' And only then does Plato proceed to proffer the two 'arguments' which I have outlined.

Glaucon's last remark may be taken as an indication that Plato was conscious of what he was doing in this 'lengthy preface'. I cannot interpret it as anything but an attempt—it proved to be highly successful—to lull the reader's critical faculties, and, by means of a dramatic display of verbal fireworks, to divert his attention from the intellectual poverty of this masterly piece of dialogue. One is tempted to think that Plato knew its weakness, and how to hide it.

V

The problem of individualism and collectivism is closely related to that of equality and inequality. Before going on to discuss it, a few terminological remarks seem to be necessary.

The term 'individualism' can be used (according to the *Oxford Dictionary*) in two different ways: (*a*) in opposition to collectivism, and (*b*) in opposition to altruism. There is no other word to express the former meaning, but several synonyms for the latter, for example 'egoism' or 'selfishness'. This is why in what follows I shall use the term 'individualism' *exclusively* in sense (*a*), using terms like 'egoism' or 'selfishness' if sense (*b*) is intended. A little table may be useful:

(*a*) *Individualism*	is opposed to	(*a′*) *Collectivism.*
(*b*) *Egoism*	is opposed to	(*b′*) *Altruism.*

Now these four terms describe certain attitudes, or demands, or decisions, or proposals, for codes of normative laws. Though necessarily vague, they can, I believe, be easily illustrated by examples and so be used with a precision sufficient for our present purpose. Let us begin with collectivism[26], since this attitude is already familiar to us from our discussion of Plato's holism. His demand that the individual should subserve the interests of the whole, whether this be the universe, the city, the tribe, the race, or any other collective body, was illustrated in the last chapter by a few passages. To quote one of these again, but more fully[27]: 'The part exists for the sake of the whole, but the whole does not exist for the sake of the part ... You are created for the sake of the whole and not the whole for the sake of you.' This quotation not only illustrates holism and collectivism, but also conveys its strong emotional appeal of which Plato was conscious (as can be seen from the preamble to the passage). The appeal is to various feelings, e.g. the longing to belong to a group or a tribe; and one factor in it is the moral appeal for altruism and against selfishness, or egoism. Plato suggests that if you cannot sacrifice your interests for the sake of the whole, then you are selfish.

Now a glance at our little table will show that this is not so. Collectivism is not opposed to egoism, nor is it identical with altruism or unselfishness. Collective or group egoism, for instance class egoism, is a very common thing (Plato knew[28] this very well), and this shows clearly enough that collectivism as such is not opposed to selfishness. On the other hand, an anti-collectivist, i.e. an individualist, can, at the same time, be an altruist; he can be ready to make sacrifices in order to help other individuals. One of the best examples of this attitude is perhaps Dickens. It would be difficult to say which is the stronger, his passionate hatred of selfishness or his passionate interest in individuals with all their human weaknesses; and this attitude is combined with a dislike, not only of what we now call collective bodies or collectives[29], but even of a genuinely devoted altruism, if directed towards anonymous groups rather than concrete individuals. (I remind the reader of

Mrs. Jellyby in *Bleak House*, 'a lady devoted to public duties'.) These illustrations, I think, explain sufficiently clearly the meaning of our four terms; and they show that any of the terms in our table can be combined with either of the two terms that stand in the other line (which gives four possible combinations).

Now it is interesting that for Plato, and for most Platonists, an altruistic individualism (as for instance that of Dickens) cannot exist. According to Plato, the only alternative to collectivism is egoism; he simply identifies all altruism with collectivism, and all individualism with egoism. This is not a matter of terminology, of mere words, for instead of four possibilities, Plato recognized only two. This has created considerable confusion in speculation on ethical matters, even down to our own day.

Plato's identification of individualism with egoism furnishes him with a powerful weapon for his defence of collectivism as well as for his attack upon individualism. In defending collectivism, he can appeal to our humanitarian feeling of unselfishness; in his attack, he can brand all individualists as selfish, as incapable of devotion to anything but themselves. This attack, although aimed by Plato against individualism in our sense, i.e. against the rights of human individuals, reaches of course only a very different target, egoism. But this difference is constantly ignored by Plato and by most Platonists.

Why did Plato try to attack individualism? I think he knew very well what he was doing when he trained his guns upon this position, for individualism, perhaps even more than equalitarianism, was a stronghold in the defences of the new humanitarian creed. The emancipation of the individual was indeed the great spiritual revolution which had led to the breakdown of tribalism and to the rise of democracy. Plato's uncanny sociological intuition shows itself in the way in which he invariably discerned the enemy wherever he met him.

Individualism was part of the old intuitive idea of justice. That justice is not, as Plato would have it, the health and harmony of the state, but rather a certain way of treating individuals, is emphasized by Aristotle, it will be remembered, when he says 'justice is something that pertains to persons'[30]. This individualistic element had been emphasized by the generation of Pericles. Pericles himself made it clear that the laws must guarantee equal justice 'to all alike in their private disputes'; but he went further. 'We do not feel called upon', he said, 'to nag at our neighbour if he chooses to go his own way.' (Compare this with Plato's remark[31] that the state does not produce men 'for the purpose of letting them loose, each to go his own way ...'.) Pericles insists that this individualism must be linked with altruism: 'We are taught … never to forget that we must protect the injured'; and his speech culminates in a description of the young Athenian who grows up 'to a happy versatility, and to self-reliance.'

This individualism, united with altruism, has become the basis of our western civilization. It is the central doctrine of Christianity ('love your neighbour', say the Scriptures, not 'love your tribe'); and it is the core of all ethical doctrines which have grown from our civilization and stimulated it. It is also, for instance, Kant's central practical doctrine ('always recognize that human individuals are ends, and do not use them as mere means to your ends'). There is no other thought which has been so powerful in the moral development of man.

Plato was right when he saw in this doctrine the enemy of his caste state; and he hated it more than any other of the 'subversive' doctrines of his time. In order to show this even more clearly, I shall quote two passages from the *Laws*[32] whose truly astonishing hostility towards the individual is, I think, too little appreciated. The first of them is famous as a reference to the *Republic*, whose 'community of women and children and property' it discusses. Plato describes here the constitution of the *Republic* as 'the highest form of the state'. In this highest state, he tells us, 'there is common property of wives, of children, and of all chattels. And everything possible has been done to eradicate from our life everywhere and in every way all that is private and individual. So far as it can be done, even those things which nature herself has made private and individual have somehow become the common property of all. Our very eyes and ears and hands seem to see, to hear, and to act, as if they belonged not to individuals but to the community. All men are moulded to be unanimous in the utmost degree in bestowing praise and blame, and they even rejoice and grieve about the same things, and at the same time. And all the laws are perfected for unifying the city to the utmost.' Plato goes on to say that 'no man can find a better criterion of the highest excellence of a state than the principles just expounded'; and he describes such a state as 'divine', and as the 'model' or 'pattern' or 'original' of the state, i.e. as its Form or Idea. This is Plato's own view of the *Republic*, expressed at a time when he had given up hope of realizing his political ideal in all its glory.

The second passage, also from the *Laws*, is, if possible, even more outspoken. It should be emphasized that the passage deals primarily with military expeditions and with military discipline, but Plato leaves no doubt that these same militarist principles should be adhered to not only in war, but also 'in peace, and from the earliest childhood on'. Like other totalitarian militarists and admirers of Sparta, Plato urges that the all-important requirements of military discipline must be paramount, even in peace, and that they must determine the whole life of all citizens; for not only the full citizens (who are all soldiers) and the children, but also the very beasts must spend their whole life in a state of permanent and total mobilization[33]. 'The greatest principle of all', he writes, 'is that nobody, whether male or female, should ever be without a leader. Nor should the mind of anybody be habituated to letting him do anything at all on his own initiative, neither out of zeal, nor even playfully. But in war and in the midst of peace—to his leader he shall direct his eye, and follow him faithfully. And even in the smallest matters he should stand under leadership. For example, he should get up, or move, or wash, or take his meals[34] ... only if he has been told to do so ... In a word, he should teach his soul, by long habit, never to dream of acting independently, and to become utterly incapable of it. In this way the life of all will be spent in total community. There is no law, nor will there ever be one, which is superior to this, or better and more effective in ensuring salvation and victory in war. *And in times of peace, and from the earliest childhood on* should it be fostered—this habit of ruling others, and of being ruled by others. And every trace of anarchy should be utterly eradicated from *all the life of all the men*, and even of the wild beasts which are subject to men.'

These are strong words. Never was a man more in earnest in his hostility towards the individual. And this hatred is deeply rooted in the fundamental dualism of Plato's philosophy; he hated the individual and his freedom just as he hated the varying particular experiences, the variety of the changing world of sensible things. In the field of politics, the individual is to Plato the Evil One himself.

This attitude, anti-humanitarian and anti-Christian as it is, has been consistently idealized. It has been interpreted as humane, as unselfish, as altruistic, and as Christian. E. B. England, for instance, calls[35] the first of these two passages from the *Laws* 'a vigorous denunciation of selfishness'. Similar words are used by Barker, when discussing Plato's theory of justice. He says that Plato's aim was 'to replace selfishness and civil discord by harmony', and that 'the old harmony of the interests of the State and the individual ... is thus restored in the teachings of Plato; but restored on a new and higher level, because it has been elevated into a conscious sense of harmony'. Such statements and countless similar ones can be easily explained if we remember Plato's identification of individualism with egoism; for all these Platonists believe that anti-individualism is the same as selflessness. This illustrates my contention that this identification had the effect of a successful piece of anti-humanitarian propaganda, and that it has confused speculation on ethical matters down to our own time. But we must also realize that those who, deceived by this identification and by high-sounding words, exalt Plato's reputation as a teacher of morals and announce to the world that his ethics is the nearest approach to Christianity before Christ, are preparing the way for totalitarianism and especially for a totalitarian, anti-Christian interpretation of Christianity. And this is a dangerous thing, for there have been times when Christianity was dominated by totalitarian ideas. There was an Inquisition; and, in another form, it may come again.

It may therefore be worth while to mention some further reasons why guileless people have persuaded themselves of the humaneness of Plato's intentions. One is that when preparing the ground for his collectivist doctrines, Plato usually begins by quoting a maxim or proverb (which seems to be of Pythagorean origin): 'Friends have in common all things they possess.'[36] This is, undoubtedly, an unselfish, high-minded and excellent sentiment. Who could suspect that an argument starting from such a commendable assumption would arrive at a wholly anti-humanitarian conclusion? Another and important point is that there are many genuinely humanitarian sentiments expressed in Plato's dialogues, particularly in those written before the *Republic* when he was still under the influence of Socrates. I mention especially Socrates' doctrine, in the *Gorgias*, that it is worse to do injustice than to suffer it. Clearly, this doctrine is not only altruistic, but also individualistic; for in a collectivist theory of justice like that of the *Republic*, injustice is an act against the state, not against a particular man, and though a man may commit an act of injustice, only the collective can suffer from it. But in the *Gorgias* we find nothing of the kind. The theory of justice is a perfectly normal one, and the examples of injustice given by 'Socrates' (who has here probably a good deal of the real Socrates in him) are such as boxing a man's ears, injuring, or killing him. Socrates' teaching that it is better to suffer such acts than to do them is indeed very similar to Christian teaching, and his doctrine of justice fits in excellently with the spirit of Pericles. (An attempt to interpret this will be made in chapter 10.)

Now the *Republic* develops a new doctrine of justice which is not merely incompatible with such an individualism, but utterly hostile towards it. But a reader may easily believe that Plato is still holding fast to the doctrine of the *Gorgias*. For in the *Republic*, Plato frequently alludes to the doctrine that it is better to suffer than to commit injustice, in spite of the fact that this is simply nonsense from the point of view of the collectivist theory of justice proffered in this work. Furthermore, we hear in the *Republic* the opponents of 'Socrates' giving voice to the opposite theory, that it is good and pleasant to inflict injustice, and bad to suffer it. Of course, every humanitarian is repelled by such cynicism, and when Plato formulates his aims through the mouth of Socrates: 'I fear to commit a sin if I permit such evil talk about Justice in my presence, without doing my utmost to defend her'[37], then the trusting reader is convinced of Plato's good intentions, and ready to follow him wherever he goes.

The effect of this assurance of Plato's is much enhanced by the fact that it follows, and is contrasted with, the cynical and selfish speeches[38] of Thrasymachus, who is depicted as a political desperado of the worst kind. At the same time, the reader is led to identify individualism with the views of Thrasymachus, and to think that Plato, in his fight against it, is fighting against all the subversive and nihilistic tendencies of his time. But we should not allow ourselves to be frightened by an individualist bogy such as Thrasymachus (there is a great similarity between his portrait and the modern collectivist bogy of 'bolshevism') into accepting another more real and more dangerous because less obvious form of barbarism. For Plato replaces Thrasymachus' doctrine that the individual's might is right by the equally barbaric doctrine that right is everything that furthers the stability and the might of the state.

To sum up. Because of his radical collectivism, Plato is not even interested in those problems which men usually call the problems of justice, that is to say, in the impartial weighing of the contesting claims of individuals. Nor is he interested in adjusting the individual's claims to those of the state. For the individual is altogether inferior. 'I legislate with a view to what is best for the whole state', says Plato, '... for I justly place the interests of the individual on an inferior level of value.'[39] He is concerned solely with the collective whole as such, and justice, to him, is nothing but the health, unity, and stability of the collective body.

VI

So far, we have seen that humanitarian ethics demands an equalitarian and individualistic interpretation of justice; but we have not yet outlined the humanitarian view of the state as such. On the other hand, we have seen that Plato's theory of the state is totalitarian; but we have not yet explained the application of this theory to the ethics of the individual. Both these tasks will be undertaken now, the second first; and I shall begin by analysing the third of Plato's arguments in his 'discovery' of justice, an argument which has so far been sketched only very roughly. Here is Plato's third argument[40]:

'Now see whether you agree with me', says Socrates. 'Do you think it would do much harm to the city if a carpenter started making shoes and a shoemaker carpentering?'—'Not very much.'—'But should one who is by nature a worker, or a member of the money-earning class … manage to get into the warrior class; or should a warrior get into the guardians' class without being worthy of it; then this kind of change and of underhand plotting would mean the downfall of the city?'—'Most definitely it would.'—'We have three classes in our city, and I take it that any such plotting or changing from one class to another is a great crime against the city, and may rightly be denounced as the utmost wickedness?'—'Assuredly.'—'But you will certainly declare that utmost wickedness towards one's own city is injustice?'—'Certainly.'—'Then this is injustice. And conversely, we shall say that when each class in the city attends to its own business, the money-earning class as well as the auxiliaries and the guardians, then this will be justice.'

Now if we look at this argument, we find (*a*) the sociological assumption that any relaxing of the rigid caste system must lead to the downfall of the city; (*b*) the constant reiteration of the one argument that what harms the city is injustice; and (*c*) the inference that the opposite is justice. Now we may grant here the sociological assumption (*a*) since it is Plato's ideal to arrest social change, and since he means by 'harm' anything that may lead to change; and it is probably quite true that social change can be arrested only by a rigid caste system. And we may further grant the inference (*c*) that the opposite of injustice is justice. Of greater interest, however, is (*b*); a glance at Plato's argument will show that his whole trend of thought is dominated by the question: does this thing harm the city? Does it do much harm or little harm? He constantly reiterates that what threatens to harm the city is morally wicked and unjust.

We see here that Plato recognizes only one ultimate standard, the interest of the state. Everything that furthers it is good and virtuous and just; everything that threatens it is bad and wicked and unjust. Actions that serve it are moral; actions that endanger it, immoral. In other words, Plato's moral code is strictly utilitarian; it is a code of collectivist or political utilitarianism. *The criterion of morality is the interest of the state.* Morality is nothing but political hygiene.

This is the collectivist, the tribal, the totalitarian theory of morality: 'Good is what is in the interest of my group; or my tribe; or my state.' It is easy to see what this morality implied for international relations: that the state itself can never be wrong in any of its actions, as long as it is strong; that the state has the right, not only to do violence to its citizens, should that lead to an increase of strength, but also to attack other states, provided it does so without weakening itself. (This inference, the explicit recognition of the amorality of the state, and consequently the defence of moral nihilism in international relations, was drawn by Hegel.)

From the point of view of totalitarian ethics, from the point of view of collective utility, Plato's theory of justice is perfectly correct. To keep one's place is a virtue. It is that civil virtue which corresponds exactly to the military virtue of discipline. And this virtue plays exactly that rôle which 'justice' plays in Plato's system of virtues. For the cogs in the great clockwork of the state can show 'virtue' in two ways. First, they must be fit for their task, by virtue of their size, shape, strength, etc.; and secondly, they must be fitted each into its right place and must retain that place. The first type of virtues, fitness for a specific task, will lead to a differentiation, in accordance with the specific task of the cog. Certain cogs will be virtuous, i.e. fit, only if they are ('by their nature') large; others if they are strong; and others if they are smooth. But the virtue of keeping to one's place will be common to all of them; and it will at the same time be a virtue of the whole: that of being properly fitted together—of being in harmony. To this universal virtue Plato gives the name 'justice'. This procedure is perfectly consistent and it is fully justified from the point of view of totalitarian morality. If the individual is nothing but a cog, then ethics is nothing but the study of how to fit him into the whole.

I wish to make it clear that I believe in the sincerity of Plato's totalitarianism. His demand for the unchallenged domination of one class over the rest was uncompromising, but his ideal was not the maximum exploitation of the working classes by the upper class; it was the stability of the whole. The reason, however, which he gives for the need to keep the exploitation within limits, is again purely utilitarian. It is the interest of stabilizing the class rule. Should the guardians try to get too much, he argues, then they will in the end have nothing at all. 'If they are not satisfied with a life of stability and security, … and are tempted, by their power, to appropriate for themselves all the wealth of the city, then surely they are bound to find out how wise Hesiod was when he said, "the half is more than the whole".'[41] But we must realize that even this tendency to restrict the exploitation of class privileges is a fairly common ingredient of totalitarianism. Totalitarianism is not simply amoral. It is the morality of the closed society—of the group, or of the tribe; it is not individual selfishness, but it is collective selfishness.

Considering that Plato's third argument is straightforward and consistent, the question may be asked why he needed the 'lengthy preface' as well as the two preceding arguments. Why all this uneasiness? (Platonists will of course reply that this uneasiness exists only in my imagination. That may be so. But the irrational character of the passages can hardly be explained away.) The answer to this question is, I believe, that Plato's collective clockwork would hardly have appealed to his readers if it had been presented to them in all its barrenness and meaninglessness. Plato was uneasy because he knew and feared the strength and the moral appeal of the forces he tried to break. He did not dare to challenge them, but tried to win them over for his own purposes. Whether we witness in Plato's writings a cynical and conscious attempt to employ the moral sentiments of the new humanitarianism for his own purposes, or whether we witness rather a tragic attempt to persuade his own better conscience of the evils of individualism, we shall never know. My personal impression is that the latter is the case, and that this inner conflict is the main secret of Plato's fascination. I think that Plato was moved to the depths of his soul by the new ideas, and especially by the great individualist Socrates and his martyrdom. And I think that he fought against this influence upon himself as well as upon others with all the might of his unequalled intelligence, though not always openly. This explains also why from time to time, amid all his totalitarianism, we find some humanitarian ideas. And it explains why it was possible for philosophers to represent Plato as a humanitarian.

A strong argument in support of this interpretation is the way in which Plato treated, or rather, maltreated, the humanitarian and rational theory of the state, a theory which had been developed for the first time in his generation.

In a clear presentation of this theory, the *language of political demands or of political proposals* (cp. chapter 5, III) should be used; that is to say, we should not try to answer the essentialist question: What is the state, what is its true nature, its real meaning? Nor should we try to answer the historicist question: How did the state originate, and what is the origin of political obligation? We should rather put our question in this way: What do we demand from a state? What do we propose to consider as the legitimate aim of state activity? And in order to find out what our fundamental political demands are, we may ask: Why do we prefer living in a well-ordered state to living without a state, i.e. in anarchy? This way of asking our question is a rational one. It is a question which a technologist must try to answer before he can proceed to the construction or reconstruction of any political institution. For only if he knows what he wants can he decide whether a certain institution is or is not well adapted to its function.

Now if we ask our question in this way, the reply of the humanitarian will be: What I demand from the state is protection; not only for myself, but for others too. I demand protection for my own freedom and for other people's. I do not wish to live at the mercy of anybody who has the larger fists or the bigger guns. In other words, I wish to be protected against aggression from other men. I want the difference between aggression and defence to be recognized, and defence to be supported by the organized power of the state. (The defence is one of a *status quo*, and the principle proposed amounts to this—that the *status quo* should not be changed by violent means, but only according to law, by compromise or arbitration, except where there is no legal procedure for its revision.) I am perfectly ready to see my own freedom of action somewhat curtailed by the state, provided I can obtain protection of that freedom which remains, since I know that some limitations of my freedom are necessary; for instance, I must give up my 'freedom' to attack, if I want the state to support defence against any attack. But I demand that the fundamental purpose of the state should not be lost sight of; I mean, the protection of that freedom which does not harm other citizens. Thus I demand that the state must limit the freedom of the citizens as equally as possible, and not beyond what is necessary for achieving an equal limitation of freedom.

Something like this will be the demand of the humanitarian, of the equalitarian, of the individualist. It is a demand which permits the social technologist to approach political problems rationally, i.e. from the point of view of a fairly clear and definite aim.

Against the claim that an aim like this can be formulated sufficiently clearly and definitely, many objections have been raised. It has been said that once it is recognized that freedom must be limited, the whole principle of freedom breaks down, and the question what limitations are necessary and what are wanton cannot be decided rationally, but only by authority. But this objection is due to a muddle. It mixes up the fundamental question of what we want from a state with certain important technological difficulties in the way of the realization of our aims. It is certainly difficult to determine exactly the degree of freedom that can be left to the citizens without endangering that freedom whose protection is the task of the state. But that something like an approximate determination of that degree is possible is proved by experience, i.e. by the existence of democratic states. In fact, this process of approximate determination is one of the main tasks of legislation in democracies. It is a difficult process, but its difficulties are certainly not such as to force upon us a change in our fundamental demands. These are, stated very briefly, that the state should be considered as a society for the prevention of crime, i.e. of aggression. And the whole objection that it is hard to know where freedom ends and crime begins is answered, in principle, by the famous story of the hooligan who protested that, being a free citizen, he could move his fist in any direction he liked; whereupon the judge wisely replied: 'The freedom of the movement of your fists is limited by the position of your neighbour's nose.'

The view of the state which I have sketched here may be called 'protectionism'. The term 'protectionism' has often been used to describe tendencies which are opposed to freedom. Thus the economist means by protectionism the policy of protecting certain industrial interests against competition; and the moralist means by it the demand that officers of the state shall establish a moral tutelage over the population. Although the political theory which I call protectionism is not connected with any of these tendencies, and although it is fundamentally a liberal theory, I think that the name may be used to indicate that, though liberal, it has nothing to do with the *policy of strict non-intervention* (often, but not quite correctly, called '*laissez-faire*'). Liberalism and state-interference are not opposed to each other. On the contrary, any kind of freedom is clearly impossible unless it is guaranteed by the state[42]. A certain amount of state control in education, for instance, is necessary, if the young are to be protected from a neglect which would make them unable to defend their freedom, and the state should see that all educational facilities are available to everybody. But too much state control in educational matters is a fatal danger to freedom, since it must lead to indoctrination. As already indicated, the important and difficult question of the limitations of freedom cannot be solved by a cut and dried formula. And the fact that there will always be borderline cases must be welcomed, for without the stimulus of political problems and political struggles of this kind, the citizens' readiness to fight for their freedom would soon disappear, and with it, their freedom. (Viewed in this light, the alleged clash between freedom and security, that is, a security guaranteed by the state, turns out to be a chimera. For there is no freedom if it is not secured by the state; and conversely, only a state which is controlled by free citizens can offer them any reasonable security at all.)

Stated in this way, the protectionist theory of the state is free from any elements of historicism or essentialism. It does not say that the state originated as an association of individuals with a protectionist aim, or that any actual state in history was ever consciously ruled in accordance with this aim. And it says nothing about the essential nature of the state, or about a natural right to freedom. Nor does it say anything about the way in which states actually function. It formulates a political *demand*, or more precisely, a *proposal* for the adoption of a certain policy. I suspect, however, that many conventionalists who have described the state as originating from an association for the protection of its members, intended to express this very demand, though they did it in a clumsy and misleading language—the language of historicism. A similar misleading way of expressing this demand is to assert that it is essentially the function of the state to protect its members; or to assert that the state is to be defined as an association for mutual protection. All these theories must be translated, as it were, into the language of demands or proposals for political actions before they can be seriously discussed. Otherwise, endless discussions of a merely verbal character are unavoidable.

An example of such a translation may be given. A criticism of what I call protectionism has been proffered by Aristotle[43], and repeated by Burke, and by many modern Platonists. This criticism asserts that protectionism takes too mean a view of the tasks of the state which is (using Burke's words) 'to be looked upon with other reverence, because it is not a partnership in things subservient only to the gross animal existence of a temporary and perishable nature'. In other words, the state is said to be something higher or nobler than an association with rational ends; it is an object of worship. It has higher tasks than the protection of human beings and their rights. It has moral tasks. 'To take care of virtue is the business of a state which truly deserves this name', says Aristotle. If we try to translate this criticism into the language of political demands, then we find that these critics of protectionism want two things. First, they wish to make the state an object of worship. From our point of view, there is nothing to say against this wish. It is a religious problem; and the state-worshippers must solve for themselves how to reconcile their creed with their other religious beliefs, for example, with the First Commandment. The second demand is political. In practice, this demand would simply mean that officers of the state should be concerned with the morality of the citizens, and that they should use their power not so much for the protection of the citizens' freedom as for the control of their moral life. In other words, it is the demand that the realm of legality, i.e. of state-enforced norms, should be increased at the expense of the realm of morality proper, i.e. of norms enforced not by the state but by our own moral decisions—by our conscience. Such a demand or proposal can be rationally discussed; and it can be said against it that those who raise such demands apparently do not see that this would be the end of the individual's moral responsibility, and that it would not improve but destroy morality. It would replace personal responsibility by tribalistic taboos and by the totalitarian irresponsibility of the individual. Against this whole attitude, the individualist must maintain that the morality of states (if there is any such thing) tends to be considerably lower than that of the average citizen, so that it is much more desirable that the morality of the state should be controlled by the citizens than the opposite. What we need and what we want is to moralize politics, and not to politicize morals.

It should be mentioned that, from the protectionist point of view, the existing democratic states, though far from perfect, represent a very considerable achievement in social engineering of the right kind. Many forms of crime, of attack on the rights of human individuals by other individuals, have been practically suppressed or very considerably reduced, and courts of law administer justice fairly successfully in difficult conflicts of interest. There are many who think that the extension of these methods[44] to international crime and international conflict is only a Utopian dream; but it is not so long since the institution of an effective executive for upholding civil peace appeared Utopian to those who suffered under the threats of criminals, in countries where at present civil peace is quite successfully maintained. And I think that the engineering problems of the control of international crime are really not so difficult, once they are squarely and rationally faced. If the matter is presented clearly, it will not be hard to get people to agree that protective institutions are necessary, both on a regional and on a world-wide scale. Let the state-worshippers continue to worship the state, but demand that the institutional technologists be allowed not only to improve its internal machinery, but also to build up an organization for the prevention of international crime.

VII

Returning now to the history of these movements, it seems that the protectionist theory of the state was first proffered by the Sophist Lycophron, a pupil of Gorgias. It has already been mentioned that he was (like Alcidamas, also a pupil of Gorgias) one of the first to attack the theory of natural privilege. That he held the theory which I have called 'protectionism' is recorded by Aristotle, who speaks about him in a manner which makes it very likely that he originated it. From the same source we learn that he formulated it with a clarity which has hardly been attained by any of his successors.

Aristotle tells us that Lycophron considered the law of the state as a 'covenant by which men assure one another of justice' (and that it has not the power to make citizens good or just). He tells us furthermore[45] that Lycophron looked upon the state as an instrument for the protection of its citizens against acts of injustice (and for permitting them peaceful intercourse, especially exchange), demanding that the state should be a 'co-operative association for the prevention of crime'. It is interesting that there is no indication in Aristotle's account that Lycophron expressed his theory in a historicist form, i.e. as a theory concerning the historical origin of the state in a social contract. On the contrary, it emerges clearly from Aristotle's context that Lycophron's theory was solely concerned with the end of the state; for Aristotle argues that Lycophron has not seen that the essential end of the state is to make its citizens virtuous. This indicates that Lycophron interpreted this end rationally, from a technological point of view, adopting the demands of equalitarianism, individualism, and protectionism.

In this form, Lycophron's theory is completely secure from the objections to which the traditional historicist theory of the social contract is exposed. It is often said, for instance by Barker[46], that the contract theory 'has been met by modern thinkers point by point'. That may be so; but a survey of Barker's points will show that they certainly do not meet the theory of Lycophron, in whom Barker sees (and in this point I am inclined to agree with him) the probable founder of the earliest form of a theory which has later been called the contract theory. Barker's points can be set down as follows: (*a*) There was, historically, never a contract; (*b*) the state was, historically, never instituted; (*c*) laws are not conventional, but arise out of tradition, superior force, perhaps instinct, etc.; they are customs before they become codes; (*d*) the strength of the laws does not lie in the sanctions, in the protective power of the state which enforces them, but in the individual's readiness to obey them, i.e. in the individual's moral will.

It will be seen at once that objections (*a*), (*b*), and (*c*), which in themselves are admittedly fairly correct (although there have been some contracts) concern the theory only in its historicist form and are irrelevant to Lycophron's version. We therefore need not consider them at all. Objection (*d*), however, deserves closer consideration. What can be meant by it? The theory attacked stresses the 'will', or better the decision of the individual, more than any other theory; in fact, the word 'contract' suggests an agreement by 'free will'; it suggests, perhaps more than any other theory, that the strength of the laws lies in the individual's readiness to accept and to obey them. How, then, can (*d*) be an objection against the contract theory? The only explanation seems to be that Barker does not think the contract to spring from the 'moral will' of the individual, but rather from a selfish will; and this interpretation is the more likely as it is in keeping with Plato's criticism. But one need not be selfish in order to be a protectionist. Protection need not mean self-protection; many people insure their lives with the aim of protecting others and not themselves, and in the same way they may demand state protection mainly for others, and to a lesser degree (or not at all) for themselves. The fundamental idea of protectionism is: protect the weak from being bullied by the strong. This demand has been raised not only by the weak, but often by the strong also. It is, to say the least of it, misleading to suggest that it is a selfish or an immoral demand.

Lycophron's protectionism is, I think, free of all these objections. It is the most fitting expression of the humanitarian and equalitarian movement of the Periclean age. And yet, we have been robbed of it. It has been handed down to later generations only in a distorted form; as the historicist theory of the origin of the state in a social contract; or as an essentialist theory claiming that the true nature of the state is that of a convention; and as a theory of selfishness, based on the assumption of the fundamentally immoral nature of man. All this is due to the overwhelming influence of Plato's authority.

VIII

There can be little doubt that Plato knew Lycophron's theory well, for he was (in all likelihood) Lycophron's younger contemporary. And, indeed, this theory can be easily identified with one which is mentioned first in the *Gorgias* and later in the *Republic*. (In neither place does Plato mention its author; a procedure often adopted by him when his opponent was alive.) In the *Gorgias*, the theory is expounded by Callicles, an ethical nihilist like the Thrasymachus of the *Republic*. In the *Republic*, it is expounded by Glaucon. In neither case does the speaker identify himself with the theory he presents.

The two passages are in many respects parallel. Both present the theory in a historicist form, i.e. as a theory of the origin of 'justice'. Both present it as if its logical premises were necessarily selfish and even nihilistic; i.e. as if the protectionist view of the state was upheld only by those who would *like* to inflict injustice, but are too weak to do so, and who *therefore* demand that the strong should not do so either; a presentation which is certainly not fair, since the only necessary premise of the theory is the demand that crime, or injustice, should be suppressed.

So far, the two passages in the *Gorgias* and in the *Republic* run parallel, a parallelism which has often been commented upon. But there is a tremendous difference between them which has, so far as I know, been overlooked by commentators. It is this. In the *Gorgias*, the theory is presented by Callicles as one which he opposes; and since he also opposes Socrates, the protectionist theory is, by implication, not attacked but rather defended by Plato. And, indeed, a closer view shows that Socrates upholds several of its features against the nihilist Callicles. But in the *Republic*, the same theory is presented by Glaucon as an elaboration and development of the views of Thrasymachus, i.e. of the nihilist who takes here the place of Callicles; in other words, the theory is presented as nihilist, and Socrates as the hero who victoriously destroys this devilish doctrine of selfishness.

Thus the passages in which most commentators find a similarity between the tendencies of the *Gorgias* and the *Republic* reveal, in fact, a complete change of front. In spite of Callicles' hostile presentation, the tendency of the *Gorgias* is favourable to protectionism; but the *Republic* is violently against it.

Here is an extract from Callicles' speech in the *Gorgias*[47]: 'The laws are made by the great mass of the people which consists mainly of the weak men. And they make the laws … in order to protect themselves and their interests. Thus they deter the stronger men … and all others who might get the better of them, from doing so; … and they mean by the word "injustice" the attempt of a man to get the better of his neighbours; and being aware of their inferiority, they are, I should say, only too glad if they can obtain equality.' If we look at this account and eliminate what is due to Callicles' open scorn and hostility, then we find all the elements of Lycophron's theory: equalitarianism, individualism, and protection against injustice. Even the reference to the 'strong' and to the 'weak' who are aware of their inferiority fits the protectionist view very well indeed, provided the element of caricature is allowed for. It is not at all unlikely that Lycophron's doctrine explicitly raised the demand that the state should protect the weak, a demand which is, of course, anything but ignoble. (The hope that this demand will one day be fulfilled is expressed by the Christian teaching: 'The meek shall inherit the earth.')

Callicles himself does not like protectionism; he is in favour of the 'natural' rights of the stronger. It is very significant that Socrates, in his argument against Callicles, comes to the rescue of protectionism; for he connects it with his own central thesis—that it is better to suffer injustice than to inflict it. He says, for instance[48]: 'Are not the many of the opinion, as you were lately saying, that justice is equality? And also that it is more disgraceful to inflict injustice than to suffer it?' And later: '… nature itself, and not only convention, affirms that to inflict injustice is more disgraceful than to suffer it, and that justice is equality.' (In spite of its individualistic and equalitarian and protectionist tendencies, the *Gorgias* also exhibits some leanings which are strongly anti-democratic. The explanation may be that Plato when writing the *Gorgias* had not yet developed his totalitarian theories; although his sympathies were already anti-democratic, he was still under Socrates' influence. How anybody can think that the *Gorgias* and the *Republic* can be both at the same time true accounts of Socrates' opinions, I fail to understand.)

Let us now turn to the *Republic*, where Glaucon presents protectionism as a logically more stringent but ethically unchanged version of Thrasymachus' nihilism. 'My theme', says Glaucon[49], 'is the origin of justice, and what sort of thing it really is. According to some it is by nature an excellent thing to inflict injustice upon others, and a bad thing to suffer it. But they hold that the badness of suffering injustice much exceeds the desirability of inflicting it.

For a time, then, men will inflict injustice on one another, and of course suffer it, and they will get a good taste of both. But ultimately, those who are not strong enough to repel it, or to enjoy inflicting it, decide that it is more profitable for them to join in a contract, mutually assuring one another that no one should inflict injustice, or suffer it. This is the way in which laws were established ... And this is the nature and the origin of justice, according to that theory.'

As far as its rational content goes, this is clearly the same theory; and the way in which it is represented also resembles in detail[50] Callicles' speech in the *Gorgias*. And yet, Plato has made a complete change of front. The protectionist theory is now no longer defended against the allegation that it is based on cynical egoism; on the contrary. Our humanitarian sentiments, our moral indignation, already aroused by Thrasymachus' nihilism, are utilized for turning us into enemies of protectionism. This theory, whose humanitarian character has been indicated in the *Gorgias*, is now made by Plato to appear as anti-humanitarian, and indeed, as the outcome of the repulsive and most unconvincing doctrine that injustice is a very good thing—for those who can get away with it. And he does not hesitate to rub this point in. In an extensive continuation of the passage quoted, Glaucon elaborates in much detail the allegedly necessary assumptions or premises of protectionism. Among these he mentions, for instance, the view that the inflicting of injustice is 'the best of all things'[51]; that justice is established only because many men are too weak to commit crimes; and that to the individual citizen, a life of crime would be most profitable. And 'Socrates', i.e. Plato, vouches explicitly[52] for the authenticity of Glaucon's interpretation of the theory presented. By this method, Plato seems to have succeeded in persuading most of his readers, and at any rate all Platonists, that the protectionist theory here developed is identical with the ruthless and cynical selfishness of Thrasymachus[53]; and, what is more important, that all forms of individualism amount to the same, namely, selfishness. But it was not only his admirers he persuaded; he even succeeded in persuading his opponents, and especially the adherents of the contract theory. From Carneades[54] to Hobbes, they not only adopted his fatal historicist presentation, but also Plato's assurances that the basis of their theory was an ethical nihilism.

Now it must be realized that the elaboration of its allegedly selfish basis is the whole of Plato's argument against protectionism; and considering the space taken up by this elaboration, we may safely assume that it was not his reticence which made him proffer no better argument, but the fact that he had none. Thus protectionism had to be dismissed by an appeal to our moral sentiments—as an affront against the idea of justice, and against our feelings of decency.

This is Plato's method of dealing with a theory which was not only a dangerous rival of his own doctrine, but also representative of the new humanitarian and individualistic creed, i.e. the arch-enemy of everything that was dear to Plato. The method is clever; its astonishing success proves it. But I should not be fair if I did not frankly admit that Plato's method appears to me dishonest. For the theory attacked does not need any assumption more immoral than that injustice is evil, i.e. that it should be avoided, and brought under control. And Plato knew quite well that the theory was not based on selfishness, for in the *Gorgias* he had presented it not as identical with the nihilistic theory from which it is 'derived' in the *Republic*, but as opposed to it.

Summing up, we can say that Plato's theory of justice, as presented in the *Republic* and later works, is a conscious attempt to get the better of the equalitarian, individualistic, and protectionist tendencies of his time, and to re-establish the claims of tribalism by developing a totalitarian moral theory. At the same time, he was strongly impressed by the new humanitarian morality; but instead of combating equalitarianism with arguments, he avoided even discussing it. And he successfully enlisted the humanitarian sentiments, whose strength he knew so well, in the cause of the totalitarian class rule of a naturally superior master race.

These class prerogatives, he claimed, are necessary for upholding the stability of the state. They constitute therefore the essence of justice. Ultimately, this claim is based upon the argument that justice is useful to the might, health, and stability of the state; an argument which is only too similar to the modern totalitarian definition: right is whatever is useful to the might of my nation, or my class, or my party.

But this is not yet the whole story. By its emphasis on class prerogative, Plato's theory of justice puts the problem 'Who should rule?' in the centre of political theory. His reply to this question was that the wisest, and the best, should rule. Does not this excellent reply modify the character of his theory?

7

THE PRINCIPLE OF LEADERSHIP

The wise shall lead and rule, and the ignorant shall follow.

PLATO.

Certain objections[1] to our interpretation of Plato's political programme have forced us into an investigation of the part played, within this programme, by such moral ideas as Justice, Goodness, Beauty, Wisdom, Truth, and Happiness. The present and the two following chapters are to continue this analysis, and the part played by the idea of Wisdom in Plato's political philosophy will occupy us next.

We have seen that Plato's idea of justice demands, fundamentally, that the natural rulers should rule and the natural slaves should slave. It is part of the historicist demand that the state, in order to arrest all change, should be a copy of its Idea, or of its true 'nature'. This theory of justice indicates very clearly that Plato saw the fundamental problem of politics in the question: *Who shall rule the state?*

I

It is my conviction that by expressing the problem of politics in the form 'Who should rule?' or 'Whose will should be supreme?', etc., Plato created a lasting confusion in political philosophy. It is indeed analogous to the confusion he created in the field of moral philosophy by his identification, discussed in the last chapter, of collectivism and altruism. It is clear that once the question 'Who should rule?' is asked, it is hard to avoid some such reply as 'the best' or 'the wisest' or 'the born ruler' or 'he who masters the art of ruling' (or, perhaps, 'The General Will' or 'The Master Race' or 'The Industrial Workers' or 'The People'). But such a reply, convincing as it may sound—for who would advocate the rule of 'the worst' or 'the greatest fool' or 'the born slave'?—is, as I shall try to show, quite useless.

First of all, such a reply is liable to persuade us that some fundamental problem of political theory has been solved. But if we approach political theory from a different angle, then we find that far from solving any fundamental problems, we have merely skipped over them, by assuming that the question 'Who should rule?' is fundamental. For even those who share this assumption of Plato's admit that political rulers are not always sufficiently 'good' or 'wise' (we need not worry about the precise meaning of these terms), and that it is not at all easy to get a government on whose goodness and wisdom one can implicitly rely. If that is granted, then we must ask whether political thought should not face from the beginning the possibility of bad government; whether we should not prepare for the worst leaders, and hope for the best. But this leads to a new approach to the problem of politics, for it forces us to replace the question: *Who should rule?* by the new[2] question: *How can we so organize political institutions that bad or incompetent rulers can be prevented from doing too much damage?*

Those who believe that the older question is fundamental, tacitly assume that political power is 'essentially' unchecked. They assume that someone has the power—either an individual or a collective body, such as a class. And they assume that he who has the power can, very nearly, do what he wills, and especially that he can strengthen his power, and thereby approximate it further to an unlimited or unchecked power. They assume that political power is, essentially, sovereign. If this assumption is made, then, indeed, the question 'Who is to be the sovereign?' is the only important question left.

I shall call this assumption the *theory of (unchecked) sovereignty*, using this expression not for any particular one of the various theories of sovereignty, proffered more especially by such writers as Bodin, Rousseau, or Hegel, but for the more general assumption that political power is practically unchecked, or for the demand that it ought to be so; together with the implication that the main question left is to get this power into the best hands. This theory of sovereignty is tacitly assumed in Plato's approach, and has played its rôle ever since. It is also implicitly assumed, for instance, by those modern writers who believe that the main problem is: Who should dictate? The capitalists or the workers?

Without entering into a detailed criticism, I wish to point out that there are serious objections against a rash and implicit acceptance of this theory. Whatever its speculative merits may appear to be, it is certainly a very unrealistic assumption. No political power has ever been unchecked, and as long as men remain human (as long as the 'Brave New World' has not materialized), there can be no absolute and unrestrained political power. So long as one man cannot accumulate enough physical power in his hands to dominate all others, just so long must he depend upon his helpers. Even the most powerful tyrant depends upon his secret police, his henchmen and his hangmen. This dependence means that his power, great as it may be, is not unchecked, and that he has to make concessions, playing one group off against another. It means that there are other political forces, other powers besides his own, and that he can exert his rule only by utilizing and pacifying them. This shows that even the extreme cases of sovereignty are never cases of pure sovereignty. They are never cases in which the will or the interest of one man (or, if there were such a thing, the will or the interest of one group) can achieve his aim directly, without giving up some of it in order to enlist powers which he cannot conquer. And in an overwhelming number of cases, the limitations of political power go much further than this.

I have stressed these empirical points, not because I wish to use them as an argument, but merely in order to avoid objections. My claim is that every theory of sovereignty omits to face a more fundamental question—the question, namely, whether we should not strive towards institutional control of the rulers by balancing their powers against other powers. This *theory of checks and balances* can at least claim careful consideration. The only objections to this claim, as far as I can see, are (*a*) that such a control is *practically* impossible, or (*b*) that it is *essentially* inconceivable since political power is essentially sovereign[3]. Both of these dogmatic objections are, I believe, refuted by the facts; and with them fall a number of other influential views (for instance, the theory that the only alternative to the dictatorship of one class is that of another class).

In order to raise the question of institutional control of the rulers, we need not assume more than that governments are not always good or wise. But since I have said something about historical facts, I think I should confess that I feel inclined to go a little beyond this assumption. I am inclined to think that rulers have rarely been above the average, either morally or intellectually, and often below it. And I think that it is reasonable to adopt, in politics, the principle of preparing for the worst, as well as we can, though we should, of course, at the same time try to obtain the best. It appears to me madness to base all our political efforts upon the faint hope that we shall be successful in obtaining excellent, or even competent, rulers. Strongly as I feel in these matters, I must insist, however, that my criticism of the theory of sovereignty does not depend on these more personal opinions.

Apart from these personal opinions, and apart from the above mentioned empirical arguments against the general theory of sovereignty, there is also a kind of logical argument which can be used to show the inconsistency of any of the particular forms of the theory of sovereignty; more precisely, the logical argument can be given different but analogous forms to combat the theory that the wisest should rule, or else the theories that the best, or the law, or the majority, etc., should rule. One particular form of this logical argument is directed against a too naïve version of liberalism, of democracy, and of the principle that the majority should rule; and it is somewhat similar to the well-known '*paradox of freedom*' which has been used first, and with success, by Plato. In his criticism of democracy, and in his story of the rise of the tyrant, Plato raises implicitly the following question: What if it is the will of the people that they should not rule, but a tyrant instead? The free man, Plato suggests, may exercise his absolute freedom, first by defying the laws and ultimately by defying freedom itself and by clamouring for a tyrant[4]. This is not just a far-fetched possibility; it has happened a number of times; and every time it has happened, it has put in a hopeless intellectual position all those democrats who adopt, as the ultimate basis of their political creed, the principle of the majority rule or a similar form of the principle of sovereignty. On the one hand, the principle they have adopted demands from them that they should oppose any but the majority rule, and therefore the new tyranny; on the other hand, the same principle demands from them that they should accept any decision reached by the majority, and thus the rule of the new tyrant. The inconsistency of their theory must, of course, paralyse their actions[5]. Those of us democrats who demand the institutional control of the rulers by the ruled, and especially the right of dismissing the government by a majority vote, must therefore base these demands upon better grounds than a self-contradictory theory of sovereignty. (That this is possible will be briefly shown in the next section of this chapter.)

Plato, we have seen, came near to discovering the paradoxes of freedom and of democracy. But what Plato and his followers overlooked is that all the other forms of the theory of sovereignty give rise to analogous inconsistencies. *All theories of sovereignty are paradoxical*. For instance, we may have selected 'the wisest' or 'the best' as a ruler. But 'the wisest' in his wisdom may find that not he but 'the best' should rule, and 'the best' in his goodness may perhaps decide that 'the majority' should rule. It is important to notice that even that form of the theory of sovereignty which demands the 'Kingship of the Law' is open to the same objection. This, in fact, has been seen very early, as Heraclitus' remark[6] shows: 'The law can demand, too, that the will of One Man must be obeyed.'

In summing up this brief criticism, one can, I believe, assert that the theory of sovereignty is in a weak position, both empirically and logically. The least that can be demanded is that it must not be adopted without careful consideration of other possibilities.

II

And indeed, it is not difficult to show that a theory of democratic control can be developed which is free of the paradox of sovereignty. The theory I have in mind is one which does not proceed, as it were, from a doctrine of the intrinsic goodness or righteousness of a majority rule, but rather from the baseness of tyranny; or more precisely, it rests upon the decision, or upon the adoption of the proposal, to avoid and to resist tyranny.

For we may distinguish two main types of government. The first type consists of governments of which we can get rid without bloodshed—for example, by way of general elections; that is to say, the social institutions provide means by which the rulers may be dismissed by the ruled, and the social traditions[7] ensure that these institutions will not easily be destroyed by those who are in power. The second type consists of governments which the ruled cannot get rid of except by way of a successful revolution—that is to say, in most cases, not at all. I suggest the term 'democracy' as a short-hand label for a government of the first type, and the term 'tyranny' or 'dictatorship' for the second. This, I believe, corresponds closely to traditional usage. But I wish to make clear that no part of my argument depends on the choice of these labels; and should anybody reverse this usage (as is frequently done nowadays), then I should simply say that I am in favour of what he calls 'tyranny', and object to what he calls 'democracy'; and I should reject as irrelevant any attempt to discover what 'democracy' 'really' or 'essentially' means, for example, by translating the term into 'the rule of the people'. (For although 'the people' may influence the actions of their rulers by the threat of dismissal, they never rule themselves in any concrete, practical sense.)

If we make use of the two labels as suggested, then we can now describe, as the principle of a democratic policy, the proposal to create, develop, and protect, political institutions for the avoidance of tyranny. This principle does not imply that we can ever develop institutions of this kind which are faultless or foolproof, or which ensure that the policies adopted by a democratic government will be right or good or wise—or even necessarily better or wiser than the policies adopted by a benevolent tyrant. (Since no such assertions are made, the paradox of democracy is avoided.) What may be said, however, to be implied in the adoption of the democratic principle is the conviction that the acceptance of even a bad policy in a democracy (as long as we can work for a peaceful change) is preferable to the submission to a tyranny, however wise or benevolent. Seen in this light, the theory of democracy is not based upon the principle that the majority should rule; rather, the various equalitarian methods of democratic control, such as general elections and representative government, are to be considered as no more than well-tried and, in the presence of a widespread traditional distrust of tyranny, reasonably effective institutional safeguards against tyranny, always open to improvement, and even providing methods for their own improvement.

He who accepts the principle of democracy in this sense is therefore not bound to look upon the result of a democratic vote as an authoritative expression of what is right. Although he will accept a decision of the majority, for the sake of making the democratic institutions work, he will feel free to combat it by democratic means, and to work for its revision. And should he live to see the day when the majority vote destroys the democratic institutions, then this sad experience will tell him only that there does not exist a foolproof method of avoiding tyranny. But it need not weaken his decision to fight tyranny, nor will it expose his theory as inconsistent.

III

Returning to Plato, we find that by his emphasis upon the problem 'who should rule', he implicitly assumed the general theory of sovereignty. The question of an institutional control of the rulers, and of an institutional balancing of their powers, is thereby eliminated without ever having been raised. The interest is shifted from institutions to questions of personnel, and the most urgent problem now becomes that of selecting the natural leaders, and that of training them for leadership.

In view of this fact some people think that in Plato's theory, the welfare of the state is ultimately an ethical and spiritual matter, depending on persons and personal responsibility rather than on the construction of impersonal institutions. I believe that this view of Platonism is superficial. *All long-term politics are institutional*. There is no escape from that, not even for Plato. The principle of leadership does not replace institutional problems by problems of personnel, it only creates new institutional problems. As we shall see, it even burdens the institutions with a task which goes beyond what can be reasonably demanded from a mere institution, namely, with *the task of selecting the future leaders*. It would be therefore a mistake to think that the opposition between the theory of balances and the theory of sovereignty corresponds to that between institutionalism and personalism. Plato's principle of leadership is far removed from a pure personalism since it involves the working of institutions; and indeed it may be said that a pure personalism is impossible. But it must be said that a pure institutionalism is impossible also. Not only does the construction of institutions involve important personal decisions, but the functioning of even the best institutions (such as democratic checks and balances) will always depend, to a considerable degree, on the persons involved. Institutions are like fortresses. They must be well designed *and* manned.

This distinction between the personal and the institutional element in a social situation is a point which is often missed by the critics of democracy. Most of them are dissatisfied with democratic institutions because they find that these do not necessarily prevent a state or a policy from falling short of some moral standards or of some political demands which may be urgent as well as admirable. But these critics misdirect their attacks; they do not understand what democratic institutions may be expected to do, and what the alternative to democratic institutions would be. Democracy (using this label in the sense suggested above) provides the institutional framework for the reform of political institutions. It makes possible the reform of institutions without using violence, and thereby the use of reason in the designing of new institutions and the adjusting of old ones. It cannot provide reason. The question of the intellectual and moral standard of its citizens is to a large degree a personal problem. (The idea that this problem can be tackled, in turn, by an institutional eugenic and educational control is, I believe, mistaken; some reasons for my belief will be given below.) It is quite wrong to blame democracy for the political shortcomings of a democratic state. We should rather blame ourselves, that is to say, the citizens of the democratic state. In a non-democratic state, the only way to achieve reasonable reforms is by the violent overthrow of the government, and the introduction of a democratic framework. Those who criticize democracy on any 'moral' grounds fail to distinguish between personal and institutional problems. It rests with us to improve matters. The democratic institutions cannot improve themselves. The problem of improving them is always a problem for *persons* rather than for institutions. But if we want improvements, we must make clear which *institutions* we want to improve.

There is another distinction within the field of political problems corresponding to that between persons and institutions. It is the one between the problems of the day and the problems of the future. While the problems of the day are largely personal, the building of the future must necessarily be institutional. If the political problem is approached by asking 'Who should rule?', and if Plato's principle of leadership is adopted—that is to say, the principle that the best should rule—then the problem of the future must take the form of designing institutions for the selection of future leaders.

This is one of the most important problems in Plato's theory of education. In approaching it I do not hesitate to say that Plato utterly corrupted and confused the theory and practice of education by linking it up with his theory of leadership. The damage done is, if possible, even greater than that inflicted upon ethics by the identification of collectivism with altruism, and upon political theory by the introduction of the principle of sovereignty. Plato's assumption that it should be the task of education (or more precisely, of the educational institutions) to select the future leaders, and to train them for leadership, is still largely taken for granted. By burdening these institutions with a task which must go beyond the scope of any institution, Plato is partly responsible for their deplorable state. But before entering into a general discussion of his view of the task of education, I wish to develop, in more detail, his theory of leadership, the leadership of the wise.

IV

I think it most likely that this theory of Plato's owes a number of its elements to the influence of Socrates. One of the fundamental tenets of Socrates was, I believe, his moral intellectualism. By this I understand (*a*) his identification of goodness and wisdom, his theory that nobody acts against his better knowledge, and that lack of knowledge is responsible for all moral mistakes; (*b*) his theory that moral excellence can be taught, and that it does not require any particular moral faculties, apart from the universal human intelligence.

Socrates was a moralist and an enthusiast. He was the type of man who would criticize any form of government for its short-comings (and indeed, such criticism would be necessary and useful for any government, although it is possible only under a democracy) but he recognized the importance of being loyal to the laws of the state. As it happened, he spent his life largely under a democratic form of government, and as a good democrat he found it his duty to expose the incompetence and windbaggery of some of the democratic leaders of his time. At the same time, he opposed any form of tyranny; and if we consider his courageous behaviour under the Thirty Tyrants then we have no reason to assume that his criticism of the democratic leaders was inspired by anything like anti-democratic leanings[8]. It is not unlikely that he demanded (like Plato) that the best should rule, which would have meant, in his view, the wisest, or those who knew something about justice. But we must remember that by 'justice' he meant equalitarian justice (as indicated by the passages from the *Gorgias* quoted in the last chapter), and that he was not only an equalitarian but also an individualist—perhaps the greatest apostle of an individualistic ethics of all time. And we should realize that, if he demanded that the wisest men should rule, he clearly stressed that he did not mean the learned men; in fact, he was sceptical of all professional learnedness, whether it was that of the philosophers of the past or of the learned men of his own generation, the Sophists. The wisdom he meant was of a different kind. It was simply the realization: how little do I know! Those who did not know this, he taught, knew nothing at all. (This is the true scientific spirit. Some people still think, as Plato did when he had established himself as a learned Pythagorean sage[9], that Socrates' agnostic attitude must be explained by the lack of success of the science of his day. But this only shows that they do not understand this spirit, and that they are still possessed by the pre-Socratic magical attitude towards science, and towards the scientist, whom they consider as a somewhat glorified shaman, as wise, learned, initiated. They judge him by the amount of knowledge in his possession, instead of taking, with Socrates, his awareness of what he does not know as a measure of his scientific level as well as of his intellectual honesty.)

It is important to see that this Socratic intellectualism is decidedly equalitarian. Socrates believed that everyone can be taught; in the *Meno*, we see him teaching a young slave a version[10] of the now so-called theorem of Pythagoras, in an attempt to prove that any uneducated slave has the capacity to grasp even abstract matters. And his intellectualism is also anti-authoritarian. A technique, for instance• rhetoric, may perhaps be dogmatically taught by an expert, according to Socrates; but real knowledge, wisdom, and also virtue, can be taught only by a method which he describes as a form of midwifery. Those eager to learn may be helped to free themselves from their prejudice; thus they may learn self-criticism, and that truth is not easily attained. But they may also learn to make up their minds, and to rely, critically, on their decisions, and on their insight. In view of such teaching, it is clear how much the Socratic demand (if he ever raised this demand) that the best, i.e. the intellectually honest, should rule, differs from the authoritarian demand that the most learned, or from the aristocratic demand that the best, i.e. the most noble, should rule. (Socrates' belief that even courage is wisdom can, I think, be interpreted as a direct criticism of the aristocratic doctrine of the nobly born hero.)

But this moral intellectualism of Socrates is a two-edged sword. It has its equalitarian and democratic aspect, which was later developed by Antisthenes. But it has also an aspect which may give rise to strongly anti-democratic tendencies. Its stress upon the need for enlightenment, for education, might easily be misinterpreted as a demand for *authoritarianism*. This is connected with a question which seems to have puzzled Socrates a great deal: that those who are not sufficiently educated, and thus not wise enough to know their deficiencies, are just those who are in the greatest need of education. Readiness to learn in itself proves the possession of wisdom, in fact all the wisdom claimed by Socrates for himself; for he who is ready to learn knows how little he knows. The uneducated seems thus to be in need of an authority to wake him up, since he cannot be expected to be self-critical. But this one element of authoritarianism was wonderfully balanced in Socrates' teaching by the emphasis that the authority must not claim more than that. The true teacher can prove himself only by exhibiting that self-criticism which the uneducated lacks. 'Whatever authority I may have rests solely upon my knowing how little I know': this is the way in which Socrates might have justified his mission to stir up the people from their dogmatic slumber. This educational mission he believed to be also a political mission. He felt that the way to improve the political life of the city was to educate the citizens to self-criticism. In this sense he claimed to be 'the only politician of his day'[11], in opposition to those others who flatter the people instead of furthering their true interests.

This Socratic identification of his educational and political activity could easily be distorted into the Platonic and Aristotelian demand that the state should look after the moral life of its citizens. And it can easily be used for a dangerously convincing proof that all democratic control is vicious. For how can those whose task it is to educate be judged by the uneducated? How can the better be controlled by the less good? But this argument is, of course, entirely un-Socratic. It assumes an authority of the wise and learned man, and goes far beyond Socrates' modest idea of the teacher's authority as founded solely on his consciousness of his own limitations. State-authority in these matters is liable to achieve, in fact, the exact opposite of Socrates' aim. It is liable to produce dogmatic self-satisfaction and massive intellectual complacency, instead of critical dissatisfaction and eagerness for improvement. I do not think that it is unnecessary to stress this danger which is seldom clearly realized. Even an author like Crossman, who, I believe, understood the true Socratic spirit, agrees[12] with Plato in what he calls Plato's third criticism of Athens: '*Education, which should be the major responsibility of the State*, had been left to individual caprice … Here again was a task which should be entrusted only to the man of proven probity. The future of any State depends on the younger generation, and it is therefore madness to allow the minds of children to be moulded by individual taste and force of circumstances. Equally disastrous had been the State's *laissez-faire* policy with regard to teachers and schoolmasters and sophist-lecturers.'[13] But the Athenian state's *laissez-faire* policy, criticized by Crossman and Plato, had the invaluable result of enabling certain sophist-lecturers to teach, and especially the greatest of them all, Socrates. And when this policy was later dropped, the result was Socrates' death. This should be a warning that state control in such matters is dangerous, and that the cry for the 'man of proven probity' may easily lead to the suppression of the best. (Bertrand Russell's recent suppression is a case in point.) But as far as basic principles are concerned, we have here an instance of the deeply rooted prejudice that the only alternative to *laissez-faire* is full state responsibility. I certainly believe that it is the responsibility of the state to see that its citizens are given an education enabling them to participate in the life of the community, and to make use of any opportunity to develop their special interests and gifts; and the state should certainly also see (as Crossman rightly stresses) that the lack of 'the individual's capacity to pay' should not debar him from higher studies. This, I believe, belongs to the state's protective functions. To say, however, that 'the future of the state depends on the younger generation, and that it is therefore madness to allow the minds of children to be moulded by individual taste', appears to me to open wide the door to totalitarianism. State interest must not be lightly invoked to defend measures which may endanger the most precious of all forms of freedom, namely, intellectual freedom. And although I do not advocate '*laissez-faire* with regard to teachers and schoolmasters', I believe that this policy is infinitely superior to an authoritative policy that gives officers of the state full powers to mould minds, and to control the teaching of science, thereby backing the dubious authority of the expert by that of the state, ruining science by the customary practice of teaching it as an authoritative doctrine, and destroying the scientific spirit of inquiry—the spirit of the search for truth, as opposed to the belief in its possession.

I have tried to show that Socrates' intellectualism was fundamentally equalitarian and individualistic, and that the element of authoritarianism which it involved was reduced to a minimum by Socrates' intellectual modesty and his scientific attitude. The intellectualism of Plato is very different from this. The Platonic 'Socrates' of the *Republic*[14] is the embodiment of an unmitigated authoritarianism. (Even his self-deprecating remarks are not based upon awareness of his limitations, but are rather an ironical way of asserting his superiority.) His educational aim is not the awakening of self-criticism and of critical thought in general. It is, rather, indoctrination—the moulding of minds and of souls which (to repeat a quotation from the *Laws*[15]) are 'to become, by long habit, utterly incapable of doing anything at all independently'. And Socrates' great equalitarian and liberating idea that it is possible to reason with a slave, and that there is an intellectual link between man and man, a medium of universal understanding, namely, 'reason', this idea is replaced by a demand for an educational monopoly of the ruling class, coupled with the strictest censorship, even of oral debates.

Socrates had stressed that he was not wise; that he was not in the possession of truth, but that he was a searcher, an inquirer, a lover of truth. This, he explained, is expressed by the word 'philosopher', i.e. the lover of wisdom, and the seeker for it, as opposed to 'Sophist', i.e. the professionally wise man. If ever he claimed that statesmen should be philosophers, he could only have meant that, burdened with an excessive responsibility, they should be searchers for truth, and conscious of their limitations.

How did Plato convert this doctrine? At first sight, it might appear that he did not alter it at all, when demanding that the sovereignty of the state should be invested in the philosophers; especially since, like Socrates, he defined philosophers as lovers of truth. But the change made by Plato is indeed tremendous. His lover is no longer the modest seeker, he is the proud possessor of truth. A trained dialectician, he is capable of intellectual intuition, i.e. of seeing, and of communicating with, the eternal, the heavenly Forms or Ideas. Placed high above all ordinary men, he is 'god-like, if not … divine'[16], both in his wisdom and in his power. Plato's ideal philosopher approaches both to omniscience and to omnipotence. He is the Philosopher-King. It is hard, I think, to conceive a greater contrast than that between the Socratic and the Platonic ideal of a philosopher. It is the contrast between two worlds—the world of a modest, rational individualist and that of a totalitarian demi-god.

Plato's demand that the wise man should rule—the possessor of truth, the 'fully qualified philosopher'[17]—raises, of course, the problem of selecting and educating the rulers. In a purely personalist (as opposed to an institutional) theory, this problem might be solved simply by declaring that the wise ruler will in his wisdom be wise enough to choose the best man for his successor. This is not, however, a very satisfactory approach to the problem. Too much would depend on uncontrolled circumstances; an accident may destroy the future stability of the state. But the attempt to control circumstances, to foresee what might happen and to provide for it, must lead here, as everywhere, to the abandonment of a purely personalist solution, and to its replacement by an institutional one. As already stated, the attempt to plan for the future must always lead to institutionalism.

V

The institution which according to Plato has to look after the future leaders can be described as the educational department of the state. It is, from a purely political point of view, by far the most important institution within Plato's society. It holds the keys to power. For this reason alone it should be clear that at least the higher grades of education are to be directly controlled by the rulers. But there are some additional reasons for this. The most important is that only 'the expert and … the man of proven probity', as Crossman puts it, which in Plato's view means only the very wisest adepts, that is to say, the rulers themselves, can be entrusted with the final initiation of the future sages into the higher mysteries of wisdom. This holds, above all, for dialectics, i.e. the art of intellectual intuition, of visualizing the divine originals, the Forms or Ideas, of unveiling the Great Mystery behind the common man's everyday world of appearances.

What are Plato's institutional demands regarding this highest form of education? They are remarkable. He demands that only those who are past their prime of life should be admitted. 'When their bodily strength begins to fail, and when they are past the age of public and military duties, then, and only then, should they be permitted to enter at will the sacred field …'[18] namely, the field of the highest dialectical studies. Plato's reason for this amazing rule is clear enough. He is afraid of the power of thought. 'All great things are dangerous'[19] is the remark by which he introduces the confession that he is afraid of the effect which philosophic thought may have upon brains which are not yet on the verge of old age. (All this he puts into the mouth of Socrates, who died in defence of his right of free discussion with the young.) But this is exactly what we should expect if we remember that Plato's fundamental aim was to arrest political change. In their youth, the members of the upper class shall fight. When they are too old to think independently, they shall become dogmatic students to be imbued with wisdom and authority in order to become sages themselves and to hand on their wisdom, the doctrine of collectivism and authoritarianism, to future generations.

It is interesting that in a later and more elaborate passage which attempts to paint the rulers in the brightest colours, Plato modifies his suggestion. Now[20] he allows the future sages to begin their preparatory dialectical studies at the age of thirty, stressing, of course, 'the need for great caution' and the dangers of 'insubordination ... which corrupts so many dialecticians'; and he demands that 'those to whom the use of arguments may be permitted must possess disciplined and well-balanced natures'. This alteration certainly helps to brighten the picture. But the fundamental tendency is the same. For, in the continuation of this passage, we hear that the future leaders must not be initiated into the higher philosophical studies—into the dialectic vision of the essence of the Good—before they reach, having passed through many tests and temptations, the age of fifty.

This is the teaching of the *Republic*. It seems that the dialogue *Parmenides*[21] contains a similar message, for here Socrates is depicted as a brilliant young man who, having dabbled successfully in pure philosophy, gets into serious trouble when asked to give an account of the more subtle problems of the theory of ideas. He is dismissed by the old Parmenides with the admonition that he should train himself more thoroughly in the art of abstract thought before venturing again into the higher field of philosophical studies. It looks as if we had here (among other things) Plato's answer—'Even a Socrates was once too young for dialectics'—to his pupils who pestered him for an initiation which he considered premature.

Why is it that Plato does not wish his leaders to have originality or initiative? The answer, I think, is clear. He hates change and does not want to see that re-adjustments may become necessary. But this explanation of Plato's attitude does not go deep enough. In fact, we are faced here with a fundamental difficulty of the leader principle. The very idea of selecting or educating future leaders is self-contradictory. You may solve the problem, perhaps, to some degree in the field of bodily excellence. Physical initiative and bodily courage are perhaps not so hard to ascertain. But the secret of intellectual excellence is the spirit of criticism; it is intellectual independence. And this leads to difficulties which must prove insurmountable for any kind of authoritarianism. The authoritarian will in general select those who obey, who believe, who respond to his influence. But in doing so, he is bound to select mediocrities. For he excludes those who revolt, who doubt, who dare to resist his influence. Never can an authority admit that the intellectually courageous, i.e. those who dare to defy his authority, may be the most valuable type. Of course, the authorities will always remain convinced of their ability to detect initiative. But what they mean by this is only a quick grasp of their intentions, and they will remain for ever incapable of seeing the difference. (Here we may perhaps penetrate the secret of the particular difficulty of selecting capable military leaders. The demands of military discipline enhance the difficulties discussed, and the methods of military advancement are such that those who do dare to think for themselves are usually eliminated. Nothing is less true, as far as intellectual initiative is concerned, than the idea that those who are good in obeying will also be good in commanding[22]. Very similar difficulties arise in political parties: the 'Man Friday' of the party leader is seldom a capable successor.)

We are led here, I believe, to a result of some importance, and to one which can be generalized. Institutions for the selection of the outstanding can hardly be devised. Institutional selection may work quite well for such purposes as Plato had in mind, namely for arresting change. But it will never work well if we demand more than that, for it will always tend to eliminate initiative and originality, and, more generally, qualities which are unusual and unexpected. This is not a criticism of political institutionalism. It only re-affirms what has been said before, that we should always prepare for the worst leaders, although we should try, of course, to get the best. But it is a criticism of the tendency to burden institutions, especially educational institutions, with the impossible task of selecting the best. This should never be made their task. This tendency transforms our educational system into a race-course, and turns a course of studies into a hurdle-race. Instead of encouraging the student to devote himself to his studies for the sake of studying, instead of encouraging in him a real love for his subject and for inquiry[23], he is encouraged to study for the sake of his personal career; he is led to acquire only such knowledge as is serviceable in getting him over the hurdles which he must clear for the sake of his advancement. In other words, even in the field of science, our methods of selection are based upon an appeal to personal ambition of a somewhat crude form. (It is a natural reaction to this appeal if the eager student is looked upon with suspicion by his colleagues.) The impossible demand for an institutional selection of intellectual leaders endangers the very life not only of science, but of intelligence.

It has been said, only too truly, that Plato was the inventor of both our secondary schools and our universities. I do not know a better argument for an optimistic view of mankind, no better proof of their indestructible love for truth and decency, of their originality and stubbornness and health, than the fact that this devastating system of education has not utterly ruined them. In spite of the treachery of so many of their leaders, there are quite a number, old as well as young, who are decent, and intelligent, and devoted to their task. 'I sometimes wonder how it was that the mischief done was not more clearly perceptible,' says Samuel Butler[24], 'and that the young men and women grew up as sensible and goodly as they did, in spite of the attempts almost deliberately made to warp and stunt their growth. Some doubtless received damage, from which they suffered to their life's end; but many seemed little or none the worse, and some almost the better. The reason would seem to be that the natural instinct of the lads in most cases so absolutely rebelled against their training, that do what the teachers might they could never get them to pay serious heed to it.'

It may be mentioned here that, in practice, Plato did not prove too successful as a selector of political leaders. I have in mind not so much the disappointing outcome of his experiment with Dionysius the Younger, tyrant of Syracuse, but rather the participation of Plato's Academy in Dio's successful expedition against Dionysius. Plato's famous friend Dio was supported in this adventure by a number of members of Plato's Academy. One of them was Callippus, who became Dio's most trusted comrade. After Dio had made himself tyrant of Syracuse he ordered Heraclides, his ally (and perhaps his rival), to be murdered. Shortly afterwards he was himself murdered by Callippus who usurped the tyranny, which he lost after thirteen months. (He was, in turn, murdered by the Pythagorean philosopher Leptines.) But this event was not the only one of its kind in Plato's career as a teacher. Clearchus, one of Plato's (and of Isocrates') disciples, made himself tyrant of Heraclea after having posed as a democratic leader. He was murdered by his relation, Chion, another member of Plato's Academy. (We cannot know how Chion, whom some represent as an idealist, would have developed, since he was soon killed.) These and a few similar experiences of Plato's[25]—who could boast a total of at least nine tyrants among his one-time pupils and associates—throw light on the peculiar difficulties connected with the selection of men who are to be invested with absolute power. It is hard to find a man whose character will not be corrupted by it. As Lord Acton says—all power corrupts, and absolute power corrupts absolutely.

To sum up. Plato's political programme was much more institutional than personalist; he hoped to arrest political change by the institutional control of succession in leadership. The control was to be educational, based upon an authoritarian view of learning—upon the authority of the learned expert, and 'the man of proven probity'. This is what Plato made of Socrates' demand that a responsible politician should be a lover of truth and of wisdom rather than an expert, and that he was wise only[26] if he knew his limitations.

8

THE PHILOSOPHER KING

> And the state will erect monuments ... to commemorate them. And sacrifices will be offered to them as demigods, ... as men who are blessed by grace, and godlike.
>
> PLATO.

The contrast between the Platonic and the Socratic creed is even greater than I have shown so far. Plato, I have said, followed Socrates in his definition of the philosopher. 'Whom do you call true philosophers?—Those who love truth', we read in the *Republic*[1]. But he himself is not quite truthful when he makes this statement. He does not really believe in it, for he bluntly declares in other places that it is one of the royal privileges of the sovereign to make full use of lies and deceit: 'It is the business of the rulers of the city, if it is anybody's, to tell lies, deceiving both its enemies and its own citizens for the benefit of the city; and no one else must touch this privilege.'[2]

'For the benefit of the city', says Plato. Again we find that the appeal to the principle of collective utility is the ultimate ethical consideration. Totalitarian morality overrules everything, even the definition, the Idea, of the philosopher. It need hardly be mentioned that, by the same principle of political expediency, the ruled are to be forced to tell the truth. 'If the ruler catches *anyone else* in a lie ... then he will punish him for introducing a practice which injures and endangers the city ...'[3] Only in this slightly unexpected sense are the Platonic rulers—the philosopher kings—lovers of truth.

I

Plato illustrates this application of his principle of collective utility to the problem of truthfulness by the example of the physician. The example is well chosen, since Plato likes to visualize his political mission as one of the healer or saviour of the sick body of society. Apart from this, the rôle which he assigns to medicine throws light upon the totalitarian character of Plato's city where state interest dominates the life of the citizen from the mating of his parents to his grave. Plato interprets medicine as a form of politics, or as he puts it himself, he 'regards Aesculapius, the god of medicine, as a politician'[4]. Medical art, he explains, must not consider the prolongation of life as its aim, but only the interest of the state. 'In all properly ruled communities, each man has his particular work assigned to him in the state. This he must do, and no one has time to spend his life in falling ill and getting cured.' Accordingly, the physician has 'no right to attend to a man who cannot carry out his ordinary duties; for such a man is useless to himself and to the state'. To this is added the consideration that such a man might have 'children who would probably be equally sick', and who also would become a burden to the state. (In his old age, Plato mentions medicine, in spite of his increased hatred of individualism, in a more personal vein. He complains of the doctor who treats even free citizens as if they were slaves, 'issuing his orders like a tyrant whose will is law, and then rushing off to the next slave-patient'[5], and he pleads for more gentleness and patience in medical treatment, at least for those who are not slaves.) Concerning the use of lies and deceit, Plato urges that these are 'useful only as a medicine'[6]; but the ruler of the state, Plato insists, must not behave like some of those 'ordinary doctors' who have not the courage to administer strong medicines. The philosopher king, a lover of truth as a philosopher, must, as a king, be 'a more courageous man', since he must be determined 'to administer a great many lies and deceptions'—for the benefit of the ruled, Plato hastens to add. Which means, as we already know, and as we learn here again from Plato's reference to medicine, 'for the benefit of the state'. (Kant remarked once in a very different spirit that the sentence 'Truthfulness is the best policy' might indeed be questionable, whilst the sentence 'Truthfulness is better than policy' is beyond dispute[7].)

What kind of lies has Plato in mind when he exhorts his rulers to use strong medicine? Crossman rightly emphasizes that Plato means 'propaganda, the technique of controlling the behaviour of … the bulk of the ruled majority'[8]. Certainly, Plato had these first in his mind; but when Crossman suggests that the propaganda lies were only intended for the consumption of the ruled, while the rulers should be a fully enlightened intelligentsia, then I cannot agree. I think, rather, that Plato's complete break with anything resembling Socrates' intellectualism is nowhere more obvious than in the place where he twice expresses his hope that even *the rulers themselves*, at least after a few generations, might be induced to believe his greatest propaganda lie; I mean his racialism, his Myth of Blood and Soil, known as the Myth of the Metals in Man and of the Earthborn. Here we see that Plato's utilitarian and totalitarian principles overrule everything, even the ruler's privilege of knowing, and of demanding to be told, the truth. The motive of Plato's wish that the rulers themselves should believe in the propaganda lie is his hope of increasing its wholesome effect, i.e. of strengthening the rule of the master race, and ultimately, of arresting all political change.

II

Plato introduces his Myth of Blood and Soil with the blunt admission that it is a fraud. 'Well then', says the Socrates of the *Republic*, 'could we perhaps fabricate one of those very handy lies which indeed we mentioned just recently? With the help of one single lordly lie we may, if we are lucky, persuade even the rulers themselves—but at any rate the rest of the city.'[9] It is interesting to note the use of the term 'persuade'. To persuade somebody to believe a lie means, more precisely, to mislead or to hoax him; and it would be more in tune with the frank cynicism of the passage to translate 'we may, if we are lucky, hoax even the rulers themselves'. But Plato uses the term 'persuasion' very frequently, and its occurrence here throws some light on other passages. It may be taken as a warning that in similar passages he may have propaganda lies in his mind; more especially where he advocates that the statesman should rule 'by means of both persuasion and force'[10].

After announcing his 'lordly lie', Plato, instead of proceeding directly to the narration of his Myth, first develops a lengthy preface, somewhat similar to the lengthy preface which precedes his discovery of justice; an indication, I think, of his uneasiness. It seems that he did not expect the proposal which follows to find much favour with his readers. The Myth itself introduces two ideas. The first is to strengthen the defence of the mother country; it is the idea that the warriors of his city are autochthonous, 'born of the earth of their country', and ready to defend their country which is their mother. This old and well-known idea is certainly not the reason for Plato's hesitation (although the wording of the dialogue cleverly suggests it). The second idea, however, 'the rest of the story', is the myth of racialism: 'God … has put gold into those who are capable of ruling, silver into the auxiliaries, and iron and copper into the peasants and the other producing classes.'[11] These metals are hereditary, they are racial characteristics. In this passage, in which Plato, hesitatingly, first introduces his racialism, he allows for the possibility that children may be born with an admixture of another metal than those of their parents; and it must be admitted that he here announces the following rule: if in one of the lower classes 'children are born with an admixture of gold and silver, they shall ... be appointed guardians, and ... auxiliaries'. But this concession is rescinded in later passages of the *Republic* (and also in the *Laws*), especially in the story of the Fall of Man and of the Number[12], partially quoted in chapter 5 above. From this passage we learn that *any* admixture of one of the base metals must be excluded from the higher classes. The possibility of admixtures and corresponding changes in status therefore only means that nobly born but degenerate children may be pushed down, and not that any of the base born may be lifted up. The way in which any mixing of metals must lead to destruction is described in the concluding passage of the story of the Fall of Man: 'Iron will mingle with silver and bronze with gold, and from this mixture variation will be born and absurd irregularity; and whenever these are born they will beget struggle and hostility. And this is how we must describe the ancestry and birth of Dissension, wherever she arises'[13]. It is in this light that we must consider that the Myth of the Earthborn concludes with the cynical fabrication of a prophecy by a fictitious oracle 'that the city must perish when guarded by iron and copper'[14]. Plato's reluctance to proffer his racialism at once in its more radical form indicates, I suppose, that he knew how much it was opposed to the democratic and humanitarian tendencies of his time.

If we consider Plato's blunt admission that his Myth of Blood and Soil is a propaganda lie, then the attitude of the commentators towards the Myth is somewhat puzzling. Adam, for instance, writes: 'Without it, the present sketch of a state would be incomplete. We require some guarantee for the permanence of the city ...; and nothing could be more in keeping with the *prevailing moral and religious spirit* of Plato's ... education than that he should find that guarantee in *faith rather than in reason*.'[15] I agree (though this is not quite what Adam meant) that nothing is more in keeping with Plato's totalitarian morality than his advocacy of propaganda lies. But I do not quite understand how the religious and idealistic commentator can declare, by implication, that religion and faith are on the level of an opportunist lie. As a matter of fact, Adam's comment is reminiscent of Hobbes' conventionalism, of the view that the tenets of religion, although not true, are a most expedient and indispensable political device. And this consideration shows us that Plato, after all, was more of a conventionalist than one might think. He does not even stop short of establishing a religious faith 'by convention' (we must credit him with the frankness of his admission that it is only a fabrication), while the reputed conventionalist Protagoras at least believed that the laws, which are our making, are made with the help of divine inspiration. It is hard to understand why those of Plato's commentators[16] who praise him for fighting against the subversive conventionalism of the Sophists, and for establishing a spiritual naturalism ultimately based on religion, fail to censure him for making a convention, or rather an invention, the ultimate basis of religion. In fact, Plato's attitude towards religion as revealed by his 'inspired lie' is practically identical with that of Critias, his beloved uncle, the brilliant leader of the Thirty Tyrants who established an inglorious blood-régime in Athens after the Peloponnesian war. Critias, a poet, was the first to glorify propaganda lies, whose invention he described in forceful verses eulogizing the wise and cunning man who fabricated religion, in order to 'persuade' the people, i.e. to threaten them into submission.[17]

> 'Then came, it seems, that wise and cunning man,
> The first inventor of the fear of gods . . .
> He framed a tale, a most alluring doctrine,
> Concealing truth by veils of lying lore.
> He told of the abode of awful gods,
> Up in revolving vaults, whence thunder roars
> And lightning's fearful flashes blind the eye . . .
> He thus encircled men by bonds of fear;
> Surrounding them by gods in fair abodes,
> He charmed them by his spells, and daunted them—
> And lawlessness turned into law and order.

In Critias' view, religion is nothing but the lordly lie of a great and clever statesman. Plato's views are strikingly similar, both in the introduction of the Myth in the *Republic* (where he bluntly admits that the Myth is a lie) and in the *Laws* where he says that the installation of rites and of gods is 'a matter for a great thinker'[18].—But is this the whole truth about Plato's religious attitude? Was he nothing but an opportunist in this field, and was the very different spirit of his earlier works merely Socratic?

There is of course no way of deciding this question with certainty, though I feel, intuitively, that there may sometimes be a more genuine religious feeling expressed even in the later works. But I believe that wherever Plato considers religious matters in their relation to politics, his political opportunism sweeps all other feelings aside. Thus Plato demands, in the *Laws*, the severest punishment even for honest and honourable people[19] if their opinions concerning the gods deviate from those held by the state. Their souls are to be treated by a Nocturnal Council of inquisitors[20], and if they do not recant or if they repeat the offence, the charge of impiety means death. Has he forgotten that Socrates had fallen a victim to that very charge?

That it is mainly state interest which inspires these demands, rather than interest in the religious faith as such, is indicated by Plato's central religious doctrine. The gods, he teaches in the *Laws*, punish severely all those on the wrong side in the conflict between good and evil, a conflict which is explained as that between collectivism and individualism[21]. And the gods, he insists, take an active interest in men, they are not merely spectators. It is impossible to appease them. Neither through prayers nor through sacrifices can they be moved to abstain from punishment[22]. The political interest behind this teaching is clear, and it is made even clearer by Plato's demand that the state must suppress all doubt about any part of this politico-religious dogma, and especially about the doctrine that the gods never abstain from punishment.

Plato's opportunism and his theory of lies makes it, of course, difficult to interpret what he says. How far did he believe in his theory of justice? How far did he believe in the truth of the religious doctrines he preached? Was he perhaps himself an atheist, in spite of his demand for the punishment of other (lesser) atheists? Although we cannot hope to answer any of these questions definitely, it is, I believe, difficult, and methodologically unsound, not to give Plato at least the benefit of the doubt. And especially the fundamental sincerity of his belief that there is an urgent need to arrest all change can, I think, hardly be questioned. (I shall return to this in chapter 10.) On the other hand, we cannot doubt that Plato subjects the Socratic love of truth to the more fundamental principle that the rule of the master class must be strengthened.

It is interesting, however, to note that Plato's theory of truth is slightly less radical than his theory of justice. Justice, we have seen, is defined, practically, as that which serves the interest of his totalitarian state. It would have been possible, of course, to define the concept of truth in the same utilitarian or pragmatist fashion. The Myth is true, Plato could have said, since anything that serves the interest of my state must be believed and therefore must be called 'true'; and there must be no other criterion of truth. In theory, an analogous step has actually been taken by the pragmatist successors of Hegel; in practice, it has been taken by Hegel himself and his racialist successors. But Plato retained enough of the Socratic spirit to admit candidly that he was lying. The step taken by the school of Hegel was one that could never have occurred, I think, to any companion of Socrates[23].

III

So much for the rôle played by the Idea of Truth in Plato's best state. But apart from Justice and Truth, we have still to consider some further Ideas, such as Goodness, Beauty, and Happiness, if we wish to remove the objections, raised in chapter 6, against our interpretation of Plato's political programme as purely totalitarian, and as based on historicism. An approach to the discussion of these Ideas, and also to that of Wisdom, which has been partly discussed in the last chapter, can be made by considering the somewhat negative result reached by our discussion of the Idea of Truth. For this result raises a new problem: Why does Plato demand that the philosophers should be kings or the kings philosophers, if he defines the philosopher as a lover of truth, insisting, on the other hand, that the king must be 'more courageous', and use lies?

The only reply to this question is, of course, that Plato has, in fact, something very different in mind when he uses the term 'philosopher'. And indeed, we have seen in the last chapter that his philosopher is not the devoted seeker for wisdom, but its proud possessor. He is a learned man, a sage. What Plato demands, therefore, is the rule of learnedness—*sophocracy*, if I may so call it. In order to understand this demand, we must try to find what kind of functions make it desirable that the ruler of Plato's state should be a possessor of knowledge, a 'fully qualified philosopher', as Plato says. The functions to be considered can be divided into two main groups, namely those connected with the *foundation* of the state, and those connected with its *preservation*.

IV

The first and the most important function of the philosopher king is that of the city's founder and lawgiver. It is clear why Plato needs a philosopher for this task. If the state is to be stable, then it must be a true copy of the divine Form or Idea of the State. But only a philosopher who is fully proficient in the highest of sciences, in dialectics, is able to see, and to copy, the heavenly Original. This point receives much emphasis in the part of the *Republic* in which Plato develops his arguments for the sovereignty of the philosophers[24]. Philosophers 'love to see the truth', and a real lover always loves to see the whole, not merely the parts. Thus he does not love, as ordinary people do, sensible things and their 'beautiful sounds and colours and shapes', but he wants 'to see, and to admire the real nature of beauty'—the Form or Idea of Beauty. *In this way, Plato gives the term philosopher a new meaning*, that of a lover and a seer of the divine world of Forms or Ideas. As such, the philosopher is the man who may become the founder of a virtuous city[25]: 'The philosopher who has communion with the divine' may be 'overwhelmed by the urge to realize ... his heavenly vision', of the ideal city and of its ideal citizens. He is like a draughtsman or a painter who has 'the divine as his model'. Only true philosophers can 'sketch the ground-plan of the city', for they alone can see the original, and can copy it, by 'letting their eyes wander to and fro, from the model to the picture, and back from the picture to the model'.

As 'a painter of constitutions'[26], the philosopher must be helped by the light of goodness and of wisdom. A few remarks will be added concerning these two ideas, and their significance for the philosopher in his function as a founder of the city.

Plato's *Idea of the Good* is the highest in the hierarchy of Forms. It is the sun of the divine world of Forms or Ideas, which not only sheds light on all the other members, but is the source of their existence[27]. It is also the source or cause of all knowledge and all truth[28]. The power of seeing, of appreciating, of knowing the Good is thus indispensable[29] to the dialectician. Since it is the sun and the source of light in the world of Forms, it enables the philosopher-painter to discern his objects. Its function is therefore of the greatest importance for the founder of the city. But this purely formal information is all we get. Plato's Idea of the Good nowhere plays a more direct ethical or political rôle; never do we hear which deeds are good, or produce good, apart from the well-known collectivist moral code whose precepts are introduced without recourse to the Idea of Good. Remarks that the Good is the aim, that it is desired by every man[30], do not enrich our information. This empty formalism is still more marked in the *Philebus*, where the Good is identified[31] with the Idea of 'measure' or 'mean'. And when I read the report that Plato, in his famous lecture 'On the Good', disappointed an uneducated audience by defining the Good as 'the class of the determinate conceived as a unity', then my sympathy is with the audience. In the *Republic*, Plato says frankly[32] that he cannot explain what he means by 'the Good'. The only practical suggestion we ever get is the one mentioned at the beginning of chapter 4—that good is everything that preserves, and evil everything that leads to corruption or degeneration. ('Good' does not, however, seem to be here the Idea of Good, but rather a property of things which makes them resemble the ideas.) Good is, accordingly, an unchanging, an arrested state of things; it is the state of things at rest.

This does not seem to carry us very far beyond Plato's political totalitarianism; and the analysis of Plato's *Idea of Wisdom* leads to equally disappointing results. Wisdom, as we have seen, does not mean to Plato the Socratic insight into one's own limitations; nor does it mean what most of us would expect, a warm interest in, and a helpful understanding of, humanity and human affairs. Plato's wise men, highly preoccupied with the problems of a superior world, 'have no time to look down at the affairs of men ...; they look upon, and hold fast to, the ordered and the measured'. It is the right kind of learning that makes a man wise: 'Philosophic natures are lovers of that kind of learning which reveals to them a reality that exists for ever and is not harassed by generation and degeneration.' It does not seem that Plato's treatment of wisdom can carry us beyond the ideal of arresting change.

V

Although the analysis of the functions of the city's founder has not revealed any new ethical elements in Plato's doctrine, it has shown that there is a definite reason why the founder of the city must be a philosopher. But this does not fully justify the demand for the permanent sovereignty of the philosopher. It only explains why the philosopher must be the first lawgiver, but not why he is needed as the permanent ruler, especially since none of the later rulers must introduce any change. For a full justification of the demand that the philosophers should rule, we must therefore proceed to analyse the tasks connected with the city's preservation.

We know from Plato's sociological theories that the state, once established, will continue to be stable as long as there is no split in the unity of the master class. The bringing up of that class is, therefore, the great preserving function of the sovereign, and a function which must continue as long as the state exists. How far does it justify the demand that a philosopher must rule? To answer this question, we distinguish again, within this function, between two different activities: the supervision of education, and the supervision of eugenic breeding.

Why should the director of education be a philosopher? Why is it not sufficient, once the state and its educational system are established, to put an experienced general, a soldier-king, in charge of it? The answer that the educational system must provide not only soldiers but philosophers, and therefore needs philosophers as well as soldiers as supervisors, is obviously unsatisfactory; for if no philosophers were needed as directors of education and as permanent rulers, then there would be no need for the educational system to produce new ones. The requirements of the educational system cannot as such justify the need for philosophers in Plato's state, or the postulate that the rulers must be philosophers. This would be different, of course, if Plato's education had an individualistic aim, apart from its aim to serve the interest of the state; for example, the aim to develop philosophical faculties for their own sake. But when we see, as we did in the preceding chapter, how frightened Plato was of permitting anything like independent thought[33]; and when we now see that the ultimate theoretical aim of this philosophic education was merely a 'Knowledge of the Idea of the Good' which is incapable of giving an articulate account of this Idea, then we begin to realize that this cannot be the explanation. And this impression is strengthened if we remember chapter 4, where we have seen that Plato also demanded restrictions in the Athenian 'musical' education. The great importance which Plato attaches to a philosophical education of the rulers must be explained by other reasons—by reasons which must be purely political.

The main reason I can see is the need for increasing to the utmost the authority of the rulers. If the education of the auxiliaries functions properly, there will be plenty of good soldiers. Outstanding military faculties may therefore be insufficient to establish an unchallenged and unchallengeable authority. This must be based on higher claims. Plato bases it upon the claims of supernatural, mystical powers which he develops in his leaders. They are not like other men. They belong to another world, they communicate with the divine. Thus the philosopher king seems to be, partly, a copy of a tribal priest-king, an institution which we have mentioned in connection with Heraclitus. (The institution of tribal priest-kings or medicine-men or shamans seems also to have influenced the old Pythagorean sect, with their surprisingly naïve tribal taboos. Apparently, most of these were dropped even before Plato. But the claim of the Pythagoreans to a supernatural basis of their authority remained.) Thus Plato's philosophical education has a definite political function. *It puts a mark on the rulers, and it establishes a barrier between the rulers and the ruled.* (This has remained a major function of 'higher' education down to our own time.) Platonic wisdom is acquired largely for the sake of establishing a permanent political class rule. It can be described as political 'medicine', giving mystic powers to its possessors, the medicine-men.[34]

But this cannot be the full answer to our question of the functions of the philosopher in the state. It means, rather, that the question why a philosopher is needed has only been shifted, and that we would have now to raise the analogous question of the practical political functions of the shaman or the medicine-man. Plato must have had some definite aim when he devised his specialized philosophic training. We must look for a permanent function of the ruler, analogous to the temporary function of the lawgiver. The only hope of discovering such a function seems to be in the field of breeding the master race.

VI

The best way to find out why a philosopher is needed as a permanent ruler is to ask the question: What happens, according to Plato, to a state which is not permanently ruled by a philosopher? Plato has given a clear answer to this question. If the guardians of the state, even of a very perfect one, are unaware of Pythagorean lore and of the Platonic Number, then the race of the guardians, and with it the state, must degenerate.

Racialism thus takes up a more central part in Plato's political programme than one would expect at first sight. Just as the Platonic racial or nuptial Number provides the setting for his descriptive sociology, 'the setting in which Plato's Philosophy of History is framed' (as Adam puts it), so it also provides the setting of Plato's political demand for the sovereignty of the philosophers. After what has been said in chapter 4 about the graziers' or cattle breeders' background of Plato's state, we are perhaps not quite unprepared to find that his *king* is a breeder king. But it may still surprise some that his *philosopher* turns out to be a philosophic breeder. The need for scientific, for mathematico-dialectical and philosophical breeding is not the least of the arguments behind the claim for the sovereignty of the philosophers.

It has been shown in chapter 4 how the problem of obtaining a pure breed of human watch-dogs is emphasized and elaborated in the earlier parts of the *Republic*. But so far we have not met with any plausible reason why only a genuine and fully qualified philosopher should be a proficient and successful political breeder. And yet, as every breeder of dogs or horses or birds knows, rational breeding is impossible without a pattern, an aim to guide him in his efforts, an ideal which he may try to approach by the methods of mating and of selecting. Without such a standard, he could never decide which offspring is 'good enough'; he could never speak of the difference between 'good offspring' and 'bad offspring'. But this standard corresponds exactly to a Platonic Idea of the race which he intends to breed.

Just as only the true philosopher, the dialectician, can see, according to Plato, the divine original of the city, so it is only the dialectician who can see that other divine original—the Form or Idea of Man. Only he is capable of copying this model, of calling it down from Heaven to Earth[35], and of realizing it here. It is a kingly Idea, this Idea of Man. It does not, as some have thought, represent what is common to all men; it is not the universal concept 'man'. It is, rather, the godlike original of man, an unchanging superman; it is a super-Greek, and a super-master. The philosopher must try to realize on earth what Plato describes as the race of 'the most constant, the most virile, and, within the limits of possibilities, the most beautifully formed men … : nobly born, and of awe-inspiring character'[36]. It is to be a race of men and women who are 'godlike if not divine … sculptured in perfect beauty'[37]—a lordly race, destined by nature to kingship and mastery.

We see that the two fundamental functions of the philosopher king are analogous: he has to copy the divine original of the city, and he has to copy the divine original of man. He is the only one who is able, and who has the urge, 'to realize, in the individual as well as in the city, his heavenly vision'[38].

Now we can understand why Plato drops his first hint that a more than ordinary excellence is needed in his rulers in the same place where he first claims that the principles of animal breeding must be applied to the race of men. We are, he says, most careful in breeding animals. 'If you did not breed them in this way, don't you think that the race of your birds or your dogs would quickly degenerate?' When inferring from this that man must be bred in the same careful way, 'Socrates' exclaims: 'Good heavens! … What surpassing excellence we shall have to demand from our rulers, if the same principles apply to the race of men!'[39] This exclamation is significant; it is one of the first hints that the rulers may constitute a class of 'surpassing excellence' with status and training of their own; and it thus prepares us for the demand that they ought to be philosophers. But the passage is even more significant in so far as it directly leads to Plato's demand that it must be the duty of the rulers, as doctors of the race of men, to administer lies and deception. Lies are necessary, Plato asserts, 'if your herd is to reach highest perfection'; for this needs 'arrangements that must be kept secret from all but the rulers, if we wish to keep the herd of guardians really free from disunion'. Indeed, the appeal (quoted above) to the rulers for more courage in administering lies as a medicine is made in this connection; it prepares the reader for the next demand, considered by Plato as particularly important. He decrees[40] that the rulers should fabricate, for the purpose of mating the young auxiliaries, 'an ingenious system of balloting, so that the persons who have been disappointed … may blame their bad luck, and not the rulers', who are, secretly, to engineer the ballot. And immediately after this despicable advice for dodging the admission of responsibility (by putting it into the mouth of Socrates, Plato libels his great teacher), 'Socrates' makes a suggestion[41] which is soon taken up and elaborated by Glaucon and which we may therefore call the *Glauconic Edict*. I mean the brutal law[42] which imposes on everybody of either sex the duty of submitting, for the duration of a war, to the wishes of the brave: 'As long as the war lasts, … nobody may say "No" to him. Accordingly, if a soldier wishes to make love to anybody, whether male or female, this law will make him more eager to carry off the price of valour.' The state, it is carefully pointed out, will thereby obtain two distinct benefits—more heroes, owing to the incitement, and again more heroes, owing to the increased numbers of children from heroes. (The latter benefit, as the most important one from the point of view of a long-term racial policy, is put into the mouth of 'Socrates'.)

VII

No special philosophical training is required for this kind of breeding. Philosophical breeding, however, plays its main part in counteracting the dangers of degeneration. In order to fight these dangers, a fully qualified philosopher is needed, i.e. one who is trained in pure mathematics (including solid geometry), pure astronomy, pure harmonics, and, the crowning achievement of all, in dialectics. Only he who knows the secrets of mathematical eugenics, of the Platonic Number, can bring back to man, and preserve for him, the happiness enjoyed before the Fall[43]. All this should be borne in mind when, after the announcement of the Glauconic Edict (and after an interlude dealing with the natural distinction between Greeks and Barbarians, corresponding, according to Plato, to that between masters and slaves), the doctrine is enunciated which Plato carefully marks as his central and most sensational political demand—the sovereignty of the philosopher king. This demand alone, he teaches, can put an end to the evils of social life; to the evil rampant in states, i.e. *political instability*, as well as to its more hidden cause, the evil rampant in the members of the race of men, i.e. *racial degeneration*. This is the passage.[44]

'Well,' says Socrates, 'I am now about to dive into that topic which I compared before to the greatest wave of all. Yet I must speak, even though I foresee that this will bring upon me a deluge of laughter. Indeed, I can see it now, this very wave, breaking over my head into an uproar of laughter and defamation ...'—'Out with the story!' says Glaucon. 'Unless,' says Socrates, 'unless, in their cities, philosophers are vested with the might of kings, or those now called kings and oligarchs become genuine and fully qualified philosophers; and unless these two, political might and philosophy, are fused (while the many who nowadays follow their natural inclination for only one of these two are suppressed by force), unless this happens, my dear Glaucon, there can be no rest; and the evil will not cease to be rampant in the cities—nor, I believe, in the race of men.' (To which Kant wisely replied: 'That kings should become philosophers, or philosophers kings, is not likely to happen; nor would it be desirable, since the possession of power invariably debases the free judgement of reason. It is, however, indispensable that a king—or a kingly, i.e. self-ruling, people—should *not suppress* philosophers but leave them the right of public utterance.'[45])

This important Platonic passage has been quite appropriately described as the key to the whole work. Its last words, 'nor, I believe, in the race of men', are, I think, an afterthought of comparatively minor importance in this place. It is, however, necessary to comment upon them, since the habit of idealizing Plato has led to the interpretation[46] that Plato speaks here about 'humanity', extending his promise of salvation from the scope of the cities to that of 'mankind as a whole'. It must be said, in this connection, that the ethical category of 'humanity' as something that transcends the distinction of nations, races, and classes, is entirely foreign to Plato. In fact, we have sufficient evidence of Plato's hostility towards the equalitarian creed, a hostility which is seen in his attitude towards Antisthenes[47], an old disciple and friend of Socrates. Antisthenes also belonged to the school of Gorgias, like Alcidamas and Lycophron, whose equalitarian theories he seems to have extended into the doctrine of the brotherhood of all men, and of the universal empire of men[48]. This creed is attacked in the *Republic* by correlating the natural inequality of Greeks and Barbarians to that of masters and slaves; and it so happens that this attack is launched[49] immediately before the key passage we are here considering. For these and other reasons[50], it seems safe to assume that Plato, when speaking of the evil rampant in the race of men, alluded to a theory with which his readers would be sufficiently acquainted at this place, namely, to his theory that the welfare of the state depends, ultimately, upon the 'nature' of the individual members of the ruling class; and that their nature, and the nature of their race, or offspring, is threatened, in turn, by the evils of an individualistic education, and, more important still, by racial degeneration. Plato's remark, with its clear allusion to the opposition between divine rest and the evil of change and decay, foreshadows the story of the Number and the Fall of Man[51].

It is very appropriate that Plato should allude to his racialism in this key passage in which he enunciates his most important political demand. For without the 'genuine and fully qualified philosopher', trained in all those sciences which are prerequisite to eugenics, the state is lost. In his story of the Number and the Fall of Man, Plato tells us that one of the first and fatal sins of omission committed by the degenerate guardians will be their loss of interest in eugenics, in watching and testing the purity of the race: 'Hence rulers will be ordained who are altogether unfit for their task as guardians; namely, to watch, and to test, the metals in the races (which are Hesiod's races as well as yours), gold and silver and bronze and iron.'[52]

It is ignorance of the mysterious nuptial Number which leads to all that. But the Number was undoubtedly Plato's own invention. (It presupposes pure harmonics, which in turn presupposes solid geometry, a new science at the time when the *Republic* was written.) Thus we see that nobody but Plato himself knew the secret of, and held the key to, true guardianship. But this can mean only one thing. The philosopher king is Plato himself, and the *Republic* is Plato's own claim for kingly power—to the power which he thought his due, uniting in himself, as he did, both the claims of the philosopher and of the descendant and legitimate heir of Codrus the martyr, the last of Athens' kings, who, according to Plato, had sacrificed himself 'in order to preserve the kingdom for his children'.

VIII

Once this conclusion has been reached, many things which otherwise would remain unrelated become connected and clear. It can hardly be doubted, for instance, that Plato's work, full of allusions as it is to contemporary problems and characters, was meant by its author not so much as a theoretical treatise, but as a topical political manifesto. 'We do Plato the gravest of wrongs', says A. E. Taylor, 'if we forget that the *Republic* is no mere collection of theoretical discussions about government ... but a serious project of practical reform put forward by an Athenian ..., set on fire, like Shelley, with a "passion for reforming the world".'[53] This is undoubtedly true, and we could have concluded from this consideration alone that, in describing his philosopher kings, Plato must have thought of some of the contemporary philosophers. But in the days when the *Republic* was written, there were in Athens only three outstanding men who might have claimed to be philosophers: Antisthenes, Isocrates, and Plato himself. If we approach the *Republic* with this in mind, we find at once that, in the discussion of the characteristics of the philosopher kings, there is a lengthy passage which is clearly marked out by Plato as containing personal allusions. It begins[54] with an unmistakable allusion to a popular character, namely Alcibiades, and ends by openly mentioning a name (that of Theages), and with a reference of 'Socrates' to himself[55]. Its upshot is that only very few can be described as true philosophers, eligible for the post of philosopher king. The nobly born Alcibiades, who was of the right type, deserted philosophy, in spite of Socrates' attempts to save him. Deserted and defenceless, philosophy was claimed by unworthy suitors. Ultimately, 'there is left only a handful of men who are worthy of being associated with philosophy'. From the point of view we have reached, we would have to expect that the 'unworthy suitors' are Antisthenes and Isocrates and their school (and that they are the same people whom Plato demands to have 'suppressed by force', as he says in the key passage of the philosopher king). And, indeed, there is some independent evidence corroborating this expectation[56]. Similarly, we should expect that the 'handful of men who are worthy' includes Plato and, perhaps, some of his friends (possibly Dio); and, indeed, a continuation of this passage leaves little doubt that Plato speaks here of himself: 'He who belongs to this small band ... can see the madness of the many, and the general corruption of all public affairs. The philosopher ... is like a man in a cage of wild beasts. He will not share the injustice of the many, but his power does not suffice for continuing his fight alone, surrounded as he is by a world of savages. He would be killed before he could do any good, to his city or to his friends ... Having duly considered all these points, he will hold his peace, and confine his efforts to his own work ...'[57]. The strong resentment expressed in these sour and most un-Socratic[58] words marks them clearly as Plato's own. For a full appreciation, however, of this personal confession, it must be compared with the following: 'It is not in accordance with nature that the skilled navigator should beg the unskilled sailors to accept his command; nor that the wise man should wait at the doors of the rich ... But the true and natural procedure is that the sick, whether rich or poor, should hasten to the doctor's door. Likewise should those who need to be ruled besiege the door of him who can rule; and never should a ruler beg them to accept his rule, if he is any good at all.' Who can miss the sound of an immense personal pride in this passage? Here am I, says Plato, your natural ruler, the philosopher king who knows how to rule. If you want me, you must come to me, and if you insist, I may become your ruler. But I shall not come begging to you.

Did he believe that they would come? Like many great works of literature, the *Republic* shows traces that its author experienced exhilarating and extravagant hopes of success[59], alternating with periods of despair. Sometimes, at least, Plato hoped that they would come; that the success of his work, the fame of his wisdom, would bring them along. Then again, he felt that they would only be incited to furious attacks; that all he would bring upon himself was 'an uproar of laughter and defamation'—perhaps even death.

Was he ambitious? He was reaching for the stars—for god-likeness. I sometimes wonder whether part of the enthusiasm for Plato is not due to the fact that he gave expression to many secret dreams[60]. Even where he argues against ambition, we cannot but feel that he is inspired by it. The philosopher, he assures us[61], is not ambitious; although 'destined to rule, he is the least eager for it'. But the reason given is—that his status is too high.

He who has had communion with the divine may descend from his heights to the mortals below, sacrificing himself for the sake of the interest of the state. He is not eager; but as a natural ruler and saviour, he is ready to come. The poor mortals need him. Without him the state must perish, for he alone knows the secret of how to preserve it—the secret of arresting degeneration.

I think we must face the fact that behind the sovereignty of the philosopher king stands the quest for power. The beautiful portrait of the sovereign is a self-portrait. When we have recovered from the shock of this finding, we may look anew at the awe-inspiring portrait; and if we can fortify ourselves with a small dose of Socrates' irony then we may cease to find it so terrifying. We may begin to discern its human, indeed, its only too human features. We may even begin to feel a little sorry for Plato, who had to be satisfied with establishing the first professorship, instead of the first kingship, of philosophy; who could never realize his dream, the kingly Idea which he had formed after his own image. Fortified by our dose of irony, we may even find, in Plato's story, a melancholy resemblance to that innocent and unconscious little satire on Platonism, the story of the *Ugly Dachshund*, of Tono, the Great Dane, who forms his kingly Idea of 'Great Dog' after his own image (but who happily finds in the end that he is Great Dog himself)[62].

What a monument of human smallness is this idea of the philosopher king. What a contrast between it and the simplicity and humaneness of Socrates, who warned the statesman against the danger of being dazzled by his own power, excellence, and wisdom, and who tried to teach him what matters most—that we are all frail human beings. What a decline from this world of irony and reason and truthfulness down to Plato's kingdom of the sage whose magical powers raise him high above ordinary men; although not quite high enough to forgo the use of lies, or to neglect the sorry trade of every shaman—the selling of spells, of breeding spells, in exchange for power over his fellow-men.

9

AESTHETICISM, PERFECTIONISM, UTOPIANISM

'Everything has got to be smashed to start with. Our whole damned civilization has got to go, before we can bring any decency into the world.'

'Mourlan', in DU GARD'S *Les Thibaults*.

Inherent in Plato's programme there is a certain approach towards politics which, I believe, is most dangerous. Its analysis is of great practical importance from the point of view of rational social engineering. The Platonic approach I have in mind can be described as that of *Utopian engineering*, as opposed to another kind of social engineering which I consider as the only rational one, and which may be described by the name of *piecemeal engineering*. The Utopian approach is the more dangerous as it may seem to be the obvious alternative to an out-and-out historicism—to a radically historicist approach which implies that we cannot alter the course of history; at the same time, it appears to be a necessary complement to a less radical historicism, like that of Plato, which permits human interference.

The Utopian approach may be described as follows. Any rational action must have a certain aim. It is rational in the same degree as it pursues its aim consciously and consistently, and as it determines its means according to this end. To choose the end is therefore the first thing we have to do if we wish to act rationally; and we must be careful to determine our real or ultimate ends, from which we must distinguish clearly those intermediate or partial ends which actually are only means, or steps on the way, to the ultimate end. If we neglect this distinction, then we must also neglect to ask whether these partial ends are likely to promote the ultimate end, and accordingly, we must fail to act rationally. These principles, if applied to the realm of political activity, demand that we must determine our ultimate political aim, or the Ideal State, before taking any practical action. Only when this ultimate aim is determined, in rough outline at least, only when we are in possession of something like a blueprint of the society at which we aim, only then can we begin to consider the best ways and means for its realization, and to draw up a plan for practical action. These are the necessary preliminaries of any practical political move that can be called rational, and especially of social engineering.

This, in brief, is the methodological approach which I call Utopian engineering[1]. It is convincing and attractive. In fact, it is just the kind of methodological approach to attract all those who are either unaffected by historicist prejudices or reacting against them. This makes it only the more dangerous, and its criticism the more imperative.

Before proceeding to criticize Utopian engineering in detail, I wish to outline another approach to social engineering, namely, that of piecemeal engineering. It is an approach which I think to be methodologically sound. The politician who adopts this method may or may not have a blueprint of society before his mind, he may or may not hope that mankind will one day realize an ideal state, and achieve happiness and perfection on earth. But he will be aware that perfection, if at all attainable, is far distant, and that every generation of men, and therefore also the living, have a claim; perhaps not so much a claim to be made happy, for there are no institutional means of making a man happy, but a claim not to be made unhappy, where it can be avoided. They have a claim to be given all possible help, if they suffer. The piecemeal engineer will, accordingly, adopt the method of searching for, and fighting against, the greatest and most urgent evils of society, rather than searching for, and fighting for, its greatest ultimate good[2]. This difference is far from being merely verbal. In fact, it is most important. It is the difference between a reasonable method of improving the lot of man, and a method which, if really tried, may easily lead to an intolerable increase in human suffering. It is the difference between a method which can be applied at any moment, and a method whose advocacy may easily become a means of continually postponing action until a later date, when conditions are more favourable. And it is also the difference between the only method of improving matters which has so far been really successful, at any time, and in any place (Russia included, as will be seen), and a method which, wherever it has been tried, has led only to the use of violence in place of reason, and if not to its own abandonment, at any rate to that of its original blueprint.

In favour of his method, the piecemeal engineer can claim that a systematic fight against suffering and injustice and war is more likely to be supported by the approval and agreement of a great number of people than the fight for the establishment of some ideal. The existence of social evils, that is to say, of social conditions under which many men are suffering, can be comparatively well established. Those who suffer can judge for themselves, and the others can hardly deny that they would not like to change places. It is infinitely more difficult to reason about an ideal society. Social life is so complicated that few men, or none at all, could judge a blueprint for social engineering on the grand scale; whether it be practicable; whether it would result in a real improvement; what kind of suffering it may involve; and what may be the means for its realization. As opposed to this, blueprints for piecemeal engineering are comparatively simple. They are blueprints for single institutions, for health and unemployed insurance, for instance, or arbitration courts, or anti-depression budgeting[3], or educational reform. If they go wrong, the damage is not very great, and a re-adjustment not very difficult. They are less risky, and for this very reason less controversial. But if it is easier to reach a reasonable agreement about existing evils and the means of combating them than it is about an ideal good and the means of its realization, then there is also more hope that by using the piecemeal method we may get over the very greatest practical difficulty of all reasonable political reform, namely, the use of reason, instead of passion and violence, in executing the programme. There will be a possibility of reaching a reasonable compromise and therefore of achieving the improvement by democratic methods. ('Compromise' is an ugly word, but it is important for us to learn its proper use. *Institutions* are inevitably the result of a compromise with circumstances, interests, etc., though as *persons* we should resist influences of this kind.)

As opposed to that, the Utopian attempt to realize an ideal state, using a blueprint of society as a whole, is one which demands a strong centralized rule of a few, and which therefore is likely to lead to a dictatorship[4]. This I consider a criticism of the Utopian approach; for I have tried to show, in the chapter on the Principle of Leadership, that an authoritarian rule is a most objectionable form of government. Some points not touched upon in that chapter furnish us with even more direct arguments against the Utopian approach. One of the difficulties faced by a benevolent dictator is to find whether the effects of his measures agree with his good intentions (as de Tocqueville saw clearly more than a hundred years ago[5]). The difficulty arises out of the fact that authoritarianism must discourage criticism; accordingly, the benevolent dictator will not easily hear of complaints concerning the measures he has taken. But without some such check, he can hardly find out whether his measures achieve the desired benevolent aim. The situation must become even worse for the Utopian engineer. The reconstruction of society is a big undertaking which must cause considerable inconvenience to many, and for a considerable span of time. Accordingly, the Utopian engineer will have to be deaf to many complaints; in fact, it will be part of his business to suppress unreasonable objections. (He will say, like Lenin, 'You can't make an omelette without breaking eggs.') But with it, he must invariably suppress reasonable criticism also. Another difficulty of Utopian engineering is related to the *problem of the dictator's successor*. In chapter 7 I have mentioned certain aspects of this problem. Utopian engineering raises a difficulty analogous to but even more serious than the one which faces the benevolent tyrant who tries to find an equally benevolent successor (see note 25 to chapter 7). The very sweep of such a Utopian undertaking makes it improbable that it will realize its ends during the lifetime of one social engineer, or group of engineers. And if the successors do not pursue the same ideal, then all the sufferings of the people for the sake of the ideal may have been in vain.

A generalization of this argument leads to a further criticism of the Utopian approach. This approach, it is clear, can be of practical value only if we assume that the original blueprint, perhaps with certain adjustments, remains the basis of the work until it is completed. But that will take some time. It will be a time of revolutions, both political and spiritual, and of new experiments and experience in the political field. It is therefore to be expected that ideas and ideals will change. What had appeared the ideal state to the people who made the original blueprint, may not appear so to their successors. If that is granted, then the whole approach breaks down. The method of first establishing an ultimate political aim and then beginning to move towards it is futile if we admit that the aim may be considerably changed during the process of its realization. It may at any moment turn out that the steps so far taken actually lead away from the realization of the new aim. And if we change our direction according to the new aim, then we expose ourselves to the same risk again. In spite of all the sacrifices made, we may never get anywhere at all. Those who prefer one step towards a distant ideal to the realization of a piecemeal compromise should always remember that if the ideal is very distant, it may even become difficult to say whether the step taken was towards or away from it. This is especially so if the course should proceed by zigzag steps, or, in Hegel's jargon, 'dialectically', or if it is not clearly planned at all. (This bears upon the old and somewhat childish question of how far the end can justify the means. Apart from claiming that no end could ever justify all means, I think that a fairly concrete and realizable end may justify temporary measures which a more distant ideal never could[6].)

We see now that the Utopian approach can be saved only by the Platonic belief in one absolute and unchanging ideal, together with two further assumptions, namely (*a*) that there are rational methods to determine once and for all what this ideal is, and (*b*) what the best means of its realization are. Only such far-reaching assumptions could prevent us from declaring the Utopian methodology to be utterly futile. But even Plato himself and the most ardent Platonists would admit that (*a*) is certainly not true; that there is no rational method for determining the ultimate aim, but, if anything, only some kind of intuition. Any difference of opinion between Utopian engineers must therefore lead, in the absence of rational methods, to the use of power instead of reason, i.e. to violence. If any progress in any definite direction is made at all, then it is made in spite of the method adopted, not because of it. The success may be due, for instance, to the excellence of the leaders; but we must never forget that excellent leaders cannot be produced by rational methods, but only by luck.

It is important to understand this criticism properly; I do not criticize the ideal by claiming that an ideal can never be realized, that it must always remain a Utopia. This would not be a valid criticism, for many things have been realized which have once been dogmatically declared to be unrealizable, for instance, the establishment of institutions for securing civil peace, i.e. for the prevention of crime *within* the state; and I think that, for instance, the establishment of corresponding institutions for the prevention of international crime, i.e. armed aggression or blackmail, though often branded as Utopian, is not even a very difficult problem[7]. What I criticize under the name Utopian engineering recommends the reconstruction of society as a whole, i.e. very sweeping changes whose practical consequences are hard to calculate, owing to our limited experiences. It claims to plan rationally for the whole of society, although we do not possess anything like the factual knowledge which would be necessary to make good such an ambitious claim. We cannot possess such knowledge since we have insufficient practical experience in this kind of planning, and knowledge of facts must be based upon experience. At present, the sociological knowledge necessary for large-scale engineering is simply non-existent.

In view of this criticism, the Utopian engineer is likely to grant the need for practical experience, and for a social technology based upon practical experiences. But he will argue that we shall never know more about these matters if we recoil from making social experiments which alone can furnish us with the practical experience needed. And he might add that Utopian engineering is nothing but the application of the experimental method to society. Experiments cannot be carried out without involving sweeping changes. They must be on a large scale, owing to the peculiar character of modern society with its great masses of people. An experiment in socialism, for instance, if confined to a factory, or to a village, or even to a district, would never give us the kind of realistic information which we need so urgently.

Such arguments in favour of Utopian engineering exhibit a prejudice which is as widely held as it is untenable, namely, the prejudice that social experiments must be on a 'large scale', that they must involve the whole of society if they are to be carried out under realistic conditions. But piecemeal social experiments can be carried out under realistic conditions, in the midst of society, in spite of being on a 'small scale', that is to say, without revolutionizing the whole of society. In fact, we are making such experiments all the time. The introduction of a new kind of life-insurance, of a new kind of taxation, of a new penal reform, are all social experiments which have their repercussions through the whole of society without remodelling society as a whole. Even a man who opens a new shop, or who reserves a ticket for the theatre, is carrying out a kind of social experiment on a small scale; and all our knowledge of social conditions is based on experience gained by making experiments of this kind. The Utopian engineer we are opposing is right when he stresses that an experiment in socialism would be of little value if carried out under laboratory conditions, for instance, in an isolated village, since what we want to know is how things work out in society under normal social conditions. But this very example shows where the prejudice of the Utopian engineer lies. He is convinced that we must recast the whole structure of society, when we experiment with it; and he can therefore conceive a more *modest* experiment only as one that recasts the whole structure of a *small* society. But the kind of experiment from which we can learn most is the alteration of one social institution at a time. For only in this way can we learn how to fit institutions into the framework of other institutions, and how to adjust them so that they work according to our intentions. And only in this way can we make mistakes, and learn from our mistakes, without risking repercussions of a gravity that must endanger the will to future reforms. Furthermore, the Utopian method must lead to a dangerous dogmatic attachment to a blueprint for which countless sacrifices have been made. Powerful interests must become linked up with the success of the experiment. All this does not contribute to the rationality, or to the scientific value, of the experiment. But the piecemeal method permits repeated experiments and continuous readjustments. In fact, it might lead to the happy situation where politicians begin to look out for their own mistakes instead of trying to explain them away and to prove that they have always been right. This—and not Utopian planning or historical prophecy—would mean the introduction of scientific method into politics, since the whole secret of scientific method is a readiness to learn from mistakes[8].

These views can be corroborated, I believe, by comparing social and, for instance, mechanical engineering. The Utopian engineer will of course claim that mechanical engineers sometimes plan even very complicated machinery as a whole, and that their blueprints may cover, and plan in advance, not only a certain kind of machinery, but even the whole factory which produces this machinery. My reply would be that the mechanical engineer can do all this because he has sufficient experience at his disposal, i.e. theories developed by trial and error. But this means that he can plan because he has made all kinds of mistakes already; or in other words, because he relies on experience which he has gained by applying piecemeal methods. His new machinery is the result of a great many small improvements. He usually has a model first, and only after a great number of piecemeal adjustments to its various parts does he proceed to a stage where he could draw up his final plans for the production. Similarly, his plan for the production of his machine incorporates a great number of experiences, namely, of piecemeal improvements made in older factories. The wholesale or large-scale method works only where the piecemeal method has furnished us first with a great number of detailed experiences, and even then only within the realm of these experiences. Few manufacturers would be prepared to proceed to the production of a new engine on the basis of a blueprint alone, even if it were drawn up by the greatest expert, without first making a model and 'developing' it by little adjustments as far as possible.

It is perhaps useful to contrast this criticism of Platonic Idealism in politics with Marx's criticism of what he calls 'Utopianism'. What is common to Marx's criticism and mine is that both demand more realism. We both believe that Utopian plans will never be realized in the way they were conceived, because hardly any social action ever produces precisely the result expected. (This does not, in my opinion, invalidate the piecemeal approach, because here we may learn—or rather, we ought to learn—and change our views, while we act.) But there are many differences. In arguing against Utopianism, Marx condemns in fact *all* social engineering—a point which is rarely understood. He denounces the faith in a rational planning of social institutions as altogether unrealistic, since society must grow according to the laws of history and not according to our rational plans. All we can do, he asserts, is to lessen the birthpangs of the historical processes. In other words, he adopts a radically historicist attitude, opposed to all social engineering. But there is one element within Utopianism which is particularly characteristic of Plato's approach and which Marx does not oppose, although it is perhaps the most important of those elements which I have attacked as unrealistic. It is the sweep of Utopianism, its attempt to deal with society as a whole, leaving no stone unturned. It is the conviction that one has to go to the very root of the social evil, that nothing short of a complete eradication of the offending social system will do if we wish to 'bring any decency into the world' (as Du Gard says). It is, in short, its uncompromising *radicalism*. (The reader will notice that I am using this term in its original and literal sense—not in the now customary sense of a 'liberal progressivism', but in order to characterize an attitude of 'going to the root of the matter'.) Both Plato and Marx are dreaming of the apocalyptic revolution which will radically transfigure the whole social world.

This sweep, this extreme radicalism of the Platonic approach (and of the Marxian as well) is, I believe, connected with its æstheticism, i.e. with the desire to build a world which is not only a little better and more rational than ours, but which is free from all its ugliness: not a crazy quilt, an old garment badly patched, but an entirely new gown, a really beautiful new world[9]. This æstheticism is a very understandable attitude; in fact, I believe most of us suffer a little from such dreams of perfection. (Some reasons why we do so will, I hope, emerge from the next chapter.) But this æsthetic enthusiasm becomes valuable only if it is bridled by reason, by a feeling of responsibility, and by a humanitarian urge to help. Otherwise it is a dangerous enthusiasm, liable to develop into a form of neurosis or hysteria.

Nowhere do we find this æstheticism more strongly expressed than in Plato. Plato was an artist; and like many of the best artists, he tried to visualize a model, the 'divine original' of his work, and to 'copy' it faithfully. A good number of the quotations given in the last chapter illustrate this point. What Plato describes as dialectics is, in the main, the intellectual intuition of the world of pure beauty. His trained philosophers are men who 'have seen the truth of what is beautiful and just, and good'[10], and can bring it down from heaven to earth. Politics, to Plato, is the Royal Art. It is an art—not in a metaphorical sense in which we may speak about the art of handling men, or the art of getting things done, but in a more literal sense of the word. It is an art of composition, like music, painting, or architecture. The Platonic politician composes cities, for beauty's sake.

But here I must protest. I do not believe that human lives may be made the means for satisfying an artist's desire for self-expression. We must demand, rather, that every man should be given, if he wishes, the right to model his life himself, as far as this does not interfere too much with others. Much as I may sympathize with the æsthetic impulse, I suggest that the artist might seek expression in another material. Politics, I demand, must uphold equalitarian and individualistic principles; dreams of beauty have to submit to the necessity of helping men in distress, and men who suffer injustice; and to the necessity of constructing institutions to serve such purposes[11].

It is interesting to observe the close relationship between Plato's utter radicalism, the demand for sweeping measures, and his æstheticism. The following passages are most characteristic. Plato, speaking about 'the philosopher who has communion with the divine', mentions first that he will be 'overwhelmed by the urge … to realize his heavenly vision in individuals as well as in the city',—a city which 'will never know happiness unless its draughtsmen are artists who have the divine as their model'. Asked about the details of their draughtsmanship, Plato's 'Socrates' gives the following striking reply: 'They will take as their canvas a city and the characters of men, and they will, first of all, *make their canvas clean*—by no means an easy matter. But this is just the point, you know, where they will differ from all others. They will not start work on a city nor on an individual (nor will they draw up laws) unless they are given a clean canvas, or have cleaned it themselves.'[12]

The kind of thing Plato has in mind when he speaks of canvas-cleaning is explained a little later. 'How can that be done?' asks Glaucon. 'All citizens above the age of ten', Socrates answers, 'must be expelled from the city and deported somewhere into the country; and the children who are now free from the influence of the manners and habits of their parents must be taken over. They must be educated in the ways [of true philosophy], and according to the laws, which we have described.' (The philosophers are not, of course, among the citizens to be expelled: they remain as educators, and so do, presumably, those non-citizens who must keep them going.) In the same spirit, Plato says in the *Statesman* of the royal rulers who rule in accordance with the Royal Science of Statesmanship: 'Whether they happen to rule by law or without law, over willing or unwilling subjects; … and whether they purge the state for its good, by killing or by deporting [or 'banishing'] some of its citizens …—so long as they proceed according to science and justice, and preserve … the state and make it better than it was, this form of government must be declared the only one that is right.'

This is the way in which the artist-politician must proceed. This is what canvas-cleaning means. He must eradicate the existing institutions and traditions. He must purify, purge, expel, banish, and kill. ('Liquidate' is the terrible modern term for it.) Plato's statement is indeed a true description of the uncompromising attitude of all forms of out-and-out radicalism—of the æstheticist's refusal to compromise. The view that society should be beautiful like a work of art leads only too easily to violent measures. But all this radicalism and violence is both unrealistic and futile. (This has been shown by the example of Russia's development. After the economic breakdown to which the canvas-cleaning of the so-called 'war communism' had led, Lenin introduced his 'New Economic Policy', in fact a kind of piecemeal engineering, though without the conscious formulation of its principles or of a technology. He started by restoring most of the features of the picture which had been eradicated with so much human suffering. Money, markets, differentiation of income, and private property—for a time even private enterprise in production—were reintroduced, and only after this basis was re-established began a new period of reform[13].)

In order to criticize the foundations of Plato's æsthetic radicalism, we may distinguish two different points.

The first is this. What some people have in mind who speak of our 'social system', and of the need to replace it by another 'system', is very similar to a picture painted on a canvas which has to be wiped clean before one can paint a new one. But there are some great differences. One of them is that the painter and those who co-operate with him as well as the institutions which make their life possible, his dreams and plans for a better world, and his standards of decency and morality, are all part of the social system, i.e. of the picture to be wiped out. If they were really to clean the canvas, they would have to destroy themselves, and their Utopian plans. (And what follows then would probably not be a beautiful copy of a Platonic ideal but chaos.) The political artist clamours, like Archimedes, for a place outside the social world on which he can take his stand, in order to lever it off its hinges. But such a place does not exist; and the social world must continue to function during any reconstruction. This is the simple reason why we must reform its institutions little by little, until we have more experience in social engineering.

This leads us to the more important second point, to the irrationalism which is inherent in radicalism. In all matters, we can only learn by trial and error, by making mistakes and improvements; we can never rely on inspiration, although inspirations may be most valuable as long as they can be checked by experience. Accordingly, *it is not reasonable to assume that a complete reconstruction of our social world would lead at once to a workable system.* Rather we should expect that, owing to lack of experience, many mistakes would be made which could be eliminated only by a long and laborious process of small adjustments; in other words, by that rational method of piecemeal engineering whose application we advocate. But those who dislike this method as insufficiently radical would have again to wipe out their freshly constructed society, in order to start anew with a clean canvas; and since the new start, for the same reasons, would not lead to perfection either, they would have to repeat this process without ever getting anywhere. Those who admit this and are prepared to adopt our more modest method of piecemeal improvements, but only after the first radical canvas-cleaning, can hardly escape the criticism that their first sweeping and violent measures were quite unnecessary.

Aestheticism and radicalism must lead us to jettison reason, and to replace it by a desperate hope for political miracles. This irrational attitude which springs from an intoxication with dreams of a beautiful world is what I call Romanticism[14]. It may seek its heavenly city in the past or in the future; it may preach 'back to nature' or 'forward to a world of love and beauty'; but its appeal is always to our emotions rather than to reason. Even with the best intentions of making heaven on earth it only succeeds in making it a hell—that hell which man alone prepares for his fellow-men.

The Background of Plato's Attack

10

THE OPEN SOCIETY AND ITS ENEMIES

He will restore us to our original nature, and heal us, and make us happy and blessed.

PLATO.

There is still something missing from our analysis. The contention that Plato's political programme is purely totalitarian, and the objections to this contention which were raised in chapter 6, have led us to examine the part played, within this programme, by such moral ideas as Justice, Wisdom, Truth, and Beauty. The result of this examination was always the same. We found that the rôle of these ideas is important, but that they do not lead Plato beyond totalitarianism and racialism. But one of these ideas we have still to examine: that of Happiness. It may be remembered that we quoted Crossman in connection with the belief that Plato's political programme is fundamentally a 'plan for the building of a perfect state in which every citizen is really happy', and that I described this belief as a relic of the tendency to idealize Plato. If called upon to justify my opinion, I should not have much difficulty in pointing out that Plato's treatment of happiness is exactly analogous to his treatment of justice; and especially, that it is based upon the same belief that society is 'by nature' divided into classes or castes. True happiness[1], Plato insists, is achieved only by justice, i.e. by keeping one's place. The ruler must find happiness in ruling, the warrior in warring; and, we may infer, the slave in slaving. Apart from that, Plato says frequently that what he is aiming at is neither the happiness of individuals nor that of any particular class in the state, but only the happiness of the whole, and this, he argues, is nothing but the outcome of that rule of justice which I have shown to be totalitarian in character. That only this justice can lead to any true happiness is one of the main theses of the *Republic*.

In view of all this, it seems to be a consistent and hardly refutable interpretation of the material to present Plato as a totalitarian party-politician, unsuccessful in his immediate and practical undertakings, but in the long run only too successful[2] in his propaganda for the arrest and overthrow of a civilization which he hated. But one only has to put the matter in this blunt fashion in order to feel that there is something seriously amiss with this interpretation. At any rate, so I felt, when I had formulated it. I felt perhaps not so much that it was untrue, but that it was defective. I therefore began to search for evidence which would refute this interpretation[3]. However, in every point but one, this attempt to refute my interpretation was quite unsuccessful. The new material made the identity between Platonism and totalitarianism only the more manifest.

The one point in which I felt that my search for a refutation had succeeded concerned Plato's hatred of tyranny. Of course, there was always the possibility of explaining this away. It would have been easy to say that his indictment of tyranny was mere propaganda. Totalitarianism often professes a love for 'true' freedom, and Plato's praise of freedom as opposed to tyranny sounds exactly like this professed love. In spite of this, I felt that certain of his observations on tyranny[4], which will be mentioned later in this chapter, were sincere. The fact, of course, that 'tyranny' usually meant in Plato's day a form of rule based on the support of the masses made it possible to claim that Plato's hatred of tyranny was consistent with my original interpretation. But I felt that this did not remove the need for modifying my interpretation. I also felt that the mere emphasis on Plato's fundamental sincerity was quite insufficient to accomplish this modification. No amount of emphasis could offset the general impression of the picture. A new picture was needed which would have to include Plato's sincere belief in his mission as healer of the sick social body, as well as the fact that he had seen more clearly than anybody else before or after him what was happening to Greek society. Since the attempt to reject the identity of Platonism and totalitarianism had not improved the picture, I was ultimately forced to modify my interpretation of totalitarianism itself. In other words, my attempt to understand Plato by analogy with modern totalitarianism led me, to my own surprise, to modify my view of totalitarianism. It did not modify my hostility, but it ultimately led me to see that the strength of both the old and the new totalitarian movements rested on the fact that they attempted to answer a very real need, however badly conceived this attempt may have been.

In the light of my new interpretation, it appears to me that Plato's declaration of his wish to make the state and its citizens happy is not merely propaganda. I am ready to grant his fundamental benevolence[5]. I also grant that he was right, to a limited extent, in the sociological analysis on which he based his promise of happiness. To put this point more precisely: I believe that Plato, with deep sociological insight, found that his contemporaries were suffering under a severe strain, and that this strain was due to the social revolution which had begun with the rise of democracy and individualism. He succeeded in discovering the main causes of their deeply rooted unhappiness—social change, and social dissension—and he did his utmost to fight them. There is no reason to doubt that one of his most powerful motives was to win back happiness for the citizens. For reasons discussed later in this chapter, I believe that the medico-political treatment which he recommended, the arrest of change and the return to tribalism, was hopelessly wrong. But the recommendation, though not practicable as a therapy, testifies to Plato's power of diagnosis. It shows that he knew what was amiss, that he understood the strain, the unhappiness, under which the people were labouring, even though he erred in his fundamental claim that by leading them back to tribalism he could lessen the strain, and restore their happiness.

It is my intention to give in this chapter a very brief survey of the historical material which induced me to hold such opinions. A few critical remarks on the method adopted, that of historical interpretation, will be found in the last chapter of the book. It will therefore suffice here if I say that I do not claim scientific status for this method, since the tests of an historical interpretation can never be as rigorous as those of an ordinary hypothesis. The interpretation is mainly a *point of view*, whose value lies in its fertility, in its power to throw light upon the historical material, to lead us to find new material, and to help us to rationalize and to unify it. What I am going to say here is therefore not meant as a dogmatic assertion, however boldly I may perhaps sometimes express my opinions.

I

Our Western civilization originated with the Greeks. They were, it seems, the first to make the step from tribalism to humanitarianism. Let us consider what that means.

The early Greek tribal society resembles in many respects that of peoples like the Polynesians, the Maoris for instance. Small bands of warriors, usually living in fortified settlements, ruled by tribal chiefs or kings, or by aristocratic families, were waging war against one another on sea as well as on land. There were, of course, many differences between the Greek and the Polynesian ways of life, for there is, admittedly, no uniformity in tribalism. There is no standardized 'tribal way of life'. It seems to me, however, that there are some characteristics that can be found in most, if not all, of these tribal societies. I mean their magical or irrational attitude towards the customs of social life, and the corresponding rigidity of these customs.

The magical attitude towards social custom has been discussed before. Its main element is the lack of distinction between the customary or conventional regularities of social life and the regularities found in 'nature'; and this often goes together with the belief that both are enforced by a supernatural will. The rigidity of the social customs is probably in most cases only another aspect of the same attitude. (There are some reasons to believe that this aspect is even more primitive, and that the supernatural belief is a kind of rationalization of the fear of changing a routine—a fear which we can find in very young children.) When I speak of the rigidity of tribalism I do not mean that no changes can occur in the tribal ways of life. I mean rather that the comparatively infrequent changes have the character of religious conversions or revulsions, or of the introduction of new magical taboos. They are not based upon a rational attempt to improve social conditions. Apart from such changes—which are rare—taboos rigidly regulate and dominate all aspects of life. They do not leave many loop-holes. There are few problems in this form of life, and nothing really equivalent to moral problems. I do not mean to say that a member of a tribe does not sometimes need much heroism and endurance in order to act in accordance with the taboos. What I mean is that he will rarely find himself in the position of doubting how he ought to act. The right way is always determined, though difficulties must be overcome in following it. It is determined by taboos, by magical tribal institutions which can never become objects of critical consideration. Not even a Heraclitus distinguishes clearly between the institutional laws of tribal life and the laws of nature; both are taken to be of the same magical character. Based upon the collective tribal tradition, the institutions leave no room for personal responsibility. The taboos that establish some form of group-responsibility may be the forerunner of what we call personal responsibility, but they are fundamentally different from it. They are not based upon a principle of reasonable accountability, but rather upon magical ideas, such as the idea of appeasing the powers of fate.

It is well known how much of this still survives. Our own ways of life are still beset with taboos; food taboos, taboos of politeness, and many others. And yet, there are some important differences. In our own way of life there is, between the laws of the state on the one hand and the taboos we habitually observe on the other, an ever-widening field of personal decisions, with its problems and responsibilities; and we know the importance of this field. Personal decisions may lead to the alteration of taboos, and even of political laws which are no longer taboos. The great difference is the possibility of rational reflection upon these matters. Rational reflection begins, in a way, with Heraclitus[6]. With Alcmaeon, Phaleas and Hippodamus, with Herodotus and the Sophists, the quest for the 'best constitution' assumes, by degrees, the character of a problem which can be rationally discussed. And in our own time, many of us make rational decisions concerning the desirability or otherwise of new legislation, and of other institutional changes; that is to say, decisions based upon an estimate of possible consequences, and upon a conscious preference for some of them. We recognize rational personal responsibility.

In what follows, the magical or tribal or collectivist society will also be called the *closed society*, and the society in which individuals are confronted with personal decisions, the *open society*.

A closed society at its best can be justly compared to an organism. The so-called organic or biological theory of the state can be applied to it to a considerable extent. A closed society resembles a herd or a tribe in being a semi-organic unit whose members are held together by semi-biological ties—kinship, living together, sharing common efforts, common dangers, common joys and common distress. It is still a concrete group of concrete individuals, related to one another not merely by such abstract social relationships as division of labour and exchange of commodities, but by concrete physical relationships such as touch, smell, and sight. And although such a society may be based on slavery, the presence of slaves need not create a fundamentally different problem from that of domesticated animals. Thus those aspects are lacking which make it impossible to apply the organic theory successfully to an open society.

The aspects I have in mind are connected with the fact that, in an open society, many members strive to rise socially, and to take the places of other members. This may lead, for example, to such an important social phenomenon as class struggle. We cannot find anything like class struggle in an organism. The cells or tissues of an organism, which are sometimes said to correspond to the members of a state, may perhaps compete for food; but there is no inherent tendency on the part of the legs to become the brain, or of other members of the body to become the belly. Since there is nothing in the organism to correspond to one of the most important characteristics of the open society, competition for status among its members, the so-called organic theory of the state is based on a false analogy. The closed society, on the other hand, does not know much of such tendencies. Its institutions, including its castes, are sacrosanct—taboo. The organic theory does not fit so badly here. It is therefore not surprising to find that most attempts to apply the organic theory to our society are veiled forms of propaganda for a return to tribalism[7].

As a consequence of its loss of organic character, an open society may become, by degrees, what I should like to term an 'abstract society'. It may, to a considerable extent, lose the character of a concrete or real group of men, or of a system of such real groups. This point which has been rarely understood may be explained by way of an exaggeration. We could conceive of a society in which men practically never meet face to face—in which all business is conducted by individuals in isolation who communicate by typed letters or by telegrams, and who go about in closed motor-cars. (Artificial insemination would allow even propagation without a personal element.) Such a fictitious society might be called a 'completely abstract or depersonalized society'. Now the interesting point is that our modern society resembles in many of its aspects such a completely abstract society. Although we do not always drive alone in closed motor cars (but meet face to face thousands of men walking past us in the street) the result is very nearly the same as if we did—we do not establish as a rule any personal relation with our fellow-pedestrians. Similarly, membership of a trade union may mean no more than the possession of a membership card and the payment of a contribution to an unknown secretary. There are many people living in a modern society who have no, or extremely few, intimate personal contacts, who live in anonymity and isolation, and consequently in unhappiness. For although society has become abstract, the biological make-up of man has not changed much; men have social needs which they cannot satisfy in an abstract society.

Of course, our picture is even in this form highly exaggerated. There never will be or can be a completely abstract or even a predominantly abstract society—no more than a completely rational or even a predominantly rational society. Men still form real groups and enter into real social contacts of all kinds, and try to satisfy their emotional social needs as well as they can. But most of the social groups of a modern open society (with the exception of some lucky family groups) are poor substitutes, since they do not provide for a common life. And many of them do not have any function in the life of the society at large.

Another way in which the picture is exaggerated is that it does not, so far, contain any of the gains made—only the losses. But there are gains. Personal relationships of a new kind can arise where they can be freely entered into, instead of being determined by the accidents of birth; and with this, a new individualism arises. Similarly, spiritual bonds can play a major rôle where the biological or physical bonds are weakened; etc. However this may be, our example, I hope, will have made plain what is meant by a more abstract society in contradistinction to a more concrete or real social group; and it will have made it clear that our modern open societies function largely by way of abstract relations, such as exchange or co-operation. (It is the analysis of these abstract relations with which modern social theory, such as economic theory, is mainly concerned. This point has not been understood by many sociologists, such as Durkheim, who never gave up the dogmatic belief that society must be analysed in terms of real social groups.)

In the light of what has been said, it will be clear that the transition from the closed to the open society can be described as one of the deepest revolutions through which mankind has passed. Owing to what we have described as the biological character of the closed society, this transition must be felt deeply indeed. Thus when we say that our Western civilization derives from the Greeks, we ought to realize what it means. It means that the Greeks started for us that great revolution which, it seems, is still in its beginning—the transition from the closed to the open society.

II

Of course, this revolution was not made consciously. The breakdown of tribalism, of the closed societies of Greece, may be traced back to the time when population growth began to make itself felt among the ruling class of landed proprietors. This meant the end of 'organic' tribalism. For it created social tension within the closed society of the ruling class. At first, there appeared to be something like an 'organic' solution of this problem, the creation of daughter cities. (The 'organic' character of this solution was underlined by the magical procedures followed in the sending out of colonists.) But this ritual of colonization only postponed the breakdown. It even created new danger spots wherever it led to cultural contacts; and these, in turn, created what was perhaps the worst danger to the closed society—commerce, and a new class engaged in trade and seafaring. By the sixth century B.C., this development had led to the partial dissolution of the old ways of life, and even to a series of political revolutions and reactions. And it had led not only to attempts to retain and to arrest tribalism by force, as in Sparta, but also to that great spiritual revolution, the invention of critical discussion, and, in consequence, of thought that was free from magical obsessions. At the same time we find the first symptoms of a new uneasiness. *The strain of civilization was beginning to be felt.*

This strain, this uneasiness, is a consequence of the breakdown of the closed society. It is still felt even in our day, especially in times of social change. It is the strain created by the effort which life in an open and partially abstract society continually demands from us—by the endeavour to be rational, to forgo at least some of our emotional social needs, to look after ourselves, and to accept responsibilities. We must, I believe, bear this strain as the price to be paid for every increase in knowledge, in reasonableness, in co-operation and in mutual help, and consequently in our chances of survival, and in the size of the population. It is the price we have to pay for being human.

The strain is most closely related to the problem of the tension between the classes which is raised for the first time by the breakdown of the closed society. The closed society itself does not know this problem. At least to its ruling members, slavery, caste, and class rule are 'natural' in the sense of being unquestionable. But with the breakdown of the closed society, this certainty disappears, and with it all feeling of security. The tribal community (and later the 'city') is the place of security for the member of the tribe. Surrounded by enemies and by dangerous or even hostile magical forces, he experiences the tribal community as a child experiences his family and his home, in which he plays his definite part; a part he knows well, and plays well. The breakdown of the closed society, raising as it does the problems of class and other problems of social status, must have had the same effect upon the citizens as a serious family quarrel and the breaking up of the family home is liable to have on children[8]. Of course, this kind of strain was felt by the privileged classes, now that they were threatened, more strongly than by those who had formerly been suppressed; but even the latter felt uneasy. They also were frightened by the breakdown of their 'natural' world. And though they continued to fight their struggle, they were often reluctant to exploit their victories over their class enemies who were supported by tradition, the *status quo*, a higher level of education, and a feeling of natural authority.

In this light we must try to understand the history of Sparta, which successfully tried to arrest these developments, and of Athens, the leading democracy.

Perhaps the most powerful cause of the breakdown of the closed society was the development of sea-communications and commerce. Close contact with other tribes is liable to undermine the feeling of necessity with which tribal institutions are viewed; and trade, commercial initiative, appears to be one of the few forms in which individual initiative[9] and independence can assert itself, even in a society in which tribalism still prevails. These two, seafaring and commerce, became the main characteristics of Athenian imperialism, as it developed in the fifth century B.C. And indeed they were recognized as the most dangerous developments by the oligarchs, the members of the privileged, or of the formerly privileged, classes of Athens. It became clear to them that the trade of Athens, its monetary commercialism, its naval policy, and its democratic tendencies were parts of one single movement, and that it was impossible to defeat democracy without going to the roots of the evil and destroying both the naval policy and the empire. But the naval policy of Athens was based upon its harbours, especially the Piraeus, the centre of commerce and the stronghold of the democratic party; and strategically, upon the walls which fortified Athens, and later, upon the Long Walls which linked it to the harbours of the Piraeus and Phalerum. Accordingly, we find that for more than a century the empire, the fleet, the harbour, and the walls were hated by the oligarchic parties of Athens as the symbols of the democracy and as the sources of its strength which they hoped one day to destroy.

Much evidence of this development can be found in Thucydides' *History of the Peloponnesian War*, or rather, of the two great wars of 431–421 and 419–403 B.C., between Athenian democracy and the arrested oligarchic tribalism of Sparta. When reading Thucydides we must never forget that his heart was not with Athens, his native city. Although he apparently did not belong to the extreme wing of the Athenian oligarchic clubs who conspired throughout the war with the enemy, he was certainly a member of the oligarchic party, and a friend neither of the Athenian people, the demos, who had exiled him, nor of its imperialist policy. (I do not intend to belittle Thucydides, the greatest historian, perhaps, who ever lived. But however successful he was in making sure of the facts he records, and however sincere his efforts to be impartial, his comments and moral judgements represent an interpretation, a point of view; and in this we need not agree with him.) I quote first from a passage describing Themistocles' policy in 482 B.C., half a century before the Peloponnesian war: 'Themistocles also persuaded the Athenians to finish the Piraeus ... Since the Athenians had now taken to the sea, he thought that they had a great opportunity for building an empire. He was the first who dared to say that they should make the sea their domain ...'[10] Twenty-five years later, 'the Athenians began to build their Long Walls to the sea, one to the harbour of Bhalerum, the other to the Piraeus'[11]. But this time, twenty-six years before the outbreak of the Peloponnesian war, the oligarchic party was fully aware of the meaning of these developments. We hear from Thucydides that they did not shrink even from the most blatant treachery. As sometimes happens with oligarchs, class interest superseded their patriotism. An opportunity offered itself in the form of a hostile Spartan expeditionary force operating in the north of Athens, and they determined to conspire with Sparta against their own country. Thucydides writes: 'Certain Athenians were privately making overtures to them' (i.e. to the Spartans) '*in the hope that they would put an end to the democracy*, and to the building of the Long Walls. But the other Athenians ... suspected their design against democracy.' The loyal Athenian citizens therefore went out to meet the Spartans, but were defeated. It appears, however, that they had weakened the enemy sufficiently to prevent him from joining forces with the fifth columnists within their own city. Some months later, the Long Walls were completed, which meant that the democracy could enjoy security as long as it upheld its naval supremacy.

This incident throws light on the tenseness of the class situation in Athens, even twenty-six years before the outbreak of the Peloponnesian war, during which the situation became much worse. It also throws light on the methods employed by the subversive and pro-Spartan oligarchic party. Thucydides, one must note, mentions their treachery only in passing, and he does not censure them, although in other places he speaks most strongly against class struggle and party spirit. The next passages quoted, written as a general reflection on the Corcyraean Revolution of 427 B.C., are interesting, first as an excellent picture of the class situation; secondly, as an illustration of the strong words Thucydides could find when he wanted to describe analogous tendencies on the side of the democrats of Corcyra. (In order to judge his lack of impartiality we must remember that in the beginning of the war Corcyra had been one of Athens' democratic allies, and that the revolt had been started by the oligarchs.) Moreover, the passage is an excellent expression of the feeling of a general social breakdown: 'Nearly the whole Hellenic world', writes Thucydides, 'was in commotion. In every city, the leaders of the democratic and of the oligarchic parties were trying hard, the one to bring in the Athenians, the other the Lacedaemonians ... The tie of party was stronger than the tie of blood ... The leaders on either side used specious names, the one party professing to uphold the constitutional equality of the many, the other the wisdom of the nobility; in reality they made the public interest their price, professing, of course, their devotion to it. They used any conceivable means for getting the better of one another, and committed the most monstrous crimes ... This revolution gave birth to every form of wickedness in Hellas ... Everywhere prevailed an attitude of perfidious antagonism. There was no word binding enough, no oath terrible enough, to reconcile enemies. Each man was strong only in the conviction that nothing was secure.'[12]

The full significance of the attempt of the Athenian oligarchs to accept the help of Sparta and stop the building of the Long Walls can be gauged when we realize that this treacherous attitude had not changed when Aristotle wrote his *Politics*, more than a century later. We hear there about an oligarchic oath, which, Aristotle said, 'is now in vogue'. This is how it runs: 'I promise to be an enemy of the people, and to do my best to give them bad advice!'[13] It is clear that we cannot understand the period without remembering this attitude.

I mentioned above that Thucydides himself was an anti-democrat. This becomes clear when we consider his description of the Athenian empire, and the way it was hated by the various Greek states. Athens' rule over its empire, he tells us, was felt to be no better than a tyranny, and all the Greek tribes were afraid of her. In describing public opinion at the outbreak of the Peloponnesian war, he is mildly critical of Sparta and very critical of Athenian imperialism. 'The general feeling of the peoples was strongly on the side of the Lacedaemonians; for they maintained that they were the liberators of Hellas. Cities and individuals were eager to assist them … , and the general indignation against the Athenians was intense. Some were longing to be liberated from Athens, others fearful of falling under its sway.'[14] It is most interesting that this judgement of the Athenian empire has become, more or less, the official judgement of 'History', i.e. of most of the historians. Just as the philosophers find it hard to free themselves from Plato's point of view, so are the historians bound to that of Thucydides. As an example I may quote Meyer (the best German authority on this period), who simply repeats Thucydides when he says: 'The sympathies of the educated world of Greece were … turned away from Athens.'[15]

But such statements are only expressions of the anti-democratic point of view. Many facts recorded by Thucydides—for instance, the passage quoted which describes the attitude of the democratic and oligarchic party leaders—show that Sparta was 'popular' not among the peoples of Greece but only among the oligarchs; among the 'educated', as Meyer puts it so nicely. Even Meyer admits that 'the democratically minded masses hoped in many places for her victory'[16], i.e. for the victory of Athens; and Thucydides' narrative contains many instances which prove Athens' popularity among the democrats and the suppressed. But who cares for the opinion of the uneducated masses? If Thucydides and the 'educated' assert that Athens was a tyrant, then she was a tyrant.

It is most interesting that the same historians who hail Rome for her achievement, the foundation of a universal empire, condemn Athens for her attempt to achieve something better. The fact that Rome succeeded where

Athens failed is not a sufficient explanation of this attitude. They do not really censure Athens for her failure, since they loathe the very idea that her attempt might have been successful. Athens, they believe, was a ruthless democracy, a place ruled by the uneducated, who hated and suppressed the educated, and were hated by them in turn. But this view—the myth of the cultural intolerance of democratic Athens—makes nonsense of the known facts, and above all of the astonishing spiritual productivity of Athens in this particular period. Even Meyer must admit this productivity. 'What Athens produced in this decade', he says with characteristic modesty, 'ranks equal with one of the mightiest decades of German literature.'[17] Pericles, who was the democratic leader of Athens at this time, was more than justified when he called her 'The School of Hellas'.

I am far from defending everything that Athens did in building up her empire, and I certainly do not wish to defend wanton attacks (if such have occurred), or acts of brutality; nor do I forget that Athenian democracy was still based on slavery[18]. But it is necessary, I believe, to see that tribalist exclusiveness and self-sufficiency could be superseded only by some form of imperialism. And it must be said that certain of the imperialist measures introduced by Athens were rather liberal. One very interesting instance is the fact that Athens offered, in 405 B.C., to her ally, the Ionian island Samos, 'that the Samians should be Athenians from now on; and that both cities should be one state; and that the Samians should order their internal affairs as they chose, and retain their laws.'[19] Another instance is Athens' method of taxing her empire. Much has been said about these taxes, or tributes, which have been described—very unjustly, I believe—as a shameless and tyrannical way of exploiting the smaller cities. In an attempt to evaluate the significance of these taxes, we must, of course, compare them with the volume of the trade which, in return, was protected by the Athenian fleet. The necessary information is given by Thucydides, from whom we learn that the Athenians imposed upon their allies, in 413 B.C., 'in place of the tribute, a duty of 5 per cent. on all things imported and exported by sea; and they thought that this would yield more'[20]. This measure, adopted under severe strain of war, compares favourably, I believe, with the Roman methods of centralization. The Athenians, by this method of taxation, became interested in the development of allied trade, and so in the initiative and independence of the various members of their empire. Originally, the Athenian empire had developed out of a league of equals. In spite of the temporary predominance of Athens, publicly criticized by some of her citizens (cp. Aristophanes' *Lysistrata*), it seems probable that her interest in the development of trade would have led, in time, to some kind of federal constitution.

At least, we know in her case of nothing like the Roman method of 'transferring' the cultural possessions from the empire to the dominant city, i.e. of looting. And whatever one might say against plutocracy, it is preferable to a rule of looters[21].

This favourable view of Athenian imperialism can be supported by comparing it with the Spartan methods of handling foreign affairs. They were determined by the ultimate aim that dominated Sparta's policy, by its attempt to arrest all change and to return to tribalism. (This is impossible, as I shall contend later on. Innocence once lost cannot be regained, and an artificially arrested closed society, or a cultivated tribalism, cannot equal the genuine article.) The principles of Spartan policy were these. (1) Protection of its arrested tribalism: shut out all foreign influences which might endanger the rigidity of tribal taboos.—(2) Anti-humanitarianism: shut out, more especially, all equalitarian, democratic, and individualistic ideologies.—(3) Autarky: be independent of trade.—(4) Anti-universalism or particularism: uphold the differentiation between your tribe and all others; do not mix with inferiors.—(5) Mastery: dominate and enslave your neighbours.—(6) But do not become too large: 'The city should grow only as long as it can do so without impairing its unity'[22], and especially, without risking the introduction of universalistic tendencies.—If we compare these six principal tendencies with those of modern totalitarianism, then we see that they agree fundamentally, with the sole exception of the last. The difference can be described by saying that modern totalitarianism appears to have imperialist tendencies. But this imperialism has no element of a tolerant universalism, and the world-wide ambitions of the modern totalitarians are imposed upon them, as it were, against their will. Two factors are responsible for this. The first is the general tendency of all tyrannies to justify their existence by saving the state (or the people) from its enemies—a tendency which must lead, whenever the old enemies have been successfully subdued, to the creation or invention of new ones. The second factor is the attempt to carry into effect the closely related points (2) and (5) of the totalitarian programme. Humanitarianism, which, according to point (2), must be kept out, has become so universal that, in order to combat it effectively at home, it must be destroyed all over the world. But our world has become so small that everybody is now a neighbour, so that, to carry out point (5), everybody must be dominated and enslaved. But in ancient times, nothing could have appeared more dangerous to those who adopted a particularism like Sparta's, than Athenian imperialism, with its inherent tendency to develop into a commonwealth of Greek cities, and perhaps even into a universal empire of man.

Summing up our analysis so far, we can say that the political and spiritual revolution which had begun with the breakdown of Greek tribalism reached its climax in the fifth century, with the outbreak of the Peloponnesian war. It had developed into a violent class war, and, at the same time, into a war between the two leading cities of Greece.

III

But how can we explain the fact that outstanding Athenians like Thucydides stood on the side of reaction against these new developments? Class interest is, I believe, an insufficient explanation; for what we have to explain is the fact that, while many of the ambitious young nobles became active, although not always reliable, members of the democratic party, some of the most thoughtful and gifted resisted its attraction. The main point seems to be that although the open society was already in existence, although it had, in practice, begun to develop new values, new equalitarian standards of life, there was still something missing, especially for the 'educated'. The new faith of the open society, its only possible faith, humanitarianism, was beginning to assert itself, but was not yet formulated. For the time being, one could not see much more than class war, the democrats' fear of the oligarchic reaction, and the threat of further revolutionary developments. The reaction against these developments had therefore much on its side—tradition, the call for defending old virtues, and the old religion. These tendencies appealed to the feelings of most men, and their popularity gave rise to a movement to which, although it was led and used for their own ends by the Spartans and their oligarchic friends, many upright men must have belonged, even at Athens. From the slogan of the movement, 'Back to the state of our forefathers', or 'Back to the old paternal state', derives the term 'patriot'. It is hardly necessary to insist that the beliefs popular among those who supported this 'patriotic' movement were grossly perverted by those oligarchs who did not shrink from handing over their own city to the enemy, in the hope of gaining support against the democrats. Thucydides was one of the representative leaders of this movement for the 'paternal state'[23], and though he probably did not support the treacherous acts of the extreme anti-democrats, he could not disguise his sympathies with their fundamental aim—to arrest social change, and to fight the universalistic imperialism of the Athenian democracy and the instruments and symbols of its power, the navy, the walls, and commerce. (In view of Plato's doctrines concerning commerce, it may be interesting to note how great the fear of commercialism was. When after his victory over Athens in 404 B.C. the

Spartan king, Lysander, returned with great booty, the Spartan 'patriots', i.e. the members of the movement for the 'paternal state', tried to prevent the import of gold; and though it was ultimately admitted, its possession was limited to the state, and capital punishment was imposed on any citizen found in possession of precious metals. In Plato's *Laws*, very similar procedures are advocated[24]).

Although the 'patriotic' movement was partly the expression of the longing to return to more stable forms of life, to religion, decency, law and order, it was itself morally rotten. Its ancient faith was lost, and was largely replaced by a hypocritical and even cynical exploitation of religious sentiments.[25] Nihilism, as painted by Plato in the portraits of Callicles and Thrasymachus, could be found if anywhere among the young 'patriotic' aristocrats who, if given the opportunity, became leaders of the democratic party. The clearest exponent of this nihilism was perhaps the oligarchic leader who helped to deal the death-blow at Athens, Plato's uncle Critias, the leader of the Thirty Tyrants.[26]

But at this time, in the same generation to which Thucydides belonged, there rose a new faith in reason, freedom and the brotherhood of all men—the new faith, and, as I believe, the only possible faith, of the open society.

IV

This generation which marks a turning point in the history of mankind, I should like to call the Great Generation; it is the generation which lived in Athens just before, and during, the Peloponnesian war.[27] There were great conservatives among them, like Sophocles, or Thucydides. There were men among them who represent the period of transition; who were wavering, like Euripides, or sceptical, like Aristophanes. But there was also the great leader of democracy, Pericles, who formulated the principle of equality before the law and of political individualism, and Herodotus, who was welcomed and hailed in Pericles' city as the author of a work that glorified these principles. Protagoras, a native of Abdera who became influential in Athens, and his countryman Democritus must also be counted among the Great Generation. They formulated the doctrine that human institutions of language, custom, and law are not of the magical character of taboos but man-made, not natural but conventional, insisting, at the same time, that we are responsible for them. Then there was the school of Gorgias—Alcidamas, Lycophron and Antisthenes, who developed the fundamental tenets of anti-slavery, of a rational protectionism, and of anti-nationalism, i.e. the creed of the universal empire of men. And there was, perhaps the greatest of all,

Socrates, who taught the lesson that we must have faith in human reason, but at the same time beware of dogmatism; that we must keep away both from misology[28], the distrust of theory and of reason, and from the magical attitude of those who make an idol of wisdom; who taught, in other words, that the spirit of science is criticism.

Since I have not so far said much about Pericles, and nothing at all about Democritus, I may use some of their own words in order to illustrate the new faith. First Democritus: 'Not out of fear but out of a feeling of what is right should we abstain from doing wrong … Virtue is based, most of all, upon respecting the other man … Every man is a little world of his own … We ought to do our utmost to help those who have suffered injustice … To be good means to do no wrong; and also, not to want to do wrong … It is good deeds, not words, that count … The poverty of a democracy is better than the prosperity which allegedly goes with aristocracy or monarchy, just as liberty is better than slavery … The wise man belongs to all countries, for the home of a great soul is the whole world.' To him is due also that remark of a true scientist: 'I would rather find a single causal law than be the king of Persia!'[29]

In their humanitarian and universalistic emphasis some of these fragments of Democritus sound, although they are of earlier date, as if they were directed against Plato. The same impression is conveyed, only much more strongly, by Pericles' famous funeral oration, delivered at least half a century before the *Republic* was written. I have quoted two sentences from this oration in chapter 6, when discussing equalitarianism[30], but a few passages may be quoted here more fully in order to give a clearer impression of its spirit. 'Our political system does not compete with institutions which are elsewhere in force. We do not copy our neighbours, but try to be an example. Our administration favours the many instead of the few: this is why it is called a democracy. The laws afford equal justice to all alike in their private disputes, but we do not ignore the claims of excellence. When a citizen distinguishes himself, then he will be called to serve the state, in preference to others, not as a matter of privilege, but as a reward of merit; and poverty is no bar … The freedom we enjoy extends also to ordinary life; we are not suspicious of one another, and do not nag our neighbour if he chooses to go his own way … But this freedom does not make us lawless. We are taught to respect the magistrates and the laws, and never to forget that we must protect the injured. And we are also taught to observe those unwritten laws whose sanction lies only in the universal feeling of what is right …

'Our city is thrown open to the world; we never expel a foreigner … We are free to live exactly as we please, and yet we are always ready to face any danger ... We love beauty without indulging in fancies, and although we try to improve our intellect, this does not weaken our will ... To admit one's poverty is no disgrace with us; but we consider it disgraceful not to make an effort to avoid it. An Athenian citizen does not neglect public affairs when attending to his private business ... We consider a man who takes no interest in the state not as harmless, but as useless; and *although only a few may originate a policy, we are all able to judge it*. We do not look upon discussion as a stumbling-block in the way of political action, but as an indispensable preliminary to acting wisely ... We believe that happiness is the fruit of freedom and freedom that of valour, and we do not shrink from the dangers of war ... To sum up, I claim that Athens is the School of Hellas, and that the individual Athenian grows up to develop a happy versatility, a readiness for emergencies, and self-reliance.'[31]

These words are not merely a eulogy on Athens; they express the true spirit of the Great Generation. They formulate the political programme of a great equalitarian individualist, of a democrat who well understands that democracy cannot be exhausted by the meaningless principle that 'the people should rule', but that it must be based on faith in reason, and on humanitarianism. At the same time, they are an expression of true patriotism, of just pride in a city which had made it its task to set an example; which became the school, not only of Hellas, but, as we know, of mankind, for millennia past and yet to come.

Pericles' speech is not only a programme. It is also a defence, and perhaps even an attack. It reads, as I have already hinted, like a direct attack on Plato. I do not doubt that it was directed, not only against the arrested tribalism of Sparta, but also against the totalitarian ring or 'link' at home; against the movement for the paternal state, the Athenian 'Society of the Friends of Laconia' (as Th. Gomperz called them in 1902[32]). The speech is the earliest[33] and at the same time perhaps the strongest statement ever made in opposition to this kind of movement. Its importance was felt by Plato, who caricatured Pericles' oration half a century later in the passages of the *Republic*[34] in which he attacks democracy, as well as in that undisguised parody, the dialogue called *Menexenus or the Funeral Oration*[35]. But the Friends of Laconia whom Pericles attacked retaliated long before Plato. Only five or six years after Pericles' oration, a pamphlet on the *Constitution of Athens*[36] was published by an unknown author (possibly Critias), now usually called the 'Old Oligarch'. This ingenious pamphlet, the oldest extant treatise on political theory, is, at the same time, perhaps the oldest monument of the desertion of mankind by its intellectual leaders. It is a ruthless attack upon Athens, written no doubt by one of her best brains. Its central idea, an idea which became an article of faith with Thucydides and Plato, is the close connection between naval imperialism and democracy. And it tries to show that there can be no compromise in a conflict between two worlds[37], the worlds of democracy and of oligarchy; that only the use of ruthless violence, of total measures, including the intervention of allies from outside (the Spartans), can put an end to the unholy rule of freedom. This remarkable pamphlet was to become the first of a practically infinite sequence of works on political philosophy which were to repeat more or less, openly or covertly, the same theme down to our own day. Unwilling and unable to help mankind along their difficult path into an unknown future which they have to create for themselves, some of the 'educated' tried to make them turn back into the past. Incapable of leading a new way, they could only make themselves leaders of the *perennial revolt against freedom*. It became the more necessary for them to assert their superiority by fighting against equality as they were (using Socratic language) misanthropists and misologists—incapable of that simple and ordinary generosity which inspires faith in men, and faith in human reason and freedom. Harsh as this judgement may sound, it is just, I fear, if it is applied to those intellectual leaders of the revolt against freedom who came after the Great Generation, and especially after Socrates. We can now try to see them against the background of our historical interpretation.

The rise of philosophy itself can be interpreted, I think, as a response to the breakdown of the closed society and its magical beliefs. It is an attempt to replace the lost magical faith by a rational faith; it modifies the tradition of passing on a theory or a myth by founding a new tradition—the tradition of challenging theories and myths and of critically discussing them[38]. (A significant point is that this attempt coincides with the spread of the so-called Orphic sects whose members tried to replace the lost feeling of unity by a new mystical religion.) The earliest philosophers, the three great Ionians and Pythagoras, were probably quite unaware of the stimulus to which they were reacting. They were the representatives as well as the unconscious antagonists of a social revolution. The very fact that they founded schools or sects or orders, i.e. new social institutions or rather concrete groups with a common life and common functions, and modelled largely after those of an idealized tribe, proves that they were reformers in the social field, and therefore, that they were reacting to certain social needs. That they reacted to these needs and to their own sense of drift, not by imitating Hesiod in inventing a historicist myth of destiny and decay[39], but by inventing the tradition of criticism and discussion, and with it the art of thinking rationally, is one of the inexplicable facts which stand at the beginning of our civilization. But even these rationalists reacted to the loss of the unity of tribalism in a largely emotional way. Their reasoning gives expression to their feeling of drift, to the strain of a development which was about to create our individualistic civilization. One of the oldest expressions of this strain goes back to Anaximander[40], the second of the Ionian philosophers. Individual existence appeared to him as *hubris*, as an impious act of injustice, as a wrongful act of usurpation, for which individuals must suffer, and do penance. The first to become conscious of the social revolution and the struggle of classes was Heraclitus. How he rationalized his feeling of drift by developing the first anti-democratic ideology and the first historicist philosophy of change and destiny, has been described in the second chapter of this book. Heraclitus was the first conscious enemy of the open society.

Nearly all these early thinkers were labouring under a tragic and desperate strain[41]. The only exception is perhaps the monotheist Xenophanes[42], who carried his burden courageously. We cannot blame them for their hostility towards the new developments in the way in which we may, to some extent, blame their successors. The new faith of the open society, the faith in man, in equalitarian justice, and in human reason, was perhaps beginning to take shape, but it was not yet formulated.

V

The greatest contribution to this faith was to be made by Socrates, who died for it. Socrates was not a leader of Athenian democracy, like Pericles, or a theorist of the open society, like Protagoras. He was, rather, a critic of Athens and of her democratic institutions, and in this he may have borne a superficial resemblance to some of the leaders of the reaction against the open society. But there is no need for a man who criticizes democracy and democratic institutions to be their enemy, although both the democrats he criticizes, and the totalitarians who hope to profit from any disunion in the democratic camp, are likely to brand him as such. There is a fundamental difference between a democratic and a totalitarian criticism of democracy. Socrates' criticism was a democratic one, and indeed of the kind that is the very life of democracy. (Democrats who do not see the difference between a friendly and a hostile criticism of democracy are themselves imbued with the totalitarian spirit. Totalitarianism, of course, cannot consider any criticism as friendly, since every criticism of such an authority must challenge the principle of authority itself.)

I have already mentioned some aspects of Socrates' teaching: his intellectualism, i.e. his equalitarian theory of human reason as a universal medium of communication; his stress on intellectual honesty and self-criticism; his equalitarian theory of justice, and his doctrine that it is better to be a victim of injustice than to inflict it upon others. I think it is this last doctrine which can help us best to understand the core of his teaching, his creed of individualism, his belief in the human individual as an end in himself.

The closed society, and with it its creed that the tribe is everything and the individual nothing, had broken down. Individual initiative and self-assertion had become a fact. Interest in the human individual as individual, and not only as tribal hero and saviour, had been aroused[43]. But a philosophy which makes man the centre of its interest began only with Protagoras. And the belief that there is nothing more important in our life than other individual men, the appeal to men to respect one another and themselves, appears to be due to Socrates.

Burnet has stressed[44] that it was Socrates who created the conception of the *soul*, a conception which had such an immense influence upon our civilization. I believe that there is much in this view, although I feel that its formulation may be misleading, especially the use of the term 'soul'; for Socrates seems to have kept away from metaphysical theories as much as he could. His appeal was a moral appeal, and his theory of individuality (or of the 'soul', if this word is preferred) is, I think, a moral and not a metaphysical doctrine. He was fighting, with the help of this doctrine, as always, against self-satisfaction and complacency. He demanded that individualism should not be merely the dissolution of tribalism, but that the individual should prove worthy of his liberation. This is why he insisted that man is not merely a piece of flesh—a body. There is more in man, a divine spark, reason; and a love of truth, of kindness, humaneness, a love of beauty and of goodness. It is these that make a man's life worth while. But if I am not merely a 'body', what am I, then? You are, first of all, intelligence, was Socrates' reply. It is your reason that makes you human; that enables you to be more than a mere bundle of desires and wishes; that makes you a self-sufficient individual and entitles you to claim that you are an end in yourself. Socrates' saying 'care for your souls' is largely an appeal for *intellectual* honesty, just as the saying 'know thyself' is used by him to remind us of our intellectual limitations.

These, Socrates insisted, are the things that matter. And what he criticized in democracy and democratic statesmen was their inadequate realization of these things. He criticized them rightly for their lack of intellectual honesty, and for their obsession with power-politics[45]. With his emphasis upon the human side of the political problem, he could not take much interest in institutional reform. It was the immediate, the personal aspect of the open society in which he was interested. He was mistaken when he considered himself a politician; he was a teacher.

But if Socrates was, fundamentally, the champion of the open society, and a friend of democracy, why, it may be asked, did he mix with anti-democrats? For we know that among his companions were not only Alcibiades, who for a time went over to the side of Sparta, but also two of Plato's uncles, Critias who later became the ruthless leader of the Thirty Tyrants, and Charmides who became his lieutenant.

There is more than one reply to this question. First we are told by Plato that Socrates' attack upon the democratic politicians of his time was carried out partly with the purpose of exposing the selfishness and lust for power of the hypocritical flatterers of the people, more particularly, of the young aristocrats who posed as democrats, but who looked upon the people as mere instruments of their lust for power[46]. This activity made him, on the one hand, attractive to some at least of the enemies of democracy; on the other hand it brought him into contact with ambitious aristocrats of that very type. And here enters a second consideration. Socrates, the moralist and individualist, would never merely attack these men. He would, rather, take a real interest in them, and he would hardly give them up without making a serious attempt to convert them. There are many allusions to such attempts in Plato's dialogues. We have reason, and this is a third consideration, to believe that Socrates, the teacher-politician, even went out of his way to attract young men and to gain influence over them, especially when he considered them open to conversion, and thought that some day they might possibly hold offices of responsibility in their city. The outstanding example is, of course, Alcibiades, singled out from his very childhood as the great future leader of the Athenian empire. And Critias' brilliancy, ambition and courage made him one of the few likely competitors of Alcibiades. (He co-operated with Alcibiades for a time, but later turned against him. It is not at all improbable that the temporary co-operation was due to Socrates' influence.) From all we know about Plato's own early and later political aspirations, it is more than likely that his relations with Socrates were of a similar kind[47]. Socrates, though one of the leading spirits of the open society, was not a party man. He would have worked in any circle where his work might have benefited his city. If he took interest in a promising youth he was not to be deterred by oligarchic family connections.

But these connections were to cause his death. When the great war was lost, Socrates was accused of having educated the men who had betrayed democracy and conspired with the enemy to bring about the downfall of Athens.

The history of the Peloponnesian war and the fall of Athens is still often told, under the influence of Thucydides' authority, in such a way that the defeat of Athens appears as the ultimate proof of the moral weaknesses of the democratic system. But this view is merely a tendentious distortion, and the well-known facts tell a very different story. The main responsibility for the lost war rests with the treacherous oligarchs who continuously conspired with Sparta. Prominent among these were three former disciples of Socrates, Alcibiades, Critias, and Charmides. After the fall of Athens in 404 B.C. the two latter became the leaders of the Thirty Tyrants, who were no more than a puppet government under Spartan protection. The fall of Athens, and the destruction of the walls, are often presented as the final results of the great war which had started in 431 B.C. But in this presentation lies a major distortion; for the democrats fought on. At first only seventy strong, they prepared under the leadership of Thrasybulus and Anytus the liberation of Athens, where Critias was meanwhile killing scores of citizens; during the eight months of his reign of terror the death-roll contained 'rather a greater number of Athenians than the Peloponnesians had killed during the last ten years of war'[48]. But after eight months (in 403 B.C.) Critias and the Spartan garrison were attacked and defeated by the democrats, who established themselves in the Piraeus, and both of Plato's uncles lost their lives in the battle. Their oligarchic followers continued for a time the reign of terror in the city of Athens itself, but their forces were in a state of confusion and dissolution. Having proved themselves incapable of ruling, they were ultimately abandoned by their Spartan protectors, who concluded a treaty with the democrats. The peace re-established democracy in Athens. Thus the democratic form of government had proved its superior strength under the most severe trials, and even its enemies began to think it invincible. (Nine years later, after the battle of Cnidus, the Athenians could re-erect their walls. The defeat of democracy had turned into victory.)

As soon as the restored democracy had re-established normal legal conditions[49], a case was brought against Socrates. Its meaning was clear enough; he was accused of having had his hand in the education of the most pernicious enemies of the state, Alcibiades, Critias, and Charmides. Certain difficulties for the prosecution were created by an amnesty for all political crimes committed before the re-establishment of the democracy. The charge could not therefore openly refer to these notorious cases. And the prosecutors probably sought not so much to punish Socrates for the unfortunate political events of the past which, as they knew well, had happened against his intentions; their aim was, rather, to prevent him from continuing his teaching, which, in view of its effects, they could hardly regard otherwise than as dangerous to the state. For all these reasons, the charge was given the vague and rather meaningless form that Socrates was corrupting the youth, that he was impious, and that he had attempted to introduce novel religious practices into the state. (The latter two charges undoubtedly expressed, however clumsily, the correct feeling that in the ethico-religious field he was a revolutionary.) Because of the amnesty, the 'corrupted youth' could not be more precisely named, but everybody knew, of course, who was meant[50]. In his defence, Socrates insisted that he had no sympathy with the policy of the Thirty, and that he had actually risked his life by defying their attempt to implicate him in one of their crimes. And he reminded the jury that among his closest associates and most enthusiastic disciples there was at least one ardent democrat, Chaerephon, who fought against the Thirty (and who was, it appears, killed in battle)[51].

It is now usually recognized that Anytus, the democratic leader who backed the prosecution, did not intend to make a martyr of Socrates. The aim was to exile him. But this plan was defeated by Socrates' refusal to compromise his principles. That he wanted to die, or that he enjoyed the rôle of martyr, I do not believe[52]. He simply fought for what he believed to be right, and for his life's work. He had never intended to undermine democracy. In fact, he had tried to give it the faith it needed. This had been the work of his life. It was, he felt, seriously threatened. The betrayal of his former companions let his work and himself appear in a light which must have disturbed him deeply. He may even have welcomed the trial as an opportunity to prove that his loyalty to his city was unbounded.

Socrates explained this attitude most carefully when he was given an opportunity to escape. Had he seized it, and become an exile, everybody would have thought him an opponent of democracy. So he stayed, and stated his reasons. This explanation, his last will, can be found in Plato's *Crito*[53]. It is simple. If I go, said Socrates, I violate the laws of the state. Such an act would put me in opposition to the laws, and prove my disloyalty. It would do harm to the state. Only if I stay can I put beyond doubt my loyalty to the state, with its democratic laws, and prove that I have never been its enemy. There can be no better proof of my loyalty than my willingness to die for it.

Socrates' death is the ultimate proof of his sincerity. His fearlessness, his simplicity, his modesty, his sense of proportion, his humour never deserted him. 'I am the gadfly that God has attached to this city', he said in his *Apology*, 'and all day long and in all places I am always fastening upon you, arousing and persuading and reproaching you. You would not readily find another like me, and therefore I should advise you to spare me ... If you strike at me, as Anytus advises you, and rashly put me to death, then you will remain asleep for the rest of your lives, unless God in his care sends you another gadfly'[54]. He showed that a man could die, not only for fate and fame and other grand things of this kind, but also for the freedom of critical thought, and for a self-respect which has nothing to do with self-importance or sentimentality.

VI

Socrates had only *one* worthy successor, his old friend Antisthenes, the last of the Great Generation. Plato, his most gifted disciple, was soon to prove the least faithful. He betrayed Socrates, just as his uncles had done. These, besides betraying Socrates, had also tried to implicate him in their terrorist acts, but they did not succeed, since he resisted. Plato tried to implicate Socrates in his grandiose attempt to construct the theory of the arrested society; and he had no difficulty in succeeding, for Socrates was dead.

I know of course that this judgement will seem outrageously harsh, even to those who are critical of Plato[55]. But if we look upon the *Apology* and the *Crito* as Socrates' last will, and if we compare these testaments of his old age with Plato's testament, the *Laws*, then it is difficult to judge otherwise. Socrates had been condemned, but his death was not intended by the initiators of the trial. Plato's *Laws* remedy this lack of intention. Here he elaborates coolly and carefully the theory of inquisition. Free thought, criticism of political institutions, teaching new ideas to the young, attempts to introduce new religious practices or even opinions, are all pronounced capital crimes. In Plato's state, Socrates might have never been given the opportunity of defending himself publicly; and he certainly would have been handed over to the secret Nocturnal Council for the purpose of 'attending' to his diseased soul, and finally for punishing it.

I cannot doubt the fact of Plato's betrayal, nor that his use of Socrates as the main speaker of the *Republic* was the most successful attempt to implicate him. But it is another question whether this attempt was conscious.

In order to understand Plato we must visualize the whole contemporary situation. After the Peloponnesian war, the strain of civilization was felt as strongly as ever. The old oligarchic hopes were still alive, and the defeat of Athens had even tended to encourage them. The class struggle continued. Yet Critias' attempt to destroy democracy by carrying out the programme of the Old Oligarch had failed. It had not failed through lack of determination; the most ruthless use of violence had been unsuccessful, in spite of favourable circumstances in the shape of powerful support from victorious Sparta. Plato felt that a complete reconstruction of the programme was needed. The Thirty had been beaten in the realm of power politics largely because they had offended the citizens' sense of justice. The defeat had been largely a moral defeat. The faith of the Great Generation had proved its strength. The Thirty had nothing of this kind to offer; they were moral nihilists. The programme of the Old Oligarch, Plato felt, could not be revived without basing it upon another faith, upon a persuasion which re-affirmed the old values of tribalism, opposing them to the faith of the open society. *Men must be taught that justice is inequality*, and that the tribe, the collective, stands higher than the individual[56]. But since Socrates' faith was too strong to be challenged openly, Plato was driven to re-interpret it as a faith in the closed society. This was difficult; but it was not impossible. For had not Socrates been killed by the democracy? Had not democracy lost any right to claim him? And had not Socrates always criticized the anonymous multitude as well as its leaders for their lack of wisdom? It was not so very difficult, moreover, to re-interpret Socrates as having recommended the rule of the 'educated', the learned philosophers. In this interpretation, Plato was much encouraged when he discovered that it was also part of the ancient Pythagorean creed; and most of all, when he found, in Archytas of Tarentum, a Pythagorean sage as well as a great and successful statesman. Here, he felt, was the solution of the riddle. Had not Socrates himself encouraged his disciples to participate in politics? Did this not mean that he wanted the enlightened, the wise, to rule? What a difference between the crudity of the ruling mob of Athens and the dignity of an Archytas! Surely Socrates, who had never stated his solution of the constitutional problem, must have had Pythagoreanism in mind.

In this way Plato may have found that it was possible to give by degrees a new meaning to the teaching of the most influential member of the Great Generation, and to persuade himself that an opponent whose overwhelming strength he would never have dared to attack directly, was an ally. This, I believe, is the simplest interpretation of the fact that Plato retained Socrates as his main speaker even after he had departed so widely from his teaching that he could no longer deceive himself about this deviation[57]. But it is not the whole story. He felt, I believe, in the depth of his soul, that Socrates' teaching was very different indeed from this presentation, and that he was betraying Socrates. And I think that Plato's continuous efforts to make Socrates re-interpret himself are at the same time Plato's efforts to quiet his own bad conscience. By trying again and again to prove that his teaching was only the logical development of the true Socratic doctrine, he tried to persuade himself that he was not a traitor.

In reading Plato we are, I feel, witnesses of an inner conflict, of a truly titanic struggle in Plato's mind. Even his famous 'fastidious reserve, the suppression of his own personality'[58], or rather, the attempted suppression—for it is not at all difficult to read between the lines—is an expression of this struggle. And I believe that Plato's influence can partly be explained by the fascination of this conflict between two worlds in one soul, a struggle whose powerful repercussions upon Plato can be felt under that surface of fastidious reserve. This struggle touches our feelings, for it is still going on within ourselves. Plato was the child of a time which is still our own. (We must not forget that it is, after all, only a century since the abolition of slavery in the United States, and even less since the abolition of serfdom in Central Europe.) Nowhere does this inner struggle reveal itself more clearly than in Plato's theory of the soul. That Plato, with his longing for unity and harmony, visualized the structure of the human soul as analogous to that of a class-divided society[59] shows how deeply he must have suffered.

Plato's greatest conflict arises from the deep impression made upon him by the example of Socrates, but his own oligarchic inclinations strive only too successfully against it. In the field of rational argument, the struggle is conducted by using the argument of Socrates' humanitarianism against itself. What appears to be the earliest example of this kind can be found in the *Euthyphro*[60]. I am not going to be like Euthyphro, Plato assures himself; I shall never take it upon myself to accuse my own father, my own venerated ancestors, of having sinned against a law and a humanitarian morality which is on the level of vulgar piety. Even if they took human life, it was, after all, only the lives of their own serfs, who are no better than criminals; and it is not my task to judge them. Did not Socrates show how hard it is to know what is right and wrong, pious and impious? And was he not himself prosecuted for impiety by these so-called humanitarians? Other traces of Plato's struggle can, I believe, be found in nearly every place where he turns against humanitarian ideas, especially in the *Republic*. His evasiveness and his resort to scorn in combating the equalitarian theory of justice, his hesitant preface to his defence of lying, to his introduction of racialism, and to his definition of justice, have all been mentioned in previous chapters. But perhaps the clearest expression of the conflict can be found in the *Menexenus*, that sneering reply to Pericles' funeral oration. Here, I feel, Plato gives himself away. In spite of his attempt to hide his feelings behind irony and scorn, he cannot but show how deeply he was impressed by Pericles' sentiments. This is how Plato makes his 'Socrates' maliciously describe the impression made upon him by Pericles' oration: 'A feeling of exultation stays with me for more than three days; not until the fourth or fifth day, and not without an effort, do I come to my senses and realize where I am.'[61] Who can doubt that Plato reveals here how seriously he was impressed by the creed of the open society, and how hard he had to struggle to come to his senses and to realize where he was—namely, in the camp of its enemies?

VII

Plato's strongest argument in this struggle was, I believe, sincere: According to the humanitarian creed, he argued, we should be ready to help our neighbours. The people need help badly, they are unhappy, they labour under a severe strain, a sense of drift. There is no certainty, no security[62] in life, when everything is in flux. I am ready to help them. But I cannot make them happy without going to the root of the evil.

And he found the root of the evil. It is the 'Fall of Man', the breakdown of the closed society. This discovery convinced him that the Old Oligarch and his followers had been fundamentally right in favouring Sparta against Athens, and in aping the Spartan programme of arresting change. But they had not gone far enough; their analysis had not been carried sufficiently deep. They had not been aware of the fact, or had not cared for it, that even Sparta showed signs of decay, in spite of its heroic effort to arrest all change; that even Sparta had been half-hearted in her attempts at controlling breeding in order to eliminate the causes of the Fall, the 'variations' and 'irregularities' in the number as well as the quality of the ruling race[63]. (Plato realized that population increase was one of the causes of the Fall.) Also, the Old Oligarch and his followers had thought, in their superficiality, that with the help of a tyranny, such as that of the Thirty, they would be able to restore the good old days. Plato knew better. The great sociologist saw clearly that these tyrannies were supported by, and that they were kindling in their turn, the modern revolutionary spirit; that they were forced to make concessions to the equalitarian cravings of the people; and that they had indeed played an important part in the breakdown of tribalism. Plato hated tyranny. Only hatred can see as sharply as he did in his famous description of the tyrant. Only a genuine enemy of tyranny could say that tyrants must 'stir up one war after another in order to make the people feel the need of a general', of a saviour from extreme danger. Tyranny, Plato insisted, was not the solution, nor any of the current oligarchies. Although it is imperative to keep the people in their place, their suppression is not an end in itself. The end must be the complete return to nature, a complete cleaning of the canvas.

The difference between Plato's theory on the one hand, and that of the Old Oligarch and the Thirty on the other, is due to the influence of the Great Generation. Individualism, equalitarianism, faith in reason and love of freedom were new, powerful, and, from the point of view of the enemies of the open society, dangerous sentiments that had to be fought. Plato had himself felt their influence, and, within himself, he had fought them. His answer to the Great Generation was a truly great effort. It was an effort to close the door which had been opened, and to arrest society by casting upon it the spell of an alluring philosophy, unequalled in depth and richness. In the political field he added but little to the old oligarchic programme against which Pericles had once argued[64]. But he discovered, perhaps unconsciously, the great secret of the revolt against freedom, formulated in our own day by Pareto[65]; '*To take advantage of sentiments, not wasting one's energies in futile efforts to destroy them.*' Instead of showing his hostility to reason, he charmed all intellectuals with his brilliance, flattering and thrilling them by his demand that the learned should rule. Although arguing against justice he convinced all righteous men that he was its advocate. Not even to himself did he fully admit that he was combating the freedom of thought for which Socrates had died; and by making Socrates his champion he persuaded all others that he was fighting for it. Plato thus became, unconsciously, the pioneer of the many propagandists who, often in good faith, developed the technique of appealing to moral, humanitarian sentiments, for anti-humanitarian, immoral purposes. And he achieved the somewhat surprising effect of convincing even great humanitarians of the immorality and selfishness of their creed[66]. I do not doubt that he succeeded in persuading himself. He transfigured his hatred of individual initiative, and his wish to arrest all change, into a love of justice and temperance, of a heavenly state in which everybody is satisfied and happy and in which the crudity of money-grabbing[67] is replaced by laws of generosity and friendship. This dream of unity and beauty and perfection, this æstheticism and holism and collectivism, is the product as well as the symptom of the lost group spirit of tribalism[68]. It is the expression of, and an ardent appeal to, the sentiments of those who suffer from the strain of civilization. (It is part of the strain that we are becoming more and more painfully aware of the gross imperfections in our life, of personal as well as of institutional imperfection; of avoidable suffering, of waste and of unnecessary ugliness; and at the same time of the fact that it is not impossible for us to do something about all this, but that such improvements would be just as hard to achieve as they are important. This awareness increases the strain of personal responsibility, of carrying the cross of being human.)

VIII

Socrates had refused to compromise his personal integrity. Plato, with all his uncompromising canvas-cleaning, was led along a path on which he compromised his integrity with every step he took. He was forced to combat free thought, and the pursuit of truth. He was led to defend lying, political miracles, tabooistic superstition, the suppression of truth, and ultimately, brutal violence. In spite of Socrates' warning against misanthropy and misology, he was led to distrust man and to fear argument. In spite of his own hatred of tyranny, he was led to look to a tyrant for help, and to defend the most tyrannical measures. By the internal logic of his anti-humanitarian aim, the internal logic of power, he was led unawares to the same point to which once the Thirty had been led, and at which, later, his friend Dio arrived, and others among his numerous tyrant-disciples[69]. He did not succeed in arresting social change. (Only much later, in the dark ages, was it arrested by the magic spell of the Platonic-Aristotelian essentialism.) Instead, he succeeded in binding himself, by his own spell, to powers which once he had hated.

The lesson which we thus should learn from Plato is the exact opposite of what he tries to teach us. It is a lesson which must not be forgotten. Excellent as Plato's sociological diagnosis was, his own development proves that the therapy he recommended is worse than the evil he tried to combat. Arresting political change is not the remedy; it cannot bring happiness. We can never return to the alleged innocence and beauty of the closed society[70]. Our dream of heaven cannot be realized on earth. Once we begin to rely upon our reason, and to use our powers of criticism, once we feel the call of personal responsibilities, and with it, the responsibility of helping to advance knowledge, we cannot return to a state of implicit submission to tribal magic. For those who have eaten of the tree of knowledge, paradise is lost. The more we try to return to the heroic age of tribalism, the more surely do we arrive at the Inquisition, at the Secret Police, and at a romanticized gangsterism. Beginning with the suppression of reason and truth, we must end with the most brutal and violent destruction of all that is human[71]. *There is no return to a harmonious state of nature. If we turn back, then we must go the whole way—we must return to the beasts.*

It is an issue which we must face squarely, hard though it may be for us to do so. If we dream of a return to our childhood, if we are tempted to rely on others and so be happy, if we shrink from the task of carrying our cross, the cross of humaneness, of reason, of responsibility, if we lose courage and flinch from the strain, then we must try to fortify ourselves with a clear understanding of the simple decision before us. We can return to the beasts. But if we wish to remain human, then there is only one way, the way into the open society. We must go on into the unknown, the uncertain and insecure, using what reason we may have to plan as well as we can for both security *and* freedom.

ADDENDA

I

PLATO AND GEOMETRY (1957)

In the second edition of this book, I made a lengthy addition to note 9 to chapter 6 (pp. 248 to 253). The historical hypothesis propounded in this note was later amplified in my paper 'The Nature of Philosophical Problems and Their Roots in Science' (*British Journal for the Philosophy of Science*, **3**, 1952, pp. 124 ff.; now also in my *Conjectures and Refutations*). It may be restated as follows: (1) the discovery of the irrationality of the square root of two which led to the breakdown of the Pythagorean programme of reducing geometry and cosmology (and presumably all knowledge) to arithmetic, produced a crisis in Greek mathematics; (2) Euclid's *Elements* are not a textbook of geometry, but rather the final attempt of the Platonic School to resolve this crisis by reconstructing the whole of mathematics and cosmology *on a geometrical basis*, in order to deal with the problem of irrationality systematically rather than *ad hoc*, thus inverting the Pythagorean programme of arithmetization; (3) it was Plato who first conceived the programme later carried out by Euclid: it was Plato who first recognized the need for a reconstruction; who chose geometry as the new basis, and the geometrical method of proportion as the new method; who drew up the programme for a *geometrization of mathematics*, including arithmetic, astronomy, and cosmology; and who became the founder of the geometrical picture of the world, and thereby also the founder of modern science—of the science of Copernicus, Galileo, Kepler, and Newton.

I suggested that the famous inscription over the door of Plato's Academy (p. 248, (2)) alluded to this programme of geometrization. (That it was intended to announce an *inversion of the Pythagorean programme* seems likely in view of Archytas, fragment A, Diels-Kranz.)

In the middle of the last paragraph on p. 249 I suggested 'that Plato was *one of the first to develop a specifically geometrical method* aiming at rescuing what could be rescued ... from the breakdown of Pythagoreanism'; and I described this suggestion as 'a highly uncertain historical hypothesis'. I no longer think that the hypothesis is so very uncertain. On the contrary, I now feel that a re-reading of Plato, Aristotle, Euclid, and Proclus, in the light of this hypothesis, would produce as much corroborating evidence as one could expect. In addition to the confirming evidence referred to in the paragraph quoted, I now wish to add that already the *Gorgias* (451a/b; c; 453e) takes the discussion of 'odd' and 'even' as characteristic of arithmetic, thereby, clearly identifying arithmetic with Pythagorean number theory, while characterizing the geometer as the man who adopts the method of proportions (465b/c). Moreover, in the passage from the *Gorgias* (508a) Plato speaks not only of geometrical equality (cp. note 48 to chapter 8) but he also states implicitly the principle which he was later to develop fully in the *Timaeus*: that the cosmic order is a *geometrical order*. Incidentally, the *Gorgias* also proves that the word '*alogos*' was not associated in Plato's mind with irrational numbers, since 465a says that even a technique, or art, must not be *alogos*; which would hold *a fortiori* for a science such as geometry. I think we may simply translate '*alogos*' as 'alogical'. (Cp. also *Gorgias* 496a/b; and 522e.) The point is important for the interpretation of the title of Democritus's lost book, mentioned earlier on p. 249.

My paper on 'The Nature of Philosophical Problems' (see above) contains some further suggestions concerning Plato's *geometrization of arithmetic* and of cosmology in general (his inversion of the Pythagorean programme), and his theory of forms.

Added in 1961

Since this *addendum* was first published in 1957, in the third edition of this book, I have found, almost by accident, some interesting corroboration of the historical hypothesis formulated above, in the first paragraph under (2). It is a passage in Proclus' commentaries to the First Book of Euclid's Elements (ed. Friedlein, 1873, Prologus ii, p. 71, 2–5) from which it becomes clear that there existed a tradition according to which Euclid's elements were a Platonic cosmology, a treatment of the problems of the *Timaeus*.

II

THE DATING OF THE *THEAETETUS* (1961)

There is a hint in note 50 (6), to chapter 8, p. 281, that 'the *Theaetetus* is perhaps (as against the usual assumption) earlier than the *Republic*'. This suggestion was made to me by the late Dr. Robert Eisler in a conversation not long before his death in 1949. But since he did not tell me any more about his conjecture than that it was partly based on *Theaetetus* 174e, f.—the crucial passage whose post-*Republican* dating did not seem to me to fit into my theory—I felt that there was not sufficient evidence for it, and that it was too *ad hoc* to justify me in publicly saddling Eisler with the responsibility for it.

However, I have since found quite a number of independent arguments in favour of an earlier dating of the *Theaetetus*, and I therefore wish now to acknowledge Eisler's original suggestion.

Since Eva Sachs (cp. *Socrates*, **5**, 1917, 531 f.) established that the proem of the *Theaetetus*, as we know it, was written after 369, the conjecture of a Socratic core and an early dating involves another—that of an earlier lost edition, revised by Plato after Theaetetus' death. The latter conjecture was proposed independently by various scholars, even before the discovery of a papyrus (ed. by Diels, *Berlin, Klassikerhefte*, **2**, 1905) that contains part of a *Commentary to the Theaetetus* and refers to two distinct editions. The following arguments seem to support both conjectures.

(1) Certain passages in Aristotle seem to allude to the *Theaetetus*: they fit the text of the *Theaetetus* perfectly, and they claim, at the same time, that the ideas there expressed belong to Socrates rather than to Plato. The passages I have in mind are the ascription to Socrates of the invention of *induction* (*Metaphysics* 1078b17–33; cp. 987b1 and 1086b3) which, I think, is an allusion to Socrates' *maieutic* (developed at length in the *Theaetetus*), his method of helping the pupil to perceive the true essence of a thing through purging his mind of his false prejudices; and the further ascription to Socrates of the attitude so strongly expressed again and again in the *Theaetetus*: 'Socrates used to ask questions and not to answer them; for he used to confess that he did not know' (*Soph. El.* 183b7). (These passages are discussed, in a different context, in my lecture *On the Sources of Knowledge and of Ignorance, Proceedings of the British Academy*, **46**, 1960 (see especially p. 50) which is also separately published by Oxford University Press and is now included in my *Conjectures and Refutations*.)

(2) The *Theaetetus* has a surprisingly inconclusive ending, even though it turns out that it was so planned and prepared almost from the beginning. (In fact, as an attempt to solve the problem of knowledge which it ostensibly tries to do, this beautiful dialogue is a complete failure.) But endings

of a similarly inconclusive nature are known to be characteristic of a number of early dialogues.

(3) 'Know thyself' is interpreted, as in the *Apology*, as 'Know how little you know'. In his final speech Socrates says 'After this, *Theaetetus* ... you will be less harsh and gentler to your associates, for you will have the wisdom not to think that you know what you do not know. So much my art [of *maieutic*] can accomplish; nor do I know any of the things that are known by others ...'

(4) That ours is a second edition, revised by Plato, seems likely, especially in view of the fact that the Introduction to the dialogue (142a to the end of 143c) which might well have been added as a memorial to a great man, actually contradicts a passage which may have survived the revision of the earlier edition of this dialogue; I mean its very end which, like a number of other early dialogues, alludes to Socrates' trial as imminent. The contradiction consists in the fact that Euclid, who appears as a character in the Introduction and who narrates how the dialogue came to be written down, tells us (142c/d, 143a) that he went repeatedly to Athens (from Megara, presumably), using every time the opportunity of checking his notes with Socrates, and making '*corrections*' here and there. This is told in a way which makes it quite clear that the dialogue itself must have taken place *at least* several months before Socrates' trial and death; but this is inconsistent with the ending of the dialogue. (I have not seen any reference to this point, but I cannot imagine that it has not been discussed by some Platonist.) It may even be that the reference to 'corrections', in 143a, and also the much discussed description of the 'new style' in 143b–c (see for example C. Ritter's *Plato*, vol. I, 1910, pp. 220 f.) were introduced in order to explain some deviations of the revised edition from the original edition. (This would make it possible to place the *revised* edition even after the *Sophist*.)

III

REPLY TO A CRITIC (1961)

I have been asked to say something in reply to the critics of this volume. But before doing so, I should like to thank again those whose criticism has helped me to improve the book in various ways.

Of the others—those I have come across—I feel reluctant to say much. In attacking Plato I have, as I now realize, offended and hurt many Platonists, and I am sorry for this. Still, I have been surprised by the violence of some of the reactions.

I think most of the defenders of Plato have denied facts which, it seems to me, cannot be seriously denied. This is true even of the best of them: Professor Ronald B. Levinson in his monumental book (645 closely printed pages) *In Defense of Plato*.

In trying to answer Professor Levinson I have before me two tasks of very unequal importance. The less important task—defending myself against a number of accusations—will be tackled first (in section A), so that the more important task—replying to Professor Levinson's defence of Plato (in section B)—will not be too much obscured by my personal defence.

A

The portrait of myself painted by Professor Levinson has caused me to doubt the truth of my own portrait of Plato; for if it is possible to derive from a living author's book so distorted an image of his doctrines and intentions, what hope can there be of producing anything like a true portrait of an author born almost twenty-four centuries ago?

Yet how can I defend myself against being identified with the supposed original of the portrait painted by Professor Levinson? All I can do is to show that some at least of the mistranslations, misrepresentations, and distortions of Plato with which Professor Levinson charges me are really non-existent. And even this I can only do by analysing two or three representative samples, taken at random from hundreds: there seem to be more such charges in the book than there are pages. Thus all I can do is to prove that some at least of the most violent accusations levelled against me are baseless.

I should have liked to do this without raising any counter-accusation of misquotation, etc.; but as this has turned out to be impossible, I wish to make it quite clear that I now see that Professor Levinson, like other Platonists, must have found my book not only exasperating, but almost sacrilegious. And since I am that man by whom the offence cometh, I must not complain if I am bitterly denounced.

So let us examine a few of the relevant passages.

Professor Levinson writes (p. 273, note 72) of me: 'As with others of whom he disapproves, so here with Critias, Popper has further blackened his character by exaggeration. For the verses cited represent religion, though a fabrication, as being aimed at the general good of society, not at the selfish benefit of the cunning fabricator himself'.

Now if this means anything, it must mean that I have asserted, or at least hinted, in the passages quoted by Professor Levinson (that is, pp. 179 and

140 of A, which corresponds to pp. 183–184, and pp. 142–143 of E[1]) that Critias' verses which I have quoted represent religion not only as a fabrication, but as a fabrication 'aimed ... at the selfish benefit of the cunning fabricator himself.'

I deny that I either asserted, or even hinted at, anything of the kind. On the contrary, my concern has been to point out that the 'general good of society' is one of the dominant preoccupations of Plato, and that his attitude in this respect 'is practically identical with that of Critias'. The basis of my criticism is clearly announced at the beginning of chapter 8 (second paragraph) where I write: '"For the benefit of the city", says Plato. Again we find that the appeal to the principle of collective utility is the ultimate ethical consideration.'

What I assert is that this moral principle which posits 'the general good of society' as a moral aim, is not good enough as a basis of ethics; for example, that it leads to lying—'for the general good of society' or 'for the benefit of the city'. In other words, I try to show that ethical collectivism is mischievous, and that it corrupts. But I nowhere interpret Critias' quoted verses in the sense alleged by Professor Levinson. I should be inclined to ask 'Who blackens whose character by exaggeration?', were it not for the fact that I recognize that the severity of my attack was a provocation which excuses Professor Levinson's charges. But it does not make them true.

A second example is this. Professor Levinson writes (pp. 354 f.): 'One of Popper's most extravagant assertions is that Plato had viewed as a "favourable circumstance" the presence in Athens of Spartan troops, summoned to assist the Thirty in maintaining themselves and their iniquitous regime and had felt no other emotion than approval at the thought of Athens beneath the Spartan yoke; he would have been prepared, we are led to suppose, to summon them again, if their presence could aid him in achieving his neo-oligarchical revolution. There is no text which Popper can cite in support of such a charge; it arises solely from his picture of Plato as a third head upon the double-headed monster he has created, called "the Old Oligarch and Critias"; it is guilt by association, the very ultimate example of the witch-hunt technique.'

To this my reply is: if this is one of my 'most extravagant assertions', then I cannot have made any extravagant assertions. For this assertion was never made by me; nor does it fit into the picture which I have of Plato, and which I have tried—not wholly successfully, it seems—to convey.

[1] 'A' stands in this *Addendum* for the American editions of 1950 and 1956; 'E' for the present edition and for the English editions from 1932 on.

I do believe that Plato was led, by his distrust of the common man, and by his ethical collectivism, to approve of violence; but I simply never have made any assertion about Plato even faintly similar to the one which Professor Levinson here asserts, somewhat extravagantly, that I have made. There is therefore no text which Professor Levinson can cite in support of his charge that I have made this assertion: it arises solely from his picture of Popper as a third head upon the double-headed monster of Otto Neurath and J. A. Lauwerys which Professor Levinson has created; and as to 'guilt by association', I can only refer to Professor Levinson's p. 441. There he is 'helped towards answering this question'—the question of 'the predisposing cause that leads Popper chronically to indulge these sinister imaginings'—by associating me with 'an older compatriot of Popper's, the late versatile Austrian philosopher and sociologist, Otto Neurath'. (In fact neither Neurath nor I had any sympathy for the other's philosophy, as emerges only too clearly from Neurath's and my own writings; Neurath, for example, defended Hegel, and attacked both Kantianism and my own praise of Kant. Of Neurath's attack on Plato I heard for the first time when I read about it in Professor Levinson's book; and I have not yet seen Neurath's relevant papers.)

But to return to my alleged 'extravagant assertion': what I actually said (p. 195E = 190A) about Plato's feelings is almost the opposite of what Professor Levinson (p. 354) reports. I did not at all suggest that Plato viewed as a 'favourable circumstance' the presence in Athens of Spartan troops, or that he 'felt no other emotion than approval at the thought of Athens beneath the Spartan yoke'. What I tried to convey, and what I said, was that the Thirty Tyrants had failed 'in spite of favourable circumstances in the shape of powerful support from victorious Sparta'; and I suggested that Plato saw the cause of their failure—just as I do—in the moral failure of the Thirty. I wrote: 'Plato felt that a complete reconstruction of the programme was needed. The Thirty had been beaten in the realm of power politics largely because they had offended the citizens' sense of justice. The defeat had been largely a moral defeat.'

This is all I say here of Plato's feelings. (I say twice 'Plato felt'.) I suggest that the failure of the Thirty induced a partial moral conversion in Plato—though not a sufficiently far-reaching one. There is no suggestion here of those feelings which Professor Levinson makes me attribute to Plato; and I would never have dreamt that anybody could read this into my text.

I certainly do attribute to Plato a measure of sympathy with the Thirty Tyrants and especially with their pro-Spartan aims. But this is of course something completely different from the 'extravagant assertions' which Professor Levinson attributes to me. I can only say that I did suggest that he admired his uncle Critias, the leader of the Thirty. I did suggest that he was in sympathy with some of Critias' aims and views. But I also said that he considered the oligarchy of the Thirty as a moral failure, and that this led him to reconstruct his collectivist morality.

It will be seen that my answer to two of Professor Levinson's charges has taken up almost as much space as the charges themselves. This is unavoidable; and I must therefore confine myself to only two further examples (out of hundreds), both connected with my alleged mistranslations of Plato's text.

The first is Professor Levinson's allegation that I worsen, or exaggerate, Plato's text. 'Popper, however, as before, employs the unfavourable word "deport" in his translation, in place of "send out",' writes Professor Levinson on p. 349, note 244. But this is simply a mistake—Professor Levinson's mistake. If he looks at the passage again, he will find that I employ the word 'deport' where his translation—or rather Fowler's—uses 'banish'. (The part of the passage in which Fowler's translation uses 'send out' simply does not occur in my quotation but is replaced by dots.)

As a consequence of this mistake, it turns out that, in this context, Professor Levinson's remark 'as before' is highly appropriate. For before the passage just discussed he writes of me (p. 348, note 243): 'Popper reënforces his interpretation [p. 166E = p. 162A] of the Platonic passage [*Rep.* 540e/541a] by slight inaccuracies in the translation, tending to give the impression of greater scorn or violence in Plato's attitude. Thus he translates "send away" (*apopempō*) as "expel and deport" ...' Now first of all, there is another of Professor Levinson's slips here (which makes two in two consecutive footnotes); for Plato does *not* use here the word '*apopempō*', but the word '*ekpempō*'. This certainly does not make much difference; yet '*ekpempō*' has, at any rate, the '*ex*' of '*expel*'; and one of its dictionary meanings is 'to drive away' and another 'to send away in disgrace' (or 'to send away with the collateral notion of disgrace' as my edition of Liddell and Scott has it). The word is a somewhat stronger form of '*pempō*'—'to send off', 'to dispatch'—which, if used in connection with Hades ('to send to Hades') 'commonly means to send a living man to Hades, i.e. to kill him'. (I am quoting Liddell and Scott. Nowadays some people might even 'commonly' say 'to dispatch him'. Closely related is the meaning intended when Phaedrus tells us in Plato's *Symposium* 179e—a passage referred to by Professor Levinson on p. 348—that the gods, redeeming and honouring Achilles for his valour and his love of Patroclus, 'sent him to the Islands of the Blessed'—while Homer sent him to Hades.) It seems obvious that neither of the translations 'expel' or 'deport' is open to criticism here on scholarly grounds. Yet Professor Levinson is open to criticism when he quotes me as writing 'expel and deport' for I do not use the words in this way. (He would have been at least technically correct had he quoted me 'must be expelled ...

and deported': the three dots make some difference here, for to write 'expel and deport' *could* be an attempt to exaggerate, by way of 're-enforcing' the one expression with the other. Thus this slight inaccuracy tends to re-enforce my alleged misdeed—my alleged re-enforcing of my interpretation of this Platonic passage by slight inaccuracies in my translation.)

But anyhow, this case amounts to nothing. For take the passage in Shorey's translation. (Shorey is, rightly, accepted as an authority by Professor Levinson.) 'All inhabitants above the age of ten', Shorey translates, 'they [the 'philosophers' who have become 'masters of the state'] will send out into the fields, and they will take over the children, remove them from the manners and habits of their parents, and bring them up in their own customs and laws which will be such as we have described.' Now does this not say exactly what I said (though perhaps not quite as clearly as I did on my p. 166E = 162A)? For who can believe that the 'sending out' of 'all the inhabitants above the age of ten' can be anything but a violent expulsion and deportation? Would they just meekly go, leaving their children behind, when 'sent out', if they were not threatened, and compelled, by the 'philosophers' who have become 'masters of the state'? (Professor Levinson's suggestion, p. 349, that they are sent to 'their ... country estates, outside the city proper' is supported by him, ironically enough, with a reference to the *Symposium* 179e and the 'Islands of the Blessed', the place to which Achilles was sent by the gods—or more precisely by Apollo's or Paris's arrow. *Gorgias*, 526c, would have been a more appropriate reference.)

In all this, there is an important principle involved. I mean the principle that *there is no such thing as a literal translation*; that all translations are interpretations; and that we always have to take the context into account, and even parallel passages.

That the passages with which (on p. 166E = p. 162A) I have associated the one just quoted may indeed be so associated is confirmed by Shorey's own footnotes: he refers, especially, to the passage which I have called the 'canvas-cleaning' passage, and to the 'kill-and-banish' passage from the *Statesman*, 293c–e. 'Whether they happen to rule by law or without law, over willing or unwilling subjects; ... and whether they purge the state for its good, by killing or by deporting [or, as Professor Levinson translates with Fowler, 'by killing or banishing'; see above] some of its citizens ... this form of government must be declared to be the only one that is right.' (See my text, p. 166E = p. 162A.)

Professor Levinson quotes (p. 349) part of this passage more fully than I do. *Yet he omits to quote that part which I quoted as its commencement*, 'Whether they happen to rule by law or without law, over willing or unwilling subjects'. The point is interesting, because it fits Professor Levinson's attempt to make the kill-and-banish passage appear in an almost innocent light. Immediately after quoting the passage, Professor Levinson writes: 'Fair interpretation of this stated principle [I do not see any 'principle' here stated, unless it is that all is permitted if it is done *for the benefit of the state*] requires at least a brief indication of the general pattern of the dialogue.' In the course of this 'brief indication' of Plato's aims and tendencies, we hear—without a direct quotation from Plato—that 'Other traditional and currently accepted criteria, such as whether rule be exercised ... *over willing or unwilling subjects, or in accord or not in accord with law*, are rejected as irrelevant or non-essential'. The words from Professor Levinson's passage which I have here italicized will be seen to be a near-quotation of the commencement (not quoted by Professor Levinson) of my own quotation from Plato's kill-and-banish passage. Yet this commencement appears now in a very harmless light: no longer are the rulers told to kill and banish '*with or without law*', as I indicated; and Professor Levinson's readers get the impression that this question is here merely dismissed as a side issue—as '*irrelevant*' to the problem in hand.

But Plato's readers, and even the participants in his dialogue, get a different impression. Even the 'Younger Socrates', who intervened just before (after the commencement of the passage as quoted by me) with the one exclamation 'Excellent!' is shocked by the lawlessness of the proposed killing; for immediately after the enunciation of the kill-and-banish principle (perhaps it really is a 'principle', after all) he says, in Fowler's translation (the italics are of course mine): 'Everything else that you have said seems reasonable; but that government [and such hard measures, too, it is implied] *should be carried out without laws* is a hard saying.'

I think that this remark proves that the commencement of my quotation—'by law or *without law*'—is really meant by Plato to be part of his kill-and-banish principle; that I was right in commencing the quotation where I did; and that Professor Levinson is simply mistaken when he suggests that 'with or without law' is here merely intended to mean that this is a question which is here 'rejected as irrelevant' to the essence of the problem in hand.

In interpreting the kill-and-banish passage, Professor Levinson is clearly deeply disturbed; yet at the end of his elaborate attempt to defend Plato by comparing his practices with our own he arrives at the following view of the passage: 'Looked at in this context, Plato's statesman, with his apparent readiness to kill, banish, and enslave, where we should prescribe either the penitentiary, at one end, or psychiatric social service, at the other, loses much of his sanguinary coloration.'

Now I do not doubt that Professor Levinson is a genuine humanitarian—a democrat and a liberal. But is it not perturbing to see that a genuine humanitarian, in his eagerness to defend Plato, can be led to compare in this fashion our admittedly very faulty penal practices and our no less faulty social services with the avowedly *lawless* killing and banishing (and enslaving) of citizens by the 'true statesman'—a good and wise man—'for the benefit of the city'? Is this not a frightening example of the spell which Plato casts over many of his readers, and of the danger of Platonism?

There is too much of this—all mixed with accusations against a largely imaginary Popper—for me to deal with. But I wish to say that I regard Professor Levinson's book not only as a very sincere attempt to defend Plato, but also as an attempt to see Plato in a new light. And though I have found only one passage—and quite an unimportant one—which has led me to think that, *in this place*, I interpreted Plato's text (though not his meaning) somewhat too freely, I do not wish to create the impression that Professor Levinson's is not a very good and interesting book—especially if we forget all about the scores of places where 'Popper' is quoted, or (as I have shown) slightly misquoted, and very often radically misunderstood.

But more important than these personal questions is the question: how far does Professor Levinson's defence of Plato succeed?

B

I have learnt that when faced with a new attack on my book by a defender of Plato it is best to disregard the smaller points and to look for answers to the following five cardinal points.

(1) How is my assertion met that the *Republic* and the *Laws* condemn the Socrates of the *Apology* (as pointed out in chapter 10, second paragraph of section vi)? As explained in a note (note 55 to chapter 10) the assertion was in effect made by Grote, and supported by Taylor. If it is fair—and I think it is—then it supports also my assertion mentioned in my next point, (2).

(2) How is my assertion met that Plato's anti-liberal and anti-humanitarian attitude cannot possibly be explained by the alleged fact that better ideas were not known to him, or that he was, for those days, *comparatively* liberal and humanitarian?

(3) How is my assertion met that Plato (for example in the canvas-cleaning passage of the *Republic* and in the kill-and-banish passage of the *Statesman*) encouraged his rulers to use ruthless violence 'for the benefit of the state'?

(4) How is my assertion met that Plato established for his philosopher kings the duty and privilege of using lies and deceit for the benefit of the

city, especially in connection with racial breeding, and that he was one of the founding fathers of racialism?

(5) What is said in answer to my quotation of the passage from the *Laws* used as a motto for *The Spell of Plato* on p. 7 (and, as announced at the beginning of the Notes on p. 203, 'discussed in some detail in notes 33 and 34 to chapter 6')?

I often tell my students that what I say about Plato is—necessarily—merely an interpretation, and that I should not be surprised if Plato (should I ever meet his shade) were to tell me, and to establish to my satisfaction, that it is a misrepresentation; but I usually add that he would have quite a task to explain away a number of the things he had said.

Has Professor Levinson succeeded on Plato's behalf in this task, regarding any of the five points mentioned above?

I really do not think he has.

(1′) As to the first point, I ask anybody in doubt to read carefully the text of the last speech made by the Athenian Stranger in book X of the *Laws* (907d down to, say, 909d). The legislation there discussed is concerned with the type of crime of which Socrates was accused. My contention is that, while Socrates had a way out (most critics think, in view of the evidence of the *Apology*, that he would probably have escaped death had he been willing to accept banishment), Plato's *Laws* do not make any such provision. I shall quote from a passage in Bury's translation (which seems to be acceptable to Levinson) of this very long speech. After classifying his 'criminals' (that is, those guilty of 'impiety' or 'the disease of atheism': the translation is Bury's; *cp.* 908c), the Athenian Stranger discusses first 'those who, though they utterly disbelieve the existence of gods, possess by nature a just character … and … are incapable of being induced to commit unjust actions'. (908b–c; this is almost a portrait—of course an unconscious one—of Socrates, apart from the important fact that he does not seem to have been an atheist, though accused of impiety and unorthodoxy.) About these Plato says:

'… those criminals … being devoid of evil disposition and character, shall be placed by the judge according to law in the reformatory for a period of not less than five years, during which time no other of the citizens shall hold intercourse with them save only those who take part in the nocturnal assembly, and they shall company with them [I should translate 'they shall attend to them'] to minister to their soul's salvation by admonition …' Thus the 'good' among the impious men get a minimum of five years of solitary confinement, only relieved by 'attention' to their sick souls from the members of the Nocturnal Council. '… and when the period of their incarceration has expired, if any of them seems to be reformed, he shall dwell with those who are reformed, but if not, and if he be convicted again on a like charge, he shall be punished by death.'

I have nothing to add to this.

(2′) The second point is perhaps the most important from Professor Levinson's point of view: it is one of his main claims that I am mistaken in my assertion that there were humanitarians—better ones than Plato—among those whom I have called the 'Great Generation'.

He asserts, in particular, that my picture of Socrates as a man very different from Plato in this respect is quite fictitious.

Now I have devoted a very long footnote (note 56 to chapter 10), in fact quite an essay, to this problem—the *Socratic Problem*; and I do not see any reason to change my views on it. But I wish to say here that I have received support in this historical conjecture of mine about the *Socratic Problem*, from a Platonic scholar of the eminence of Richard Robinson; support which is the more significant as Robinson castigates me severely (and perhaps justly) for the tone of my attack on Plato. Nobody who reads his review of my book (*Philosophical Review*, **60**, 1951) can accuse him of undue partiality for me; and Professor Levinson quotes him approvingly (p. 20) for speaking of my 'rage to blame' Plato. But although Professor Levinson (in a footnote on p. 20) refers to Richard Robinson as 'mingling praise and blame in his extensive review of the *Open Society*', and although (in another footnote, on p. 61) he rightly refers to Robinson as an authority about 'the growth of Plato's logic from its Socratic beginnings through its middle period', Professor Levinson never tells his readers that Robinson agrees not only with my main accusations against Plato, but also, more especially, with my conjectural solution of the *Socratic Problem*. (Incidentally, Robinson also agrees that my quotation mentioned here in point (5) is correct; see below.)

Since Robinson, as we have heard, 'mingles praise and blame', some of his readers (anxious to find confirmation for their 'rage to blame' me) may have overlooked the praise contained in the surprising last sentence of the following forceful passage from his review (p. 494):

'Dr. Popper holds that Plato perverted the teaching of Socrates . . . To him Plato is a very harmful force in politics but Socrates a very beneficial one. Socrates died for the right to talk freely to the young; but in the *Republic* Plato makes him take up an attitude of condescension and distrust towards them. Socrates died for truth and free speech; but in the *Republic* "Socrates" advocates lying. Socrates was intellectually modest; but in the *Republic* he is a dogmatist. Socrates was an individualist; but in the *Republic* he is a radical collectivist. And so on.

'What is Dr. Popper's evidence for the views of the real Socrates? It is drawn exclusively from Plato himself, from the early dialogues, and primarily from the *Apology*. Thus the angel of light with whom he contrasts the demon Plato is known to us only from the demon's own account! Is this absurd?

'It is not absurd, in my opinion, but entirely correct.'

This passage shows that at least one scholar, admitted by Professor Levinson to be an authority on Plato, has found that my view on the *Socratic Problem* is not absurd.

But even if my conjectural solution of the *Socratic Problem* should be mistaken, there is plenty of evidence left for the existence of humanitarian tendencies in this period.

Concerning the speech of Hippias, to be found in Plato's *Protagoras*, 337e (see above p. 70; Professor Levinson seems for once not to object to my translation; see his p. 144), Professor Levinson writes (p. 147): 'We must begin by assuming that Plato is here reflecting faithfully a well-known sentiment of Hippias.' So far Professor Levinson and I agree. But we disagree completely about the relevance of Hippias' speech. On this I have now even stronger views than those I expressed in the text of this volume. (Incidentally, I don't think I ever asserted that there was evidence that Hippias was an opponent of slavery; what I said of him was that 'this spirit was bound up with the Athenian movement against slavery'; thus Professor Levinson's elaborate argument that I am not justified 'in including him [Hippias] among the opponents of slavery' is pointless.)

I now see Hippias' speech as a manifesto—the first perhaps—of a humanitarian faith which inspired the ideas of the Enlightenment and the French Revolution: that all men are brothers, and that it is conventional, man-made, law and custom which divide them and which are the source of much avoidable unhappiness; so that it is not impossible for men to make things better by a change in the laws—by legal reform. These ideas also inspired Kant. And Schiller speaks of conventional law as 'the fashion' which sternly ('*streng*')—Beethoven says 'insolently' ('*frech*')—divides mankind.

As to slavery, my main contention is that the *Republic* contains evidence of the existence of tendencies in Athens which may be described as opposition to slavery. Thus the 'Socrates' of the *Republic* (563b) says, in a speech satirizing Athenian democracy (I quoted it in chapter 4, ii, p. 43E = p. 44A; but I am here using Shorey's translation): 'And the climax of popular liberty ... is attained in such a city when the purchased slaves, male and female, are no less free than the owners who paid for them.'

Shorey has a number of cross-references to this passage (see footnote below); but the passage speaks for itself. Levinson says of this passage elsewhere (p. 176): 'Let us contribute the just-quoted passage to help fill the modest inventory of Plato's social sins', and on the next page he refers to it when he speaks of 'Another instance of Platonic *hauteur*'. But this is no answer to my contention that, taken together with a second passage from the *Republic* quoted in my text (p. 43E = p. 44A), this first passage supplies evidence of an anti-slavery movement. The second passage (which follows in Plato immediately after an elaboration of the first, here quoted at the end of the preceding paragraph) reads in Shorey's translation (*Republic* 563d; the previous passage was *Republic* 563b): 'And do you know that the sum total of all these items ... is that they render the souls of the citizens so sensitive that they chafe at the slightest suggestion of servitude [I translated 'slavery'] and will not endure it?'

How does Professor Levinson deal with this evidence? First, by separating the two passages: the first he does not discuss until p. 176, long after he has smashed to bits (on p. 153) my alleged evidence concerning an anti-slavery movement. The second he dismisses on p. 153 as a grotesque mistranslation of mine; for he writes there: 'Yet it is all a mistake; though Plato uses the word *douleia* (slavery or servitude), it bears *only a figurative allusion* [my italics] to slavery in the usual sense.'

This may sound plausible when the passage is divorced from its immediate predecessor (only mentioned by Professor Levinson more than twenty pages later, where he explains it by Plato's *hauteur*); but in its context—in connection with Plato's complaint about the licentious behaviour of slaves (and even of animals)—there can be no doubt whatever that, in addition to the meaning which Professor Levinson correctly ascribes to the passage, the passage also bears a second meaning which takes '*douleia*' quite literally; for it says, and it means, that the free democratic citizens cannot stand slavery in any form—not only do they not submit themselves to any suggestion of servitude (not even to laws, as Plato goes on to say), but they have become so tender-hearted that they cannot bear 'even the slightest suggestion of servitude'—such as the slavery of 'purchased slaves, male or female'.

Professor Levinson (p. 153, after discussing Plato's second passage) asks: 'in the light of the evidence ... what, then, can fairly be said to remain standing in Popper's case ...? The simplest answer is "Nothing," if words are taken in anything like their literal sense.' Yet his own case rests upon taking '*douleia*', in a context which clearly refers to slavery, not in its literal sense but as 'only a figurative allusion', as he himself has put it a few lines earlier.[2]

[2] Added in 1965. That the word '*douleia*' in the passage in question (*Republic* 563d) bears this literal meaning (*in addition* to the figurative meaning which Professor Levinson correctly attributes to it) is confirmed by Shorey, the great Platonist and open enemy of democracy, whom Professor Levinson considers an authority on Plato's text. (I can often agree with Shorey's interpretation of Plato because he rarely tries to humanize or liberalize Plato's text.) For in a footnote which Shorey attaches to the word 'servitude' (*douleia*) in his translation of *Republic* 563d, he refers to two parallel passages: *Gorgias* 491e, and *Laws* 890a. The first of these

And yet, he says of the grotesque 'mistake' I made in translating '*douleia*' literally: 'This misreading has borne fruit in the preface to Sherwood Anderson's play *Barefoot in Athens* ... where the unsuspecting playwright, following Popper' (Professor Levinson asserts on p. 24 that 'the Andersonian version of Plato plainly bespeaks a close and docile reading of Popper', but he gives no evidence for this strange accusation) 'passes on to his readers in turn the allusion, and declares flatly ... as on Plato's own authority, that the Athenians ... "advocate[d] the manumission of all slaves" ...'

Now this remark of Maxwell (*not* Sherwood) Anderson's may well be an exaggeration. But where have I said anything similar to this? And what is the worth of a case if, in its defence, the defender has to exaggerate the views of his opponent, or blacken them by associating them with the (alleged) guilt of some 'docile' reader? (See also the Index to this volume, under 'Slavery'.)

(3′) My contention that Plato encouraged his rulers to use ruthless and lawless violence, though it is combated by Professor Levinson, is nowhere really denied by him, as will be seen from his discussion of the 'kill-and-banish' passage of the *Statesman* mentioned in this *Addendum* towards the end of section A. All he denies is that a number of other passages in the *Republic*—the canvas-cleaning passages—are similar, as both Shorey and I think. Apart from this, he tries to derive comfort and moral support from some of our modern violent practices—a comfort which, I fear, will be diminished if he re-reads the passage of the *Statesman* together with its commencement, quoted by me, but first omitted by Professor Levinson, and later dismissed as irrelevant.

(4′) As to Plato's racialism, and his injunction to his rulers to use lies and deceit for the benefit of the state, I wish to remind my readers, before entering into any discussion with Professor Levinson, of Kant's saying (see

reads in W. R. M. Lamb's translation (Loeb Edition): 'For how can a man be happy if he is a slave to anybody at all?' Here the phrase 'to be a slave' has, like the one in the *Republic*, not only the figurative meaning 'to submit oneself' but also the literal meaning; indeed, the whole point is the merging of the two meanings. The passage from the *Laws* 890a (an elaborate attack on certain Sophists of the Great Generation) reads in Bury's translation (Loeb Edition) as follows: 'these teachers [who corrupt the young men] attract them towards the life ... "according to nature" which consists in being master over the rest, in reality [*alētheia*], instead of being a slave to others, according to legal convention.' Plato clearly alludes here among others to those Sophists (p. 70E = p. 70A and note 13 to chapter 5) who taught that men cannot be slaves 'by nature' or 'in truth', but only 'by legal convention' (by legal fiction). Thus Shorey connects the crucial passage of the *Republic* by this reference at least indirectly to the great classical discussion of the *theory of slavery* ('slavery' in the literal sense).

p. 139E = p. 137A) that though '*truthfulness is the best policy*' might be questionable, '*truthfulness is better than policy*' is beyond dispute.

Professor Levinson writes (p. 434, referring to my pp. 138 ff. E = pp. 136 ff. A, and especially to p. 150E = p. 148A) very fairly: 'First of all, we must agree that the use of lies in certain circumstances is *advocated* [my italics] in the *Republic* for purposes of government ...' This, after all, is my main point. No attempt to play it down or to diminish its significance—and no counter-attack on my alleged exaggerations—should be allowed to obscure this admission.

Professor Levinson also admits, in the same place, that 'there can be no doubt that some use of the persuasive art of speech would be required to make the auxiliaries "blame chance and not the rulers" when they are told [see my p. 150E = p. 148A] that the fall of the lot has determined their marriages, whereas really these are engineered by the rulers for eugenic reasons'.

This was my second main point.

Professor Levinson continues (pp. 434 f.; my italics): 'In this instance we have the only sanctioning by Plato of an outright practical lie,[3] to be told, to be sure, for benevolent reasons (and only for such purposes does Plato sanction the telling), but a lie and nothing more. We, like Popper, find this policy distasteful. This lie, then, *and any others like it* which Plato's *rather general permission* might justify, constitute such basis as exists for Popper's charge that Plato proposes to use "lying propaganda" in his city.'

Is this not enough? Let us assume that I was wrong in my other points (which, of course, I deny), does not all this at least excuse my suspicion that Plato would not have scrupled to make some further use of his 'rather general permission' of 'the use of lies'—especially in view of the fact that he actually '*advocated*' the 'use of lies' as Professor Levinson has it?

Moreover, the lying is here used in connection with 'eugenics', or more precisely, with *the breeding of the master race*—the race of the guardians.

In defending Plato against my accusation that he was a racialist Professor Levinson tries to compare him favourably with some 'notorious' modern totalitarian racialists whose names I have tried to keep out of my book. (And

[3] It is by no means the only instance, as may be seen from my chapter 8. The passage quoted in the text to note 2, for example (*Rep.*, 389b), is a different instance from the passage (*Rep.*, 460a) which Professor Levinson has in mind. There are several other passages. See *Rep.*, 415d and especially *Tim.*, 18e, which prove that Plato finds his instruction to lie of sufficient importance to be included in the very brief summary of the *Republic*. (See also *Laws*, 663d down to 664b.)

I shall continue to do so.) He says of these (p. 541; my italics) that their 'breeding schedule' 'was primarily intended to *preserve the purity of the master race*, an aim which we have been at some pains to show Plato did not share.'

Did he not? Was my quotation from one of the main eugenic discussions of the *Republic* (460c) perhaps a mistranslation? I wrote (p. 51E = p. 52A); I am here introducing new italics):

'"*The race of the guardians must be kept pure*", says Plato (in defence of infanticide) when developing the racialist argument that we breed animals with great care while neglecting our own race, an argument which has been repeated ever since.'

Is my translation wrong? Or my assertion that this has been, ever since Plato, the main argument of racialists and breeders of the master race? Or are the guardians not the masters of Plato's best city?

As to my translation, Shorey puts it a little differently; I shall quote from his translation (the italics are mine) also the preceding sentence (referring to infanticide): '... the offspring of the inferior, and any of those of the other sort who are born defective, they [the rulers] will properly dispose of in secret, so that no one will know what has become of them. "That is the condition," he said, "*of preserving the purity of the guardian's breed*."'

It will be seen that Shorey's last sentence is slightly weaker than mine. But the difference is trifling, and does not affect my thesis. And at any rate, I stick to my translation. 'At all events the breed of the guardians must be preserved pure' or 'If at all events [as we agree] the purity of the breed of the guardians must be preserved' would be a translation which, using some of Shorey's words, brings out precisely the same meaning as my translation in the body of the book (p. 51E = p. 52A) and here repeated.

I cannot see, therefore, what the difference is between Professor Levinson's formulation of that 'notorious ... breeding schedule' of the totalitarians, and Plato's formulation of his own breeding aims. Whatever minor difference there may be is irrelevant to the central question.

As to the problem whether Plato allowed—very exceptionally—a mingling of his races (which would be the consequence of promoting a member of the lower race), opinions may differ. I still believe that what I said is true. But I cannot see that it would make any difference if exceptions were permitted. (Even those modern totalitarians to whom Professor Levinson alludes permitted exceptions.)

(5′) I have been repeatedly and severely attacked for quoting—or rather misquoting—a passage from the *Laws* which I have taken as one of the two mottos of *The Spell of Plato* (the other and contrasting passage is from Pericles' funeral oration). These mottos were printed by my American publishers on the jacket of the American edition; the English editions have no such advertisement. As is usual with jackets, I was not consulted by the publishers about them. (But I certainly have no objection to my American publishers' choice: why should they not print my mottos—or anything else I wrote in the book—on their jackets?)

My translation and interpretation of this passage has been pronounced to be correct by Richard Robinson, as mentioned above; but others went so far as to ask me whether I had not consciously tried to hide its identity, in order to make it impossible for my readers to check the text! And this although I have taken more trouble, I think, than most authors to make it possible for my readers to check any passage quoted or referred to. Thus I have a reference to my mottos at the beginning of my notes—although it is somewhat unusual to make references to one's mottos.

The main accusation against me for using this passage is that I do not say, or do not emphasize sufficiently, that it refers to military matters. But here I have testimony in my favour from Professor Levinson himself who writes (p. 531, footnote; my italics):

'Popper, in citing this passage in his text, p. 102 [= p. 103E] *duly emphasizes* its reference to military matters.'

Thus this charge is answered. However, Professor Levinson continues: '… but [Popper] protests simultaneously that Plato means the same "militarist principles" to be adhered to in peace as well as in war, and that they are to be applied to every area of peaceful existence rather than simply to the program of military training. He then quotes the passage with perverse mistranslations which tend to obscure its military reference …' and so on.

Now the first charge here is that I 'protest simultaneously' that Plato means these militarist principles to be adhered to in peace as well as in war. Indeed I have said so—quoting Plato: *it is Plato who says so*. Should I have suppressed it? Plato says, in Bury's translation of which Professor Levinson approves (though I prefer mine: I ask my readers whether there is any difference of *meaning* between them, as distinct from one of clarity; see p. 103E = p. 102A): '… nor should anyone, whether at work or in play, grow habituated in mind to acting alone and on his own initiative, but he should *live always* both in war *and peace*, with his eyes fixed constantly on his commander …' (*Laws*, Loeb Library, vol. ii, p. 477; my italics).

And later (p. 479):

'This task of ruling, and of being ruled by, others must be practised *in peace* from earliest childhood …'

As to mistranslation, I can only say that there is practically no difference between my translation and Bury's—except that I have broken up Plato's two very long sentences which, as they stand, are not quite easy to follow. Professor Levinson says (p. 531) that I have 'made great and illegitimate use' of this passage; and he continues: 'His journalistic misapplication of a selection from it on the dust cover' [the publishers' advertisement; see above] 'and on the title page of Part I of his book will be dissected in our note, where we also print the passage in full.'

The dissection of my 'journalistic misapplication' in this note consists, apart from some alleged 'corrections' of my translation which I do not accept, mainly of the same charge—that I have printed the passage on the jacket and in other important places. For Professor Levinson writes (p. 532; italics mine):

'This small unfairness is entirely eclipsed, however, by what Popper has done with the passage elsewhere. On the title page of Part I of his book, and also on the dust jacket' [who is unfair to whom?] '*he prints* a carefully chosen selection drawn from it, and beside it prints, as its very antithesis, a sentence drawn from Pericles' funeral oration … *This is to print in parallel a political ideal and a proposed military regulation*; yet Popper has not only failed to apprise the reader of this selection of its military reference, but employing the same mistranslations, has deleted absolutely all those parts of the passage which would reveal the fact.'

My answer to this is very simple. (*a*) The mistranslations are non-existent. (*b*) I have tried to show at length that the passage, in spite of its military reference, formulates, like the Pericles passage (which incidentally also has some, though less, military reference), *a political ideal*—that is, Plato's political ideal.

I have seen no valid reason to change my belief that I am right in holding that this passage—like so many similar passages in the *Laws*—formulates Plato's political ideal. But whether this belief of mine is true or not, I have certainly given strong reasons for it (reasons which Professor Levinson fails to undermine). And since I have done so, and since Professor Levinson does not at all question the fact that I believe that I have done so, it constitutes neither a 'small unfairness' nor a great one if I try to present the passage as what I believe it to be: Plato's own description of his political ideal—of his totalitarian and militaristic ideal state.

As to my mistranslations, I shall confine myself to the one which Professor Levinson finds important enough to discuss in his text (as distinct from his footnote). He writes, on p. 533:

'A further objection concerns Popper's use of the word "leader." Plato uses "*archōn*", the same word he employs for officials of the state and for military commanders; it is clearly the latter, or the directors of the athletic contests, whom he has here in mind.'

Clearly, there is no case for me to answer. (Should I have perhaps translated 'director'?) Anybody who consults a Greek dictionary can ascertain that '*archōn*', in its most basic meaning, is properly and precisely rendered by the English word '*leader*' (or the Latin '*dux*' or the Italian '*il duce*'). The word is described, by Liddell and Scott, as a participle of the verb '*archō*' whose fundamental meaning, according to these authorities, is 'to be first', either 'in point of Time', or 'in point of Place or Station'. In this second sense the first meanings given are: '*to lead, rule, govern, command, be leader or commander*'. Accordingly we find, under *archōn*, '*a ruler, commander, captain*; also, with respect to Athens, *the chief magistrates at Athens*, nine in number.' This should suffice to show that 'leader' is not a mistranslation, provided it fits the text. That it does can be seen from Bury's own version in which, it will be remembered, the passage is rendered as follows: 'but he should live always, both in war and peace, with his eyes fixed constantly on his *commander* and *following his lead*'. In fact, '*leader*' fits the text only too well: it is the horrifying fittingness of the word which has produced Professor Levinson's protest. Since he is unable to see Plato as an advocate of totalitarian leadership, he feels that it must be my 'perverse mistranslations' (p. 531) which are to be blamed for the horrifying associations which this passage evokes.

But I assert that it is Plato's text, and Plato's thought, which is horrifying. I am, as is Professor Levinson, shocked by the 'leader', and all that this term connotes. Yet these connotations must not be played down if we wish to understand the appalling implications of the Platonic ideal state. These I set out to bring home, as well as I could.

It is perfectly true that in my comments I have stressed the fact that, although the passage refers to military expeditions, Plato leaves no doubt that its principles are to apply to the whole life of his soldier-citizens. It is no answer to say that a Greek citizen was, and had to be, a soldier; for this is true of Pericles and the time of his funeral oration (for soldiers fallen in battle) at least as much as of Plato and the time of his *Laws*.

This is the point which my mottos were meant to bring out as clearly as possible. This made it necessary to cut out one clause from this unwieldy passage, thereby omitting (as indicated by the insertion of dots) some of those references to military matters which would have obscured my main point: I mean the fact that the passage has a general application, *to war and to peace*, and that many Platonists have misread it, and missed its point, because of its length and obscure formulation, and because of their anxiety to idealize Plato. This is how the case stands. Yet I am accused in this context by Professor Levinson (p. 532) of using 'tactics' which 'make it necessary to check in merciless detail every one of Popper's citations from the Platonic text', in order to 'reveal how far from the path of objectivity and fairness Popper has been swept'.

Faced with these accusations and allegations, and with suspicions cast upon me, I can only try to defend myself. But I am conscious of the principle that no man ought to be judge in his own cause. It is for this reason that I wish here to quote what Richard Robinson says (on p. 491 of *The Philosophical Review*, **60**) about this Platonic passage, and about my translation of it. It should be remembered that Robinson is 'mingling praise with blame' in his review of my book, and that part of the blame consists in the assertion that my translations of Plato are biased. Yet he writes:

'Biased though they are, they should certainly not be disregarded. They draw attention to real and important features of Plato's thought that are usually overlooked. In particular, Dr. Popper's show piece, the horrible passage from *Laws* 942 about never acting on one's own, is correctly translated. (It might be urged that Plato intended this to apply only to the military life of his citizens, and it is true that the passage begins as a prescription for army discipline; but by the end Plato is clearly wishing to extend it to all life; cf. "the anarchy must be removed from all the life of all the men" [*Laws*, 942d 1]).'

I feel that I should add nothing to Robinson's statement.

To sum up. I cannot possibly attempt to answer even a fraction of the charges Professor Levinson has brought against me. I have tried to answer only a few of them, bearing in mind, as well as I could, that more important than the problem of who is unfair to whom is the question whether or not my assertions about Plato have been refuted. I have tried to give reasons for my belief that they have not been refuted. But I repeat that no man ought to be judge in his own cause: I must leave it to my readers to decide.

Yet I do not wish to end this long discussion without reaffirming my conviction of Plato's overwhelming intellectual achievement. My opinion that he was the greatest of all philosophers has not changed. Even his moral and political philosophy is, as an intellectual achievement, without parallel, though I find it morally repulsive, and indeed horrifying. As to his physical cosmology, I have changed my mind between the first and second edition (more precisely, between the first English edition and the first American edition) of this book; and I have tried to give reasons why I now think that he is the founder of *the geometrical theory of the world*; a theory whose importance has continuously increased down the ages. His literary powers I should think it presumptuous to praise. What my critics have shown is, I believe, that Plato's greatness makes it all the more important to fight his moral and political philosophy, and to warn those who may fall under his magic spell.

IV (1965)

In note 31 to Chapter 3 I mentioned a number of works which seemed to me to anticipate my views of Plato's politics. Since writing this note I have read Diana Spearman's great attack, of 1939, on appeasers and dictators, *Modern Dictatorship*. Her chapter, 'The Theory of Autocracy', contains one of the deepest and most penetrating, and at the same time one of the briefest analyses of Plato's political theory that I have seen.

Volume II

The High Tide of Prophecy: Hegel, Marx, and the Aftermath

To the débâcle of liberal science can be traced the moral schism of the modern world which so tragically divides enlightened men.

WALTER LIPPMANN.

THE HIGH TIDE OF PROPHECY

The Rise of Oracular Philosophy

11

THE ARISTOTELIAN ROOTS OF HEGELIANISM

The task of writing a history of the ideas in which we are interested—of historicism and its connection with totalitarianism—will not be attempted here. The reader will remember, I hope, that I do not even try to give more than a few scattered remarks which may throw light on the background of the modern version of these ideas. The story of their development, more particularly during the period from Plato to Hegel and Marx, could not possibly be told while keeping the size of the book within reasonable limits. I shall therefore not attempt a serious treatment of Aristotle, except in so far as his version of Plato's essentialism has influenced the historicism of Hegel, and thereby that of Marx. The restriction to those ideas of Aristotle with which we have become acquainted in our criticism of Plato, Aristotle's great master, does not, however, create as serious a loss as one might fear at first sight. For Aristotle, in spite of his stupendous learning and his astonishing scope, was not a man of striking originality of thought. What he added to the Platonic store of ideas was, in the main, systematization and a burning interest in empirical and especially in biological problems. To be sure, he is the inventor of logic, and for this and his other achievements, he amply deserves what he himself claimed (at the end of his *Sophistic Refutations*)—our warm thanks, and our pardon for his shortcomings. Yet for readers and admirers of Plato these shortcomings are formidable.

I

In some of Plato's latest writings, we can find an echo of the contemporary political developments in Athens—of the consolidation of democracy. It seems that even Plato began to doubt whether some form of democracy had not come to stay. In Aristotle, we find indications that he did not doubt any longer. Although he is no friend of democracy, he accepts it as unavoidable, and is ready to compromise with the enemy.

An inclination to compromise, strangely mixed with an inclination to find fault with his predecessors and contemporaries (and with Plato in particular), is one of the outstanding characteristics of Aristotle's encyclopædic writings. They show no trace of the tragic and stirring conflict that is the motive of Plato's work. Instead of Plato's flashes of penetrating insight, we find dry systematization and the love, shared by so many mediocre writers of later times, for settling any question whatever by issuing a 'sound and balanced judgement' that does justice to everybody; which means, at times, by elaborately and solemnly missing the point. This exasperating tendency which is systematized in Aristotle's famous 'doctrine of the mean' is one of the sources of his so often forced and even fatuous criticism of Plato[1]. An example of Aristotle's lack of insight, in this case of historical insight (he also was a historian), is the fact that he acquiesced in the apparent democratic consolidation just when it had been superseded by the imperial monarchy of Macedon; a historical event which happened to escape his notice. Aristotle, who was, as his father had been, a courtier at the Macedonian court, chosen by Philip to be the teacher of Alexander the Great, seems to have underrated these men and their plans; perhaps he thought he knew them too well. 'Aristotle sat down to dinner with Monarchy without becoming aware of it', is Gomperz's appropriate comment.[2]

Aristotle's thought is entirely dominated by Plato's. Somewhat grudgingly, he followed his great teacher as closely as his temperament permitted, not only in his general political outlook but practically everywhere. So he endorsed, and systematized, Plato's naturalistic theory of slavery[3]: 'Some men are by nature free, and others slaves; and for the latter, slavery is fitting as well as just ... A man who is by nature not his own, but another's, is by nature a slave ... Hellenes do not like to call themselves slaves, but confine this term to barbarians ... The slave is totally devoid of any faculty of reasoning', while free women have just a very little of it. (We owe to Aristotle's criticisms and denunciations most of our knowledge of the Athenian movement against slavery. By arguing against the fighters for freedom, he preserved some of their utterances.) In some minor points

Aristotle slightly mitigates Plato's theory of slavery, and duly censures his teacher for being too harsh. He could neither resist an opportunity for criticizing Plato, nor one for a compromise, not even if it was a compromise with the liberal tendencies of his time.

But the theory of slavery is only one of Plato's many political ideas to be adopted by Aristotle. Especially his theory of the Best State, as far as we know it, is modelled upon the theories of the *Republic* and the *Laws*; and his version throws considerable light on Plato's. Aristotle's Best State is a compromise between three things, a romantic Platonic aristocracy, a 'sound and balanced' feudalism, and some democratic ideas; but feudalism has the best of it. With the democrats, Aristotle holds that all citizens should have the right to participate in the government. But this, of course, is not meant to be as radical as it sounds, for Aristotle explains at once that not only slaves but all members of the producing classes are excluded from citizenship. Thus he teaches with Plato that the working classes must not rule and the ruling classes must not work, nor earn any money. (But they are supposed to have plenty.) They own the land, but must not work it themselves. Only hunting, war, and similar hobbies are considered worthy of the feudal rulers. Aristotle's fear of any form of money earning, i.e. of all professional activities, goes perhaps even further than Plato's. Plato had used the term 'banausic'[4] to describe a plebeian, abject, or depraved state of mind. Aristotle extends the disparaging use of the term so as to cover all interests which are not pure hobbies. In fact, his use of the term is very near to our use of the term 'professional', more especially in the sense in which it disqualifies in an amateur competition, but also in the sense in which it applies to any specialized expert, such as a physician. For Aristotle, every form of professionalism means a loss of caste. A feudal gentleman, he insists[5], must never take too much interest in 'any occupation, art or science ... There are also some *liberal arts*, that is to say, arts which a gentleman may acquire, but always only to a certain degree. For if he takes too much interest in them, then these evil effects will follow', namely, he will become proficient, like a professional, and lose caste. This is Aristotle's idea of a *liberal education*, the idea, unfortunately not yet obsolete[6], of a gentleman's education, as opposed to the education of a slave, serf, servant, or professional man. It is in the same vein that he repeatedly insists that 'the first principle of all action is leisure'[7]. Aristotle's admiration and deference for the leisured classes seems to be the expression of a curious feeling of uneasiness. It looks as if the son of the Macedonian court physician was troubled by the question of his own social position, and especially by the possibility that he might lose caste because of his own scholarly interests which might be considered professional. 'One is tempted to believe', says Gomperz[8], 'that he feared to hear such denunciations from his aristocratic friends … It is indeed strange to see that one of the greatest scholars of all time, if not the greatest, does not wish to be a professional scholar. He would rather be a dilettante, and a man of the world …' Aristotle's feelings of inferiority have, perhaps, still another basis, apart from his wish to prove his independence of Plato, apart from his own 'professional' origin, and apart from the fact that he was, undoubtedly, a professional 'sophist' (he even taught rhetoric). For with Aristotle, Platonic philosophy gives up her great aspirations, her claims to power. From this moment, it could continue only as a teaching profession. And since hardly anybody but a feudal lord had the money and the leisure for studying philosophy, all that philosophy could aspire to was to become an annex to the traditional education of a gentleman. With this more modest aspiration in view, Aristotle finds it very necessary to persuade the feudal gentleman that philosophical speculation and contemplation may become a most important part of his 'good life'; for it is the happiest and noblest and the most refined method of whiling away one's time, if one is not occupied with political intrigues or by war. It is the best way of spending one's leisure since, as Aristotle himself puts it, 'nobody … would arrange a war for that purpose'[9].

It is plausible to assume that such a courtier's philosophy will tend to be optimistic, since it will hardly be a pleasant pastime otherwise. And indeed, in its optimism lies the one important adjustment made by Aristotle in his systematization[10] of Platonism. Plato's sense of drift had expressed itself in his theory that all change, at least in certain cosmic periods, must be for the worse; all change is degeneration. Aristotle's theory admits of changes which are improvements; thus change may be progress. Plato had taught that all development starts from the original, the perfect Form or Idea, so that the developing thing must lose its perfection in the degree in which it changes and in which its similarity to the original decreases. This theory was given up by his nephew and successor, Speusippus, as well as by Aristotle. But Aristotle censured Speusippus' arguments as going too far, since they implied a general biological evolution towards higher forms. Aristotle, it seems, was opposed to the much-discussed evolutionary biological theories of his time[11]. But the peculiar optimistic twist which he gave to Platonism was an outcome of biological speculation also. It was based upon the idea of a *final cause*.

According to Aristotle, one of the four causes of anything—also of any movement or change—is the final cause, or the end towards which the movement aims. In so far as it is an aim or a desired end, the final cause is also *good*. It follows from this that some *good* may not only be the starting point of a movement (as Plato had taught, and as Aristotle admitted[12]) but that some good must also stand at its end. And this is particularly important for anything that has a beginning in time, or, as Aristotle puts it, for anything that comes into being. *The Form or essence of anything developing is identical with the purpose or end or final state towards which it develops.* Thus we obtain after all, in spite of Aristotle's disclaimer, something very closely resembling Speusippus' adjustment of Platonism. The Form or Idea, which is still, with Plato, considered to be good, stands at the end, instead of the beginning. This characterizes Aristotle's substitution of optimism for pessimism.

Aristotle's teleology, i.e. his stress upon the end or aim of change as its final cause, is an expression of his predominantly *biological* interests. It is influenced by Plato's biological theories[13], and also by Plato's extension of his theory of justice to the universe. For Plato did not confine himself to teaching that each of the different classes of citizens has its natural place in society, a place to which it belongs and for which it is naturally fitted; he also tried to interpret the world of physical bodies and their different classes or kinds on similar principles. He tried to explain the weight of heavy bodies, like stones, or earth, and their tendency to fall, as well as the tendency of air and fire to rise, by the assumption that they strive to retain, or to regain, the place inhabited by their kind. Stones and earth fall because they strive to be where most stones and earth are, and where they belong, in the just order of nature; air and fire rise because they strive to be where air and fire (the heavenly bodies) are, and where they belong, in the just order of nature[14]. This theory of motion appealed to the zoologist Aristotle; it combines easily with the theory of final causes, and it allows an explanation of all motion as being analogous with the canter of horses keen to return to their stables. He developed it as his famous theory of *natural places*. Everything if removed from its own natural place has a natural tendency to return to it.

Despite some alterations, Aristotle's version of Plato's essentialism shows only unimportant differences. Aristotle insists, of course, that unlike Plato he does not conceive the Forms or Ideas as existing apart from sensible things. But in so far as this difference is important, it is closely connected with the adjustment in the theory of change. For one of the main points in Plato's theory is that he must consider the Forms or essences or originals (or fathers) as existing prior to, and therefore apart from, sensible things, since these move further and further away from them. Aristotle makes sensible things move towards their final causes or ends, and these he identifies[15] with their Forms or essences. And as a biologist, he assumes that sensible things carry potentially within themselves the seeds, as it were, of their final states, or of their essences. This is one of the reasons why he can say that the Form or essence is *in* the thing, not, as Plato said, prior and external to it. For Aristotle, all movement or change means the realization (or 'actualization') of some of the potentialities inherent in the essence of a thing[16]. It is, for example, an essential potentiality of a piece of timber, that it can float on water, or that it can burn; these potentialities remain inherent in its essence even if it should never float or burn. But if it does, then it realizes a potentiality, and thereby changes or moves. Accordingly, the essence, which embraces all the potentialities of a thing, is something like its internal source of change or motion. This Aristotelian essence or Form, this 'formal' or 'final' cause, is therefore practically identical with Plato's 'nature' or 'soul'; and this identification is corroborated by Aristotle himself. 'Nature', he writes[17] in the *Metaphysics*, 'belongs also to the same class as potentiality; for it is a principle of movement inherent in the thing itself.' On the other hand, he defines the 'soul' as the 'first entelechy of a living body', and since 'entelechy', in turn, is explained as the Form, or the formal cause, considered as a motive force[18], we arrive, with the help of this somewhat complicated terminological apparatus, back at Plato's original point of view: that the soul or nature is something akin to the Form or Idea, but inherent in the thing, and its principle of motion. (When Zeller praised Aristotle for his 'definite use and comprehensive development of a scientific terminology'[19], I think he must have felt a bit uneasy in using the word 'definite'; but the comprehensiveness is to be admitted, as well as the most deplorable fact that Aristotle, by using this complicated and somewhat pretentious jargon, fascinated only too many philosophers; so that, as Zeller puts it, 'for thousands of years he showed philosophy her way'.)

Aristotle, who was a historian of the more encyclopædic type, made no direct contribution to historicism. He adhered to a more restricted version of Plato's theory that floods and other recurring catastrophes destroy the human race from time to time, leaving only a few survivors.[20] But he does not seem, apart from this, to have interested himself in the problem of historical trends. In spite of this fact, it may be shown here how his theory of change lends itself to historicist interpretations, and that it contains all the elements needed for elaborating a grandiose historicist philosophy. (This opportunity was not fully exploited before Hegel.) Three historicist doctrines which directly follow from Aristotle's essentialism may be distinguished. (1) Only if a person or a state develops, and only by way of its history, can we get to *know* anything about its 'hidden, undeveloped essence' (to use a phrase of Hegel's[21]). This doctrine leads later, first of all, to the adoption of an historicist method; that is to say, of the principle that we can obtain any knowledge of social entities or essences only by applying the historical method, by studying social changes. But the doctrine leads further (especially when connected with Hegel's moral positivism which identifies the known as well as the real with the good) to the worship of History and its exaltation as the Grand Theatre of Reality as well as the World's Court of Justice. (2) Change, by revealing what is hidden in the undeveloped essence, can only make apparent the essence, the potentialities, the seeds, which from the beginning have inhered in the changing object. This doctrine leads to the historicist idea of an historical fate or an inescapable essential destiny; for, as Hegel[22] showed later, 'what we call principle, aim, *destiny*' is nothing but the 'hidden undeveloped essence'. This means that whatever may befall a man, a nation, or a state, must be considered to emanate from, and to be understandable through, the essence, the real thing, the real 'personality' that manifests itself in this man, this nation, or this state. 'A man's fate is immediately connected with his own being; it is something which, indeed, he may fight against, but which is really a part of his own life.' This formulation (due to Caird[23]) of Hegel's theory of fate is clearly the historical and romantic counterpart of Aristotle's theory that all bodies seek their own 'natural places'. It is, of course, no more than a bombastic expression of the platitude, that what befalls a man depends not only on his external circumstances, but also on himself, on the way he reacts to them. But the naïve reader is extremely pleased with his ability to understand, and to feel the truth of this depth of wisdom that needs to be formulated with the help of such thrilling words as 'fate' and especially 'his own being'. (3) In order to become real or actual, the essence must unfold itself in change. This doctrine assumes later, with Hegel, the following form[24]: 'That which exists for itself only, is … a mere potentiality: it has not yet emerged into Existence … It is only by activity that the Idea is actualized.' Thus if I wish to 'emerge into Existence' (surely a very modest wish), then I must 'assert my personality'. This still rather popular theory leads, as Hegel sees clearly, to a new justification of the theory of slavery. For self-assertion means[25], in so far as one's relations to others are concerned, the attempt to dominate them. Indeed, Hegel points out that all personal relations can thus be reduced to the fundamental relation of master and slave, of domination and submission. Each must strive to assert and prove himself, and he who has not the nature, the courage, and the general capacity for preserving his independence, must be reduced to servitude. This charming theory of personal relations has, of course, its counterpart in Hegel's theory of international relations. Nations must assert themselves on the Stage of History; it is their duty to attempt the domination of the World.

All these far-reaching historicist consequences, which will be approached from a different angle in the next chapter, were slumbering for more than twenty centuries, 'hidden and undeveloped', in Aristotle's essentialism. Aristotelianism was more fertile and promising than most of its many admirers know.

II

> The chief danger to our philosophy, apart from laziness and woolliness, is scholasticism, ... which is treating what is vague as if it were precise . . .
>
> F. P. RAMSEY.

We have reached a point from which we could without delay proceed to an analysis of the historicist philosophy of Hegel, or, at any rate, to the brief comments upon the developments between Aristotle and Hegel and upon the rise of Christianity that conclude, as section III, the present chapter. As a kind of digression, however, I shall next discuss a more technical problem, Aristotle's *essentialist method of Definitions*.

The problem of definitions and of the 'meaning of terms' does not directly bear upon historicism. But it has been an inexhaustible source of confusion and of that particular kind of verbiage which, when combined with historicism in Hegel's mind, has bred that poisonous intellectual disease of our own time which I call *oracular philosophy*. And it is the most important source of Aristotle's regrettably still prevailing intellectual influence, of all that verbal and empty scholasticism that haunts not only the Middle Ages, but our own contemporary philosophy; for even a philosophy as recent as that of L. Wittgenstein[26] suffers, as we shall see, from this influence. The development of thought since Aristotle could, I think, be summed up by saying that every discipline, as long as it used the Aristotelian method of definition, has remained arrested in a state of empty verbiage and barren scholasticism, and that the degree to which the various sciences have been able to make any progress depended on the degree to which they have been able to get rid of this essentialist method. (This is why so much of our 'social science' still belongs to the Middle Ages.) The discussion of this method will have to be a little abstract, owing to the fact that the problem has been so thoroughly muddled by Plato and Aristotle, whose influence has given rise to such deep-rooted prejudices that the prospect of dispelling them does not seem very bright. In spite of all that, it is perhaps not without interest to analyse the source of so much confusion and verbiage.

Aristotle followed Plato in distinguishing between *knowledge* and *opinion*[27]. Knowledge, or science, according to Aristotle, may be of two kinds—either demonstrative or intuitive. *Demonstrative knowledge* is also a knowledge of 'causes'. It consists of statements that can be demonstrated—the conclusions—together with their syllogistic demonstrations (which exhibit the 'causes' in their 'middle terms'). *Intuitive knowledge* consists in grasping the 'indivisible form' or essence or essential nature of a thing (if it is 'immediate', i.e. if its 'cause' is identical with its essential nature); it is the originative source of all science since it grasps the original basic premises of all demonstrations.

Undoubtedly, Aristotle was right when he insisted that we must not attempt to prove or demonstrate *all* our knowledge. Every proof must proceed from premises; the proof as such, that is to say, the derivation from the premises, can therefore never finally settle the truth of any conclusion, but only show that the conclusion must be true *provided* the premises are true. If we were to demand that the premises should be proved in their turn, the question of truth would only be shifted back by another step to a new set of premises, and so on, to infinity. It was in order to avoid such an infinite regress (as the logicians say) that Aristotle taught that we must assume that there are premises which are indubitably true, and which do not need any proof; and these he called 'basic premises'. If we take for granted the methods by which we derive conclusions from these basic premises, then we could say that, according to Aristotle, the whole of scientific knowledge is contained in the basic premises, and that it would all be ours if only we could obtain an encyclopædic list of the basic premises. But how to obtain these basic premises? Like Plato, Aristotle believed that we obtain all knowledge ultimately by an intuitive grasp of the essences of things. 'We can know a thing only by knowing its essence', Aristotle writes[28], and 'to know a thing is to know its essence'. A 'basic premise' is, according to him, nothing but a statement describing the essence of a thing. But such a statement is just what he calls[29] a definition. Thus *all 'basic premises of proofs' are definitions*.

What does a definition look like? An example of a definition would be: 'A puppy is a young dog.' The subject of such a definition-sentence, the term 'puppy', is called the *term to be defined* (or *defined term*); the words 'young dog' are called the *defining formula*. As a rule, the defining formula is longer and more complicated than the defined term, and sometimes very much so. Aristotle considers[30] the term to be defined as a name of the essence of a thing, and the defining formula as the description of that essence. And he insists that the defining formula must give an exhaustive description of the essence or the essential properties of the thing in question; thus a statement like 'A puppy has four legs', although true, is not a satisfactory definition, since it does not exhaust what may be called the essence of puppiness, but holds true of a horse also; and similarly the statement 'A puppy is brown', although it may be true of some, is not true of all puppies; and it describes what is not an essential but merely an accidental property of the defined term.

But the most difficult question is how we can get hold of definitions or basic premises, and make sure that they are correct—that we have not erred, not grasped the wrong essence. Although Aristotle is not very clear on this point[31], there can be little doubt that, in the main, he again follows Plato. Plato taught[32] that we can grasp the Ideas with the help of some kind of unerring *intellectual intuition*; that is to say, we visualize or look at them with our 'mental eye', a process which he conceived as analogous to seeing, but dependent purely upon our intellect, and excluding any element that depends upon our senses. Aristotle's view is less radical and less inspired than Plato's, but in the end it amounts to the same[33]. For although he teaches that we arrive at the definition only after we have made many observations, he admits that sense-experience does not in itself grasp the universal essence, and that it cannot, therefore, fully determine a definition. Eventually he simply postulates that we possess an intellectual intuition, a mental or intellectual faculty which enables us unerringly to grasp the essences of things, and to know them. And he further assumes that if we know an essence intuitively, we must be capable of describing it and therefore of defining it. (His arguments in the *Posterior Analytic* in favour of this theory are surprisingly weak. They consist merely in pointing out that our knowledge of the basic premises cannot be demonstrative, since this would lead to an infinite regress, and that the basic premises must be at least as true and as certain as the conclusions based upon them. 'It follows from this', he writes, 'that there cannot be demonstrative knowledge of the primary premises; and since nothing but intellectual intuition can be more true than demonstrative knowledge, it follows that it must be intellectual intuition that grasps the basic premises.' In the *De Anima*, and in the theological part of the *Metaphysics*, we find more of an argument; for here we have a *theory* of intellectual intuition—that it comes into contact with its object, the essence, and that it even becomes one with its object. 'Actual knowledge is identical with its object.')

Summing up this brief analysis, we can give, I believe, a fair description of the Aristotelian ideal of perfect and complete knowledge if we say that he saw the ultimate aim of all inquiry in the compilation of an encyclopædia containing the intuitive definitions of all essences, that is to say, their names together with their defining formulæ; and that he considered the progress of knowledge as consisting in the gradual accumulation of such an encyclopædia, in expanding it as well as in filling up the gaps in it and, of course, in the syllogistic derivation from it of 'the whole body of facts' which constitute demonstrative knowledge.

Now there can be little doubt that all these essentialist views stand in the strongest possible contrast to the methods of modern science. (I have the empirical sciences in mind, not perhaps pure mathematics.) First, although in science we do our best to find the truth, we are conscious of the fact that we can never be sure whether we have got it. We have learned in the past, from many disappointments, that we must not expect finality. And we have learned not to be disappointed any longer if our scientific theories are overthrown; for we can, in most cases, determine with great confidence which of any two theories is the better one. We can therefore know that we are making progress; and it is this knowledge that to most of us atones for the loss of the illusion of finality and certainty. In other words, we know that our scientific theories must always remain hypotheses, but that, in many important cases, we can find out whether or not a new hypothesis is superior to an old one. For if they are different, then they will lead to different predictions, which can often be tested experimentally; and on the basis of such a crucial experiment, we can sometimes find out that the new theory leads to satisfactory results where the old one breaks down. Thus we can say that in our search for truth, we have replaced scientific certainty by scientific progress. And this view of scientific method is corroborated by the development of science. For science does not develop by a gradual encyclopædic accumulation of essential information, as Aristotle thought, but by a much more revolutionary method; it progresses by bold ideas, by the advancement of new and very strange theories (such as the theory that the earth is not flat, or that 'metrical space' is not flat), and by the overthrow of the old ones.

But this view of scientific method means[34] that in science there is no '*knowledge*', in the sense in which Plato and Aristotle understood the word, in the sense which implies finality; in science, we never have sufficient reason for the belief that we have attained the truth. What we usually call 'scientific knowledge' is, as a rule, not knowledge in this sense, but rather information regarding the various competing hypotheses and the way in which they have stood up to various tests; it is, using the language of Plato and Aristotle, information concerning the latest, and the best tested, scientific '*opinion*'. This view means, furthermore, that we have no proofs in science (excepting, of course, pure mathematics and logic). In the empirical sciences, which alone can furnish us with information about the world we live in, proofs do not occur, if we mean by 'proof' an argument which establishes once and for ever the truth of a theory. (What may occur, however, are refutations of scientific theories.) On the other hand, pure mathematics and logic, which permit of proofs, give us no information about the world, but only develop the means of describing it. Thus we could say (as I have pointed out elsewhere[35]): 'In so far as scientific statements refer to the world of experience, they must be refutable; and, in so far as they are irrefutable, they do not refer to the world of experience.' But although proof does not play any part in the empirical sciences, argument still does[36]; indeed, its part is at least as important as that played by observation and experiment.

The rôle of definitions in science, especially, is also very different from what Aristotle had in mind. Aristotle taught that in a definition we have first pointed to the essence—perhaps by naming it—and that we then describe it with the help of the defining formula; just as in an ordinary sentence like 'This puppy is brown', we first point to a certain thing by saying 'this puppy', and then describe it as 'brown'. And he taught that by thus describing the essence to which the term points which is to be defined, we determine or explain the *meaning*[37] of the term also. Accordingly, the definition may at one time answer two very closely related questions. The one is 'What is it?', for example, 'What is a puppy?'; it asks what the essence is which is denoted by the defined term. The other is 'What does it mean?', for example, 'What does "puppy" mean?'; it asks for the meaning of a term (namely, of the term that denotes the essence). In the present context, it is not necessary to distinguish between these two questions; rather, it is important to see what they have in common; and I wish, especially, to draw attention to the fact that both *questions are raised by the term that stands, in the definition, on the left side and answered by the defining formula which stands on the right side.* This fact characterizes the essentialist view, from which the scientific method of definition radically differs.

While we may say that the essentialist interpretation reads a definition 'normally', that is to say, from the *left to the right*, we can say that *a definition, as it is normally used in modern science, must be read back to front, or from the right to the left;* for it starts with the defining formula, and asks for a short label to it. Thus the scientific view of the definition 'A puppy is a young dog' would be that it is an answer to the question '*What shall we call* a young dog?' rather than an answer to the question '*What is* a puppy?'. (Questions like '*What is* life?' or '*What is* gravity?' do not play any rôle in science.) The scientific use of definitions, characterized by the approach 'from the right to the left', may be called its *nominalist* interpretation, as opposed to its Aristotelian or *essentialist* interpretation[38]. In modern science, only[39] nominalist definitions occur, that is to say, shorthand symbols or labels are introduced in order to cut a long story short. And we can at once see from this that definitions do *not* play any very important part in science. For shorthand symbols can always, of course, be replaced by the longer expressions, the defining formula, for which they stand. In some cases this would make our scientific language very cumbersome; we should waste time and paper. But we should never lose the slightest piece of factual information. Our 'scientific knowledge', in the sense in which this term may be properly used, remains entirely unaffected if we eliminate all definitions; the only effect is upon our language, which would lose, not precision[40], but merely brevity. (This must not be taken to mean that in science there cannot be an urgent practical need for introducing definitions, for brevity's sake.) There could hardly be a greater contrast than that between this view of the part played by definitions, and Aristotle's view. For Aristotle's essentialist definitions are the principles from which all our knowledge is derived; they thus contain all our knowledge; and they serve to substitute a long formula for a short one. As opposed to this, the scientific or nominalist definitions do not contain any knowledge whatever, not even any 'opinion'; they do nothing but introduce new arbitrary shorthand labels; they cut a long story short.

In practice, these labels are of the greatest usefulness. In order to see this, we only need to consider the extreme difficulties that would arise if a bacteriologist, whenever he spoke of a certain strain of bacteria, had to repeat its whole description (including the methods of dyeing, etc., by which it is distinguished from a number of similar species). And we may also understand, by a similar consideration, why it has so often been forgotten, even by scientists, that scientific definitions must be read 'from the right to the left', as explained above. For most people, when first studying a science, say bacteriology, must try to find out the meanings of all these new technical terms with which they are faced. In this way, they really *learn* the definition 'from the left to the right', substituting, as if it were an essentialist definition, a very long story for a very short one. But this is merely a psychological accident, and a teacher or writer of a textbook may indeed proceed quite differently; that is to say, he may introduce a technical term only after the need for it has arisen[41].

So far I have tried to show that the scientific or nominalist use of definitions is entirely different from Aristotle's essentialist method of definitions. But it can also be shown that the essentialist view of definitions is simply untenable in itself. In order not to prolong this digression unduly[42], I shall criticize two only of the essentialist doctrines; two doctrines which are of significance because some influential modern schools are still based upon them. One is the esoteric doctrine of intellectual intuition, and the other the very popular doctrine that 'we must define our terms', if we wish to be precise.

Aristotle held with Plato that we possess a faculty, intellectual intuition, by which we can visualize essences and find out which definition is the correct one, and many modern essentialists have repeated this doctrine. Other philosophers, following Kant, maintain that we do not possess anything of the sort. My opinion is that we can readily admit that we possess something which may be described as 'intellectual intuition'; or more precisely, that certain of our intellectual experiences may be thus described. Everybody who 'understands' an idea, or a point of view, or an arithmetical method, for instance, multiplication, in the sense that he has 'got the feel of it', might be said to understand that thing intuitively; and there are countless intellectual experiences of that kind. But I would insist, on the other hand, that these experiences, important as they may be for our scientific endeavours, can never serve to establish the truth of any idea or theory, however strongly somebody may feel, intuitively, that it must be true, or that it is 'self-evident'[43]. Such intuitions cannot even serve as an argument, although they may encourage us to look for arguments. For somebody else may have just as strong an intuition that the same theory is false. The way of science is paved with discarded theories which were once declared self-evident; Francis Bacon, for example, sneered at those who denied the self-evident truth that the sun and the stars rotated round the earth, which was obviously at rest. Intuition undoubtedly plays a great part in the life of a scientist, just as it does in the life of a poet. It leads him to his discoveries. But it may also lead him to his failures. And it always remains his private affair, as it were. Science does not ask how he has got his ideas, it is only interested in arguments that can be tested by everybody. The great mathematician, Gauss, described this situation very neatly once when he exclaimed: 'I have got my result; but I do not know yet how to get it.' All this applies, of course, to Aristotle's doctrine of intellectual intuition of so-called essences[44], which was propagated by Hegel, and in our own time by E. Husserl and his numerous pupils; and it indicates that the 'intellectual intuition of essences' or 'pure phenomenology', as Husserl calls it, is a method of neither science nor philosophy. (The much debated question whether it is a new invention, as the pure phenomenologists think, or perhaps a version of Cartesianism or Hegelianism, can be easily decided; it is a version of Aristotelianism.)

The second doctrine to be criticized has even more important connections with modern views; and it bears especially upon the problem of verbalism. Since Aristotle, it has become widely known that one cannot prove all statements, and that an attempt to do so would break down because it would lead only to an infinite regression of proofs. But neither he[45] nor, apparently, a great many modern writers seem to realize that the analogous attempt to define the meaning of all our terms must, in the same way, lead to an infinite regression of definitions. The following passage from Crossman's *Plato To-Day* is characteristic of a view which by implication is held by many contemporary philosophers of repute, for example, by Wittgenstein[46]: '... if we do not know precisely the meanings of the words we use, we cannot discuss anything profitably. Most of the futile arguments on which we all waste time are largely due to the fact that we each have our own vague meanings for the words we use and assume that our opponents are using them in the same senses. If we defined our terms to start with, we could have far more profitable discussions. Again, we have only to read the daily papers to observe that propaganda (the modern counterpart of rhetoric) depends largely for its success on confusing the meaning of the terms. If politicians were compelled by law to define any term they wished to use, they would lose most of their popular appeal, their speeches would be shorter, and many of their disagreements would be found to be purely verbal.' This passage is very characteristic of one of the prejudices which we owe to Aristotle, of the prejudice that language can be made more precise by the use of definitions. Let us consider whether this can really be done.

First, we can see clearly that if 'politicians' (or anybody else) 'were compelled by law to define any term they wished to use', their speeches would not be shorter, but infinitely long. For a definition cannot establish the meaning of a term any more than a logical derivation[47] can establish the truth of a statement; both can only shift this problem back. The derivation shifts the problem of truth back to the premises, the definition shifts the problem of meaning back to the defining terms (i.e., the terms that make up the defining formula). But these, for many reasons[48], are likely to be just as vague and confusing as the terms we started with; and in any case, we should have to go on to define them in turn; which leads to new terms which too must be defined. And so on, to infinity. One sees that the demand that all our terms should be defined is just as untenable as the demand that all our statements should be proved.

At first sight this criticism may seem unfair. It may be said that what people have in mind, if they demand definitions, is the elimination of the ambiguities so often connected with words such as[49] 'democracy', 'liberty', 'duty', 'religion', etc.; that it is clearly impossible to define all our terms, but possible to define some of these more dangerous terms and to leave it at that; and that the defining terms have just to be accepted, i.e., that we must stop after a step or two in order to avoid an infinite regression. This defence, however, is untenable. Admittedly, the terms mentioned are much misused.

But I deny that the attempt to define them can improve matters. It can only make matters worse. That by 'defining their terms' even once, and leaving the defining terms undefined, the politicians would not be able to make their speeches shorter, is clear; for any essentialist definition, i.e. one that 'defines our terms' (as opposed to the nominalist one which introduces new technical terms), means the substitution of a long story for a short one, as we have seen. Besides, the attempt to define terms would only increase the vagueness and confusion. For since we cannot demand that all the defining terms should be defined in their turn, a clever politician or philosopher could easily satisfy the demand for definitions. If asked what he means by 'democracy', for example, he could say 'the rule of the general will' or 'the rule of the spirit of the people'; and since he has now given a definition, and so satisfied the highest standards of precision, nobody will dare to criticize him any longer. And, indeed, how could he be criticized, since the demand that 'rule' or 'people' or 'will' or 'spirit' should be defined in their turn, puts us well on the way to an infinite regression so that everybody would hesitate to raise it? But should it be raised in spite of all that, then it can be equally easily satisfied. On the other hand, a quarrel about the question whether the definition was correct, or true, can only lead to an empty controversy about words.

Thus the essentialist view of definition breaks down, even if it does not, with Aristotle, attempt to establish the 'principles' of our knowledge, but only makes the apparently more modest demand that we should 'define the meaning of our terms'.

But undoubtedly, the demand that we speak clearly and without ambiguity is very important, and must be satisfied. Can the nominalist view satisfy it? And can nominalism escape the infinite regression?

It can. For the nominalist position there is no difficulty which corresponds to the infinite regression. As we have seen, science does not use definitions in order to determine the meaning of its terms, but only in order to introduce handy shorthand labels. And it does not depend on definitions; all definitions can be omitted without loss to the information imparted. It follows from this that in science, *all the terms that are really needed must be undefined terms*. How then do the sciences make sure of the meanings of their terms? Various replies to this question have been suggested[50], but I do not think that any of them are satisfactory. The situation seems to be this. Aristotelianism and related philosophies have told us for such a long time how important it is to get a precise knowledge of the meaning of our terms that we are all inclined to believe it. And we continue to cling to this creed in spite of the unquestionable fact that philosophy, which for twenty centuries has worried about the meaning of its terms, is not only full of verbalism but also appallingly vague and ambiguous, while a science like physics which worries hardly at all about terms and their meaning, but about facts instead, has achieved great precision. This, surely, should be taken as indicating that, under Aristotelian influence, the importance of the meaning of terms has been grossly exaggerated. But I think that it indicates even more. For not only does this concentration on the problem of meaning fail to establish precision; it is itself the main source of vagueness, ambiguity, and confusion.

In science, we take care that the statements we make should never *depend* upon the meaning of our terms. Even where the terms are defined, we never try to derive any information from the definition, or to base any argument upon it. This is why our terms make so little trouble. We do not overburden them. We try to attach to them as little weight as possible. We do not take their 'meaning' too seriously. We are always conscious that our terms are a little vague (since we have learned to use them only in practical applications) and we reach precision not by reducing their penumbra of vagueness, but rather by keeping well within it, by carefully phrasing our sentences in such a way that the possible shades of meaning of our terms do not matter. This is how we avoid quarrelling about words.

The view that the precision of science and of scientific language depends upon the precision of its terms is certainly very plausible, but it is none the less, I believe, a mere prejudice. The precision of a language depends, rather, just upon the fact that it takes care not to burden its terms with the task of being precise. A term like 'sand-dune' or 'wind' is certainly very vague. (How many inches high must a little sand-hill be in order to be called 'sand-dune'? How quickly must the air move in order to be called 'wind'?) However, for many of the geologist's purposes, these terms are quite sufficiently precise; and for other purposes, when a higher degree of differentiation is needed, he can always say 'dunes between 4 and 30 feet high' or 'wind of a velocity of between 20 and 40 miles an hour'. And the position in the more exact sciences is analogous. In physical measurements, for instance, we always take care to consider the range within which there may be an error; and precision does not consist in trying to reduce this range to nothing, or in pretending that there is no such range, but rather in its explicit recognition.

Even where a term has made trouble, as for instance the term 'simultaneity' in physics, it was not because its meaning was unprecise or ambiguous, but rather because of some intuitive theory which induced us to burden the term with too much meaning, or with too 'precise' a meaning, rather than with too little. What Einstein found in his analysis of simultaneity was that, when speaking of simultaneous events, physicists made a false assumption which would have been unchallengeable were there signals of infinite velocity. The fault was not that they did not mean anything, or that their meaning was ambiguous, or the term not precise enough; what Einstein found was, rather, that the elimination of a theoretical assumption, unnoticed so far because of its intuitive self-evidence, was able to remove a difficulty which had arisen in science. Accordingly, he was not really concerned with a question of the meaning of a term, but rather with the truth of a theory. It is very unlikely that it would have led to much if someone had started, apart from a definite physical problem, to improve the concept of simultaneity by analysing its 'essential meaning', or even by analysing what physicists 'really mean' when they speak of simultaneity.

I think we can learn from this example that we should not attempt to cross our bridges before we come to them. And I also think that the preoccupation with questions concerning the meaning of terms, such as their vagueness or their ambiguity, can certainly not be justified by an appeal to Einstein's example. Such a preoccupation rests, rather, on the assumption that much depends upon the meaning of our terms, and that we operate with this meaning; and therefore it must lead to verbalism and scholasticism. From this point of view, we may criticize a doctrine like that of Wittgenstein[51], who holds that while science investigates matters of fact, it is the business of philosophy to clarify the meaning of terms, thereby purging our language, and eliminating linguistic puzzles. It is characteristic of the views of this school that they do not lead to any chain of argument that could be rationally criticized; the school therefore addresses its subtle analyses[52] exclusively to the small esoteric circle of the initiated. This seems to suggest that any preoccupation with meaning tends to lead to that result which is so typical of Aristotelianism: scholasticism and mysticism.

Let us consider briefly how these two typical results of Aristotelianism have arisen. Aristotle insisted that demonstration or proof, and definition, are the two fundamental methods of obtaining knowledge. Considering the doctrine of proof first, it cannot be denied that it has led to countless attempts to prove more than can be proved; medieval philosophy is full of this scholasticism and the same tendency can be observed, on the Continent, down to Kant. It was Kant's criticism of all attempts to prove the existence of God which led to the romantic reaction of Fichte, Schelling, and Hegel. The new tendency is to discard proofs, and with them, any kind of rational argument. With the romantics, a new kind of dogmatism becomes fashionable, in philosophy as well as in the social sciences. It confronts us with its dictum. And we can *take it or leave it*. This romantic period of an oracular philosophy, called by Schopenhauer the 'age of dishonesty', is described by him as follows[53]: 'The character of honesty, that spirit of undertaking an inquiry together with the reader, which permeates the works of all previous philosophers, disappears here completely. Every page witnesses that these so-called philosophers do not attempt to teach, but to bewitch the reader.'

A similar result was produced by Aristotle's doctrine of definition. First it led to a good deal of hairsplitting. But later, philosophers began to feel that one cannot argue about definitions. In this way, essentialism not only encouraged verbalism, but it also led to the disillusionment with argument, that is, with reason. Scholasticism and mysticism and despair in reason, these are the unavoidable results of the essentialism of Plato and Aristotle. And Plato's open revolt against freedom becomes, with Aristotle, a secret revolt against reason.

As we know from Aristotle himself, essentialism and the theory of definition met with strong opposition when they were first proposed, especially from Socrates' old companion Antisthenes, whose criticism seems to have been most sensible[54]. But this opposition was unfortunately defeated. The consequences of this defeat for the intellectual development of mankind can hardly be overrated. Some of them will be discussed in the next chapter. With this I conclude my digression, the criticism of the Platonic-Aristotelian theory of definition.

III

It will hardly be necessary again to stress the fact that my treatment of Aristotle is most sketchy—much more so than my treatment of Plato. The main purpose of what has been said about both of them is to show the rôle they have played in the rise of historicism and in the fight against the open society, and to show their influence on problems of our own time—on the rise of the oracular philosophy of Hegel, the father of modern historicism and totalitarianism. The developments between Aristotle and Hegel cannot be treated here at all. In order to do anything like justice to them, at least another volume would be needed. In the remaining few pages of this chapter I shall, however, attempt to indicate how this period might be interpreted in terms of the conflict between the open and the closed society.

The conflict between the Platonic-Aristotelian speculation and the spirit of the Great Generation, of Pericles, of Socrates, and of Democritus, can be traced throughout the ages. This spirit was preserved, more or less purely, in the movement of the Cynics who, like the early Christians, preached the brotherhood of man, which they connected with a monotheistic belief in the fatherhood of God. Alexander's empire as well as that of Augustus was influenced by these ideas which had first taken shape in the imperialist Athens of Pericles, and which had always been stimulated by the contact between West and East. It is very likely that these ideas, and perhaps the Cynic movement itself, influenced the rise of Christianity also.

In its beginning, Christianity, like the Cynic movement, was opposed to the highbrow Platonizing Idealism and intellectualism of the 'scribes', the learned men. ('Thou hast hid these things from the wise and prudent and hast revealed them unto the babes.') I do not doubt that it was, in part, a protest against what may be described as Jewish Platonism in the wider sense[55], the abstract worship of God and His Word. And it was certainly a protest against Jewish tribalism, against its rigid and empty tribal taboos, and against its tribal exclusiveness which expressed itself, for example, in the doctrine of the chosen people, i.e. in an interpretation of the deity as a tribal god. Such an emphasis upon tribal laws and tribal unity appears to be characteristic not so much of a primitive tribal society as of a desperate attempt to restore and arrest the old forms of tribal life; and in the case of Jewry, it seems to have originated as a reaction to the impact of the Babylonian conquest on Jewish tribal life. But side by side with this movement towards greater rigidity we find another movement which apparently originated at the same time, and which produced humanitarian ideas that resembled the response of the Great Generation to the dissolution of Greek tribalism. This process, it appears, repeated itself when Jewish independence was ultimately destroyed by Rome. It led to a new and deeper schism between these two possible solutions, the return to the tribe, as represented by orthodox Jewry, and the humanitarianism of the new sect of Christians, which embraced barbarians (or gentiles) as well as slaves. We can see from the *Acts*[56] how urgent these problems were, the social problem as well as the national problem. And we can see this from the development of Jewry as well; for its conservative part reacted to the same challenge by another movement towards arresting and petrifying their tribal form of life, and by clinging to their 'laws' with a tenacity which would have won the approval of Plato. It can hardly be doubted that this development was, like that of Plato's ideas, inspired by a strong antagonism to the new creed of the open society; in this case, of Christianity.

But the parallelism between the creed of the Great Generation, especially of Socrates, and that of early Christianity goes deeper. There is little doubt that the strength of the early Christians lay in their moral courage. It lay in the fact that they refused to accept Rome's claim 'that it was entitled to compel its subjects to act against their conscience'[57]. The Christian martyrs who rejected the claims of might to set the standards of right suffered for the same cause for which Socrates had died.

It is clear that these matters changed very considerably when the Christian faith itself became powerful in the Roman empire. The question arises whether this official recognition of the Christian Church (and its later organization after the model of Julian the Apostate's Neo-Platonic Anti-Church[58]) was not an ingenious political move on the part of the ruling powers, designed to break the tremendous moral influence of an equalitarian religion—a religion which they had in vain attempted to combat by force as well as by accusations of atheism and impiety. In other words, the question arises whether (especially after Julian) Rome did not find it necessary to apply Pareto's advice, 'to take advantage of sentiments, not wasting one's energies in futile efforts to destroy them'. This question is hard to answer; but it certainly cannot be dismissed by appealing (as Toynbee does[59]) to our 'historical sense that warns us against attributing', to the period of Constantine and his followers, '... motives that are anachronistically cynical', that is to say, motives that are more in keeping with our own 'modern Western attitude to life'. For we have seen that such motives are openly and 'cynically', or more precisely, shamelessly, expressed as early as in the fifth century B.C., by Critias, the leader of the Thirty Tyrants; and similar statements can be found frequently during the history of Greek philosophy[60]. However this may be, it can hardly be doubted that with Justinian's persecution of non-Christians, heretics, and philosophers (A.D. 529), the dark ages began. The Church followed in the wake of Platonic-Aristotelian totalitarianism, a development that culminated in the Inquisition. The theory of the Inquisition, more especially, can be described as purely Platonic. It is set out in the last three books of the *Laws*, where Plato shows that it is the duty of the shepherd rulers to protect their sheep at all costs by preserving the rigidity of the laws and especially of religious practice and theory, even if they have to kill the wolf, who may admittedly be an honest and honourable man whose diseased conscience unfortunately does not permit him to bow to the threats of the mighty.

It is one of the characteristic reactions to the strain of civilization in our own time that the allegedly 'Christian' authoritarianism of the Middle Ages has, in certain intellectualist circles, become one of the latest fashions of the day[61]. This, no doubt, is due not only to the idealization of an indeed more 'organic' and 'integrated' past, but also to an understandable revulsion against modern agnosticism which has increased this strain beyond measure. Men believed God to rule the world. This belief limited their responsibility. The new belief that they had to rule it themselves created for many a well-nigh intolerable burden of responsibility. All this has to be admitted. But I do not doubt that the Middle Ages were, even from the point of view of Christianity, not better ruled than our Western democracies. For we can read in the Gospels that the founder of Christianity was questioned by a certain 'doctor of the law' about a criterion by which to distinguish between a true and a false interpretation of His words. To this He replied by telling the parable of the priest and the Levite who both, seeing a wounded man in great distress, 'passed by on the other side', while the Samaritan bound up his wounds, and looked after his material needs. This parable, I think, should be remembered by those 'Christians' who long not only for a time when the Church suppressed freedom and conscience, but also for a time in which, under the eye and with the authority of the Church, untold oppression drove the people to despair. As a moving comment upon the suffering of the people in those days and, at the same time, upon the 'Christianity' of the now so fashionable romantic medievalism which wants to bring these days back, a passage may be quoted here from H. Zinsser's book, *Rats, Lice, and History*,[62] in which he speaks about epidemics of dancing mania in the Middle Ages, known as 'St. John's dance', 'St. Vitus' dance', etc. (I do not wish to invoke Zinsser as an authority on the Middle Ages—there is no need to do so since the facts at issue are hardly controversial. But his comments have the rare and peculiar touch of the practical Samaritan—of a great and humane physician.) 'These strange seizures, though not unheard of in earlier times, became common during and immediately after the dreadful miseries of the Black Death. For the most part, the dancing manias present none of the characteristics which we associate with epidemic infectious diseases of the nervous system. They seem, rather, like *mass hysterias, brought on by terror and despair, in populations oppressed, famished, and wretched to a degree almost unimaginable to-day*. To the miseries of constant war, political and social disintegration, there was added the dreadful affliction of inescapable, mysterious, and deadly disease. Mankind stood helpless as though trapped in a world of terror and peril against which there was no defence. God and the devil were living conceptions to the men of those days who cowered under the afflictions which they believed imposed by supernatural forces. For those who broke down under the strain there was no road of escape except to the inward refuge of mental derangement which, under the circumstances of the times, took the direction of religious fanaticism.' Zinsser then goes on to draw some parallels between these events and certain reactions of our time in which, he says, 'economic and political hysterias are substituted for the religious ones of the earlier times'; and after this, he sums up his characterization of the people who lived in those days of authoritarianism as 'a terror-stricken and wretched population, which had broken down under the stress of almost incredible hardship and danger'. Is it necessary to ask which attitude is more Christian, one that longs to return to the 'unbroken harmony and unity' of the Middle Ages, or one that wishes to use reason in order to free mankind from pestilence and oppression?

But some part at least of the authoritarian Church of the Middle Ages succeeded in branding such practical humanitarianism as 'worldly', as characteristic of 'Epicureanism', and of men who desire only to 'fill their bellies like the beasts'. The terms 'Epicureanism', 'materialism', and 'empiricism', that is to say, the philosophy of Democritus, one of the greatest of the Great Generation, became in this way the synonyms of wickedness, and the tribal Idealism of Plato and Aristotle was exalted as a kind of Christianity before Christ. Indeed, this is the source of the immense authority of Plato and Aristotle, even in our own day, that their philosophy was adopted by medieval authoritarianism. But it must not be forgotten that, outside the totalitarian camp, their fame has outlived their practical influence upon our lives. And although the name of Democritus is seldom remembered, his science as well as his morals still live with us.

12

HEGEL AND THE NEW TRIBALISM

> The philosophy of Hegel, then, was . . . a scrutiny of thought so profound that it was for the most part unintelligible . . .
>
> J. H. STIRLING.

I

Hegel, the source of all contemporary historicism, was a direct follower of Heraclitus, Plato, and Aristotle. Hegel achieved the most miraculous things. A master logician, it was child's play for his powerful dialectical methods to draw real physical rabbits out of purely metaphysical silk-hats. Thus, starting from Plato's *Timaeus* and its number-mysticism, Hegel succeeded in 'proving' by purely philosophical methods (114 years after Newton's *Principia*) that the planets must move according to Kepler's laws. He even accomplished[1] the deduction of the actual position of the planets, thereby proving that no planet could be situated between Mars and Jupiter (unfortunately, it had escaped his notice that such a planet had been discovered a few months earlier). Similarly, he proved that magnetizing iron means increasing its weight, that Newton's theories of inertia and of gravity *contradict* each other (of course, he could not foresee that Einstein would show the *identity* of inert and gravitating mass), and many other things of this kind. That such a surprisingly powerful philosophical method was taken seriously can be only partially explained by the backwardness of German natural science in those days. For the truth is, I think, that it was not at first taken really seriously by serious men (such as Schopenhauer, or J. F. Fries), not at any rate by those scientists who, like Democritus[2], 'would rather find a single causal law than be the king of Persia'. Hegel's fame was made by those who prefer a quick initiation into the deeper secrets of this world to the laborious technicalities of a science which, after all, may only disappoint them by its lack of power to unveil all mysteries. For they soon found out that nothing could be applied with such ease to any problem whatsoever, and at the same time with such impressive (though only apparent) difficulty, and with such quick and sure but imposing success, nothing could be used as cheaply and with so little scientific training and knowledge, and nothing would give such a spectacular scientific air, as did Hegelian *dialectics*, the mystery method that replaced 'barren formal logic'. Hegel's success was the beginning of the 'age of dishonesty' (as Schopenhauer[3] described the period of German Idealism) and of the 'age of irresponsibility' (as K. Heiden characterizes the age of modern totalitarianism); first of intellectual, and later, as one of its consequences, of moral irresponsibility; of a new age controlled by the magic of high-sounding words, and by the power of jargon.

In order to discourage the reader beforehand from taking Hegel's bombastic and mystifying cant too seriously, I shall quote some of the amazing details which he discovered about sound, and especially about the relations between sound and heat. I have tried hard to translate this gibberish from Hegel's *Philosophy of Nature*[4] as faithfully as possible; he writes: '§302. Sound is the change in the specific condition of segregation of the material parts, and in the negation of this condition;—merely an *abstract* or an ideal *ideality*, as it were, of that specification. But this change, accordingly, is itself immediately the negation of the material specific subsistence; which is, therefore, *real ideality* of specific gravity and cohesion, i.e.—*heat*. The heating up of sounding bodies, just as of beaten or rubbed ones, is the appearance of heat, originating conceptually together with sound.' There are some who still believe in Hegel's sincerity, or who still doubt whether his secret might not be profundity, fullness of thought, rather than emptiness. I should like them to read carefully the last sentence—the only intelligible one—of this quotation, because in this sentence, Hegel gives himself away. For clearly it means nothing but: 'The heating up of sounding bodies ... is heat ... together with sound.' The question arises whether Hegel deceived himself, hypnotized by his own inspiring jargon, or whether he boldly set out to deceive and bewitch others. I am satisfied that the latter was the case, especially in view of what Hegel wrote in one of his letters. In this letter, dated a few years before the publication of his *Philosophy of Nature*, Hegel referred to another *Philosophy of Nature*, written by his former friend Schelling: 'I have had too much to do ... with mathematics ... differential calculus, chemistry',

Hegel boasts in this letter (but this is just bluff), 'to let myself be taken in by the humbug of the Philosophy of Nature, by this philosophizing without knowledge of fact ... and by the treatment of *mere fancies, even imbecile fancies, as ideas*.' This is a very fair characterization of Schelling's method, that is to say, of that audacious way of bluffing which Hegel himself copied, or rather aggravated, as soon as he realized that, if it reached its proper audience, it meant success.

In spite of all this it seems improbable that Hegel would ever have become the most influential figure in German philosophy without the authority of the Prussian state behind him. As it happened, he became the first official philosopher of Prussianism, appointed in the period of feudal 'restoration' after the Napoleonic wars. Later, the state also backed his pupils (Germany had, and still has, only state-controlled Universities), and they in their turn backed one another. And although Hegelianism was officially renounced by most of them, Hegelianizing philosophers have dominated philosophical teaching and thereby indirectly even the secondary schools of Germany ever since. (Of German-speaking Universities, those of Roman Catholic Austria remained fairly unmolested, like islands in a flood.) Having thus become a tremendous success on the continent, Hegelianism could hardly fail to obtain support in Britain from those who, feeling that such a powerful movement must after all have something to offer, began to search for what Stirling called *The Secret of Hegel*. They were attracted, of course, by Hegel's 'higher' idealism and by his claims to 'higher' morality, and they were also somewhat afraid of being branded as immoral by the chorus of the disciples; for even the more modest Hegelians claimed[5] of their doctrines that 'they are acquisitions which must ... ever be reconquered in the face of assault from the powers eternally hostile to spiritual and moral values'. Some really brilliant men (I am thinking mainly of McTaggart) made great efforts in constructive idealistic thought, well above the level of Hegel; but they did not get very far beyond providing targets for equally brilliant critics. And one can say that outside the continent of Europe, especially in the last twenty years, the interest of philosophers in Hegel has slowly been vanishing.

But if that is so, why worry any more about Hegel? The answer is that Hegel's influence has remained a most powerful force, in spite of the fact that scientists never took him seriously, and that (apart from the 'evolutionists'[6]) many philosophers are beginning to lose interest in him. Hegel's influence, and especially that of his cant, is still very powerful in moral and social philosophy and in the social and political sciences (with the sole exception of economics). Especially the philosophers of history, of politics, and of education are still to a very large extent under its sway. In politics, this is shown most drastically by the fact that the Marxist extreme left wing, as well as the conservative centre, and the fascist extreme right, all base their political philosophies on Hegel; the left wing replaces the war of nations which appears in Hegel's historicist scheme by the war of classes, the extreme right replaces it by the war of races; but both follow him more or less consciously. (The conservative centre is as a rule less conscious of its indebtedness to Hegel.)

How can this immense influence be explained? My main intention is not so much to explain this phenomenon as to combat it. But I may make a few explanatory suggestions. For some reason, philosophers have kept around themselves, even in our day, something of the atmosphere of the magician. Philosophy is considered as a strange and abstruse kind of thing, dealing with those mysteries with which religion deals, but not in a way which can be 'revealed unto babes' or to common people; it is considered to be too profound for that, and to be the religion and theology of the intellectuals, of the learned and wise. Hegelianism fits these views admirably; it is exactly what this kind of popular superstition supposes philosophy to be. It knows all about everything. It has a ready answer to every question. And indeed, who can be sure that the answer is not true?

But this is not the main reason for Hegel's success. His influence, and the need to combat it, can perhaps be better understood if we briefly consider the general historical situation.

Medieval authoritarianism began to dissolve with the Renaissance. But on the Continent, its political counterpart, medieval feudalism, was not seriously threatened before the French Revolution. (The Reformation had only strengthened it.) The fight for the open society began again only with the ideas of 1789; and the feudal monarchies soon experienced the seriousness of this danger. When in 1815 the reactionary party began to resume its power in Prussia, it found itself in dire need of an ideology. Hegel was appointed to meet this demand, and he did so by reviving the ideas of the first great enemies of the open society, Heraclitus, Plato, and Aristotle. Just as the French Revolution rediscovered the perennial ideas of the Great Generation and of Christianity, freedom, equality, and the brotherhood of all men, so Hegel rediscovered the Platonic ideas which lie behind the perennial revolt against freedom and reason. Hegelianism is the renaissance of tribalism. The historical significance of Hegel may be seen in the fact that he represents the 'missing link', as it were, between Plato and the modern form of totalitarianism. Most of the modern totalitarians are quite unaware that their ideas can be traced back to Plato. But many know of their indebtedness to Hegel, and all of them have been brought up in the close atmosphere of Hegelianism. They have been taught to worship the state, history, and the nation. (My view of Hegel presupposes, of course, that he interpreted Plato's teaching in the same way as I did here, that is to say, as totalitarian, to use this modern label; and indeed, it can be shown[7], from his criticism of Plato in the *Philosophy of Law*, that Hegel's interpretation agrees with ours.)

In order to give the reader an immediate glimpse of Hegel's Platonizing worship of the state, I shall quote a few passages, even before I begin the analysis of his historicist philosophy. These passages show that Hegel's radical collectivism depends as much on Plato as it depends on Frederick William III, king of Prussia in the critical period during and after the French Revolution. Their doctrine is that the state is everything, and the individual nothing; for he owes everything to the state, his physical as well as his spiritual existence. This is the message of Plato, of Frederick William's Prussianism, and of Hegel. 'The Universal is to be found in the State', Hegel writes[8]. 'The State is the Divine Idea as it exists on earth … We must therefore worship the State as the manifestation of the Divine on earth, and consider that, if it is difficult to comprehend Nature, it is infinitely harder to grasp the Essence of the State … The State is the march of God through the world … The State must be comprehended as an organism … To the complete State belongs, essentially, consciousness and thought. The State knows what it wills … The State is real; and … true reality is necessary. What is real is eternally necessary … The State … exists for its own sake … The State is the actually existing, realized moral life.' This selection of utterances may suffice to show Hegel's Platonism and his insistence upon the absolute moral authority of the state, which overrules all personal morality, all conscience. It is, of course, a bombastic and hysterical Platonism, but this only makes more obvious the fact that it links Platonism with modern totalitarianism.

One could ask whether by these services and by his influence upon history, Hegel has not proved his genius. I do not think this question very important, since it is only part of our romanticism that we think so much in terms of 'genius'; and apart from that, I do not believe that success proves anything, or that history is our judge[9]; these tenets are rather part of Hegelianism. But as far as Hegel is concerned, I do not even think that he was talented. He is an indigestible writer. As even his most ardent apologists must admit[10], his style is 'unquestionably scandalous'. And as far as the content of his writing is concerned, he is supreme only in his outstanding lack of originality. There is nothing in Hegel's writing that has not been said better before him. There is nothing in his apologetic method that is not borrowed from his apologetic forerunners[11]. But he devoted these borrowed thoughts and methods with singleness of purpose, though without a trace of brilliancy, to one aim: to fight against the open society, and thus to serve his employer, Frederick William of Prussia. Hegel's confusion and debasement of reason is partly necessary as a means to this end, partly a more accidental but very natural expression of his state of mind. And the whole story of Hegel would indeed not be worth relating, were it not for its more sinister consequences, which show how easily a clown may be a 'maker of history'. The tragi-comedy of the rise of 'German Idealism', in spite of the hideous crimes to which it has led, resembles a comic opera much more than anything else; and these beginnings may help to explain why it is so hard to decide of its latter-day heroes whether they have escaped from the stage of Wagner's Grand Teutonic Operas or from Offenbach's farces.

My assertion that Hegel's philosophy was inspired by ulterior motives, namely, by his interest in the restoration of the Prussian government of Frederick William III, and that it cannot therefore be taken seriously, is not new. The story was well known to all who knew the political situation, and it was freely told by the few who were independent enough to do so. The best witness is Schopenhauer, himself a Platonic idealist and a conservative if not a reactionary[12], but a man of supreme integrity who cherished truth beyond anything else. There can be no doubt that he was as competent a judge in philosophical matters as could be found at the time. Schopenhauer, who had the pleasure of knowing Hegel personally and who suggested[13] the use of Shakespeare's words, 'such stuff as madmen tongue and brain not', as the motto of Hegel's philosophy, drew the following excellent picture of the master: 'Hegel, installed from above, by the powers that be, as the certified Great Philosopher, was a flat-headed, insipid, nauseating, illiterate charlatan, who reached the pinnacle of audacity in scribbling together and dishing up the craziest mystifying nonsense. This nonsense has been noisily proclaimed as immortal wisdom by mercenary followers and readily accepted as such by all fools, who thus joined into as perfect a chorus of admiration as had ever been heard before. The extensive field of spiritual influence with which Hegel was furnished by those in power has enabled him to achieve the intellectual corruption of a whole generation.' And in another place, Schopenhauer describes the political game of Hegelianism as follows: 'Philosophy, brought afresh to repute by Kant … had soon to become a tool of interests; of state interests from above, of personal interests from below … The driving forces of this movement are, contrary to all these solemn airs and assertions, not ideal; they are very real purposes indeed, namely personal, official, clerical, political, in short, material interests … Party interests are vehemently agitating the pens of so many pure lovers of wisdom … Truth is certainly the last thing they have in mind … Philosophy is misused, from the side of the state as a tool, from the other side as a means of gain … Who can really believe that truth also will thereby come to light, just as a by-product? … *Governments make of philosophy a means of serving their state interests, and scholars make of it a trade* …' Schopenhauer's view of Hegel's status as the paid agent of the Prussian government is, to mention only one example, corroborated by Schwegler, an admiring disciple[14] of Hegel. Schwegler says of Hegel: 'The fullness of his fame and activity, however, properly dates only from his call to Berlin in 1818. Here there rose up around him a numerous, widely extended, and … exceedingly active school; here too, he acquired, from his connections with the Prussian bureaucracy, political influence for himself as well as the recognition of his system as the official philosophy; not always to the advantage of the inner freedom of his philosophy, or of its moral worth.' Schwegler's editor, J. H. Stirling[15], the first British apostle of Hegelianism, of course defends Hegel against Schwegler by warning his readers not to take too literally 'the little hint of Schwegler's against … the philosophy of Hegel as a state-philosophy'. But a few pages later, Stirling quite unintentionally confirms Schwegler's representation of the facts as well as the view that Hegel himself was aware of the party-political and apologetic function of his philosophy. (The evidence quoted[16] by Stirling shows that Hegel expressed himself rather cynically on this function of his philosophy.) And a little later, Stirling unwittingly gives away the 'secret of Hegel' when he proceeds to the following poetic as well as prophetic revelations[17], alluding to the lightning attack made by Prussia on Austria in 1866, the year before he wrote: 'Is it not indeed to Hegel, and especially his philosophy of ethics and politics, that Prussia owes that mighty life and organization she is now rapidly developing? Is it not indeed the grim Hegel that is the centre of that organization which, maturing counsel in an invisible brain, strikes, lightning-like, with a hand that is weighted from the mass? But as regards the value of this organization, it will be more palpable to many, should I say, that, while in constitutional England, Preference-holders and Debenture-holders are ruined by the prevailing commercial immorality, the ordinary owners of Stock in Prussian Railways can depend on a safe average of 8.33 per cent. This, surely, is saying something for Hegel at last!

'The fundamental outlines of Hegel must now, I think, be evident to every reader. I have gained much from Hegel …' Stirling continues his eulogy. I too hope that Hegel's outlines are now evident, and I trust that what Stirling had gained was saved from the menace of the commercial immorality prevailing in an un-Hegelian and constitutional England.

(Who could resist mentioning in this context the fact that Marxist philosophers, always ready to point out how an opponent's theory is affected by his class interest, habitually fail to apply this method to Hegel? Instead of denouncing him as an apologist for Prussian absolutism, they regret[18] that the works of the originator of dialectics, and especially his works on logic, are not more widely read in Britain—in contrast to Russia, where the merits of Hegel's philosophy in general, and of his logic in particular, are officially recognized.)

Returning to the problem of Hegel's political motives, we have, I think, more than sufficient reason to suspect that his philosophy was influenced by the interests of the Prussian government by which he was employed. But under the absolutism of Frederick William III, such an influence implied more than Schopenhauer or Schwegler could know; for only in the last decades have the documents been published that show the clarity and consistency with which this king insisted upon the complete subordination of all learning to state interest. 'Abstract sciences', we read in his educational programme[19], 'that touch only the academic world, and serve only to enlighten this group, are of course without value to the welfare of the State; it would be foolish to restrict them entirely, but it is healthy to keep them within proper limits.' Hegel's call to Berlin in 1818 came during the high tide of reaction, during the period which began with the king's purging his government of the reformers and national liberals who had contributed so much to his success in the 'War of Liberation'. Considering this fact, we may ask whether Hegel's appointment was not a move to 'keep philosophy within proper limits', so as to enable her to be healthy and to serve 'the welfare of the State', that is to say, of Frederick William and his absolute rule. The same question is suggested to us when we read what a great admirer says[20] of Hegel: 'And in Berlin he remained till his death in 1831, the acknowledged dictator of one of the most powerful philosophic schools in the history of thought.' (I think we should substitute 'lack of thought' for 'thought', because I cannot see what a dictator could possibly have to do with the history of thought, even if he were a dictator of philosophy. But otherwise, this revealing passage is only too true. For example, the concerted efforts of this powerful school succeeded, by a conspiracy of silence, in concealing from the world for forty years the very fact of Schopenhauer's existence.) We see that Hegel may indeed have had the power to 'keep philosophy within proper limits', so that our question may be quite to the point.

In what follows, I shall try to show that Hegel's whole philosophy can be interpreted as an emphatic answer to this question; an answer in the affirmative, of course. And I shall try to show how much light is thrown upon

Hegelianism if we interpret it in this way, that is to say, as an apology for Prussianism. My analysis will be divided into three parts, to be treated in sections II, III, and IV of this chapter. Section II deals with Hegel's historicism and moral positivism, together with the rather abstruse theoretical background of these doctrines, his dialectic method and his so-called philosophy of identity. Section III deals with the rise of nationalism. In section IV, a few words will be said on Hegel's relation to Burke. And section V deals with the dependence of modern totalitarianism upon the doctrines of Hegel.

II

I begin my analysis of Hegel's philosophy with a general comparison between Hegel's historicism and that of Plato.

Plato believed that the Ideas or essences exist *prior* to the things in flux, and that the trend of all developments can be explained as a movement away from the perfection of the Ideas, and therefore as a descent, as a movement towards decay. The history of states, especially, is one of degeneration; and ultimately this degeneration is due to the racial degeneration of the ruling class. (We must here remember the close relationship between the Platonic notions of 'race', 'soul', 'nature', and 'essence'[21].) Hegel believes, with Aristotle, that the Ideas or essences are *in* the things in flux; or more precisely (as far as we can treat a Hegel with precision), Hegel teaches that they are identical with the things in flux: 'Everything actual is an Idea', he says[22]. But this does not mean that the gulf opened up by Plato between the essence of a thing and its sensible appearance is closed; for Hegel writes: 'Any mention of Essence implies that we distinguish it from the Being' (of the thing); '... upon the latter, as compared with Essence, we rather look as mere appearance or semblance ... Everything has an Essence, we have said; that is, things are not what they immediately show themselves to be.' Also like Plato and Aristotle, Hegel conceives the essences, at least those of organisms (and therefore also those of states), as souls, or 'Spirits'.

But unlike Plato, Hegel does not teach that the trend of the development of the world in flux is a descent, away from the Idea, towards decay. Like Speusippus and Aristotle, Hegel teaches that the general trend is rather towards the Idea; it is progress. Although he says[23], with Plato, that 'the perishable thing has its basis in Essence, and originates from it', Hegel insists, in opposition to Plato, that even the essences develop. In Hegel's world, as in Heraclitus', *everything* is in flux; and the essences, originally introduced by Plato in order to obtain something stable, are not exempted.

But this flux is not decay. Hegel's historicism is optimistic. His essences and Spirits are, like Plato's souls, self-moving; they are self-developing, or, using more fashionable terms, they are 'emerging' and 'self-creating'. And they propel themselves in the direction of an Aristotelian 'final cause', or, as Hegel puts it[24], towards a 'self-realizing and self-realized final cause in itself'. This final cause or end of the development of the essences is what Hegel calls 'The absolute Idea' or 'The Idea'. (This Idea is, Hegel tells us, rather complex: it is, all in one, the Beautiful; Cognition and Practical Activity; Comprehension; the Highest Good; and the Scientifically Contemplated Universe. But we really need not worry about minor difficulties such as these.) We can say that Hegel's world of flux is in a state of 'emergent' or 'creative evolution'[25]; each of its stages contains the preceding ones, from which it originates; and each stage supersedes all previous stages, approaching nearer and nearer to perfection. The general law of development is thus one of progress; but, as we shall see, not of a simple and straightforward, but of a 'dialectic' progress.

As previous quotations have shown, the collectivist Hegel, like Plato, visualizes the state as an organism; and following Rousseau who had furnished it with a collective 'general will', Hegel furnishes it with a conscious and thinking essence, its 'reason' or 'Spirit'. This Spirit, whose 'very essence is activity' (which shows its dependence on Rousseau), is at the same time the collective *Spirit of the Nation* that forms the state.

To an essentialist, knowledge or understanding of the state must clearly mean knowledge of its essence or Spirit. And as we have seen[26] in the last chapter, we can know the essence and its 'potentialities' only from its 'actual' history. Thus we arrive at the fundamental position of historicist method, that the way of obtaining knowledge of social institutions such as the state is to study its history, or the history of its 'Spirit'. And the other two historicist consequences developed in the last chapter follow also. The Spirit of the nation determines its hidden historical destiny; and every nation that wishes 'to emerge into existence' must assert its individuality or soul by entering the 'Stage of History', that is to say, by fighting the other nations; the object of the fight is world domination. We can see from this that Hegel, like Heraclitus, believes that war is the father and king of all things. And like Heraclitus, he believes that war is just: 'The History of the World is the World's court of justice', writes Hegel. And like Heraclitus, Hegel generalizes this doctrine by extending it to the world of nature, interpreting the contrasts and oppositions of things, the polarity of opposites, etc., as a kind of war, and as a moving force of natural development. And like Heraclitus, Hegel believes in the unity or identity of opposites; indeed, the unity of opposites plays such an important part in the evolution, in the 'dialectical' progress, that we can describe these two Heraclitean ideas, the war of opposites, and their unity or identity, as the main ideas of Hegel's *dialectics*.

So far, this philosophy appears as a tolerably decent and honest historicism, although one that is perhaps a little unoriginal[27]; and there seems to be no reason to describe it, with Schopenhauer, as charlatanism. But this appearance begins to change if we now turn to an analysis of Hegel's dialectics. For he proffers this method with an eye to Kant, who, in his attack upon metaphysics (the violence of these attacks may be gauged from the motto to my 'Introduction'), had tried to show that all speculations of this kind are untenable. Hegel never attempted to refute Kant. He bowed, and twisted Kant's view into its opposite. This is how Kant's 'dialectics', the attack upon metaphysics, was converted into Hegelian 'dialectics', the main tool of metaphysics.

Kant, in his *Critique of Pure Reason*, asserted under the influence of Hume that pure speculation or reason, whenever it ventures into a field in which it cannot possibly be checked by experience, is liable to get involved in contradictions or 'antinomies' and to produce what he unambiguously described as 'mere fancies'; 'nonsense'; 'illusions'; 'a sterile dogmatism'; and 'a superficial pretension to the knowledge of everything'[28]. He tried to show that to every metaphysical assertion or *thesis*, concerning for example the beginning of the world in time, or the existence of God, there can be contrasted a counter-assertion or *antithesis*; and both, he held, may proceed from the same assumptions, and can be proved with an equal degree of 'evidence'. In other words, when leaving the field of experience, our speculation can have no scientific status, since to every argument there must be an equally valid counter-argument. Kant's intention was to stop once and forever the 'accursed fertility' of the scribblers on metaphysics. But unfortunately, the effect was very different. What Kant stopped was only the attempts of the scribblers to use rational argument; they only gave up the attempt to teach, but not the attempt to bewitch the public (as Schopenhauer puts it[29]). For this development, Kant himself undoubtedly bears a very considerable share of the blame; for the obscure style of his work (which he wrote in a great hurry, although only after long years of meditation) contributed considerably to a further lowering of the low standard of clarity in German theoretical writing[30].

None of the metaphysical scribblers who came after Kant made any attempt to refute him[31]; and Hegel, more particularly, even had the audacity to patronize Kant for 'reviving the name of Dialectics, which he restored to their post of honour'. He taught that Kant was quite right in pointing out the antinomies, but that he was wrong to worry about them. It just lies in the nature of reason that it must contradict itself, Hegel asserted; and it is not a weakness of our human faculties, but it is the very essence of all rationality that it must work with contradictions and antinomies; for this is just the way in which *reason develops*. Hegel asserted that Kant had analysed reason as if it were something static; that he forgot that mankind develops, and with it, our social heritage. But what we are pleased to call our own reason is nothing but the product of this social heritage, of the historical development of the social group in which we live, the nation. This development proceeds *dialectically*, that is to say, in a three-beat rhythm. First a *thesis* is proffered; but it will produce criticism, it will be contradicted by opponents who assert its opposite, an *antithesis*; and in the conflict of these views, a *synthesis* is attained, that is to say, a kind of unity of the opposites, a compromise or a reconciliation on a higher level. The synthesis absorbs, as it were, the two original opposite positions, by superseding them; it reduces them to components of itself, thereby negating, elevating, and preserving them. And once the synthesis has been established, the whole process can repeat itself on the higher level that has now been reached. This is, in brief, the three-beat rhythm of progress which Hegel called the 'dialectic triad'.

I am quite prepared to admit that this is not a bad description of the way in which a critical discussion, and therefore also scientific thought, may sometimes progress. For all criticism consists in pointing out some contradictions or discrepancies, and scientific progress consists largely in the elimination of contradictions wherever we find them. This means, however, that science proceeds on the assumption that *contradictions are impermissible and avoidable*, so that the discovery of a contradiction forces the scientist to make every attempt to eliminate it; and indeed, once a contradiction is admitted, all science must collapse[32]. But Hegel derives a very different lesson from his dialectic triad. Since contradictions are the means by which science progresses, he concludes that contradictions are not only permissible and unavoidable but also highly desirable. This is a Hegelian doctrine which must destroy all argument and all progress. For if contradictions are unavoidable and desirable, there is no need to eliminate them, and so all progress must come to an end.

But this doctrine is just one of the main tenets of Hegelianism. Hegel's intention is to operate freely with all contradictions. 'All things are contradictory in themselves', he insists[33], in order to defend a position which means the end not only of all science, but of all rational argument. And the reason why he wishes to admit contradictions is that he wants to stop rational argument, and with it scientific and intellectual progress. By making argument and criticism impossible, he intends to make his own philosophy proof against all criticism, so that it may establish itself as a *reinforced dogmatism*, secure from every attack, and the unsurmountable summit of all philosophical development. (We have here a first example of a typical *dialectical twist*; the idea of progress, popular in a period which leads to Darwin, but not in keeping with conservative interests, is twisted into its opposite, that of a development which has arrived at an end—an arrested development.)

So much for Hegel's dialectic triad, one of the two pillars on which his philosophy rests. The significance of the theory will be seen when I proceed to its application.

The other of the two pillars of Hegelianism is his so-called *philosophy of identity*. It is, in its turn, an application of dialectics. I do not intend to waste the reader's time by attempting to make sense of it, especially since I have tried to do so elsewhere[34]; for in the main, the philosophy of identity is nothing but shameless equivocation, and, to use Hegel's own words, it consists of nothing but 'fancies, even imbecile fancies'. It is a maze in which are caught the shadows and echoes of past philosophies, of Heraclitus, Plato, and Aristotle, as well as of Rousseau and Kant, and in which they now celebrate a kind of witches' sabbath, madly trying to confuse and beguile the naïve onlooker. The leading idea, and at the same time the link between Hegel's dialectics and his philosophy of identity, is Heraclitus' doctrine of the unity of opposites. 'The path that leads up and the path that leads down are identical', Heraclitus had said, and Hegel repeats this when he says: 'The way west and the way east are the same.' This Heraclitean doctrine of the identity of opposites is applied to a host of reminiscences from the old philosophies which are thereby 'reduced to components' of Hegel's own system. Essence and Idea, the one and the many, substance and accident, form and content, subject and object, being and becoming, everything and nothing, change and rest, actuality and potentiality, reality and appearance, matter and spirit, all these ghosts from the past seem to haunt the brain of the Great Dictator while he performs his dance with his balloon, with his puffed-up and fictitious problems of God and the World. But there is method in this madness, and even Prussian method. For behind the apparent confusion there lurk the interests of the absolute monarchy of Frederick William. The philosophy of identity serves to justify the existing order. Its main upshot is an *ethical and juridical positivism*, the doctrine that what is, is good, since there can be no standards but existing standards; it is the doctrine that *might is right*.

How is this doctrine derived? Merely by a series of equivocations. Plato, whose Forms or Ideas, as we have seen, are entirely different from 'ideas in the mind', had said that the Ideas alone are real, and that perishable things are unreal. Hegel adopts from this doctrine the equation *Ideal* = *Real*. Kant talked, in his dialectics, about the 'Ideas of pure Reason', using the term 'Idea' in the sense of 'ideas in the mind'. Hegel adopts from this the doctrine that the Ideas are something mental or spiritual or rational, which can be expressed in the equation *Idea* = *Reason*. Combined, these two equations, or rather equivocations, yield *Real* = *Reason*; and this allows Hegel to maintain that everything that is reasonable must be real, and everything that is real must be reasonable, and that the development of reality is the same as that of reason. And since there can be no higher standard in existence than the latest development of Reason and of the Idea, everything that is now real or actual exists by necessity, and must be reasonable as well as good[35]. (Particularly good, as we shall see, is the actually existing Prussian state.)

This is the philosophy of identity. Apart from ethical positivism a theory of truth also comes to light, just as a byproduct (to use Schopenhauer's words). And a very convenient theory it is. All that is reasonable is real, we have seen. This means, of course, that all that is reasonable must conform to reality, and therefore must be true. Truth develops in the same way as reason develops, and everything that appeals to reason in its latest stage of development must also be true for that stage. In other words, everything that seems certain to those whose reason is up to date, must be true. Self-evidence is the same as truth. Provided you are up to date, all you need is to believe in a doctrine; this makes it, by definition, true. In this way, the opposition between what Hegel calls 'the Subjective', i.e. belief, and 'the Objective', i.e. truth, is turned into an identity; and this unity of opposites explains scientific knowledge also. 'The Idea is the union of Subjective and Objective ... Science presupposes that the separation between itself and Truth is already cancelled.'[36]

So much on Hegel's philosophy of identity, the second pillar of wisdom on which his historicism is built. With its erection, the somewhat tiresome work of analysing Hegel's more abstract doctrines comes to an end. The rest of this chapter will be confined to the practical political applications made by Hegel of these abstract theories. And these practical applications will show us more clearly the apologetic purpose of all his labours.

Hegel's dialectics, I assert, are very largely designed to pervert the ideas of 1789. Hegel was perfectly conscious of the fact that the dialectic method can be used for twisting an idea into its opposite. 'Dialectics', he writes[37], 'are no novelty in philosophy. Socrates ... used to simulate the wish for some clearer knowledge about the subject under discussion, and after putting all sorts of questions with that intention, he brought those with whom he conversed round to the opposite of what their first impression had pronounced correct.' As a description of Socrates' intentions, this statement of Hegel's is perhaps not very fair (considering that Socrates' main aim was the exposure of cocksureness rather than the conversion of people to the opposite of what they believed before); but as a statement of Hegel's own intention, it is excellent, even though in practice Hegel's method turns out to be more clumsy than his programme indicates.

As a first example of this use of dialectics, I shall select the problem of *freedom of thought*, of the independence of science, and of the standards of objective truth, as treated by Hegel in the *Philosophy of Law* (§ 270). He begins with what can only be interpreted as a demand for freedom of thought, and for its protection by the state: 'The state', he writes, 'has ... thought as its essential principle. Thus freedom of thought, and science, can originate only in the state; it was the Church that burnt Giordano Bruno, and forced Galileo to recant ... Science, therefore, must seek protection from the state, since ... the aim of science is knowledge of objective truth.' After this promising start which we may take as representing the 'first impressions' of his opponents, Hegel proceeds to bring them 'to the opposite of what their first impressions pronounced correct', covering his change of front by another sham attack on the Church: 'But such knowledge does, of course, not always conform with the standards of science, it may degenerate into mere opinion ...; and for these opinions ... it' (i.e. science) 'may raise the same pretentious demand as the Church—the demand to be free in its opinions and convictions.' Thus the demand for freedom of thought, and of the claim of science to judge for itself, is described as 'pretentious'; but this is merely the first step in Hegel's twist. We next hear that, if faced with subversive opinions, 'the state must protect objective truth'; which raises the fundamental question: who is to judge what is, and what is not, objective truth? Hegel replies: 'The state has, in general, ... to make up its own mind concerning what is to be considered as objective truth.' With this reply, freedom of thought, and the claims of science to set its own standards, give way, finally, to their opposites.

As a second example of this use of dialectics, I select Hegel's treatment of the demand for a *political constitution*, which he combines with his treatment of *equality* and *liberty*. In order to appreciate the problem of the constitution, it must be remembered that Prussian absolutism knew no constitutional law (apart from such principles as the full sovereignty of the king) and that the slogan of the campaign for democratic reform in the various German principalities was that the prince should 'grant the country a constitution'. But Frederick William agreed with his councillor Ancillon in the conviction that he must never give way to 'the hotheads, that very active and loud-voiced group of persons who for some years have set themselves up as the nation and have cried for a constitution'[38]. And although, under great pressure, the king promised a constitution, he never fulfilled his word. (There is a story that an innocent comment on the king's 'constitution' led to the dismissal of his unfortunate court-physician.) Now how does Hegel treat this ticklish problem? 'As a living mind', he writes, 'the state is an organized whole, articulated into various agencies ... The *constitution* is this articulation or organization of state power ... The constitution is existent *justice* ... Liberty and equality are ... the final aims and results of the constitution.' This, of course, is only the introduction. But before proceeding to the dialectical transformation of the demand for a constitution into one for an absolute monarchy, we must first show how Hegel transforms the two 'aims and results', liberty and equality, into their opposites.

Let us first see how Hegel twists equality into inequality: 'That the citizens are equal before the law', Hegel admits[39], 'contains a great truth. But expressed in this way, it is only a tautology; it only states in general that a legal status exists, that the laws rule. But to be more concrete, the citizens ... are equal before the law only in the points in which they are equal *outside the law* also. *Only that equality which they possess in property, age, ... etc., can deserve equal treatment before the law* ... The laws themselves ... presuppose unequal conditions ... It should be said that it is just the great development and maturity of form in modern states which produces the supreme concrete inequality of individuals in actuality.'

In this outline of Hegel's twist of the 'great truth' of equalitarianism into its opposite, I have radically abbreviated his argument; and I must warn the reader that I shall have to do the same throughout the chapter; for only in this way is it at all possible to present, in a readable manner, his verbosity and the flight of his thoughts (which, I do not doubt, is pathological[40]).

We may consider liberty next. 'As regards liberty', Hegel writes, 'in former times, the legally defined rights, the private as well as public rights of a city, etc., were called its "liberties". Really, every genuine law is a liberty; for it contains a reasonable principle ...; which means, in other words, that it embodies a liberty ...' Now this argument which tries to show that 'liberty' is the same as 'a liberty' and therefore the same as 'law', from which it follows that the more laws, the more liberty, is clearly nothing but a clumsy statement (clumsy because it relies on a kind of pun) of the paradox of freedom, first discovered by Plato, and briefly discussed above[41]; a paradox that can be expressed by saying that unlimited freedom leads to its opposite, since without its protection and restriction by law, freedom must lead to a tyranny of the strong over the weak. This paradox, vaguely restated by Rousseau, was solved by Kant, who demanded that the freedom of each man should be restricted, but not beyond what is necessary to safeguard an equal degree of freedom for all. Hegel of course knows Kant's solution, but he does not like it, and he presents it, without mentioning its author, in the following disparaging way: 'To-day, nothing is more familiar than the idea that each must restrict his liberty in relation to the liberty of others; that the state is a condition of such reciprocal restrictions; and that the laws are restrictions. But', he goes on to criticize Kant's theory, 'this expresses the kind of outlook that views freedom as casual good-pleasure and self-will.' With this cryptic remark, Kant's equalitarian theory of justice is dismissed.

But Hegel himself feels that the little jest by which he equates liberty and law is not quite sufficient for his purpose; and somewhat hesitatingly he turns back to his original problem, that of the constitution. 'The term political liberty', he says[42], 'is often used to mean a formal participation in the public affairs of the state by … those who otherwise find their chief function in the particular aims and business of civil society' (in other words, by the ordinary citizen). 'And it has … become a custom to give the title "constitution" only to that side of the state which establishes such participation … , and to regard a state in which this is not formally done as a state without a constitution.' Indeed, this has become a custom. But how to get out of it? By a merely verbal trick—by a definition: 'About this use of the term, the only thing to say is that by a constitution we must understand the determination of laws in general, that is to say, of liberties …' But again, Hegel himself feels the appalling poverty of the argument, and in despair he dives into a collectivist mysticism (of Rousseau's making) and into historicism[43]: 'The question "To whom … belongs the power of making a constitution?" is the same as "Who has to make the Spirit of a Nation?". Separate your idea of a constitution', Hegel exclaims, 'from that of a collective Spirit, as if the latter exists, or has existed, without a constitution, and your fancy proves how superficially you have apprehended the nexus' (namely, that between the Spirit and the constitution). '… It is the indwelling Spirit and the history of the Nation—which only is that Spirit's history—by which constitutions have been and are made.' But this mysticism is still too vague to justify absolutism. One must be more specific; and Hegel now hastens to be so: 'The really living totality,' he writes, 'that which preserves, and continually produces, the State and its constitution, is the *Government* … In the Government, regarded as an organic totality, the Sovereign Power or Principate is … the all-sustaining, all-decreeing Will of the State, its highest Peak and all-pervasive Unity. In the perfect form of the State in which each and every element ... has reached its free existence, this will is that of *one actual decreeing Individual* (not merely of a majority in which the unity of the decreeing will has no *actual* existence); it is *monarchy*. The monarchical constitution is therefore the constitution of developed reason; and all other constitutions belong to lower grades of the development and the self-realization of reason.' And to be still more specific, Hegel explains in a parallel passage of his *Philosophy of Law*—the foregoing quotations are all taken from his *Encyclopædia*—that 'ultimate decision ... *absolute* self-determination constitutes the power of the prince as such', and that 'the *absolutely decisive* element in the whole ... is a single individual, the monarch.'

Now we have it. How can anybody be so stupid as to demand a 'constitution' for a country that is blessed with an absolute monarchy, the highest possible grade of all constitutions anyway? Those who make such demands obviously know not what they do and what they are talking about, just as those who demand freedom are too blind to see that in the Prussian absolute monarchy, 'each and every element has reached its free existence'. In other words, we have here Hegel's absolute dialectical proof that Prussia is the 'highest peak', and the very stronghold, of freedom; that its absolutist constitution is the goal (not as some might think, the gaol) towards which humanity moves; and that its government preserves and keeps, as it were, the purest spirit of freedom—in concentration.

Plato's philosophy, which once had claimed mastership in the state, becomes with Hegel its most servile lackey.

These despicable services[44], it is important to note, were rendered voluntarily. There was no totalitarian intimidation in those happy days of absolute monarchy; nor was the censorship very effective, as countless liberal publications show. When Hegel published his *Encyclopædia* he was professor in Heidelberg. And immediately after the publication, he was called to Berlin to become, as his admirers say, the 'acknowledged dictator' of philosophy. But, some may contend, all this, even if it is true, does not prove anything against the excellence of Hegel's dialectic philosophy, or against his greatness as a philosopher. To this contention, Schopenhauer's reply has already been given: 'Philosophy is misused, from the side of the state as a tool, from the other side as a means of gain. *Who can really believe that truth also will thereby come to light, just as a by-product?*'

These passages give us a glimpse of the way in which Hegel's dialectic method is applied in practice. I now proceed to the combined application of dialectics and the philosophy of identity.

Hegel, we have seen, teaches that everything is in flux, even essences. Essences and Ideas and Spirits develop; and their development is, of course, self-moving and dialectical[45]. And the latest stage of every development must be reasonable, and therefore good and true, for it is the apex of all past developments, superseding all previous stages. (Thus things can only get better and better.) Every real development, since it is a real process, must, according to the philosophy of identity, be a rational and reasonable process. It is clear that this must hold for history also.

Heraclitus had maintained that there is a hidden reason in history. For Hegel, history becomes an open book. The book is pure apologetics. By its appeal to the wisdom of Providence it offers an apology for the excellence of Prussian monarchism; by its appeal to the excellence of Prussian monarchism it offers an apology for the wisdom of Providence.

History is the development of something real. According to the philosophy of identity, it must therefore be something rational. The evolution of the real world, of which history is the most important part, is taken by Hegel to be 'identical' with a kind of logical operation, or with a process of reasoning. History, as he sees it, is the thought process of the 'Absolute Spirit' or 'World Spirit'. It is the manifestation of this Spirit. It is a kind of huge dialectical syllogism[46]; reasoned out, as it were, by Providence. The syllogism is the plan which Providence follows; and the logical conclusion arrived at is the end which Providence pursues—the perfection of the world. 'The only thought', Hegel writes in his *Philosophy of History*, 'with which Philosophy approaches History, is the simple conception of Reason; it is the doctrine that Reason is the Sovereign of the World, and that the History of the World, therefore, presents us with a *rational process*. This conviction and intuition is ... no hypothesis in the domain of Philosophy. It is there proven ... that Reason ... is *Substance*; as well as *Infinite Power*; ... *Infinite Matter* ...; *Infinite Form* ...; *Infinite Energy* ... That this "Idea" or "Reason" is the *True*, the *Eternal*, the absolutely *Powerful Essence*; that it reveals itself in the World, and that in that World nothing else is revealed but this and its honour and glory—this is a thesis which, as we have said, has been proved in Philosophy, and is here regarded as demonstrated.' This gush does not carry us far. But if we look up the passage in 'Philosophy' (i.e., in his *Encyclopædia*) to which Hegel refers, then we see a little more of his apologetic purpose. For here we read: 'That History, and above all Universal History, is founded on an essential and actual aim, which *actually* is, and will be, *realized in it*—the Plan of Providence; that, in short, there is Reason in History, must be decided on strictly philosophical grounds, and thus shown to be essential and in fact necessary.' Now since the aim of Providence 'actually is realized' in the results of history, it might be suspected that this realization has taken place in the actual Prussia. And so it has; we are even shown how this aim is reached, in three dialectical steps of the historical development of reason, or, as Hegel says, of 'Spirit', whose 'life … is a cycle of progressive embodiments'[47]. The first of these steps is Oriental despotism, the second is formed by the Greek and Roman democracies and aristocracies, and the third, and highest, is the Germanic Monarchy, which of course is an absolute monarchy. And Hegel makes it quite clear that he does not mean a Utopian monarchy of the future: 'Spirit … has no past, no future,' he writes, 'but is essentially *now*; this necessarily implies that the present form of the Spirit contains and surpasses all earlier steps.'

But Hegel can be even more outspoken than that. He subdivided the third period of history, Germanic Monarchy, or 'the German World', into three divisions too, of which he says[48]: 'First, we have to consider *Reformation* in itself—the all-enlightening *Sun*, following on that blush of dawn which we observed at the termination of the medieval period; next, the unfolding of that state of things which succeeded the Reformation; and lastly, Modern Times, dating from the end of the last century', i.e. the period from 1800 down to 1830 (the last year in which these lectures were delivered). And Hegel proves again that this present Prussia is the pinnacle and the stronghold and the goal of freedom. 'On the Stage of Universal History', Hegel writes 'on which we can observe and grasp it, Spirit displays itself in its most concrete reality.' And the essence of Spirit, Hegel teaches, is freedom. 'Freedom is the sole truth of Spirit.' Accordingly, the development of Spirit must be the development of freedom, and the highest freedom must have been achieved in those thirty years of the Germanic Monarchy which represent the last subdivision of historical development. And indeed, we read[49]: 'The German Spirit is the Spirit of the new World. Its aim is the realization of absolute Truth as the unlimited self-determination of Freedom.' And after a eulogy of Prussia, the government of which, Hegel assures us, 'rests with the official world, whose apex is the personal decision of the Monarch; for a final decision is, as shown above, an absolute necessity', Hegel reaches the crowning conclusion of his work: 'This is the point', he says, 'which consciousness has attained, and these are the principal phases of that form in which Freedom has realized itself; for the History of the World is nothing but the development of the Idea of Freedom … That the History of the World … is the realization of Spirit, this is the true Theodicy, the justification of God in History … What has happened and is happening … is essentially His Work …'

I ask whether I was not justified when I said that Hegel presents us with an apology for God and for Prussia at the same time, and whether it is not clear that the state which Hegel commands us to worship as the Divine Idea on earth is not simply Frederick William's Prussia from 1800 to 1830. And I ask whether it is possible to outdo this despicable perversion of everything that is decent; a perversion not only of reason, freedom, equality, and the other ideas of the open society, but also of a sincere belief in God, and even of a sincere patriotism.

I have described how, starting from a point that appears to be progressive and even revolutionary, and proceeding by that general dialectical method of twisting things which by now will be familiar to the reader, Hegel finally reaches a surprisingly conservative result. At the same time, he connects his philosophy of history with his ethical and juridical positivism, giving the latter a kind of historicist justification. History is our judge. Since History and Providence have brought the existing powers into being, their might must be right, even Divine right.

But this moral positivism does not fully satisfy Hegel. He wants more. Just as he opposes liberty and equality, so he opposes the brotherhood of man, humanitarianism, or, as he says, 'philanthropy'. Conscience must be replaced by blind obedience and by a romantic Heraclitean ethics of fame and fate, and the brotherhood of man by a *totalitarian nationalism*. How this is done will be shown in section III and especially[50] in section IV of this chapter.

III

I now proceed to a very brief sketch of a rather strange story—the story of the *rise of German nationalism*. Undoubtedly the tendencies denoted by this term have a strong affinity with the revolt against reason and the open society. Nationalism appeals to our tribal instincts, to passion and to prejudice, and to our nostalgic desire to be relieved from the strain of individual responsibility which it attempts to replace by a collective or group responsibility. It is in keeping with these tendencies that we find that the oldest works on political theory, even that of the Old Oligarch, but more markedly those of Plato and of Aristotle, express decidedly nationalist views; for these works were written in an attempt to combat the open society and the new ideas of imperialism, cosmopolitanism, and equalitarianism[51]. But this early development of a nationalist political theory stops short with Aristotle. With Alexander's empire, genuine tribal nationalism disappears for ever from political practice, and for a long time from political theory. From Alexander onward, all the civilized states of Europe and Asia were empires, embracing populations of infinitely mixed origin. European civilization and all the political units belonging to it have remained international or, more precisely, inter-tribal ever since. (It seems that about as long before Alexander as Alexander was before us, the empire of ancient Sumer had created the first international civilization.) And what holds good of political practice holds good of political theory; until about a hundred years ago, the Platonic-Aristotelian nationalism had practically disappeared from political doctrines. (Of course, tribal and parochial feelings were always strong.) When nationalism was revived a hundred years ago, it was in one of the most mixed of all the thoroughly mixed regions of Europe, in Germany, and especially in Prussia with its largely Slav population. (It is not well known that barely a century ago, Prussia, with its then predominantly Slav population, was not considered a German state at all; though its kings, who as princes of Brandenburg were 'Electors' of the German Empire, were considered German princes. At the Congress of Vienna, Prussia was registered as a 'Slav kingdom'; and in 1830 Hegel still spoke[52] even of Brandenburg and Mecklenburg as being populated by 'Germanized Slavs'.)

Thus it is only a short time since the *principle of the national state* was reintroduced into political theory. In spite of this fact, it is so widely accepted in our day that it is usually taken for granted, and very often unconsciously so. It now forms, as it were, an implicit assumption of popular political thought. It is even considered by many to be the basic postulate of political ethics, especially since Wilson's well-meant but less well-considered principle of national self-determination. How anybody who had the slightest knowledge of European history, of the shifting and mixing of all kinds of tribes, of the countless waves of peoples who had come forth from their original Asian habitat and split up and mingled when reaching the maze of peninsulas called the European continent, how anybody who knew this could ever have put forward such an inapplicable principle, is hard to understand. The explanation is that Wilson, who was a sincere democrat (and Masaryk also, one of the greatest of all fighters for the open society[53]), fell a victim to a movement that sprang from the most reactionary and servile political philosophy that had ever been imposed upon meek and long-suffering mankind. He fell a victim to his upbringing in the metaphysical political theories of Plato and of Hegel, and to the nationalist movement based upon them.

The *principle of the national state*, that is to say, the political demand that the territory of every state should coincide with the territory inhabited by one nation, is by no means so self-evident as it seems to appear to many people to-day. Even if anyone knew what he meant when he spoke of nationality, it would be not at all clear why nationality should be accepted as a fundamental political category, more important for instance than religion, or birth within a certain geographical region, or loyalty to a dynasty, or a political creed like democracy (which forms, one might say, the uniting factor of multi-lingual Switzerland). But while religion, territory, or a political creed can be more or less clearly determined, nobody has ever been able to explain what he means by a nation, in a way that could be used as a basis for practical politics. (Of course, if we say that a nation is a number of people who live or have been born in a certain state, then everything is clear; but this would mean giving up the principle of the national state which demands that the state should be determined by the nation, and not the other way round.) None of the theories which maintain that a nation is united by a common origin, or a common language, or a common history, is acceptable, or applicable in practice. The principle of the national state is not only inapplicable but it has never been clearly conceived. It is a myth. It is an irrational, a romantic and Utopian dream, a dream of naturalism and of tribal collectivism.

In spite of its inherent reactionary and irrational tendencies, modern nationalism, strangely enough, was in its short history before Hegel a revolutionary and liberal creed. By something like an historical accident—the invasion of German lands by the first national army, the French army under Napoleon, and the reaction caused by this event—it had made its way into the camp of freedom. It is not without interest to sketch the history of this development, and of the way in which Hegel brought nationalism back into the totalitarian camp where it had belonged from the time when Plato first maintained that Greeks are related to barbarians like masters to slaves.

Plato, it will be remembered[54], unfortunately formulated his fundamental political problem by asking: Who should rule? Whose will should be law? Before Rousseau, the usual answer to this question was: The prince. Rousseau gave a new and most revolutionary answer. Not the prince, he maintained, but the people should rule; not the will of one man but the will of all. In this way, he was led to invent the people's will, the collective will, or the 'general will', as he called it; and the people, once endowed with a will, had to be exalted into a super-personality; 'in relation to what is external to it' (i.e. in relation to other peoples), Rousseau says, 'it becomes one single being, one individual'. There was a good deal of romantic collectivism in this invention, but no tendency towards nationalism. But Rousseau's theories clearly contained the germ of nationalism, whose most characteristic doctrine is that the various nations must be conceived as personalities. And a great practical step in the nationalist direction was made when the French Revolution inaugurated a people's army, based on national conscription.

One of the next to contribute to the theory of nationalism was J. G. Herder, a former pupil and at the time a personal friend of Kant. Herder maintained that a good state should have natural borders, namely those which coincide with the places inhabited by its 'nation'; a theory which he first proffered in his *Ideas towards a Philosophy of the History of Mankind* (1785). 'The most natural state', he wrote[55], 'is a state composed of a single people with a single national character ... A people is a natural growth like a family, only spread more widely ... As in all human communities, ... so, in the case of the state, the natural order is the best—that is to say, the order in which everyone fulfils that function for which nature intended him.' This theory, which tries to give an answer to the problem of the 'natural' borders of the state[56], an answer that only raises the new problem of the 'natural' borders of the nation, did not at first exert much influence. It is interesting to see that Kant at once realized the dangerous irrational romanticism in this work of Herder's, of whom he made a sworn enemy by his outspoken criticism. I shall quote a passage from this criticism, because it excellently sums up, once and for all, not only Herder, but also the later oracular philosophers like Fichte, Schelling, Hegel, together with all their modern followers: 'A sagacity quick in picking up analogies', Kant wrote, 'and an imagination audacious in the use it makes of them are combined with a capability for enlisting emotions and passions in order to obtain interest for its object—an object that is always veiled in mystery. These emotions are easily mistaken for the efforts of powerful and profound thoughts, or at least of deeply significant allusions; and they thus arouse higher expectations than cool judgement would find justified ... Synonyms are passed off as explanations, and allegories are offered as truths.'

It was Fichte who provided German nationalism with its first theory. The borders of a nation, he contended, are determined by language. (This does not improve matters. Where do differences of dialect become differences of language? How many different languages do the Slavs or the Teutons speak, or are the differences merely dialects?)

Fichte's opinions had a most curious development, especially if we consider that he was one of the founders of German nationalism. In 1793, he defended Rousseau and the French Revolution, and in 1799 he still declared[57]: 'It is plain that from now on the French Republic alone can be the fatherland of the upright man, that he can devote his powers to this country alone of all, since not only the dearest hopes of humanity but also its very existence are bound up with the victory of France ... I dedicate myself and all my abilities to the Republic.' It may be noted that when Fichte made these remarks he was negotiating for a university position in Mainz, a place then controlled by the French. 'In 1804', E. N. Anderson writes in his interesting study on nationalism, 'Fichte ... was eager to leave Prussian service and to accept a call from Russia. The Prussian government had not appreciated him to the desired financial extent and he hoped for more recognition from Russia, writing to the Russian negotiator that if the government would make him a member of the St. Petersburg Academy of Science and pay him a salary of not less than four hundred roubles, "I would be theirs until death" … Two years later', Anderson continues, 'the transformation of Fichte the cosmopolitan into Fichte the nationalist was completed.'

When Berlin was occupied by the French, Fichte left, out of patriotism; an act which, as Anderson says 'he did not allow … to remain unnoticed by the Prussian king and government'. When A. Mueller and W. von Humboldt had been received by Napoleon, Fichte wrote indignantly to his wife: 'I do not envy Mueller and Humboldt; I am glad that I did not obtain that shameful honour … It makes a difference to one's conscience *and apparently also to one's later success* if … one has openly shown devotion to the good cause.' On this, Anderson comments: 'As a matter of fact, he did profit; undoubtedly his call to the University of Berlin resulted from this episode. This does not detract from the patriotism of his act, but merely places it in its proper light.' To all this we must add that Fichte's career as a philosopher was from the beginning based on a fraud. His first book was published anonymously, when Kant's philosophy of religion was expected, under the title *Critique of All Revelation*. It was an extremely dull book, which did not prevent it from being a clever copy of Kant's style; and everything was set in motion, including rumours, to make people believe that it was Kant's work. The matter appears in its right light if we realize that Fichte only obtained a publisher through the kindheartedness of Kant (who was never able to read more than the first few pages of the book). When the press extolled Fichte's work as one of Kant's, Kant was forced to make a public statement that the work was Fichte's, and Fichte, upon whom fame had suddenly descended, was made professor in Jena. But Kant was later forced to make another declaration, in order to dissociate himself from this man, a declaration in which occur the words[58]: 'May God protect us from our friends. From our enemies, we can try to protect ourselves.'

These are a few episodes in the career of the man whose 'windbaggery' has given rise to modern nationalism as well as to modern Idealist philosophy, erected upon the perversion of Kant's teaching. (I follow Schopenhauer in distinguishing between Fichte's 'windbaggery' and Hegel's 'charlatanry', although I must admit that to insist on this distinction is perhaps a little pedantic.) The whole story is interesting mainly because of the light it throws upon the 'history of philosophy' and upon 'history' in general. I mean not only the perhaps more humorous than scandalous fact that such clowns are taken seriously, and that they are made the objects of a kind of worship, of solemn although often boring studies (and of examination papers to match). I mean not only the appalling fact that the windbag Fichte and the charlatan Hegel are treated on a level with men like Democritus, Pascal, Descartes, Spinoza, Locke, Hume, Kant, J. S. Mill, and Bertrand Russell, and that their moral teaching is taken seriously and perhaps even considered superior to that of these other men. But I mean that many of these eulogist historians of philosophy, unable to discriminate between thought and fancy, not to mention good and bad, dare to pronounce that their history is our judge, or that their history of philosophy is an implicit criticism of the different 'systems of thought'. For it is clear, I think, that their adulation can only be an implicit criticism of their histories of philosophy, and of that pomposity and conspiracy of noise by which the business of philosophy is glorified. It seems to be a law of what these people are pleased to call 'human nature' that bumptiousness grows in direct proportion to deficiency of thought and inversely to the amount of service rendered to human welfare.

At the time when Fichte became the apostle of nationalism, an instinctive and revolutionary nationalism was rising in Germany as a reaction to the Napoleonic invasion. (It was one of those typical tribal reactions against the expansion of a super-national empire.) The people demanded democratic reforms which they understood in the sense of Rousseau and of the French Revolution, but which they wanted without their French conquerors. They turned against their own princes and against the emperor at the same time. This early nationalism arose with the force of a new religion, as a kind of cloak in which a humanitarian desire for freedom and equality was clad. 'Nationalism', Anderson writes[59], 'grew as orthodox Christianity declined, replacing the latter with belief in a mystical experience of its own.' It is the mystical experience of community with the other members of the oppressed tribe, an experience which replaced not only Christianity but especially the feeling of trust and loyalty to the king which the abuses of absolutism had destroyed. It is clear that such an untamed new and democratic religion was a source of great irritation, and even of danger, to the ruling class, and especially to the king of Prussia. How was this danger to be met? After the wars of liberation, Frederick William met it first by dismissing his nationalist advisers, and then by appointing Hegel. For the French Revolution had proved the influence of philosophy, a point duly emphasized by Hegel (since it is the basis of his own services): 'The Spiritual', he says[60], 'is now the essential basis of the potential fabric, and *Philosophy* has thereby become dominant. It has been said that the French Revolution resulted from

Philosophy, and it is not without reason that Philosophy has been described as World Wisdom; Philosophy is not only Truth in and for itself … but also Truth as exhibited in worldly matters. We should not, therefore, contradict the assertion that the Revolution received its first impulse from Philosophy.' This is an indication of Hegel's insight into his immediate task, to give a counter impulse; an impulse, though not the first, by which philosophy might strengthen the forces of reaction. Part of this task was the perversion of the ideas of freedom, equality, etc. But perhaps an even more urgent task was the taming of the revolutionary nationalist religion. Hegel fulfilled this task in the spirit of Pareto's advice 'to take advantage of sentiments, not wasting one's energies in futile efforts to destroy them'. He tamed nationalism not by outspoken opposition but by transforming it into a well-disciplined Prussian authoritarianism. And it so happened that he brought back a powerful weapon into the camp of the closed society, where it fundamentally belonged.

All this was done rather clumsily. Hegel, in his desire to please the government, sometimes attacked the nationalists much too openly. 'Some men', he wrote[61] in the *Philosophy of Law*, 'have recently begun to talk of the "sovereignty of the people" in opposition to the sovereignty of the monarch. But when it is contrasted with the sovereignty of the monarch, then the phrase "sovereignty of the people" turns out to be merely one of those confused notions which arise from a wild idea of the "people". Without its monarch … the people are just a formless multitude.' Earlier, in the *Encyclopædia*, he wrote: 'The aggregate of private persons is often spoken of as the *nation*. But such an aggregate is a rabble, not a people; and with regard to it, it is the one aim of the state that a nation should *not* come into existence, to power and action, as such an aggregate. Such a condition of a nation is a condition of lawlessness, demoralization, brutishness. In it, the nation would only be a shapeless wild blind force, like that of a stormy elemental sea, which however is not self-destructive, as the nation—a spiritual element—would be. Yet one can often hear such a condition described as pure freedom.' There is here an unmistakable allusion to the liberal nationalists, whom the king hated like the plague. And this is even clearer when we see Hegel's reference to the early nationalists' dreams of rebuilding the German empire: 'The fiction of an Empire', he says in his eulogy of the latest developments in Prussia, 'has utterly vanished. It is broken into Sovereign States.' His anti-liberal tendencies induced Hegel to refer to England as the most characteristic example of a nation in the bad sense. 'Take the case of England,' he writes, 'which, because private persons have a predominant share in public affairs, has been regarded as having the freest of all constitutions. Experience shows that that country, as compared with the other civilized states of Europe, is the most backward in civil and criminal legislation, in the law and liberty of property, and in arrangements for the *arts and sciences*, and that objective freedom or rational right is *sacrificed* to formal[62] right and particular private interest: and that this happens even in the institutions and possessions dedicated to religion.' An astonishing statement indeed, especially when the 'arts and sciences' are considered, for nothing could have been more backward than Prussia, where the University of Berlin had been founded only under the influence of the Napoleonic wars, and with the idea, as the king said[63], that 'the state must replace with intellectual prowess what it has lost in physical strength'. A few pages later, Hegel forgets what he has said about the arts and sciences in England; for he speaks there of 'England, where the art of historical writing has undergone a process of purification and arrived at a firmer and more mature character'.

We see that Hegel knew that his task was to combat the liberal and even the imperialist leanings of nationalism. He did it by persuading the nationalists that their collectivist demands are automatically realized by an almighty state, and that all they need do is to help to strengthen the power of the state. 'The Nation State is Spirit in its substantive rationality and immediate actuality', he writes[64]; 'it is therefore the absolute power on earth ... The state is the Spirit of the People itself. The actual State is animated by this spirit, in all its particular affairs, its Wars, and its Institutions ... The self-consciousness of one particular Nation is the vehicle for the ... development of the collective spirit; ... in it, the Spirit of the Time invests its Will. Against this Will, the other national minds have no rights: *that* Nation dominates the World.' It is thus the nation and its spirit and its will that act on the stage of history. History is the contest of the various national spirits for world domination. From this it follows that the reforms advocated by the liberal nationalists are unnecessary, since the nation and its spirit are the leading actors anyway; besides, 'every nation ... has the constitution which is appropriate to it and belongs to it'. (Juridical positivism.) We see that Hegel replaces the liberal elements in nationalism not only by a Platonic-Prussianist worship of the state, but also by a worship of history, of historical success. (Frederick William had been successful against Napoleon.) In this way, Hegel not only began a new chapter in the history of nationalism, but he also provided nationalism with a new theory. Fichte, we have seen, had provided it with the theory that it was based on language. Hegel introduced the *historical theory of the nation*. A nation, according to Hegel, is united by a spirit that acts in history. It is united by the common foe, and by the comradeship of the wars it has fought. (It has been said that a race is a collection of men united not by their origin but by a common error in regard to their origin. In a similar way, we could say that a nation in Hegel's sense is a number of men united by a common error in regard to their history.) It is clear how this theory is connected with Hegel's historicist essentialism. The history of a nation is the history of its essence or 'Spirit', asserting itself on the 'Stage of History'.

In concluding this sketch of the rise of nationalism, I may make a remark on the events down to the foundation of Bismarck's German empire. Hegel's policy had been to take advantage of nationalist sentiments, instead of wasting energy in futile efforts to destroy them. But sometimes this celebrated technique appears to have rather strange consequences. The medieval conversion of Christianity into an authoritarian creed could not fully suppress its humanitarian tendencies; again and again, Christianity breaks through the authoritarian cloak (and is persecuted as heresy). In this way, Pareto's advice not only serves to neutralize tendencies that endanger the ruling class, but can also unintentionally help to preserve these very tendencies. A similar thing happened to nationalism. Hegel had tamed it, and had tried to replace German nationalism by a Prussian nationalism. But by thus 'reducing nationalism to a component' of his Prussianism (to use his own jargon) Hegel 'preserved' it; and Prussia found itself forced to proceed on the way of taking advantage of the sentiments of German nationalism. When it fought Austria in 1866 it had to do so in the name of German nationalism, and under the pretext of securing the leadership of 'Germany'. And it had to advertise the vastly enlarged Prussia of 1871 as the new 'German Empire', a new 'German Nation'—welded by war into a unit, in accordance with Hegel's historical theory of the nation.

IV

In our own time, Hegel's hysterical historicism is still the fertilizer to which modern totalitarianism owes its rapid growth. Its use has prepared the ground, and has educated the intelligentsia to intellectual dishonesty, as will be shown in section V of this chapter. We have to learn the lesson that intellectual honesty is fundamental for everything we cherish.

But is this all? And is it just? Is there nothing in the claim that Hegel's greatness lies in the fact that he was the creator of a new, of a historical way of thinking—of a new historical sense?

Many of my friends have criticized me for my attitude towards Hegel, and for my inability to see his greatness. They were, of course, quite right, since I was indeed unable to see it. (I am so still.) In order to remedy this fault, I made a fairly systematic inquiry into the question, Wherein lies Hegel's greatness?

The result was disappointing. No doubt, Hegel's talk about the vastness and greatness of the historical drama created an atmosphere of interest in history. No doubt, his vast historicist generalizations, periodizations, and interpretations fascinated some historians and challenged them to produce valuable and detailed historical studies (which nearly invariably showed the weakness of Hegel's findings as well as of his method). But was this challenging influence the achievement of either a historian or a philosopher? Was it not, rather, that of a propagandist? Historians, I found, tend to value Hegel (if at all) as a philosopher, and philosophers tend to believe that his contributions (if any) were to the understanding of history. But historicism is not history, and to believe in it reveals neither historical understanding nor historical sense. And if we wish to evaluate Hegel's greatness, as a historian or as a philosopher, we should not ask ourselves whether some people found his vision of history inspiring, but whether there was much truth in this vision.

I found only one idea which was important and which might be claimed to be implicit in Hegel's philosophy. It is the idea which leads Hegel to attack abstract rationalism and intellectualism which does not appreciate the indebtedness of reason to tradition. It is a certain awareness of the fact (which, however, Hegel forgets in his Logic) that men cannot start with a blank, creating a world of thought from nothing; but that their thoughts are, largely, the product of an intellectual inheritance.

I am ready to admit that this is an important point, and one which might be found in Hegel if one is willing to search for it. But I deny that it was Hegel's own contribution. It was the common property of the Romantics. That all social entities are products of history; not inventions, planned by reason, but formations emerging from the vagaries of historical events, from the interplay of ideas and interests, from sufferings and from passions, all this is older than Hegel. It goes back to Edmund Burke, whose appreciation of the significance of tradition for the functioning of all social institutions had immensely influenced the political thought of the German Romantic Movement. The trace of his influence can be found in Hegel, but only in the exaggerated and untenable form of an historical and evolutionary relativism—in the form of the dangerous doctrine that what is believed to-day is, in fact, true to-day, and in the equally dangerous corollary that what was true yesterday (*true*, and not merely 'believed') may be false to-morrow—a doctrine which, surely, is not likely to encourage an appreciation of the significance of tradition.

V

I now proceed to the last part of my treatment of Hegelianism, to the analysis of the dependence of the new tribalism or totalitarianism upon the doctrines of Hegel.

If it were my aim to write a history of the rise of totalitarianism, I should have to deal with Marxism first; for fascism grew partly out of the spiritual and political breakdown of Marxism. (And, as we shall see, a similar statement may be made about the relationship between Leninism and Marxism.) Since my main issue, however, is historicism, I propose to deal with Marxism later, as the purest form of historicism that has so far arisen, and to tackle fascism first.

Modern totalitarianism is only an episode within the perennial revolt against freedom and reason. From older episodes it is distinguished not so much by its ideology, as by the fact that its leaders succeeded in realizing one of the boldest dreams of their predecessors; they made the revolt against freedom a popular movement. (Its popularity, of course, must not be overrated; the intelligentsia are only a part of the people.) It was made possible only by the breakdown, in the countries concerned, of another popular movement, Social Democracy or the democratic version of Marxism, which in the minds of the working people stood for the ideas of freedom and equality. When it became obvious that it was not just by chance that this movement had failed in 1914 to make a determined stand against war; when it became clear that it was helpless to cope with the problems of peace, most of all with unemployment and economic depression; and when, at last, this movement defended itself only half-heartedly against fascist aggression, then the belief in the value of freedom and in the possibility of equality was seriously threatened, and the perennial revolt against freedom could by hook or by crook acquire a more or less popular backing.

The fact that fascism had to take over part of the heritage of Marxism accounts for the one 'original' feature of fascist ideology, for the one point in which it deviates from the traditional make-up of the revolt against freedom. The point I have in mind is that fascism has not much use for an open appeal to the supernatural. Not that it is necessarily atheistic or lacking in mystical or religious elements. But the spread of agnosticism through Marxism led to a situation in which no political creed aiming at popularity among the working class could bind itself to any of the traditional religious forms. This is why fascism added to its official ideology, in its early stages at least, some admixture of nineteenth-century evolutionist materialism.

Thus the formula of the fascist brew is in all countries the same: Hegel plus a dash of nineteenth-century materialism (especially Darwinism in the somewhat crude form given to it by Haeckel[65]). The 'scientific' element in racialism can be traced back to Haeckel, who was responsible, in 1900, for a prize-competition whose subject was: 'What can we learn from the principles of Darwinism in respect of the internal and political development of a state?' The first prize was allotted to a voluminous racialist work by W. Schallmeyer, who thus became the grandfather of racial biology. It is interesting to observe how strongly this materialist racialism, despite its very different origin, resembles the naturalism of Plato. In both cases, the basic idea is that degeneration, particularly of the upper classes, is at the root of political decay (read: of the advance of the open society). Moreover, the modern myth of Blood and Soil has its exact counterpart in Plato's Myth of the Earthborn. Nevertheless, not 'Hegel + Plato', but 'Hegel + Haeckel' is the formula of modern racialism. As we shall see, Marx replaced Hegel's 'Spirit' by matter, and by material and economic interests. In the same way, racialism substitutes for Hegel's 'Spirit' something material, the quasi-biological conception of Blood or Race. Instead of 'Spirit', Blood is the self-developing essence; instead of 'Spirit', Blood is the Sovereign of the world, and displays itself on the Stage of History; and instead of its 'Spirit', the Blood of a nation determines its essential destiny.

The transubstantiation of Hegelianism into racialism or of Spirit into Blood does not greatly alter the main tendency of Hegelianism. It only gives it a tinge of biology and of modern evolutionism. The outcome is a materialistic and at the same time mystical religion of a self-developing biological essence, very closely reminiscent of the religion of creative evolution (whose prophet was the Hegelian[66] Bergson), a religion which G. B. Shaw, more prophetically than profoundly, once characterized as 'a faith which complied with the first condition of all religions that have ever taken hold of humanity: namely, that it must be … a *meta-biology*'. And indeed, this new religion of racialism clearly shows a *meta*-component and a *biology*-component, as it were, or Hegelian mystical metaphysics and Haeckelian materialist biology.

So much about the difference between modern totalitarianism and Hegelianism. In spite of its significance from the point of view of popularity, this difference is unimportant so far as their main political tendencies are concerned. But if we now turn to the similarities, then we get another picture. Nearly all the more important ideas of modern totalitarianism are directly inherited from Hegel, who collected and preserved what A. Zimmern calls[67] the 'armoury of weapons for authoritarian movements'. Although most of these weapons were not forged by Hegel himself, but discovered by him in the various ancient war treasuries of the perennial revolt against freedom, it is undoubtedly his effort which rediscovered them and placed them in the hands of his modern followers. Here is a brief list of some of the most precious of these ideas. (I omit Platonic totalitarianism and tribalism, which have already been discussed, as well as the theory of master and slave.)

(*a*) Nationalism, in the form of the historicist idea that the state is the incarnation of the Spirit (or now, of the Blood) of the state-creating nation (or race); one chosen nation (now, the chosen race) is destined for world domination. (*b*) The state as the natural enemy of all other states must assert its existence in war. (*c*) The state is exempt from any kind of moral obligation; history, that is, historical success, is the sole judge; collective utility is the sole principle of personal conduct; propagandist lying and distortion of the truth is permissible. (*d*) The 'ethical' idea of war (total and collectivist), particularly of young nations against older ones; war, fate and fame as most desirable goods. (*e*) The creative rôle of the Great Man, the world-historical personality, the man of deep knowledge and great passion (now, the principle of leadership). (*f*) The ideal of the heroic life ('live dangerously') and of the 'heroic man' as opposed to the petty bourgeois and his life of shallow mediocrity.

This list of spiritual treasures is neither systematic nor complete. All of them are part and parcel of an old patrimony. And they were stored up, and made ready for use, not only in the works of Hegel and his followers, but also in the minds of an intelligentsia fed exclusively for three long generations on such debased spiritual food, early recognized by Schopenhauer[68] as an 'intelligence-destroying pseudo-philosophy' and as a 'mischievous and criminal misuse of language'. I now proceed to a more detailed examination of the various points in this list.

(*a*) According to modern totalitarian doctrines, the state as such is not the highest end. This is, rather, the Blood, and the People, the Race. The higher races possess the power to create states. The highest aim of a race or nation is to form a mighty state which can serve as a powerful instrument of its self-preservation. This teaching (but for the substitution of Blood for Spirit) is due to Hegel, who wrote[69]: 'In the existence of a *Nation*, the substantial aim is to be a State and preserve itself as such. A Nation that has not formed itself into a State—*a mere Nation*—has strictly speaking no history, like the Nations … which existed in a condition of savagery. What happens to a Nation … has its essential significance in relation to the State.' The state which is thus formed is to be totalitarian, that is to say, its might must permeate and control the whole life of the people in all its functions: 'The

State is therefore the basis and centre of all the concrete elements in the life of a people: of Art, Law, Morals, Religion, and Science ... The substance that ... exists in that concrete reality which is the state, is the Spirit of the People itself. The actual State is animated by this Spirit in all its particular affairs, in its Wars, Institutions, etc.' Since the state must be powerful, it must contest the powers of other states. It must assert itself on the 'Stage of History', must prove its peculiar essence or Spirit and its 'strictly defined' national character by its historical deeds, and must ultimately aim at world domination. Here is an outline of this historicist essentialism in Hegel's words: 'The very essence of Spirit is activity; it actualizes its potentiality, and makes itself its own deed, its own work ... Thus it is with the Spirit of a Nation; it is a Spirit having strictly defined characteristics which exist and persist ... in the events and transitions that make up its history. That is its work—that is what this particular Nation *is*. Nations are what their deeds are ... A Nation is moral, virtuous, vigorous, as long as it is engaged in realizing its grand objects ... The constitutions under which World-Historical Peoples have reached their culminations are peculiar to them ... Therefore, from ... the political institutions of the ancient World-Historical Peoples, nothing can be learned ... Each particular National Genius is to be treated as only One Individual in the process of Universal History.' The Spirit or National Genius must finally prove itself in World-Domination: 'The self-consciousness of a particular Nation ... is the objective actuality in which the Spirit of the Time invests its Will. Against this absolute Will the other particular national minds have no rights: *that* Nation dominates the World ...'

But Hegel not only developed the historical and totalitarian theory of nationalism, he also clearly foresaw the psychological possibilities of nationalism. He saw that nationalism answers a need—the desire of men to find and to know their definite place in the world, and to belong to a powerful collective body. At the same time he exhibits that remarkable characteristic of German nationalism, its strongly developed feelings of inferiority (to use a more recent terminology), especially towards the English. And he consciously appeals, with his nationalism or tribalism, to those feelings which I have described (in chapter 10) as the *strain of civilization*: 'Every Englishman', Hegel writes[70], 'will say: We are the men who navigate the ocean, and who have the commerce of the world; to whom the East Indies belong and their riches ... The relation of the individual man to that Spirit is ... that it ... enables him to have a definite place in the world—to be *something*. For he finds in ... the people to which he belongs an already established, firm world ... with which he has to incorporate himself. In this its work, and therefore its world, the Spirit of the people enjoys its existence and finds satisfaction.'

(*b*) A theory common to both Hegel and his racialist followers is that the state by its very essence can exist only through its contrast to other individual states. H. Freyer, one of the leading sociologists of present-day Germany, writes[71]: 'A being that draws itself round its own core creates, even unintentionally, the boundary-line. And the frontier—even though it be unintentionally—creates the enemy.' Similarly Hegel: 'Just as the individual is not a real person unless related to other persons so the State is no real individuality unless related to other States ... The relation of one particular State to another presents ... the most shifting play of ... passions, interests, aims, talents, virtues, power, injustice, vice, and mere external chance. It is a play in which even the Ethical Whole, the Independence of the State, is exposed to accident.' Should we not, therefore, attempt to regulate this unfortunate state of affairs by adopting Kant's plans for the establishment of eternal peace by means of a federal union? Certainly not, says Hegel, commenting on Kant's plan for peace: 'Kant proposed an alliance of princes', Hegel says rather inexactly (for Kant proposed a federation of what we now call democratic states), 'which should settle the controversies of States; and the Holy Alliance probably aspired to be an institution of this kind. The State, however, is an individual; and in individuality, negation is essentially contained. A number of States may constitute themselves into a family, but this confederation, as an individuality, must create opposition and so beget an enemy.' For in Hegel's dialectics, negation equals limitation, and therefore means not only the boundary-line, the frontier, but also the creation of an opposition, of an enemy: 'The fortunes and deeds of States in their relation to one another reveal the dialectic of the finite nature of these Spirits.' These quotations are taken from the *Philosophy of Law*; yet in his earlier *Encyclopædia*, Hegel's theory anticipates the modern theories, for instance that of Freyer, even more closely: 'The final aspect of the State is to appear in immediate actuality as a single nation ... As a single individual it is exclusive of other like individuals. In their mutual relations, waywardness and chance have a place ... This independency ... reduces disputes between them to terms of mutual violence, to a *state of war* ... It is this state of war in which the omnipotence of the State manifests itself ...' Thus the Prussian historian Treitschke only shows how well he understands Hegelian dialectic essentialism when he repeats: 'War is not only a practical necessity, it is also a theoretical necessity, an exigency of logic. The concept of the State implies the concept of war, for the essence of the State is Power. The State is the People organized in sovereign Power.'

(*c*) The State *is* the Law, the moral law as well as the juridical law. Thus it cannot be subject to any other standard, and especially not to the yardstick of civil morality. Its historical responsibilities are deeper. Its only judge is the History of the World. The only possible standard of a judgement upon the state is the world historical *success* of its actions. And this success, the power and expansion of the state, must overrule all other considerations in the private life of the citizens; right is what serves the might of the state. This is the theory of Plato; it is the theory of modern totalitarianism; and it is the theory of Hegel: it is the Platonic-Prussian morality. 'The State', Hegel writes[72], 'is the realization of the ethical Idea. It is the ethical Spirit as revealed, self-conscious, substantial Will.' Consequently, there can be no ethical idea above the state. 'When the particular Wills of the States can come to no agreement, their controversy can be decided only by war. What offence shall be regarded as a breach of treaty, or as a violation of respect and honour, must remain indefinite ... The State may identify its infinitude and honour with every one of its aspects.' For '... the relation among States fluctuates, and no judge exists to adjust their differences.' In other words: 'Against the State there is no power to decide what is ... right ... States ... may enter into mutual agreements, but they are, at the same time, superior to these agreements' (i.e. they need not keep them)...'Treaties between states ... depend ultimately on the particular sovereign wills, and for that reason, they must remain unreliable.'

Thus only *one* kind of 'judgement' can be passed on World-Historical deeds and events: their result, their success. Hegel can therefore identify[73] 'the essential *destiny*—the absolute *aim*, or, what amounts to the same—the true *result* of the World's History'. To be successful, that is, to emerge as the strongest from the dialectical struggle of the different National Spirits for power, for world-domination, is thus the only and ultimate aim and the only basis of judgement; or as Hegel puts it more poetically: 'Out of this dialectic rises the universal Spirit, the unlimited World-Spirit, pronouncing its judgement—and its judgement is the highest—upon the finite Nations of the World's History; for the History of the World is the World's court of justice.'

Freyer has very similar ideas, but he expresses them more frankly[74]: 'A manly, a bold tone prevails in history. He who has the grip has the booty. He who makes a faulty move is done for ... he who wishes to hit his mark must know how to shoot.' But all these ideas are, in the last instance, only repetitions of Heraclitus: 'War ... proves some to be gods and others to be mere men, by turning the latter into slaves and the former into masters ... . War is just.' According to these theories, there can be no moral difference between a war in which we are attacked, and one in which we attack our neighbours; the only possible difference is success. F. Haiser, author of the book *Slavery: Its*

Biological Foundation and Moral Justification (1923), a prophet of a master race and of a master morality, argues: 'If we are to defend ourselves, then there must also be aggressors ...; if so, why then should we not be the aggressors ourselves?' But even this doctrine (its predecessor is Clausewitz's famous doctrine that an attack is always the most effective defence) is Hegelian; for Hegel, when speaking about offences that lead to war, not only shows the necessity for a 'war of defence' to turn into a 'war of conquest', but he informs us that some states which have a strong individuality 'will naturally be more inclined to irritability', in order to find an occasion and a field for what he euphemistically calls 'intense activity'.

With the establishment of historical success as the sole judge in matters relating to states or nations, and with the attempt to break down such moral distinctions as those between attack and defence, it becomes necessary to argue against the morality of conscience. Hegel does it by establishing what he calls 'true morality or rather social virtue' in opposition to 'false morality'. Needless to say, this 'true morality' is the Platonic totalitarian morality, combined with a dose of historicism, while the 'false morality' which he also describes as 'mere formal rectitude' is that of personal conscience. 'We may fairly', Hegel writes[75], 'establish the true principles of morality, or rather of social virtue, in opposition to false morality; for the History of the World occupies a higher ground than that morality which is personal in character—the conscience of individuals, their particular will and mode of action ... What the absolute aim of Spirit requires and accomplishes, what Providence does, transcends ... the imputation of good and bad motives ... Consequently it is only formal rectitude, deserted by the living Spirit and by God, which those who take their stand upon ancient right and order maintain.' (That is to say, the moralists who refer, for example, to the New Testament.) 'The deeds of Great Men, of the Personalities of World History, ... must not be brought into collision with irrelevant moral claims. *The Litany of private virtues, of modesty, humility, philanthropy, and forbearance*, must not be raised against them. The History of the World can, in principle, entirely ignore the circle within which morality ... lies.' Here, at last, we have the perversion of the third of the ideas of 1789, that of fraternity, or, as Hegel says, of philanthropy, together with the ethics of conscience. This Platonic-Hegelian historicist moral theory has been repeated over and over again. The famous historian E. Meyer, for example, speaks of the 'flat and moralizing evaluation, which judges great political undertakings with the yardstick of civil morality, ignoring the deeper, the truly moral factors of the State and of historical responsibilities'.

When such views are held, then all hesitation regarding propagandist lying and distortion of the truth must disappear, particularly if it is successful in furthering the power of the state. Hegel's approach to this problem, however, is rather subtle: 'A great mind has publicly raised the question', he writes[76], 'whether it is permissible to deceive the People. The answer is that the People will not permit themselves to be deceived concerning their substantial basis' (F. Haiser, the master moralist, says: 'no error is possible where the racial soul dictates') 'but it deceives *itself*', Hegel continues, 'about the way it knows this … Public opinion deserves therefore to be esteemed as much as to be despised … Thus to be independent of public opinion is the first condition of achieving anything great … And great achievements are certain to be subsequently recognized and accepted by public opinion …' In brief, it is always success that counts. If the lie was successful, then it was no lie, since the People were not deceived concerning their substantial basis.

(*d*) We have seen that the State, particularly in its relation to other states, is exempt from morality—it is a-moral. We may therefore expect to hear that war is not a moral evil, but morally neutral. However, Hegel's theory defies this expectation; it implies that war is good in itself. 'There is an ethical element in war', we read[77]. 'It is necessary to recognize that the Finite, such as property and life, is accidental. This necessity appears first under the form of a force of nature, for all things finite are mortal and transient. In the ethical order, in the State, however, … this necessity is exalted to a work of freedom, to an ethical law … War … now becomes an element … of … right … War has the deep meaning that by it the ethical health of a nation is preserved and their finite aims uprooted … War protects the people from the corruption which an everlasting peace would bring upon it. History shows phases which illustrate how successful wars have checked internal unrest … . These Nations, torn by internal strife, win peace at home as a result of war abroad.' This passage, taken from the *Philosophy of Law*, shows the influence of Plato's and Aristotle's teaching on the 'dangers of prosperity'; at the same time, the passage is a good instance of the identification of the moral with the healthy, of ethics with political hygiene, or of right with might; this leads directly, as will be seen, to the identification of virtue and vigour, as the following passage from Hegel's *Philosophy of History* shows. (It follows immediately after the passage already mentioned, dealing with nationalism as a means of getting over one's feelings of inferiority, and thereby suggests that even a war can be an appropriate means to that noble end.) At the same time, the modern theory of the virtuous aggressiveness of the young or have-not countries against the wicked old possessor countries is clearly implied. 'A Nation', Hegel writes, 'is moral, virtuous, vigorous while it is engaged in realizing its grand objects … But this having been attained, the activity displayed by the Spirit of the People … is no longer needed … The Nation can still accomplish much in war and peace … but the living substantial soul itself may be said to have ceased its activity … The Nation lives the same kind of life as the individual when passing from maturity to old age … This mere *customary life* (the watch wound up and going of itself) is that which brings on natural death … Thus perish individuals, thus perish peoples by a natural death … A people can only die a violent death when it has become naturally dead in itself.' (The last remarks belong to the decline-and-fall tradition.)

Hegel's ideas on war are surprisingly modern; he even visualizes the moral consequences of mechanization; or rather, he sees in mechanical warfare the consequences of the ethical Spirit of totalitarianism or collectivism[78]: 'There are different kinds of bravery. The courage of the animal, or the robber, the bravery that arises from a sense of honour, chivalrous bravery, are not yet the true forms of bravery. In civilized nations true bravery consists in the readiness to give oneself wholly to the service of the State so that the individual counts but as *one among many*.' (An allusion to universal conscription.) 'Not personal valour is significant; the important aspect lies in *self-subordination to the universal*. This higher form causes … bravery to appear more mechanical … Hostility is directed not against separate individuals, but against a hostile whole' (here we have an anticipation of the principle of *total war*); '… personal valour appears as impersonal. This principle has caused the invention of the gun; it is not a chance invention …' In a similar vein, Hegel says of the invention of gunpowder: 'Humanity needed it, and it made its appearance forthwith.' (How kind of Providence!)

It is thus purest Hegelianism when the philosopher E. Kaufmann, in 1911, argues against the Kantian ideal of a community of free men: 'Not a community of men of free will but a *victorious war* is the social ideal … it is in war that the State displays its true nature'[79]; or when E. Banse, the famous 'military scientist', writes in 1933: 'War means the highest intensification … of all spiritual energies of an age … it means the utmost effort of the people's Spiritual power … Spirit and Action linked together. Indeed, war provides the basis on which the human soul may manifest itself at its fullest height … Nowhere else can the Will … of the Race … rise into being thus integrally as in war.' And General Ludendorff continues in 1935: 'During the years of the so-called peace, politics … have only a meaning inasmuch as they prepare for total war.' He thus only formulates more precisely an idea voiced by the famous essentialist philosopher Max Scheler in 1915: 'War means the State in its most actual growth and rise: it means politics.' The same Hegelian doctrine is reformulated by Freyer in 1935: 'The State, from the first moment of its existence, takes its stand in the sphere of war … War is not only the most perfect form of State activity, it is the very element in which the State is embedded; war delayed, prevented, disguised, avoided, must of course be included in the term.' But the boldest conclusion is drawn by F. Lenz, who, in his book *The Race as the Principle of Value*, tentatively raises the question: 'But if humanity were to be the goal of morality, then have not *we*, after all, taken the wrong side?' and who, of course, immediately dispels this absurd suggestion by replying: 'Far be it from us to think that humanity should condemn war: nay, it is war that condemns humanity.' This idea is linked up with historicism by E. Jung, who remarks: 'Humanitarianism, or the idea of mankind ... is no regulator of history.' But it was Hegel's predecessor, Fichte, called by Schopenhauer the 'wind-bag', who must be credited with the original anti-humanitarian argument. Speaking of the word 'humanity', Fichte wrote: 'If one had presented, to the German, instead of the Roman word "*humaneness*" its proper translation, the word "*manhood*", then ... he would have said: "It is after all not so very much to be a man instead of a wild beast!" This is how a German would have spoken—in a manner which would have been impossible for a Roman. For in the German language, "manhood" has remained a merely phenomenal notion; it has never become a super-phenomenal idea, as it did among the Romans. Whoever might attempt to smuggle, cunningly, this alien Roman symbol' (viz., the word 'humaneness') 'into the language of the Germans, would thereby manifestly debase their ethical standards ...' Fichte's doctrine is repeated by Spengler, who writes: 'Manhood is either a zoological expression or an empty word'; and also by Rosenberg, who writes: 'Man's inner life became debased when ... an alien motive was impressed upon his mind: salvation, humanitarianism, and the culture of humanity.'

Kolnai, to whose book I am deeply indebted for a great deal of material to which I would otherwise have had no access, says[80] most strikingly: 'All of us ... who stand for ... rational, civilized methods of government and social organization, agree that war is in itself an evil ...' Adding that in the opinion of most of us (except the pacifists) it might become, under certain circumstances, a necessary evil, he continues: 'The nationalist attitude is different, though it need not imply a desire for perpetual or frequent warfare. It sees in a war a good rather than an evil, even if it be a dangerous good, like an exceedingly heady wine that is best reserved for rare occasions of high festivity.' War is not a common and abundant evil but a precious though rare good:—this sums up the views of Hegel and of his followers.

One of Hegel's feats was the revival of the Heraclitean idea of fate; and he insisted[81] that this glorious Greek idea of fate as expressive of the essence of a person, or of a nation, is opposed to the nominalist Jewish idea of universal laws, whether of nature, or of morals. The essentialist doctrine of fate can be derived (as shown in the last chapter) from the view that the essence of a nation can reveal itself only in its history. It is not 'fatalistic' in the sense that it encourages inactivity; 'destiny' is not to be identified with 'predestination'. The opposite is the case. Oneself, one's real essence, one's innermost soul, the stuff one is made of (will and passion rather than reason) are of decisive importance in the formation of one's fate. Since Hegel's amplification of this theory, the idea of fate or destiny has become a favourite obsession, as it were, of the revolt against freedom. Kolnai rightly stresses the connection between racialism (it is fate that makes one a member of one's race) and hostility to freedom: 'The principle of Race', Kolnai says[82], 'is meant to embody and express the utter negation of human freedom, the denial of equal rights, a challenge in the face of mankind.' And he rightly insists that racialism tends 'to oppose *Liberty* by *Fate*, individual consciousness by the compelling urge of the Blood beyond control and argument'. Even this tendency is expressed by Hegel, although as usual in a somewhat obscure manner: 'What we call *principle, aim, destiny*, or the nature or idea of Spirit', Hegel writes, 'is a hidden, undeveloped essence, which *as such*—however true in itself—is not completely real ... The motive power that ... gives them ... existence is the *need, instinct, inclination and passion* of men.' The modern philosopher of total education, E. Krieck, goes further in the direction of fatalism: 'All rational will and activity of the individual is confined to his everyday life; beyond this range he can only achieve a higher destiny and fulfilment in so far as he is gripped by superior powers of fate.' It sounds like personal experience when he continues: 'Not through his own rational scheming will he be made a creative and relevant being, only through forces that work above and beneath him, that do not originate in his own self but sweep and work their way through his self ...' (But it is an unwarranted generalization of the most intimate personal experiences when the same philosopher thinks that not only 'the epoch of "objective" or "free" science is ended', but also that of 'pure reason'.)

Together with the idea of fate, its counterpart, that of fame is also revived by Hegel: 'Individuals ... are *instruments* ... What they personally gain ... through the individual share they take in the substantial business (prepared and appointed independently of them) is ... *Fame*, which is their reward.'[83] And Stapel, a propagator of the new paganized Christianity, promptly repeats: 'All great deeds were done for the sake of fame or glory.' But this 'Christian' moralist is even more radical than Hegel: 'Metaphysical glory is the one true morality', he teaches, and the 'Categorical Imperative' of this one true morality runs accordingly: 'Do such deeds as spell glory!'

(*e*) Yet glory cannot be acquired by everybody; the religion of glory implies anti-equalitarianism—it implies a religion of 'Great Men'. Modern racialism accordingly 'knows no equality between souls, no equality between men'[84] (Rosenberg). Thus there are no obstacles to adopting the Leader Principle from the arsenal of the perennial revolt against freedom, or as Hegel calls it, the idea of the World Historical Personality. This Idea is one of Hegel's favourite themes. In discussing the blasphemous 'question whether it is permissible to deceive a people' (see above), he says: 'In public opinion all is false and true, but to discover the truth in it is the business of the Great Man. The Great Man of his time is *he who expresses the will of his time; who tells his time what it wills; and who carries it out*. He acts according to the inner Spirit and Essence of his time, which he realizes. And he who does not understand *how to despise public opinion*, as it makes itself heard here and there, will never accomplish anything great.' This excellent description of the Leader—the Great Dictator—as a publicist is combined with an elaborate myth of the Greatness of the Great Man, that consists in his being the foremost instrument of the Spirit in history. In this discussion of 'Historical Men—World Historical Individuals' Hegel says: 'They were practical, political men. But at the same time they were thinking men, who had an insight into the requirements of the time—into what was ripe for development ... World Historical Men—the Heroes of an epoch—must therefore be recognized as its clear-sighted ones; *their* deeds, *their* words are the best of that time ... It was they who best understood affairs; from whom others learned, and approved, or at least acquiesced in—their policy. For the Spirit which has taken this fresh step in History is the inmost soul of all individuals; but in a state of unconsciousness which aroused the Great Men ... Their fellows, therefore, follow those Soul-Leaders, for they feel the irresistible power of their own inner Spirit thus embodied.' But the Great Man is not only the man of greatest understanding and wisdom but also the Man of Great Passions—foremost, of course, of political passions and ambitions. He is thereby able to arouse passions in others. 'Great Men have formed purposes to satisfy themselves, not others ... They are Great Men because they willed and accomplished something great ... Nothing Great in the World has been accomplished without *passion* ... *This may be called the cunning of reason—that it sets the passions to work for itself* ... Passion, it is true, is not quite the suitable word for what I wish to express. I mean here nothing more than human activity as resulting from *private* interests—particular, or if you will, self-seeking designs—with the qualification that the whole energy of will and character is devoted to their attainment ... Passions, private aims, and the satisfaction of selfish desires are ... most effective springs of action. Their power lies in the fact that they respect none of the limitations which justice and morality would impose on them; and that these natural impulses have a more direct influence over their fellow-men than the artificial and tedious discipline that tends to order and self-restraint, law and morality.' From Rousseau onwards, the Romantic school of thought realized that man is not mainly rational. But while the humanitarians cling to rationality as an aim, the revolt against reason exploits this psychological insight into the irrationality of man for its political aims. The fascist appeal to 'human nature' is to our passions, to our collectivist mystical needs, to 'man the unknown'. Adopting Hegel's words just quoted, this appeal may be called the *cunning of the revolt against reason*. But the height of this cunning is reached by Hegel in this boldest dialectical twist of his. While paying lip-service to rationalism, while talking more loudly about 'reason' than any man before or after him, he ends up in irrationalism; in an apotheosis not only of passion, but of brutal force: 'It is', Hegel writes, 'the absolute interest of Reason that this Moral Whole' (i.e. the State) 'should exist; and herein lies the justification and merit of heroes, the founders of States—however cruel they may have been ... Such men may treat other great and even sacred interests inconsiderately ... But so mighty a form must trample down many an innocent flower; it must crush to pieces many an object on its path.'

(f) The conception of man as being not so much a rational as an heroic animal was not invented by the revolt against reason; it is a typical tribalist ideal. We have to distinguish between this ideal of the Heroic Man and a more reasonable respect for heroism. Heroism is, and always will be, admirable; but our admiration should depend, I think, very largely on our appreciation of the cause to which the hero has devoted himself. The heroic element in gangsterism, I think, deserves little appreciation. But we should admire Captain Scott and his party, and if possible even more, the heroes of X-ray or of Yellow Fever research; and certainly those who defend freedom.

The tribal ideal of the Heroic Man, especially in its fascist form, is based upon different views. It is a direct attack upon those things which make heroism admirable to most of us—such things as the furthering of civilization. For it is an attack on the idea of civil life itself; this is denounced as shallow and materialistic, because of the idea of security which it cherishes. *Live dangerously!* is its imperative; the cause for which you undertake to follow this imperative is of secondary importance; or as W. Best says[85]: 'Good fighting as such, not a "good cause" ... is the thing that turns the scale ... It merely matters *how*, not for what object we fight'. Again we find that this argument is an elaboration of Hegelian ideas: 'In peace', Hegel writes, 'civil life becomes more extended, every sphere is hedged in ... and at last all men stagnate ... From the pulpits much is preached concerning the insecurity, vanity, and instability of temporal things, and yet everyone ... thinks that he, at least, will manage to hold on to his possessions ... It is necessary to recognize ... property and life as accidental ... Let insecurity finally come in the form of Hussars with glistening sabres, and show its earnest activity!' In another place, Hegel paints a gloomy picture of what he calls 'mere customary life'; he seems to mean by it something like the normal life of a civilized community: 'Custom is activity without opposition ... in which fullness and zest is out of the question—a merely external and sensuous' (i.e. what some people in our day like to call 'materialist') 'existence which has ceased to throw itself enthusiastically into its object ... , an existence without intellect or vitality.' Hegel, always faithful to his historicism, bases his anti-utilitarian attitude (in distinction to Aristotle's utilitarian comments upon the 'dangers of prosperity') on his interpretation of history: 'The History of the World is no theatre of happiness. Periods of happiness are blank pages in it, for they are periods of harmony.' Thus, liberalism, freedom and reason are, as usual, objects of Hegel's attacks. The hysterical cries: We want our history! We want our destiny! We want our fight! We want our chains! resound through the edifice of Hegelianism, through this stronghold of the closed society and of the revolt against freedom.

In spite of Hegel's, as it were, official optimism, based on his theory that what is rational is real, there are features in him to which one can trace the *pessimism* which is so characteristic of the more intelligent among the modern racial philosophers; not so much, perhaps, of the earlier ones (as Lagarde, Treitschke, or Moeller van den Bruck) but of those who came after Spengler, the famous historicist. Neither Spengler's biological holism, intuitive understanding, Group-Spirit and Spirit of the Age, nor even his Romanticism, helps this fortune-teller to escape a very pessimistic outlook. An element of blank despair is unmistakable in the 'grim' activism that is left to those who foresee the future and feel instrumental in its arrival. It is interesting to observe that this gloomy view of affairs is equally shared by both wings of the racialists, the 'Atheist' as well as the 'Christian' wing.

Stapel, who belongs to the latter (but there are others, for example Gogarten), writes[86]: 'Man is under the sway of original sin in his totality ... The Christian knows that it is strictly impossible for him to live except in sin ... Therefore he steers clear of the pettiness of moral hair-splitting ... An ethicized Christianity is a counter-Christianity through and through ... God has made this world perishable, it is doomed to destruction. May it, then, go to the dogs according to destiny! Men who imagine themselves capable of making it better, who want to create a "higher" morality, are starting a ridiculous petty revolt against God ... The hope of Heaven does not mean the expectation of a happiness of the blessed; it means obedience and War-Comradeship.' (The return to the tribe.) 'If God orders His man to go to hell, then his sworn adherent ... will accordingly go to hell ... If He allots to him eternal pain, this has to be borne too ... Faith is but another word for victory. It is victory that the Lord demands ...'

A very similar spirit lives in the work of the two leading philosophers of contemporary Germany, the 'existentialists' Heidegger and Jaspers, both originally followers of the essentialist philosophers Husserl and Scheler. Heidegger has gained fame by reviving the Hegelian *Philosophy of Nothingness*: Hegel had 'established' the theory[87] that 'Pure Being' and 'Pure Nothingness' are identical; he had said that if you try to think out the notion of a *pure* being, you must abstract from it all particular 'determinations of an object', and therefore, as Hegel puts it—'nothing remains'. (This Heraclitean method might be used for proving all kinds of pretty identities, such as that of pure wealth and pure poverty, pure mastership and pure servitude, pure Aryanism and pure Judaism.) Heidegger ingeniously applies the Hegelian theory of Nothingness to a practical Philosophy of Life, or of 'Existence'. Life, Existence, can be understood only by understanding Nothingness. In his *What is Metaphysics?* Heidegger says: 'The enquiry should be into the Existing or else into—nothing; ... into the existing alone, and beyond it into—*Nothingness*.' The enquiry into nothingness ('Where do we search for Nothingness? Where can we find Nothingness?') is made possible by the fact that 'we know Nothingness'; we know it through fear: 'Fear reveals Nothingness.'

Fear; the fear of nothingness; the anguish of death; these are the basic categories of Heidegger's Philosophy of Existence; of a life whose true meaning it is[88] 'to be cast down into existence, directed towards death'. Human existence is to be interpreted as a 'Thunderstorm of Steel'; the 'determined existence' of a man is 'to be a self, passionately free to die ... in full self-consciousness and anguish'. But these gloomy confessions are not entirely without their comforting aspect. The reader need not be quite overwhelmed by Heidegger's passion to die. For the will to power and the will to live appear to be no less developed in him than in his master, Hegel. 'The German University's Will to the Essence', Heidegger writes in 1933, 'is a Will to Science; it is a Will to the historico-spiritual mission of the German Nation, as a Nation experiencing itself in its State. Science and German Destiny must attain Power, especially in the essential Will.' This passage, though not a monument of originality or clarity, is certainly one of loyalty to his masters; and those admirers of Heidegger who in spite of all this continue to believe in the profundity of his 'Philosophy of Existence' might be reminded of Schopenhauer's words: 'Who can really believe that truth also will come to light, just as a by-product?' And in view of the last of Heidegger's quotations, they should ask themselves whether Schopenhauer's advice to a dishonest guardian has not been successfully administered by many educationists to many promising youths, inside and outside of Germany. I have in mind the passage: 'Should you ever intend to dull the wits of a young man and to incapacitate his brains for any kind of thought whatever, then you cannot do better than give him Hegel to read. For these monstrous accumulations of words that annul and contradict one another drive the mind into tormenting itself with vain attempts to think anything whatever in connection with them, until finally it collapses from sheer exhaustion. Thus any ability to think is so thoroughly destroyed that the young man will ultimately mistake empty and hollow verbiage for real thought. A guardian fearing that his ward might become too intelligent for his schemes might prevent this misfortune by innocently suggesting the reading of Hegel.'

Jaspers declares[89] his nihilist tendencies more frankly even, if that is possible, than Heidegger. Only when you are faced with Nothingness, with annihilation, Jaspers teaches, will you be able to experience and appreciate Existence. In order to live in the essential sense, one must live in a crisis. In order to taste life one has not only to risk, but to lose!—Jaspers carries the historicist idea of change and destiny recklessly to its most gloomy extreme. All things must perish; everything ends in failure: in this way does the historicist law of development present itself to his disillusioned intellect. But face destruction—and you will get the thrill of your life! Only in the 'marginal situations', on the edge between existence and nothingness, do we really live. The bliss of life always coincides with the end of its intelligibility, particularly with extreme situations of the body, above all with bodily danger. You cannot taste life without tasting failure. Enjoy yourself perishing!

This is the philosophy of the gambler—of the gangster. Needless to say, this demoniac 'religion of Urge and Fear, of the Triumphant or else the Hunted Beast' (Kolnai[90]), this absolute nihilism in the fullest sense of the word, is not a popular creed. It is a confession characteristic of an esoteric group of intellectuals who have surrendered their reason, and with it, their humanity.

There is another Germany, that of the ordinary people whose brains have not been poisoned by a devastating system of higher education. But this 'other' Germany is certainly not that of her thinkers. It is true, Germany had also some 'other' thinkers (foremost among them, Kant); however, the survey just finished is not encouraging, and I fully sympathize with Kolnai's remark[91]: 'Perhaps it is not … a paradox to solace our despair at German culture with the consideration that, after all, there is another Germany of Prussian Generals besides the Germany of Prussian Thinkers.'

VI

I have tried to show the identity of Hegelian historicism with the philosophy of modern totalitarianism. This identity is seldom clearly enough realized. Hegelian historicism has become the language of wide circles of intellectuals, even of candid 'anti-fascists' and 'leftists'. It is so much a part of their intellectual atmosphere that, for many, it is no more noticeable, and its appalling dishonesty no more remarkable, than the air they breathe. Yet some racial philosophers are fully conscious of their indebtedness to Hegel. An example is H. O. Ziegler, who in his study, *The Modern Nation*, rightly describes[92] the introduction of Hegel's (and A. Mueller's) idea of 'collective Spirits conceived as Personalities', as the 'Copernican revolution in the Philosophy of the Nation'. Another illustration of this awareness of the significance of Hegelianism, which might specially interest British readers, can be found in the judgements passed in a recent German history of British philosophy (by R. Metz, 1935). A man of the excellence of T. H. Green is here criticized, not of course because he was influenced by Hegel, but because he 'fell back into the typical individualism of the English … He shrank from such radical consequences as Hegel has drawn'. Hobhouse, who fought bravely against Hegelianism, is contemptuously described as representing 'a typical form of bourgeois liberalism, defending itself against the omnipotence of the State because it feels its freedom threatened thereby'—a feeling which to some people might appear well founded. Bosanquet of course is praised for his genuine Hegelianism. But the significant fact is that this is all taken perfectly seriously by most of the British reviewers.

I mention this fact mainly because I wish to show how difficult and, at the same time, how urgent it is to continue Schopenhauer's fight against this shallow cant (which Hegel himself accurately fathomed when describing his own philosophy as of 'the most lofty depth'). At least the new generation should be helped to free themselves from this intellectual fraud, the greatest, perhaps, in the history of our civilization and its quarrels with its enemies. Perhaps they will live up to the expectations of Schopenhauer, who in 1840 prophesied[93] that 'this colossal mystification will furnish posterity with an inexhaustible source of sarcasm'. (So far the great pessimist has proved a wild optimist concerning posterity.) The Hegelian farce has done enough harm. We must stop it. We must speak—even at the price of soiling ourselves by touching this scandalous thing which, unfortunately without success, was so clearly exposed a hundred years ago. Too many philosophers have neglected Schopenhauer's incessantly repeated warnings; they neglected them not so much at their own peril (they did not fare badly) as at the peril of those whom they taught, and at the peril of mankind.

It seems to me a fitting conclusion to this chapter if I leave the last word to Schopenhauer, the anti-nationalist who said of Hegel a hundred years ago: 'He exerted, not on philosophy alone but on all forms of German literature, a devastating, or more strictly speaking, a stupefying, one could also say, a pestiferous, influence. To combat this influence forcefully and on every occasion is the duty of everybody who is able to judge independently. *For if we are silent, who will speak?*'

Marx's Method

13

MARX'S SOCIOLOGICAL DETERMINISM

> The collectivists ... have the zest for progress, the sympathy for the poor, the burning sense of wrong, the impulse for great deeds, which have been lacking in latter-day liberalism. But their science is founded on a profound misunderstanding ... , and their actions, therefore, are deeply destructive and reactionary. So men's hearts are torn, their minds divided, they are offered impossible choices.
>
> WALTER LIPPMANN.

It has always been the strategy of the revolt against freedom 'to take advantage of sentiments, not wasting one's energies in futile efforts to destroy them'[1]. The most cherished ideas of the humanitarians were often loudly acclaimed by their deadliest enemies, who in this way penetrated into the humanitarian camp under the guise of allies, causing disunion and thorough confusion. This strategy has often been highly successful, as is shown by the fact that many genuine humanitarians still revere Plato's idea of 'justice', the medieval idea of 'Christian' authoritarianism, Rousseau's idea of the 'general will', or Fichte's and Hegel's ideas of 'national freedom'.[2] Yet this method of penetrating dividing and confusing the humanitarian camp and of building up a largely unwitting and therefore doubly effective intellectual fifth column achieved its greatest success only after Hegelianism had established itself as the basis of a truly humanitarian movement: of Marxism, so far the purest, the most developed and the most dangerous form of historicism.

It is tempting to dwell upon the similarities between Marxism, the Hegelian left-wing, and its fascist counterpart. Yet it would be utterly unfair to overlook the difference between them. Although their intellectual origin is nearly identical, there can be no doubt of the humanitarian impulse of Marxism. Moreover, in contrast to the Hegelians of the right-wing, Marx made an honest attempt to apply rational methods to the most urgent problems of social life. The value of this attempt is unimpaired by the fact that it was, as I shall try to show, largely unsuccessful. Science progresses through trial *and* error. Marx tried, and although he erred in his main doctrines, he did not try in vain. He opened and sharpened our eyes in many ways. A return to pre-Marxian social science is inconceivable. All modern writers are indebted to Marx, even if they do not know it. This is especially true of those who disagree with his doctrines, as I do; and I readily admit that my treatment, for example of Plato[3] and Hegel, bears the stamp of his influence.

One cannot do justice to Marx without recognizing his sincerity. His open-mindedness, his sense of facts, his distrust of verbiage, and especially of moralizing verbiage, made him one of the world's most influential fighters against hypocrisy and pharisaism. He had a burning desire to help the oppressed, and was fully conscious of the need for proving himself in deeds, and not only in words. His main talents being theoretical, he devoted immense labour to forging what he believed to be scientific weapons for the fight to improve the lot of the vast majority of men. His sincerity in his search for truth and his intellectual honesty distinguish him, I believe, from many of his followers (although unfortunately he did not altogether escape the corrupting influence of an upbringing in the atmosphere of Hegelian dialectics, described by Schopenhauer as 'destructive of all intelligence'[4]). Marx's interest in social science and social philosophy was fundamentally a practical interest. He saw in knowledge a means of promoting the progress of man[5].

Why, then, attack Marx? In spite of his merits, Marx was, I believe, a false prophet. He was a prophet of the course of history, and his prophecies did not come true; but this is not my main accusation. It is much more important that he misled scores of intelligent people into believing that historical prophecy is the scientific way of approaching social problems. Marx is responsible for the devastating influence of the historicist method of thought within the ranks of those who wish to advance the cause of the open society.

But is it true that Marxism is a pure brand of historicism? Are there not some elements of social technology in Marxism? The fact that Russia is making bold and often successful experiments in social engineering has led many to infer that Marxism, as the science or creed which underlies the Russian experiment, must be a kind of social technology, or at least favourable to it. But nobody who knows anything about the history of Marxism can make this mistake. Marxism is a purely historical theory, a theory which aims at predicting the future course of economic and power-political developments and especially of revolutions. As such, it certainly did not furnish the basis of the policy of the Russian Communist Party after its rise to political power. Since Marx had practically forbidden all social technology, which he denounced as Utopian[6], his Russian disciples found themselves at first entirely unprepared for their great tasks in the field of social engineering. As Lenin was quick to realize, Marxism was unable to help in matters of practical economics. 'I do not know of any socialist who has dealt with these problems', said Lenin[7], after his rise to power; 'there was nothing written about such matters in the Bolshevik textbooks, or in those of the Mensheviks.' After a period of unsuccessful experiment, the so-called 'period of war-communism', Lenin decided to adopt measures which meant in fact a limited and temporary return to private enterprise. This so-called NEP (New Economic Policy) and the later experiments—five-year plans, etc.—have nothing whatever to do with the theories of 'Scientific Socialism' once propounded by Marx and Engels. Neither the peculiar situation in which Lenin found himself before he introduced the NEP, nor his achievements, can be appreciated without due consideration of this point. The vast economic researches of Marx did not even touch the problems of a constructive economic policy, for example, economic planning. As Lenin admits, *there is hardly a word on the economics of socialism to be found in Marx's work*—apart from such useless[8] slogans as 'from each according to his ability, to each according to his needs'. The reason is that the economic research of Marx is completely subservient to his historical prophecy. But we must say even more. Marx strongly emphasized the opposition between his purely historicist method and any attempt to make an economic analysis with a view to rational planning. Such attempts he denounced as Utopian, and as illegitimate. In consequence, Marxists did not even study what the so-called 'bourgeois economists' attained in this field. They were by their training even less prepared for constructive work than some of the 'bourgeois economists' themselves.

Marx saw his specific mission in the freeing of socialism from its sentimental, moralist, and visionary background. Socialism was to be developed from its Utopian stage to its scientific stage[9]; it was to be based upon the scientific method of analysing cause and effect, and upon scientific prediction. And since he assumed prediction in the field of society to be the same as historical prophecy, scientific socialism was to be based upon a study of historical causes and historical effects, and finally upon the prophecy of its own advent.

Marxists, when they find their theories attacked, often withdraw to the position that Marxism is primarily not so much a doctrine as a method. They say that even if some particular part of the doctrines of Marx, or of some of his followers, were superseded, his method would still remain unassailable. I believe that it is quite correct to insist that Marxism is, fundamentally, a method. But it is wrong to believe that, as a method, it must be secure from attacks. The position is, simply, that whoever wishes to judge Marxism has to probe it and to criticize it as a method, that is to say, he must measure it by methodological standards. He must ask whether it is a fruitful method or a poor one, i.e. whether or not it is capable of furthering the task of science. The standards by which we must judge the Marxist method are thus of a practical nature. By describing Marxism as purest historicism, I have indicated that I hold the Marxist method to be very poor indeed[10].

Marx himself would have agreed with such a practical approach to the criticism of his method, for he was one of the first philosophers to develop the views which later were called 'pragmatism'. He was led to this position, I believe, by his conviction that a scientific background was urgently needed by the practical politician, which of course meant the socialist politician. Science, he taught, should yield practical results. Always look at the fruits, the practical consequences of a theory! They tell something even of its scientific structure. A philosophy or a science that does not yield practical results merely interprets the world we live in; but it can and it should do more; it should change the world. 'The philosophers', wrote Marx[11] early in his career, 'have only interpreted the world in various ways; the point however is to change it.' It was perhaps this pragmatic attitude that made him anticipate the important methodological doctrine of the later pragmatists that the most characteristic task of science is not to gain knowledge of past facts, but to predict the future.

This stress on scientific prediction, in itself an important and progressive methodological discovery, unfortunately led Marx astray. For the plausible argument that science can predict the future only if the future is predetermined—if, as it were, the future is present in the past, telescoped in it—led him to adhere to the false belief that a rigidly scientific method must be based on a rigid determinism. Marx's 'inexorable laws' of nature and of historical development show clearly the influence of the Laplacean atmosphere and that of the French Materialists. But the belief that the terms 'scientific' and 'determinist' are, if not synonymous, at least inseparably connected, can now be said to be one of the superstitions of a time that has not yet entirely passed away[12]. Since I am interested mainly in questions of method, I am glad that, when discussing its methodological aspect, it is quite unnecessary to enter into a dispute concerning the metaphysical problem of determinism. For whatever may be the outcome of such metaphysical controversies as, for example, the bearing of the Quantum theory on 'free-will', one thing, I should say, is settled. No kind of determinism, whether it be expressed as the principle of the uniformity of nature or as the law of universal causation, can be considered any longer a necessary assumption of scientific method; for physics, the most advanced of all sciences, has shown not only that it can do without such assumptions, but also that to some extent it contradicts them. Determinism is not a necessary pre-requisite of a science which can make predictions. Scientific method cannot, therefore, be said to favour the adoption of strict determinism. Science can be rigidly scientific without this assumption. Marx, of course, cannot be blamed for having held the opposite view, since the best scientists of his day did the same.

It must be noted that it is not so much the abstract, theoretical doctrine of determinism which led Marx astray, but rather the practical influence of this doctrine upon his view of scientific method, upon his view of the aims and possibilities of a social science. The abstract idea of 'causes' which 'determine' social developments is as such quite harmless as long as it does not lead to historicism. And indeed, there is no reason whatever why this idea should lead us to adopt a historicist attitude towards social institutions, *in strange contrast to the obviously technological attitude taken up by everybody, and especially by determinists, towards mechanical or electrical machinery*. There is no reason why we should believe that, of all sciences, social science is capable of realizing the age-old dream of revealing what the future has in store for us. This belief in scientific fortune-telling is not founded on determinism alone; its other foundation is the confusion between *scientific prediction*, as we know it from physics or astronomy, and *large-scale historical prophecy*, which foretells in broad lines the main tendencies of the future development of society. These two kinds of prediction are very different (as I have tried to show elsewhere[13]), and the scientific character of the first is no argument in favour of the scientific character of the second.

Marx's historicist view of the aims of social science greatly upset the pragmatism which had originally led him to stress the predictive function of science. It forced him to modify his earlier view that science should, and that it could, change the world. For if there was to be a social science, and accordingly, historical prophecy, the main course of history must be predetermined, and neither good-will nor reason had power to alter it. All that was left to us in the way of reasonable interference was to make sure, by historical prophecy, of the impending course of development, and to remove the worst obstacles in its path. 'When a society has discovered',

Marx writes in *Capital*[14], 'the natural law that determines its own movement, ... even then it can neither overleap the natural phases of its evolution, nor shuffle them out of the world by a stroke of the pen. But this much it can do; it can shorten and lessen its birth-pangs.' These are the views that led Marx to denounce as 'Utopianists' all who looked upon social institutions with the eyes of the social engineer, holding them to be amenable to human reason and will, and to be a possible field of rational planning. These 'Utopianists' appeared to him to attempt with fragile human hands to steer the colossal ship of society against the natural currents and storms of history. All a scientist could do, he thought, was to forecast the gusts and vortices ahead. The practical service he could achieve would thus be confined to issuing a warning against the next storm that threatened to take the ship off the right course (the right course was of course the left!) or to advising the passengers as to the side of the boat on which they had better assemble. Marx saw the real task of scientific socialism in the annunciation of the impending socialist millennium. Only by way of this annunciation, he holds, can scientific socialist teaching contribute to bringing about a socialist world, whose coming it can further by making men conscious of the impending change, and of the parts allotted to them in the play of history. Thus scientific socialism is not a social technology; it does not teach the ways and means of constructing socialist institutions. Marx's views of the relation between socialist theory and practice show the purity of his historicist views.

Marx's thought was in many respects a product of his time, when the remembrance of that great historical earthquake, the French Revolution, was still fresh. (It was revived by the revolution of 1848.) Such a revolution could not, he felt, be planned and staged by human reason. But it could have been foreseen by a historicist social science; sufficient insight into the social situation would have revealed its causes. That this historicist attitude was rather typical of the period can be seen from the close similarity between the historicism of Marx and that of J.S. Mill. (It is analogous to the similarity between the historicist philosophies of their predecessors, Hegel and Comte.) Marx did not think very highly of 'bourgeois economists such as ... J.S. Mill'[15] whom he viewed as a typical representative of 'an insipid, brainless syncretism'. Although it is true that in some places Marx shows a certain respect for the 'modern tendencies' of the 'philanthropic economist' Mill, it seems to me that there is ample circumstantial evidence against the conjecture that Marx was directly influenced by Mill's (or rather by Comte's) views on the methods of social science. The agreement between the views of Marx and of Mill is therefore the more striking. Thus when Marx says in the preface to *Capital*, 'It is the ultimate aim of this work to lay bare the ... law of motion of modern society'[16], he might be said to carry out Mill's programme: 'The fundamental problem ... of the social science, is to find the law according to which any state of society produces the state which succeeds it and takes its place.' Mill distinguished fairly clearly the possibility of what he called 'two kinds of sociological inquiry', the first closely corresponding to what I call social technology, the second corresponding to historicist prophecy, and he took sides with the latter, characterizing it as the 'general Science of Society by which the conclusions of the other and more special kind of inquiry must be limited and controlled'. This general science of society is based upon the principle of causality, in accordance with Mill's view of scientific method; and he describes this causal analysis of society as the 'Historical Method'. Mill's 'states of society'[17] with 'properties ... changeable ... from age to age' correspond exactly to Marxist 'historical periods', and Mill's optimistic belief in progress resembles Marx's, although it is of course much more naïve than its dialectical counterpart. (Mill thought that the type of movement 'to which human affairs must conform ... must be ... one or the other' of two possible astronomical movements, viz., 'an orbit' or 'a trajectory'. Marxist dialectics is less certain of the simplicity of the laws of historical development; it adopts a combination, as it were, of Mill's two movements—something like a wave or a corkscrew movement.)

There are more similarities between Marx and Mill; for example, both were dissatisfied with *laissez-faire* liberalism, and both tried to provide better foundations for carrying into practice the fundamental idea of liberty. But in their views on the method of sociology, there is one very important difference. Mill believed that the study of society, in the last analysis, must be reducible to psychology; that the laws of historical development must be explicable in terms of *human nature*, of the 'laws of the mind', and in particular, of its progressiveness. 'The progressiveness of the human race', says Mill, 'is the foundation on which a method of ... social science has been ... erected, far superior to ... the modes ... previously ... prevalent ...'[18] The theory that sociology must in principle be reducible to social psychology, difficult though the reduction may be because of the complications arising from the interaction of countless individuals, has been widely held by many thinkers; indeed, it is one of the theories which are often simply taken for granted. I shall call this approach to sociology (methodological) *psychologism*[19]. Mill, we can now say, believed in psychologism. But Marx challenged it. 'Legal relationships', he asserted[20], 'and the various political structures cannot ... be explained by ... what has been called the general "progressiveness of the human mind".' To have questioned psychologism is perhaps the greatest achievement of Marx as a sociologist. By doing so he opened the way to the more penetrating conception of a specific realm of sociological laws, and of a sociology which was at least partly autonomous.

In the following chapters, I shall explain some points of Marx's method, and I shall try always to emphasize especially such of his views as I believe to be of lasting merit. Thus I shall deal next with Marx's attack on psychologism, i.e. with his arguments in favour of an autonomous social science, irreducible to psychology. And only later shall I attempt to show the fatal weakness and the destructive consequences of his historicism.

14

THE AUTONOMY OF SOCIOLOGY

A concise formulation of Marx's opposition to psychologism[1], i.e. to the plausible doctrine that all laws of social life must be ultimately reducible to the psychological laws of 'human nature', is his famous epigram: 'It is not the consciousness of man that determines his existence—rather, it is his social existence that determines his consciousness.'[2] The function of the present chapter as well as of the two following ones is mainly to elucidate this epigram. And I may state at once that in developing what I believe to be Marx's anti-psychologism, I am developing a view to which I subscribe myself.

As an elementary illustration, and a first step in our examination, we may refer to the problem of the so-called rules of exogamy, i.e. the problem of explaining the wide distribution, among the most diverse cultures, of marriage laws apparently designed to prevent inbreeding. Mill and his psychologistic school of sociology (it was joined later by many psycho-analysts) would try to explain these rules by an appeal to 'human nature', for instance to some sort of instinctive aversion against incest (developed perhaps through natural selection, or else through 'repression'); and something like this would also be the naïve or popular explanation. Adopting the point of view expressed in Marx's epigram, however, one could ask whether it is not the other way round, that is to say, whether the apparent instinct is not rather a product of education, the effect rather than the cause of the social rules and traditions demanding exogamy and forbidding incest[3]. It is clear that these two approaches correspond exactly to the very ancient problem whether social laws are 'natural' or 'conventional' (dealt with at length in chapter 5). In a question such as the one chosen here as an illustration, it would be difficult to determine which of the two theories is the correct one, the explanation of the traditional social rules by instinct or the explanation of an apparent instinct by traditional social rules. The possibility of deciding such questions by experiment has, however, been shown in a similar case, that of the apparently instinctive aversion to snakes. This aversion has a greater semblance of being instinctive or 'natural' in that it is exhibited not only by men but also by all anthropoid apes and by most monkeys as well. But experiments seem to indicate that this fear is conventional. It appears to be a product of education, not only in the human race but also for instance in chimpanzees, since[4] both young children and young chimpanzees who have not been taught to fear snakes do not exhibit the alleged instinct. This example should be taken as a warning. We are faced here with an aversion which is apparently universal, even beyond the human race. But although from the fact that a habit is not universal we might perhaps argue against its being based on an instinct (but even this argument is dangerous since there are social customs enforcing the suppression of instincts), we see that the converse is certainly not true. The universal occurrence of a certain behaviour is not a decisive argument in favour of its instinctive character, or of its being rooted in 'human nature'.

Such considerations may show how naïve it is to assume that all social laws must be derivable, in principle, from the psychology of 'human nature'. But this analysis is still rather crude. In order to proceed one step further, we may try to analyse more directly the main thesis of psychologism, the doctrine that, society being the product of interacting minds, social laws must ultimately be reducible to psychological laws, since the events of social life, including its conventions, must be the outcome of motives springing from the minds of individual men.

Against this doctrine of psychologism, the defenders of an autonomous sociology can advance *institutionalist* views[5]. They can point out, first of all, that no action can ever be explained by motive alone; if motives (or any other psychological or behaviourist concepts) are to be used in the explanation, then they must be supplemented by a reference to the general situation, and especially to the environment. In the case of human actions, this environment is very largely of a social nature; thus our actions cannot be explained without reference to our social environment, to social institutions and to their manner of functioning. It is therefore impossible, the institutionalist may contend, to reduce sociology to a psychological or behaviouristic analysis of our actions; rather, every such analysis presupposes sociology, which therefore cannot wholly depend on psychological analysis. Sociology, or at least a very important part of it, must be autonomous.

Against this view, the followers of psychologism may retort that they are quite ready to admit the great importance of environmental factors, whether natural or social; but the structure (they may prefer the fashionable word 'pattern') of the social environment, as opposed to the natural environment, is man-made; and therefore it must be explicable in terms of human nature, in accordance with the doctrine of psychologism. For instance, the characteristic institution which economists call 'the market', and whose functioning is the main object of their studies, can be derived in the last analysis from the psychology of 'economic man', or, to use Mill's phraseology, from the psychological 'phenomena … of the pursuit of wealth'[6]. Moreover, the followers of psychologism insist that it is because of the peculiar psychological structure of human nature that institutions play such an important rôle in our society, and that, once established, they show a tendency to become a traditional and a comparatively fixed part of our environment. Finally—and this is their decisive point—the *origin as well as the development* of traditions must be explicable in terms of human nature. When tracing back traditions and institutions to their origin, we must find that their introduction is explicable in psychological terms, since they have been introduced by man for some purpose or other, and under the influence of certain motives. And even if these motives have been forgotten in the course of time, then that forgetfulness, as well as our readiness to put up with institutions whose purpose is obscure, is in its turn based on human nature. Thus 'all phenomena of society are phenomena of human nature'[7], as Mill said; and 'the Laws of the phenomena of society are, and can be, nothing but the laws of the actions and passions of human beings', that is to say, 'the laws of individual human nature. Men are not, when brought together, converted into another kind of substance …'[8]

This last remark of Mill's exhibits one of the most praiseworthy aspects of psychologism, namely, its sane opposition to collectivism and holism, its refusal to be impressed by Rousseau's or Hegel's romanticism—by a general will or a national spirit, or perhaps, by a group mind. Psychologism is, I believe, correct only in so far as it insists upon what may be called 'methodological individualism' as opposed to 'methodological collectivism'; it rightly insists that the 'behaviour' and the 'actions' of collectives, such as states or social groups, must be reduced to the behaviour and to the actions of human individuals. But the belief that the choice of such an individualistic method implies the choice of a psychological method is mistaken (as will be shown below in this chapter), even though it may appear very convincing at first sight. And that psychologism as such moves on rather dangerous ground, apart from its commendable individualistic method, can be seen from some further passages of Mill's argument. For they show that *psychologism is forced to adopt historicist methods*. The attempt to reduce the facts of our social environment to psychological facts forces us into speculations about origins and developments. When analysing Plato's sociology, we had an opportunity of gauging the dubious merits of such an approach to social science (compare chapter 5). In criticizing Mill, we shall now try to deal it a decisive blow.

It is undoubtedly Mill's psychologism which forces him to adopt a historicist method; and he is even vaguely aware of the barrenness or poverty of historicism, since he tries to account for this barrenness by pointing out the difficulties arising from the tremendous complexity of the interaction of so many individual minds. 'While it is ... imperative', he says, '... never to introduce any generalization ... into the social sciences until sufficient grounds can be pointed out in human nature, I do not think any one will contend that it would have been possible, setting out from the principle of human nature and from the general circumstances of the position of our species, to determine *a priori* the order in which human development must take place, and to predict, consequently, the general facts of history up to the present time.'[9] The reason he gives is that 'after the first few terms of the series, the influence exercised over each generation by the generations which preceded it becomes ... more and more preponderant over all other influences'. (In other words, the social environment becomes a dominant influence.) 'So long a series of actions and reactions ... could not possibly be computed by human faculties ...'

This argument, and especially Mill's remark on 'the first few terms of the series', are a striking revelation of the weakness of the psychologistic version of historicism. If all regularities in social life, the laws of our social environment, of all institutions, etc., are ultimately to be explained by, and reduced to, the 'actions and passions of human beings', then such an approach forces upon us not only the idea of historico-causal development, but also the idea of the *first steps* of such a development. For the stress on the psychological origin of social rules or institutions can only mean that they can be traced back to a state when their introduction was dependent solely upon psychological factors, or more precisely, when it was independent of any established social institutions. Psychologism is thus forced, whether it likes it or not, to operate with the idea of a *beginning of society*, and with the idea of a human nature and a human psychology as they existed prior to society. In other words, Mill's remark concerning the 'first few terms of the series' of social development is not an accidental slip, as one might perhaps believe, but the appropriate expression of the desperate position forced upon him.

It is a desperate position because this theory of a pre-social human nature which explains the foundation of society—a psychologistic version of the 'social contract'—is not only an historical myth, but also, as it were, a methodological myth. It can hardly be seriously discussed, for we have every reason to believe that man or rather his ancestor was social prior to being human (considering, for example, that language presupposes society). But this implies that social institutions, and with them, typical social regularities or sociological laws[10], must have existed prior to what some people are pleased to call 'human nature', and to human psychology. If a reduction is to be attempted at all, it would therefore be more hopeful to attempt a reduction or interpretation of psychology in terms of sociology than the other way round.

This brings us back to Marx's epigram at the beginning of this chapter. Men—i.e. human minds, the needs, the hopes, fears, and expectations, the motives and aspirations of human individuals—are, if anything, the product of life in society rather than its creators. It must be admitted that the structure of our social environment is man-made in a certain sense; that its institutions and traditions are neither the work of God nor of nature, but the results of human actions and decisions, and alterable by human actions and decisions. But this does not mean that they are all consciously designed, and explicable in terms of needs, hopes, or motives. On the contrary, even those which arise as the result of conscious and intentional human actions are, as a rule, *the indirect, the unintended and often the unwanted by-products of such actions*. 'Only a minority of social institutions are consciously designed, while the vast majority have just "grown", as the undesigned results of human actions', as I have said before[11]; and we can add that even most of the few institutions which were consciously and successfully designed (say, a newly founded University, or a trade union) do not turn out according to plan—again because of the unintended social repercussions resulting from their intentional creation. For their creation affects not only many other social institutions but also 'human nature'—hopes, fears, and ambitions, first of those more immediately involved, and later often of all members of the society. One of the consequences of this is that the moral values of a society—the demands and proposals recognized by all, or by very nearly all, of its members—are closely bound up with its institutions and traditions, and that they cannot survive the destruction of the institutions and traditions of a society (as indicated in chapter 9 when we discussed the 'canvas-cleaning' of the radical revolutionary).

All this holds most emphatically for the more ancient periods of social development, i.e. for the closed society, in which the conscious design of institutions is a most exceptional event, if it happens at all. To-day, things may begin to be different, owing to our slowly increasing knowledge of society, i.e. owing to the study of the unintended repercussions of our plans and actions; and one day, men may even become the conscious creators of an open society, and thereby of a greater part of their own fate. (Marx entertained this hope, as will be shown in the next chapter.) But all this is partly a matter of degree, and although we may learn to foresee many of the unintended consequences of our actions (the main aim of all social technology), there will always be many which we did not foresee.

The fact that psychologism is forced to operate with the idea of a psychological origin of society constitutes in my opinion a decisive argument against it. But it is not the only one. Perhaps the most important criticism of psychologism is that it fails to understand the main task of the explanatory social sciences.

This task is not, as the historicist believes, the prophecy of the future course of history. It is, rather, the discovery and explanation of the less obvious dependences within the social sphere. It is the discovery of the difficulties which stand in the way of social action—the study, as it were, of the unwieldiness, the resilience or the brittleness of the social stuff, of its resistance to our attempts to mould it and to work with it.

In order to make my point clear, I shall briefly describe a theory which is widely held but which assumes what I consider the very opposite of the true aim of the social sciences; I call it the '*conspiracy theory of society*'. It is the view that an explanation of a social phenomenon consists in the discovery of the men or groups who are interested in the occurrence of this phenomenon (sometimes it is a hidden interest which has first to be revealed), and who have planned and conspired to bring it about.

This view of the aims of the social sciences arises, of course, from the mistaken theory that, whatever happens in society—especially happenings such as war, unemployment, poverty, shortages, which people as a rule dislike—is the result of direct design by some powerful individuals and groups. This theory is widely held; it is older even than historicism (which, as shown by its primitive theistic form, is a derivative of the conspiracy theory). In its modern forms it is, like modern historicism, and a certain modern attitude towards 'natural laws', a typical result of the secularization of a religious superstition. The belief in the Homeric gods whose conspiracies explain the history of the Trojan War is gone. The gods are abandoned. But their place is filled by powerful men or groups—sinister pressure groups whose wickedness is responsible for all the evils we suffer from—such as the Learned Elders of Zion, or the monopolists, or the capitalists, or the imperialists.

I do not wish to imply that conspiracies never happen. On the contrary, they are typical social phenomena. They become important, for example, whenever people who believe in the conspiracy theory get into power. And people who sincerely believe that they know how to make heaven on earth are most likely to adopt the conspiracy theory, and to get involved in a counter-conspiracy against non-existing conspirators. For the only explanation of their failure to produce their heaven is the evil intention of the Devil, who has a vested interest in hell.

Conspiracies occur, it must be admitted. But the striking fact which, in spite of their occurrence, disproves the conspiracy theory is that few of these conspiracies are ultimately successful. *Conspirators rarely consummate their conspiracy*.

Why is this so? Why do achievements differ so widely from aspirations? Because this is usually the case in social life, conspiracy or no conspiracy. Social life is not only a trial of strength between opposing groups: it is action within a more or less resilient or brittle framework of institutions and traditions, and it creates—apart from any conscious counter-action—many unforeseen reactions in this framework, some of them perhaps even unforeseeable.

To try to analyse these reactions and to foresee them as far as possible is, I believe, the main task of the social sciences. It is the task of analysing the unintended social repercussions of intentional human actions—those repercussions whose significance is neglected both by the conspiracy theory and by psychologism, as already indicated. An action which proceeds precisely according to intention does not create a problem for social science (except that there may be a need to explain why in this particular case no unintended repercussions occurred). One of the most primitive economic actions may serve as an example in order to make the idea of unintended consequences of our actions quite clear. If a man wishes urgently to buy a house, we can safely assume that he does not wish to raise the market price of houses. But the very fact that he appears on the market as a buyer will tend to raise market prices. And analogous remarks hold for the seller. Or to take an example from a very different field, if a man decides to insure his life, he is unlikely to have the intention of encouraging some people to invest their money in insurance shares. But he will do so nevertheless. We see here clearly that not all consequences of our actions are intended consequences; and accordingly, that the conspiracy theory of society cannot be true because it amounts to the assertion that all results, even those which at first sight do not seem to be intended by anybody, are the intended results of the actions of people who are interested in these results.

The examples given do not refute psychologism as easily as they refute the conspiracy theory, for one can argue that it is the sellers' *knowledge* of a buyer's presence in the market, and their *hope* of getting a higher price—in other words, psychological factors—which explain the repercussions described. This, of course, is quite true; but we must not forget that this knowledge and this hope are not ultimate data of human nature, and that they are, in their turn, explicable in terms of the *social situation*—the market situation.

This social situation is hardly reducible to motives and to the general laws of 'human nature'. Indeed, the interference of certain 'traits of human nature', such as our susceptibility to propaganda, may sometimes lead to deviations from the economic behaviour just mentioned. Furthermore, if the social situation is different from the one envisaged, then it is possible that the consumer, by the action of buying, may indirectly contribute to a cheapening of the article; for instance, by making its mass-production more profitable. And although this effect happens to further his interest as a consumer, it may have been caused just as involuntarily as the opposite effect, and altogether under precisely similar psychological conditions. It seems clear that the social situations which may lead to such widely different unwanted or unintended repercussions must be studied by a social science which is not bound to the prejudice that 'it is imperative never to introduce any generalization into the social sciences until sufficient grounds can be pointed out in human nature', as Mill said[12]. They must be studied by an autonomous social science.

Continuing this argument against psychologism we may say that our actions are to a very large extent explicable in terms of the situation in which they occur. Of course, they are never fully explicable in terms of the situation alone; an explanation of the way in which a man, when crossing a street, dodges the cars which move on it may go beyond the situation, and may refer his motives, to an 'instinct' of self-preservation, or to his wish to avoid pain, etc. But this 'psychological' part of the explanation is very often trivial, as compared with the detailed determination of his action by what we may call the *logic of the situation*; and besides, it is impossible to include all psychological factors in the description of the situation. The analysis of situations, the situational logic, plays a very important part in social life as well as in the social sciences. It is, in fact, the method of economic analysis. As to an example outside economics, I refer to the 'logic of power'[13], which we may use in order to explain the moves of power politics as well as the working of certain political institutions. The method of applying a situational logic to the social sciences is not based on any psychological assumption concerning the rationality (or otherwise) of 'human nature'. On the contrary: when we speak of 'rational behaviour' or of 'irrational behaviour' then we mean behaviour which is, or which is not, in accordance with the logic of that situation. In fact, the psychological analysis of an action in terms of its (rational or irrational) motives presupposes—as has been pointed out by Max Weber[14]—that we have previously developed some standard of what is to be considered as rational in the situation in question.

My arguments against psychologism should not be misunderstood[15]. They are not, of course, intended to show that psychological studies and discoveries are of little importance for the social scientist. They mean, rather, that psychology—the psychology of the individual—is one of the social sciences, even though it is not the basis of all social science. Nobody would deny the importance for political science of psychological facts such as the craving for power, and the various neurotic phenomena connected with it. But 'craving for power' is undoubtedly a social notion as well as a psychological one: we must not forget that, if we study, for example, the first appearance in childhood of this craving, then we study it in the setting of a certain social institution, for example, that of our modern family. (The Eskimo family may give rise to rather different phenomena.) Another psychological fact which is significant for sociology, and which raises grave political and institutional problems, is that to live in the haven of a tribe, or of a 'community' approaching a tribe, is for many men an emotional necessity (especially for young people who, perhaps in accordance with a parallelism between ontogenetic and phylogenetic development, seem to have to pass through a tribal or 'American-Indian' stage). That my attack on psychologism is not intended as an attack on all psychological considerations may be seen from the use I have made (in chapter 10) of such a concept as the 'strain of civilization' which is partly the result of this unsatisfied emotional need. This concept refers to certain feelings of uneasiness, and is therefore a psychological concept. But at the same time, it is a sociological concept also; for it characterizes these feelings not only as unpleasant and unsettling, etc., but relates them to a certain social situation, and to the contrast between an open and a closed society. (Many psychological concepts such as ambition or love have an analogous status.) Also, we must not overlook the great merits which psychologism has acquired by advocating a methodological individualism and by opposing a methodological collectivism; for it lends support to the important doctrine that all social phenomena, and especially the functioning of all social institutions, should always be understood as resulting from the decisions, actions, attitudes, etc., of human individuals, and that we should never be satisfied by an explanation in terms of so-called 'collectives' (states, nations, races, etc.). The mistake of psychologism is its presumption that this methodological individualism in the field of social science implies the programme of reducing all social phenomena and all social regularities to psychological phenomena and psychological laws. The danger of this presumption is its inclination towards historicism, as we have seen. That it is unwarranted is shown by the need for a theory of the unintended social repercussions of our actions, and by the need for what I have described as the logic of social situations.

In defending and developing Marx's view that the problems of society are irreducible to those of 'human nature', I have permitted myself to go beyond the arguments actually propounded by Marx. Marx did not speak of 'psychologism', nor did he criticize it systematically; nor was it Mill whom he had in mind in the epigram quoted at the beginning of this chapter. The force of this epigram is directed, rather, against 'idealism', in its Hegelian form. Yet so far as the problem of the psychological nature of society is concerned, Mill's psychologism can be said to coincide with the idealist theory combated by Marx[16]. As it happened, however, it was just the influence of another element in Hegelianism, namely Hegel's Platonizing collectivism, his theory that the state and the nation is more 'real' than the individual who owes everything to them, that led Marx to the view expounded in this chapter. (An instance of the fact that one can sometimes extract a valuable suggestion even from an absurd philosophical theory.) Thus, historically, Marx developed certain of Hegel's views concerning the superiority of society over the individual, and used them as arguments against other views of Hegel. Yet since I consider Mill a worthier opponent than Hegel, I have not kept to the history of Marx's ideas, but have tried to develop them in the form of an argument against Mill.

15

ECONOMIC HISTORICISM

To see Marx presented in this way, that is to say, as an opponent of any psychological theory of society, may possibly surprise some Marxists as well as some anti-Marxists. For there seem to be many who believe in a very different story. Marx, they think, taught the all-pervading influence of the economic motive in the life of men; he succeeded in explaining its overpowering strength by showing that 'man's overmastering need was to get the means of living'[1]; he thus demonstrated the fundamental importance of such categories as the profit motive or the motive of class interest for the actions not only of individuals but also of social groups; and he showed how to use these categories for explaining the course of history. Indeed, they think that the very essence of Marxism is the doctrine that *economic motives* and especially *class interest* are the driving forces of history, and that it is precisely this doctrine to which the name '*materialistic interpretation of history*' or '*historical materialism*' alludes, a name by which Marx and Engels tried to characterize the essence of their teaching.

Such opinions are very common; but I have no doubt that they misinterpret Marx. Those who admire him for having held them, I may call Vulgar Marxists (alluding to the name 'Vulgar Economist' given by Marx to certain of his opponents[2]). The average Vulgar Marxist believes that Marxism lays bare the sinister secrets of social life by revealing the hidden motives of greed and lust for material gain which actuate the powers behind the scenes of history; powers that cunningly and consciously create war, depression, unemployment, hunger in the midst of plenty, and all the other forms of social misery, in order to gratify their vile desires for profit. (And the Vulgar Marxist is sometimes seriously concerned with the problem of reconciling the claims of Marx with those of Freud and Adler; and if he does not choose the one or the other of them, he may perhaps decide that hunger, love and lust for power[3] are the Three Great Hidden Motives of Human Nature brought to light by Marx, Freud, and Adler, the Three Great Makers of the modern man's philosophy. . . .)

Whether or not such views are tenable and attractive, they certainly seem to have very little to do with the doctrine which Marx called 'historical materialism'. It must be admitted that he sometimes speaks of such psychological phenomena as greed and the profit motive, etc., but never in order to explain history. He interpreted them, rather, as symptoms of the corrupting influence of the *social system*, i.e. of a system of institutions developed during the course of history; as effects rather than causes of corruption; as repercussions rather than moving forces of history. Rightly or wrongly, he saw in such phenomena as war, depression, unemployment, and hunger in the midst of plenty, not the result of a cunning conspiracy on the part of 'big business' or of 'imperialist war-mongers', but the unwanted social consequences of actions, directed towards different results, by agents who are caught in the network of the social system. He looked upon the human actors on the stage of history, including the 'big' ones, as mere puppets, irresistibly pulled by economic wires—by historical forces over which they have no control. The stage of history, he taught, is set in a social system which binds us all; it is set in the 'kingdom of necessity'. (But one day the puppets will destroy this system and attain the 'kingdom of freedom'.)

This doctrine of Marx's has been abandoned by most of his followers—perhaps for propagandist reasons, perhaps because they did not understand him—and a Vulgar Marxist Conspiracy Theory has very largely replaced the ingenious and highly original Marxian doctrine. It is a sad intellectual come-down, this come-down from the level of *Capital* to that of *The Myth of the 20th Century*.

Yet such was Marx's own philosophy of history, usually called 'historical materialism'. It will be the main theme of these chapters. In the present chapter, I shall explain in broad outlines its 'materialist' or economic emphasis; after that, I shall discuss in more detail the rôle of class war and class interest and the Marxist conception of a 'social system'.

I

The exposition of Marx's economic historicism[4] can be conveniently linked up with our comparison between Marx and Mill. Marx agrees with Mill in the belief that social phenomena must be explained historically, and that we must try to understand any historical period as a historical product of previous developments. The point where he departs from Mill is, as we have seen, Mill's psychologism (corresponding to Hegel's idealism). This is replaced in Marx's teaching by what he calls *materialism*.

Much has been said about Marx's materialism that is quite untenable. The often repeated claim that Marx does not recognize anything beyond the 'lower' or 'material' aspects of human life is an especially ridiculous distortion. (It is another repetition of that most ancient of all reactionary libels against the defenders of freedom, Heraclitus' slogan that 'they fill their bellies like the beasts'[5].) But in this sense, Marx cannot be called a materialist at all, even though he was strongly influenced by the eighteenth-century French Materialists, and even though he used to call himself a materialist, which is well in keeping with a good number of his doctrines. For there are some important passages which can hardly be interpreted as materialistic. The truth is, I think, that he was not much concerned with purely philosophical issues—less than Engels or Lenin, for instance—and that it was mainly the sociological and methodological side of the problem in which he was interested.

There is a well-known passage in *Capital*[6], where Marx says that 'in Hegel's writing, dialectics stands on its head; one must turn it the right way up again …' Its tendency is clear. Marx wished to show that the 'head', i.e. human thought, is not itself the basis of human life but rather a kind of superstructure, on a physical basis. A similar tendency is expressed in the passage: 'The ideal is nothing other than the material when it has been transposed and translated inside the human head.' But it has not, perhaps, been sufficiently recognized that these passages do not exhibit a radical form of materialism; rather, they indicate a certain leaning towards a dualism of body and mind. It is, so to speak, a practical dualism. Although, theoretically, mind was to Marx apparently only another *form* (or another aspect, or perhaps an epi-phenomenon) of matter, in practice it is different from matter, since it is *another* form of it. The passages quoted indicate that although our feet have to be kept, as it were, on the firm ground of the material world, our heads—and Marx thought highly of human heads—are concerned with thoughts or ideas. In my opinion, Marxism and its influence cannot be appreciated unless we recognize this dualism.

Marx loved freedom, real freedom (not Hegel's 'real freedom'). And as far as I am able to see he followed Hegel's famous equation of freedom with spirit, in so far as he believed that we can be free only as spiritual beings. At the same time he recognized in practice (as a practical dualist) that we are spirit *and* flesh, and, realistically enough, that the flesh is the fundamental one of these two. This is why he turned against Hegel, and why he said that Hegel puts things upside down. But although he recognized that the material world and its necessities are fundamental, he did not feel any love for the 'kingdom of necessity', as he called a society which is in bondage to its material needs. He cherished the spiritual world, the 'kingdom of freedom', and the spiritual side of 'human nature', as much as any Christian dualist; and in his writings there are even traces of hatred and contempt for the material. What follows may show that this interpretation of Marx's views can be supported by his own text.

In a passage of the third volume of *Capital*[7], Marx very aptly describes the material side of social life, and especially its economic side, that of production and consumption, as an extension of human metabolism, i.e. of man's exchange of matter with nature. He clearly states that our freedom must always be limited by the necessities of this metabolism. All that can be achieved in the direction of making us more free, he says, is 'to conduct this metabolism rationally, … with a minimum expenditure of energy and under conditions most dignified and adequate to human nature. Yet it will still remain the kingdom of necessity. Only outside and beyond it can that development of human faculties begin which constitutes an end in itself—the true kingdom of freedom. But this can flourish only on the ground occupied by the kingdom of necessity, which remains its basis …' Immediately before this, Marx says: 'The kingdom of freedom actually begins only where drudgery, enforced by hardship and by external purposes, ends; it thus lies, quite naturally, beyond the sphere of proper material production.' And he ends the whole passage by drawing a practical conclusion which clearly shows that it was his sole aim to open the way into that non-materialist kingdom of freedom for all men alike: 'The shortening of the labour day is the fundamental pre-requisite.'

In my opinion this passage leaves no doubt regarding what I have called the dualism of Marx's practical view of life. With Hegel he thinks that freedom is the aim of historical development. With Hegel he identifies the realm of freedom with that of man's mental life. But he recognizes that we are not purely spiritual beings; that we are not fully free, nor capable of ever achieving full freedom, unable as we shall always be to emancipate ourselves entirely from the necessities of our metabolism, and thus from productive toil. All we can achieve is to improve upon the exhausting and undignified conditions of labour, to make them more worthy of man, to equalize them, and to reduce drudgery to such an extent that *all of us can be free for some part of our lives*. This, I believe, is the central idea of Marx's 'view of life'; central also in so far as it seems to me to be the most influential of his doctrines.

With this view, we must now combine the methodological determinism which has been discussed above (in chapter 13). According to this doctrine, the scientific treatment of society, and scientific historical prediction, are possible only in so far as society is determined by its past. But this implies that science can deal only with the kingdom of necessity. If it were possible for men ever to become perfectly free, then historical prophecy, and with it, social science, would come to an end. 'Free' spiritual activity as such, if it existed, would lie beyond the reach of science, which must always ask for causes, for determinants. It can therefore deal with our mental life only in so far as our thoughts and ideas are caused or determined or necessitated by the 'kingdom of necessity', by the material, and especially by the economic conditions of our life, by our metabolism. Thoughts and ideas can be treated scientifically only by considering, on the one hand, the material conditions under which they originated, i.e. the economic conditions of the life of the men who originated them, and on the other hand, the material conditions under which they were assimilated, i.e. the economic conditions of the men who adopted them. Hence from the scientific or causal point of view, thoughts and ideas must be treated as 'ideological superstructures on the basis of economic conditions'. Marx, in opposition to Hegel, contended that the clue to history, even to the history of ideas, is to be found in the development of the relations between man and his natural environment, the material world; that is to say, in his economic life, and not in his spiritual life. This is why we may describe Marx's brand of historicism as *economism*, as opposed to Hegel's idealism or to Mill's psychologism. But it signifies a complete misunderstanding if we identify Marx's economism with that kind of materialism which implies a depreciatory attitude towards man's mental life. Marx's vision of the 'kingdom of freedom', i.e. of a partial but equitable liberation of men from the bondage of their material nature, might rather be described as idealistic.

Considered in this way, the Marxist view of life appears to be consistent enough; and I believe that such apparent contradictions and difficulties as have been found in its partly determinist and partly libertarian view of human activities disappear.

II

The bearing of what I have called Marx's dualism and his scientific determinism on his view of history is plain. Scientific history, which to him is identical with social science as a whole, must explore the laws according to which man's exchange of matter with nature develops. Its central task must be the explanation of the development of the conditions of production. Social relationships have historical and scientific significance only in proportion to the degree in which they are bound up with the productive process—affecting it, or perhaps affected by it. 'Just as the savage must wrestle with nature in order to satisfy his needs, to keep alive, and to reproduce, so must the civilized man; and he must continue to do so in all forms of society and under all possible forms of production. This kingdom of necessity expands with its development, and so does the range of human needs. Yet at the same time, there is an expansion of the productive forces which satisfy these needs.'[8] This, in brief, is Marx's view of man's history.

Similar views are expressed by Engels. The expansion of modern means of production, according to Engels, has created 'for the first time … the possibility of securing for every member of society … an existence not only … sufficient from a material point of view, but also … warranting the … development and exercise of his physical and mental faculties'[9]. With this, freedom becomes possible, i.e. the emancipation from the flesh. 'At this point … man finally cuts himself off from the animal world, leaves … animal existence behind him and enters conditions which are really human.' Man is in fetters exactly in so far as he is dominated by economics; when 'the domination of the product over producers disappears …, man … becomes, for the first time, the conscious and real master of nature, by becoming master of his own social environment … Not until then will man himself, in full consciousness, make his own history … It is humanity's leap from the realm of necessity into the realm of freedom.'

If now again we compare Marx's version of historicism with that of Mill, then we find that Marx's economism can easily solve the difficulty which I have shown to be fatal to Mill's psychologism. I have in mind the rather monstrous doctrine of a beginning of society which can be explained in psychological terms—a doctrine which I have described as the psychologistic version of the social contract. This idea has no parallel in Marx's theory. To replace the priority of psychology by the priority of economics creates no analogous difficulty, since 'economics' covers man's metabolism, the exchange of matter between man and nature. Whether this metabolism has always been socially organized, even in pre-human times, or whether it was once dependent solely on the individual, can be left an open question. No more is assumed than that the science of society must coincide with the history of the development of the economic conditions of society, usually called by Marx 'the conditions of production'.

It may be noted, in parentheses, that the Marxist term 'production' was certainly intended to be used in a wide sense, covering the whole economic process, including distribution and consumption. But these latter never received much attention from Marx and the Marxists. Their prevailing interest remained production in the narrow sense of the word. This is just another example of the naïve historico-genetic attitude, of the belief that science must only ask for causes, so that, even in the realm of man-made things, it must ask 'Who has made it?' and 'What is it made of?' rather than 'Who is going to use it?' and 'What is it made for?'

III

If we now proceed to a criticism as well as to an appreciation of Marx's 'historical materialism', or of so much of it as has been presented so far, then we may distinguish two different aspects. The first is historicism, the claim that the realm of social sciences coincides with that of the historical or evolutionary method, and especially with historical prophecy. This claim, I think, must be dismissed. The second is economism (or 'materialism'), i.e. the claim that the economic organization of society, the organization of our exchange of matter with nature, is fundamental for all social institutions and especially for their historical development. This claim, I believe, is perfectly sound, so long as we take the term 'fundamental' in an ordinary vague sense, not laying too much stress upon it. In other words, there can be no doubt that practically all social studies, whether institutional or historical, may profit if they are carried out with an eye to the 'economic conditions' of society. Even the history of an abstract science such as mathematics is no exception[10]. In this sense, Marx's economism can be said to represent an extremely valuable advance in the methods of social science.

But, as I said before, we must not take the term 'fundamental' too seriously. Marx himself undoubtedly did so. Owing to his Hegelian upbringing, he was influenced by the ancient distinction between 'reality' and 'appearance', and by the corresponding distinction between what is 'essential' and what is 'accidental'. His own improvement upon Hegel (and Kant) he was inclined to see in the identification of 'reality' with the material world[11] (including man's metabolism), and of 'appearance' with the world of thoughts or ideas. Thus all thoughts and ideas would have to be explained by reducing them to the underlying essential reality, i.e. to economic conditions. This philosophical view is certainly not much better[12] than any other form of essentialism. And its repercussions in the field of method must result in an over-emphasis upon economism. For *although the general importance of Marx's economism can hardly be overrated, it is very easy to overrate the importance of the economic conditions in any particular case.* Some knowledge of economic conditions may contribute considerably, for example, to a history of the problems of mathematics, but a knowledge of the problems of mathematics themselves is much more important for that purpose; and it is even possible to write a very good history of mathematical problems without referring at all to their 'economic background'. (In my opinion, the 'economic conditions' or the 'social relations' of science are themes which can easily be overdone, and which are liable to degenerate into platitude.)

This, however, is only a minor example of the danger of over-stressing economism. Often it is sweepingly interpreted as the doctrine that all social development depends upon that of economic conditions, and especially upon the development of the physical means of production. But such a doctrine is palpably false. There is an interaction between economic conditions and ideas, and not simply a unilateral dependence of the latter on the former. If anything, we might even assert that certain 'ideas', those which constitute our knowledge, are more fundamental than the more complex material means of production, as may be seen from the following consideration. Imagine that our economic system, including all machinery and all social organizations, was destroyed one day, but that technical and scientific knowledge was preserved. In such a case it might conceivably not take very long before it was reconstructed (on a smaller scale, and after many had starved). But imagine *all knowledge* of these matters to disappear, while the material things were preserved. This would be tantamount to what would happen if a savage tribe occupied a highly industrialized but deserted country. It would soon lead to the complete disappearance of all the material relics of civilization.

It is ironical that the history of Marxism itself furnishes an example that clearly falsifies this exaggerated economism. Marx's *idea* 'Workers of all countries, unite!' was of the greatest significance down to the eve of the Russian Revolution, and it had its influence upon economic conditions. But with the revolution, the situation became very difficult, simply because, as Lenin himself admitted, there were no further constructive ideas. (See chapter 13.) Then Lenin had some new ideas which may be briefly summarized in the slogan: 'Socialism is the dictatorship of the proletariat, plus the widest introduction of the most modern electrical machinery.' It was this new idea that became the basis of a development which changed the whole economic and material background of one-sixth of the world. In a fight against tremendous odds, uncounted material difficulties were overcome, uncounted material sacrifices were made, in order to alter, or rather, to build up from nothing, the conditions of production. And the driving power of this development was the enthusiasm for an *idea*. This example shows that in certain circumstances, ideas may revolutionize the economic conditions of a country, instead of being moulded by these conditions. Using Marx's terminology, we could say that he had underrated the power of the kingdom of freedom and its chances of conquering the kingdom of necessity.

The glaring contrast between the development of the Russian Revolution and Marx's metaphysical theory of an economic reality and its ideological appearance can best be seen from the following passages: 'In considering such revolutions', Marx writes, 'it is necessary always to distinguish between the material revolution in the economic conditions of production, which fall within the scope of exact scientific determination, and the juridical, political, religious, æsthetic, or philosophic—in a word, ideological forms of appearance …'[13] In Marx's view, it is vain to expect that any important change can be achieved by the use of legal or political means; a *political revolution* can only lead to one set of rulers giving way to another set—a mere exchange of the persons who act as rulers. Only the evolution of the underlying essence, the economic reality, can produce any essential or real change—a *social revolution*. And only when such a social revolution has become a reality, only then can a political revolution be of any significance. But even in this case, the political revolution is only the outward expression of the essential or real change that has occurred before. In accordance with this theory, Marx asserts that every social revolution develops in the following way. The material conditions of production grow and mature until they begin to conflict with the social and legal relations, outgrowing them like clothes, until they burst. 'Then an epoch of social revolution opens', Marx writes. 'With the change in the economic foundation, the whole vast superstructure is more or less rapidly transformed … New, more highly productive relationships' (within the superstructure) 'never come into being before the material conditions for their existence have been brought to maturity within the womb of the old society itself.' In view of this statement, it is, I believe, impossible to identify the Russian Revolution with the social revolution prophesied by Marx; it has, in fact, no similarity with it whatever[14].

It may be noted in this connection that Marx's friend, the poet H. Heine, thought very differently about these matters. 'Mark this, ye proud men of action', he writes; 'ye are nothing but unconscious instruments of the men of thought who, often in humblest seclusion, have appointed you to your inevitable task. Maximilian Robespierre was merely the hand of Jean-Jacques Rousseau …'[15] (Something like this might perhaps be said of the relationship between Lenin and Marx.) We see that Heine was, in Marx's terminology, an idealist, and that he applied his idealistic interpretation of history to the French Revolution, which was one of the most important instances used by Marx in favour of his economism, and which indeed seemed to fit this doctrine not so badly—especially if we compare it now with the Russian Revolution. Yet in spite of this heresy, Heine remained Marx's friend[16]; for in those happy days, excommunication for heresy was still rather uncommon among those who fought for the open society, and tolerance was still tolerated.

My criticism of Marx's 'historical materialism' must certainly not be interpreted as expressing any preference for Hegelian 'idealism' over Marx's 'materialism'; I hope I have made it clear that in this conflict between idealism and materialism my sympathies are with Marx. What I wish to show is that Marx's 'materialist interpretation of history', valuable as it may be, must not be taken too seriously; that we must regard it as nothing more than a most valuable suggestion to us to consider things in their relation to their economic background.

16

THE CLASSES

An important place among the various formulations of Marx's 'historical materialism' is occupied by his (and Engels') statement: 'The history of all hitherto existing society is a history of class struggle.'[1] The tendency of this statement is clear. It implies that history is propelled and the fate of man determined by the war of classes and not by the war of nations (as opposed to the views of Hegel and of the majority of historians). In the causal explanation of historical developments, including national wars, class interest must take the place of that allegedly national interest which, in reality, is only the interest of a nation's ruling class. But over and above this, class struggle and class interest are capable of explaining phenomena which traditional history may in general not even attempt to explain. An example of such a phenomenon which is of great significance for Marxist theory is the historical trend towards increasing productivity. Even though it may perhaps record such a trend, traditional history, with its fundamental category of military power, is quite unable to explain this phenomenon. Class interest and class war, however, can explain it fully, according to Marx; indeed, a considerable part of *Capital* is devoted to the analysis of the mechanism by which, within the period called by Marx 'capitalism', an increase in productivity is brought about by these forces.

How is the doctrine of class war related to the institutionalist doctrine of the autonomy of sociology discussed above[2]? At first sight it may seem that these two doctrines are in open conflict, for in the doctrine of class war, a fundamental part is played by class interest, which apparently is a kind of *motive*. But I do not think that there is any serious inconsistency in this part of Marx's theory. And I should even say that nobody has understood Marx, and particularly that major achievement of his, anti-psychologism, who does not see how it can be reconciled with the theory of class struggle. We need not assume, as Vulgar Marxists do, that class interest must be interpreted psychologically. There may be a few passages in Marx's own writings that savour a little of this Vulgar Marxism, but wherever he makes serious use of anything like class interest, he always means a thing within the realm of autonomous sociology, and not a psychological category. He means a thing, a situation, and not a state of mind, a thought, or a feeling of being interested in a thing. It is simply that thing or that social institution or situation which is advantageous to a class. The interest of a class is simply everything that furthers its power or its prosperity.

According to Marx, class interest in this institutional, or, if we may say so, 'objective', sense exerts a decisive influence on human minds. Using Hegelian jargon, we might say that the objective interest of a class becomes conscious in the subjective minds of its members; it makes them class-interested and class-conscious, and it makes them act accordingly. Class interest as an institutional or objective social situation, and its influence upon human minds, is described by Marx in the epigram which I have quoted (at the beginning of chapter 14): 'It is not the consciousness of man that determines his existence—rather, it is his social existence that determines his consciousness.' To this epigram we need add only the remark that it is, more precisely, the place where man stands in society, his class situation, by which, according to Marxism, his consciousness is determined.

Marx gives some indication of how this process of determination works. As we learned from him in the last chapter, we can be free only in so far as we emancipate ourselves from the productive process. But now we shall learn that, in any hitherto existing society, we were not free even to that extent. For how could we, he asks, emancipate ourselves from the productive process? Only by making others do the dirty work for us. We are thus forced to use them as means for our ends; we must degrade them. We can buy a greater degree of freedom only at the cost of enslaving other men, by splitting mankind into *classes*; the ruling class gains freedom at the cost of the ruled class, the slaves. But this fact has the consequence that the members of the ruling class must pay for their freedom by a new kind of bondage. They are *bound* to oppress and to fight the ruled, if they wish to preserve their own freedom and their own status; they are compelled to do this, since he who does not do so ceases to belong to the ruling class. Thus the rulers are determined by their class situation; they cannot escape from their social relation to the ruled; they are bound to them, since they are bound to the social metabolism. Thus all, rulers as well as ruled, are caught in the net, and forced to fight one another. According to Marx, it is this bondage, this determination, which brings their struggle within the reach of scientific method, and of scientific historical prophecy; which makes it possible to treat the history of society scientifically, as the history of class struggle. This social net in which the classes are caught, and forced to struggle against one another, is what Marxism calls the economic structure of society, or the social system.

According to this theory, social systems or class systems change with the conditions of production, since on these conditions depends the way in which the rulers can exploit and fight the ruled. To every particular period of economic development corresponds a particular social system, and a historical period is best characterized by its social system of classes; this is why we speak of 'feudalism', 'capitalism', etc. 'The hand-mill', Marx writes[3], 'gives you a society with the feudal lord; the steam-mill gives you a society with the industrial capitalist.' The class relations that characterize the social system are independent of the individual man's will. The social system thus resembles a vast machine in which the individuals are caught and crushed. 'In the social production of their means of existence', Marx writes[4], 'men enter into definite and unavoidable relations which are independent of their will. These productive relationships correspond to the particular stage in the development of their material productive forces. The system of all these productive relationships constitutes the economic structure of society', i.e. the social system.

Although it has a kind of logic of its own, this social system works blindly, not reasonably. Those who are caught in its machinery are, in general, blind too—or nearly so. They cannot even foresee some of the most important repercussions of their actions. One man may make it impossible for many to procure an article which is available in large quantities; he may buy just a trifle and thereby prevent a slight decrease of price at a critical moment. Another may in the goodness of his heart distribute his riches, but by thus contributing to a lessening of the class struggle, he may cause a delay in the liberation of the oppressed. Since it is quite impossible to foresee the more remote social repercussions of our actions, since we are one and all caught in the network, we cannot seriously attempt to cope with it. We obviously cannot influence it from outside; but blind as we are, we cannot even make any plan for its improvement from within. Social engineering is impossible, and a social technology therefore useless. We cannot impose our interests upon the social system; instead, the system forces upon us what we are led to *believe* to be our interests. It does so by forcing us to act in accordance with our class interest. It is vain to lay on the individual, even on the individual 'capitalist' or 'bourgeois', the blame for the injustice, for the immorality of social conditions, since it is this very system of conditions that forces the capitalist to act as he does. And it is also vain to hope that circumstances may be improved by improving men; rather, men will be better if the system in which they live is better. 'Only in so far', Marx writes in *Capital*[5], 'as the capitalist is personified capital does he play a historical rôle ... But exactly to that extent, his motive is not to obtain and to enjoy useful commodities, but to increase the production of commodities for exchange' (his real historical task). 'Fanatically bent upon the expansion of value, he ruthlessly drives human beings to produce for production's sake ... With the miser, he shares the passion for wealth. But what is a kind of mania in the miser is in the capitalist the effect of the social mechanism in which he is only a driving-wheel ... Capitalism subjects any individual capitalist to the immanent laws of capitalist production, laws which are external and coercive. Without respite, competition forces him to extend his capital for the sake of maintaining it.'

This is the way in which, according to Marx, the social system determines the actions of the individual; the ruler as well as the ruled; capitalist or bourgeois as well as proletarian. It is an illustration of what has been called above the 'logic of a social situation'. To a considerable degree, all the actions of a capitalist are 'a mere function of the capital which, through his instrumentality, is endowed with will and consciousness', as Marx puts it[6], in his Hegelian style. But this means that the social system determines their thoughts too; for thoughts, or ideas, are partly *instruments* of actions, and partly—that is, if they are publicly expressed—an important *kind* of social action; for in this case, they are immediately aimed at influencing the actions of other members of the society. By thus determining human thoughts, the social system, and especially the 'objective interest' of a class, becomes conscious in the subjective minds of its members (as we said before in Hegelian jargon[7]). Class struggle, as well as competition between the members of the same class, are the means by which this is achieved.

We have seen why, according to Marx, social engineering, and consequently, a social technology, are impossible; it is because the causal chain of dependence binds us to the social system, and not *vice versa*. But although we cannot alter the social system at will[8], capitalists as well as workers are bound to contribute to its transformation, and to our ultimate liberation from its fetters. By driving 'human beings to produce for production's sake'[9], the capitalist coerces them 'to develop the forces of social productivity, and to create those material conditions of production which alone can form the material bases of a higher type of society whose fundamental principle is the full and free development of every human individual.' In this way, even the members of the capitalist class must play their rôle on the stage of history and further the ultimate coming of socialism.

In view of subsequent arguments, a linguistic remark may be added here on the Marxist terms usually translated by the words 'class-conscious' and 'class consciousness'. These terms indicate, first of all, the result of the process analysed above, by which the objective class situation (class interest as well as class struggle) gains consciousness in the minds of its members, or, to express the same thought in a language less dependent on Hegel, by which members of a class become conscious of their class situation. Being class-conscious, they know not only their place but their true class interest as well. But over and above this, the original German word used by Marx suggests something which is usually lost in the translation. The term is derived from, and alludes to, a common German word which became part of Hegel's jargon. Though its literal translation would be 'self-conscious', this word has even in common use rather the meaning of being *conscious of one's worth and powers*, i.e. of being proud and fully assured of oneself, and even self-satisfied. Accordingly, the term translated as 'class-conscious' means in German not simply this, but rather, 'assured or proud of one's class', and bound to it by the consciousness of the need for solidarity. This is why Marx and the Marxists apply it nearly exclusively to the workers, and hardly ever to the 'bourgeoisie'. The class-conscious proletarian—this is the worker who is not only aware of his class situation, but who is also class-proud, fully assured of the historical mission of his class, and believing that its unflinching fight will bring about a better world.

How does he know that this will happen? Because being class-conscious, he must be a Marxist. The Marxist theory itself and its scientific prophecy of the advent of socialism are part and parcel of the historical process by which the class situation 'emerges into consciousness', establishing itself in the minds of the workers.

II

My criticism of Marx's theory of the classes, as far as its historicist emphasis goes, follows the lines taken up in the last chapter. The formula 'all history is a history of class struggle' is very valuable as a suggestion that we should look into the important part played by class struggle in power politics as well as in other developments; this suggestion is the more valuable since Plato's brilliant analysis of the part played by class struggle in the history of Greek city states was only rarely taken up in later times. But again, we must not, of course, take Marx's word 'all' too seriously. Not even the history of class issues is always a history of class struggle in the Marxian sense, considering the important part played by dissension within the classes themselves. Indeed, the divergence of interests within both the ruling and the ruled classes goes so far that Marx's theory of classes must be considered as a dangerous over-simplification, even if we admit that the issue between the rich and the poor is always of fundamental importance. One of the great themes of medieval history, the fight between popes and emperors, is an example of dissension within the ruling class. It would be palpably false to interpret this quarrel as one between exploiter and exploited. (Of course, one can widen Marx's concept 'class' so as to cover this and similar cases, and narrow the concept 'history', until ultimately Marx's doctrine becomes trivially true—a mere tautology; but this would rob it of any significance.)

One of the dangers of Marx's formula is that if taken too seriously, it misleads Marxists into interpreting all political conflicts as struggles between exploiters and exploited (or else as attempts to cover up the 'real issue', the underlying class conflict). As a consequence there were Marxists, especially in Germany, who interpreted a war such as the First World War as one between the revolutionary or 'have-not' Central Powers and an alliance of conservative or 'have' countries—a kind of interpretation which might be used to excuse any aggression. This is only one example of the danger inherent in Marx's sweeping historicist generalization.

On the other hand, his attempt to use what may be called the 'logic of the class situation' to explain the working of the institutions of the industrial system seems to me admirable, in spite of certain exaggerations and the neglect of some important aspects of the situation; admirable, at least, as a sociological analysis of that stage of the industrial system which Marx has mainly in mind: the system of 'unrestrained capitalism' (as I shall call it[10]) of one hundred years ago.

17

THE LEGAL AND THE SOCIAL SYSTEM

We are now ready to approach what is probably the most crucial point in our analysis as well as in our criticism of Marxism; it is Marx's theory of the state and—paradoxical as it may sound to some—of the impotence of all politics.

I

Marx's theory of the state can be presented by combining the results of the last two chapters. The legal or juridico-political system—the system of legal institutions enforced by the state—has to be understood, according to Marx, as one of the superstructures erected upon, and giving expression to, the actual productive forces of the economic system; Marx speaks[1] in this connection of 'juridical and political superstructures'. It is not, of course, the only way in which the economic or material reality and the relations between the classes which correspond to it make their appearance in the world of ideologies and ideas. Another example of such a superstructure would be, according to Marxist views, the prevailing moral system. This, as opposed to the legal system, is not enforced by state power, but sanctioned by an ideology created and controlled by the ruling class. The difference is, roughly, one between persuasion and force (as Plato[2] would have said); and it is the state, the legal or political system, which uses force. It is, as Engels[3] puts it, 'a special repressive force' for the coercion of the ruled by the rulers. 'Political power, properly so called,' says the *Manifesto*[4], 'is merely the organized power of one class for oppressing the other.' A similar description is given by Lenin[5]: 'According to Marx, the state is an organ of class *domination*, an organ for the oppression of one class by another; its aim is the creation of an "order" which legalizes and perpetuates this oppression ...' The state, in brief, is just part of the machinery by which the ruling class carries on its struggle.

Before proceeding to develop the consequences of this view of the state, it may be pointed out that it is partly an institutional and partly an essentialist theory. It is institutional in so far as Marx tries to ascertain what practical functions legal institutions have in social life. But it is essentialist in so far as Marx neither inquires into the variety of ends which these institutions may possibly serve (or be made to serve), nor suggests what institutional reforms are necessary in order to make the state serve those ends which he himself might deem desirable. Instead of making his demands or proposals concerning the functions which he wants the state, the legal institutions or the government to perform, he asks, '*What is* the state?'; that is to say, he tries to discover the *essential* function of legal institutions. It has been shown before[6] that such a typically essentialist question cannot be answered in a satisfactory way; yet this question, undoubtedly, is in keeping with Marx's essentialist and metaphysical approach which interprets the field of ideas and norms as the appearance of an economic reality.

What are the consequences of this theory of the state? The most important consequence is that all politics, all legal and political institutions as well as all political struggles, can never be of primary importance. *Politics are impotent*. They can never alter decisively the economic reality. The main if not the only task of any enlightened political activity is to see that the alternations in the juridico-political cloak keep pace with the changes in the social reality, that is to say, in the means of production and in the relations between the classes; in this way, such difficulties as must arise if politics lag behind these developments can be avoided. Or in other words, political developments are either superficial, unconditioned by the deeper reality of the social system, in which case they are doomed to be unimportant, and can never be of real help to the suppressed and exploited; or else they give expression to a change in the economic background and the class situation, in which case they are of the character of volcanic eruptions, of complete revolutions which can perhaps be foreseen, as they arise from the social system, and whose ferocity might then be mitigated by non-resistance to the eruptive forces, but which can be neither caused nor suppressed by political action.

These consequences show again the unity of Marx's historicist system of thought. Yet considering that few movements have done as much as Marxism to stimulate interest in political action, the theory of the fundamental impotence of politics appears somewhat paradoxical. (Marxists might, of course, meet this remark with either of two arguments. The one is that in the theory expounded, political action *has* its function; for even though the workers' party cannot, by its actions, improve the lot of the exploited masses, its fight awakens class consciousness and thereby prepares for the revolution. This would be the argument of the radical wing. The other argument, used by the moderate wing, asserts that there may exist historical periods in which political action can be directly helpful; the periods, namely, in which the forces of the two opposing classes are approximately in equilibrium. In such periods, political effort and energy may be decisive in achieving very significant improvements for the workers.—It is clear that this second argument sacrifices some of the fundamental positions of the theory, but without realizing this, and consequently without going to the root of the matter.)

It is worth noting that according to Marxist theory, the workers' party can hardly make political mistakes of any importance, as long as the party continues to play its assigned rôle, and to press the claims of the workers energetically. For political mistakes cannot materially affect the actual class situation, and even less the economic reality on which everything else ultimately depends.

Another important consequence of the theory is that, in principle, all government, even democratic government, is a dictatorship of the ruling class over the ruled. 'The executive of the modern state', says the *Manifesto*[7], 'is merely a committee for managing the economic affairs of the whole bourgeoisie …' What we call a democracy is, according to this theory, nothing but that form of class dictatorship which happens to be most convenient in a certain historical situation. (This doctrine does not agree very well with the class equilibrium theory of the moderate wing mentioned above.) And just as the state, under capitalism, is a dictatorship of the bourgeoisie, so, after the social revolution, it will at first be a dictatorship of the proletariat. But this proletarian state must lose its function as soon as the resistance of the old bourgeoisie has broken down. For the proletarian revolution leads to a one-class society, and therefore to a classless society in which there can be no class-dictatorship. Thus the state, deprived of any function, must disappear. '*It withers away*', as Engels said[8].

II

I am very far from defending Marx's theory of the state. His theory of the impotence of all politics, more particularly, and his view of democracy, appear to me to be not only mistakes, but fatal mistakes. But it must be admitted that behind these grim as well as ingenious theories, there stood a grim and depressing experience. And although Marx, in my opinion, failed to understand the future which he so keenly wished to foresee, it seems to me that even his mistaken theories are proof of his keen sociological insight into the conditions of his own time, and of his invincible humanitarianism and sense of justice.

Marx's theory of the state, in spite of its abstract and philosophical character, undoubtedly furnishes an enlightening interpretation of his own historical period. It is at least a tenable view that the so-called 'industrial revolution' developed at first mainly as a revolution of the 'material means of production', i.e. of machinery; that this led, next, to a transformation of the class structure of society, and thus to a new social system; and that political revolutions and other transformations of the legal system came only as a third step. Even though this Marxist interpretation of the 'rise of capitalism' has been challenged by historians who were able to lay bare some of its deep-lying ideological foundations (which were perhaps not quite unsuspected by Marx[9], although destructive to his theory), there can be little doubt about the value of the Marxist interpretation as a first approximation, and about the service rendered to his successors in this field. And even though some of the developments studied by Marx were deliberately fostered by legislative measures, and indeed made possible only by legislation (as Marx himself says[10]), it was he who first discussed the influence of economic developments and economic interests upon legislation, and the function of legislative measures as weapons in the class struggle, and especially as means for the creation of a 'surplus population', and with it, of the industrial proletariat.

It is clear from many of Marx's passages that these observations confirmed him in his belief that the juridico-political system is a mere 'superstructure'[11] on the social, i.e. the economic, system; a theory which, although undoubtedly refuted by subsequent experience[12], not only remains interesting, but also, I suggest, contains a grain of truth.

But it was not only Marx's general views of the relations between the economic and the political system that were in this way influenced by his historical experience; his views on liberalism and democracy, more particularly, which he considered to be nothing but veils for the dictatorship of the bourgeoisie, furnished an interpretation of the social situation of his time which appeared to fit only too well, corroborated as it was by sad experience. For Marx lived, especially in his younger years, in a period of the most shameless and cruel exploitation. And this shameless exploitation was cynically defended by hypocritical apologists who appealed to the principle of human freedom, to the right of man to determine his own fate, and to enter freely into any contract he considers favourable to his interests.

Using the slogan 'equal and free competition for all', the unrestrained capitalism of this period resisted successfully all labour legislation until the year 1833, and its practical execution for many years more[13]. The consequence was a life of desolation and misery which can hardly be imagined in our day. Especially the exploitation of women and children led to incredible suffering. Here are two examples, quoted from Marx's *Capital*: 'William Wood, 9 years old, was 7 years and 10 months when he began to work ... He came to work every day in the week at 6 a.m., and left off about 9 p.m ... ' 'Fifteen hours of labour for a child 7 years old!' exclaims an official report[14] of the Children's Employment Commission of 1863. Other children were forced to start work at 4 a.m., or to work throughout the night until 6 a.m., and it was not unusual for children of only six years to be forced to a daily toil of 15 hours.—'Mary Anne Walkley had worked without pause 26½ hours, together with sixty other girls, thirty of them in one room ... A doctor, Mr. Keys, called in too late, testified before the coroner's jury that "Mary Anne Walkley had died from long hours of work in an overcrowded workroom ... " Wishing to give this gentleman a lecture in good manners, the coroner's jury brought in a verdict to the effect that "the deceased had died of apoplexy, but there is reason to fear that her death had been accelerated by overwork in an overcrowded workroom".'[15] Such were the conditions of the working class even in 1863, when Marx was writing *Capital*; his burning protest against these crimes, which were then tolerated, and sometimes even defended, not only by professional economists but also by churchmen, will secure him forever a place among the liberators of mankind.

In view of such experiences, we need not wonder that Marx did not think very highly of liberalism, and that he saw in parliamentary democracy nothing but a veiled dictatorship of the bourgeoisie. And it was easy for him to interpret these facts as supporting his analysis of the relationship between the legal and the social system. According to the legal system, equality and freedom were established, at least approximately. But what did this mean in reality! Indeed, we must not blame Marx for insisting that the economic facts alone are 'real' and that the legal system may be a mere superstructure, a cloak for this reality, and an instrument of class domination.

The opposition between the legal and the social system is most clearly developed in *Capital*. In one of its theoretical parts (treated more fully in chapter 20), Marx approaches the analysis of the capitalist economic system by using the simplifying and idealizing assumption that the legal system is perfect in every respect. Freedom, equality before the law, justice, are all assumed to be guaranteed to everybody. There are no privileged classes before the law. Over and above that, he assumes that not even in the economic realm is there any kind of 'robbery'; he assumes that a 'just price' is paid for all commodities, including the labour power which the worker sells to the capitalist on the labour market. The price for all these commodities is 'just', in the sense that all commodities are bought and sold in proportion to the average amount of labour needed for their reproduction (or using Marx's terminology, they are bought and sold according to their true 'value'[16]). Of course, Marx knows that all this is an over-simplification, for it is his opinion that the workers are hardly ever treated as fairly as that; in other words, that they are usually cheated. But arguing from these idealized premises, he attempts to show that even under so excellent a legal system, the economic system would function in such a way that the workers would not be able to enjoy their freedom. In spite of all this 'justice', they would not be very much better off than slaves[17]. For if they are poor, they can only sell themselves, their wives and their children on the labour market, for as much as is necessary for the reproduction of their labour power. That is to say, for the whole of their labour power, they will not get more than the barest means of existence. This shows that exploitation is not merely robbery. It cannot be eliminated by merely legal means. (And Proudhon's criticism that 'property is theft' is much too superficial[18].)

In consequence of this, Marx was led to hold that the workers cannot hope much from the improvement of a legal system which as everybody knows grants to rich and poor alike the freedom of sleeping on park benches, and which threatens them alike with punishment for the attempt to live 'without visible means of support'. In this way Marx arrived at what may be termed (in Hegelian language) the distinction between *formal* and *material* freedom. Formal[19] or legal freedom, although Marx does not rate it low, turns out to be quite insufficient for securing to us that freedom which he considered to be the aim of the historical development of mankind. What matters is real, i.e. economic or material, freedom. This can be achieved only by an equal emancipation from drudgery. For this emancipation, 'the shortening of the labour day is the fundamental prerequisite'.

III

What have we to say to Marx's analysis? Are we to believe that politics, or the framework of legal institutions, are intrinsically impotent to remedy such a situation, and that only a complete social revolution, a complete change of the 'social system', can help? Or are we to believe the defenders of an unrestrained 'capitalist' system who emphasize (rightly, I think) the tremendous benefit to be derived from the mechanism of free markets, and who conclude from this that a truly free labour market would be of the greatest benefit to all concerned?

I believe that the injustice and inhumanity of the unrestrained 'capitalist system' described by Marx cannot be questioned; but it can be interpreted in terms of what we called, in a previous chapter[20], the *paradox of freedom*. Freedom, we have seen, defeats itself, if it is unlimited. Unlimited freedom means that a strong man is free to bully one who is weak and to rob him of his freedom. This is why we demand that the state should limit freedom to a certain extent, so that everyone's freedom is protected by law. Nobody should be at the *mercy* of others, but all should have a *right* to be protected by the state.

Now I believe that these considerations, originally meant to apply to the realm of brute-force, of physical intimidation, must be applied to the economic realm also. Even if the state protects its citizens from being bullied by physical violence (as it does, in principle, under the system of unrestrained capitalism), it may defeat our ends by its failure to protect them from the misuse of economic power. In such a state, the economically strong is still free to bully one who is economically weak, and to rob him of his freedom. Under these circumstances, unlimited economic freedom can be just as self-defeating as unlimited physical freedom, and economic power may be nearly as dangerous as physical violence; for those who possess a surplus of food can force those who are starving into a 'freely' accepted servitude, without using violence. And assuming that the state limits its activities to the suppression of violence (and to the protection of property), a minority which is economically strong may in this way exploit the majority of those who are economically weak.

If this analysis is correct[21], then the nature of the remedy is clear. It must be a *political* remedy—a remedy similar to the one which we use against physical violence. We must construct social institutions, enforced by the power of the state, for the protection of the economically weak from the economically strong. The state must see to it that nobody need enter into an inequitable arrangement out of fear of starvation, or economic ruin.

This, of course, means that the principle of non-intervention, of an unrestrained economic system, has to be given up; if we wish freedom to be safeguarded, then we must demand that the policy of unlimited economic freedom be replaced by the planned economic intervention of the state. We must demand that unrestrained *capitalism* give way to an *economic interventionism*[22].

And this is precisely what has happened. The economic system described and criticized by Marx has everywhere ceased to exist. It has been replaced, not by a system in which the state begins to lose its functions and consequently 'shows signs of withering away', but by various interventionist systems, in which the functions of the state in the economic realm are extended far beyond the protection of property and of 'free contracts'. (This development will be discussed in the next chapters.)

IV

I should like to characterize the point here reached as the most central point in our analysis. It is only here that we can begin to realize the significance of the clash between historicism and social engineering, and its effect upon the policy of the friends of the open society.

Marxism claims to be more than a science. It does more than make a historical prophecy. It claims to be the basis for practical political action. It criticizes existing society, and it asserts that it can lead the way to a better world. But according to Marx's own theory, we cannot at will alter the economic reality by, for example, legal reforms. Politics can do no more than 'shorten and lessen the birth-pangs'.[23] This, I think, is an extremely poor political programme, and its poverty is a consequence of the third-rate place which it attributes to political power in the hierarchy of powers. For according to Marx, the real power lies in the evolution of machinery; next in importance is the system of economic class-relationships; and the least important influence is that of politics.

A directly opposite view is implied in the position we have reached in our analysis. It considers political power as fundamental. Political power, from this point of view, can control economic power. This means an immense extension of the field of political activities. We can ask what we wish to achieve and how to achieve it. We can, for instance, develop a rational political programme for the protection of the economically weak. We can make laws to limit exploitation. We can limit the working day; but we can do much more. By law, we can insure the workers (or better still, all citizens) against disability, unemployment, and old age. In this way we can make impossible such forms of exploitation as are based upon the helpless economic position of a worker who must yield to anything in order not to starve. And when we are able by law to guarantee a livelihood to everybody willing to work, and there is no reason why we should not achieve that, then the protection of the freedom of the citizen from economic fear and economic intimidation will approach completeness. From this point of view, political power is the key to economic protection. Political power and its control is everything. Economic power must not be permitted to dominate political power; if necessary, it must be fought and brought under control by political power.

From the point of view reached, we can say that Marx's disparaging attitude towards political power not only means that he neglects to develop a theory of the most important potential means of bettering the lot of the economically weak, but also that he neglected the greatest potential danger to human freedom. His naïve view that, in a classless society, state power would lose its function and 'wither away' shows very clearly that he never grasped the paradox of freedom, and that he never understood the function which state power could and should perform, in the service of freedom and humanity. (Yet this view of Marx stands witness to the fact that he was, ultimately, an individualist, in spite of his collectivist appeal to class consciousness.) In this way, the Marxian view is analogous to the liberal belief that all we need is 'equality of opportunity'. We certainly need this. But it is not enough. It does not protect those who are less gifted, or less ruthless, or less lucky, from becoming objects of exploitation for those who are more gifted, or ruthless, or lucky.

Moreover, from the point of view we have reached, what Marxists describe disparagingly as 'mere formal freedom' becomes the basis of everything else. This 'mere formal freedom', i.e. democracy, the right of the people to judge and to dismiss their government, is the only known device by which we can try to protect ourselves against the misuse of political power[24]; it is the control of the rulers by the ruled. And since political power can control economic power, political democracy is also the only means for the control of economic power by the ruled. Without democratic control, there can be no earthly reason why any government should not use its political and economic power for purposes very different from the protection of the freedom of its citizens.

V

It is the fundamental rôle of 'formal freedom' which is overlooked by Marxists who think that formal democracy is not enough and wish to supplement it by what they usually call 'economic democracy'; a vague and utterly superficial phrase which obscures the fact that 'merely formal freedom' is the only guarantee of a democratic economic policy.

Marx discovered the significance of economic power; and it is understandable that he exaggerated its status. He and the Marxists see economic power everywhere. Their argument runs: he who has the money has the power; for if necessary, he can buy guns and even gangsters. But this is a roundabout argument. In fact, it contains an admission that the man who has the gun has the power. And if he who has the gun becomes aware of this, then it may not be long until he has both the gun and the money. But under an unrestrained capitalism, Marx's argument applies, to some extent; for a rule which develops institutions for the control of guns and gangsters but not of the power of money is liable to come under the influence of this power. In such a state, an uncontrolled gangsterism of wealth may rule. But Marx himself, I think, would have been the first to admit that this is not true of all states; that there have been times in history when, for example, all exploitation was looting, directly based upon the power of the mailed fist. And to-day there will be few to support the naïve view that the 'progress of history' has once and for all put an end to these more direct ways of exploiting men, and that, once formal freedom has been achieved, it is impossible for us to fall again under the sway of such primitive forms of exploitation.

These considerations would be sufficient for refuting the dogmatic doctrine that economic power is more fundamental than physical power, or the power of the state. But there are other considerations as well. As has been rightly emphasized by various writers (among them Bertrand Russell and Walter Lippmann[25]), it is only the active intervention of the state—the protection of property by laws backed by physical sanctions—which makes of wealth a potential source of power; for without this intervention, a man would soon be without his wealth. Economic power is therefore entirely dependent on political and physical power. Russell gives historical examples which illustrate this dependence, and sometimes even helplessness, of wealth: 'Economic power within the state,' he writes[26], 'although ultimately derived from law and public opinion, easily acquires a certain independence. It can influence law by corruption and public opinion by propaganda. It can put politicians under obligations which interfere with their freedom. It can threaten to cause a financial crisis. *But there are very definite limits to what it can achieve.* Cæsar was helped to power by his creditors, who saw no hope of repayment except through his success; but when he had succeeded he was powerful enough to defy them. Charles V borrowed from the Fuggers the money required to buy the position of Emperor, but when he had become Emperor he snapped his fingers at them and they lost what they had lent.'

The dogma that economic power is at the root of all evil must be discarded. Its place must be taken by an understanding of the dangers of *any* form of uncontrolled power. Money as such is not particularly dangerous. It becomes dangerous only if it can buy power, either directly, or by enslaving the economically weak who must sell themselves in order to live.

We must think in these matters in even more materialist terms, as it were, than Marx did. We must realize that the control of physical power and of physical exploitation remains the central political problem. In order to establish this control, we must establish 'merely formal freedom'. Once we have achieved this, and have learned how to use it for the control of political power, everything rests with us. We must not blame anybody else any longer, nor cry out against the sinister economic demons behind the scenes. For in a democracy, we hold the keys to the control of the demons. We can tame them. We must realize this and use the keys; we must construct institutions for the democratic control of economic power, and for our protection from economic exploitation.

Much has been made by Marxists of the possibility of buying votes, either directly or by buying propaganda. But closer consideration shows that we have here a good example of the power-political situation analysed above. Once we have achieved formal freedom, we can control vote-buying in every form. There are laws to limit the expenditure on electioneering, and it rests entirely with us to see that much more stringent laws of this kind are introduced[27]. The legal system can be made a powerful instrument for its own protection. In addition, we can influence public opinion, and insist upon a much more rigid moral code in political matters. All this we can do; but we must first realize that social engineering of this kind is our task, that it is in our power, and that we must not wait for economic earthquakes miraculously to produce a new economic world for us, so that all we shall have to do will be to unveil it, to remove the old political cloak.

VI

Of course, in practice Marxists never fully relied on the doctrine of the impotence of political power. So far as they had an opportunity to act, or to plan action, they usually assumed, like everybody else, that political power can be used for the control of economic power. But their plans and actions were never based on a clear refutation of their original theory, nor upon any well-considered view of that most fundamental problem of all politics: the control of the controller, of the dangerous accumulation of power represented in the state. They never realized the full significance of democracy as the only known means to achieve this control.

As a consequence they never realized the danger inherent in a policy of increasing the power of the state. Although they abandoned more or less unconsciously the doctrine of the impotence of politics, they retained the view that state power presents no important problem, and that it is bad only if it is in the hands of the bourgeoisie. They did not realize that *all* power, and political power at least as much as economic power, is dangerous. Thus they retained their formula of the dictatorship of the proletariat. They did not understand the principle (cp. chapter 8) that all large-scale politics must be institutional, not personal; and when clamouring for the extension of state powers (in contrast to Marx's view of the state) they never considered that the wrong persons might one day get hold of these extended powers. This is part of the reason why, as far as they proceeded to consider state-intervention, they planned to give the state practically limitless powers in the economic realm. They retained Marx's holistic and Utopian belief that only a brand-new 'social system' can improve matters.

I have criticized this Utopian and Romantic approach to social engineering in a previous chapter (chapter 9). But I wish to add here that economic intervention, even the piecemeal methods advocated here, will tend to increase the power of the state. Interventionism is therefore extremely dangerous. This is not a decisive argument against it; state power must always remain a dangerous though necessary evil. But it should be a warning that if we relax our watchfulness, and if we do not strengthen our democratic institutions while giving more power to the state by interventionist 'planning', then we may lose our freedom. And if freedom is lost, everything is lost, including 'planning'. For why should plans for the welfare of the people be carried out if the people have no power to enforce them? Only freedom can make security secure.

We thus see that there is not only a paradox of freedom but also a paradox of state planning. If we plan too much, if we give too much power to the state, then freedom will be lost, and that will be the end of planning.

Such considerations lead us back to our plea for piecemeal, and against Utopian or holistic, methods of social engineering. And they lead us back to our demand that measures should be planned to fight concrete evils rather than to establish some ideal good. State intervention should be limited to what is really necessary for the protection of freedom.

But it is not enough to say that our solution should be a minimum solution; that we should be watchful; and that we should not give more power to the state than is necessary for the protection of freedom. These remarks may raise problems, but they do not show a way to a solution. It is even conceivable that there is no solution; that the acquisition of new economic powers by a state—whose powers, as compared to those of its citizens, are always dangerously great—will make it irresistible. So far, we have shown neither that freedom can be preserved, nor how it can be preserved.

Under these circumstances it may be useful to remember our considerations of chapter 7 concerning the question of the control of political power and the paradox of freedom.

VII

The important distinction which we made there was that between persons and institutions. We pointed out that, while the political question of the day may demand a personal solution, all long-term policy—and especially all democratic long-term policy—must be conceived in terms of impersonal institutions. And we pointed out that, more especially, the problem of controlling the rulers, and of checking their powers, was in the main an institutional problem—the problem, in short, of designing institutions for preventing even bad rulers from doing too much damage.

Analogous considerations will apply to the problem of the control of the economic power of the state. What we shall have to guard against is an increase in the power of the rulers. We must guard against persons and against their arbitrariness. Some types of institution may confer arbitrary powers upon a person; but other types will deny them to that person.

If we look upon our labour legislation from this point of view, then we shall find both types of institution. Many of these laws add very little power to the executive organs of the state. It is conceivable, to be sure, that the laws against child labour, for example, may be misused, by a civil servant, to intimidate, and to dominate over, an innocent citizen. But dangers of this kind are hardly serious if compared with those which are inherent in a legislation that confers upon the rulers discretionary powers, such as the power of directing labour[28]. Similarly, a law establishing that a citizen's misuse of his property should be punished by its forfeiture will be incomparably less dangerous than one which gives the rulers, or the servants of the state, discretionary powers of requisitioning a citizen's property.

We thus arrive at a distinction between two entirely different methods[29] by which the economic intervention of the state may proceed. The first is that of designing a 'legal framework' of protective institutions (laws restricting the powers of the owner of an animal, or of a landowner, are an example). The second is that of empowering organs of the state to act—within certain limits—as they consider necessary for achieving the ends laid down by the rulers for the time being. We may describe the first procedure as 'institutional' or 'indirect' intervention, and the second as 'personal' or 'direct' intervention. (Of course, intermediate cases exist.)

There can be no doubt, from the point of view of democratic control, which of these methods is preferable. The obvious policy for all democratic intervention is to make use of the first method wherever this is possible, and to restrict the use of the second method to cases for which the first method is inadequate. (Such cases exist. The classical example is the Budget—this expression of the Chancellor's discretion and sense of what is equitable and just. And it is conceivable although highly undesirable that a counter-cycle measure may have to be of a similar character.)

From the point of view of piecemeal social engineering, the difference between the two methods is highly important. Only the first, the institutional method, makes it possible to make adjustments in the light of discussion and experience. It alone makes it possible to apply the method of trial and error to our political actions. It is long-term; yet the permanent legal framework can be slowly changed, in order to make allowances for unforeseen and undesired consequences, for changes in other parts of the framework, etc. It alone allows us to find out, by experience and analysis, what we actually were doing when we intervened with a certain aim in mind. Discretionary decisions of the rulers or civil servants are outside these rational methods. They are short-term decisions, transitory, changing from day to day, or at best, from year to year. As a rule (the Budget is the great exception) they cannot even be publicly discussed, both because necessary information is lacking, and because the principles on which the decision is taken are obscure. If they exist at all, they are usually not institutionalized, but part of an internal departmental tradition.

But it is not only in this sense that the first method can be described as rational and the second as irrational. It is also in an entirely different and highly important sense. The legal framework can be known and understood by the individual citizen; and it should be designed to be so understandable. Its functioning is predictable. It introduces a factor of certainty and security into social life. When it is altered, allowances can be made, during a transitional period, for those individuals who have laid their plans in the expectation of its constancy.

As opposed to this, the method of personal intervention must introduce an ever-growing element of unpredictability into social life, and with it will develop the feeling that social life is irrational and insecure. The use of discretionary powers is liable to grow quickly, once it has become an accepted method, since adjustments will be necessary, and adjustments to discretionary short-term decisions can hardly be carried out by institutional means. This tendency must greatly increase the irrationality of the system, creating in many the impression that there are hidden powers behind the scenes, and making them susceptible to the conspiracy theory of society with all its consequences—heresy hunts, national, social, and class hostility.

In spite of all this, the obvious policy of preferring where possible the institutional method is far from being generally accepted. The failure to accept it is, I suppose, due to different reasons. One is that it needs a certain detachment to embark on the long-term task of re-designing the 'legal framework'. But governments live from hand to mouth, and discretionary powers belong to this style of living—quite apart from the fact that rulers are inclined to love those powers for their own sake. But the most important reason is, undoubtedly, that the significance of the distinction between the two methods is not understood. The way to its understanding is blocked to the followers of Plato, Hegel, and Marx. They will never see that the old question 'Who shall be the rulers?' must be superseded by the more real one 'How can we tame them?'

VIII

If we now look back at Marx's theory of the impotence of politics and of the power of historical forces, then we must admit that it is an imposing edifice. It is the direct result of his sociological method; of his economic historicism, of the doctrine that the development of the economic system, or of man's metabolism, determines his social and political development. The experience of his time, his humanitarian indignation, and the need of bringing to the oppressed the consolation of a prophecy, the hope, or even the certainty, of their victory, all this is united in one grandiose philosophic system, comparable or even superior to the holistic systems of Plato and Hegel. It is only due to the accident that he was not a reactionary that the history of philosophy takes so little notice of him and assumes that he was mainly a propagandist. The reviewer of *Capital* who wrote: 'At the first glance ... we come to the conclusion that the author is one of the greatest among the idealist philosophers, in the German, that is to say, the bad sense of the word "idealist". But in actual fact, he is enormously more realistic than any of his predecessors ...'[30], this reviewer hit the nail on the head. Marx was the last of the great holistic system builders. We should take care to leave it at that, and not to replace his by another Great System. What we need is not holism. It is piecemeal social engineering.

With this, I conclude my critical analysis of Marx's philosophy of the *method* of social science, of his economic determinism as well as of his prophetic historicism. The final test of a method, however, must be its practical results. I therefore proceed now to a more detailed examination of the main result of his method, the prophecy of the impending advent of a classless society.

Marx's Prophecy

18

THE COMING OF SOCIALISM

I

Economic historicism is the method applied by Marx to an analysis of the impending changes in our society. According to Marx, every particular social system must destroy itself, simply because it must create the forces which produce the next historical period. A sufficiently penetrating analysis of the feudal system, undertaken shortly before the industrial revolution, might have led to the detection of the forces which were about to destroy feudalism, and to the prediction of the most important characteristics of the coming period, capitalism. Similarly, an analysis of the development of capitalism might enable us to detect the forces which work for its destruction, and to predict the most important characteristics of the new historical period which lies ahead of us. For there is surely no reason to believe that capitalism, of all social systems, will last for ever. On the contrary, the material conditions of production, and with them, the ways of human life, have never changed so quickly as they have done under capitalism. By changing its own foundations in this way, capitalism is bound to transform itself, and to produce a new period in the history of mankind.

According to Marx's method, the principles of which have been discussed above, the fundamental or essential[1] forces which will destroy or transform capitalism must be searched for in the evolution of the material means of production. Once these fundamental forces have been discovered, it is possible to trace their influence upon the social relationships between classes as well as upon the juridical and political systems.

The analysis of the fundamental economic forces and the suicidal historical tendencies of the period which he called 'capitalism' was undertaken by Marx in *Capital*, the great work of his life. The historical period and the economic system he dealt with was that of western Europe and especially England, from about the middle of the eighteenth century to 1867 (the year of the first publication of *Capital*). The 'ultimate aim of this work', as Marx explained in his preface[2], was 'to lay bare the economic law of motion of modern society', in order to prophesy its fate. A secondary aim[3] was the refutation of the apologists of capitalism, of the economists who presented the laws of the capitalist mode of production as if they were inexorable laws of nature, declaring with Burke: 'The laws of commerce are the laws of nature, and therefore the laws of God.' Marx contrasted these allegedly inexorable laws with those which he maintained to be the only inexorable laws of society, namely, its laws of development; and he tried to show that what the economists declared to be eternal and immutable laws were in fact merely temporary regularities, doomed to be destroyed together with capitalism itself.

Marx's historical prophecy can be described as a closely knit argument. But *Capital* elaborates only what I shall call the 'first step' of this argument, the analysis of the fundamental economic forces of capitalism and their influence upon the relations between the classes. The 'second step', which leads to the conclusion that a social revolution is inevitable, and the 'third step', which leads to the prediction of the emergence of a classless, i.e. socialist, society, are only sketched. In this chapter, I shall first explain more clearly what I call the three steps of the Marxist argument, and then discuss the third of these steps in detail. In the two following chapters, I shall discuss the second and the first steps. To reverse the order of the steps in this way turns out to be best for a detailed critical discussion; the advantage lies in the fact that it is then easier to assume without prejudice the truth of the premises of each step in the argument, and to concentrate entirely upon the question whether the conclusion reached in this particular step follows from its premises. Here are the three steps.

In the *first step* of his argument, Marx analyses the method of capitalist production. He finds that there is a tendency towards an *increase in the productivity* of work, connected with technical improvements as well as with what he calls the increasing *accumulation* of the means of production. Starting from here, the argument leads him to the conclusion that in the realm of the social relations between the classes this tendency must lead to the accumulation of more and more wealth in fewer and fewer hands; that is to say, the conclusion is reached that there will be a tendency towards an *increase of wealth and misery*; of wealth in the ruling class, the bourgeoisie, and of misery in the ruled class, the workers. This first step will be treated in chapter 20 ('Capitalism and Its Fate').

In the *second step* of the argument, the result of the first step is taken for granted. From it, two conclusions are drawn; first, that all classes except a small ruling bourgeoisie and a large exploited working class are bound to disappear, or to become insignificant; secondly, that the increasing tension between these two classes must lead to a *social revolution*. This step will be analysed in chapter 19 ('The Social Revolution').

In the *third step* of the argument, the conclusions of the second step are taken for granted in their turn; and the final conclusion reached is that, after the victory of the workers over the bourgeoisie, there will be a society consisting of one class only, and, therefore, a classless society, a society without exploitation; that is to say, *socialism*.

II

I now proceed to the *discussion of the third step*, of the final prophecy of the coming of socialism.

The main premises of this step, to be criticized in the next chapter but here to be taken for granted, are these: the development of capitalism has led to the elimination of all classes but two, a small bourgeoisie and a huge proletariat; and the increase of misery has forced the latter to revolt against its exploiters. The conclusions are, first, that the workers must win the struggle, secondly that, by eliminating the bourgeoisie, they must establish a classless society, since only one class remains.

Now I am prepared to grant that the first conclusion follows from the premises (in conjunction with a few premises of minor importance which we need not question). Not only is the number of the bourgeoisie small, but their physical existence, their 'metabolism', depends upon the proletariat. The exploiter, the drone, starves without the exploited; in any case, if he destroys the exploited then he ends his own career as a drone. Thus he cannot win; he can, at the best, put up a prolonged struggle. The worker, on the other hand, does not depend for his material subsistence on his exploiter; once the worker revolts, once he has decided to challenge the existing order, the exploiter has no essential social function any longer. The worker can destroy his class enemy without endangering his own existence. Accordingly, there is only one outcome possible. The bourgeoisie will disappear.

But does the second conclusion follow? Is it true that the workers' victory must lead to a classless society? I do not think so. From the fact that of two classes only one remains, it does not follow that there will be a classless society. *Classes are not like individuals*, even if we admit that they behave nearly like individuals so long as there are *two* classes who are joined in battle. The unity or solidarity of a class, according to Marx's own analysis, is part of their class consciousness[4], which in turn is very largely a product of the class struggle. There is no earthly reason why the individuals who form the proletariat should retain their class unity once the pressure of the struggle against the common class enemy has ceased. Any latent conflict of interests is now likely to divide the formerly united proletariat into new classes, and to develop into a new class struggle. (The principles of dialectics would suggest that a new antithesis, a new class antagonism, must soon develop. Yet, of course, dialectics is sufficiently vague and adaptable to explain anything at all, and therefore a classless society also, as a dialectically necessary synthesis of an antithetical development[5].)

The most likely development is, of course, that those actually in power at the moment of victory—those of the revolutionary leaders who have survived the struggle for power and the various purges, together with their staff—will form a *New Class: the new ruling class of the new society*, a kind of new aristocracy or bureaucracy[6]; and it is most likely that they will attempt to hide this fact. This they can do, most conveniently, by retaining as much as possible of the revolutionary ideology, taking advantage of these sentiments instead of wasting their time in efforts to destroy them (in accordance with Pareto's advice to all rulers). And it seems likely enough that they will be able to make fullest use of the revolutionary ideology if at the same time they exploit the fear of counter-revolutionary developments. In this way, the revolutionary ideology will serve them for apologetic purposes: it will serve them both as a vindication of the use they make of their power, and as a means of stabilizing it; in short, as a new 'opium for the people'.

Something of this kind are the events which, on Marx's own premises, are likely to happen. Yet it is not my task here to make historical prophecies (or to interpret the past history of many revolutions). I merely wish to show that Marx's conclusion, the prophecy of the coming of a classless society, does not follow from the premises. The third step of Marx's argument must be pronounced to be inconclusive.

More than this I do not maintain. I do not think, more particularly, that it is possible to prophesy that socialism will not come, or to say that the premises of the argument make the introduction of socialism very unlikely. It is, for instance, possible that the prolonged struggle and the enthusiasm of victory may contribute to a feeling of solidarity strong enough to continue until laws preventing exploitation and the misuse of power are established.

(The establishment of institutions for the democratic control of the rulers is the only guarantee for the elimination of exploitation.) The chances of founding such a society will depend, in my opinion, very largely upon the devotion of the workers to the ideas of socialism and freedom, as opposed to the immediate interests of their class. These are matters which cannot be easily foreseen; all that can certainly be said is that class struggle as such does not always produce lasting solidarity among the oppressed. There are examples of such solidarity and great devotion to the common cause; but there are also examples of groups of workers who pursue their particular group interest even where it is in open conflict with the interest of the other workers, and with the idea of the solidarity of the oppressed. Exploitation need not disappear with the bourgeoisie, since it is quite possible that groups of workers may obtain privileges which amount to an exploitation of less fortunate groups[7].

We see that a whole host of possible historical developments may follow upon a victorious proletarian revolution. There are certainly too many possibilities for the application of the method of historical prophecy. And in particular it must be emphasized that it would be most unscientific to close our eyes to some possibilities because we do not like them. Wishful thinking is apparently a thing that cannot be avoided. But it should not be mistaken for scientific thinking. And we should also recognize that the allegedly scientific prophecy provides, for a great number of people, a form of escape. It provides an escape from our present responsibilities into a future paradise; and it provides the fitting complement of this paradise by overstressing the helplessness of the individual in face of what it describes as the overwhelming and demoniacal economic forces of the present moment.

III

If we now look a little more closely at these forces, and at our own present economic system, then we can see that our theoretical criticism is borne out by experience. But we must be on our guard against misinterpreting experience in the light of the Marxist prejudice that 'socialism' or 'communism' is the only alternative and the only possible successor to 'capitalism'. Neither Marx nor anybody else has ever shown that socialism, in the sense of a classless society, of 'an association in which the free development of each is the warrant for the free development of all'[8], is the only possible alternative to the ruthless exploitation of that economic system which he first described a century ago (in 1845), and to which he gave the name 'capitalism'[9]. And indeed, if anybody were attempting to prove that socialism is the only possible successor to Marx's unrestrained 'capitalism', then we could simply refute him by pointing to historical facts. For *laissez-faire* has disappeared from the face of the earth, but it has not been replaced by a socialist or communist system as Marx understood it. Only in the Russian sixth of the earth do we find an economic system where, in accordance with Marx's prophecy, the means of production are owned by the state, whose political might however shows, in opposition to Marx's prophecy, no inclination to wither away. But all over the earth, organized political power has begun to perform far-reaching economic functions. *Unrestrained capitalism* has given way to a new historical period, to our own period of political *interventionism*, of the economic interference of the state. Interventionism has assumed various forms. There is the Russian variety; there is the fascist form of totalitarianism; and there is the democratic interventionism of England, of the United States, and of the 'Smaller Democracies', led by Sweden[10], where the technology of democratic intervention has reached its highest level so far. The development which led to this intervention started in Marx's own day, with British factory legislation. It made its first decisive advances with the introduction of the 48-hour week, and later with the introduction of unemployment insurance and other forms of social insurance. How utterly absurd it is to identify the economic system of the modern democracies with the system Marx called 'capitalism' can be seen at a glance, by comparing it with his 10-point programme for the communist revolution. If we omit the rather insignificant points of this programme (for instance, '4. Confiscation of the property of all emigrants and rebels'), then we can say that in the democracies most of these points have been put into practice, either completely, or to a considerable degree; and with them, many more important steps, which Marx had never thought of, have been made in the direction of social security. I mention only the following points in his programme: 2. A heavy progressive or graduated income tax. (Carried out.) 3. Abolition of all right of inheritance. (Largely realized by heavy death duties. Whether more would be desirable is at least doubtful.) 6. Central control by the state of the means of communication and transport. (For military reasons this was carried out in Central Europe before the war of 1914, without very beneficial results. It has also been achieved by most of the Smaller Democracies.) 7. Increase in the number and size of factories and instruments of production owned by the state ... (Realized in the Smaller Democracies; whether this is always very beneficial is at least doubtful.) 10. Free education for all children in public (i.e. state) schools. Abolition of children's factory labour in its present form ... (The first demand is fulfilled in the Smaller Democracies, and to some extent practically everywhere; the second has been exceeded.)

A number of points in Marx's programme[11] (for instance: '1. Abolition of all property in land') have not been realized in the democratic countries. This is why Marxists rightly claim that these countries have not established 'socialism'. But if they infer from this that these countries are still 'capitalist' in Marx's sense, then they only demonstrate the dogmatic character of their presupposition that there is no further alternative. This shows how it is possible to be blinded by the glare of a preconceived system. Not only is Marxism a bad guide to the future, but it also renders its followers incapable of seeing what is happening before their own eyes, in their own historical period, and sometimes even with their own co-operation.

IV

But it could be asked whether this criticism speaks in any way against the method of large-scale historical prophecy as such. Could we not, in principle, so strengthen the premises of the prophetic argument as to obtain a valid conclusion? Of course we could do this. It is always possible to obtain any conclusion we like if only we make our premises sufficiently strong. But the situation is such that, for nearly every large-scale historical prophecy, we would have to make such assumptions concerning moral and other factors of the kind called by Marx 'ideological' as are beyond our ability to reduce to economic factors. But Marx would have been the first to admit that this would be a highly unscientific proceeding. His whole method of prophecy depends on the assumption that ideological influences need not be treated as independent and unpredictable elements, but that they are reducible to, and dependent on, observable economic conditions, and therefore predictable.

It is sometimes admitted even by certain unorthodox Marxists that the coming of socialism is not merely a matter of historical development; Marx's statement that 'we can shorten and lessen the birth-pangs' of the coming of socialism is sufficiently vague to be interpreted as stating that a mistaken policy might delay the advent of socialism even for centuries, as compared with the proper policy which would shorten the time of the development to a minimum. This interpretation makes it possible even for Marxists to admit that it will depend largely upon ourselves whether or not the outcome of a revolution will be a socialist society; that is to say, it will depend upon our aims, upon our devotion and sincerity, and upon our intelligence, in other words, upon moral or 'ideological' factors. Marx's prophecy, they may add, is a great source of moral encouragement, and it is therefore likely to further the development of socialism. What Marx really tries to show is that there are only two possibilities: that a terrible world should continue forever, or that a better world should eventually emerge; and it is hardly worth our while to contemplate the first alternative seriously. Therefore Marx's prophecy is fully justified. For the more clearly men realize that they can achieve the second alternative, the more surely will they make a decisive leap from capitalism to socialism; but a more definite prophecy cannot be made.

This is an argument which admits the influence of irreducible moral and ideological factors upon the course of history, and with it, the inapplicability of the Marxist method. Concerning that part of the argument which tries to defend Marxism, we must repeat that nobody has ever shown that there are only two possibilities, 'capitalism' and 'socialism'. With the view that we should not waste our time in contemplating the eternal continuation of a very unsatisfactory world, I quite agree. But the alternative need not be to contemplate the prophesied advent of a better world, or to assist its birth by propaganda and other irrational means, perhaps even by violence. It can be, for instance, the development of a technology for the immediate improvement of the world we live in, the development of a method for piecemeal engineering, for democratic intervention[12]. Marxists would of course contend that this kind of intervention is impossible since history cannot be made according to rational plans for improving the world. But this theory has very strange consequences. For if things cannot be improved by the use of reason, then it would be indeed an historical or political miracle if the irrational powers of history by themselves were to produce a better and more rational world[13].

Thus we are thrown back to the position that moral and other ideological factors which do not fall within the scope of scientific prophecy exert a far-reaching influence upon the course of history. One of these unpredictable factors is just the influence of social technology and of political intervention in economic matters. The social technologist and the piecemeal engineer may plan the construction of new institutions, or the transformation of old ones; they may even plan the ways and means of bringing these changes about; but 'history' does not become more predictable by their doing so. For they do not plan for the whole of society, nor can they know whether their plans will be carried out; in fact, they will hardly ever be carried out without great modification, partly because our experience grows during construction, partly because we must compromise[14]. Thus Marx was quite right when he insisted that 'history' cannot be planned on paper. But *institutions* can be planned; and they are being planned. Only by planning[15], step by step, for institutions to safeguard freedom, especially freedom from exploitation, can we hope to achieve a better world.

V

In order to show the practical political significance of Marx's historicist theory, I intend to illustrate each of the three chapters dealing with the three steps of his prophetic argument by a few remarks on the effects of his historical prophecy upon recent European history. For these effects have been far-reaching, because of the influence exercised, in Central and Eastern Europe, by the two great Marxist parties, the Communists and the Social Democrats.

Both these parties were entirely unprepared for such a task as the transformation of society. The Russian Communists, who found themselves first within reach of power, went ahead, entirely unaware of the grave problems and the immensity of sacrifice as well as of suffering which lay ahead. The Social Democrats of Central Europe, whose chance came a little later, shrank for many years from the responsibilities which the Communists had so readily taken upon themselves. They doubted, probably rightly, whether any people but that of Russia, which had been most savagely oppressed by Tsarism, would have stood up to the sufferings and sacrifices demanded from them by revolution, civil war, and a long period of at first often unsuccessful experiments. Moreover, during the critical years from 1918 to 1926, the outcome of the Russian experiment appeared to them most uncertain. And, indeed, there was surely no basis for judging its prospects. One can say that the split between the Central European Communists and Social Democrats was one between those Marxists who had a kind of irrational faith in the final success of the Russian experiment, and those who were, more reasonably, sceptical of it. When I say 'irrational' and 'more reasonably', I judge them by their own standard, by Marxism; for according to Marxism, the proletarian revolution should have been the final outcome of industrialization, and not *vice versa*[16]; and it should have come first in the highly industrialized countries, and only much later in Russia[17].

This remark is not, however, intended as a defence of the Social Democratic leaders[18] whose policy was fully determined by the Marxist prophecy, by their implicit belief that socialism must come. But this belief was often combined, in the leaders, with a hopeless scepticism concerning their own immediate functions and tasks, and what lay immediately ahead[19]. They had learned from Marxism to organize the workers, and to inspire them with a truly wonderful faith in their task, the liberation of mankind[20]. But they were unable to prepare for the realization of their promises. They had learned their textbooks well, they knew all about 'scientific socialism', and they knew that the preparation of recipes for the future was unscientific

Utopianism. Had not Marx himself ridiculed a follower of Comte who had criticized him in the *Revue Positiviste* for his neglect of practical programmes? 'The *Revue Positiviste* accuses me', Marx had said[21] scornfully, 'of a metaphysical treatment of economics, and further—you would hardly guess it—of confining myself to a merely critical analysis of actual facts, instead of prescribing recipes (Comtist ones, perhaps?) for the kitchen in which the future is cooked.' Thus the Marxist leaders knew better than to waste their time on such matters as technology. 'Workers of all countries, unite!'—that exhausted their practical programme. When the workers of their countries were united, when there was an opportunity of assuming the responsibility of government and laying the foundations for a better world, when their hour had struck, they left the workers high and dry. The leaders did not know what to do. They waited for the promised suicide of capitalism. After the inevitable capitalist collapse, when things had gone thoroughly wrong, when everything was in dissolution and the risk of discredit and disgrace to themselves considerably diminished, then they hoped to become the saviours of mankind. (And, indeed, we should keep in mind the fact that the success of the Communists in Russia was undoubtedly made possible, in part, by the terrible things that had happened before their rise to power.) But when the great depression, which they first welcomed as the promised collapse, was running its course, they began to realize that the workers were growing tired of being fed and put off with interpretations of history[22]; that it was not enough to tell them that according to the infallible scientific socialism of Marx fascism was definitely the last stand of capitalism before its impending collapse. The suffering masses needed more than that. Slowly the leaders began to realize the terrible consequences of a policy of waiting and hoping for the great political miracle. But it was too late. Their opportunity was gone.

These remarks are very sketchy. But they give some indication of the practical consequences of Marx's prophecy of the coming of socialism.

19

THE SOCIAL REVOLUTION

The second step of Marx's prophetic argument has as its most relevant premise the assumption that capitalism must lead to an increase of wealth and misery; of wealth in the numerically declining bourgeoisie, and of misery in the numerically increasing working class. This assumption will be criticized in the next chapter but is here taken for granted. The conclusions drawn from it can be divided into two parts. The first part is a prophecy concerning the development of the *class structure* of capitalism. It affirms that all classes apart from the bourgeoisie and the proletariat, and especially the so-called middle classes, are bound to disappear, and that, in consequence of the increasing tension between the bourgeoisie and the proletariat, the latter will become increasingly class-conscious and united. The second part is the prophecy that this tension cannot possibly be removed, and that it will lead to a proletarian *social revolution*.

I believe that neither of the two conclusions follows from the premise. My criticism will be, in the main, similar to that propounded in the last chapter; that is to say, I shall try to show that Marx's argument neglects a great number of possible developments.

I

Let us consider at once the *first conclusion*, i.e. the prophecy that all classes are bound to disappear, or to become insignificant, except the bourgeoisie and the proletariat whose class consciousness and solidarity must increase. It must be admitted that the premise, Marx's theory of increasing wealth and misery, provides indeed for the disappearance of a certain middle class, that of the weaker capitalists and the petty bourgeoisie. 'Each capitalist lays many of his fellows low', as Marx puts it[1]; and these fellow capitalists may indeed be reduced to the position of wage-earners, which for Marx is the same as proletarians. This movement is part of the increase of wealth, the accumulation of more and more capital, and its concentration and centralization in fewer and fewer hands. An analogous fate is meted out to 'the lower strata of the middle class', as Marx says[2]. 'The small tradespeople, shopkeepers, and retired tradesmen generally, the handicraftsmen and the peasants, all these sink gradually into the proletariat; partly because their small capital, insufficient as it is for the scale on which modern industry is conducted, is overwhelmed in the competition with the bigger capitalists; partly because their specialized skill is rendered worthless by new means of production. Thus the proletariat is recruited from all classes of the population.' This description is certainly fairly accurate, especially so far as handicrafts are concerned; and it is also true that many proletarians come from peasant stock.

But admirable as Marx's observations are, the picture is defective. The movement he investigated is an industrial movement; his 'capitalist' is the industrial capitalist, his 'proletarian' the industrial worker. And in spite of the fact that many industrial workers come from peasant stock, this does not mean that the farmers and peasants, for instance, are all gradually reduced to the position of industrial workers. Even the agricultural labourers are not necessarily united with the industrial workers by a common feeling of solidarity and class consciousness. 'The dispersion of the rural workers over large areas', Marx admits[3], 'breaks down their power of resistance at the very time when the concentration of capital in a few hands increases the power of resistance of the urban workers.' This hardly suggests unification in one class-conscious whole. It shows, rather, that there is at least a possibility of division, and that the agricultural worker might sometimes be too dependent upon his master, the farmer or peasant, to make common cause with the industrial proletariat. But that farmers or peasants may easily choose to support the bourgeoisie rather than the workers was mentioned by Marx himself[4]; and a workers' programme such as the one of the *Manifesto*[5], whose first demand is the 'abolition of all property in land', is hardly designed to counteract this tendency.

This shows that it is at least possible that the rural middle classes may not disappear, and that the rural proletariat may not merge with the industrial proletariat. But this is not all. Marx's own analysis shows that it is vitally important for the bourgeoisie to foment division among the wage-earners; and as Marx himself has seen, this might be achieved in at least two ways. One way is the creation of a *new* middle class, of a privileged group of wage-earners who would feel superior to the manual worker[6] and at the same time dependent upon the rulers' mercy. The other way is the utilization of that lowest stratum of society which Marx christened the 'rabble-proletariat'. This is, as pointed out by Marx, the recruiting ground for criminals who may be ready to sell themselves to the class enemy. Increasing misery must tend, as he admits, to swell the numbers of this class; a development which will hardly contribute to the solidarity of all the oppressed.

But even the solidarity of the class of industrial workers is not a necessary consequence of increasing misery. Admittedly, increasing misery must produce resistance, and it is even likely to produce rebellious outbreaks. But the assumption of our argument is that the misery cannot be alleviated until victory has been won in the social revolution. This implies that the resisting workers will be beaten again and again in their fruitless attempts to better their lot. But such a development need not make the workers class-conscious in the Marxist sense[7], i.e. proud of their class and assured of their mission; it may make them, rather, class-conscious in the sense of being conscious of the fact that they belong to a beaten army. And it probably will do so, if the workers do not find strength in the realization that their numbers as well as their potential economic powers continue to grow. This might be the case if, as Marx prophesied, all classes, apart from their own and that of the capitalists, were to show a tendency to disappear. But since, as we have seen, this prophecy need not come true, it is possible that the solidarity of even the industrial workers may be undermined by defeatism.

Thus, as opposed to Marx's prophecy which insists that there must develop a neat division between two classes, we find that on his own assumptions, the following class structure may possibly develop: (1) bourgeoisie, (2) big landed proprietors, (3) other landowners, (4) rural workers, (5) new middle class, (6) industrial workers, (7) rabble proletariat. (Any other combination of these classes may, of course, develop too.) And we find, furthermore, that such a development may possibly undermine the unity of (6).

We can say, therefore, that the first conclusion of the second step in Marx's argument does not follow. But as in my criticism of the third step, here also I must say that I do not intend to replace Marx's prophecy by another one. I do not assert that the prophecy cannot come true, or that the alternative developments I have described will come to pass. I only assert that they may come to pass. (And, indeed, this possibility can hardly be denied by members of the radical Marxist wings who use the accusation of treachery, bribery, and insufficient class solidarity as favourite devices for explaining away developments which do not conform to the prophetic schedule.) That such things may happen should be clear to anybody who has observed the development which has led to fascism, in which all the possibilities I have mentioned played a part. But the mere possibility is sufficient to destroy the first conclusion reached in the second step of Marx's argument.

This of course affects the *second conclusion*, the prophecy of the coming social revolution. But before I can enter into a criticism of the way in which this prophecy is arrived at, it is necessary to discuss at some length the rôle played by it within the whole argument, as well as Marx's use of the term 'social revolution'.

II

What Marx meant when he spoke of the *social revolution* seems at first sight clear enough. His 'social revolution of the proletariat' is a *historical concept*. It denotes the more or less rapid transition from the historical period of capitalism to that of socialism. In other words, it is the name of a transitional period of class struggle between the two main classes, down to the ultimate victory of the workers. When asked whether the term 'social revolution' implied a violent civil war between the two classes, Marx answered[8] that this was not necessarily implied, adding, however, that the prospects of avoiding civil war were, unfortunately, not very bright. And he might have added further that, from the point of view of historical prophecy, the question appears to be perhaps not quite irrelevant, but at any rate of secondary importance. Social life is violent, Marxism insists, and the class war claims its victims every day[9]. What really matters is the result, socialism. To achieve this result is the essential characteristic of the 'social revolution'.

Now if we could take it as established, or as intuitively certain, that capitalism will be followed by socialism, then this explanation of the term 'social revolution' might be quite satisfactory. But since we must make use of the doctrine of social revolution as a part of that scientific argument by which we try to establish the coming of socialism, the explanation is very unsatisfactory indeed. If in such an argument we try to characterize the social revolution as the transition to socialism, then the argument becomes as circular as that of the doctor who was asked to justify his prediction of the death of a patient, and had to confess that he knew neither the symptoms nor anything else of the malady—only that it would turn into a 'fatal malady'. (If the patient did not die, then it was not yet the 'fatal malady'; and if a revolution does not lead to socialism, then it is not yet the 'social revolution'.) We can also give to this criticism the simple form that in none of the three steps of the prophetic argument must we assume anything whatever that is deduced only in a later step.

These considerations show that, for a proper reconstruction of Marx's argument, we must find such a characterization of the social revolution as does not refer to socialism, and as permits the social revolution to play its part in this argument as well as possible. A characterization which fulfils these conditions appears to be this. The social revolution is an attempt of a largely united proletariat to conquer complete political power, undertaken with the firm resolution not to shrink from violence, should violence be necessary for achieving this aim, and to resist any effort of its opponents to regain political influence. This characterization is free from the difficulties just mentioned; it fits the third step of the argument in so far as this third step is valid, giving it that degree of plausibility which the step undoubtedly possesses; and it is, as will be shown, in agreement with Marxism, and especially with its historicist tendency to avoid a definite[10] statement about whether or not violence will actually be used in this phase of history.

But although if regarded as an historical prophecy the proposed characterization is indefinite about the use of violence, it is important to realize that it is not so from a moral or legal point of view. Considered from such a point of view, the characterization of the social revolution here proposed undoubtedly makes of it a *violent uprising*; for the question whether or not violence is actually used is less significant than the intention; and we have assumed a firm resolution not to shrink from violence should it be necessary for achieving the aims of the movement. To say that the resolution not to shrink from violence is decisive for the character of the social revolution as a violent uprising is in agreement not only with the moral or legal point of view, but also with the ordinary view of the matter. For if a man is determined to use violence in order to achieve his aims, then we may say that to all intents and purposes he adopts a violent attitude, whether or not violence is actually used in a particular case. Admittedly, in trying to predict a future action of this man, we should have to be just as indefinite as Marxism, stating that we do not know whether or not he will actually resort to force. (Thus our characterization agrees in this point with the Marxist view.) But this lack of definiteness clearly disappears if we do not attempt historical prophecy, but try to characterize his attitude in the ordinary way.

Now I wish to make it quite clear that it is this prophecy of a possibly violent revolution which I consider, from the point of view of practical politics, by far the most harmful element in Marxism; and I think it will be better if I briefly explain the reason for my opinion before I proceed with my analysis.

I am not in all cases and under all circumstances against a violent revolution. I believe with some medieval and Renaissance Christian thinkers who taught the admissibility of tyrannicide that there may indeed, under a tyranny, be no other possibility, and that a violent revolution may be justified. But I also believe that any such revolution should have as its *only* aim the establishment of a democracy; and by a democracy I do not mean something as vague as 'the rule of the people' or 'the rule of the majority', but a set of institutions (among them especially general elections, i.e. the right of the people to dismiss their government) which permit public control of the rulers and their dismissal by the ruled, and which make it possible for the ruled to obtain reforms without using violence, even against the will of the rulers. In other words, the use of violence is justified only under a tyranny which makes reforms without violence impossible, and it should have only one aim, that is, to bring about a state of affairs which makes reforms without violence possible.

I do not believe that we should ever attempt to achieve more than that by violent means. For I believe that such an attempt would involve the risk of destroying all prospects of reasonable reform. The prolonged use of violence may lead in the end to the loss of freedom, since it is liable to bring about not a dispassionate rule of reason, but the rule of the strong man. A violent revolution which tries to attempt more than the destruction of tyranny is at least as likely to bring about another tyranny as it is likely to achieve its real aims.

There is only one further use of violence in political quarrels which I should consider justified. I mean the resistance, once democracy has been attained, to any attack (whether from within or without the state) against the democratic constitution and the use of democratic methods. Any such attack, especially if it comes from the government in power, or if it is tolerated by it, should be resisted by all loyal citizens, even to the use of violence. In fact, the working of democracy rests largely upon the understanding that a government which attempts to misuse its powers and to establish itself as a tyranny (or which tolerates the establishment of a tyranny by anybody else) outlaws itself, and that the citizens have not only a right but also a duty to consider the action of such a government as a crime, and its members as a dangerous gang of criminals. But I hold that such violent resistance to attempts to overthrow democracy should be unambiguously defensive. No shadow of doubt must be left that the only aim of the resistance is to save democracy. A threat of making use of the situation for the establishment of a counter-tyranny is just as criminal as the original attempt to introduce a tyranny; the use of such a threat, even if made with the candid intention of saving democracy by deterring its enemies, would therefore be a very bad method of defending democracy; indeed, such a threat would confuse the ranks of its defenders in an hour of peril, and would therefore be likely to help the enemy.

These remarks indicate that a successful democratic policy demands from the defenders the observance of certain rules. A few such rules will be listed later in this chapter; here I only wish to make it clear why I consider the Marxist attitude towards violence one of the most important points to be dealt with in any analysis of Marx.

III

According to their interpretation of the social revolution, we may distinguish between two main groups of Marxists, a radical wing and a moderate wing (corresponding roughly, but not precisely[11], to the Communist and the Social Democratic parties).

Marxists often decline to discuss the question whether or not a violent revolution would be 'justified'; they say that they are not moralists, but scientists, and that they do not deal with speculations about what ought to be, but with the facts of what is or will be. In other words, they are historical prophets who confine themselves to the question of what will happen. But let us assume that we have succeeded in persuading them to discuss the justification of the social revolution. In this case, I believe that we should find all Marxists agreeing, in principle, with the old view that violent revolutions are justified only if they are directed against a tyranny. From here on, the opinions of the two wings differ.

The radical wing insists that, according to Marx, all class rule is necessarily a dictatorship, i.e. a tyranny[12]. A real democracy can therefore be attained only by the establishment of a classless society, by overthrowing, if necessary violently, the capitalist dictatorship. The moderate wing does not agree with this view, but insists that democracy can to some extent be realized even under capitalism, and that it is therefore possible to conduct the social revolution by peaceful and gradual reforms. But even this moderate wing insists that such a peaceful development is uncertain; it points out that it is the bourgeoisie which is likely to resort to force, if faced with the prospect of being defeated by the workers on the democratic battlefield; and it contends that in this case the workers would be justified in retaliating, and in establishing their rule by violent means[13]. Both wings claim to represent the true Marxism of Marx, and in a way, both are right. For, as mentioned above, Marx's views in this matter were somewhat ambiguous, because of his historicist approach; over and above this, he seems to have changed his views during the course of his life, starting as a radical and later adopting a more moderate position[14].

I shall examine the *radical position* first, since it appears to me the only one which fits in with *Capital* and the whole trend of Marx's prophetic argument. For it is the main doctrine of *Capital* that the antagonism between capitalist and worker must necessarily increase, and that there is no compromise possible, so that capitalism can only be destroyed, not improved. It will be best to quote the fundamental passage of *Capital* in which Marx finally sums up the 'historical tendency of capitalist accumulation'. He writes[15]: 'Along with the steady decrease in the number of capitalist magnates who usurp and monopolize all the advantages of this development, there grows the extent of misery, oppression, servitude, degradation, and exploitation; but at the same time, there rises the rebellious indignation of the working class which is steadily growing in number, and which is being disciplined, unified, and organized by the very mechanism of the capitalist method of production. Ultimately, the monopoly of capital becomes a fetter upon the mode of production which has flourished with it, and under it. Both the centralization in a few hands of the means of production, and the social organization of labour, reach a point where their capitalist cloak becomes a strait-jacket. It bursts asunder. The hour of capitalist private property has struck. The expropriators are expropriated.'

In view of this fundamental passage, there can be little doubt that the core of Marx's teaching in *Capital* was the impossibility of reforming capitalism, and the prophecy of its violent overthrow; a doctrine corresponding to that of the radical wing. And this doctrine fits into our prophetic argument as well as can be. For if we grant not only the premise of the second step but the first conclusion as well, then the prophecy of the social revolution would indeed follow, in accordance with the passage we have quoted from *Capital*. (And the victory of the workers would follow too, as pointed out in the last chapter.) Indeed, it seems hard to envisage a fully united and class-conscious working class which would not in the end, if their misery cannot be mitigated by any other means, make a determined attempt to overthrow the social order. But this does not, of course, save the second conclusion. For we have already shown that the first conclusion is invalid; and from the premise alone, from the theory of increasing wealth and misery, the inevitability of the social revolution cannot be derived. As pointed out in our analysis of the first conclusion, all we can say is that rebellious outbreaks may be unavoidable; but since we can be sure neither of class unity nor of a developed class consciousness among the workers, we cannot identify such outbreaks with the social revolution. (They need not be victorious either, so that the assumption that they represent the social revolution would not fit in with the third step.)

As opposed to the radical position which at least fits quite well into the prophetic argument, the *moderate position* destroys it completely. But as was said before, it too has the support of Marx's authority. Marx lived long enough to see reforms carried out which, according to his theory, should have been impossible. But it never occurred to him that these improvements in the workers' lot were at the same time refutations of his theory. His ambiguous historicist view of the social revolution permitted him to interpret these reforms as its prelude[16] or even as its beginning. As Engels tells us[17], Marx reached the conclusion that in England, at any rate, 'the inevitable social revolution might be effected entirely by peaceful and legal means. He certainly never forgot to add that he hardly expected the English ruling class to submit, without a "pro-slavery rebellion", to this peaceful and legal revolution'. This report agrees with a letter[18] in which Marx wrote, only three years before his death: 'My party … considers an English revolution not *necessary* but—according to historic precedents—*possible*.' It should be noted that in the first at least of these statements, the theory of the 'moderate wing' is clearly expressed; the theory, namely, that should the ruling class not submit, violence would be unavoidable.

These moderate theories seem to me to destroy the whole prophetic argument[19]. They imply the possibility of a compromise, of a gradual reform of capitalism, and therefore, of a decreasing class-antagonism. But the sole basis of the prophetic argument is the assumption of an increasing class-antagonism. There is no logical necessity why a gradual reform, achieved by compromise, should lead to the complete destruction of the capitalist system; why the workers, who have learned by experience that they can improve their lot by gradual reform, should not prefer to stick to this method, even if it does not yield 'complete victory', i.e. the submission of the ruling class; why they should not compromise with the bourgeoisie and leave it in possession of the means of production rather than risk all their gains by making demands liable to lead to violent clashes. Only if we assume that 'the proletarians have nothing to lose but their fetters'[20], only if we assume that the law of increasing misery is valid, or that it at least makes improvements impossible, only then can we prophesy that the workers will be forced to make an attempt to overthrow the whole system. An evolutionary interpretation of the 'social revolution' thus destroys the whole Marxist argument, from the first step to the last; all that is left of Marxism would be the historicist approach. If an historical prophecy is still attempted, then it must be based upon an entirely new argument.

If we try to construct such a modified argument in accordance with Marx's later views and with those of the moderate wing, preserving as much of the original theory as possible, then we arrive at an argument based entirely upon the claim that the working class represents now, or will one day represent, the *majority* of the people. The argument would run like this. Capitalism will be transformed by a 'social revolution', by which we now mean nothing but the advance of the class struggle between capitalists and workers. This revolution may either proceed by gradual and democratic methods, or it may be violent, or it may be gradual and violent in alternate stages. All this will depend upon the resistance of the bourgeoisie. But in any case, and particularly if the development is a peaceful one, it must end with the workers assuming 'the position of the ruling class'[21], as the *Manifesto* says; they must 'win the battle of democracy'; for 'the proletarian movement is the self-conscious independent movement of the immense majority, in the interest of the immense majority'.

It is important to realize that even in this moderate and modified form, the prediction is untenable. The reason is this. The theory of increasing misery must be given up if the possibility of gradual reform is admitted; but with it, even the semblance of a justification for the assertion that the industrial workers must one day form the 'immense majority' disappears. I do not wish to imply that this assertion would really follow from the Marxist theory of increasing misery, since this theory has never taken sufficient heed of the farmers and peasants. But if the law of increasing misery, supposed to reduce the middle class to the level of the proletariat, is invalid, then we must be prepared to find that a very considerable middle class continues to exist (or that a new middle class has arisen) and that it may co-operate with the other non-proletarian classes against a bid for power by the workers; and nobody can say for certain what the outcome of such a contest would be. Indeed, statistics no longer show any tendency for the number of industrial workers to increase in relation to the other classes of the population. There is, rather, the opposite tendency, in spite of the fact that the accumulation of instruments of production continues. This fact alone refutes the validity of the modified prophetic argument. All that remains of it is the important observation (which is, however, not up to the pretentious standards of a historicist prophecy) that social reforms are carried out largely[22] under the pressure of the oppressed, or (if this term is preferred) under the pressure of class struggle; that is to say, that the emancipation of the oppressed will be largely the achievement of the oppressed themselves[23].

IV

The prophetic argument is untenable, and irreparable, in all its interpretations, whether radical or moderate. But for a full understanding of this situation, it is not enough to refute the modified prophecy; it is also necessary to examine the *ambiguous attitude towards the problem of violence* which we can observe in both the radical and the moderate Marxist parties. This attitude has, I assert, a considerable influence upon the question whether or not the 'battle of democracy' will be won; for wherever the moderate Marxist wing has won a general election, or come close to it, one of the reasons seems to have been that they attracted large sections of the middle class. This was due to their humanitarianism, to their stand for freedom and against oppression. But the *systematic ambiguity* of their attitude towards violence not only tends to neutralize this attraction, but it also directly furthers the interest of the anti-democrats, the anti-humanitarians, the fascists.

There are two closely connected ambiguities in the Marxist doctrine, and both are important from this point of view. The one is an ambiguous attitude towards violence, founded upon the historicist approach. The other is the ambiguous way in which Marxists speak about 'the conquest of political power by the proletariat', as the *Manifesto* puts it[24]. What does this mean? It may mean, and it is sometimes so interpreted, that the workers' party has the harmless and obvious aim of every democratic party, that of obtaining a majority, and of forming a government. But it may mean, and it is often hinted by Marxists that it does mean, that the party, once in power, intends to entrench itself in this position; that is to say, that it will use its majority vote in such a way as to make it very difficult for others ever to regain power by ordinary democratic means. The difference between these two interpretations is most important. If a party which is at a certain time in the minority plans to suppress the other party, whether by violence or by means of a majority vote, then it recognizes by implication the right of the present majority party to do the same. It loses any moral right to complain about oppression; and, indeed, it plays into the hands of those groups within the present ruling party who wish to suppress the opposition by force.

I may call these two ambiguities briefly *the ambiguity of violence* and *the ambiguity of power-conquest*. Both are rooted not only in the vagueness of the historicist approach, but also in the Marxist theory of the state. If the state is, essentially, a class tyranny, then, on the one hand, violence is permissible, and on the other, all that can be done is to replace the dictatorship of the bourgeoisie by that of the proletariat. To worry much about formal democracy merely shows lack of historical sense; after all 'democracy is …

only one of the stages in the course of the historical development', as Lenin says[25].

The two ambiguities play their rôle in the tactical doctrines of both the radical and the moderate wings. This is understandable, since the systematic use of the ambiguity enables them to extend the realm from which prospective followers may be recruited. This is a tactical advantage which may, however, easily lead to a disadvantage at the most critical moment; it may lead to a split whenever the most radical members think that the hour has struck for taking violent action. The way in which the radical wing may make a systematic use of the ambiguity of violence may be illustrated by the following extracts taken from Parkes' recent critical dissection of Marxism[26]. 'Since the Communist Party of the United States now declares not only that it does not now advocate revolution, but also that it never did advocate revolution, it may be advisable to quote a few sentences from the program of the Communist International (drafted in 1928).' Parkes then quotes among others the following passages from this programme: 'The Conquest of power by the proletariat does not mean peacefully "capturing" the ready-made bourgeois state by means of parliamentary majority ... The conquest of power ... is the violent overthrow of bourgeois power, the destruction of the capitalist state apparatus ... The Party ... is confronted with the task of leading the masses to a direct attack upon the bourgeois state. This is done by ... propaganda ... and ... mass action ... This mass action includes ... finally, the general strike conjointly with armed insurrection ... The latter form ... which is the supreme form, must be conducted according to the rules of war ...' One sees, from these quotations, that this part of the programme is quite unambiguous; but this does not prevent the party from making a systematic use of the ambiguity of violence, withdrawing, if the tactical situation[27] demands it, towards a non-violent interpretation of the term 'social revolution'; and this in spite of the concluding paragraph of the *Manifesto*[28] (which is retained by the programme of 1928): 'The Communists disdain to conceal their views and aims. They openly declare that their aims can be attained only by the forcible overthrow of all the existing social conditions ...'

But the way in which the moderate wing has systematically used the ambiguity of violence as well as that of power-conquest is even more important. It has been developed especially by Engels, on the basis of Marx's more moderate views quoted above, and it has become a tactical doctrine which has greatly influenced later developments. The doctrine I have in mind might be presented as follows[29]: We Marxists much prefer a peaceful and democratic development towards socialism, if we can have it. But as political realists we foresee the probability that the bourgeoisie will not quietly stand by when we are within reach of attaining the majority. They will rather attempt to destroy democracy. In this case, we must not flinch, but fight back, and conquer political power. And since this development is a probable one, we must prepare the workers for it; otherwise we should betray our cause. Here is one of Engels' passages[30] on the matter: 'For the moment ... legality ... is working so well in our favour that we should be mad to abandon it as long as it lasts. It remains to be seen whether it will not be the bourgeoisie ... which will abandon it first in order to crush us with violence. *Take the first shot, gentlemen of the bourgeoisie!* Never doubt it, they will be the first to fire. One fine day the ... bourgeoisie will grow tired of ... watching the rapidly increasing strength of socialism, and will have recourse to illegality and violence.' What will happen then is left systematically ambiguous. And this ambiguity is used as a threat; for in later passages, Engels addresses the 'gentlemen of the bourgeoisie' in the following way: 'If ... you break the constitution ... then the Social Democratic Party is free to act, or to refrain from acting, against you—whatever it likes best. What it is going to do, however, it will hardly give away to you to-day!'

It is interesting to see how widely this doctrine differs from the original conception of Marxism which predicted that the revolution would come as the result of the increasing pressure of capitalism upon the workers, and not as the result of the increasing pressure of a successful working-class movement upon capitalists. This most remarkable change of front[31] shows the influence of the actual social development which turned out to be one of decreasing misery. But Engels' new doctrine, which leaves the revolutionary, or more precisely, the counter-revolutionary, initiative to the ruling class, is tactically absurd, and doomed to failure. The original Marxist theory taught that the workers' revolution will break out at the depth of a depression, i.e. at a moment when the political system is weakened by the breakdown of the economic system, a situation which would contribute greatly to the victory of the workers. But if the 'gentlemen of the bourgeoisie' are invited to take the first shot, is it conceivable that they will be stupid enough not to choose their moment wisely? Will they not make proper preparations for the war they are going to wage? And since, according to the theory, they hold the power, will such a preparation not mean the mobilization of forces against which the workers can have no slightest chance of victory? Such criticism cannot be met by amending the theory so that the workers should not wait until the other side strikes but try to anticipate them, since, on its own assumption, it must always be easy for those in power to be ahead in their preparations—to prepare rifles, if the workers prepare sticks, guns if they prepare rifles, dive bombers if they prepare guns, etc.

V

But this criticism, practical as it is, and corroborated by experience, is only superficial. The main defects of the doctrine lie deeper. The criticism I now wish to offer attempts to show that both the presupposition of the doctrine and its tactical consequences are such that they are likely to *produce* exactly that anti-democratic reaction of the bourgeoisie which the theory predicts, yet claims (with ambiguity) to abhor: the strengthening of the anti-democratic element in the bourgeoisie, and, in consequence, civil war. And we know that this may lead to defeat, and to fascism.

The criticism I have in mind is, briefly, that Engels' tactical doctrine, and, more generally, the ambiguities of violence and of power-conquest, make the working of democracy impossible, once they are adopted by an important political party. I base this criticism on the contention that democracy can work only if the main parties adhere to a view of its functions which may be summarized in some rules such as these (cp. also section II of chapter 7):

1 Democracy cannot be fully characterized as the rule of the majority, although the institution of general elections is most important. For a majority might rule in a tyrannical way. (The majority of those who are less than 6 ft. high may decide that the minority of those over 6ft. shall pay all taxes.) In a democracy, the powers of the rulers must be limited; and the criterion of a democracy is this: In a democracy, the rulers—that is to say, the government—can be dismissed by the ruled without bloodshed. Thus if the men in power do not safeguard those institutions which secure to the minority the possibility of working for a peaceful change, then their rule is a tyranny.

2 We need only distinguish between two forms of government, viz. such as possess institutions of this kind, and all others; i.e. democracies and tyrannies.

3 A consistent democratic constitution should exclude only one type of change in the legal system, namely a change which would endanger its democratic character.

4 In a democracy, the full protection of minorities should not extend to those who violate the law, and especially not to those who incite others to the violent overthrow of the democracy[32].

5 A policy of framing institutions to safeguard democracy must always proceed on the assumption that there may be anti-democratic tendencies latent among the ruled as well as among the rulers.

6 If democracy is destroyed, all rights are destroyed. Even if certain economic advantages enjoyed by the ruled should persist, they would persist only on sufferance[33].
7 Democracy provides an invaluable battle-ground for any reasonable reform, since it permits reform without violence. But if the preservation of democracy is not made the first consideration in any particular battle fought out on this battle-ground, then the latent anti-democratic tendencies which are always present (and which appeal to those who suffer under the strain of civilization, as we called it in chapter 10) may bring about a breakdown of democracy. If an understanding of these principles is not yet developed, its development must be fought for. The opposite policy may prove fatal; it may bring about the loss of the most important battle, the battle for democracy itself.

As opposed to such a policy, that of Marxist parties can be characterized as one of *making the workers suspicious of democracy*. 'In reality the state is nothing more', says Engels[34], 'than a machine for the oppression of one class by another, and this holds for a democratic republic no less than for a monarchy.' But such views must produce:

(*a*) A policy of blaming democracy for all the evils which it does not prevent, instead of recognizing that the democrats are to be blamed, and the opposition usually no less than the majority. (Every opposition has the majority it deserves.)
(*b*) A policy of educating the ruled to consider the state not as theirs, but as belonging to the rulers.
(*c*) A policy of telling them that there is only one way to improve things, that of the *complete conquest of power*. But this neglects the one really important thing about democracy, that it checks and balances power.

Such a policy amounts to doing the work of the enemies of the open society; it provides them with an unwitting fifth column. And against the *Manifesto* which says[35] ambiguously: 'The first step in the revolution of the working class is to raise the proletariat to the position of the ruling class—to win the battle of democracy', I assert that if this is accepted as the first step, then the battle of democracy will be lost.

These are the general consequences of Engels' tactical doctrines, and of the ambiguities grounded in the theory of the social revolution. Ultimately, they are merely the last consequences of Plato's way of posing the problem of politics by asking 'who should rule the state?' (cp. chapter 7). It is high time for us to learn that the question '*who* is to wield the power in the state?' matters only little as compared with the question '*how* is the power wielded?' and '*how much* power is wielded?' We must learn that in the long run, all political problems are institutional problems, problems of the legal framework rather than of persons, and that progress towards more equality can be safeguarded only by the institutional control of power.

VI

As in the previous chapter, I shall now illustrate the second step by showing something of the way in which the prophecy has influenced recent historical developments. All political parties have some sort of 'vested interest' in their opponent's unpopular moves. They live by them and are therefore liable to dwell upon, to emphasize, and even to look forward to them. They may even encourage the political mistakes of their opponents as long as they can do so without becoming involved in the responsibility for them. This, together with Engels' theory, has led some Marxist parties to look forward to the political moves made by their opponents against democracy. Instead of fighting such moves tooth and nail, they were pleased to tell their followers: 'See what these people do. That is what they call democracy. That is what they call freedom and equality! Remember it when *the day of reckoning* comes.' (An ambiguous phrase which may refer to election day or to the day of revolution.) This policy of letting one's opponents expose themselves must, if extended to moves against democracy, lead to disaster. It is a policy of talking big and doing nothing in the face of real and increasing danger to democratic institutions. It is a policy of talking war and acting peace; and it taught the fascists the invaluable method of talking peace and acting war.

There is no doubt about the way in which the ambiguity just mentioned played into the hands of those fascist groups who wanted to destroy democracy. For we must reckon with the possibility that there will be such groups, and that their influence within the so-called bourgeoisie will depend largely on the policy adopted by the workers' parties.

For instance, let us consider more closely the use made in the political struggle of the threat of revolution or even of *political* strikes (as opposed to wage disputes, etc.). As explained above, the decisive question here would be whether such means are used as offensive weapons or solely for the defence of democracy. Within a democracy, they would be justified as a purely defensive weapon, and when resolutely applied in connection with a defensive and unambiguous demand they have been successfully used in this way. (Remember the quick breakdown of Kapp's putsch.) But if used as an offensive weapon they must lead to a strengthening of the anti-democratic tendencies in the opponent's camp, since they clearly make democracy unworkable. Furthermore, such use must make the weapon ineffective for defence. If you use the whip even when the dog is good, then it won't work if you need it to deter him from being bad. The defence of democracy must consist in making anti-democratic experiments too costly for those who try them; much more costly than a democratic compromise ... The use by the workers of any kind of non-democratic pressure is likely to lead to a similar, or even to an anti-democratic, counterpressure—to provoke a move against democracy. Such an anti-democratic move on the part of the rulers is, of course, a much more serious and dangerous thing than a similar move on the part of the ruled. It would be the task of the workers to fight this dangerous move resolutely, to stop it in its inconspicuous beginnings. But how can they now fight in the name of democracy? Their own anti-democratic action must provide their enemies, and those of democracy, with an opportunity.

The facts of the development described can, if one wishes, be interpreted differently; they may lead to the conclusion that democracy is 'no good'. This is indeed a conclusion which many Marxists have drawn. After having been defeated in what they believed to be the democratic struggle (which they had lost in the moment they formulated their tactical doctrine), they said: 'We have been too lenient, too humane—next time we will make a really bloody revolution!' It is as if a man who loses a boxing match should conclude: boxing is no good—I should have used a club ... The fact is that the Marxists taught the theory of class war to the workers, but the practice of it to the reactionary diehards of the bourgeoisie. Marx talked war. His opponents listened attentively; then they began to talk peace and accuse the workers of belligerency; this charge the Marxists could not deny, since class war was their slogan. And the fascists acted.

So far, the analysis mainly covers certain more 'radical' Social Democratic parties who based their policy entirely upon Engels' ambiguous tactical doctrine. The disastrous effects of Engels' tactics were increased in their case by the lack of a practical programme discussed in the last chapter. But the Communists too adopted the tactics here criticized in certain countries and at certain periods, especially where the other workers' parties, for instance the Social Democrats or the Labour Party, observed the democratic rules.

But the position was different with the Communists in so far as they had a programme. It was: 'Copy Russia!' This made them more definite in their revolutionary doctrines as well as in their assertion that democracy merely means the dictatorship of the bourgeoisie[36]. According to this assertion, not much could be lost and something would be gained if that hidden dictatorship became an open one, apparent to all; for this could only bring the revolution nearer[37]. They even hoped that a totalitarian dictatorship in Central Europe would speed up matters. After all, since the revolution was bound to come, fascism could only be one of the means of bringing it about; and this was more particularly so since the revolution was clearly long overdue. Russia had already had it in spite of its backward economic conditions. Only the vain hopes created by democracy[38] were holding it back in the more advanced countries. Thus the destruction of democracy through the fascists could only promote the revolution by achieving the ultimate disillusionment of the workers in regard to democratic methods. With this, the radical wing of Marxism[39] felt that it had discovered the 'essence' and the 'true historical rôle' of fascism. Fascism was, essentially, *the last stand of the bourgeoisie*. Accordingly, the Communists did not fight when the fascists seized power. (Nobody expected the Social Democrats to fight.) For the Communists were sure that the proletarian revolution was overdue and that the fascist interlude, necessary for its speeding up[40], could not last longer than a few months. Thus no action was required from the Communists. They were harmless. There was never a 'communist danger' to the fascist conquest of power. As Einstein once emphasized, of all organized groups of the community, it was only the Church, or rather a section of the Church, which seriously offered resistance.

20

CAPITALISM AND ITS FATE

According to Marxist doctrine, capitalism is labouring under inner contradictions that threaten to bring about its downfall. A minute analysis of these contradictions and of the historical movement which they force upon society constitutes the first step of Marx's prophetic argument. This step is not only the most important of his whole theory, it is also the one on which he spent most of his labour, since practically the whole of the three volumes of *Capital* (over 2,200 pages in the original edition[1]) is devoted to its elaboration. It is also the least abstract step of the argument since it is based upon a descriptive analysis, supported by statistics, of the economic system of his time—that of unrestrained capitalism[2]. As Lenin puts it: 'Marx deduces the inevitability of the transformation of capitalist society into socialism wholly and exclusively from *the economic law of the movement of contemporary society*.'

Before proceeding to explain in some detail the first step of Marx's prophetic argument, I shall try to describe its main ideas in the form of a very brief outline.

Marx believes that capitalist competition forces the capitalist's hand. It forces the capitalist to accumulate capital. By doing so, he works against his own long-term economic interests (since the accumulation of capital is liable to bring about a fall of his profits). But although working against his own personal interest, he works in the interest of the historical development; he works, unwittingly, for economic progress, and for socialism. This is due to the fact that accumulation of capital means (*a*) increased productivity; increase of wealth; and concentration of wealth in a few hands; (*b*) increase of pauperism and misery; the workers are kept on subsistence or starvation wages, mainly by the fact that the surplus of workers, called the 'industrial reserve army', keeps the wages on the lowest possible level. The trade cycle prevents, for any length of time, the absorption of the surplus of workers by the growing industry. This cannot be altered by the capitalists, even if they wish to do so; for the falling rate of their profits makes their own economic position much too precarious for any effective action. In this way, capitalist accumulation turns out to be a suicidal and self-contradictory process, even though it fosters the technical, economic, and historical progress towards socialism.

I

The premises of the first step are the laws of capitalist competition, and of the accumulation of the means of production. The conclusion is the law of increasing wealth and misery. I begin my discussion with an explanation of these premises and conclusions.

Under capitalism, competition between the capitalists plays an important rôle. 'The battle of competition', as analysed by Marx in *Capital*[3], is carried out by selling the commodities produced, if possible at a lower price than the competitor could afford to accept. 'But the cheapness of a commodity', Marx explains, 'depends in its turn, other things being equal, upon the productivity of labour; and this, again, depends on the scale of production.' For production on a very large scale is in general capable of employing more specialized machinery, and a greater quantity of it; this increases the productivity of the workers, and permits the capitalist to produce, and to sell, at a lower price. 'Large capitalists, therefore, get the better of small ones … Competition always ends with the downfall of many lesser capitalists and with the transition of their capital into the hands of the conqueror.' (This movement is, as Marx points out, much accelerated by the credit system.)

According to Marx's analysis, the process described, *accumulation due to competition*, has two different aspects. One of them is that the capitalist is forced to accumulate or concentrate more and more capital, in order to survive; this means in practice investing more and more capital in more and more as well as newer and newer machinery, thus continually increasing the *productivity* of his workers. The other aspect of the accumulation of capital is the *concentration* of more and more wealth in the hands of the various capitalists, and of the capitalist class; and along with it goes the reduction in the number of capitalists, a movement called by Marx the *centralization*[4] of capital (in contradistinction to mere accumulation or concentration).

Now three of these terms, competition, accumulation, and increasing productivity, indicate the fundamental tendencies of all capitalist production, according to Marx; they are the tendencies to which I alluded when I described the *premise* of the first step as 'the laws of capitalist competition and of accumulation'. The fourth and the fifth terms, however, concentration and centralization, indicate a tendency which forms one part of the *conclusion* of the first step; for they describe a tendency towards a continuous increase of wealth, and its centralization in fewer and fewer hands. The other part of the conclusion, however, the law of increasing misery, is only reached by a much more complicated argument. But before beginning an explanation of this argument, I must first explain this second conclusion itself.

The term 'increasing misery' may mean, as used by Marx, two different things. It may be used in order to describe the extent of misery, indicating that it is spread over an increasing number of people; or it may be used in order to indicate an increase in the intensity of the suffering of the people. Marx undoubtedly believed that misery was growing both in extent and in intensity. This, however, is more than he needed in order to carry his point. For the purpose of the prophetic argument, a wider interpretation of the term 'increasing misery' would do just as well (if not better[5]); an interpretation, namely, according to which the extent of misery increases, while its intensity may or may not increase, but at any rate does not show any marked decrease.

But there is a further and much more important comment to be made. Increasing misery, to Marx, involves fundamentally an *increasing exploitation of the employed workers; not only in numbers but also in intensity*. It must be admitted that in addition it involves an increase in the suffering as well as in the numbers of the unemployed, called[6] by Marx the (relative) 'surplus population' or the 'industrial reserve army'. But the function of the unemployed, in this process, is to exert pressure upon the employed workers, thus assisting the capitalists in their efforts to make profit out of the employed workers, to exploit them. 'The industrial reserve army', Marx writes[7], 'belongs to capitalism just as if its members had been reared by the capitalists at their own cost. For its own varying needs, capital creates an ever-ready supply of exploitable human material … During periods of depression and of semi-prosperity, the industrial reserve army keeps up its pressure upon the ranks of the employed workers; and during periods of excessive production and boom, it serves to bridle their aspirations.' Increasing misery, according to Marx, is essentially the increasing exploitation of labour power; and since labour power of the unemployed is not exploited, they can serve in this process only as unpaid assistants of the capitalists in the exploitation of the employed workers. The point is important since later Marxists have often referred to unemployment as one of the empirical facts that verify the prophecy that misery tends to increase; but unemployment can be claimed to corroborate Marx's theory only if it occurs together with increased exploitation of the employed workers, i.e. with long hours of work and with low real wages.

This may suffice to explain the term 'increasing misery'. But it is still necessary to explain the *law* of increasing misery which Marx claimed to have discovered. By this I mean the doctrine of Marx on which the whole prophetic argument hinges; namely, the doctrine that capitalism cannot possibly afford to decrease the misery of the workers, since the mechanism of capitalist accumulation keeps the capitalist under a strong economic pressure which he is forced to pass on to the workers if he is not to succumb. This is why the capitalists cannot compromise, why they cannot meet any important demand of the workers, even if they wished to do so; this is why 'capitalism cannot be reformed but can only be destroyed'[8]. It is clear that this law is the decisive conclusion of the first step. The other conclusion, the law of increasing wealth, would be a harmless matter, if only it were possible for the increase of wealth to be shared by the workers. Marx's contention that this is impossible will therefore be the main subject of our critical analysis. But before proceeding to a presentation and criticism of Marx's arguments in favour of this contention, I may briefly comment on the first part of the conclusion, the theory of increasing wealth.

The tendency towards the accumulation and concentration of wealth, which Marx observed, can hardly be questioned. His theory of increasing productivity is also, in the main, unexceptionable. Although there may be limits to the beneficial effects exerted by the growth of an enterprise upon its productivity, there are hardly any limits to the beneficial effects of the improvement and accumulation of machinery. But in regard to the tendency towards the centralization of capital in fewer and fewer hands, matters are not quite so simple. Undoubtedly, there is a tendency in that direction, and we may grant that under an unrestrained capitalist system there are few counteracting forces. Not much can be said against this part of Marx's analysis as a description of an unrestrained capitalism. But considered as a prophecy, it is less tenable. For we know that now there are many means by which legislation can intervene. Taxation and death duties can be used most effectively to counteract centralization, and they have been so used. And anti-trust legislation can also be used, although perhaps with less effect. To evaluate the force of Marx's prophetic argument we must consider the possibility of great improvements in this direction; and as in previous chapters, I must declare that the argument on which Marx bases this prophecy of centralization or of a decrease in the number of capitalists is inconclusive.

Having explained the main premises and conclusions of the first step, and having disposed of the first conclusion, we can now concentrate our attention entirely upon Marx's derivation of the other conclusion, the prophetic law of increasing misery. Three different trends of thought may be distinguished in his attempts to establish this prophecy. They will be dealt with in the next four sections of this chapter under the headings: II: the theory of value; III: the effect of the surplus population upon wages; IV: the trade cycle; V: the effects of the falling rate of profit.

II

Marx's *theory of value*, usually considered by Marxists as well as by anti-Marxists as a corner-stone of the Marxist creed, is in my opinion one of its rather unimportant parts; indeed, the sole reason why I am going to treat of it, instead of proceeding at once to the next section, is that it is generally held to be important, and that I cannot defend my reasons for differing from this opinion without discussing the theory. But I wish to make it clear at once that in holding that the theory of value is a redundant part of Marxism, I am defending Marx rather than attacking him. For there is little doubt that the many critics who have shown that the theory of value is very weak in itself are in the main perfectly right. But even if they were wrong, it would only strengthen the position of Marxism if it could be established that its decisive historico-political doctrines can be developed entirely independently of such a controversial theory.

The idea of the so-called *labour theory of value*[9], adapted by Marx for his purposes from suggestions he found in his predecessors (he refers especially to Adam Smith and David Ricardo), is simple enough. If you need a carpenter, you must pay him by the hour. If you ask him why a certain job is more expensive than another one, he will point out that there is more work in it. In addition to the labour, you must pay of course for the timber. But if you go into this a little more closely, then you find that you are, indirectly, paying for the labour involved in foresting, felling, transporting, sawing, etc. This consideration suggests the general theory that you have to pay for the job, or for any commodity you may buy, roughly in proportion to the amount of work in it, i.e. to the number of labour hours necessary for its production.

I say 'roughly' because the actual prices fluctuate. But there is, or so at least it appears, always something more stable behind these prices, a kind of average price about which the actual prices oscillate[10], christened the 'exchange-value' or, briefly, the 'value' of the thing. Using this general idea,

Marx defined the *value* of a commodity as the average number of labour hours necessary for its production (or for its reproduction).

The next idea, that of the *theory of surplus value*, is nearly as simple. It too was adapted by Marx from his predecessors. (Engels asserts[11]—perhaps mistakenly, but I shall follow his presentation of the matter—that Marx's main source was Ricardo.) The theory of surplus value is an attempt, within the limits of the labour theory of value, to answer the question: 'How does the capitalist make his profit?' If we assume that the commodities produced in his factory are sold on the market at their true value, i.e. according to the number of labour hours necessary for their production, then the only way in which the capitalist can make a profit is by paying his workers less than the full value of their product. Thus the wages received by the worker represent a value which is not equal to the number of hours he has worked. And we can accordingly divide his working day into two parts, the hours he has spent in producing value equivalent to his wages and the hours he has spent in producing value for the capitalist[12]. And correspondingly, we can divide the whole value produced by the worker into two parts, the value equal to his wages, and the rest, which is called *surplus value*. This surplus value is appropriated by the capitalist and is the sole basis for his *profit*.

So far, the story is simple enough. But now there arises a theoretical difficulty. The whole value theory has been introduced in order to explain the actual prices at which all commodities are exchanged; and it is still assumed that the capitalist is able to obtain on the market the full value of his product, i.e. a price that corresponds to the total number of hours spent on it. But it looks as if the worker does not get the full price of the commodity which he sells to the capitalist on the labour market. It looks as if he is cheated, or robbed; at any rate, as if he is not paid according to the general law assumed by the value theory, namely, that *all* actual prices paid are, at least in a first approximation, determined by the value of the commodity. (Engels says that the problem was realized by the economists who belonged to what Marx called 'the school of Ricardo'; and he asserts[13] that their inability to solve it led to the breakdown of this school.) There appeared what seemed a rather obvious solution of the difficulty. The capitalist possesses a monopoly of the means of production, and this superior economic power can be used for bullying the worker into an agreement which violates the law of value. But this solution (which I consider quite a plausible description of the situation) utterly destroys the labour theory of value. For it now turns out that certain prices, namely, wages, do not correspond to their values, not even in a first approximation. And this opens up the possibility that this may be true of other prices for similar reasons.

Such was the situation when Marx entered the scene in order to save the labour theory of value from destruction. With the help of another simple but brilliant idea he succeeded in showing that the theory of surplus value was not only compatible with the labour theory of value but that it could also be rigidly deduced from the latter. In order to achieve this deduction, we have only to ask ourselves: what is, precisely, the commodity which the worker sells to the capitalist? Marx's reply is: not his labour *hours*, but his whole labour *power*. What the capitalist buys or hires on the labour market is the labour *power* of the worker. Let us assume, tentatively, that this commodity is sold at its true value. What is its value? According to the definition of value, the value of labour *power* is the average number of labour *hours* necessary for its production or reproduction. But this is, clearly, nothing but the number of hours necessary for producing the worker's (and his family's) *means of subsistence*.

Marx thus arrived at the following result. The true value of the worker's whole labour power is equal to the labour hours needed for producing the means of his subsistence. Labour power is sold for this price to the capitalist. If the worker is able to work longer than that, then his surplus labour belongs to the buyer or hirer of his power. The greater the productivity of labour, that is to say, the more a worker can produce per hour, the fewer hours will be needed for the production of his subsistence, and the more hours remain for his exploitation. This shows that the basis of capitalist exploitation is a *high productivity of labour*. If the worker could produce in a day no more than his own daily needs, then exploitation would be impossible without violating the law of value; it would be possible only by means of cheating, robbery, or murder. But once the productivity of labour has, by the introduction of machinery, risen so high that one man can produce much more than he needs, capitalist exploitation becomes possible. It is possible even in a capitalist society which is 'ideal' in the sense that every commodity, including labour power, is bought and sold at its true value. In such a society, the injustice of exploitation does not lie in the fact that the worker is not paid a 'just price' for his labour power, but rather in the fact that he is so poor that he is forced to sell his labour power, while the capitalist is rich enough to buy labour power in great quantities, and to make profit out of it.

By this derivation[14] of the theory of surplus value, Marx saved the labour theory of value from destruction for the time being; and in spite of the fact that I regard the whole 'value problem' (in the sense of an 'objective' true value round which the prices oscillate) as irrelevant, I am very ready to admit that this was a theoretical success of the first order. But Marx had done more than save a theory originally advanced by 'bourgeois economists'.

With one stroke, he gave a theory of exploitation and a theory explaining why the workers' wages tend to oscillate about the subsistence (or starvation) level. But the greatest success was that he could now give an explanation, one in keeping with his economic theory of the legal system, of the fact that the capitalist mode of production tended to adopt the legal cloak of liberalism. For the new theory led him to the conclusion that once the introduction of new machinery had multiplied the productivity of labour, there arose the possibility of a new form of exploitation which used a free market instead of brutal force, and which was based on the 'formal' observance of justice, equality before the law, and freedom. The capitalist system, he asserted, was not only a system of 'free competition', but it was also 'maintained by the exploitation of the labour of others, but of labour which, *in a formal sense*, is free'[15].

It is impossible for me to enter here into a detailed account of the really astonishing number of further applications made by Marx of his value theory. But it is also unnecessary, since my criticism of the theory will show the way in which the value theory can be eliminated from all these investigations. I am now going to develop this criticism; its three main points are (*a*) that Marx's value theory does not suffice to explain exploitation, (*b*) that the additional assumptions which are necessary for such an explanation turn out to be sufficient, so that the theory of value turns out to be redundant, (*c*) that Marx's theory of value is an essentialist or metaphysical one.

(*a*) The fundamental law of the theory of value is the law that the prices of practically all commodities, including wages, are determined by their values, or more precisely, that they are at least in a first approximation proportional to the labour hours necessary for their production. Now this 'law of value', as I may call it, at once raises a problem. Why does it hold? Obviously, neither the buyer nor the seller of the commodity can see, at a glance, how many hours are necessary for its production; and even if they could, it would not explain the law of value. For it is clear that the buyer simply buys as cheaply as he can, and that the seller charges as much as he can get. This, it appears, must be one of the fundamental assumptions of any theory of market prices. In order to explain the law of value, it would be our task to show why the buyer is unlikely to succeed in buying below, and the seller in selling above, the 'value' of a commodity. This problem was seen more or less clearly by those who believed in the labour theory of value, and their reply was this. For the purpose of simplification, and in order to obtain a first approximation, let us assume perfectly free competition, and for the same reason let us consider only such commodities as can be manufactured in practically unlimited quantities (if only the labour were available). Now let us assume that the price of such a commodity is above its value; this would mean that excessive profits can be made in this particular branch of production. It would encourage various manufacturers to produce this commodity, and competition would lower the price. The opposite process would lead to an increase in the price of a commodity which is sold below its value. Thus there will be oscillations of price, and these will tend to centre about the values of commodities. In other words, it is a mechanism of *supply and demand* which, under free competition, tends to give force[16] to the law of value.

Such considerations as these can be found frequently in Marx, for instance, in the third volume of *Capital*[17], where he tries to explain why there is a tendency for all profits in the various branches of manufacture to approximate, and adjust themselves, to a certain average profit. And they are also used in the first volume, especially in order to show why wages are kept low, near subsistence level, or, what amounts to the same, just above starvation level. It is clear that with wages below this level, the workers would actually starve, and the supply of labour power on the labour market would disappear. But as long as men live, they will reproduce; and Marx attempts to show in detail (as we shall see in section IV), why the mechanism of capitalist accumulation must create a surplus population, an industrial reserve army. Thus as long as wages are just above starvation level there will always be not only a sufficient but even an excessive supply of labour power on the labour market; and it is this excessive supply which, according to Marx, prevents the rise of wages[18]: 'The industrial reserve army keeps up its pressure upon the ranks of the employed workers; ... thus surplus population is the background in front of which there operates the law of supply and demand of labour. Surplus population restricts the range within which this law is permitted to operate to such limits as best suit the capitalist greed for exploitation and domination.'

(*b*) Now this passage shows that Marx himself realized the necessity of backing up the law of value by a more concrete theory; a theory which shows, in any particular case, how the *laws of supply and demand* bring about the effect which has to be explained; for instance, starvation wages. But if these laws are sufficient to explain these effects, then we do not need the labour theory of value at all, whether or not it may be tenable as a first approximation (which I do not think it is). Furthermore, as Marx realized, the laws of supply and demand are necessary for explaining all those cases in which there is no free competition, and in which his law of value is therefore clearly out of operation; for instance, where a monopoly can be used to keep prices constantly above their 'values'. Marx considered such cases as exceptions, which is hardly the right view; but however this may be, the case of monopolies shows not only that the laws of supply and demand are necessary to supplement his law of value, but also that they are more generally applicable.

On the other hand, it is clear that the laws of supply and demand are not only necessary but also sufficient to explain all the phenomena of 'exploitation' which Marx observed—the phenomena, more precisely, of the misery of the workers side by side with the wealth of the entrepreneurs—if we assume, as Marx did, a free labour market as well as a chronically excessive supply of labour. (Marx's theory of this excessive supply will be discussed more fully in section IV below.) As Marx shows, it is clear enough that the workers will be forced, under such circumstances, to work long hours at low wages, in other words, to permit the capitalist to 'appropriate the best part of the fruits of their labour'. And in this trivial argument, which is part of Marx's own, there is no need even to mention 'value'.

Thus the value theory turns out to be a completely redundant part of Marx's theory of exploitation; and this holds independently of the question whether or not the value theory is true. But the part of Marx's theory of exploitation which remains after the value theory is eliminated is undoubtedly correct, provided we accept the doctrine of surplus population. It is unquestionably true that (in the absence of a redistribution of wealth through the state) the existence of a surplus population must lead to starvation wages, and to provocative differences in the standard of living.

(What is not so clear, and not explained by Marx either, is why the supply of labour should continue to exceed the demand. For if it is so profitable to 'exploit' labour, how is it, then, that the capitalists are not forced, by competition, to try to raise their profits by employing more labour? In other words, why do they not compete against each other on the labour market, thereby raising the wages to the point where they begin to become no longer sufficiently profitable, so that it is no longer possible to speak of exploitation? Marx would have answered—see section V, below—'Because competition forces them to invest more and more capital in machinery, so that they cannot increase that part of their capital which they use for wages'. But this answer is unsatisfactory since even if they spend their capital on machinery, they can do so only by buying labour to build machinery, or by causing others to buy such labour, thus increasing the demand for labour. It appears, for such reasons, that the phenomena of 'exploitation' which Marx observed were due, not, as he believed, to the mechanism of a perfectly competitive market, but to other factors—especially to a mixture of low productivity and imperfectly competitive markets. But a detailed and satisfactory explanation[19] of the phenomena appears still to be missing.)

(*c*) Before leaving this discussion of the value theory and the part played by it in Marx's analysis, I wish to comment briefly upon another of its aspects. The whole idea—which was not Marx's invention—that there is something *behind* the prices, an objective or real or true value of which prices are only a 'form of appearance'[20], shows clearly enough the influence of Platonic Idealism with its distinction between a hidden essential or true reality, and an accidental or delusive appearance. Marx, it must be said, made a great effort[21] to destroy this mystical character of objective 'value', but he did not succeed. He tried to be realistic, to accept only something observable and important—labour hours—as the reality which appears in the form of price; and it cannot be questioned that the number of labour hours necessary for producing a commodity, i.e. its Marxian 'value', is an important thing. And in a way, it surely is a purely verbal problem whether or not we should call these labour hours the 'value' of the commodity. But such a terminology may become most misleading and strangely unrealistic, especially if we assume with Marx that the productivity of labour increases. For it has been pointed out by Marx himself[22] that, with increasing productivity, the value of all commodities decreases, and that an increase is therefore possible in real wages as well as real profits, i.e. in the commodities consumed by workers and by capitalists respectively, together with a decrease in the 'value' of wages and of profits, i.e. in the hours spent on them. Thus wherever we find real progress, such as shorter working hours and a greatly improved standard of living of the workers (quite apart from a higher income in money[23], even if calculated in gold), then the workers could at the same time bitterly complain that the Marxian 'value', the real essence or substance of their income, is dwindling away, since the labour hours necessary for its production have been reduced. (An analogous complaint might be made by the capitalists.) All this is admitted by Marx himself; and it shows how misleading the value terminology must be, and how little it represents the real social experience of the workers. In the labour theory of value, the Platonic 'essence' has become entirely divorced from experience[24]...

III

After eliminating Marx's labour theory of value and his theory of surplus value, we can, of course, still retain his analysis (see the end of (*a*) in section II) of the pressure exerted by the *surplus population* upon the wages of the employed workers. It cannot be denied that, if there is a free labour market *and* a surplus population, i.e. widespread and chronic unemployment (and there can be no doubt that unemployment played its rôle in Marx's time and ever since), then wages cannot rise above starvation wages; and under the same assumption, together with the doctrine of accumulation developed above, Marx, although not justified in proclaiming a law of increasing misery, was right in asserting that, in a world of high profits and increasing wealth, starvation wages and a life of misery might be the permanent lot of the workers.

I think that, even if Marx's analysis was defective, his effort to explain the phenomenon of 'exploitation' deserves the greatest respect. (As mentioned at the end of (*b*) in the foregoing section, no really satisfactory theory seems to exist even now.) It must be said, of course, that Marx was wrong when he prophesied that the conditions which he observed were to be permanent if not changed by a revolution, and even more when he prophesied that they would get worse. The facts have refuted these prophecies. Moreover, even if we could admit the validity of his analysis for an unrestrained, a non-interventionist system, even then would his prophetic argument be inconclusive. For the tendency towards increasing misery operates, according to Marx's own analysis, only under a system in which the labour market is free—in a perfectly unrestrained capitalism. But once we admit the possibility of trade unions, of collective bargaining, of strikes, then the assumptions of the analysis are no longer applicable, and the whole prophetic argument breaks down. According to Marx's own analysis, we should have to expect that such a development would either be suppressed, or that it would be equivalent to a social revolution. For collective bargaining can oppose capital by establishing a kind of monopoly of labour; it can prevent the capitalist from using the industrial reserve army for the purpose of keeping wages down; and in this way it can force the capitalists to content themselves with lower profits. We see here why the cry 'Workers, unite!' was, from a Marxian point of view, indeed the only possible reply to an unrestrained capitalism.

But we see, too, why this cry must open up the whole problem of state interference, and why it is likely to lead to the end of the unrestrained system, and to a new system, *interventionism*[25], which may develop in very different directions. For it is almost inevitable that the capitalists will contest the workers' right to unite, maintaining that unions must endanger the freedom of competition on the labour market. Non-interventionism thus faces the problem (it is part of the paradox of freedom[26]): Which freedom should the state protect? The freedom of the labour market, or the freedom of the poor to unite? Whichever decision is taken, it leads to state intervention, to the use of organized political power, of the state as well as of unions, in the field of economic conditions. It leads, under all circumstances, to an extension of the economic responsibility of the state, whether or not this responsibility is consciously accepted. And this means that the assumptions on which Marx's analysis is based must disappear.

The derivation of the historical law of increasing misery is thus invalid. All that remains is a moving description of the misery of the workers which prevailed a hundred years ago, and a valiant attempt to explain it with the help of what we may call, with Lenin[27], Marx's 'economic law of the movement of contemporary society' (that is, of the unrestrained capitalism of a hundred years ago). But in so far as it is meant as an historical prophecy, and in so far as it is used to deduce the 'inevitability' of certain historical developments, the derivation is invalid.

IV

The significance of Marx's analysis rests very largely upon the fact that a surplus population actually existed at his time, and down to our own day (a fact which has hardly received a really satisfactory explanation yet, as I said before). So far, however, we have not yet discussed Marx's argument in support of his contention that it is the mechanism of capitalist production itself that always produces the surplus population which it needs for keeping down the wages of the employed workers. But this theory is not only ingenious and interesting in itself; it contains at the same time Marx's *theory of the trade cycle* and of general depressions, a theory which clearly bears upon the prophecy of the crash of the capitalist system because of the intolerable misery which it must produce. In order to make as strong a case for Marx's theory as I can, I have altered it slightly[28] (namely, by introducing a distinction between two kinds of machinery, the one for the mere extension, and the other for the intensification, of production). But this alteration need not arouse the suspicion of Marxist readers; for I am not going to criticize the theory at all.

The amended theory of surplus population and of the trade cycle may be outlined as follows. The accumulation of capital means that the capitalist spends part of his profits on new machinery; this may also be expressed by saying that only a part of his real profits consists in goods for consumption, while part of it consists in machines. These machines, in turn, may be intended either for the *expansion* of industry, for new factories, etc., or they may be intended for *intensifying* production by increasing the productivity of labour in the existing industries. The former kind of machinery makes possible an increase of employment, the latter kind has the effect of making workers superfluous, of 'setting the workers at liberty' as this process was called in Marx's day. (Nowadays it is sometimes called 'technological unemployment'.) Now the mechanism of capitalist production, as envisaged by the amended Marxist theory of the trade cycle, works roughly like this. If we assume, to start with, that for some reason or other there is a general expansion of industry, then a part of the industrial reserve army will be absorbed, the pressure upon the labour market will be relieved, and wages will show a tendency to rise. A period of prosperity begins. But the moment wages rise, certain mechanical improvements which intensify production and which were previously unprofitable because of the low wages may become profitable (even though the cost of such machinery will begin to rise). Thus more machinery will be produced of the kind that 'sets the workers at liberty'. As long as these machines are only in the process of being produced, prosperity continues, or increases. But once the new machines are themselves beginning to produce, the picture changes. (This change is, according to Marx, accentuated by a fall in the rate of profit, to be discussed under (v), below.) Workers will be 'set at liberty', i.e. condemned to starvation. But the disappearance of many consumers must lead to a collapse of the home market. In consequence, great numbers of machines in the expanded factories become idle (the less efficient machinery first), and this leads to a further increase of unemployment and a further collapse of the market. The fact that much machinery now lies idle means that much capital has become worthless, that many capitalists cannot fulfil their obligations; thus a financial crisis develops, leading to complete stagnation in the production of capital goods, etc. But while the depression (or, as Marx calls it, the 'crisis') takes its course, the conditions are ripening for a recovery. These conditions mainly consist in the growth of the industrial reserve army and the consequent readiness of the workers to accept starvation wages. At very low wages, production becomes profitable even at the low prices of a depressed market; and once production starts, the capitalist begins again to accumulate, to buy machinery. Since wages are very low, he will find that it is not yet profitable to use new machinery (perhaps invented in the meanwhile) of the type which sets the workers at liberty. At first he will rather buy machinery with the plan of extending production. This leads slowly to an extension of employment and to a recovery of the home market. Prosperity is coming once again. Thus we are back at our starting point. The cycle is closed, and the process can start once more.

This is the amended Marxist theory of unemployment and of the trade cycle. As I have promised, I am not going to criticize it. The theory of trade cycles is a very difficult affair, and we certainly do not yet know enough about it (at least I don't). It is very likely that the theory outlined is incomplete, and, especially, that such aspects as the existence of a monetary system based partly upon credit creation, and the effects of hoarding, are not sufficiently taken into account. But however this may be, the trade cycle is a fact which cannot easily be argued away, and it is one of the greatest of Marx's merits to have emphasized its significance as a social problem. But although all this must be admitted, we may criticize the prophecy which Marx attempts to base upon his theory of the trade cycle. First of all, he asserts that depressions will become increasingly worse, not only in their scope but also in the intensity of the workers' suffering. But he gives no argument to support this (apart, perhaps, from the theory of the fall in the rate of profit, which will be discussed presently). And if we look at actual developments, then we must say that terrible as are the effects and especially the psychological effects of unemployment even in those countries where the workers are now insured against it, there is no doubt that the workers' sufferings were incomparably worse in Marx's day. But this is not my main point.

In Marx's day, nobody ever thought of that technique of state intervention which is now called 'counter cycle policy'; and, indeed, such a thought must be utterly foreign to an unrestrained capitalist system. (But even before Marx's time, we find the beginning of doubts about, and even of investigations into, the wisdom of the credit policy of the Bank of England during a depression[29].) Unemployment insurance, however, means intervention, and therefore an increase in the responsibility of the state, and it is likely to lead to experiments in counter cycle policy. I do not maintain that these experiments must necessarily be successful (although I do believe that the problem may in the end prove not so very difficult, and that Sweden[30], in particular, has already shown what can be done in this field). But I wish to assert most emphatically that the belief that it is impossible to abolish unemployment by piecemeal measures is on the same plane of dogmatism as the numerous physical proofs (proffered by men who lived even later than Marx) that the problems of aviation would always remain insoluble. When the Marxists say, as they sometimes do, that Marx has proved the uselessness of a counter cycle policy and of similar piecemeal measures, then they simply do not speak the truth; Marx investigated an unrestrained capitalism, and he never dreamt of interventionism. He therefore never investigated the possibility of a systematic interference with the trade cycle, much less did he offer a proof of its impossibility. It is strange to find that the same people who complain of the irresponsibility of the capitalists in the face of human suffering are irresponsible enough to oppose, with dogmatic assertions of this kind, experiments from which we may learn how to relieve human suffering (how to become masters of our social environment, as Marx would have said), and how to control some of the unwanted social repercussions of our actions. But the apologists of Marxism are quite unaware of the fact that in the name of their own vested interests they are fighting against progress; they do not see that it is the danger of any movement like Marxism that it soon comes to represent all kinds of vested interests, and that there are intellectual investments, as well as material ones.

Another point must be stated here. Marx, as we have seen, believed that unemployment was fundamentally a gadget of the capitalist mechanism with the function of keeping wages low, and of making the exploitation of the employed workers easier; increasing misery always involved for him increasing misery of the employed workers too; and this is just the whole point of the plot. But even if we assume that this view was justified in his day, as a prophecy it has been definitely refuted by later experience. The standard of living of employed workers has risen everywhere since Marx's day; and (as Parkes[31] has emphasized in his criticism of Marx) the real wages of *employed* workers tend even to increase during a depression (they did so, for example, during the last great depression), owing to a more rapid fall in prices than in wages. This is a glaring refutation of Marx, especially since it proves that the main burden of unemployment insurance was borne not by the workers, but by the entrepreneurs, who therefore lost directly through unemployment, instead of profiting indirectly, as in Marx's scheme.

V

None of the Marxist theories so far discussed do even seriously attempt to prove the point which is the most decisive one within the first step; namely, that accumulation keeps the capitalist under a strong economic pressure which he is forced, on pain of his own destruction, to pass on to the workers; so that capitalism can only be destroyed, but not reformed. An attempt to prove this point is contained in that theory of Marx's which aims at establishing the law *that the rate of profit tends to fall*.

What Marx calls the rate of profit corresponds to the rate of interest; it is the percentage of the yearly average of capitalist profit over the whole invested capital. This rate, Marx says, tends to fall owing to the rapid growth of capital investments; for these must accumulate more quickly than profits can rise.

The argument by which Marx attempts to prove this is again rather ingenious. Capitalist competition, as we have seen, forces the capitalists to make investments that increase the productivity of labour. Marx even admitted that by this increase in productivity they render a great service to mankind[32]:

'It is one of the civilizing aspects of capitalism that it exacts surplus value in a manner and under circumstances which are more favourable than previous forms (such as slavery, serfdom, etc.) to the development of the productive powers, as well as to the social conditions for a reconstruction of society on a higher plane. For this, it even creates the elements; ... for the quantity of useful commodities produced in any given span of time depends upon the productivity of labour.' But this service to mankind is not only rendered without any intention by the capitalists; the action to which they are forced by competition also runs counter to their own interests, for the following reason.

The capital of any industrialist can be divided into two parts. One is invested in land, machinery, raw materials, etc. The other is used for wages. Marx calls the first part 'constant capital' and the second 'variable capital'; but since I consider this terminology rather misleading, I shall call the two parts 'immobilized capital' and 'wage capital'. The capitalist, according to Marx, can profit only by exploiting the workers; in other words, by using his wage capital. Immobilized capital is a kind of a dead weight which he is forced by competition to carry on with, and even to increase continually. This increase is not, however, accompanied by a corresponding increase in his profits; only an extension of the wage capital could have this wholesome effect. But the general tendency towards an increase in productivity means that the material part of capital increases relatively to its wage part. Therefore, the total capital increases also, and without a compensating increase in profits; that is to say, the rate of profit must fall.

Now this argument has been often questioned; indeed, it was attacked, by implication, long before Marx[33]. In spite of these attacks, I believe that there may be something in Marx's argument; especially if we take it together with his theory of the trade cycle. (I shall return to this point briefly in the next chapter.) But what I wish to question here is the bearing of this argument upon the theory of increasing misery.

Marx sees this connection as follows. If the rate of profit tends to fall, then the capitalist is faced with destruction. All he can do is to attempt to 'take it out of the workers', i.e. to increase exploitation. This he can do by extending working hours; speeding up work; lowering wages; raising the workers' cost of living (inflation); exploiting more women and children. The inner contradictions of capitalism, based on the fact that competition and profit-making are in conflict, develop here into a climax. First, they force the capitalist to accumulate and to increase productivity, and so reduce the rate of profit. Next, they force him to increase exploitation to an intolerable degree, and with it the tension between the classes. Thus compromise is impossible.

The contradictions cannot be removed. They must finally seal the fate of capitalism.

This is the main argument. But can it be conclusive? We must remember that increased productivity is the very basis of capitalist exploitation; only if the worker can produce much more than he needs for himself and his family can the capitalist appropriate surplus labour. Increased productivity, in Marx's terminology, means increased surplus labour; it means both an increased number of hours available to the capitalist, and on top of this, an increased number of commodities produced per hour. It means, in other words, a greatly increased profit. This is admitted by Marx[34]. He does not hold that profits are dwindling; he only holds that the total capital increases much more quickly than the profits, so that the *rate* of profit falls.

But if this is so, there is no reason why the capitalist should labour under an economic pressure which he is forced to pass on to the workers, whether he likes it or not. It is true, probably, that he does not like to see a fall in his rate of profit. But as long as his income does not fall, but, on the contrary, rises, there is no real danger. The situation for a successful average capitalist will be this: he sees his income rise quickly, and his capital still more quickly; that is to say, his savings rise more quickly than the part of his income which he consumes. I do not think that this is a situation which must force him to desperate measures, or which makes a compromise with the workers impossible. On the contrary, it seems to me quite tolerable.

It is true, of course, that the situation contains an element of danger. Those capitalists who speculate on the assumption of a constant or of a rising rate of profit may get into trouble; and things such as these may indeed contribute to the trade cycle, accentuating the depression. But this has little to do with the sweeping consequences which Marx prophesied.

This concludes my analysis of the third and last argument, propounded by Marx in order to prove the law of increasing misery.

VI

In order to show how completely wrong Marx was in his prophecies, and at the same time how justified he was in his glowing protest against the hell of an unrestrained capitalism as well as in his demand, 'Workers, unite!', I shall quote a few passages from the chapter of *Capital* in which he discusses the 'General Law of Capitalist Accumulation'[35]. 'In factories … young male workers are used up in masses before they reach the age of manhood; after that, only a very small proportion remains useful for industry, so that they are constantly dismissed in large numbers. They then form part of the floating surplus population which grows with the growth of industry ... Labour power is so quickly used up by capital that the middle-aged worker is usually a worn-out man ... Dr. Lee, medical officer of health, declared not long ago "that the average age at death of the Manchester upper middle class was 38, while the average age at death of the labouring class was 17; while at Liverpool those figures were represented as 35 against 15 ..." ... The exploitation of working-class children puts a premium upon their production ... The higher the productivity of labour ... the more precarious become the worker's conditions of existence ... Within the capitalist system, all the methods for raising the social productivity of labour ... are transformed into means of domination and of exploitation; they mutilate the worker into a fragment of a human being, they degrade him to a mere cog in the machine, they make work a torture, ... and drag his wife and children beneath the wheels of the capitalist Juggernaut ... *It follows that to the degree in which capital accumulates, the worker's condition must deteriorate, whatever his payment may be* ... the greater the social wealth, the amount of capital at work, the extent and energy of its growth, ... the larger is the surplus population ... The size of the industrial reserve army grows as the power of wealth grows. But ... the larger the industrial reserve army, the larger are the masses of the workers whose misery is relieved only by an increase in the agony of toil; and ... the larger is the number of those who are officially recognized as paupers. *This is the absolute and general law of capitalist accumulation* ... The accumulation of wealth at the one pole of society involves at the same time an accumulation of misery, of the agony of toil, of slavery, ignorance, brutalization, and of moral degradation, at the opposite pole ...'

Marx's terrible picture of the economy of his time is only too true. But his law that misery must increase together with accumulation does not hold. Means of production have accumulated and the productivity of labour has increased since his day to an extent which even he would hardly have thought possible. But child labour, working hours, the agony of toil, and the precariousness of the worker's existence, have not increased; they have declined. I do not say that this process must continue. There is no law of progress, and everything will depend on ourselves. But the actual situation is briefly and fairly summed up by Parkes[36] in one sentence: 'Low wages, long hours, and child labour have been characteristic of capitalism not, as Marx predicted, in its old age, but in its infancy.'

Unrestrained capitalism is gone. Since the day of Marx, democratic interventionism has made immense advances, and the improved productivity of labour—a consequence of the accumulation of capital—has made it possible virtually to stamp out misery. This shows that much has been achieved, in spite of undoubtedly grave mistakes, and it should encourage us to believe that more can be done. For much remains to be done and to be undone. Democratic interventionism can only make it possible. It rests with us to do it.

I have no illusions concerning the force of my arguments. Experience shows that Marx's prophecies were false. But experience can always be explained away. And, indeed, Marx himself, and Engels, began with the elaboration of an *auxiliary hypothesis* designed to explain why the law of increasing misery does not work as they expected it to do. According to this hypothesis, the tendency towards a falling rate of profit, and with it, increasing misery, is counteracted by the effects of *colonial exploitation*, or, as it is usually called, by 'modern imperialism'. Colonial exploitation, according to this theory, is a method of passing on economic pressure to the colonial proletariat, a group which, economically as well as politically, is weaker still than the industrial proletariat at home. 'Capital invested in colonies', Marx writes[37], 'may yield a higher rate of profit for the simple reason that the rate of profit is higher there where capitalist development is still in a backward stage, and for the added reason that slaves, coolies, etc., permit a better exploitation of labour. I can see no reason why these higher rates of profit …, when sent home, should not enter there as elements into the average rate of profit, and, in proportion, contribute to keeping it up.' (It is worth mentioning that the main idea behind this theory of 'modern' imperialism can be traced back for more than 160 years, to Adam Smith, who said of colonial trade that it 'has necessarily contributed to keep up the rate of profit'.) Engels went one step further than Marx in his development of the theory. Forced to admit that in Britain the prevailing tendency was not towards an increase in misery but rather towards a considerable improvement, he hints that this may be due to the fact that Britain 'is exploiting the whole world'; and he scornfully assails 'the British working class' which, instead of suffering as he expected them to do, 'is actually becoming more and more bourgeois'. And he continues[38]: 'It seems that this most bourgeois of all nations wants to bring matters to such a pass as to have a bourgeois aristocracy and a bourgeois proletariat *side by side* with the bourgeoisie.' Now this change of front on Engels' part is at least as remarkable as that other one of his which I mentioned in the last chapter[39]; and like that, it was made under the influence of a social development which turned out to be one of decreasing misery. Marx blamed capitalism for 'proletarianizing the middle class and the lower bourgeoisie', and for reducing the workers to pauperism. Engels now blames the system—it is still blamed—for making bourgeois out of workers. But the nicest touch in Engels' complaint is the indignation that makes him call the British who behave so inconsiderately as to falsify Marxist prophecies 'this most bourgeois of all nations'. According to Marxist doctrine, we should expect from the 'most bourgeois of all nations' a development of misery and class tension to an intolerable degree; instead, we hear that the opposite takes place. But the good Marxist's hair rises when he hears of the incredible wickedness of a capitalist system that transforms good proletarians into bad bourgeois; quite forgetting that Marx showed that the wickedness of the system consisted solely in the fact that it was working the other way round. Thus we read in Lenin's analysis[40] of the evil causes and dreadful effects of modern British imperialism: 'Causes: (1) exploitation of the whole world by this country; (2) its monopolistic position in the world market; (3) its colonial monopoly. Effects: (1) *bourgeoisification of a part of the British proletariat*; (2) a part of the proletariat permits itself to be led by people who are bought by the bourgeoisie, or who are at least paid by it.' Having given such a pretty Marxist name, 'the bourgeoisification of the proletariat', to a hateful tendency—hateful mainly because it did not fit in with the way the world should go according to Marx—Lenin apparently believes that it has become a Marxist tendency. Marx himself held that the more quickly the whole world could go through the necessary historical period of capitalist industrialization, the better, and he was therefore inclined to support[41] imperialist developments. But Lenin came to a very different conclusion. Since Britain's possession of colonies was the reason why the workers at home followed 'leaders bought by the bourgeoisie' instead of the Communists, he saw in the colonial empire a potential trigger or fuse. A revolution there would make the law of increasing misery operative at home, and a revolution at home would follow. Thus the colonies were the place from which the fire would spread …

I do not believe that the auxiliary hypothesis whose history I have sketched can save the law of increasing misery; for this hypothesis is itself refuted by experience. There are countries, for instance the Scandinavian democracies, Czechoslovakia, Canada, Australia, New Zealand, to say nothing of the United States, in which a democratic interventionism secured to the workers a high standard of living, in spite of the fact that colonial exploitation had no influence there, or was at any rate far too unimportant to support the hypothesis. Furthermore, if we compare certain countries that 'exploit' colonies, like Holland and Belgium, with Denmark, Sweden, Norway, and Czechoslovakia which do not 'exploit' colonies, we do not find that the industrial *workers* profited from the possession of colonies, for the situation of the working classes in all those countries was strikingly similar. Furthermore, although the misery imposed upon the natives through colonization is one of the darkest chapters in the history of civilization, it cannot be asserted that their misery has tended to increase since the days of Marx. The exact opposite is the case; things have greatly improved. And yet, increasing misery would have to be very noticeable there if the auxiliary hypothesis and the original theory were both correct.

VII

As I did with the second and third steps in the previous chapters, I shall now illustrate the first step of Marx's prophetic argument by showing something of its practical influence upon the tactics of Marxist parties.

The Social Democrats, under the pressure of obvious facts, tacitly dropped the theory that the intensity of misery increases; but their whole tactics remained based upon the assumption that the law of the increasing extent of misery was valid, that is to say, that the numerical strength of the industrial proletariat must continue to increase. This is why they based their policy exclusively upon representing the interests of the industrial workers, at the same time firmly believing that they were representing, or would very soon represent, 'the great majority of the population'[42]. They never doubted the assertion of the *Manifesto* that 'All previous historical movements were movements of minorities ... The proletarian movement is the self-conscious, independent movement of the immense majority, in the interest of the immense majority.' They waited confidently, therefore, for the day when the class consciousness and class assuredness of the industrial workers would win them the majority in the elections. 'There can be no doubt as to who will be victorious in the end—the few exploiters, or the immense majority, the workers.' They did not see that the industrial workers nowhere formed a majority, much less an 'immense majority', and that statistics no longer showed any tendency towards an increase in their numbers. They did not understand that the existence of a democratic workers' party was fully justified only as long as such a party was prepared to compromise or even to co-operate with other parties, for instance with some party representing the peasants, or the middle classes. And they did not see that, if they wanted to rule the state solely as the representatives of the majority of the population, they would have to change their whole policy and cease to represent mainly or exclusively the industrial workers. Of course, it is no substitute for this change of policy to assert naïvely that the proletarian policy as such may simply bring (as Marx said[43]) 'the rural producers under the intellectual leadership of the central towns of their districts, there securing to them, in the industrial worker, the *natural trustee* of their interests ...'

The position of the Communist parties was different. They strictly adhered to the theory of increasing misery, believing in an increase not only of its extent but also of its intensity, once the causes of the temporary bourgeoisification of the workers were removed. This belief contributed considerably to what Marx would have called 'the inner contradictions' of their policy.

The tactical situation seems simple enough. Thanks to Marx's prophecy, the Communists knew for certain that misery must soon increase. They also knew that the party could not win the confidence of the workers without fighting for them, and with them, for an improvement of their lot. These two fundamental assumptions clearly determined the principles of their general tactics. Make the workers demand their share, back them up in every particular episode in their unceasing fight for bread and shelter. Fight with them tenaciously for the fulfilment of their practical demands, whether economic or political. Thus you will win their confidence. At the same time, the workers will learn that it is impossible for them to better their lot by these petty fights, and that nothing short of a wholesale revolution can bring about an improvement. For all these petty fights are bound to be unsuccessful; we know from Marx that the capitalists simply *cannot* continue to compromise and that, ultimately, misery *must* increase. Accordingly, the only result—but a valuable one—of the workers' daily fight against their oppressors is an increase in their class consciousness; it is that feeling of unity which can be won only in battle, together with a desperate knowledge that only revolution can help them in their misery. When this stage is reached, then the hour has struck for the final show-down.

This is the theory and the Communists acted accordingly. At first they support the workers in their fight to improve their lot. But, contrary to all expectations and prophecies, the fight is successful. The demands are granted. Obviously, the reason is that they had been too modest. Therefore one must demand more. But the demands are granted again[44]. And as misery decreases, the workers become less embittered, more ready to bargain for wages than to plot for revolution.

Now the Communists find that their policy must be reversed. Something must be done to bring the law of increasing misery into operation. For instance, colonial unrest must be stirred up (even where there is no chance of a successful revolution), and with the general purpose of counteracting the bourgeoisification of the workers, a policy fomenting catastrophes of all sorts must be adopted. But this new policy destroys the confidence of the workers. The Communists lose their members, with the exception of those who are inexperienced in real political fights. They lose exactly those whom they describe as the 'vanguard of the working class'; their tacitly implied principle: 'The worse things are, the better they are, since misery must precipitate revolution', makes the workers suspicious—the better the application of this principle, the worse are the suspicions entertained by the workers. For they are realists; to obtain their confidence, one must work to improve their lot.

Thus the policy must be reversed again: one is forced to fight for the immediate betterment of the workers' lot and to hope at the same time for the opposite.

With this, the 'inner contradictions' of the theory produce the last stage of confusion. It is the stage when it is hard to know who is the traitor, since treachery may be faithfulness and faithfulness treachery. It is the stage when those who followed the party not simply because it appeared to them (rightly, I am afraid) as the only vigorous movement with humanitarian ends, but especially because it was a movement based on a scientific theory, must either leave it, or sacrifice their intellectual integrity; for they must now learn to believe blindly in some authority. Ultimately, they must become mystics—hostile to reasonable argument.

It seems that it is not only capitalism which is labouring under inner contradictions that threaten to bring about its downfall …

21

AN EVALUATION OF THE PROPHECY

The arguments underlying Marx's historical prophecy are invalid. His ingenious attempt to draw prophetic conclusions from observations of contemporary economic tendencies failed. The reason for this failure does not lie in any insufficiency of the empirical basis of the argument. Marx's sociological and economic analyses of contemporary society may have been somewhat one-sided, but in spite of their bias, they were excellent in so far as they were descriptive. The reason for his failure as a prophet lies entirely in the poverty of historicism as such, in the simple fact that even if we observe to-day what appears to be a historical tendency or trend, we cannot know whether it will have the same appearance to-morrow.

We must admit that Marx saw many things in the right light. If we consider only his prophecy that the system of unrestrained capitalism, as he knew it, was not going to last much longer, and that its apologists who thought it would last forever were wrong, then we must say that he was right. He was right, too, in holding that it was largely the 'class struggle', i.e. the association of the workers, that was going to bring about its transformation into a new economic system. But we must not go so far as to say that Marx predicted that new system, interventionism[1], under another name, socialism. The truth is that he had no inkling of what was lying ahead. What he called 'socialism' was very dissimilar from any form of interventionism, even from the Russian form; for he strongly believed that the impending development would diminish the influence, political as well as economic, of the state, while interventionism has increased it everywhere.

Since I am criticizing Marx and, to some extent, praising democratic piecemeal interventionism (especially of the institutional kind explained in section VII to chapter 17), I wish to make it clear that I feel much sympathy with Marx's hope for a decrease in state influence. It is undoubtedly the greatest danger of interventionism—especially of any direct intervention—that it leads to an increase in state power and in bureaucracy. Most interventionists do not mind this, or they close their eyes to it, which increases the danger. But I believe that once the danger is faced squarely, it should be possible to master it. For this is again merely a problem of social technology and of social piecemeal engineering. But it is important to tackle it early, for it constitutes a danger to democracy. We must plan for freedom, and not only for security, if for no other reason than that only freedom can make security secure.

But let us return to Marx's prophecy. One of the historical tendencies which he claimed to have discovered seems to be of a more persistent character than the others; I mean the tendency towards the accumulation of the means of production, and especially towards increasing the productivity of labour. It seems indeed that this tendency will continue for some time, provided, of course, that we continue to keep civilization going. But Marx did not merely recognize this tendency and its 'civilizing aspects', he also saw its inherent dangers. More especially, he was one of the first (although he had some predecessors, for instance, Fourier[2]) to emphasize the connection between 'the development of the productive forces' in which he saw[3] 'the historical mission and justification of capital', and that most destructive phenomenon of the credit system—a system which seems to have encouraged the rapid rise of industrialism—the *trade cycle*.

Marx's own theory of the trade cycle (discussed in section IV of the last chapter) may perhaps be paraphrased as follows: even if it is true that the inherent laws of the free market produce a tendency towards full employment, it is also true that every single approach towards full employment, i.e. towards a shortage of labour, stimulates inventors and investors to create and to introduce new labour-saving machinery, thereby giving rise (first to a short boom and then) to a new wave of unemployment and depression. Whether there is any truth in this theory, and how much, I do not know. As I said in the last chapter, the theory of the trade cycle is a rather difficult subject, and one upon which I do not intend to embark. But since Marx's contention that the increase of productivity is one of the factors contributing to the trade cycle seems to me important, I may be permitted to develop some rather obvious considerations in its support.

The following list of possible developments is, of course, quite incomplete; but it is constructed in such a way that whenever the productivity of labour increases, then at least one of the following developments, and possibly many at a time, must commence and must proceed in a degree sufficient to balance the increase in productivity.

(A) Investments increase, that is to say, such capital goods are produced as strengthen the power for producing other goods. (Since this leads to a further increase of productivity, it cannot *alone* balance its effects for any length of time.)

(B) Consumption increases—the standard of living rises:
- (*a*) that of the whole population;
- (*b*) that of certain parts of it (for instance, of a certain class).

(C) Labour time decreases:
- (*a*) the daily labour hours are reduced;
- (*b*) the number of people who are not industrial workers increases, and especially
- (b_1) the number of scientists, physicians, artists, businessmen, etc., increases.

....

- (b_2) the number of unemployed workers increases.

(D) The quantity of goods produced but not consumed increases:
- (*a*) consumption goods are destroyed;
- (*b*) capital goods are not used (factories are idle);
- (*c*) goods, other than consumption goods and goods of the type (A), are produced, for instance, arms;
- (*d*) labour is used to destroy capital goods (and thereby to reduce productivity).

I have listed these developments—the list could, of course, be elaborated—in such a way that down to the dotted line, i.e. down to (C, b_1), the developments as such are generally recognized as desirable, whilst from (C, b_2) onward come those which are generally taken to be undesirable; they indicate depression, the manufacture of armaments, and war.

Now it is clear that since (A) alone cannot restore the balance for good, although it may be a very important factor, one or several of the other developments must set in. It seems, further, reasonable to assume that if no institutions exist which guarantee that the desirable developments proceed in a degree sufficient to balance the increased productivity, some of the undesirable developments will begin. But all of these, with the possible exception of armament production, are of such a character that they are likely to lead to a sharp reduction of (A), which must severely aggravate the situation.

I do not think that such considerations as the above are able to 'explain' armament or war in any sense of the word, although they may explain the success of totalitarian states in fighting unemployment. Nor do I think that they are able to 'explain' the trade cycle, although they may perhaps contribute something to such an explanation, in which problems of credit and money are likely to play a very important part; for the reduction of (A), for instance, may be equivalent to the hoarding of such savings as would otherwise probably be invested—a much-discussed and important factor[4]. And it is not quite impossible that the Marxist law of the falling rate of profit (if this law is at all tenable[5]) may also give a hint for the explanation of hoarding; for assuming that a period of quick accumulation may lead to such a fall, this might discourage investments and encourage hoarding, and reduce (A).

But all this would not be a theory of the trade cycle. Such a theory would have a different task. Its main task would be to explain why the institution of the free market, as such a very efficient instrument for equalizing supply and demand, does not suffice to prevent depressions[6], i.e. overproduction or underconsumption. In other words, we should have to show that the buying and selling on the market produces, as one of the unwanted social repercussions[7] of our actions, the trade cycle. The Marxist theory of the trade cycle has precisely this aim in view; and the considerations sketched here regarding the effects of a general tendency towards increasing productivity can at the best only supplement this theory.

I am not going to pronounce judgement on the merits of all these speculations upon the trade cycle. But it seems to me quite clear that they are most valuable even if in the light of modern theories they should by now be entirely superseded. The mere fact that Marx treated this problem extensively is greatly to his credit. This much at least of his prophecy has come true, for the time being; the tendency towards an increase of productivity continues: the trade cycle also continues, and its continuation is likely to lead to interventionist counter-measures and therefore to a further restriction of the free market system; a development which conforms to Marx's prophecy that the trade cycle would be one of the factors that must bring about the downfall of the unrestrained system of capitalism. And to this, we must add that other piece of successful prophecy, namely, that the association of the workers would be another important factor in this process.

In view of this list of important and largely successful prophecies, is it justifiable to speak of the poverty of historicism? If Marx's historical prophecies have been even partially successful, then we should certainly not dismiss his method lightly. But a closer view of Marx's successes shows that *it was nowhere his historicist method which led him to success, but always the methods of institutional analysis.* Thus it is not an historicist but a typical institutional analysis which leads to the conclusion that the capitalist is forced by competition to increase productivity. It is an institutional analysis on which Marx bases his theory of the trade cycle and of surplus population. And even the theory of class struggle is institutional; it is part of the mechanism by which the distribution of wealth as well as of power is controlled, a mechanism which makes possible collective bargaining in the widest sense. Nowhere in these analyses do the typical historicist 'laws of historical development', or stages, or periods, or tendencies, play any part whatever. On the other hand, none of Marx's more ambitious historicist conclusions, none of his 'inexorable laws of development' and his 'stages of history which cannot be leaped over', has ever turned out to be a successful prediction. Marx was successful *only* in so far as he was analysing institutions and their functions. And the opposite is true also: none of his more ambitious and sweeping historical prophecies falls within the scope of institutional analysis. Wherever the attempt is made to back them up by such an analysis, the derivation is invalid. Indeed, compared with Marx's own high standards, the more sweeping prophecies are on a rather low intellectual level. They contain not only a lot of wishful thinking, they are also lacking in political imagination. Roughly speaking, Marx shared the belief of the progressive industrialist, of the 'bourgeois' of his time: the belief in a law of progress. But this naïve historicist optimism, of Hegel and Comte, of Marx and Mill, is no less superstitious than a pessimistic historicism like that of Plato and Spengler. And it is a very bad outfit for a prophet, since it must bridle historical imagination. Indeed, it is necessary to recognize as one of the principles of any unprejudiced view of politics that everything is possible in human affairs; and more particularly that no conceivable development can be excluded on the grounds that it may violate the so-called tendency of human progress, or any other of the alleged laws of 'human nature'. 'The fact of progress', writes[8] H. A. L. Fisher, 'is written plain and large on the page of history; but progress is not a law of nature. The ground gained by one generation may be lost by the next.'

In accordance with the principle that everything is possible it may be worth while to point out that Marx's prophecies might well have come true. A faith like the progressivist optimism of the nineteenth century can be a powerful political force; it can help to bring about what it has predicted. Thus even a correct prediction must not be accepted too readily as a corroboration of a theory, and of its scientific character. It may rather be a consequence of its religious character and a proof of the force of the religious faith which it has been able to inspire in men. And in Marxism more particularly the religious element is unmistakable. In the hour of their deepest misery and degradation, Marx's prophecy gave the workers an inspiring belief in their mission, and in the great future which their movement was to prepare for the whole of mankind. Looking back at the course of events from 1864 to 1930, I think that but for the somewhat accidental fact that Marx discouraged research in social technology, European affairs might possibly have developed, under the influence of this prophetic religion, towards a socialism of a non-collectivist type. A thorough preparation for social engineering, for planning for freedom, on the part of the Russian Marxists as well as those in Central Europe, might possibly have led to an unmistakable success, convincing to all friends of the open society. But this would not have been a corroboration of a scientific prophecy. It would have been the result of a religious movement—the result of the faith in humanitarianism, combined with a critical use of our reason for the purpose of changing the world.

But things developed differently. The prophetic element in Marx's creed was dominant in the minds of his followers. It swept everything else aside, banishing the power of cool and critical judgement and destroying the belief that by the use of reason we may change the world. All that remained of Marx's teaching was the oracular philosophy of Hegel, which in its Marxist trappings threatens to paralyse the struggle for the open society.

Marx's Ethics

22

THE MORAL THEORY OF HISTORICISM

The task which Marx set himself in *Capital* was to discover inexorable laws of social development. It was not the discovery of economic laws which would be useful to the social technologist. It was neither the analysis of the economic conditions which would permit the realization of such socialist aims as just prices, equal distribution of wealth, security, reasonable planning of production and, above all, freedom, nor was it an attempt to analyse and to clarify these aims.

But although Marx was strongly opposed to Utopian technology as well as to any attempt at a moral justification of socialist aims, his writings contained, by implication, an ethical theory. This he expressed mainly by moral evaluations of social institutions. After all, Marx's condemnation of capitalism is fundamentally a moral condemnation. The *system is condemned*, for the cruel injustice inherent in it which is combined with full 'formal' justice and righteousness. The system is condemned, because by forcing the exploiter to enslave the exploited it robs both of their freedom. Marx did not combat wealth, nor did he praise poverty. He hated capitalism, not for its accumulation of wealth, but for its oligarchical character; he hated it because in this system wealth means political power in the sense of power over other men. Labour power is made a commodity; that means that men must sell themselves on the market. Marx hated the system because it resembled slavery.

By laying such stress on the moral aspect of social institutions, Marx emphasized our responsibility for the more remote social repercussions of our actions; for instance, of such actions as may help to prolong the life of socially unjust institutions.

But although *Capital* is, in fact, largely a treatise on social ethics, these ethical ideas are never represented as such. They are expressed only by implication, but not the less forcibly on that account, since the implications are very obvious. Marx, I believe, avoided an explicit moral theory, because he hated preaching. Deeply distrustful of the moralist, who usually preaches water and drinks wine, Marx was reluctant to formulate his ethical convictions explicitly. The principles of humanity and decency were for him matters that needed no discussion, matters to be taken for granted. (In this field, too, he was an optimist.) He attacked the moralists because he saw them as the sycophantic apologists of a social order which he felt to be immoral; he attacked the eulogists of liberalism because of their self-satisfaction, because of their identification of freedom with the formal liberty then existing within a social system which destroyed freedom. Thus, by implication, he admitted his love for freedom; and in spite of his bias, as a philosopher, for holism, he was certainly not a collectivist, for he hoped that the state would 'wither away'. Marx's faith, I believe, was fundamentally a faith in the open society.

Marx's attitude towards Christianity is closely connected with these convictions, and with the fact that a hypocritical defence of capitalist exploitation was in his day characteristic of official Christianity. (His attitude was not unlike that of his contemporary Kierkegaard, the great reformer of Christian ethics, who exposed[1] the official Christian morality of his day as anti-Christian and anti-humanitarian hypocrisy.) A typical representative of this kind of Christianity was the High Church priest J. Townsend, author of *A Dissertation on the Poor Laws, by a Wellwisher of Mankind*, an extremely crude apologist for exploitation whom Marx exposed. 'Hunger', Townsend begins his eulogy[2], 'is not only a peaceable, silent, unremitted pressure but, as the most natural motive of industry and labour, it calls forth the most powerful exertions.' In Townsend's 'Christian' world order, everything depends (as Marx observes) upon making hunger permanent among the working class; and Townsend believes that this is indeed the divine purpose of the principle of the growth of population; for he goes on: 'It seems to be a law of nature that the poor should be to a certain degree improvident, so that there may always be some to fulfil the most servile, the most sordid, the most ignoble offices in the community. The stock of human happiness is thereby much increased, whilst the more delicate ... are left at liberty without interruption to pursue those callings which are suited to their various dispositions.' And the 'delicate priestly sycophant', as Marx called him for this remark, adds that the Poor Law, by helping the hungry, 'tends to destroy the harmony and beauty, the symmetry and order, of that system which God and nature have established in the world.'

If this kind of 'Christianity' has disappeared to-day from the face of the better part of our globe, it is in no small degree due to the moral reformation brought about by Marx. I do not suggest that the reform of the Church's attitude towards the poor in England did not commence long before Marx had any influence in England; but he influenced this development especially on the Continent, and the rise of socialism had the effect of strengthening it in England also. His influence on Christianity may be perhaps compared with Luther's influence on the Roman Church. Both were a challenge, both led to a counter-reformation in the camps of their enemies, to a revision and re-valuation of their ethical standards. Christianity owes not a little to Marx's influence if it is to-day on a different path from the one it was pursuing only thirty years ago. It is even partly due to Marx's influence that the Church has listened to the voice of Kierkegaard, who, in his *Book of the Judge*, described his own activity as follows[3]: 'He whose task it is to produce a corrective idea, has only to study, precisely and deeply, the rotten parts of the existing order—and then, in the most partial way possible, to stress the opposite of it.' ('Since that is so', he adds, 'an apparently clever man will easily raise the objection of partiality against the corrective idea—and he will make the public believe that this was the whole truth about it.') In this sense one might say that the early Marxism, with its ethical rigour, its emphasis on deeds instead of mere words, was perhaps the most important corrective idea of our time[4]. This explains its tremendous moral influence.

The demand that men should prove themselves in deeds is especially marked in some of Marx's earlier writings. This attitude, which might be described as his *activism*, is most clearly formulated in the last of his *Theses on Feuerbach*[5]: 'The philosophers have only interpreted the world in various ways; the point however is to *change* it.' But there are many other passages which show the same 'activist' tendency; especially those in which Marx speaks of socialism as the 'kingdom of freedom', a kingdom in which man would become the 'master of his own social environment'. Marx conceived of socialism as a period in which we are largely free from the irrational forces that now determine our life, and in which human reason can actively control human affairs. Judging by all this, and by Marx's general moral and emotional attitude, I cannot doubt that, if faced with the alternative '*are we to be the makers of our fate, or shall we be content to be its prophets?*' he would have decided to be a maker and not merely a prophet.

But as we already know, these strong 'activist' tendencies of Marx's are counteracted by his historicism. Under its influence, he became mainly a prophet. He decided that, at least under capitalism, we must submit to 'inexorable laws' and to the fact that all we can do is 'to shorten and lessen the birth-pangs' of the 'natural phases of its evolution'[6]. There is a wide gulf between Marx's activism and his historicism, and this gulf is further widened by his doctrine that we must submit to the purely irrational forces of history. For since he denounced as Utopian any attempt to make use of our reason in order to plan for the future, *reason can have no part in bringing about a more reasonable world*. I believe that such a view cannot be defended, and must lead to mysticism. But I must admit that there seems to be a theoretical possibility of bridging this gulf, although I do not consider the bridge to be sound. This bridge, of which there are only rough plans to be found in the writings of Marx and Engels, I call their *historicist moral theory*[7].

Unwilling to admit that their own ethical ideas were in any sense ultimate and self-justifying, Marx and Engels preferred to look upon their humanitarian aims in the light of a theory which explains them as the product, or the reflection, of social circumstances. Their theory can be described as follows. If a social reformer, or a revolutionary, believes that he is inspired by a hatred of 'injustice', and by a love for 'justice', then he is largely a victim of illusion (like anybody else, for instance the apologists of the old order). Or, to put it more precisely, his moral ideas of 'justice' and 'injustice' are by-products of the social and historical, development. But they are by-products of an important kind, since they are part of the mechanism by which the development propels itself. To illustrate this point, there are always at least two ideas of 'justice' (or of 'freedom' or of 'equality'), and these two ideas differ very widely indeed. The one is the idea of 'justice' as the ruling class understands it, the other, the same idea as the oppressed class understands it. These ideas are, of course, products of the class situation, but at the same time they play an important part in the class struggle—they have to provide both sides with that good conscience which they need in order to carry on their fight.

This theory of morality may be characterized as historicist because it holds that all moral categories are dependent on the historical situation; it is usually described as *historical relativism* in the field of ethics. From this point of view, it is an incomplete question to ask: Is it right to act in this way? The complete question would run like this: Is it right, in the sense of fifteenth-century feudal morality, to act in this way? Or perhaps: Is it right, in the sense of nineteenth-century proletarian morality, to act in this way? This historical relativism was formulated by Engels as follows[8]: 'What morality is preached to us to-day? There is first Christian-feudal morality, inherited from past centuries; and this again has two main subdivisions, Roman Catholic and Protestant moralities, each of which in turn has no lack of further subdivisions, from the Jesuit-Catholic and Orthodox-Protestant to loose "advanced" moralities. Alongside of these, we find the modern bourgeois morality, and with it, too, the proletarian morality of the future …'

But this so-called 'historical relativism' by no means exhausts the historicist character of the Marxist theory of morals. Let us imagine we could ask those who hold such a theory, for instance Marx himself: Why do you act in the way you do? Why would you consider it distasteful and repulsive, for instance, to accept a bribe from the bourgeoisie for stopping your revolutionary activities? I do not think that Marx would have liked to answer such a question; he would probably have tried to evade it, asserting perhaps that he just acted as he pleased, or as he felt compelled to. But all this does not touch our problem. It is certain that in the practical decisions of his life Marx followed a very rigorous moral code; it is also certain that he demanded from his collaborators a high moral standard. Whatever the terminology applied to these things may be, the problem which faces us is how to find a reply which he might have possibly made to the question: Why do you act in such a way? Why do you try, for instance, to help the oppressed? (Marx did not himself belong to this class, either by birth or by upbringing or by his way of living.)

If pressed in this way, Marx would, I think, have formulated his moral belief in the following terms, which form the core of what I call his historicist moral theory. As a social scientist (he might have said) I know that our moral ideas are weapons in the class struggle. As a scientist, I can consider them without adopting them. But as a scientist I find also that I cannot avoid taking sides in this struggle; that any attitude, even aloofness, means taking sides in some way or other. My problem thus assumes the form: Which side shall I take? When I have chosen a certain side, then I have, of course, also decided upon my morality. I shall have to adopt the moral system necessarily bound up with the interests of the class which I have decided to support. But before making this fundamental decision, I have not adopted any moral system at all, provided I can free myself from the moral tradition of my class; but this, of course, is a necessary prerequisite for making any conscious and rational decision regarding the competing moral systems. Now since a decision is 'moral' only in relation to some previously accepted moral code, my fundamental decision can be no 'moral' decision at all. But it can be a *scientific* decision. For as a social scientist, I am able to see what is going to happen. I am able to see that the bourgeoisie, and with it its system of morals, is bound to disappear, and that the proletariat, and with it a new system of morals, is bound to win. I see that this development is inevitable. It would be madness to attempt to resist it, just as it would be madness to attempt to resist the law of gravity. This is why my fundamental decision is in favour of the proletariat and of its morality. And this decision is based only on scientific foresight, on scientific historical prophecy. Although itself not a moral decision, since it is not based on any system of morality, it leads to the adoption of a certain system of morality. To sum up, my fundamental decision is not (as you suspected) the sentimental decision to help the oppressed, but the scientific and rational decision not to offer vain resistance to the developmental laws of society. Only after I have made this decision am I prepared to accept, and to make full use of, those moral sentiments which are necessary weapons in the fight for what is bound to come in any case. In this way, I adopt the facts of the coming period as the standards of my morality. And in this way, I solve the apparent paradox that a more reasonable world will come without being planned by reason; for according to my moral standards now adopted, the future world must be better, and therefore more reasonable. And I also bridge the gap between my activism and my historicism. For it is clear that even though I have discovered the natural law that determines the movement of society, I cannot shuffle the natural phases of its evolution out of the world by a stroke of the pen. But this much I can do. I can actively assist in shortening and lessening its birth-pangs.

This, I think, would have been Marx's reply, and it is this reply which to me represents the most important form of what I have called 'historicist moral theory'. It is this theory to which Engels alludes when he writes[9]: 'Certainly, that morality which contains the greatest number of elements that are going to last is the one which, within the present time, represents the overthrow of the present time; it is the one which represents the future; it is the proletarian morality ... According to this conception, the ultimate causes of all social changes and political revolutions are not increasing insight into justice; they are to be sought not in the *philosophy* but in the *economics* of the epoch concerned. The growing realization that existing social institutions are irrational and unjust is only a symptom ...' It is the theory of which a modern Marxist says: 'In founding socialist aspirations on a rational economic law of social development, *instead of justifying them on moral grounds*, Marx and Engels proclaimed socialism a historical necessity.'[10] It is a theory which is very widely held; but it has rarely been formulated clearly and explicitly. Its criticism is therefore more important than might be realized at first sight.

First, it is clear enough that the theory depends largely on the possibility of correct historical prophecy. If this is questioned—and it certainly must be questioned—then the theory loses most of its force. But for the purpose of analysing it, I shall assume at first that historical foreknowledge is an established fact; and I shall merely stipulate that this historical foreknowledge is limited; I shall stipulate that we have foreknowledge for, say, the next 500 years, a stipulation which should not restrict even the boldest claims of Marxist historicism.

Now let us first examine the claim of historicist moral theory that the fundamental decision in favour of, or against, one of the moral systems in question is itself not a moral decision; that it is not based on any moral consideration or sentiment, but on a scientific historical prediction. This claim is, I think, untenable. In order to make this quite clear, it will suffice to make explicit the imperative, or principle of conduct, implied in this fundamental decision. It is the following principle: Adopt the moral system of the future! or: Adopt the moral system held by those whose actions are most useful for bringing about the future! Now it seems clear to me that even on the assumption that we know exactly what the next 500 years will be like, it is not at all necessary for us to adopt such a principle. It is, to give an example, at least conceivable that some humanitarian pupil of Voltaire who foresaw in 1764 the development of France down to, say, 1864 might have disliked the prospect; it is at least conceivable that he would have decided that this development was rather distasteful and that he was not going to adopt the moral standards of Napoleon III as his own. I shall be faithful to my humanitarian standards, he might have said, I shall teach them to my pupils; perhaps they will survive this period, perhaps some day they will be victorious. It is likewise at least conceivable (I do not assert more, at present) that a man who to-day foresees with certainty that we are heading for a period of slavery, that we are going to return to the cage of the arrested society, or even that we are about to return to the beasts, may nevertheless decide not to adopt the moral standards of this impending period but to contribute as well as he can to the survival of his humanitarian ideals, hoping perhaps for a resurrection of his morality in some dim future.

All that is, at least, conceivable. It may perhaps not be the 'wisest' decision to make. But the fact that such a decision is excluded neither by foreknowledge nor by any sociological or psychological law shows that the first claim of historicist moral theory is untenable. Whether we should accept the morality of the future just because it is the morality of the future, this in itself is just a moral problem. The fundamental decision cannot be derived from any knowledge of the future.

In previous chapters I have mentioned *moral positivism* (especially that of Hegel), the theory that there is no moral standard but the one which exists; that what is, is reasonable and good; and therefore, that *might is right*. The practical aspect of this theory is this. A moral criticism of the existing state of affairs is impossible, since this state itself determines the moral standard of things. Now the historicist moral theory we are considering is nothing but another form of moral positivism. For it holds that *coming might is right*. The future is here substituted for the present—that is all. And the practical aspect of the theory is this. A moral criticism of the coming state of affairs is impossible, since this state determines the moral standard of things. The difference between 'the present' and 'the future' is here, of course, only a matter of degree. One can say that the future starts to-morrow, or in 500 years, or in 100. *In their theoretical structure there is no difference between moral conservatism, moral modernism, and moral futurism*. Nor is there much to choose between them in regard to moral sentiments. If the moral futurist criticizes the cowardice of the moral conservative who takes sides with the powers that be, then the moral conservative can return the charge; he can say that the moral futurist is a coward since he takes sides with the powers that will be, with the rulers of to-morrow.

I feel sure that, had he considered these implications, Marx would have repudiated historicist moral theory. Numerous remarks and numerous actions prove that it was not a scientific judgement but a moral impulse, the wish to help the oppressed, the wish to free the shamelessly exploited and miserable workers, which led him to socialism. I do not doubt that it is this moral appeal that is the secret of the influence of his teaching. And the force of this appeal was tremendously strengthened by the fact that he did not preach morality in the abstract. He did not pretend to have any right to do so. Who, he seems to have asked himself, lives up to his own standard, provided it is not a very low one? It was this feeling which led him to rely, in ethical matters, on under-statements, and which led him to the attempt to find in prophetic social science an authority in matters of morals more reliable than he felt himself to be.

Surely, in Marx's practical ethics such categories as freedom and equality played the major rôle. He was, after all, one of those who took the ideals of 1789 seriously. And he had seen how shamelessly a concept like 'freedom' could be twisted. This is why he did not preach freedom in words—why he preached it in action. He wanted to improve society and improvement meant to him more freedom, more equality, more justice, more security, higher standards of living, and especially that shortening of the working day which at once gives the workers *some* freedom. It was his hatred of hypocrisy, his reluctance to speak about these 'high ideals', together with his amazing optimism, his trust that all this would be realized in the near future, which led him to veil his moral beliefs behind historicist formulations.

Marx, I assert, would not seriously have defended moral positivism in the form of moral futurism if he had seen that it implies the recognition of future might as right. But there are others who do not possess his passionate love of humanity, who are moral futurists just because of these implications, i.e. opportunists wishing to be on the winning side. Moral futurism is widespread to-day. Its deeper, non-opportunist basis is probably the belief that goodness must 'ultimately' triumph over wickedness. But moral futurists forget that we are not going to live to witness the 'ultimate' outcome of present events. 'History will be our judge!' What does this mean? That *success* will judge. The worship of success and of future might is the highest standard of many who would never admit that present might is right. (They quite forget that the present is the future of the past.) The basis of all this is a half-hearted compromise between a moral optimism and a moral scepticism. It seems to be hard to believe in one's conscience. And it seems to be hard to resist the impulse to be on the winning side.

All these critical remarks are consistent with the assumption that we can predict the future for the next, say, 500 years. But if we drop this entirely fictitious assumption, then historicist moral theory loses all its plausibility. And we must drop it. For there is no prophetic sociology to help us in selecting a moral system. We cannot shift our responsibility for such a selection on to anybody, not even on to 'the future'.

Marx's historicist moral theory is, of course, only the result of his view concerning the method of social science, of his *sociological determinism*, a view which has become rather fashionable in our day. All our opinions, it is said, including our moral standards, depend upon society and its historical state. They are the products of society or of a certain class situation. Education is defined as a special process by which the community attempts to 'pass on' to its members 'its culture including the standards by which it would have them to live'[11], and the 'relativity of educational theory and practice to a prevailing order' is emphasized. Science, too, is said to depend on the social stratum of the scientific worker, etc.

A theory of this kind which emphasizes the sociological dependence of our opinions is sometimes called *sociologism*; if the historical dependence is emphasized, it is called *historism*. (Historism must not, of course, be mixed up with historicism.) Both sociologism and historism, in so far as they maintain the determination of scientific knowledge by society or history, will be discussed in the next two chapters. In so far as sociologism bears upon moral theory, a few remarks may be added here. But before going into any detail, I wish to make quite clear my opinion concerning these Hegelianizing theories. I believe that they chatter trivialities clad in the jargon of oracular philosophy.

Let us examine this moral 'sociologism'. That man, and his aims, are *in a certain sense* a product of society is true enough. But it is also true that society is a product of man and of his aims and that it may become increasingly so. The main question is: Which of these two aspects of the relations between men and society is more important? Which is to be stressed?

We shall understand sociologism better if we compare it with the analogous 'naturalistic' view that man and his aims are a product of heredity and environment. Again we must admit that this is true enough. But it is also quite certain that man's environment is to an increasing extent a product of him and his aims (to a limited extent, the same might be said even of his heredity). Again we must ask: which of the two aspects is more important, more fertile? The answer may be easier if we give the question the following more practical form. We, the generation now living, and our minds, our opinions, are largely the product of our parents, and of the way they have brought us up. But the next generation will be, to a similar extent, a product of ourselves, of our actions and of the way in which we bring them up. Which of the two aspects is the more important one for us to-day?

If we consider this question seriously, then we find that the decisive point is that our minds, our opinions, though largely dependent on our upbringing are not totally so. If they were totally dependent on our upbringing, if we were incapable of self-criticism, of learning from our own way of seeing things, from our experience, then, of course, the way we have been brought up by the last generation would determine the way in which we bring up the next. But it is quite certain that this is not so. Accordingly, we can concentrate our critical faculties on the difficult problem of bringing up the next generation in a way which we consider better than the way in which we have been brought up ourselves.

The situation stressed so much by sociologism can be dealt with in an exactly analogous way. That our minds, our views, are in a way a product of 'society' is trivially true. The most important part of our environment is its social part; thought, in particular, is very largely dependent on social intercourse; language, the medium of thought, is a social phenomenon. But it simply cannot be denied that we can examine thoughts, that we can criticize them, improve them, and further that we can change and improve our physical environment according to our changed, improved thoughts. And the same is true of our social environment.

All these considerations are entirely independent of the metaphysical 'problem of free will'. Even the indeterminist admits a certain amount of dependence on heredity and on environmental, especially social, influence. On the other hand, the determinist must agree that our views and actions are not fully and solely determined by heredity, education, and social influences. He has to admit that there are other factors, for instance, the more 'accidental' experiences accumulated during one's life, and that these also exert their influence. Determinism or indeterminism, as long as they remain within their metaphysical boundaries, do not affect our problem. But the point is that they may trespass beyond these boundaries; that metaphysical determinism, for instance, may encourage sociological determinism or 'sociologism'. But in this form, the theory can be confronted with experience. And experience shows that it is certainly false.

Beethoven, to take an instance from the field of æsthetics, which has a certain similarity to that of ethics, is surely to some extent a *product* of musical education and tradition, and many who take an interest in him will be impressed by this aspect of his work. The more important aspect, however, is that he is also a *producer* of music, and thereby of musical tradition and education. I do not wish to quarrel with the metaphysical determinist who would insist that every bar Beethoven wrote was determined by some combination of hereditary and environmental influences. Such an assertion is empirically entirely insignificant, since no one could actually 'explain' a single bar of his writing in this way. The important thing is that everyone admits that what he wrote can be explained neither by the musical works of his predecessors, nor by the social environment in which he lived, nor by his deafness, nor by the food which his housekeeper cooked for him; not, in other words, by any definite set of environmental influences or circumstances open to empirical investigation, or by anything we could possibly know of his heredity.

I do not deny that there are certain interesting sociological aspects of Beethoven's work. It is well known, for instance, that the transition from a small to a large symphony orchestra is connected, in some way, with a socio-political development. Orchestras cease to be the private hobbies of princes, and are at least partly supported by a middle class whose interest in music greatly increases. I am willing to appreciate any sociological 'explanation' of this sort, and I admit that such aspects may be worthy of scientific study. (After all, I myself have attempted similar things in this book, for instance, in my treatment of Plato.)

What then, more precisely, is the object of my attack? It is the exaggeration and generalization of any aspect of this kind. If we 'explain' Beethoven's symphony orchestra in the way hinted above, we have explained very little. If we describe Beethoven as representing the bourgeoisie in the process of emancipating itself, we say very little, even if it is true. Such a function could most certainly be combined with the production of bad music (as we see from Wagner). We cannot attempt to explain Beethoven's genius in this way, or in any way at all.

I think that Marx's own views could likewise be used for an empirical refutation of sociological determinism. For if we consider in the light of this doctrine the two theories, activism and historicism, and their struggle for supremacy in Marx's system, then we will have to say that historicism would be a view more fitting for a conservative apologist than for a revolutionary or even a reformer. And, indeed, historicism was used by Hegel with that tendency. The fact that Marx not only took it over from Hegel, but in the end permitted it to oust his own activism, may thus show that the side a man takes in the social struggle need not always determine his intellectual decisions. These may be determined, as in Marx's case, not so much by the true interest of the class he supported as by accidental factors, such as the influence of a predecessor, or perhaps by shortsightedness. Thus in this case, sociologism may further our understanding of Hegel, but the example of Marx himself exposes it as an unjustified generalization. A similar case is Marx's underrating of the significance of his own moral ideas; for it cannot be doubted that the secret of his religious influence was in its moral appeal, that his criticism of capitalism was effective mainly as a moral criticism. Marx showed that a social system can as such be unjust; that if the system is bad, then all the righteousness of the individuals who profit from it is a mere sham righteousness, is mere hypocrisy. For our responsibility extends to the system, to the institutions which we allow to persist.

It is this moral radicalism of Marx which explains his influence; and that is a hopeful fact in itself. This moral radicalism is still alive. It is our task to keep it alive, to prevent it from going the way which his political radicalism will have to go. 'Scientific' Marxism is dead. Its feeling of social responsibility and its love for freedom must survive.

The Aftermath

23

THE SOCIOLOGY OF KNOWLEDGE

> Rationality, in the sense of an appeal to a universal and impersonal standard of truth, is of supreme importance ..., not only in ages in which it easily prevails, but also, and even more, in those less fortunate times in which it is despised and rejected as the vain dream of men who lack the virility to kill where they cannot agree.
>
> BERTRAND RUSSELL.

It can hardly be doubted that Hegel's and Marx's historicist philosophies are characteristic products of their time—a time of social change. Like the philosophies of Heraclitus and Plato, and like those of Comte and Mill, Lamarck and Darwin, they are philosophies of change, and they witness to the tremendous and undoubtedly somewhat terrifying impression made by a changing social environment on the minds of those who live in this environment. Plato reacted to this situation by attempting to arrest all change. The more modern social philosophers appear to react very differently, since they accept, and even welcome, change; yet this love of change seems to me a little ambivalent. For even though they have given up any hope of arresting change, as historicists they try to predict it, and thus to bring it under rational control; and this certainly looks like an attempt to tame it. Thus it seems that, to the historicist, change has not entirely lost its terrors.

In our own time of still more rapid change, we even find the desire not only to predict change, but to control it by centralized large-scale planning. These holistic views (which I have criticized in *The Poverty of Historicism*) represent a compromise, as it were, between Platonic and Marxian theories.

Plato's will to arrest change, combined with Marx's doctrine of its inevitability, yield, as a kind of Hegelian 'synthesis', the demand that since it cannot be entirely arrested, change should at least be 'planned', and controlled by the state whose power is to be vastly extended.

An attitude like this may seem, at first sight, to be a kind of rationalism; it is closely related to Marx's dream of the 'realm of freedom' in which man is for the first time master of his own fate. But as a matter of fact, it occurs in closest alliance with a doctrine which is definitely opposed to rationalism (and especially to the doctrine of the rational unity of mankind; see chapter 24), one which is well in keeping with the irrationalist and mystical tendencies of our time. I have in mind the Marxist doctrine that our opinions, including our moral and scientific opinions, are determined by class interest, and more generally by the social and historical situation of our time. Under the name of 'sociology of knowledge' or 'sociologism', this doctrine has been developed recently (especially by M. Scheler and K. Mannheim[1]) as a theory of the social determination of scientific knowledge.

The sociology of knowledge argues that scientific thought, and especially thought on social and political matters, does not proceed in a vacuum, but in a socially conditioned atmosphere. It is influenced largely by unconscious or subconscious elements. These elements remain hidden from the thinker's observing eye because they form, as it were, the very place which he inhabits, his *social habitat*. The social habitat of the thinker determines a whole system of opinions and theories which appear to him as unquestionably true or self-evident. They appear to him as if they were logically and trivially true, such as, for example, the sentence 'all tables are tables'. This is why he is not even aware of having made any assumptions at all. But that he has made assumptions can be seen if we compare him with a thinker who lives in a very different social habitat; for he too will proceed from a system of apparently unquestionable assumptions, but from a very different one; and it may be so different that no intellectual bridge may exist and no compromise be possible between these two systems. Each of these different socially determined systems of assumptions is called by the sociologists of knowledge a *total ideology*.

The sociology of knowledge can be considered as a Hegelian version of Kant's theory of knowledge. For it continues on the lines of Kant's criticism of what we may term the 'passivist' theory of knowledge. I mean by this the theory of the empiricists down to and including Hume, a theory which may be described, roughly, as holding that knowledge streams into us through our senses, and that error is due to our interference with the sense-given material, or to the associations which have developed within it; the best way of avoiding error is to remain entirely passive and receptive. Against this receptacle theory of knowledge (I usually call it the 'bucket theory of the mind'), Kant[2] argued that knowledge is not a collection of gifts received by our senses and stored in the mind as if it were a museum, but that it is very largely the result of our own mental activity; that we must most actively engage ourselves in searching, comparing, unifying, generalizing, if we wish to attain knowledge. We may call this theory the 'activist' theory of knowledge. In connection with it, Kant gave up the untenable ideal of a science which is free from any kind of presuppositions. (That this ideal is even self-contradictory will be shown in the next chapter.) He made it quite clear that we cannot start from nothing, and that we have to approach our task equipped with a system of presuppositions which we hold without having tested them by the empirical methods of science; such a system may be called a 'categorial apparatus'[3]. Kant believed that it was possible to discover the one true and unchanging categorial apparatus, which represents as it were the necessarily unchanging framework of our intellectual outfit, i.e. human 'reason'. This part of Kant's theory was given up by Hegel, who, as opposed to Kant, did not believe in the unity of mankind. He taught that man's intellectual outfit was constantly changing, and that it was part of his social heritage; accordingly the development of man's reason must coincide with the historical development of his society, i.e. of the nation to which he belongs. This theory of Hegel's, and especially his doctrine that all knowledge and all truth is 'relative' in the sense of being determined by history, is sometimes called 'historism' (in contradistinction to 'historicism', as mentioned in the last chapter). The sociology of knowledge or 'sociologism' is obviously very closely related to or nearly identical with it, the only difference being that, under the influence of Marx, it emphasizes that the historical development does not produce one uniform 'national spirit', as Hegel held, but rather several and sometimes opposed 'total ideologies' within one nation, according to the class, the social stratum, or the social habitat, of those who hold them.

But the likeness to Hegel goes further. I have said above that according to the sociology of knowledge, no intellectual bridge or compromise between different total ideologies is possible. But this radical scepticism is not really meant quite as seriously as it sounds. There is a way out of it, and the way is analogous to the Hegelian method of superseding the conflicts which preceded him in the history of philosophy. Hegel, a spirit freely poised above the whirlpool of the dissenting philosophies, reduced them all to mere components of the highest of syntheses, of his own system. Similarly, the sociologists of knowledge hold that the 'freely poised intelligence' of an intelligentsia which is only loosely anchored in social traditions may be able to avoid the pitfalls of the total ideologies; that it may even be able to see through, and to unveil, the various total ideologies and the hidden motives and other determinants which inspire them. Thus the sociology of knowledge believes that the highest degree of objectivity can be reached by the freely poised intelligence analysing the various hidden ideologies and their anchorage in the unconscious. The way to true knowledge appears to be the unveiling of unconscious assumptions, a kind of psycho-therapy, as it were, or if I may say so, a *socio-therapy*. Only he who has been socio-analysed or who has socio-analysed himself, and who is freed from this social complex, i.e. from his social ideology, can attain to the highest synthesis of objective knowledge.

In a previous chapter, when dealing with 'Vulgar Marxism' I mentioned a tendency which can be observed in a group of modern philosophies, the tendency to unveil the hidden motives behind our actions. The sociology of knowledge belongs to this group, together with psycho-analysis and certain philosophies which unveil the 'meaninglessness' of the tenets of their opponents[4]. The popularity of these views lies, I believe, in the ease with which they can be applied, and in the satisfaction which they confer on those who see through things, and through the follies of the unenlightened. This pleasure would be harmless, were it not that all these ideas are liable to destroy the intellectual basis of any discussion, by establishing what I have called[5] a 'reinforced dogmatism'. (Indeed, this is something rather similar to a 'total ideology'.) Hegelianism does it by declaring the admissibility and even fertility of contradictions. But if contradictions need not be avoided, then any criticism and any discussion becomes impossible since criticism always consists in pointing out contradictions either within the theory to be criticized, or between it and some facts of experience. The situation with psycho-analysis is similar: the psycho-analyst can always explain away any objections by showing that they are due to the repressions of the critic. And the philosophers of meaning, again, need only point out that what their opponents hold is meaningless, which will always be true, since 'meaninglessness' can be so defined that any discussion about it is by definition without meaning[6]. Marxists, in a like manner, are accustomed to explain the disagreement of an opponent by his class bias, and the sociologists of knowledge by his total ideology. Such methods are both easy to handle and good fun for those who handle them. But they clearly destroy the basis of rational discussion, and they must lead, ultimately, to anti-rationalism and mysticism.

In spite of these dangers, I do not see why I should entirely forgo the fun of handling these methods. For just like the psycho-analysts, the people to whom psycho-analysis applies best,[7] the socio-analysts invite the application of their own methods to themselves with an almost irresistible hospitality. For is not their description of an intelligentsia which is only loosely anchored in tradition a very neat description of their own social group? And is it not also clear that, assuming the theory of total ideologies to be correct, it would be part of every total ideology to believe that one's own group was free from bias, and was indeed that body of the elect which alone was capable of objectivity? Is it not, therefore, to be expected, always assuming the truth of this theory, that those who hold it will unconsciously deceive themselves by producing an amendment to the theory in order to establish the objectivity of their own views? Can we, then, take seriously their claim that by their sociological self-analysis they have reached a higher degree of objectivity; and their claim that socio-analysis can cast out a total ideology? But we could even ask whether the whole theory is not simply the expression of the class interest of this particular group; of an intelligentsia only loosely anchored in tradition, though just firmly enough to speak Hegelian as their mother tongue.

How little the sociologists of knowledge have succeeded in socio-therapy, that is to say, in eradicating their own total ideology, will be particularly obvious if we consider their relation to Hegel. For they have no idea that they are just repeating him; on the contrary, they believe not only that they have outgrown him, but also that they have successfully seen through him, socio-analysed him; and that they can now look at him, not from any particular social habitat, but objectively, from a superior elevation. This palpable failure in self-analysis tells us enough.

But, all joking apart, there are more serious objections. The sociology of knowledge is not only self-destructive, not only a rather gratifying object of socio-analysis, it also shows an astounding failure to understand precisely its main subject, the *social aspects of knowledge*, or rather, of scientific method. It looks upon science or knowledge as a process in the mind or 'consciousness' of the individual scientist, or perhaps as the product of such a process. If considered in this way, what we call scientific objectivity must indeed become completely ununderstandable, or even impossible; and not only in the social or political sciences, where class interests and similar hidden motives may play a part, but just as much in the natural sciences. Everyone who has an inkling of the history of the natural sciences is aware of the passionate tenacity which characterizes many of its quarrels. No amount of political partiality can influence political theories more strongly than the partiality shown by some natural scientists in favour of their intellectual offspring. If scientific objectivity were founded, as the sociologistic theory of knowledge naïvely assumes, upon the individual scientist's impartiality or objectivity, then we should have to say good-bye to it. Indeed, we must be in a way more radically sceptical than the sociology of knowledge; for there is no doubt that we are all suffering under our own system of prejudices (or 'total ideologies', if this term is preferred); that we all take many things as self-evident, that we accept them uncritically and even with the naïve and cocksure belief that criticism is quite unnecessary; and scientists are no exception to this rule, even though they may have superficially purged themselves from some of their prejudices in their particular field. But they have not purged themselves by socio-analysis or any similar method; they have not attempted to climb to a higher plane from which they can understand, socio-analyse, and expurgate their ideological follies. For by making their minds more 'objective' they could not possibly attain to what we call 'scientific objectivity'. No, what we usually mean by this term rests on different grounds[8]. It is a matter of scientific method. And, ironically enough, objectivity is closely bound up with the *social aspect of scientific method*, with the fact that science and scientific objectivity do not (and cannot) result from the attempts of an individual scientist to be 'objective', but from the *friendly-hostile co-operation of many scientists*. Scientific objectivity can be described as the inter-subjectivity of scientific method. But this social aspect of science is almost entirely neglected by those who call themselves sociologists of knowledge.

Two aspects of the method of the natural sciences are of importance in this connection. Together they constitute what I may term the 'public character of scientific method'. First, there is something approaching *free criticism*. A scientist may offer his theory with the full conviction that it is unassailable. But this will not impress his fellow-scientists and competitors; rather it challenges them: they know that the scientific attitude means criticizing everything, and they are little deterred even by authorities. Secondly, scientists try to avoid talking at cross-purposes. (I may remind the reader that I am speaking of the natural sciences, but a part of modern economics may be included.) They try very seriously to speak one and the same language, even if they use different mother tongues. In the natural sciences this is achieved by recognizing experience as the impartial arbiter of their controversies. When speaking of 'experience' I have in mind experience of a 'public' character, like observations, and experiments, as opposed to experience in the sense of more 'private' æsthetic or religious experience; and an experience is 'public' if everybody who takes the trouble can repeat it. In order to avoid speaking at cross-purposes, scientists try to express their theories in such a form that they can be tested, i.e. refuted (or else corroborated) by such experience.

This is what constitutes scientific objectivity. Everyone who has learned the technique of understanding and testing scientific theories can repeat the experiment and judge for himself. In spite of this, there will always be some who come to judgements which are partial, or even cranky. This cannot be helped, and it does not seriously disturb the working of the various *social institutions* which have been designed to further scientific objectivity and criticism; for instance the laboratories, the scientific periodicals, the congresses. This aspect of scientific method shows what can be achieved by institutions designed to make public control possible, and by the open expression of public opinion, even if this is limited to a circle of specialists. Only political power, when it is used to suppress free criticism, or when it fails to protect it, can impair the functioning of these institutions, on which all progress, scientific, technological, and political, ultimately depends.

In order to elucidate further still this sadly neglected aspect of scientific method, we may consider the idea that it is advisable to characterize science by its methods rather than by its results.

Let us first assume that a clairvoyant produces a book by dreaming it, or perhaps by automatic writing. Let us assume, further, that years later as a result of recent and revolutionary scientific discoveries, a great scientist (who has never seen that book) produces one precisely the same. Or to put it differently, we assume that the clairvoyant 'saw' a scientific book which could not then have been produced by a scientist owing to the fact that many relevant discoveries were still unknown at that date. We now ask: is it advisable to say that the clairvoyant produced a scientific book? We may assume that, if submitted at the time to the judgement of competent scientists, it would have been described as partly ununderstandable, and partly fantastic; thus we shall have to say that the clairvoyant's book was not when written a scientific work, since it was not the result of scientific method. I shall call such a result, which, though in agreement with some scientific results, is not the product of scientific method, a piece of 'revealed science'.

In order to apply these considerations to the problem of the publicity of scientific method, let us assume that Robinson Crusoe succeeded in building on his island physical and chemical laboratories, astronomical observatories, etc., and in writing a great number of papers, based throughout on observation and experiment. Let us even assume that he had unlimited time at his disposal, and that he succeeded in constructing and in describing scientific systems which actually coincide with the results accepted at present by our own scientists. Considering the character of this Crusonian science, some people will be inclined, at first sight, to assert that it is real science and not 'revealed science'. And, no doubt, it is very much more like science than the scientific book which was revealed to the clairvoyant, for Robinson Crusoe applied a good deal of scientific method. And yet, I assert that this Crusonian science is still of the 'revealed' kind; that there is an element of scientific method missing, and consequently, that the fact that Crusoe arrived at our results is nearly as accidental and miraculous as it was in the case of the clairvoyant. For there is nobody but himself to check his results; nobody but himself to correct those prejudices which are the unavoidable consequence of his peculiar mental history; nobody to help him to get rid of that strange blindness concerning the inherent possibilities of our own results which is a consequence of the fact that most of them are reached through comparatively irrelevant approaches. And concerning his scientific papers, it is only in attempts to explain his work to *somebody who has not done it* that he can acquire the discipline of clear and reasoned communication which too is part of scientific method. In one point—a comparatively unimportant one—is the 'revealed' character of the Crusonian science particularly obvious; I mean Crusoe's discovery of his 'personal equation' (for we must assume that he made this discovery), of the characteristic personal reaction-time affecting his astronomical observations. Of course it is conceivable that he discovered, say, changes in his reaction-time, and that he was led, in this way, to make allowances for it. But if we compare this way of finding out about reaction-time, with the way in which it was discovered in 'public' science—through the contradiction between the results of various observers—then the 'revealed' character of Robinson Crusoe's science becomes manifest.

To sum up these considerations, it may be said that what we call 'scientific objectivity' is not a product of the individual scientist's impartiality, but a product of the social or public character of scientific method; and the individual scientist's impartiality is, so far as it exists, not the source but rather the result of this socially or institutionally organized objectivity of science.

Both[9] Kantians and Hegelians make the same mistake of assuming that our presuppositions (since they are, to start with, undoubtedly indispensable instruments which we need in our active 'making' of experiences) can neither be changed by decision nor refuted by experience; that they are above and beyond the scientific methods of testing theories, constituting as they do the basic presuppositions of all thought. But this is an exaggeration, based on a misunderstanding of the relations between theory and experience in science. It was one of the greatest achievements of our time when Einstein showed that, in the light of experience, we may question and revise our pre-suppositions regarding even space and time, ideas which had been held to be necessary presuppositions of all science, and to belong to its 'categorial apparatus'. Thus the sceptical attack upon science launched by the sociology of knowledge breaks down in the light of scientific method. The empirical method has proved to be quite capable of taking care of itself.

But it does so not by eradicating our prejudices all at once; it can eliminate them only one by one. The classical case in point is again Einstein's discovery of our prejudices regarding time. Einstein did not set out to discover prejudices; he did not even set out to criticize our conceptions of space and time. His problem was a concrete problem of physics, the re-drafting of a theory that had broken down because of various experiments which in the light of the theory seemed to contradict one another. Einstein together with most physicists realized that this meant that the theory was false. And he found that if we alter it in a point which had so far been held by everybody to be self-evident and which had therefore escaped notice, then the difficulty could be removed. In other words, he just applied the methods of scientific criticism and of the invention and elimination of theories, of trial and error. But this method does not lead to the abandonment of all our prejudices; rather, we can discover the fact that we had a prejudice only after having got rid of it.

But it certainly has to be admitted that, at any given moment, our scientific theories will depend not only on the experiments, etc., made up to that moment, but also upon prejudices which are taken for granted, so that we have not become aware of them (although the application of certain logical methods may help us to detect them). At any rate, we can say in regard to this incrustation that science is capable of learning, of breaking down some of its crusts. The process may never be perfected, but there is no fixed barrier before which it must stop short. Any assumption can, in principle, be criticized. And that anybody may criticize constitutes scientific objectivity.

Scientific results are 'relative' (if this term is to be used at all) only in so far as they are the results of a certain stage of scientific development and liable to be superseded in the course of scientific progress. But this does not mean that *truth* is 'relative'. If an assertion is true, it is true for ever[10]. It only means that most scientific results have the character of hypotheses, i.e. statements for which the evidence is inconclusive, and which are therefore liable to revision at any time. These considerations (with which I have dealt more fully elsewhere[11]), though not necessary for a criticism of the sociologists, may perhaps help to further the understanding of their theories. They also throw some light, to come back to my main criticism, on the important rôle which co-operation, intersubjectivity, and the publicity of method play in scientific criticism and scientific progress.

It is true that the social sciences have not yet fully attained this publicity of method. This is due partly to the intelligence-destroying influence of Aristotle and Hegel, partly perhaps also to their failure to make use of the social instruments of scientific objectivity. Thus they are really 'total ideologies', or putting it differently, some social scientists are unable, and even unwilling, to speak a common language. But the reason is not class interest, and the cure is not a Hegelian dialectical synthesis, nor self-analysis. The only course open to the social sciences is to forget all about the verbal fireworks and to tackle the practical problems of our time with the help of the theoretical methods which are fundamentally the same in *all* sciences. I mean the methods of trial and error, of inventing hypotheses which can be practically tested, and of submitting them to practical tests. *A social technology is needed whose results can be tested by piecemeal social engineering.*

The cure here suggested for the social sciences is diametrically opposed to the one suggested by the sociology of knowledge. Sociologism believes that it is not their unpractical character, but rather the fact that practical and theoretical problems are too much intertwined in the field of social and political knowledge, that creates the methodological difficulties of these sciences. Thus we can read in a leading work on the sociology of knowledge[12]: 'The peculiarity of political knowledge, as opposed to "exact" knowledge, lies in the fact that knowledge and will, or the rational element and the range of the irrational, are inseparably and essentially intertwined.' To this we can reply that 'knowledge' and 'will' are, in a certain sense, always inseparable; and that this fact need not lead to any dangerous entanglement. No scientist can know without making an effort, without taking an interest; and in his effort there is usually even a certain amount of self-interest involved. The engineer studies things mainly from a practical point of view. So does the farmer. Practice is not the enemy of theoretical knowledge but the most valuable incentive to it. Though a certain amount of aloofness may be becoming to the scientist, there are many examples to show that it is not always important for a scientist to be thus disinterested. But it *is* important for him to remain in touch with reality, with practice, for those who overlook it have to pay by lapsing into scholasticism. Practical application of our findings is thus the means by which we may eliminate irrationalism from social science, and not any attempt to separate knowledge from 'will'.

As opposed to this, the sociology of knowledge hopes to reform the social sciences by making the social scientists aware of the social forces and ideologies which unconsciously beset them. But the main trouble about prejudices is that there is no such direct way of getting rid of them. For how shall we ever know that we have made any progress in our attempt to rid ourselves from prejudice? Is it not a common experience that those who are most convinced of having got rid of their prejudices are most prejudiced? The idea that a sociological or a psychological or an anthropological or any other study of prejudices may help us to rid ourselves of them is quite mistaken; for many who pursue these studies are full of prejudice; and not only does self-analysis not help us to overcome the unconscious determination of our views, it often leads to even more subtle self-deception. Thus we can read in the same work on the sociology of knowledge[13] the following references to its own activities: 'There is an increasing tendency towards making conscious the factors by which we have so far been unconsciously ruled … Those who fear that our increasing knowledge of determining factors may paralyse our decisions and threaten "freedom" should put their minds at rest. For only he is truly determined who does not know the most essential determining factors but acts immediately under the pressure of determinants unknown to him.' Now this is clearly just a repetition of a pet idea of Hegel's which Engels naïvely repeated when he said[14]: 'Freedom is the appreciation of necessity.' And it is a reactionary prejudice. For are those who act under the pressure of well-known determinants, for example, of a political tyranny, made free by their knowledge? Only Hegel could tell us such tales. But that the sociology of knowledge preserves this particular prejudice shows clearly enough that there is no possible short-cut to rid us of our ideologies. (Once a Hegelian, always a Hegelian.) Self-analysis is no substitute for those practical actions which are necessary for establishing the democratic institutions which alone can guarantee the freedom of critical thought, and the progress of science.

24

ORACULAR PHILOSOPHY AND THE REVOLT AGAINST REASON

Marx was a rationalist. With Socrates, and with Kant, he believed in human reason as the basis of the unity of mankind. But his doctrine that our opinions are determined by class interest hastened the decline of this belief. Like Hegel's doctrine that our ideas are determined by national interests and traditions, Marx's doctrine tended to undermine the rationalist belief in reason. Thus threatened both from the right and from the left, a rationalist attitude to social and economic questions could hardly resist when historicist prophecy and oracular irrationalism made a frontal attack on it. This is why the conflict between rationalism and irrationalism has become the most important intellectual, and perhaps even moral, issue of our time.

I

Since the terms 'reason' and 'rationalism' are vague, it will be necessary to explain roughly the way in which they are used here. First, they are used in a wide sense[1]; they are used to cover not only intellectual activity but also observation and experiment. It is necessary to keep this remark in mind, since 'reason' and 'rationalism' are often used in a different and more narrow sense, in opposition not to 'irrationalism' but to 'empiricism'; if used in this way, rationalism extols intelligence above observation and experiment, and might therefore be better described as 'intellectualism'. But when I speak here of 'rationalism', I use the word always in a sense which includes 'empiricism' as well as 'intellectualism'; just as science makes use of experiments as well as of thought. Secondly, I use the word 'rationalism' in order to indicate, roughly, an attitude that seeks to solve as many problems as possible by an appeal to reason, i.e. to clear thought and experience, rather than by an appeal to emotions and passions. This explanation, of course, is not very satisfactory, since all terms such as 'reason' or 'passion' are vague; we do not possess 'reason' or 'passions' in the sense in which we possess certain physical organs, for example, brains or a heart, or in the sense in which we possess certain 'faculties', for example, the power of speaking, or of gnashing our teeth. In order therefore to be a little more precise, it may be better to explain rationalism in terms of practical attitudes or behaviour. We could then say that rationalism is an attitude of readiness to listen to critical arguments and to learn from experience. It is fundamentally an attitude of admitting that '*I may be wrong and you may be right, and by an effort, we may get nearer to the truth*'. It is an attitude which does not lightly give up hope that by such means as argument and careful observation, people may reach some kind of agreement on many problems of importance; and that, even where their demands and their interests clash, it is often possible to argue about the various demands and proposals, and to reach—perhaps by arbitration—a compromise which, because of its equity, is acceptable to most, if not to all. In short, the rationalist attitude, or, as I may perhaps label it, the 'attitude of reasonableness', is very similar to the scientific attitude, to the belief that in the search for truth we need co-operation, and that, with the help of argument, we can in time attain something like objectivity.

It is of some interest to analyse this resemblance between this attitude of reasonableness and that of science more fully. In the last chapter, I tried to explain the social aspect of scientific method with the help of the fiction of a scientific Robinson Crusoe. An exactly analogous consideration can show the social character of reasonableness, as opposed to intellectual gifts, or cleverness. Reason, like language, can be said to be a product of social life. A Robinson Crusoe (marooned in early childhood) might be clever enough to master many difficult situations; but he would invent neither language nor the art of argumentation. Admittedly, we often argue with ourselves; but we are accustomed to do so only because we have learned to argue with others, and because we have learned in this way that the argument counts, rather than the person arguing. (This last consideration cannot, of course, tip the scales when we argue with ourselves.) Thus we can say that we owe our reason, like our language, to intercourse with other men.

The fact that the rationalist attitude considers the argument rather than the person arguing is of far-reaching importance. It leads to the view that we must recognize everybody with whom we communicate as a potential source of argument and of reasonable information; it thus establishes what may be described as the 'rational unity of mankind'.

In a way, our analysis of 'reason' may be said to resemble slightly that of Hegel and the Hegelians, who consider reason as a social product and indeed as a kind of department of the soul or the spirit of society (for example, of the nation, or the class) and who emphasize, under the influence of Burke, our indebtedness to our social heritage, and our nearly complete dependence on it. Admittedly, there is some similarity. But there are very considerable differences also. Hegel and the Hegelians are collectivists. They argue that, since we owe our reason to 'society'—or to a certain society such as a nation—'society' is everything and the individual nothing; or that whatever value the individual possesses is derived from the collective, the real carrier of all values. As opposed to this, the position presented here does not assume the existence of collectives; if I say, for example, that we owe our reason to 'society', then I always mean that we owe it to certain concrete individuals—though perhaps to a considerable number of anonymous individuals—and to our intellectual intercourse with them. Therefore, in speaking of a 'social' theory of reason (or of scientific method), I mean more precisely that the theory is an *inter-personal* one, and never that it is a collectivist theory. Certainly we owe a great deal to tradition, and tradition is very important, but the term 'tradition' also has to be analysed into concrete personal relations[2]. And if we do this, then we can get rid of that attitude which considers every tradition as sacrosanct, or as valuable in itself, replacing this by an attitude which considers traditions as valuable or pernicious, as the case may be, according to their influence upon individuals. We thus may realize that each of us (by way of example and criticism) may contribute to the growth or the suppression of such traditions.

The position here adopted is very different from the popular, originally Platonic, view of reason as a kind of 'faculty', which may be possessed and developed by different men in vastly different degrees. Admittedly, intellectual gifts may be different in this way, and they may contribute to reasonableness; but they need not. Clever men may be very unreasonable; they may cling to their prejudices and may not expect to hear anything worth while from others. According to our view, however, we not only owe our reason to others, but we can never excel others in our reasonableness in a way that would establish a claim to authority; authoritarianism and rationalism in our sense cannot be reconciled, since argument, which includes criticism, and the art of listening to criticism, is the basis of reasonableness. Thus rationalism in our sense is diametrically opposed to all those modern Platonic dreams of brave new worlds in which the growth of reason would be controlled or 'planned' by some superior reason. Reason, like science, grows by way of mutual criticism; the only possible way of 'planning' its growth is to develop those institutions that safeguard the freedom of this criticism, that is to say, the freedom of thought. It may be remarked that Plato, even though his theory is authoritarian, and demands the strict control of the growth of human reason in his guardians (as has been shown especially in chapter 8), pays tribute, *by his manner of writing*, to our inter-personal theory of reason; for most of his earlier dialogues describe arguments conducted in a very reasonable spirit.

My way of using the term 'rationalism' may become a little clearer, perhaps, if we distinguish between a true rationalism and a false or a pseudo-rationalism. What I shall call the 'true rationalism' is the rationalism of Socrates. It is the awareness of one's limitations, the intellectual modesty of those who know how often they err, and how much they depend on others even for this knowledge. It is the realization that we must not expect too much from reason; that argument rarely settles a question, although it is the only means for learning—not to see clearly, but to see more clearly than before.

What I shall call 'pseudo-rationalism' is the intellectual intuitionism of Plato. It is the immodest belief in one's superior intellectual gifts, the claim to be initiated, to know with certainty, and with authority. According to Plato, opinion—even 'true opinion', as we can read in the *Timaeus*[3]—'is shared by all men; but reason' (or 'intellectual intuition') 'is shared only by the gods, and by very few men'. This authoritarian intellectualism, this belief in the possession of an infallible instrument of discovery, or an infallible method, this failure to distinguish between a man's intellectual powers and his indebtedness to others for all he can possibly know or understand, this pseudo-rationalism is often called 'rationalism', but it is diametrically opposed to what we call by this name.

My analysis of the rationalist attitude is undoubtedly very incomplete, and, I readily admit, a little vague; but it will suffice for our purpose. In a similar way I shall now describe irrationalism, indicating at the same time how an irrationalist is likely to defend it.

The irrationalist attitude may be developed along the following lines. Though perhaps recognizing reason and scientific argument as tools that may do well enough if we wish to scratch the surface of things, or as means to serve some irrational end, the irrationalist will insist that 'human nature' is in the main not rational. Man, he holds, is more than a rational animal, and also less. In order to see that he is less, we need only consider how small is the number of men who are capable of argument; this is why, according to the irrationalist, the majority of men will always have to be tackled by an appeal to their emotions and passions rather than by an appeal to their reason. But man is also more than just a rational animal, since all that really matters in his life goes beyond reason. Even the few scientists who take reason and science seriously are bound to their rationalist attitude merely because they love it. Thus even in these rare cases, it is the emotional make-up of man and not his reason that determines his attitude. Moreover, it is his intuition, his mystical insight into the nature of things, rather than his reasoning which makes a great scientist. Thus rationalism cannot offer an adequate interpretation even of the apparently rational activity of the scientist. But since the scientific field is exceptionally favourable to a rationalist interpretation, we must expect that rationalism will fail even more conspicuously when it tries to deal with other fields of human activity. And this expectation, so the irrationalist will continue his argument, proves to be quite accurate. Leaving aside the lower aspects of human nature, we may look to one of its highest, to the fact that man can be creative. It is the small creative minority of men who really matter; the men who create works of art or of thought, the founders of religions, and the great statesmen. These few exceptional individuals allow us to glimpse the real greatness of man. But although these leaders of mankind know how to make use of reason for their purposes, they are never men of reason. Their roots lie deeper—deep in their instincts and impulses, and in those of the society of which they are parts. Creativeness is an entirely irrational, a mystical faculty …

II

The issue between rationalism and irrationalism is of long standing. Although Greek philosophy undoubtedly started off as a rationalist undertaking, there were streaks of mysticism even in its first beginnings. It is (as hinted in chapter 10) the yearning for the lost unity and shelter of tribalism which expresses itself in these mystical elements within a fundamentally rational approach[4]. An open conflict between rationalism and irrationalism broke out for the first time in the Middle Ages, as the opposition between scholasticism and mysticism. (It is perhaps not without interest that rationalism flourished in the former Roman provinces, while men from the 'barbarian' countries were prominent among the mystics.) In the seventeenth, eighteenth, and nineteenth centuries, when the tide of rationalism, of intellectualism, and of 'materialism' was rising, irrationalists had to pay some attention to it, to argue against it; and by exhibiting its limitations, and exposing the immodest claims and dangers of pseudo-rationalism (which they did not distinguish from rationalism in our sense), some of these critics, notably Burke, have earned the gratitude of all true rationalists. But the tide has now turned, and 'profoundly significant allusions ... and allegories' (as Kant puts it) have become the fashion of the day. An oracular irrationalism has established (especially with Bergson and the majority of German philosophers and intellectuals) the habit of ignoring or at best deploring the existence of such an inferior being as a rationalist. To them the rationalists—or the 'materialists', as they often say—and especially, the rationalist scientist, are the poor in spirit, pursuing soulless and largely mechanical activities[5], and completely unaware of the deeper problems of human destiny and of its philosophy. And the rationalists usually reciprocate by dismissing irrationalism as sheer nonsense. Never before has the break been so complete. And the break in the diplomatic relations of the philosophers proved its significance when it was followed by a break in the diplomatic relations of the states.

In this issue, I am entirely on the side of rationalism. This is so much the case that even where I feel that rationalism has gone too far I still sympathize with it, holding as I do that an excess in this direction (as long as we exclude the intellectual immodesty of Plato's pseudo-rationalism) is harmless indeed as compared with an excess in the other. In my opinion, the only way in which excessive rationalism is likely to prove harmful is that it tends to undermine its own position and thus to further an irrationalist reaction. It is only this danger which induces me to examine the claims of an excessive rationalism more closely and to advocate a modest and self-critical rationalism which recognizes certain limitations. Accordingly, I shall distinguish in what follows between two rationalist positions, which I label 'critical rationalism' and 'uncritical rationalism' or 'comprehensive rationalism'. (This distinction is independent of the previous one between a 'true' and a 'false' rationalism, even though a 'true' rationalism in my sense will hardly be other than critical.)

Uncritical or comprehensive rationalism can be described as the attitude of the person who says 'I am not prepared to accept anything that cannot be defended by means of argument or experience'. We can express this also in the form of the principle that any assumption which cannot be supported either by argument or by experience is to be discarded[6]. Now it is easy to see that this principle of an uncritical rationalism is inconsistent; for since it cannot, in its turn, be supported by argument or by experience, it implies that it should itself be discarded. (It is analogous to the paradox of the liar[7], i.e. to a sentence which asserts its own falsity.) Uncritical rationalism is therefore logically untenable; and since a purely logical argument can show this, uncritical rationalism can be defeated by its own chosen weapon, argument.

This criticism may be generalized. Since all argument must proceed from assumptions, it is plainly impossible to demand that all assumptions should be based on argument. The demand raised by many philosophers that we should start with no assumption whatever and never assume anything about 'sufficient reason', and even the weaker demand that we should start with a very small set of assumptions ('categories'), are both in this form inconsistent. For they themselves rest upon the truly colossal assumption that it is possible to start without, or with only a few assumptions, and still to obtain results that are worth while. (Indeed, this principle of avoiding all presuppositions is not, as some may think, a counsel of perfection, but a form of the paradox of the liar[8].)

Now all this is a little abstract, but it may be restated in connection with the problem of rationalism in a less formal way. The rationalist attitude is characterized by the importance it attaches to argument and experience. But neither logical argument nor experience can establish the rationalist attitude; for only those who are ready to consider argument or experience, and who have therefore adopted this attitude already, will be impressed by them. That is to say, a rationalist attitude must be first adopted if any argument or experience is to be effective, and it cannot therefore be based upon argument or experience. (And this consideration is quite independent of the question whether or not there exist any convincing rational arguments which favour the adoption of the rationalist attitude.) We have to conclude from this that no rational argument will have a rational effect on a man who does not want to adopt a rational attitude. Thus a comprehensive rationalism is untenable.

But this means that whoever adopts the rationalist attitude does so because he has adopted, consciously or unconsciously, some proposal, or decision, or belief, or behaviour; an adoption which may be called 'irrational'. Whether this adoption is tentative or leads to a settled habit, we may describe it as an irrational *faith in reason*. So rationalism is necessarily far from comprehensive or self-contained. This has frequently been overlooked by rationalists who thus exposed themselves to a beating in their own field and by their own favourite weapon whenever an irrationalist took the trouble to turn it against them. And indeed it did not escape the attention of some enemies of rationalism that one can always refuse to accept arguments, either all arguments or those of a certain kind; and that such an attitude can be carried through without becoming logically inconsistent. This led them to see that the uncritical rationalist who believes that rationalism is self-contained and can be established by argument must be wrong. Irrationalism is logically superior to uncritical rationalism.

Then why not adopt irrationalism? Many who started as rationalists but were disillusioned by the discovery that a too comprehensive rationalism defeats itself have indeed practically capitulated to irrationalism. (This is what has happened to Whitehead[9], if I am not quite mistaken.) But such panic action is entirely uncalled for. Although an uncritical and comprehensive rationalism is logically untenable, and although a comprehensive irrationalism is logically tenable, this is no reason why we should adopt the latter. For there are other tenable attitudes, notably that of critical rationalism which recognizes the fact that the fundamental rationalist attitude results from an (at least tentative) act of faith—from faith in reason. Accordingly, our choice is open. We may choose some form of irrationalism, even some radical or comprehensive form. But we are also free to choose a critical form of rationalism, one which frankly admits its origin in an irrational decision (and which, to that extent, admits a certain priority of irrationalism).

III

The choice before us is not simply an intellectual affair, or a matter of taste. It is a moral decision[10] (in the sense of chapter 5). For the question whether we adopt some more or less radical form of irrationalism, or whether we adopt that minimum concession to irrationalism which I have termed 'critical rationalism', will deeply affect our whole attitude towards other men, and towards the problems of social life. It has already been said that rationalism is closely connected with the belief in the unity of mankind. Irrationalism, which is not bound by any rules of consistency, may be combined with any kind of belief, including a belief in the brotherhood of man; but the fact that it may easily be combined with a very different belief, and especially the fact that it lends itself easily to the support of a romantic belief in the existence of an elect body, in the division of men into leaders and led, into natural masters and natural slaves, shows clearly that a moral decision is involved in the choice between it and a critical rationalism.

As we have seen before (in chapter 5), and now again in our analysis of the uncritical version of rationalism, arguments cannot *determine* such a fundamental moral decision. But this does not imply that our choice cannot be *helped* by any kind of argument whatever. On the contrary, whenever we are faced with a moral decision of a more abstract kind, it is most helpful to analyse carefully the consequences which are likely to result from the alternatives between which we have to choose. For only if we can visualize these consequences in a concrete and practical way, do we really know what our decision is about; otherwise we decide blindly. In order to illustrate this point, I may quote a passage from Shaw's *Saint Joan*. The speaker is the Chaplain; he has stubbornly demanded Joan's death; but when he sees her at the stake, he breaks down: 'I meant no harm. I did not know what it would be like ... I did not know what I was doing ... If I had known, I would have torn her from their hands. You don't know. You haven't seen: it is so easy to talk when you don't know. You madden yourself with words ... But when it is brought home to you; when you see the thing you have done; when it is blinding your eyes, stifling your nostrils, tearing your heart, then—then—O God, take away this sight from me!' There were, of course, other figures in Shaw's play who knew exactly what they were doing, and yet decided to do it; and who did not regret it afterwards. Some people dislike seeing their fellow men burning at the stake, and others do not. This point (which was neglected by many Victorian optimists) is important, for it shows that a rational analysis of the consequences of a decision does not make the decision rational; the consequences do not determine our decision; it is always we who decide. But an analysis of the concrete consequences, and their clear realization in what we call our 'imagination', makes the difference between a blind decision and a decision made with open eyes; and since we use our imagination very little[11], we only too often decide blindly. This is especially so if we are intoxicated by an oracular philosophy, one of the most powerful means of maddening ourselves with words—to use Shaw's expression.

The rational and imaginative analysis of the consequences of a moral theory has a certain analogy in scientific method. For in science, too, we do not accept an abstract theory because it is convincing in itself; we rather decide to accept or reject it after we have investigated those concrete and practical consequences which can be more directly tested by experiment. But there is a fundamental difference. In the case of a scientific theory, our decision depends upon the results of experiments. If these confirm the theory, we may accept it until we find a better one. If they contradict the theory, we reject it. But in the case of a moral theory, we can only confront its consequences with our conscience. And while the verdict of experiments does not depend upon ourselves, the verdict of our conscience does.

I hope I have made it clear in which sense the analysis of consequences may influence our decision without determining it. And in presenting the consequences of the two alternatives between which we must decide, rationalism and irrationalism, I warn the reader that I shall be partial. So far, in presenting the two alternatives of the moral decision before us—it is, in many senses, the most fundamental decision in the ethical field—I have tried to be impartial, although I have not hidden my sympathies. But now I am going to present those considerations of the consequences of the two alternatives which appear to me most telling, and by which I myself have been influenced in rejecting irrationalism and accepting the faith in reason.

Let us examine the consequences of irrationalism first. The irrationalist insists that emotions and passions rather than reason are the mainsprings of human action. To the rationalist's reply that, though this may be so, we should do what we can to remedy it, and should try to make reason play as large a part as it possibly can, the irrationalist would rejoin (if he condescends to a discussion) that this attitude is hopelessly unrealistic. For it does not consider the weakness of 'human nature', the feeble intellectual endowment of most and their obvious dependence upon emotions and passions.

It is my firm conviction that this irrational emphasis upon emotion and passion leads ultimately to what I can only describe as crime. One reason for this opinion is that this attitude, which is at best one of resignation towards the irrational nature of human beings, at worst one of scorn for human reason, must lead to an appeal to violence and brutal force as the ultimate arbiter in any dispute. For if a dispute arises, then this means that those more constructive emotions and passions which might in principle help to get over it, reverence, love, devotion to a common cause, etc., have shown themselves incapable of solving the problem. But if that is so, then what is left to the irrationalist except the appeal to other and less constructive emotions and passions, to fear, hatred, envy, and ultimately, to violence? This tendency is very much strengthened by another and perhaps even more important attitude which also is in my opinion inherent in irrationalism, namely, the stress on the inequality of men.

It cannot, of course, be denied that human individuals are, like all other things in our world, in very many respects very unequal. Nor can it be doubted that this inequality is of great importance and even in many respects highly desirable[12]. (The fear that the development of mass production and collectivization may react upon men by destroying their inequality or individuality is one of the nightmares[13] of our times.) But all this simply has no bearing upon the question whether or not we should decide to treat men, especially in political issues, as equals, or as much like equals as is possible; that is to say, as possessing equal rights, and equal claims to equal treatment; and it has no bearing upon the question whether we ought to construct political institutions accordingly. 'Equality before the law' is *not a fact but a political demand*[14] *based upon a moral decision*; and it is quite independent of the theory—which is probably false—that 'all men are born equal'. Now I do not intend to say that the adoption of this humanitarian attitude of impartiality is a direct consequence of a decision in favour of rationalism. But a tendency towards impartiality is closely related to rationalism, and can hardly be excluded from the rationalist creed. Again, I do not intend to say that an irrationalist could not consistently adopt an equalitarian or impartial attitude; and even if he could not do so consistently, he is not bound to be consistent. But I do wish to stress the fact that the irrationalist attitude can hardly avoid becoming entangled with the attitude that is opposed to equalitarianism. This fact is connected with its emphasis upon emotions and passions; for we cannot feel the same emotions towards everybody. Emotionally, we all divide men into those who are near to us, and those who are far from us. The division of mankind into friend and foe is a most obvious emotional division; and this division is even recognized in the Christian commandment, 'Love thy enemies!' Even the best Christian who really lives up to this commandment (there are not many, as is shown by the attitude of the average good Christian towards 'materialists' and 'atheists'), even he cannot feel equal love for all men. We cannot really love 'in the abstract'; we can love only those whom we know. Thus the appeal even to our best emotions, love and compassion, can only tend to divide mankind into different categories. And this will be more true if the appeal is made to lesser emotions and passions. Our 'natural' reaction will be to divide mankind into friend and foe; into those who belong to our tribe, to our emotional community, and those who stand outside it; into believers and unbelievers; into compatriots and aliens; into class comrades and class enemies; and into leaders and led.

I have mentioned before that the theory that our thoughts and opinions are dependent upon our class situation, or upon our national interests, must lead to irrationalism. I now wish to emphasize the fact that the opposite is also true. The abandonment of the rationalist attitude, of the respect for reason and argument and the other fellow's point of view, the stress upon the 'deeper' layers of human nature, all this must lead to the view that thought is merely a somewhat superficial manifestation of what lies within these irrational depths. It must nearly always, I believe, produce an attitude which considers the person of the thinker instead of his thought. It must produce the belief that 'we think with our blood', or 'with our national heritage', or 'with our class'. This view may be presented in a materialist form or in a highly spiritual fashion; the idea that we 'think with our race' may perhaps be replaced by the idea of elect or inspired souls who 'think by

God's grace'. I refuse, on moral grounds, to be impressed by these differences; for the decisive similarity between all these intellectually immodest views is that they do not judge a thought on its own merits. By thus abandoning reason, they split mankind into friends and foes; into the few who share in reason with the gods, and the many who don't (as Plato says); into the few who stand near and the many who stand far; into those who speak the untranslatable language of our own emotions and passions and those whose tongue is not our tongue. Once we have done this, political equalitarianism becomes practically impossible.

Now the adoption of an anti-equalitarian attitude in political life, i.e. in the field of problems concerned with the power of man over man, is just what I should call criminal. For it offers a justification of the attitude that different categories of people have different rights; that the master has the right to enslave the slave; that some men have the right to use others as their tools. Ultimately, it will be used, as in Plato[15], to justify murder.

I do not overlook the fact that there are irrationalists who love mankind, and that not all forms of irrationalism engender criminality. But I hold that he who teaches that not reason but love should rule opens the way for those who rule by hate. (Socrates, I believe, saw something of this when he suggested[16] that mistrust or hatred of argument is related to mistrust or hatred of man.) Those who do not see this connection at once, who believe in a direct rule of emotional love, should consider that love as such certainly does not promote impartiality. And it cannot do away with conflict either. That love as such may be unable to settle a conflict can be shown by considering a harmless test case, which may pass as representative of more serious ones. Tom likes the theatre and Dick likes dancing. Tom lovingly insists on going to a dance while Dick wants for Tom's sake to go to the theatre. This conflict cannot be settled by love; rather, the greater the love, the stronger will be the conflict. There are only two solutions; one is the use of emotion, and ultimately of violence, and the other is the use of reason, of impartiality, of reasonable compromise. All this is not intended to indicate that I do not appreciate the difference between love and hate, or that I think that life would be worth living without love. (And I am quite prepared to admit that the Christian idea of love is not meant in a purely emotional way.) But I insist that no emotion, not even love, can replace the rule of institutions controlled by reason.

This, of course, is not the only argument against the idea of a rule of love. Loving a person means wishing to make him happy. (This, by the way, was Thomas Aquinas' definition of love.) But of all political ideals, that of making the people happy is perhaps the most dangerous one. It leads invariably to the attempt to impose our scale of 'higher' values upon others, in order to make them realize what seems to us of greatest importance for their happiness; in order, as it were, to save their souls. It leads to Utopianism and Romanticism. We all feel certain that everybody would be happy in the beautiful, the perfect community of our dreams. And no doubt, there would be heaven on earth if we could all love one another. But, as I have said before (in chapter 9), the attempt to make heaven on earth invariably produces hell. It leads to intolerance. It leads to religious wars, and to the saving of souls through the inquisition. And it is, I believe, based on a complete misunderstanding of our moral duties. It is our duty to help those who need our help; but it cannot be our duty to make others happy, since this does not depend on us, and since it would only too often mean intruding on the privacy of those towards whom we have such amiable intentions. The political demand for piecemeal (as opposed to Utopian) methods corresponds to the decision that the fight against suffering must be considered a duty, while the right to care for the happiness of others must be considered a privilege confined to the close circle of their friends. In their case, we may perhaps have a certain right to try to impose our scale of values—our preferences regarding music, for example. (And we may even feel it our duty to open to them a world of values which, we trust, can so much contribute to their happiness.) This right of ours exists only if, and because, they can get rid of us; because friendships can be ended. But the use of political means for imposing our scale of values upon others is a very different matter. Pain, suffering, injustice, and their prevention, these are the eternal problems of public morals, the 'agenda' of public policy (as Bentham would have said). The 'higher' values should very largely be considered as 'non-agenda', and should be left to the realm of *laissez-faire*. Thus we might say: help your enemies; assist those in distress, even if they hate you; but love only your friends.

This is only part of the case against irrationalism, and of the consequences which induce me to adopt the opposite attitude, that is, a critical rationalism. This latter attitude with its emphasis upon argument and experience, with its device 'I may be wrong and you may be right, and by an effort we may get nearer to the truth', is, as mentioned before, closely akin to the scientific attitude. It is bound up with the idea that everybody is liable to make mistakes, which may be found out by himself, or by others, or by himself with the assistance of the criticism of others. It therefore suggests the idea that nobody should be his own judge, and it suggests the idea of impartiality. (This is closely related to the idea of 'scientific objectivity' as analysed in the previous chapter.) Its faith in reason is not only a faith in our own reason, but also—and even more—in that of others. Thus a rationalist, even if he believes himself to be intellectually superior to others, will reject all claims to authority[17] since he is aware that, if his intelligence is superior to that of others (which is hard for him to judge), it is so only in so far as he is capable of learning from criticism as well as from his own and other people's mistakes, and that one can learn in this sense only if one takes others and their arguments seriously. Rationalism is therefore bound up with the idea that the other fellow has a right to be heard, and to defend his arguments. It thus implies the recognition of the claim to tolerance, at least[18] of all those who are not intolerant themselves. One does not kill a man when one adopts the attitude of first listening to his arguments. (Kant was right when he based the 'Golden Rule' on the idea of reason. To be sure, it is impossible to prove the rightness of any ethical principle, or even to argue in its favour in just the manner in which we argue in favour of a scientific statement. Ethics is not a science. But although there is no 'rational scientific basis' of ethics, there is an ethical basis of science, and of rationalism.) Also the idea of impartiality leads to that of responsibility; we have not only to listen to arguments, but we have a duty to respond, to answer, where our actions affect others. Ultimately, in this way, rationalism is linked up with the recognition of the necessity of social institutions to protect freedom of criticism, freedom of thought, and thus the freedom of men. And it establishes something like a moral obligation towards the support of these institutions. This is why rationalism is closely linked up with the political demand for practical social engineering—piecemeal engineering, of course—in the humanitarian sense, with the demand for the rationalization of society[19], for planning for freedom, and for its control by reason; not by 'science', not by a Platonic, a pseudo-rational authority, but by that Socratic reason which is aware of its limitations, and which therefore respects the other man and does not aspire to coerce him—not even into happiness. The adoption of rationalism implies, moreover, that there is a common medium of communication, a common language of reason; it establishes something like a moral obligation towards that language, the obligation to keep up its standards of clarity[20] and to use it in such a way that it can retain its function as the vehicle of argument. That is to say, to use it plainly; to use it as an instrument of rational communication, of significant information, rather than as a means of 'self-expression', as the vicious romantic jargon of most of our educationists has it. (It is characteristic of the modern romantic hysteria that it combines a Hegelian collectivism concerning 'reason' with an excessive individualism concerning 'emotions': thus the emphasis on language as a means of self-expression instead of a means of communication. Both attitudes, of course, are parts of the revolt against reason.) And it implies the recognition that mankind is united by the fact that our different mother tongues, in so far as they are rational, can be translated into one another. It recognizes the unity of human reason.

A few remarks may be added concerning the relation of the rationalist attitude to the attitude of readiness to use what is usually called 'imagination'. It is frequently assumed that imagination has a close affinity with emotion and therefore with irrationalism, and that rationalism rather tends towards an unimaginative dry scholasticism. I do not know whether such a view may have some psychological basis, and I rather doubt it. But my interests are institutional rather than psychological, and from an institutional point of view (as well as from that of method) it appears that rationalism must encourage the use of imagination because it needs it, while irrationalism must tend to discourage it. The very fact that rationalism is critical, whilst irrationalism must tend towards dogmatism (where there is no argument, nothing is left but full acceptance or flat denial), leads in this direction. Criticism always demands a certain degree of imagination, whilst dogmatism suppresses it. Similarly, scientific research and technical construction and invention are inconceivable without a very considerable use of imagination; one must offer something new in these fields (as opposed to the field of oracular philosophy where an endless repetition of impressive words seems to do the trick). At least as important is the part played by imagination in the practical application of equalitarianism and of impartiality. The basic attitude of the rationalist, 'I may be wrong and you may be right', demands, when put into practice, and especially when human conflicts are involved, a real effort of our imagination. I admit that the emotions of love and compassion may sometimes lead to a similar effort. But I hold that it is humanly impossible for us to love, or to suffer with, a great number of people; nor does it appear to me very desirable that we should, since it would ultimately destroy either our ability to help or the intensity of these very emotions. But reason, supported by imagination, enables us to understand that men who are far away, whom we shall never see, are like ourselves, and that their relations to one another are like our relations to those we love. A direct emotional attitude towards the abstract whole of mankind seems to me hardly possible. We can love mankind only in certain concrete individuals. But by the use of thought and imagination, we may become ready to help all who need our help.

All these considerations show, I believe, that the link between rationalism and humanitarianism is very close, and certainly much closer than the corresponding entanglement of irrationalism with the anti-equalitarian and anti-humanitarian attitude. I believe that as far as possible this result is corroborated by experience. A rationalist attitude seems to be usually combined with a basically equalitarian and humanitarian outlook; irrationalism, on the other hand, exhibits in most cases at least some of the anti-equalitarian tendencies described, even though it may often be associated with humanitarianism also. My point is that the latter connection is anything but well founded.

IV

I have tried to analyse those consequences of rationalism and irrationalism which induce me to decide as I do. I wish to repeat that the decision is largely a moral decision. It is the decision to try to take argument seriously. This is the difference between the two views; for irrationalism will use reason too, but without any feeling of obligation; it will use it or discard it as it pleases. But I believe that the only attitude which I can consider to be morally right is one which recognizes that we owe it to other men to treat them and ourselves as rational.

Considered in this way, my counter-attack upon irrationalism is a moral attack. The intellectualist who finds our rationalism much too commonplace for his taste, and who looks out for the latest esoteric intellectual fashion, which he discovers in the admiration of medieval mysticism, is not, one fears, doing his duty by his fellow men. He may think himself and his subtle taste superior to our 'scientific age', to an 'age of industrialization' which carries its brainless division of labour and its 'mechanization' and 'materialization' even into the field of human thought[21]. But he only shows that he is incapable of appreciating the moral forces inherent in modern science. The attitude I am attacking can perhaps be illustrated by the following passage which I take from A. Keller[22]; a passage that seems to me a typical expression of this romantic hostility towards science: 'We seem to be entering upon a new era where the human soul is regaining its mystical and religious faculties, and protesting, by inventing new myths, against the materialization and mechanization of life. The mind suffered when it had to serve humanity as technician, as chauffeur; it is reawakening again as poet and prophet, obeying the command and leadership of dreams which seem to be quite as wise and reliable as, but more inspiring and stimulating than, intellectual wisdom and scientific programmes. The myth of revolution is a reaction against the unimaginative banality and conceited self-sufficiency of bourgeois society and of an old tired culture. It is the adventure of men who have lost all security and are embarking on dreams instead of concrete facts.'

In analysing this passage I wish first, but only in passing, to draw attention to its typical historicist character and to its moral futurism[23] ('entering a new era', 'old and tired culture', etc.). But more important even than to realize the technique of the word-magic which the passage uses is to ask whether what it says is true. Is it true that our soul protests against the materialization and mechanization of our life, that it protests against the progress we have made in the fight against the untold suffering through hunger and pestilence which characterized the Middle Ages? Is it true that the mind suffered when it had to serve humanity as a technician, and was it happier to serve as a serf or a slave? I do not intend to belittle the very serious problem of purely mechanical work, of a drudgery which is felt to be meaningless, and which destroys the creative power of the workers; but the only practical hope lies, not in a return to slavery and serfdom, but in an attempt to make machinery take over this mechanical drudgery. Marx was right in insisting that increased productivity is the only reasonable hope of humanizing labour, and of further shortening the labour day. (Besides, I do not think that the mind always suffers when it has to serve humanity as a technician; I suspect that often enough, the 'technicians', including the great inventors and the great scientists, rather enjoyed it, and that they were just as adventurous as the mystics.) And who believes that the 'command and leadership of dreams', as dreamt by our contemporary prophets, dreamers, and leaders, are really 'quite as wise and reliable as intellectual wisdom and scientific programmes'? But we need only turn to the 'myth of revolution', etc., in order to see more clearly what we are facing here. It is a typical expression of the romantic hysteria and the radicalism produced by the dissolution of the tribe and by the strain of civilization (as I have described it in chapter 10). This kind of 'Christianity' which recommends the creation of myth as a substitute for Christian responsibility is a tribal Christianity. It is a Christianity that refuses to carry the cross of being human. Beware of these false prophets! What they are after, without being aware of it, is the lost unity of tribalism. And the return to the closed society which they advocate is the return to the cage, and to the beasts[24].

It may be useful to consider how the adherents of this kind of romanticism are likely to react to such criticism. Arguments will hardly be offered; since it is impossible to discuss such profundities with a rationalist, the most likely reaction will be a high-handed withdrawal, combined with the assertion that there is no language common to those whose souls have not yet 'regained their mystical faculties', and those whose souls possess such faculties. Now this reaction is analogous to that of the psycho-analyst (mentioned in the last chapter) who defeats his opponents not by replying to their arguments but by pointing out that their repressions prevent them from accepting psycho-analysis. It is analogous also to that of the socio-analyst who points out that the total ideologies of his opponents prevent them from accepting the sociology of knowledge. This method, as I admitted before, is good fun for those who practise it. But we can see here more clearly that it must lead to the irrational division of men into those who are near to us and those who are far from us. This division is present in every religion, but it is comparatively harmless in Mohammedanism, Christianity, or the rationalist faith, which all see in every man a potential convert, and the same may be said of psycho-analysis, which sees in every man a potential object of treatment (only that in the last case the fee for conversion constitutes a serious obstacle). But the division is getting less harmless when we proceed to the sociology of knowledge. The socio-analyst claims that only certain intellectuals can get rid of their total ideology, can be freed from 'thinking with their class'; he thus gives up the idea of a potential rational unity of man, and delivers himself body and soul to irrationalism. And this situation gets very much worse when we proceed to the biological or naturalist version of this theory, to the racial doctrine that we 'think with our blood' or that we 'think with our race'. But at least as dangerous, since more subtle, is the same idea when it appears in the cloak of a religious mysticism; not in the mysticism of the poet or musician, but in that of the Hegelianizing intellectualist who persuades himself and his followers that their thoughts are endowed, because of special grace, with 'mystical and religious faculties' not possessed by others, and who thus claim that they 'think by God's grace'. This claim with its gentle allusion to those who do not possess God's grace, this attack upon the potential spiritual unity of mankind, is, in my opinion, as pretentious, blasphemous and anti-Christian, as it believes itself to be humble, pious, and Christian.

As opposed to the intellectual irresponsibility of a mysticism which escapes into dreams and of an oracular philosophy which escapes into verbiage, modern science enforces upon our intellect the discipline of practical tests. Scientific theories can be tested by their practical consequences. The scientist, in his own field, is responsible for what he says; you can know him by his fruits, and thus distinguish him from the false prophets[25]. One of the few who have appreciated this aspect of science is the Christian philosopher J. Macmurray (with whose views on historical prophecy I widely disagree, as will be seen in the next chapter): 'Science itself', he says[26], 'in its own specific fields of research, employs a method of understanding which restores the broken integrity of theory and practice.' This, I believe, is why science is such an offence in the eyes of mysticism, which evades practice by creating myths instead. 'Science, in its own field,' says Macmurray in another place, 'is the product of Christianity, and its most adequate expression so far; … its capacity for co-operative progress, which knows no frontiers of race or nationality or sex, its ability to predict, and its ability to control, are the fullest manifestations of Christianity that Europe has yet seen.' I fully agree with this, for I too believe that our Western civilization owes its rationalism, its faith in the rational unity of man and in the open society, and especially its scientific outlook, to the ancient Socratic and Christian belief in the brotherhood of all men, and in intellectual honesty and responsibility. (A frequent argument against the morality of science is that many of its fruits have been used for bad purposes, for instance, in war. But this argument hardly deserves serious consideration. There is nothing under the sun which cannot be misused, and which has not been misused. Even love can be made an instrument of murder; and pacifism can be made one of the weapons of an aggressive war. On the other hand, it is only too obvious that it is irrationalism and not rationalism that has the responsibility for all national hostility and aggression. There have been only too many aggressive religious wars, both before and after the Crusades, but I do not know of any war waged for a 'scientific' aim, and inspired by scientists.)

It will have been observed that in the passages quoted, Macmurray emphasizes that what he appreciates is science 'in its own specific fields of research'. I think that this emphasis is particularly valuable. For nowadays one often hears, usually in connection with the mysticism of Eddington and Jeans, that modern science, as opposed to that of the nineteenth century, has become more humble, in that it now recognizes the mysteries of this world. But this opinion, I believe, is entirely on the wrong track. Darwin and Faraday, for instance, sought for truth as humbly as anybody, and I do not doubt that they were much more humble than the two great contemporary astronomers mentioned. For great as these are 'in their own specific fields of research', they do not, I believe, prove their humility by extending their activities to the field of philosophical mysticism[27]. Speaking more generally, however, it may indeed be the case that scientists are becoming more humble, since the progress of science is largely by way of the discovery of errors, and since, in general, the more we know, the more clearly we realize what we do not know. (The spirit of science is that of Socrates[28].)

Although I am mainly concerned with the moral aspect of the conflict between rationalism and irrationalism, I feel that I should briefly touch upon a more 'philosophical' aspect of the problem; but I wish to make it clear that I consider this aspect as of minor importance here. What I have in mind is the fact that the critical rationalist can turn the tables upon the irrationalist in another way as well. He may contend that the irrationalist who prides himself on his respect for the more profound mysteries of the world and his understanding of them (as opposed to the scientist who just scratches its surface) in fact neither respects nor understands its mysteries, but satisfies himself with cheap rationalizations. For what is a myth if not an attempt to rationalize the irrational? And who shows greater reverence for mystery, the scientist who devotes himself to discovering it step by step, always ready to submit to facts, and always aware that even his boldest achievement will never be more than a stepping-stone for those who come after him, or the mystic who is free to maintain anything because he need not fear any test? But in spite of this dubious freedom, the mystics endlessly repeat the same thing. (It is always the myth of the lost tribal paradise, the hysterical refusal to carry the cross of civilization[29].) All mystics, as F. Kafka, the mystical poet, wrote[30] in despair, 'set out to say ... that the incomprehensible is incomprehensible, and that we knew before'. And the irrationalist not only tries to rationalize what cannot be rationalized, but he also gets hold of the wrong end of the stick altogether. For it is the particular, the unique and concrete individual, which cannot be approached by rational methods, and not the abstract universal. Science can describe general types of landscape, for example, or of man, but it can never exhaust one single individual landscape, or one single individual man. The universal, the typical, is not only the domain of reason, but it is also largely the product of reason, in so far as it is the product of scientific abstraction. But the unique individual and his unique actions and experiences and relations to other individuals can never be fully rationalized[31]. And it appears to be just this irrational realm of unique individuality which makes human relations important. Most people would feel, for example, that what makes their lives worth living would largely be destroyed if they themselves, and their lives, were in no sense unique but in all and every respect typical of a class of people, so that they repeated exactly all the actions and experiences of all other men who belong to this class. It is the uniqueness of our experiences which, in this sense, makes our lives worth living, the unique experience of a landscape, of a sunset, of the expression of a human face. But since the day of Plato, it has been a characteristic of all mysticism that it transfers this feeling of the irrationality of the unique individual, and of our unique relations to individuals, to a different field, namely, to the field of abstract universals, a field which properly belongs to the province of science. That it is this feeling which the mystic tries to transfer can hardly be doubted. It is well known that the terminology of mysticism, the mystical union, the mystical intuition of beauty, the mystical love, have in all times been borrowed from the realm of relations between individual men, and especially from the experience of sexual love. Nor can it be doubted that this feeling is transferred by mysticism to the abstract universals, to the essences, to the Forms or Ideas. It is again the lost unity of the tribe, the wish to return into the shelter of a patriarchal home and to make its limits the limits of our world, which stands behind this mystical attitude. 'The feeling of the world as a limited whole is the mystical feeling', says[32] Wittgenstein. But this holistic and universalistic irrationalism is misplaced. The 'world' and the 'whole' and 'nature', all these are abstractions and products of our reason. (This makes the difference between the mystical philosopher and the artist who does not rationalize, who does not use abstractions, but who creates, in his imagination, concrete individuals and unique experiences.) To sum up, mysticism attempts to rationalize the irrational, and at the same time it seeks the mystery in the wrong place; and it does so because it dreams of the collective[33], and the union of the elect, since it dares not face the hard and practical tasks which those must face who realize that every individual is an end in himself.

The nineteenth-century conflict between science and religion appears to me to be superseded[34]. Since an 'uncritical' rationalism is inconsistent, the problem cannot be the choice between knowledge and faith, but only between two kinds of faith. The new problem is: which is the right faith and which is the wrong faith? What I have tried to show is that the choice with which we are confronted is between a faith in reason and in human individuals and a faith in the mystical faculties of man by which he is united to a collective; and that this choice is at the same time a choice between an attitude that recognizes the unity of mankind and an attitude that divides men into friends and foes, into masters and slaves.

Enough has been said, for the present purpose, to explain the terms 'rationalism' and 'irrationalism', as well as my motives in deciding in favour of rationalism, and the reason why I see in the irrational and mystical intellectualism which is at present so fashionable the subtle intellectual disease of our time. It is a disease which need not be taken too seriously, and it is not more than skin-deep. (Scientists, with very few exceptions, are particularly free from it.) But in spite of its superficiality, it is a dangerous disease, because of its influence in the field of social and political thought.

V

In order to illustrate the danger, I shall briefly criticize two of the most influential irrationalist authorities of our time. The first of them is

A. N. Whitehead, famous for his work in mathematics, and for his collaboration with the greatest contemporary rationalist philosopher, Bertrand Russell[35]. Whitehead considers himself a rationalist philosopher too; but so did Hegel, to whom Whitehead owes a great deal; indeed, he is one of the few Neo-Hegelians who know how much they owe to Hegel[36] (as well as to Aristotle). Undoubtedly, he owes it to Hegel that he has the courage, in spite of Kant's burning protest, to build up grandiose metaphysical systems with a royal contempt for argument.

Let us consider first one of the few rational arguments offered by Whitehead in his *Process and Reality*, the argument by which he defends his speculative philosophical method (a method which he calls 'rationalism'). 'It has been an objection to speculative philosophy', he writes[37], 'that it is over-ambitious. Rationalism, it is admitted, is the method by which advance is made within the limits of particular sciences. It is, however, held that this limited success must not encourage attempts to frame ambitious schemes expressive of the general nature of things. One alleged justification of this criticism is ill-success; European thought is represented as littered with metaphysical problems, abandoned and unreconciled ... [But] *the same criterion would fasten ill-success upon science*. We no more retain the physics of the seventeenth century than we do the Cartesian philosophy of the century ... The proper test is not that of finality, but of progress.' Now this is in itself certainly a perfectly reasonable and even plausible argument; but is it valid? The obvious objection against it is that while physics progresses, metaphysics does not. In physics, there is a 'proper test of progress', namely the test of experiment, of practice. We can say why modern physics is better than the physics of the seventeenth century. Modern physics stands up to a great number of practical tests which utterly defeat the older systems. And the obvious objection against speculative metaphysical systems is that the progress they claim seems to be just as imaginary as anything else about them. This objection is very old; it dates back to Bacon, Hume, and Kant. We read, for example, in Kant's *Prolegomena*[38], the following remarks concerning the alleged progress of metaphysics: 'Undoubtedly there are many who, like myself, have been unable to find that this science has progressed by so much as a finger-breadth in spite of so many beautiful things which have long been published on this subject. Admittedly, we may find an attempt to sharpen a definition, or to supply a lame proof with new crutches, and thus to patch up the crazy quilt of metaphysics, or to give it a new pattern; but this is not what the world needs. We are sick of metaphysical assertions. We want to have definite criteria by which we may distinguish dialectical fancies ... from truth.' Whitehead is probably aware of this classical and obvious objection; and it looks as if he remembers it when in the sentence following the one quoted last he writes: 'But the main objection dating from the sixteenth century and receiving final expression from Francis Bacon, is the uselessness of philosophic speculation.' Since it was the experimental and practical uselessness of philosophy to which Bacon objected, it looks as if Whitehead here had our point in mind. But he does not follow it up. He does not reply to the obvious objection that this practical uselessness destroys his point that speculative philosophy, like science, is justified by the progress it makes. Instead, he contents himself with switching over to an entirely different problem, namely, the well-known problem 'that there are no brute, self-contained matters of fact', and that all science must make use of thought, since it must generalize, and interpret, the facts. On this consideration he bases his defence of metaphysical systems: 'Thus the understanding of the immediate brute fact requires its metaphysical interpretation …' Now this may be so, or it may not be so. But it is certainly an entirely different argument from the one he began with. 'The proper test is … progress', in science as well as in philosophy: this is what we originally heard from Whitehead. But no answer to Kant's obvious objection is forthcoming. Instead, Whitehead's argument, once on the track of the problem of universality and generality, wanders off to such questions as the (Platonic) collectivist theory of morality[39]: 'Morality of outlook is inseparably conjoined with generality of outlook. The antithesis between the general good and the individual interest can be abolished only when the individual is such that its interest is the general good …'

Now this was a sample of rational argument. But rational arguments are rare indeed. Whitehead has learned from Hegel how to avoid Kant's criticism that speculative philosophy only supplies new crutches for lame proofs. This Hegelian method is simple enough. We can easily avoid crutches as long as we avoid proofs and arguments altogether. Hegelian philosophy does not argue; it decrees. It must be admitted that, as opposed to Hegel, Whitehead does not pretend to offer the final truth. He is not a dogmatic philosopher in the sense that he presents his philosophy as an indisputable dogma; he even emphasizes its imperfections. But like all Neo-Hegelians, he adopts the dogmatic method of laying down his philosophy without argument. We can take it or leave it. But we cannot discuss it. (We are indeed faced with 'brute facts'; not with Baconian brute facts of experience, but with the brute facts of a man's metaphysical inspiration.) In order to illustrate this 'method of take it or leave it', I shall quote just one passage from *Process and Reality*; but I must warn my readers that, although I have tried to select the passage fairly, they should not form an opinion without reading the book itself.

Its last part, entitled 'Final Interpretations', consists of two chapters, 'The Ideal Opposites' (where, for instance, 'Permanence and Flux' occurs, a well-known patch from Plato's system; we have dealt with it under the name 'Change and Rest'), and 'God and the World'. I quote from this latter chapter. The passage is introduced by the two sentences: 'The final summary can only be expressed in terms of a group of antitheses, whose apparent self-contradiction depends on neglect of the diverse categories of existence. In each antithesis there is a shift of meaning which converts the opposition into a contrast.' This is the introduction. It prepares us for an 'apparent contradiction', and tells us that this 'depends' on some neglect. This seems to indicate that by avoiding that neglect we may avoid the contradiction. But how this is to be achieved, or what is, more precisely, in the author's mind, we are not told. We have just to take it or leave it. Now I quote the first two of the announced 'antitheses' or 'apparent self-contradictions' which are also stated without a shadow of argument: 'It is as true to say that God is permanent and the World fluent as that the World is permanent and God fluent.—It is as true to say that God is one and the World many, as that the World is one and God many.'[40] Now I am not going to criticize these echoes of Greek philosophical fancies; we may indeed take it for granted that the one is just 'as true' as the other. But we have been promised an 'apparent self-contradiction'; and I should like to know where a self-contradiction appears here. For to me not even the appearance of a contradiction is apparent. A self-contradiction would be, for instance, the sentence: 'Plato is happy and Plato is not happy', and all the sentences of the same 'logical form' (that is to say, all sentences obtained from the foregoing by substituting a proper name for 'Plato' and a property word for 'happy'). But the following sentence is clearly not a contradiction: 'It is as true to say that Plato is happy to-day as it is to say that he is unhappy to-day' (for since Plato is dead, the one is indeed 'as true' as the other); and no other sentence of the same or a similar form can be called self-contradictory, even if it happens to be false. This is only to indicate why I am at a loss as to this purely logical aspect of the matter, the 'apparent self-contradictions'. And I feel that way about the whole book. I just do not understand what its author wished it to convey. Very likely, this is my fault and not his. I do not belong to the number of the elect, and I fear that many others are in the same position. This is just why I claim that the method of the book is irrational. It divides mankind into two parts, a small number of the elect, and the large number of the lost. But lost as I am, I can only say that, as I see it, Neo-Hegelianism no longer looks like that old crazy quilt with a few new patches, so vividly described by Kant; rather it looks now like a bundle of a few old patches which have been torn from it.

I leave it to the careful student of Whitehead's book to decide whether it has stood up to its own 'proper test', whether it shows progress as compared with the metaphysical systems of whose stagnation Kant complained; provided he can find the criteria by which to judge such progress. And I will leave it to the same student to judge the appropriateness of concluding these remarks with another of Kant's comments upon metaphysics[41]: 'Concerning metaphysics in general, and the views I have expressed on their value, I admit that my formulations may here or there have been insufficiently conditional and cautious. Yet I do not wish to hide the fact that I can only look with repugnance and even with something like hate upon the puffed-up pretentiousness of all these volumes filled with wisdom, such as are fashionable nowadays. For I am fully satisfied that the wrong way has been chosen; that the accepted methods must endlessly increase these follies and blunders; and that even the complete annihilation of all these fanciful achievements could not possibly be as harmful as this fictitious science with its accursed fertility.'

The second example of contemporary irrationalism with which I intend to deal here is A. J. Toynbee's *A Study of History*. I wish to make it clear that I consider this a most remarkable and interesting book, and that I have chosen it because of its superiority to all other contemporary irrationalist and historicist works I know of. I am not competent to judge Toynbee's merits as a historian. But as opposed to other contemporary historicist and irrationalist philosophers, he has much to say that is most stimulating and challenging; I at least have found him so, and I owe to him many valuable suggestions. I do not accuse him of irrationalism in his own field of historical research. For where it is a question of comparing evidence in favour of or against a certain historical interpretation, he uses unhesitatingly a fundamentally rational method of argument. I have in mind, for instance, his comparative study of the authenticity of the Gospels as historical records, with its negative results[42]; although I am not able to judge his evidence, the rationality of the method is beyond question, and this is the more admirable as Toynbee's general sympathies with Christian orthodoxy might have made it hard for him to defend a view which, to say the least, is unorthodox[43]. I also agree with many of the political tendencies expressed in his work, and most emphatically with his attack upon modern nationalism, and the tribalist and 'archaist', i.e. culturally reactionary tendencies, which are connected with it.

The reason why, in spite of all this, I single out Toynbee's monumental historicist work in order to charge it with irrationality, is that only when we see the effects of this poison in a work of such merit do we fully appreciate its danger.

What I must describe as Toynbee's irrationalism expresses itself in various ways. One of them is that he yields to a widespread and dangerous fashion of our time. I mean the fashion of not taking arguments seriously, and at their face value, at least tentatively, but of seeing in them nothing but a way in which deeper irrational motives and tendencies express themselves. It is the attitude of socio-analysis, criticized in the last chapter; the attitude of looking at once for the unconscious motives and determinants in the social habitat of the thinker, instead of first examining the validity of the argument itself.

This attitude may be justified to a certain extent, as I have tried to show in the two previous chapters; and this is especially so in the case of an author who does not offer any arguments, or whose arguments are obviously not worth looking into. But if no attempt is made to take serious arguments seriously, then I believe that we are justified in making the charge of irrationalism; and we are even justified in retaliating, by adopting the same attitude towards the procedure. Thus I think that we have every right to make the socio-analytical diagnosis that Toynbee's neglect to take serious arguments seriously is representative of a twentieth-century intellectualism which expresses its disillusionment, or even despair, of reason, and of a rational solution of our social problems, by an escape into a religious mysticism[44].

As an example of the refusal to take serious arguments seriously, I select Toynbee's treatment of Marx. My reasons for this selection are the following. First, it is a topic which is familiar to myself as well as to the reader of this book. Secondly, it is a topic on which I agree with Toynbee in most of its practical aspects. His main judgements on Marx's political and historical influence are very similar to results at which I have arrived by more pedestrian methods; and it is indeed one of the topics whose treatment shows his great historical intuition. Thus I shall hardly be suspected of being an apologist for Marx if I defend Marx's rationality against Toynbee. For this is the point on which I disagree: Toynbee treats Marx (as he treats everybody) not as a rational being, a man who offers arguments for what he teaches. Indeed, the treatment of Marx, and of his theories, only exemplifies the general impression conveyed by Toynbee's work that arguments are an unimportant mode of speech, and that the history of mankind is a history of emotions, passions, religions, irrational philosophies, and perhaps of art and poetry; but that it has nothing whatever to do with the history of human reason or of human science. (Names like Galileo and Newton, Harvey and Pasteur, do not play any part in the first six volumes[45] of Toynbee's historicist study of the life-cycle of civilizations.)

Regarding the points of similarity between Toynbee's and my general views of Marx, I may remind the reader of my allusions, in chapter 1, to the analogy between the chosen people and the chosen class; and in various other places, I have commented critically upon Marx's doctrines of historical necessity, and especially of the inevitability of the social revolution. These ideas are linked together by Toynbee with his usual brilliance: 'The distinctively Jewish ... inspiration of Marxism', he writes[46], 'is the apocalyptic vision of a violent revolution which is inevitable because it is the decree ... of God himself, and which is to invert the present rôles of Proletariat and Dominant Minority in ... a reversal of rôles which is to carry the Chosen People, at one bound, from the lowest to the highest place in the Kingdom of This World. Marx has taken the Goddess "Historical Necessity" in place of Yahweh for his omnipotent deity, and the internal proletariat of the modern Western World in place of Jewry; and his Messianic Kingdom is conceived as a Dictatorship of the Proletariat. But the salient features of the traditional Jewish apocalypse protrude through this threadbare disguise, and it is actually the pre-Rabbinical Maccabæan Judaism that our philosopher-impresario is presenting in modern Western costume ...' Now there is certainly not much in this brilliantly phrased passage with which I do not agree, as long as it is intended as nothing more than an interesting analogy. But if it is intended as a serious analysis (or part of it) of Marxism, then I must protest; Marx, after all, wrote *Capital*, studied *laissez-faire* capitalism, and made serious and most important contributions to social science, even if much of them has been superseded. And, indeed, Toynbee's passage is intended as a serious analysis; he believes that his analogies and allegories contribute to a serious appreciation of Marx; for in an Annex to this passage (from which I have quoted only an important part) he treats, under the title[47] 'Marxism, Socialism, and Christianity', what he considers to be likely objections of a Marxist to this 'account of the Marxian Philosophy'. This Annex itself is also undoubtedly intended as a serious discussion of Marxism, as can be seen by the fact that its first paragraph commences with the words 'The advocates of Marxism will perhaps protest that ...' and the second with the words: 'In attempting to reply to a Marxian protest on such lines as these ...' But if we look more closely into this discussion, then we find that none of the rational arguments or claims of Marxism is even mentioned, let alone examined. Of Marx's theories and of the question whether they are true or false we do not hear a word. The one additional problem raised in the Annex is again one of historical origin; for the Marxist opponent envisaged by Toynbee does not protest, as any Marxist in his senses would, that it is Marx's claim to have based an old idea, socialism, upon a new, namely a rational and scientific, basis; instead, he 'protests' (I am quoting Toynbee) 'that in a rather summary account of Marxian Philosophy ... we have made a show of analysing this into a Hegelian and a Jewish and a Christian constituent element without having said a word about the most characteristic … part of Marx's message … Socialism, the Marxian will tell us, is the essence of the Marxian way of life; *it is an original element in the Marxian system which cannot be traced to a Hegelian or a Christian or a Jewish or any other pre-Marxian source*'. This is the protest put by Toynbee into the mouth of a Marxist, although any Marxist, even if he has read nothing but the *Manifesto*, must know that Marx himself as early as in 1847 distinguished about seven or eight different 'pre-Marxian sources' of socialism, and among them also those which he labelled 'Clerical' or 'Christian' socialism, and that he never dreamt of having discovered socialism, but only claimed that he had made it rational; or, as Engels expresses it, that he had developed socialism from a Utopian idea into a science[48]. But Toynbee neglects all that. 'In attempting', he writes, 'to reply to a Marxian protest on such lines as these, we shall readily admit the humaneness and constructiveness of the ideal for which socialism stands, as well as the importance of the part which this ideal plays in the Marxian "ideology"; but we shall find ourselves unable to accept *the Marxian contention that Socialism is Marx's original discovery*. We shall have to point out, on our part, that there is a Christian socialism which was practised as well as preached before the Marxian Socialism was ever heard of; and, when our turn comes for taking the offensive, we shall … maintain that the Marxian Socialism is derived from the Christian tradition …' Now I would certainly never deny this derivation, and it is quite clear that every Marxist could admit it without sacrificing the tiniest bit of his creed; for the Marxist creed is not that Marx was the inventor of a humane and constructive ideal but that he was the scientist who by purely rational means showed that socialism will come, and in what way it will come.

How, I ask, can it be explained that Toynbee discusses Marxism on lines which have nothing whatever to do with its rational claims? The only explanation I can see is that the Marxist claim to rationality has no meaning whatever for Toynbee. He is interested only in the question of how it originated as a religion. Now I should be the last to deny its religious character. But the method of treating philosophies or religions entirely from the point of view of their historical origin and environment, an attitude described in the previous chapters as *historism* (and to be distinguished from historicism), is, to say the least, very one-sided; and how much this method is liable to produce irrationalism can be seen from Toynbee's neglect of, if not contempt for, that important realm of human life which we have here described as rational.

In an assessment of Marx's influence, Toynbee arrives at the conclusion[49] that 'the verdict of History may turn out to be that a re-awakening of the

Christian social conscience has been the one great positive achievement of Karl Marx'. Against this assessment, I have certainly not much to say; perhaps the reader will remember that I too have emphasized[50] Marx's moral influence upon Christianity. I do not think that, as a final appraisal, Toynbee takes sufficiently into account the great moral idea that the exploited should emancipate themselves, instead of waiting for acts of charity on the part of the exploiters; but this, of course, is just a difference of opinion, and I would not dream of contesting Toynbee's right to his own opinion, which I consider very fair. But I should like to draw attention to the phrase 'the verdict of history may turn out', with its implied historicist moral theory, and even moral futurism[51]. For I hold that we cannot and must not evade deciding in such matters for ourselves; and that if we are not able to pass a verdict, neither will history.

So much about Toynbee's treatment of Marx. Concerning the more general problem of his historism or historical relativism, it may be said that he is well aware of it, although he does not formulate it as a general principle of the historical determination of *all* thought, but only as a restricted principle applicable to *historical* thought; for he explains[52] that he takes 'as the starting point … the axiom that all historical thought is inevitably relative to the particular circumstances of the thinker's own time and place. This is a law of Human Nature from which no human genius can be exempt.' The analogy of this historism with the sociology of knowledge is rather obvious; for 'the thinker's own time and place' is clearly nothing but the description of what may be called his 'historical habitat', by analogy with the 'social habitat' described by the sociology of knowledge. The difference, if any, is that Toynbee confines his 'law of Human Nature' to historical thought, which seems to me a slightly strange and perhaps even unintentional restriction; for it is somewhat improbable that there should be a 'law of Human Nature from which no human genius can be exempt' holding not for thought in general but only for historical thought.

With the undeniable but rather trivial kernel of truth contained in such a historism or sociologism I have dealt in the last two chapters, and I need not repeat what I have said there. But as regards criticism, it may be worth while to point out that Toynbee's sentence, if freed from its restriction to historical thought, could hardly be considered an 'axiom' since it would be paradoxical. (It would be another[53] form of the paradox of the liar; for if no genius is exempt from expressing the fashions of his social habitat then this contention itself may be merely an expression of the fashion of its author's social habitat, i.e. of the relativistic fashion of our own day.) This remark has not only a formal-logical significance. For it indicates that historism or historio-analysis can be applied to historism itself, and this is indeed a permissible way of dealing with an idea *after* it has been criticized by way of rational argument. Since historism has been so criticized, I may now risk a historio-analytical diagnosis, and say that historism is a typical though slightly obsolescent product of our time; or more precisely, of the typical backwardness of the social sciences of our time. It is the typical reaction to interventionism and to a period of rationalization and industrial co-operation; a period which, perhaps more than any other in history, demands the practical application of rational methods to social problems. A social science which cannot quite meet these demands is therefore inclined to defend itself by producing elaborate attacks upon the applicability of science to such problems. Summing up my historio-analytical diagnosis, I venture to suggest that Toynbee's historism is an apologetic anti-rationalism, born out of despair of reason, and trying to escape into the past, as well as into prophecy of the future[54]. If anything then historism must be understood as an historical product.

This diagnosis is corroborated by many features of Toynbee's work. An example is his stress upon the superiority of other-worldliness over action which will influence the course of this world. So he speaks, for instance, of Mohammed's 'tragic worldly success', saying that the opportunity which offered itself to the prophet of taking action in this world was 'a challenge to which his spirit failed to rise. In accepting … he was renouncing the sublime rôle of the nobly-honoured prophet and contenting himself with the commonplace rôle of the magnificently successful statesman.' (In other words, Mohammed succumbed to a temptation which Jesus resisted.) Ignatius Loyola, accordingly, wins Toynbee's approval for turning from a soldier into a saint[55]. One may ask, however, whether this saint did not become a successful statesman too? (But if it is a question of Jesuitism, then, it seems, all is different: this form of statesmanship is sufficiently other-worldly.) In order to avoid misunderstandings, I wish to make it clear that I myself would rate many saints higher than most, or very nearly all, statesmen I know of, for I am generally not impressed by political success. I quote this passage only as a corroboration of my historio-analytical diagnosis: that this historism of a modern historical prophet is a philosophy of escape.

Toynbee's anti-rationalism is prominent in many other places. For instance, in an attack upon the rationalistic conception of tolerance he uses categories like 'nobleness' as opposed to 'lowness' instead of arguments. The passage deals with the opposition between the merely 'negative' avoidance of violence, on rational grounds, and the true non-violence of other-worldliness, hinting that these two are instances of 'meanings … which are …

positively antithetical to one another'[56]. Here is the passage I have in mind: 'At its lowest the practice of Non-Violence may express nothing more noble and more constructive than a cynical disillusionment with ... violence ... previously practised *ad nauseam* ... A notorious example of Non-Violence of this unedifying kind is the religious tolerance in the Western World from the seventeenth century ... down to our day.' It is difficult to resist the temptation to retaliate by asking—using Toynbee's own terminology—whether this edifying attack upon Western democratic religious tolerance expresses anything more noble or more constructive than a cynical disillusionment with reason; whether it is not a notorious example of that anti-rationalism which has been, and unfortunately still is, fashionable in our Western World, and which has been practised *ad nauseam*, especially from the time of Hegel, down to our day?

Of course, my historio-analysis of Toynbee is not a serious criticism. It is only an unkind way of retaliating, of paying historism back in its own coin. My fundamental criticism is on very different lines, and I should certainly be sorry if by dabbling in historism I were to become responsible for making this cheap method more fashionable than it is already.

I do not wish to be misunderstood. I feel no hostility towards religious mysticism (only towards a militant anti-rationalist intellectualism) and I should be the first to fight any attempt to oppress it. It is not I who advocate religious intolerance. But I claim that faith in reason, or rationalism, or humanitarianism, or humanism, has the same right as any other creed to contribute to an improvement of human affairs, and especially to the control of international crime and the establishment of peace. 'The humanist', Toynbee writes[57], 'purposely concentrates all his attention and effort upon ... bringing human affairs under human control. Yet ... the unity of mankind can never be established in fact except within a framework of the unity of the superhuman whole of which Humanity is a part ...; and our Modern Western school of humanists have been peculiar, as well as perverse, in planning to reach Heaven by raising a titanic Tower of Babel on terrestrial foundations ...' Toynbee's contention, if I understand him rightly, is that there is no chance for the humanist to bring international affairs under the control of human reason. Appealing to the authority of Bergson[58], he claims that only allegiance to a superhuman whole can save us, and that there is no way for human reason, no 'terrestrial road', as he puts it, by which tribal nationalism can be superseded. Now I do not mind the characterization of the humanist's faith in reason as 'terrestrial', since I believe that it is indeed a principle of rationalist politics that we cannot make heaven on earth[59]. But humanism is, after all, a faith which has proved itself in deeds, and which has proved itself as well, perhaps, as any other creed. And although I think, with most humanists, that Christianity, by teaching the fatherhood of God, may make a great contribution to establishing the brotherhood of man, I also think that those who undermine man's faith in reason are unlikely to contribute much to this end.

Conclusion

25

HAS HISTORY ANY MEANING?

I

In approaching the end of this book, I wish again to remind the reader that these chapters were not intended as anything like a full history of historicism; they are merely scattered marginal notes to such a history, and rather personal notes to boot. That they form, besides, a kind of critical introduction to the philosophy of society and of politics, is closely connected with this character of theirs, for historicism is a social and political and moral (or, shall I say, immoral) philosophy, and it has been as such most influential since the beginning of our civilization. It is therefore hardly possible to comment on its history without discussing the fundamental problems of society, of politics, and of morals. But such a discussion, whether it admits it or not, must always contain a strong personal element. This does not mean that much in this book is purely a matter of opinion; in the few cases where I am explaining my personal proposals or decisions in moral and political matters, I have always made the personal character of the proposal or decision clear. It rather means that the selection of the subject matter treated is a matter of personal choice to a much greater extent than it would be, say, in a scientific treatise.

In a way, however, this difference is a matter of degree. Even a science is not merely a 'body of facts'. It is, at the very least, a collection, and as such it is dependent upon the collector's interests, upon a point of view. In science, this point of view is usually determined by a scientific theory; that is to say, we select from the infinite variety of facts, and from the infinite variety of aspects of facts, those facts and those aspects which are interesting because they are connected with some more or less preconceived scientific theory. A certain school of philosophers of scientific method[1] have concluded from considerations such as these that science always argues in a circle, and 'that we find ourselves chasing our own tails', as Eddington puts it, since we can only get out of our factual experience what we have ourselves put into it, in the form of our theories. But this is not a tenable argument. Although it is, in general, quite true that we select only facts which have a bearing upon some preconceived theory, it is not true that we select only such facts as confirm the theory and, as it were, repeat it; the method of science is rather to look out for facts which may refute the theory. This is what we call testing a theory—to see whether we cannot find a flaw in it. But although the facts are collected with an eye upon the theory, and will confirm it as long as the theory stands up to these tests, they are more than merely a kind of empty repetition of a preconceived theory. They confirm the theory only if they are the results of unsuccessful attempts to overthrow its predictions, and therefore a telling testimony in its favour. So it is, I hold, the possibility of overthrowing it, or its falsifiability, that constitutes the possibility of testing it, and therefore the scientific character of a theory; and the fact that all tests of a theory are attempted falsifications of predictions derived with its help, furnishes the clue to scientific method[2]. This view of scientific method is corroborated by the history of science, which shows that scientific theories are often overthrown by experiments, and that the overthrow of theories is indeed the vehicle of scientific progress. The contention that science is circular cannot be upheld.

But one element of this contention remains true; namely, that all scientific descriptions of facts are highly selective, that they always depend upon theories. The situation can be best described by comparison with a searchlight (the 'searchlight theory of science', as I usually call it in contradistinction to the 'bucket theory of the mind'[3]). What the searchlight makes visible will depend upon its position, upon our way of directing it, and upon its intensity, colour, etc.; although it will, of course, also depend very largely upon the things illuminated by it. Similarly, a scientific description will depend, largely, upon our point of view, our interests, which are as a rule connected with the theory or hypothesis we wish to test; although it will also depend upon the facts described. Indeed, the theory or hypothesis could be described as the crystallization of a point of view. For if we attempt to formulate our point of view, then this formulation will, as a rule, be what one sometimes calls a working hypothesis; that is to say, a provisional assumption whose function is to help us to select, and to order, the facts. But we should be clear that there cannot be any theory or hypothesis which is not, in this sense, a working hypothesis, and does not remain one. For no theory is final, and every theory helps us to select and order facts. This selective character of all description makes it in a certain sense 'relative'; but only in the sense that we would offer not this but another description, if our point of view were different. It may also affect our *belief* in the truth of the description; but it does not affect the question of the truth or falsity of the description; truth is not 'relative' in this sense[4].

The reason why all description is selective is, roughly speaking, the infinite wealth and variety of the possible aspects of the facts of our world. In order to describe this infinite wealth, we have at our disposal only a finite number of finite series of words. Thus we may describe as long as we like: our description will always be incomplete, a mere selection, and a small one at that, of the facts which present themselves for description. This shows that it is not only impossible to avoid a selective point of view, but also wholly undesirable to attempt to do so; for if we could do so, we should get not a more 'objective' description, but only a mere heap of entirely unconnected statements. But, of course, a point of view is inevitable; and the naïve attempt to avoid it can only lead to self-deception, and to the uncritical application of an unconscious point of view[5]. All this is true, most emphatically, in the case of *historical description*, with its 'infinite subject matter', as Schopenhauer[6] calls it. Thus in history no less than in science, we cannot avoid a point of view; and the belief that we can must lead to self-deception and to lack of critical care. This does not mean, of course, that we are permitted to falsify anything, or to take matters of truth lightly. Any particular historical description of facts will be simply true or false, however difficult it may be to decide upon its truth or falsity.

So far, the position of history is analogous to that of the natural sciences, for example, that of physics. But if we compare the part played by a 'point of view' in history with that played by a 'point of view' in physics, then we find a great difference. In physics, as we have seen, the 'point of view' is usually presented by a physical theory which can be tested by searching for new facts. In history, the matter is not quite so simple.

II

Let us first consider a little more closely the rôle of the theories in a natural science such as physics. Here, theories have several connected tasks. They help to unify science, and they help to explain as well as to predict events. Regarding explanation and prediction, I may perhaps quote from one of my own publications[7]: 'To give a *causal explanation* of a certain event means to derive deductively a statement (it will be called a *prognosis*) which describes that event, using as premises of the deduction some *universal laws* together with certain singular or specific sentences which we may call *initial conditions*. For example, we can say that we have given a causal explanation of the breaking of a certain thread if we find that this thread was capable of carrying one pound only, and that a weight of two pounds was put on it. If we analyse this causal explanation, then we find that two different constituents are involved in it. (1) We assume some hypotheses of the character of universal laws of nature; in our case, perhaps: "Whenever a certain thread undergoes a tension exceeding a certain maximum tension which is characteristic for that particular thread, then it will break." (2) We assume some specific statements (the initial conditions) pertaining to the particular event in question; in our case, we may have the two statements: "For this thread, the characteristic maximum tension at which it is liable to break is equal to a one-pound weight" and "The weight put on this thread was a two-pound weight." Thus we have two different kinds of statements which together yield a complete causal explanation, viz.: (1) *universal statements of the character of natural laws*, and (2) *specific statements pertaining to the special case in question, the initial conditions*. Now from the universal laws (1), we can deduce with the help of the initial conditions (2) the following specific statement (3): "This thread will break." This conclusion (3) we may also call a specific *prognosis*.—The initial conditions (or more precisely, the situation described by them) are usually spoken of as the *cause* of the event in question, and the prognosis (or rather, the event described by the prognosis) as the effect: for example, we say that the putting of a weight of two pounds on a thread capable of carrying one pound only was the cause of the breaking of the thread.'

From this analysis of causal explanation, we can see several things. One is that we can never speak of cause and effect in an absolute way, but that an event is a cause of another event, which is its effect, relative to some universal law. However, these universal laws are very often so trivial (as in our own example) that as a rule we take them for granted, instead of making conscious use of them. A second point is that the use of a theory for the purpose of *predicting* some specific event is just another aspect of its use for the purpose of *explaining* such an event. And since we test a theory by comparing the events predicted with those actually observed, our analysis also shows how theories can be *tested*. Whether we use a theory for the purpose of explanation, or prediction, or of testing, depends on our interest, and on what propositions we take as given or assumed.

Thus in the case of the so-called theoretical or *generalizing sciences* (such as physics, biology, sociology, etc.) we are predominantly interested in the universal laws or hypotheses. We wish to know whether they are true, and since we can never directly make sure of their truth, we adopt the method of eliminating the false ones. Our interest in the specific events, for example in experiments which are described by the initial conditions and prognoses, is somewhat limited; we are interested in them mainly as means to certain ends, means by which we can test the universal laws, which latter are considered as interesting in themselves, and as unifying our knowledge.

In the case of applied sciences, our interest is different. The engineer who uses physics in order to build a bridge is predominantly interested in a prognosis: whether or not a bridge of a certain kind described (by the initial conditions) will carry a certain load. For him, the universal laws are means to an end and taken for granted.

Accordingly, pure and applied generalizing sciences are respectively interested in testing universal hypotheses, and in predicting specific events. But there is a further interest, that in explaining a specific or particular event. If we wish to explain such an event, for example, a certain road accident, then we usually tacitly assume a host of rather trivial universal laws (such as that a bone breaks under a certain strain, or that any motor-car colliding in a certain way with any human body will exert a strain sufficient to break a bone, etc.), and are interested, predominantly, in the initial conditions or in the cause which, together with these trivial universal laws, would explain the event in question. We then usually assume certain initial conditions hypothetically, and attempt to find some further evidence in order to find out whether or not these hypothetically assumed initial conditions are true; that is to say, we test these specific hypotheses by deriving from them (with the help of some other and usually equally trivial universal laws) new predictions which can be confronted with observable facts.

Very rarely do we find ourselves in the position of having to worry about the universal laws involved in such an explanation. It happens only when we observe some new or strange kind of event, such as an unexpected chemical reaction. If such an event gives rise to the framing and testing of new hypotheses, then it is interesting mainly from the point of view of some generalizing science. But as a rule, if we are interested in specific events and their explanation, we take for granted all the many universal laws which we need.

Now the sciences which have this interest in specific events and in their explanation may, in contradistinction to the generalizing sciences, be called the *historical sciences*.

This view of history makes it clear why so many students of history and its method insist that it is the particular event that interests them, and not any so-called universal historical laws. For from our point of view, there can be no historical laws. Generalization belongs simply to a different line of interest, sharply to be distinguished from that interest in specific events and their causal explanation which is the business of history. Those who are interested in laws must turn to the generalizing sciences (for example, to sociology). Our view also makes it clear why history has so often been described as 'the events of the past as they actually did happen'. This description brings out quite well the specific interest of the student of history, as opposed to a student of a generalizing science, even though we shall have to raise certain objections against it. And our view explains why, in history, we are confronted, much more than in the generalizing sciences, with the problems of its 'infinite subject matter'. For the theories or universal laws of generalizing science introduce unity as well as a 'point of view'; they create, for every generalizing science, its problems, and its centres of interest as well as of research, of logical construction, and of presentation. But in history we have no such unifying theories; or, rather, the host of trivial universal laws we use are taken for granted; they are practically without interest, and totally unable to bring order into the subject matter. If we explain, for example, the first division of Poland in 1772 by pointing out that it could not possibly resist the combined power of Russia, Prussia, and Austria, then we are tacitly using some trivial universal law such as: 'If of two armies which are about equally well armed and led, one has a tremendous superiority in men, then the other never wins.' (Whether we say here 'never' or 'hardly ever' does not make, for our purposes, as much difference as it does for the Captain of H.M.S. *Pinafore*.) Such a law might be described as a law of the sociology of military power; but it is too trivial ever to raise a serious problem for the students of sociology, or to arouse their attention. Or if we explain Cæsar's decision to cross the Rubicon by his ambition and energy, say, then we are using some very trivial psychological generalizations which would hardly ever arouse the attention of a psychologist. (As a matter of fact, most historical explanation makes tacit use, not so much of trivial sociological and psychological laws, but of what I have called, in chapter 14, the *logic of the situation*; that is to say, besides the initial conditions describing personal interests, aims, and other situational factors, such as the information available to the person concerned, it tacitly assumes, as a kind of first approximation, the trivial general law that sane persons as a rule act more or less rationally.)

III

We see, therefore, that those universal laws which historical explanation uses provide no selective and unifying principle, no 'point of view' for history. In a very limited sense such a point of view may be provided by confining history to a history of something; examples are the history of power politics, or of economic relations, or of technology, or of mathematics. But as a rule, we need further selective principles, points of view which are at the same time centres of interest. Some of these are provided by preconceived ideas which in some way resemble universal laws, such as the idea that what is important for history is the character of the 'Great Men', or the 'national character', or moral ideas, or economic conditions, etc. Now it is important to see that many 'historical theories' (they might perhaps be better described as 'quasi-theories') are in their character vastly different from scientific theories. For in history (including the historical natural sciences such as historical geology) the facts at our disposal are often severely limited and cannot be repeated or implemented at our will. And they have been collected in accordance with a preconceived point of view; the so-called 'sources' of history record only such facts as appeared sufficiently interesting to record, so that the sources will often contain only such facts as fit in with preconceived theory. And if no further facts are available, it will often not be possible to test this theory or any other subsequent theory. Such untestable historical theories can then rightly be charged with being circular in the sense in which this charge has been unjustly brought against scientific theories. I shall call such historical theories, in contradistinction to scientific theories, '*general interpretations*'.

Interpretations are important since they represent a point of view. But we have seen that a point of view is always inevitable, and that, in history, a theory which can be tested and which is therefore of scientific character can only rarely be obtained. Thus we must not think that a general interpretation can be confirmed by its agreement even with all our records; for we must remember its circularity, as well as the fact that there will always be a number of other (and perhaps incompatible) interpretations that agree with the same records, and that we can rarely obtain new data able to serve as do crucial experiments in physics[8]. Historians often do not see any other interpretation which fits the facts as well as their own does; but if we consider that even in the field of physics, with its larger and more reliable stock of facts, new crucial experiments are needed again and again because the old ones are all in keeping with both of two competing and incompatible theories (consider the eclipse-experiment which is needed for deciding between Newton's and Einstein's theories of gravitation), then we shall give up the naïve belief that any definite set of historical records can ever be interpreted in one way only.

But this does not mean, of course, that all interpretations are of equal merit. First, there are always interpretations which are not really in keeping with the accepted records; secondly, there are some which need a number of more or less plausible auxiliary hypotheses if they are to escape falsification by the records; next, there are some that are unable to connect a number of facts which another interpretation can connect, and in so far 'explain'. There may accordingly be a considerable amount of progress even within the field of historical interpretation. Furthermore, there may be all kinds of intermediate stages between more or less universal 'points of view' and those specific or singular historical hypotheses mentioned above, which in the explanation of historical events play the rôle of hypothetical initial conditions rather than of universal laws. Often enough, these can be tested fairly well and are therefore comparable to scientific theories. But some of these specific hypotheses closely resemble those universal quasi-theories which I have called interpretations, and may accordingly be classed with these, as 'specific interpretations'. For the evidence in favour of such a specific interpretation is often enough just as circular in character as the evidence in favour of some universal 'point of view'. For example, our only authority may give us just that information regarding certain events which fits with his own specific interpretation. Most specific interpretations of these facts we may attempt will then be circular in the sense that they must fit in with that interpretation which was used in the original selection of facts. If, however, we can give to such material an interpretation which radically deviates from that adopted by our authority (and this is certainly so, for example, in our interpretation of Plato's work), then the character of our interpretation may perhaps take on some semblance to that of a scientific hypothesis. But fundamentally, it is necessary to keep in mind the fact that it is a very dubious argument in favour of a certain interpretation that it can be easily applied, and that it explains all we know; for only if we can look out for counter examples can we test a theory. (This point is nearly always overlooked by the admirers of the various 'unveiling philosophies', especially by the psycho-, socio-, and historio-analysts; they are often seduced by the ease with which their theories can be applied everywhere.)

I said before that interpretations may be incompatible; but as long as we consider them merely as crystallizations of points of view, then they are not. For example, the interpretation that man steadily progresses (towards the open society or some other aim) is incompatible with the interpretation that he steadily slips back or retrogresses. But the 'point of view' of one who looks on human history as a history of progress is not necessarily incompatible with that of one who looks on it as a history of retrogression; that is to say, we could write a history of human progress towards freedom (containing, for example, the story of the fight against slavery) and another history of human retrogression and oppression (containing perhaps such things as the impact of the white race upon the coloured races); and these two histories need not be in conflict; rather, they may be complementary to each other, as would be two views of the same landscape seen from two different points. This consideration is of considerable importance. For since each generation has its own troubles and problems, and therefore its own interests and its own point of view, it follows that each generation has a right to look upon and re-interpret history in its own way, which is complementary to that of previous generations. After all, we study history because we are interested in it[9], and perhaps because we wish to learn something about our own problems. But history can serve neither of these two purposes if, under the influence of an inapplicable idea of objectivity, we hesitate to present historical problems from our point of view. And we should not think that our point of view, if consciously and critically applied to the problem, will be inferior to that of a writer who naïvely believes that he does not interpret, and that he has reached a level of objectivity permitting him to present 'the events of the past as they actually did happen'. (This is why I believe that even such admittedly personal comments as can be found in this book are justified, since they are in keeping with historical method.) The main thing is to be conscious of one's point of view, and critical, that is to say, to avoid, as far as this is possible, unconscious and therefore uncritical bias in the presentation of the facts. In every other respect, the interpretation must speak for itself; and its merits will be its fertility, its ability to elucidate the facts of history, as well as its topical interest, its ability to elucidate the problems of the day.

To sum up, there can be no history of 'the past as it actually did happen'; there can only be historical interpretations, and none of them final; and every generation has a right to frame its own. But not only has it a right to frame its own interpretations, it also has a kind of obligation to do so; for there is indeed a pressing need to be answered. We want to know how our troubles are related to the past, and we want to see the line along which we may progress towards the solution of what we feel, and what we choose, to be our main tasks. It is this need which, if not answered by rational and fair means, produces historicist interpretations. Under its pressure the historicist substitutes for a rational question: 'What are we to choose as our most urgent problems, how did they arise, and along what roads may we proceed to solve them?' the irrational and apparently factual question: 'Which way are we going? What, in essence, is the part that history has destined us to play?'

But am I justified in refusing to the historicist the right to interpret history in his own way? Have I not just proclaimed that anybody has such a right? My answer to this question is that historicist interpretations are of a peculiar kind. Those interpretations which are needed, and justified, and one or other of which we are bound to adopt, can, I have said, be compared to a searchlight. We let it play upon our past, and we hope to illuminate the present by its reflection. As opposed to this, the historicist interpretation may be compared to a searchlight which we direct upon ourselves. It makes it difficult if not impossible to see anything of our surroundings, and it paralyses our actions. To translate this metaphor, the historicist does not recognize that it is we who select and order the facts of history, but he believes that 'history itself', or the 'history of mankind', determines, by its inherent laws, ourselves, our problems, our future, and even our point of view. Instead of recognizing that historical interpretation should answer a need arising out of the practical problems and decisions which face us, the historicist believes that in our desire for historical interpretation, there expresses itself the profound intuition that by contemplating history we may discover the secret, the essence of human destiny. Historicism is out to find The Path on which mankind is destined to walk; it is out to discover The Clue to History (as J. Macmurray calls it), or The Meaning of History.

IV

But is there such a clue? *Is there a meaning in history?*

I do not wish to enter here into the problem of the meaning of 'meaning'; I take it for granted that most people know with sufficient clarity what they mean when they speak of the 'meaning of history' or of the 'meaning or purpose of life'[10]. And in this sense, in the sense in which the question of the meaning of history is asked, I answer: *History has no meaning*.

In order to give reasons for this opinion, I must first say something about that 'history' which people have in mind when they ask whether it has meaning. So far, I have myself spoken about 'history' as if it did not need any explanation. That is no longer possible; for I wish to make it clear that *'history' in the sense in which most people speak of it simply does not exist*; and this is at least one reason why I say that it has no meaning.

How do most people come to use the term 'history'? (I mean 'history' in the sense in which we say of a book that it is *about* the history of Europe—not in the sense in which we say that it is a history of Europe.) They learn about it in school and at the University. They read books about it. They see what is treated in the books under the name 'history of the world' or 'the history of mankind', and they get used to looking upon it as a more or less definite series of facts. And these facts constitute, they believe, the history of mankind.

But we have already seen that the realm of facts is infinitely rich, and that there must be selection. According to our interests, we could, for instance, write about the history of art; or of language; or of feeding habits; or of typhus fever (see Zinsser's *Rats, Lice, and History*). Certainly, none of these is the history of mankind (nor all of them taken together). What people have in mind when they speak of the history of mankind is, rather, the history of the Egyptian, Babylonian, Persian, Macedonian, and Roman empires, and so on, down to our own day. In other words: They speak about the *history of mankind*, but what they mean, and what they have learned about in school, is the *history of political power*.

There is no history of mankind, there is only an indefinite number of histories of all kinds of aspects of human life. And one of these is the history of political power. This is elevated into the history of the world. But this, I hold, is an offence against every decent conception of mankind. It is hardly better than to treat the history of embezzlement or of robbery or of poisoning as the history of mankind. For *the history of power politics is nothing but the history of international crime and mass murder* (including, it is true, some of the attempts to suppress them). This history is taught in schools, and some of the greatest criminals are extolled as its heroes.

But is there really no such thing as a universal history in the sense of a concrete history of mankind? There can be none. This must be the reply of every humanitarian, I believe, and especially that of every Christian. A concrete history of mankind, if there were any, would have to be the history of all men. It would have to be the history of all human hopes, struggles, and sufferings. For there is no one man more important than any other. Clearly, this concrete history cannot be written. We must make abstractions, we must neglect, select. But with this we arrive at the many histories; and among them, at that history of international crime and mass murder which has been advertised as the history of mankind.

But why has just the history of power been selected, and not, for example, that of religion, or of poetry? There are several reasons. One is that power affects us all, and poetry only a few. Another is that men are inclined to worship power. But there can be no doubt that the worship of power is one of the worst kinds of human idolatries, a relic of the time of the cage, of human servitude. The worship of power is born of fear, an emotion which is rightly despised. A third reason why power politics has been made the core of 'history' is that those in power wanted to be worshipped and could enforce their wishes. Many historians wrote under the supervision of the emperors, the generals and the dictators.

I know that these views will meet with the strongest opposition from many sides, including some apologists for Christianity; for although there is hardly anything in the New Testament to support this doctrine, it is often considered a part of the Christian dogma that God reveals Himself in history; that history has meaning; and that its meaning is the purpose of God. Historicism is thus held to be a necessary element of religion. But I do not admit this. I contend that this view is pure idolatry and superstition, not only from the point of view of a rationalist or humanist but from the Christian point of view itself.

What is behind this theistic historicism? With Hegel, it looks upon history—political history—as a stage, or rather, as a kind of lengthy Shakespearian play; and the audience conceive either the 'great historical personalities', or mankind in the abstract, as the heroes of the play. Then they ask, 'Who has written this play?' And they think that they give a pious answer when they reply, 'God'. But they are mistaken. Their answer is pure blasphemy, for the play was (and they know it) written not by God, but, under the supervision of generals and dictators, by the professors of history.

I do not deny that it is as justifiable to interpret history from a Christian point of view as it is to interpret it from any other point of view; and it should certainly be emphasized, for example, how much of our Western aims and ends, humanitarianism, freedom, equality, we owe to the influence of Christianity. But at the same time, the only rational as well as the only Christian attitude even towards the history of freedom is that we are ourselves responsible for it, in the same sense in which we are responsible for what we make of our lives, and that only our conscience can judge us and not our worldly success. The theory that God reveals Himself and His judgement in history is indistinguishable from the theory that worldly success is the ultimate judge and justification of our actions; it comes to the same thing as the doctrine that history will judge, that is to say, that future might is right; it is the same as what I have called 'moral futurism'[11]. To maintain that God reveals Himself in what is usually called 'history', in the history of international crime and of mass murder, is indeed blasphemy; for what really happens within the realm of human lives is hardly ever touched upon by this cruel and at the same time childish affair. The life of the forgotten, of the unknown individual man; his sorrows and his joys, his suffering and death, this is the real content of human experience down the ages. If that could be told by history, then I should certainly not say that it is blasphemy to see the finger of God in it. But such a history does not and cannot exist; and all the history which exists, our history of the Great and the Powerful, is at best a shallow comedy; it is the opera buffa played by the powers behind reality (comparable to Homer's opera buffa of the Olympian powers behind the scene of human struggles). It is what one of our worst instincts, the idolatrous worship of power, of success, has led us to believe to be real. And in this not even man-made, but man-faked 'history', some Christians dare to see the hand of God! They dare to understand and to know what He wills when they impute to Him their petty historical interpretations! 'On the contrary', says K. Barth, the theologian, in his *Credo*, 'we have to begin with the admission … that all that we think we know when we say "God" does not reach or comprehend Him …, but always one of our self-conceived and self-made idols, whether it is "spirit" or "nature", "fate" or "idea" …'[12] (It is in keeping with this attitude that Barth characterizes the 'Neo-Protestant doctrine of the revelation of God in history' as 'inadmissible' and as an encroachment upon 'the kingly office of Christ'.) But it is, from the Christian point of view, not only arrogance that underlies such attempts; it is, more specifically, an anti-Christian attitude. For Christianity teaches, if anything, that worldly success is not decisive. Christ 'suffered under Pontius Pilate'. I am quoting Barth again: 'How does Pontius Pilate get into the Credo? The simple answer can at once be given: it is a matter of date.' Thus the man who was successful, who represented the historical power of that time, plays here the purely technical rôle of indicating when these events happened. And what were these events? They had nothing to do with power-political success, with 'history'. They were not even the story of an unsuccessful non-violent nationalist revolution (*à la* Gandhi) of the Jewish people against the Roman conquerors. The events were nothing but the sufferings of a man. Barth insists that the word 'suffers' refers to the whole of the life of Christ and not only to His death; he says[13]: 'Jesus *suffers*. Therefore He does not conquer. He does not triumph. He has no success … He achieved nothing except … His crucifixion. The same could be said of His relationship to His people and to His disciples.' My intention in quoting Barth is to show that it is not only my 'rationalist' or 'humanist' point of view from which the worship of historical success appears as incompatible with the spirit of Christianity. What matters to Christianity is not the historical deeds of the powerful Roman conquerers but (to use a phrase of Kierkegaard's[14]) 'what a few fishermen have given the world'. And yet all theistic interpretation of history attempts to see in history as it is recorded, i.e. in the history of power, and in historical success, the manifestation of God's will.

To this attack upon the 'doctrine of the revelation of God in history', it will probably be replied that it is success, His success after His death, by which Christ's unsuccessful life on earth was finally revealed to mankind as the greatest spiritual victory; that it was the success, the fruits of His teaching which proved it and justified it, and by which the prophecy 'The last shall be first and the first last' has been verified. In other words, that it was the historical success of the Christian Church through which the will of God manifested itself. But this is a most dangerous line of defence. Its implication that the worldly success of the Church is an argument in favour of Christianity clearly reveals lack of faith. The early Christians had no worldly encouragement of this kind. (They believed that conscience must judge power[15], and not the other way round.) Those who hold that the history of the success of Christian teaching reveals the will of God should ask themselves whether this success was really a success of the spirit of Christianity; and whether this spirit did not triumph at the time when the Church was persecuted, rather than at the time when the Church was triumphant. Which Church incorporated this spirit more purely, that of the martyrs, or the victorious Church of the Inquisition?

There seem to be many who would admit much of this, insisting as they do that the message of Christianity is to the meek, but who still believe that this message is one of historicism. An outstanding representative of this view is J. Macmurray, who, in *The Clue to History*, finds the essence of Christian teaching in historical prophecy, and who sees in its founder the discoverer of a dialectical law of 'human nature'. Macmurray holds[16] that, according to this law, political history must inevitably bring forth 'the socialist commonwealth of the world. The fundamental law of human nature cannot be broken … It is the meek who will inherit the earth.' But this historicism, with its substitution of certainty for hope, must lead to a moral futurism. 'The law *cannot* be broken.' So we can be sure, on psychological grounds, that whatever we do will lead to the same result; that even fascism must, in the end, lead to that commonwealth; so that the final outcome does not depend upon our moral decision, and that there is no need to worry over our responsibilities. If we are told that we can be *certain*, on scientific grounds, that 'the last will be first and the first last', what else is this but the substitution of historical prophecy for conscience? Does not this theory come dangerously close (certainly against the intentions of its author) to the admonition: 'Be wise, and take to heart what the founder of Christianity tells you, for he was a great psychologist of human nature and a great prophet of history. Climb in time upon the band-waggon of the meek; for according to the inexorable scientific laws of human nature, this is the surest way to come out on top!' Such a clue to history implies the worship of success; it implies that the meek will be justified because they will be on the winning side. It translates Marxism, and especially what I have described as Marx's historicist moral theory, into the language of a psychology of human nature, and of religious prophecy. It is an interpretation which, by implication, sees the greatest achievement of Christianity in the fact that its founder was a forerunner of Hegel—a superior one, admittedly.

My insistence that success should not be worshipped, that it cannot be our judge, and that we should not be dazzled by it, and in particular, my attempts to show that in this attitude I concur with what I believe to be the true teaching of Christianity, should not be misunderstood. They are not intended to support the attitude of 'other-worldliness' which I have criticized in the last chapter[17]. Whether Christianity is other-worldly, I do not know, but it certainly teaches that the only way to prove one's faith is by rendering practical (and worldly) help to those who need it. And it is certainly possible to combine an attitude of the utmost reserve and even of contempt towards worldly success in the sense of power, glory, and wealth, with the attempt to do one's best in this world, and to further the ends one has decided to adopt with the clear purpose of making them succeed; not for the sake of success or of one's justification by history, but for their own sake.

A forceful support of some of these views, and especially of the incompatibility of historicism and Christianity, can be found in Kierkegaard's criticism of Hegel. Although Kierkegaard never freed himself entirely from the Hegelian tradition in which he was educated[18], there was hardly anybody who recognized more clearly what Hegelian historicism meant. 'There were', Kierkegaard wrote[19], 'philosophers who tried, before Hegel, to explain ... history. And providence could only smile when it saw these attempts. But providence did not laugh outright, for there was a human, honest sincerity about them. But Hegel—! Here I need Homer's language. How did the gods roar with laughter! Such a horrid little professor who has simply seen through the necessity of anything and everything there is, and who now plays the whole affair on his barrel-organ: listen, ye gods of Olympus!' And Kierkegaard continues, referring to the attack[20] by the atheist Schopenhauer upon the Christian apologist Hegel: 'Reading Schopenhauer has given me more pleasure than I can express. What he says is perfectly true; and then—it serves the Germans right—he is as rude as only a German can be.' But Kierkegaard's own expressions are nearly as blunt as Schopenhauer's; for Kierkegaard goes on to say that Hegelianism, which he calls 'this brilliant spirit of putridity', is the 'most repugnant of all forms of looseness'; and he speaks of its 'mildew of pomposity', its 'intellectual voluptuousness', and its 'infamous splendour of corruption'.

And, indeed, our intellectual as well as our ethical education is corrupt. It is perverted by the admiration of brilliance, of the way things are said, which takes the place of a critical appreciation of the things that are said (and the things that are done). It is perverted by the romantic idea of the splendour of the stage of History on which we are the actors. We are educated to act with an eye to the gallery.

The whole problem of educating man to a sane appreciation of his own importance relative to that of other individuals is thoroughly muddled by these ethics of fame and fate, by a morality which perpetuates an educational system that is still based upon the classics with their romantic view of the history of power and their romantic tribal morality which goes back to Heraclitus; a system whose ultimate basis is the worship of power. Instead of a sober combination of individualism and altruism (to use these labels again[21])—that is to say, instead of a position like 'What really matters are human individuals, but I do not take this to mean that it is I who matter very much'—a romantic combination of egoism and collectivism is taken for granted. That is to say, the importance of the self, of its emotional life and its 'self-expression', is romantically exaggerated; and with it, the tension between the 'personality' and the group, the collective. This takes the place of the other individuals, the other men, but does not admit of reasonable personal relations. 'Dominate or submit' is, by implication, the device of this attitude; either be a Great Man, a Hero wrestling with fate and earning fame ('the greater the fall, the greater the fame', says Heraclitus), or belong to 'the masses' and submit yourself to leadership and sacrifice yourself to the higher cause of your collective. There is a neurotic, an hysterical element in this exaggerated stress on the importance of the tension between the self and the collective, and I do not doubt that this hysteria, this reaction to the strain of civilization, is the secret of the strong emotional appeal of the ethics of hero-worship, of the ethics of domination and submission[22].

At the bottom of all this there is a real difficulty. While it is fairly clear (as we have seen in chapters 9 and 24) that the politician should limit himself to fighting against evils, instead of fighting for 'positive' or 'higher' values, such as happiness, etc., the teacher, in principle, is in a different position. Although he should not *impose* his scale of 'higher' values upon his pupils, he certainly should try to *stimulate* their interest in these values. He should care for the souls of his pupils. (When Socrates told his friends to care for their souls, *he* cared for them.) Thus there is certainly something like a romantic or æsthetic element in education, such as should not enter politics. But though this is true in principle, it is hardly applicable to our educational system. For it presupposes a relation of friendship between teacher and pupil, a relation which, as emphasized in chapter 24, each party must be free to end. (Socrates chose his companions, and they him.) The very number of pupils makes all this impossible in our schools. Accordingly, attempts to impose higher values not only become unsuccessful, but it must be insisted that they lead to *harm*—to something much more concrete and public than the ideals aimed at. And the principle that those who are entrusted to us must, before anything else, not be harmed, should be recognized to be just as fundamental for education as it is for medicine. 'Do no harm' (and, therefore, 'give the young what they most urgently need, in order to become independent of us, and to be able to choose for themselves') would be a very worthy aim for our educational system, and one whose realization is somewhat remote, even though it sounds modest. Instead, 'higher' aims are the fashion, aims which are typically romantic and indeed nonsensical, such as 'the full development of the personality'.

It is under the influence of such romantic ideas that individualism is still identified with egoism, as it was by Plato, and altruism with collectivism (i.e. with the substitution of group egoism for the individualist egoism). But this bars the way even to a clear formulation of the main problem, the problem of how to obtain a sane appreciation of one's own importance in relation to other individuals. Since it is felt, and rightly so, that we have to aim at something beyond our own selves, something to which we can devote ourselves, and for which we may make sacrifices, it is concluded that this must be the collective, with its 'historical mission'. Thus we are told to make sacrifices, and, at the same time, assured that we shall make an excellent bargain by doing so. We shall make sacrifices, it is said, but we shall thereby obtain honour and fame. We shall become 'leading actors', heroes on the Stage of History; for a small risk we shall gain great rewards. This is the dubious morality of a period in which only a tiny minority counted, and in which nobody cared for the common people. It is the morality of those who, being political or intellectual aristocrats, have a chance of getting into the textbooks of history. It cannot possibly be the morality of those who favour justice and equalitarianism; for historical fame cannot be just, and it can be attained only by a very few. The countless number of men who are just as worthy, or worthier, will always be forgotten.

It should perhaps be admitted that the Heraclitean ethics, the doctrine that the higher reward is that which only posterity can offer, may in some way perhaps be slightly superior to an ethical doctrine which teaches us to look out for reward now. But it is not what we need. We need an ethics which defies success and reward. And such an ethics need not be invented. It is not new. It has been taught by Christianity, at least in its beginnings. It is, again, taught by the industrial as well as by the scientific co-operation of our own day. The romantic historicist morality of fame, fortunately, seems to be on the decline. The Unknown Soldier shows it. We are beginning to realize that sacrifice may mean just as much, or even more, when it is made anonymously. Our ethical education must follow suit. We must be taught to do our work; to make our sacrifice for the sake of this work, and not for praise or the avoidance of blame. (The fact that we all need some encouragement, hope, praise, and even blame, is another matter altogether.) We must find our justification in our work, in what we are doing ourselves, and not in a fictitious 'meaning of history'.

History has no meaning, I contend. But this contention does not imply that all we can do about it is to look aghast at the history of political power, or that we must look on it as a cruel joke. For we can interpret it, with an eye to those problems of power politics whose solution we choose to attempt in our time. We can interpret the history of power politics from the point of view of our fight for the open society, for a rule of reason, for justice, freedom, equality, and for the control of international crime. Although history has no ends, we can impose these ends of ours upon it; and *although history has no meaning, we can give it a meaning.*

It is the problem of nature and convention which we meet here again[23]. Neither nature nor history can tell us what we ought to do. Facts, whether those of nature or those of history, cannot make the decision for us, they cannot determine the ends we are going to choose. It is we who introduce purpose and meaning into nature and into history. Men are not equal; but we can decide to fight for equal rights. Human institutions such as the state are not rational, but we can decide to fight to make them more rational. We ourselves and our ordinary language are, on the whole, emotional rather than rational; but we can try to become a little more rational, and we can train ourselves to use our language as an instrument not of self-expression (as our romantic educationists would say) but of rational communication[24]. History itself—I mean the history of power politics, of course, not the non-existent story of the development of mankind—has no end nor meaning, but we can decide to give it both. We can make it our fight for the open society and against its enemies (who, when in a corner, always protest their humanitarian sentiments, in accordance with Pareto's advice); and we can interpret it accordingly. Ultimately, we may say the same about the 'meaning of life'. It is up to us to decide what shall be our purpose in life, to determine our ends[25].

This dualism of facts and decisions[26] is, I believe, fundamental. Facts as such have no meaning; they can gain it only through our decisions.

Historicism is only one of many attempts to get over this dualism; it is born of fear, for it shrinks from realizing that we bear the ultimate responsibility even for the standards we choose. But such an attempt seems to me to represent precisely what is usually described as superstition. For it assumes that we can reap where we have not sown; it tries to persuade us that if we merely fall into step with history everything will and must go right, and that no fundamental decision on our part is required; it tries to shift our responsibility on to history, and thereby on to the play of demoniac powers beyond ourselves; it tries to base our actions upon the hidden intentions of these powers, which can be revealed to us only in mystical inspirations and intuitions; and it thus puts our actions and ourselves on the moral level of a man who, inspired by horoscopes and dreams, chooses his lucky number in a lottery[27]. Like gambling, historicism is born of our despair in the rationality and responsibility of our actions. It is a debased hope and a debased faith, an attempt to replace the hope and the faith that springs from our moral enthusiasm and the contempt for success by a certainty that springs from a pseudo-science; a pseudoscience of the stars, or of 'human nature', or of historical destiny.

Historicism, I assert, is not only rationally untenable, it is also in conflict with any religion that teaches the importance of conscience. For such a religion must agree with the rationalist attitude towards history in its emphasis on our supreme responsibility for our actions, and for their repercussions upon the course of history. True, we need hope; to act, to live without hope goes beyond our strength. But we do *not* need more, and we must not be given more. We do not need certainty. Religion, in particular, should not be a substitute for dreams and wish-fulfilment; it should resemble neither the holding of a ticket in a lottery, nor the holding of a policy in an insurance company. The historicist element in religion is an element of idolatry, of superstition.

This emphasis upon the dualism of facts and decisions determines also our attitude towards such ideas as 'progress'. If we think that history progresses, or that we are bound to progress, then we commit the same mistake as those who believe that history has a meaning that can be discovered in it and need not be given to it. For to progress is to move towards some kind of end, towards an end which exists for us as human beings. 'History' cannot do that; only we, the human individuals, can do it; we can do it by defending and strengthening those democratic institutions upon which freedom, and with it progress, depends. And we shall do it much better as we become more fully aware of the fact that progress rests with us, with our watchfulness, with our efforts, with the clarity of our conception of our ends, and with the realism[28] of their choice.

Instead of posing as prophets we must become the makers of our fate. We must learn to do things as well as we can, and to look out for our mistakes. And when we have dropped the idea that the history of power will be our judge, when we have given up worrying whether or not history will justify us, then one day perhaps we may succeed in getting power under control. In this way we may even justify history, in our turn. It badly needs a justification.

ADDENDA

I

FACTS, STANDARDS, AND TRUTH: A FURTHER CRITICISM OF RELATIVISM (1961)

The main philosophical malady of our time is an intellectual and moral relativism, the latter being at least in part based upon the former. By relativism—or, if you like, scepticism—I mean here, briefly, the theory that the choice between competing theories is arbitrary; since either, there is no such thing as objective truth; or, if there is, no such thing as a theory which is true or at any rate (though perhaps not true) nearer to the truth than another theory; or, if there are two or more theories, no ways or means of deciding whether one of them is better than another.

In this *addendum*[1] I shall first suggest that a dose of Tarski's theory of truth (see also the references to A. Tarski in the Index of this book), stiffened perhaps by my own theory of getting nearer to the truth, may go a long way towards curing this malady, though I admit that some other remedies might also be required, such as the non-authoritarian theory of knowledge which I have developed elsewhere.[2] I shall also try to show (in sections 12 ff. below) that the situation in the realm of standards—especially in the moral and political field—is somewhat analogous to that obtaining in the realm of facts.

[1] I am deeply indebted to Dr. William W. Bartley's incisive criticism which not only helped me to improve chapter 24 of this book (especially page 231) but also induced me to make important changes in the present *addendum*.

[2] See for example 'On the Sources of Knowledge and of Ignorance', now the Introduction to my *Conjectures and Refutations* and, more especially, Chapter 10 of that book; also, of course, my *The Logic of Scientific Discovery*.

1. Truth

Certain arguments in support of relativism arise from the question, asked in the tone of the assured sceptic who knows for certain that there is no answer: '*What is truth?*' But Pilate's question can be answered in a simple and reasonable way—though hardly in a way that would have satisfied him—as follows: an assertion, proposition, statement, or belief, is true if, and only if, it corresponds to the facts.

Yet what do we mean by saying that a statement corresponds to the facts? Though to our sceptic or relativist this second question may seem just as unanswerable as the first, it actually can be equally readily answered. The answer is not difficult—as one might expect if one reflects upon the fact that every judge assumes that the witness knows what truth (in the sense of correspondence with the facts) means. Indeed, the answer turns out to be almost trivial.

In a way it is trivial—that is, once we have learnt from Tarski that the problem is one in which we *refer to or speak about* statements and facts and some relationship of correspondence holding between statement and facts; and that, therefore, the solution must also be one that *refers to or speaks about* statements and facts, and some relation between them. Consider the following:

The statement 'Smith entered the pawnshop shortly after 10.15' corresponds to the facts if, and only if, Smith entered the pawnshop shortly after 10.15.

When we read this italicized paragraph, what is likely to strike us first is its triviality. But never mind its triviality: if we look at it again, and more carefully, we see (1) that it refers to a statement, and (2) to some facts; and (3) that it can therefore state the very obvious conditions which we should expect to hold whenever we wish to say that the statement referred to corresponds to the facts referred to.

Those who think that this italicized paragraph is too trivial or too simple to contain anything interesting should be reminded of the fact, already referred to, that since everybody knows what truth, or correspondence with the facts, means (as long as he does not allow himself to speculate about it) this must be, in a sense, a trivial matter.

That the idea formulated in the italicized paragraph is correct, may be brought out by the following second italicized paragraph.

The assertion made by the witness, 'Smith entered the pawnshop shortly after 10.15' is true if and only if Smith entered the pawnshop shortly after 10.15.

It is clear that this second italicized paragraph is again very trivial. Nevertheless, it states in full the conditions for applying the predicate 'is true' to any statement made by a witness.

Some people might think that a better way to formulate the paragraph would be the following:

The assertion made by the witness 'I saw that Smith entered the pawnshop shortly after 10.15' is true if and only if the witness saw that Smith entered the pawnshop shortly after 10.15.

Comparing this third italicized paragraph with the second we see that while the second gives the conditions for the truth of a statement about Smith and what he did, the third gives the conditions for the truth of a statement about the witness and what he did (or saw). But this is the only difference between the two paragraphs: both state the full conditions for the truth of the two different statements which are quoted in them.

It is a rule of *giving evidence* that eye-witnesses should confine themselves to stating what they *actually saw*. Compliance with this rule may sometimes make it easier for the judge to *distinguish* between true evidence and false evidence. Thus the third italicized paragraph may perhaps be said to have some advantages over the second, if regarded from the point of view of truth-*seeking* and truth-*finding*.

But it is essential for our present purpose not to mix up questions of actual truth-seeking or truth-finding (i.e. epistemological or methodological questions) with the question of what we mean, or what we intend to say, when we speak of truth, or of correspondence with the facts (the logical or ontological question of truth). Now from the latter point of view, the third italicized paragraph has no advantage whatever over the second. Each of them states to the full the conditions for the truth of the statement to which it refers.

Each, therefore, answers the question—'What is truth?' in precisely the same way; though each does it only indirectly, by giving *the conditions for the truth for a certain statement*—and each for a different statement.

2. Criteria

It is decisive to realize that knowing what truth means, or under what conditions a statement is called true, is not the same as, and must be clearly distinguished from, possessing a means of deciding—a *criterion* for deciding—whether a given statement is true or false.

The distinction I am referring to is a very general one, and it is of considerable importance for an assessment of relativism, as we shall see.

We may know, for example, what we mean by 'good meat' and by 'meat gone bad'; but we may not know how to tell the one from the other, at least in some cases: it is this we have in mind when we say that we have no *criterion* of the 'goodness' of good meat. Similarly, every doctor knows, more or less, what he means by 'tuberculosis'; but he may not always recognize it. And even though there may be (by now) batteries of tests which amount almost to a decision method,—that is to say, to a *criterion*—sixty years ago there certainly were no such batteries of tests at the disposal of doctors, and no criterion. But doctors knew then very well what they meant—a lung infection due to a certain kind of microbe.

Admittedly, a criterion—a definite method of decision—if we could obtain one, might make everything clearer and more definite and more precise. It is therefore understandable that some people, hankering after precision, demand criteria. And if we can get them, the demand may be reasonable.

But it would be a mistake to believe that, before we have a criterion for deciding whether or not a man is suffering from tuberculosis, the phrase '*X* is suffering from tuberculosis' is meaningless; or that, before we have a criterion of the goodness or badness of meat, there is no point in considering whether or not a piece of meat has gone bad; or that, before we have a reliable lie-detector, we do not know what we mean when we say that *X* is deliberately lying, and should therefore not even consider this 'possibility', since it is no possibility at all, but meaningless; or that, before we have a criterion of truth, we do not know what we mean when we say of a statement that it is true.

Thus those who insist that, without a criterion—a reliable test—for tuberculosis, or lying, or truth, we cannot mean anything by the words 'tuberculosis' or 'lying' or 'true', are certainly mistaken. In fact, construction of a battery of tests for tuberculosis, or for lying, comes *after* we have established—perhaps only roughly—what we mean by 'tuberculosis' or by 'lying'.

It is clear that in the course of developing tests for tuberculosis, we may learn a lot more about this illness; so much, perhaps, that we may say that the very meaning of the term 'tuberculosis' has changed under the influence of our new knowledge, and that after the establishment of the criterion the meaning of the term is no longer the same as before. Some, perhaps, may even say that 'tuberculosis' can now be defined in terms of the criterion. But this does not alter the fact that we meant something before—though we may, of course, have known less about the thing. Nor does it alter the fact that there are few diseases (if any) for which we have either a criterion or a clear definition, and that few criteria (if any) are reliable. (But if they are not reliable, we had better not call them 'criteria'.)

There may be no criterion which helps us to establish whether a pound note is, or is not, genuine. But should we find two pound notes with the same serial number, we should have good reasons to assert, even in the absence of a criterion, that one of them at least is a forgery; and this assertion would clearly not be made meaningless by the absence of a criterion of genuineness.

To sum up, the theory that in order to determine what a word means we must establish a criterion for its correct use, or for its correct application, is mistaken: we practically never have such a criterion.

3. Criterion philosophies

The view just rejected—the view that we must have criteria in order to know what we are talking about, whether it is tuberculosis, lying, or existence, or meaning, or truth—is the overt or implicit basis of many philosophies. A philosophy of this kind may be called a '*criterion philosophy*'.

Since the basic demand of a criterion philosophy cannot as a rule be met, it is clear that the adoption of a criterion-philosophy will, in many cases, lead to disappointment, and to relativism or scepticism.

I believe that it is the demand for a *criterion of truth* which has made so many people feel that the question 'What is truth?' is unanswerable. *But the absence of a criterion of truth does not render the notion of truth non-significant any more than the absence of a criterion of health renders the notion of health non-significant. A sick man may seek health even though he has no criterion for it. An erring man may seek truth even though he has no criterion for it.*

And both may simply seek health, or truth, without much bothering about the meanings of these terms which they (and others) understand well enough for their purposes.

One immediate result of Tarski's work on truth is the following theorem of logic: *there can be no general criterion of truth* (except with respect to certain artificial language systems of a somewhat impoverished kind).

This result can be exactly established; and its establishment makes use of the notion of truth as correspondence with the facts.

We have here an interesting and philosophically very important result (important especially in connection with the problem of an authoritarian theory of knowledge[3]). But this result has been established with the help of a notion—in this case the notion of truth—for which we have no criterion. The unreasonable demand of the criterion-philosophies that we should not

[3] For a description and criticism of authoritarian (or non-fallibilist) theories of knowledge see especially sections v, vi, and x. ff.. of the Introduction to my *Conjectures and Refutations*.

take a notion seriously before a criterion has been established would therefore, if adhered to in this case, have for ever prevented us from attaining a logical result of great philosophical interest.

Incidentally, the result that there can be no general criterion of truth is a direct consequence of the still more important result (which Tarski obtained by combining Gödel's undecidability theorem with his own theory of truth) that there can be no general criterion of truth even for the comparatively narrow field of number theory, or for any science which makes full use of arithmetic. It applies *a fortiori* to truth in any extra-mathematical field in which unrestricted use is made of arithmetic.

4. Fallibilism

All this shows not only that some still fashionable forms of scepticism and relativism are mistaken, but also that they are obsolete; that they are based on a logical confusion—between the meaning of a term and the criterion of its proper application—although the means for clearing up this confusion have been readily available for some thirty years.

It must be admitted, however, that there is a kernel of truth in both scepticism and relativism. The kernel of truth is just that there exists no general criterion of truth. But this does not warrant the conclusion that the choice between competing theories is arbitrary. It merely means, quite simply, that we can always err in our choice—that we can always miss the truth, or fall short of the truth; that certainty is not for us (nor even knowledge that is highly probable, as I have shown in various places, for example in chapter 10 of *Conjectures and Refutations*); that we are fallible.

This, for all we know, is no more than the plain truth. There are few fields of human endeavour, if any, which seem to be exempt from human fallibility. What we once thought to be well-established, or even certain, may later turn out to be not quite correct (but this means false), and in need of correction.

A particularly impressive example of this is the discovery of heavy water, and of heavy hydrogen (*deuterium*, first separated by Harold C. Urey in 1931). Prior to this discovery, nothing more certain and more settled could be imagined in the field of chemistry than our knowledge of water (H_2O) and of the chemical elements of which it is composed. Water was even used for the 'operational' definition of the gramme, the unit standard of mass of the 'absolute' metric system; it thus formed one of the basic units of experimental physical measurements. This illustrates the fact that our knowledge of water was believed to be so well established that it could be used as the firm basis of all other physical measurements. But after the discovery of heavy water, it was realized that what had been believed to be a chemically pure compound was actually a mixture of chemically indistinguishable but physically very different compounds, with very different densities, boiling points, and freezing points—though for the definitions of all these points, 'water' had been used as a standard base.

This historical incident is typical; and we may learn from it that we cannot foresee which parts of our scientific knowledge may come to grief one day. Thus the belief in scientific certainty and in the authority of science is just wishful thinking: *science is fallible, because science is human*.

But the fallibility of our knowledge—or the thesis that all knowledge is guesswork, though some consists of guesses which have been most severely tested—must not be cited in support of scepticism or relativism. From the fact that we can err, and that a criterion of truth which might save us from error does not exist, it does not follow that the choice between theories is arbitrary, or non-rational: that we cannot learn, or get nearer to the truth: that our knowledge cannot grow.

5. Fallibilism and the growth of knowledge

By 'fallibilism' I mean here the view, or the acceptance of the fact, that we may err, and that the quest for certainty (or even the quest for high probability) is a mistaken quest. But this does not imply that the quest for truth is mistaken. On the contrary, the idea of error implies that of truth as the standard of which we may fall short. It implies that, though we may seek for truth, and though we may even find truth (as I believe we do in very many cases), we can never be quite certain that we have found it. There is always a possibility of error; though in the case of some logical and mathematical proofs, this possibility may be considered slight.

But fallibilism need in no way give rise to any sceptical or relativist conclusions. This will become clear if we consider that all the *known* historical examples of human fallibility—including all the *known* examples of miscarriage of justice—are *examples of the advance of our knowledge*. Every discovery of a mistake constitutes a real advance in our knowledge. As Roger Martin du Gard says in *Jean Barois*, 'it is something if we know where truth is not to be found'.

For example, although the discovery of heavy water showed that we were badly mistaken, this was not only an advance in our knowledge, but it was in its turn connected with other advances, and it produced many further advances. *Thus we can learn from our mistakes*.

This fundamental insight is, indeed, the basis of all epistemology and methodology; for it gives us a hint how to learn more systematically, how to advance more quickly (not necessarily in the interests of technology: for each individual seeker after truth, the problem of how to hasten one's advance is most urgent). This hint, very simply, is that *we must search for our mistakes*—or in other words, that *we must try to criticize our theories*.

Criticism, it seems, is the only way we have of detecting our mistakes, and of learning from them in a systematic way.

6. Getting nearer to the truth

In all this, the idea of the growth of knowledge—of getting nearer to the truth—is decisive. Intuitively, this idea is as clear as the idea of truth itself. A statement is true if it corresponds to the facts. It is nearer to the truth than another statement if it corresponds to the facts more closely than the other statement.

But though this idea is intuitively clear enough, and its legitimacy is hardly questioned by ordinary people or by scientists, it has, like the idea of truth, been attacked as illegitimate by some philosophers (for example quite recently by W. V. Quine[4]). It may therefore be mentioned here that, combining two analyses of Tarski, I have recently been able to give a 'definition' of the idea of approaching truth in the purely logical terms of Tarski's theory. (I simply combined the ideas of truth and of content, obtaining the idea of the truth-content of a statement *a*, i.e. the class of all true statements following from *a*, and its falsity content, which can be defined, roughly, as its content minus its truth content. We can then say that a statement *a* gets nearer to the truth than a statement *b* if and only if its truth content has increased without an increase in its falsity content; see chapter 10 of my *Conjectures and Refutations*.) There is therefore no reason whatever to be sceptical about the notion of getting nearer to the truth, or of the advancement of knowledge. And though we may always err, we have in many cases (especially in cases of crucial tests deciding between two theories) a fair idea of whether or not we have in fact got nearer to the truth.

It should be very clearly understood that the idea of one statement *a* getting nearer to the truth than another statement *b* in no way interferes with the idea that every statement is either true or false, and that there is no third possibility. It only takes account of the fact that there may be a lot of truth in a false statement. If I say 'It is half past three—too late to catch the

[4] See W. V. Quine, *Word and Object*, 1959, p. 23.

3.35' then my statement might be false because it was not too late for the 3.35 (since the 3.35 happened to be four minutes late). But there was still a lot of truth—of true information—in my statement; and though I might have added 'unless indeed the 3.35 is late (which it rarely is)', and thereby added to its truth-content, this additional remark might well have been taken as understood. (My statement might also have been false because it was only 3.28 not 3.30, when I made it. But even then there was a lot of truth in it.)

A theory like Kepler's which describes the track of the planets with remarkable accuracy may be said to contain a lot of true information, even though it is a false theory because deviations from Kepler's ellipses do occur. And Newton's theory (even though we may assume here that it is false) contains, for all we know, a staggering amount of true information—much more than Kepler's theory. Thus Newton's theory is a better approximation than Kepler's—it gets nearer to the truth. But this does not make it true: it can be nearer to the truth and it can, at the same time, be a false theory.

7. Absolutism

The idea of a philosophical absolutism is rightly repugnant to many people since it is, as a rule, combined with a dogmatic and authoritarian claim to possess the truth, or a criterion of truth.

But there is another form of absolutism—a fallibilistic absolutism—which indeed rejects all this: it merely asserts that our mistakes, at least, are absolute mistakes, in the sense that if a theory deviates from the truth, it is simply false, even if the mistake made was less glaring than that in another theory. Thus the notions of truth, and of falling short of the truth, can represent absolute standards for the fallibilist. This kind of absolutism is completely free from any taint of authoritarianism. And it is a great help in serious critical discussions. Of course, it can be criticized in its turn, in accordance with the principle that *nothing is exempt from criticism*. But at least at the moment it seems to me unlikely that criticism of the (logical) theory of truth and the theory of getting nearer to the truth will succeed.

8. Sources of knowledge

The principle that *everything is open to criticism* (from which this principle itself is not exempt) leads to a simple solution of the problem of the sources of knowledge, as I have tried to show elsewhere (see the Introduction to my *Conjectures and Refutations*). It is this: every 'source'—tradition, reason, imagination, observation, or what not—is admissible and may be used, *but none has any authority*.

This denial of authority to the sources of knowledge attributes to them a role very different from that which they were supposed to play in past and present epistemologies. But it is part of our critical and fallibilist approach: every source is welcome, but no statement is immune from criticism, whatever its 'source' may be. Tradition, more especially, which both the intellectualists (Descartes) and the empiricists (Bacon) tended to reject, can be admitted by us as one of the most important 'sources', since almost all that we learn (from our elders, in school, from books) stems from it. I therefore hold that anti-traditionalism must be rejected as futile. Yet traditionalism—which stresses the authority of traditions—must be rejected too; not as futile, but as mistaken—just as mistaken as any other epistemology which accepts some source of knowledge (intellectual intuition, say, or sense intuition) as an authority, or a guarantee, or a criterion, of truth.

9. Is a critical method possible?

But if we really reject any claim to authority, of any particular source of knowledge, how can we then criticize any theory? Does not all criticism proceed from some assumptions? *Does not the validity of any criticism, therefore, depend upon the truth of these assumptions?* And what is the good of criticizing a theory if the criticism should turn out to be invalid? Yet in order to show that it is valid, must we not establish, or justify, its assumptions? And is not the establishment or the justification of any assumption just the thing which everybody attempts (though often in vain) and which I here declare to be impossible? But if it is impossible, is not then (valid) criticism impossible too?

I believe that it is this series of questions or objections which has largely barred the way to a (tentative) acceptance of the point of view here advocated: as these questions show, one may easily be led to believe that the critical method is, logically considered, in the same boat with all other methods: since it cannot work without making assumptions, it would have to establish or justify those assumptions; yet the whole point of our argument was that we cannot establish or justify anything as certain, or even as probable, but have to content ourselves with theories which withstand criticism.

Obviously, these objections are very serious. They bring out the importance of our principle that nothing is exempt from criticism, or should be held to be exempt from criticism—not even this principle of the critical method itself.

Thus these objections constitute an interesting and important criticism of my position. But this criticism can in its turn be criticized; and it can be refuted.

First of all, even if we were to admit that all criticism starts from certain assumptions, this would not necessarily mean that, for it to be valid criticism, these assumptions must be established and justified. For the assumptions may, for example, be part of the theory against which the criticism is directed. (In this case we speak of 'immanent criticism'.) Or they may be assumptions which would be generally found acceptable, even though they do not form part of the theory criticized. In this case the criticism would amount to pointing out that the theory criticized contradicts (unknown to its defenders) some generally accepted views. This kind of criticism may be very valuable even when it is unsuccessful; for it may lead the defenders of the criticized theory to question those generally accepted views, and this may lead to important discoveries. (An interesting example is the history of Dirac's theory of anti-particles.)

Or they may be assumptions which are of the nature of a competing theory (in which case the criticism may be called 'transcendent criticism', in contradistinction to 'immanent criticism'): the assumptions may be, for example, hypotheses, or guesses, which can be independently criticized and tested. In this case the criticism offered would amount to a challenge to carry out certain crucial tests in order to decide between two competing theories.

These examples show that the important objections raised here against my theory of criticism are based upon the untenable dogma that criticism, in order to be 'valid', must proceed from assumptions which are established or justified.

Moreover, criticism may be important, enlightening, and even fruitful, without being valid: the arguments used in order to reject some invalid criticism may throw a lot of new light upon a theory, and can be used as a (tentative) argument in its favour; and of a theory which can thus defend itself against criticism we may well say that it is supported by critical arguments.

Quite generally, we may say that valid criticism of a theory consists in pointing out that a theory does not succeed in solving the *problems* which it was supposed to solve; and if we look at criticism in this light then it certainly need not be dependent on any particular set of assumptions (that is, it can be 'immanent'), even though it may well be that some assumptions which were foreign to the theory under discussion (that is, some 'transcendent' assumptions) inspired it to start with.

10. Decisions

From the point of view here developed, theories are not, in general, capable of being established or justified; and although they may be supported by critical arguments, this support is never conclusive. Accordingly, we shall frequently have to make up our minds whether or not these critical arguments are strong enough to justify the *tentative* acceptance of the theory—or in other words, whether the theory seems preferable, in the light of the critical discussion, to the competing theories.

In this sense, *decisions* enter into the critical method. But it is always a tentative decision, and a decision subject to criticism.

As such it should be contrasted with what has been called 'decision' or 'leap in the dark' by some irrationalist or anti-rationalist or existentialist philosophers. These philosophers, probably under the impact of the argument (rejected in the preceding section) of the impossibility of criticism without presuppositions, developed the theory that all our tenets must be based on some fundamental decision—on some leap in the dark. It must be a decision, a leap, which we take with closed eyes, as it were; for as we cannot 'know' without assumptions, without already having taken up a fundamental position, this fundamental position cannot be taken up on the basis of knowledge. It is, rather, a choice—but a kind of fateful and almost irrevocable choice, one which we take blindly, or by instinct, or by chance, or by the grace of God.

Our rejection of the objections presented in the preceding section shows that the irrationalist view of decisions is an exaggeration as well as an overdramatization. Admittedly, we must decide. But unless we decide against listening to argument and reason, against learning from our mistakes, and against listening to others who may have objections to our views, our decisions need not be final; not even the decision to consider criticism. (It is only in its decision *not* to take an irrevocable leap into the darkness of irrationality that rationalism may be said not to be self-contained, in the sense of chapter 24.)

I believe that the critical theory of knowledge here sketched throws some light upon the great problems of all theories of knowledge: how it is that we know so much and so little; and how it is that we can lift ourselves slowly out of the swamp of ignorance—by our own bootstraps, as it were. We do so by working with guesses, and by improving upon our guesses, through criticism.

11. Social and political problems

The theory of knowledge sketched in the preceding sections of this *addendum* seems to me to have important consequences for the evaluation of the social situation of our time, a situation influenced to a large extent by the decline of authoritarian religion. This decline has led to a widespread relativism and nihilism: to the decline of all beliefs, even the belief in human reason, and thus in ourselves.

But the argument here developed shows that there are no grounds whatever for drawing such desperate conclusions. The relativistic and the nihilistic (and even the 'existentialistic') arguments are all based on faulty reasoning. In this they show, incidentally, that these philosophies actually do accept reason, but are unable to use it properly; in their own terminology we might say that they fail to understand 'the human situation', and especially man's ability to grow, intellectually and morally.

As a striking illustration of this misunderstanding—of desperate consequences drawn from an insufficient understanding of the epistemological situation—I will quote a passage from one of Nietzsche's *Tracts Against the Times* (from section 3 of his essay on Schopenhauer).

> This was the first danger in whose shadow Schopenhauer grew up: isolation. The second was: despair of finding the truth. This latter danger is the constant companion of every thinker who sets out from Kant's philosophy; that is if he is a real man, a living human being, able to suffer and yearn, and not a mere rattling automaton, a mere thinking and calculating machine ... Though I am reading everywhere that [owing to Kant] ... a revolution has started in all fields of thought, I cannot believe that this is so as yet ... But should Kant one day begin to exert a more general influence, then we shall find that this will take the form of a creeping and destructive scepticism and relativism; and only the most active and the most noble of minds ... will instead experience that deep emotional shock, and that despair of truth, which was felt for example by Heinrich von Kleist ... 'Recently', he wrote, in his moving way, 'I have become acquainted with the philosophy of Kant; and I must tell you of a thought of which I need not be afraid that it will shake you as deeply and as painfully as it shook me:—It is impossible for us to decide whether that to which we appeal as truth is in truth the truth, or whether it merely seems to us so. If it is the latter, then all that truth to which we may attain here will be as nothing after our death, and all our efforts to produce and acquire something that might survive us must be in vain.—If the sharp point of this thought does not pierce your heart, do not smile at one who feels wounded by it in the holiest depth of his soul. My highest, my only aim has fallen to the ground, and I have none left.'

I agree with Nietzsche that Kleist's words are moving; and I agree that Kleist's reading of Kant's doctrine that it is impossible to attain any knowledge of things in themselves is straightforward enough, even though it conflicts with Kant's own intentions; for Kant believed in the possibility of science, and of finding the truth. (It was only the need to explain the paradox of the existence of an *a priori* science of nature which led him to adopt that subjectivism which Kleist rightly found shocking.) Moreover, Kleist's despair is at least partly the result of disappointment—of seeing the downfall of an over-optimistic belief in a simple criterion of truth (such as self-evidence). Yet whatever may be the history of this philosophic despair, it is not called for. Though truth is not self-revealing (as Cartesians and Baconians thought), though certainty may be unattainable, the human situation with respect to knowledge is far from desperate. On the contrary, it is exhilarating: here we are, with the immensely difficult task before us of getting to know the beautiful world we live in, and ourselves; and fallible though we are we nevertheless find that our powers of understanding, surprisingly, are almost adequate for the task—more so than we ever dreamt in our wildest dreams. We really do learn from our mistakes, by trial and error. And at the same time we learn how little we know—as when, in climbing a mountain; every step upwards opens some new vista into the unknown, and new worlds unfold themselves of whose existence we knew nothing when we began our climb.

Thus we can *learn*, we can *grow* in knowledge, even if we can never *know*—that is, know for certain. Since we can learn, there is no reason for despair of reason; and since we can never know, there are no grounds here for smugness, or for conceit over the growth of our knowledge.

It may be said that this new way of knowing is too abstract and too sophisticated to replace the loss of authoritarian religion. This may be true. But we must not underrate the power of the intellect and the intellectuals. It was the intellectuals—the 'second-hand dealers in ideas', as F. A. Hayek calls them—who spread relativism, nihilism, and intellectual despair. There is no reason why some intellectuals—some more enlightened intellectuals—should not eventually succeed in spreading the good news that the nihilist ado was indeed about nothing.

12. Dualism of facts and standards

In the body of this book I spoke about the *dualism of facts and decisions*, and I pointed out, following L. J. Russell (see note 5 (3) to chapter 5, vol. i, p. 234), that this dualism may be described as one of propositions and proposals. The latter terminology has the advantage of reminding us that both propositions, which state facts, and proposals, which propose policies, including principles or standards of policy, are open to rational discussion. Moreover, a decision—one, say, concerning the adoption of a principle of conduct—reached after the discussion of a proposal, may well be tentative, and it may be in many respects very similar to a decision to adopt (also tentatively), as the best available hypothesis, a proposition which states a fact.

There is, however, an important difference here. For the proposal to adopt a policy or a standard, its discussion, and the decision to adopt it, may be said to *create* this policy or this standard. On the other hand, the proposal of a hypothesis, its discussion, and the decision to adopt it—or to accept a proposition—does not, in the same sense, create a fact. This, I suppose, was the reason why I thought that the term 'decision' would be able to express the contrast between the acceptance of policies or standards, and the acceptance of facts. Yet there is no doubt that it would have been clearer had I spoken of a *dualism of facts and policies*, or of a *dualism of facts and standards*, rather than of a dualism of facts and decisions.

Terminology apart, the important thing is the irreducible dualism itself: whatever the facts may be, and whatever the standards may be (for example, the principles of our policies), the first thing is to distinguish the two, and to see clearly why standards cannot be reduced to facts.

13. Proposals and propositions

There is, then, a decisive asymmetry between standards and facts: through the decision to accept a proposal (at least tentatively) we create the corresponding standard (at least tentatively); yet through the decision to accept a proposition we do *not* create the corresponding fact.

Another asymmetry is that standards always *pertain to* facts, and that facts are *evaluated by* standards; these are relations which cannot be simply turned round.

Whenever we are faced with a fact—and more especially, with a fact which we may be able to change—we can ask whether or not it complies with certain standards. It is important to realize that this is very far from being the same as asking whether we like it; for although we may often adopt standards which correspond to our likes or dislikes, and although our likes and dislikes may play an important role in inducing us to adopt or reject some proposed standard, there will as a rule be many other possible standards which we have not adopted; and it will be possible to judge, or evaluate, the facts by any of them. This shows that the relationship of evaluation (of some questionable fact by some adopted or rejected standard) is, logically considered, totally different from a person's psychological relation (which is not a standard but a fact), of like or dislike, to the fact in question, or to the standard in question. Moreover, our likes and dislikes are facts which can be evaluated like any other facts.

Similarly, the fact that a certain standard has been adopted or rejected by some person or by some society must, as a fact, be distinguished from *any* standard, including the adopted or rejected standard. And since it is a fact (and an alterable fact) it may be judged or evaluated by some (other) standards.

These are a few reasons why standards and facts, and therefore proposals and propositions, should be clearly and decisively distinguished. Yet once they have been distinguished, we may look not only at the dissimilarities of facts and standards but also at their similarities.

First, both proposals and propositions are alike in that we can discuss them, criticize them, and come to some decision about them. Secondly, there is some kind of regulative idea about both. In the realm of facts it is the idea of correspondence between a statement or a proposition and a fact; that is to say, the idea of truth. In the realm of standards, or of proposals, the regulative idea may be described in many ways, and called by many terms, for example, by the terms 'right' or 'good'. We may say of a proposal that it is right (or wrong) or perhaps good (or bad); and by this we may mean, perhaps, that it corresponds (or does not correspond) to certain standards which we have decided to adopt. But we may also say of a standard that it is right or wrong, or good or bad, or valid or invalid, or high or low; and by this we may mean, perhaps, that the corresponding proposal should or should not be accepted. It must therefore be admitted that the logical situation of the regulative ideas, of 'right', say, or 'good', is far less clear than that of the idea of correspondence to the facts.

As pointed out in the book, this difficulty is a logical one and cannot be got over by the introduction of a religious system of standards. The fact that God, or any other authority, commands me to do a certain thing is no guarantee that the command is right. It is I who must decide whether to accept the standards of any authority as (morally) good or bad. God is good only if His commandments are good; it would be a grave mistake—in fact an immoral adoption of authoritarianism—to say that His commandments are good simply because they are His, unless we have first decided (at our own risk) that He can only demand good or right things of us.

This is Kant's idea of autonomy, as opposed to heteronomy.

Thus no appeal to authority, not even to religious authority, can get us out of the difficulty that the regulative idea of absolute 'rightness' or 'goodness' differs in its logical status from that of absolute truth; and we have to admit the difference. This difference is responsible for the fact, alluded to above, that in a sense we *create* our standards by proposing, discussing, and adopting them.

All this must be admitted; nevertheless we may take the idea of absolute truth—of correspondence to the facts—as a kind of model for the realm of standards, in order to make it clear to ourselves that, just as we may *seek* for absolutely true propositions in the realm of facts or at least for propositions which come nearer to the truth, so we may *seek* for absolutely right or valid proposals in the realm of standards—or at least for better, or more valid, proposals.

However, it would be a mistake, in my opinion, to extend this attitude beyond the *seeking* to the *finding*. For though we should seek for absolutely right or valid proposals, we should never persuade ourselves that we have definitely found them; for clearly, there cannot be a *criterion of absolute rightness*—even less than a criterion of absolute truth. The maximization of happiness *may* have been intended as a criterion. On the other hand I certainly never recommended that we adopt the minimization of misery as a criterion, though I think that it is an improvement on some of the ideas of utilitarianism. I also suggested that the reduction of avoidable misery belongs to the agenda of public policy (which does not mean that any question of public policy is to be decided by a calculus of minimizing misery) while the maximization of one's happiness should be left to one's private endeavour. (I quite agree with those critics of mine who have shown that if used as a *criterion*, the minimum misery principle would have absurd consequences; and I expect that the same may be said about any other moral criterion.)

But although we have no criterion of absolute rightness, we certainly can make progress in this realm. As in the realm of facts, we can make discoveries. That cruelty is always 'bad'; that it should always be avoided where possible; that the golden rule is a good standard which can perhaps even be improved by doing unto others, wherever possible, as *they* want to be done by: these are elementary and extremely important examples of discoveries in the realm of standards.

These discoveries create standards, we might say, out of nothing: as in the field of factual discovery, we have to lift ourselves by our own bootstraps. This is the incredible fact: that we can learn; by our mistakes, and by criticism; and that we can learn in the realm of standards just as well as in the realm of facts.

14. Two wrongs do not make two rights

Once we have accepted the absolute theory of truth it is possible to answer an old and serious yet deceptive argument in favour of relativism, of both the intellectual and the evaluative kind, by making use of the analogy between true facts and valid standards. The deceptive argument I have in mind appeals to the discovery that other people have ideas and beliefs which differ widely from ours. Who are we to insist that ours are the right ones? Already Xenophanes sang, 2500 years ago (Diels-Kranz, B, 16, 15):

> The Ethiops say that their gods are flat-nosed and black,
> While the Thracians say that theirs have blue eyes and red hair.
> Yet if cattle or horses or lions had hands and could draw,
> And could sculpture like men, then the horses would draw their gods
> Like horses, and cattle like cattle; and each they would shape
> Bodies of gods in the likeness, each kind, of their own.

So each of us sees his gods, and his world, from his own point of view, according to his tradition and his upbringing; and none of us is exempt from this subjective bias.

This argument has been developed in various ways; and it has been argued that our race, or our nationality, or our historical background, or our historical period, or our class interest, or our social habitat, or our language, or our personal background knowledge, is an insurmountable, or an almost insurmountable, barrier to objectivity.

The facts on which this argument is based must be admitted; and indeed, we can never rid ourselves of bias. There is, however, no need to accept the argument itself, or its relativistic conclusions. For first of all, we can, in stages, get rid of some of this bias, by means of critical thinking and especially of listening to criticism. For example, Xenophanes doubtless was helped, by his own discovery, to see things in a less biased way. Secondly, it is a fact that people with the most divergent cultural backgrounds can enter into fruitful discussion, provided they are interested in getting nearer to the truth, and are ready to listen to each other, and to learn from each other. This shows that, though there are cultural and linguistic barriers, they are not insurmountable.

Thus it is of the utmost importance to profit from Xenophanes' discovery in every field; to give up cocksureness, and become open to criticism. Yet it is also of the greatest importance not to mistake this discovery, this step towards criticism, for a step towards relativism. If two parties disagree, this may mean that one is wrong, or the other, or both: this is the view of the criticist. It does not mean, as the relativist will have it, that both may be equally right. They may be equally wrong, no doubt, though they need not be. But anybody who says that to be equally wrong means to be equally right is merely playing with words, or with metaphors.

It is a great step forward to learn to be self-critical; to learn to think that the other fellow may be right—more right than we ourselves. But there is a great danger involved in this: we may think that both, the other fellow and we ourselves, may be right. But this attitude, modest and self-critical as it may appear to us, is neither as modest nor as self-critical as we may be inclined to think; for it is more likely that both, we ourselves and the other fellow, are wrong. Thus self-criticism should not be an excuse for laziness and for the adoption of relativism. And as two wrongs do not make a right, two wrong parties to a dispute do not make two right parties.

15. 'Experience' and 'intuition' as sources of knowledge

The fact that we can learn from our mistakes, and through criticism, in the realm of standards as well as in the realm of facts, is of fundamental importance. But is the appeal to criticism sufficient? Do we not have to appeal to the authority of experience or (especially in the realm of standards) of intuition?

In the realm of facts, we do not merely criticize our theories, we criticize them by an appeal to experimental and observational *experience*. It is a serious mistake, however, to believe that we can appeal to anything like an *authority* of experience, though philosophers, particularly empiricist philosophers, have depicted sense perception, and especially sight, as a source of knowledge which furnishes us with definite 'data' out of which our experience is composed. I believe that this picture is totally mistaken. For even our experimental and observational experience does not consist of 'data'. Rather, it consists of a web of guesses—of conjectures, expectations, hypotheses, with which there are interwoven accepted, traditional, scientific, and unscientific, lore and prejudice. There simply is no such thing as *pure* experimental and observational experience—experience untainted by expectation and theory. There are no pure 'data', no empirically given 'sources of knowledge' to which we can appeal, in our criticism. 'Experience', whether ordinary or scientific experience, is much more like what Oscar Wilde had in mind in *Lady Windermere's Fan*, Act iii:

Dumby:	Experience is the name everyone gives to their mistakes.
Cecil Graham:	One shouldn't commit any.
Dumby:	Life would be very dull without them.

Learning from our mistakes—without which life would indeed be dull—is also the meaning of 'experience' which is implied in Dr. Johnson's famous joke about 'the triumph of hope over experience'; or in C. C. King's remark (in his *Story of the British Army*, 1897, p. 112): 'But the British leaders were to learn … in the "only school fools learn in, that of experience".'

It seems, then, that at least some of the ordinary uses of 'experience' agree much more closely with what I believe to be the character of both 'scientific experience' and 'ordinary empirical knowledge' than with the traditional analyses of the philosophers of the empiricist schools. And all this seems to agree also with the original meaning of '*empeiria*' (from '*peiraō*'—to try, to test, to examine) and thus of '*experientia*' and '*experimentum*'. Yet it must not be held to constitute an argument; neither one from ordinary usage nor one from origin. It is intended only to illustrate my logical analysis of the structure of experience. According to this analysis, experience, and more especially scientific experience, is the result of usually mistaken guesses, of testing them, and of learning from our mistakes. Experience (in this sense) is not a 'source of knowledge'; nor does it carry any authority.

Thus criticism which appeals to experience is not of an authoritative character. It does not consist in contrasting dubious results with established ones, or with 'the evidence of our senses' (or with 'the given'). It consists, rather, in comparing some dubious results with others, often equally dubious, which may, however, be taken as unproblematic for the moment, although they may at any time be challenged as new doubts arise, or else because of some inkling or conjecture; an inkling or a conjecture, for example, that a certain experiment may lead to a new discovery.

Now the situation in acquiring knowledge about standards seems to me altogether analogous.

Here, too, philosophers have looked for the authoritative *sources* of this knowledge, and they found, in the main, two: feelings of pleasure and pain, or a moral sense or a moral intuition for what is right or wrong (analogous to perception in the epistemology of factual knowledge), or, alternatively, a source called 'practical reason' (analogous to 'pure reason', or to a faculty of 'intellectual intuition', in the epistemology of factual knowledge). And quarrels continually raged over the question whether all, or only some, of these authoritative sources of moral knowledge existed.

I think that this problem is a pseudo-problem. The main point is not the question of the 'existence' of any of these faculties—a very vague and dubious psychological question—but whether these may be authoritative 'sources of knowledge' providing us with 'data' or other definite starting-points for our constructions or, at least, with a definite frame of reference for our criticism. I deny that we have any authoritative sources of this kind, either in the epistemology of factual knowledge or in the epistemology of the knowledge of standards. And I deny that we need any such definite frame of reference for our criticism.

How do we learn about standards? How, in this realm, do we learn from our mistakes? First we learn to imitate others (incidentally, we do so by trial and error), and so learn to look upon standards of behaviour as if they consisted of fixed, 'given' rules. Later we find (also by trial and error) that we are making mistakes—for example, that we may hurt people. We may thus learn the golden rule; but soon we find that we may misjudge a man's attitude, his background knowledge, his aims, his standards; and we may learn from our mistakes to take care even beyond the golden rule.

Admittedly, such things as sympathy and imagination may play an important rôle in this development; but they are not authoritative sources of knowledge—no more than any of our sources in the realm of the knowledge of facts. And though something like an intuition of what is right and what is wrong may also play an important rôle in this development, it is, again, not an authoritative source of knowledge. For we may see to-day very clearly that we are right, and yet learn to-morrow that we made a mistake.

'Intuitionism' is the name of a philosophical school which teaches that we have some faculty or capacity of intellectual intuition allowing us to 'see' the truth; so that what we have seen to be true must indeed be true. It is thus a theory of some authoritative source of knowledge. Anti-intuitionists have usually denied the existence of this source of knowledge while asserting, as a rule, the existence of some other source such as sense-perception. My view is that both parties are mistaken, for two reasons. First, I assert that there exists something like an intellectual intuition which makes us feel, most convincingly, that we see the truth (a point denied by the opponents of intuitionism). Secondly, I assert that this intellectual intuition, though in a way indispensable, often leads us astray in the most dangerous manner. Thus we do not, in general, see the truth when we are most convinced that we see it; and we have to learn, through mistakes, to distrust these intuitions.

What, then, are we to trust? What are we to accept? The answer is: whatever we accept we should trust only tentatively, always remembering that we are in possession, at best, of partial truth (or rightness), and that we are bound to make at least some mistake or misjudgement somewhere—not only with respect to facts but also with respect to the adopted standards; secondly, we should trust (even tentatively) our intuition only if it has been arrived at as the result of many attempts to use our imagination; of many mistakes, of many tests, of many doubts, and of searching criticism.

It will be seen that this form of anti-intuitionism (or some may say, perhaps, of intuitionism) is radically different from the older forms of anti-intuitionism. And it will be seen that there is one essential ingredient in this theory: the idea that we may fall short—perhaps always—of some standard of absolute truth, or of absolute rightness, in our opinions as well as in our actions.

It may be objected to all this that, whether or not my views on the nature of ethical knowledge and ethical experience are acceptable, they are still 'relativist' or 'subjectivist'. For they do not *establish* any absolute moral standards: at best they show that the idea of an absolute standard is a regulative idea, of use to those who are already converted—who are already eager to learn about, and search for, true or valid or good moral standards. My reply is that even the 'establishment'—say, by means of pure logic—of an absolute standard, or a system of ethical norms, would make no difference in this respect. For assuming we have succeeded in logically proving the validity of an absolute standard, or a system of ethical norms, so that we could logically prove to somebody how he ought to act: even then he might take no notice; or else he might reply: 'I am not in the least interested in your "ought", or in your moral rules—no more so than in your logical proofs, or, say, in your higher mathematics.' Thus even a logical proof cannot alter the fundamental situation that only he who is prepared to take these things seriously and to learn about them will be impressed by ethical (or any other) arguments. You cannot force anybody by arguments to take arguments seriously, or to respect his own reason.

16. The dualism of facts and standards and the idea of liberalism

The dualism of facts and standards is, I contend, one of the bases of the liberal tradition. For an essential part of this tradition is the recognition of the injustice that does exist in this world, and the resolve to try to help those who are its victims. This means that there is, or that there may be, a conflict, or at least a gap, between facts and standards: facts may fall short of right (or valid or true) standards—especially those social or political facts which consist in the actual acceptance and enforcement of some code of justice.

To put it in another way, liberalism is based upon the dualism of facts and standards in the sense that it believes in searching for ever better standards, especially in the field of politics and of legislation.

But this dualism of facts and standards has been rejected by some relativists who have opposed it with arguments like the following:

(1) The acceptance of a proposal—and thus of a standard—is a social or political or historical fact.

(2) If an accepted standard is judged by another, not yet accepted standard, and found wanting, then this judgement (whoever may have made it) is also a social or political or historical fact.

(3) If a judgement of this kind becomes the basis of a social or political movement, then this is also a historical fact.

(4) If this movement is successful, and if in consequence the old standards are reformed or replaced by new standards, then this is also a historical fact.

(5) Thus—so argues the relativist or moral positivist—we never have to transcend the realm of facts, if only we include in it social or political or historical facts: there is no dualism of facts and standards.

I consider this conclusion (5) *to be mistaken*. It does not follow from the premises (1) to (4) whose truth I admit. The reason for rejecting (5) is very simple: we can always ask whether a development as here described—a social movement based upon the acceptance of a programme for the reform of certain standards—was 'good' or 'bad'. In raising this question, we re-open the gulf between standards and facts which the monistic argument (1) to (5) attempts to close.

From what I have just said, it may be rightly inferred that the monistic position—*the philosophy of the identity of facts and standards*—is dangerous; for even where it does not identify standards with existing facts—even where it does not identify present might and right—it leads necessarily to the identification of future might and right. Since the question whether a certain movement for reform is right or wrong (or good or bad) cannot be raised, according to the monist, except in terms of another movement with opposite tendencies, nothing can be asked except the question which of these opposite movements succeeded, in the end, in establishing its standards as a matter of social or political or historical fact.

In other words, the philosophy here described—the attempt to 'transcend' the dualism of facts and standards and to erect a monistic system, a world of facts only—leads to *the identification of standards either with established might or with future might*: it leads to a moral positivism, or to a moral historicism, as described and discussed in chapter 22 of this book.

17. Hegel again

My chapter on Hegel has been much criticized. Most of the criticism I cannot accept, because it fails to answer my main objections against Hegel—that his philosophy exemplifies, if compared with that of Kant (I still find it almost sacrilegious to put these two names side by side), a terrible decline in intellectual sincerity and intellectual honesty; that his philosophical arguments are not to be taken seriously; and that his philosophy was a major factor in bringing about the 'age of intellectual dishonesty', as Konrad Heiden called it, and in preparing for that contemporary *trahison des clercs* (I am alluding to Julien Benda's great book) which has helped to produce two world wars so far.

It should not be forgotten that I looked upon my book as my war effort: believing as I did in the responsibility of Hegel and the Hegelians for much of what happened in Germany, I felt that it was my task, as a philosopher, to show that this philosophy was a pseudo-philosophy.

The time at which the book was written may perhaps also explain my optimistic assumption (which I could attribute to Schopenhauer) that the stark realities of the war would show up the playthings of the intellectuals, such as relativism, as what they were, and that this verbal spook would disappear.

I certainly was too optimistic. Indeed, it seems that most of my critics took some form of relativism so much for granted that they were quite unable to believe that I was really in earnest in rejecting it.

I admit that I made some factual mistakes: Mr. H. N. Rodman, of Harvard University, has told me that I was mistaken in writing 'two years' in the third line from the bottom of p. 266, and that I ought to have written 'four years'. He also told me that there are, in his opinion, a number of more serious—if less clear-cut—historical errors in the chapter, and that some of my attributions of ulterior motives to Hegel are, in his opinion, historically unjustified.

Such things are very much to be regretted, although they have happened to better historians than I. But the question of real importance is this: do these mistakes affect my assessment of Hegel's philosophy, and of its disastrous influence?

My own answer to the question is: 'No.' It is his philosophy which has led me to look upon Hegel as I do, not his biography. In fact, I am still surprised that serious philosophers were offended by my admittedly partly playful attack upon a philosophy which I am still unable to take seriously. I tried to express this by the scherzo-style of my Hegel chapter, hoping to expose the ridiculous in this philosophy which I can only regard with a mixture of contempt and horror.

All this was clearly indicated in my book; also the fact that I neither could[5] nor wished to spend unlimited time upon deep researches into the history

[5] See my Introduction and my Preface to the Second Edition.

of a philosopher whose work I abhor. As it was, I wrote about Hegel in a manner which assumed that few would take him seriously. And although this manner was lost upon my Hegelian critics, who were decidedly not amused, I still hope that some of my readers got the joke.

But all this is comparatively unimportant. What may be important is the question whether my attitude towards Hegel's philosophy was justified. It is a contribution towards an answer to this question which I wish to make here.

I think most Hegelians will admit that one of the fundamental motives and intentions of Hegel's philosophy is precisely to replace and 'transcend' the dualistic view of facts and standards which had been presented by Kant, and which was the philosophical basis of the idea of liberalism and of social reform.

To transcend this dualism of facts and standards is the decisive aim of Hegel's *philosophy of identity*—the identity of the ideal and the real, of right and might. All standards are historical: they are *historical facts*, stages in the development of reason, which is the same as the development of the ideal and of the real. There is nothing but fact; and some of the social or historical facts are, at the same time, standards.

Now Hegel's argument was, fundamentally, the one I stated (and criticized) here in the preceding section—although Hegel presented it in a surpassingly vague, unclear, and specious form. Moreover, I contend that this identity philosophy (despite some 'progressivist' suggestions, and some mild expressions of sympathy with various 'progressive' movements which it contained) played a major role in the downfall of the liberal movement in Germany; a movement which, under the influence of Kant's philosophy, had produced such important liberal thinkers as Schiller and Wilhelm von Humboldt, and such important works as Humboldt's *Essay towards the Determination of the Limits of the Powers of the State*.

This is my first and fundamental accusation. My second accusation, closely connected with the first, is that Hegel's identity philosophy, by contributing to historicism and to an identification of might and right, encouraged totalitarian modes of thought.

My third accusation is that Hegel's argument (which admittedly required of him a certain degree of subtlety, though not more than a great philosopher might be expected to possess) was full of logical mistakes and of tricks, presented with pretentious impressiveness. This undermined and eventually lowered the traditional standards of intellectual responsibility and honesty. It also contributed to the rise of totalitarian philosophizing and, even more serious, to the lack of any determined intellectual resistance to it.

These are my principal objections to Hegel stated, I believe, fairly clearly in chapter 12. But I certainly did not analyse the fundamental issue—the philosophy of identity of facts and standards—quite as clearly as I ought to have done. So I hope I have made amends in this addendum—not to Hegel, but to those who may have been harmed by him.

18. Conclusion

In ending my book once again, I am as conscious as ever of its imperfections. In part, these imperfections are a consequence of its scope, which transcends what I should consider as my more professional interests. In part they are simply a consequence of my personal fallibility: it is not for nothing that I am a fallibilist.

But though I am very conscious of my personal fallibility, even as it affects what I am going to say now, I do believe that a fallibilist approach has much to offer to the social philosopher. By recognizing the essentially critical and therefore revolutionary character of all human thought—of the fact that we learn from our mistakes, rather than by the accumulation of data—and by recognizing on the other hand that almost all the problems as well as the (non-authoritative) sources of our thought are rooted in traditions, and that it is almost always traditions which we criticize, a critical (and progressive) fallibilism may provide us with a much-needed perspective for the evaluation of both, tradition and revolutionary thought. Even more important, it can show us that the role of thought is to carry out revolutions by means of critical debates rather than by means of violence and of warfare; that it is the great tradition of Western rationalism to fight our battles with words rather than with swords. This is why our Western civilization is an essentially pluralistic one, and why monolithic social ends would mean the death of freedom: of the freedom of thought, of the free search for truth, and with it, of the rationality and the dignity of man.

II

NOTE ON SCHWARZSCHILD'S BOOK ON MARX (1965)

Some years after I wrote this book, Leopold Schwarzschild's book on Marx, *The Red Prussian* (translated by Margaret Wing: London 1948) became known to me. There is no doubt in my mind that Schwarzschild looks at Marx with unsympathetic and even hostile eyes, and that he often paints him in the darkest possible colours. But even though the book may be not always fair, it contains documentary evidence, especially from the Marx–Engels correspondence, which shows that Marx was less of a humanitarian, and less of a lover of freedom, than he is made to appear in my book. Schwarzschild describes him as a man who saw in 'the proletariat' mainly an instrument for his own personal ambition. Though this may put the matter more harshly than the evidence warrants, it must be admitted that the evidence itself is shattering.

Notes

General Remarks. The text of the book is self-contained and may be read without these Notes. However, a considerable amount of material which is likely to interest all readers of the book will be found here, as well as some references and controversies which may not be of general interest. Readers who wish to consult the Notes for the sake of this material may find it convenient first to read without interruption through the text of a chapter, and then to turn to the Notes.

I wish to apologize for the perhaps excessive number of cross-references which have been included for the benefit of those readers who take a special interest in one or other of the side issues touched upon (such as Plato's preoccupation with racialism, or the Socratic Problem). Knowing that war conditions would make it impossible for me to read the proofs, I decided to refer not to pages but to note numbers. Accordingly, references to the text have been indicated by notes such as: 'cp. text to note 24 to chapter 3', etc. War conditions also restricted library facilities, making it impossible for me to obtain a number of books, some recent and some not, which would have been consulted in normal circumstances.

Notes which make use of material which was not available to me when writing the manuscript for the first edition of this book (and other notes which I wish to characterize as having been added to the book since 1943) are enclosed by asterisks; not all new additions to the notes have, however, been so marked.

NOTE TO INTRODUCTION

For Kant's motto, see note 41 to chapter 24, and text.

The terms '*open society*' and '*closed society*' were first used, to my knowledge, by Henri Bergson, in *Two Sources of Morality and Religion* (Engl. ed., 1935). In spite of a considerable difference (due to a fundamentally different approach to nearly every problem of philosophy) between Bergson's way of using these terms and mine, there is a certain similarity also, which I wish to acknowledge. (Cp. Bergson's characterization of the closed society, *op. cit.*, p. 229, as 'human society fresh from the hands of nature'.) The main difference, however, is this. My terms indicate, as it were, a *rationalist distinction*;

the closed society is characterized by the belief in magical taboos, while the open society is one in which men have learned to be to some extent critical of taboos, and to base decisions on the authority of their own intelligence (after discussion). Bergson, on the other hand, has a kind of *religious distinction* in mind. This explains why he can look upon his open society as the product of a mystical intuition, while I suggest (in chapters 10 and 24) that mysticism may be interpreted as an expression of the longing for the lost unity of the closed society, and therefore as a reaction against the rationalism of the open society. From the way my term 'The Open Society' is used in chapter 10, it may be seen that there is some resemblance to Graham Wallas' term 'The Great Society'; but my term may cover a 'small society' too, as it were, like that of Periclean Athens, while it is perhaps conceivable that a 'Great Society' may be arrested and thereby closed. There is also, perhaps, a similarity between my 'open society' and the term used by Walter Lippmann as the title of his most admirable book, *The Good Society* (1937). See also note 59 (2) to chapter 10 and notes 29, 32, and 58 to chapter 24, and text.

Notes to Volume I

NOTES TO CHAPTER ONE

For Pericles' motto, see note 31 to chapter 10, and text. Plato's motto is discussed in some detail in notes 33 and 34 to chapter 6, and text.

1. I use the term 'collectivism' only for a doctrine which emphasizes the significance of some collective or group, for instance, 'the state' (or a certain state; or a nation; or a class) as against that of the individual. The problem of collectivism versus individualism is explained more fully in chapter 6, below; see especially notes 26 to 28 to that chapter, and text.—Concerning 'tribalism', cp. chapter 10, and especially note 38 to that chapter (list of Pythagorean tribal taboos).
2. This means that the interpretation does not convey any empirical information, as shown in my *The Logic of Scientific Discovery*.
3. One of the features which the doctrines of the chosen people, the chosen race, and the chosen class have in common is that they originated, and became important, as reactions against some kind of oppression. The doctrine of the chosen people became important at the time of the foundation of the Jewish church, i.e. during the Babylonian captivity; Count Gobineau's theory of the Aryan master race was a reaction of the aristocratic emigrant to the claim that the French Revolution had successfully expelled the Teutonic masters. Marx's prophecy of the victory of the proletariat is his reply to one of the most sinister periods of oppression and exploitation in modern history. Compare with these matters chapter 10, especially note 39, and chapter 17, especially notes 13–15, and text.

* One of the briefest and best summaries of the historicist creed can be found in the radically historicist pamphlet which is quoted more fully at the end of note 12 to chapter 9, entitled *Christians in the Class Struggle*, by Gilbert Cope, Foreword by the Bishop of Bradford. ('Magnificat' Publication No. 1, Published by the Council of Clergy and Ministers for Common Ownership, 1942, 28, Maypole Lane, Birmingham 14.) Here we read, on pp. 5–6: 'Common to all these views is a certain quality of "inevitability plus freedom". Biological evolution, the class conflict succession, the

action of the Holy Spirit—all three are characterized by a definite motion towards an end. That motion may be hindered or deflected for a time by deliberate human action, but its gathering momentum cannot be dissipated, and though the final stage is but dimly apprehended, ...' it is 'possible to know enough about the process to help forward or to delay the inevitable flow. In other words, the natural laws of what we observe to be "progress" are sufficiently ... understood by men so that they can ... either ... make efforts to arrest or divert the main stream—efforts which may seem to be successful for a time, but which are in fact foredoomed to failure.'*

4. Hegel said that, in his Logic, he had preserved the whole of Heraclitus' teaching. He also said that he owed everything to Plato. *It may be worth mentioning that Ferdinand von Lassalle, one of the founders of the German social democratic movement (and, like Marx, a Hegelian), wrote two volumes on Heraclitus.*

NOTES TO CHAPTER TWO

1. The question 'What is the world made of?' is more or less generally accepted as the fundamental problem of the early Ionian philosophers. If we assume that they viewed the world as an edifice, the question of the ground-plan of the world would be complementary to that of its building material. And indeed, we hear that Thales was not only interested in the stuff the world is made of, but also in descriptive astronomy and geography, and that Anaximander was the first to draw up a ground-plan, i.e. a map of the earth. Some further remarks on the Ionian school (and especially on Anaximander as predecessor of Heraclitus) will be found in chapter 10; cp. notes 38–40 to that chapter, especially note 39.

* According to R. Eisler, *Weltenmantel und Himmelszelt*, p. 693, Homer's feeling of destiny ('moira') can be traced back to oriental astral mysticism which deifies time, space, and fate. According to the same author (*Revue de Synthèse Historique*, 41, app., p. 16 f.), Hesiod's father was a native of Asia Minor, and the sources of his idea of the Golden Age, and the metals in man, are oriental. (Cp. on this question Eisler's forthcoming posthumous study of Plato, Oxford 1950.) Eisler also shows (*Jesus Basileus*, vol. II, 618 f.) that the idea of the world as a totality of things ('cosmos') goes back to Babylonian political theory. The idea of the world as an edifice (a house or tent) is treated in his *Weltenmantel*.*

2. See Diels, *Die Vorsokratiker*, 5th edition, 1934 (abbreviated here as 'D5'), fragment 124; cp. also D5, vol. II, p. 423, lines 21 f. (The interpolated negation seems to me methodologically as unsound as the attempt of certain authors to discredit the fragment altogether; apart from this, I follow Rüstow's emendation.) For the two other quotations in this paragraph, see Plato, *Cratylus*, 401d, 402a/b.

   My interpretation of the teaching of Heraclitus is perhaps different from that commonly assumed at present, for instance from that of Burnet. Those who may feel doubtful whether it is at all tenable are referred to my notes, especially the present note and notes 6, 7, and 11, in which I am dealing with Heraclitus' natural philosophy, having confined my text to a presentation of the historicist aspect of Heraclitus' teaching and to his social philosophy. I further refer them to the evidence of chapters 4 to 9, and especially of chapter 10, in whose light Heraclitus' philosophy, as I see it, appears as a somewhat typical reaction to the social revolution which he witnessed. Cp. also the notes 39 and 59 to that chapter (and text), and the general criticism of Burnet's and Taylor's methods in note 56.

As indicated in the text, I hold (with many others, for instance, with Zeller and Grote) that the doctrine of universal flux is the central doctrine of Heraclitus. As opposed to this, Burnet holds that this 'is hardly the central point in the system' of Heraclitus (cp. *Early Greek Philosophy*, 2nd ed., 163). But a close inspection of his arguments (158 f.) leaves me quite unconvinced that Heraclitus' fundamental discovery was the abstract metaphysical doctrine 'that wisdom is not the knowledge of many things, but the perception of the underlying unity of warring opposites', as Burnet puts it. The unity of opposites is certainly an important part of Heraclitus' teaching, but it can be derived (as far as such things can be derived; cp. note 11 to this chapter, and the corresponding text) from the more concrete and intuitively understandable theory of flux; and the same can be said of Heraclitus' doctrine of the fire (cp. note 7 to this chapter).

Those who suggest, with Burnet, that the doctrine of universal flux was not new, but anticipated by the earlier Ionians, are, I feel, unconscious witnesses to Heraclitus' originality; for they fail now, after 2,400 years, to grasp his main point. They do not see the difference between a flux or circulation *within* a vessel or an edifice or a cosmic framework, i.e. *within a totality of things* (part of the Heraclitean theory can indeed be understood in this way, but only that part of it which is not very original; see below), and a universal flux which embraces everything, even the vessel, the framework itself (cp. Lucian in D5 I, p. 190) and which is described by Heraclitus' denial of the existence of any fixed thing whatever. (In a way, Anaximander had made a beginning by dissolving the framework, but there was still a long way from this to the theory of universal flux. Cp. also note 15 (4) to chapter 3.)

The doctrine of universal flux forces Heraclitus to attempt an explanation of the *apparent stability* of the things in this world, and of other typical regularities. This attempt leads him to the development of subsidiary theories, especially to his doctrine of fire (cp. note 7 to this chapter) and of natural laws (cp. note 6). It is in this explanation of the apparent stability of the world that he makes much use of the theories of his predecessors by developing their theory of rarefaction and condensation, together with their doctrine of the revolution of the heavens, into a general theory of the circulation of matter, and of periodicity. But this part of his teaching, I hold, is not central to it, but subsidiary. It is, so to speak, apologetic, for it attempts to reconcile the new and revolutionary doctrine of flux with common experience as well as with the teaching of his predecessors. I believe, therefore, that he is not a mechanical materialist who teaches something like the conservation and circulation of matter and of energy; this view seems to me to be excluded by his magical attitude towards laws as well as by his theory of the unity of opposites which emphasizes his mysticism.

My contention that the universal flux is the central theory of Heraclitus is, I believe, corroborated by Plato. The overwhelming majority of his explicit references to Heraclitus (*Crat.*, 401d, 402a/b, 411, 437ff., 440; *Theaet.*, 153c/d, 160d, 177c, 179d f., 182a ff., 183a ff., cp. also *Symp.*, 207d, *Phil.*, 43a; cp. also Aristotle's *Metaphysics*, 987a33, 1010a13, 1078b13) witness to the tremendous impression made by this central doctrine upon the thinkers of that period. These straightforward and clear testimonies are much stronger than the admittedly interesting passage which does not mention Heraclitus' name (*Soph.*, 242d f., quoted already, in connection with Heraclitus, by Ueberweg and Zeller), on which Burnet attempts to base his interpretation. (His other witness, Philo Judaeus, cannot count much as against the evidence of Plato and Aristotle.) But even this passage agrees completely with our interpretation. (With regard to Burnet's somewhat wavering judgement concerning the value of this passage, cp. note 56(7) to chapter 10.) Heraclitus' discovery that the world is not the totality of *things* but of events or *facts* is not at all trivial; this can be perhaps gauged by the fact that Wittgenstein has found it necessary to reaffirm it quite recently: 'The world is the totality of facts, *not of things*.' (Cp. *Tractatus Logico-Philosophicus*, 1921/22, sentence 1.1; italics mine.)

To sum up. I consider the doctrine of universal flux as fundamental, and as emerging from the realm of Heraclitus' social experiences. All other doctrines of his are in a way subsidiary to it. The doctrine of fire (cp. Aristotle's *Metaphysics*, 984a7, 1067a2; also 989a2, 996a9, 1001a15; *Physics*, 205a3) I consider to be his central doctrine in the field of natural philosophy; it is an attempt to reconcile the doctrine of flux with our experience of stable things, a link with the older theories of circulation, and it leads to a theory of laws. And the doctrine of the unity of opposites I consider as something less central and more abstract, as a forerunner of a kind of logical or methodological theory (as such it inspired Aristotle to formulate his law of contradiction), and as linked to his mysticism.

3. W. Nestle, *Die Vorsokratiker* (1905), 35.
4. In order to facilitate the identification of the fragments quoted, I give the numbers of Bywater's edition (adopted, in his English translation of the fragments, by Burnet, *Early Greek Philosophy*), and also the numbers of Diels' 5th edition.

   Of the eight passages quoted in the present paragraph, (1) and (2) are from the fragments B 114 (= Bywater, and Burnet), D5 121 (= Diels, 5th edition). The others are from the fragments: (3) B 111, D5 29; cp. Plato's *Republic*, 586a/b ... (4): B 111, D5 104 ... (5): B 112, D5 39 (cp. D5, vol. I, p. 65, Bias, 1) ... (6): B 5, D5 17 ... (7): B 110, D5 33 ... (8): B 100, D5 44.
5. The three passages quoted in this paragraph are from the fragments: (1) and (2): cp. B 41, D5 91; for (1) cp. also note 2 to this chapter; (3): D5 74.
6. The two passages are B 21, D5 31; and B 22, D5 90.
7. For Heraclitus' 'measures' (or laws, or periods), see B 20, 21, 23, 29; D5 30, 31, 94. (D 31 brings 'measure' and 'law' (*logos*) together.)

   The five passages quoted later in this paragraph are from the fragments: (1): D5, vol. I, p. 141, line 10. (Cp. *Diog. Laert.*, IX, 7.) ... (2): B 29, D5 94 (cp. note 2 to chapter 5) ... (3): B 34, D5 100 ... (4): B 20, D5 30 ... (5): B 26, D5 66.

   (1) The idea of law is *correlative* to that of change or flux, since only laws or regularities within the flux can explain the apparent stability of the world. The most typical regularities within the changing world known to man are the natural periods: the day, the moon-month, and the year (the seasons). Heraclitus' theory of law is, I believe, logically intermediate between the comparatively modern views of 'causal laws' (held by Leucippus and especially by Democritus) and Anaximander's dark powers of fate. Heraclitus' laws are still 'magical', i.e. he has not yet distinguished between abstract causal regularities and laws enforced, like taboos, by sanctions (with this, cp. chapter 5, note 2). It appears that his theory of fate was connected with a theory of a 'Great Year' or 'Great Cycle' of 18,000 or 36,000 ordinary years. (Cp. for instance J. Adam's edition of *The Republic of Plato*, vol. II, 303.) I certainly

do not think that this theory is an indication that Heraclitus did not really believe in a universal flux, but only in various circulations which always re-established the stability of the framework; but I think it possible that he had difficulties in conceiving a law of change, and even of fate, other than one involving a certain amount of periodicity. (Cp. also note 6 to chapter 3.)

(2) Fire plays a central rôle in Heraclitus' philosophy of nature. (There may be some Persian influence here.) The flame is the obvious symbol of a flux or *process which appears in many respects as a thing.* It thus explains the experience of stable things, and reconciles this experience with the doctrine of flux. This idea can easily be extended to living bodies which are like flames, only burning more slowly. Heraclitus teaches that *all* things are in flux, *all* are like fire; their flux has only different 'measures' or laws of motion. The 'bowl' or 'trough' in which the fire burns will be in a much slower flux than the fire, but it will be in flux nevertheless. It changes, it has its fate and its laws, it must be burned into by the fire, and consumed, even if it takes a longer time before its fate is fulfilled. Thus, 'in its advance, the fire will judge and convict everything' (B 26, D5 66).

Accordingly, the fire is the symbol and the explanation of the apparent rest of things in spite of their real state of flux. But it is also a symbol of the transmutation of matter from one stage (fuel) into another. It thus provides the link between Heraclitus' intuitive theory of nature and the theories of rarefaction and condensation, etc., of his predecessors. But its flaring up and dying down, in accordance with the measure of fuel provided, is also an instance of a law. If this is combined with some form of periodicity, then it can be used to explain the regularities of natural periods, such as days or years. (This trend of thought renders it unlikely that Burnet is right in disbelieving the traditional reports of Heraclitus' belief in a periodical conflagration, which was probably connected with his Great Year; cp. Aristotle, *Physics*, 205a3 with D5 66.)

8. The thirteen passages quoted in this paragraph are from the fragments. (1): B 10, D5 123 ... (2): B 11, D5 93 ... (3): B 16, D5 40 ... (4): B 94, D5 73 ... (5): B 95, D5 89 ... with (4) and (5), cp. Plato's *Republic*, 476c f., and 520c ... (6): B 6, D5 19 ... (7): B 3, D5 34 ... (8): B 19, D5 41 ... (9): B 92, D5 2 ... (10): B 91a, D5 113 ... (11): B 59, D5 10 ... (12): B 65, D5 32 ... (13): B 28, D5 64.

9. More consistent than most moral historicists, Heraclitus is also an ethical and juridical positivist (for this term, cp. chapter 5): 'All things are, to the gods, fair and good and right; men, however, have taken up some things as wrong, and some as right.' (D5 102, B 61; see passage (8) in note 11.) That he was the first juridical positivist is attested by Plato (*Theaet.*, 177c/d). On moral and juridical positivism in general, cp. chapter 5 (text to notes 14–18) and chapter 22.

10. The two passages quoted in this paragraph are: (1): B 44, D5 53 ... (2): B 62, D5 80.

11. The nine passages quoted in this paragraph are: (1): B 39, D5 126 ... (2): B 104, D5 111 ... (3): B 78, D5 88 ... (4): B 45, D5 51 ... (5): D5 8 ... (6): B 69, D5 60 ... (7): B 50, D5 59 ... (8): B 61, D5 102 (cp. note 9) ... (9): B 57, D5 58. (Cp. Aristotle, *Physics*, 185b20.)

Flux or change must be the transition from one stage or property or position to another. In so far as flux presupposes something that changes, this something must remain identically the same, even though it assumes an opposite stage or property or position. This links the theory of flux to that of the unity of opposites (cp. Aristotle, *Metaphysics*, 1005b25, 1024a24 and 34, 1062a32, 1063a25) as well as the doctrine of the oneness of all things; they are all only different phases or appearances of the one changing something (of fire).

Whether 'the path that leads up' and 'the path that leads down' were originally conceived as an ordinary path leading first up a mountain, and later down again (or perhaps: leading up from the point of view of the man who is down, and down from that of the man who is up), and whether this metaphor was only later applied to the processes of circulation, to the path that leads up from earth through water (perhaps liquid fuel in a bowl?) to the fire, and down again from the fire through the water (rain?) to earth; or whether Heraclitus' path up and down was originally applied by him to this process of circulation of matter; all this can of course not be decided. (But I think that the first alternative is more likely in view of the great number of similar ideas in Heraclitus' fragments: cp. the text.)

12. The four passages are: (1): B 102, D5 24 ... (2): B 101, D5 25 (a closer version which more or less preserves Heraclitus' pun is: 'Greater death wins greater destiny.' Cp. also Plato's *Laws*, 903 d/e; contrast with *Rep.* 617 d/e) ... (3): B 111, D5 29 (part of the continuation is quoted above; see passage (3) in note 4) ... (4): B 113, D5 49.
13. It seems very probable (cp. Meyer's *Gesch. d. Altertums*, esp. vol. I) that such characteristic teachings as that of the chosen people originated in this period, which produced several other religions of salvation besides the Jewish.
14. Comte, who in France developed a historicist philosophy not very dissimilar from Hegel's Prussian version, tried, like Hegel, to stem the revolutionary tide. (Cp. F. A. von Hayek, *The Counter-Revolution of Science, Economica*, N.S. vol. VIII, 1941, pp. 119 ff., 281 ff.) For Lassalle's interest in Heraclitus, see note 4 to chapter 1.—It is interesting to note, in this connection, the parallelism between the history of historicist and of evolutionary ideas. They originated in Greece with the semi-Heraclitean Empedocles (for Plato's version, see note 1 to chapter 11), and they were revived, in England as well as in France, in the time of the French Revolution.

NOTES TO CHAPTER THREE

1. With this explanation of the term oligarchy, cp. also the end of notes 44 and 57 to chapter 8.
2. Cp. especially note 48 to chapter 10.
3. Cp. the end of chapter 7, esp. note 25, and chapter 10, esp. note 69.
4. Cp. *Diogenes Laert.*, III, 1.—Concerning Plato's family connections, and especially the alleged descent of his father's family from Codrus, 'and even from the God Poseidon', see G. Grote, *Plato and other Companions of Socrates* (edn 1875), vol. I, 114. (See, however, the similar remark on Critias' family, i.e. on that of Plato's mother, in E. Meyer, *Geschichte des Altertums*, vol. V, 1922, p. 66.) Plato says of Codrus in the *Symposium* (208d): 'Do you suppose that Alcestis, ... or Achilles, ... or that your own Codrus would have sought death—*in order to save the kingship for his children*—had they not expected to win that immortal memory of their virtue in which indeed we keep them?' Plato praises Critias' (i.e. his mother's) family in the early *Charmides* (157e ff.) and in the late *Timaeus* (20e), where the family is traced back to the Athenian ruler (*archōn*) Dropides, the friend of Solon.
5. The two autobiographical quotations which follow in this paragraph are from the *Seventh Letter* (325). Plato's authorship of the *Letters* has been questioned by some

eminent scholars (perhaps without sufficient foundation; I think Field's treatment of this problem very convincing; cp. note 57 to chapter 10; on the other hand, even the *Seventh Letter* looks to me a little suspicious—it repeats too much what we know from the *Apology*, and says too much what the occasion requires). I have therefore taken care to base my interpretation of Platonism mainly on some of the most famous dialogues; it is, however, in general agreement with the *Letters*. For the reader's convenience, a list of those Platonic dialogues which are frequently mentioned in the text may be given here, in what is their probable historical order; cp. note 56 (8) to chapter 10. *Crito—Apology—Euthyphro; Protagoras—Meno—Gorgias; Cratylus—Menexenus—Phaedo; Republic; Parmenides—Theaetetus; Sophist—Statesman* (or *Politicus*)—*Philebus; Timaeus—Critias; Laws*.

6. (1) That *historical* developments may have a *cyclic* character is nowhere very clearly stated by Plato. It is, however, alluded to in at least four dialogues, namely in the *Phaedo*, in the *Republic*, in the *Statesman* (or *Politicus*), and in the *Laws*. In all these places, Plato's theory may possibly allude to Heraclitus' Great Year (cp. note 6 to chapter 2). It may be, however, that the allusion is not to Heraclitus directly, but rather to Empedocles, whose theory (cp. also Aristotle, *Met.*, 1000a25 f.) Plato considered as merely a 'milder' version of the Heraclitean theory of the unity of all flux. He expresses this in a famous passage of the *Sophist* (242e f.). According to this passage, and to Aristotle (*De Gen. Corr.*, B, 6., 334a6), there is a historical cycle embracing a period in which love rules, and a period in which Heraclitus' strife rules; and Aristotle tells us that, according to Empedocles, the present period is 'now a period of the reign of Strife, as it was formerly one of Love'. This insistence that the flux of our own cosmic period is a kind of strife, and therefore bad, is in close accordance both with Plato's theories and with his experiences.

The length of the Great Year is, probably, the period of time after which *all* heavenly bodies return to the same positions relative to each other as were held by them at the moment from which the period is reckoned. (This would make it the smallest common multiple of the periods of the 'seven planets'.)

(2) The passage in the *Phaedo* mentioned under (1) alludes first to the Heraclitean theory of change leading from one state to its opposite state, or from one opposite to the other: 'that which becomes less must once have been greater ...' (70e/71a). It then proceeds to indicate a cyclic law of development: 'Are there not two processes which are ever going on, from one extreme to its opposite, and back again ...?' (*loc. cit.*). And a little later (72a/b) the argument is put like this: 'If the development were in a straight line only, and there were no compensation or cycle in nature, ... then, in the end, all things would take on the same properties ... and there would be no further development.' It appears that the general tendency of the *Phaedo* is more optimistic (and shows more faith in man and in human reason) than that of the later dialogues, but there are no direct references to human historical development.

(3) Such references are, however, made in the *Republic* where, in Books VIII and IX, we find an elaborate description of historical decay treated here in chapter 4. This description is introduced by Plato's Story of the Fall of Man and of the Number, which will here be discussed more fully in chapters 5 and 8. J. Adam, in his edition of *The Republic of Plato* (1902, 1921), rightly calls this story 'the setting in which Plato's "Philosophy of History" is framed' (vol. II, 210). This story does not contain any explicit statement on the cyclic character of history, but it contains a few rather

mysterious hints which, according to Aristotle's (and Adam's) interesting but uncertain interpretation, are possibly allusions to the Heraclitean Great Year, i.e. to the cyclic development. (Cp. note 6 to chapter 2, and Adam, *op. cit.*, vol. II, 303; the remark on Empedocles made there, 303f., needs correction; see (1) in this note, above.)

(4) There is, furthermore, the myth in the *Statesman* (268e–274c). According to this myth, God himself steers the world for half a cycle of the great world period. When he lets go, then the world, which so far has moved forward, begins to roll back again. Thus we have two half-periods or half-cycles in the full cycle, a forward movement led by God constituting the good period without war or strife, and a backward movement when God abandons the world, which is a period of increasing disorganization and strife. It is, of course, the period in which we live. Ultimately, things will become so bad that God will take the wheel again, and reverse the motion, in order to save the world from utter destruction.

This myth shows great resemblances to Empedocles' myth mentioned in (1) above, and probably also to Heraclitus' Great Year.—Adam (*op. cit.*, vol. II, 296 f.) also points out the similarities with Hesiod's story. *One of the points which allude to Hesiod is the reference to a Golden Age of Cronos; and it is important to note that the men of this age are earth-born. This establishes a point of contact with the Myth of the Earth-born, and of the metals in man, which plays a rôle in the *Republic* (414b ff. and 546e f.); this rôle is discussed below in chapter 8. The Myth of the Earth-born is also alluded to in the *Symposium* (191b); possibly the allusion is to the popular claim that the Athenians are 'like grasshoppers'—autochthonous (cp. notes 32 (1)e to chapter 4 and 11 (2) to chapter 8).*

When, however, later in the *Statesman* (302b ff.) the six forms of imperfect government are ordered according to their degree of imperfection, there is no indication any longer to be found of a cyclic theory of history. Rather, the six forms, which are all degenerate copies of the perfect or best state (*Statesman*, 293d/e; 297c; 303b), appear all as steps in the process of degeneration; i.e. both here and in the *Republic* Plato confines himself, when it comes to more concrete historical problems, to that part of the cycle which leads to decay.

* (5) Analogous remarks hold for the *Laws*. Something like a cyclic theory is sketched in Book III, 676b/c–677b, where Plato turns to a more detailed analysis of the beginning of one of the cycles; and in 678e and 679c, this beginning turns out to be a Golden Age, so that the further story again becomes one of deterioration.—It may be mentioned that Plato's doctrine, that the planets are gods, together with the doctrine that the gods influence human lives (and with his belief that cosmic forces are at work in history), played an important part in the astrological speculations of the neo-Platonists. All three doctrines can be found in the *Laws* (see, for example, 821b–d and 899b; 899d–905d; 677a ff.). Astrology, it should be realized, shares with historicism the belief in a determinate destiny which can be predicted; and it shares with some important versions of historicism (especially with Platonism and Marxism) the belief that, notwithstanding the possibility of predicting the future, we have some influence upon it, especially if we actually know what is coming.*

(6) Apart from these scanty allusions, there is hardly anything to indicate that Plato took the upward or forward part of the cycle seriously. But there are many remarks, apart from the elaborate description in the *Republic* and that quoted in (5),

which show that he believed very seriously in the downward movement, in the decay of history. We must consider, especially, the *Timaeus*, and the *Laws*.

(7) In the *Timaeus* (42b f., 90e ff., and especially 91d f.; cp. also the *Phaedrus*, 248d f.), Plato describes what may be called the origin of species by degeneration (cp. text to note 4 to chapter 4, and note 11 to chapter 11): men degenerate into women, and later into lower animals.

(8) In Book III of the *Laws* (cp. also Book IV, 713a ff.; see however the short allusion to a cycle mentioned above) we have a rather elaborate theory of historical decay, largely analogous to that in the *Republic*. See also the next chapter, especially notes 3, 6, 7, 27, 31, and 44.

7. A similar opinion of Plato's political aims is expressed by G. C. Field, *Plato and His Contemporaries* (1930), p. 91: 'The chief aim of Plato's philosophy may be regarded as the attempt to re-establish standards of thought and conduct for a civilization that seemed on the verge of dissolution.' See also note 3 to chapter 6, and text.

8. I follow the majority of the older and a good number of contemporary authorities (e.g. G. C. Field, F. M. Cornford, A. K. Rogers) in believing, against John Burnet and A. E. Taylor, that the theory of Forms or Ideas is nearly entirely Plato's, and not Socrates', in spite of the fact that Plato puts it into the mouth of Socrates as his main speaker. Though Plato's dialogues are our only first-rate source for Socrates' teaching, it is, I believe, possible to distinguish in them between 'Socratic', i.e. historically true, and 'Platonic' features of Plato's speaker 'Socrates'. The so-called *Socratic Problem* is discussed in chapters 6, 7, 8, and 10; cp. especially note 56 to chapter 10.

9. The term 'social engineering' seems to have been used first by Roscoe Pound, in his *Introduction to the Philosophy of Law* (1922, p. 99; *Bryan Magee tells me now that the Webbs used it almost certainly before 1922.*) He uses the term in the 'piecemeal' sense. In another sense it is used by M. Eastman, *Marxism: Is it Science?* (1940). I read Eastman's book after the text of my own book was written; my term 'social engineering' is, accordingly, used without any intention of alluding to Eastman's terminology. As far as I can see, he advocates the approach which I criticize in chapter 9 under the name 'Utopian social engineering'; cp. note 1 to that chapter.—See also note 18 (3) to chapter 5. As the first social engineer one might describe the town-planner Hippodamus of Miletus. (Cp. Aristotle's *Politics* 1276b22, and R. Eisler, *Jesus Basileus*, II, p. 754.)

The term 'social technology' has been suggested to me by C. G. F. Simkin.—I wish to make it clear that in discussing problems of method, my main emphasis is upon gaining practical institutional experience. Cp. chapter 9, especially text to note 8 to that chapter. For a more detailed analysis of the problems of method connected with social engineering and social technology, see my *The Poverty of Historicism* (2nd edition, 1960), part III.

10. The quoted passage is from my *The Poverty of Historicism*, p. 65. The 'undesigned results of human actions' are more fully discussed below, in chapter 14, see especially note 11 and text.

11. I believe in a dualism of facts and decisions or demands (or of 'is' and 'ought'); in other words, I believe in the impossibility of reducing decisions or demands to facts, although they can, of course, be treated as facts. More on this point will be said in chapters 5 (text to notes 4–5), 22, and 24.

12. Evidence in support of this interpretation of Plato's theory of the best state will be supplied in the next three chapters; I may refer, in the meanwhile, to *Statesman*, 293d/e; 297c; *Laws*, 713b/c; 739d/e; *Timaeus*, 22d ff., especially 25e and 26d.
13. Cp. Aristotle's famous report, partly quoted later in this chapter (see especially note 25 to this chapter, and the text).
14. This is shown in Grote's *Plato*, vol. III, note *u* on pp. 267 f.
15. The quotations are from the *Timaeus*, 50c/d and 51e–52b. The simile which describes the Forms or Ideas as the fathers, and Space as the mother, of the sensible things, is important and has far-reaching connections. Cp. also notes 17 and 19 to this chapter, and note 59 to chapter 10.

(1) It resembles Hesiod's *myth of chaos*, the yawning gap (space; receptacle) which corresponds to the mother, and the God Eros, who corresponds to the father or to the Ideas. Chaos is the origin, and the question of the causal explanation (chaos = cause) remains for a long time one of origin (archē) or birth or generation.

(2) The mother or Space corresponds to the indefinite or boundless of Anaximander and of the Pythagoreans. The Idea, which is male, must therefore correspond to the definite (or limited) of the Pythagoreans. For the definite, as opposed to the boundless, the male, as opposed to the female, the light, as opposed to the dark, and the good, as opposed to the bad, all belong to the same side in the *Pythagorean table of opposites*. (Cp. Aristotle's *Metaphysics*, 986a22 f.) We also can therefore expect to see the Ideas associated with light and goodness. (Cp. end of note 32 to chapter 8.)

(3) The Ideas are boundaries or limits, they are definite, as opposed to indefinite Space, and impress or imprint (cp. note 17 (2) to this chapter) themselves like rubber-stamps, or better, like moulds, upon Space (which is not only space but at the same time Anaximander's unformed matter—stuff without property), thus generating sensible things. *J. D. Mabbott has kindly drawn my attention to the fact that the Forms or Ideas, according to Plato, do not impress themselves upon Space but are, rather, impressed or imprinted upon it by the Demiurge. Traces of the theory that the Forms are 'causes both of being and of generation (or becoming)' can be found already in the *Phaedo* (100d), as Aristotle points out (in *Metaphysics* 1080a2).*

(4) In consequence of the act of generation, Space, i.e. the receptacle, begins to labour, so that all things are set in motion, in a Heraclitean or Empedoclean flux which is really universal in so far as the movement or flux extends even to the framework, i.e. (boundless) space itself. (For the late Heraclitean idea of the receptacle, cp. the *Cratylus*, 412d.)

(5) This description is also reminiscent of Parmenides' 'Way of Delusive Opinion', in which the world of experience and of flux is created by the mingling of two opposites, the light (or hot or fire) and the dark (or cold or earth). It is clear that Plato's Forms or Ideas would correspond to the former, and Space or what is boundless to the latter; especially if we consider that Plato's pure space is closely akin to indeterminate matter.

(6) The opposition between the determinate and indeterminate seems also to correspond, especially after the all-important discovery of the irrationality of the square root of two, to the opposition between the rational and the irrational. But since Parmenides identifies the rational with being, this would lead to an

interpretation of Space or the irrational as non-being. In other words, the Pythagorean table of opposites is to be extended to cover rationality, as opposed to irrationality, and being, as opposed to non-being. (This agrees with *Metaphysics*, 1004b27, where Aristotle says that 'all the contraries are reducible to being and non-being'; 1072a31, where one side of the table—that of being—is described as the object of (rational) thought; and 1093b13, where the powers of certain numbers—presumably in opposition to their roots—are added to this side. This would further explain Aristotle's remark in *Metaphysics*, 986b27; and it would perhaps not be necessary to assume, as F. M. Cornford does in his excellent article 'Parmenides' Two Ways', *Class. Quart.*, XVII, 1933, p. 108, that Parmenides, fr. 8, 53/54, 'has been misinterpreted by Aristotle and Theophrastus' for if we expand the table of opposites in this way, Cornford's most convincing interpretation of the crucial passage of fr. 8 becomes compatible with Aristotle's remark.)

(7) Cornford has explained (*op. cit.*, 100) that there are three 'ways' in Parmenides, the way of Truth, the way of Not-being, and the way of Seeming (or, if I may call it so, of delusive opinion). He shows (101) that they correspond to three regions discussed in the *Republic*, the perfectly real and rational world of the Ideas, the perfectly unreal, and the world of opinion (based on the perception of things in flux). He has also shown (102) that in the *Sophist*, Plato modifies his position. To this, some comments may be added from the point of view of the passages in the *Timaeus* to which this note is appended.

(8) The main difference between the Forms or Ideas of the *Republic* and those of the *Timaeus* is that in the former, the Forms (and also God; cp. *Rep.*, 380d) are petrified, so to speak, while in the latter, they are deified. In the former, they bear a much closer resemblance to the Parmenidean One (cp. Adam's note to *Rep.*, 380d28, 31), than in the latter. This development leads to the *Laws*, where the Ideas are largely replaced by souls. The decisive difference is that the Ideas become more and more the starting points of motion and causes of generation, or as the *Timaeus* puts it, fathers of the moving things. The greatest contrast is perhaps between the *Phaedo*, 79e: 'The soul is infinitely more like the unchangeable; even the most stupid person would not deny that' (cp. also *Rep.*, 585c, 609b f.), and the *Laws*, 895e/896a (cp. *Phaedrus*, 245c ff.): 'What is the definition of that which is named "soul"? Can we imagine any other definition than ... "The motion that moves itself"?' The transition between these two positions is, perhaps, provided by the *Sophist* (which introduces the Form or Idea of motion itself) and by the *Timaeus*, 35a, which describes the 'divine and unchanging' Forms and the changing and corruptible bodies. This seems to explain why, in the *Laws* (cp. 894d/e), the motion of the soul is said to be '*first in origin and power*' and why the soul is described (966e) as 'the most ancient and divine of all things whose motion is an ever-flowing source of real existence'. (Since, according to Plato, *all living things* have souls, it may be claimed that he admitted the presence of an at least partly formal principle in things; a point of view which is very close to Aristotelianism, especially in the presence of the primitive and widespread belief that all things are alive.) (Cp. also note 7 to chapter 4.)

(9) In this development of Plato's thought, a development whose driving force is to explain the world of flux with the help of the Ideas, i.e. to make the break between the world of reason and the world of opinion at least understandable, even though it cannot be bridged, the *Sophist* seems to play a decisive rôle. Apart from making

room, as Cornford mentions (*op. cit.*, 102), for the plurality of Ideas, it presents them, in an argument against Plato's own earlier position (248a ff.): (*a*) as active causes, which may interact, for example, with mind; (*b*) as unchanging in spite of that, although there is now an Idea of motion in which all moving things participate and which is not at rest; (*c*) as capable of mingling with one another. It further introduces 'Not-being', identified in the *Timaeus* with Space (cp. Cornford, *Plato's Theory of Knowledge*, 1935, note to 247), and thus makes it possible for the Ideas to mingle with it (cp. also *Philolaus*, fr. 2, 3, 5, Diels[5]), and to produce the world of flux with its characteristic intermediate position between the being of Ideas and the not-being of Space or matter.

(10) Ultimately, I wish to defend my contention in the text that the Ideas are not only outside space, but also outside time, though they are in contact with the world at the beginning of time. This, I believe, makes it easier to understand how they act without being in motion; for all motion or flux is in space and time. Plato, I believe, assumes that time has a beginning. I think that this is the most direct interpretation of *Laws*, 721c: 'the race of man is twin-born with all time', considering the many indications that Plato believed man to be created as one of the first creatures. (In this point, I disagree slightly with Cornford, *Plato's Cosmology*, 1937, p. 145, and pp. 26 ff.)

(11) To sum up, the Ideas are earlier and better than their changing and decaying copies, and are themselves not in flux. (See also note 3 to chapter 4.)

16. Cp. note 4 to this chapter.

17. (1) The rôle of the gods in the *Timaeus* is similar to the one described in the text. Just as the Ideas stamp out things, so the gods form the *bodies* of men. Only the human *soul* is created by the Demiurge himself who also creates the world and the gods. (For another hint that the gods are patriarchs, see *Laws*, 713c/d.) Men, the weak, degenerate children of gods, are then liable to further degeneration; cp. note 6(7) to this chapter, and 37–41 to chapter 5.

(2) In an interesting passage of the *Laws* (681b; cp. also note 32 (1, a) to chapter 4) we find another allusion to the parallelism between the relation *Idea—things* and the relation *parent—children*. In this passage, the origin of law is explained by the influence of tradition, and more especially, by the transmission of a rigid order from the parents to the children; and the following remark is made: 'And they (the parents) would be sure to stamp upon their children, and upon their children's children, their own cast of mind.'

18. Cp. note 49, especially (3), to chapter 8.

19. Cp. *Timaeus*, 31a. The term which I have freely translated by 'superior thing which is their prototype' is a term frequently used by Aristotle with the meaning 'universal' or 'generic term'. It means a 'thing which is general' or 'surpassing' or 'embracing' and I suspect that it originally means 'embracing' or 'covering' in the sense in which a mould embraces or covers what it moulds.

20. Cp. *Republic*, 597c. See also 596a (and Adam's second note to 596a5): 'For we are in the habit, you will remember, of postulating a Form or Idea—one for each group of many particular things to which we apply the same name.'

21. There are innumerable passages in Plato; I mention only the *Phaedo* (e.g. 79a), the *Republic*, 544a, the *Theaetetus* (152d/e, 179d/e), the *Timaeus* (28b/c, 29c/d, 51d f.). Aristotle mentions it in *Metaphysics*, 987a32; 999a25–999b10; 1010a6–15; 1078b15; see also notes 23 and 25 to this chapter.

22. Parmenides taught, as Burnet puts it (*Early Greek Philosophy2*, 208), that 'what is ... is finite, spherical, motionless, corporeal', i.e. that the world is a full globe, a whole without any parts, and that 'there is nothing beyond it'. I am quoting Burnet because (*a*) his description is excellent and (*b*) it destroys his own interpretation (*E.G.P.*, 208–11) of what Parmenides calls the 'Opinion of the Mortals' (or the Way of Delusive Opinion). For Burnet dismisses there all the interpretations of Aristotle, Theophrastus, Simplicius, Gomperz, and Meyer, as 'anachronisms' or 'palpable anachronisms', etc. Now the interpretation dismissed by Burnet is practically the same as the one here proposed in the text; namely, that Parmenides believed in a world of reality behind this world of appearance. Such a dualism, which would allow Parmenides' description of the world of appearance to claim at least some kind of adequacy, is dismissed by Burnet as hopelessly anachronistic. I suggest, however, that if Parmenides had believed solely in his unmoving world, and not at all in the changing world, then he would have been really mad (as Empedocles hints). But in fact there is an indication of a similar dualism already in Xenophanes, fragm. 23–6, if confronted with fragm. 34 (esp. 'But all may have their fancy opinions'), so that we can hardly speak of an anachronism.—As indicated in note 15 (6–7), I follow Cornford's interpretation of Parmenides. (See also note 41 to chapter 10.)
23. Cp. Aristotle's *Metaphysics*, 1078b23; the next quotation is: *op. cit.*, 1078b19.
24. This valuable comparison is due to G. C. Field, *Plato and His Contemporaries*, 211.
25. The preceding quotation is from Aristotle, *Metaphysics*, 1078b15; the next from *op. cit.*, 987b7.
26. In Aristotle's analysis (in *Metaphysics*, 987a30–b18) of the arguments which led to the theory of Ideas (cp. also note 56 (6) to chapter 10), we can distinguish the following steps: (*a*) Heraclitus' flux, (*b*) the impossibility of true knowledge of things in flux, (*c*) the influence of Socrates' ethical essences, (*d*) the Ideas as objects of true knowledge, (*e*) the influence of the Pythagoreans, (*f*) the 'mathematicals' as intermediate objects.—((*e*) and (*f*) I have not mentioned in the text, where I have mentioned instead (*g*) the Parmenidean influence.)

It may be worth while to show how these steps can be identified in Plato's own work, where he expounds his theory; especially in the *Phaedo* and in the *Republic*, in the *Theaetetus* and in the *Sophist*, and in the *Timaeus*.

(1) In the *Phaedo*, we find indications of all the points up to and including (*e*). In 65a–66a, the steps (*d*) and (*c*) are prominent, with an allusion to (*b*). In 70e step (*a*), Heraclitus' theory appears, combined with an element of Pythagoreanism (*e*). This leads to 74a ff., and to a statement of step (*d*). 99–100 is an approach to (*d*) through (*c*), etc. For (*a*) to (*d*), cp. also the *Cratylus*, 439c ff.

In the *Republic*, it is of course especially Book VI that corresponds closely to Aristotle's report. (*a*) In the beginning of Book VI, 485a/b (cp. 527a/b), the Heraclitean flux is referred to (and contrasted with the unchanging world of Forms). Plato there speaks of 'a reality which exists for ever and *is exempt from generation and degeneration*'. (Cp. notes 2 (2) and 3 to chapter 4 and note 33 to chapter 8, and text.) The steps (*b*), (*d*) and especially (*f*) play a rather obvious rôle in the famous Simile of the Line (*Rep.*, 509c–511e; cp. Adam's notes, and his appendix I to Book VII); Socrates' ethical influence, i.e. step (*c*), is of course alluded to throughout the *Republic*. It plays an important rôle within the Simile of the Line and especially immediately before, i.e. in 508b ff., where the rôle of the good is emphasized; see in particular 508b/c: 'This is what I maintain regarding the offspring of the good. What the good has begotten in its own likeness is, in the intelligible world, related to reason (and its objects) in the same way as, in the visible world', that which is the offspring of the sun, 'is related to sight (and its objects).' Step (*e*) is implied in (*f*), but more fully developed in Book VII, in the famous *Curriculum* (cp. especially 523a–527c), which is largely based on the Simile of the Line in Book VI.

(2) In the *Theaetetus*, (*a*) and (*b*) are treated extensively; (*c*) is mentioned in 174b and 175c. In the *Sophist*, all the steps, including (*g*), are mentioned, only (*e*) and (*f*) being left out; see especially 247a (step (*c*)); 249c (step (*b*)); 253d/e (step (*d*)). In the *Philebus*, we find indications of all steps except perhaps (*f*); steps (*a*) to (*d*) are especially emphasized in 59a–c.

(3) In the *Timaeus*, all the steps mentioned by Aristotle are indicated, with the possible exception of (*c*), which is alluded to only indirectly in the introductory recapitulation of the contents of the *Republic*, and in 29d. Step (*e*) is, as it were, alluded to throughout, since 'Timaeus' is a 'western' philosopher and strongly influenced by Pythagoreanism. The other steps occur twice in a form almost completely parallel to Aristotle's account; first briefly in 28a–29d, and later, with more elaboration, in 48e–55c. Immediately after (*a*), i.e. a Heraclitean description (49a ff.; cp. Cornford, *Plato's Cosmology*, 178) of the world in flux, the argument (*b*) is raised (51c–e) that if we are right in distinguishing between reason (or true knowledge) and mere opinion, we must admit the existence of the unchangeable Forms; these are (in 51e f.) introduced next in accordance with step (*d*). The Heraclitean flux then comes again (as labouring space), but this time it is *explained*, as a consequence of the act of generation. And as a next step (*f*) appears, in 53c. (I suppose that the 'lines and planes and solids' mentioned by Aristotle in *Metaphysics*, 992b13, refer to 53c ff.)

(4) It seems that this parallelism between the *Timaeus* and Aristotle's report has not been sufficiently emphasized so far; at least, it is not used by G. C. Field in his excellent and convincing analysis of Aristotle's report (*Plato and His Contemporaries*, 202 ff.). But it would have strengthened Field's arguments (arguments, however, which hardly need strengthening, since they are practically conclusive) against Burnet's and Taylor's views that the Theory of Ideas is Socratic (cp. note 56 to chapter 10). For in the *Timaeus*, Plato does not put this theory into the mouth of Socrates, a fact which according to Burnet's and Taylor's principles should prove that it was not Socrates' theory. (They avoid this inference by claiming that 'Timaeus' is a Pythagorean, and that he develops not Plato's philosophy but his own. But Aristotle knew Plato personally for twenty years and should have been able to judge these matters; and he wrote his *Metaphysics* at a time when members of the Academy could have contradicted his presentation of Platonism.)

(5) Burnet writes, in *Greek Philosophy*, 1, 155 (cp. also p. xliv of his edition of the *Phaedo*, 1911): 'the theory of forms in the sense in which it is maintained in the *Phaedo* and *Republic* is wholly absent from what we may fairly regard the most distinctively Platonic of the dialogues, those, namely, in which Socrates is no longer the chief speaker. In that sense it is never even mentioned in any dialogue later than the *Parmenides* ... with the single exception of the *Timaeus* (51c), where the speaker is a Pythagorean.' But if it is maintained in the *Timaeus* in the sense in which it is maintained in the *Republic*, then it is certainly so maintained in the *Sophist*, 257d/e; and in the *Statesman*, 269c/d; 286a; 297b/c, and c/d; 301a and e; 302e; and 303b;

and in the *Philebus*, 15a f., and 59a–d; and in the *Laws*, 713b, 739d/e, 962c f., 963c ff., and, most important, 965c (cp. *Philebus*, 16d), 965d, and 966a; see also the next note. (Burnet believes in the genuineness of the *Letters*, especially the *Seventh*; but the theory of Ideas is maintained there in 342a ff.; see also note 56 (5, d) to chapter 10.)

27. Cp. *Laws*, 895d–e. I do not agree with England's note (in his edition of the *Laws*, vol. II, 472) that 'the word "essence" will not help us'. True, if we meant by 'essence' some important sensible part of the sensible thing (which might perhaps be purified and produced by some distillation), then 'essence' would be misleading. But the word 'essential' is widely used in a way which corresponds very well indeed with what we wish to express here; something opposed to the accidental or unimportant or changing empirical aspect of the thing, whether it is conceived as dwelling in that thing, or in a metaphysical world of Ideas.

I am using the term '*essentialism*' in opposition to 'nominalism', in order to avoid, and to replace, the misleading traditional term 'realism', wherever it is opposed (not to 'idealism' but) to 'nominalism'. (See also note 26 ff. to chapter 11, and text, and especially note 38.)

On Plato's application of his essentialist method, for instance, as mentioned in the text, to the theory of the soul, see *Laws*, 895e f., quoted in note 15 (8) to this chapter, and chapter 5, especially note 23. See also, for instance, *Meno*, 86d/e, and *Symposium*, 199c/d.

28. On the theory of causal explanation, cp. my *The Logic of Scientific Discovery*, especially section 12, pp. 59 ff. See also note 6 to chapter 25, below.

29. The theory of language here indicated is that of Semantics, as developed especially by A. Tarski and R. Carnap. Cp. Carnap, *Introduction to Semantics*, 1942, and note 23 to chapter 8.

30. The theory that while the physical sciences are based on a methodological nominalism, the social sciences must adopt essentialist ('realistic') methods, has been made clear to me by K. Polanyi (in 1925); he pointed out, at that time, that a reform of the methodology of the social sciences might conceivably be achieved by abandoning this theory.—The theory is held, to some extent, by most sociologists, especially by J. S. Mill (for instance, *Logic*, VI, ch. VI, 2; see also his historicist formulations, e.g. in VI, ch. X, 2, last paragraph: 'The fundamental problem ... of the social science is to find the laws according to which any state of society produces the state which succeeds it ...'), K. Marx (see below); M. Weber (cp., for example, his definitions in the beginning of *Methodische Grundlagen der Soziologie*, in *Wirtschaft und Gesellschaft*, I, and in *Ges. Aufsaetze zur Wissenschaftslehre*), G. Simmel, A. Vierkandt, R. M. MacIver, and many more.—The philosophical expression of all these tendencies is E. Husserl's 'Phaenomenology', a systematic revival of the methodological essentialism of Plato and Aristotle. (See also chapter 11, especially note 44.)

The opposite, the *nominalist* attitude in sociology, can be developed, I think, only as a technological theory of social *institutions*.

In this context, I may mention how I came to trace historicism back to Plato and Heraclitus. In analysing historicism, I found that it needs what I call now methodological essentialism; i.e. I saw that the typical arguments in favour of essentialism are bound up with historicism (cp. my *The Poverty of Historicism*). This led me to consider the history of essentialism. I was struck by the parallelism between

Aristotle's report and the analysis which I had carried out originally without any reference to Platonism. In this way, I was reminded of the rôles of both Heraclitus and Plato in this development.

31. R. H. S. Crossman's *Plato To-day* (1937) was the first book (apart from G. Grote's *Plato*) I have found to contain a political interpretation of Plato which is partly similar to my own. See also notes 2–3 to chapter 6, and text. *Since then I have found that similar views of Plato have been expressed by various authors. C. M. Bowra (*Ancient Greek Literature*, 1933) is perhaps the first; his brief but thorough criticism of Plato (pp. 186–90) is as fair as it is penetrating. The others are W. Fite (*The Platonic Legend*, 1934); B. Farrington (*Science and Politics in the Ancient World*, 1939); A. D. Winspear (*The Genesis of Plato's Thought*, 1940); and H. Kelsen (*Platonic Justice*, 1933; now in *What is Justice?*, 1957, and *Platonic Love*, in *The American Imago*, vol. 3, 1942).*

NOTES TO CHAPTER FOUR

1. Cp. *Republic*, 608e. See also note 2 (2) to this chapter.
2. In the *Laws*, the soul—'the most ancient and divine of all things in motion' (966e)—is described as the 'starting point of all motion' (895b). (1) With the Platonic theory, Aristotle contrasts his own, according to which the 'good' thing is not the starting point, but rather the end or aim of change since 'good' *means* a thing aimed at—*the final cause of change*. Thus he says of the Platonists, i.e. of 'those who believe in Forms', that they agree with Empedocles (they speak 'in the same way' as Empedocles) in so far as they 'do not speak as if anything came to pass *for the sake of these*' (i.e. of things which are 'good') 'but as if all *movement started from them*'. And he points out that 'good' means therefore to the Platonists not 'a cause *qua* good', i.e. an aim, but that 'it is only incidentally a good'. Cp. *Metaphysics*, 988a35 and b8 ff. and 1075a, 34/35. This criticism sounds as if Aristotle had sometimes held views similar to those of Speusippus, which is indeed Zeller's opinion; see note 11 to chapter 11.

   (2) Concerning the *movement towards corruption*, mentioned in the text in this paragraph, and its general significance in the Platonic philosophy, we must keep in mind the general opposition between the world of unchanging things or Ideas, and the world of sensible things in flux. Plato often expresses this opposition as one between the world of unchanging things and the world of *corruptible* things, or between *things that are ungenerated, and those that* are generated and are doomed to *degenerate*, etc.; see, for instance, *Republic*, 485a/b, quoted in note 26(1) to chapter 3 and in text to note 33 to chapter 8; *Republic*, 508d–e; 527a/b; and *Republic*, 546a, quoted in text to note 37 to chapter 5: 'All things that have been generated must degenerate' (or decay). That this problem of the *generation and corruption* of the world of things in flux was an important part of the Platonic School tradition is indicated by the fact that Aristotle devoted a separate treatise to this problem. Another interesting indication is the way in which Aristotle talked about these matters in the introduction to his *Politics*, contained in the concluding sentences of the *Nicomachean Ethics* (1181b/15): 'We shall try to ... find what it is that *preserves or corrupts* the cities ...' This passage is significant not only as a general formulation of what Aristotle considered the main problem of his *Politics*, but also because of its

striking similarity to an important passage in the *Laws*, viz. 676a, and 676b/c quoted below in text to notes 6 and 25 to this chapter. (See also notes 1, 3, and 24/25 to this chapter; see note 32 to chapter 8, and the passage from the *Laws* quoted in note 59 to chapter 8.)

3. This quotation is from the *Statesman*, 269d. (See also note 23 to this chapter.) For the hierarchy of motions, see *Laws*, 893c–895b. For the theory that perfect things (divine 'natures'; cp. the next chapter) can only become less perfect when they change, see especially *Republic*, 380e–381c—in many ways (note the examples in 380e) a parallel passage to *Laws*, 797d. The quotations from Aristotle are from the *Metaphysics*, 988b3, and from *De Gen. et Corr.*, 335b14. The last four quotations in this paragraph are from Plato's *Laws*, 904c f., and 797d. See also note 24 to this chapter, and text. (It is possible to interpret the remark about the evil objects as another allusion to a cyclic development, as discussed in note 6 to chapter 2, i.e. as an allusion to the belief that the trend of the development must reverse, and that things must begin to improve, once the world has reached the lowest depth of evilness.

* Since my interpretation of the Platonic theory of change and of the passages from the *Laws* has been challenged, I wish to add some further comments, especially on the two passages (1) *Laws*, 904c, f, and (2) 797d.

(1) The passage *Laws*, 904c, 'the less significant is the beginning decline in their level of rank' may be translated more literally 'the less significant is the beginning movement *down* in the level of rank'. It seems to me certain, from the context, that '*down* the level of rank' is meant rather than '*as to* level of rank', which clearly is also a possible translation. (My reason is not only the whole dramatic context, down from 904a, but also more especially the series '*kata* ... *kata* ... *katō*' which, in a passage of gathering momentum, must colour the meaning of at least the second '*kata*'.—Concerning the word I translate by 'level', this *may*, admittedly, mean not only 'plane' but also 'surface'; and the word I translate by 'rank' *may* mean 'space'; yet Bury's translation: 'the smaller the change of character, the less is the movement over surface in space' does not seem to me to yield much meaning in this context.)

(2) The continuation of this passage (*Laws*, 798) is most characteristic. It demands that 'the lawgiver must contrive, by whatever means at his disposal ['by hook or by crook', as Bury well translates], a method which ensures for his state that the whole soul of every one of its citizens will, from reverence and fear, resist any change of any of the things that are established of old'. (Plato includes, explicitly, things which other lawgivers consider 'mere matters of play'—such, as, for example, changes in the games of children.)

(3) In general, the main evidence for my interpretation of Plato's theory of change—apart from a great number of minor passages referred to in the various notes in this chapter and the preceding one—is of course found in the historical or evolutionary passages of *all* the dialogues which contain such passages, especially the *Republic* (the decline and fall of the state from its near-perfect or Golden Age in Books VIII and IX), the *Statesman* (the theory of the Golden Age and its decline), the *Laws* (the story of the primitive patriarchy and of the Dorian conquest, and the story of the decline and fall of the Persian Empire), the *Timaeus* (the story of evolution by degeneration, which occurs twice, and the story of the Golden Age of Athens, which is continued in the *Critias*).

To this evidence Plato's frequent references to Hesiod must be added, and the undoubted fact that Plato's synthetic mind was not less keen than that of Empedocles (whose period of strife is the one ruling *now*; cp. Aristotle, *De Gen. et Corr.*, 334a, b) in conceiving human affairs in a cosmic setting (*Statesman, Timaeus*).

(4) Ultimately, I may perhaps refer to general psychological considerations. On the one hand the fear of innovation (illustrated by many passages in the *Laws*, e.g. 758c/d) and, on the other hand, the idealization of the past (such as found in Hesiod or in the story of the lost paradise) are frequent and striking phenomena. It is perhaps not too far-fetched to connect the latter, or even both, with the idealization of one's childhood—one's home, one's parents, and with the nostalgic wish to return to these early stages of one's life, to one's origin. There are many passages in Plato in which he takes it for granted that the original state of affairs, or original nature, is a state of blessedness. I refer only to the speech of Aristophanes in the *Symposium*; here it is taken for granted that the urge and the suffering of passionate love is sufficiently explained if it is shown that it derives from this nostalgia, and similarly, that the feelings of sexual gratification can be explained as those of a gratified nostalgia. Thus Plato says of Eros (*Symposium*, 193d): 'He will restore us *to our original nature* (see also 191d) and heal us and make us happy and blessed.' The same thought underlies many remarks such as the following from the *Philebus* (16c): 'The men of old ... were better than we are now, and ... lived nearer to the gods ...' All this indicates the view that our unhappy and unblessed state is a consequence of the development which makes us different from our original nature—our Idea; and it further indicates that the development is one from a state of goodness and blessedness to a state where goodness and blessedness are being lost; but this means that the development is one of increasing corruption. Plato's theory of *anamnesis*—the theory that all knowledge is re-cognition or re-collection of the knowledge we had in our pre-natal past is part of the same view: in the past there resides not only the good, the noble, and the beautiful, but also all wisdom. Even the ancient change or motion is better than secondary motion; for in the *Laws* the soul is said to be (895b) '*the starting point* of all motions the *first* to arise in things at rest ... the most ancient and potent motion', and (966c) 'the most ancient and divine of all things'. (Cp. note 15 (8) to chapter 3.)

As pointed out before (cp. especially note 6 to chapter 3), the doctrine of an historical and cosmic tendency towards decay appears to be combined, in Plato, with a doctrine of an historical and cosmic cycle. (The period of decay, probably, is a part of this cycle.)*

4. Cp. *Timaeus*, 91d–92b/c. See also note 6 (7) to chapter 3 and note 11 to chapter 11.
5. See the beginning of chapter 2 above, and note 6 (1) to chapter 3. It is not a mere accident that Plato mentions Hesiod's story of 'metals' when discussing his own theory of historical decay (*Rep.*, 546e/547a, esp. notes 39 and 40 to chapter 5); he clearly wishes to indicate how well his theory fits in with, and explains, that of Hesiod.
6. The historical part of the *Laws* is in Books Three and Four (see note 6(5) and (8) to chapter 3). The two quotations in the text are from the beginning of this part, i.e. *Laws*, 676a. For the parallel passages mentioned, see *Republic*, 369b, f. ('The birth of a city ...') and 545d ('How will our city be changed ...').

It is often said that the *Laws* (and the *Statesman*) are less hostile towards democracy than the *Republic*, and it must be admitted that Plato's general tone is in fact less hostile (this is perhaps due to the increasing inner strength of democracy; see chapter 10 and the beginning of chapter 11). But the only practical concession made to democracy in the *Laws* is that political officers are to be elected, by the members of the ruling (i.e. the military) class; and since all important changes in the laws of the state are forbidden anyway (cp., for instance, the quotations in note 3 of this chapter), this does not mean very much. The fundamental tendency remains pro-Spartan, and this tendency was, as can be seen from Aristotle's *Politics*, II, 6, 17 (1265b), compatible with a so-called 'mixed' constitution. In fact, Plato in the *Laws* is, if anything, more hostile towards the spirit of democracy, i.e. towards the idea of the freedom of the individual, than he is in the *Republic*; cp. especially the text to notes 32 and 33 to chapter 6 (i.e. *Laws*, 739c, ff., and 942a, f.) and to notes 19–22 to chapter 8 (i.e. *Laws*, 903c–909a).—See also next note.

7. It seems likely that it was largely this difficulty of explaining the first change (or the Fall of Man) that led Plato to transform his theory of Ideas, as mentioned in note 15 (8) to chapter 3; viz., to transform the Ideas into causes and active powers, capable of mingling with some of the other Ideas (cp. *Sophist*, 252e, ff.), and of rejecting the remaining ones (*Sophist*, 223c), and thus to transform them into something like gods, as opposed to the *Republic* which (cp. 380d) petrifies even the gods into unmoving and unmoved Parmenidean beings. An important turning point is, apparently, the *Sophist*, 248e–249c (note especially that here the Idea of motion is not at rest). The transformation seems to solve at the same time the difficulty of the so-called 'third man'; for if the Forms are, as in the *Timaeus*, fathers, then there is no 'third man' necessary to explain their similarity to their offspring.

   Regarding the relation of the *Republic* to the *Statesman* and to the *Laws*, I think that Plato's attempt in the two latter dialogues to trace the origin of human society further and further back is likewise connected with the difficulties inherent in the problem of the first change. That it is difficult to conceive of a change overtaking a perfect city is clearly stated in *Republic*, 546a; Plato's attempt in the *Republic* to solve it will be discussed in the next chapter (cp. text to notes 37–40 to chapter 5). In the *Statesman*, Plato adopts the theory of a cosmic catastrophe which leads to the change from the (Empedoclean) half-circle of love to the present period, the half-circle of strife. This idea seems to have been dropped in the *Timaeus*, in order to be replaced by a theory (retained in the *Laws*) of more limited catastrophes, such as floods, which may destroy civilizations, but apparently do not affect the course of the universe. (It is possible that this solution of the problem was suggested to Plato by the fact that in 373–372 B.C., the ancient city of Helice was destroyed by earthquake and flood.) The earliest form of society, removed in the *Republic* only by one single step from the still existing Spartan state, is thrust back to a more and more distant past. Although Plato continues to believe that the first settlement must be the best city, he now discusses societies prior to the first settlement, i.e. nomad societies, 'hill shepherds'. (Cp. especially note 32 to this chapter.)

8. The quotation is from Marx–Engels, *The Communist Manifesto*; cp. *A Handbook of Marxism* (edited by E. Burns, 1935), 22.

9. The quotation is from Adam's comments on Book VIII of the *Republic*; see his edition, vol. II, 198, note to 544a3.

10. Cp. *Republic*, 544c.
11. (1) As opposed to my contention that Plato, like many modern sociologists since Comte, tries to outline the typical stages of social development, most critics take Plato's story merely as a somewhat dramatic presentation of a purely logical classification of constitutions. But this not only contradicts what Plato says (cp. Adam's note to *Rep.*, 544c19, *op. cit.*, vol. II, 199), but it is also against the whole spirit of Plato's logic, according to which the essence of a thing is to be understood by its original nature, i.e. by its historical origin. And we must not forget that he uses the same word, 'genus', to mean a class in the logical sense and a race in the biological sense. The logical 'genus' is still identical with the 'race', in the sense of 'offspring of the same parent'. (With this, cp. notes 15–20 to chapter 3, and text, as well as notes 23–24 to chapter 5, and text, where the equation *nature* = *origin* = *race* is discussed.) Accordingly, there is every reason for taking what Plato says at its face value; for even if Adam were right when he says (*loc. cit.*) that Plato intends to give a 'logical order', this order would for him be at the same time that of a typical historical development. Adam's remark (*loc. cit.*) that the order 'is primarily determined by psychological and not by historical considerations' turns, I believe, against him. For he himself points out (for instance, *op. cit.*, vol. II, 195, note to 543a, ff.) that Plato 'retains throughout ... the analogy between the Soul and the City'. According to Plato's political theory of the soul (which will be discussed in the next chapter), the psychological history must run parallel to the social history, and the alleged opposition between psychological and historical considerations disappears, turning into another argument in favour of our interpretation.

    (2) Exactly the same reply could be made if somebody should argue that Plato's order of the constitution is, fundamentally, not a logical but an ethical one; for the ethical order (and the aesthetic order as well) is, in Plato's philosophy, indistinguishable from the historical order. In this connection, it may be remarked that this historicist view provides Plato with a theoretical background for Socrates' eudemonism, i.e. for the theory that goodness and happiness are identical. This theory is developed, in the *Republic* (cp. especially 580b), in the form of the doctrine that goodness and happiness, or badness and unhappiness, are proportional; and so they must be, if the degree of the goodness as well as of the happiness of a man is to be measured by the degree in which he resembles our original blessed nature—the perfect Idea of man. (The fact that Plato's theory leads, in this point, to a theoretical justification of an apparently paradoxical Socratic doctrine may well have helped Plato to convince himself that he was only expounding the true Socratic creed; see text to notes 56/57 to chapter 10.)

    (3) Rousseau took over Plato's classification of institutions (*Social Contract*, Book II, ch. VII, Book III, ch. III ff., cp. also ch. X). It seems however that he was not directly influenced by Plato when he revived the Platonic Idea of a primitive society (cp., however, notes 1 to chapter 6 and 14 to chapter 9); but a direct product of the Platonic Renaissance in Italy was Sanazzaro's most influential *Arcadia*, with its revival of Plato's idea of a blessed primitive society of Greek (Dorian) hill shepherds. (For this idea of Plato's, cp. text to note 32 to this chapter.) Thus *Romanticism* (cp. also chapter 9) is historically indeed an offspring of Platonism.

    (4) How far the modern historicism of Comte and Mill, and of Hegel and Marx, is influenced by the theistic historicism of Giambattista Vico's *New Science* (1725) is

very hard to say: Vico himself was undoubtedly influenced by Plato, as well as by St. Augustine's *De Civitate Dei* and Machiavelli's *Discourses on Livy*. Like Plato (cp. ch. 5), Vico identified the 'nature' of a thing with its 'origin' (cp. *Opere*, Ferrari's second edn, 1852–4, vol. V, p. 99); and he believed that all nations must pass through the same course of development, according to one universal law. His 'nations' (like Hegel's) may thus be said to be one of the links between Plato's 'Cities' and Toynbee's 'Civilizations'.

12. Cp. *Republic*, 549c/d; the next quotations are *op. cit.*, 550d–e, and later, *op. cit.*, 551a/b.
13. Cp. *op. cit.*, 556e. (This passage should be compared with Thucydides, III, 82–4, quoted in chapter 10, text to note 12.) The next quotation is *op. cit.*, 557a.
14. For Pericles' democratic programme, see text to note 31, chapter 10, note 17 to chapter 6, and note 34 to chapter 10.
15. Adam, in his edition of *The Republic of Plato*, vol. II, 240, note to 559d22. (The italics in the second quotation are mine.) Adam admits that 'the picture is doubtless somewhat exaggerated'; but he leaves little doubt that he thinks it is, fundamentally, true 'for all time'.
16. Adam, *loc. cit.*
17. This quotation is from *Republic*, 560d (for this and the next quotation, cp. Lindsay's translation); the next two quotations are from the same work, 563 a–b, and d. (See also Adam's note to 563d25.) It is significant that Plato appeals here to the institution of private property, severely attacked in other parts of the *Republic*, as if it were an unchallenged principle of justice. It seems that when the property bought is a slave, an appeal to the lawful right of the buyer is adequate.

    Another attack upon democracy is that 'it tramples under foot' the educational principle that 'no one can grow up to be a good man unless his earliest years were given to noble games'. (*Rep.*, 558b; see Lindsay's translation; cp. note 68 to chapter 10.) See also the attacks upon equalitarianism quoted in note 14 to chapter 6.

* For Socrates' attitude towards his young companions see most of the earlier dialogues, but also the *Phaedo*, where Socrates' 'pleasant, kind, and respectful manner in which he listened to the young man's criticism' is described. For Plato's contrasting attitude, see text to notes 19–21 to chapter 7; see also the excellent lectures by H. Cherniss, *The Riddle of the Early Academy* (1945), especially pp. 70 and 79 (on the *Parmenides* 135c–d), and cp. notes 18–21 to chapter 7, and text.

18. Slavery (see the preceding note) and the Athenian movement against it will be further discussed in chapters 5 (notes 13 and text), 10, and 11; see also note 29 to the present chapter. Like Plato, Aristotle (e.g. in *Pol.*, 1313b11, 1319b20; and in his *Constitution of Athens*, 59, 5) testifies to Athens' liberality towards slaves; and so does the Pseudo-Xenophon (cp. his *Const. of Athens*, I, 10 f.)
19. Cp. *Republic*, 577a, f.; see Adam's notes to 577a5 and b12 (*op. cit.*, vol. II, 332 f.). See now also the *Addendum III* (Reply to a Critic), especially pp. 330 f.
20. *Republic*, 566e; cp. note 63 to chapter 10.
21. Cp. *Statesman* (*Politicus*), 301c/d. Although Plato distinguishes six types of debased states, he does not introduce any new terms; the names 'monarchy' (or 'kingship') and 'aristocracy' are used in the *Republic* (445d) of the best state itself, and not of the relatively best forms of debased states, as in the *Statesman*.

22. Cp. *Republic*, 544d.
23. Cp. *Statesman*, 297c/d: 'If the government I have mentioned is the only true original, then the others' (which are 'only copies of this'; cp. 297b/c) 'must use its laws, and write them down; this is the only way in which they can be preserved'. (Cp. note 3 to this chapter, and note 18 to chapter 7.) 'And any violation of the laws should be punished with death, and the most severe punishments; and this is very just and good, although, of course, only the second best thing.' (For the origin of the laws, cp. note 32 (1, a) to this chapter, and note 17 (2) to chapter 3.) And in 300e/301a, f., we read: 'The nearest approach of these lower forms of government to the true government ... is to follow these written laws and customs ... When the rich rule and imitate the true Form, then the government is called aristocracy; and when they do not heed the (ancient) laws oligarchy,' etc. It is important to note that not lawfulness or lawlessness in the abstract, but the preservation of the ancient institutions of the original or perfect state is the criterion of the classification. (This is in contrast to Aristotle's *Politics*, 1292a, where the main distinction is whether or not '*the law* is supreme', or, for instance, *the mob*.)
24. The passage, *Laws*, 709e–714a, contains several allusions to the *Statesman*; for instance, 710d–e, which introduces, following Herodotus III, 80–82, the *number of rulers* as the principle of classification; the enumerations of the forms of government in 712c and d; and 713b, ff., i.e. the myth of the perfect state in the day of Cronos, 'of which the best of our present states are imitations'. In view of these allusions, I little doubt that Plato intended his theory of the fitness of tyranny for Utopian experiments to be understood as a kind of continuation of the story of the *Statesman* (and thus also of the *Republic*).—The quotations in this paragraph are from the *Laws*, 709e, and 710c/d; the 'remark from the *Laws* quoted above' is 797d, quoted in the text to note 3, in this chapter. (I agree with E. B. England's note to this passage, in his edition of *The Laws of Plato*, 1921, vol. II, 258, that it is Plato's principle that '*change is detrimental* to the power ... of anything', and therefore also to the power of evil; but I do not agree with him 'that change *from* bad', viz., to good, is too self-evident to be mentioned as an exception; it is *not* self-evident from the point of view of Plato's doctrine of the evil nature of change. See also next note.)
25. Cp. *Laws*, 676b/c (cp. 676a quoted in the text to note 6). In spite of Plato's doctrine that 'change is detrimental' (cp. the end of the last note), E. B. England interprets these passages on change and revolution by giving them an optimistic or progressive meaning. He suggests that the object of Plato's search is what 'we might call "the secret of political vitality"'. (Cp. *op. cit.*, vol. I, 344.) And he interprets this passage on the search for the true cause of (detrimental) change as dealing with a search for 'the cause and nature of the *true development* of a state, i.e. of its *progress towards perfection*'. (Italics his; cp. vol. I, 345.) This interpretation cannot be correct, for the passage in question is an introduction to a story of political decline; but it shows how much the tendency to idealize Plato and to represent him as a progressivist blinds even such an excellent critic to his own finding, namely, that Plato believed change to be detrimental.
26. Cp. *Republic*, 545d (see also the parallel passage 465b). The next quotation is from the *Laws*, 683e. (Adam in his edition of the *Republic*, vol. II, 203, note to 545d21, refers to this passage in the *Laws*.) England, in his edition of the *Laws*, vol. I, 360 f., note to 683e5, mentions *Republic*, 609a, but neither 545d nor 465b, and supposes

that the reference is 'to a *previous* discussion, or one recorded in a lost dialogue'. I do not see why Plato should not be alluding to the *Republic*, by using the fiction that some of its topics have been discussed by the present interlocutors. As Cornford says, in Plato's last group of dialogues there is 'no motive to keep up the illusion that the conversations had really taken place'; and he is also right when he says that Plato 'was not the slave of his own fictions'. (Cp. Cornford, *Plato's Cosmology*, pp. 5 and 4.) Plato's law of revolutions was rediscovered, without reference to Plato, by V. Pareto; cp. his *Treatise on General Sociology*, §§ 2054, 2057, 2058. (At the end of § 2055, there is also a theory of arresting history.) Rousseau also rediscovered the law. (*Social Contract*, Book III, ch. X.)

27. (1) It may be worth noting that the intentionally non-historical traits of the best state, especially the rule of the philosophers, are not mentioned by Plato in the summary at the beginning of the *Timaeus*, and that in Book VIII of the *Republic* he assumes that the rulers of the best state are not versed in Pythagorean number-mysticism; cp. *Republic*, 546c/d, where the rulers are said to be ignorant of these matters. (Cp. also the remark, *Rep.*, 543d/544a, according to which the best state of Book VIII can still be surpassed, namely, as Adam says, by the city of Books V–VII—the ideal city in heaven.)

In his book, *Plato's Cosmology*, pp. 6 ff., Cornford reconstructs the outlines and contents of Plato's unfinished trilogy, *Timaeus—Critias—Hermocrates*, and shows how they are related to the historical parts of the *Laws* (Book III). This reconstruction is, I think, a valuable corroboration of my theory that Plato's view of the world was fundamentally historical, and that his interest in 'how it generated' (and how it decays) is linked with his theory of Ideas, and indeed based on it. But if that is so, then there is no reason why we should assume that the later books of the *Republic* 'started from the question how it' (i.e. the city) 'might be realized in the *future* and sketched its possible decline through lower forms of politics' (Cornford, *op. cit.*, 6; italics mine); instead we should look upon the Books VIII and IX of the *Republic*, in view of their close parallelism with the Third Book of the *Laws*, as a simplified historical sketch of the actual decline of the ideal city of the *past*, and as an explanation of the origin of the existing states, analogous to the greater task set by Plato for himself in the *Timaeus*, in the unfinished trilogy, and in the *Laws*.

(2) In connection with my remark, later in the paragraph, that Plato 'certainly knew that he did not possess the necessary data', see for instance *Laws*, 683d, and England's note to 683d2.

(3) To my remark, further down in the paragraph, that Plato recognized the Cretan and Spartan societies as petrified or *arrested* forms (and to the remark in the next paragraph that Plato's best state is not only a class state but a *caste state*) the following may be added. (Cp. also note 20 to this chapter, and 24 to chapter 10.)

In *Laws*, 797d (in the introduction to the 'important pronouncement', as England calls it, quoted in the text to note 3 to this chapter), Plato makes it perfectly clear that his Cretan and Spartan interlocutors are aware of the 'arrested' character of their social institutions; Clenias, the Cretan interlocutor, emphasizes that he is anxious to listen to any defence of the archaic character of a state. A little later (799a), and in the same context, a direct reference is made to the Egyptian method of arresting the development of institutions; surely a clear indication that Plato recognized a tendency in Crete and Sparta parallel to that of Egypt, namely, to arrest all social change.

In this context, a passage in the *Timaeus* (see especially 24a–b) seems important. In this passage, Plato tries to show (*a*) that a class division very similar to that of the *Republic* was established in Athens at a very ancient period of its pre-historical development, and (*b*) that these institutions were closely akin to the caste system of Egypt (whose arrested caste institutions he assumes to have derived from his ancient Athenian state). Thus Plato himself acknowledges by implication that the ideal ancient and perfect state of the *Republic* is a caste state. It is interesting that Crantor, first commentator on the *Timaeus*, reports, only two generations after Plato, that Plato had been accused of deserting the Athenian tradition, and of becoming a disciple of the Egyptians. (Cp. Gomperz, *Greek Thinkers*, Germ. ed., II, 476.) Crantor alludes perhaps to Isocrates' *Busiris*, 8, quoted in note 3 to chapter 13.

For the problem of the castes in the *Republic*, see furthermore notes 31 and 32 (I, d) to this chapter, note 40 to chapter 6, and notes 11–14 to chapter 8. A. E. Taylor, *Plato: The Man and His Work*, p. 269 f., forcefully denounces the view that Plato favoured a caste state.

28. Cp. *Republic*, 416a. The problem is considered more fully in this chapter, text to note 35. (For the problem of caste, mentioned in the next paragraph, see notes 27 (3) and 31 to this chapter.)

29. For Plato's advice against legislating for the common people with their 'vulgar market quarrels', etc., see *Republic*, 425b–427a/b; especially 425d–e and 427a. These passages, of course, attack Athenian democracy, and all 'piecemeal' legislation in the sense of chapter 9. *That this is so is also seen by Cornford, *The Republic of Plato* (1941); for he writes, in a note to a passage in which Plato recommends Utopian engineering (it is *Republic* 500d, f., the recommendation of 'canvas-cleaning' and of a romantic radicalism; cp. note 12 to chapter 9, and text): 'Contrast the piecemeal tinkering at reform satirized at 425e …'. Cornford does not seem to like piecemeal reforms, and he seems to prefer Plato's methods; but his and my interpretation of Plato's intentions seem to coincide.*

The four quotations further down in this paragraph are from the *Republic*, 371d/e; 463a–b ('supporters' and 'employers'); 549a; and 471b/c. Adam comments (*op. cit.*, vol. I, 97, note to 371e32): 'Plato does not admit slave labour in his city, unless perhaps in the persons of barbarians.' I agree that Plato opposes in the *Republic* (469b–470c) the enslavement of Greek prisoners of war; but he goes on (in 471b–c) to encourage that of barbarians by Greeks, and especially by the citizens of his best city. (This appears to be also the opinion of Tarn; cp. note 13(2) to chapter 15.) And Plato violently attacked the Athenian movement against slavery, and insisted on the legal rights of property when the property was a slave (cp. text to notes 17 and 18 to this chapter). As is shown also by the third quotation (from *Rep.*, 548e/549a) in the paragraph to which this note is appended, he did *not* abolish slavery in his best city. (See also *Rep.*, 590c/d, where he defends the demand that the coarse and vulgar should be the slaves of the best man.) A. E. Taylor is therefore wrong when he twice asserts (in his *Plato*, 1908 and 1914, pp. 197 and 118) that Plato implies 'that there is no class of slaves in the community'. For similar views in Taylor's *Plato: The Man and His Work* (1926), cp. end of note 27 to this chapter.

Plato's treatment of slavery in the *Statesman* throws, I think, much light on his attitude in the *Republic*. For here, too, he does not speak much about slaves, although he clearly assumes that there are slaves in his state. (See his characteristic remark, 289b/c, that 'all property in tame animals, except slaves' has been already dealt with; and a similarly characteristic remark, 309a, that true kingscraft 'makes slaves of those who wallow in ignorance and abject humility'. The reason why Plato does not say very much about the slaves is quite clear from 289c, ff., especially 289d/e. He does not see a major distinction between 'slaves and other servants', such as labourers, tradesmen, merchants (i.e. all 'banausic' persons who earn money; cp. note 4 to chapter 11); slaves are distinguished from the others merely as 'servants acquired by purchase'. In other words, he is so high above the baseborn that it is hardly worth his while to bother about subtle differences. All this is very similar to the *Republic*, only a little more explicit. (See also note 57 (2) to chapter 8.)

For Plato's treatment of slavery in the *Laws*, see especially G. R. Morrow, 'Plato and Greek Slavery' (*Mind*, N.S., vol. 48, 186–201; see also p. 402), an article which gives an excellent and critical survey of the subject, and reaches a very just conclusion, although the author is, in my opinion, still a little biased in favour of Plato. (The article does not perhaps sufficiently stress the fact that in Plato's day an anti-slavery movement was well on the way; cp. note 13 to chapter 5.)

30. The quotation is from Plato's summary of the *Republic* in the *Timaeus* (18c/d).—With the remark concerning the lack of novelty of the suggested community of women and children, compare Adam's edition of *The Republic of Plato*, vol. I, p. 292 (note to 457b, ff.) and p. 308 (note to 463c17), as well as pp. 345–55, esp. 354; with the Pythagorean element in Plato's communism, cp. *op. cit.*, p. 199, note to 416d22. (For the precious metals, see note 24 to chapter 10. For the common meals, see note 34 to chapter 6; and for the communist principle in Plato and his successors, note 29 (2) to chapter 5, and the passages mentioned there.)

31. The passage quoted is from *Republic*, 434b/c. In demanding a caste state, Plato hesitates for a long time. This is quite apart from the 'lengthy preface' to the passage in question (which will be discussed in chapter 6; cp. notes 24 and 40 to that chapter); for when first speaking about these matters, in 415a, ff., he speaks as though a rise from the lower to the upper classes were permissible, provided that in the lower classes 'children were born with an admixture of gold and silver' (415c), i.e. of upper class blood and virtue. But in 434b–d, and, even more clearly, in 547a, this permission is, in effect, withdrawn; and in 547a *any* admixture of the metals is declared an impurity which must be fatal to the state. See also text to notes 11–14 to chapter 8 (and note 27 (3) to the present chapter).

32. Cp. the *Statesman*, 271e. The passages in the *Laws* about the primitive nomadic shepherds and their patriarchs are 677e–680e. The passage quoted is *Laws*, 680e. The passage quoted next is from the Myth of the Earthborn, *Republic*, 415d/e. The concluding quotation of the paragraph is from *Republic*, 440d.—It may be necessary to add some comments on certain remarks in the paragraph to which this note is appended.

(1) It is stated in the text that it is not very clearly explained how the 'settlement' came about. Both in the *Laws* and in the *Republic* we first hear (see (*a*) and (*c*), below) of a kind of agreement or social contract (for the social contract, cp. note 29 to chapter 5 and notes 43–54 to chapter 6, and text), and later (see (*b*) and (*c*), below) of a forceful subjugation.

(*a*) In the *Laws*, the various tribes of hill shepherds settle in the plains after having joined together to form larger war bands whose laws are arrived at by an agreement or contract, made by arbiters vested with royal powers (681b and c/d; for the origin of the laws described in 681b, cp. note 17 (2) to chapter 3). But now Plato becomes evasive. Instead of describing how these bands settle in Greece, and how the Greek cities were founded, Plato switches over to Homer's story of the foundation of Troy, and to the Trojan war. From there, Plato says, the Achaeans returned under the name of Dorians, and 'the rest of the story ... is part of Lacedaemonian history' (682e) 'for we have reached the settlement of Lacedaemon' (682e/683a). So far we have heard nothing about the manner of this settlement, and there follows at once a further digression (Plato himself speaks about the 'roundabout track of the argument') until we get ultimately (in 683c/d) the 'hint' mentioned in the text; see (*b*).

(*b*) The statement in the text that we get a hint that the Dorian 'settlement' in the Peloponnese was in fact a violent subjugation, refers to the *Laws* (683c/d), where Plato introduces what are actually his first historical remarks on Sparta. He says that he begins at the time when the whole of the Peloponnese was 'practically subjugated' by the Dorians. In the *Menexenus* (whose genuineness can hardly be doubted; cp. note 35 to chapter 10) there is in 245c an allusion to the fact that the Peloponnesians were 'immigrants from abroad' (as Grote puts it: cp. his *Plato*, III, p. 5).

(*c*) In the *Republic* (369b) the city is founded by workers with a view to the advantages of a division of labour and of co-operation, in accordance with the contract theory.

(*d*) But later (in *Rep.*, 415d/e; see the quotation in the text, to this paragraph) we get a description of the triumphant invasion of a warrior class of somewhat mysterious origin—the 'earthborn'. The decisive passage of this description states that the earthborn must look round to find for their camp the most suitable spot (literally) 'for keeping down those within', i.e. for keeping down those already living in the city, i.e. for *keeping down the inhabitants*.

(*e*) In the *Statesman* (271a, f.) these 'earthborn' are identified with the very early nomad hill shepherds of the pre-settlement period. Cp. also the allusion to the autochthonous grasshoppers in the *Symposium*, 191b; cp. note 6 (4) to chapter 3, and 11 (2) to chapter 8.

(*f*) To sum up, it seems that Plato had a fairly clear idea of the Dorian conquest, which he preferred, for obvious reasons, to veil in mystery. It also seems that there was a tradition that the conquering war hordes were of nomad descent.

(2) With the remark later in the text in this paragraph regarding Plato's 'continuous emphasis' on the fact that *ruling is shepherding*, cp., for instance, the following passages: *Republic*, 343b, where the idea is introduced; 345c, f., where, in the form of the simile of the good shepherd, it becomes one of the central topics of the investigation; 375a–376b, 404a, 440d, 451b–e, 459a–460c, and 466c–d (quoted in note 30 to chapter 5), where the auxiliaries are likened to sheep-dogs and where their breeding and education are discussed accordingly; 416a, ff., where the problem of the wolves without and within the state is introduced; cp. furthermore the *Statesman*, where the idea is continued over many pages, especially 261d–276d. With regard to the *Laws*, I may refer to the passage (694e), where Plato says of Cyrus that he had acquired for his sons 'cattle and sheep and many herds of men and other animals'. (Cp. also *Laws*, 735, and *Theaet.*, 174d.)

(3) With all this, cp. also A. J. Toynbee, *A Study of History*, esp. vol. III, pp. 32 (n. 1), where A. H. Lybyer, *The Government of the Ottoman Empire*, etc., is quoted, 33 (n. 2), 50–100; see more especially his remark on the conquering nomads (p. 22) who 'deal with ... men', and on Plato's 'human watchdogs' (p. 94, n. 2). I have been much stimulated by Toynbee's brilliant ideas and much encouraged by many of his remarks which I take as corroborating my interpretations, and which I can value the more highly the more Toynbee's and my fundamental assumptions seem to disagree. I also owe to Toynbee a number of terms used in my text, especially 'human cattle', 'human herd' and 'human watch-dog'.

Toynbee's *Study of History* is, from my point of view, a model of what I call historicism; I need not say much more to express my fundamental disagreement with it; and a number of special points of disagreement will be discussed at various places (cp. notes 43 and 45 (2) to this chapter, notes 7 and 8 to chapter 10, and chapter 24; also, my criticism of Toynbee in chapter 24, and in *The Poverty of Historicism*, p. 110 ff.). But it contains a wealth of interesting and stimulating ideas. Regarding Plato, Toynbee emphasizes a number of points in which I can follow him, especially that Plato's best state is inspired by his experience of social revolutions and by his wish to arrest all change, and that it is a kind of arrested Sparta (which itself was also arrested). In spite of these points of agreement, there is even in the interpretation of Plato a fundamental disagreement between Toynbee's views and my own. Toynbee regards Plato's best state as a typical (reactionary) Utopia, while I interpret its major part, in connection with what I consider as Plato's general theory of change, as an attempt to reconstruct a primitive form of society. Nor do I think that Toynbee would agree with my interpretation of Plato's story of the period prior to the settlement, and of the settlement itself, outlined in this note and the text; for Toynbee says (*op. cit.*, vol. III, 80) that 'the Spartan society was not of nomadic origin'. Toynbee strongly emphasizes (*op. cit.*, III, 50 ff.) the peculiar character of the Spartan society, which, he says, was arrested in its development owing to a superhuman effort to keep down their 'human cattle'. But I think that this emphasis on the peculiar situation of Sparta makes it difficult to understand the similarities between the institutions of Sparta and Crete which Plato found so striking (*Rep.*, 544c; *Laws*, 683a). These, I believe, can be explained only as arrested forms of very ancient tribal institutions, which must be considerably older than the effort of the Spartans in the second Messenian war (about 650–620 B.C.; cp. Toynbee, *op. cit.*, III, 53). Since the conditions of the survival of these institutions were so very different in the two localities, their similarity is a strong argument in favour of their being primitive and against an explanation by a factor which affects only one of them.

* For problems of the Dorian Settlement, see also R. Eisler in *Caucasia*, vol. V, 1928, especially p. 113, note 84, where the term 'Hellenes' is translated as the 'settlers', and 'Greeks' as the 'graziers'—i.e. the cattle-breeders or nomads. The same author has shown (*Orphisch-Dionisische Mysteriengedanken*, 1925, p. 58, note 2) that the idea of the God-Shepherd is of Orphic origin. At the same place, the sheep-dogs of God (*Domini Canes*) are mentioned.*

33. The fact that education is in Plato's state a class prerogative has been overlooked by some enthusiastic educationists who credit Plato with the idea of making education independent of financial means; they do not see that the evil is the class prerogative

as such, and that it is comparatively unimportant whether this prerogative is based upon the possession of money or upon any other criterion by which membership of the ruling class is determined. Cp. notes 12 and 13 to chapter 7, and text. Concerning the carrying of arms, see also *Laws*, 753b.

34. Cp. *Republic*, 460c. (See also note 31 to this chapter.) Regarding Plato's recommendation of infanticide, see Adam, *op. cit.*, vol. I, p. 299, note to 460c18, and pp. 357 ff. Although Adam rightly insists that Plato was in favour of infanticide, and although he rejects as 'irrelevant' all attempts 'to acquit Plato of sanctioning' such a dreadful practice, he tries to excuse Plato by pointing out 'that the practice was widely prevalent in ancient Greece'. But it was not so in Athens. Plato chooses throughout to prefer the ancient Spartan barbarism and racialism to the enlightenment of Pericles' Athens; and for this choice he must be held responsible. For a hypothesis explaining the Spartan practice, see note 7 to chapter 10 (and text); see also the cross-references given there.

    The later quotations in this paragraph which favour applying the principles of animal breeding to man are from *Republic*, 459b (cp. note 39 to chapter 8, and text); those on the analogy between dogs and warriors, etc., from the *Republic*, 404a; 375a; 376a/b; and 376b. See also note 40 (2) to chapter 5, and the next note here.

35. The two quotations before the note number are both from *Republic*, 375b. The next following quotation is from 416a (cp. note 28 to this chapter); the remaining ones are from 375c–e. The problem of blending opposite 'natures' (or even Forms; cp. notes 18–20 and 40 (2) to chapter 5, and text and note 39 to chapter 8) is one of Plato's favourite topics. (In the *Statesman*, 283e, f., and later in Aristotle, it merges into the doctrine of the mean.)

36. The quotations are from *Republic*, 410c; 410d; 410e; 411e/412a and 412b.

37. In the *Laws* (680b, ff.) Plato himself treats Crete with some irony because of its barbarous ignorance of literature. This ignorance extends even to Homer, whom the Cretan interlocutor does not know, and of whom he says: 'foreign poets are very little read by Cretans'. ('But they are read in Sparta', rejoins the Spartan interlocutor.) For Plato's preference for Spartan customs, see also note 34 to chapter 6, and the text to note 30 to the present chapter.

38. For Plato's view on Sparta's treatment of the human cattle, see note 29 to this chapter, *Republic*, 548e/549a, where the timocratic man is compared with Plato's brother Glaucon: 'He would be harder' (than Glaucon) 'and less musical'; the continuation of this passage is quoted in the text to note 29.—Thucydides reports (IV, 80) the treacherous murder of the 2,000 helots; the best of the helots were selected for death by a promise of freedom. It is almost certain that Plato knew Thucydides well, and we can be sure that he had in addition more direct sources of information.

    For Plato's views on Athens' slack treatment of slaves, see note 18 to this chapter.

39. Considering the decidedly anti-Athenian and therefore anti-literary tendency of the *Republic*, it is a little difficult to explain why so many educationists are so enthusiastic about Plato's educational theories. I can see only three likely explanations. Either they do not understand the *Republic*, in spite of its most outspoken hostility towards the then existing Athenian literary education; or they are simply flattered by Plato's rhetorical emphasis upon the political power of education, just as so many philosophers are, and even some musicians (see text to note 41); or both.

It is also difficult to see how lovers of Greek art and literature can find encouragement in Plato, who, especially in the Tenth Book of the *Republic*, launched a most violent attack against all poets and tragedians, and especially against Homer (and even Hesiod). See *Republic*, 600a, where Homer is put below the level of a good technician or mechanic (who would be generally despised by Plato as banausic and depraved; cp. *Rep.*, 495e and 590c, and note 4 to chapter 11); *Republic*, 600c, where Homer is put below the level of the Sophists Protagoras and Prodicus (see also Gomperz, *Greek Thinkers*, German edn, II, 401); and *Republic*, 605a/b, where poets are bluntly forbidden to enter into any well-governed city.

These clear expressions of Plato's attitude, however, are usually passed over by the commentators, who dwell, on the other hand, on remarks like the one made by Plato in preparing his attack on Homer ('... though love and admiration for Homer hardly allow me to say what I have to say'; *Rep.*, 595b). Adam comments on this (note to 595b11) by saying that 'Plato speaks with real feeling'; but I think that Plato's remark only illustrates a method fairly generally adopted in the *Republic*, namely, that of making some concession to the reader's sentiments (cp. chapter 10, especially text to note 65) before the main attack upon humanitarian ideas is launched.

40. For the rigid censorship aimed at class discipline, see *Republic*, 377e, ff., and especially 378c: 'Those who are to be the guardians of our city ought to consider it the most pernicious crime to quarrel easily with one another.' It is interesting that Plato does not state this political principle at once, when introducing his theory of censorship in 376e, ff., but that he speaks first only of truth, beauty, etc. The censorship is further tightened up in 595a, ff., especially 605a/b (see the foregoing note, and notes 18–22 to chapter 7, and text). For the rôle of censorship in the *Laws*, see 801c/d.—See also the next note.

For Plato's forgetfulness of his principle (*Rep.*, 410c–412b, see note 36 to this chapter) that music has to strengthen the gentle element in man as opposed to the fierce, see especially 399a, f., where modes of music are demanded which do not make men soft, but are 'fit for men who are warriors'. Cp. also the next note, (2).—It must be made clear that Plato has not 'forgotten' a *previously* announced principle, but only that principle to which his discussion is going to lead up.

41. (1) For Plato's attitude towards music, especially music proper, see, for instance, *Republic*, 397b, ff.; 398e, ff.; 400a, ff.; 410b, 424b, f., 546d. *Laws*, 657e, ff.; 673a, 700b, ff., 798d, ff., 801d, ff., 802b, ff., 816c. His attitude is, fundamentally, that one must 'beware of changing to a new mode of music; this endangers everything' since 'any change in the style of music always leads to a change in the most important institutions of the whole state. So says Damon, and I believe him.' (*Rep.*, 424c.) Plato, as usual, follows the Spartan example. Adam (*op. cit.*, vol. I, p. 216, note to 424c20; italics mine; cp. also his references) says that 'the connection between musical and political changes ... was recognized universally throughout Greece, and *particularly at Sparta*, where ... Timotheus had his lyre confiscated for adding to it four new strings'. That Sparta's procedure inspired Plato cannot be doubted; its universal recognition throughout Greece, and especially in Periclean Athens, is most improbable. (Cp. (2) of this note.)

(2) In the text I have called Plato's attitude towards music (cp. especially *Rep.*, 398e, ff.) superstitious and backward if compared with 'a more enlightened contemporary criticism'. The criticism I have in mind is that of the anonymous writer,

probably a musician of the fifth (or the early fourth) century, the author of an address (possibly an Olympian oration) which is now known as the thirteenth piece of Grenfell and Hunt, *The Hibeh Papyri*, 1906, pp. 45 ff. It seems possible that the writer is one of 'the various musicians who criticize Socrates' (i.e. the 'Socrates' of Plato's *Republic*), mentioned by Aristotle (in the equally superstitious passage of his *Politics*, 1342b, where he repeats most of Plato's arguments); but the criticism of the anonymous author goes much further than Aristotle indicates. Plato (and Aristotle) believed that certain musical modes, for instance, the 'slack' Ionian and Lydian modes, made people soft and effeminate, while others, especially the Dorian mode, made them brave. This view is attacked by the anonymous author. 'They say', he writes, 'that some modes produce temperate and others just men; others, again, heroes, and others cowards.' He brilliantly exposes the silliness of this view by pointing out that some of the most war-like of the Greek tribes use modes reputed to produce cowards, while certain professional (opera) singers habitually sing in the 'heroic' mode without ever showing signs of becoming heroes. This criticism might have been directed against the Athenian musician Damon, often quoted by Plato as an authority, a friend of Pericles (who was liberal enough to tolerate a pro-Spartan attitude in the field of artistic criticism). But it might easily have been directed against Plato himself. For Damon, see Diels[5]; for a hypothesis concerning the anonymous author, see *ibid.*, vol. II, p. 334, note.

(3) In view of the fact that I am attacking a 'reactionary' attitude towards music, I may perhaps remark that my attack is in no way inspired by a personal sympathy for 'progress' in music. In fact, I happen to like old music (the older the better) and to dislike modern music intensely (especially most works written since the day when Wagner began to write music). I am altogether against 'futurism', whether in the field of art or of morals (cp. chapter 22, and note 19 to chapter 25). But I am also against imposing one's likes and dislikes upon others, and against censorship in such matters. We can love and hate, especially in art, without favouring legal measures for suppressing what we hate, or for canonizing what we love.

42. Cp. *Republic*, 537a; and 466e–467e.

The characterization of modern totalitarian education is due to A. Kolnai, *The War against the West* (1938), p. 318.

43. Plato's remarkable theory that the state, i.e. centralized and organized political power, originates through a conquest (the subjugation of a sedentary agricultural population by nomads or hunters) was, as far as I know, first re-discovered (if we discount some remarks by Machiavelli) by Hume in his criticism of the historical version of the contract theory (cp. his *Essays, Moral, Political, and Literary*, vol. II, 1752, Essay XII, *Of the Original Contract*):—'Almost all the governments', Hume writes, 'which exist at present, or of which there remains any record in story, have been founded originally, either on usurpation or conquest, or both ...' And he points out that for 'an artful and bold man ..., it is often easy ..., by employing sometimes violence, sometimes false pretences, to establish his dominion over a people a hundred times more numerous than his partizans ... By such arts as these, many governments have been established; and this is all the *original contract*, which they have to boast of.' The theory was next revived by Renan, in *What is a Nation?* (1882), and by Nietzsche in his *Genealogy of Morals* (1887); see the third German edition of 1894, p. 98. The latter writes of the origin of the 'state' (without reference to Hume):

'Some horde of blonde beasts, a conquering master race with a war-like organization … lay their terrifying paws heavily upon a population which is perhaps immensely superior in—numbers … This is the way in which the "state" originates upon earth; I think that the sentimentality which lets it originate with a "contract", is dead.' This theory appeals to Nietzsche because he likes these blonde beasts. But it has also been proffered more recently by F. Oppenheimer (*The State*, transl. Gitterman, 1914, p. 68); by a Marxist, K. Kautsky (in his book on *The Materialist Interpretation of History*); and by W. C. Macleod (*The Origin and History of Politics*, 1931). I think it very likely that something of the kind described by Plato, Hume, and Nietzsche has happened in many, if not in all, cases. I am speaking only about 'states' in the sense of organized and even centralized political power.

I may mention that Toynbee has a very different theory. But before discussing it, I wish first to make it clear that from the anti-historicist point of view, the question is of no great importance. It is perhaps interesting in itself to consider how 'states' originated, but it has no bearing whatever upon the sociology of states, as I understand it, i.e. upon political technology (see chapters 3, 9, and 25).

Toynbee's theory does not confine itself to 'states' in the sense of organized and centralized political power. He discusses, rather, the 'origin of *civilizations*'. But here begins the difficulty; for some of his 'civilizations' are states (as here described), some are groups or sequences of states, and some are societies like that of the Eskimos, which are not states; and if it is questionable whether 'states' originate according to one single scheme, then it must be even more doubtful when we consider a class of such diverse social phenomena as the early Egyptian and Mesopotamian states and their institutions and technique on the one side, and the Eskimo way of living on the other.

But we may concentrate on Toynbee's description (*A Study of History*, vol. I, pp. 305 ff.) of the origin of the Egyptian and Mesopotamian 'civilizations'. His theory is that the challenge of a difficult jungle environment rouses a response from ingenious and enterprising leaders; they lead their followers into the valleys which they begin to cultivate, and found states. This (Hegelian and Bergsonian) theory of the creative genius as a cultural and political leader appears to me most romantic. If we take Egypt, then we must look, first of all, for the origin of the caste system. This, I believe, is most likely the result of conquests, just as in India where every new wave of conquerors imposed a new caste upon the old ones. But there are other arguments. Toynbee himself favours a theory which is probably correct, namely, that animal breeding and especially animal training is a later, a more advanced and a more difficult stage of development than mere agriculture, and that this advanced step is taken by the nomads of the steppe. But in Egypt we find both agriculture and animal breeding, and the same holds for most of the early 'states' (though not for all the American ones, I gather). This seems to be a sign that these states contain a nomadic element; and it seems only natural to venture the hypothesis that this element is due to nomad invaders imposing their rule, a caste rule, upon the original agricultural population. This theory disagrees with Toynbee's contention (*op. cit.*, III, 23 f.) that nomad-built states usually wither away very quickly. But the fact that many of the early caste states go in for the breeding of animals has to be explained somehow.

The idea that nomads or even hunters constituted the original upper class is corroborated by the age-old and still surviving upper-class tradition according to which war, hunting, and horses are the symbols of the leisured classes; a tradition which formed the basis of Aristotle's ethics and politics, and which is still alive, as Veblen (*The Theory of the Leisure Class*) and Toynbee have shown; and to this evidence we can perhaps add the animal breeder's belief in racialism, and especially in the racial superiority of the upper class. The latter belief which is so pronounced in caste states and in Plato and in Aristotle is held by Toynbee to be 'one of the ... sins of our ... modern age' and 'something alien from the Hellenic genius' (*op. cit.*, III, 93). But although many Greeks may have developed beyond racialism, it seems likely that Plato's and Aristotle's theories are based on old traditions; especially in view of the fact that racial ideas played such a rôle in Sparta.

44. Cp. *Laws*, 694a–698a.

45. (1) Spengler's *Decline of the West* is not in my opinion to be taken seriously. But it is a symptom; it is the theory of one who believes in an upper class which is facing defeat. Like Plato, Spengler tries to show that 'the world' is to be blamed, with its general law of decline and death. And like Plato, he demands (in his sequel, *Prussianism and Socialism*) a new order, a desperate experiment to stem the forces of history, a regeneration of the Prussian ruling class by the adoption of a 'socialism' or communism, and of economic abstinence.—Concerning Spengler, I largely agree with L. Nelson, who published his criticism under a long ironical title whose beginning may be translated: 'Witchcraft: Being an Initiation into the Secrets of Oswald Spengler's Art of Fortune Telling, and a Most Evident Proof of the Irrefutable Truth of His Soothsaying', etc. I think that this is a just characterization of Spengler. Nelson, I may add, was one of the first to oppose what I call historicism (following here Kant in his criticism of Herder; cp. chapter 12, note 56).

(2) My remark that Spengler's is not the last *Decline and Fall* is meant especially as an allusion to Toynbee. Toynbee's work is so superior to Spengler's that I hesitate to mention it in the same context; but the superiority is due mainly to Toynbee's wealth of ideas and to his superior knowledge (which manifests itself in the fact that he does not, as Spengler does, deal with everything under the sun at the same time). But the aim and method of the investigation is similar. It is most decidedly historicist. (Cp. my criticism of Toynbee in *The Poverty of Historicism*, pp. 110 ff.) And it is, fundamentally, Hegelian (although I do not see that Toynbee is aware of this fact). His 'criterion of the growth of civilizations' which is 'progress towards self-determination' shows this clearly enough; for Hegel's law of progress towards 'self-consciousness' and 'freedom' can be only too easily recognized. (Toynbee's Hegelianism seems to come somehow through Bradley, as may be seen, for instance, by his remarks on relations, *op. cit.*, III, 223: 'The very concept of "relations" between "things" or "beings" involves' a 'logical contradiction ... How is this contradiction to be transcended?' (I cannot enter here into a discussion of the problem of relations. But I may state dogmatically that all problems concerning relations can be reduced, by certain simple methods of modern logic, to problems concerning properties, or classes; in other words, *peculiar philosophical difficulties concerning relations do not exist*. The method mentioned is due to N. Wiener and K. Kuratowski; see Quine, *A System of Logistic*, 1934, pp. 16 ff.). Now I do not believe that to classify a work as belonging to a certain school is to dismiss it; but in the case of Hegelian historicism I think that it is so, for reasons to be discussed in the second volume of this book.

Concerning Toynbee's historicism, I wish to make it especially clear that I doubt very much indeed whether civilizations are born, grow, break down, and die. I am obliged to stress this point because I myself use some of the terms used by Toynbee, in so far as I speak of the 'breakdown' and of the 'arresting' of societies. But I wish to make it clear that my term 'breakdown' refers not to all kinds of civilizations but to one particular kind of phenomenon—to the *feeling* of bewilderment connected with the dissolution of the magical or tribal 'closed society'. Accordingly, I do not believe, as Toynbee does, that Greek society suffered 'its breakdown' in the period of the Peloponnesian war; and I find the symptoms of the breakdown which Toynbee describes much earlier. (Cp. with this notes 6 and 8 to chapter 10, and text.) Regarding 'arrested' societies, I apply this term exclusively, either to a society that clings to its magical forms through closing itself up, by force, against the influence of an open society, or to a society that attempts to *return to the tribal cage*.

Also I do not think that our Western civilization is just one member of a species. I think that there are many closed societies who may suffer all kinds of fates; but an 'open society' can, I suppose, only go on, or be arrested and forced back into the cage, i.e. to the beasts. (Cp. also chapter 10, especially the last note.)

(3) Regarding the Decline and Fall stories, I may mention that nearly all of them stand under the influence of Heraclitus' remark: 'They fill their bellies like the beasts', and of Plato's theory of the low animal instincts. I mean to say that they all try to show that the decline is due to an adoption (by the ruling class) of these 'lower' standards which are allegedly natural to the working classes. In other words, and putting the matter crudely but bluntly, the theory is that civilizations, like the Persian and the Roman empires, decline owing to overfeeding. (Cp. note 19 to chapter 10.)

NOTES TO CHAPTER FIVE

1. The 'charmed circle' is a quotation from Burnet, *Greek Philosophy*, I, 106, where similar problems are treated. I do not, however, agree with Burnet that 'in early days the regularity of human life had been far more clearly apprehended than the even course of nature'. This presupposes the establishment of a differentiation which, I believe, is characteristic of a later period, i.e. the period of the dissolution of the 'charmed circle of law and custom'. Moreover, natural periods (the seasons, etc.; cp. note 6 to chapter 2, and Plato (?), *Epinomis*, 978d, ff.) must have been apprehended in very early days.—For the distinction between natural and normative laws, see esp. note 18 (4) to this chapter.
2. *Cp. R. Eisler, *The Royal Art of Astrology*. Eisler says that the peculiarities of the movement of the planets were interpreted, by the Babylonian 'tablet writers who produced the Library of Assurbanipal' (*op. cit.*, 288), as 'dictated by the "laws" or "decisions" ruling "heaven and earth" (*pirishtē shamē u irsiti*), pronounced by the creator god at the beginning' (*ibid.*, 232 f.). And he points out (*ibid.*, 288) that the idea of 'universal laws' (of nature) originates with this 'mythological ... concept of ... "decrees of heaven and earth" ...'*

   For the passage from Heraclitus, cp. D5, B 29, and note 7 (2) to chapter 2; also note 6 to that chapter, and text. See also Burnet, *loc. cit.*, who gives a different interpretation; he thinks that 'when the regular course of nature began to be observed, no better name could be found for it than Right or Justice ... which properly meant the unchanging custom that guided human life.' I do not believe that the term meant first something social and was then extended, but I think that both social and natural regularities ('order') were originally undifferentiated, and interpreted as magical.

3. The opposition is expressed sometimes as one between 'nature' and 'law' (or 'norm' or 'convention'), sometimes as one between 'nature' and the 'positing' or 'laying down' (viz., of normative laws), and sometimes as one between 'nature' and 'art', or 'natural' and 'artificial'.

   The antithesis between nature and convention is often said (on the authority of *Diogenes Laertius*, II, 16 and 4; *Doxogr.*, 564b) to have been introduced by Archelaus, who is said to have been the teacher of Socrates. But I think that, in the *Laws*, 690b, Plato makes it clear enough that he considers 'the Theban poet Pindar' to be the originator of the antithesis (cp. notes 10 and 28 to this chapter). Apart from Pindar's fragments (quoted by Plato; see also Herodotus, III, 38), and some remarks by Herodotus (*loc. cit.*), one of the earliest original sources preserved is the Sophist Antiphon's fragments *On Truth* (see notes 11 and 12 to this chapter). According to Plato's *Protagoras*, the Sophist Hippias seems to have been a pioneer of similar views (see note 13 to this chapter). But the most influential early treatment of the problem seems to have been that of Protagoras himself, although he may possibly have used a different terminology. (It may be mentioned that Democritus dealt with the antithesis which he applied also to such social 'institutions' as language; and Plato did the same in the *Cratylus*, e.g. 384e.)

4. A very similar point of view can be found in Russell's 'A Free Man's Worship' (in *Mysticism and Logic*); and in the last chapter of Sherrington's *Man on His Nature*.

5. (1) Positivists will reply, of course, that the reason why norms cannot be derived from factual propositions is that norms are meaningless; but this shows only that (with Wittgenstein's *Tractatus*) they define 'meaning' arbitrarily in such a way that only factual propositions are 'meaningful'. (See also my *The Logic of Scientific Discovery*, pp. 35 ff. and 51 f.) The followers of 'psychologism', on the other hand, will try to explain imperatives as expressions of emotions, norms as habits, and standards as points of view. But although the habit of not stealing certainly is a fact, it is necessary, as explained in the text, to distinguish this fact from the corresponding norm.—On the question of the logic of norms, I fully agree with most of the views expressed by K. Menger in his book, *Moral, Wille und Weltgestaltung*, 1935. He is one of the first, I believe, to develop the foundations of a *logic of norms*. I may perhaps express here my opinion that the reluctance to admit that norms are something important and irreducible is one of the main sources of the intellectual and other weaknesses of the more 'progressive' circles in our present time.

   (2) Concerning my contention that it is impossible to derive a sentence stating a norm or decision from a sentence stating a fact, the following may be added. In analysing the relations between sentences and facts, we are moving in that field of logical inquiry which A. Tarski has called *Semantics* (cp. note 29 to chapter 3 and note 23 to chapter 8). One of the fundamental concepts of semantics is the concept of *truth*. As shown by Tarski, it is possible (within what Carnap calls a semantical system) to derive a descriptive statement like 'Napoleon died on St. Helena' from the statement 'Mr. A said that Napoleon died on St. Helena', in conjunction with the further

statement that what Mr. A said was *true*. (And if we use the term 'fact' in such a wide sense that we not only speak about the fact described by a sentence but also about the *fact that this sentence is true*, then we could even say that it is possible to derive 'Napoleon died on St. Helena' from the two 'facts' that Mr. A said it, and that he spoke the truth.) Now there is no reason why we should not proceed in an exactly analogous fashion in the realm of norms. We might then introduce, in correspondence to the concept of truth, the concept of the *validity or rightness* of a norm. This would mean that a certain norm *N* could be derived (in a kind of semantic of norms) from a sentence stating that *N* is valid or right; or in other words, the norm or commandment 'Thou shalt not steal' would be considered as equivalent to the assertion 'The norm "Thou shalt not steal" is valid or right'. (And again, if we use the term 'fact' in such a wide sense that we speak about the *fact that a norm is valid or right*, then we could even derive norms from facts. This, however, does not impair the correctness of our considerations in the text which are concerned solely with the impossibility of deriving norms from psychological or sociological or similar, i.e. non-semantic, facts.)

* (3) In my first discussion of these problems, I spoke of norms or decisions but never of *proposals*. The proposal to speak, instead, of 'proposals' is due to L. J. Russell; see his paper 'Propositions and Proposals', in the *Library of the Tenth International Congress of Philosophy* (Amsterdam, August 11–18, 1948), vol. I, *Proceedings of the Congress*. In this important paper, statements of fact or 'propositions' are distinguished from suggestions for the adoption of a line of conduct (of a certain policy, or of certain norms, or of certain aims or ends), and the latter are called 'proposals'. The great advantage of this terminology is that, as everybody knows, one can *discuss* a proposal, while it is not so clear whether, and in which sense, one can discuss a decision or a norm; thus by talking of 'norms' or 'decisions', one is liable to support those who say that these things are beyond discussion (either above it, as some dogmatic theologians or metaphysicians may say, or—as nonsensical—below it, as some positivists may say).

Adopting Russell's terminology, we could say that a proposition may be *asserted* or *stated* (or a hypothesis *accepted*) while a proposal is *adopted*; and we shall distinguish the *fact of its adoption* from the *proposal* which has been adopted.

Our dualistic thesis then becomes the thesis that *proposals are not reducible to facts* (or to statements of facts, or to propositions) *even though they pertain to facts*.*

6. Cp. also the last note (71) to chapter 10.

Although my own position is, I believe, clearly enough implied in the text, I may perhaps briefly formulate what seem to me the most important principles of humanitarian and equalitarian ethics.

(1) Tolerance towards all who are not intolerant and who do not propagate intolerance. (For this exception, cp. what is said in notes 4 and 6 to chapter 7.) This implies, especially, that the moral decisions of others should be treated with respect, as long as such decisions do not conflict with the principle of tolerance.

(2) The recognition that all moral urgency has its basis in the urgency of suffering or pain. I suggest, for this reason, to replace the utilitarian formula 'Aim at the greatest amount of happiness for the greatest number', or briefly, 'Maximize happiness', by the formula 'The least amount of avoidable suffering for all', or briefly, 'Minimize suffering'. Such a simple formula can, I believe, be made one of the fundamental principles (admittedly not the only one) of public policy. (The principle

'Maximize happiness', in contrast, seems to be apt to produce a benevolent dictatorship.) We should realize that from the moral point of view suffering and happiness must not be treated as symmetrical; that is to say, the promotion of happiness is in any case much less urgent than the rendering of help to those who suffer, and the attempt to prevent suffering. (The latter task has little to do with 'matters of taste', the former much.) Cp. also note 2 to chapter 9.

(3) The fight against tyranny; or in other words, the attempt to safeguard the other principles by the institutional means of a legislation rather than by the benevolence of persons in power. (Cp. section 11 of chapter 7.)

7. Cp. Burnet, *Greek Philosophy*, I, 117.—Protagoras' doctrine referred to in this paragraph is to be found in Plato's dialogue *Protagoras*, 322a, ff.; cp. also the *Theaetetus*, esp. 172b (see also note 27 to this chapter).

The difference between Platonism and Protagoreanism can perhaps be briefly expressed as follows:

(Platonism.) There is an inherent 'natural' order of justice in the world, i.e. the original or first order in which nature was created. Thus the past is good, and any development leading to new norms is bad.

(Protagoreanism.) Man is the moral being in this world. Nature is neither moral nor immoral. Thus it is possible for man also to improve things.—It is not unlikely that Protagoras was influenced by Xenophanes, one of the first to express the attitude of the open society, and to criticize Hesiod's historical pessimism: 'In the beginning, the Gods did not show to man all he was wanting; but in the course of time, he may search for the better, and find it.' (Cp. Diels[5], 18.) It seems that Plato's nephew and successor Speusippus returned to this progressive view (cp. Aristotle's *Metaphysics*, 1072b30 and note 11 to chapter 11) and that the Academy adopted with him a more liberal attitude in the field of politics also.

Concerning the relation of the doctrine of Protagoras to the tenets of religion, it may be remarked that he believed God to work through man. I do not see how this position can contradict that of Christianity. Compare with it for instance K. Barth's statement (*Credo*, 1936, p. 188): 'The Bible is a *human* document' (i.e. man is God's instrument).

8. Socrates' advocacy of the autonomy of ethics (closely related to his insistence that problems of nature do not matter) is expressed especially in his doctrine of the self-sufficiency or autarky of the 'virtuous' individual. That this theory contrasts strongly with Plato's views of the individual will be seen later; cp. especially notes 25 to this chapter and 36 to the next, and text. (Cp. also note 56 to chapter 10.)

9. We cannot, for instance, construct institutions which work independently of how they are being 'manned'. With these problems, cp. chapter 7 (text to notes 7–8, 22–23), and especially chapter 9.

10. For Plato's discussion of Pindar's naturalism, see esp. *Gorgias*, 484b; 488b; *Laws*, 690b (quoted below in this chapter; cp. note 28); 714e/715a; cp. also 890a/b. (See also Adam's note to *Rep.*, 359c20.)

11. Antiphon uses the term which, in connection with Parmenides and Plato, I have translated above by 'delusive opinion' (cp. note 15 to chapter 3); and he likewise opposes it to 'truth'. Cp. also Barker's translation in *Greek Political Theory*, I—*Plato and His Predecessors* (1918), 83.

12. See Antiphon, *On Truth*; cp. Barker, *op. cit.*, 83–5. See also next note, (2).

13. Hippias is quoted in Plato's *Protagoras*, 337e. For the next four quotations, cp. (1) Euripides *Ion*, 854 ff.; and (2) his *Phoenissae*, 538; cp. also Gomperz, *Greek Thinkers* (German edn, I, 325); and Barker, *op. cit.*, 75; cp. also Plato's violent attack upon Euripides in *Republic*, 568a–d. Furthermore (3) Alcidamas in *Schol. to Aristotle's Rhet.*, I, 13, 1373b18. (4) Lycophron in Aristotle's *Fragm.*, 91 (Rose); (cp. also the Pseudo-Plutarch, *De Nobil.*, 18.2). For the Athenian movement against slavery, cp. text to note 18 to chapter 4, and note 29 (with further references) to the same chapter; also note 18 to chapter 10 and *Addendum III* (Reply to a Critic), especially pp. 330 f.

(1) It is worth nothing that most Platonists show little sympathy with this equalitarian movement. Barker, for instance, discusses it under the heading 'General Iconoclasm'; cp. *op. cit.*, 75. (See also the second quotation from Field's *Plato* quoted in text to note 3, chapter 6.) This lack of sympathy is due, undoubtedly, to Plato's influence.

(2) For Plato's and Aristotle's anti-equalitarianism mentioned in the text, next paragraph, cp. also especially note 49 (and text) to chapter 8, and notes 3–4 (and text) to chapter 11.

This anti-equalitarianism and its devastating effects has been clearly described by W. W. Tarn in his excellent paper 'Alexander the Great and the Unity of Mankind' (*Proc. of the British Acad.*, XIX, 1933, pp. 123 ff.). Tarn recognizes that in the fifth century, there may have been a movement towards 'something better than the hard-and-fast division of Greeks and barbarians; but', he says, 'this had no importance for history, *because anything of the sort was strangled by the idealist philosophies.* Plato and Aristotle left no doubt about their views. Plato said that all barbarians were enemies by nature; it was proper to wage war upon them, even to the point of enslaving ... them. Aristotle said that all barbarians were slaves by nature ...' (p. 124, italics mine). I fully agree with Tarn's appraisal of the pernicious anti-humanitarian influence of the idealist philosophers, i.e. of Plato and Aristotle. I also agree with Tarn's emphasis upon the immense significance of equalitarianism, of the idea of the unity of mankind (cp. *op. cit.*, p. 147). The main point in which I cannot fully agree is Tarn's estimate of the fifth-century equalitarian movement, and of the early cynics. He may or may not be right in holding that the historical influence of these movements was small in comparison with that of Alexander. But I believe that he would have rated these movements more highly if he had only followed up the parallelism between the cosmopolitan and the anti-slavery movement. The parallelism between the relations *Greeks: barbarians* and *free men: slaves* is clearly enough shown by Tarn in the passage here quoted; and if we consider the unquestionable strength of the movement against slavery (see esp. note 18 to chapter 4) then the scattered remarks against the distinction between Greeks and barbarians gain much in significance. Cp. also Aristotle, *Politics*, III, 5, 7 (1278a); IV (VI), 4, 16 (1319b); and III, 2, 2 (1275b). See also note 48 to chapter 8, and the reference to E. Badian at the end of that note.

14. For the theme 'return to the beasts', cp. chapter 10, note 71, and text.

15. For Socrates' doctrine of the soul, see text to note 44 to chapter 10.

16. The term 'natural right' in an equalitarian sense came to Rome through the Stoics (there is the influence of Antisthenes to be considered; cp. note 48 to chapter 8) and was popularized by Roman Law (cp. *Institutiones*, II, 1, 2; I, 2, 2). It is used by Thomas Aquinas also (*Summa*, II, 91, 2). The confusing use of the term 'natural law' instead

of 'natural right' by modern Thomists is to be regretted, as well as the small emphasis they put upon equalitarianism.

17. The monistic tendency which first led to the attempt to interpret norms as natural has recently led to the opposite attempt, namely, to interpret natural laws as conventional. This (physical) type of *conventionalism* has been based, by Poincaré, on the recognition of the conventional or verbal character of definitions. Poincaré, and more recently Eddington, point out that we define natural entities by the laws they obey. From this the conclusion is drawn that these laws, i.e. the laws of nature, are definitions, i.e. verbal conventions. Cp. Eddington's letter in *Nature*, 148 (1941), 141: 'The elements' (of physical theory) '... can only be defined ... by the laws they obey; so that we find ourselves chasing our own tails in a purely formal system.'—An analysis and a criticism of this form of conventionalism can be found in my *The Logic of Scientific Discovery*, especially pp. 78 ff.

18. (1) The hope of getting some argument or theory to share our responsibilities is, I believe, one of the basic motives of 'scientific' ethics. 'Scientific' ethics is in its absolute barrenness one of the most amazing of social phenomena. What does it aim at? At telling us what we ought to do, i.e. at constructing a code of norms upon a scientific basis, so that we need only look up the index of the code if we are faced with a difficult moral decision? This clearly would be absurd; quite apart from the fact that if it could be achieved, it would destroy all personal responsibility and therefore all ethics. Or would it give scientific criteria of the truth and falsity of moral judgements, i.e. of judgements involving such terms as 'good' or 'bad'? But it is clear that moral *judgements* are absolutely irrelevant. Only a scandal-monger is interested in judging people or their actions; 'judge not' appears to some of us one of the fundamental and much too little appreciated laws of humanitarian ethics. (We may have to disarm and to imprison a criminal in order to prevent him from repeating his crimes, but too much of moral judgement and especially of moral indignation is always a sign of hypocrisy and pharisaism.) Thus an ethics of moral judgements would be not only irrelevant but indeed an immoral affair. The all-importance of moral problems rests, of course, on the fact that we can act with intelligent foresight, and that we can ask ourselves what our aims ought to be, i.e. how we ought to act.

Nearly all moral philosophers who have dealt with the problem of how we ought to act (with the possible exception of Kant) have tried to answer it either by reference to 'human nature' (as did even Kant, when he referred to human reason) or to the nature of 'the good'. The first of these ways leads nowhere, since all actions possible to us are founded upon 'human nature', so that the problem of ethics could also be put by asking which elements in human nature I ought to approve and to develop, and which sides I ought to suppress or to control. But the second of these ways also leads nowhere; for given an analysis of 'the good' in form of a sentence like: 'The good is such and such' (or 'such and such is good'), we would always have to ask: What about it? Why should this concern me? Only if the word 'good' is used in an ethical sense, i.e. only if it is used to mean 'that which I ought to do', could I derive from the information '*x* is good' the conclusion that I ought to do *x*. In other words, if the word 'good' is to have any ethical significance at all, it must be defined as 'that which I (or we) ought to do (or to promote)'. But if it is so defined, then its whole meaning is exhausted by the defining phrase, and it can in every context be replaced by this phrase, i.e. the introduction of the term 'good' cannot materially contribute to our problem. (Cp. also note 49 (3) to chapter 11.)

All the discussions about the definition of the good, or about the possibility of defining it, are therefore quite useless. They only show how far 'scientific' ethics is removed from the urgent problems of moral life. And they thus indicate that 'scientific' ethics is a form of escape, and escape from the realities of moral life, i.e. from our moral responsibilities. (In view of these considerations, it is not surprising to find that the beginning of 'scientific' ethics, in the form of ethical naturalism, coincides in time with what may be called the discovery of personal responsibility. Cp. what is said in chapter 10, text to notes 27–38 and 55–7, on the open society and the Great Generation.)

(2) It may be fitting in this connection to refer to a particular form of the escape from responsibility discussed here, as exhibited especially by the juridical positivism of the Hegelian school, as well as by a closely allied spiritual naturalism. That the problem is still significant may be seen from the fact that an author of the excellence of Catlin remains on this important point (as on a number of others) dependent upon Hegel; and my analysis will take the form of a criticism of Catlin's arguments in favour of spiritual naturalism, and against the distinction between laws of nature and normative laws (cp. G. E. G. Catlin, *A Study of the Principles of Politics*, 1930, pp. 96–99).

Catlin begins by making a clear distinction between the laws of nature and 'laws ... which human legislators make'; and he admits that, at first sight the phrase 'natural law', if applied to norms, 'appears to be patently unscientific, since it seems to fail to make a distinction between that human law which requires enforcement and the physical laws which are incapable of breach'. But he tries to show that it only *appears* to be so, and that 'our criticism' of this way of using the term 'natural law' was 'too hasty'. And he proceeds to a clear statement of spiritual naturalism, i.e. to a distinction between 'sound law' which is 'according to nature', and other law: 'Sound law, then, involves a formulation of human tendencies, or, in brief, is a copy of the "natural" law to be "found" by political science. Sound law is in this sense emphatically found and not made. It is a copy of natural social law' (i.e. of what I called 'sociological laws'; cp. text to note 8 to this chapter). And he concludes by insisting that in so far as the legal system becomes more rational, its rules 'cease to assume the character of arbitrary commands and become mere deductions drawn from the primary social laws' (i.e. from what I should call 'sociological laws').

(3) This is a very strong statement of spiritual naturalism. Its criticism is the more important as Catlin combines his doctrine with a theory of 'social engineering' which may perhaps at first sight appear similar to the one advocated here (cp. text to note 9 to chapter 3 and text to notes 1–3 and 8–11 to chapter 9). Before discussing it, I wish to explain why I consider Catlin's view to be dependent on Hegel's positivism. Such an explanation is necessary, because Catlin uses his naturalism in order to distinguish between 'sound' and other law; in other words, he uses it in order to distinguish between 'just' and 'unjust' law; and this distinction certainly does not look like positivism, i.e. the recognition of the existing law as the sole standard of justice. In spite of all that, I believe that Catlin's views are very close to positivism; my reason being that he believes that only 'sound' law can be effective, and in so far 'existent' in precisely Hegel's sense. For Catlin says that when our legal

code is not 'sound', i.e. not in accordance with the laws of human nature, then 'our statute remains paper'. This statement is purest positivism; for it allows us to deduce from the fact that a certain code is not only 'paper' but successfully enforced, that it is 'sound'; or in other words, that all legislation which does not turn out to be merely paper is a copy of human nature and therefore just.

(4) I now proceed to a brief criticism of the argument proffered by Catlin against the distinction between (*a*) laws of nature which cannot be broken, and (*b*) normative laws, which are man-made, i.e. enforced by sanctions; a distinction which he himself makes so very clearly at first. Catlin's argument is a twofold one. He shows (a') that laws of nature also are man-made, in a certain sense, and that they can, in a sense, be broken; and (b') that in a certain sense normative laws cannot be broken. I begin with (a'). 'The natural laws of the physicist', writes Catlin, 'are not brute facts, they are rationalizations of the physical world, whether superimposed by man or justified because the world is inherently rational and orderly.' And he proceeds to show that natural laws 'can be nullified' when 'fresh facts' compel us to recast the law. My reply to this argument is this. A statement intended as a formulation of a law of nature is certainly man-made. We *make* the hypothesis that there is a certain invariable regularity, i.e. we describe the supposed regularity with the help of a statement, the natural law. But, as scientists, we are prepared to learn from nature that we have been wrong; we are prepared to recast the law if fresh facts which contradict our hypothesis show that *our supposed law was no law, since it has been broken*. In other words, by accepting nature's nullification, the scientist shows that he accepts a hypothesis only as long as it has not been falsified; which is the same as to say that he regards a law of nature as a rule which cannot be broken, since he accepts the breaking of his rule as proof that his rule did not formulate a law of nature. Furthermore: although the hypothesis is man-made, we may be unable to prevent its falsification. This shows that, by creating the hypothesis, we have not created the regularity which it is intended to describe (although we did create a new set of problems, and may have suggested new observations and interpretations). (b') 'It is not true', says Catlin, 'that the criminal "breaks" the law when he does the forbidden act ... the statute does not say: "Thou canst not"; it says, "Thou shalt not, or this punishment will be inflicted." As command', Catlin continues, 'it may be broken, but as law, in a very real sense, it is only broken when the punishment is not inflicted ... So far as the law is perfected and its sanctions executed, ... it approximates to physical law.' The reply to this is simple. In whichever sense we speak of 'breaking' the law, the juridical law *can* be broken; no verbal adjustment can alter that. Let us accept Catlin's view that a criminal cannot 'break' the law, and that it is only 'broken' if the criminal does not receive the punishment prescribed by the law. But even from this point of view, the law *can* be broken; for instance, by officers of the state who refuse to punish the criminal. And even in a state where all sanctions are, *in fact*, executed, the officers *could*, if they chose, prevent such execution, and so 'break' the law in Catlin's sense. (That they would thereby 'break' the law in the ordinary sense, also, i.e. that they would become criminals, and that they might ultimately perhaps be punished is quite another question.) In other words: A normative law is always enforced *by men* and by their sanctions, and it is therefore fundamentally different from a hypothesis. Legally, we can enforce the suppression of murder, or of acts of kindness; of falsity, or of truth; of justice, or of injustice. But we

cannot force the sun to alter its course. No amount of argument can bridge this gap.

19. The 'nature of happiness and misery' is referred to in the *Theaetetus*, 175c. For the close relationship between 'nature' and 'Form' or 'Idea', cp. especially *Republic*, 597a–d, where Plato first discusses the Form or Idea of a bed, and then refers to it as 'the bed which exists by nature, and which was made by God' (597b). In the same place, he proffers the corresponding distinction between the 'artificial' (or the 'fabricated' thing, which is an 'imitation') and 'truth'. Cp. also Adam's note to *Republic*, 597b10 (with the quotation from Burnet given there), and the notes to 476b13, 501b9, 525c15; furthermore *Theaetetus*, 174b (and Cornford's note 1 to p. 85 in his *Plato's Theory of Knowledge*). See also Aristotle's *Metaphysics*, 1015a14.

20. For Plato's attack upon art, see the last book of the *Republic*, and especially the passages *Republic*, 600a–605b, mentioned in note 39 to chapter 4.

21. Cp. notes 11, 12 and 13 to this chapter, and text. My contention that Plato agrees at least partly with Antiphon's naturalist theories (although he does not, of course, agree with Antiphon's equalitarianism) will appear strange to many, especially to the readers of Barker, *op. cit.* And it may surprise them even more to hear the opinion that the main disagreement was not so much a theoretical one, but rather one of moral practice, and that Antiphon and not Plato was morally in the right, as far as the practical issue of equalitarianism is concerned. (For Plato's agreement with Antiphon's principle that nature is true and right, see also text to notes 23 and 28, and note 30 to this chapter.)

22. These quotations are from *Sophist*, 266b and 265e. But the passage also contains (265c) a criticism (similar to *Laws*, quoted in text to notes 23 and 30 in this chapter) of what may be described as a materialist interpretation of naturalism such as was held, perhaps, by Antiphon; I mean 'the belief ... that nature ... generates without intelligence'.

23. Cp. *Laws*, 892a and c. For the doctrine of the affinity of the soul to the Ideas, see also note 15 (8) to chapter 3. For the affinity of 'natures' and 'souls', see Aristotle's *Metaphysics*, 1015a14, with the passages of the *Laws* quoted, and with 896d/e: 'the soul dwells in all things that move ...'

Compare further especially the following passages in which 'natures' and 'souls' are used in a way that is obviously synonymous: *Republic*, 485a/b, 485e/486a and d, 486b ('nature'); 486b and d ('soul'), 490e/491a (both), 491b (both), and many other places (cp. also Adam's note to 370a7). The affinity is directly stated in 490b(10). For the affinity between 'nature' and 'soul' and 'race', cp. 501e where the phrase 'philosophic natures' or 'souls' found in analogous passages is replaced by 'race of philosophers'.

There is also an affinity between 'soul' or 'nature' and the social class or caste; see for instance *Republic*, 435b. The connection between caste and race is fundamental, for from the beginning (415a), caste is identified with race.

'Nature' is used in the sense of 'talent' or 'condition of the soul' in *Laws*, 648d, 650b, 655e, 710b, 766a, 875c. The priority and superiority of nature over art is stated in *Laws*, 889a, ff. For 'natural' in the sense of 'right', or 'true', see *Laws*, 686d and 818e, respectively.

24. Cp. the passages quoted in note 32 (1), (*a*) and (*c*), to chapter 4.

25. The Socratic doctrine of autarky is mentioned in *Republic*, 387d/e (cp. *Apology*, 41c, ff., and Adam's note to *Rep.*, 387d25). This is only one of the few scattered passages

reminiscent of Socratic teaching; but it is in direct contradiction to the main doctrine of the *Republic*, as it is expounded in the text (see also note 36 to chapter 6, and text); this may be seen by contrasting the quoted passage with 369c, ff., and very many similar passages.

26. Cp. for instance the passage quoted in the text to note 29 to chapter 4. For the 'rare and uncommon natures', cp. *Republic*, 491a/b, and many other passages, for instance *Timaeus*, 51e: 'reason is shared by the gods with very few men'. For the 'social habitat', see 491d (cp. also chapter 23).

    While Plato (and Aristotle; cp. especially note 4 to chapter 11, and text) insisted that manual work is degrading, Socrates seems to have adopted a very different attitude. (Cp. Xenophon, *Memorabilia*, II, 7; 7–10; Xenophon's story is, to some extent, corroborated by Antisthenes' and Diogenes' attitude towards manual work; cp. also note 56 to chapter 10.)

27. See especially *Theaetetus*, 172b (cp. also Cornford's comments on this passage in *Plato's Theory of Knowledge*). See also note 7 to this chapter. The elements of conventionalism in Plato's teaching may perhaps explain why the *Republic* was said, by some who still possessed Protagoras' writings, to resemble these. (Cp. *Diogenes Laertius*, III, 37.) For Lycophron's contract theory, see notes 43–54 to chapter 6 (especially note 46), and text.

28. Cp. *Laws*, 690b/c; see note 10 to this chapter. Plato mentions Pindar's naturalism also in *Gorgias*, 484b, 488b; *Laws*, 714c, 890a. For the opposition between 'external compulsion' on the one hand, and (*a*) 'free action', (*b*) 'nature', on the other, cp. also *Republic*, 603c, and *Timaeus*, 64d. (Cp. also *Rep.*, 466c–d, quoted in note 30 to this chapter.)

29. Cp. *Republic*, 369b–c. This is part of the *contract theory*. The next quotation, which is the first statement of the *naturalist principle* in the perfect state, is 370a/b–c. (Naturalism is in the *Republic* first mentioned by Glaucon in 358e, ff.; but this is, of course, not Plato's own doctrine of naturalism.)

    (1) For the further development of the naturalistic principle of the division of labour and the part played by this principle in Plato's theory of justice, cp. especially text to notes 6, 23 and 40 to chapter 6.

    (2) For a modern radical version of the naturalistic principle, see Marx's formula of the communist society (adopted from Louis Blanc): 'From each according to his ability: to each according to his needs!' (Cp. for instance *A Handbook of Marxism*, E. Burns, 1935, p. 752; and note 8 to chapter 13; see also note 3 to chapter 13, and note 48 to chapter 24, and text.)

    For the historical roots of this 'principle of communism', see Plato's maxim 'Friends have in common all things they possess' (see note 36 to chapter 6, and text; for Plato's communism see also notes 34 to chapter 6 and 30 to chapter 4, and text), and compare these passages with the *Acts*: 'And all that believed were together, and had all things in common; ... and parted them to all men, as every man had need' (2, 44–45).—'Neither was there any among them that lacked: for ... distribution was made unto every man according as he had need' (4, 34–35).

30. See note 23, and text. The quotations in the present paragraph are all from the *Laws*: (1) 889, a–d (cp. the very similar passage in the *Theaetetus*, 172b); (2) 896c–e; (3) 890e/891a.

For the next paragraph in the text (i.e. for my contention that Plato's naturalism is incapable of solving practical problems) the following may serve as an illustration. Many naturalists have contended that men and women are 'by nature' different, both physically and spiritually, and that they should therefore fulfil different functions in social life. Plato, however, uses the same naturalistic argument to prove the opposite; for, he argues, are not dogs of both sexes useful for watching as well as hunting? 'Do you agree', he writes (*Rep.*, 466c–d), 'that women ... must participate with men in guarding as well as in hunting, as it is with dogs; ... and that in so doing, they will be acting in the most desirable manner, since this will be not contrary to nature, but in accordance with the natural relations of the sexes?' (See also text to note 28 to this chapter; for the dog as ideal guardian, cp. chapter 4, especially note 32 (2), and text.)

31. For a brief criticism of the biological theory of the state, see note 7 to chapter 10, and text. *For the oriental origin of the theory, see R. Eisler, *Revue de Synthèse Historique*, vol. 41, p. 15.*
32. For some applications of Plato's political theory of the soul, and for the inferences drawn from it, see notes 58–9 to chapter 10, and text. For the fundamental methodological analogy between city and individual, see especially *Republic*, 368e, 445c, 577c. For Alcmaeon's political theory of the human individual, or of human physiology, cp. note 13 to chapter 6.
33. Cp. *Republic*, 423, b and d.
34. This quotation as well as the next is from G. Grote, *Plato and the Other Companions of Socrates* (1875), vol. III, 124.—The main passages of the *Republic* are 439c, f. (the story of Leontius); 571c, f. (the bestial part versus the reasoning part); 588c (the Apocalyptic Monster; cp. the 'Beast' which possesses a Platonic Number, in the *Revelation* 13, 17 and 18); 603d and 604b (man at war with himself). See also *Laws*, 689a–b, and notes 58–9 to chapter 10.
35. Cp. *Republic*, 519e, f. (cp. also note 10 to chapter 8); the next two quotations are both from the *Laws*, 903c. (I have reversed their order.) It may be mentioned that the 'whole' referred to in these two passages ('*pan*' and '*holon*') is not the *state* but the *world*; yet there is no doubt that the underlying tendency of this cosmological holism is a political holism; cp. *Laws*, 903d–e (where the physician and craftsman is associated with the statesman), and the fact that Plato often uses '*holon*' (especially the plural of it) to mean 'state' as well as 'world'. Furthermore, the first of these two passages (in my order of quoting) is a shorter version of *Republic*, 420b–421c; the second of *Republic*, 520b, ff. ('We have created you for the sake of the state, as well as for your own sake.') Further *passages on holism or collectivism* are: *Republic*, 424a, 449e, 462a, f., *Laws*, 715b, 739c, 875a, f., 903b, 923b, 942a, f. (See also notes 31/32 to chapter 6.) For the remark in this paragraph that Plato spoke of the state as an organism, cp. *Republic*, 462c, and *Laws*, 964e, where the state is even compared with the human *body*.
36. Cp. Adam in his edition of the *Republic*, vol. II, 303; see also note 3 to chapter 4, and text.
37. This point is emphasized by Adam, *op. cit.*, note 546a, b7, and pp. 288 and 307. The next quotation in this paragraph is *Republic*, 546a; cp. *Republic*, 485a/b, quoted in note 26 (1) to chapter 3 and in text to note 33 to chapter 8.
38. This is the main point in which I must deviate from Adam's interpretation. I believe Plato to indicate that the philosopher king of Books VI–VII, whose main interest is

in the things that are not generated and do not decay (*Rep.*, 485b; see the last note and the passages there referred to), obtains with his mathematical and dialectical training the knowledge of the Platonic Number and with it the means of arresting social degeneration and thereby the decay of the state. See especially the text to note 39.

The quotations that follow in this paragraph are: 'keeping pure the race of the guardians'; cp. *Republic*, 460c, and text to note 34 to chapter 4. 'A city thus constituted, etc.': 546a.

The reference to Plato's distinction, in the field of mathematics, acoustics, and astronomy, between *rational knowledge* and delusive opinion based upon *experience or perception* is to *Republic*, 523a, ff., 525d, ff. (where '*calculation*' is discussed; see especially 526a); 527d, ff., 529b, f., 531a, ff. (down to 534a and 537d); see also 509d–511e.

39. * I have been blamed for 'adding' the words (which I never placed in quotation marks) 'lacking a purely rational method'; but in view of *Rep.*, 523a to 537d, it seems to me clear that Plato's reference to '*perception*' implies just this contrast.* The quotations in this paragraph are from *Rep.*, 546b, ff. Note that, throughout this passage, it is '*The Muses*' who speak through the mouth of 'Socrates'.

In my interpretation of the Story of the Fall and the Number, I have carefully avoided the difficult, undecided, and perhaps undecidable problem of the computation of the Number itself. (It may be undecidable since Plato may not have revealed his secret in full.) I confine my interpretation entirely to the passages immediately before and after the one that describes the Number itself; these passages are, I believe, clear enough. In spite of that, my interpretation deviates, as far as I know, from previous attempts.

(1) The crucial statement on which I base my interpretation is (*A*) that the guardians work by '*calculation aided by perception*'. Next to this, I am using the statements (*B*) that they will not '*accidentally hit* upon (the correct way of) obtaining good offspring'; (*C*) that they will '*blunder*, and beget children in the wrong way'; (*D*) that they are '*ignorant*' of such matters (that is, such matters as the Number).

Regarding (*A*), it should be clear to every careful reader of Plato that such a reference to perception is intended to express a criticism of the method in question. This view of the passage under consideration (546a, f.) is supported by the fact that it comes so soon after the passages 523a–537d (see the end of the last note), in which the opposition between pure rational knowledge and opinion based on perception is one of the main themes, and in which, more especially, the term 'calculation' is used in a context emphasizing the opposition between rational knowledge and experience, while the term 'perception' (see also 511c/d) is given a definite technical and deprecatory sense. (Cp. also, for instance, Plutarch's wording in his discussion of this opposition: in his *Life of Marcellus*, 306.) I am therefore of the opinion, and this opinion is enforced by the context, especially by (*B*), (*C*), (*D*), that Plato's remark (*A*) implies (*a*) that 'calculation based upon perception' is a poor method, and (*b*) that there are better methods, namely the methods of mathematics and dialectics, which yield pure rational knowledge. The point I am trying to elaborate is, indeed, so plain, that I should not have troubled so much about it were it not for the fact that even Adam has missed it. In his note to 546a, b7, he interprets 'calculation' as a reference to the rulers' task of determining the number of marriages they should permit, and 'perception' as the means by which they 'decide what couples should be joined, what children be reared, etc.'. That is to say, Adam takes Plato's remark to be a simple description and not as a polemic against the weakness of the empirical method. Accordingly, he relates neither the statement (*C*) that the rulers will 'blunder' nor the remark (*D*) that they are 'ignorant' to the fact that they use empirical methods. (The remark (*B*) that they will not 'hit' upon the right method 'by accident' would simply be left untranslated, if we follow Adam's suggestion.)

In interpreting our passage we must keep it in mind that in Book VIII, immediately before the passage in question, Plato returns to the question of the first city of Books II to IV. (See Adam's notes to 449a, ff., and 543a, ff.) But the guardians of this city are neither mathematicians nor dialecticians. Thus they have no idea of the purely rational methods emphasized so much in Book VII, 525–534. In this connection, the import of the remarks on perception, i.e. on the poverty of empirical methods, and on the resulting ignorance of the guardians, is unmistakable.

The statement (*B*) that the rulers will not 'hit accidentally upon' (the correct way of) 'obtaining good offspring, or none at all', is perfectly clear in my interpretation. Since the rulers have merely empirical methods at their disposal, it would be only a lucky accident if they did hit upon a method whose determination needs mathematical or other rational methods. Adam suggests (note to 546a, b7) the translation: 'none the more will they by calculation together with perception obtain good offspring'; and only in brackets, he adds: 'lit. hit the obtaining of'. I think that his failure to make any sense of the 'hit' is a consequence of his failure to see the implications of (*A*).

The interpretation here suggested makes (*C*) and (*D*) perfectly understandable; and Plato's remark that his Number is 'master over better or worse birth', fits in perfectly. It may be remarked that Adam does not comment on (*D*), i.e. the ignorance, although such a comment would be most necessary in view of his theory (note to 546d22) that 'the number is not a nuptial ... number', and that it has no technical eugenic meaning.

That the meaning of the Number is indeed technical and eugenic is, I think, clear, if we consider that the passage containing the Number is enclosed in passages containing references to eugenic knowledge, or rather, lack of eugenic knowledge. Immediately before the Number, (*A*), (*B*), (*C*), occur, and immediately afterwards, (*D*), as well as the story of the bride and bridegroom and their degenerate offspring. Besides, (*C*) before the Number and (*D*) after the Number refer to each other; for (*C*), the 'blunder', is connected with a reference to 'begetting in the wrong way', and (*D*), the 'ignorance', is connected with an exactly analogous reference, viz., 'uniting bride and bridegroom in the wrong manner'. (See also next note.)

The last point in which I must defend my interpretation is my contention that those who *know* the Number thereby obtain the power to influence 'better or worse births'. This does not of course follow from Plato's statement that the Number itself has such power; for if Adam's interpretation is right, then the Number regulates the births because it determines an unalterable period after which degeneration is bound to set in. But I assert that Plato's references to 'perception', to 'blunder' and to 'ignorance' as the immediate cause of the eugenic mistakes would be pointless if he did not mean that, had they possessed an adequate knowledge of the appropriate mathematical and purely rational methods, the guardians would not have blundered. But this makes the inference inevitable that the Number has a *technical* eugenic meaning, and that its knowledge is the key to the power of arresting degeneration. (This inference also seems to me the only one compatible with all we know about this type of superstition; all astrology, for instance, involves the apparently somewhat contradictory conception that the knowledge of our fate may help us to influence this fate.)

I think that the rejection of the explanation of the Number as a secret breeding taboo arises from a reluctance to credit Plato with such crude ideas, however clearly he may express them. In other words, they arise from the tendency to idealize Plato.

(2) In this connection, I must refer to an article by A. E. Taylor, 'The Decline and Fall of The State in *Republic*, VIII' (*Mind*, N.S. 48, 1939, pp. 23 ff.). In this article, Taylor attacks Adam (in my opinion not justly), and argues against him: 'It is true, of course, that the decay of the ideal State is expressly said in 546b to begin when the ruling class "beget children out of due season" ... But this need not mean, and in my opinion does not mean, that Plato is concerning himself here with problems of the hygiene of reproduction. The main thought is the simple one that if, like everything of man's making, the State carries the seeds of its own dissolution within it, this must, of course, mean that sooner or later the persons wielding supreme power will be inferior to those who preceded them' (pp. 25 ff.). Now this interpretation seems to me not only untenable, in view of Plato's fairly definite statements, but also a typical example of the attempt to eliminate from Plato's writing such embarrassing elements as racialism or superstition. Adam began by denying that the Number has technical eugenic importance, and by asserting that it is not a 'nuptial number', but merely a cosmological period. Taylor now continues by denying that Plato is here at all interested in 'problems of the hygiene of the reproduction'. But Plato's passage is thronged with allusions to these problems, and Taylor himself admits two pages before (p. 23) that it is 'nowhere suggested' that the Number 'is a determinant of anything but the "better and worse births"'. Besides, not only the passage in question but the whole of the *Republic* (and similarly the *Statesman*, especially 310b, 310e) is simply full of emphasis upon the 'problems of the hygiene of reproduction'. Taylor's theory that Plato, when speaking of the 'human creature' (or, as Taylor puts it, of a 'thing of human generation'), means *the state*, and that Plato wishes to allude to the fact that the state is the creation of a human lawgiver, is, I think, without support in Plato's text. The whole passage begins with a reference to the things of the sensible world in flux, to the things that are generated and that decay (see notes 37 and 38 to this chapter), and more especially, to living things, plants as well as animals, and to their racial problems. Besides, a thing 'of man's making' would, if emphasized by Plato in such a context, mean an 'artificial' thing which is inferior because it is 'twice removed' from reality. (Cp. text to notes 20–23 to this chapter, and the whole Tenth Book of the *Republic* down to the end of 608b.) Plato would never expect anybody to interpret the phrase 'a thing of man's making' as meaning the perfect, the 'natural' state; rather he would expect them to think of something very inferior (like poetry; cp. note 39 to chapter 4). The phrase which Taylor translates 'thing of human generation' is usually simply translated by 'human creature', and this removes all difficulties.

(3) Assuming that my interpretation of the passage in question is correct, a suggestion may be made with the intention of connecting Plato's belief in the significance of racial degeneration with his repeated advice that the number of the

members of the ruling class should be kept constant (advice that shows that the sociologist Plato understood the unsettling effect of population increase). Plato's way of thinking, described at the end of the present chapter (cp. text to note 45; and note 37 to chapter 8), especially the way he opposes The One monarch, The Few timocrats, to The Many who are nothing but a mob, may have suggested to him the belief that *an increase in numbers is equivalent to a decline in quality*. (Something on these lines is indeed suggested in the *Laws*, 710d.) If this hypothesis is correct, then he may easily have concluded *that population increase is interdependent with, or perhaps even caused by, racial degeneration*. Since population increase was in fact the main cause of the instability and dissolution of the early Greek tribal societies (cp. notes 6, 7, and 63 to chapter 10, and text), this hypothesis would explain why Plato believed that the 'real' cause was racial degeneration (in keeping with his general theories of 'nature', and of 'change').

40. (1) Or 'at the wrong time'. Adam insists (note to 546d22) that we must not translate 'at the wrong time' but 'inopportunely'. I may remark that my interpretation is quite independent of this question; it is fully compatible with 'inopportunely' or 'wrongly' or 'at the wrong time' or 'out of due season'. (The phrase in question means, originally, something like 'contrary to the proper measure'; usually it means 'at the wrong time'.)

* (2) Concerning Plato's remarks about 'mingling' and 'mixture', it may be observed that Plato seems to have held a primitive but popular theory of heredity (apparently still held by race-horse breeders) according to which the offspring is an even mixture or blend of the characters or 'natures' of his two parents, and that their characters, or natures, or 'virtues' (stamina, speed, etc., or, according to the *Republic*, the *Statesman*, and the *Laws*, gentleness, fierceness, boldness, self-restraint, etc.) are mixed in him in proportion to the number of ancestors (grandparents, great-grandparents, etc.) who possessed these characters. Accordingly, the art of breeding is one of a judicious and scientific—mathematical or harmonious—blending or mixing of natures. See especially the *Statesman*, where the royal craft of statesmanship or herdsmanship is likened to that of weaving, and where the kingly weaver must blend boldness with self-restraint. (See also *Republic*, 375c–e, and 410c, ff.; *Laws*, 731b; and notes 34 f. to chapter 4; 13 and 39 f. to chapter 8; and text.)*

41. For Plato's law of social revolutions, see especially note 26 to chapter 4, and text.

42. The term 'meta-biology' is used by G. B. Shaw in this sense, i.e. as denoting a kind of religion. (Cp. the preface to *Back to Methuselah*; see also note 66 to chapter 12.)

43. Cp. Adam's note to *Republic*, 547a 3.

44. For a criticism of what I call 'psychologism' in the method of sociology, cp. text to note 19 to chapter 13 and chapter 14, where Mill's still popular methodological psychologism is discussed.

45. It has often been said that Plato's thought must not be squeezed into a 'system'; accordingly, my attempts in this paragraph (and not only in this paragraph) to show the systematic unity of Plato's thought, which is obviously based on the Pythagorean table of opposites, will probably arouse criticism. But I believe that such a systematization is a necessary test of any interpretation. Those who believe that they do not need an interpretation, and that they can 'know' a philosopher or his work, and take him just 'as he was', or his work just 'as it was', are mistaken. They cannot but interpret both the man and his work; but since they are not aware of the fact that

they interpret (that their view is coloured by tradition, temperament, etc.), their interpretation must necessarily be naïve and uncritical. (Cp. also chapter 10 (notes 1–5 and 56), and chapter 25.) A critical interpretation, however, must take the form of a rational reconstruction, and must be systematic; it must try to reconstruct the philosopher's thought as a consistent edifice. Cp. also what A. C. Ewing says of Kant (*A Short Commentary on Kant's Critique of Pure Reason*, 1938, p. 4): '... we ought to start with the assumption that a great philosopher is not likely to be always contradicting himself, and consequently, wherever there are two interpretations, one of which will make Kant consistent and the other inconsistent, prefer the former to the latter, if reasonably possible.' This surely applies also to Plato, and even to interpretation in general.

NOTES TO CHAPTER SIX

1. Cp. note 3 to chapter 4 and text, especially the end of that paragraph. Furthermore, note 2 (2) to that chapter. Concerning the formula *Back to Nature*, I wish to draw attention to the fact that Rousseau was greatly influenced by Plato. Indeed, a glance at the *Social Contract* will reveal a wealth of analogies especially with those Platonic passages on naturalism which have been commented upon in the last chapter. Cp. especially note 14 to chapter 9. There is also an interesting similarity between *Republic*, 591a, ff. (and *Gorgias*, 472e, ff., where a similar idea occurs in an individualist context), and Rousseau's (and Hegel's) famous theory of punishment. (Barker, *Greek Political Theory*, I, 388 ff., rightly emphasizes Plato's influence upon Rousseau. But he does not see the strong element of romanticism in Plato; and it is not generally appreciated that the rural romanticism which influenced both France and Shakespeare's England through the medium of Sanazzaro's *Arcadia*, has its origin in Plato's Dorian shepherds; cp. notes 11 (3), 26, and 32 to chapter 4, and note 14 to chapter 9.)
2. Cp. R. H. S. Crossman, *Plato To-Day* (1937), 132; the next quotation is from p. 111. This interesting book (like the works of Grote and T. Gomperz) has greatly encouraged me to develop my rather unorthodox views on Plato, and to follow them up to their rather unpleasant conclusions. For the quotations from C. E. M. Joad, cp. his *Guide to the Philosophy of Morals and Politics* (1938), 661, and 660. I may also refer here to the very interesting remarks on Plato's views on justice by C. L. Stevenson, in his article 'Persuasive Definitions' (*Mind*, N.S., vol. 47, 1938, pp. 331 ff.).
3. Cp. Crossman, *op. cit.*, 132 f. The next two quotations are: Field, *Plato*, etc., 91; cp. similar remarks in Barker, *Greek Political Theory*, etc. (see note 13 to chapter 5).

   The idealization of Plato has played a considerable part in the debates on the genuineness of the various works transmitted under his name. Many of them have been rejected by some of the critics simply because they contained passages which did not fit in with their idealized view of Plato. A rather naïve as well as typical expression of this attitude can be found in Davies' and Vaughan's 'Introductory Notice' (cp. the Golden Treasury edition of the *Republic*, p. vi): 'Mr. Grote, in his zeal to take Plato down from his super-human pedestal, may be somewhat too ready to attribute to him the compositions which have been judged unworthy of so divine a philosopher.' It does not seem to occur to the writers that their judgement of Plato should depend on what he wrote, and not vice versa; and that, if these compositions are genuine *and* unworthy, Plato was not quite so divine a philosopher. (For Plato's divinity, see also Simplicius in *Arist. de coelo*, 32b44, 319a15, etc.)

4. The formulation of (*a*) emulates one of Kant's, who describes a *just constitution* as 'a constitution that achieves *the greatest possible freedom of human individuals* by framing the laws in such a way that *the freedom of each can co-exist with that of all others*' (*Critique of Pure Reason*[2], 373); see also his *Theory of Right*, where he says: 'Right (or justice) is the sum total of the conditions which are necessary for everybody's free choice to co-exist with that of everybody else, in accordance with a general law of liberty.' Kant believed that this was the aim pursued by Plato in the *Republic*; from which we may see that Kant was one of the many philosophers who either were deceived by Plato or who idealized him by imputing to him their own humanitarian ideas. I may remark, in this connection, that Kant's ardent liberalism is very little appreciated in English and American writings on political philosophy (in spite of Hastie's *Kant's Principles of Politics*). He is only too often claimed to be a forerunner of Hegel; but in view of the fact that he recognized in the romanticism of both Herder and Fichte a doctrine diametrically opposed to his own, this claim is grossly unjust to Kant, and there can be no doubt that he would have strongly resented it. It is the tremendous influence of Hegelianism that led to a wide acceptance of this, I believe, completely untenable claim.
5. Cp. text to notes 32/33 to chapter 5.
6. Cp. text to notes 25–29, chapter 5. The quotations in the present paragraph are: (1) *Republic*, 433a; (2) *Republic*, 434a/b; (3) *Republic*, 441d. With Plato's statement, in the first quotation, 'we have repeated over and again', cp. also esp. *Republic*, 397e, where the theory of justice is carefully prepared, and, of course, *Republic*, 369b–c, quoted in text to note 29, chapter 5. See also notes 23 and 40 to the present chapter.
7. As pointed out in chapter 4 (note 18 and text, and note 29), Plato does not say much about slaves in the *Republic*, although what he says is significant enough; but he dispels all doubts about his attitude in the *Laws* (cp. especially G. R. Morrow's article in *Mind*, referred to in note 29 to chapter 4).
8. The quotations are from Barker, *Greek Political Theory*, I, p. 180. Barker states (pp. 176 f.) that 'Platonic Justice' is 'social justice', and correctly emphasizes its holistic nature. He mentions (178 f.) the possible criticism that this formula does 'not ... touch the essence of what men generally mean by justice', i.e. 'a principle for dealing with the clash of wills', i.e. justice as pertaining to individuals. But he thinks that 'such an objection is beside the point', and that Plato's idea is 'not a matter of law' but 'a conception of social morality' (179); and he goes on to assert that this treatment of justice corresponded, in a way, to the current Greek ideas of justice: 'Nor was Plato, in conceiving justice in this sense, very far removed from the current ideas in Greece.' He does not even mention that there exists some evidence to the contrary, as here discussed in the next notes, and text.
9. Cp. *Gorgias*, 488e, ff.; the passage is more fully quoted and discussed in section VIII below (see note 48 to this chapter, and text). For Aristotle's theory of slavery, see note 3 to chapter II and text. The quotations from Aristotle in this paragraph are: (1) and (2) *Nicom. Ethics*, V, 4, 7, and 8; (3) *Politics*, III, 12, 1 (1282b; see also notes 20 and 30 to this chapter. The passage contains a reference to the *Nicom. Eth.*); (4) *Nicom. Ethics*, V, 4, 9; (5) *Politics*, IV (VI), 2, 1 (1317b).—In the *Nicom. Ethics*, V, 3, 7 (cp. also *Pol.*, III, 9, 1; 1280a), Aristotle also mentions that the meaning of 'justice' varies in

democratic, oligarchic, and aristocratic states, according to their different ideas of 'merit'. *(What follows here was first added in the American edition of 1950.)

For Plato's views, in the *Laws*, on *political justice and equality*, see especially the passage on the two kinds of equality (*Laws*, 757b–d) quoted below under (1). For the fact, mentioned here in the text, that not only virtue and breeding but also wealth should count in the distribution of honours and of spoils (and even size and good looks), see *Laws*, 744c, quoted in note 20 (1) to the present chapter, where other relevant passages are also discussed.

(1) In the *Laws*, 757b–d, Plato discusses '*two kinds of equality*'. 'The one of these ... is equality of measure, weight, or number [i.e. numerical or arithmetical equality]; but the truest and best equality ... distributes more to the greater and less to the smaller, giving each his due measure, in *accordance with nature* ... By granting the greater honour to those who are superior in virtue, and the lesser honour to those who are inferior in virtue and breeding, *it distributes to each what is proper, according to this principle of [rational] proportions*. And this is precisely what we shall call "*political justice*". And whoever may found a state must make this the sole aim of his legislation ... : this justice alone which, as stated, is *natural equality*, and which is distributed, as the situation requires, to unequals.' This second of the two equalities which constitutes what Plato here calls 'political justice' (and what Aristotle calls 'distributive justice'), and which is described by Plato (and Aristotle) as '*proportionate equality*'—the truest, best, and most natural equality—was later called 'geometrical' (*Gorgias* 508a; see also 465b/c, and Plutarch, *Moralia* 719b, f.), as opposed to the lower and democratic '*arithmetical*' equality. On this identification, the remarks under (2) may throw some light.

(2) According to tradition (see *Comm. in Arist. Graeca, pars* XV, Berlin, 1897, p. 117, 29, and *pars* XVIII, Berlin, 1900, p. 118, 18), an inscription over the door of Plato's academy said: 'Nobody untrained in geometry may enter my house!' I suspect that the meaning of this is not merely an emphasis upon the importance of mathematical studies, but that it means: 'Arithmetic (i.e. more precisely, Pythagorean number theory) is not enough; you must know geometry!' And I shall attempt to sketch the reasons which make me believe that the latter phrase adequately sums up one of Plato's most important contributions to science. See also *Addendum*, p. 319.

As is now generally believed, the earlier Pythagorean treatment of geometry adopted a method somewhat similar to the one nowadays called 'arithmetization'. Geometry was treated as part of the theory of integers (or 'natural' numbers, i.e. of numbers composed of monads or 'indivisible units'; cp. *Republic*, 525e) and of their '*logoi*', i.e. their 'rational' proportions. For example, the Pythagorean rectangular triangles were those with sides in such rational proportions. (Examples are 3:4:5; or 5:12:13.) A general formula ascribed to Pythagoras is this: $2n + 1: 2n(n + 1): 2n(n + 1) + 1$. But this formula, derived from the '*gnomōn*', is not general enough, as the example 8:15:17 shows. A *general formula*, from which the Pythagorean can be obtained by putting $m = n + 1$, is this: $m^2 - n^2: 2mn: m^2 + n^2$ (where $m > n$). Since this formula is a close consequence of the so-called 'Theorem of Pythagoras' (if taken together with that kind of Algebra which seems to have been known to the early Pythagoreans), and since this formula was, apparently, not only unknown to Pythagoras but even to Plato (who proposed, according to Proclus, another non-general formula), it seems that the 'Theorem of Pythagoras' was not known, in its general form, to either Pythagoras or even to Plato. (See for a less radical view on this matter T. Heath, *A History of Greek Mathematics*, 1921, vol. I, pp. 80–2. The formula described by me as 'general' is essentially that of Euclid; it can be obtained from Heath's unnecessarily complicated formula on p. 82 by first obtaining the three sides of the triangle and by multiplying them by $2/mn$, and then by substituting in the result m and n and p and q.)

The discovery of the irrationality of the square root of two (alluded to by Plato in the *Greater Hippias* and in the *Meno*; cp. note 10 to chapter 8; see also Aristotle, *Anal. Priora*, 41a26 f.) destroyed the Pythagorean programme of 'arithmetizing' geometry, and with it, it appears, the vitality of the Pythagorean Order itself. The tradition that this discovery was at first kept secret is, it seems, supported by the fact that Plato still calls the irrational at first '*arrhētos*', i.e. the secret, the unmentionable mystery; cp. the *Greater Hippias*, 303b/c; *Republic*, 546c. (A later term is 'the non-commensurable'; cp. *Theaetetus*, 147c, and *Laws*, 820c. The term '*alogos*' seems to occur first in Democritus, who wrote two books *On Illogical Lines and Atoms* (or *and Full Bodies*) which are lost; Plato knew the term, as proved by his somewhat disrespectful allusion to Democritus' title in the *Republic*, 534d, but never used it himself as a synonym for '*arrhētos*'. The first extant and indubitable use in this sense is in Aristotle's *Anal. Post.*, 76b9. See also T. Heath, *op. cit.*, vol. I, pp. 84 f., 156 f. and my first *Addendum* on p. 319, below.)

It appears that the breakdown of the Pythagorean programme, i.e. of the arithmetical method of geometry, led to the development of the axiomatic method of Euclid, that is to say, of a new method which was on the one side designed to rescue, from the breakdown, what could be rescued (including the method of rational proof), and on the other side to accept the irreducibility of geometry to arithmetic. Assuming all this, it would seem highly probable that Plato's role in the transition from the older Pythagorean method to that of Euclid was an exceedingly important one—in fact, that Plato was *one of the first to develop a specifically geometrical method* aiming at rescuing what could be rescued from, and at cutting the losses of, the breakdown of Pythagoreanism. Much of this must be considered as a highly uncertain historical hypothesis, but some confirmation may be found in Aristotle, *Anal. Post.*, 76b9 (mentioned above), especially if this passage is compared with the *Laws*, 818c, 895e (even and odd), and 819e/820a, 820c (incommensurable). The passage reads: 'Arithmetic assumes the meaning of "odd" and "even", geometry that of "irrational" ...' (Or 'incommensurable'; cp. *Anal. Priora*, 41a26 f., 50a37. See also *Metaphysics*, 983a20, 1061b1–3, where the problem of irrationality is treated as if it were the *proprium* of geometry, and 1089a, where, as in *Anal. Post.*, 76b40, there is an allusion to the 'square foot' method of the *Theaetetus*, 147d.) Plato's great interest in the problem of irrationality is shown especially in two of the passages mentioned above, the *Theaetetus*, 147c–148a, and *Laws*, 819d–822d, where Plato declares that he is ashamed of the Greeks for not being alive to the great problem of incommensurable magnitudes.

Now I suggest that the 'Theory of the Primary Bodies' (in the *Timaeus*, 53c to 62c, and perhaps even down to 64a; see also *Republic*, 528b–d) was part of Plato's answer to the challenge. It preserves, on the one hand, the atomistic character of Pythagoreanism—the indivisible units ('monads') which also play a role in the school of the Atomists—and it introduces, on the other hand, the irrationalities (of the square roots of two and three) whose admission into the world had become unavoidable. It does so by taking two of the offending rectangular triangles—the one which is half of a square and incorporates the square root of two, and the one which is half of an equilateral triangle and incorporates the square root of three—as the units of which everything else is composed. Indeed, the doctrine that these two irrational triangles are the limits (*peras*; cp. *Meno*, 75d–76a) or Forms of all elementary physical bodies may be said to be one of the central physical doctrines of the *Timaeus*.

All this would suggest that the warning against those untrained in geometry (an allusion to it may perhaps be found in the *Timaeus*, 54a) might have had the more pointed significance mentioned above, and that it may have been connected with the belief that geometry is something of higher importance than is arithmetic. (Cp. *Timaeus*, 31c.) And this, in turn, would explain why Plato's 'proportionate equality', said by him to be something more aristocratic than the democratic arithmetical or numerical equality, was later identified with the 'geometrical equality', mentioned by Plato in the *Gorgias*, 508a (cp. note 48 to this chapter), and why (for example by Plutarch, *loc. cit.*) arithmetic and geometry were associated with democracy and Spartan aristocracy respectively—in spite of the fact, then apparently forgotten, that the Pythagoreans had been as aristocratically minded as Plato himself; that their programme had stressed arithmetic; and that 'geometrical', in their language, is the name of a certain kind of numerical (i.e. arithmetical) proportion.

(3) In the *Timaeus*, Plato needs for the construction of the Primary Bodies an Elementary Square and an Elementary Equilateral Triangle. These two, in turn, are composed of two different kinds of *sub-elementary triangles*—the half-square which incorporates $\sqrt{2}$, and the half-equilateral which incorporates $\sqrt{3}$ respectively. The question why he chooses these two sub-elementary triangles, instead of the Square and the Equilateral itself, has been much discussed; and similarly a second question—see below under (4)—why he constructs his Elementary Squares out of four sub-elementary half-squares instead of two, and the Elementary Equilateral out of six sub-elementary half-equilaterals instead of two. (See the first two of the three figures below.)

Concerning the first of these two questions, it seems to have been generally overlooked that Plato, with his burning interest in the problem of irrationality, would not have introduced the two irrationalities $\sqrt{2}$ and $\sqrt{3}$ (which he explicitly mentions in 54b) *had he not been anxious to introduce precisely these irrationalities as irreducible elements into his world.* (Cornford, *Plato's Cosmology*, pp. 214 and 231 ff., gives a long discussion of both questions, but the common solution which he offers for both—his 'hypothesis' as he calls it on p. 234—appears to me quite unacceptable; had Plato wanted to achieve some 'grading' like the one discussed by Cornford—note that there is no hint in Plato that anything smaller than what Cornford calls 'Grade B' exists—it would have been sufficient to divide into two the *sides* of the *Elementary Squares* and Equilaterals of what Cornford calls 'Grade B', building each of them up from four elementary figures *which do not contain any irrationalities.*) But if Plato was anxious to introduce these irrationalities into the world, as the sides of sub-elementary triangles of which everything else is composed, then he must have believed that he could, in this way, solve a problem; and this problem, I suggest, was that of 'the nature of (the commensurable and) the uncommensurable' (*Laws*, 820c). This problem, clearly, was particularly hard to solve on the basis of a cosmology which made use of anything like atomistic ideas, since irrationals are not multiples of any unit able to measure rationals; but if the unit measures themselves contain sides in 'irrational ratios', then the great paradox might be solved; for then they can measure both, and the existence of irrationals was no longer incomprehensible or 'irrational'.

But Plato knew that there were more irrationalities than √2 and √3, for he mentions in the *Theaetetus* the discovery of an infinite sequence of irrational square roots (he also speaks, 148b, of 'similar considerations concerning solids', but this need not refer to cubic roots but could refer to the cubic diagonal, i.e. to √3); and he also mentions in the *Greater Hippias* (303b–c; cp. Heath, *op. cit.*, 304) the fact that by adding (or otherwise composing) irrationals, other irrational numbers may be obtained (but also rational numbers—probably an allusion to the fact that, for example, 2 minus √2 is irrational; for this number, plus √2, gives of course a rational number). In view of these circumstances it appears that, if Plato wanted to solve the problem of irrationality by way of introducing his elementary triangles, he must have thought that all irrationals (or at least their multiples) can be composed by adding up (*a*) units; (*b*) √2; (*c*) √3; and multiples of these. This, of course, would have been a mistake, but we have every reason to believe that no disproof existed at the time; and the proposition that there are only two kinds of atomic irrationalities—the diagonals of the squares and of cubes—and that all other irrationalities are commensurable relative to (*a*) the unit; (*b*) √2; and (*c*) √3, has a certain amount of plausibility in it if we consider the relative character of irrationalities. (I mean the fact that we may say with equal justification that the diagonal of a square with unit side is irrational or that the side of a square with a unit diagonal is irrational. We should also remember that Euclid, in Book X, def. 2, still calls all incommensurable square roots 'commensurable by their squares'.) Thus Plato may well have believed in this proposition, even though he could not possibly have been in the possession of a valid proof of his conjecture. (A disproof was apparently first given by Euclid.) Now there is undoubtedly a reference to some unproved conjecture in the very passage in the *Timaeus* in which Plato refers to the reason for choosing his sub-elementary triangles, for he writes (*Timaeus*, 53c/d): 'all triangles are derived from two, each having one right angle ... ; of these triangles, one [the half-square] has on either side half of a right angle, ... and equal sides; the other [the scalene] ... has unequal sides. These two we assume as the first principles ... according to an account which combines likelihood [or likely conjecture] with necessity [proof]. Principles which are still further removed than these are known to heaven, and to such men as heaven favours.' And later, after explaining that there is an endless number of scalene triangles, of which 'the best' must be selected, and after explaining that he takes the half-equilateral as the best, Plato says (*Timaeus*, 54a/b; Cornford had to emend the passage in order to fit it into his interpretation; cp. his note 3 to p. 214): 'The reason is too long a story; but if anybody puts this matter to the test, and proves that it has this property, then the prize is his, with all our good will.' Plato does not say clearly what 'this property' means; it must be a (provable or refutable) mathematical property which justifies that, having chosen the triangle incorporating √2, the choice of that incorporating √3 is 'the best'; and I think that, in view of the foregoing considerations, the property which he had in mind was the conjectured relative rationality of the other irrationals, i.e. relative to the unit, and the square roots of two and three.

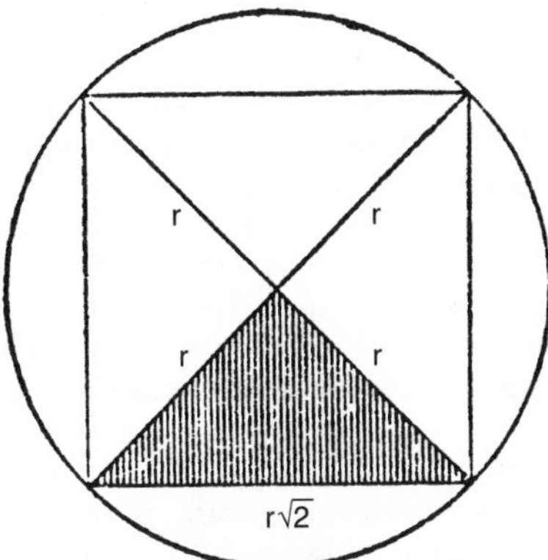

Plato's Elementary Square, composed of four sub-elementary isosceles rectangular triangles

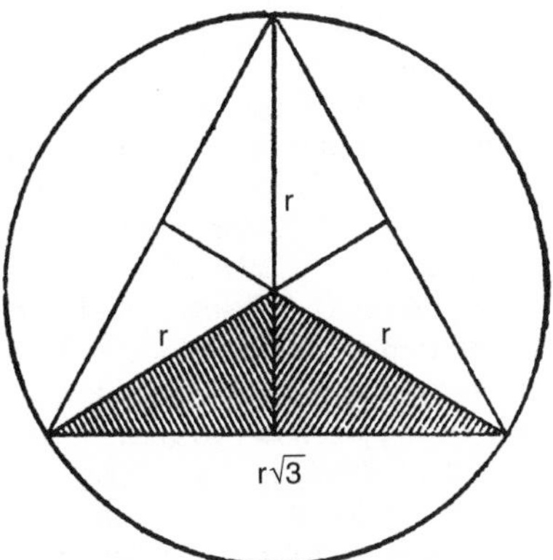

Plato's Elementary Equilateral, composed of six sub-elementary scalene rectangular triangles

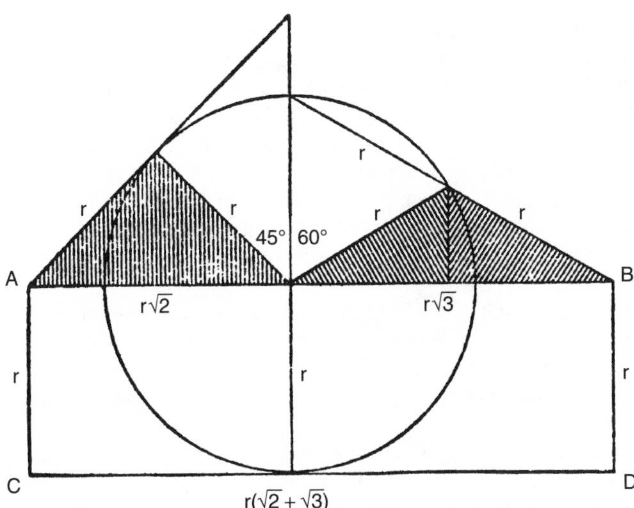

The rectangle ABCD has an area exceeding that of the circle by less than 1½ pro mille

(4) An additional reason for our interpretation, although one for which I do not find any further evidence in Plato's text, may perhaps emerge from the following consideration. It is a curious fact that $\sqrt{2} + \sqrt{3}$ very nearly approximates p. (Cp. E. Borel, *Space and Time*, 1926, 1960, p. 216; my attention was drawn to this fact, in a different context, by W. Marinelli.) The excess is less than 0.0047, i.e. less than

1½ pro mille of π, and a better approximation to π was hardly known at the time. A kind of explanation of this curious fact is that the arithmetical mean of the areas of the circumscribed hexagon and the inscribed octagon is a good approximation of the area of the circle. Now it appears, on the one hand, that Bryson operated with the means of circumscribed and inscribed polygons (cp. Heath, *op. cit.*, 224), and we know, on the other hand (from the *Greater Hippias*), that Plato was interested in the adding of irrationals, so that he must have added $\sqrt{2} + \sqrt{3}$. There are thus two ways by which Plato may have found out the approximate equation $\sqrt{2} + \sqrt{3} \approx \pi$, and the second of these ways seems almost inescapable. It seems a plausible hypothesis that Plato knew of this equation, but was unable to prove whether or not it was a strict equality or only an approximation.

But if this is so, then we can perhaps answer the 'second question' mentioned above under (3), i.e. the question why Plato composed his elementary square of four sub-elementary triangles (half-squares) instead of two, and his elementary equilateral of six sub-elementary triangles (half-equilaterals) instead of two. If we look at the first two of the figures above, then we see that this construction emphasizes the centre of the circumscribed and inscribed circles, and, in both cases, the radii of the circumscribed circle. (In the case of the equilateral, the radius of the inscribed circle appears also; but it seems that Plato had that of the circumscribed circle in mind, since he mentions it, in his description of the method of composing the equilateral, as the 'diagonal'; cp. the *Timaeus*, 54d/e; cp. also 54b.)

If we now draw these two circumscribed circles, or more precisely, if we inscribe the elementary square and equilateral into a circle with the radius r, then we find that the sum of the sides of these two figures approximates rp; in other words, Plato's construction suggests one of the simplest approximate solutions of the squaring of the circle, as our three figures show. In view of all this, it may easily be the case that Plato's conjecture and his offer of 'a prize with all our good will', quoted above under (3), involved not only the general problem of the commensurability of the irrationalities, but also the special problem whether $\sqrt{2} + \sqrt{3}$ squares the unit circle.

I must again emphasize that no direct evidence is known to me to show that this was in Plato's mind; but if we consider the indirect evidence here marshalled, then the hypothesis does perhaps not seem too far-fetched. I do not think that it is more so than Cornford's hypothesis; and if true, it would give a better explanation of the relevant passages.

(5) If there is anything in our contention, developed in section (2) of this note, that Plato's inscription meant 'Arithmetic is not enough; you must know geometry!' and in our contention that this emphasis was connected with the discovery of the irrationality of the square roots of 2 and 3, then this might throw some light on the Theory of Ideas, and on Aristotle's much debated reports. It would explain why, in view of this discovery, the Pythagorean view that things (forms, shapes) are numbers, and moral ideas ratios of numbers, had to disappear—perhaps to be replaced, as in the *Timaeus*, by the doctrine that the elementary forms, or limits ('peras'; cp. the passage from the *Meno*, 75d–76a, referred to above), or shapes, or ideas of things, are triangles. But it would also explain why, one generation later, the Academy could return to the Pythagorean doctrine. Once the shock caused by the discovery of irrationality had worn off, mathematicians began to get used to the idea

that *the irrationals must be numbers*, in spite of everything, since they stand in the elementary relations of greater or less to other (rational) numbers. This stage reached, the reasons against Pythagoreanism disappeared, although the theory that shapes are numbers or ratios of numbers meant, after the admission of irrationals, something different from what it had meant before (a point which possibly was not fully appreciated by the adherents of the new theory). See also *Addendum I*, p. 319.*

10. The well-known representation of Themis as blindfolded, i.e. disregarding the suppliant's station, and as carrying scales, i.e. as distributing equality or as balancing the claims and interests of the contesting individuals, is a symbolic representation of the equalitarian idea of justice. This representation cannot, however, be used here as an argument in favour of the contention that this idea was current in Plato's time; for, as Prof. E. H. Gombrich kindly informs me, it dates from the Renaissance, and is inspired by a passage in Plutarch's *De Iside et Osiride*, but not by classical Greece. *On the other hand, the representation of Dikē with scales is classical (for such a representation, by Timochares, one generation after Plato, see R. Eisler, *The Royal Art of Astrology*, 1946, pp. 100, 266, and Plate 5), and goes back, probably, to Hesiod's identification of the constellation of Virgo with Dikē (in view of the neighbouring scales). And in view of the other evidence given here to show the association of Justice or Dikē with distributive equality, the scales are likely to mean the same as in the case of Themis.*
11. *Republic*, 440c–d. The passage concludes with a characteristic sheep-dog metaphor: 'Or else, until he has been called back, and calmed down, by the voice of his own reason, like a dog by his shepherd?' Cp. note 32 (2) to chapter 4.
12. Plato, in fact, implies this when he twice presents Socrates as rather doubtful where he should now look out for justice. (Cp. 368b, ff., 432b, ff.)
13. Adam obviously overlooks (under the influence of Plato) the equalitarian theory in his note to *Republic*, 331e, ff., where he, probably correctly, says that 'the view that Justice consists in doing good to friends and harm to enemies, is a faithful reflection of prevalent Greek morality'. But he is wrong when he adds that this was 'an all but universal view'; for he forgets his own evidence (note to 561e28), which shows that equality before the laws ('isonomy') 'was the proud claim of democracy'. See also notes 14 and 17 to this chapter.

    One of the oldest (if not the oldest) reference to 'isonomy' is to be found in a fragment due to Alcmaeon the physician (early fifth century; see Diels[5], chapter 24, fr. 4); he speaks of isonomy as a condition of health, and opposes it to 'monarchy'—the dominance of one over many. Here we have a political theory of the body, or more precisely, of human physiology. Cp. also notes 32 to chapter 5 and 59 to chapter 10.
14. A passing reference to *equality* (similar to that in the *Gorgias*, 483c/d; see also this note, below, and note 47 to this chapter) is made in Glaucon's speech in *Republic*, 359c; but the issue is not taken up. (For this passage cp. note 50 to this chapter.)

    In Plato's abusive attack upon democracy (see text to notes 14–18, chapter 4), three scornful jocular references to equalitarianism occur. The *first* is a remark to the effect that democracy 'distributes equality to equals and to unequals alike' (558c; cp. Adam's note to 558c16; see also note 21 to this chapter); this is intended as an ironical criticism. (Equality has been connected with democracy before, viz. in the description of the democratic revolution; cp. *Rep.*, 557a, quoted in the text to note 13, chapter 4.) The *second* characterizes the 'democratic man' as gratifying all his desires 'equally', whether they may be good or bad; he is therefore called an 'equalitarianist' ('isonomist'), a punning allusion to the idea of 'equal laws for all' or 'equality before the law' ('isonomy'; cp. notes 13 and 17 to this chapter). This pun occurs in *Republic*, 561e. The way for it is well paved, since the word 'equal' has already been used three times (*Rep.*, 561b and c) to characterize an attitude of the man to whom all desires and whims are 'equal'. The *third* of these cheap cracks is an appeal to the reader's imagination, typical even nowadays of this kind of propaganda: 'I nearly forgot to mention the great role played by these famous "equal laws", and by this famous "liberty", in the interrelations between men and women ...' (*Rep.*, 563b).

Besides the evidence of the importance of equalitarianism mentioned here (and in the text to notes 9–10 to this chapter), we must consider especially Plato's own testimony in (1) the *Gorgias*, where he writes (488e/489a; see also notes 47, 48, and 50 to the present chapter): 'Does not the multitude (i.e. here: the majority of the people) believe ... that justice is equality?'

(2) The *Menexenus* (238e–239a; see note 19 to this chapter, and text). The passages in the *Laws* on equality are later than the *Republic*, and cannot be used as testimony for Plato's awareness of the issue when writing the *Republic*; but see text to notes 9, 20 and 21 to this chapter.

15. Plato himself says, in connection with the *third* remark (563b; cp. the last note): 'Shall we utter whatever rises to our lips?'; by which he apparently wishes to indicate that he does not see any reason to suppress the joke.

16. I believe that Thucydides' (II, 37 ff.) version of Pericles' oration can be taken as practically authentic. In all likelihood, he was present when Pericles spoke; and in any case he would have reconstructed it as faithfully as possible. There is much reason to believe that in those times it was not extraordinary for a man to learn another's oration even by heart (cp. Plato's *Phaedrus*), and a faithful reconstruction of a speech of this kind is indeed not as difficult as one might think. Plato knew the oration, taking either Thucydides' version or another source, which must have been extremely similar to it, as authentic. Cp. also notes 31 and 34/35 to chapter 10. (It may be mentioned here that early in his career, Pericles had made rather dubious concessions to the popular tribal instincts and to the equally popular group egoism of the people; I have in mind the legislation concerning citizenship in 451 B.C. But later he revised his attitude towards these matters, probably under the influence of such men as Protagoras.)

17. Cp. *Herodotus*, III, 80, and especially the eulogy on 'isonomy', i.e. equality before the law (III, 80, 6); see also notes 13 and 14 to this chapter. The passage from Herodotus, which influenced Plato in other ways also (cp. note 24 to chapter 4), is one which Plato ridicules in the *Republic* just as he ridicules Pericles' oration; cp. note 14 to chapter 4, and 34 to chapter 10.

18. Even the naturalist Aristotle does not always refer to this naturalistic version of equalitarianism; for instance, his formulation of the principles of democracy in *Politics*, 1317b (cp. note 9 to this chapter, and text), is quite independent of it. But it is perhaps even more interesting that in the *Gorgias*, in which the opposition of nature and convention plays such an important rôle, Plato presents equalitarianism

without burdening it with the dubious theory of the natural equality of all men (see 488e/489a, quoted in note 14 to this chapter, and 483d, 484a, and 508a).

19. Cp. *Menexenus*, 238e/239a. The passage immediately follows a clear allusion to Pericles' oration (viz., to the second sentence quoted in the text to note 17, in this chapter).—It seems not improbable that the reiteration of the term 'equal birth' in that passage is meant as a scornful allusion to the 'low' birth of Pericles' and Aspasia's sons, who were recognized as Athenian citizens only by special legislation in 429 B.C. (Cp. E. Meyer, *Gesch. d. Altertums*, vol. IV, p. 14, note to No. 392, and p. 323, No. 558.)

It has been held (even by Grote; cp. his *Plato*, III, p. 11) that Plato in the *Menexenus*, 'in his own rhetorical discourse, ... drops the ironical vein', i.e. that the middle part of the *Menexenus*, from which the quotation in the text is taken, is not meant ironically. But in view of the quoted passage on equality, and in view of Plato's open scorn in the *Republic* when he deals with this point (cp. note 14 to this chapter), this opinion seems to me untenable. And it appears to me equally impossible to doubt the ironical character of the passage immediately preceding the one quoted in the text where Plato says of Athens (cp. 238c/d): 'In this time *as well as at present* ... our government was always an aristocracy ... ; though it is sometimes called a democracy, it is really an aristocracy, that is to say, a rule of the best, with the approval of the many ...' In view of Plato's hatred of democracy, this description needs no further comment. *Another undoubtedly ironical passage is 245c–d (cp. note 48 to chapter 8) where 'Socrates' praises Athens for its consistent hatred of foreigners and barbarians. Since elsewhere (in the *Republic*, 562e, f., quoted in note 48 to chapter 8) in an attack on democracy—and this means Athenian democracy—Plato scorns Athens because of its liberal treatment of foreigners, his praise in the *Menexenus* cannot be anything but irony; again the liberality of Athens is ridiculed by a pro-Spartan partisan. (Strangers were forbidden to reside in Sparta, by a law of Lycurgus; cp. Aristophanes' *Birds*, 1012.) It is interesting, in this connection, that in the *Menexenus* (236a; cp. note 15 (1) to chapter 10) where 'Socrates' is an orator who attacks Athens, Plato says of 'Socrates' that he was a pupil of the oligarchic party leader Antiphon the Orator (of Rhamnus; not to be confused with Antiphon the Sophist, who was an Athenian); especially in view of the fact that 'Socrates' produces a parody of a speech recorded by Thucydides, who in fact seems to have been a pupil of Antiphon whom he greatly admired.* For the genuineness of the *Menexenus*, see also note 35 to chapter 10.

20. *Laws*, 757a; cp. the whole passage, 757a–e, of which the main parts are quoted above, in note 9 (1) to this chapter.

(1) For what I call the standard objection against equalitarianism, cp. also *Laws*, 744b, ff. 'It would be excellent if everybody could ... have all things equal; but since this is impossible ...', etc. The passage is especially interesting in view of the fact that Plato is often described as an enemy of plutocracy by many writers who judge him only by the *Republic*. But in this important passage of the *Laws* (i.e. 744b, ff.) Plato demands that 'political offices, and contributions, as well as distributions, should be proportional to the value of a citizen's wealth. And they should depend not only on his virtue or that of his ancestors or on the size of his body and his good looks, but also upon his wealth or his poverty. In this way, a man will receive honours and offices as equitably as possible, i.e. in proportion to his wealth,

although according to a principle of unequal distribution.' *The doctrine of the unequal distribution of honour and, we may assume, of spoils, in proportion to wealth and bodily size, is probably a residue from the heroic age of conquest. The wealthy who are heavily and expensively armed, and those who are strong, contribute more to the victory than the others. (The principle was accepted in Homeric times, and it can be found, as R. Eisler assures me, in practically all known cases of conquering war hordes.)* The basic idea of this attitude, viz., that it is unjust to treat unequals equally, can be found, in a passing remark, as early as the *Protagoras*, 337a (see also *Gorgias*, 508a, f., mentioned in notes 9 and 48 to this chapter); but Plato did not make much use of the idea before writing the *Laws*.

(2) For Aristotle's elaboration of these ideas, cp. esp. his *Politics*, III, 9, 1, 1280a (see also 1282b–1284b and 1301b29), where he writes: 'All men cling to justice of some kind, but their conceptions are imperfect, and do not embrace the whole Idea. For example, justice is thought (by democrats) to be equality; and so it is, although it is not equality for all, but only for equals. And justice is thought (by oligarchs) to be inequality; and so it is, although it is not inequality for all, but only for unequals.' Cp. also *Nichom. Eth.*, 1131b27, 1158b30 ff.

(3) Against all this anti-equalitarianism, I hold, with Kant, that it must be the principle of all morality that no man should consider himself more valuable than any other person. And I assert that this principle is the only one acceptable, considering the notorious impossibility of judging oneself impartially. I am therefore at a loss to understand the following remark of an excellent writer like Catlin (*Principles*, 314): 'There is something profoundly immoral in the morality of Kant which endeavours to roll all personalities level ... and which ignores the Aristotelian precept to render equals to equals and unequals to unequals. One man has not socially the same rights as another ... The present writer would by no means be prepared to deny that ... there is something in "blood".' Now I ask: If there were something in 'blood', or in inequality of talents, etc.; and even if it were worth while to waste one's time in assessing these differences; and even if one could assess them; why, then, should they be made the ground of greater rights and not only of heavier duties? (Cp. text to notes 31/32 to chapter 4.) I fail to see the profound immorality of Kant's equalitarianism. And I fail to see on what Catlin bases his moral judgement, since he considers morals to be a matter of taste. Why should Kant's 'taste' be profoundly immoral? (It is also the Christian 'taste'.) The only reply to this question that I can think of is that Catlin judges from his positivistic point of view (cp. note 18 (2) to chapter 5), and that he thinks the Christian and Kantian demand immoral because it contradicts the positively enforced moral valuations of our contemporary society.

(4) One of the best answers ever given to all these anti-equalitarianists is due to Rousseau. I say this in spite of my opinion that his romanticism (cp. note 1 to this chapter) was one of the most pernicious influences in the history of social philosophy. But he was also one of the few really brilliant writers in this field. I quote one of his excellent remarks from the *Origin of Inequality* (see, for instance, the Everyman edition of the *Social Contract*, p. 174; the italics are mine); and I wish to draw the reader's attention to the dignified formulation of the last sentence of this passage. 'I conceive that there are two kinds of inequality among the human species; one, which I call natural or physical because it is established by nature, and consists in a

difference of age, health, bodily strength, and the qualities of the mind or of the soul; and another, which may be called moral or political inequality, because it depends on a kind of convention, and is established, or at least authorized, by the consent of men. This latter consists of the different privileges, which some men enjoy ... ; such as that of being more rich, more honoured, or more powerful ... It is useless to ask what is the source of natural inequality, because that question is answered by the simple definition of the word. Again, *it is still more useless to inquire whether there is any essential connection between the two inequalities*; for this would be only asking, in other words, whether those who command are necessarily better than those who obey, and whether strength of body or of mind, or wisdom, or virtue, are always found ... in proportion to the power or wealth of a man; *a question fit perhaps to be discussed by slaves in the hearing of their masters, but highly unbecoming to reasonable and free men in search of the truth*.'

21. *Republic*, 558c; cp. note 14 to this chapter (the first passage in the attack on democracy).
22. *Republic*, 433b. Adam, who also recognizes that the passage is intended as an argument, tries to reconstruct the argument (note to 433b11); but he confesses that 'Plato seldom leaves so much to be mentally supplied in his reasoning'.
23. *Republic*, 433e/434a.—For a continuation of the passage, cp. text to note 40 to this chapter; for the preparation for it in earlier parts of the *Republic*, see note 6 to this chapter.—Adam comments on the passage which I call the 'second argument' as follows (note to 433e35): 'Plato is looking for a point of contact between his own view of Justice and the popular judicial meaning of the word ...' (See the passage quoted in the next paragraph in the text.) Adam tries to defend Plato's argument against a critic (Krohn) who saw, though perhaps not very clearly, that there was something wrong with it.
24. The quotations in this paragraph are from *Republic*, 430d, ff.
25. This device seems to have been successful even with a keen critic such as Gomperz, who, in his brief criticism (*Greek Thinkers*, Book V, II, 10; Germ. edn, vol. II, pp. 378/379), fails to mention the weaknesses of the argument; and he even says, commenting upon the first two books (V, II, 5; p. 368): 'An exposition follows which might be described as a miracle of clarity, precision, and genuine scientific character ...', adding that Plato's interlocutors Glaucon and Adeimantus, 'driven by their burning enthusiasm ... dismiss and forestall all superficial solutions'.

    For my remarks on temperance, in the next paragraph of the text, see the following passage from Davies' and Vaughan's 'Analysis' (cp. the Golden Treasury edition of the *Republic*, p. xviii; italics mine): 'The essence of temperance is restraint. The essence of political temperance lies in recognizing *the right of the governing body to the allegiance and obedience of the governed*.' This may show that my interpretation of Plato's idea of temperance is shared (though expressed in a different terminology) by followers of Plato. I may add that 'temperance', i.e. being satisfied with one's place, is a virtue in which all three classes share, although it is the only virtue in which the workers may participate. Thus the virtue attainable by the workers or money-earners is temperance; the virtues attainable by the auxiliaries are temperance and courage; by the guardians, temperance, courage, and wisdom.

    The 'lengthy preface', also quoted in the next paragraph, is from *Republic*, 432b, ff.
26. On the term 'collectivism', a terminological comment may be made here. What

H. G. Wells calls 'collectivism' has nothing to do with what I call by that name. Wells is an individualist (in my sense of the word), as is shown especially by his *Rights of Man* and his *Common Sense of War and Peace*, which contain very acceptable formulations of the demands of an equalitarian individualism. But he also believes, rightly, in the rational planning of political institutions, with the aim of furthering the freedom and the welfare of individual human beings. This he calls 'collectivism'; to describe what I believe to be the same thing as his 'collectivism', I should use an expression like: 'rational institutional planning for freedom'. This expression may be long and clumsy, but it avoids the danger that 'collectivism' may be interpreted in the anti-individualistic sense in which it is often used, not only in the present book.

27. *Laws*, 903c; cp. text to note 35, chapter 5. The 'preamble' mentioned in the text ('But he needs ... some words of counsel to act as a charm upon him', etc.) is *Laws*, 903b.

28. There are innumerable places in the *Republic* and in the *Laws* where Plato gives a warning against unbridled group egoism; cp., for instance, *Republic*, 519e, and the passages referred to in note 41 to this chapter.

    Regarding the identity often alleged to exist between collectivism and altruism, I may refer, in this connection, to the very pertinent question of Sherrington, who asks in *Man on His Nature* (p. 388): 'Are the shoal and the herd altruism?'

29. For Dickens' mistaken contempt of Parliament, cp. also note 23 to chapter 7.

30. Aristotle's *Politics*, III, 12, 1 (1282b); cp. text to notes 9 and 20, to this chapter. (Cp. also Aristotle's remark in *Pol.*, III, 9, 3, 1280a, to the effect that justice pertains to persons as well as to things.) With the quotation from Pericles later in this paragraph, cp. text to note 16 to this chapter, and to note 31 to chapter 10.

31. This remark is from a passage (*Rep.*, 519e, f.) quoted in the text to note 35 to chapter 5.

32. The important passages from the *Laws* quoted (1) in the present and (2) in the next paragraph are:

    (1) *Laws*, 739c, ff. Plato refers here to the *Republic*, and apparently especially to *Republic*, 462a ff., 424a, and 449e. (A list of passages on collectivism and holism can be found in note 35 to chapter 5. On his communism, see note 29 (2) to chapter 5 and other places there mentioned.) The passage here quoted begins, characteristically, with a quotation of the Pythagorean maxim 'Friends have in common all things they possess'. Cp. note 36 and text; also the 'common meals' mentioned in note 34.

    (2) *Laws*, 942a, f.; see next note. Both these passages are referred to as anti-individualistic by Gomperz (*op. cit.*, vol. II, 406). See also *Laws*, 807d/e.

33. Cp. note 42, chapter 4, and text.—The quotation which follows in the present paragraph is *Laws*, 942a, f. (see the preceding note).

    We must not forget that military education in the *Laws* (as in the *Republic*) is obligatory for all those allowed to carry arms, i.e. for all citizens—for all those who have anything like civil rights (cp. *Laws*, 753b). All others are 'banausic', if not slaves (cp. *Laws*, 741e and 743d, and note 4 to chapter 11).

    It is interesting that Barker, who hates militarism, believes that Plato held similar views (*Greek Political Theory*, 298–301). It is true that Plato did not eulogize war, and that he even spoke against war. But many militarists have talked peace and practised war; and Plato's state is ruled by the military caste, i.e. by the wise ex-soldiers. This remark is as true for the *Laws* (cp. 753b) as it is for the *Republic*.

34. Strictest legislation about meals—especially '*common meals*'—and also about drinking habits plays a considerable part in Plato; cp., for instance, *Republic*, 416e, 458c, 547d/e; *Laws*, 625e, 633a (where the obligatory common meals are said to be instituted with a view to war), 762b, 780–783, 806c, f, 839c, 842b. Plato always emphasizes the importance of common meals, in accordance with Cretan and Spartan customs. Interesting also is the preoccupation of Plato's uncle Critias with these matters. (Cp. Diels[2], Critias, fr. 33.)

    With the allusion to the anarchy of the 'wild beasts', at the end of the present quotation, cp. also *Republic*, 563c.
35. Cp. E. B. England's edition of the *Laws*, vol. I, p. 514, note to 739b8 ff. The quotations from Barker are from *op. cit.*; pp. 149 and 148. Countless similar passages can be found in the writings of most Platonists. See however Sherrington's remark (cp. note 28 to this chapter) that it is hardly correct to say that a shoal or a herd is inspired by altruism. Herd instinct and tribal egoism, and the appeal to these instincts, should not be mixed up with unselfishness.
36. Cp. *Republic*, 424a, 449c; *Phaedrus*, 279c; *Laws*, 739c; see note 32 (1). (Cp. also *Lysis*, 207c, and Euripides, *Orest.*, 725.) For the possible connection of this principle with early Christian and Marxian communism, see note 29 (2) to chapter 5.

    Regarding the individualistic theory of justice and injustice of the *Gorgias*, cp. for instance the examples given in the *Gorgias*, 468b, ff., 508d/e. These passages probably still show Socratic influence (cp. note 56 to chapter 10). Socrates' individualism is most clearly expressed in his famous doctrine of the self-sufficiency of the good man; a doctrine which is mentioned by Plato in the *Republic* (387d/e) in spite of the fact that it flatly contradicts one of the main theses of the *Republic*, viz., that the state alone can be self-sufficient. (Cp. chapter 5, note 25, and the text to that and the following notes.)
37. *Republic*, 368b/c.
38. Cp. especially *Republic*, 344a, ff.
39. Cp. *Laws*, 923b.
40. *Republic*, 434a–c. (Cp. also text to note 6 and note 23 to this chapter, and notes 27 (3) and 31 to chapter 4.)
41. *Republic*, 466b/c. Cp. also the *Laws*, 715b/c, and many other passages against the anti-holistic misuse of class prerogatives. See also note 28 to this chapter, and note 25 (4) to chapter 7.
42. The problem here alluded to is that of the '*paradox of freedom*'; cp. note 4 to chapter 7.—For the problem of state control in education, see note 13 to chapter 7.
43. Cp. Aristotle, *Politics*, III, 9, 6 ff. (1280a). Cp. Burke, *French Revolution* (edn 1815; vol. V, 184; the passage is aptly quoted by Jowett in his notes to the passage of Aristotle's; see his edition of Aristotle's *Politics*, vol. II, 126).

    The quotation from Aristotle later in the paragraph is *op. cit.*, III, 9, 8, (1280b).

    Field, for instance, proffers a similar criticism (in his *Plato and His Contemporaries*, 117): 'There is no question of the city and its laws exercising any educative effect on the moral character of its citizens.' However, Green has clearly shown (in his *Lectures on Political Obligation*) that it is impossible for the state to enforce morality by law. He would certainly have agreed with the formula: 'We want to moralize politics, and not to politicize morals.' (See end of this paragraph in the text.) Green's view is foreshadowed by Spinoza (*Tract. Theol. Pol.*, chapter 20): 'He who seeks to regulate everything by law is more likely to encourage vice than to smother it.'

44. I consider the analogy between civil peace and international peace, and between ordinary crime and international crime, as fundamental for any attempt to get international crime under control. For this analogy and its limitations as well as for the poverty of the historicist method in such problems, cp. note 7 to chapter 9.

* Among those who consider rational methods for the establishment of international peace as a Utopian dream, H. J. Morgenthau may be mentioned (cp. his book, *Scientific Man versus Power Politics*, English edition, 1947). Morgenthau's position can be summed up as that of a disappointed historicist. He realizes that historical predictions are impossible; but since he assumes (with, for example, the Marxists) that the field of applicability of *reason* (or of the scientific method) is limited to the field of *predictability*, he concludes from the unpredictability of historical events that reason is inapplicable to the field of international affairs.

The conclusion does not follow, because scientific prediction and prediction in the sense of historical prophecy are not the same. (None of the natural sciences, with practically the sole exception of the theory of the solar system, attempts anything resembling historical prophecy.) The task of the social sciences is not to predict 'trends' or 'tendencies' of development, nor is this the task of the natural sciences. 'The best the so-called "social laws" can do is exactly the best the so-called "natural laws" can do, namely, to indicate certain *trends* ... Which conditions will actually occur and help one particular *trend* to materialize, neither the natural nor the social sciences are able to foretell. Nor are they able to forecast with more than a high degree of probability that in the presence of certain conditions a certain trend will materialize', writes Morgenthau (pp. 120 ff.; italics mine). But the natural sciences do not attempt the prediction of trends, and only historicists believe that they, and the social sciences, have such aims. Accordingly, the realization that these aims are not realizable will disappoint only the historicist. 'Many ... political scientists, however, claim that they can ... actually ... predict social events with a high degree of certainty. In fact, they ... are the victims of ... delusions', writes Morgenthau. I certainly agree; but this merely shows that historicism is to be repudiated. To assume, however, that the repudiation of historicism means the repudiation of rationalism in politics reveals a fundamentally historicist prejudice—the prejudice, namely, that historical prophecy is the basis of any rational politics. (I have mentioned this view as characteristic of historicism in the beginning of chapter 1.)

Morgenthau ridicules all attempts to bring power under the control of reason, and to suppress war, as springing from a rationalism and scientism which is inapplicable to society by its very essence. But clearly, he proves too much. Civil peace has been established in many societies, in spite of that essential lust for power which, according to Morgenthau's theory, should prevent it. He admits the fact, of course, but does not see that it destroys the theoretical basis of his romantic contentions.*

45. The quotation is from Aristotle's *Politics*, III, 9, 8, (1280).

(1) I say in the text 'furthermore' because I believe that the passages alluded to in the text, i.e. *Politics*, III, 9, 6, and III, 9, 12, are likely to represent Lycophron's views also. My reasons for believing this are the following. From III, 9, 6, to III, 9, 12, Aristotle is engaged in a criticism of the doctrine I have called protectionism. In III,

9, 8, quoted in the text, he directly attributes to Lycophron a concise and perfectly clear formulation of this doctrine. From Aristotle's other references to Lycophron (see (2) in this note), it is probable that Lycophron's age was such that he must have been, if not the first, at least one of the first to formulate protectionism. Thus it seems reasonable to assume (although it is anything but certain) that the whole attack upon protectionism, i.e. III, 9, 6, to III, 9, 12, is directed against Lycophron, and that the various but equivalent formulations of protectionism are all his. (It may also be mentioned that Plato describes protectionism as a 'common view' in *Rep.*, 358c.)

Aristotle's objections are all intended to show that the protectionist theory is unable to account for the local as well as the internal unity of the state. It overlooks, he holds (III, 9, 6), the fact that the state exists for the sake of the good life in which neither slaves nor beasts can have a share (i.e. for the good life of the virtuous landed proprietor, for everybody who earns money is by his 'banausic' occupation prevented from citizenship). It also overlooks the *tribal unity* of the 'true' state which is (III, 9, 12) 'a community of well-being in families, and an *aggregation of families*, for the sake of a complete and self-sufficient life ... established among men who live in the same place, and *who intermarry*'.

(2) For Lycophron's equalitarianism, see note 13 to chapter 5.—Jowett (in *Aristotle's Politics*, II, 126) describes Lycophron as 'an obscure rhetorician'; but Aristotle must have thought otherwise, since in his extant writings he mentions Lycophron at least six times. (In *Pol.*, *Rhet.*, *Fragm.*, *Metaph.*, *Phys.*, *Soph. El.*)

It is unlikely that Lycophron was much younger than Alcidamas, his colleague in Gorgias' school, since his equalitarianism would hardly have attracted so much attention if it had become known after Alcidamas had succeeded Gorgias as the head of the school. Lycophron's epistemological interests (mentioned by Aristotle in *Metaphysics*, 1045b9, and *Physics*, 185b27) are also a case in point, since they make it probable that he was a pupil of Gorgias' earlier period, i.e. before Gorgias confined himself practically exclusively to rhetoric. Of course, any opinion on Lycophron must be highly speculative, owing to the scanty information we have.

46. Barker, *Greek Political Theory*, I, p. 160. For Hume's criticism of the historical version of the contract theory, see note 43 to chapter 4. Concerning Barker's further contention (p. 161) that Plato's justice, as opposed to that of the contract theory, is not 'something external', but rather, internal to the soul, I may remind the reader of Plato's frequent recommendations of most severe sanctions by which justice may be achieved; he always recommends the use of 'persuasion *and force*' (cp. notes 5, 10 and 18 to chapter 8). On the other hand, some modern democratic states have shown that it is possible to be liberal and lenient without increasing criminality.

With my remark that Barker sees in Lycophron (as I do) the originator of the contract theory, cp. Barker, *op. cit.*, p. 63: 'Protagoras did not anticipate the Sophist Lycophron in founding the doctrine of Contract.' (Cp. with this the text to note 27 to chapter 5.)

47. Cp. *Gorgias*, 483b, f.
48. Cp. *Gorgias*, 488e–489b; see also 527b.

From the way in which Socrates replies here to Callicles, it seems possible that the historical Socrates (cp. note 56 to chapter 10) may have countered the arguments in support of a biological naturalism of Pindar's type by arguing like this: If it is natural that the stronger should rule, then it is also natural that equality should rule, since the multitude which shows its strength by the fact that it rules demands equality. In other words, he may have shown the empty, ambiguous character of the naturalistic demand. And his success might have inspired Plato to proffer his own version of naturalism.

I do not wish to assert that Socrates' later remark (508a) on 'geometrical equality' must necessarily be interpreted as anti-equalitarian, i.e. why it must mean the same as the 'proportionate equity' of the *Laws*, 744b, ff., and 757a–e (cp. notes 9 and 20 (1) to this chapter). This is what Adam suggests in his second note to *Republic*, 558c15. But perhaps there is something in his suggestion; for the 'geometrical' equality of the *Gorgias*, 508a, seems to allude to Pythagorean problems (cp. note 56 (6) to chapter 10; see also the remarks in that note on the *Cratylus*) and may well be an allusion to 'geometrical proportions'.

49. *Republic*, 358e. Glaucon disclaims the authorship in 358c. In reading this passage, the reader's attention is easily distracted by the issue 'nature versus convention', which plays a major rôle in this passage as well as in Callicles' speech in the *Gorgias*. However, Plato's major concern in the *Republic* is not to defeat conventionalism, but to denounce the rational protectionist approach as selfish. (That the conventionalist contract theory was not Plato's main enemy emerges from notes 27–28 to chapter 5, and text.)
50. If we compare Plato's presentation of protectionism in the *Republic* with that in the *Gorgias*, then we find that it is indeed the same theory, although in the *Republic* much less emphasis is laid on *equality*. But even equality is mentioned, although only in passing, viz., in *Republic*, 359c: 'Nature ..., by conventional law, is twisted round and compelled by force to honour equality.' This remark increases the similarity with Callicles' speech. (See *Gorgias*, esp. 483c/d.) But as opposed to the *Gorgias*, Plato drops equality at once (or rather, he does not even take the issue up) and never returns to it; which makes it only the more obvious that he was at pains to avoid the problem. Instead, Plato revels in the description of the cynical egoism which he presents as the only source from which protectionism springs. (For Plato's silence on equalitarianism, cp. especially note 14 to this chapter, and text.) A. E. Taylor, *Plato: The Man and His Work* (1926), p. 268, contends that while Callicles starts from 'nature', Glaucon starts from 'convention'.
51. Cp. *Republic*, 359a; my further allusions in the text are to 359b, 360d, ff.; see also 358c. For the 'rubbing in', cp. 359a–362c, and the elaboration down to 367e. Plato's description of the nihilistic tendencies of protectionism fills altogether nine pages in the Everyman edition of the *Republic*; an indication of the significance Plato attached to it. (There is a parallel passage in the *Laws*, 890a, f.)
52. When Glaucon has finished his presentation, Adeimantus takes his place (with a very interesting and indeed most pertinent challenge to Socrates to criticize utilitarianism), yet not until Socrates has stated that he thinks Glaucon's presentation an excellent one (362d). Adeimantus' speech is an amendment of Glaucon's, and it reiterates the claim that what I call protectionism derives from Thrasymachus' nihilism (see especially 367a, ff.). After Adeimantus, Socrates himself speaks, full of admiration for Glaucon as well as Adeimantus, because their belief in justice is unshaken in spite of the fact that *they presented the case for injustice so excellently*, i.e. the theory that it is good to inflict injustice as long as one can 'get away with it'. By

emphasizing the excellence of the arguments proffered by Glaucon and Adeimantus, 'Socrates' (i.e. Plato) implies that these arguments are a fair presentation of the views discussed; and he ultimately states his own theory, not in order to show that Glaucon's representation needs emendation, but, as he emphasizes, in order to show that, contrary to the opinions of the protectionists, justice is good, and injustice evil. (It should not be forgotten—cp. note 49 to this chapter—that Plato's attack is not directed against the contract theory as such but solely against protectionism; for the contract theory is soon (*Rep.*, 369b–c; cp. text to note 29 to chapter 5) adopted by Plato himself, at least partially; including the theory that people 'gather into settlements' because 'every one expects in this way to further his own interests'.)

It must also be mentioned that the passage culminates with the impressive remark of 'Socrates' quoted in the text to note 37 to this chapter. This shows that Plato combats protectionism only by presenting it as an immoral and indeed unholy form of egoism.

Finally, in forming our judgement on Plato's procedure, we must not forget that Plato likes to argue against rhetoric and sophistry; and indeed, that he is the man who by his attacks on the 'Sophists' created the bad associations connected with that word. I believe that we therefore have every reason to censor him when he himself makes use of rhetoric and sophistry in place of argument. (Cp. also note 10 to chapter 8.)

53. We may take Adam and Barker as representative of the Platonists mentioned here. Adam says (note to 358e, ff.) of Glaucon that he resuscitates Thrasymachus' theory, and he says (note to 373a, ff.) of Thrasymachus that his is 'the same theory which is afterwards (in 358e, ff.) represented by Glaucon'. Barker says (*op. cit.*, 159) of the theory which I call protectionism and which he calls 'pragmatism', that it is 'in the same spirit as Thrasymachus'.

54. That the great sceptic Carneades believed in Plato's presentation can be seen from Cicero (*De Republica*, III, 8; 13; 23), where Glaucon's version is presented, practically without alteration, as the theory adopted by Carneades. (See also text to notes 65 and 66 and note 56 to chapter 10.)

    In this connection I may express my opinion, that one can find a great deal of comfort in the fact that anti-humanitarians have always found it necessary to appeal to our humanitarian sentiments; and also in the fact that they have frequently succeeded in persuading us of their sincerity. It shows that they are well aware that these sentiments are deeply rooted in most of us, and that the despised 'many' are too good, too candid, and too guileless, rather than too bad; while they are even ready to be told by their often unscrupulous 'betters' that they are unworthy and materialistically minded egoists who only want to 'fill their bellies like the beasts'.

NOTES TO CHAPTER SEVEN

The motto to this chapter is from the *Laws*, 690b. (Cp. note 28 to chapter 5.)

1. Cp. text to notes 2/3 to chapter 6.
2. Similar ideas have been expressed by J. S. Mill; thus he writes in his *Logic* (1st edn, p. 557 f.): 'Although the actions of rulers are by no means wholly determined by their selfish interests, it is as security against those selfish interests that constitutional

checks are required.' Similarly he writes in *The Subjection of Women* (p. 251 of the Everyman edition; italics mine): 'Who doubts that there may be great goodness, and great happiness and great affection, under the absolute government of a good man? Meanwhile *laws and institutions require to be adapted, not to good men, but to bad*.' Much as I agree with the sentence in italics, I feel that the admission contained in the first part of the sentence is not really called for. (Cp. especially note 25 (3) to this chapter.) A similar admission may be found in an excellent passage of his *Representative Government* (1861; see especially p. 49) where Mill combats the Platonic ideal of the philosopher king because, *especially if his rule should be a benevolent one*, it will involve the 'abdication' of the ordinary citizen's will, and ability, to judge a policy.

It may be remarked that this admission of J. S. Mill's was part of an attempt to resolve the conflict between James Mill's *Essay on Government* and 'Macaulay's famous attack' on it (as J. S. Mill calls it; cp. his *Autobiography*, chapter V, One Stage Onward; 1st edition, 1873, pp. 157–61; Macaulay's criticisms were first published in the *Edinburgh Review*, March 1829, June 1829, and October 1829). This conflict played a great rôle in J. S. Mill's development; his attempt to resolve it determined, indeed, the ultimate aim and character of his *Logic* ('the principal chapters of what I afterwards published on the Logic of the Moral Sciences') as we hear from his *Autobiography*.

The resolution of the conflict between his father and Macaulay which J. S. Mill proposes is this. He says that his father was right in believing that politics was a deductive science, but wrong in believing that 'the type of deduction (was) that of ... pure geometry', while Macaulay was right in believing that it was more experimental than this, but wrong in believing that it was like 'the purely experimental method of chemistry'. The true solution according to J. S. Mill (*Autobiography*, pp. 159 ff.) is this: the appropriate method of politics is the deductive one of dynamics—a method which, he believes, is characterized by the summation of effects as exemplified in the 'principle of the Composition of Forces'. (That this idea of J. S. Mill survived at any rate down to 1937 is shown in my *The Poverty of Historicism*, p. 63.)

I do not think that there is very much in this analysis (which is based, apart from other things, upon a misinterpretation of dynamics and chemistry). Yet so much would seem to be defensible.

James Mill, like many before and after him, tried to 'deduce the science of government from the principles of human nature' as Macaulay said (towards the end of his first paper), and Macaulay was right, I think, to describe this attempt as 'utterly impossible'. Also, Macaulay's method could perhaps be described as more empirical, in so far as he made full use of historical facts for the purpose of refuting J. Mill's dogmatic theories. But the method which he practised has nothing to do with that of chemistry or with that which J. S. Mill believed to be the method of chemistry (or with the Baconian inductive method which, irritated by J. Mill's syllogisms, Macaulay praised). It was simply the method of rejecting invalid logical demonstrations in a field in which nothing of interest can be logically demonstrated, and of discussing theories and possible situations, in the light of alternative theories and of alternative possibilities, and of factual historical evidence. One of the main points at issue was that J. Mill believed that he had demonstrated the necessity for monarchy and aristocracy to produce a rule of terror—a point which was easily refuted by examples. J. S. Mill's two passages quoted at the beginning of this note show the influence of this refutation.

Macaulay always emphasized that he only wanted to reject Mill's proofs, and not to pronounce on the truth or falsity of his alleged conclusions. This alone should have made it clear that he did not attempt to practise the inductive method which he praised.

3. Cp. for instance E. Meyer's remark (*Gesch. d. Altertums*, V, p. 4) that 'power is, in its very essence, indivisible'.

4. Cp. *Republic*, 562b–565e. In the text, I am alluding especially to 562c: 'Does not the excess' (of liberty) 'bring men to such a state that they badly want a tyranny?' Cp. furthermore 563d/e: 'And in the end, as you know well enough, they just do not take any notice of the laws, whether written or unwritten, since they want to have no despot of any kind over them. This then is the origin out of which tyranny springs.' (For the beginning of this passage, see note 19 to chapter 4.)

Other remarks of Plato's on the *paradoxes of freedom and of democracy* are: *Republic*, 564a: 'Then too much freedom is liable to change into nothing else but too much slavery, in the individual as well as in the state ... Hence it is reasonable to assume that tyranny is enthroned by no other form of government than by democracy. Out of what I believe is the greatest possible excess of freedom springs what is the hardest and most savage form of slavery.' See also *Republic*, 565c/d: 'And are not the common people in the habit of making one man their champion or party leader, and of exalting his position and making him great?'—'This is their habit.'—'Then it seems clear that whenever a tyranny grows up, this democratic party-leadership is the origin from which it springs.'

The so-called *paradox of freedom* is the argument that freedom in the sense of absence of any restraining control must lead to very great restraint, since it makes the bully free to enslave the meek. This idea is, in a slightly different form, and with a very different tendency, clearly expressed by Plato.

Less well known is the *paradox of tolerance*: unlimited tolerance must lead to the disappearance of tolerance. If we extend unlimited tolerance even to those who are intolerant, if we are not prepared to defend a tolerant society against the onslaught of the intolerant, then the tolerant will be destroyed, and tolerance with them.—In this formulation, I do not imply, for instance, that we should always suppress the utterance of intolerant philosophies; as long as we can counter them by rational argument and keep them in check by public opinion, suppression would certainly be most unwise. But we should claim the *right* to suppress them if necessary even by force; for it may easily turn out that they are not prepared to meet us on the level of rational argument, but begin by denouncing all argument; they may forbid their followers to listen to rational argument, because it is deceptive, and teach them to answer arguments by the use of their fists or pistols. We should therefore claim, in the name of tolerance, the right not to tolerate the intolerant. We should claim that any movement preaching intolerance places itself outside the law, and we should consider incitement to intolerance and persecution as criminal, in the same way as we should consider incitement to murder, or to kidnapping, or to the revival of the slave trade, as criminal.

Another of the less well-known paradoxes is the *paradox of democracy*, or more precisely, of majority-rule; i.e. the possibility that the majority may decide that a tyrant should rule. That Plato's criticism of democracy can be interpreted in the way sketched here, and that the principle of majority-rule may lead to self-contradictions, was first suggested, as far as I know, by Leonard Nelson (cp. note 25 (2) to this chapter). I do not think, however, that Nelson, who, in spite of his passionate humanitarianism and his ardent fight for freedom, adopted much of Plato's political theory, and especially Plato's principle of leadership, was aware of the fact that analogous arguments can be raised against all the different particular forms of the *theory of sovereignty*.

All these paradoxes can easily be avoided if we frame our political demands in the way suggested in section ii of this chapter, or perhaps in some such manner as this. We demand a government that rules according to the principles of equalitarianism and protectionism; that tolerates all who are prepared to reciprocate, i.e. who are tolerant; that is controlled by, and accountable to, the public. And we may add that some form of majority vote, together with institutions for keeping the public well informed, is the best, though not infallible, means of controlling such a government. (No infallible means exist.) Cp. also chapter 6, the last four paragraphs in the text prior to note 42; text to note 20 to chapter 17; note 7 (4) to chapter 24; and note 6 to the present chapter.

5. Further remarks on this point will be found in chapter 19, below.

6. Cp. passage (7) in note 4 to chapter 2.

The following remarks on the *paradoxes of freedom and of sovereignty* may possibly appear to carry the argument too far; since, however, the arguments discussed in this place are of a somewhat formal character, it may be just as well to make them more watertight, even if it involves something approaching hair-splitting. Moreover, my experience in debates of this kind leads me to expect that the defenders of the leader-principle, i.e. of the sovereignty of the best or the wisest, may actually offer the following counter-argument: (*a*) if 'the wisest' should decide that the majority should rule, then he was not really wise. As a further consideration they may support this by the assertion (*b*) that a wise man would never establish a principle which might lead to contradictions, like that of majority-rule. My reply to (*b*) would be that we need only to alter this decision of the 'wise' man in such a way that it becomes free from contradictions. (For instance, he could decide in favour of a government bound to rule according to the principle of equalitarianism and protectionism, and controlled by majority vote. This decision of the wise man would give up the sovereignty-principle; and since it would thereby become free from contradictions, it may be made by a 'wise' man. But of course, this would not free the principle that the wisest should rule from *its* contradictions. The other argument, namely (*a*), is a different matter. It comes dangerously close to defining the 'wisdom' or 'goodness' of a politician in such a way that he is called 'wise' or 'good' only if he is determined not to give up his power. And indeed, the only sovereignty-theory which is free from contradictions would be the theory which demands that only a man who is absolutely determined to cling to his power should rule. Those who believe in the leader-principle should frankly face this logical consequence of their creed. If freed from contradictions it implies, not the rule of the best or wisest, but the rule of the strong man, of the man of power. (Cp. also note 7 to chapter 24.)

7 *Cp. my lecture 'Towards a Rational Theory of Tradition' (first published in *The Rationalist Yearbook*, 1949; now in my *Conjectures and Refutations*), where I try to

show that traditions play a kind of intermediate and intermediary rôle between *persons* (and personal decisions) and *institutions*.*

8. For Socrates' behaviour under the Thirty, see *Apology*, 32c. The Thirty tried to implicate Socrates in their crimes, but he resisted. This would have meant death to him if the rule of the Thirty had continued a little longer. Cp. also notes 53 and 56 to chapter 10.

   For the contention, later in the paragraph, that wisdom means knowing the limitations of one's knowledge, see the *Charmides*, 167a, 170a, where the meaning of 'know thyself' is explained in this way; the *Apology* (cp. especially 23a–b) exhibits a similar tendency (of which there is still an echo in the *Timaeus*, 72a). For the important modification in the interpretation of 'know thyself' which takes place in the *Philebus*, see note 26 to the present chapter. (Cp. also note 15 to chapter 8.)
9. Cp. Plato's *Phaedo*, 96–99. The *Phaedo* is, I believe, still partly Socratic, but very largely Platonic. The story of his philosophical development told by the Socrates of the *Phaedo* has given rise to much discussion. It is, I believe, an authentic autobiography neither of Socrates nor of Plato. I suggest that it is simply *Plato's interpretation* of Socrates' development. Socrates' attitude towards science (an attitude which combined the keenest interest in rational argument with a kind of modest agnosticism) was incomprehensible to Plato. He tried to explain it by referring to the backwardness of Athenian science in Socrates' day, as opposed to Pythagoreanism. Plato thus presents this agnostic attitude in such a way that it is no longer justified in the light of his newly acquired Pythagoreanism. (And he tries to show how much the new metaphysical theories of the soul would have appealed to Socrates' burning interest in the individual; cp. notes 44 and 56 to chapter 10, and note 58 to chapter 8.)
10. It is the version that involves the square root of two, and the problem of irrationality; i.e. it is the very problem that precipitated the dissolution of Pythagoreanism. By refuting the Pythagorean arithmetization of geometry, it gave rise to the specific deductive-geometrical methods which we know from Euclid. (Cp. note 9 (2) to chapter 6.) The use of this problem in the *Meno* might be connected with the fact that there is a tendency in some parts of this dialogue to 'show off' the author's (hardly Socrates') acquaintance with the 'latest' philosophical developments and methods.
11. *Gorgias*, 521d, f.
12. Cp. Crossman, *Plato To-Day*, 118. 'Faced by these three cardinal errors of Athenian Democracy ...'—How truly Crossman understands Socrates may be seen from *op. cit.*, 93: 'All that is good in our Western culture has sprung from this spirit, whether it is found in scientists, or priests, or politicians, or quite ordinary men and women who have refused to prefer political falsehoods to simple truth ... in the end, their example is the only force which can break the dictatorship of force and greed ... Socrates showed that philosophy is nothing else than conscientious objection to prejudice and unreason.'
13. Cp. Crossman, *op. cit.*, 117 f. (first group of italics mine). It seems that Crossman has for the moment forgotten that, in Plato's state, education is a class monopoly. It is true that in the *Republic* the possession of money is not a key to higher education. But this is quite unimportant. The important point is that only the members of the ruling class are educated. (Cp. note 33 to chapter 4.) Besides, Plato was, at least

in his later life, anything but an opponent of plutocracy, which he much preferred to a classless or equalitarian society: cp. the passage from the *Laws*, 744b, ff., quoted in note 20 (1) to chapter 6. For the problem of state control in education, cp. also note 42 to that chapter, and notes 39–41, chapter 4.

14. Burnet takes (*Greek Philosophy*, I, 178) the *Republic* to be purely Socratic (or even pre-Socratic—a view which may be nearer to the truth; cp. especially A. D. Winspear, *The Genesis of Plato's Thought*, 1940). But he does not even seriously attempt to reconcile this opinion with an important statement which he quotes from Plato's *Seventh Letter* (326a, cp. *Greek Philosophy*, I, 218) which he believes to be authentic. Cp. note 56 (5, d) to chapter 10.
15. *Laws*, 942c, quoted more fully in text to note 33, chapter 6.
16. *Republic*, 540c.
17. Cp. the quotations from the *Republic*, 473c–e, quoted in text to note 44, chapter 8.
18. *Republic*, 498b/c. Cp. the *Laws*, 634d/e, in which Plato praises the Dorian law that 'forbids any young man to question which of the laws are right and which are wrong, and makes them all unanimous in proclaiming that the laws are all good'. Only an old man may criticize a law, adds the old writer; and even he may do so only when no young man can hear him. See also text to note 21 to this chapter, and notes 17, 23 and 40 to chapter 4.
19. *Republic*, 497d.
20. *Op. cit.*, 537c. The next quotations are from 537d–e, and 539d. The 'continuation of this passage' is 540b–c. Another most interesting remark is 536c–d, where Plato says that the persons selected (in the previous passage) for dialectical studies are decidedly too old for learning new subjects.
21. * Cp. H. Cherniss, *The Riddle of the Early Academy*, p. 79; and the *Parmenides*, 135c–d.*

    Grote, the great democrat, strongly comments on this point (i.e. on the 'brighter' passages of the *Republic*, 537c–540): 'The dictum forbidding dialectic debate with youth ... is decidedly anti-Socratic ... It belongs indeed to the case of Meletus and Anytus, in their indictment against Socrates ... It is identical with their charge against him, of corrupting the youth ... And when we find him (= Plato) forbidding all such discourse at an earlier age than thirty years—we remark as a singular coincidence that this is the exact prohibition which Critias and Charicles actually imposed upon Socrates himself, during the short-lived dominion of the Thirty Oligarchs at Athens.' (Grote, *Plato, and the Other Companions of Socrates*, edn 1875, vol. III, 239.)
22. The idea, contested in the text, that those who are good in obeying will also be good in commanding is Platonic. Cp. *Laws*, 762e.

    Toynbee has admirably shown how successfully a Platonic system of educating rulers may work—in an arrested society; cp. *A Study of History*, III, especially 33 ff.; cp. notes 32 (3) and 45 (2) to chapter 4.
23. Some may perhaps ask how an individualist can demand devotion to any cause, and especially to such an abstract cause as scientific inquiry. But such a question would only reveal the old mistake (discussed in the foregoing chapter), the identification of individualism and egoism. An individualist can be unselfish, and he can devote himself not only to the help of individuals, but also to the development of the institutional means for helping other people. (Apart from that, I do not think that devotion should be *demanded*, but only that it should be *encouraged*.) I believe that devotion to certain institutions, for instance, to those of a democratic state,

and even to certain traditions, may fall well within the realm of individualism, provided that the humanitarian aims of these institutions are not lost sight of. Individualism must not be identified with an anti-institutional personalism. This is a mistake frequently made by individualists. They are right in their hostility to collectivism, but they mistake institutions for collectives (which claim to be aims in themselves), and therefore become anti-institutional personalists; which leads them dangerously close to the leader-principle. (I believe that this partly explains Dickens' hostile attitude towards Parliament.) For my terminology ('individualism' and 'collectivism') see text to notes 26–29 to chapter 6.

24. Cp. Samuel Butler, *Erewhon* (1872), p. 135 of the Everyman's edition.

25. Cp. for these events: Meyer, *Gesch. d. Altertums*, V, pp. 522–525, and 488f.; see also note 69 to chapter 10. The Academy was notorious for breeding tyrants. Among Plato's pupils were Chairon, later the tyrant of Pellene; Eurastus and Coriscus, the tyrants of Skepsis (near Atarneus); and Hermias, later tyrant of Atarneus and Assos. (Cp. *Athen.*, XI, 508, and Strabo, XIII, 610.) Hermias was, according to some sources, a direct pupil of Plato's; according to the so-called 'Sixth Platonic Letter', whose authenticity is questionable, he was perhaps only an admirer of Plato's, ready to accept his advice. Hermias became a patron of Aristotle, and of the third head of the Academy, Plato's pupil Xenocrates.

For Perdiccas III, and his relations to Plato's pupil Euphacus, see *Athen.*, XI, 508 ff., where Callippus is also referred to as Plato's pupil.

(1) Plato's lack of success as an educator is not very surprising if we look at the principles of education and selection developed in the First Book of the *Laws* (from 637d and especially 643a: 'Let me define the nature and meaning of education' to the end of 650b). For in this long passage he shows that there is one great instrument of educating, or rather, of selecting the man one can trust. It is wine, drunkenness, which will loose his tongue, and give you an idea of what he is really like. 'What is more fitting than to make use of wine, first of all to test the character of a man, and secondly, to train him? What is cheaper, and less objectionable?' (649d/e). So far, I have not seen the method of drinking discussed by any of the educationists who glorify Plato. This is strange, for the method is still widely in use, even though it is perhaps no longer so cheap, especially in the universities.

(2) In fairness to the leader-principle, it must be admitted, however, that others have been more fortunate than Plato in their selection. Leonard Nelson (cp. note 4 to this chapter), for instance, who believed in this principle, seems to have had a unique power both of attracting and of selecting a number of men and women who have remained true to their cause, in the most trying and tempting circumstances. But theirs was a better cause than Plato's; it was the humanitarian idea of freedom and equalitarian justice. *(Some of Nelson's essays have just been published in an English translation, by Yale University Press, under the title *Socratic Method and Critical Philosophy*, 1949. The very interesting introductory essay is by Julius Kraft.)*

(3) There remains this fundamental weakness in the theory of the benevolent dictator, a theory still flourishing even among some democrats. I have in mind the theory of the leading personality whose intentions are for the best for his people and who can be trusted. Even if that theory were in order; even if we believe that a man can continue, without being controlled or checked, in such an attitude: how can we

assume that he will detect a successor of the same rare excellence? (Cp. also notes 3 and 4 to chapter 9, and note 69 to chapter 10.)

(4) Concerning the problem of power, mentioned in the text, it is interesting to compare the *Gorgias* (525e, f.) with the *Republic* (615d, f.). The two passages are closely parallel. But the *Gorgias* insists that the greatest criminals are *always* 'men who come from the class which possesses power'; private persons may be bad, it is said, but not incurable. In the *Republic*, this clear warning against the corrupting influence of power is omitted. Most of the greatest sinners are still tyrants; but, it is said, 'there are also some private people among them'. (In the *Republic*, Plato relies on self-interest which, he trusts, will prevent the guardians from misusing their power; cp. *Rep.*, 466b/c, quoted in text to note 41, chapter 6. It is not quite clear why self-interest should have such a beneficial effect on guardians, but not on tyrants.)

26. * In the early (Socratic) dialogues (e.g. in the *Apology* and the *Charmides*; cp. note 8 to the present chapter, note 15 to chapter 8 and note 56 (5) to chapter 10), the saying 'know thyself' is interpreted as 'know how little you know'. The late (Platonic) dialogue *Philebus*, however, introduces a subtle but very important change. At first (48c/d, f.), the saying is here interpreted, by implication, in the same way; for the many who do not know themselves are said to be 'claiming, ... and lying, that they are wise'. But this interpretation is now developed as follows. Plato divides men into two classes, the weak and the powerful. The ignorance and folly of the weak man is described as laughable, while '*the ignorance of the strong*' is 'appropriately called "evil" and "hateful" ...'. But this implies the Platonic doctrine that *he who wields power ought to be wise rather than ignorant* (or that only he who is wise ought to wield power); in opposition to the original Socratic doctrine that (everybody, and especially) *he who wields power ought to be aware of his ignorance.* (There is, of course, no suggestion in the *Philebus* that 'wisdom' in its turn ought to be interpreted as 'awareness of one's limitations'; on the contrary, wisdom involves here an expert knowledge of Pythagorean teaching, and of the Platonic Theory of Forms, as developed in the *Sophist*.)*

NOTES TO CHAPTER EIGHT

With the motto for this chapter, taken from *Republic* 540c–d, cp. note 37 to this chapter, and note 12 to chapter 9, where the passage is quoted more fully.

1. *Republic*, 475e; cp. for instance also 485c, f., 501c.
2. *Op. cit.*, 389b, f.
3. *Op. cit.*, 389c/d; cp. also *Laws*, 730b, ff.
4. With this and the three following quotations, cp. *Republic*, 407e and 406c. See also *Statesman*, 293a, f., 295b–296e, etc.
5. Cp. *Laws*, 720c. It is interesting to note that the passage (718c–722b) serves to introduce the idea that the statesman should use *persuasion*, together with force (722b); and since by 'persuasion' of the masses, Plato means largely lying propaganda—cp. notes 9 and 10 to this chapter and the quotation from *Republic*, 414b/c, quoted there in the text—it turns out that Plato's thought in our passage from the *Laws*, in spite of this novel gentleness, is still pervaded by the old associations—the doctor-politician administering lies. Later on (*Laws*, 857c/d), Plato complains about an

opposite type of doctor: one who talks too much philosophy to his patient, instead of concentrating on the cure. It seems likely enough that Plato reports here some of his experiences when he fell ill while writing the *Laws*.

6. *Republic*, 389b.—With the following short quotations cp. *Republic*, 459c.
7. Cp. Kant, *On Eternal Peace*, Appendix. (*Werke*, ed. Cassirer, 1914, vol. VI, 457.) Cp. M. Campbell Smith's translation (1903), pp. 162 ff.
8. Cp. Crossman, *Plato To-Day* (1937), 130; cp. also the immediately preceding pages. It seems that Crossman still believes that lying propaganda was intended only for the consumption of the ruled, and that Plato intended to educate the rulers to a full use of their critical faculties; for I find now (in *The Listener*, vol. 27, p. 750) that he writes: 'Plato believed in free speech, free discussion only for the select few.' But the fact is that he did not believe in it at all. Both in the *Republic* and in the *Laws* (cp. the passages quoted in notes 18–21 to chapter 7, and text), he expresses his fear lest anybody who is not yet on the verge of old age should think or speak freely, and thus endanger the rigidity of the arrested doctrine, and therefore the petrifaction of the arrested society. See also the next two notes.
9. *Republic*, 414b/c. In 414d, Plato reaffirms his hope of persuading 'the rulers themselves and the military class, and then the rest of the city', of the truth of his lie. Later he seems to have regretted his frankness; for in the *Statesman*, 269b, ff. (see especially 271b; cp. also note 6 (4) to chapter 3), he speaks as if he believed in the truth of the same Myth of the Earthborn which, in the *Republic*, he had been reluctant (see note 11 to this chapter) to introduce even as a lordly 'lie'.

* What I translate as a 'lordly lie' is usually translated 'noble lie' or 'noble falsehood' or even 'spirited fiction'.

The literal translation of the word '*gennaios*' which I now translate by 'lordly' is 'high born' or 'of noble descent'. Thus 'lordly lie' is at least as literal as 'noble lie', but it avoids the associations which the term 'noble lie' might suggest, and which are in no way warranted by the situation, viz. a lie by which a man nobly takes something upon himself which endangers him—such as Tom Sawyer's lie by which he takes Becky's guilt upon himself and which Judge Thatcher (in chapter XXXV) describes as 'a noble, a generous, a magnanimous lie'. There is no reason whatever why the 'lordly lie' should be considered in this light; thus the translation 'noble lie' is just one of the typical attempts at idealizing Plato.—Cornford translates 'a ... bold flight of invention', and argues in a footnote against the translation 'noble lie'; he gives passages where '*gennaios*' means 'on a generous scale'; and indeed, 'big lie' or 'grand lie' would be a perfectly appropriate translation. But Cornford at the same time argues against the use of the term 'lie'; he describes the myth as 'Plato's harmless allegory' and argues against the idea that Plato 'would countenance lies, for the most part ignoble, now called propaganda'; and in the next footnote he says: 'Note that the Guardians themselves are to accept this allegory, if possible. It is not "propaganda" foisted on the masses by the Rulers.' But all these attempts at idealization fail. Plato himself makes it quite clear that the lie is one for which one ought to feel ashamed; see the last quotation in note 11, below. (In the first edition of this book, I translated 'inspired lie', alluding to its 'high birth', and suggested 'ingenious lie' as an alternative; this was criticized both as too free and as tendentious by some of my Platonic friends. But Cornford's 'bold flight of invention' takes '*gennaios*' in precisely the same sense.)

See also notes 10 and 18 to this chapter.*

10. Cp. *Republic*, 519e, f., quoted in the text to note 35 to chapter 5; on *persuasion and force*, see also *Republic*, 366d, discussed in the present note, below, and the passages referred to in notes 5 and 18 to this chapter.

The Greek word ('peithō'; its personification is an alluring goddess, an attendant of Aphroditē) usually translated by *persuasion* can mean (*a*) 'persuasion by fair means' and (*b*) 'talking over by foul means', i.e. 'make-believe' (see below, sub. (D), i.e. *Rep.*, 414c), and sometimes it means even 'persuasion by gifts', i.e. bribery (see below, sub. (D), i.e. *Rep.*, 390e). Especially in the phrase 'persuasion and force', the term 'persuasion' is often (*Rep.* 548b) interpreted in sense (*a*), and the phrase is often (and often appropriately) translated 'by fair means or foul' (cp. Davies' and Vaughan's translation 'by fair means or foul', of the passage (C), *Rep.*, 365d, quoted below). I believe, however, that Plato, when recommending 'persuasion and force' as instruments of political technique, uses the words in a more literal sense, and that he recommends the use of rhetorical propaganda together with violence. (Cp. *Laws*, 661c, 711c, 722b, 753a.)

The following passages are significant for Plato's use of the term 'persuasion' in sense (*b*), and especially in connection with political propaganda. (*A*) *Gorgias*, 453a to 466a, especially 454b–455a; *Phaedrus*, 260b, ff., *Theaetetus*, 201a; *Sophist*, 222c; *Statesman*, 296b, ff., 304c/d; *Philebus*, 58a. In all these passages, persuasion (the 'art of persuasion' as opposed to the 'art of imparting true knowledge') is associated with rhetoric, make-believe, and propaganda. In the *Republic*, 364b, f., especially 364e–365d (cp. *Laws*, 909b), deserves attention. (*B*) In 364e ('they persuade', i.e. mislead into believing, 'not only individuals, but whole cities'), the term is used much in the same sense as in 414b/c (quoted in the text to note 9, this chapter), the passage of the 'lordly lie'. (*C*) 365d is interesting because it uses a term which Lindsay translates very aptly by 'cheating' as a kind of paraphrase for 'persuading'. ('In order not to be caught ... we have the masters of persuasion at our disposal; ... thus by *persuasion and force*, we shall escape punishment. But, it may be objected, one cannot *cheat, or force*, the gods ...') Furthermore (*D*) in *Republic*, 390e, f., the term 'persuasion' is used in the sense of bribery. (This must be an old use; the passage is supposed to be a quotation from Hesiod. It is interesting that Plato, who so often argues against the idea that men can 'persuade' or bribe the gods, makes some concession to it in the next passage, 399a/b.) Next we come to 414b/c, the passage of the 'lordly lie'; immediately after this passage, in 414c (cp. also the next note in this chapter), 'Socrates' makes the cynical remark (*E*): 'It would need much persuading to make anybody believe in this story.' Lastly, I may mention (*F*) *Republic*, 511d and 533e, where Plato speaks of persuasion or belief or faith (the root of the Greek word for 'persuasion' is the same as that of our 'faith') as a lower cognitive faculty of the soul, corresponding to the formation of (delusive) opinion about things in flux (cp. note 21 to chapter 3, and especially the use of 'persuasion' in *Tim.*, 51e), as opposed to rational knowledge of the unchanging Forms. For the problem of 'moral' persuasion, see also chapter 6, especially notes 52/54 and text, and chapter 10, especially text to notes 56 and 65, and note 69.

11. *Republic*, 415a. The next quotation is from 415c. (See also the *Cratylus*, 398a.) Cp. notes 12–14 to the present chapter and text, and notes 27 (3), 29, and 31 to chapter 4.

(1) For my remark in the text, earlier in this paragraph, concerning Plato's uneasiness, see *Republic*, 414c–d, and last note, (*E*): 'It would need much persuading to make anybody believe in this story,' says Socrates.—'You seem to be rather reluctant to tell it,' replies Glaucon.—'You will understand my reluctance', says Socrates, 'when I have told it.'—'Speak and don't be frightened', says Glaucon. This dialogue introduces what I call the *first idea of the Myth* (proffered by Plato in the *Statesman* as a true story; cp. note 9 to this chapter; see also *Laws*, 740a). As mentioned in the text, Plato suggests that it is this 'first idea' which is the reason for his hesitation, for Glaucon replies to this idea: 'Not without reason were you so long ashamed to tell your lie.' No similar rhetorical remark is made after Socrates has told 'the rest of the story', i.e., the Myth of Racialism.

* (2) Concerning the autochthonous warriors, we must remember that the Athenian nobility claimed (as opposed to the Dorians) to be the aborigines of their country, born of the earth 'like grasshoppers' (as Plato says in the *Symposium*, 191b; see also end of note 52 to the present chapter). It has been suggested to me by a friendly critic that Socrates' uneasiness, and Glaucon's comment that Socrates had reason to be ashamed, mentioned here under (1), is to be interpreted as an ironical allusion of Plato's to the Athenians who, in spite of their claim to be autochthonous, did not defend their country as they would defend a mother. But this ingenious suggestion does not appear to me a tenable one. Plato, with his openly admitted preference of Sparta, would be the last to charge the Athenians with lack of patriotism; and there would be no justice in such a charge, for in the Peloponnesian war, the Athenian democrats never gave in to Sparta (as will be shown in chapter 10), while Plato's own beloved uncle Critias did give in, and became the leader of a puppet government under the protection of the Spartans. If Plato intended to allude ironically to an inadequate defence of Athens, then it could be only an allusion to the Peloponnesian war, and thus a criticism of Critias—the last person whom Plato would criticize in this way.

(3) Plato calls his Myth a 'Phoenician lie'. A suggestion which may explain this is due to R. Eisler. He points out that the Ethiopians, Greeks (the silver mines), Sudanese, and Syrians (Damascus) were in the Orient described, respectively, as golden, silver, bronze, and iron races, and that this description was utilized in Egypt for purposes of political propaganda (cp. also Daniel, ii. 31–45); and he suggests that the story of these four races was brought to Greece in Hesiod's time by the Phoenicians (as might be expected), and that Plato alludes to this fact.*

12. The passage is from the *Republic*, 546a, ff.; cp. text to notes 36–40 to chapter 5. The intermixture of classes is clearly forbidden in 434c also; cp. notes 27 (3), 31 and 34 to chapter 4, and note 40 to chapter 6.

    The passage from the *Laws* (930d–e) contains the principle that the child of a mixed marriage inherits the caste of his lesser parent.

13. *Republic*, 547a. (For the mixture theory of heredity, see also text to note 39/40 to chapter 5, especially 40 (2), and to notes 39–43, and 52, to the present chapter.)
14. *Op. cit.*, 415c.
15. Cp. Adam's note to *Republic*, 414b, ff., italics mine. The great exception is Grote (*Plato, and the Other Companions of Socrates*, London, 1875, III, 240), who sums up the spirit of the *Republic*, and its opposition to that of the *Apology*: 'In the ... Apology, we find Socrates confessing his own ignorance ... But the Republic presents him in

a new character ... He is himself on the throne of King Nomos: the infallible authority, temporal as well as spiritual, from which all public sentiment emanates, and by whom orthodoxy is determined ... He now expects every individual to fall into the place, and contract the opinions, prescribed by authority; *including among these opinions deliberate ethical and political fictions*, such as about the ... earthborn men ... Neither the Socrates of the Apology, nor his negative Dialectic, could be allowed to exist in the Platonic Republic.' (Italics mine; see also Grote, *op. cit.*, p. 188.)

The doctrine that *religion is opium for the people*, although not in this particular formulation, turns out to be one of the tenets of Plato and the Platonists. (Cp. also note 17 and text, and especially note 18 to this chapter.) It is, apparently, one of the more esoteric doctrines of the school, i.e. it may be discussed only by sufficiently elderly members (cp. note 18 to chapter 7) of the upper class. But those who let the cat out of the bag are prosecuted for atheism by the idealists.

16. For instance Adam, Barker, Field.
17. Cp. Diels, *Vorsokratiker*[5], Critias fragm. 25. (I have picked about eleven characteristic lines out of more than forty.)—It may be remarked that the passage commences with a sketch of the social contract (which even somewhat resembles Lycophron's equalitarianism; cp. note 45 to chapter 6). On Critias, cp. especially note 48 to chapter 10. Since Burnet has suggested that the poetic and dramatic fragments known under the name of Critias should be attributed to the grandfather of the leader of the Thirty, it should be noted that Plato attributes to the latter poetic gifts in the *Charmides*, 157e; and in 162d, he alludes even to the fact that Critias was a dramatist. (Cp. also Xenophon's *Memorabilia*, I, iv, 18.)
18. Cp. the *Laws*, 909e. It seems that Critias' view later even became part of the Platonic school tradition, as indicated by the following passage from Aristotle's *Metaphysics* (1074b3) which at the same time provides another example of the use of the term 'persuasion' for 'propaganda' (cp. notes 5 and 10 to this chapter). 'The rest ... has been added in the form of a myth, with a view to the persuasion of the mob, and to legal and general (political) expediency ...' Cp. also Plato's attempt in the *Statesman*, 271a, f., to argue in favour of the truth of a myth in which he certainly did not believe. (See notes 9 and 15 to this chapter.)
19. *Laws*, 908b.
20. *Op. cit.*, 909a.
21. For the conflict between good and evil, see *op. cit.*, 904–906. See especially 906a/b (justice versus injustice; 'justice' means here, still, the collectivist justice of the *Republic*). Immediately preceding is 903c, a passage quoted above in the text to note 35 to chapter 5 and to note 27 to chapter 6. See also note 32 to the present chapter.
22. *Op. cit.*, 905d–907b.
23. The paragraph to which this note is appended indicates my adherence to an 'absolutist' theory of truth which is in accordance with the common idea that *a statement is true if* (and only if) *it agrees with the facts* it describes. This 'absolute' or 'correspondence theory of truth' (which goes back to Aristotle) was first clearly developed by A. Tarski (*Der Wahrheitsbegriff in den formalisierten Sprachen*, Polish edn 1933, German translation 1936), and is the basis of a theory of logic called by him Semantics (cp. note 29 to chapter 3 and note 5 (2) to chapter 5); see also R. Carnap's *Introduction to Semantics*, 1942, which develops the theory of truth in detail. I am

quoting from p. 28: 'It is especially to be noticed that the concept of truth in the sense just explained—we may call it the semantical concept of truth—is fundamentally different from concepts like "believed", "verified", "highly confirmed", etc.'—A similar, though undeveloped view can be found in my *Logik der Forschung* (translated, 1959, as *The Logic of Scientific Discovery*), section 84; this was written before I became acquainted with Tarski's Semantics, which is the reason why my theory is only rudimentary. The pragmatist theory of truth (which derives from Hegelianism) was criticized by Bertrand Russell from the point of view of an absolutist theory of truth as early as 1907; and recently he has shown the connection between a relativist theory of truth and the creed of fascism. See Russell, *Let the People Think*, pp. 77, 79.

24. Especially *Rep.*, 474c–502d. The following quotation is *Rep.*, 475e.
25. For the seven quotations which follow, in this paragraph, see: (1) and (2), *Republic*, 476b; (3), (4), (5), *op. cit.*, 500d–e; (6) and (7): *op. cit.*, 501a/b; with (7), cp. also the parallel passage, *op. cit.*, 484c. See, furthermore, *Sophist*, 253d/e; *Laws*, 964a–966a (esp. 965b/c).
26. Cp. *op. cit.*, 501c.
27. Cp. especially *Republic*, 509a, f.—See 509b: 'The sun induces the sensible things to generate' (although he is not himself involved in the process of generation); similarly, 'you may say of the objects of rational knowledge that not only do they owe it to the Good that they can be known, but their reality and even their essence flows from it; although the Good is not itself an essence but transcends even essences in dignity and power.' (With 509b, cp. Aristotle, *De Gen. et Corr.*, 336a 15, 31, and *Phys.*, 194b 13.)—In 510b, the Good is described as the absolute origin (not merely postulated or assumed), and in 511b, it is described as 'the first origin of everything'.
28. Cp. especially *Republic*, 508b, ff.—See 508b/c: 'What the Good has begotten in its own likeness' (viz. *truth*) 'is the link, in the intelligible world between reason and its objects' (i.e. the Ideas) 'in the same way as, in the visible world, that thing' (viz. *light* which is the offspring of the sun) 'which is the link between sight and its objects' (i.e. sensible things).
29. Cp. *op. cit.*, 505a; 534b, ff.
30. Cp. *op. cit.*, 505d.
31. *Philebus*, 66a.
32. *Republic*, 506d, ff., and 509–511.

The definition of the Good, here quoted, as 'the class of the determinate (or finite, or limited) conceived as a unity' is, I believe, not so hard to understand, and is in full agreement with others of Plato's remarks. The 'class of the determinate' is the class of the Forms or Ideas, conceived as male principles, or progenitors, as opposed to the female, unlimited or indeterminate space (cp. note 15 (2) to chapter 3). These Forms or primogenitors are, of course, good, in so far as they are ancient and unchanging originals, and in so far as each of them is one as opposed to the many sensible things which it generates. If we conceive the class or race of the progenitors as many, then they are not absolutely good; thus the absolute Good can be visualized if we conceive them as a unity, as One—as the One primogenitor. (Cp. also Arist., *Met.*, 988a 10.)

Plato's Idea of the Good is practically empty. It gives us no indication of what is good, in a moral sense, i.e. what we ought to do. As can be seen especially from notes 27 and 28 to this chapter, all we hear is that the Good is highest in the realm of Form or Ideas, a kind of super-Idea, from which the Ideas originate, and receive their existence. All we could possibly derive from this is that the Good is unchangeable and prior or primary and therefore ancient (cp. note 3 to chapter 4), and One Whole; and, therefore, that those things participate in it which do not change, i.e., the good is what preserves (cp. notes 2 and 3 to chapter 4), and what is ancient, especially the ancient laws (cp. note 23 to chapter 4, note 7, paragraph on Platonism, to chapter 5, and note 18 to chapter 7), and that holism is good (cp. note 21 to the present chapter); i.e., we are again thrown back, in practice, to totalitarian morality (cp. text to notes 40/41 to chapter 6).

If the *Seventh Letter* is genuine, then we have there (314b/c) another statement by Plato that his doctrine of the Good cannot be formulated; for he says of this doctrine: 'It is not capable of expression like other branches of study.' (Cp. also note 57 to chapter 10.)

It is again Grote who clearly saw and criticized the emptiness of the Platonic Idea or Form of Good. After asking what this Good is, he says (*Plato*, III, 241 f.): 'This question is put ... But unfortunately it remains unanswered ... In describing the condition of other men's minds—that they divine a Real Good ... do everything in order to obtain it, but puzzle themselves in vain to grasp and determine what it is—he' (Plato) 'has unconsciously described the condition of his own.' It is surprising to see how few modern writers have taken any notice of Grote's excellent criticism of Plato.

For the quotations in the next paragraph of the text, see (1): *Republic*, 500b–c; (2): *op. cit.*, 485a/b. This second passage is very interesting. It is, as Adam reaffirms (note to 485b9), the first passage in which 'generation' and 'degeneration' are employed in this half-technical sense. It refers to the flux, and to Parmenides' changeless entities. And it introduces the main argument in favour of the rule of the philosophers. See also note 26 (1) to chapter 3 and note 2 (2) to chapter 4. In the *Laws*, 689c–d, when discussing the 'degeneration' (688c) of the Dorian kingdom brought about by the 'worst ignorance' (the ignorance, namely, of not knowing how to obey those who are rulers by nature; see 689b), Plato explains what he means by wisdom: only such wisdom as aims at the greatest unity or 'unisonity' entitles a man to authority. And the term 'unisonity' is explained in the *Republic*, 591b and d, as the harmony of the ideas of justice (i.e. of keeping one's place) and of temperance (of being satisfied with it). Thus we are again thrown back to our starting point.

33. *A critic of this passage asserted that he could find no trace, in Plato, of any fear of independent thought. But we should remember Plato's insistence on censorship (see notes 40 and 41 to chapter 4) and his prohibition of higher dialectical studies for anybody under 50 years of age in the *Republic* (see notes 19 to 21 to chapter 7), to say nothing of the *Laws* (see note 18 to chapter 7, and many other passages).*

34. For the problem of the priest caste, see the *Timaeus*, 24a. In a passage which clearly alludes to the best or 'ancient' state of the *Republic*, the priest caste takes the place of the 'philosophic race' of the *Republic*. Cp. also the attacks on priests (and even on Egyptian priests), diviners, and shamans, in the *Statesman*, 290c, f.; see also note 57 (2) to chapter 8, and note 29 to chapter 4.

    The remark of Adam's, quoted in the text in the paragraph after the next, is from his note to *Republic*, 547a3 (quoted above in text to note 43 to chapter 5).

35. Cp. for instance *Republic*, 484c, 500e, ff.

36. *Republic*, 535a/b. All that Adam says (cp. his note to 535b8) about the term which I have translated by 'awe-inspiring' supports the usual view that the term means 'stern' or 'awful', especially in the sense of 'inspiring terror'. Adam's suggestion that we translate 'masculine' or 'virile' follows the general tendency to tone down what Plato says, and it clashes strangely with *Theaetetus* 149a. Lindsay translates: 'of ... sturdy morals'.
37. *Op. cit.*, 540c; see also 500c–d: 'the philosopher himself ... becomes godlike', and note 12 to chapter 9, where 540c, f., is quoted more fully.—It is most interesting to note how Plato transforms the Parmenidian One when arguing in favour of an aristocratic hierarchy. The opposition *one—many* is not preserved, but gives rise to a system of grades: the one Idea—the few who come close to it—the more who are their helpers—the many, i.e. the mob (this division is fundamental in the *Statesman*). As opposed to this, Antisthenes' monotheism preserves the original Eleatic opposition between the One (God) and the Many (whom he probably considered as brothers because of their equal distance from God).—Antisthenes was influenced by Parmenides through Zeno's influence upon Gorgias. Probably there was also the influence of Democritus, who had taught: 'The wise man belongs to all countries alike, for the home of a great soul is the whole world.'
38. *Republic*, 500d.
39. The quotations are from *Republic*, 459b, and ff.; cp. also notes 34 f. to chapter 4, and especially 40 (2) to chapter 5. Cp. also the three similes of the *Statesman*, where the ruler is compared with (1) the shepherd, (2) the doctor, (3) the weaver whose functions are explained as those of a man who blends characters by skilful breeding (310b, f.).
40. *Op. cit.*, 460a. My statement that Plato considers this law very important is based on the fact that Plato mentions it in the outline of the *Republic* in the *Timaeus*, 18d/e.
41. *Op. cit.*, 460b. The 'suggestion is taken up' in 468c; see the next note.
42. *Op. cit.*, 468c. Though it has been denied by my critics, my translation is correct, and so is my remark about 'the latter benefit'. Shorey calls the passage 'deplorable'.
43. For the Story of the Number and the Fall, cp. notes 13 and 52 to this chapter, notes 39/40 to chapter 5, and text.
44. *Republic*, 473c–e. Note the opposition between (divine) *rest*, and the *evil*, i.e. change in the form of corruption, or degeneration. Concerning the term translated here by 'oligarchs' cp. the end of note 57, below. It is equivalent to 'hereditary aristocrats'.

The phrase which, for stylistic reasons, I have put in brackets, is important, for in it *Plato demands the suppression of all 'pure' philosophers* (and unphilosophical politicians). A more literal translation of the phrase would be this: 'while the many' (who have) 'natures' (disposed or gifted) 'for drifting along, nowadays, in one alone of these two, *are eliminated by force*'. Adam admits that the meaning of Plato's phrase is 'that Plato refuses to sanction the exclusive pursuit of knowledge'; but his suggestion that we soften the meaning of the last words of the phrase by translating: 'are forcibly debarred from *exclusively* pursuing either' (italics his; cp. note to 473d24, vol. I, 330, of his edn of the *Republic*) has no foundation in the original,—only in his tendency to idealize Plato. The same holds for Lindsay's translation ('are forcibly debarred from this behaviour').—Whom does Plato wish to suppress? I believe that 'the many' whose limited or incomplete talents or 'natures' Plato condemns here are identical (as far as philosophers are concerned) with the 'many whose natures are incomplete', mentioned in *Republic*, 495d; and also with the 'many' (professed philosophers) 'whose wickedness is inevitable', mentioned in 489e (cp. also 490e/491a); cp. notes 47, 56, and 59 to this chapter (and note 23 to chapter 5). The attack is, therefore, directed on the one hand against the 'uneducated' democratic politicians, on the other hand most probably mainly against the half-Thracian Antisthenes, the 'uneducated bastard', the equalitarian philosopher; cp. note 47, below.

45. Kant, *On Eternal Peace*, Second Supplement (*Werke*, ed. Cassirer, 1914, vol. VI, 456). Italics mine; I have also abbreviated the passage. (The 'possession of power' may well allude to Frederick the Great.)

46. Cp. for instance Gomperz, *Greek Thinkers*, V, 12, 2 (German edn, vol. II^2, 382); or Lindsay's translation of the *Republic*. (For a criticism of this interpretation, cp. note 50, below.)

47. It must be admitted that Plato's attitude towards Antisthenes raises a highly speculative problem; this is of course connected with the fact that very little is known about Antisthenes from first-rate sources. Even the old Stoic tradition that the Cynic school or movement can be traced back to Antisthenes is at present often questioned (cp., for instance, G. C. Field's *Plato*, 1930, or D. R. Dudley, *A History of Cynicism*, 1937) although perhaps not on quite sufficient grounds (cp. Fritz's review of the last-mentioned book in *Mind*, vol. 47, p. 390). In view of what we know, especially from Aristotle, about Antisthenes, it appears to me highly probable that there are many allusions to him in Plato's writings; and even the one fact that Antisthenes was, apart from Plato, the only member of Socrates' inner circle who taught philosophy at Athens, would be a sufficient justification for searching Plato's work for such allusions. Now it seems to me rather probable that a series of attacks in Plato's work first pointed out by Duemmler (especially *Rep.*, 495d/e, mentioned below in note 56 to this chapter; *Rep.*, 535e, f., *Soph.*, 251b–e) represents these allusions. There is a definite resemblance (or so at least it appears to me) between these passages and Aristotle's scornful attacks on Antisthenes. Aristotle, who mentions Antisthenes' name, speaks of him as of a simpleton, and he speaks of 'uneducated people such as the Antistheneans' (cp. note 54 to chapter 11). Plato, in the passages mentioned, speaks in a similar way, but more sharply. The first passage I have in mind is from the *Sophist*, 251b, f., which corresponds very closely indeed to Aristotle's first passage. Regarding the two passages from the *Republic*, we must remember that, according to the tradition, Antisthenes was a 'bastard' (his mother came from barbarian Thrace), and that he taught in the Athenian gymnasium reserved for 'bastards'. Now we find, in *Republic*, 535e, f. (cp. end of note 52 to this chapter), an attack which is so specific that an individual person must be intended. Plato speaks of 'people who dabble in philosophy without being restrained by a feeling of their own unworthiness', and he contends that 'the baseborn should be debarred' from doing so. He speaks of the people as 'unbalanced' (or 'skew' or 'limping') in their love of work and of relaxation; and becoming more personal, he alludes to somebody with a 'crippled soul' who, though he loves truth (as a Socratic would), does not attain it, since he 'wallows in ignorance' (probably because he does not accept the theory of Forms); and he warns the city not to trust such limping 'bastards'. I think it likely that Antisthenes is the object of this undoubtedly personal attack; the admission that the enemy loves truth seems to me an especially strong

argument, occurring as it does in an attack of extreme violence. But if this passage refers to Antisthenes, then it is very likely that a very similar passage refers to him also, viz. *Republic*, 495d/e, where Plato again describes his victim as possessing a disfigured or crippled soul as well as body. He insists in this passage that the object of his contempt, in spite of aspiring to be a philosopher, is so depraved that he is not even ashamed of doing degrading ('banausic'; cp. note 4 to chapter 11) manual labour. Now we know of Antisthenes that he recommended manual labour, which he held in high esteem (for Socrates' attitude, cp. Xenophon, *Mem.*, II, 7, 10), and that he practised what he taught; a further strong argument that the man with the crippled soul is Antisthenes.

Now in the same passage, *Republic*, 495d, there is also a remark about 'the many whose natures are incomplete', and who nevertheless aspire to philosophy. This seems to refer to the same group (the 'Antistheneans' of Aristotle) of 'many natures' whose suppression is demanded in *Republic*, 473c–e, discussed in note 44 to this chapter.—Cp. also *Republic*, 489e, mentioned in notes 59 and 56 to this chapter.

48. We know (from Cicero, *De Natura Deorum*, and Philodemus, *De Pietate*) that Antisthenes was a monotheist; and the form in which he expressed his monotheism (there is only One God 'according to nature', i.e., to truth, although there are many 'according to convention') shows that he had in mind the opposition *nature—convention* which, in the mind of a former member of the school of Gorgias and contemporary of Alcidamas and Lycophron (cp. note 13 to chapter 5), must have been connected with *equalitarianism*.

This in itself does not of course establish the conclusion that the half-barbarian Antisthenes believed in the brotherhood of Greeks and barbarians. Yet it seems to me extremely likely that he did.

W. W. Tarn (*Alexander the Great and the Unity of Mankind*; cp. note 13 (2) to chapter 5) has tried to show—I once thought successfully—that the idea of the unity of mankind can be traced back at least to Alexander the Great. I think that by a very similar line of reasoning, we can trace it back farther; to Diogenes, Antisthenes, and even to Socrates and the 'Great Generation' of the Periclean age (cp. note 27 to chapter 10, and text). This seems, even without considering the more detailed evidence, likely enough; for a cosmopolitan idea can be expected to occur as a corollary of such imperialist tendencies as those of the Periclean age (cp. *Rep.*, 494c/d, mentioned in note 50 (5) to this chapter, and the *First Alcibiades*, 105b, ff.; see also text to notes 9–22, 36 and 47 to chapter 10). This is especially likely if other equalitarian tendencies exist. I do not intend to belittle the significance of Alexander's deeds, but the ideas ascribed to him by Tarn seem to me, in a way, a renaissance of some of the best ideas of fifth-century Athenian imperialism. See also *Addendum III*, pp. 329 f.

Proceeding to details, I may first say that there is strong evidence that at least in Plato's (and Aristotle's) time, the problem of equalitarianism was clearly seen to be concerned with two fully analogous distinctions, that between *Greeks and barbarians* on the one side and that between *masters* (*or free men*) *and slaves* on the other; cp. with this note 13 to chapter 5. Now we have very strong evidence that the fifth-century Athenian movement against slavery was not confined to a few intellectualists like Euripides, Alcidamas, Lycophron, Antiphon, Hippias, etc., but that it had considerable practical success. This evidence is contained in the unanimous reports of the enemies of Athenian democracy (especially the 'Old Oligarch', Plato, Aristotle; cp. notes 17, 18 and 29 to chapter 4, and 36 to chapter 10).

If we now consider in this light the admittedly scanty available evidence for the existence of *cosmopolitism*, it appears, I believe, reasonably strong—*provided that we include the attacks of the enemies of this movement among the evidence*. In other words, we must make full use of the attacks of the Old Oligarch, of Plato, and of Aristotle against the humanitarian movement, if we wish to assess its real significance. Thus the Old Oligarch (2, 7) attacks Athens for an eclectic cosmopolitan way of life. Plato's attacks on cosmopolitan and similar tendencies, although not frequent, are especially valuable. (I have in mind passages like *Rep.*, 562e/563a—'citizens, resident aliens, and strangers from abroad, are all on a footing of equality'—a passage which should be compared with the ironical description in *Menexenus*, 245c–d, in which Plato sarcastically eulogizes Athens for its consistent hatred of barbarians; *Rep.*, 494c/d; of course, the passage *Rep.*, 469b–471c, must be considered in this context too. See also end of note 19 to chapter 6.) Whether or not Tarn is right on Alexander, he hardly does full justice to the various extant statements of this fifth-century movement, for instance to Antiphon (cp. p. 149, note 6 of his paper) or Euripides or Hippias, or Democritus (cp. note 29 to chapter 10), or to Diogenes (p. 150, note 12) and Antisthenes. I do not think that Antiphon wanted only to stress the biological kinship between men, for he was undoubtedly a social reformer; and 'by nature' meant to him 'in truth'. It therefore seems to me practically certain that he attacked the distinction between Greeks and barbarians as being fictitious. Tarn comments on Euripides' fragment which states that a noble man can range the world like an eagle the air by remarking that 'he knew that an eagle has a permanent home-rock'; but this remark does not do full justice to the fragment; for in order to be a cosmopolitan, one need not give up one's permanent home. In the light of all this, I do not see why Diogenes' meaning was purely 'negative' when he replied to the question 'where are you from?' by saying that he was a cosmopolite, a citizen of the whole world; especially if we consider that a similar answer ('I am a man of the world') is reported of Socrates, and another ('The wise man belongs to all countries, for the home of a great soul is the whole world'; cp. Diels[5], fr. 247; genuineness questioned by Tarn and Diels) of Democritus.

Antisthenes' monotheism also must be considered in the light of this evidence. There is no doubt that this monotheism was not of the Jewish, i.e. tribal and exclusive, type. (Should the story of *Diog. Laert.*, VI, 13, that Antisthenes taught in the Cynosarges, the gymnasium for 'bastards', be true, then he must have deliberately emphasized his own mixed and barbarian descent.) Tarn is certainly right when he points out (p. 145) that Alexander's monotheism was connected with his idea of the unity of mankind. But the same should be said of the Cynic ideas, which were influenced, as I believe (see the last note), by Antisthenes, and in this way by Socrates. (Cp. especially the evidence of Cicero, *Tuscul*, V., 37, and of Epictetus, I, 9, 1, with *D.L.*, VI, 2, 63–71; also *Gorgias*, 492e, with *D.L.*, VI, 105. See also Epictetus, III, 22 and 24.)

All this made it once appear to me not too unlikely that Alexander may have been genuinely inspired, as the tradition reports, by Diogenes' ideas; and thus by the equalitarian tradition. But in view of E. Badian's criticism of Tarn (*Historia*, 7, 1958, pp. 425 ff.) I feel now inclined to reject Tarn's claim; but not, of course, my views on the fifth-century movement.

49. Cp. *Republic*, 469b–471c, especially 470b–d, and 469b/c. Here indeed we have (cp. the next note) a trace of something like the introduction of a new ethical whole, more embracing than the city; namely the unity of Hellenic superiority. As was to be expected (see the next note (1) (*b*)), Plato elaborates the point in some detail. *(Cornford justly summarizes this passage when he says that Plato 'expresses no humanitarian sympathies extending beyond the borders of Hellas'; cp. *The Republic of Plato*, 1941, p. 165.)*

50. In this note, further arguments are collected bearing on the interpretation of *Republic*, 473e, and the *problem of Plato's humanitarianism*. I wish to express my thanks to my colleague, Prof. H. D. Broadhead, whose criticism has greatly helped me to complete and clarify my argument.

(1) One of Plato's standard topics (cp. the methodological remarks, *Rep.*, 368e, 445c, 577c, and note 32 to chapter 5) is the opposition and comparison between the individual and the whole, i.e. the city. The introduction of a new whole, even more comprehensive than the city, viz. mankind, would be a most important step for a holist to take; it would need (*a*) preparation and (*b*) elaboration. (*a*) Instead of such a preparation we get the above mentioned passage on the opposition between Greeks and barbarians (*Rep.*, 469b–471c). (*b*) Instead of an elaboration, we find, if anything, a withdrawal of the ambiguous expression 'race of men'. First, in the immediate continuation of the key passage under consideration, i.e. of the passage of the philosopher king (*Rep.*, 473d/e), there occurs a paraphrase of the questionable expression, in form of a summary or winding up of the whole speech; and in this paraphrase, Plato's standard opposition, *city—individual*, replaces that of *city—human race*. The paraphrase reads: 'No other constitution can establish a state of happiness, neither in *private* affairs nor in those of the city.' Secondly, a similar result is found if we analyse the six repetitions or variations (viz. 487e, 499b, 500e, 501e, 536a–b, discussed in note 52 below, and the summary 540d/e with the afterthought 541b) of the key passage under consideration (i.e. of *Rep.*, 473d/e). In two of them (487e, 500e) the city alone is mentioned; in all the others, Plato's standard opposition *city—individual* again replaces that of *city—human race*. Nowhere is there a further allusion to the allegedly Platonic idea that sophocracy alone can save, not only the suffering *cities*, but all suffering *mankind*.—In view of all this it seems clear that in *all* these places only his standard opposition lingered in Plato's mind (without, however, the wish to give it any prominence in this connection), probably in the sense that sophocracy alone can attain the stability and the happiness—the divine rest—of any *state*, as well as that of all its *individual citizens and their progeny* (in which otherwise evil must grow—the evil of degeneration).

(2) The term 'human' ('anthrōpinos') is used by Plato, as a rule, either in opposition to 'divine' (and, accordingly, sometimes in a slightly disparaging sense, especially if the limitations of human knowledge or human art are to be stressed, cp. *Timaeus*, 29c/d; 77a, or *Sophist*, 266c, 268d, or *Laws*, 691e, f., 854a), or in a *zoological* sense, in opposition, or with reference to, animals, for example, eagles. Nowhere except in the early Socratic dialogues (for one further exception, see this note under (6), below) do I find this term (or the term 'man') used in a humanitarian sense, i.e. indicating something that transcends the distinction of nation, race, or class. Even a 'mental' use of the term 'human' is rare. (I have in mind a use such as in *Laws*, 737b: 'a humanly impossible piece of folly'.) In fact, the extreme nationalist views of

Fichte and Spengler, quoted in chapter 12, text to note 79, are a pointed expression of the Platonic usage of the term 'human', as signifying a zoological rather than a moral category. A number of Platonic passages indicating this and similar usages may be given: *Republic*, 365d; 486a; 459b/c; 514b; 522c; 606e, f. (where Homer as a guide to human affairs is opposed to the composer of hymns to the gods); 620b.—*Phaedo*, 82b.—*Cratylus*, 392b.—*Parmenides*, 134e.—*Theaetetus*, 107b.—*Crito*, 46e.—*Protagoras*, 344c.—*Statesman*, 274d (the shepherd of the human flock who is a god, not a man).—*Laws* 673d; 688d; 737b (890b is perhaps another example of a disparaging use—'the men' seems here nearly equivalent with 'the many').

(3) It is of course true that Plato assumes a *Form or Idea of Man*; but it is a mistake to think that it represents what all men have in common; rather, it is an aristocratic ideal of a proud super-Greek; and on this is based a belief, not in the brotherhood of men, but in a hierarchy of 'natures', aristocratic or slavish, in accordance with their greater or lesser likeness to the original, the ancient primogenitor of the human race. (The Greeks are more like him than any other race.) Thus 'intelligence is shared by the gods with only a very few men' (*Tim.*, 51e; cp. Aristotle, in the text to note 3, chapter 11).

(4) The 'City in Heaven' (*Rep.*, 592b) and its citizens are, as Adam rightly points out, not Greek; but this does not imply that they belong to 'humanity' as he thinks (note to 470e30, and others); they are rather super-exclusive, super-Greek (they are 'above' the Greek city of 470e, ff.)—more remote from the barbarians than ever. (This remark does not imply that the idea of the City in Heaven—as those of the Lion in Heaven, for example, and of other constellations—may not have been of oriental origin.)

(5) Finally, it may be mentioned that the passage 499c/d rescinds the distinction between Greeks and barbarians no more than that between the past, the present, and the future: Plato tries here to give drastic expression to a sweeping generalization in regard to time and space; he wishes to say no more than: 'If at any time whatever, or if at any place whatever' (we may add: even in such an extremely unlikely place as a barbarian country) 'such a thing did happen, then ...' The remark, *Republic*, 494c/d, expresses a similar, though stronger, feeling of being faced with something approaching impious absurdity, a feeling here aroused by Alcibiades' hopes for a universal empire of Greeks and foreigners. (I agree with the views expressed by Field, *Plato and His Contemporaries*, 130, note 1, and by Tarn; cp. note 13 (2) to chapter 5.)

To sum up, I am unable to find anything but hostility towards the humanitarian idea of a unity of mankind which transcends race and class, and I believe that those who find the opposite idealize Plato (cp. note 3 to chapter 6, and text) and fail to see the link between his aristocratic and anti-humanitarian exclusiveness and his theory of Ideas. See also this chapter, notes 51, 52, and 57, below.

*(6) There is, to my knowledge, only one real exception, one passage which stands in flagrant contrast to all this. In a passage (*Theaetetus*, 174e, f.), designed to illustrate the broad-mindedness and the universalistic outlook of the philosopher, we read: 'Every man has had countless ancestors, and among them are in any case rich and poor, kings and slaves, barbarians and Greeks.' I do not know how to reconcile this interesting and definitely humanitarian passage—its emphasis on the

parallelism master *v.* slave and Greek *v.* barbarian is reminiscent of all those theories which Plato opposes—with Plato's other views. Perhaps it is, like so much in the *Gorgias*, Socratic; and the *Theaetetus* is perhaps (as against the usual assumption) earlier than the *Republic*. See also my *Addendum II* p. 320.*

51. The allusion is, I believe, to two places in the Story of the Number where Plato (by speaking of 'your race') refers to the race of men: 'concerning your own race' (546a/b; cp. note 39 to chapter 5, and text) and 'testing the metals within your races' (546d/e, f.; cp. notes 39 and 40 to chapter 5, and the next passage). Cp. also the arguments in note 52 to this chapter, concerning a 'bridge' between the two passages, i.e. the key passage of the philosopher king, and the Story of the Number.

52. *Republic*, 546d/e, f. The passage quoted here is part of the Story of the Number and the Fall of Man, 546a–547a, quoted in text to notes 39/40 to chapter 5; see also notes 13 and 43 to the present chapter.—My contention (cp. text to the last note) that the remark in the key passage of the philosopher king, *Republic*, 473e (cp. notes 44 and 50 to this chapter), foreshadows the Story of the Number, is strengthened by the observation that there exists a bridge, as it were, between the two passages. The Story of the Number is undoubtedly foreshadowed by *Republic*, 536a/b, a passage which, on the other hand, may be described as the converse (and so as a variation) of the philosopher king passage; for it says in effect that the worst must happen if the wrong men are selected as rulers, and it even finishes up with a direct reminiscence of the great wave: 'if we take men of another kind ... then we shall bring down upon philosophy another deluge of laughter'. This clear reminiscence is, I believe, an indication that Plato was conscious of the character of the passage (which proceeds, as it were, from the end of 473c–e back to its beginning), which shows what must happen if the advice given in the passage of the philosopher king is neglected. Now this 'converse' passage (536a/b) may be described as a bridge between the 'key passage' (473e) and the 'Number-passage' (546a, ff.); for it contains unambiguous references to racialism, foreshadowing the passage (546d, f.) on the same subject to which the present note is appended. (This may be interpreted as additional evidence that racialism was in Plato's mind, and alluded to, when he wrote the passage of the philosopher king.) I now quote the beginning of the 'converse' passage (536a/b): 'We must distinguish carefully between the trueborn and the bastard. For if an individual or a city does not know how to look upon matters such as these, they will quite innocently accept the services of the unbalanced (or limping) bastards in any capacity; perhaps as friends, or even as rulers.' (Cp. also note 47 to this chapter.)

For something like an explanation of Plato's preoccupation with matters of racial degeneration and racial breeding, see text to notes 6, 7, and 63 to chapter 10, in connection with note 39 (3) and 40 (2) to chapter 5.

*For the passage about Codrus the martyr, quoted in the next paragraph of the text, see the *Symposium*, 208d, quoted more fully in note 4 to chapter 3.—R. R. Eisler (*Caucasica*, 5, 1928, p. 129, note 237) asserts that 'Codrus' is a pre-Hellenic word for 'king'. This would give some further colour to the tradition that Athens' nobility was autochthonous. (See note 11 (2) to this chapter; 52 to chapter 8; and *Republic* 368a and 580b/c.)*

53. A. E. Taylor, *Plato* (1908, 1914), pp. 122 f. I agree with this interesting passage as far as it is quoted in the text. I have, however, omitted the word 'patriot' after 'Athenian'

since I do not fully agree with this characterization of Plato in the sense in which it is used by Taylor. For Plato's 'patriotism' cp. text to notes 14–18 to chapter 4. For the term 'patriotism', and the 'paternal state', cp. notes 23–26 and 45 to chapter 10.

54. *Republic*, 494b: 'But will not one who is of this type be first in everything, from childhood on?'
55. *Op. cit.*, 496c: 'Of my own spiritual sign, I need not speak.'
56. Cp. what Adam says in his edn of the *Republic*, notes to 495d23 and 495e31, and my note 47 to the present chapter. (See also note 59 to this chapter.)
57. *Republic*, 496c–d; cp. the *Seventh Letter*, 325d. (I do not think that Barker, *Greek Political Theory*, I, 107, n. 2, makes a good guess when he says of the passage quoted that 'it is possible ... that Plato is thinking of the Cynics'. The passage certainly does not refer to Antisthenes; and Diogenes, whom Barker must have in mind, was hardly famous when it was written, quite apart from the fact that Plato would not have referred to him in this way.)

(1) Earlier in the same passage of the *Republic*, there is another remark which may be a reference to Plato himself. Speaking of the small band of the worthy and those who belong to it, he mentions 'a nobly-born and well-bred character who was saved by flight' (or 'by exile'; saved, that is, from the fate of Alcibiades, who became a victim of flattery and deserted Socratic philosophy). Adam thinks (note to 496b9) that 'Plato was hardly exiled'; but the flight to Megara of Socrates' disciples after the death of their master may well stand out in Plato's memory as one of the turning-points of his life. That the passage refers to Dio is hardly possible since Dio was about 40 when he went into exile, and therefore well beyond the critical youthful age; and there was not (as in Plato's case) a parallelism with the Socratic companion Alcibiades (quite apart from the fact that Plato had resisted Dio's banishment, and had tried to get it rescinded). If we assume that the passage refers to Plato, then we shall have to assume the same of 502a: 'Who will doubt the possibility that kings or aristocrats may have a descendant who is a born philosopher?'; for the continuation of that passage is so similar to the previous one that they seem to refer to the same 'nobly-born character'. This interpretation of 502a is probable in itself, for we must remember that Plato always showed his family pride, for instance, in the eulogy on his father and on his brothers, whom he calls 'divine'. (*Rep.*, 368a; I cannot agree with Adam, who takes the remark as ironical; cp. also the remark on Plato's alleged ancestor Codrus in *Symp.*, 208d, together with his alleged descent from Attica's tribal kings.) If this interpretation is adopted, the reference in 499b–c to 'rulers, kings, or their sons', which fits Plato perfectly (he was not only a Codride, but also a descendant of the ruler Dropides), would have to be considered in the same light, i.e. as a preparation for 502a. But this would solve another puzzle. I have in mind 499b and 502a. It is difficult, if not impossible, to interpret these passages as attempts to flatter the younger Dionysius, since such an interpretation could hardly be reconciled with the unmitigated violence and the admittedly (576a) personal background of Plato's attacks (572–580) upon the older Dionysius. It is important to note that Plato speaks in all three passages (473d, 499b, 502a) about hereditary kingdoms (which he opposes so strongly to tyrannies) and about 'dynasties'; but we know from Aristotle's *Politics*, 1292b2 (cp. Meyer, *Gesch. d. Altertums*, V, p. 56) and 1293a11, that 'dynasties' are hereditary oligarchic families, and therefore not so much the families of a tyrant like Dionysius, but rather what we call now *aristocratic*

families, like that of Plato himself. Aristotle's statement is supported by Thucydides, IV, 78, and Xenophon, *Hellenica*, V, 4, 46. (These arguments are directed against Adam's second note to 499b13.) See also note 4 to chapter 3.

* (2) Another important passage which contains a revealing self-reference is to be found in the *Statesman*. Here the essential characteristic of the royal statesman is assumed (258b, 292c) to be his *knowledge or science*; and the result is another plea for sophocracy: 'The only right government is that in which the rulers are true Masters of Science' (293c). And Plato proves that 'the man who possesses the Royal Science, *whether he rules or does not rule*, must, as our argument shows, be proclaimed royal' (292e/293a). Plato certainly claimed to possess the Royal Science; accordingly, this passage implies unequivocally that he considered himself a 'man who must be proclaimed royal'. This illuminating passage must not be neglected in any attempt to interpret the *Republic*. (The Royal Science, of course, is again that of the romantic pedagogue and breeder of a master class which must provide the fabric for covering and holding together the other classes—the slaves, labourers, clerks, etc., discussed in 289c, ff. The task of the Royal Science is thus described as that of 'interweaving' (blending, mixing) 'of the characters of temperate and courageous men, when they have been drawn together, by kingscraft, into a community life of unanimity and friendship'. See also notes 40 (2) to chapter 5; 29 to chapter 4; and note 34 to the present chapter.)*

58. In a famous passage in the *Phaedo* (89d) Socrates warns against misanthropy or hatred of men (with which he compares misology or distrust in rational argument). See also note 28 and 56 to chapter 10, and note 9 to chapter 7.

The next quotation in this paragraph is from *Republic*, 489b/c.—The connection with the previous passages is more obvious if the whole of 488 and 489 is considered, and especially the attack in 489e upon the 'many' philosophers whose wickedness is inevitable, i.e. the same 'many' and 'incomplete natures' whose suppression is discussed in notes 44 and 47 to this chapter.

An indication that Plato had once dreamt of becoming the philosopher king and saviour of Athens can be found, I believe, in the *Laws*, 704a–707c, where Plato tries to point out the moral dangers of the sea, of seafaring, trade, and imperialism. (Cp. Aristotle, *Pol.*, 1326b–1327a, and my notes 9–22 and 36 to chapter 10, and text.)

See especially *Laws*, 704d: 'If the city were to be built on the coast, and well supplied with natural harbours ... then it would need a mighty saviour, and indeed, a super-human legislator, to make her escape variability and degeneration.' Does this not read as if Plato wanted to show that his failure in Athens was due to the super-human difficulties created by the geography of the place? (But in spite of all disappointments—cp. note 25 to chapter 7—Plato still believes in the method of winning over a tyrant; cp. *Laws*, 710c/d, quoted in text to note 24 to chapter 4.)

59. There is a passage (beginning in *Republic*, 498d/e; cp. note 12 to chapter 9) in which Plato even expresses his hope that 'the many' may change their minds and accept philosophers as rulers, once they have learned (perhaps from the *Republic*?) to distinguish between the genuine philosopher and the pseudo-philosopher.

With the last two lines of the paragraph in the text, cp. *Republic*, 473e–474a, and 517a/b.

60. Sometimes such dreams have even been openly confessed. F. Nietzsche, *The Will to Power* (ed. 1911, Book IV, Aphor. 958; the reference is to *Theages*, 125e/126a),

writes: 'In Plato's *Theages* it is written: "Every one of us wants to be the lord of all men, if it were only possible—and most of all he would like to be the Lord God Himself." This is the spirit which must come again.' I need not comment upon Nietzsche's political views; but there are other philosophers, Platonists, who have naïvely hinted that if a Platonist were, by some lucky accident, to gain power in a modern state, he would move towards the Platonic Ideal, and leave things at least nearer perfection than he found them. '... men born into an "oligarchy" or "democracy"', we read (in the context this may well be an allusion to England in 1939), with the ideals of Platonic philosophers and finding themselves, by some fortunate turn of circumstance, possessed of supreme political power, would certainly try to actualise the Platonic State, and even if they were not completely successful, as they might be, would at least leave the commonwealth nearer to that model than they found it.' (Quoted from A. E. Taylor, 'The Decline and Fall of the State in *Republic*, VIII', *Mind*, N.S. 48, 1939, p. 31.) The argument in the next chapter is directed against such romantic dreams.

* A searching analysis of the Platonic lust for power can be found in H. Kelsen's brilliant article *Platonic Love (The American Imago*, vol. III, 1942, pp. 1 ff.).*

61. *Op. cit.*, 520a–521c, the quotation is from 520d.
62. Cp. G. B. Stern, *The Ugly Dachshund*, 1938.

NOTES TO CHAPTER NINE

The motto, from *Les Thibaults*, by Roger Martin du Gard, is quoted from p. 575 of the English edition (*Summer 1914*, London, 1940).

1 My description of Utopian social engineering seems to coincide with that kind of social engineering advocated by M. Eastman in *Marxism: is it Science?*; see especially pp. 22 ff. I have the impression that Eastman's views represent the swing of the pendulum from historicism to Utopian engineering. But I may possibly be mistaken, and what Eastman really has in mind may be more in the direction of what I call piecemeal engineering. Roscoe Pound's conception of 'social engineering' is clearly 'piecemeal'; cp. note 9 to chapter 3. See also note 18 (3) to chapter 5.

2. I believe that there is, from the ethical point of view, no symmetry between suffering and happiness, or between pain and pleasure. Both the greatest happiness principle of the Utilitarians and Kant's principle 'Promote other people's happiness ... ' seem to me (at least in their formulations) wrong on this point which, however, is not completely decidable by rational argument. (For the irrational aspect of ethical beliefs, see note 11 to the present chapter, and for the rational aspect, sections II and especially III of chapter 24). In my opinion (cp. note 6 (2) to chapter 5) human suffering makes a direct moral appeal, namely, the appeal for help, while there is no similar call to increase the happiness of a man who is doing well anyway. (A further criticism of the Utilitarian formula 'Maximize pleasure' is that it assumes, in principle, a continuous pleasure-pain scale which allows us to treat degrees of pain as negative degrees of pleasure. But, from the moral point of view, pain cannot be outweighed by pleasure, and especially not one man's pain by another man's pleasure. Instead of the greatest happiness for the greatest number, one should demand, more modestly, the least amount of avoidable suffering for all; and further,

that unavoidable suffering—such as hunger in times of an unavoidable shortage of food—should be distributed as equally as possible.) There is some kind of analogy between this view of ethics and the view of scientific methodology which I have advocated in my *The Logic of Scientific Discovery*. It adds to clarity in the field of ethics if we formulate our demands negatively, i.e. if we demand the elimination of suffering rather than the promotion of happiness. Similarly, it is helpful to formulate the task of scientific method as the elimination of false theories (from the various theories tentatively proffered) rather than the attainment of established truths.

3. A very good example of this kind of piecemeal engineering, or perhaps of the corresponding piecemeal technology, are C. G. F. Simkin's two articles on 'Budgetary Reform' in the Australian *Economic Record* (1941, pp. 192 ff., and 1942, pp. 16 ff.). I am glad to be able to refer to these two articles since they make conscious use of the methodological principles which I advocate; they thus show that these principles are useful in the practice of technological research.

   I do not suggest that piecemeal engineering cannot be bold, or that it must be confined to 'smallish' problems. But I think that the degree of complication which we can tackle is governed by the degree of our experience gained in conscious and systematic piecemeal engineering.

4. This view has recently been emphasized by F. A. von Hayek in various interesting papers (cp. for instance his *Freedom and the Economic System*, Public Policy Pamphlets, Chicago, 1939). What I call 'Utopian engineering' corresponds largely, I believe, to what Hayek would call 'centralized' or 'collectivist' planning. Hayek himself recommends what he calls 'planning for freedom'. I suppose he would agree that this would take the character of 'piecemeal engineering'. One could, I believe, formulate Hayek's objections to collectivist planning somewhat like this. If we try to construct society according to a blueprint, then we may find that we cannot incorporate individual freedom in our blueprint; or if we do, that we cannot realize it. The reason is that centralized economic planning eliminates from economic life one of the most important functions of the individual, namely his function as a chooser of the product, as a free consumer. In other words, Hayek's criticism belongs to the realm of social technology. He points out a certain technological impossibility, namely that of drafting a plan for a society which is at once economically centralized *and* individualistic.

* Readers of Hayek's *The Road to Serfdom* (1944) may feel puzzled by this note; for Hayek's attitude in this book is so explicit that no room is left for the somewhat vague comments of my note. But my note was printed before Hayek's book was published; and although many of his leading ideas were foreshadowed in his earlier writings, they were not yet quite as explicit as in *The Road to Serfdom*. And many ideas which, as a matter of course, we now associate with Hayek's name were unknown to me when I wrote my note.

In the light of what I know now about Hayek's position, my summary of it does not appear to me to be mistaken, although it is, no doubt, an understatement of his position. The following modifications may perhaps put the matter right.

(*a*) Hayek would not himself use the word 'social engineering' for any political activity which he would be prepared to advocate. He objects to this term because it is associated with a general tendency which he has called 'scientism'—the naïve belief that the methods of the natural sciences (or, rather, what many people believe to be the methods of the natural sciences) must produce similarly impressive results in the social field. (Cp. Hayek's two series of articles, *Scientism and the Study of Society, Economica*, IX–XI 1942–44, and *The Counter-revolution of Science, ibid.*, VIII, 1941.)

If by 'scientism' we mean a tendency to ape, in the field of social science, what are supposed to be the methods of the natural sciences, then *historicism can be described as a form of scientism*. A typical and influential scientistic argument in favour of historicism is, in brief, this: 'We can predict eclipses; why should we not be able to predict revolutions?'; or, in a more elaborate form: 'The task of science is to predict; thus the task of the social sciences must be to make social, i.e. historical, predictions.' I have tried to refute this kind of argument (cp. my *The Poverty of Historicism*, and 'Prediction and Prophecy, and their Significance for Social Theory', *Proceedings of the Xth International Congress of Philosophy, Amsterdam*, 1948; now in my *Conjectures and Refutations*); and in this sense, I am opposed to scientism.

But if by 'scientism' we should mean the view that the methods of the social sciences are, to a very considerable extent, the same as those of the natural sciences, then I should be obliged to plead 'guilty' to being an adherent of 'scientism'; indeed, I believe that the similarity between the social and the natural sciences can even be used for correcting wrong ideas about the natural sciences by showing that these are much more similar to the social sciences than is generally supposed.

It is for this reason that I have continued to use Roscoe Pound's term 'social engineering' in Roscoe Pound's sense, which as far as I can see, is free of that 'scientism' which, I think, must be rejected.

Terminology apart, I still think that Hayek's views can be interpreted as favourable to what I call 'piecemeal engineering'. On the other hand, Hayek has given a much clearer formulation of his views than my old outline indicates. The part of his views which corresponds to what I should call 'social engineering' (in Pound's sense) is his suggestion that there is an urgent need, in a free society, to reconstruct what he describes as its '*legal framework*'.*

5. Bryan Magee has drawn my attention to what he rightly calls 'de Tocqueville's superbly put argument' in *L'ancien régime*.

6. The problem whether or not a good end justifies bad means seems to arise out of such cases as whether one should lie to a sick man in order to set his mind at rest; or whether one should keep a people in ignorance in order to make them happy; or whether one should begin a long and bloody civil war in order to establish a world of peace and beauty.

In all these cases the action contemplated is to bring about first a more immediate result (called 'the means') which is considered an evil, in order that a secondary result (called 'the end') may be brought about which is considered a good.

I think that in all such cases three different kinds of questions arise.

(*a*) How far are we entitled to assume that the means will in fact lead to the expected end? Since the means are the more immediate result, they will in most cases be the more certain result of the contemplated action, and the end, which is more remote, will be less certain.

The question here raised is a factual question rather than one of moral valuations. It is the question whether, as a matter of fact, the assumed causal connection between the means and the end can be relied upon; and one might therefore reply that, if the assumed causal connection does not hold, the case was simply not one of means and ends.

This may be true. But in practice, the point here considered contains what is perhaps the most important moral issue. For although the question (whether the contemplated means will bring about the contemplated end) is a factual one, *our attitude towards this question raises some of the most fundamental moral problems*—the problem whether we ought to rely, in such cases, on our conviction that such a causal connection holds; or in other words, whether we ought to rely, dogmatically, on causal theories, or whether we should adopt a sceptical attitude towards them, especially where the immediate result of our action is, in itself, considered evil.

This question is perhaps not so important in the first of our three examples, but it is so in the two others. Some people may feel very certain that the causal connections assumed in these two cases hold; but the connection may be a very remote one; and even the emotional certainty of their belief may itself be the result of an attempt to suppress their doubts. (The issue, in other words, is that between the fanatic and the rationalist in the Socratic sense—the man who tries to know his intellectual limitations.) The issue will be the more important the greater the evil of 'the means'. However that may be, to educate oneself so as to adopt an attitude of scepticism towards one's causal theories, and one of intellectual modesty, is, without doubt, one of the most important moral duties.

But let us assume that the assumed causal connection holds, or in other words, that there is a situation in which one can properly speak of means and ends. Then we have to distinguish between two further questions, (*b*) and (*c*).

(*b*) Assuming that the causal relation holds, and that we can be reasonably certain of it, the problem becomes, in the main, one of choosing the lesser of two evils—that of the contemplated means and that which must arise if these means are not adopted. In other words, the best of ends do not as such justify bad means, but the attempt to avoid results may justify actions which are in themselves producing bad results. (Most of us do not doubt that it is right to cut off a man's limb in order to save his life.)

In this connection it may become very important that we are not really able to assess the evils in question. Some Marxists, for example (cp. note 9 to chapter 19), believe that there would be far less suffering involved in a violent social revolution than in the chronic evils inherent in what they call 'Capitalism'. But even assuming that this revolution leads to a better state of affairs—how can they evaluate the suffering in the one state and in the other? Here, again, a factual question arises, and it is again our duty not to over-estimate our factual knowledge. Besides, granted that the contemplated means will on balance improve the situation—have we ascertained whether other means would not achieve better results, at a lesser price?

But the same example raises another very important question. Assuming, again, that the sum total of suffering under 'Capitalism' would, if it continues for several generations, outweigh the suffering of civil war—can we condemn one generation to suffer for the sake of later generations? (There is a great difference between sacrificing oneself for the sake of others, and between sacrificing others—or oneself *and* others—for some such end.)

(*c*) The third point of importance is that we must not think that the so-called 'end', as a final result, is more important than the intermediate result, the 'means'. This idea, which is suggested by such sayings as 'All is well that ends well', is most misleading. First, the so-called 'end' is hardly ever the end of the matter. Secondly, the means are not, as it were, superseded once the end is achieved. For example, 'bad' means, such as a new powerful weapon used in war for the sake of victory, may, after this 'end' is achieved, create new trouble. In other words, even if something can be correctly described as a means to an end, it is, very often, much more than this. It produces other results apart from the end in question; and what we have to balance is not the (past or present) means against (future) ends, but the total results, as far as they can be foreseen, of one course of action against those of another. These results spread over a period of time which includes intermediate results; and the contemplated 'end' will not be the last to be considered.

7. (1) I believe that the parallelism between the institutional problems of civil and of international peace is most important. Any international organization which has legislative, administrative and judicial institutions *as well as an armed executive which is prepared to act* should be as successful in upholding international peace as are the analogous institutions within the state. But it seems to me important not to expect more. We have been able to reduce crime within the states to something comparatively unimportant, but we have not been able to stamp it out entirely. Therefore we shall, for a long time to come, need a police force which is ready to strike, and which sometimes does strike. Similarly, I believe that we must be prepared for the probability that we may not be able to stamp out international crime. If we declare that our aim is to make war impossible once and for all, then we may undertake too much, with the fatal result that we may not have a force which is ready to strike when these hopes are disappointed. The failure of the League of Nations to take action against aggressors was, at least in the case of the attack on Manchukuo, due largely to the general feeling that the League had been established in order to end *all* wars and not to wage them. This shows that propaganda for ending *all* wars is self-defeating. We must end international anarchy, and be ready to go to war against any international crime. (Cp. especially H. Mannheim, *War and Crime*, 1941; and A. D. Lindsay, 'War to End War', in *Background and Issues*, 1940.)

But it is also important to search for the weak spot in the analogy between civil and international peace, that is to say, for the point where the analogy breaks down. In the case of civil peace, upheld by the state, there is the individual citizen to be protected by the state. The citizen is, as it were, a 'natural' unit or atom (although there is a certain 'conventional' element even in the conditions of citizenship). On the other hand, the members or units or atoms of our international order will be states. But a state can never be a 'natural' unit like the citizen; *there are no natural boundaries to a state*. The boundaries of a state change, and can be defined only by applying the principle of a *status quo*; and since every *status quo* must refer to an arbitrarily chosen date, the determination of the boundaries of a state is purely conventional.

The attempt to find some 'natural' boundaries for states, and accordingly, to look upon the state as a 'natural' unit, leads to the *principle of the national state* and to the romantic fictions of nationalism, racialism, and tribalism. But this principle is not 'natural', and the idea that there exist natural units like nations, or linguistic or racial groups, is entirely fictitious. Here, if anywhere, we should learn from history; for since the dawn of history, men have been continually mixed, unified, broken up, and mixed again; and this cannot be undone, even if it were desirable.

There is a second point in which the analogy between civil and international peace breaks down. The state must protect the individual citizen, its units or atoms; but the international organization also must ultimately protect human individuals, and not its units or atoms, i.e. states or nations.

The complete renunciation of the principle of the national state (a principle which owes its popularity solely to the fact that it appeals to tribal instincts and that it is the cheapest and surest method by which a politician who has nothing better to offer can make his way), and the recognition of the necessarily conventional demarcation of *all* states, together with the further insight that *human individuals and not states or nations must be the ultimate concern even of international organizations*, will help us to realize clearly, and to get over, the difficulties arising from the breakdown of our fundamental analogy. (Cp. also chapter 12, notes 51–64 and text, and note 2 to chapter 13.)

(2) It seems to me that the remark that human individuals must be recognized to be the ultimate concern not only of international organizations, but of all politics, international as well as 'national' or parochial, has important applications. We must realize that *we can treat individuals fairly, even if we decide to break up the power-organization of an aggressive state* or 'nation' to which these individuals belong. It is a widely held prejudice that the destruction and control of the military, political and even of the economic power of a state or 'nation' implies misery or subjugation for its individual citizens. But this prejudice is as unwarranted as it is dangerous.

It is unwarranted provided that an international organization protects the citizens of the thus weakened state against exploitation of their political and military weakness. The only damage to the individual citizen that cannot be avoided is one to his national pride; and if we assume that he was a citizen of an aggressor country, then this is a damage which will be unavoidable in any case, provided the aggression has been warded off.

The prejudice that we cannot distinguish between the treatment of a state and of its individual citizens is also very dangerous, for when it comes to the problem of dealing with an aggressor country, it necessarily creates two factions in the victorious countries, viz., the faction of those who demand harsh treatment and those who demand leniency. As a rule, both overlook the possibility of treating a state harshly, and, at the same time, its citizens leniently.

But if this possibility is overlooked, then the following is likely to happen. Immediately after the victory the aggressor state *and* its citizens will be treated comparatively harshly. But the state, the power-organization, will probably not be treated as harshly as might be reasonable because of a reluctance to treat innocent individuals harshly, that is to say, because the influence of the faction for leniency will make itself felt somehow. In spite of this reluctance, it is likely that individuals will suffer beyond what they deserve. After a short time, therefore, a reaction is likely to occur in the victorious countries. Equalitarian and humanitarian tendencies are likely to strengthen the faction for leniency until the harsh policy is reversed. But this development is not only likely to give the aggressor state a chance for a new aggression; it will also provide it with the weapon of the moral indignation of one who has been wronged, while the victorious countries are likely to become afflicted with the diffidence of those who feel that they may have done wrong.

This very undesirable development must in the end lead to a new aggression. It can be avoided if, and only if, from the start, a clear distinction is made between the aggressor state (and those responsible for its acts) on the one hand, and its citizens on the other hand. Harshness towards the aggressor state, and even the radical destruction of its power apparatus, will not produce this moral reaction of humanitarian feelings in the victorious countries if it is combined with a policy of fairness towards the individual citizens.

But is it possible to break the political power of a state without injuring its citizens indiscriminately? In order to prove that this is possible I shall construct an example of a policy which breaks the political and military power of an aggressor state without violating the interests of its individual citizens.

The fringe of the aggressor country, including its sea-coast and its main (not all) sources of water power, coal, and steel, could be severed from the state, and administered as an international territory, never to be returned. Harbours as well as the raw materials could be made accessible to the citizens of the state for their legitimate economic activities, without imposing any economic disadvantages on them, on the condition that they *invite* international commissions to control the proper use of these facilities. Any use which may help to build up a new war potential is forbidden, and if there is reason for suspicion that the internationalized facilities and raw materials may be so used, their use has at once to be stopped. It then rests with the suspect party to *invite* and to facilitate a thorough investigation, and to offer satisfactory guarantees for a proper use of its resources.

Such a procedure would not eliminate the possibility of a new attack but it would force the aggressor state to make its attack on the internationalized territories prior to building up a new war potential. Thus such an attack would be hopeless provided the other countries have retained and developed their war potential. Faced with this situation the former aggressor state would be forced to change its attitude radically, and adopt one of co-operation. It would be forced to *invite* the international control of its industry and to facilitate the investigation of the international controlling authority (instead of obstructing them) because only such an attitude would guarantee its use of the facilities needed by its industries; and such a development would be likely to take place without any further interference with the internal politics of the state.

The danger that the internationalization of these facilities might be misused for the purpose of exploiting or of humiliating the population of the defeated country can be counteracted by international legal measures that provide for courts of appeal, etc.

This example shows that it is not impossible to treat a state harshly and its citizens leniently.

* (I have left parts (1) and (2) of this note exactly as they were written in 1942. Only in part (3), which is non-topical, have I made an addition, after the first two paragraphs.)*

(3) But is such an engineering approach towards the problem of peace scientific? Many will contend, I am sure, that a truly scientific attitude towards the problems of war and peace must be different. They will say that *we must first study the causes of*

war. We must study the forces that lead to war, and also those that may lead to peace. It has been recently claimed, for instance, that 'lasting peace' can come only if we consider fully the 'underlying dynamic forces' in society that may produce war or peace. In order to find out these forces, we must, of course, study history. In other words, we must approach the problem of peace by a historicist method, and not by a technological method. This, it is claimed, is the only scientific approach.

The historicist may, with the help of history, show that the causes of war can be found in the clash of economic interests; or in the clash of classes; or of ideologies, for instance, freedom versus tyranny; or in the clash of races, or of nations, or of imperialisms, or of militarist systems; or in hate; or in fear; or in envy; or in the wish to take revenge; or in all these things together, and in countless others. And he will thereby show that the task of removing these causes is extremely difficult. And he will show that there is no point in constructing an international organization, as long as we have not removed the causes of war, for instance the economic causes, etc.

Similarly, psychologism may argue that the causes of war are to be found in 'human nature', or, more specifically, in its aggressiveness, and that the way to peace is that of preparing for other outlets for aggression. (The reading of thrillers has been suggested in all seriousness—in spite of the fact that some of our late dictators were addicted to them.)

I do not think that these methods of dealing with this important problem are very promising. And I do not believe, more especially, in the plausible argument that in order to establish peace we must ascertain the cause or the causes of war.

Admittedly, there are cases where the method of searching for the causes of some evil, and of removing them, may be successful. If I feel a pain in my foot I may find that it is caused by a pebble and remove it. But we must not generalize from this. The method of removing pebbles does not even cover all cases of pains in my foot. In some such cases I may not find 'the cause'; and in others I may be unable to remove it.

In general, the method of removing causes of some undesirable event is applicable only if we know a short list of necessary conditions (i.e. a list of conditions such that the event in question never happens except if one at least of the conditions on the list is present) and if all of these conditions can be controlled, or, more precisely, prevented. (It may be remarked that necessary conditions are hardly what one describes by the vague term 'causes'; they are, rather, what are usually called 'contributing causes'; as a rule, where we speak of 'causes' we mean a set of sufficient conditions.) But I do not think that we can hope to construct such a list of the necessary conditions of war. Wars have broken out under the most varying circumstances. Wars are not simple phenomena, such as, perhaps, thunderstorms. There is no reason to believe that by calling a vast variety of phenomena 'wars', we ensure that they are all 'caused' in the same way.

All this shows that the apparently unprejudiced and convincingly scientific approach, the study of the 'causes of war', is, in fact, not only prejudiced, but also liable to bar the way to a reasonable solution; it is, in fact, pseudo-scientific.

How far should we get if, instead of introducing laws and a police force, we approached the problem of criminality 'scientifically', i.e. by trying to find out what precisely are the causes of crime? I do not imply that we cannot here or there discover important factors contributing to crime or to war, and that we cannot avert much harm in this way; but this can well be done after we have got crime under control, i.e. after we have introduced our police force. On the other hand, the study of economic, psychological, hereditary, moral, etc., 'causes' of crime, and the attempt to remove these causes, would hardly have led us to find out that a police force (which does not remove the cause) can bring crime under control. Quite apart from the vagueness of such phrases as 'the cause of war', the whole approach is anything but scientific. It is as if one insisted that it is unscientific to wear an overcoat when it is cold; and that we should rather study the causes of cold weather, and remove them. Or, perhaps, that lubricating is unscientific, since we should rather find out the causes of friction and remove them. This latter example shows, I believe, the absurdity of the apparently scientific criticism; for just as lubrication certainly reduces the 'causes' of friction, so an international police force (or another armed body of this kind) may reduce an important 'cause' of war, namely the hope of 'getting away with it'.

8. I have tried to show this in my *The Logic of Scientific Discovery*. I believe, in accordance with the methodology outlined, that systematic piecemeal engineering will help us to build an empirical social technology, reached by the method of trial and error. Only in this way, I believe, can we begin to build an empirical social science. The fact that such a social science hardly exists so far, and that the historical method is incapable of furthering it much, is one of the strongest arguments against the possibility of large-scale or Utopian social engineering. See also my *The Poverty of Historicism*.

9. For a very similar formulation, see John Carruthers' lecture *Socialism & Radicalism* (published as a pamphlet by the Hammersmith Socialist Society, London, 1894). He argues in a typical manner against piecemeal reform: 'Every palliative measure brings its own evil with it, and the evil is generally greater than that it was intended to cure. Unless we make up our minds to have a new garment altogether, we must be prepared to go in rags, for patching will not improve the old one.' (It should be noted that by 'radicalism', used by Carruthers in the title of his lecture, he means about the opposite of what is meant here. Carruthers advocates an uncompromising programme of canvas-cleaning and attacks 'radicalism', i.e. the programme of 'progressive' reforms advocated by the 'radical liberals'. This use of the term 'radical' is, of course, more customary than mine; nevertheless, the term means originally 'going to the root'—of the evil, for instance—or 'eradicating the evil'; and there is no proper substitute for it.)

For the quotations in the next paragraph of the text (the 'divine original' which the artist-politician must 'copy'), see *Republic*, 500e/501a. See also notes 25 and 26 to chapter 8.

In Plato's Theory of Forms are, I believe, elements which are of great importance for the understanding, and for the theory, of art. This aspect of Platonism is treated by J. A. Stewart, in his book *Plato's Doctrine of Ideas* (1909), 128 ff. I believe, however, that he stresses too much the object of pure contemplation (as opposed to that 'pattern' which the artist not only visualizes, but which he labours to reproduce, on his canvas).

10. *Republic*, 520c. For the 'Royal Art', see especially the *Statesman*; cp. note 57 (2) to chapter 8.

11. It has often been said that ethics is only a part of aesthetics, since ethical questions are ultimately a matter of taste. (Cp. for instance G. E. G. Catlin, *The Science and Methods of Politics*, 315 ff.) If by saying this, no more is meant than that ethical problems cannot be solved by the rational methods of science, I agree. But we must not overlook the vast difference between moral 'problems of taste' and problems of taste in aesthetics. If I dislike a novel, a piece of music, or perhaps a picture, I need not read it, or listen to it, or look at it. Aesthetic problems (with the possible exception of architecture) are largely of a private character, but ethical problems concern men, and their lives. To this extent, there is a fundamental difference between them.

12. For this and the preceding quotations, cp. *Republic*, 500d–501a (italics mine); cp. also notes 29 (end) to chapter 4, and 25, 26, 37, 38 (especially 25 and 38) to chapter 8.

The two quotations in the next paragraph are from the *Republic*, 541a, and from the *Statesman*, 293c–e.

It is interesting (because it is, I believe, characteristic of the hysteria of romantic radicalism with its *hubris*—its ambitious arrogance of godlikeness) to see that both passages of the *Republic*—the canvas-cleaning of 500d, ff., and the purge of 541a—are preceded by reference to the godlikeness of the philosophers; cp. 500c–d, 'the philosopher becomes ... godlike himself', and 540c–d (cp. note 37 to chapter 8 and text), 'And the state will erect monuments, at the expense of the public, to commemorate them; and sacrifices will be offered to them, as demigods, ... or at least as men who are blessed by grace, and godlike.'

It is also interesting (for the same reasons) that the first of these passages is preceded by the passage (498d/e, f.; see note 59 to chapter 8) in which Plato expresses his hope that philosophers may become, as rulers, acceptable even to 'the many'.

* Concerning the term 'liquidate' the following modern outburst of radicalism may be quoted: 'Is it not obvious that if we are to have socialism—real and permanent socialism—all the fundamental opposition must be "liquidated" (i.e. rendered politically inactive by disfranchisement, and if necessary by imprisonment)?' This remarkable rhetorical question is printed on p. 18 of the still more remarkable pamphlet *Christians in the Class Struggle*, by Gilbert Cope, with a Foreword by the Bishop of Bradford. (1942; for the historicism of this pamphlet, see note 3 to chapter 1.) The Bishop, in his Foreword, denounces 'our present economic system' as 'immoral and un-Christian', and he says that 'when something is so plainly the work of the devil ... nothing can excuse a minister of the Church from working for its destruction'. Accordingly, he recommends the pamphlet 'as a lucid and penetrating analysis'.

A few more sentences may be quoted from the pamphlet. 'Two parties may ensure partial democracy, but a full democracy can be established only by a single party ... ' (p. 17).—'In the period of transition ... the workers ... must be led and organized by a single party which tolerates the existence of no other party fundamentally opposed to it ...' (p. 19).—'Freedom in the socialist state means that no one is allowed to attack the principle of common ownership, but everyone is encouraged to work for its more effective realization and operation ... The important matter of how the opposition is to be nullified depends upon the methods used by the opposition itself' (p. 18).

Most interesting of all is perhaps the following argument (also to be found on p. 18) which deserves to be read carefully: 'Why is it possible to have a socialist party in a capitalist country if it is not possible to have a capitalist party in a socialist state? The answer is simply that the one is a movement involving all the productive forces of a great majority against a small minority, while the other is an attempt of a minority to restore their position of power and privilege by renewed exploitation of the majority.' In other words, a ruling 'small minority' can afford to be tolerant, while a 'great majority' cannot afford to tolerate a 'small minority'. This simple answer is indeed a model of 'a lucid and penetrating analysis', as the Bishop puts it.*

13. Cp. for this development also chapter 13, especially note 7, and text.
14. It seems that romanticism, in literature as well as in philosophy, may be traced back to Plato. It is well known that Rousseau was directly influenced by him (cp. note 1 to chapter 6). Rousseau also knew Plato's *Statesman* (cp. the *Social Contract*, Book II, ch. VII, and Book III, ch. VI) with its eulogy of the early hill-shepherds. But apart from this direct influence, it is probable that Rousseau derived his pastoral romanticism and love for primitivity indirectly from Plato; for he was certainly influenced by the Italian Renaissance, which had rediscovered Plato, and especially his naturalism and his dreams of a perfect society of primitive shepherds (cp. notes 11 (3) and 32 to chapter 4 and note 1 to chapter 6).—It is interesting that Voltaire recognized at once the dangers of Rousseau's romantic obscurantism; just as Kant was not prevented by his admiration for Rousseau from recognizing this danger when he was faced with it in Herder's 'Ideas' (cp. also note 56 to chapter 12, and text).

NOTES TO CHAPTER TEN

This chapter's motto is taken from the *Symposium*, 193d.

1 Cp. *Republic*, 419a, ff., 421b, 465c, ff., and 519e; see also chapter 6, especially sections II and IV.
2. I am thinking not only of the medieval attempts to arrest society, attempts that were based on the Platonic theory that the rulers are responsible for the souls, the spiritual welfare of the ruled (and on many practical devices developed by Plato in the *Republic* and in the *Laws*), but I am thinking also of many later developments.
3. I have tried, in other words, to apply as far as possible the method which I have described in my *The Logic of Scientific Discovery*.
4. Cp. especially *Republic*, 566e; see also below, note 63 to this chapter.
5. In my story there should be 'no villains ... Crime is not interesting ... It is what men do at their best, with good intentions ... that really concerns us'. I have tried as far as possible to apply this methodological principle to my interpretation of Plato. (The formulation of the principle quoted in this note I have taken from G. B. Shaw's Preface to *Saint Joan*; see the first sentences in the section 'Tragedy, not Melodrama'.)
6. For Heraclitus, see chapter 2. For Alcmaeon's and Herodotus' theories of isonomy, see notes 13, 14, and 17, to chapter 6. For Phaleas of Chalcedon's economic equalitarianism, see Aristotle's *Politics*, 1266a, and Diels[5], chapter 39 (also on Hippodamus). For Hippodamus of Miletus, see Aristotle's *Politics*, 1267b22, and note 9 to chapter 3. Among the first political theorists, we must, of course, also

count the Sophists, Protagoras, Antiphon, Hippias, Alcidamas, Lycophron; Critias (cp. Diels[5], fr. 6, 30–38, and note 17 to chapter 8), and the Old Oligarch (if these were two persons); and Democritus.

For the terms 'closed society' and 'open society', and their use in a somewhat similar sense by Bergson, see the Note to the Introduction. My characterization of the closed society as magical and of the open society as rational and critical of course makes it impossible to apply these terms without idealizing the society in question. The magical attitude has by no means disappeared from our life, not even in the most 'open' societies so far realized, and I think it unlikely that it can ever completely disappear. In spite of this, it seems to be possible to give some useful criterion of the transition from the closed society to the open. The transition takes place when social institutions are first consciously recognized as man-made, and when their conscious alteration is discussed in terms of their suitability for the achievement of human aims or purposes. Or, putting the matter in a less abstract way, the closed society breaks down when the supernatural awe with which the social order is considered gives way to active interference, and to the conscious pursuit of personal or group interests. It is clear that cultural contact through civilization may engender such a breakdown, and, even more, the development of an impoverished, i.e. landless, section of the ruling class.

I may mention here that I do not like to speak of 'social breakdown' in a general way. I think that the breakdown of a closed society, as described here, is a fairly clear affair, but in general the term 'social breakdown' seems to me to convey very little more than that the observer does not like the course of the development he describes. I think that the term is much misused. But I admit that, with or without reason, the member of a certain society might have the feeling that 'everything is breaking down'. There is little doubt that to the members of the *ancien régime* or of the Russian nobility, the French or the Russian revolution must have appeared as a complete social breakdown; but to the new rulers it appeared very differently.

Toynbee (cp. *A Study of History*, V, 23–35; 338) describes 'the appearance of schism in the body social' as a criterion of a society which has broken down. Since schism, in the form of class disunion, undoubtedly occurred in Greek society long before the Peloponnesian war, it is not quite clear why he holds that this war (and not the breakdown of tribalism) marks what he describes as the breakdown of Hellenic civilization. (Cp. also note 45 (2) to chapter 4, and note 8 to the present chapter.)

Concerning the similarity between the Greeks and the Maoris, some remarks can be found in Burnet's *Early Greek Philosophy*[2], especially pp. 2 and 9.

7. I owe this criticism of the organic theory of the state, together with many other suggestions, to J. Popper-Lynkeus; he writes (*Die allgemeine Nährpflicht*, 2nd edn, 1923, pp. 71 f.): 'The excellent Menenius Agrippa ... persuaded the insurgent plebs to return' (to Rome) 'by telling them his simile of the body's members who rebelled against the belly ... Why did not one of them say: "Right, Agrippa! If there must be a belly, then we, the plebs, want to be the belly from now on; and you ... may play the rôle of the members!"' (For the simile, see Livy II, 32, and Shakespeare's *Coriolanus*, Act 1, Scene 1.) It is perhaps interesting to note that even a modern and apparently progressive movement like 'Mass-Observation' makes propaganda for the organic theory of society (on the cover of its pamphlet, *First Year's Work*, 1937–38). See also note 31 to chapter 5.

On the other hand, it must be admitted that the tribal 'closed society' has something like an 'organic' character, just because of the absence of social tension. The fact that such a society may be based on slavery (as it was the case with the Greeks) does not create in itself a social tension, because slaves sometimes form no more part of society than its cattle; their aspirations and problems do not necessarily create anything that is felt by the rulers as a problem within society. *Population growth*, however, does create such a problem. In Sparta, which did not send out colonies, it led first to the subjugation of neighbouring tribes for the sake of winning their territory, and then to a conscious effort to arrest all change by measures that included the control of population increase through the institution of infanticide, birth control, and homosexuality. All this was seen quite clearly by Plato, who always insisted (perhaps under the influence of Hippodamus) on the need for a fixed number of citizens, and who recommended in the *Laws* colonization and birth control, as he had earlier recommended homosexuality (explained in the same way in Aristotle's *Politics*, 1272a23) as means for keeping the population constant; see *Laws*, 740d–741a, and 838e. (For Plato's recommendation of infanticide in the *Republic*, and for similar problems, see especially note 34 to chapter 4; furthermore, notes 22 and 63 to chapter 10, and 39 (3) to chapter 5.)

Of course, all these practices are far from being completely explicable in rational terms; and the Dorian homosexuality, more especially, is closely connected with the practice of war, and with the attempts to recapture, in the life of the war horde, an emotional satisfaction which had been largely destroyed by the breakdown of tribalism; see especially the 'war horde composed of lovers', glorified by Plato in the *Symposium*, 178e. In the *Laws*, 636b, f., 836b/c, Plato deprecates homosexuality (cp., however, 838e).

8. I suppose that what I call the 'strain of civilization' is similar to the phenomenon which Freud had in mind when writing *Civilization and its Discontents*. Toynbee speaks of a Sense of Drift (*A Study of History*, V, 412 ff.), but he confines it to 'ages of disintegration', while I find my strain very clearly expressed in Heraclitus (in fact, traces can be found in Hesiod)—long before the time when, according to Toynbee, his 'Hellenic society' begins to 'disintegrate'. Meyer speaks of the disappearance of 'The status of birth, which had determined every man's place in life, his civil and social rights and duties, together with the security of earning his living' (*Geschichte des Altertums*, III, 542). This gives an apt description of the strain in Greek society of the fifth century B.C.

9. Another profession of this kind which led to comparative intellectual independence, was that of a wandering bard. I am thinking here mainly of Xenophanes, the progressivist; cp. the paragraph on 'Protagoreanism' in note 7 to chapter 5. (Homer also may be a case in point.) It is clear that this profession was accessible to very few men.

I happen to have no personal interest in matters of commerce, or in commercially minded people. But the influence of commercial initiative seems to me rather important. It is hardly an accident that the oldest known civilization, that of Sumer, was, as far as we know, a commercial civilization with strong democratic features; and that the arts of writing and arithmetic, and the beginnings of science, were closely connected with its commercial life. (Cp. also text to note 24 to this chapter.)

10. *Thucydides*, I, 93 (I mostly follow Jowett's translation). For the problem of Thucydides' bias, cp. note 15 (1) to this chapter.

11. This and the next quotation: *op. cit.*, I, 107. Thucydides' story of the treacherous oligarchs can hardly be recognized in Meyer's apologetic version (*Gesch. d. Altertums*, III, 594), in spite of the fact that he has no better sources; it is simply distorted beyond recognition. (For Meyer's partiality, see note 15 (2) to the present chapter.)—For a similar treachery (in 479 B.C. on the eve of Plataea) cp. Plutarch's *Aristides*, 13.
12. *Thucydides*, III, 82–84. The following conclusion of the passage is characteristic of the element of individualism and humanitarianism present in Thucydides, a member of the Great Generation (see below, and note 27 to this chapter) and, as mentioned above, a moderate: 'When men take revenge, they are reckless; they do not consider the future, and do not hesitate to annul those common laws of humanity on which every individual must rely for his own deliverance should he ever be overtaken by calamity; they forget that in their own hour of need they will look for them in vain.' For a further discussion of Thucydides' bias see note 15 (1) to this chapter.
13. Aristotle, *Politics*, VIII, (V), 9, 10/11; 1310a. Aristotle does not agree with such open hostility; he thinks it wiser that 'true Oligarchs should *affect* to be advocates of the people's cause'; and he is anxious to give them good advice: 'They should take, or they should at least *pretend* to take, the opposite line, by including in their oath the pledge: I shall do no harm to the people.'
14. *Thucydides*, II, 9.
15. Cp. E. Meyer, *Geschichte des Altertums*, IV (1915), 368.

(1) In order to judge Thucydides' alleged impartiality, or rather, his involuntary bias, one must compare his treatment of the most important affair of Plataea which marked the outbreak of the first part of the Peloponnesian war (Meyer, following Lysias, calls this part the Archidamian war; cp. Meyer, *Gesch. d. Altertums*, IV, 307, and V, p. vii) with his treatment of the Melian affair, Athens' first aggressive move in the second part (the war of Alcibiades). The Archidamian war broke out with an attack on democratic Plataea—a lightning attack made without declaration of war by Thebes, a partner of totalitarian Sparta, whose friends inside Plataea, the oligarchic fifth column, had by night opened the doors of Plataea to the enemy. Though most important as the immediate cause of the war, the incident is comparatively briefly related by Thucydides (II, 1–7); he does not comment upon the moral aspect, apart from calling 'the affair of Plataea a glaring violation of the thirty years truce'; but he censures (II, 5) the democrats of Plataea for their harsh treatment of the invaders, and even expresses doubts whether they did not break an oath. This method of presentation contrasts strongly with the famous and most elaborate, though of course fictitious, Melian Dialogue (*Thuc.*, V, 85–113) in which Thucydides tries to brand Athenian imperialism. Shocking as the Melian affair seems to have been (Alcibiades may have been responsible; cp. Plutarch, *Alc.*, 16), the Athenians did *not* attack without warning, and tried to negotiate before using force.

Another case in point, bearing on Thucydides' attitude, is his eulogy (in VIII, 68) of the oligarchic party leader, the orator Antiphon (who is mentioned in Plato's *Menexenus*, 236a, as a teacher of Socrates; cp. end of note 19 to chapter 6).

(2) E. Meyer is one of the greatest modern authorities on this period. But to appreciate his point of view one must read the following scornful remarks on democratic governments (there are a great many passages of this kind): 'Much more

important' (viz., than to arm) 'was it to continue the entertaining game of party-quarrels, and to secure unlimited freedom, as interpreted by everybody according to his particular interests.' (V, 61.) But is it more, I ask, than an 'interpretation according to his particular interests' when Meyer writes: 'The wonderful freedom of democracy, and of her leaders, have manifestly proved their inefficiency.' (V, 69.) About the Athenian democratic leaders who in 403 B.C. refused to surrender to Sparta (and whose refusal was later even justified by success—although no such justification is necessary), Meyer says: 'Some of these leaders might have been honest fanatics; ... they might have been so utterly incapable of any sound judgement that they really believed' (what they said, namely:) 'that Athens must never capitulate.' (IV, 659.) Meyer censures other historians in the strongest terms for being biased. (Cp. e.g. the notes in V, 89 and 102, where he defends the older tyrant Dionysius against allegedly biased attacks, and 113 bottom to 114 top, where he is also exasperated by some anti-Dionysian 'parroting historians'.) Thus he calls Grote 'an English radical leader', and his work 'not a history, but an apology for Athens', and he proudly contrasts himself with such men: 'It will hardly be possible to deny that we have become more impartial in questions of politics, and that we have arrived thereby at a more correct and more comprehensive historical judgement.' (All this in III, 239.)

Behind Meyer's point of view stands—Hegel. This explains everything (as will be clear, I hope, to readers of chapter 12). Meyer's Hegelianism becomes obvious in the following remark, which is an unconscious but nearly literal quotation from Hegel; it is in III, 256, when Meyer speaks of a 'flat and moralizing evaluation, which judges great political undertakings with the yardstick of civil morality' (Hegel speaks of 'the litany of private virtues'), 'ignoring the deeper, the truly moral factors of the state, and of historical responsibilities'. (This corresponds exactly to the passages from Hegel quoted in chapter 12, below; cp. note 75 to chapter 12.) I wish to use this opportunity once more to make it clear that I do not pretend to be impartial in my historical judgement. Of course I do what I can to ascertain the relevant facts. But I am aware that my evaluations (like anybody else's) must depend entirely on my point of view. This I admit, although I fully believe in my point of view, i.e. that my evaluations are right.

16. Cp. Meyer, *op. cit.*, IV, 367.
17. Cp. Meyer, *op. cit.*, IV, 464.
18. It must however be kept in mind that, as the reactionaries complained. slavery was in Athens on the verge of dissolution. Cp. the evidence mentioned in notes 17, 18 and 29 to chapter 4; furthermore, notes 13 to chapter 5, 48 to chapter 8, and 27–37 to the present chapter.
19. Cp. Meyer, *op. cit.*, IV, 659.

Meyer comments upon this move of the Athenian democrats: 'Now when it was too late they made a move towards a political constitution which later helped Rome ... to lay the foundations of its greatness.' In other words, instead of crediting the Athenians with a constitutional invention of the first order, he reproaches them; and the credit goes to Rome, whose conservatism is more to Meyer's taste.

The incident in Roman history to which Meyer alludes is Rome's alliance, or federation, with Gabii. But immediately before, and on the very page on which Meyer describes this federation (in V, 135) we can read also: 'All these towns, when incorporated with Rome, lost their existence ... without even receiving a political organization of the type of Attica's "demes".' A little later, in V, 147, Gabii is again referred to, and Rome in her generous 'liberality' again contrasted with Athens; but at the turn of the same page Meyer reports without criticism Rome's looting and total destruction of Veii, which meant the end of Etruscan civilization.

The worst perhaps of all these Roman destructions is that of Carthage. It took place at a moment when Carthage was no longer a danger to Rome, and it robbed Rome, and us, of most valuable contributions which Carthage could have made to civilization. I only mention the great treasures of geographical information which were destroyed there. (The story of the decline of Carthage is not unlike that of the fall of Athens in 404 B.C., discussed in this chapter below; see note 48. The oligarchs of Carthage preferred the fall of their city to the victory of democracy.)

Later, under the influence of Stoicism, derived indirectly from Antisthenes, Rome began to develop a very liberal and humanitarian outlook. It reached the height of this development in those centuries of peace after Augustus (cp. for instance Toynbee, *A Study of History*, V, pp. 343–346), but it is here that some romantic historians see the beginning of her decline.

Regarding this decline itself, it is, of course, naïve and romantic to believe, as many still do, that it was due to the degeneration caused by long-continued peace, or to demoralization, or to the superiority of the younger barbarian peoples, etc.; in brief, to over-feeding. (Cp. note 45 (3) to chapter 4.) The devastating result of violent epidemics (cp. H. Zinsser, *Rats, Lice, and History*, 1937, pp. 131 ff.) and the unchecked and progressive exhaustion of the soil, and with it a breakdown of the agricultural basis of the Roman economic system (cp. V. G. Simkhovitch, 'Hay and History', and 'Rome's Fall Reconsidered', in *Towards the Understanding of Jesus*, 1927), seem to have been some of the main causes. Cp. also W. Hegemann, *Entlarvte Geschichte* (1934).

20. *Thucydides*, VII, 28; cp. Meyer, *op. cit.*, IV, 535. The important remark that 'this would yield more' enables us, of course, to fix an approximate upper limit for the ratio between the taxes previously imposed and the volume of trade.
21. This is an allusion to a grim little pun which I owe to P. Milford: 'A Plutocracy is preferable to a Lootocracy.'
22. Plato, *Republic*, 423b. For the problem of keeping the size of the population constant, cp. note 7, above.
23. Cp. Meyer, *Geschichte des Altertums*, IV, 577.
24. *Op. cit.*, V, 27. Cp. also note 9 to this chapter, and text to note 30 to chapter 4. *For the passage from the *Laws*, see 742a–c. Plato elaborates here the Spartan attitude. He lays down 'a law that forbids private citizens to possess any gold or silver ... Our citizens should be allowed only such coins as are legal tender among ourselves, but valueless elsewhere ... For the sake of an expeditionary force, or official visit abroad, such as embassies or other necessary missions ... it is necessary that the state should always possess Hellenic (gold) coinage. And if a private citizen should ever be obliged to go abroad, he may do so, provided he has duly obtained permission from the magistrates. And should he have, upon his return, any foreign money left, then he must surrender it to the state, and accept its equivalent in home currency. And should anybody be found to keep it, then it must be confiscated, and he who imported it, and anybody who failed to inform against him, should be liable to

curses and condemnations, and, in addition, to a fine of not less than the amount of the money involved.' Reading this passage, one wonders whether one does not wrong Plato in describing him as a reactionary who copied the laws of the totalitarian township of Sparta; for here he anticipates by more than 2000 years the principles and practices which nowadays are nearly universally accepted as sound policy by the most progressive Western European democratic governments (who, like Plato, hope that some other government will look after the 'Universal Hellenic gold currency').

A later passage (*Laws*, 950d) has, however, less of a liberal Western ring. 'First, no man under forty years shall obtain permission for going abroad to whatever place it may be. Secondly, nobody shall obtain such permission in a private capacity: in a public capacity, permission may be granted only to heralds, ambassadors, and to certain missions of inspection ... And *these men, after their return, will teach the young that the political institutions of other countries are inferior to their own*.'

Similar laws are laid down for the reception of strangers. For 'intercommunication between states necessarily results in a mixing of characters ... and in importing novel customs; and this must cause the greatest harm to people who enjoy ... the right laws' (949e/950a).*

25. This is admitted by Meyer (*op. cit.*, IV, 433 f.), who in a very interesting passage says of the two parties: 'each of them claims that it defends "the paternal state" ... , and that the opponent is infected with the modern spirit of selfishness and revolutionary violence. In reality, both are infected ... The traditional customs and religion are more deeply rooted in the democratic party; its aristocratic enemies who fight under the flag of the restoration of the ancient times, are ... entirely modernized.' Cp. also *op. cit.*, V, 4 f., 14, and the next note.
26. From Aristotle's *Athenian Constitution*, ch. 34, §3, we learn that the Thirty Tyrants professed at first what appeared to Aristotle a 'moderate' programme, viz., that of the 'paternal state'.—For the nihilism and the modernity of Critias, cp. his theory of religion discussed in chapter 8 (see especially note 17 to that chapter) and note 48 to the present chapter.
27. It is most interesting to contrast Sophocles' attitude towards the new faith with that of Euripides. Sophocles complains (cp. Meyer, *op. cit.*, IV, 111): 'It is wrong that ... the lowly born should flourish, while the brave and nobly born are unfortunate.' Euripides replies (with Antiphon; cp. note 13 to chapter 5) that the distinction between the nobly and the low born (especially slaves) is merely verbal: 'The name alone brings shame upon the slave.'—For the humanitarian element in Thucydides, cp. the quotation in note 12 to this chapter. For the question how far the Great Generation was connected with cosmopolitan tendencies, see the evidence marshalled in note 48 to chapter 8—especially the hostile witnesses, i.e. the Old Oligarch, Plato, and Aristotle.
28. 'Misologists', or haters of rational argument, are compared by Socrates to 'misanthropists', or haters of men; cp. the *Phaedo*, 89c. In contrast, cp. Plato's misanthropic remark in the *Republic*, 496c–d (cp. notes 57 and 58 to chapter 8).
29. The quotations in this paragraph are from Democritus' fragments, Diels, *Vorsokratiker*[5], fragments number 41; 179; 34; 261; 62; 55; 251; 247 (genuineness questioned by Diels and by Tarn, cp. note 48 to chapter 8); 118.
30. Cp. text to note 16, chapter 6.

31. Cp. *Thucydides*, II, 37–41. Cp. also the remarks in note 16 to chapter 6.
32. Cp. T. Gomperz, *Greek Thinkers*, Book V, ch. 13, 3 (Germ. edn, II, 407).
33. Herodotus' work with its pro-democratic tendency (cp. for example, III, 80) appeared about a year or two after Pericles' oration (cp. Meyer, *Gesch. d. Altertums*, IV, 369).
34. This has been pointed out for instance by T. Gomperz, *Greek Thinkers*, V, 13, 2 (Germ. edn, II, 406 f.); the passages in the *Republic* to which he draws attention are: 557d and 561c, ff. The similarity is undoubtedly intentional. Cp. also Adam's edition of the *Republic*, vol. II, 235, note to 557d26. See also the *Laws*, 699d/e, ff., and 704d–707d. For a similar observation regarding Herodotus III, 80, see note 17 to chapter 6.
35. Some hold the *Menexenus* to be spurious, but I believe that this shows only their tendency to idealize Plato. The *Menexenus* is vouched for by Aristotle, who quotes a remark from it as due to the 'Socrates of the Funeral Dialogue' (*Rhetoric*, I, 9, 30 = 1367b8; and III, 14, 11 = 1415b30). See especially also end of note 19 to chapter 6; also note 48 to chapter 8 and notes 15 (1) and 61 to the present chapter.
36. The Old Oligarch's (or the Pseudo-Xenophon's) *Constitution of Athens* was published in 424 B.C. (according to Kirchhoff, quoted by Gomperz, *Greek Thinkers*, Germ. edn, I, 477). For its attribution to Critias, cp. J. E. Sandys, *Aristotle's Constitution of Athens*, Introduction IX, especially note 3. See also notes 18 and 48 to this chapter. Its influence upon Thucydides is, I think, noticeable in the passages quoted in notes 10 and 11 to this chapter. For its influence upon Plato, see especially note 59 to chapter 8, and *Laws*, 704a–707d. (Cp. Aristotle, *Politics*, 1326b–1327a; Cicero, *De Republica*, II, 3 and 4.)
37. I am alluding to M. M. Rader's book, *No Compromise—The Conflict between Two Worlds* (1939), an excellent criticism of the ideology of fascism.

    With the allusion, later in this paragraph, to Socrates' warning against misanthropy and misology, cp. note 28, above.
38. *(1) For the theory that what may be called 'the invention of critical thought' consists in the foundation of a new tradition—the tradition of critically discussing the traditional myths and theories—see my 'Towards a Rational Theory of Tradition,' *The Rationalist Annual*, 1949; now in *Conjectures and Refutations*. (Only such a new tradition can explain the fact that, in the Ionian School, the three first generations produced three different philosophies.)*

    (2) Schools (especially Universities) have retained certain aspects of tribalism ever since. But we must think not only of their emblems, or of the Old School Tie with all its social implications of caste, etc., but also of the patriarchal and authoritarian character of so many schools. It was not just an accident that Plato, when he had failed to re-establish tribalism, founded a school instead; nor is it an accident that schools are so often bastions of reaction, and school teachers dictators in pocket edition.

    As an illustration of the tribalistic character of these early schools, I give here a list of some of the taboos of the early Pythagoreans. (The list is from Burnet's *Early Greek Philosophy*², 106, who takes it from Diels; cp. *Vorsokratiker*⁵, vol. I, pp. 97 ff.; but see also Aristoxenus' evidence in *op. cit.*, p. 101.) Burnet speaks of 'genuine taboos of a thoroughly primitive type'.—To abstain from beans.—Not to pick up what has fallen.—Not to touch a white cock.—Not to break bread.—Not to step over a crossbar.—Not to stir the fire with iron.—Not to eat from a whole loaf.—Not to pluck a garland.—Not to sit on a quart measure.—Not to eat the heart.—Not to walk on highways.—Not to let the swallows share one's roof.—When the pot is taken off the fire, not to leave the mark of it in the ashes, but to stir them together.—Not to look in a mirror beside a light.—After rising from the bedclothes, to roll them together and to smooth out the impress of the body.

39. An interesting parallelism to this development is the destruction of tribalism through the Persian conquests. This social revolution led, as Meyer points out (*op. cit.*, vol. III, 167 ff.), to the emergence of a number of prophetic, i.e. in our terminology, of historicist, religions of destiny, degeneration, and salvation, among them that of the 'chosen people', the Jews (cp. chapter 1).

    Some of these religions were also characterized by the doctrine that the creation of the world is not yet concluded, but still going on. This must be compared with the early Greek conception of the world as an edifice and with the Heraclitean destruction of this conception, described in chapter 2 (see note 1 to that chapter). It may be mentioned here that even Anaximander felt uneasy about the edifice. His stress upon the boundless or indeterminate or indefinite character of the building-material may have been the expression of a feeling that the building may possess no definite framework, that it may be in flux (cp. next note).

    The development of the Dionysian and the Orphic mysteries in Greece is probably dependent upon the religious development of the east (cp. *Herodotus*, II, 81). Pythagoreanism, as is well known, had much in common with Orphic teaching, especially regarding the theory of the soul (see also note 44 below). But Pythagoreanism had a definitely 'aristocratic' flavour, as opposed to the Orphic teaching which represented a kind of 'proletarian' version of this movement. Meyer (*op. cit.*, III, p. 428, § 246) is probably right when he describes the beginnings of philosophy as a rational counter-current against the movement of the mysteries; cp. Heraclitus' attitude in these matters (fragm. 5, 14, 15; and 40, 129, Diels[5]; 124–129; and 16–17, Bywater). He hated the mysteries *and* Pythagoras; the Pythagorean Plato despised the mysteries. (*Rep.*, 364e, f.; cp. however Adam's Appendix IV to Book IX of the *Republic*, vol. II, 378 ff., of his edition.)

40. For Anaximander (cp. the preceding note), see Diels[5], fragm. 9: 'The origin of things ... is some indeterminate (or boundless) nature; ... out of those things from which existing things are generated, into these they dissolve again, by necessity. For they do penance to one another for their offence (or injustice), according to the order of time.' That individual existence appeared to Anaximander as *injustice* was the interpretation of Gomperz (*Greek Thinkers*, Germ. edn, vol. I, p. 46; note the similarity to Plato's theory of justice); but this interpretation has been severely criticized.

41. Parmenides was the first to seek his salvation from this strain by interpreting his dream of the arrested world as a revelation of true reality, and the world of flux in which he lived as a dream. 'The real being is indivisible. It is always an integrated whole, which never breaks away from its order; it never disperses, and thus need not re-unite.' (D5, fragm. 4.) For Parmenides, cp. also note 22 to chapter 3, and text.

42. Cp. note 9 to the present chapter (and note 7 to chapter 5).

43. Cp. Meyer, *Geschichte des Altertums*, III, 443, and IV, 120 f.

44. J. Burnet, 'The Socratic Doctrine of the Soul', *Proceedings of the British Academy*, VIII (1915/16), 235 ff. I am the more anxious to stress this partial agreement since I

cannot agree with Burnet in most of his other theories, especially those that concern Socrates' relations to Plato; his opinion in particular that Socrates is politically the more reactionary of the two (*Greek Philosophy*, I, 210) appears to me untenable. Cp. note 56 to this chapter.

Regarding the Socratic doctrine of the soul, I believe that Burnet is right in insisting that the saying 'care for your souls' is Socratic; for this saying expresses Socrates' moral interests. But I think it highly improbable that Socrates held any metaphysical theory of the soul. The theories of the *Phaedo*, the *Republic*, etc., seem to me undoubtedly Pythagorean. (For the Orphic-Pythagorean theory that the body is the tomb of the soul, cp. Adam, Appendix IV to Book IX of the *Republic*; see also note 39 to this chapter.) And in view of Socrates' clear statement in the *Apology*, 19c, that he had 'nothing whatever to do with such things' (i.e. with speculations on nature; see note 56 (5) to this chapter), I strongly disagree with Burnet's opinion that Socrates was a Pythagorean; and also with the opinion that he held any definite metaphysical doctrine of the 'nature' of the soul.

I believe that Socrates' saying 'care for your souls' is an expression of his moral (and intellectual) individualism. Few of his doctrines seem to be so well attested as his individualistic theory of the moral self-sufficiency of the virtuous man. (See the evidence mentioned in notes 25 to chapter 5 and 36 to chapter 6.) But this is most closely connected with the idea expressed in the sentence 'care for your souls'. In his emphasis on self-sufficiency, Socrates wished to say: They can destroy your body, but they cannot destroy your moral integrity. If the latter is your main concern, they cannot do any really serious harm to you.

It appears that Plato, when becoming acquainted with the Pythagorean metaphysical theory of the soul, felt that Socrates' moral attitude needed a metaphysical foundation, especially a theory of survival. He therefore substituted for 'they cannot destroy your moral integrity' the idea of the indestructibility of the soul. (Cp. also notes 9f. to chapter 7.)

Against my interpretation, it may be contended by both metaphysicians and positivists that there can be no such moral and non-metaphysical idea of the soul as I ascribe to Socrates, since any way of speaking of the soul must be metaphysical. I do not think that I have much hope of convincing Platonic metaphysicians; but I shall attempt to show positivists (or materialists, etc.) that they too believe in a 'soul', in a sense very similar to that which I attribute to Socrates, and that most of them value that 'soul' more highly than the body.

First of all, even positivists may admit that we can make a perfectly empirical and 'meaningful', although somewhat unprecise, distinction between 'physical' and 'psychical' maladies. In fact, this distinction is of considerable practical importance for the organization of hospitals, etc. (It is quite probable that one day it may be superseded by something more precise, but that is a different question.) Now most of us, even positivists, would, if we had to choose, prefer a mild physical malady to a mild form of insanity. Even positivists would moreover probably prefer a lengthy and in the end incurable physical illness (provided it was not too painful, etc.) to an equally lengthy period of incurable insanity, and perhaps even to a period of curable insanity. In this way, I believe, we can say without using metaphysical terms that they care for their 'souls' more than for their 'bodies'. (Cp. *Phaedo*, 82d: they 'care for their souls and are not servants of their bodies'; see also *Apology*, 29d–30b.) And this way of speaking would be quite independent of any theory they might have concerning the 'soul'; even if they should maintain that, in the last analysis, it is only part of the body, and all insanity only a physical malady, our conclusion would still hold. (It would come to something like this: that they value their brains more highly than other parts of their bodies.)

We can now proceed to a similar consideration of an idea of the 'soul' which is closer still to the Socratic idea. Many of us are prepared to undergo considerable physical hardship for the sake of purely intellectual ends. We are, for example, ready to suffer in order to advance scientific knowledge; and also for the sake of furthering our own intellectual development, i.e. for the sake of attaining 'wisdom'. (For Socrates' intellectualism, cp. for instance the *Crito*, 44d/e, and 47b.) Similar things could be said of the furthering of moral ends, for instance, equalitarian justice, peace, etc. (Cp. *Crito*, 47e/48a, where Socrates explains that he means by 'soul' that part of us which is 'improved by justice and depraved by injustice'.) And many of us would say, with Socrates, that these things are more important to us than things like health, even though we like to be in good health. And many may even agree with Socrates that the possibility of adopting such an attitude is what makes us proud to be men, and not animals.

All this, I believe, can be said without any reference to a metaphysical theory of the 'nature of the soul'. And I see no reason why we should attribute such a theory to Socrates in the face of his clear statement that he had nothing to do with speculations of that sort.

45. In the *Gorgias*, which is, I believe, Socratic in parts (although the Pythagorean elements which Gomperz has noted show, I think, that it is largely Platonic; cp. note 56 to this chapter), Plato puts into the mouth of Socrates an attack on 'the ports and ship-yards and walls' of Athens, and on the tributes or taxes imposed upon her allies. These attacks, as they stand, are certainly Plato's, which may explain why they sound very much like those of the oligarchs. But I think it quite possible that Socrates may have made similar remarks, in his anxiety to stress the things which, in his opinion, mattered most. But he would, I believe, have loathed the idea that his moral criticism could be turned into treacherous oligarchic propaganda against the open society, and especially, against its representative, Athens. (For the question of Socrates' loyalty, cp. esp. note 53 to this chapter, and text.)

46. The typical figures, in Plato's works, are Callicles and Thrasymachus. Historically, the nearest realizations are perhaps Theramenes and Critias; Alcibiades also, whose character and deeds, however, are very hard to judge.

47. The following remarks are highly speculative and do not bear upon my arguments.

I consider it possible that the basis of the *First Alcibiades* is Plato's own conversion by Socrates, i.e. that Plato may in this dialogue have chosen the figure of Alcibiades to hide himself. There might have been a strong inducement for him to tell the story of his conversion; for Socrates, when accused of being responsible for the misdeeds of Alcibiades, Critias, and Charmides (see below), had referred, in his defence before the court, to Plato as a living example, and as a witness, of his true educational influence. It seems not unlikely that Plato with his urge to literary testimony felt that he had to tell the tale of Socrates' relations with himself, a tale which he could not tell in court (cp. Taylor, *Socrates*, note 1 to p. 105). By using Alcibiades' name and the special circumstances surrounding him (e.g. his ambitious political dreams which might well have been similar to those of Plato before his conversion) he would attain his apologetic purpose (cp. text to notes 49–50), showing that Socrates' moral influence in general, and in particular on Alcibiades, was very different from what his prosecutors maintained it to be. I think it not unlikely that the *Charmides* is also, largely, a self-portrait. (It is not without interest to note that Plato himself undertook similar conversions, but as far as we can judge, in a different way; not so much by direct personal moral appeal, but rather by an institutional teaching of Pythagorean mathematics, as a pre-requisite for the dialectical intuition of the Idea of the Good. Cp. the stories of his attempted conversion of the younger Dionysius.) For the *First Alcibiades* and related problems, see also Grote's *Plato*, I, especially pp. 351–355.

48. Cp. Meyer, *Geschichte des Altertums*, V, 38 (and Xenophon's *Hellenica*, II, 4, 22). In the same volume, on pp. 19–23 and 36–44 (see especially p. 36) can be found all the evidence needed for justifying the interpretation given in the text. The *Cambridge Ancient History* (1927, vol. V; cp. especially pp. 369 ff.) gives a very similar interpretation of the events.

It may be added that the number of full citizens killed by the Thirty during the eight months of terror approached probably 1,500, which is, as far as we know, not much less than one-tenth (probably about 8 per cent.) of the total number of full citizens left after the war, or 1 per cent. per month—an achievement hardly surpassed even in our own day.

Taylor writes of the Thirty (*Socrates*, Short Biographies, 1937, p. 100, note 1): 'It is only fair to remember that these men probably "lost their heads" under the temptation presented by their situation. Critias had previously been known as a man of wide culture whose political leanings were decidedly democratic.' I believe that this attempt to minimize the responsibility of the puppet government, and especially of Plato's beloved uncle, must fail. We know well enough what to think of the shortlived democratic sentiments professed in those days at suitable occasions by the young aristocrats. Besides, Critias' father (cp. Meyer, vol. IV, p. 579, and *Lys.*, 12, 43, and 12, 66), and probably Critias himself, had belonged to the oligarchy of the Four Hundred; and Critias' extant writings show his treacherous pro-Spartan leanings as well as his oligarchic outlook (cp., for instance, Diels[5], 45) and his blunt nihilism (cp. note 17 to chapter 8) and his ambition (cp. Diels[5], 15; cp. also Xenophon's *Memorabilia*, I, 2, 24; and his *Hellenica*, II, 3, 36 and 47). But the decisive point is that he simply tried to give consistent effect to the programme of the 'Old Oligarch', the author of the Pseudo-Xenophontic *Constitution of Athens* (cp. note 36 to the present chapter): to eradicate democracy; and to make a determined attempt to do so with Spartan help, should Athens be defeated. The degree of violence used is the logical result of the situation. It does not indicate that Critias lost his head; rather, that he was very well aware of the difficulties, i.e. of the democrats' still formidable power of resistance.

Meyer, whose great sympathy for Dionysius I proves that he is at least not prejudiced *against* tyrants, says about Critias (*op. cit.*, V, p. 17), after a sketch of his amazingly opportunistic political career, that 'he was just as unscrupulous as Lysander', the Spartan conqueror, and therefore the appropriate head of Lysander's puppet government.

It seems to me that there is a striking similarity between the characters of Critias, the soldier, æsthete, poet, and sceptical companion of Socrates, and of Frederick II of Prussia, called 'the Great', who also was a soldier, an æsthete, a poet, and a sceptical disciple of Voltaire, as well as one of the worst tyrants and most ruthless oppressors in modern history. (On Frederick, cp. W. Hegemann, *Entlarvte Geschichte*, 1934; see especially p. 90 on his attitude towards religion, reminiscent of that of Critias.)

49. This point is very well explained by Taylor, *Socrates*, Short Biographies, 1937, p. 103, who follows here Burnet's note to Plato's *Euthyphro*, 4c, 4.—The only point in which I feel inclined to deviate, but only very slightly, from Taylor's excellent treatment (*op. cit.*, 103, 120) of Socrates' trial is in the interpretation of the tendencies of the charge, especially of the charge concerning the introduction of 'novel religious practices' (*op. cit.*, 109 and 111 f.).

50. Evidence to show this can be found in Taylor's *Socrates*, 113–115; cp. especially 115, note 1, where *Aeschines*, I, 173, is quoted: 'You put Socrates the Sophist to death because he was shown to have educated Critias.'

51. It was the policy of the Thirty to implicate as many people in their acts of terrorism as they could; cp. the excellent remarks by Taylor in *Socrates*, 101 f. (especially note 3 to p. 101). For Chaerephon, see note 56, (5) e_6 to the present chapter.

52. As Crossman and other do; cp. Crossman, *Plato To-Day*, 91/92. I agree in this point with Taylor, *Socrates*, 116; see also his notes 1 and 2 to that page.

That the plan of the prosecution was not to make a martyr of Socrates; that the trial could have been avoided, or managed differently, had Socrates been prepared to compromise, i.e. to leave Athens, or even to promise to keep quiet, all this seems fairly clear in view of Plato's (or Socrates') allusions in the *Apology* as well as in the *Crito*. (Cp. *Crito*, 45e and especially 52b/c, where Socrates says that he would have been permitted to emigrate had he offered to do so at the trial.)

53. Cp. especially *Crito*, 53b/c, where Socrates explains that, if he were to accept the opportunity for escape, he would confirm his judges in their belief; for he who corrupts the laws is likely to corrupt the young also.

The *Apology* and *Crito* were probably written not long after Socrates' death. The *Crito* (possibly the earlier of the two) was perhaps written upon Socrates' request that his motives in declining to escape should be made known. Indeed, such a wish may have been the first inspiration of the Socratic dialogues. T. Gomperz (*Greek Thinkers*, V, 11, 1, Germ. edn, II, 358) believes the *Crito* to be of later date and explains its tendency by assuming that it was Plato who was anxious to stress his loyalty. 'We do not know' writes Gomperz, 'the immediate situation to which this small dialogue owes its existence; but it is hard to resist the impression that Plato is here most interested in defending himself and his group against the suspicion of harbouring revolutionary views.' Although Gomperz's suggestion would easily fit into my general interpretation of Plato's views, I feel that the *Crito* is much more likely to be Socrates' defence than Plato's. But I agree with Gomperz's interpretation of its tendency. Socrates had certainly the greatest interest in defending himself against a suspicion which endangered his life's work.—Regarding this interpretation of the contents of the *Crito*, I again agree fully with Taylor (*Socrates*, 124 f.). But the loyalty of the *Crito* and its contrast to the obvious disloyalty of the *Republic* which quite openly takes sides with Sparta against Athens seems to refute Burnet's and Taylor's view that the *Republic* is Socratic, and that Socrates was more strongly opposed to democracy than Plato. (Cp. note 56 to this chapter.)

Concerning Socrates' affirmation of his loyalty to democracy, cp. especially the following passages of the *Crito*: 51d/e, where the democratic character of the laws is stressed, i.e. the possibility that the citizen might change the laws without violence, by rational argument (as Socrates puts it, he may try to convince the laws);—52b, f., where Socrates insists that he has no quarrel with the Athenian constitution;—53c/d, where he describes not only virtue and justice but especially institutions and laws (those of Athens) as the best things among men;—54c, where he says that he may be a victim of men, but insists that he is not a victim of the laws.

In view of all these passages (and especially of *Apology*, 32c; cp. note 8 to chapter 7), we must, I believe, discount the one passage which looks very different, viz. 52e, where Socrates by implication praises the constitutions of Sparta and Crete. Considering especially 52b/c, where Socrates said that he was not curious to know other states *or their laws*, one may be tempted to suggest that the remark on Sparta and Crete in 52e is an interpolation, made by somebody who attempted to reconcile the *Crito* with later writings, especially with the *Republic*. Whether that is so or whether the passage is a Platonic addition, it seems extremely unlikely that it is Socratic. One need only remember Socrates' anxiety not to do anything which might be interpreted as pro-Spartan, an anxiety of which we know from Xenophon's *Anabasis*, III, 1, 5. There we read that 'Socrates feared that he' (i.e. his friend, the young Xenophon—another of the young black sheep) 'might be blamed for being disloyal; for Cyrus was known to have assisted the Spartans in the war against Athens.' (This passage is certainly much less suspect than the *Memorabilia*; there is no influence of Plato here, and Xenophon actually accuses himself, by implication, of having taken his obligations to his country too lightly, and of having deserved his banishment, mentioned in *op. cit.*, V, 3, 7, and VII, 7, 57.)

54. *Apology*, 30e/31a.
55. Platonists, of course, would all agree with Taylor who says in the last sentence of his *Socrates*: 'Socrates had just one "successor"—Plato.' Only Grote seems sometimes to have held views similar to those stated in the text; what he says, for instance, in the passage quoted here in note 21 to chapter 7 (see also note 15 to chapter 8) can be interpreted as at least an expression of doubt whether Plato did not betray Socrates. Grote makes it perfectly clear that the *Republic* (not only the *Laws*) would have furnished the theoretical basis for condemning the Socrates of the *Apology*, and that this Socrates would never have been tolerated in Plato's best state. And he even points out that Plato's theory agrees with the practical treatment meted out to Socrates by the Thirty. (An example showing that the perversion of his master's teaching by a pupil is a thing that can succeed, even if the master is still alive, famous, and protests in public, can be found in note 58 to chapter 12.)

For the remarks on the *Laws*, made later in this paragraph, see especially the passages of the *Laws* referred to in notes 19–23 to chapter 8. Even Taylor, whose opinions on these questions are diametrically opposed to those presented here (see also the next note), admits: 'The person who first proposed to make false opinions in theology an offence against the state, was Plato himself, in the tenth Book of the *Laws*.' (Taylor, *op. cit.*, 108, note 1.)

In the text, I contrast especially Plato's *Apology* and *Crito* with his *Laws*. The reason for this choice is that nearly everybody, even Burnet and Taylor (see the next note), would agree that the *Apology* and the *Crito* represent the *Socratic* doctrine, and that the *Laws* may be described as *Platonic.* It seems to me therefore very difficult to understand how Burnet and Taylor could possibly defend their opinion that Socrates' attitude towards democracy was more hostile than Plato's. (This opinion is expressed in Burnet's *Greek Philosophy*, I, 209 f., and in Taylor's *Socrates*, 150 f., and 170 f.) I have seen no attempt to defend this view of Socrates, who fought for freedom (cp. especially note 53 to this chapter) and died for it, and of Plato, who wrote the *Laws*.

Burnet and Taylor hold this strange view because they are committed to the opinion that the *Republic* is Socratic and not Platonic; and because it may be said that the *Republic* is slightly less anti-democratic than the Platonic *Statesman* and the *Laws*. But the differences between the *Republic* and the *Statesman* as well as the *Laws* are very slight indeed, especially if not only the first books of the *Laws* are considered but also the last; in fact, the agreement of doctrine is rather closer than one would expect in two books separated by at least one decade, and probably by three or more, and most dissimilar in temperament and style (see note 6 to chapter 4, and many other places in this book where the similarity, if not identity, between the doctrines of the *Laws* and the *Republic* is shown). There is not the slightest internal difficulty in assuming that the *Republic* and the *Laws* are both *Platonic*; but Burnet's and Taylor's own admission that their theory leads to the conclusion that Socrates was not only an enemy of democracy but even a greater enemy than Plato shows the difficulty if not absurdity of their view that not only the *Apology* and the *Crito* are Socratic but the *Republic* as well. For all these questions, see also the next note, and the *Addenda*, III, B(2), below.

56. I need hardly say that this sentence is an attempt to sum up my interpretation of the historical rôle of Plato's theory of justice (for the moral failure of the Thirty, cp. Xenophon's *Hellenica*, II, 4, 40–42); and particularly of the main political doctrines of the *Republic*; an interpretation which tries to explain the contradictions among the early dialogues, especially the *Gorgias*, and the *Republic*, as arising from the fundamental difference between the views of Socrates and those of the later Plato. The cardinal importance of the question which is usually called the *Socratic Problem* may justify my entering here into a lengthy and partly methodological debate.

(1) The older solution of the Socratic Problem assumed that a group of the Platonic dialogues, especially the *Apology* and the *Crito*, is Socratic (i.e., in the main historically correct, and intended as such) while the majority of the dialogues are Platonic, including many of those in which Socrates is the main speaker, as for instance the *Phaedo* and the *Republic*. The older authorities justified this opinion often by referring to an 'independent witness', Xenophon, and by pointing out the similarity between the Xenophontic Socrates and the Socrates of the 'Socratic' group of dialogues, and the dissimilarities between the Xenophontic 'Socrates' and the 'Socrates' of the Platonic group of dialogues. The metaphysical theory of Forms or Ideas, more especially, was usually considered Platonic.

(2) Against this view, an attack was launched by J. Burnet, who was supported by A. E. Taylor. Burnet denounced the argument on which the 'older solution' (as I call it) is based as circular and unconvincing. It is not sound, he held, to select a group of dialogues solely because the theory of Forms is less prominent in them, to call them Socratic, and then to say that the theory of Forms was not Socrates' but Plato's invention. And it is not sound to claim Xenophon as an independent witness

since we have no reason whatever to believe in his independence, and good reason to believe that he must have known a number of Plato's dialogues when he commenced writing the *Memorabilia*. Burnet demanded that we should proceed from the assumption that *Plato really meant what he said*, and that, when he made Socrates pronounce a certain doctrine, he believed, and wished his readers to believe, that this doctrine was characteristic of Socrates' teaching.

(3) Although Burnet's views on the Socratic Problem appear to me untenable, they have been most valuable and stimulating. A bold theory of this kind, even if it is false, always means progress; and Burnet's books are full of bold and most unconventional views on his subject. This is the more to be appreciated as a historical subject always shows a tendency to become stale. But much as I admire Burnet for his brilliant and bold theories, and much as I appreciate their salutary effect, I am, considering the evidence available to me, unable to convince myself that these theories are tenable. In his invaluable enthusiasm, Burnet was, I believe, not always critical enough towards his own ideas. This is why others have found it necessary to criticize these ideas instead.

Regarding the Socratic Problem, I believe with many others that the view which I have described as the 'older solution' is fundamentally correct. This view has lately been well defended, against Burnet and Taylor, especially by G. C. Field (*Plato and His Contemporaries*, 1930) and A. K. Rogers (*The Socratic Problem*, 1933); and many other scholars seem to adhere to it. In spite of the fact that the arguments so far offered appear to me convincing, I may be permitted to add to them, using some results of the present book. But before proceeding to criticize Burnet, I may state that it is to Burnet that we owe our insight into the following principle of method. *Plato's evidence is the only first-rate evidence available to us*; all other evidence is secondary. (Burnet has applied this principle to Xenophon; but we must apply it also to Aristophanes, whose evidence was rejected by Socrates himself, in the *Apology*; see under (5), below.)

(4) Burnet explains that it is his method to assume 'that Plato really meant what he said'. According to this methodological principle, Plato's 'Socrates' must be intended as a *portrait of the historical Socrates*. (Cp. *Greek Philosophy*, I, 128, 212 f., and note on p. 349/50; cp. Taylor's *Socrates*, 14 f., 32 f., 153.) I admit that Burnet's methodological principle is a sound starting point. But I shall try to show, under (5), that the facts are such that they soon force *everybody* to give it up, including Burnet and Taylor. They are forced, like all others, to *interpret* what Plato says. But while others become conscious of this fact, and therefore careful and critical in their interpretations, it is inevitable that those who cling to the belief that they do not interpret Plato but simply accept what he said make it impossible for themselves to examine their interpretations critically.

(5) The facts that make Burnet's methodology inapplicable and force him and all others to interpret what Plato said, are, of course, the contradictions in Plato's alleged portrait of Socrates. Even if we accept the principle that we have no better evidence than Plato's, we are forced by the internal contradictions in his writing not to take him at his word, and to give up the assumption that he 'really meant what he said'. If a witness involves himself in contradictions, then we cannot accept his testimony without interpreting it, even if he is the best witness available. I give first only three examples of such internal contradictions.

(*a*) The Socrates of the *Apology* very impressively repeats three times (18b–c; 19c–d; 23d) that he is not interested in natural philosophy (and therefore not a Pythagorean): 'I know nothing, neither much nor little, about such things', he said (19c); 'I, men of Athens, have nothing whatever to do with such things' (i.e. with speculations about nature). Socrates asserts that many who are present at the trial could testify to the truth of this statement; they have heard him speak, but neither in few nor in many words has anybody ever heard him speak about matters of natural philosophy. (*Ap.*, 19, c–d.) On the other hand, we have (*a′*) the *Phaedo* (cp. especially 108d, f., with the passages of the *Apology* referred to) and the *Republic*. In these dialogues, Socrates appears as a Pythagorean philosopher of 'nature'; so much so that both Burnet and Taylor could say that he was in fact a leading member of the Pythagorean school of thought. (Cp. Aristotle, who says of the Pythagoreans 'their discussions ... are all about nature'; see *Metaphysics*, end of 989b.)

Now I hold that (*a*) and (*a′*) flatly contradict each other; and this situation is made worse by the fact that the dramatic date of the *Republic* is earlier and that of the *Phaedo* later than that of the *Apology*. This makes it impossible to reconcile (*a*) with (*a′*) by assuming that Socrates either gave up Pythagoreanism in the last years of his life, between the *Republic* and the *Apology*, or that he was converted to Pythagoreanism in the last month of his life.

I do not pretend that there is no way of removing this contradiction by some assumption or *interpretation*. Burnet and Taylor may have reasons, perhaps even good reasons, for trusting the *Phaedo* and the *Republic* rather than the *Apology*. (But they ought to realize that, assuming the correctness of Plato's portrait, any doubt of Socrates' veracity in the *Apology* makes of him one who lies for the sake of saving his skin.) Such questions, however, do not concern me at the moment. My point is rather that in accepting evidence (*a′*) as against (*a*), Burnet and Taylor are forced to abandon their fundamental methodological assumption 'that Plato really meant what he said'; they must interpret.

But interpretations made unawares must be uncritical; this can be illustrated by the use made by Burnet and Taylor of Aristophanes' evidence. They hold that Aristophanes' jests would be pointless if Socrates had not been a natural philosopher. But it so happens that Socrates (I always assume, with Burnet and Taylor, that the *Apology* is historical) foresaw this very argument. In his apology, he warned his judges against precisely this very interpretation of Aristophanes, insisting most earnestly (*Ap.*, 19c, ff.; see also 20c–e) that he had neither little nor much to do with natural philosophy, but simply nothing at all. Socrates felt as if he were fighting against shadows in this matter, against the shadows of the past (*Ap.*, 18d–e); but we can now say that he was also fighting the shadows of the future. For when he challenged his fellow-citizens to come forward—those who believed Aristophanes and dared to call Socrates a liar—*not one came*. It was 2,300 years before some Platonists made up their minds to answer his challenge.

It may be mentioned, in this connection, that Aristophanes, a moderate anti-democrat, attacked Socrates as a 'sophist', and that most of the sophists were democrats.

(*b*) In the *Apology* (40c, ff.) Socrates takes up an agnostic attitude towards the problem of survival; (*b′*) the *Phaedo* consists mainly of elaborate proofs of the immortality of the soul. This difficulty is discussed by Burnet (in his edition of the *Phaedo*, 1911, pp. xlviii ff.), in a way which does not convince me at all. (Cp. notes 9 to chapter 7, and 44 to the present chapter.) But whether he is right or not, his own discussion proves that he is forced to give up his methodological principle and to *interpret* what Plato says.

(*c*) The Socrates of the *Apology* holds that the wisdom even of the wisest consists in the realization of how little he knows, and that, accordingly, the Delphian saying 'know thyself' must be interpreted as 'know thy limitations'; and he implies that the rulers, more than anybody else, ought to know their limitations. Similar views can be found in other early dialogues. But the main speakers of the *Statesman* and the *Laws* propound the doctrine that the powerful ought to be wise; and by wisdom they no longer mean a knowledge of one's limitations, but rather the initiation into the deeper mysteries of dialectic philosophy—the intuition of the world of Forms or Ideas, or the training in the Royal Science of politics. The same doctrine is expounded, in the *Philebus*, even as part of a discussion of the Delphian saying. (Cp. note 26 to chapter 7.)

(*d*) Apart from these three flagrant contradictions, I may mention two further contradictions which could easily be neglected by those who do not believe that the *Seventh Letter* is genuine, but which seem to me fatal to Burnet who maintains that the *Seventh Letter* is authentic. Burnet's view (untenable even if we neglect this letter; cp. for the whole question note 26 (5) to chapter 3) that Socrates *but not Plato* held the theory of Forms, is contradicted in 342a, ff., of this letter; and his view that the *Republic*, more especially, is Socratic, in 326a (cp. note 14 to chapter 7). Of course, all these difficulties could be removed, but only by interpretation.

(*e*) There are a number of similar although at the same time more subtle and more important contradictions which have been discussed at some length in previous chapters, especially in chapters 6, 7 and 8. I may sum up the most important of these.

(e_1) The attitude towards men, especially towards the young, changes in Plato's portrait in a way which cannot be Socrates' development. Socrates died for the right to talk freely to the young, whom he loved. But in the *Republic*, we find him taking up an attitude of condescension and distrust which resembles the disgruntled attitude of the Athenian Stranger (admittedly Plato himself) in the *Laws* and the general distrust of mankind expressed so often in this work. (Cp. text to notes 17–18 to chapter 4; 18–21 to chapter 7; and 57–58 to chapter 8.)

(e_2) The same sort of thing can be said about Socrates' attitude towards truth and free speech. He died for it. But in the *Republic*, 'Socrates' advocates lying; in the admittedly Platonic *Statesman*, a lie is offered as truth, and in the *Laws*, free thought is suppressed by the establishment of an Inquisition. (Cp. the same places as before, and furthermore notes 1–23 and 40–41 to chapter 8; and note 55 to the present chapter.)

(e_3) The Socrates of the *Apology* and some other dialogues is intellectually modest; in the *Phaedo*, he changes into a man who is assured of the truth of his metaphysical speculations. In the *Republic*, he is a dogmatist, adopting an attitude not far removed from the petrified authoritarianism of the *Statesman* and of the *Laws*. (Cp. text to notes 8–14 and 26 to chapter 7; 15 and 33 to chapter 8; and (*c*) in the present note.)

(e_4) The Socrates of the *Apology* is an individualist; he believes in the self-sufficiency of the human individual. In the *Gorgias*, he is still an individualist. In the

Republic, he is a radical collectivist, very similar to Plato's position in the *Laws*. (Cp. notes 25 and 35 to chapter 5; text to notes 26, 32, 36 and 48–54 to chapter 6 and note 45 to the present chapter.)

(e_5) Again we can say similar things about Socrates' equalitarianism. In the *Meno*, he recognizes that a slave participates in the general intelligence of all human beings, and that he can be taught even pure mathematics; in the *Gorgias*, he defends the equalitarian theory of justice. But in the *Republic*, he despises workers and slaves and is as much opposed to equalitarianism as is Plato in the *Timaeus* and in the *Laws*. (Cp. the passages mentioned under (e_4); furthermore, notes 18 and 29 to chapter 4; note 10 to chapter 7, and note 50 (3) to chapter 8, where *Timaeus*, 51e, is quoted.)

(e_6) The Socrates of the *Apology* and *Crito* is loyal to Athenian democracy. In the *Meno* and in the *Gorgias* (cp. note 45 to this chapter) there are suggestions of a *hostile* criticism; in the *Republic* (and, I believe, in the *Menexenus*), he is an open enemy of democracy; and although Plato expresses himself more cautiously in the *Statesman* and in the beginning of the *Laws*, his political tendencies in the later part of the *Laws* are admittedly (cp. text to note 32 to chapter 6) identical with those of the 'Socrates' of the *Republic*. (Cp. notes 53 and 55 to the present chapter and notes 7 and 14–18 to chapter 4.)

The last point may be further supported by the following. It seems that Socrates, in the *Apology*, is not merely loyal to Athenian democracy, but that he appeals directly to the democratic party by pointing out that Chaerephon, one of the most ardent of his disciples, belonged to their ranks. Chaerephon plays a decisive part in the *Apology*, since by approaching the Oracle, he is instrumental in Socrates' recognition of his mission in life, and thereby ultimately in Socrates' refusal to compromise with the Demos. Socrates introduces this important person by emphasizing the fact (*Apol.*, 20e/21a) that Chaerephon was not only his friend, but also a friend of the people, whose exile he shared, and with whom he returned (presumably, he participated in the fight against the Thirty); that is to say, Socrates chooses as the main witness for his defence an ardent democrat. (There is some independent evidence for Chaerephon's sympathies, such as in Aristophanes' *Clouds*, 104, 501 ff. Chaerephon's appearance in the *Charmides* may be intended to create a kind of balance; the prominence of Critias and Charmides would otherwise create the impression of a pro-Thirty manifesto.) Why does Socrates emphasize his intimacy with a militant member of the democratic party? We cannot assume that this was merely special pleading, intended to move his judges to be more merciful: the whole spirit of his apology is against this assumption. The most likely hypothesis is that Socrates, by pointing out that he had disciples in the democratic camp, intended to deny, by implication, the charge (which also was only implied) that he was a follower of the aristocratic party and a teacher of tyrants. The spirit of the *Apology* excludes the assumption that Socrates was pleading friendship with a democratic leader without being truly sympathetic with the democratic cause. And the same conclusion must be drawn from the passage (*Apol.*, 32b–d) in which he emphasizes his faith in democratic legality, and denounces the Thirty in no uncertain terms.

(6) It is simply the internal evidence of the Platonic dialogues which forces us to assume that they are not entirely historical. We must therefore attempt to interpret

this evidence, by proffering theories which can be critically compared with the evidence, using the method of trial and error. Now we have very strong reason to believe that the *Apology* is in the main historical, for it is the only dialogue which describes a public occurrence of considerable importance and well known to a great number of people. On the other hand, we know that the *Laws* are Plato's latest work (apart from the doubtful *Epinomis*), and that they are frankly 'Platonic'. It is, therefore, the simplest assumption that the dialogues will be historical or Socratic so far as they agree with the tendencies of the *Apology*, and Platonic where they contradict these tendencies. (This assumption brings us practically back to the position which I have described above as the 'older solution' of the Socratic Problem.)

If we consider the tendencies mentioned above under (e_1) to (e_6), we find that we can easily order the most important of the dialogues in such a way that for any single one of these tendencies the similarity with the Socratic *Apology* decreases and that with the Platonic *Laws* increases. This is the series.

Apology and *Crito*—*Meno*—*Gorgias*—*Phaedo*—*Republic*—*Statesman*—*Timaeus*—*Laws*.

Now the fact that this series orders the dialogues according to *all* the tendencies (e_1) to (e_6) is in itself a corroboration of the theory that we are here faced with a development in Plato's thought. But we can get quite independent evidence. 'Stylometric' investigations show that our series agrees with the chronological order in which Plato wrote the dialogues. Lastly, the series, at least up to the *Timaeus*, exhibits also a continually increasing interest in Pythagoreanism (and Eleaticism). This must therefore be another tendency in the development of Plato's thought.

A very different argument is this. We know, from Plato's own testimony in the *Phaedo*, that Antisthenes was one of Socrates' most intimate friends; and we also know that Antisthenes claimed to preserve the true Socratic creed. It is hard to believe that Antisthenes would have been a friend of the Socrates of the *Republic*. Thus we must find a common point of departure for the teaching of Antisthenes and Plato; and this common point we find in the Socrates of the *Apology* and *Crito*, and in *some* of the doctrines put into the mouth of the 'Socrates' of the *Meno*, *Gorgias*, and *Phaedo*.

These arguments are entirely independent of any work of Plato's which has ever been seriously doubted (as the *Alcibiades I* or the *Theages* or the *Letters*). They are also independent of the testimony of Xenophon. They are based solely upon the internal evidence of some of the most famous Platonic dialogues. But they agree with this secondary evidence, especially with the *Seventh Letter*, where in a sketch of his own mental development (325 f.), Plato even refers, unmistakably, to the key passage of the *Republic* as *his own central discovery*: 'I had to state ... that ... never will the race of men be saved from its plight before either the race of the genuine and true philosophers gains political power, or the ruling men in the cities become genuine philosophers, by the grace of God.' (326a; cp. note 14 to chapter 7, and (*d*) in this note, above.) I cannot see how it is possible to accept, with Burnet, this letter as genuine without admitting that the central doctrine of the *Republic* is Plato's, not Socrates'; that is to say, without giving up the fiction that Plato's portrait of Socrates in the *Republic* is historical. (For further evidence, cp. for instance Aristotle, *Sophist. El.*, 183b7: 'Socrates raised questions, but gave no answers; for he confessed that he did not know.' This agrees with the *Apology*, but hardly with the *Gorgias*, and certainly not with the *Phaedo* or the *Republic*. See furthermore Aristotle's famous report on the history of the theory of Ideas, admirably discussed by Field, *op. cit.*; cp. also note 26 to chapter 3.)

(7) Against evidence of this character, the type of evidence used by Burnet and Taylor can have little weight. The following is an example. As evidence for his opinion that Plato was politically more moderate than Socrates, and that Plato's family was rather 'Whiggish', Burnet uses the argument that a member of Plato's family was named 'Demos'. (Cp. *Gorg.*, 481d, 513b.—It is not, however, certain, although probable, that Demos' father Pyrilampes here mentioned is really identical with Plato's uncle and stepfather mentioned in *Charm.*, 158a, and *Parm.*, 126b, i.e. that Demos was a relation of Plato's.) What weight can this have, I ask, compared with the historical record of Plato's two tyrant uncles; with the extant political fragments of Critias (which remain in the family even if Burnet is right, which he hardly is, in attributing them to his grandfather; cp. *Greek Phil.*, I, 338, note 1, with *Charmides*, 157e and 162d, where the poetical gifts of Critias the tyrant are alluded to); with the fact that Critias' father had belonged to the Oligarchy of the Four Hundred (*Lys.*, 12, 66); and with Plato's own writings which combine family pride with not only anti-democratic but even anti-Athenian tendencies? (Cp. the eulogy, in *Timaeus*, 20a, of an enemy of Athens like Hermocrates of Sicily, father-in-law of the older Dionysius.) The purpose behind Burnet's argument is, of course, to strengthen the theory that the *Republic* is Socratic. Another example of bad method may be taken from Taylor, who argues (*Socrates*, note 2 on p. 148 f.; cp. also p. 162) in favour of the view that the *Phaedo* is Socratic (cp. my note 9 to chapter 7): 'In the *Phaedo* [72e] ... the doctrine that "learning is just recognition" is expressly said by Simmias' (this is a slip of Taylor's pen; the speaker is Cebes) 'speaking to Socrates, to be "the doctrine *you* are so constantly repeating". Unless we are willing to regard the *Phaedo* as a gigantic and unpardonable mystification, this seems to me proof that the theory really belongs to Socrates.' (For a similar argument, see Burnet's edition of the *Phaedo*, p. xii, end of chapter ii.) On this I wish to make the following comments: (*a*) It is here *assumed* that Plato considered himself a *historian* when writing this passage, for otherwise his statement would not be 'a gigantic and unpardonable mystification'; in other words, the most questionable and the most central point of the theory is assumed. (*b*) But even if Plato had considered himself a historian (I do not think that he did), the expression 'a gigantic ... etc.' seems to be too strong. Taylor, not Plato, puts 'you' in italics. Plato might only have wished to indicate that he is going to assume that the readers of the dialogue are acquainted with this theory. Or he might have intended to refer to the *Meno*, and thus to himself. (This last explanation is I think almost certainly true, in view of *Phaedo*, 73a, f., with the allusion to diagrams.) Or his pen might have slipped, for some reason or other. Such things are bound to occur, even to historians. Burnet, for example, has to explain Socrates' Pythagoreanism; to do this he makes Parmenides a Pythagorean rather than a pupil of Xenophanes, of whom he writes (*Greek Philosophy*, I, 64): 'the story that he founded the Eleatic school seems to be derived from a playful remark of Plato's which would also prove Homer to have been a Heraclitean.' To this, Burnet adds the footnote: 'Plato, *Soph.*, 242d. See *E. Gr. Ph.*[2], p. 140'. Now I believe that this statement of a historian clearly implies four things, (1) that the passage of Plato which refers to Xenophanes is playful, i.e. not meant seriously, (2) that this

playfulness manifests itself in the reference to Homer, that is, (3) by remarking that he was a Heraclitean, which would, of course, be a very playful remark since Homer lived long before Heraclitus, and (4) that there is no other serious evidence connecting Xenophanes with the Eleatic School. But none of these four implications can be upheld. For we find, (1) that the passage in the *Sophist* (242d) which refers to Xenophanes is not playful, but that it is recommended by Burnet himself, in the methodological appendix to his *Early Greek Philosophy*, as important and as full of valuable historical information; (2) that it contains no reference at all to Homer; and (3) that another passage which contains this reference (*Theaet.*, 179d/e; cp. 152d/e, 160d) with which Burnet mistakenly identified *Sophist*, 242d, in *Greek Philosophy*, I (the mistake is not made in his *Early Greek Philosophy*[2]), does not refer to Xenophanes; nor does it call Homer a Heraclitean, but it says the opposite, namely, that some of Heraclitus' ideas are as old as Homer (which is, of course, much less playful); and (4), there is a clear and important passage in Theophrastus (*Phys. op.*, fragm. 8 = Simplicius, *Phys.*, 28, 4) ascribing to Xenophanes a number of opinions which we know Parmenides shared with him and linking him with Parmenides—to say nothing of D.L. ix, 21–3, or of Timaeus ap. Clement *Strom* 1, 64, 2. This heap of misunderstandings, misinterpretations, misquotations, and misleading omissions (for the created myth, see Kirk and Raven, p. 265) can be found in one single historical remark of a truly great historian such as Burnet. From this we must learn that such things do happen, even to the best of historians: all men are fallible. (A more serious example of this kind of fallibility is the one discussed in note 26 (5) to chapter 3.)

(8) The chronological order of those Platonic dialogues which play a rôle in these arguments is here assumed to be nearly the same as that of the stylometric list of Lutoslawski (*The Origin and Growth of Plato's Logic*, 1897). A list of those dialogues which play a rôle in the text of this book will be found in note 5 to chapter 3. It is drawn up in such a way that there is more uncertainty of date within each group than between the groups. A minor deviation from the stylometric list is the position of the *Euthyphro* which for reasons of its content (discussed in text to note 60 to this chapter) appears to me to be probably later than the *Crito*; but this point is of little importance. (Cp. also note 47 to this chapter.)

57. There is a famous and rather puzzling passage in the *Second Letter* (314c): 'There is no writing of Plato nor will there ever be. What goes by his name really belongs to Socrates turned young and handsome.' The most likely solution of this puzzle is that the passage, if not the whole letter, is spurious. (Cp. Field, *Plato and His Contemporaries*, 200 f., where he gives an admirable summary of the reasons for suspecting the letter, and especially the passages '312d–313c and possibly down to 314c'; concerning 314c, an additional reason is, perhaps, that the forger might have intended to allude to, or to give his interpretation of, a somewhat similar remark in the *Seventh Letter*, 341b/c, quoted in note 32 to chapter 8.) But if for a moment we assume with Burnet (*Greek Philosophy*, I, 212) that the passage is genuine, then the remark 'turned young and handsome' certainly raises a problem, especially as it cannot be taken literally since Socrates is presented in all the Platonic dialogues as old and ugly (the only exception is the *Parmenides*, where he is hardly handsome, although still young). If genuine, the puzzling remark would mean that Plato quite intentionally gave an idealized and not an historical account of Socrates; and it

would fit our interpretation quite well to see that Plato was indeed conscious of re-interpreting Socrates as a young and handsome aristocrat who is, of course, Plato himself. (Cp. also note 11 (2) to chapter 4, note 20 (1) to chapter 6, and note 50 (3) to chapter 8.)

58. I am quoting from the first paragraph of Davies' and Vaughan's introduction to their translation of the *Republic*. Cp. Crossman, *Plato To-Day*, 96.

59. (1) The 'division' or 'split' in Plato's soul is one of the most outstanding impressions of his work, and especially of the *Republic*. Only a man who had to struggle hard to uphold his self-control or the rule of his reason over his animal instincts could emphasize this point as much as Plato did; cp. the passages referred to in note 34 to chapter 5, especially the story of the beast in man (*Rep.*, 588c), which is probably of Orphic origin, and in notes 15 (1)–(4), 17, and 19 to chapter 3, which not only show an astonishing similarity with psycho-analytical doctrines, but might also be claimed to exhibit strong symptoms of repression. (See also the beginning of Book IX, 571d and 575a, which sound like an exposition of the doctrine of the Oedipus Complex. On Plato's attitude to his mother, some light is perhaps thrown by *Republic*, 548e–549d, especially in view of the fact that in 548e his brother Glaucon is identified with the son in question.) *An excellent statement of the conflicts in Plato, and an attempt at a psychological analysis of his will to power, are made by H. Kelsen in *The American Imago*, vol. 3, 1942, pp. 1–110, and Werner Fite, *The Platonic Legend*, 1939.*

Those Platonists who are not prepared to admit that from Plato's longing and clamouring for unity and harmony and unisonity, we may conclude that he was himself disunited and disharmonious, may be reminded that this way of arguing was invented by Plato. (Cp. *Symposium*, 200a, f., where Socrates argues that it is a necessary and not a probable inference that he who loves or desires does not possess what he loves and desires.)

What I have called Plato's *political theory of the soul* (see also text to note 32 to chapter 5), i.e. the division of the soul according to the class-divided society, has long remained the basis of most psychologies. It is the basis of psycho-analysis too. According to Freud's theory, what Plato had called the ruling part of the soul tries to uphold its tyranny by a 'censorship', while the rebellious proletarian animal-instincts, which correspond to the social underworld, really exercise a hidden dictatorship; for they determine the policy of the apparent ruler.—Since Heraclitus' 'flux' and 'war', the realm of social experience has strongly influenced the theories, metaphors, and symbols by which we interpret the physical world around us (and ourselves) to ourselves. I mention only Darwin's adoption, under the influence of Malthus, of the theory of social competition.

(2) A remark may be added here on *mysticism*, in its relation to the closed and open society, and to the strain of civilization.

As McTaggart has shown, in his excellent study *Mysticism* (see his *Philosophical Studies*, edited by S. V. Keeling, 1934, esp. pp. 47 ff.), the fundamental ideas of mysticism are two: (*a*) the doctrine of the *mystic union*, i.e. the assertion that there is a greater unity in the world of realities than that which we recognize in the world of ordinary experience, and (*b*) the doctrine of the *mystic intuition*, i.e. the assertion that there is a way of knowing which 'brings the known into closer and more direct relation with what is known' than is the relation between the knowing subject and the known object in ordinary experience. McTaggart rightly asserts (p. 48) that 'of these two characteristics the mystic unity is the more fundamental', since the mystic intuition is 'an example of the mystic unity'. We may add that a third characteristic, less fundamental still, is (*c*) the *mystic love*, which is an example of mystic unity *and* mystic intuition.

Now it is interesting (and this has not been seen by McTaggart) that in the history of Greek Philosophy, the doctrine of the mystic unity was first clearly asserted by Parmenides in his holistic doctrine of the one (cp. note 41 to the present chapter); next by Plato, who added an elaborate doctrine of mystic intuition and communion with the divine (cp. chapter 8), of which doctrine there are just the very first beginnings in Parmenides; next by Aristotle, e.g. in *De Anima*, 425b30 f.: 'The actual hearing and the actual sound are merged into one'; cp. *Rep.* 507c, ff., 430a20, and 431a1: 'Actual knowledge is identical with its object' (see also *De Anima*, 404b16, and *Metaphysics*, 1072b20 and 1075a2, and cp. Plato's *Timaeus*, 45b–c, 47a–d; *Meno*, 81a, ff.; *Phaedo*, 79d); and next by the Neo-Platonists, who elaborated the doctrine of the mystic love, of which only the beginning can be found in Plato (for example, in his doctrine, *Rep.*, 475 ff., that the philosopher *loves* truth, which is closely connected with the doctrines of holism and the philosopher's communion with the divine truth).

In view of these facts and of our historical analysis, we are led to interpret mysticism as one of the typical reactions to the breakdown of the closed society; a reaction which, *in its origin*, was directed against the open society, and which may be described as an escape into the dream of a paradise in which the tribal unity reveals itself as the unchanging reality.

This interpretation is in direct conflict with that of Bergson in his *Two Sources of Morality and Religion*; for Bergson asserts that it is mysticism which makes the leap from the closed to the open society.

* But it must of course be admitted (as Jacob Viner very kindly pointed out to me in a letter) that mysticism is versatile enough to work in any political direction; and even among the apostles of the open society, mystics and mysticism have their representatives. It is the mystic inspiration of a better, a less divided, world which undoubtedly inspired not only Plato, but also Socrates.*

It may be remarked that in the nineteenth century, especially in Hegel and Bergson, we find an *evolutionary mysticism*, which, by extolling change, seems to stand in direct opposition to Parmenides' and Plato's hatred of change. And yet, the underlying experience of these two forms of mysticism seems to be the same, as shown by the fact that an over-emphasis on change is common to both. Both are reactions to the frightening experience of social change: the one combined with the hope that change may be arrested; the other with a somewhat hysterical (and undoubtedly ambivalent) acceptance of change as real, essential and welcome.—Cp. also notes 32–33 to chapter 11, 36 to chapter 12, and 4, 6, 29, 32 and 58 to chapter 24.

60. The *Euthyphro*, an early dialogue, is usually interpreted as an unsuccessful attempt of Socrates to define piety. Euthyphro himself is the caricature of a popular 'pietist' who knows exactly what the gods wish. To Socrates' question 'What is piety and what is impiety?' he is made to answer: 'Piety is acting as I do! That is to say, prosecuting any one guilty of murder, sacrilege, or of any similar crime, whether he be

your father or your mother ...; while not to prosecute them is impiety' (5, d/e). Euthyphro is presented as prosecuting his father for having murdered a serf. (According to the evidence quoted by Grote, *Plato*, I, note to p. 312, every citizen was bound by Attic law to prosecute in such cases.)

61. *Menexenus*, 235b. Cp. note 35 to this chapter, and the end of note 19 to chapter 6.
62. The claim that if you want security you must give up liberty has become a mainstay of the revolt against freedom. But nothing is less true. There is, of course, no absolute security in life. But what security can be attained depends on our own watchfulness, enforced by institutions to help us watch—i.e. by *democratic institutions* which are devised (using Platonic language) to enable the herd to watch, and to judge, their watch-dogs.
63. With the 'variations' and 'irregularities', cp. *Republic*, 547a, quoted in the text to notes 39 and 40 to chapter 5. Plato's obsession with the problems of propagation and birth control may perhaps be explained in part by the fact that he understood the implications of population growth. Indeed (cp. text to note 7 to this chapter) the 'Fall', the loss of the tribal paradise, is caused by a 'natural' or 'original' fault of man, as it were: by a maladjustment in his natural rate of breeding. Cp. also notes 39 (3) to ch. 5, and 34 to ch. 4. With the next quotation further below in this paragraph, cp. *Republic*, 566e, and text to note 20 to chapter 4.—Crossman, whose treatment of the period of tyranny in Greek history is excellent (cp. *Plato To-Day*, 27–30), writes: 'Thus it was the tyrants who really created the Greek *State*. They broke down the old tribal organization of primitive aristocracy ...' (*op. cit.*, 29). This explains why Plato hated tyranny, perhaps even more than freedom: cp. *Republic*, 577c.—(See, however, note 69 to this chapter.) His passages on tyranny, especially 565–568, are a brilliant sociological analysis of a consistent power-politics. I should like to call it the first attempt towards a *logic of power*. (I chose this term in analogy to F. A. von Hayek's use of the term *logic of choice* for the pure economic theory.)—The logic of power is fairly simple, and has often been applied in a masterly way. The opposite kind of politics is much more difficult; partly because the logic of anti-power politics, i.e. the *logic of freedom*, is hardly understood yet.
64. It is well known that most of Plato's political proposals, including the proposed communism of women and children, were 'in the air' in the Periclean period. Cp. the excellent summary in Adam's edition of the *Republic*, vol. I, p. 354 f., *and A. D. Winspear, *The Genesis of Plato's Thought*, 1940.*
65. Cp. V. Pareto, *Treatise on General Sociology*, §1843 (English translation: *The Mind and Society*, 1935, vol. III, pp. 1281); cp. note 1 to chapter 13, where the passage is quoted more fully.
66. Cp. the effect which Glaucon's presentation of Lycophron's theory had on Carneades (cp. note 54 to chapter 6), and later, on Hobbes. The professed 'a-morality' of so many Marxists is also a case in point. Leftists frequently believe in their own immorality. (This, although not much to the point, is sometimes more modest and more pleasant than the dogmatic self-righteousness of many reactionary moralists.)
67. *Money* is one of the symbols as well as one of the difficulties of the open society. There is no doubt that we have not yet mastered the rational control of its use; its greatest misuse is that it can buy political power. (The most direct form of this misuse is the institution of the slave-market; but just this institution is defended in *Republic*, 563b; cp. note 17 to chapter 4; and in the *Laws*, Plato is not opposed to the

political influence of wealth; cp. note 20 (1) to chapter 6.) From the point of view of an individualistic society, money is fairly important. It is part of the institution of the (partially) *free market*, which gives the consumer some measure of control over production. Without some such institution, the producer may control the market to such a degree that he ceases to produce for the sake of consumption, while the consumer consumes largely for the sake of production.—The sometimes glaring misuse of money has made us rather sensitive, and Plato's opposition between money and friendship is only the first of many conscious or unconscious attempts to utilize these sentiments for the purpose of political propaganda.

68. The group-spirit of tribalism is, of course, not entirely lost. It manifests itself, for instance, in the most valuable experiences of *friendship and comradeship*; also, in youthful tribalistic movements like the boy-scouts (or the German Youth Movement), and in certain clubs and adult societies, as described, for instance, by Sinclair Lewis in *Babbitt*. The importance of this perhaps most universal of all emotional and æsthetic experiences must not be underrated. Nearly all social movements, totalitarian as well as humanitarian, are influenced by it. It plays an important rôle in war, and is one of the most powerful weapons of the revolt against freedom; admittedly also in peace, and in revolts against tyranny, but in these cases its humanitarianism is often endangered by its romantic tendencies.—A conscious and not unsuccessful attempt to revive it for the purpose of arresting society and of perpetuating a class rule seems to have been the English Public School System. ('No one can grow up to be a good man unless his earliest years were given to noble games' is its motto, taken from *Republic*, 558b.)

Another product and symptom of the loss of the tribalistic group-spirit is, of course, Plato's emphasis upon the analogy between politics and medicine (cp. chapter 8, especially note 4), an emphasis which expresses the feeling that the body of society is sick, i.e. the feeling of strain, of drift. 'From the time of Plato on, the minds of political philosophers seem to have recurred to this comparison between medicine and politics,' says G. E. G. Catlin (*A Study of the Principles of Politics*, 1930, note to 458, where Thomas Aquinas, G. Santayana, and Dean Inge are quoted to support his statement; cp. also the quotations in *op. cit.*, note to 37, from Mill's *Logic*). Catlin also speaks most characteristically (*op. cit.*, 459) of 'harmony' and of the 'desire for protection, whether assured by the mother or by society'. (Cp. also note 18 to chapter 5.)

69. Cp. chapter 7 (note 24 and text; see *Athen.*, XI, 508) for the names of nine such disciples of Plato (including the younger Dionysius and Dio). I suppose that Plato's repeated insistence upon the use, not only of force, but of '*persuasion* and force' (cp. *Laws*, 722b, and notes 5, 10, and 18 to chapter 8), was meant as a criticism of the tactics of the Thirty, whose propaganda was indeed primitive. But this would imply that Plato was well aware of Pareto's recipe for utilizing sentiments instead of fighting them. That Plato's friend Dio (cp. note 25 to chapter 7) ruled Syracuse as a tyrant is admitted even by Meyer in his defence of Dio whose fate he explains, in spite of his admiration for Plato as a politician, by pointing out the 'gulf between' (the Platonic) 'theory and practice' (*op. cit.*, V, 999). Meyer says of Dio (*loc. cit.*), 'The ideal king had become, externally, indistinguishable from the contemptible tyrant.' But he believes that, internally as it were, Dio remained an idealist, and that he suffered deeply when political necessity forced murder (especially that of his ally

Heraclides) and similar measures upon him. I think, however, that Dio acted according to Plato's theory; a theory which, by the logic of power, drove Plato in the *Laws* to admit even the goodness of tyranny (709e, ff.; at the same place, there may also be a suggestion that the débâcle of the Thirty was due to their great number: Critias alone would have been all right).

70. The tribal paradise is, of course, a myth (although some primitive people, most of all the Eskimos, seem to be happy enough). There may have been no sense of drift in the closed society, but there is ample evidence of other forms of fear—fear of demoniac powers behind nature. The attempt to revive this fear, and to use it against the intellectuals, the scientists, etc., characterizes many late manifestations of the revolt against freedom. It is to the credit of Plato, the disciple of Socrates, that it never occurred to him to present his enemies as the offspring of the sinister demons of darkness. In this point, he remained enlightened. He had little inclination to idealize the evil which was to him simply debased, or degenerate, or impoverished goodness. (Only in one passage in the *Laws*, 896e and 898c, there is what may be a suggestion of an abstract idealization of the evil.)

71. A final note may be added here in connection with my remark on *the return to the beasts*. Since the intrusion of Darwinism into the field of human problems (an intrusion for which Darwin should not be blamed) there have been many 'social zoologists' who have proved that the human race is bound to degenerate physically, because insufficient physical competition, and the possibility of protecting the body by the efforts of the mind, prevent natural selection from acting upon our bodies. The first to formulate this idea (not that he believed in it) was Samuel Butler, who wrote: 'The one serious danger which this writer' (an Erewhonian writer) 'apprehended was that the machines' (and, we may add, civilization in general) 'would so ... lessen the severity of competition, that many persons of inferior physique would escape detection and transmit their inferiority to their descendants.' (*Erewhon*, 1872; cp. Everyman's edition, p. 161.) The first as far as I know to write a bulky volume on this theme was W. Schallmayer (cp. note 65 to chapter 12), one of the founders of modern racialism. In fact, Butler's theory has been continually rediscovered (especially by 'biological naturalists' in the sense of chapter 5, above). According to some modern writers (see, for example, G. H. Estabrooks, *Man: The Mechanical Misfit*, 1941), man made the decisive mistake when he became civilized, and especially when he began to help the weak; before this, he was an almost perfect man-beast; but civilization, with its artificial methods of protecting the weak, leads to degeneration, and therefore must ultimately destroy itself. In reply to such arguments, we should, I think, first admit that man is likely to disappear one day from this world; but we should add that this is also true of even the most perfect beasts, to say nothing of those which are only 'almost perfect'. The theory that the human race might live a little longer if it had not made the fatal mistake of helping the weak is most questionable; but even if it were true—is mere length of survival of the race really all we want? Or is the almost perfect man-beast so eminently valuable that we should prefer a prolongation of his existence (he did exist for quite a long time, anyway) to our experiment of helping the weak?

Mankind, I believe, has not done so badly. In spite of the treason of some of its intellectual leaders, in spite of the stupefying effects of Platonic methods in education and the devastating results of propaganda, there have been some surprising successes. Many weak men have been helped, and for nearly a hundred years slavery has been practically abolished. Some say it will soon be re-introduced. I feel more optimistic; and, after all, it will depend on ourselves. But even if all this should be lost again, and even if we had to return to the almost perfect man-beast, this would not alter the fact that once upon a time (even if the time was short), slavery did disappear from the face of the earth. This achievement and its memory may, I believe, compensate some of us for all our misfits, mechanical or otherwise; and it may even compensate some of us for the fatal mistake made by our forefathers when they missed the golden opportunity of arresting all change—of returning to the cage of the closed society and establishing, for ever and ever, a perfect zoo of almost perfect monkeys.

Notes to Volume II

NOTES TO CHAPTER ELEVEN

1. That Aristotle's criticism of Plato is very frequently, and in important places, unmerited, has been admitted by many students of the history of philosophy. It is one of the few points in which even the admirers of Aristotle find it difficult to defend him, since usually they are admirers of Plato as well. Zeller, to quote just one example, comments (cp. *Aristotle and the Earlier Peripatetics*, English translation by Costelloe and Muirhead, 1897, II, 261, n. 2), upon the distribution of land in Aristotle's Best State: 'There is a similar plan in Plato's *Laws*, 745c seqq.; Aristotle, however, in *Politics* 1265b24 considers Plato's arrangement, merely on account of a trifling difference, highly objectionable.' A similar remark is made by G. Grote, *Aristotle* (Ch. XIV, end of second paragraph). In view of many criticisms of Plato which strongly suggest that envy of Plato's originality is part of his motive, Aristotle's much-admired solemn assurance (*Nicomachean Ethics*, I, 6, 1) that the sacred duty of giving preference to truth forces him to sacrifice even what is most dear to him, namely, his love for Plato, sounds to me somewhat hypocritical.
2. Cp. Th. Gomperz, *Greek Thinkers* (I am quoting from the German edition, III, 298, i.e. Book 7, Ch. 31, § 6). See especially Aristotle's *Politics*, 1313a.

   G. C. Field (in *Plato and His Contemporaries*, 114 f.) defends Plato and Aristotle against the 'reproach ... that, with the possibility, and, in the case of the latter, the actuality of this' (i.e. the Macedonian conquest) 'before their eyes, they ... say nothing of these new developments'. But Field's defence (perhaps directed against Gomperz) is unsuccessful, in spite of his strong comments upon those who make such a reproach. (Field says: 'this criticism betrays ... a singular lack of understanding.') Of course, it is correct to claim, as Field does, 'that a hegemony like that exercised by Macedon ... was no new thing'; but Macedon was in Plato's eyes at least half-barbarian and therefore a natural enemy. Field is also right in saying that 'the destruction of independence by Macedon' was not a complete one; but did Plato or Aristotle foresee that it was not to become complete? I believe that a defence like Field's cannot possibly succeed, simply because it would have to prove too much; namely, that the significance of Macedon's threat could not have been clear, at the time, to any observer; but this is disproved, of course, by the example of Demosthenes. The question is: why did Plato, who like Isocrates had taken some interest in pan-Hellenic nationalism (cp. notes 48–50 to chapter 8, *Rep.*, 470, and the *Eighth Letter*, 353e, which Field claims to be 'certainly genuine') and who was apprehensive of a 'Phœnician and Oscan' threat to Syracuse, why did he ignore Macedon's threat to Athens? A likely reply to the corresponding question concerning Aristotle is: because he belonged to the pro-Macedonian party. A reply in Plato's case is suggested by Zeller (*op. cit.*, II, 41) in his defence of Aristotle's right to support Macedon: 'So satisfied was Plato of the intolerable character of the existing political position that he advocated sweeping changes.' ('Plato's follower', Zeller continues, referring to Aristotle, 'could the less evade the same convictions, since he had a keener insight into men and things ...') In other words, the answer might be that Plato's hatred of Athenian democracy exceeded so much even his pan-Hellenic nationalism that he was, like Isocrates, looking forward to the Macedonian conquest.

3. This and the following three quotations are from Aristotle's *Politics*, 1254b–1255a; 1254a; 1255a; 1260a.—See also: 1252a, f. (I, 2, 2–5); 1253b, ff. (I, 4, 386, and especially I, 5); 1313b (V, 11, 11). Furthermore: *Metaphysics*, 1075a, where freemen and slaves are also opposed 'by nature'. But we find also the passage: 'Some slaves have the souls of freemen, and others their bodies' (*Politics*, 1254b). Cp. with Plato's *Timaeus*, 51e, quoted in note 50 (2), to chapter 8.—For a trifling mitigation, and a typically 'balanced judgement' of Plato's *Laws*, see *Politics*, 1260b: 'Those' (this is a somewhat typical Aristotelian way of referring to Plato) 'are wrong who forbid us even to converse with slaves and say that we should only use the language of command; for slaves must be admonished' (Plato had said, in *Laws*, 777e, that they should not be admonished) 'even more than children.' Zeller, in his long list of the personal virtues of Aristotle (*op. cit.*, I, 44), mentions his 'nobility of principles' and his 'benevolence to slaves'. I cannot help remembering the perhaps less noble but certainly more benevolent principle put forward much earlier by Alcidamas and Lycophron, namely, that there should be no slaves at all. W. D. Ross (*Aristotle*, 2nd ed., 1930, pp. 241 ff.) defends Aristotle's attitude towards slavery by saying: 'Where to us he seems reactionary, he may have seemed revolutionary to them', viz., to his contemporaries. In support of this view, Ross mentions Aristotle's doctrine that Greek should not enslave Greek. But this doctrine was hardly very revolutionary since Plato had taught it, probably half a century before Aristotle. And that Aristotle's views were indeed reactionary can be best seen from the fact that he repeatedly finds it necessary to defend them against the doctrine that no man is a slave by nature, and further from his own testimony to the anti-slavery tendencies of the Athenian democracy.

An excellent statement on Aristotle's *Politics* can be found in the beginning of Chapter XIV of G. Grote's *Aristotle*, from which I quote a few sentences: 'The scheme ... of government proposed by Aristotle, in the two last books of his *Politics*, as representing his own ideas of something like perfection, is evidently founded upon the *Republic* of Plato: from whom he differs in the important circumstance of not admitting either community of property or community of wives and children. Each of these philosophers recognizes one separate class of inhabitants, relieved from all private toil and all money-getting employments, and constituting exclusively the citizens of the commonwealth. This small class is in effect *the city—the commonwealth*: the remaining inhabitants are not a part of the commonwealth, they are only appendages to it—indispensable indeed, but still appendages, in the same manner as slaves or cattle.' Grote recognizes that Aristotle's Best State, where it deviates from the *Republic*, largely copies Plato's *Laws*. Aristotle's dependence upon Plato is prominent even where he expresses his acquiescence in the victory of democracy; cp. especially *Politics*, III, 15; 11–13; 1286b (a parallel passage is IV, 13; 10; 1297b). The passage ends by saying of democracy: 'No other form of government appears to be possible any longer'; but this result is reached by an argument that follows very closely Plato's story of the decline and fall of the state in Books VIII–IX of the *Republic*; and this in spite of the fact that Aristotle criticizes Plato's story severely (for instance in V, 12; 1316a, f.).

4. Aristotle's use of the word 'banausic' in the sense of 'professional' or 'money earning' is clearly shown in *Politics*, VIII, 6, 3 ff. (1340b) and especially 15 f. (1341b). Every professional, for example a flute player, and of course every artisan or labourer, is 'banausic', that is to say, not a free man, not a citizen, even though he is not a real slave; the status of a 'banausic' man is one of 'partial or limited slavery' (*Politics*, I, 14; 13; 1260a/b). The word '*banausos*' derives, I gather, from a pre-Hellenic word for 'fire-worker'. Used as an attribute it means that a man's origin and caste 'disqualify him from prowess in the field'. (Cp. Greenidge, quoted by Adam in his edition of the *Republic*, note to 495e30.) It may be translated by 'low-caste', 'cringing', 'degrading', or in some contexts by 'upstart'. Plato used the word in the same sense as Aristotle. In the *Laws* (741e and 743d), the term '*banausia*' is used to describe the depraved state of a man who makes money by means other than the hereditary possession of land. See also the *Republic*, 495e and 590c. But if we remember the tradition that Socrates was a mason; and Xenophon's story (*Mem.* II, 7); and Antisthenes' praise of hard work; and the attitude of the Cynics; then it seems unlikely that Socrates agreed with the aristocratic prejudice that money earning must be degrading. (The *Oxford English Dictionary* proposes to render 'banausic' as 'merely mechanical, proper to a mechanic', and quotes Grote, *Eth. Fragm.*, vi, 227 = *Aristotle*, 2nd edn, 1880, p. 545; but this rendering is much too narrow, and Grote's passage does not justify this interpretation, which may originally rest upon a misunderstanding of Plutarch. It is interesting that in Shakespeare's *Midsummer Night's Dream* the term 'mere mechanicals' is used precisely in the sense of 'banausic' men; and this use might well be connected with a passage on Archimedes in North's translation of the *Life of Marcellus*.)

In *Mind*, vol. 47, there is an interesting discussion between A. E. Taylor and F. M. Cornford, in which the former (pp. 197 ff.) defends his view that Plato, when speaking of 'the god' in a certain passage of the *Timaeus*, may have had in mind a 'peasant cultivator' who 'serves' by bodily labour; a view which is, I think most convincingly, criticized by Cornford (pp. 329 ff.). Plato's attitude towards all 'banausic' work, and especially manual labour, bears on this problem; and when (p. 198, note) Taylor uses the argument that Plato compares his gods 'with shepherds or sheep-dogs in charge of a flock of sheep' (*Laws*, 901e, 907a), then we could point out that the activities of *nomads* and *hunters* are quite consistently considered by Plato as noble or even divine; but the sedentary 'peasant cultivator' is banausic and depraved. Cp. note 32 to chapter 4, and text.

5. The two passages that follow are from *Politics* (1337b, 4 and 5).
6. The 1939 edition of the *Pocket Oxford Dictionary* still says: 'liberal ... (of education) fit for a gentleman, of a general literary rather than technical kind'. This shows most clearly the everlasting power of Aristotle's influence.

   I admit that there is a serious problem of a professional education, that of *narrow-mindedness*. But I do not believe that a 'literary' education is the remedy; for it may create its own peculiar kind of narrow-mindedness, its peculiar snobbery. And in our day no man should be considered educated if he does not take an interest in science. The usual defence that an interest in electricity or stratigraphy need not be more enlightening than an interest in human affairs only betrays a complete lack of understanding of human affairs. For science is not merely a collection of facts about electricity, etc.; it is one of the most important spiritual movements of our day. Anybody who does not attempt to acquire an understanding of this movement cuts himself off from the most remarkable development in the history of human affairs. Our so-called Arts Faculties, based upon the theory that by means of a literary and historical education they introduce the student into the spiritual life of man, have therefore become obsolete in their present form. There can be no history of man which excludes a history of his intellectual struggles and achievements; and there can be no history of ideas which excludes the history of scientific ideas. But literary education has an even more serious aspect. Not only does it fail to educate the student, who is often to become a teacher, to an understanding of the greatest spiritual movement of his own day, but it also often fails to educate him to intellectual honesty. Only if the student experiences how easy it is to err, and how hard to make even a small advance in the field of knowledge, only then can he obtain a feeling for the standards of intellectual honesty, a respect for truth, and a disregard of authority and bumptiousness. But nothing is more necessary to-day than the spread of these modest intellectual virtues. 'The mental power', T. H. Huxley wrote in *A Liberal Education*, 'which will be of most importance in your ... life will be the power of seeing things as they are without regard to authority ... But at school and at college, you shall know of no source of truth but authority.' I admit that, unfortunately, this is true also of many courses in science, which by some teachers is still treated as if it was a 'body of knowledge', as the ancient phrase goes. But this idea will one day, I hope, disappear; for science can be taught as a fascinating part of human history—as a quickly developing growth of bold hypotheses, controlled by experiment, and by *criticism*. Taught in this way, as a part of the history of 'natural philosophy', and of the history of problems and of ideas, it could become the basis of a new liberal University education; of one whose aim, where it cannot produce experts, will be to produce at least *men who can distinguish between a charlatan and an expert*. This modest and liberal aim will be far beyond anything that our Arts Faculties nowadays achieve.
7. *Politics*, VIII, 3, 2 (1337b): 'I must repeat over and again, that the first principle of all action is leisure.' Previously, in VII, 15, 1 f. (1334a), we read: 'Since the end of individuals and of states is the same ... they should both contain the virtues of leisure ... For the proverb says truly, "There is no leisure for slaves".' Cp. also the reference in note 9 to this section, and *Metaphysics*, 1072b23.

   Concerning Aristotle's 'admiration and deference for the leisured classes', cp. for example the following passage from the *Politics*, IV (VII), 8, 4–5 (1293b/1294a): 'Birth and education as a rule go together with wealth ... The rich are already in possession of those advantages the want of which is a temptation to crime, and hence they are called noblemen and gentlemen. Now it appears to be impossible that a state should be badly governed if the best citizens rule ...' Aristotle, however, not only admires the rich, but is also, like Plato, a racialist (cp. *op. cit.*, III, 13, 2–3, 1283a): 'The nobly born are citizens in a truer sense of the word than the low born ... Those who come from better ancestors are likely to be better men, for nobility is excellence of race.'

8. Cp. Th. Gomperz, *Greek Thinkers*. (I am quoting from the German edition, vol. III, 263, i.e. book 6, ch. 27, § 7.)
9. Cp. *Nicomachean Ethics*, X, 7, 6. The Aristotelian phrase, '*the good life*', seems to have caught the imagination of many modern admirers who associate with this phrase something like a 'good life' in the Christian sense—a life devoted to help, service, and the quest for the 'higher values'. But this interpretation is the result of a mistaken idealization of Aristotle's intentions; Aristotle was exclusively concerned with the 'good life' of feudal gentlemen, and this 'good life' he did not envisage as a life of good deeds, but as a *life of refined leisure*, spent in the pleasant company of friends who are equally well situated.
10. I do not think that even the term 'vulgarization' would be too strong, considering that to Aristotle himself 'professional' means 'vulgar', and considering that he certainly made a profession of Platonic philosophy. Besides, he made it dull, as even Zeller admits in the midst of his eulogy (*op. cit.*, I, 46): 'He cannot inspire us ... at all in the same way as Plato does. His work is drier, more professional ... than Plato's has been.'
11. Plato presented in the *Timaeus* (42a f., 90e f., and especially 91d f.; see note 6 (7) to chapter 3) a general theory of the *origin of species by way of degeneration*, down from the Gods and the first man. Man first degenerates into a woman, then further to the higher and lower animals and to the plants. It is, as Gomperz says (*Greek Thinkers*, book 5, ch. 19, § 3; I am quoting from the German edition, vol. 11, 482), 'a theory of descent in the literal sense or a theory of devolution, as opposed to the modern theory of evolution which, since it assumes an ascending sequence, might be called a theory of ascent.' Plato's mythical and possibly semi-ironical presentation of this theory of descent by degeneration makes use of the Orphic and Pythagorean theory of the transmigration of the soul. All this (and the important fact that evolutionary theories which made the lower forms precede the higher were in vogue at least as early as Empedocles) must be remembered when we hear from Aristotle that Speusippus, together with certain Pythagoreans, believed in an evolutionary theory according to which the best and most divine, which are first in rank, come last in the chronological order of development. Aristotle speaks (*Met.*, 1072b30) of 'those who suppose, with the Pythagoreans and Speusippus, that supreme beauty and goodness are not present in the beginning'. From this passage we may conclude, perhaps, that some Pythagoreans had used the myth of transmigration (possibly under the influence of Xenophanes) as the vehicle of a 'theory of ascent'. This surmise is supported by Aristotle, who says (*Met.*, 1091a34): 'The mythologists seem to agree with some thinkers of the present day' (an allusion, I suppose, to Speusippus) '... who say that the good as well as the beautiful make their appearance in nature only after nature has made some progress.' It also seems as if Speusippus had taught that the world will in the course of its development become

a Parmenidian *One*—an organized and fully harmonious whole. (Cp. *Met.*, 1092a14, where a thinker who maintains that the more perfect always comes from the imperfect, is quoted as saying that 'the One itself does not yet exist'; cp. also *Met.*, 1091a11.) Aristotle himself consistently expresses, at the places quoted, his opposition to these 'theories of ascent'. His argument is that it is a complete man that produces man, and that the incomplete seed is not prior to man. In view of this attitude, Zeller can hardly be right in attributing to Aristotle what is practically the Speusippian theory. (Cp. Zeller, *Aristotle*, etc., vol. II, 28 f. A similar interpretation is propounded by H. F. Osborn, *From the Greeks to Darwin*, 1908, pp. 48–56.) We may have to accept Gomperz's interpretation, according to which Aristotle taught the *eternity and invariability of the human species and at least of the higher animals*. Thus his morphological orders must be interpreted as neither chronological nor genealogical. (Cp. *Greek Thinkers*, book 6, ch. 11, § 10, and especially ch. 13, §§ 6 f., and the notes to these passages.) But there remains, of course, the possibility that Aristotle was inconsistent in this point, as he was in many others, and that his arguments against Speusippus are due to his wish to assert his independence. See also note 6 (7) to chapter 3, and notes 2 and 4 to chapter 4.

12. Aristotle's First Mover, that is, God, is prior in time (though he is eternal) and has the predicate of goodness. For the evidence concerning the identification of formal and final cause mentioned in this paragraph, see note 15 to this chapter.
13. For Plato's biological teleology see *Timaeus*, 73a–76e. Gomperz comments rightly (*Greek Thinkers*, book 5, ch. 19, § 7; German edn, vol. II, 495 f.) that Plato's teleology is only understandable if we remember that 'animals are degenerate men, and that their organization may therefore exhibit purposes which were originally only the ends of man'.
14. For Plato's version of the theory of the *natural places*, see *Timaeus*, 60b–63a, and especially 63b f. Aristotle adopts the theory with only minor changes and explains like Plato the 'lightness' and 'heaviness' of bodies by the 'upward' and 'downward' direction of their natural movements towards their natural places; cp. for instance *Physics*, 192b13; also *Metaphysics*, 1065b10.
15. Aristotle is not always quite definite and consistent in his statements on this problem. Thus he writes in the *Metaphysics* (1044a35): 'What is the formal cause (of man)? His Essence. The final cause? His end. But *perhaps* these two are the same.' In other parts of the same work he seems to be more assured of the identity between the *Form* and the *end* of a change or movement. Thus we read (1069b/1070a): 'Everything that changes ... is changed *by* something *into* something. That by which it is changed is the immediate mover; ... that into which it is changed, the Form.' And later (1070a, 9/10): 'There are three kinds of substance: first, matter ...; secondly, the nature towards which it moves; and thirdly, the particular substance which is composed of these two.' Now since what is here called 'nature' is as a rule called 'Form' by Aristotle, and since it is here described as an end of movement, we have: *Form = end*.
16. For the doctrine that movement is the realization or actualization of potentialities, see for instance *Metaphysics*, Book IX; or 1065b17, where the term 'buildable' is used to describe a definite potentiality of a prospective house: 'When the "buildable" ... actually exists, then it is being built; and this is the process of building.' Cp. also Aristotle's *Physics*, 201b4 f.; furthermore, see Gomperz, *op. cit.*, book 6, ch. 11, § 5.

17. Cp. *Metaphysics*, 1049b5. See further Book V, ch. IV, and especially 1015a12 f., Book VII, ch. IV, especially 1029b15.
18. For the definition of the soul as the First Entelechy, see the reference given by Zeller, *op. cit.*, vol. II, p. 3, n. 1. For the meaning of Entelechy as formal cause, see *op. cit.*, vol. I, 379, note 2. Aristotle's use of this term is anything but precise. (See also *Met.*, 1035b15.) Cp. also note 19 to chapter 5, and text.
19. For this and the next quotation see Zeller, *op. cit.*, I, 46.
20. Cp. *Politics*, II, 8, 21 (1269a), with its references to Plato's various Myths of the Earthborn (*Rep.*, 414c; *Pol.*, 271a; *Tim.*, 22c; *Laws*, 677a).
21. Cp. Hegel, *Lectures on the Philosophy of History*, transl. by J. Sibree, London 1914, Introduction, 23; see also Loewenberg's *Hegel—Selections* (The Modern Student's Library), 366.—The whole Introduction, especially this and the following pages, shows clearly Hegel's dependence upon Aristotle. That Hegel was aware of it is shown by the way in which he alluded to Aristotle on p. 59 (Loewenberg's edition, 412).
22. Hegel, *op. cit.*, 23 (Loewenberg's edition, 365).
23. Cp. Caird, *Hegel* (Blackwood 1911), 26 f.
24. The next quotations are from the place referred to in notes 21 and 22.
25. For the following remarks, see *Hegel's Philosophical Propaedeutics*, 2nd Year, *Phenomenology of the Spirit*, transl. by W. T. Harris (Loewenberg's edition, 68 ff.). I deviate slightly from this translation. My remarks allude to the following interesting passages: § 23: 'The impulse of self-consciousness' ('self-consciousness' in German means also self-assertion; cp. the end of chapter 16) 'consists in this: to realize its ... "true nature" ... It is therefore ... active ... in asserting itself externally ...' § 24: 'Self-consciousness has in its culture, or movement, three stages: ... (2) *in so far as it is related to another self ... : the relation of master and slave (domination and servitude)*.' Hegel does not mention any other 'relation to another self'.—We read further: '(3) *The Relation of Master and Slave* ... § 32: In order to assert itself as free being and *to obtain recognition* as such, self-consciousness must exhibit itself to another self ... § 33: ... With the reciprocal demand for recognition there enters ... the relation of master and slave between them ... § 34: Since ... each must strive to assert and prove himself ... the one who prefers life to freedom enters into a condition of slavery, thereby showing that he has not the capacity' ('nature' would have been Aristotle's or Plato's expression) '... for his independence ... § 35: ... The one who serves is devoid of selfhood and has another self in place of his own ... The master, on the contrary, looks upon the servant as reduced, and upon his own individual will as preserved and elevated ... § 36: The individual will of the servant ... is cancelled in his fear of the master ...' etc. It is difficult to overlook an element of hysteria in this theory of human relations and their reduction to mastership and servitude. I hardly doubt that Hegel's method of burying his thoughts under heaps of words, which one must remove in order to get to his meaning (as a comparison between my various quotations and the original may show) is one of the symptoms of his hysteria; it is a kind of escape, a way of shunning the daylight. I do not doubt that this method of his would make as excellent an object for psycho-analysis as his wild dreams of domination and submission. (It must be mentioned that Hegel's dialectics—see the next chapter—carries him, at the end of § 36 here quoted, beyond the master–slave relation 'to the universal will, the transition to positive

freedom'. As will be seen from chapter 12 (especially sections II and IV), these terms are just euphemisms for the totalitarian state. Thus, mastership and servitude are very appropriately 'reduced to components' of totalitarianism.)

With Hegel's remark quoted here (cp. § 35) that the slave is the man who prefers life to freedom, compare Plato's remark (*Republic*, 387a) that free men are those who fear slavery more than death. In a sense, this is true enough; those who are not prepared to fight for their freedom will lose it. But the theory which is implied by both Plato and Hegel, and which is very popular with later authors also, is that men who give in to superior force, or who do not die rather than give in to an armed gangster, are, by nature, 'born slaves' who do not deserve to fare better. This theory, I assert, can be held only by the most violent enemies of civilization.

26. For a criticism of Wittgenstein's view that, while science investigates matters of fact, the business of philosophy is the clarification of meaning, see notes 46 and especially 51 and 52 to this chapter. (Cp. further, H. Gomperz, 'The Meanings of Meaning', in *Philosophy of Science*, vol. 8, 1941, especially p. 183.)

For the whole problem to which this digression (down to note 54 to this chapter) is devoted, viz. the problem of *methodological essentialism versus methodological nominalism*, cp. notes 27–30 to chapter 3, and text; see further especially note 38 to the present chapter.

27. For Plato's, or rather Parmenides', distinction between knowledge and opinion (a distinction which continued to be popular with more modern writers, for example with Locke and Hobbes), see notes 22 and 26 to chapter 3, and text; further, notes 19 to chapter 5, and 25–27 to chapter 8. For Aristotle's corresponding distinction, cp. for example *Metaphysics* 1039b31 and *Anal. Post.*, I, 33 (88b30 ff.); II, 19 (100b5).

For Aristotle's distinction between *demonstrative* and *intuitive* knowledge, see the last chapter of the *Anal. Post.* (II, 19, especially 100b 5–17; see also 72b 18–24, 75b31, 84a31, 90a6–91a11.) For the connection between demonstrative knowledge and the 'causes' of a thing which are 'distinct from its essential nature' and thereby require a middle term, see *op. cit.*, II, 8 (especially 93a5, 93b26). For the analogous connection between intellectual intuition and the 'indivisible form' which it grasps—the indivisible essence and individual nature which is identical with its cause—see *op. cit.*, 72b24, 77a4, 85a1, 88b35. See also *op. cit.*, 90a31: 'To know the nature of a thing is to know the reason why it is' (i.e. its cause); and 93b21: 'There are essential natures which are immediate, i.e. basic premises.'

For Aristotle's recognition that we must stop somewhere in the regression of proofs or demonstrations, and accept certain *principles* without proof, see for example *Metaphysics*, 1006a7: 'It is impossible to prove everything, for then there would arise an infinite regression ...' See also *Anal. Post.*, II, 3 (90b, 18–27).

I may mention that my analysis of Aristotle's theory of definition agrees largely with that of Grote, but partly disagrees with that of Ross. The very great difference between the interpretations of these two writers may be just indicated by two quotations, both taken from chapters devoted to the analysis of Aristotle's *Anal. Post.*, Book II. 'In the second book, Aristotle turns to consider demonstration as the instrument whereby *definition* is reached.' (Ross, *Aristotle*, 2nd edn, p. 49.) This may be contrasted with: 'The Definition can never be demonstrated, for it declares only the essence of the subject ...; whereas Demonstration assumes the essence to be known ...' (Grote, *Aristotle*, 2nd edn, 241; see also 240/241. Cp. also end of note 29 below.)

28. Cp. Aristotle's *Metaphysics*, 1031b7 and 1031b20. See also 996b20: 'We have knowledge of a thing if we know its essence.'
29. 'A definition is a statement that describes the essence of a thing' (Aristotle, *Topics*, I, 5, 101b36; VII, 3, 153a, 153a15, etc. See also *Met.*, 1042a17)—'The definition ... reveals the essential nature' (*Anal. Post.*, II, 3, 91a1).—'Definition is ... a statement of the nature of the thing' (93b28).—'Only those things have essences whose formulæ are definitions.' (*Met.*, 1030a5 f.)—'The essence, whose formula is a definition, is also called the substance of a thing.' (*Met.*, 1017b21)—'Clearly, then, the definition is the formula of the essence ...' (*Met.*, 1031a13).

    Regarding the principles, i.e. the starting points or basic premises of proofs, we must distinguish between two kinds. (1) The logical principles (cp. *Met.*, 996b25 ff.) and (2) the premises from which proofs must proceed and which cannot be proven in turn if an infinite regression is to be avoided (cp. note 27 to this chapter). The latter are definitions: 'The basic premises of proofs are definitions' (*Anal. Post.*, II, 3, 90b23; cp. 89a17, 90a35, 90b23). See also Ross, *Aristotle*, p. 45/46, commenting upon *Anal. Post.*, I, 4, 20–74a4: 'The premises of science', Ross writes (p. 46), 'will, we are told, be *per se* in either sense (*a*) or sense (*b*).' On the previous page we learn that a premise is necessary *per se* (or essentially necessary) in the senses (*a*) and (*b*) *if it rests upon a definition*.
30. 'If it has a name, then there will be a formula of its meaning', says Aristotle (*Met.*, 1030a14; see also 1030b24); and he explains that not every formula of the meaning of a name is a definition; but if the name is one of a species of a genus, then the formula will be a definition.

    It is important to note that in my use (I follow here the modern use of the word) 'definition' always refers to the whole definition sentence, while Aristotle (and others who follow him in this, e.g. Hobbes) sometimes uses the word also as a synonym for 'definiens'.

    Definitions are not of particulars, but only of universals (cp. *Met.*, 1036a28) and only of essences, i.e. of something which is the species of a genus (i.e. a *last differentia*; cp. *Met.*, 1038a19) and an indivisible form, see also *Anal. Post.* II, 13., 97b6 f.
31. That Aristotle's treatment is not very lucid may be seen from the end of note 27 to this chapter, and from a further comparison of these two interpretations. The greatest obscurity is in Aristotle's treatment of the way in which, by a process of induction, we rise to definitions that are principles; cp. especially *Anal. Post.*, II, 19, pp. 100a, f.
32. For Plato's doctrine, see notes 25–27 to chapter 8, and text.

    Grote writes (*Aristotle*, 2nd ed., 260): 'Aristotle had inherited from Plato his doctrine of an infallible Nous or Intellect, enjoying complete immunity from error.' Grote continues to emphasize that, as opposed to Plato, Aristotle does not despise observational experience, but rather assigns to his Nous (i.e. intellectual intuition) 'a position as terminus and correlate to the process of Induction' (*loc. cit.*, see also *op. cit.*, p. 577). This is so; but observational experience has apparently only the function of priming and developing our intellectual intuition for its task, the intuition of the universal essence; and, indeed, nobody has ever explained how definitions, *which are beyond error*, can be reached by induction.
33. Aristotle's view amounts to the same as Plato's in so far as there is for both, in the last instance, no possible appeal to argument. All that can be done is to assert

dogmatically of a certain definition that it is a true description of its essence; and if asked why this and no other description is true, all that remains is an appeal to the 'intuition of the essence'.

Aristotle speaks of induction in at least two senses—in a more heuristic sense of a method leading us to 'intuit the general principle' (cp. *An. Pri.*, 67a22f., 27b25–33, *An. Post.*, 71a7, 81a38–b5, 100b4 f.) and in a more empirical sense (cp. *An. Pri.*, 68b15–37, 69a16, *An. Post.*, 78a35, 81b5 ff., *Topics*, 105a13, 156a4, 157a34).

A case of an apparent contradiction, which, however, might be cleared up, is 77a4, where we read that a definition is neither universal nor particular. I suggest that the solution is not that a definition is 'not strictly a judgement at all' (as G. R. G. Mure suggests in the Oxford translation), but that it is not *simply* universal but 'commensurate', i.e. universal and *necessary*. (Cp. 73b26, 96b4, 97b25.)

For the 'argument' of *Anal. Post.* mentioned in the text, see 100b6 ff. For the mystical union of the knowing and the known in *De Anima*, see especially 425b30 f., 430a20, 431a1; the decisive passage for our purpose is 430b27 f.: 'The intuitive grasp of the definition ... of the essence is never in error ... just as ... the seeing of the special object of sight can never be in error.' For the theological passages of the *Metaphysics*, see especially 1072b20 ('contact') and 1075a2. See also notes 59 (2) to chapter 10, 36 to chapter 12, and notes 3, 4, 6, 29–32, and 58 to chapter 24.

For 'the whole body of fact' mentioned in the next paragraph, see the end of *Anal. Post.* (100b15 f.).

It is remarkable how similar the views of Hobbes (a nominalist but *not* a methodological nominalist) are to Aristotle's methodological essentialism. Hobbes too believes that definitions are the basic premises of all knowledge (as opposed to opinion).

34. I have developed this view of scientific method in my *Logic of Scientific Discovery*; see, e.g. pp. 278 ff. and pp. 315 ff., for a fuller translation from *Erkenntnis*, vol. 5 (1934) where I say: 'We shall have to get accustomed to interpreting sciences as systems of hypotheses (instead of "bodies of knowledge"), i.e. of anticipations that cannot be established, but which we use as long as they are corroborated, and of which we are not entitled to say that they are "true" or "more or less certain" or even "probable".'
35. The quotation is from my note in *Erkenntnis*, vol. 3 (1933), now retranslated in *The Logic of Scientific Discovery*, pp. 312 ff.; it is a variation and generalization of a statement on geometry made by Einstein in his *Geometry and Experience*.
36. It is, of course, not possible to estimate whether theories, argument, and reasoning, or else observation and experiment, are of greater significance for science; for science is always *theory tested by observation and experiment*. But it is certain that all those 'positivists' who try to show that science is the 'sum total of our observations', or that it is observational rather than theoretical, are quite mistaken. The rôle of theory and argument in science can hardly be overrated.—Concerning the relation between proof and logical argument in general, see note 47 to this chapter.
37. Cp. e.g. *Met.*, 1030a, 6 and 14 (see note 30 to this chapter).
38. I wish to emphasize that I speak here about *nominalism versus essentialism* in a purely methodological way. I do not take up any position towards the *metaphysical* problem of universals, i.e. towards the metaphysical problem of nominalism versus essentialism (a term which I suggest should be used instead of the traditional term

'realism'); and I certainly do not advocate a metaphysical nominalism, although I advocate a methodological nominalism. (See also notes 27 and 30 to chapter 3.)

The opposition between *nominalist and essentialist definitions* made in the text is an attempt to reconstruct the traditional distinction between 'verbal' and 'real' definitions. *My main emphasis, however, is on the question whether the definition is read from the right to the left or from the left to the right; or, in other words, whether it replaces a long story by a short one, or a short story by a long one.*

39. My contention that in science *only* nominalist definitions occur (I speak here of explicit definitions only and neither of implicit nor of recursive definitions) needs some defence. It certainly does not imply that terms are not used more or less 'intuitively' in science; this is clear if only we consider that all chains of definitions must start with *undefined* terms, whose meaning can be exemplified but not defined. Further, it seems clear that in science, especially in mathematics, we often first use a term, for instance 'dimension' or 'truth', intuitively, but proceed later to define it. But this is a rather rough description of the situation. A more precise description would be this. Some of the undefined terms used intuitively can be sometimes replaced by defined terms of which it can be shown that they fulfil the intentions with which the undefined terms have been used; that is to say, to every sentence in which the undefined terms occurred (e.g. which was interpreted as analytic) there is a corresponding sentence in which the newly defined term occurs (which follows from the definition).

One certainly can say that K. Menger has recursively defined 'Dimension' or that A. Tarski has defined 'Truth'; but this way of expressing matters may lead to misunderstandings. What has happened is that Menger gave a purely nominal definition of classes of sets of points which he labelled '*n*-dimensional', because it was possible to replace the intuitive mathematical concept '*n*-dimensional' by the new concept in all important contexts; and the same can be said of Tarski's concept 'Truth'. Tarski gave a nominal definition (or rather a method of drafting nominal definitions) which he labelled 'Truth', since a system of sentences could be derived from the definition corresponding to those sentences (like the law of the excluded middle) which had been used by many logicians and philosophers in connection with what they called 'Truth'.

40. If anything, our language would gain precision if we were to avoid definitions and take the immense trouble of always using the defining terms instead of the defined terms. For there is a source of imprecision in the current methods of definition: Carnap has developed (in 1934) what appears to be the first method of avoiding inconsistencies in a language using definitions. Cp. *Logical Syntax of Language*, 1937, §22, p. 67. (See also Hilbert-Bernays, *Grundlagen d. Math.*, 1939, II, p. 295, note 1.) Carnap has shown that in most cases a language admitting definitions will be inconsistent even if the definitions satisfy the general rules for forming definitions. The comparative practical unimportance of this inconsistency merely rests upon the fact that we can always eliminate the defined terms, replacing them by the defining terms.

41. Several examples of this method of introducing the new term only after the need has arisen may be found in the present book. Dealing, as it does, with philosophical positions, it can hardly avoid introducing, for the sake of brevity, *names* for these positions. This is the reason why I have to make use of so many 'isms'. But in many

cases these names are introduced only after the positions in question have been described.

42. In a more systematic criticism of the essentialist method, three problems might be distinguished which essentialism can neither escape nor solve. (1) The problem of distinguishing clearly between a mere verbal convention and an essentialist definition which 'truly' describes an essence. (2) The problem of distinguishing 'true' essential definitions from 'false' ones. (3) The problem of avoiding an infinite regression of definitions.—I shall briefly deal with the second and third of these problems only. The third of these problems will be dealt with in the text; for the second, see notes 44 (1) and 54 to this chapter.

43. The fact that a statement is true may sometimes help to explain why it appears to us as self-evident. This is the case with '2 + 2 = 4', or with the sentence 'the sun radiates light as well as heat'. But the opposite is clearly not the case. The fact that a sentence appears to some or even to all of us to be 'self-evident', that is to say, the fact that some or even all of us believe firmly in its truth and cannot conceive of its falsity, is no reason why it should be true. (The fact that we are unable to conceive of the falsity of a statement is in many cases only a reason for suspecting that our power of imagination is deficient or undeveloped.) It is one of the gravest mistakes if a philosophy ever offers self-evidence as an argument in favour of the truth of a sentence; yet this is done by practically all idealist philosophies. It shows that idealist philosophies are often systems of apologetics for some dogmatic beliefs.

The excuse that we are often in such a position that we must accept certain sentences for no better reason than that they are self-evident, is not valid. The principles of logic and of scientific method (especially the 'principle of induction' or the 'law of uniformity of nature') are usually mentioned as statements which we must accept, and which we cannot justify by anything but self-evidence. Even if this were so, it would be franker to say that we cannot justify them, and leave it at that. But, in fact, there is no need for a 'principle of induction'. (Cp. my *The Logic of Scientific Discovery*.) And as far as the 'principles of logic' are concerned, much has been done in recent years which shows that the self-evidence theory is obsolete. (Cp. especially Carnap's *Logical Syntax of Language* and his *Introduction to Semantics*.) See also note 44 (2).

44. (1) If we apply these considerations to the intellectual intuition of essences, then we can see that essentialism is unable to solve the problem: How can we find out whether or not a proposed definition which is formally correct is true also; and especially, how can we decide between two competing definitions? It is clear that for the methodological nominalist the answer to a question of this kind is trivial. For let us assume that somebody maintains (with the *Oxford Dictionary*) that 'A puppy is a vain, empty-headed, impertinent young man', and that he insists upon upholding this definition against somebody who clings to our previous definition. In this case, the nominalist, if he is patient enough to do so, will point out that a quarrel about labels does not interest him, since their choice is arbitrary; and he may suggest, *if there is any danger of ambiguity*, that one can easily introduce two different labels, for example 'puppy$_1$' and 'puppy$_2$'. And if a third party should support that 'A puppy is a brown dog', then the nominalist will patiently suggest the introduction of the label 'puppy$_3$'. But should the contesting parties continue to quarrel, either because somebody insists that only his puppy is the legitimate one, or because he insists

that his puppy must, at least, be labelled '$puppy_1$', then even a very patient nominalist would only shrug his shoulders. (In order to avoid misunderstandings, it should be said that *methodological nominalism* does not discuss the question of the existence of universals; Hobbes, accordingly, is not a methodological nominalist, but what I should call an ontological nominalist.)

The same trivial problem, however, raises insurmountable difficulties for the essentialist method. We have already supposed that the essentialist insists that, for instance, 'A puppy is a brown dog' is not a correct definition of the essence of 'puppiness'. How can he defend this view? Only by an appeal to his intellectual intuition of essences. But this fact has the practical consequence that the essentialist is reduced to complete helplessness, if his definition is challenged. For there are only two ways in which he can react. The one is to reiterate stubbornly that his intellectual intuition is the only true one, to which, of course, his opponent may reply in the same way, so that we reach a deadlock instead of the absolutely final and indubitable knowledge which we were promised by Aristotle. The other is to admit that his opponent's intuition may be as true as his own, but that it is of a different essence, which he unfortunately denotes by the same name. This would lead to the suggestion that two different names should be used for the two different essences, for example '$puppy_1$' and '$puppy_1$'. But this step means giving up the essentialist position altogether. For it means that we start with the defining formula and attach to it some label, i.e. that we proceed 'from the right to the left'; and it means that we shall have to attach these labels arbitrarily. This can be seen by considering that the attempt to insist that a $puppy_1$ is, essentially, a young dog, while the brown dog can only be a $puppy_2$, would clearly lead to the same difficulty which has driven the essentialist into his present dilemma. Accordingly, every definition must be considered as equally admissible (provided it is formally correct); which means, in Aristotelian terminology, that one basic premise is just as true as another (which is contrary to it) and that '*it is impossible to make a false statement*'. (This seems to have been pointed out by Antisthenes; see note 54 to this chapter.) Thus the Aristotelian claim that intellectual intuition is a source of knowledge as opposed to opinion, unerringly and indubitably true, and that it furnishes us with definitions which are the safe and necessary basic premises of all scientific deduction, is baseless in every single one of its points. And a definition turns out to be nothing but a sentence which tells us that the defined term means the same as the defining formula, and that each can be replaced by the other. Its nominalist use permits us to cut a long story short and is therefore of some practical advantage. But its essentialist use can only help us to replace a short story by a story which means the same but is much longer. This use can only encourage verbalism.

(2) For a criticism of Husserl's intuition of essences, cp. J. Kraft, *From Husserl to Heidegger* (in German, 1932). See also note 8 to chapter 24. Of all authors who hold related views, M. Weber had probably the greatest influence upon the treatment of sociological problems. He advocated for the social sciences a 'method of intuitive understanding'; and his 'ideal types' largely correspond to the essences of Aristotle and Husserl. It is worth mentioning that Weber saw, in spite of these tendencies, the inadmissibility of appeals to self-evidence. 'The fact that an interpretation possesses a high degree of self-evidence proves in itself nothing about its empirical validity' (*Ges. Aufsaetze*, 1922, p. 404); and he says quite rightly that intuitive

understanding '*must always be controlled by ordinary methods*'. (*Loc. cit.*, italics mine.) But if that is so, then it is not a characteristic method of a science of 'human behaviour' as he thinks; it also belongs to mathematics, physics, etc. And it turns out that those who believe that intuitive understanding is a method peculiar to sciences of 'human behaviour' hold such views mainly because they cannot imagine that a mathematician or a physicist could become so well acquainted with his object that he could 'get the feel of it', in the way in which a sociologist 'gets the feel' of human behaviour.

45. 'Science assumes the definitions of all its terms ...' (Ross, *Aristotle*, 44; cp. *Anal. Post.*, I, 2); see also note 30 to this chapter.

46. The following quotation is from R. H. S. Crossman, *Plato To-Day* 1937, pp. 71 f.

A very similar doctrine is expressed by M. R. Cohen and E. Nagel in their book, *An Introduction to Logic and Scientific Method* (1936), p. 232: 'Many of the disputes about the true nature of property, of religion, of law, ... would assuredly disappear if the precisely defined equivalents were substituted for these words.' (See also notes 48 and 49 to this chapter.)

The views concerning this problem expressed by Wittgenstein in his *Tractatus Logico-Philosophicus* (1921/22) and by several of his followers are not as definite as those of Crossman, Cohen, and Nagel. Wittgenstein is an anti-metaphysician. 'The book', he writes in the preface, 'deals with the problems of philosophy and shows, I believe, that the method of formulating these problems rests on the misunderstanding of the logic of our language.' He tries to show that metaphysics is 'simply nonsense' and tries to draw a limit, in our language, between sense and nonsense: 'The limit can ... be drawn in languages and what lies on the other side of the limit will be simply nonsense.' According to Wittgenstein's book, propositions have sense. They are true or false. Philosophical propositions do not exist; they only look like propositions, but are, in fact, nonsensical. The limit between sense and nonsense coincides with that between natural science and philosophy: 'The totality of true propositions is the total natural science (or the totality of the natural sciences).—Philosophy is not one of the natural sciences.' *The true task of philosophy, therefore, is not to formulate propositions; it is, rather, to clarify propositions*: 'The result of philosophy is not a number of "philosophical propositions", but to make propositions clear.' Those who do not see that, and propound philosophical propositions, talk metaphysical nonsense.

(It should be remembered, in this connection, that a sharp distinction between meaningful statements which have sense, and meaningless linguistic expressions which may look like statements but which are without sense, was first made by Russell in his attempt to solve the problems raised by the paradoxes which he had discovered. Russell's division of expressions which look like statements is threefold, since statements which may be *true* or *false*, and *meaningless* or nonsensical pseudo-statements, may be distinguished. It is important to note that this use of the terms 'meaningless' or 'senseless' partly agrees with ordinary use, but is much sharper, since ordinarily one often calls real statements 'meaningless', for example, if they are 'absurd', i.e. self-contradictory, or obviously false. Thus a statement asserting of a certain physical body that it is at the same time in two different places is not meaningless but a false statement, or one which contradicts the use of the term 'body' in classical physics; and similarly, a statement asserting of a certain electron that it has a precise place and momentum is not meaningless—as some physicists have asserted, and as some philosophers have repeated—but it simply contradicts modern physics.)

What has been said so far can be summed up as follows. Wittgenstein looks for a line of demarcation between sense and nonsense, and finds that this demarcation coincides with that between science and metaphysics, i.e. between scientific sentences and philosophical pseudo-propositions. (That he wrongly identifies the sphere of the natural sciences with that of *true* sentences shall not concern us here; see, however, note 51 to this chapter.) This interpretation of his aim is corroborated when we read: 'Philosophy limits the ... sphere of natural science.' (All sentences so far quoted are from pp. 75 and 77.)

How is the line of demarcation ultimately drawn? How can 'science' be distinguished from 'metaphysics', and thereby 'sense' from 'nonsense'? It is the reply given to this question which establishes the similarity between Wittgenstein's theory and that of Crossman and the rest. Wittgenstein implies that the terms or 'signs' used by scientists have meaning, while the metaphysician 'has given no meaning to certain signs in his propositions'; this is what he writes (pp. 187 and 189): 'The right method of philosophy would be this. To say nothing except what can be said, i.e. the propositions of natural science, i.e. something that has nothing to do with philosophy: and then always when someone else wished to say something metaphysical, to demonstrate to him that he had given no meaning to certain signs in his propositions.' In practice, this implies that we should proceed by asking the metaphysician: 'What do you mean by this word? What do you mean by that word?' In other words, *we demand a definition from him; and if it is not forthcoming, we assume that the word is meaningless.*

This theory, as will be shown in the text, overlooks the facts (*a*) that a witty and unscrupulous metaphysician every time he is asked, 'What do you mean by this word?', will quickly proffer a definition, so that the whole game develops into a trial of patience; (*b*) that the natural scientist is in no better logical position than the metaphysician; and even, if compared with a metaphysician who is unscrupulous, in a worse position.

It may be remarked that Schlick, in *Erkenntnis*, 1, p. 8, where he deals with Wittgenstein's doctrine, mentions the difficulty of an infinite regress; but the solution he suggests (which seems to lie in the direction of inductive definitions or 'constitutions', or perhaps of operationalism; cp. note 50 to this chapter) is neither clear nor able to solve the problem of demarcation. I think that certain of the intentions of Wittgenstein and Schlick in demanding a philosophy of meaning are fulfilled by that logical theory which Tarski has called 'Semantics'. But I also believe that the correspondence between these intentions and Semantics does not go far; for Semantics *propounds propositions*; it does not only 'clarify' them.—These comments upon Wittgenstein are continued in notes 51–52 to the present chapter. (See also notes 8 (2) and 32 to chapter 24; and 10 and 25 to chapter 25.)

47. It is important to distinguish between a logical deduction in general, and a proof or demonstration in particular. A *proof* or *demonstration* is a deductive argument by which the truth of the conclusion is finally established; this is how Aristotle uses the term, demanding (for example, in *Anal. Post.*, I, 4, pp. 73a, ff.) that the 'necessary' truth of the conclusion should be established; and this is how Carnap uses the term

(see especially *Logical Syntax*, § 10, p. 29, § 47, p. 171), showing that conclusions which are 'demonstrable' in this sense are 'analytically' true. (Into the problems concerning the terms 'analytic' and 'synthetic', I shall not enter here.)

Since Aristotle, it has been clear that not all logical deductions are proofs (i.e. demonstrations); there are also logical deductions which are not proofs; for example, we can deduce conclusions from admittedly false premises, and such deductions are not called proofs. Non-demonstrative deductions are called by Carnap 'derivations' (*loc. cit.*). It is interesting that a name for these non-demonstrative deductions has not been introduced earlier; it shows the preoccupation with proofs, a preoccupation which arose from the Aristotelian prejudice that 'science' or 'scientific knowledge' must establish all its statements, i.e. accept them either as self-evident premises, or prove them. But the position is this. *Outside of pure logic and pure mathematics nothing can be proved.* Arguments in other sciences (and even some within mathematics, as I. Lakatos has shown) are not proofs but merely *derivations*.

It may be remarked that there is a far-reaching parallelism between the problems of *derivation* on the one side and *definition* on the other, and between the problems of the *truth of sentences* and that of the *meaning of terms*.

A derivation starts with premises and leads to a conclusion; a definition starts (if we read it from the right to the left) with the defining terms and leads to a defined term. A derivation informs us about the truth of the conclusion, *provided* we are informed about the truth of the premises; a definition informs us about the meaning of the defined term, *provided* we are informed about the meaning of the defining terms. Thus a derivation shifts the problem of *truth* back to the premises, without ever being able to solve it; and a definition shifts the problem of *meaning* back to the defining terms, without ever being able to solve it.

48. The reason why the defining terms are likely to be rather less clear and precise than the defined terms is that they are as a rule more abstract and general. This is not necessarily true if certain modern methods of definition are employed ('definition by abstraction', a method of symbolic logic); but it is certainly true of all those definitions which Crossman can have in mind, and especially of all Aristotelian definitions (by *genus* and *differentia*).

It has been held by some positivists, especially under the influence of Locke and Hume, that it is possible to define abstract terms like those of science or of politics (see text to next note) in terms of particular, concrete observations or even of sensations. Such an 'inductive' method of definition has been called by Carnap 'constitution'. But we can say that it is impossible to 'constitute' universals in terms of particulars. (With this, cp. my *The Logic of Scientific Discovery*, especially sections 14, pp. 64 ff., and 25, p. 93; and Carnap's 'Testability and Meaning', in *Philosophy of Science*, vol. 3, 1936, pp. 419 ff., and vol. 4, pp. I ff.)

49. The examples are the same as those which Cohen and Nagel, *op. cit.*, 232 f., recommend for definition. (Cp. note 46 to this chapter.)

Some general remarks on the uselessness of essentialist definitions may be added here. (Cp. also end of note 44 (1) to this chapter.)

(1) The attempt to solve a factual problem by reference to definitions usually means the substitution of a merely verbal problem for the factual one. (There is an excellent example of this method in Aristotle's *Physics*, II, 6, towards the end.) This

may be shown for the following examples. (*a*) There is a factual problem: Can we return to the cage of tribalism? And by what means? (*b*) There is a moral problem: Should we return to the cage?

The philosopher of meaning, if faced by (*a*) or (*b*), will say: It all depends on what you mean by your vague terms; tell me how you define 'return', 'cage', 'tribalism', *and with the help of these definitions I may be able to decide your problem*. Against this, I maintain that if the decision can be made with the help of the definitions, if it follows from the definitions, then the problem so decided was merely a verbal problem; for it has been solved independently of facts or of moral decisions.

(2) An *essentialist* philosopher of meaning may do even worse, especially in connection with problem (*b*); he may suggest, for example, that it depends upon 'the essence' or 'the essential character' or perhaps upon 'the destiny' of our civilization whether or not we should try to return. (See also note 61 (2) to this chapter.)

(3) Essentialism and the theory of definition have led to an amazing development in Ethics. The development is one of increasing abstraction and loss of touch with *the basis of all ethics*—the practical moral problems, to be decided by us here and now. It leads first to the general question, 'What is good?' or 'What is the Good?'; next to 'What does "Good" mean?' and next to 'Can the problem "What does 'Good' mean?" be answered?' or 'Can "good" be defined?' G. E. Moore, who raised this last problem in his *Principia Ethica*, was certainly right in insisting that 'good' in the moral sense cannot be defined in 'naturalistic' terms. For, indeed, if we could, it would mean something like 'bitter' or 'sweet' or 'green' or 'red'; and it would be utterly irrelevant from the point of view of morality. Just as we need not attain the bitter, or the sweet, etc., there would be no reason to take any moral interest in a naturalistic 'good'. But although Moore was right in what is perhaps justly considered his main point, it may be held that an analysis of good or of any other concept or essence can in no way contribute to an ethical theory which bears upon the only relevant basis of all ethics, the immediate moral problem that must be solved here and now. Such an analysis can lead only to the substitution of a verbal problem for a moral one. (Cp. also note 18 (1) to chapter 5, especially upon the irrelevance of moral judgements.)

50. I have in mind the methods of 'constitution' (see note 48 to this chapter), 'implicit definition', 'definition by correlation', and 'operational definition'. The arguments of the 'operationalists' seem to be in the main true enough; but they cannot get over the fact that in their operational definitions, or descriptions, they need universal terms which have to be taken as undefined; and to them, the problem applies again.

A few hints or allusions may be added here concerning the way we 'use our terms'. For the sake of brevity, these hints will refer without explanation to certain technicalities; they may therefore, in the present form, not be generally understandable.

Of the so-called *implicit definitions*, especially in mathematics, Carnap has shown (*Symposion* I, 1927, 355 ff.; cp. also his *Abriss*) that they do not 'define' in the ordinary sense of this word; a system of implicit definitions cannot be considered as defining a 'model', but it defines a whole class of 'models'. Accordingly, the system of symbols defined by a system of implicit definitions cannot be considered as a system of *constants*, but they must be considered as *variables* (with a definite range, and bound by the system in a certain way to one another). I believe that there is a limited analogy between this situation and the way we 'use our terms' in science.

The analogy can be described in this way. In a branch of mathematics in which we operate with signs defined by implicit definition, the fact that these signs have no 'definite meaning' does not affect our operating with them, or the precision of our theories. Why is that so? Because we do not overburden the signs. We do not attach a 'meaning' to them, beyond that shadow of a meaning that is warranted by our implicit definitions. (And if we attach to them an intuitive meaning, then we are careful to treat this as a private auxiliary device, which must not interfere with the theory.) In this way, we try to keep, as it were, within the 'penumbra of vagueness' or of ambiguity, and to avoid touching the problem of the precise limits of this penumbra or range; and it turns out that we can achieve a great deal without discussing the meaning of these signs; for nothing *depends* on their meaning. In a similar way, I believe, we can operate with these terms whose meaning we have learned 'operationally'. We use them, as it were, so that nothing depends upon their meaning, or as little as possible. Our 'operational definitions' have the advantage of helping us to shift the problem into a field in which nothing or little depends on words. *Clear speaking is speaking in such a way that words do not matter.*

51. Wittgenstein teaches in the *Tractatus* (cp. note 46 to this chapter where further cross-references are given) that philosophy cannot propound propositions, and that all philosophical propositions are in fact senseless pseudo-propositions. Closely connected with this is his doctrine that the true task of philosophy is not to propound sentences but to clarify them: 'The object of philosophy is the logical clarification of thoughts.—Philosophy is not a theory but an activity. A philosophical work consists essentially of elucidations.' (*Op. cit.*, p. 77.)

The question arises whether this view is in keeping with Wittgenstein's fundamental aim, the destruction of metaphysics by unveiling it as meaningless nonsense. In my *The Logic of Scientific Discovery* (see especially pp. 311 ff.), I have tried to show that Wittgenstein's method leads to a merely verbal solution and that it must give rise, in spite of its apparent radicalism, not to the destruction or to the exclusion or even to the clear demarcation of metaphysics, but to their intrusion into the field of science, and to their confusion with science. The reasons for this are simple enough.

(1) Let us consider one of Wittgenstein's sentences, for example, 'philosophy is not a theory but an activity'. Surely, this is not a sentence belonging to 'total natural science (or the totality of the natural sciences)'. Therefore, according to Wittgenstein (see note 46 to this chapter), it cannot belong to 'the totality of true propositions'. On the other hand, it is not a false proposition either (since if it were, its negation would have to be true, and to belong to natural science). *Thus we arrive at the result that it must be 'meaningless' or 'senseless' or 'nonsensical'; and the same holds for most of Wittgenstein's propositions.* This consequence of his doctrine is recognized by Wittgenstein himself, for he writes (p. 189): 'My propositions are elucidatory in this way: he who understands me finally recognizes them as senseless ...' The result is important. Wittgenstein's own philosophy is senseless, and it is admitted to be so. 'On the other hand', as Wittgenstein says in his Preface, 'the truth of the thoughts communicated here seems to me unassailable and definite. I am, therefore, of the opinion that the problems have in essentials been finally solved.' This shows that we can communicate *unassailably and definitely true thoughts* by way of propositions which are admittedly nonsensical, and that we can solve problems 'finally' by propounding nonsense. (Cp. also note 8 (2, b) to chapter 24.)

Consider what this means. It means that all the metaphysical nonsense against which Bacon, Hume, Kant, and Russell have fought for centuries may now comfortably settle down, and even frankly admit that it is nonsense. (Heidegger does so; cp. note 87 to chapter 12.) For now we have a new kind of nonsense at our disposal, nonsense that communicates thoughts whose truth is unassailable and definitive; in other words, *deeply significant nonsense*.

I do not deny that Wittgenstein's thoughts are unassailable and definitive. For how could one assail them? Obviously, whatever one says against them must be philosophical and therefore nonsense. And it can be dismissed as such. We are thus faced with that kind of position which I have described elsewhere, in connection with Hegel (cp. note 33 to chapter 12) as a *reinforced dogmatism*. 'All you need', I wrote in my *Logik der Forschung* (now translated as *The Logic of Scientific Discovery*: see p. 51), p. 21, 'is to determine the conception of "sense" or of "meaning" in a suitably narrow way, and you can say of all uncomfortable questions that you cannot find any "sense" or "meaning" in them. By recognizing the problems of natural science alone as "meaningful", every debate about the concept of meaning must become nonsensical. Once enthroned, the dogma of meaning is for ever raised above the possibility of attack. It is "unassailable and definitive".'

(2) But not only does Wittgenstein's theory invite every kind of metaphysical nonsense to pose as deeply significant; it also blurs what I have called (*op. cit.*, p. 7) the *problem of demarcation*. This he does because of his naïve idea that there is something 'essentially' or 'by nature' scientific and something 'essentially' or 'by nature' metaphysical and that it is our task to discover the 'natural' demarcation between these two. 'Positivism', I may quote myself again (*op. cit.*, p. 8), 'interprets the problem of demarcation in a naturalistic way; instead of interpreting this question as one to be decided according to practical usefulness, it asks for a difference that exists "by nature", as it were, between natural science and metaphysics.' But it is clear that the philosophical or methodological task can only be to suggest and to devise a useful demarcation between these two. This can hardly be done by characterizing metaphysics as 'senseless' or 'meaningless'. First, because these terms are better fitted for giving vent to one's personal indignation about metaphysicians and metaphysical systems than for a technical characterization of a line of demarcation. Secondly, because the problem is only shifted, for we must now ask: 'What do "meaningful" and "meaningless" mean?' If 'meaningful' is only an equivalent for 'scientific', and 'meaningless' for 'non-scientific', then we have clearly made no progress. For reasons such as these I suggested (*op. cit.*, 8 ff., 21 f., 227) that we eliminate the emotive terms 'meaning', 'meaningful', 'meaningless', etc., from the methodological discussion altogether. (Recommending that we solve the problem of demarcation by using falsifiability or testability, or degrees of testability, as criterion of the empirical character of a scientific system, I suggested that it was of no advantage to introduce 'meaningful' as an emotive equivalent of 'testable'.) *In spite of my explicit refusal to regard falsifiability or testability (or anything else) as a '*criterion of meaning*', I find that philosophers frequently attribute to me the proposal to adopt this as a criterion of meaning or of 'meaningfulness'. (See, for example, *Philosophic Thought in France and in the United States*, edited by M. Farber, 1950, p. 570.)*

But even if we eliminate all reference to 'meaning' or 'sense' from Wittgenstein's theories, his solution of the problem of demarcating science from metaphysics remains most unfortunate. For since he identifies 'the totality of true propositions' with the totality of natural science, he excludes all those hypotheses from 'the sphere of natural science' which are not true. And since we can never know of a hypothesis whether or not it is true, we can never know whether or not it belongs to the sphere of natural science. The same unfortunate result, namely, a demarcation that excludes all hypotheses from the sphere of natural science, and therefore includes them in the field of metaphysics, is attained by Wittgenstein's famous 'principle of verification', as I pointed out in *Erkenntnis*, 3 (1933), p. 427. (For a hypothesis is, strictly speaking, not verifiable, and if we speak loosely, then we can say that even a metaphysical system like that of the early atomists has been verified.) Again, this conclusion has been drawn in later years by Wittgenstein himself, who, according to Schlick (cp. my *The Logic of Scientific Discovery*, note 7 to section 4), asserted in 1931 that scientific theories are 'not really propositions', i.e. not meaningful. Theories, hypotheses, that is to say, the most important of all scientific utterances, are thus thrown out of the temple of natural science, and therefore put on a level with metaphysics.

Wittgenstein's original view in the *Tractatus* can only be explained by the assumption that he overlooked the difficulties connected with the status of a scientific hypothesis which always goes *far beyond a simple enunciation of fact*; he overlooked the problem of universality or generality. In this, he followed in the footsteps of earlier positivists, notably of Comte, who wrote (cp. his *Early Essays on Social Philosophy*, edited by H. D. Hutton, 1911, p. 223; see F. A. von Hayek, *Economica*, VIII, 1941, p. 300): 'Observation of facts is the only solid basis of human knowledge ... a proposition which does not admit of being reduced to a simple enunciation of fact, special or general, can have no real and intelligible sense.' Comte, although he remained unaware of the gravity of the problem hidden behind the simple phrases 'general fact', at least *mentions* this problem, by inserting the words 'special or general'. If we omit these words, then the passage becomes a very clear and concise formulation of Wittgenstein's fundamental criterion of sense or meaning, as formulated by him in the *Tractatus* (all propositions are truth-functions of, and therefore reducible to, atomic propositions, i.e. pictures of atomic facts), and as expounded by Schlick in 1931.—Comte's criterion of meaning was adopted by J. S. Mill.

To sum up. The anti-metaphysical theory of meaning in Wittgenstein's *Tractatus*, far from helping to combat metaphysical dogmatism and oracular philosophy, represents a reinforced dogmatism that opens wide the door to the enemy, deeply significant metaphysical nonsense, and throws out, by the same door, the best friend, that is to say, scientific hypothesis.

52. It appears that irrationalism in the sense of a doctrine or creed that does not propound connected and debatable arguments but rather propounds aphorisms and dogmatic statements which must be 'understood' or else left alone, will generally tend to become the property of an esoteric circle of the initiated. And, indeed, this prognosis seems to be partly corroborated by some of the publications that come from Wittgenstein's school. (I do not wish to generalize; for example, everything I have seen of F. Waismann's writing is presented as a chain of rational and exceedingly clear arguments, and entirely free from the attitude of '*take it or leave it*'.)

Some of these esoteric publications seem to be without a serious problem; to me, they appear to be subtle for subtlety's sake. It is significant that they come from a school which started by denouncing philosophy for the barren subtlety of its attempts to deal with pseudo-problems.

I may end this criticism by stating briefly that I do not think that there is much justification for fighting metaphysics in general, or that anything worth while will result from such a fight. It is necessary to solve the problem of the demarcation of science from metaphysics. But we should recognize that many metaphysical systems have led to important scientific results. I mention only the system of Democritus; and that of Schopenhauer which is very similar to that of Freud. And some, for instance those of Plato or Malebranche or Schopenhauer, are beautiful structures of thought. But I believe, at the same time, that we should fight those metaphysical systems which tend to bewitch and to confuse us. But clearly, we should do the same even with un-metaphysical and anti-metaphysical systems, if they exhibit this dangerous tendency. And I think that we cannot do this at one stroke. We have rather to take the trouble to analyse the systems in some detail; we must show that we understand what the author means, but that what he means is not worth the effort to understand it. (It is characteristic of all these dogmatic systems and especially of the esoteric systems that their admirers assert of all critics that 'they do not understand'; but these admirers forget that understanding must lead to agreement only in the case of sentences with a trivial content. In all other cases, one can understand *and* disagree.)

53. Cp. Schopenhauer, *Grundprobleme* (4th edn, 1890, p. 147). He comments upon 'intellectually intuiting reason that makes its pronouncements from the tripod of the oracle' (hence my term 'oracular philosophy'); and he continues: 'This is the origin of that philosophic method which entered the stage immediately after Kant, of this method of mystifying and imposing upon people, of deceiving them and throwing dust in their eyes—the method of windbaggery. One day this era will be recognized by the history of philosophy as the *age of dishonesty*.' (Then follows the passage quoted in the text.) Concerning the irrationalist attitude of '*take it or leave it*', cp. also text to notes 39–40 to chapter 24.

54. Plato's theory of definition (cp. note 27 to chapter 3 and note 23 to chapter 5), which Aristotle later developed and systematized, met its main opposition (1) from Antisthenes, (2) from the school of Isocrates, especially Theopompus.

(1) Simplicius, one of the best of our sources on these very doubtful matters, presents Antisthenes (*ad Arist. Categ.*, pp. 66b, 67b) as an opponent of Plato's theory of Forms or Ideas, and in fact, of the doctrine of essentialism and intellectual intuition altogether. 'I can see a horse, Plato', Antisthenes is reported to have said, 'but I cannot see its horseness.' (A very similar argument is attributed by a lesser source, *D.L.*, VI, 53, to Diogenes the Cynic, and there is no reason why the latter should not have used it too.) I think that we may rely upon Simplicius (who appears to have had access to Theophrastus), considering that Aristotle's own testimony in the *Metaphysics* (especially in *Met.*, 1043b24) squares well with this anti-essentialism of Antisthenes.

The two passages in the *Metaphysics* in which Aristotle mentions Antisthenes' objection to the essentialist theory of definitions are both very interesting. In the first (*Met.*, 1024b32) we hear that Antisthenes raised the point discussed in note 44 (1) to this chapter; that is to say, that there is no way of distinguishing between a 'true' and a 'false' definition (of 'puppy', for example) so that two apparently contradictory definitions would only refer to two different essences, 'puppy$_1$' and 'puppy$_2$'; thus there would be no contradiction, and it would hardly be possible to speak of false sentences. 'Antisthenes', Aristotle writes about this criticism, 'showed his crudity by claiming that nothing could be described except by its proper formula, one formula for one thing; from which it followed that there could be no contradiction; and almost that it was impossible to make a false statement.' (The passage has usually been interpreted as containing Antisthenes' positive theory, instead of his criticism of the doctrine of definition. But this interpretation neglects Aristotle's context. The whole passage deals with the possibility of false definitions, i.e. with precisely that problem which gives rise, in view of the inadequacy of the theory of intellectual intuition, to the difficulties described in note 44 (1). And it is clear from Aristotle's text that he is troubled by these difficulties as well as by Antisthenes' attitude towards them.) The second passage (*Met.*, 1043b24) also agrees with the criticism of essentialist definitions developed in the present chapter. It shows that Antisthenes attacked essentialist definitions as useless, as *merely substituting a long story for a short one*; and it shows further that Antisthenes very wisely admitted that, although it is useless to *define*, it is possible to describe or to *explain* a thing by referring to the similarity it bears to a thing already known, or, if it is composite, by explaining what its parts are. 'Indeed there is', Aristotle writes, 'something in that difficulty which has been raised by the Antisthenians and other such-like uneducated people. They said that what a thing is' (or the 'what is it' of a thing) 'cannot be defined; for the so-called definition, they say, is nothing but a long formula. But they admit that it is possible to explain, for example of silver, what sort of a thing it is; for we may say that it is similar to tin.' From this doctrine it would follow, Aristotle adds, 'that it is possible to give a definition and a formula of the *composite* kind of things or substances, whether they are sensible things, or objects of intellectual intuition; but not of their primary parts ...' (In the sequel, Aristotle wanders off, trying to link this argument with his doctrine that a defining formula is *composed* of two parts, genus and differentia, which are related, and *united*, like matter and form.)

I have dealt here with this matter since it appears that the enemies of Antisthenes, for example Aristotle (cp. *Topics*, I, 104b21), cited what he said in a manner which has led to the impression that it is not Antisthenes' criticism of essentialism but rather his positive doctrine. This impression was made possible by mixing it up with another doctrine probably held by Antisthenes; I have in mind the simple doctrine that we must speak plainly, just using each term in one meaning, and that in this way we can avoid all those difficulties whose solution is unsuccessfully attempted by the theory of definitions.

All these matters are, as mentioned before, very uncertain, owing to the scantiness of our evidence. But I think that Grote is likely to be right when he characterizes 'this debate between Antisthenes and Plato' as the 'first protest of Nominalism against the doctrine of an extreme Realism' (or in our terminology, of an extreme essentialism). Grote's position may be thus defended against Field's attack (*Plato and His Contemporaries*, 167) that it is 'quite wrong' to describe Antisthenes as a nominalist.

In support of my interpretation of Antisthenes, I may mention that against the scholastic theory of definitions, very similar arguments were used by Descartes (cp. *The Philosophical Works*, translated by Haldane and Ross, 1911, vol. I, p. 317) and, less clearly, by Locke (Essay, Book III, ch. III, § 11, to ch. IV, § 6; also ch. X, §§ 4 to 11; see especially ch. IV, § 5). Both Descartes and Locke, however, remained essentialists. Essentialism itself was attacked by Hobbes (cp. note 33 above) and by Berkeley who might be described as one of the first to hold a *methodological nominalism*, quite apart from his ontological nominalism; see also note 7 (2) to chapter 25.

(2) Of other critics of the Platonic-Aristotelian theory of definition, I mention only Theopompus (quoted by Epictetus, II, 17, 4–10; see Grote, *Plato*, I, 324). I think it likely that, as opposed to the generally accepted view, Socrates himself would not have favoured the theory of definitions; what he seems to have combated was the merely verbal solution of ethical problems; and his so-called attempted definitions of ethical terms, considering their negative results, may well be attempts to destroy verbalist prejudices.

(3) I wish to add here that in spite of all my criticism I am very ready to admit Aristotle's merits. He is the founder of logic, and down to *Principia Mathematica*, all logic can be said to be an elaboration and generalization of the Aristotelian beginnings. (A new epoch in logic has indeed begun, in my opinion, though not with the so-called 'non-Aristotelian' or 'multi-valued' systems, but rather with the clear distinction between 'object-language' and 'meta-language'.) Furthermore, Aristotle has the great merit of having tried to tame idealism by his common-sense approach which insists that only individual things are 'real' (and that their 'forms' and 'matter' are only aspects or abstractions). *Yet this very approach is responsible for the fact that Aristotle does not even attempt to solve Plato's problem of universals (see notes 19 and 20 to chapter 3, and text), i.e., the problem of explaining why certain things resemble one another and others do not. For why should there not be as many different Aristotelian essences in things as there are things?*

55. The influence of Platonism especially upon the Gospel of St. John is clear; and this influence is less noticeable in the earlier Gospels, though I do not assert that it is absent. Nevertheless the Gospels exhibit a clearly anti-intellectualist and anti-philosophizing tendency. They avoid an appeal to philosophical speculation, and they are definitely against scholarship and dialectics, for instance, that of the 'scribes'; but scholarship means, in this period, interpreting the scriptures in a dialectical and philosophical sense, and especially in the sense of the Neo-Platonists.

56. The problem of nationalism and the superseding of Jewish parochial tribalism by internationalism plays a most important part in the early history of Christianity; the echoes of these struggles can be found in the *Acts* (especially 10, 15 ff.; 11, 1–18; see also *St. Matthew* 3, 9, and the polemics against tribal feeding taboos in *Acts* 10, 10–15). It is interesting that this problem turns up together with the social problem of wealth and poverty, and with that of slavery; see *Galatians* 3, 28; and especially *Acts* 5, 1–11, where the retention of private property is described as mortal sin.

The survival in the Ghettos of eastern Europe, down to 1914 and even longer, of arrested and petrified forms of Jewish tribalism is very interesting. (Cp. the way in which the Scottish tribes attempted to cling to their tribal life.)

57. The quotation is from Toynbee, *A Study of History*, vol. VI, p. 202; the passage deals with the motive for the persecution of Christianity by the Roman rulers, who were usually very tolerant in matters of religion. 'The element in Christianity', Toynbee writes, 'that was intolerable to the Imperial Government was the Christians' refusal

to accept the Government's claim that it was entitled to compel its subjects to act against their conscience ... So far from checking the propagation of Christianity, the martyrdoms proved the most effective agencies of conversion ...'

58. For Julian's Neo-Platonic Anti-Church with its Platonizing hierarchy, and his fight against the 'atheists', i.e. Christianity, cp. for example Toynbee, *op. cit.*, V, pp. 565 and 584; I may quote a passage from J. Geffken (quoted by Toynbee, *loc. cit.*): 'In Jamblichus' (a pagan philosopher and number-mystic and founder of the Syrian school of Neo-Platonists, living about A.D. 300) 'the individual religious experience ... is eliminated. Its place is taken by a mystical church with sacraments, by a scrupulous exactness in carrying out the forms of worship, by a ritual that is closely akin to magic, and by a clergy ... Julian's ideas about the elevation of the priesthood reproduce ... exactly the standpoint of Jamblichus, whose zeal for the priests, for the details of the forms of worship, and for a systematic orthodox doctrine has prepared the ground for the construction of a pagan church.' We can recognize in these principles of the Syrian Platonist and of Julian the development of the genuine Platonic (and perhaps also late Jewish; cp. note 56 to this chapter) tendency to resist the revolutionary religion of individual conscience and humaneness by arresting all change and by introducing a rigid doctrine kept pure by a philosophic priest caste and by rigid taboos. (Cp. text to notes 14 and 18–23 to chapter 7; and chapter 8, especially text to note 34.) With Justinian's prosecution of non-Christians and heretics and his suppression of philosophy in 529, the tables are turned; it is now Christianity which adopts totalitarian methods and the control of conscience by violence. The dark ages begin.
59. For Toynbee's warning against an interpretation of the rise of Christianity in the sense of Pareto's advice (for which cp. notes 65 to chapter 10 and 1 to chapter 13) see, for example, *A Study of History*, V, 709.
60. For Critias' and Plato's and Aristotle's cynical doctrine that religion is opium for the people, cp. notes 5 to 18 (especially 15 and 18) to chapter 8. (See also Aristotle's *Topics*, I, 2, 101a30 ff.) For later examples (Polybius and Strabo) see, for example, Toynbee, *op. cit.*, V, 646 f., 561. Toynbee quotes from Polybius (*Historiae*, VI, 56): 'The point in which the Roman constitution excels others most conspicuously is to be found, in my opinion, in its handling of Religion ... The Romans have managed to forge the main bond of their social order ... out of superstition.' etc. And he quotes from Strabo: 'A rabble ... cannot be induced to answer to the call of Philosophic Reason ... In dealing with people of that sort, you cannot do without superstition.' etc. In view of this long series of Platonizing philosophers who teach that religion is 'opium for the people' I fail to see how the imputation of similar motives to Constantine can be described as *anachronistic*.

    It may be mentioned that it is a formidable opponent of whom Toynbee says, by implication, that he lacks historical sense: Lord Acton. For he writes (cp. his *History of Freedom*, 1909, p. 30 f., italics mine) of Constantine's relation to the Christians: 'Constantine, in adopting their faith, intended neither to abandon his predecessor's scheme of policy nor to renounce the fascinations of arbitrary authority, *but to strengthen his throne with the support of a religion* which had astonished the world by its power of resistance ...'
61. I admire the mediæval cathedrals as much as anybody, and I am perfectly prepared to recognize the greatness and uniqueness of mediæval craftsmanship. But I believe that æstheticism must never be used as an argument against humanitarianism.

The eulogy of the Middle Ages seems to begin with the Romantic movement in Germany, and it has become fashionable with the renaissance of this Romantic movement which unfortunately we are witnessing at the present time. It is, of course, an anti-rationalist movement; it will be discussed from another point of view in chapter 24.

The two attitudes towards the Middle Ages, rationalism and anti-rationalism, correspond to two *interpretations of 'history'* (cp. chapter 25).

(1) The rationalist interpretation of history views with hope those periods in which man attempted to look upon human affairs rationally. It sees in the Great Generation and especially in Socrates, in early Christianity (down to Constantine), in the Renaissance and the period of the Enlightenment, and in modern science, parts of an often interrupted movement, the efforts of men to free themselves, to break out of the cage of the closed society, and to form an open society. It is aware that this movement does not represent a 'law of progress' or anything of that sort, but that it depends solely upon ourselves, and must disappear if we do not defend it against its antagonists as well as against laziness and indolence. This interpretation sees in the intervening periods dark ages with their Platonizing authorities, their hierarchies of priest and tribalist orders of knights.

A classical formulation of this interpretation has been made by Lord Acton (*op. cit.*, p. 1; italics mine). 'Liberty,' he writes, 'next to religion, has been the motive of good deeds and the common pretext of crime, from the sowing of the seed at Athens, two thousand five hundred and sixty years ago ... In every age its progress has been beset by its natural enemies, by ignorance and superstition, by lust of conquest and by love of ease, by the strong man's craving for power, and the poor man's craving for food. During long intervals it has been utterly arrested ... No obstacle has been so constant, or so difficult to overcome, as uncertainty and confusion touching the nature of true liberty. *If hostile interests have wrought much injury, false ideas have wrought still more.*'

It is strange how strong a feeling of darkness prevails in the dark ages. Their science and their philosophy are both obsessed by the feeling that *the truth has once been known, and has been lost.* This expresses itself in the belief in the lost secret of the ancient philosopher's stone and in the ancient wisdom of astrology no less than in the belief that an idea cannot be of any value if it is new, and that every idea needs the backing of ancient authority (Aristotle and the Bible). But the men who felt that the secret key to wisdom was lost in the past were right. For this key is faith in reason, and liberty. It is the free competition of thought, which cannot exist without freedom of thought.

(2) The other interpretation agrees with Toynbee in seeing, in Greek as well as in modern rationalism (since the Renaissance), an *aberration* from the path of faith. 'To the present writer's eye', Toynbee says (*A Study of History*, vol. V, pp. 6 f., note; italics mine), 'the common element of rationalism which may be discernible in the Hellenic and Western Civilization is not so distinctive as to mark this pair of societies off from all other representatives of the species ... If we regard the Christian element of our Western Civilization as being the essence of it, then our reversion to Hellenism might be taken to be, *not a fulfilment of the potentialities of Western Christendom, but an aberration from the proper path of Western growth—in fact, a false step which it may or may not be possible now to retrieve.*'

In contrast to Toynbee, I do not doubt for a minute that it is possible to retrieve this step and to return to the cage, to the oppressions, superstition, and pestilences, of the Middle Ages. But I believe that we had much better not do so. And I contend that what we ought to do will have to be decided by ourselves, through free decisions, and not by historicist essentialism; nor, as Toynbee holds (see also note 49 (2) to this chapter), by 'the question of what the essential Character of the Western Civilization may be'.

(The passages here quoted from Toynbee are parts of his reply to a letter from Dr. E. Bevan; and Bevan's letter, i.e. the first of his two letters quoted by Toynbee, seems to me to present very clearly indeed what I call the rationalist interpretation.)

62. See H. Zinsser, *Rats, Lice, and History* (1937), pp. 80 and 83; italics mine.

Concerning my remark in the text, at the end of this chapter, that Democritus' science and morals still live with us, I may mention that a direct historical connection leads from Democritus and Epicurus via Lucretius not only to Gassendi but undoubtedly to Locke also. 'Atoms and the void' is the characteristic phrase whose presence always reveals the influence of this tradition; and as a rule, the natural philosophy of 'atoms and the void' goes together with the moral philosophy of an altruistic hedonism or utilitarianism. In regard to hedonism and utilitarianism, I believe that it is indeed necessary to replace their principle: *maximize pleasure!* by one which is probably more in keeping with the original views of Democritus and Epicurus, more modest, and much more urgent. I mean the rule: *minimize pain!* I believe (cp. chapters 9, 24, and 25) that it is not only impossible but very dangerous to attempt to maximize the pleasure or the happiness of the people, since such an attempt must lead to totalitarianism. But there is little doubt that most of the followers of Democritus (down to Bertrand Russell, who is still interested in atoms, geometry, and hedonism) would have little quarrel with the suggested re-formulation of their pleasure principle provided it is taken for what it is meant, and not for an ethical criterion.

NOTES TO CHAPTER TWELVE

General Note to this Chapter. Wherever possible, I refer in these notes to *Selections*, i.e. to *Hegel: Selections*, edited by J. Loewenberg, 1929. (From *The Modern Student's Library of Philosophy*.) This excellent and easily accessible selection contains a great number of the most characteristic passages from Hegel, so that it was possible in many cases to choose the quotations from them. Quotations from the *Selections* will, however, be accompanied by references to editions of the original texts. Wherever possible I have referred to '*WW*', i.e. to *Hegel's Sämtliche Werke*, herausgegeben von H. Glockner, Stuttgart (from 1927 on). An important version of the *Encyclopedia*, however, which is not included in *WW*, is quoted as '*Encycl.* 1870', i.e., G. W. F. Hegel, *Encyclopädie*, herausgegeben von K. Rosenkranz, Berlin 1870. Passages from the *Philosophy of Law* (or *Philosophy of Right*) are quoted by paragraph numbers, and the letter L indicates that the passage is from the lecture notes added by Gans in his edition of 1833. I have not always adopted the wording of the translators.

1. In his Inaugural Dissertation, *De Orbitis Planetarum*, 1801. (The asteroid Ceres had been discovered on the 1st of January, 1801.)

2. Democritus, fragm., 118 (D[2]); cp. text to note 29 to chapter 10.
3. Schopenhauer, *Grundprobleme* (4th edn, 1890), p. 147; cp. note 53 to chapter 11.
4. The whole *Philosophy of Nature* is full of such definitions. H. Stafford Hatfield, for instance, translates (cp. his translation of Bavink, *The Anatomy of Modern Science*, pp. 30) Hegel's definition of heat: 'Heat is the self-restoration of matter in its formlessness, its liquidity the triumph of its abstract homogeneity over specific definiteness, its abstract, purely self-existing continuity, as negation of negation, is here set as activity.' Similar is, for example, Hegel's definition of electricity.

   For the next quotation see Hegel's *Briefe*, I, 373, quoted by Wallace, *The Logic of Hegel* (transl., pp. xiv f., italics mine).
5. Cp. Falkenberg, *History of Modern Philosophy* (6th German edn, 1908, 612; cp. the English translation by Armstrong, 1895, 632).
6. I have in mind the various philosophies of 'evolution' or 'progress' or 'emergence' such as those of H. Bergson, S. Alexander, Field-Marshal Smuts or A. N. Whitehead.
7. The passage is quoted and analysed in note 43 (2), below.
8. For the eight quotations in this paragraph, cp. *Selections*, pp. 389 (= *WW*, vi, 71), 447, 443, 446 (three quotations); 388 (two quotations) (= *WW*, xi, 70). The passages are from *The Philosophy of Law* (§§ 272L, 258L, 269L, 270L); the first and the last are from the *Philosophy of History*.

   For Hegel's holism, and for his organic theory of the state, see for example his reference to Menenius Agrippa (*Livy*, II, 32; for a criticism, see note 7 to chapter 10) in the *Philosophy of Law*, § 269L; and his classical formulation of the opposition between the power of an organized body and the powerless 'heap, or aggregate, of atomic units', at the end of § 290L (cp. also note 70 to this chapter).

   Two other very important points in which Hegel adopts Plato's political teaching are: (1) The theory of the One, the Few, and the Many; see, for example, *op. cit.*, § 273: The monarch is *one* person; the *few* enter the scene with the executive; and the *many* ... with the legislative; also the reference is to 'the many' in § 301, etc. (2) The theory of the opposition between knowledge and opinion (cp. the discussion of *op. cit.*, § 270, on *freedom of thought*, in the text between notes 37 and 38, below), which Hegel uses for characterizing public opinion as the 'opinion of the many' or even as the 'caprice of the many', cp. *op. cit.*, §§ 316 ff., and note 76, below.

   For Hegel's interesting criticism of Plato, and the even more interesting twist he gives to his own criticism, cp. note 43 (2) to this chapter.
9. For these remarks, cp. especially chapter 25.
10. Cp. *Selections*, xii (J. Loewenberg in the Introduction to the *Selections*).
11. I have in mind not only his immediate philosophical predecessors (Fichte, Schlegel, Schelling, and especially Schleiermacher), or his ancient sources (Heraclitus, Plato, Aristotle), but especially Rousseau, Spinoza, Montesquieu, Herder, Burke (cp. section IV to this chapter), and the poet Schiller. Hegel's indebtedness to Rousseau, Montesquieu (cp. *The Spirit of the Laws*, XIX, 4 f.), and Herder, for his *Spirit of the Nation*, is obvious. His relations to Spinoza are of a different character. He adopts, or rather adapts, two important ideas of the determinist Spinoza. The first is that there is no freedom but in the rational recognition of the necessity of all things, and in the power which reason, by this recognition, may exert over the passions. This idea is developed by Hegel into an identification of reason (or 'Spirit') with freedom, and of his teaching that freedom is the truth of necessity (*Selections*, 213, *Encycl.*

1870, p. 154). The second idea is Spinoza's strange moral positivism, his doctrine that might is right, an idea which he contrived to use for the fight against what he called tyranny i.e. the attempt to wield power beyond the limits of one's actual power. Spinoza's main concern being the freedom of thought, he taught that it is impossible for a ruler to force men's thoughts (for thoughts are free), and that the attempt to achieve the impossible is tyrannical. On this doctrine, he based his support of the power of the secular state (which, he naïvely hoped, would not curtail the freedom of thought) as against the Church. Hegel also supported the state against the Church, and he paid lip-service to the demand for freedom of thought whose great political significance he realized (cp. the preface to the *Phil. of Law*); but at the same time he perverted this idea, claiming that the state must decide what is true and false, and may suppress what it deems to be false (see the discussion of the *Phil. of Law*, § 270, in the text between notes 37 and 38, below). From Schiller, Hegel took (incidentally without acknowledgement or even indication that he was quoting) his famous dictum 'The history of the world is the World's court of justice'. But this dictum (at the end of § 340 of the *Phil. of Law*; cp. text to note 26) implies a good deal of Hegel's historicist political philosophy; not only his worship of success and thus of power, but also his peculiar moral positivism, and his theory of the reasonableness of history.

The question whether Hegel was influenced by Vico seems to be still open. (Weber's German translation of the *New Science* was published in 1822.)

12. Schopenhauer was an ardent admirer not only of Plato but also of Heraclitus. He believed that the mob fill their bellies like the beast; he adopted Bias' dictum 'all men are wicked' as his device; and he believed that a Platonic aristocracy was the best government. At the same time, he hated nationalism, and especially German nationalism. He was a cosmopolite. The rather repulsive expressions of his fear and hatred of the revolutionaries of 1848 can be partly explained by his apprehension that under 'mob rules' he might lose his independence, and partly by his hatred of the nationalist ideology of the movement.
13. For Schopenhauer's suggestion of this motto (taken from *Cymbeline*, Act V, Sc. 4) see his *Will in Nature* (4th edn, 1878), p. 7. The two following quotations are from his *Works* (2nd edn, 1888), vol. V, 103 f., and vol. II, pp. xvii, f. (i.e. Preface to the second edn of the *World as Will and Idea*; the italics are mine). I believe that everybody who has studied Schopenhauer must be impressed by his sincerity and truthfulness. Cp. also the judgement of Kierkegaard, quoted in the text to notes 19/20 to chapter 25.
14. Schwegler's first publication (1839) was an essay in memory of Hegel. The quotation is from his *History of Philosophy*, transl. by H. Stirling, 7th edn, p. 322.
15. 'To English readers Hegel was first introduced in the powerful statement of his principles by Dr. Hutchinson Stirling', writes E. Caird (*Hegel*, 1883, Preface, p. vi); which may show that Stirling was taken quite seriously. The following quotation is from Stirling's *Annotations* to Schwegler's *History*, p. 429. I may remark that the motto of the present chapter is taken from p. 441 of the same work.
16. Stirling writes (*op. cit.*, 441): 'The great thing at last for Hegel was a good citizen, and for him who was already that, there was to Hegel's mind no call for philosophy. Thus he tells a M. Duboc who writes to him about his difficulties with the system, that, as a good head of a house and father of a family, possessed of a faith that is firm, he has pretty well enough, and may consider anything further, in the way of

philosophy, for instance, as but ... an intellectual luxury.' Thus, according to Stirling, *Hegel was not interested in clearing up a difficulty in his system, but merely in converting 'bad' citizens into 'good' ones.*

17. The following quotation is from Stirling, *op. cit.*, 444 f. Stirling continues the last sentence quoted in the text: 'I have gained much from Hegel, and will always thankfully acknowledge that much, but my position in his regard has been simply that of one who, in making the unintelligible intelligible, would do a service to the public.' And he ends the paragraph by saying: 'My general aim ... I conceive to be identical with Hegel's ... that, namely, of a Christian philosopher.'
18. Cp., for example, *A Textbook of Marxist Philosophy*.
19. I take this passage from the most interesting study, *Nationalism and the Cultural Crisis in Prussia, 1806–1815*, by E. N. Anderson (1939), p. 270. Anderson's analysis is critical of nationalism, and he clearly recognizes the neurotic and hysterical element in it (cp., for example, pp. 6 f.). And yet I cannot entirely agree with his attitude. Led, I suppose, by the historian's desire for objectivity, he seems to me to take the nationalist movement too seriously. I cannot agree, more particularly, with his condemnation of King Frederick William for his lack of understanding of the nationalist movement. 'Frederick William lacked the capacity for appreciating greatness', Anderson writes on p. 271, 'whether in an ideal or in an action. The course into nationalism which the rising German literature and philosophy opened so brilliantly for others remained closed to him.' But by far the best of German literature and philosophy was anti-nationalistic; Kant and Schopenhauer were both anti-national, and even Goethe kept away from nationalism; and it is unjustifiable to demand of anybody, and especially of a simple, candid, conservative like the king, that he should get excited about Fichte's windbaggery. Many will fully agree with the king's judgement when he spoke (*loc. cit.*) of 'eccentric, popular scribbling'. Although I agree that the king's conservatism was very unfortunate, I feel the greatest respect for his simplicity, and his resistance to the wave of nationalist hysteria.
20. Cp. *Selections*, xi (J. Loewenberg in the Introduction to the *Selections*).
21. Cp. notes 19 to chapter 5 and 18 to chapter 11, and text.
22. For this quotation see *Selections*, 103 (= *WW*, iii, 116); for the next one, see *Selections*, 130 (= G. W. F. Hegel, *Werke*, Berlin and Leipzig 1832–1887, vol. vi, 224). For the last quotation in this paragraph, see *Selections*, 131 (= *Werke*, 1832–1887, vol. vi, 224–5).
23. Cp. *Selections*, 103 (= *WW*, iii, 103).
24. Cp. *Selections*, 128 (= *WW*, iii, 141).
25. I am alluding to Bergson, and especially to his *Creative Evolution*. (Engl. transl. by A. Mitchell, 1913.) It appears that the Hegelian character of this work is not sufficiently recognized; and, indeed, Bergson's lucidity and reasoned presentation of his thought sometimes make it difficult to realize how much his philosophy depends on Hegel. But if we consider, for example, that Bergson teaches that *the essence is change*, or if we read passages like the following (cp. *op. cit.*, 275 and 278), then there remains little doubt.

    'Essential also is the progress to reflection', writes Bergson. 'If our analysis is correct, it is consciousness, or rather super-consciousness, that is at the origin of life ... Consciousness corresponds exactly to the living being's power of choice; it is co-extensive with the fringe of possible action that surrounds real action: *consciousness is synonymous* with invention and *with freedom*.' (Italics mine.) The identification of consciousness (or Spirit) with freedom is the Hegelian version of Spinoza. This goes so far that theories can be found in Hegel which I feel inclined to describe as 'unmistakably Bergsonian'; for example, 'The very essence of Spirit is activity; it realizes its potentiality; it makes itself its own deed, its own work ...' (*Selections*, 435 = *WW*, xi, 113.)

26. Cp. notes 21 to 24 to chapter 11, and text. Another characteristic passage is this (cp. *Selections*, 409 = *WW*, xi, 89): 'The principle of *Development* involves also the existence of a latent germ of being—a capacity or potentiality striving to realize itself.'—For the quotation later in the paragraph, cp. *Selections*, 468 (i.e. *Phil. of Law*, § 340; see also note 11, above).
27. Considering, on the other hand, that even a second-hand Hegelianism, i.e. a third- or fourth-hand Fichteanism and Aristotelianism, has often been noisily acclaimed as an original achievement, it is perhaps a little hard on Hegel to say that he was unoriginal. (But cp. note 11.)
28. Cp. Kant's *Critique of Pure Reason*, 2nd edn, p. 514 (top); see also p. 518 (end of section 5); for the motto of my Introduction, see Kant's letter to Mendelssohn of April 8th, 1766.
29. Cp. note 53 to chapter 11, and text.
30. It is perhaps reasonable to assume that what one usually calls the 'spirit of a language' is very largely the *traditional standard of clarity* introduced by the great writers of that particular language. There are some further traditional standards in a language, apart from clarity, for example, standards of simplicity, of ornamentation, of brevity, etc.; but the standard of clarity is perhaps the most important of them; and it is a cultural inheritance which should be carefully guarded. Language is one of the most important institutions of social life, and its clarity is a condition of its functioning as a means of rational communication. Its use for the communication of emotions is much less important, for we can communicate a great deal of emotion without saying a word.

* It may be worth saying that Hegel, who had learned from Burke something about the importance of the historical growth of traditions, did in fact do much to destroy the intellectual tradition which Kant had founded, both by his doctrine of 'the cunning of reason' which reveals itself in passion (see notes 82, 84 and text), and by his actual method of arguing. But he did more. By his historical relativism—by his theory that truth is relative, dependent on the spirit of the age—he helped to destroy the tradition of searching for truth, and of respecting truth. See also section IV of this chapter, and my paper, 'Towards a Rational Theory of Tradition' (in *The Rationalist Annual*, 1949; now in my *Conjectures and Refutations*).*

31. Attempts to refute Kant's Dialectics (his doctrine of Antinomies) seem to be very rare. Serious criticism attempting to clarify and restate Kant's arguments can be found in Schopenhauer's *World as Will and Idea* and in J. F. Fries' *New or Anthropological Critique of Reason*, second German edn, 1828, pp. xxiv ff. I have tried to interpret Kant as holding that mere speculation cannot establish anything where experience cannot help to weed out false theories. (Cp. *Mind*, 49, 1940, p. 416; also, *Conjectures and Refutations*, pp. 326 f. In the same volume of *Mind*, pp. 204 ff., there is a careful and interesting criticism of Kant's argument by M. Fried.) For an attempt to make sense of Hegel's dialectical theory of reason as well as of his collectivist interpretation of reason (his 'objective spirit'), see the analysis of the social or

interpersonal aspect of scientific method in chapter 23, and the corresponding interpretation of 'reason' in chapter 24.

32. I have given a detailed justification of this in 'What is Dialectic?' (*Mind*, 49, pp. 403 ff.; see especially the last sentence on p. 410: also, *Conjectures and Refutations*, p. 321). See also a further note under the title, *Are Contradictions Embracing?* *This has since appeared in *Mind*, 52, 1943, pp. 47 ff. After it was written I received Carnap's *Introduction to Semantics*, 1942, where he uses the term 'comprehensive', which seems preferable to 'embracing'. See especially § 30 of Carnap's book.*

In 'What is Dialectic?' a number of problems are treated which are only touched upon in the present book; especially the transition from Kant to Hegel, Hegel's dialectics, and his philosophy of identity. Although a few statements from that paper have been repeated here, the two presentations of the problems are in the main complementary to one another. Cp. also the next notes, down to note 36.

33. Cp. *Selections*, xxviii (the German quotation; for similar quotations see *WW*, iv, 618, and *Werke* 1832–1887, vol. vi, 259). For the idea of a *reinforced dogmatism* mentioned in this paragraph, cp. 'What is Dialectic?', p. 417, and *Conjectures and Refutations*, p. 327; see also note 51 to chapter 11.

34. Cp. 'What is Dialectic?' especially from p. 414, where the problem, 'How can our mind grasp the world?' is introduced, down to p. 420 (*Conjectures and Refutations*, pp. 325–30).

35. 'Everything actual is an Idea', says Hegel. Cp. *Selections*, 103 (= *WW*, iii, 116); and from the perfection of the Idea, moral positivism follows. See also *Selections*, 388 (= *WW*, xi, 70), i.e. the last passage quoted in the text to note 8; see, furthermore, § 6 of the *Encyclopædia*, and the Preface as well as § 270L of the *Philosophy of Right*.—I need hardly add that the 'Great Dictator' in the previous paragraph is an allusion to Chaplin's film.

36. Cp. *Selections*, 103 (= *WW*, iii, 116). See also *Selections*, 128, § 107 (= *WW*, iii, 142).

Hegel's philosophy of identity shows, of course, the influence of the mystic theory of knowledge of Aristotle—the doctrine of the unity of the knowing subject and the known object. (Cp. notes 33 to chapter 11, 59–70 to chapter 10, notes 4, 6, and 29–32, and 58, to chapter 24.)

To my remarks in the text about Hegel's philosophy of identity, it may be added that Hegel believed, with most of the philosophers of his time, that logic is the theory of thinking or of reasoning. (See 'What is Dialectic?' p. 418.) This, together with the philosophy of identity, has the consequence that logic is considered as the theory of thought, or of reason, or of the Ideas or notions, or of the Real. From the further premise that thought develops dialectically, Hegel can deduce that reason, the Ideas or notions, and the Real, all develop dialectically; and he further gets *Logic = Dialectics* and *Logic = Theory of Reality*. This latter doctrine is known as Hegel's *pan-logism*.

On the other hand, Hegel can derive from these premises that notions develop dialectically, i.e. are capable of a kind of self-creation and self-development, out of nothing. (Hegel begins this development with the Idea of Being which presupposes its opposite, i.e. Nothing, and creates the transition from Nothing to Being, i.e. Becoming.) There are two motives for this attempt to develop notions out of nothing. The one is the mistaken idea that philosophy has to start without any presuppositions. (This idea has been recently reaffirmed by Husserl; it is discussed in chapter 24; cp. note 8 to that chapter, and text.) This leads Hegel to start from 'nothing'. The other motive is the hope of giving a systematic development and justification of Kant's Table of Categories. Kant had made the remark that the first two categories of each group are opposed to each other, and that the third is a kind of synthesis of the first. This remark (and the influence of Fichte) led Hegel to hope that he could derive all categories 'dialectically', out of nothing, and thereby justify the 'necessity' of all the categories.

37. Cp. *Selections*, xvi (= *Werke*, 1832–1887, vi, 153–4).
38. Cp. Anderson, *Nationalism*, etc., 294.—The king promised the constitution on May 22, 1815.—The story of the 'constitution' and the court-physician seems to have been told of most of the princes of the period (for example, of the emperor Francis I as well as his successor Ferdinand I of Austria).—The next quotation is from *Selections*, 246 f. (= *Encycl.* 1870, pp. 437–8).
39. Cp. *Selections*, 248 f. (= *Encycl.* 1870, pp. 437–8; italics partly mine).
40. Cp. note 25 to chapter 11.
41. For the *paradox of freedom*, cp. note 43 (1) below; the four paragraphs in the text before note 42 to chapter 6; notes 4 and 6 to chapter 7, and note 7 to chapter 24; and the passages in the text. (See also note 20 to chapter 17.) For Rousseau's restatement of the paradox of freedom, cp. the *Social Contract*, Book I, chapter VIII, second paragraph. For Kant's solution, cp. note 4 to chapter 6. Hegel frequently alludes to this Kantian solution (cp. Kant's *Metaphysics of Morals*, Introduction to the Theory of Law, § C; *Works*, ed. by Cassirer, VII, p. 31); for example in his *Philosophy of Law*, § 29; and § 270, where, following Aristotle and Burke (cp. note 43 to chapter 6 and text), Hegel argues against the theory (due to Lycophron and Kant) that 'the state's specific function consists in the protection of everybody's life, property, and caprice', as he sneeringly puts it.

    For the two quotations at the beginning and end of this paragraph, cp. *Selections*, 248 f., and 249 (= *Encycl.* 1870, p. 439).
42. For the quotations, cp. *Selections*, 250 (= *Encycl.* 1870, pp. 440–41).
43. (1) For the following quotations, cp. *Selections*, 251 (§ 540 = *Encycl.* 1870, p. 441); 251 f. (first sentence of § 541 = *Encycl.* 1870, p. 442); and 253 f. (beginning of § 542, italics partly mine = *Encycl.* 1870, p. 443). These are the passages from the *Encyclopædia*. The 'parallel passage' from the *Philosophy of Law* is: § 273 (last paragraph) to § 281. The two quotations are from § 275, and from § 279, end of first paragraph (italics mine). For a similarly dubious use of the paradox of freedom, cp. *Selections*, 394 (= *WW*, xi, 76): 'If the principle of regard for the individual will is recognized as the only basis of political liberty ... then we have, properly speaking, *no Constitution*.' See also *Selections*, 400 f. (= *WW*, xi, 80–81), and 449 (see the *Philosophy of Law*, § 274).

    Hegel himself summarizes his twist (*Selections*, 401 = *WW*, xi, 82): 'At an earlier stage of the discussion, we established ... *first*, the Idea of Freedom as the absolute and final aim ... We *then* recognized the State as the moral Whole and the Reality of Freedom ...' Thus we begin with freedom and end with the totalitarian state. One can hardly present the twist more cynically.

    (2) For another example of a dialectic twist, viz., that of *reason into passion and violence*, see end of (g) in section IV, below, of the present chapter (text to note 84). Particularly interesting in this connection is *Hegel's criticism of Plato*. (See also notes 7 and 8 above, and text.) Hegel, paying lip-service to all modern and 'Christian'

values, not only to freedom, but even to the 'subjective freedom' of the individual, criticizes Plato's holism or collectivism (*Phil. of Law*, § 185): 'The principle of the self-sufficient ... personality of the individual, the principle of subjective freedom, is denied its right by ... Plato. This principle dawned ... in the Christian religion and ... in the Roman World.' This criticism is excellent, and it proves that Hegel knew what Plato was about; in fact, Hegel's reading of Plato agrees very well with my own. For the untrained reader of Hegel, this passage might even prove the injustice of branding Hegel as a collectivist. But we have only to turn to § 70L of the same work in order to see that Plato's most radical collectivist saying, 'You are created for the sake of the whole, and not the whole for the sake of you', is fully subscribed to by Hegel, who writes: 'A single person, it hardly needs saying, is something subordinate, and as such he must dedicate himself to the ethical whole', i.e. the state. This is Hegel's 'individualism'.

But why, then, does he criticize Plato? Why does he emphasize the importance of 'subjective freedom'? §§ 316 and 317 of the *Philosophy of Law* give an answer to this question. Hegel is convinced that revolutions can be avoided only by granting the people, as a kind of safety valve, a certain small amount of freedom which should not go beyond an irrelevant opportunity to give vent to their feelings. Thus he writes (*op. cit.*, §§316, 317L, italics mine): 'In our day ... the principle of subjective freedom is of great importance and significance ... Everybody wishes to participate in discussions and deliberations. But once he has had his say, ... his subjectivity is gratified and *he will put up with a lot*. In France, freedom of speech has proved far less dangerous than silence imposed by force; with the latter ... men have to swallow everything, while if they are permitted to argue, they have an outlet as well as some satisfaction; *and in this way, a thing may be pushed ahead more easily*.' It must be difficult to surpass the cynicism exhibited by this discussion in which Hegel gives vent, so freely, to his feeling concerning 'subjective freedom' or, as he often calls it so solemnly, '*the principle of the modern world*'.

To sum up. Hegel agrees with Plato completely, except that he criticizes Plato's failure to provide the ruled with the illusion of 'subjective freedom'.

44. The astonishing thing is that these despicable services could be successful, that even serious people have been deceived by Hegel's dialectical method. As an example it may be mentioned that even such a critical and enlightened fighter for freedom and reason as C. E. Vaughan fell a victim to Hegel's hypocrisy, when he expressed his belief in Hegel's 'belief in freedom and progress which, *on Hegel's own showing*, is ... the essence of his creed'. (Cp. C. E. Vaughan, *Studies in the History of Political Philosophy*, vol. II, 296; italics mine.) It must be admitted that Vaughan criticized Hegel's 'undue leaning towards the established order' (p. 178); he even said of Hegel that 'no one could ... be more ready ... to assure the world that the most retrograde and oppressive institutions ... must ... be accepted as indisputably rational' (p. 295); yet he trusted 'Hegel's own showing' so much that he took features of this kind as mere 'extravagances' (p. 295), as 'shortcomings for which it is easy to allow' (p. 182). Moreover, his strongest and perfectly justified comment, that Hegel 'discovers the last word of political wisdom, the coping stone ... of history, in the Prussian Constitution' (p. 182), was not fated to be published without an antidote restoring the reader's confidence in Hegel; for the editor of Vaughan's posthumous *Studies* destroys the force of Vaughan's comment by adding in a

foot-note, with reference to a passage from Hegel which he assumes to be the one alluded to by Vaughan (he does not refer to the passage quoted here in the text to notes 47, 48, and 49), 'but perhaps the passage hardly justifies the comment ...'

45. See note 36 to this chapter. An indication of this dialectical theory may be found as early as in Aristotle's *Physics*, I, 5.

46. I am greatly indebted to E. H. Gombrich, who permitted me to adopt the main ideas of this paragraph from his excellent criticism of my presentation of Hegel (communicated to me by letter).

For Hegel's view that 'the Absolute Spirit manifests itself in the history of the world', see his *Philosophy of Law*, § 259L. For his identification of the 'Absolute Spirit' with the 'World Spirit', see *op. cit.*, § 339L. For the view that perfection is the aim of Providence, and for Hegel's attack on the (Kantian) view that the plan of Providence is inscrutable, see *op. cit.*, § 343. (For M. B. Foster's interesting counter-attacks, see note 19 to chapter 25.) For Hegel's use of (dialectical) syllogisms, see especially the *Encyclopædia*, § 181 ('the syllogism is the rational, and everything rational'); § 198, where the state is described as a triad of syllogisms; and §§ 575 to 577, where Hegel's whole system is presented as such a triad of syllogisms. According to this last passage, we might infer that 'history' is the realm of the 'second syllogism' (§ 576); cp. *Selections*, 309 f. For the first passage (from section III of the Introduction to the *Philosophy of History*), see *Selections*, 348 f.—For the next passage (from the *Encyclopædia*) see *Selections*, 262 f.

47. Cp. *Selections*, 442 (last paragraph = *WW*, xi, 119–20). The last quotation in this paragraph is from the same place.

Concerning the three steps, cp. *Selections*, 360, 362, 398 (= *WW*, xi, 44, 46, 79–80). See also Hegel's *Philosophy of History* (transl. by J. Sibree, 1857, quoted from the edition of 1914), p. 110: 'The East knew ... only that *One* is free; the Greek and the Roman World, that *some* are free; the German World knows that *All* are free. The first political form therefore which we observe in History is *Despotism*, the second *Democracy* and *Aristocracy*, the third *Monarchy*.'

(For the further treatment of the three steps, cp. *op. cit.*, pp. 117, 260, 354.)

48. For the next three quotations cp. Hegel's *Philosophy of History*, 429; *Selections*, 358, 359 (= *WW*, xi, 43–44).

The presentation in the text simplifies the matter somewhat; for Hegel first divides (*Phil. of Hist.*, 356 ff.) the Germanic World into three periods which he describes (p. 358) as the 'Kingdoms of the Father, the Son and the Spirit'; and the kingdom of the Spirit is again subdivided into the three periods mentioned in the text.

49. For the following three passages, cp. the *Philosophy of History*, pp. 354, 476, 476–7.

50. See especially text to note 75 to this chapter.

51. Cp. especially notes 48–50 to chapter 8.

52. Cp. Hegel's *Philosophy of History*, p. 418. (The translator writes: 'Germanized Sclaves'.)

53. Masaryk has been described sometimes as a 'philosopher king'. But he was certainly not a ruler of the kind Plato would have liked; for he was a democrat. He was very interested in Plato, but he idealized Plato and interpreted him democratically. His nationalism was a reaction to national oppression, and he always fought against nationalist excesses. It may be mentioned that his first printed work in the Czech language was an article on Plato's patriotism. (Cp. K. Capek's biography of Masaryk,

the chapter on his period as a university student.) Masaryk's Czechoslovakia was probably one of the best and most democratic states that ever existed; but in spite of all that, it was built on the principle of the national state, on a principle which in this world is inapplicable. An international federation in the Danube basin might have prevented much.

54. See chapter 7. For the quotation from Rousseau, later in the paragraph, cp. the *Social Contract*, book I, ch. VII (end of second paragraph). For Hegel's view concerning the doctrine of the sovereignty of the people, see the passage from § 279 of the *Philosophy of Law* quoted in text to note 61 to this chapter.

55. Cp. Herder, quoted by Zimmern, *Modern Political Doctrines* (1939), p. 165 f. (The passage quoted in my text is not characteristic of Herder's empty verbalism, which was criticized by Kant.)

56. Cp. note 7 to chapter 9.

For the two quotations from Kant, further on in this paragraph, cp. *Works* (ed. by E. Cassirer), vol. IV, p. 179; and p. 195.

57. Cp. Fichte's *Briefwechsel* (ed. Schulz, 1925), II, p. 100. The letter is partly quoted by Anderson, *Nationalism*, etc., p. 30. (Cp. also Hegemann, *Entlarvte Geschichte*, 2nd ed., 1934, p. 118.)—The next quotation is from Anderson, *op. cit.*, p. 34 f.—For the quotations in the next paragraph, cp. *op. cit.*, 36 f.; italics mine.

It may be remarked that an originally anti-German feeling is common to many of the founders of German nationalism; which shows how far nationalism is based upon a feeling of inferiority. (Cp. notes 61 and 70 to this chapter.) As an example, Anderson says (*op. cit.*, 79) about E. M. Arndt, later a famous nationalist: 'When Arndt travelled through Europe in 1798–9, he called himself a Swede because, as he said, the name German "stinks in the world"; not, he added characteristically, through the fault of the common people.' Hegemann insists rightly (*op. cit.*, 118) that the German spiritual leaders of the time turned especially against the barbarism of Prussia, and he quotes Winckelmann, who said, 'I would rather be a Turkish eunuch than a Prussian'; and Lessing, who said, 'Prussia is the most slavish country in Europe'; and he refers to Goethe, who passionately hoped that relief would come from Napoleon. And Hegemann, who is also the author of a book against Napoleon, adds: 'Napoleon was a despot; ... whatever we have to say against him, it must be admitted that by his victory of Jena he had forced the reactionary state of Frederick to introduce a few reforms that had been long overdue.'

An interesting judgement on the Germany of 1800 can be found in Kant's *Anthropology* (1800), where he deals, not quite seriously, with *national characteristics*. Kant writes (*Works*, vol. VIII, 213, 211, 212; italics mine) of the German 'His bad side is the compulsion to imitate others and *his low opinion of himself* with respect to his own originality ...; and especially a certain pedantic inclination to classify himself painstakingly in relation to other citizens, according to a system of rank and of prerogatives. In this system of rank, he is inexhaustible in the invention of titles, and thus *slavish out of pedantry* ... Of all civilized peoples, the German submits most easily and most lastingly to the government under which he happens to live, and he is further removed than any other from a love of change and from resistance to the established order. His character is a kind of phlegmatic reason.'

58. Cp. Kant's *Works*, vol. VIII, 516. Kant, who had been immediately ready to help when Fichte appealed to him as an unknown author in distress, hesitated for seven years

after the anonymous publication of Fichte's first book to speak his mind about Fichte, although he was pressed to do so from various sides, for example by Fichte himself, who posed as the fulfiller of the Kantian promise. Ultimately, Kant published his *Public Explanation Regarding Fichte*, as a reply 'to the solemn demand made by a reviewer in the name of the public', that he should speak his mind. He declared that, in his view, 'Fichte's system was totally untenable'; and he declined to have anything to do with a philosophy which consisted of 'barren subtleties'. And after praying (as quoted in the text) that God may protect us from our friends, Kant goes on to say: 'For there may be also ... fraudulent and perfidious friends who are scheming for our ruin, although they speak the language of benevolence; one cannot be sufficiently cautious in order to avoid the traps they set for us.' If Kant, a most balanced, benevolent, and conscientious person, was moved to say things such as these, then we have every reason to consider his judgement seriously. *But I have seen so far no history of philosophy which clearly states that, in Kant's opinion, Fichte was a dishonest impostor*; although I have seen many histories of philosophy that try to explain away Schopenhauer's indictments, for example, by hinting that he was envious.

But Kant's and Schopenhauer's accusations are by no means isolated. A. von Feuerbach (in a letter of January 30th, 1799; cp. Schopenhauer's *Works*, vol. V, 102) expressed himself as strongly as Schopenhauer; Schiller arrived at a similar opinion, and so did Goethe; and Nicolovius called Fichte a 'sycophant and a deceiver'. (Cp. also Hegemann, *op. cit.*, pp. 119 ff.)

It is astonishing to see that, thanks to a conspiracy of noise, a man like Fichte succeeded in perverting the teaching of his 'master', *in spite of Kant's protests, and in Kant's lifetime*. This happened only a hundred years ago and can easily be checked by anybody who takes the trouble to read Kant's and Fichte's letters, and Kant's public announcements; and it shows that my theory of Plato's perversion of the teaching of Socrates is by no means so fantastic as it may appear to Platonists. Socrates was dead then, and he had left no letters. (Were the comparison not one that does too much honour to Fichte and Hegel, one would be tempted to say: without Plato, there could have been no Aristotle; and without Fichte, no Hegel.)

59. Cp. Anderson, *op. cit.*, p. 13.
60. Cp. Hegel's *Philosophy of History*, 465. See also *Philosophy of Law*, § 258. With Pareto's advice, cp. note 1 to chapter 13.
61. Cp. *Philosophy of Law*, § 279; for the next quotation, see *Selections*, 256 f. (= *Encycl.* 1870, p. 446). The attack upon England, further below in the paragraph, follows on p. 257 (= *Encycl.* 1870, p. 447). For Hegel's reference to the German empire, cp. *Philosophy of History*, p. 475 (see also note 77 to this chapter).—Feelings of inferiority, especially in relation to England, and clever appeals to such feelings, play a considerable part in the story of the rise of nationalism; cp. also notes 57 and 70 to this chapter. For other passages on England, see the next note and note 70 to this chapter, and text. (The words 'arts and science' are italicized by me.)
62. Hegel's disparaging reference to merely 'formal' rights, to merely 'formal' freedom, to a merely 'formal' constitution, etc., is interesting, since it is the dubious source of the modern Marxist criticism of merely 'formal' democracies which offer merely 'formal' freedom. Cp. note 19 to chapter 17 and text.

A few characteristic passages in which Hegel denounces merely 'formal' freedom, etc., may be quoted here. They are all taken from the *Philosophy of History*—(p. 471):

'Liberalism sets up, in opposition to all this' (i.e. to the Prussian 'holistic' restoration), 'the atomistic principle which insists upon the sway of individual wills, maintaining that all governments should ... have their' (the people's) 'explicit sanction. In thus asserting the *formal side of Freedom*—this mere abstraction—the party in question makes it impossible firmly to establish any political organization.'—(p. 474): 'The Constitution of England is a complex of *mere particular rights* and particular privileges, ... Of institutions characterized by real freedom' (as opposed to merely formal freedom) 'there are nowhere fewer than in England. In point of private rights and the freedom of possessions they present an incredible deficiency: sufficient proof of which is afforded in the rights of primogeniture which make it necessary to provide (by purchase or otherwise) military or ecclesiastical appointments for the younger sons of the aristocracy.' See further the discussion of the French declaration of the Rights of Man and Kant's principles on pp. 462 ff. with its reference to 'nothing more than *formal* Will' and the 'principle of Freedom' that 'remained merely formal'; and contrast this, for example, with the remarks on p. 354, which show that the German Spirit is 'true' and 'absolute' freedom: 'The German Spirit is the Spirit of the new World. Its aim is the realization of absolute Truth as the unlimited self-determination of Freedom; of that Freedom which has its own absolute form itself as its purport.' If I were to use the term 'formal freedom' in a disparaging sense, then I should apply it to Hegel's 'subjective freedom', as treated by him in *Philosophy of Law*, § 317L (quoted at the end of note 43).

63. Cp. Anderson, *Nationalism*, etc., p. 279. For Hegel's reference to England (quoted in brackets at the end of this paragraph), cp. *Selections*, 263 (= *Encycl.* 1870, p. 452); see also note 70 to this chapter.

64. This quotation is from the *Philosophy of Law*, § 331. For the following two quotations, cp. *Selections*, 403 (= *WW*, xi, 84) and 267 f. (= *Encycl.* 1870, pp. 455–56). For the quotation further below (illustrating juridical positivism), cp. *Selections*, 449 (i.e. *Phil. of Law*, § 274). With the theory of world dominion, cp. also the theory of domination and submission, and of slavery, outlined in note 25 to chapter 11, and text. For the theory of national spirits or wills or geniuses asserting themselves in history, i.e. in the history of wars see text to notes 69 and 77.

In connection with the *historical theory of the nation*, cp. the following remarks of Renan (quoted by A. Zimmern in *Modern Political Doctrines*, pp. 190 f.): 'To forget and—I will venture to say—to get one's history wrong, are essential factors in the making of a nation [or, as we now know, of a totalitarian state]; and thus the advance of historical studies is often a danger to nationality ... Now it is of the essence of a nation that all individuals should have much in common, and further that they should all have forgotten much.' One would hardly believe that Renan is a nationalist; but he is, although one of the democratic type; and his nationalism is typically Hegelian; for he writes (p. 202): 'A nation is a soul, a spiritual principle.'

65. Haeckel can hardly be taken seriously as a philosopher or scientist. He called himself a free thinker, but his thinking was not sufficiently independent to prevent him from demanding in 1914 'the following fruits of victory': '(1) Emancipation from England's tyranny: (2) the invasion of the British pirate state by the German navy and army; the capture of London; (3) the partitioning of Belgium'; and so forth for quite a time. (In: *Das Monistische Jahrhundert*, 1914, No. 31/32, pp. 65 f., quoted in *Thus Spake Germany*, 270.)

W. Schallmayer's prize essay has the title: *Heredity and Selection in the Life of the Nations*. (See also note 71 to chapter 10, above.)

66. For Bergson's Hegelianism, cp. note 25 to this chapter. For Shaw's characterization of the religion of creative evolution, cp. *Back to Methuselah*, the last section of the Preface ('My Own Part in The Matter'): '... as the conception of Creative Evolution developed, I saw that we were at last within reach of a faith which complied with the first condition of all the religions that have ever taken hold of humanity: namely that it must be, first and fundamentally, a science of metabiology.'
67. Cp. A. Zimmern's excellent Introduction to his *Modern Political Doctrines*, p. xviii.—Regarding Platonic totalitarianism, cp. text to note 8 to this chapter. For the theory of master and slave, and of domination and submission, cp. note 25 to chapter 11; see also note 74 to the present chapter.
68. Cp. Schopenhauer, *Grundprobleme*, p. xix.
69. For the eight quotations in this paragraph, cp. *Selections*, 265, 402, 403, 435, 436, 399, 407, 267 f. (= *Encycl.* 1870, p. 453, *WW*, xi, 83, 84, 113–14, 81, 88, *Encycl.* pp. 455–6). Cp. also § 347 of the *Philosophy of Law*.
70. Cp. *Selections*, 435 f. (= *WW*, xi, 114). For the problem of inferiority, cp. also notes 57 and 61 to this chapter, and text. For the other passage on England, see notes 61–63, and text to this chapter. A very interesting passage (*Phil. of Law*, § 290L) containing a classical formulation of holism shows that Hegel not only thought in terms of holism or collectivism and power, but also that he saw the applicability of these principles towards the organization of the proletariat. 'The lower classes', Hegel writes, 'have been left more or less unorganized. And yet, it is of the utmost importance that they should be organized, for only in this way can they become powerful. Without organization, they are nothing but a heap, an aggregate of atoms.' Hegel comes pretty close to Marx in this passage.
71. The passage is from H. Freyer, *Pallas Athene* (1935), quoted by A. Kolnai, *The War against the West* (1938), p. 417. I am greatly indebted to Kolnai's book, which has made it possible for me to quote in the remaining part of this chapter a considerable number of authors who would otherwise have been inaccessible to me. (I have, however, not always followed the wording of Kolnai's translations.)

    For the characterization of Freyer as one of the leading sociologists of contemporary Germany, cp. F. A. von Hayek, *Freedom and the Economic System* (Public Policy Pamphlet No. 29, 2nd impression, 1940), p. 30.

    For the four passages in this paragraph from Hegel's *Philosophy of Law*, §§ 331, 340, 342L (cp. also 331 f.) and 340, see *Selections*, 466, 467, 465, 468. For the passages from the *Encyclopædia*, cp. *Selections*, 260 f. (= *Encycl.* 1870, pp. 449–50). (The last sentence quoted is a different version of the first sentence of § 546.)

    For the passage from H. von Treitschke, cp. *Thus Spake Germany* (1941), p. 60.
72. Cp. *Philosophy of Law*, § 257, i.e. *Selections*, 443. For the next three quotations, see *Philosophy of Law*, §§ 334 and 339L, i.e. *Selections*, 467. For the last quotation in this paragraph, cp. Hegel's *Philosophy of Law*, §§ 330L and 333.
73. Cp. *Selections*, 365 (= *WW*, xi, 49); italics partly mine. For the next quotation, cp. *Selections*, 468, i.e. *Philosophy of Law*, § 340.
74. Quoted by Kolnai, *op. cit.*, 418.—For Heraclitus, cp. text to note 10 to chapter 2.—For Haiser, see Kolnai, *loc. cit.*; cp. also Hegel's theory of slavery, mentioned in note 25 to chapter 11.—For the concluding quotation of this paragraph, cp. *Selections*,

467, i.e. *Philosophy of Law*, 334. For the 'war of defence' that turns into a 'war of conquest', see *op. cit.*, § 326.

75. For all the passages from Hegel in this paragraph, cp. *Selections*, 426 f. (= *WW*, xi, 105–6). (Italics mine.) For another passage expressing the postulate that world-history must overrule morals, see the *Philosophy of Law*, § 345. For E. Meyer, cp. end of note 15 (2) to chapter 10.
76. See *Philosophy of Law*, § 317 f.; cp. *Selections*, 461; for similar passages, see § 316: 'Public opinion as it exists is a continuous self-contradiction'; see also § 301, i.e. *Selections*, 456, and § 318L. (For further views of Hegel on public opinion, cp. also text to note 84 to this chapter.)—For Haiser's remark, cp. Kolnai, *op. cit.*, 234.
77. Cp. *Selections*, 464, 465, for the passages from the *Philosophy of Law*, §§ 324 and 324L. For the next passages from the *Philosophy of History*, cp. *Selections*, 436 f. (= *WW*, xi, 114–15). (The next passage quoted continues characteristically: '... naturally dead in itself, as e.g. the German Imperial Cities, the German Imperial Constitution.' With this, cp. note 61 to this chapter, and text.)
78. Cp. *Philosophy of Law*, §§ 327L and 328, i.e. *Selections*, 465 f. (Italics mine.) For the remark on gunpowder, cp. Hegel's *Philosophy of History*, p. 419.
79. For the quotations from Kaufmann, Banse, Ludendorff, Scheler, Freyer, Lenz, and Jung, cp. Kolnai, *op. cit.*, 411, 411 f., 412, 411, 417, 411, and 420.—For the quotation from J. G. Fichte's *Addresses to the German Nation* (1808), cp. the German edition of 1871 (edited by I. H. Fichte), pp. 49 f.; see also A. Zimmern, *Modern Political Doctrines*, 170 f.—For Spengler's repetition, see his *Decline of the West*, I, p. 12; for Rosenberg's repetition, cp. his *Myth of the Twentieth Century* (1935), p. 143; see also my note 50 to chapter 8, and Rader, *No Compromise* (1939), 116.
80. Cp. Kolnai, *op. cit.*, 412.
81. Cp. Caird, *Hegel* (1883), p. 26.
82. Kolnai, *op. cit.*, 438.—For the passages from Hegel, cp. *Selections*, 365 f., italics partly mine; cp. also text to note 84 to this chapter. For E. Krieck, cp. Kolnai, *op. cit.*, 65 f., and E. Krieck, *National-Political Education* (in German, 1932, p. 1; quoted in *Thus Spake Germany*, p. 53).
83. Cp. *Selections*, 268 (= *Encycl.* 1870, p. 456); for Stapel, cp. Kolnai, *op. cit.*, 292 f.
84. For Rosenberg, cp. Kolnai, *op. cit.*, 295. For Hegel's views on public opinion, cp. also text to note 76 to this chapter; for the passages quoted in the present paragraph, see *Philosophy of Law*, § 318L, i.e. *Selections*, pp. 461 (italics mine), 375, 377, 377, 378, 367/368, 380, 368, 364, 388, 380 (= *WW*, xi, 59, 60, 60, 60–61, 51–2, 63, 52, 48, 70–1, 63). (Italics partly mine.) For Hegel's eulogy of emotion and passion and self-interest, cp. also text to note 82 to this chapter.
85. For Best, cp. Kolnai, *op. cit.*, 414 f.—For the quotations from Hegel, cp. *Selections*, 464 f., 464, 465, 437 (= *WW*, xi, 115, a noteworthy similarity to Bergson), 372. (The passages from *Phil. of Law* are from §§ 324, 324L, 327L.)—For the remark on Aristotle, cp. *Pol.*, VII, 15, 3 (1334a).
86. For Stapel, cp. Kolnai, *op. cit.*, 255–257.
87. Cp. *Selections*, p. 100: 'If I neglect *all* the determinations of an object, then *nothing* remains.'—For Heidegger's *What is Metaphysics?* cp. Carnap, *Erkenntnis*, 2, 229. For Heidegger's relation to Husserl and Scheler, cp. J. Kraft, *From Husserl to Heidegger* (2nd German edn, 1957). Heidegger recognizes that his sentences are meaningless: 'Question and answer concerning nothingness are in themselves equally

nonsensical', Heidegger writes (cp. *Erkenntnis*, 2, 231). What could be said, from the point of view of Wittgenstein's *Tractatus*, against this kind of philosophy which admits that it talks nonsense—but deeply significant nonsense? (Cp. note 51 (1) to chapter 11.) G. Schneeberger, *Nachlese zu Heidegger*, 1962, contains a collection of documents on Heidegger's political activity.

88. For these quotations from Heidegger, cp. Kolnai, *op. cit.*, 221, 313.—For Schopenhauer's advice to the guardian, cp. *Works*, vol. V, p. 25 (note).

89. For Jaspers, cp. Kolnai, *op. cit.*, 270 f. Kolnai (p. 282) calls Jaspers 'Heidegger's lesser brother'. I cannot agree with that. For, as opposed to Heidegger, Jaspers has undoubtedly written books which contain much of interest, even books which contain much that is based on experience, for instance his *General Psycho-Pathology*. But I may quote here a few passages from an early work, his *Psychology of World-Views* (first published in 1919; I quote from the third German edn, 1925), which show that Jaspers' world-views were far advanced, at any rate, before Heidegger took to writing. 'To visualize the life of man, one would have to see how he lives in the Moment. The Moment is the sole reality, it is reality in itself, in the life of the soul. The Moment that has been lived is the Last, the Warm-Blooded, the Immediate, the Living, the Bodily-Present, the Totality of the Real, the only Concrete Thing ... Man finds Existence and the Absolute ultimately in the Moment alone.' (p. 112.)—(From the chapter on the *Enthusiastic Attitude*, p. 112): 'Wherever Enthusiasm is the absolute leading motive, i.e. wherever one lives in Reality and for Reality, and still dares and risks all, there one may well speak of Heroism: of heroic Love, heroic Strife, heroic Work, etc. § 5. *The Enthusiastic Attitude is Love* ...'—(Subsection 2, p. 128): '*Compassion is not Love* ...'—(p. 127): 'This is why Love is cruel, ruthless; and why it is believed in, by the genuine Lover, only if it is so.'—(pp. 256 ff.): 'III. *Single Marginal Situations* ... (A) *Strife*. Strife is a fundamental form of all Existence ... The *reactions* to the Marginal Situations of Strife are the following: ... 2. *Man's lack of understanding of the fact that Strife is Ultimate*: He skulks ...' And so on. We always find the same picture: a hysterical romanticism, combined with a brutal barbarism and the professorial pedantry of sub-sections and sub-sub-sections.

90. Cp. Kolnai, *op. cit.*, 208.

For my remark on the 'philosophy of the gambler', cp. O. Spengler (*The Hour of Decision. Germany and World-Historical Evolution.*—German edn, 1933, p. 230; quoted in *Thus Spake Germany*, 28): 'He whose sword compels victory here will be lord of the world. The dice are there, ready for this stupendous game. Who dares to throw them?'

Of the gangster philosophy, a book by the very talented author, E. von Salomon, is perhaps even more characteristic. I quote a few passages from this book, *The Outlaws* (1930; the passages quoted are from pp. 105, 73, 63, 307, 73, 367): 'Satanic lust! Am I not one with my gun? ... The first lust of man is destruction ... They shot quite indiscriminately, just because it was good fun ... We are free of the burden of plan, method or system ... What we wanted we did not know, and what we knew we did not want ... My greatest lust was always for destruction.' And so on. (Cp. also Hegemann, *op. cit.*, 171.)

91. Cp. Kolnai, *op. cit.*, 313.

92. For Ziegler, cp. Kolnai, *op. cit.*, 398.

93. This quotation is from Schopenhauer, *Grundprobleme* (4th edn, 1890), Introduction to the first edition (1840), p. xix.—Hegel's remark on 'the most lofty depth' (or 'the

most elevated depth') is from the *Jahrbuecher d. wiss. Lit.*, 1827, No. 7; it is quoted by Schopenhauer, *op. cit.*—The concluding quotation is from Schopenhauer, *op. cit.*, xviii.

NOTES TO CHAPTER THIRTEEN

General Note to the Chapters on Marx. Wherever possible, I refer in these notes to *Capital* or to *H.o.M.* or to both. I use *Capital* as abbreviation for the Everyman Double Volume Edition of K. Marx, *Capital*, translated by E. and C. Paul.—*H.o.M.* stands for *A Handbook of Marxism*, edited by E. Burns, 1935, but references to complete editions of the texts have always been added. For quotations from Marx and Engels, I refer to the Moscow standard edition (*Gesamtausgabe*, abbreviated *GA*), published from 1927 onwards and edited by D. Ryazanow and others but still incomplete. For quotations from Lenin, I refer to the *Little Lenin Library*, published by Martin Lawrence, later Lawrence and Wishart, abbreviated L.L.L. The later volumes of *Capital* are quoted as *Das Kapital* (of which vol. I was first published in 1867); the references are to vol. II, 1885, or to vol. III, part 1, and vol. III, part 2 (quoted as III/1 and III/2), both 1894. I wish to make it quite clear that although I refer where possible to the translations mentioned above, I do not always adopt their wording.

1 Cp. V. Pareto, *Treatise on General Sociology*, § 1843. (English transl.: *The Mind and Society*, 1935, vol. III, p. 1281; cp. also text to note 65 to chapter 10.) Pareto writes (pp. 1281 f.): 'The art of government lies in finding ways to take advantage of such sentiments, not wasting one's energy in futile efforts to destroy them; very frequently the sole effect of the latter course is to strengthen them. The person capable of freeing himself from the blind domination of his own sentiments will be able to utilize the sentiments of other people for his own ends ... This may be said in general of the relation between ruler and ruled. The statesman who is of greatest service to himself and to his party is the man without prejudice who knows how to profit by the prejudices of others.' The prejudices Pareto has in mind are of diverse character—nationalism, love of freedom, humanitarianism. And it may be just as well to remark that Pareto, though he has freed himself from many prejudices, has certainly not succeeded in freeing himself from all of them. This can be seen in nearly every page he writes, especially, of course, where he speaks of what he describes not inappropriately as 'the humanitarian religion'. His own prejudice is the anti-humanitarian religion. Had he seen that his choice was not between prejudice and freedom from prejudice, but only between the humanitarian prejudice and the anti-humanitarian prejudice, he might perhaps have felt a little less confident of his superiority. (For the problem of prejudices, cp. note 8 (1) to chapter 24, and text.)

Pareto's ideas concerning the 'art of government' are very old; they go back at least to Plato's uncle Critias, and have played their part in the Platonic school tradition (as pointed out in note 18 to chapter 8).

2. (1) Fichte's and Hegel's ideas led to the principle of the national state and of national self-determination, a reactionary principle in which, however, a fighter for the open society such as Masaryk sincerely believed, and which the democrat Wilson adopted. (For Wilson, cp. for instance *Modern Political Doctrines*, ed. by A. Zimmern, 1939, pp. 223 ff.) This principle is obviously inapplicable on this earth,

and especially in Europe, where the nations (i.e. linguistic groups) are so densely packed that it is quite impossible to disentangle them. The terrible effect of Wilson's attempt to apply this romantic principle to European politics should be clear by now to everybody. That the Versailles settlement was harsh, is a myth; that Wilson's principles were not adhered to, is another myth. The fact is that such principles could not be more consistently applied; and Versailles failed mainly because of the attempt to apply Wilson's inapplicable principles. (For all this, cp. note 7 to chapter 9, and text to notes 51–64 to chapter 12.)

(2) In connection with the Hegelian character of Marxism mentioned in the text in this paragraph, I give here a list of important views which Marxism takes over from Hegelianism. My treatment of Marx is not based on this list, since I do not intend to treat him just as another Hegelian, but rather as a serious investigator who can, and must, answer for himself. This is the list, ordered approximately according to the importance of the various views for Marxism.

(*a*) Historicism: The method of a science of society is the study of history, and especially of the tendencies inherent in the historical development of mankind.

(*b*) Historical relativism: What is a law in one historical period need not be a law in another historical period. (Hegel maintained that what is true in one period need not be true in another.)

(*c*) There is an inherent law of progress in historical development.

(*d*) The development is one towards more freedom and reason, although the instrumentality of bringing this about is not our reasonable planning but rather such irrational forces as our passions and our self-interests. (Hegel calls this 'the cunning of reason'.)

(*e*) Moral positivism, or in Marx's case, moral 'futurism'. (This term is explained in chapter 22.)

(*f*) Class consciousness is one of the instruments by which the development propels itself. (Hegel operates with the consciousness of the nation, the 'national Spirit' or 'national Genius'.)

(*g*) Methodological essentialism. Dialectics.

(*h*) The following Hegelian ideas play a part in Marx's writings but have become more important with later Marxists.

(h_1) The distinction between merely 'formal' freedom or merely 'formal' democracy and 'real' or 'economic' freedom or 'economic' democracy, etc.; in connection with this, there is a certain 'ambivalent' attitude towards liberalism, i.e. a mixture of love and hate.

(h_2) Collectivism.

In the following chapters, (*a*) is again the main theme. In connection with (*a*) and (*b*), see also note 13 to this chapter. For (*b*), cp. chapters 22–24. For (*c*), cp. chapters 22 and 25. For (*d*), cp. chapter 22 (and regarding Hegel's 'cunning of reason', cp. text to note 84 to chapter 12). For (*f*), cp. chapters 16 and 19. For (*g*), cp. notes 4 to the present chapter, 6 to chapter 17, 13 to chapter 15, 15 to chapter 19, and notes 20–24 to chapter 20, and text. For (h_1), cp. note 19 to chapter 17. (h_2) has its influence on Marx's anti-psychologism (cp. text to note 16 to chapter 14); it is under the influence of the Platonic-Hegelian doctrine of the superiority of the state over the individual that Marx develops his theory that even the 'consciousness' of the individual is determined by social conditions. Yet, fundamentally, Marx was an individualist; his main interest was to help suffering human individuals. Thus collectivism as such certainly does not play an important part in Marx's own writings. (Apart from his emphasis upon a collective class consciousness, mentioned under (*f*); cp., for example, note 4 to chapter 18.) But it plays its part in Marxist practice.

3. In *Capital* (387–9), Marx makes some interesting remarks both on Plato's theory of the division of labour (cp. note 29 to chapter 5 and text) and on the caste character of Plato's state. (Marx refers, however, only to Egypt and not to Sparta; cp. note 27 to chapter 4.) In this connection, Marx quotes also an interesting passage from Socrates' *Busiris*, 15 f., 224/5, where Isocrates first proffers arguments for the division of labour very similar to those of Plato (text to note 29 to chapter 5); Isocrates then continues: 'The Egyptians ... were so successful that the most celebrated philosophers who discuss such topics extol the constitution of Egypt above all others, and that the Spartans ... govern their own city in such an excellent manner because they have copied the ways of the Egyptians.' I think it most probable that Isocrates refers here to Plato; and he may in turn be referred to by Crantor, when he spoke of those who accuse Plato of becoming a disciple of the Egyptians, as mentioned in note 27 (3) to chapter 4.
4. Or, 'intelligence destroying'; cp. text to note 68 to chapter 12. For *dialectics* in general, and Hegelian dialectics in particular, cp. chapter 12, especially text to notes 28–33. With Marx's dialectics, I do not intend to deal in this book, since I have dealt with it elsewhere. (Cp. 'What is Dialectic?', *Mind*, N.S., vol. 49, 1940, pp. 403 ff.; or, revised, in *Conjectures and Refutations*, pp. 312 ff.) I consider Marx's dialectics, like Hegel's, a rather dangerous muddle; but its analysis can be avoided here, especially since the criticism of his historicism covers all that may be taken seriously in his dialectics.
5. Cp., for instance, the quotation in the text to note 11 to this chapter.
6. Utopianism is first attacked by Marx and Engels in the *Communist Manifesto*, III, 3. (Cp. *H.o.M.*, 55 ff. = *GA*, Series I, vol. 6, 553–5.) For Marx's attacks upon the 'bourgeois economists' who 'try to reconcile ... political economy with the claims of the proletariat', attacks directed especially against Mill and other members of the Comtist school, cp. especially *Capital*, 868 (against Mill; see also note 14 to this chapter), and 870 (against the Comtist *Revue Positiviste*; see also text to note 21 to chapter 18). For the whole problem of social technology versus historicism, and of piecemeal social engineering versus Utopian social engineering, cp. especially chapter 9, above. (See also the notes 9 to chapter 3; 18 (3) to chapter 5; and 1 to chapter 9; with references to M. Eastman's *Marxism: Is it Science?*)
7. (1) The two quotations from Lenin are taken from Sidney and Beatrice Webb, *Soviet Communism* (2nd edn, 1937), pp. 650 f., who say, in a note, that the second of the quotations is from a speech made by Lenin in May, 1918. It is most interesting to see how quickly Lenin grasped the situation. On the eve of his party's rise to power, in August, 1917, when he published his book *State and Revolution*, he was still a pure historicist. Not only was he as yet unaware of the most difficult problems involved in the task of constructing a new society; he even believed, with most Marxists, that the problems were non-existent, or that they would be solved by the process of history. Cp. especially the passages from *State and Revolution* in *H.o.M.*, pp. 757 f. (= Lenin, *State and Revolution*, L.L.L., vol. 14, 77–9), where Lenin emphasizes the simplicity of the problems of organization and administration in the various phases

of the evolving Communist society. 'All that is required', he writes, 'is that they should work equally, should regularly do their share of work, and should receive equal pay. The accounting and control necessary for this have been *simplified*' (italics in the original) 'by capitalism to the utmost.' They can thus be simply taken over by the workers, since these methods of control are 'within reach of anybody who can read and write, and knows the first four rules of arithmetic.' These astonishingly naïve statements are representative. (We find similar views expressed in Germany and in England; cp. this note, under (2).) They must be contrasted with Lenin's speeches made a few months later. They show how free the prophetic 'scientific socialist' was from any foreboding of the problems and disasters ahead. (I mean the disaster of the period of war-communism, that period which was the outcome of this prophetic and anti-technological Marxism.) But they show also Lenin's capability of finding, and of admitting to himself, the mistakes made. He abandoned Marxism in practice, although not in theory. Compare also Lenin's chapter V, sections 2 and 3, *H.o.M.*, pp. 742 ff. (= *State and Revolution*, 67–73), for the purely historicist, i.e. prophetic and anti-technological ('anti-Utopian', Lenin might have said; cp. p. 747 = *State and Revolution* 70–71), character of this 'scientific socialism' before its rise to power.

But when Lenin confessed that he knew no book dealing with the more constructive problems of social engineering, then he only demonstrated that Marxists, faithful to Marx's commandments, did not even read the 'Utopian stuff' of the 'professorial armchair socialists' who tried to make a beginning with these very problems; I am thinking of some of the Fabians in England and of A. Menger (e.g. *Neue Staatslehre*, 2nd edn, 1904, especially pp. 248 ff.) and J. Popper-Lynkeus in Austria. The latter developed apart from many other suggestions a technology of collective farming, and especially of giant farms of the kind later introduced in Russia (see his *Allgemeine Nährpflicht*, 1912; cp. pp. 206 ff. and 300 ff. of the 2nd edn, 1923). But he was dismissed by Marxists as a 'half-socialist'. They called him a 'half-socialist' because he envisaged a private enterprise sector in his society; he confined the economic activity of the state to the care for the basic needs of everybody—for the 'guaranteed minimum of subsistence'. Everything beyond this was to be left to a strictly competitive system.

(2) Lenin's view in *State and Revolution* quoted above is (as J. Viner has pointed out) very similar to that of John Carruthers, *Socialism and Radicalism* (cp. note 9 to chapter 9); see especially pp. 14–16. He says: 'The capitalists have invented a system of finance which, although complex, is sufficiently simple to be practically worked, and which fully instructs everyone as to the best manner of managing his factory. A very similar although greatly simpler finance would in the same way instruct the elected manager of a socialist factory how he should manage it, and he would have no more need for advice from a professional organizer than a capitalist has.'

8. This naïve naturalistic slogan is Marx's 'principle of communism' (taken over by Marx from Louis Blanc's article 'L'Organisation de travail', as Bryan Magee has kindly pointed out to me). Its origin is Platonic and early Christian (cp. note 29 to chapter 5; the *Acts*, 2, 44–45, and 4, 34–35; see also note 48 to chapter 24, and the cross-references given there). It is quoted by Lenin in *State and Revolution*; see *H.o.M.*, 752 (= *State and Revolution*, 74). Marx's 'principle of socialism', which is incorporated in

the *New Constitution* of the U.S.S.R. (1936), is slightly but significantly weaker; compare the *Article 12*: 'In the U.S.S.R.', we read there, 'the principle of socialism is realized: "From each according to his ability, to each according to his work".' The substitution of 'work' for the early Christian term 'needs' transforms a romantic and economically quite indefinite naturalistic phrase into a fairly practical but commonplace principle—and into one which even 'capitalism' may claim as its own.

9. I am alluding to the title of a famous book by Engels: 'The Development of Socialism From a Utopia Into a Science.' (The book has been published in English under the title: *Socialism: Utopian and Scientific.*)
10. See my *The Poverty of Historicism* (*Economica*, 1944: now published separately).
11. This is the eleventh of Marx's *Theses on Feuerbach* (1845), cp. *H.o.M.*, 231 (= F. Engels, *Ludwig Feuerbach und der Ausgang der Klassischen deutschen Philosophie*, J. W. Dietz, Nachf. Berlin 1946, 56). See also notes 14–16 to this chapter, and the sections 1, 17 and 18 of *The Poverty of Historicism*.
12. I do not intend to discuss here the metaphysical or the methodological problem of determinism in any detail. (A few further remarks on the problem will be found in chapter 22, below.) But I wish to point out how little adequate it is if 'determinism' and 'scientific method' are taken as synonyms. This is still done, even by a writer of the excellence and clarity of B. Malinowski. Cp., for instance, his paper in *Human Affairs* (ed. by Cattell, Cohen, and Travers, 1937), chapter XII. I fully agree with the methodological tendencies of this paper, with its plea for the application of scientific method in social science as well as with its brilliant condemnation of romantic tendencies in anthropology (cp. especially pp. 207 ff., 221–4.) But when Malinowski argues in favour of 'determinism in the study of human culture' (p. 212; cp., for instance, also p. 252), I fail to see what he means by 'determinism' if not simply 'scientific method'. This equation is, however, not tenable, and has its grave dangers, as shown in the text; for it may lead to historicism.
13. For a criticism of historicism, see *The Poverty of Historicism* (*Economica*, 1944).

    Marx may be excused for holding the mistaken belief that there is a 'natural law of historical development'; for some of the best scientists of his time (e.g. T. H. Huxley; cp. his *Lay Sermons*, 1880, p. 214) believed in the possibility of discovering a *law of evolution*. But there can be no empirical 'law of evolution'. There is a specific evolutionary hypothesis, stating that life *on earth* has developed in certain ways. But a universal or natural law of evolution would have to state a hypothesis concerning the course of development of life on *all* planets (at least). In other words, wherever we are confined to the observation of one unique process, there we cannot hope to find, and to test, a 'law of nature'. (Of course, there are laws of evolution pertaining to the development of young organisms, etc.)

    There can be *sociological laws*, and even sociological laws pertaining to the problem of progress; for example, the hypothesis that, wherever the freedom of thought, and of the communication of thought, is effectively protected by legal institutions and institutions ensuring the publicity of discussion, there will be scientific progress. (Cp. chapter 23.) But there are reasons for holding the view that we should do better not to speak of *historical laws* at all. (Cp. note 7 to chapter 25, and text.)
14. Cp. *Capital*, 864 (Preface to the First Edition. For a similar remark of Mill's, see note 16, below). At the same place, Marx also says: 'It is the ultimate aim of this work to lay bare the economic law of motion of modern society.' (For this, cp. *H.o.M.*, 374,

and text to note 16 to the present chapter.) The clash between Marx's pragmatism and his historicism becomes fairly obvious if we compare these passages with the eleventh of his *Theses on Feuerbach* (quoted in text to note 11 to this chapter). In *The Poverty of Historicism*, section 17, I have tried to make this clash more obvious by characterizing Marx's historicism in a form which is exactly analogous to his attack on Feuerbach. For we can paraphrase Marx's passage quoted in the text by saying: The historicist can only *interpret* social development, and aid it in various ways; his point, however, is that *nobody can change it*. See also chapter 22, especially text to notes 5 ff.

15. Cp. *Capital*, 469; the next three quotations are from *Capital*, 868 (Preface to the Second Edition. The translation 'shallow syncretism' is not quite in keeping with the very strong expression of the original); *op. cit.*, 673; and *op. cit.*, 830. For the 'ample circumstantial evidence' mentioned in the text, see, for instance, *op. cit.*, 105, 562, 649, 656.

16. Cp. *Capital*, 864 = *H.o.M.*, 374; cp. note 14 to this chapter. The following three quotations are from J. S. Mill, *A System of Logic* (1st edn, 1843; quoted from the 8th edn), Book VI, Chapter X; § 2 (end); § 1 (beginning); § 1 (end). An interesting passage (which says nearly the same as Marx's famous remark quoted in text to note 14) can be found in the same chapter of Mill's *Logic*, § 8. Referring to the historical method, which searches for the 'laws of social order and of social progress', Mill writes: 'By its aid we may hereafter succeed not only in looking far forward into the future history of the human race, but in determining what artificial means may be used, and to what extent, *to accelerate the natural progress in so far as it is beneficial*; to compensate for whatever may be its inherent inconveniences or disadvantages, and to guard against the dangers or accidents to which our species is exposed from the necessary incidents of its progression.' (Italics mine.) Or as Marx puts it, to 'shorten and lessen its birth-pangs'.

17. Cp. Mill, *loc. cit.*, § 2; the next remarks are from the first paragraph of § 3. The 'orbit' and the 'trajectory' are from the end of the second paragraph of § 3. When speaking of 'orbits' Mill thinks, probably, of such cyclical theories of historical development as formulated in Plato's *Statesman*, or perhaps in Machiavelli's *Discourses on Livy*.

18. Cp. Mill, *loc. cit.*, the beginning of the last paragraph of § 3.—For all these passages, cp. also notes 6–9 to chapter 14, and *The Poverty of Historicism*, sections 22, 24, 27, 28.

19. Concerning *psychologism* (the term is due to E. Husserl), I may here quote a few sentences by the excellent psychologist D. Katz; the passages are taken from his article *Psychological Needs* (Chapter III of *Human Affairs*, ed. by Cattell, Cohen, and Travers, 1937, p. 36). 'In philosophy there has been for some time a tendency to make psychology "the" fundamental basis of all other sciences ... This tendency is usually called psychologism ... But even such sciences, which, like sociology and economics, are more closely related to psychology, have a neutral nucleus which is not psychological ...' Psychologism will be discussed at length in chapter 14. Cp. also note 44 to chapter 5.

20. Cp. Marx's Preface to *A Contribution to the Critique of Political Economy* (1859), quoted in *H.o.M.*, 371 (= Karl Marx, *Zur Kritik der politischen Oekonomie*, edited by K. Kautsky, J. W. Dietz, Nachf. Berlin 1930, LIV–LV, also in *Capital*, pp. xv f.). The passage is quoted more fully in text to note 13 to chapter 15, and in text to note 3 to chapter 16; see also note 2 to chapter 14.

NOTES TO CHAPTER FOURTEEN

1 Cp. note 19 to the last chapter.

2. Cp. Marx's Preface to *A Contribution to the Critique of Political Economy*, quoted also in note 20 to chapter 13 and in text to notes 13 to chapter 15 and 4 to chapter 16; cp. *H.o.M.*, 372 = *Capital*, p. xvi. See also Marx and Engels, *German Ideology* (*H.o.M.*, 213 = *GA*, Series I, vol. v, 16): 'It is not consciousness that determines life, but life that determines consciousness.'

3. Cp. M. Ginsberg, *Sociology* (Home University Library, 130 ff.), who discusses this problem in a similar context, without, however, referring to Marx.

4. Cp. for instance, *Zoology Leaflet 10*, published by the Field Museum of Natural History, Chicago, 1929.

5. For institutionalism, cp. especially chapter 3 (text to notes 9 and 10) and chapter 9.

6. Cp. Mill, *A System of Logic*, VI; IX, § 3. (Cp. also notes 16–18 to chapter 13.)

7. Cp. Mill, *op. cit.*, VI; VI, § 2.

8. Cp. Mill, *op. cit.*, VI; VII, § 1. For the opposition between 'methodological individualism' and 'methodological collectivism', see F. A. von Hayek's *Scientism and the Study of Society*, Part II, section VII (*Economica*, 1943, pp. 41 ff.).

9. For this and the following quotation see Mill, *op. cit.*, VI; X, § 4.

10. I am using the term 'sociological laws' to denote the natural laws of social life, as opposed to its normative laws; cp. text to notes 8–9 to chapter 5.

11. Cp. note 10 to chapter 3. (The passage is from p. 122 of part II of my *The Poverty of Historicism* (*Economica*, N.S. xi, 1944), and p. 65 of the book.

I owe the suggestion that it was Marx who first conceived social theory as the study of the *unwanted social repercussions of nearly all our actions* to K. Polanyi, who emphasized this aspect of Marxism in private discussions (1924).

* (1) It should be noted, however, that in spite of the aspect of Marxism which has been just mentioned and which constitutes an important point of agreement between Marx's views on method and mine, there is a considerable disagreement between Marx's and my views about the way in which these unwanted or unintended repercussions have to be analysed. For Marx is a *methodological collectivist*. He believes that it is the 'system of economic relations' as such which gives rise to the unwanted consequences—a system of institutions which, in turn, may be explicable in terms of 'means of production', but which is not analysable in terms of individuals, their relations, and their actions. As opposed to this, I hold that institutions (and traditions) must be analysed in individualistic terms—that is to say, in terms of the relations of individuals acting in certain situations, and of the unintended consequences of their actions.

(2) The reference in the text to 'canvas-cleaning', and to chapter 9 is to notes 9 to 12, and the text, of this chapter.

(3) Concerning the remarks in the text (in the paragraph to which this note is appended, and in some of those which follow) about the unintended social repercussions of our actions, I wish to draw attention to the fact that the situation in the physical sciences (and in the field of mechanical engineering and technology) is somewhat similar. The task of technology is here also largely to inform us about unintended consequences of what we are doing (e.g. that a bridge may become too heavy if we strengthen certain of its components). But the analogy goes even

further. Our mechanical inventions do rarely turn out according to our original plans. The inventors of the motor car probably did not foresee the social repercussions of their doings, but they certainly did not foresee the purely mechanical repercussions—the many ways in which their cars broke down. And while their cars were altered in order to avoid these breakdowns, they changed beyond recognition. (And with them, some people's motives and aspirations changed also.)

(4) With my criticism of the Conspiracy Theory (pp. 94–6), cp. my *Prediction and Prophecy and their Significance for Social Theory* (in *Proceedings of the Xth International Congress of Philosophy*, 1948, vol. i, pp. 82 ff., especially p. 87 f.), and 'Towards a Rational Theory of Tradition' (*The Rationalist Annual*, 1949, pp. 36 ff., especially p. 40 f.). Both papers are now in my *Conjectures and Refutations*.*

12. See the passage from Mill cited in note 8 to this chapter.
13. Cp. note 63 to chapter 10. Important contributors to the logic of power are Plato (in Books VIII and IX of the *Republic*, and in the *Laws*), Aristotle, Machiavelli, Pareto, and many others.
14. Cp. Max Weber's *Ges. Aufsaetze zur Wissenschaftslehre* (1922), especially pp. 408 ff.

A remark may be added here concerning the often repeated assertion that the social sciences operate with a method different from that of the natural sciences, in so far as we know the 'social atoms', i.e. ourselves, by direct acquaintance, while our knowledge of physical atoms is only hypothetical. From this, it is often concluded (e.g. by Karl Menger) that the method of social science, since it makes use of our knowledge of ourselves, is psychological, or perhaps 'subjective', as opposed to the 'objective' methods of the natural sciences. To this, we may answer: There is surely no reason why we should not use any 'direct' knowledge we may have of ourselves. But such knowledge is useful in the social sciences only if we generalize, i.e. if we assume that what we know of ourselves holds good for others too. But this generalization is of a hypothetical character, and it must be tested and corrected by experience of an 'objective' kind. (Before having met anybody who does not like chocolate, some people may easily believe that everybody likes it.) Undoubtedly, in the case of 'social atoms' we are in certain ways more favourably situated than in the case of physical atoms, owing not only to our knowledge of ourselves, but also to the use of language. Yet from the point of view of scientific method, a social hypothesis suggested by self-intuition is in no different position from a physical hypothesis about atoms. The latter may also be suggested to the physicist by a kind of intuition about what atoms are like. And in both cases, this intuition is a private affair of the man who proposes the hypothesis. What is 'public', and important for science, is merely the question whether the hypotheses could be tested by experience, and whether they stood up to tests.

From this point of view, social theories are no more 'subjective' than physical ones. (And it would be clearer, for example, to speak of 'the theory of subjective values' or of 'the theory of acts of choice' than of 'the subjective theory of value': see also note 9 to chapter 20.)

15. The present paragraph has been inserted in order to avoid the misunderstanding mentioned in the text. I am indebted to Prof. E. Gombrich for drawing my attention to the possibility of such a misunderstanding.
16. Hegel contended that his 'Idea' was something existing 'absolutely', i.e. independently of anybody's thought. One might contend, therefore, that he was not a

psychologist. Yet Marx, quite reasonably, did not take seriously this 'absolute idealism' of Hegel; he rather interpreted it as a disguised *psychologism*, and combated it as such. Cp. *Capital*, 873 (italics mine): 'For Hegel, the *thought process* (which he even presents in disguise under the name "Idea" as an independent agent or subject) is the creator of the real.' Marx confines his attack to the doctrine that the thought process (or consciousness, or mind) creates the 'real'; and he shows that it does not even create the social reality (to say nothing about the material universe).

For the Hegelian theory of the dependence of the individual upon society, see (apart from section iii of chapter 12) the discussion, in chapter 23, of the social, or more precisely, the inter-personal element in scientific method, as well as the corresponding discussion, in chapter 24, of the inter-personal element in rationality.

NOTES TO CHAPTER FIFTEEN

1 Cp. Cole's Preface to *Capital*, xvi. (But see also the next note.)

2. Lenin too sometimes used the term 'Vulgar Marxists', but in a somewhat different sense.—How little Vulgar Marxism has in common with the views of Marx may be seen from Cole's analysis, *op. cit.*, xx, and from the text to notes 4 and 5 to chapter 16, and from note 17 to chapter 17.

3. According to Adler, lust for power, of course, is really nothing but the urge towards compensation for one's feelings of inferiority by proving one's superiority.

   Some Vulgar Marxists even believe that the finishing touch to the philosophy of the modern man was added by Einstein, who, so they think, discovered 'relativity' or 'relativism', i.e. that 'everything is relative'.

4. J. F. Hecker writes (*Moscow Dialogues*, p. 76) of Marx's so-called 'historical materialism': 'I would have preferred to call it "dialectical historicism" or ... something of that sort.'—I again draw the reader's attention to the fact that in this book I am not dealing with Marx's *dialectics*, since I have dealt with them elsewhere. (Cp. note 4 to chapter 13.)

5. For Heraclitus' slogan, cp. especially text to note 4 (3) to chapter 2, notes 16/17 to chapter 4, and note 25 to chapter 6.

6. Both the following quotations are from *Capital*, 873 (Epilogue to the second edn of vol. 1).

7. Cp. *Das Kapital*, vol. III/2 (1894), p. 355; i.e. chapter 48, section III, from where the following quotations are taken.

8. Cp. *Das Kapital*, vol. III/2, *loc. cit.*

9. For the quotations in this paragraph, cp. F. Engels, *Anti-Dühring*; see *H.o.M.*, 298, 299 (= F. Engels, *Herrn Eugen Duehring's* Umwaelzung der Wissenschaft, *GA* special volume, 294–5).

10. I have in mind questions concerning, for example, the influence of economic conditions (such as the need for land surveying) upon Egyptian geometry, and upon the different development of early Pythagorean geometry in Greece.

11. Cp. especially the quotation from *Capital* in note 13 to chapter 14; also the full passages from the Preface to *A Contribution to the Critique of Political Economy*, quoted only partially in the text to the next note. For the problem of Marx's essentialism, and the distinction between 'reality' and appearance, see note 13 to this chapter, and notes 6 and 16 to chapter 17.

12. But I feel inclined to say that it is a little better than an idealism of the Hegelian or Platonic brand; as I said in 'What is Dialectic?', if I were forced to choose, which, fortunately, I am not, I would choose materialism. (Cp. p. 422 of *Mind*, vol. 49, or *Conjectures and Refutations*, p. 331, where I deal with problems very similar to those dealt with here.)
13. For this and the following quotations, cp. Marx's Preface to *A Contribution to the Critique of Political Economy*, *H.o.M.*, 372 (= *Zur Kritik der politischen Oekonomie*, LV).
   Some further light is thrown upon these passages (and on the text to note 3 to chapter 16) by the *Second Observation* of part II of Marx's *Poverty of Philosophy* (cp. *H.o.M.*, 354 f. = *GA*, Series I, vol. vi, 179–80); for Marx here analyses society very clearly into *three layers*, if I may call them so. The first of these layers corresponds to 'reality' or 'essence', the second and the third to a primary and a secondary form of appearance. (This is very similar to Plato's distinction of Ideas, sensible things, and images of sensible things; cp. for the problem of Plato's essentialism chapter 3; for Marx's corresponding ideas, see also notes 8 and 16 to chapter 17.) The *first* or fundamental layer (or 'reality') is the material layer, the machinery and other material means of production that exist in society; this layer is called by Marx the material 'productive forces', or 'material productivity'. The *second* layer he calls 'productive relationship' or 'social relations'; they are dependent on the first layer: 'Social relations are closely bound up with productive forces. In acquiring new productive forces men change their mode of production; and in changing their mode of production, they change their way of earning their living—they change all their social relations.' (For the first two layers, cp. text to note 3 to chapter 16.) The *third* layer is formed by the ideologies, i.e. by legal, moral, religious, scientific ideas: 'The same men who establish their social relations in conformity with material productivity, produce also principles, ideas, and categories, in conformity with their social relations.' In terms of this analysis, we may say that in Russia the first layer was transformed in conformity with the third, a striking refutation of Marx's theory. (See also the next note.)
14. It is easy to make very general prophecies; for instance, to prophesy that, within a reasonable time, it will rain. Thus there would not be much in the prophecy that, in some decades, there will be a revolution somewhere. But, as we see, Marx said just a little more than that, and just enough to be falsified by events. Those who try to interpret this falsification away remove the last bit of empirical significance from Marx's system. It then becomes purely 'metaphysical' (in the sense of my *The Logic of Scientific Discovery*).
   How Marx conceived the general mechanism of any revolution, in accordance with his theory, is illustrated by the following description of the social revolution of the bourgeoisie (also called the 'industrial revolution'), taken from the *Communist Manifesto* (*H.o.M.*, 28; italics mine = *GA*, Series I, vol. vi, 530–31): 'The means of production and of exchange, on whose foundation the bourgeoisie built itself up, were generated in feudal society. At a certain stage in the development of the means of production and of exchange ... the feudal relations of property became no longer compatible with the *already developed productive forces*. They became so many fetters. They had to be burst asunder. And they were burst asunder.' (Cp. also text to note 11, and note 17 to chapter 17.)
15. Cp. H. Heine, *Religion and Philosophy in Germany*. (Engl. transl., 1882); here quoted from the appendix to P. Carus, *Kant's Prolegomena*, 1912, p. 267.

16. A testimony to this friendship can be found in *Capital*, at the end of footnote 2 to p. 671.

    Marx, I admit, was often intolerant. Nevertheless, I feel—but I may easily be mistaken—that he had sufficient critical sense to see the weakness of all dogmatism, and that he would have disliked the way in which his theories were converted into a set of dogmas. (See note 30 to chapter 17, and p. 425—p. 334 in *Conjectures and Refutations*—of 'What is Dialectic?' Cp. note 4 to chapter 13.) It seems, however, that Engels was prepared to tolerate the intolerance and orthodoxy of the Marxists. In his Preface to the first English translation of *Capital*, he writes (cp. *Capital*, 886) of the book that it 'is often called, on the Continent, "the Bible of the working class".' And instead of protesting against a description which converts 'scientific' socialism into a religion, Engels proceeds to show, in his comments, that *Capital* is worthy of this title, since 'the conclusions arrived at in this work are daily more and more becoming the fundamental principles of the great working-class movement' all over the world. From here there was only one step to the heresy-hunting and excommunication of those who retain the critical, i.e. scientific, spirit, the spirit which had once inspired Engels as well as Marx.

NOTES TO CHAPTER SIXTEEN

1 Cp. Marx and Engels, *The Communist Manifesto*; see *H.o.M.*, p. 22 (= *GA*, Series I, vol. vi, 525). As pointed out in chapter 4 (see text to notes 5/6 and 11/12), Plato had very similar ideas.

2. Cp. text to note 15 to chapter 14.

3. Cp. Marx, *The Poverty of Philosophy*, *H.o.M.*, 355 (= *GA*, Series I, vol. vi, 179). (The quotation is from the same place as that from which the passages quoted in note 13 to chapter 15 are taken.)

4. Cp. the preface to *A Contribution to the Critique of Political Economy*; cp. *Capital*, xvi, and *H.o.M.*, 371 f. (= *Zur Kritik der politischen Oekonomie*, LIV–LV. See also note 20 to chapter 13, note 1 to chapter 14, note 13 to chapter 15, and text.) The passage quoted here, and especially the terms 'material productive forces' and 'productive relationships' receive some light from those quoted in note 13 to chapter 15.

5. Cp. *Capital*, 650 f. See also the parallel passage on capitalist and miser in *Capital*, 138 f., = *H.o.M.*, 437; cp. also note 17 to chapter 17. In *The Poverty of Philosophy*, *H.o.M.*, 367 (= *GA*, Series I, vol. vi, 189), Marx writes: 'Although all the members of the modern bourgeoisie have the same interest in so far as they form a class against another class, they have opposite, antagonistic interests, in so far as they stand face to face with one another. This opposition of interests results from the economic conditions of their bourgeois life.'

6. *Capital*, 651.

7. This is exactly analogous to Hegel's nationalist historicism, where the true interest of the nation gains consciousness in the subjective minds of the nationals, and especially of the leader.

8. Cp. the text to note 14 to chapter 13.

9. Cp. *Capital*, 651.

10. *I originally used the term '*laissez-faire* capitalism'; but in view of the fact that '*laissez-faire*' indicates the absence of trade barriers (such as customs)—something

highly desirable, I believe—and of the fact that I consider the economic policy of non-interference of the early nineteenth century as undesirable, and even as paradoxical, I decided to change my terminology, and to use the term 'unrestrained capitalism' instead.*

NOTES TO CHAPTER SEVENTEEN

1 Cp. the Preface to *A Contribution to the Critique of Political Economy* (*H.o.M.*, 372 = *Zur Kritik der politischen Oekonomie*, LV). For the theory of the strata or layers of the 'superstructures', see the quotations in note 13 to chapter 15.

2. For Plato's recommendation of 'both persuassion and force', see, for instance, text to note 35 to chapter 5, and notes 5 and 10 to chapter 8.

3. Cp. Lenin, *State and Revolution* (*H.o.M.*, 733/4 and 735 = *State and Revolution*, 15 and 16).

4. The two quotations are from Marx–Engels, *The Communist Manifesto* (*H.o.M.*, 46 = *GA*, Series I, vol. vi, 546).

5. Cp. Lenin, *State and Revolution* (*H.o.M.*, 725 = *State and Revolution*, 8–9).

6. For the characteristic problems of a historicist essentialism, and especially for problems of the type 'What is the state?' or 'What is government?' cp. the text to notes 26–30 to chapter 3, 21–4 and 26 ff. to chapter 11 and 26 to chapter 12.

   For the *language of political demands* (or better, of *political 'proposals'*, as L. J. Russell puts it) which in my opinion must replace this kind of essentialism, cp. especially text between notes 41 and 42 to chapter 6 and note 5(3) to chapter 5. For Marx's essentialism, see especially text to note 11, and note 13, to chapter 15; note 16 to the present chapter; and notes 20–24 to chapter 20. Cp. especially the methodological remark in the third volume of *Capital* (*Das Kapital*, III/2, p. 352), quoted in note 20 to chapter 20.

7. This quotation is from the *Communist Manifesto* (*H.o.M.*, 25 = *GA*, Series I, vol. vi, 528). The text is from Engels' Preface to the first English translation of *Capital.* I quote here the whole concluding passage of this Preface; Engels speaks there about Marx's conclusion 'that at least in Europe, England is the only country where the inevitable social revolution might be effected entirely by peaceful and legal means. He certainly never forgot to add that he hardly expected the English ruling class to submit, without a "pro-slavery rebellion", to this peaceful and legal revolution'. (Cp. *Capital*, 887; see also text to note 7 to chapter 19.) This passage shows clearly that, according to Marxism, the violence or non-violence of the revolution will depend on the resistance or non-resistance of the old ruling class. Cp. also text to notes 3 ff. to chapter 19.

8. Cp. Engels, *Anti-Dühring* (*H.o.M.*, 296 = *GA*, Special volume, 292); see also the passages mentioned in note 5 to this chapter.

   The resistance of the bourgeoisie has been broken for some years in Russia; but there are no signs of the 'withering away' of the Russian state, not even in its internal organization.

   The theory of the withering away of the state is highly unrealistic, and I think that it may have been adopted by Marx and Engels mainly in order to take the wind out of their rivals' sails. The rivals I have in mind are Bakunin and the anarchists; Marx did not like to see anyone else's radicalism outdoing his own. Like Marx, they aimed at the overthrow of the existing social order, directing their attack, however, against the politico-legal, instead of the economic system. To them, the state was the fiend who had to be destroyed. But for his anarchist competitors, Marx, from his own premises, might have easily granted the possibility that the institution of the state, under socialism, might have to fulfil new and indispensable functions; namely those functions of safeguarding justice and freedom allotted to it by the great theorists of democracy.

9. Cp. *Capital*, 799.

10. In the chapter, 'Primary accumulation', Marx is, as he says (p. 801), 'not concerned ... with the purely economic causes of the agricultural revolution. Our present interest is the forcible' (i.e. political) 'means that were used to bring about the change.'

11. For the many passages, and the superstructures, cp. note 13 to chapter 15.

12. Cp. the text to the notes referred to in the last note.

13. One of the most noteworthy and valuable parts of *Capital*, a truly imperishable document of human suffering, is Chapter VIII of the First Volume, entitled 'The Working Day', in which Marx sketches the early history of labour legislation. From this well-documented chapter, the following quotations are taken.

    It must, however, be realized that this very chapter contains the material for a complete refutation of Marxist 'Scientific Socialism', which is based upon the *prophecy of ever-increasing exploitation* of the workers. No man can read this chapter of Marx without realizing that this prophecy has fortunately not come true. It is not impossible, however, that this is due, in part, to the activities of the Marxists in organizing labour; but the main contribution comes from the increased productivity of labour—in its turn, according to Marx, a result of 'Capitalist accumulation'.

14. Cp. *Capital*, 246. (See the footnote 1 to this passage.)

15. Cp. *Capital*, 257 f. Marx's comment in his footnote 1 to this page is most interesting. He shows that such cases as these were used by the pro-slavery Tory reactionaries for *propaganda for slavery*. And he shows that among others, Thomas Carlyle, the oracle (a forerunner of fascism), participated in this pro-slavery movement. Carlyle, to quote Marx, reduced 'the one great event of contemporary history, the American Civil War, to this level, that the Peter of the North wants to break the head of the Paul of the South because the Peter of the North hires his workers "by the day, and the Paul of the South hires them by the lifetime".' Marx is here quoting Carlyle's article 'Ilias Americana in Nuce' (*Macmillan's Magazine*, August, 1863). And Marx concludes: 'Thus the bubble of the Tory sympathy for the urban workers (the Tories never had any sympathy for agricultural workers) has burst at last. Inside it we find—slavery!'

    One of my reasons for quoting this passage is that I wish to emphasize Marx's complete disagreement with the belief that there is not much to choose between slavery and 'wage-slavery'. Nobody could stress more strongly than Marx the fact that the abolition of slavery (and consequently the introduction of 'wage-slavery') is a most important and necessary step in the emancipation of the oppressed. The term 'wage-slavery' is therefore dangerous and misleading; for it has been interpreted, by Vulgar Marxists, as an indication that Marx agreed with what is in fact Carlyle's appraisal of the situation.

16. Marx defines the 'value' of a commodity as the average number of labour hours necessary for its reproduction. This definition is a good illustration of his *essentialism*

(cp. note 8 to this chapter). For he introduces *value* in order to get at the essential reality which corresponds to what appears in the form of the *price* of a commodity. Price is a delusive kind of appearance. 'A thing may have a price without having value', writes Marx (*Capital*, 79; see also Cole's excellent remarks in his Introduction to *Capital*, especially pp. xxvii, ff.). A sketch of Marx's 'value theory' will be found in chapter 20. (Cp. notes 9–27 to that chapter, and text.)

17. For the problem of the 'wage-slaves', cp. end of note 15 to this chapter; also *Capital*, 155 (especially footnote 1). For Marx's analysis the results of which are briefly sketched here, see especially *Capital*, 153 ff., also the footnote 1 to p. 153; cp. also my chapter 20, below.

My presentation of Marx's analysis may be supported by quoting a statement made by Engels in his *Anti-Dühring* on the occasion of a summary of *Capital*. Engels writes (*H.o.M.*, 269 = *GA*, Special volume, 160–67): 'In other words, even if we exclude all possibility of robbery, violence, and fraud and even if we assume that all private property was originally produced by the owner's own labour; and that throughout the whole subsequent process, there was only exchange of equal values for equal values; even then the progressive development of production and exchange would necessarily bring about the present capitalist system of production; with its monopolization of the instruments of production as well as of the goods of consumption in the hands of a class weak in numbers; with its degradation into proletarian paupers of the other class comprising the immense majority; with its periodic cycle of production booms and of trade depressions; in other words, with the whole anarchy of our present system of production. The whole process is explained by purely economic causes: robbery, force, and the assumption of political interference of any kind are unnecessary at any point whatever.'

Perhaps this passage may one day convince a Vulgar Marxist that Marxism does not explain depressions by the conspiracy of 'big business'. Marx himself said (*Das Kapital*, II, 406 f., italics mine): 'Capitalist production involves conditions which, *independently of good or bad intentions*, permit only a temporary relative prosperity of the working class, and always only as a forerunner of a depression.'

18. For the doctrine 'property is theft' or 'property is robbery', cp. also Marx's remark on John Watts in *Capital*, 601, footnote 1.

19. For the Hegelian character of the distinction between merely 'formal' and 'actual' or 'real' freedom, or democracy, cp. note 62 to chapter 12. Hegel likes to attack the British constitution for its cult of merely 'formal' freedom, as opposed to the Prussian state in which 'real' freedom is 'actualized'. For the quotation at the end of this paragraph, cp. the passage quoted in the text to note 7 to chapter 15. See also notes 14 and 15 to chapter 20, and text.

20. For the *paradox of freedom* and the need for the protection of freedom by the state, cp. the four paragraphs in the text before note 42 to chapter 6, and especially notes 4 and 6 to chapter 7, and text; see also note 41 to chapter 12, and text, and note 7 to chapter 24.

21. Against this analysis, it may be said that, if we assume perfect competition between the entrepreneurs as producers, and especially as buyers of labour on the labour markets (and if we further assume that there is no 'industrial reserve army' of unemployed to exert pressure on this market), then there could be no talk of exploitation of the economically weak by the economically strong, i.e. of the workers by

the entrepreneurs. But is the assumption of perfect competition between the buyers on the labour markets at all realistic? Is it not true that, for example, on many local labour markets, there is only one buyer of any significance? Besides, we cannot assume that perfect competition would automatically eliminate the problem of unemployment, if for no other reason than because labour cannot easily be moved.

22. For the problem of economic intervention by the state, and for a characterization of our present economic system as *interventionism*, see the next three chapters, especially note 9 to chapter 18 and text. It may be remarked that *interventionism* as used here is the economic complement of what I have called in chapter 6, text to notes 24–44, political *protectionism*. (It is clear why the term 'protectionism' cannot be used instead of 'interventionism'.) See especially note 9 to chapter 18, and 25/26 to chapter 20, and text.
23. The passage is quoted more fully in the text to note 14 to chapter 13; for the contradiction between practical action and historicist determinism, see that note, and text to notes 5 ff. to chapter 22.
24. Cp. section II of chapter 7.
25. See Bertrand Russell, *Power* (1938); cp. especially pp. 123 ff.; Walter Lippmann, *The Good Society* (1937), cp. especially pp. 188 ff.
26. Russell, *Power*, pp. 128 f. Italics mine.
27. Laws to safeguard democracy are still in a rather rudimentary state of development. Very much could and should be done. The freedom of the press, for instance, is demanded because of the aim that the public should be given correct information; but viewed from this standpoint, it is a very insufficient institutional guarantee that this aim will be achieved. What good newspapers usually do at present on their own initiative, namely, giving the public all important information available, might be established as their duty, either by carefully framed laws, or by the establishment of a moral code, sanctioned by public opinion. Matters such as, for instance, the Zinovief letter, could be perhaps controlled by a law which makes it possible to nullify elections won by improper means, and which makes a publisher who neglects his duty to ascertain as well as possible the truth of published information liable for the damage done; in this case, for the expenses of a fresh election. I cannot go into details here, but it is my firm conviction that we could easily overcome the technological difficulties which may stand in the way of achieving such ends as the conduct of election campaigns largely by appeal to reason instead of passion. I do not see why we should not, for instance, standardize the size, type, etc., of the electioneering pamphlets, and eliminate placards. (This need not endanger freedom, just as reasonable limitations imposed upon those who plead before a court of justice protect freedom rather than endanger it.) The present methods of propaganda are an insult to the public as well as to the candidate. Propaganda of the kind which may be good enough for selling soap should not be used in matters of such consequence.
28. *Cp. the British 'Control of Engagement Order', 1947. The fact that this order is hardly used (it is clearly not abused) shows that legislation of even the most dangerous character is enacted without compelling need—obviously because the fundamental difference between the two types of legislation, viz. the one that establishes general rules of conduct, and the one that gives the government discretionary powers, is not sufficiently understood.*

29. *For this distinction, and for the use of the term 'legal framework', see F. A. Hayek, *The Road to Serfdom* (I am quoting from the 1st English edition, London, 1944). See, for example, p. 54, where Hayek speaks of 'the distinction ... between the creation of a *permanent framework of laws* within which productive activity is guided by individual decision, and the *direction of economic activity* by a central authority.' (Italics mine.) Hayek emphasizes the significance of the *predictability of the legal framework*; see, for example, p. 56.*

30. The review, published in the *European Messenger* of St. Petersburg, is quoted by Marx in the Preface to the 2nd edition of *Capital*. (See *Capital*, 871.)

In fairness to Marx, we must say that he did not always take his own system too seriously, and that he was quite prepared to deviate a little from his fundamental scheme; he considered it as a point of view (and as such it was certainly most important) rather than as a system of dogmas.

Thus we read, on two consecutive pages of *Capital* (832 f.), a statement which emphasizes the usual Marxist theory of the secondary character of the legal system (or of its character as a cloak, an 'appearance'), and another statement which ascribes a very important rôle to the political might of the state and raises it explicitly to the rank of a full-grown *economic force*. The first of these statements, 'The author would have done well to remember that revolutions are not made by laws', refers to the industrial revolution, and to an author who asked for the enactments by which it was effected. The second statement is a comment (and one most unorthodox from the Marxist point of view) upon the methods of accumulating capital; all these methods, Marx says, 'make use of the power of the state, which is the centralized political might of society. Might is the midwife of every old society pregnant with a new one. *It is itself an economic force*.' Up to the last sentence, which I have put in italics, the passage is clearly orthodox. But the last sentence breaks through this orthodoxy.

Engels was more dogmatic. One should compare especially one of his statements in his *Anti-Dühring* (*H.o.M.*, 277), where he writes, 'The rôle played in history by political might as opposed to economic developments is now clear.' He contends that whenever 'political might works against economic developments, then, as a rule, with only few exceptions, it succumbs; these few exceptions are isolated cases of conquest in which barbarian conquerors ... have laid waste ... productive forces which they did not know how to use'. (Compare, however, notes 13/14 to chapter 15, and text.)

The dogmatism and authoritarianism of most Marxists is a really astonishing phenomenon. It just shows that they use Marxism irrationally, as a metaphysical system. It is to be found among radicals and moderates alike. E. Burns, for example, makes (in *H.o.M.*, 374) the surprisingly naïve statement that 'refutations ... inevitably distort Marx's theories'; which seems to imply that Marx's theories are irrefutable, i.e. unscientific; for every scientific theory is refutable, and can be superseded. L. Laurat, on the other hand, in *Marxism and Democracy*, p. 226, says: 'In looking at the world in which we live, we are staggered at the almost mathematical precision with which the essential predictions of Karl Marx are being realized.'

Marx himself seems to have thought differently. I may be wrong in this, but I do believe in the sincerity of his statement (at the end of his Preface to the first edition of *Capital*; see 865): 'I welcome scientific criticism, however harsh. But in the face of the prejudices of a so-called public opinion, I shall stick to my maxim ...: Follow your course, and let them chatter!'

NOTES TO CHAPTER EIGHTEEN

1 For Marx's essentialism, and the fact that the material means of production play the part of essences in his theory, cp. especially note 13 to chapter 15. See also note 6 to chapter 17 and notes 20–24 to chapter 20, and text.

2. Cp. *Capital*, 864 = *H.o.M.*, 374, and notes 14 and 16 to chapter 13.

3. What I call the secondary aim of *Capital*, its anti-apologetic aim, includes a somewhat academic task, namely, the *critique of political economy with regard to its scientific status*. It is this latter task to which Marx alluded both in the title of the forerunner of *Capital*, namely in *A Contribution to the Critique of Political Economy*, and in the sub-title of *Capital* itself, which reads, in literal translation, *Critique of Political Economy*. For both these titles allude unmistakably to Kant's *Critique of Pure Reason*. And this title, in turn, was intended to mean: 'Critique of pure or metaphysical philosophy in regard to its scientific status'. (This is more clearly indicated by the title of the paraphrase of Kant's *Critique* which reads in an almost literal translation: *Prolegomena To Any Metaphysics Which In Future May Justly Claim Scientific Status.*) By alluding to Kant, Marx apparently wished to say: 'Just as Kant criticized the claim of metaphysics, revealing that it was *no science* but largely *apologetic theology*, so I criticize here the corresponding claims of bourgeois economics.' That the main tendency of Kant's *Critique* was, in Marx's circles, considered to be directed against apologetic theology can be seen from its representation in *Religion and Philosophy in Germany* by Marx's friend, H. Heine (cp. notes 15 and 16 to chapter 15). It is not quite without interest that, in spite of Engels' supervision, the first English translators of *Capital* translated its sub-title as *A Critical Analysis of Capitalist Production*, thus substituting an emphasis upon what I have described in the text as Marx's first aim for an allusion to his second aim.

   Burke is quoted by Marx in *Capital*, 843, note 1. The quotation is from E. Burke, *Thoughts and Details on Scarcity*, 1800, pp. 31 f.

4. Cp. my remarks on class consciousness towards the end of section I, in chapter 16.

   Concerning the continued existence of class-unity after the class struggle against the class enemy has ceased, it is, I think, hardly in keeping with Marx's assumptions, and especially with his dialectics, to assume that class consciousness is a thing that *can* be accumulated and afterwards stored, that it *can* survive the forces that produced it. But the further assumption that it *must necessarily* outlive these forces contradicts Marx's theory which looks upon consciousness as a mirror or as a product of hard social realities. And yet, this further assumption must be made by anybody who holds with Marx that the dialectic of history must lead to socialism.

   The following passage from the *Communist Manifesto* (*H.o.M.*, 46 f. = *GA*, Series I, vol. vi, 46) is particularly interesting in this context; it contains a clear statement that the class consciousness of the workers is a mere consequence of the 'force of circumstances', i.e. the pressure of the class situation; but it contains, at the same time, the doctrine criticized in the text, namely, the prophecy of the classless society. This is the passage: 'In spite of the fact that the proletariat is compelled, by the force of circumstances, to organize itself as a class during its struggle with the bourgeoisie; in spite of the fact that, by means of revolution, it makes itself the ruling class, and, as such, sweeps away by force the old conditions of production; in spite of these facts, it will sweep away, along with these conditions, also the conditions for the existence of any class antagonism and of any classes, and will thereby abolish its own supremacy as a class.—In place of the old bourgeois society, with its classes and class antagonism, we shall have an association in which the free development of each is the warrant for the free development of all.' (Cp. also text to note 8 to this chapter.) It is a beautiful belief, but it is an æsthetic and romantic belief; it is a wishful 'Utopianism', to use Marxist terminology, not a 'scientific socialism'.

Marx fought against what he called 'Utopianism', and rightly so. (Cp. chapter 9.) But since he was himself a romantic, he failed to discern the most dangerous element in Utopianism, its romantic hysteria, its æstheticist irrationalism; instead, he fought against its (admittedly most immature) attempts at rational planning, opposing to them his historicism. (Cp. note 21 to the present chapter.)

For all his acute reasoning and for all his attempts to use scientific method, Marx permitted irrational and æsthetic sentiments to usurp, in places, complete control of his thoughts. Nowadays one calls this wishful thinking. It was romantic, irrational, and even mystical wishful thinking that led Marx to assume that the collective class unity and class solidarity of the workers would last after a change in the class situation. It is thus wishful thinking, a mystical collectivism, and an irrational reaction to the strain of civilization which leads Marx to prophesy the necessary advent of socialism.

This kind of romanticism is one of the elements of Marxism which appeals most strongly to many of its followers. It is expressed, for example, most touchingly in the dedication of Hecker's *Moscow Dialogues*. Hecker speaks here of socialism as of 'a social order where the strife of class and race shall be no more, and where truth, goodness and beauty shall be the share of all'. Who would not like to have heaven on earth! And yet, it must be one of the first principles of rational politics that *we cannot make heaven on earth*. We are not going to become Free Spirits or angels at least not for the next couple of centuries or so. We are bound to this earth by our metabolism, as Marx once wisely declared; or as Christianity puts it, we are spirit *and* flesh. Thus we must be more modest. In politics and in medicine, he who promises too much is likely to be a quack. We must try to improve things, but we must get rid of the idea of a philosopher's stone, of a formula which will convert our corrupt human society into pure, lasting gold.

At the back of all this is the hope of casting out the devil from our world. Plato thought he could do it by banishing him to the lower classes, and ruling over him. The anarchists dreamt that once the state, the Political System, was destroyed, everything must turn out well. And Marx dreamt a similar dream of banishing the devil by destroying the economic system.

These remarks are not intended to imply that it is impossible to make even rapid advances, perhaps even through the introduction of comparatively small reforms, such as, for example, a reform of taxation, or a reduction of the rate of interest. I only wish to insist that we must expect every elimination of an evil to create, as its unwanted repercussion, a host of new though possibly very much lesser evils, which may be on an altogether different plane of urgency. Thus the second principle of sane politics would be: *all politics consists in choosing the lesser evil* (as the Viennese poet and critic K. Kraus put it). And politicians should be zealous in the search for the evils their actions must necessarily produce instead of concealing them, since a proper evaluation of competing evils must otherwise become impossible.

5. Although I do not intend to deal with Marx's dialectics (cp. note 4 to chapter 13), I may show that it would be possible to 'strengthen' Marx's logically inconclusive argument by so-called 'dialectical reasoning'. In accordance with this reasoning, all we need is to describe the antagonistic trends within capitalism in such a manner that socialism (for instance in the form of a totalitarian state-capitalism) appears as the necessary synthesis. The two antagonistic tendencies of capitalism can then perhaps be described thus. *Thesis*: The tendency towards the accumulation of capital in a few hands; towards industrialization and bureaucratic control of industry; towards economic and psychological levelling of the workers through the standardization of needs and desires. *Antithesis*: The increasing misery of the great masses; their increasing class consciousness in consequence of (*a*) class war, and (*b*) their increasing realization of their paramount significance within an economic system like that of an industrial society in which the working class is the only productive class, and accordingly the only essential class. (Cp. also note 15 to chapter 19, and text.)

   It is hardly necessary to show how the desired Marxist synthesis emerges; but it may be necessary to insist that a slightly changed emphasis in the description of the antagonistic tendency may lead to very different 'syntheses'; in fact, to any other synthesis one wishes to defend. For instance, one could easily present fascism as a necessary synthesis; or perhaps 'technocracy'; or else, a system of democratic interventionism.

6. *Bryan Magee writes about this passage: 'This is what *The New Class* by Djilas is all about: a fully worked out theory of the realities of the Communist revolution, written by an unrepentant Communist.'*

7. The history of the working-class movement is full of contrasts. It shows that the workers have been ready for the greatest sacrifices in their fight for the liberation of their own class, and beyond this, of mankind. But there are also many chapters telling a sorry tale of quite ordinary selfishness and of the pursuit of sectional interest to the detriment of all.

   It is certainly understandable that a trade union which obtains a great advantage for its members through solidarity and collective bargaining should try to exclude those from these benefits who are not prepared to join the union; for instance, by incorporating in their collective contracts the condition that only members of the union are to be employed. But it is a very different matter, and indeed indefensible, if a union which in this way has obtained a monopoly closes its membership list, thus keeping out fellow workers who want to join, without even establishing a just method (such as the strict adherence to a waiting list) of admitting new members. That such things can occur shows that the fact that a man is a worker does not always prevent him from forgetting all about the solidarity of the oppressed and from making full use of the economic prerogatives he may possess, i.e. from exploiting his fellow workers.

8. Cp. *The Communist Manifesto* (*H.o.M.*, 47 = *GA*, Series I, vol. vi, 546); the passage is quoted more fully in note 4 to this chapter, where Marx's romanticism is dealt with.

9. The term 'capitalism' is much too vague to be used as a name of a definite historical period. The term 'capitalism' was originally used in a disparaging sense, and it has

retained this sense ('system favouring big profits made by people who do not work') in popular usage. But at the same time it has also been used in a neutral scientific sense, but with many different meanings. In so far as, according to Marx, all accumulations of means of production may be termed 'capital', we may even say that 'capitalism' is in a certain sense synonymous with 'industrialism'. We could in this sense quite correctly describe a communist society, in which the state owns all capital, as 'state-capitalism'. For these reasons, I suggest using the name '*unrestrained capitalism*' for that period which Marx analysed and christened 'capitalism', and the name *interventionism* for our own period. The name 'interventionism' could indeed cover the three main types of social engineering in our time: the collectivist interventionism of Russia; the democratic interventionism of Sweden and the 'Smaller Democracies' and the New Deal in America; and even the fascist methods of regimented economy. What Marx called 'capitalism'—i.e. unrestrained capitalism—has completely 'withered away' in the twentieth century.

10. The Swedish 'social democrats', the party which inaugurated the Swedish experiment, had once been Marxist; but it gave up its Marxist theories shortly after its decision to accept governmental responsibilities and to embark upon a great programme of social reform. One of the aspects in which the Swedish experiment deviates from Marxism is its emphasis upon the consumer, and the rôle played by the consumer co-operatives, as opposed to the dogmatic Marxist emphasis upon production. The technological economic theory of the Swedes is strongly influenced by what Marxists would call 'bourgeois economics', while the orthodox Marxist theory of value plays no rôle in it whatever.

11. For this programme, see *H.o.M.*, 46 (= *GA*, Series I, vol. vi, 545).—With point (1), cp. text to note 15 to chapter 19.

    It may be remarked that even in one of the most radical statements ever made by Marx, the *Address to the Communist League* (1850), he considered a progressive income tax a most revolutionary measure. In the final description of revolutionary tactics towards the end of this address which culminates in the battle cry 'Revolution in permanence!' Marx says: 'If the democrats propose proportional taxation, the workers must demand progressive taxation. And should the democrats themselves declare for a moderate progressive tax, the workers must insist upon a steeply graduated tax; so steeply graduated as to cause the collapse of large capital.' (Cp. *H.o.M.*, 70, and especially note 44 to chapter 20.)

12. For my conception of piecemeal social engineering, cp. especially chapter 9. For political intervention in economic matters, and a more precise explanation of the term *interventionism*, see note 9 to this chapter and text.

13. I consider this criticism of Marxism very important. It is mentioned in sections 17/18 of my *The Poverty of Historicism*; and as stated there, it can be parried by proffering a *historicist moral theory*. But I believe that only if such a theory (cp. chapter 22, especially notes 5 ff. and text) is accepted can Marxism escape the charge that it teaches '*the belief in political miracles*'. (This term is due to Julius Kraft.) See also notes 4 and 21 to the present chapter.

14. For the problem of *compromise*, cp. a remark at the end of the paragraph to which note 3 to chapter 9 is appended. For a justification of the remark in the text, 'For they do not plan for the whole of society', see chapter 9, and my The *Poverty of Historicism, II* (especially the criticism of holism).

15. F. A. von Hayek (cp., for example, his *Freedom and the Economic System*, Chicago, 1939) insists that a centralized 'planned economy' must involve the gravest dangers to individual freedom. But he also emphasizes that *planning for freedom* is necessary. ('Planning for freedom' is also advocated by Mannheim, in his *Man and Society in an Age of Reconstruction*, 1941. But since his idea of 'planning' is emphatically *collectivistic* and *holistic*, I am convinced that it must lead to tyranny, and not to freedom; and, indeed, Mannheim's 'freedom' is the offspring of Hegel's. Cp. the end of chapter 23, and my paper quoted at the end of the preceding note.)
16. This contradiction between the Marxist historical theory and the Russian historical reality is discussed in chapter 15, notes 13/14, and text.
17. This is another contradiction between Marxist theory and historical practice; as opposed to that mentioned in the last note, this second contradiction has given rise to many discussions and attempts to explain the matter by the introduction of auxiliary hypotheses. The most important of these is the theory of imperialism and colonial exploitation. This theory asserts that the revolutionary development is frustrated in countries in which the proletarian in common with the capitalist reaps where not he but the oppressed natives of the colonies have sown. This hypothesis which is undoubtedly refuted by developments like those in the non-imperialistic Smaller Democracies will be discussed more fully in chapter 20 (text to notes 37–40).

    Many social democrats interpreted the Russian revolution, in accordance with Marx's scheme, as a belated 'bourgeois revolution', insisting that this revolution was bound up with an economic development parallel to the 'industrial revolution' in the more advanced countries. But this interpretation assumes, of course, that history must conform with the Marxist scheme. In fact, such an essentialist problem as whether the Russian revolution is a belated industrial revolution or a premature 'social revolution' is of a purely verbal character; and if it leads to difficulties within Marxism, then this shows only that Marxism has verbal difficulties in describing events which have not been foreseen by its founders.
18. The leaders were able to inspire in their followers an enthusiastic faith in their mission—to liberate mankind. But the leaders also were responsible for the ultimate failure of their politics, and the breakdown of the movement. This failure was due, very largely, to intellectual irresponsibility. The leaders had assured the workers that Marxism was a science, and that the intellectual side of the movement was in the best hands. But they never adopted a scientific, i.e. a critical, attitude towards Marxism. As long as they could apply it (and what is easier than this?), as long as they could interpret history in articles and speeches, they were intellectually satisfied. (Cp. also notes 19 and 22 to this chapter.)
19. For a number of years prior to the rise of fascism in Central Europe a very marked defeatism within the ranks of the social democratic leaders was noticeable. They began to believe that fascism was an unavoidable stage in social development. That is to say, they began to make some amendments to Marx's scheme, but they never doubted the soundness of the historicist approach; they never saw that such a question as 'Is fascism an unavoidable stage in the development of civilization?' may be totally misleading.
20. The Marxist movement in Central Europe had few precedents in history. It was a movement which, in spite of the fact that it professed atheism, can truly be called a great religious movement. (Perhaps this may impress some of those intellectuals who do not take Marxism seriously.) Of course, it was a collectivist and even a

tribalist movement, in many ways. But it was a movement of the workers to educate themselves for their great task; to emancipate themselves, to raise the standard of their interests and of their pastimes; to substitute mountaineering for alcohol, classical music for swing, serious books for thrillers. 'The emancipation of the working class can only be achieved by the workers themselves' was their belief. (For the deep impression made by this movement on some observers, see, for example, G. E. R. Gedye's *Fallen Bastions*, 1939.)

21. The quotation is from Marx's Preface to the second edition of *Capital* (cp. *Capital*, 870; cp. also note 6 to chapter 13). It shows how fortunate Marx was in his reviewers (cp. also note 30 to chapter 17, and text).

   Another most interesting passage in which Marx expresses his anti-Utopianism and historicism can be found in *The Civil War in France* (*H.o.M.*, 150, K. Marx, *Der Buergerkrieg in Frankreich*, A. Willaschek, Hamburg 1920, 65–66), where Marx says approvingly of the Paris *Commune* of 1871: 'The working class did not expect miracles from the Commune. They have no ready-made Utopias, to be introduced by the decree of the people. They know that in order to achieve their own emancipation, and with it, those higher forms to which our present society is irresistibly tending, ... they will have to pass through long struggles, through a series of historic processes, transforming circumstances and men. They have no ideals to realize, but to set free the elements of the new society with which the old collapsing bourgeois society itself is pregnant.' There are few passages in Marx which exhibit the historicist lack of plan more strikingly. 'They have to pass through long struggles ...', Marx says. But if they have no plan to realize, 'no ideals to realize', as Marx says, what are they struggling for? They 'did not expect miracles', Marx says; but he himself expected miracles in believing that the historical struggle irresistibly tends to 'higher forms' of social life. (Cp. notes 4 and 13 to the present chapter.) Marx was to a certain extent justified in his refusal to embark upon social engineering. To organize the workers was undoubtedly the most important practical task of his day. If such a suspect excuse as 'the time was not ripe for it' can ever be justly applied, it must be applied to Marx's refusal to dabble in the problems of rational institutional social engineering. (This point is illustrated by the childish character of the Utopian proposals down to and including, say, Bellamy.) But it was unfortunate that he supported this sound political intuition by a theoretical attack upon social technology. This became an excuse for his dogmatic followers to continue in the same attitude at a time when things had changed, and technology had become politically more important even than organizing the workers.

22. The Marxist leaders interpreted the events as the dialectical ups and downs of history. They thus functioned as cicerones, as guides through the hills (and valleys) of history rather than as political leaders of action. This dubious art of interpreting the terrible events of history instead of fighting them was forcefully denounced by the poet K. Kraus (mentioned in note 4 to this chapter).

NOTES TO CHAPTER NINETEEN

1. Cp. *Capital*, 846 = *H.o.M.*, 403.
2. The passage is from Marx-Engels, *The Communist Manifesto*. (Cp. *H.o.M.*, 31 = *GA*, Series I, vol. vi, 533.)
3. Cp. *Capital*, 547 = *H.o.M.*, 560 (where it is quoted by Lenin).

A remark may be made concerning the term 'concentration of capital' (which I have translated in the text 'concentration of capital in a few hands').

In the third edition of *Capital* (cp. *Capital*, 689 ff.) Marx introduced the following distinctions: (*a*) by *accumulation* of capital he means merely the growth in the total amount of capital goods, for example, within a certain region; (*b*) by *concentration* of capital he means (cp. 689/690) the normal growth of the capital in the hands of the various individual capitalists, a growth which arises from the general tendency towards accumulation and which gives them command over an increasing number of workers; (*c*) by *centralization* he means (cp. 691) that kind of growth of capital which is due to the expropriation of some capitalists by other capitalists ('one capitalist lays many of his fellows low').

In the second edition, Marx had not yet distinguished between concentration and centralization; he used the term 'concentration' in both senses (*b*) and (*c*). To show the difference, we read in the third edition (*Capital*, 691): 'Here we have genuine centralization, in contradistinction to accumulation and concentration.' In the second edition, we read at this place: 'Here we have genuine concentration, in contradistinction to accumulation.' The alteration, however, was not made throughout the book, but only in a few passages (especially pp. 690–3, and 846). In the passage here quoted in the text, the wording remained the same as in the second edition. In the passage (p. 846) quoted in the text to note 15 to this chapter, Marx replaced 'concentration' by 'centralization'.

4. Cp. Marx's *Eighteenth Brumaire* (*H.o.M.*, 123; italics mine = Karl Marx, *Der Achtzehnte Brumaire des Louis Bonaparte*, Verlag für Literatur und Politik. Wien-Berlin 1927, 28–29): 'The bourgeois republic triumphed. On its side stood the aristocracy of finance, the industrial bourgeoisie, *the middle class*, the petty bourgeoisie, the army, *the rabble proletariat*, organized as the Mobile Guard, *the intellectual lights*, the clergy, *and the rural population*. On the side of the Paris proletariat stood none but the proletariat itself.'

   For an incredibly naïve statement made by Marx concerning the 'rural producers', cp. also note 43 to chapter 20.

5. Cp. text to note 11 to chapter 18.
6. Cp. the quotation in note 4 to the present chapter, especially the reference to the middle class and to the 'intellectual lights'.

   For the 'rabble proletariat', cp. the same place and *Capital*, 711 f. (The term is there translated as 'tatterdemalion proletariat'.)

7. For the meaning of 'class consciousness' in Marx's sense, see end of section I in chapter 16.

   Apart from the possible development of a defeatist spirit, as mentioned in the text, there are other things which may undermine the class consciousness of the workers, and which may lead to disunion among the working class. Lenin, for example, mentions that imperialism may split the workers by offering them a share in its spoils; he writes (*H.o.M.*, 707 = V. I. Lenin, L.L.L., *Imperialism, the Highest State of Capitalism*, vol. xv, 96; cp. also note 40 to chapter 20): ' ... in Great Britain, the tendency of imperialism to split the workers, to strengthen the opportunists among them, and to cause temporary decay in the working-class movement, revealed itself much earlier than at the end of the nineteenth and the beginning of the twentieth centuries.'

H. B. Parkes rightly mentions in his excellent analysis, *Marxism—A Post Mortem* (1940; also published under the title *Marxism—An Autopsy*), that it is quite possible that entrepreneurs and workers may together exploit the consumer; in a protected or monopolist industry, they may share in the spoil. This possibility shows that Marx exaggerates the antagonism between the interests of the workers and entrepreneurs.

And lastly it may be mentioned that the tendency of most governments to proceed along the line of least resistance is liable to lead to the following result. Since workers and entrepreneurs are the best organized and politically most powerful groups in the community, a modern government may easily tend to satisfy both at the expense of the consumer. And it may do so without a guilty conscience; for it will persuade itself that it has done well by establishing peace between the most antagonistic parties in the community.

8. Cp. text to notes 17 and 18 to this chapter.
9. Some Marxists even dare to assert that there would be far less suffering involved in a violent social revolution than in the chronic evils inherent in what they call 'capitalism'. (Cp. L. Laurat, *Marxism and Democracy*, translated by E. Fitzgerald, 1940; p. 38, note 2; Laurat criticizes Sidney Hook, *Towards an Understanding of Marx*, for holding such views.) These Marxists do not, however, disclose the scientific basis of this estimate; or to speak more bluntly, of this utterly irresponsible piece of oracular pretence.
10. 'It should be plain without any further comment', Engels says about Marx, remembering his Hegel, 'that if things and their mutual relations are taken to be variable instead of fixed, then their mental images, their notions, will be subject to variation and transformation also; that one does not attempt to force them into the pigeonholes of rigid definitions; but that one treats them, as the case may be, according to the historical or logical character of the process by which they have been formed.' (Cp. Engels' Preface to *Das Kapital*, III/1, p. xvi.)
11. It does not correspond precisely because the Communists sometimes profess the more moderate theory, especially in those countries where this theory is not represented by the Social Democrats. Cp., for example, text to note 26 to this chapter.
12. Cp. notes 4 and 5 to chapter 17, and text; as well as note 14 to the present chapter; and contrast with notes 17 and 18 to the present chapter, and text.
13. There are, of course, positions between these two; and there are also more moderate Marxist positions: especially A. Bernstein's so-called 'revisionism'. This latter position, in fact, gives up Marxism altogether; it is nothing but the advocacy of a strictly democratic and non-violent workers' movement.
14. This development of Marx's is, of course, an interpretation, and not a very convincing one; the fact is that Marx was not very consistent, and that he used the terms 'revolution', 'force', 'violence', etc., with a systematic ambiguity. This position was partly forced upon him by the fact that history during his lifetime did not proceed according to his plan. It conformed to the Marxist theory in so far as it exhibited most clearly a tendency away from what Marx called 'capitalism', i.e. away from non-intervention. Marx frequently referred with satisfaction to this tendency, for example, in his Preface to the first edition of *Capital*. (Cp. the quotation in note 16 to the present chapter; see also the text.) On the other hand, this same tendency (towards interventionism) led to an improvement of the lot of the workers in opposition to Marx's

theory; and it thereby reduced the likelihood of a revolution. Marx's wavering and ambiguous interpretations of his own teaching are probably the result of this situation.

In order to illustrate the point, two passages may be quoted, one from an early and one from a late work of Marx. The early passage is from the *Address to the Communist League* (1850; cp. *H.o.M.*, pp. 60 ff. = *Labour Monthly*, September 1922, 136 ff.). The passage is interesting because it is practical. Marx assumes that the workers together with the bourgeois democrats have won the battle against feudalism and have set up a democratic regime. Marx insists that after having achieved this, the battle-cry of the workers must be 'Revolution in permanence!' What this means is explained in detail (p. 66): 'They must act in such a manner that the revolutionary excitement does not collapse immediately after the victory. On the contrary, they must maintain it as long as possible. Far from opposing so-called excesses, such as the sacrificing to popular revenge of hated individuals or public buildings to which hateful memories are attached, such deeds must not only be tolerated, but their direction must be taken in hand, for example's sake.' (Cp. also note 35 (1) to this chapter, and note 44 to chapter 20.)

A moderate passage which contrasts with the previous one may be chosen from Marx's *Address to the First International* (Amsterdam, 1872; cp. L. Laurat, *op. cit.*, p. 36): 'We do not deny that there are countries, such as the United States and Great Britain—if I knew your institutions better, I should perhaps add Holland—where the workers will be able to achieve their aims by peaceful means. But this is not the case in all countries.' For these more moderate views, cp. also text to notes 16–18 to the present chapter.

But the whole confusion can be found in a nutshell as early as in the final summary of the *Manifesto* where we find the following two contradictory statements, separated by one sentence only: (1) 'In short, the Communists support everywhere every revolutionary movement against the existing social and political order of things.' (This must include England, for example.) (2) Finally, they labour everywhere for the union and agreement of the democratic parties of all countries.' To make the confusion complete, the next sentences run: 'The communists disdain to conceal their views and aims. They openly declare that their ends can be attained only by the forcible overthrow of all existing social conditions.' (Democratic conditions are not excluded.)

15. Cp. *Capital*, 846 = *H.o.M.*, 403 f. (Concerning the term 'centralization', substituted in the third edition for the term 'concentration' of the second edition, cp. note 3 to the present chapter. Concerning the translation 'their capitalist cloak becomes a straitjacket', it may be remarked that a more literal translation would be: 'they become incompatible with their capitalist wrapper' or 'cloak' or slightly more freely: 'their capitalist cloak becomes intolerable'.)

This passage is strongly influenced by Hegelian *dialectics*, as is shown by its continuation. (Hegel called the *antithesis* of a *thesis* sometimes its negation, and the *synthesis* the 'negation of the negation'.) 'The capitalist method of appropriation', Marx writes, ' ... is the first negation of individual private property based upon individual labour. But with the inexorability of a law of nature, capitalist production begets its own negation. It is the negation of the negation. This second negation ... establishes ... the common ownership of the land and of the means of production.' (For a more detailed dialectical derivation of socialism, cp. note 5 to chapter 18.)

16. This was the attitude taken up by Marx in his Preface to the first edition of *Capital* (*Capital*, 865), where he says: 'Still, progress is undeniable ... The foreign representatives of the British crown ... tell us ... that in the more advanced countries of the European continent, a change in the relations between capital and labour is just as obvious and as inevitable as in England ... Mr. Wade, the vice-president of the United States of North America ... declares at public meetings that, after the abolition of slavery, a radical change in the conditions of capital and landed property comes next on the agenda!' (Cp. also note 14 to this chapter.)
17. Cp. Engels' Preface to the first English edition of *Capital*. (*Capital*, 887.) The passage is quoted more fully in note 9 to chapter 17.
18. Cp. Marx's letter to Hyndman, dated December 8th, 1880; see H. H. Hyndman, *The Record of an Adventurous Life* (1911), p. 283. Cp. also L. Laurat, *op. cit.*, 239. The passage may be quoted here more fully: 'If you say that you do not share the views of my party for England I can only reply that that party considers an English revolution not *necessary*, but—according to historic precedents—*possible*. If the unavoidable evolution turns into a revolution, it would not only be the fault of the ruling classes, but also of the working class.' (Note the ambiguity of the position.)
19. H. B. Parkes, *Marxism—A Post Mortem*, p. 101 (cp. also pp. 106 ff.), expresses a similar view; he insists that the Marxist 'belief that capitalism cannot be reformed but can only be destroyed' is one of the characteristic tenets of the Marxist theory of accumulation. 'Adopt some other theory', he says, '... and it remains possible for capitalism to be transformed by gradual methods.'
20. Cp. the end of the *Manifesto* (*H.o.M.*, 59 = *GA*, Series I, vol. vi, 557): 'The proletarians have nothing to lose but their fetters. They have a world to win.'
21. Cp. the *Manifesto* (*H.o.M.*, 45 = *GA*, Series I, vol. vi, 545); the passage is quoted more fully in text to note 35 to this chapter.—The last quotation in this paragraph is from the *Manifesto*, *H.o.M.*, 35 (= *GA*, Series I, vol. vi, 536). Cp. also note 35 to this chapter.
22. But social reforms have rarely been carried out under the pressure of those who suffer; religious movements—I include the Utilitarians—and individuals (like Dickens) may influence public opinion greatly. And Henry Ford discovered, to the astonishment of all Marxists and many 'capitalists' that a rise in wages may benefit the employer.
23. Cp. notes 18 and 21 to chapter 18.
24. Cp. *H.o.M.*, 37 (= *GA*, Series I, vol. vi, 538).
25. Cp. *The State and Revolution*, *H.o.M.*, 756 (= *State and Revolution*, 77). Here is the passage in full: 'Democracy is of great importance for the working class in its struggle for freedom against the capitalists. But democracy is by no means a limit one may not overstep; it is only one of the stages in the course of the development from feudalism to capitalism, and from capitalism, to Communism.'

    Lenin insists that democracy means only '*formal* equality'. Cp. also *H.o.M.*, 834 (= V. I. Lenin, *The Proletarian Revolution and the Renegade Kautsky*. L.L.L., vol. xviii, 34), where Lenin uses this Hegelian argument of merely 'formal' equality against Kautsky: ' ... he accepts the formal equality, which under capitalism is merely a fraud and a piece of hypocrisy at its face value as a de facto equality ...'
26. Cp. Parkes, *Marxism—A Post Mortem*, p. 219.
27. Such a tactical move is in keeping with the *Manifesto* which announces that the Communists 'labour everywhere for the union and agreement of the democratic

parties of all countries', but which announces at the same time 'that their ends can be attained only by the forcible overthrow of existing social conditions', which include democratic conditions.

But such a tactical move is also in keeping with the party programme of 1928; for this says (*H.o.M.*, 1036; italics mine = *The Programme of the Communist International*, Modern Books Ltd., London 1932, 61): 'In determining its line of tactics each Communist Party must take into account the concrete internal and external situation ... The party determines slogans ... with a view to organizing ... the masses *on the broadest possible scale.*' But this cannot be achieved without making full use of the systematic ambiguity of the term revolution.

28. Cp. *H.o.M.*, 59 and 1042 (= *GA*, Series I, vol. vi, 557, and *Programme of the Communist International*, 65); and end of note 14 to this chapter. (See also note 37.)
29. This is not a quotation but a paraphrase. Cp., for example, the passage from Engels' Preface to the first English edition of *Capital* quoted in note 9 to chapter 17. See also L. Laurat, *op. cit.*, p. 240.
30. The first of the two passages is quoted by L. Laurat, *loc. cit.*; for the second, cp. *H.o.M.*, 93 (= Karl Marx, *The Class Struggle in France 1848–1850.* Introduction by F. Engels. Co-operative Publishing Society of Foreign Workers in the U.S.S.R., Moscow 1934, 29). Italics mine.
31. Engels was partly conscious that he had been forced to a change of front since 'History has proved us wrong, and all who thought like us', as he said (*H.o.M.*, 79 = Karl Marx, *Die Klassenkampfe in Frankreich*, Vorwaerts, Berlin 1890, 8). But he was conscious mainly of one mistake: that he and Marx had overrated the speed of the development. That the development was, in fact, in a different direction, he never admitted, although he complained of it; cp. text to notes 38–9 to chapter 20, where I quote Engels' paradoxical complaint that the 'working class is actually becoming more and more bourgeois'.
32. Cp. notes 4 and 6 to chapter 7.
33. They may continue for other reasons also; for example, because the tyrant's power depends on the support of a certain section of the ruled. *But this does not mean that the tyranny must in fact be a class rule*, as the Marxists would say. For even if the tyrant is forced to bribe a certain section of the population, to grant them economic or other advantages, this does not mean that he is forced *by this section*, or that this section has the power to claim and to enforce these advantages as their right. If there are no *institutions* in existence enabling that section to enforce its influence, the tyrant may withdraw the benefits enjoyed by this section and seek support from another one.
34. Cp. *H.o.M.*, 171 (= Karl Marx, *Civil War in France*, Introduction by F. Engels. Martin Lawrence, London 1933, 19). (See also *H.o.M.*, 833 = *The Proletarian Revolution*, 33–34.)
35. Cp. *H.o.M.*, 45 (= *GA*, Series I, vol. vi, 545). See also note 21 to this chapter. Cp. further the following passage from the *Manifesto* (*H.o.M.*, 37 = *GA*, Series I, vol. vi, 538): 'The immediate aim of the Communists is the ... conquest of political power by the proletariat.'

(1) Tactical advice that must lead to the loss of the battle of democracy is given in detail by Marx in his *Address to the Communist League*. (*H.o.M.*, 67 = *Labour Monthly*, September 1922, 143; cp. also note 14 to this chapter and note 44 to chapter 20.)

Marx explains there the attitude to be taken up, after democracy has been attained, towards the democratic party with whom, according to the *Manifesto* (cp. note 14 to this chapter), the Communists have had to establish 'union and agreement'. Marx says: 'In short, from the first moment of victory, we must no longer direct our distrust against the beaten reactionary enemy, but against our former allies' (i.e. the democrats).

Marx demands that 'the arming of the whole proletariat with rifles, guns, and ammunition should be carried out at once' and that 'the workers must try to organize themselves into an independent guard, with their own chiefs and general staff'. The aim is 'that the bourgeois democratic Government not only immediately loses all backing among the workers, but from the commencement finds itself under the supervision and threats of authorities behind whom stands the entire mass of the working class'.

It is clear that this policy is bound to wreck democracy. It is bound to make the Government turn against those workers who are not prepared to abide by the law, but try to rule by threats. Marx tries to excuse his politics by prophecy (*H.o.M.*, 68 and 67 = *Labour Monthly*, Sept. 1922, 143): 'As soon as the new Government is established they will commence to fight the workers', and he says: 'In order that this party' (i.e. the democrats) 'whose betrayal of the workers will begin with the first hour of victory, should be frustrated in its nefarious work, it is necessary to organize and to arm the proletariat.' I think that his tactics would produce precisely the nefarious effect he prophesies. They would make his historical prophecy come true. Indeed, if the workers were to proceed in this way, every democrat in his senses would be forced (even if, and particularly if, he wished to promote the cause of the oppressed) to join in what Marx describes as the betrayal of the workers, and to fight against those who were out to wreck the democratic institutions for the protection of the individual from the benevolence of tyrants and Great Dictators.

I may add that the passages quoted are comparatively early utterances of Marx and that his more mature opinions were probably somewhat different, and at any rate more ambiguous. But this does not detract from the fact that these early passages had a lasting influence, and that they have often been acted upon, to the detriment of all concerned.

(2) In connection with point (*b*) in the text above, a passage from Lenin may be quoted (*H.o.M.*, 828 = *The Proletarian Revolution*, 30): '... the working class realizes perfectly well that the bourgeois parliaments are institutions *foreign* to them, that they are *instruments of the oppression* of the proletariat by the bourgeoisie, that they are institutions of the hostile class, of the exploiting minority.' It is clear that these stories did not encourage the workers to defend parliamentary democracy against the assault of the fascists.

36. Cp. Lenin, *State and Revolution* (*H.o.M.*, 744 = *State and Revolution*, 68): 'Democracy ... for the rich, that is the democracy of capitalist society ... Marx brilliantly grasped the *essence* of capitalist democracy when ... he said that the oppressed were allowed, once every few years, to decide which particular representatives of the oppressing class should ... oppress them!' See also notes 1 and 2 to chapter 17.

37. Lenin writes in *Left-Wing Communism* (*H.o.M.*, 884 f.; italics mine = V. I. Lenin, *Left-Wing Communism, An Infantile Disorder*. L.L.L. vol. xvi, 72–73): '... all attention must be concentrated on the *next* step ... on seeking out the forms of *transition or approach*

to the proletarian revolution. The proletarian vanguard has been ideologically won over ... But from this first step it is still a long way to victory ... In order that the entire class ... may take up such a position, propaganda and agitation alone are not enough. *The masses must have their own political experience*. Such is the fundamental law of all great revolutions ...: *it has been necessary ... to realize through their own painful experience ... the absolute inevitability of a dictatorship of the extreme reactionaries* ... as the only alternative to a dictatorship of the proletariat, *in order to turn them resolutely towards communism*.'

38. As is to be expected, each of the two Marxist parties tries to put the blame for their failure on the other; the one blames the other for its policy of catastrophe, and in its turn is blamed by the latter for keeping up the workers' faith in the possibility of winning the battle of democracy. It is somewhat ironical to find that Marx himself has given an excellent description which fits every detail of this method of blaming the circumstances, and especially the competing party, for one's failure. (The description was, of course, aimed by Marx against a competing leftist group of his time.) Marx writes (*H.o.M.*, 130; last group of italics mine = V. I. Lenin, *The Teachings of Karl Marx*, L.L.L. vol. i, 55): 'They do not need to consider their own resources too critically. They have merely to give the signal, and the people, with all its inexhaustible resources, will fall upon the *oppressors*. If, in the actual event, their ... powers prove to be sheer impotence, then the fault lies either with the pernicious sophists' (the other party, presumably) 'who split the *united people* into different hostile camps, or ... the whole thing has been wrecked by a detail in its execution, or else an unforeseen accident has, for the time being, spoilt the game. In any case the democrat' (or the antidemocrat) 'comes out of the most disgraceful defeat immaculate, just as he went into it innocent, *with the newly won conviction that he is destined to conquer; that neither he himself nor his party have to give up their old standpoint, but, on the contrary, conditions have to ripen, to move in his direction* ...'
39. I say 'the radical wing', for this historicist interpretation of fascism as being an inevitable stage in the inexorable development was believed in, and defended, by groups far beyond the ranks of the Communists. Even some of the leaders of the Viennese workers who offered a heroic but belated and badly organized resistance to fascism believed faithfully that fascism was a necessary step in the historical development towards socialism. Much as they hated it, they felt compelled to regard even fascism as a step forward, bringing the suffering people nearer to the ultimate goal.
40. Cp. the passage quoted in note 37 to this chapter.

NOTES TO CHAPTER TWENTY

1. The only complete English translation of the three volumes of *Capital* has nearly 2,500 pages. To these have to be added the three volumes which were published in German under the title *Theories of Surplus Value*; they contain material, largely historical, which Marx intended to use in *Capital*.
2. Cp. the opposition between an unrestrained capitalism and interventionism introduced in chapters 16 and 17. (See notes 10 to chapter 16, 22 to chapter 17 and 9 to chapter 18, and text.)

   For Lenin's statement, cp. *H.o.M.*, 561 (= *The Teachings of Karl Marx*, 29, italics mine). It is interesting that neither Lenin nor most of the Marxists appear to realize that society has changed since Marx. Lenin speaks in 1914 of 'contemporary society' as if it were Marx's as well as his contemporary society. But the *Manifesto* was published in 1848.

3. For all quotations in this paragraph, cp. *Capital*, 691.
4. Cp. the remarks on these terms made in note 3 to chapter 19.
5. It would do better because the defeatist spirit, which might endanger class consciousness (as mentioned in the text to note 7 to chapter 19), would be less likely to develop.
6. Cp. *Capital*, 697 ff.
7. The two quotations are from *Capital*, 698 and 706. The term translated by 'semi-prosperity' would be, in a more literal translation, 'medium prosperity'. I translate 'excessive production' instead of 'over-production' because Marx does *not* mean 'over-production' in the sense that more is produced than can be sold *now*, but in the sense that so much is produced that a difficulty of selling it will soon develop.
8. As Parkes puts it; cp. note 19 to chapter 19.
9. The labour theory of value is, of course, very old. My discussion of the value theory, it must be remembered, is confined to the so-called 'objective value theory'; I do not intend to criticize the 'subjective value theory' (which should perhaps better be described as the theory of subjective evaluation, or of acts of choice; cp. note 14 to chapter 14). J. Viner kindly pointed out to me that almost the only connection between Marx's value theory and Ricardo's arises out of Marx's misunderstanding of Ricardo, and that Ricardo never held that, unit for unit, labour had any more creating power than capital.
10. It appears to me certain that Marx never doubted that his 'values' *in some way* correspond to market prices. The value of a commodity, he taught, is equal to that of another one if the average number of labour hours needed for their production is the same. If one of the two commodities is *gold*, then its weight can be considered as the *price* of the other commodity, expressed in gold; and since money is based (by law) upon gold, we thus arrive at the money price of a commodity.

    The actual exchange ratios on the market, Marx teaches (see especially the important footnote 1 to p. 153 of *Capital*), will oscillate about the value ratios; and accordingly, the market price in money will also oscillate about the corresponding value ratio to gold of the commodity in question. 'If the magnitude of value is transformed into price', Marx says, a bit clumsily (*Capital*, 79; italics mine), 'then this ... relation assumes the form of an ... exchange ratio to *that commodity which functions as money*' (i.e. gold). 'In this ratio expresses itself, however, not only the magnitude of the value of the commodity, but also the ups and downs, the more or less, for which special circumstances are responsible'; in other words, prices may fluctuate. 'The possibility ... of a derivation of price from ... value is therefore inherent in the price form. This is not a defect; on the contrary, it shows that the price form is quite adequate to a method of production in which *regularities can manifest themselves only as averages of irregularities*.' It seems to me clear that the 'regularities' of which Marx speaks here are the values, and that he believes that values 'manifest themselves' (or 'assert themselves') only as averages of the actual market prices, which are therefore oscillating about the value.

    The reason why I emphasize this is that it has sometimes been denied. G. D. H. Cole, for example, writes in his 'Introduction' (*Capital*, xxv; italics mine): 'Marx ...

speaks usually as if commodities had actually a tendency, *subsequent* to temporary market fluctuations, to exchange at their "values". But he says explicitly (on page 79) that he does not mean this; and in the third volume of *Capital* he ... makes the inevitable divergence of prices and "values" abundantly clear.' But although it is true that Marx does not consider the fluctuations as merely 'temporary', he does hold that commodities have a tendency, *subject* to market fluctuations, to exchange at their 'values'; for as we have seen in the passage quoted here, and referred to by Cole, Marx does not speak of any *divergence* between value and price, but describes fluctuations and averages. The position is somewhat different in the third volume of *Capital*, where (in Chapter IX) the place of the 'value' of a commodity is taken by a new category, the 'production-price', which is the sum of its production cost plus the average rate of surplus value. But even here it remains characteristic of Marx's thinking that this new category, the production-price, is related to the actual market price as a kind of regulator of averages only. It does not determine the market price directly, but it expresses itself (just as does 'value' in the first volume) as an average about which the actual prices oscillate or fluctuate. This may be shown with the help of the following passage (*Das Kapital*, III/2, pp. 396 f.): 'The market prices rise above or fall below these regulating production-prices, but these oscillations compensate one another ... The same principle of regulative averages rules here that has been established by Quételet for social phenomena in general.' Similarly, Marx speaks there (p. 399) of the 'regulative price ..., i.e. the price about which market prices oscillate'; and on the next page, where he speaks of the influence of competition, he says that he is interested in the '*natural* price ..., i.e. the price ... that is not regulated by competition, but regulates it.' (Italics mine.) Apart from the fact that the 'natural' price clearly indicates that Marx hopes to find the essence of which the oscillating market prices are the 'forms of appearance' (cp. also note 23 to this chapter), we see that Marx consistently clings to the view that this essence, whether value or production-price, manifests itself as the *average* of the market prices. See also *Das Kapital*, III/1, 171 f.

11. Cole, *op. cit.*, xxix, says in his otherwise excellently clear statement of Marx's theory of Surplus Value that it was 'his distinctive contribution to economic doctrine'. But Engels, in his Preface to the second volume of *Capital*, has shown that this theory was not Marx's, that Marx not only never claimed that it was, but also had dealt with its history (in his *Theories of Surplus Value*; cp. note 1 to this chapter). Engels quotes from Marx's manuscript in order to show that Marx deals with Adam Smith's and Ricardo's contribution to that theory and quotes at length from the pamphlet, *The Source and Remedy of the National Difficulties*, mentioned in *Capital*, 646, in order to show that the main ideas of the doctrine, apart from the Marxian distinction between labour and labour power, can be found there. (Cp. *Das Kapital*, II, xii–xv.)
12. The first part is called by Marx (cp. *Capital*, 213 f.) *necessary labour time*, the second part *surplus labour time*.
13. Cp. Engels' Preface to the second volume of *Capital*. (*Das Kapital*, II, xxi, f.)
14. Marx's derivation of the doctrine of surplus value is of course closely connected with his criticism of 'formal' freedom, 'formal' justice, etc. Cp. especially notes 17 and 19 to chapter 17, and text. See also the text to the next note.
15. Cp. *Capital*, 845. See also the passages referred to in the foregoing note.
16. Cp. the text to note 18 (and note 10) to this chapter.

17. See especially chapter X of the third volume of *Capital*.
18. For this quotation, cp. *Capital*, 706. From the words 'thus surplus population', the passage follows immediately after the one quoted in the text to note 7 to this chapter. (I have omitted the word 'relative' before 'surplus population', since it is irrelevant in the present context, and perhaps confusing. There seems to be a misprint in the Everyman edition: 'overproduction' instead of 'surplus population'.) The quotation is of interest in connection with the problem of supply and demand, and with Marx's teaching that these must have a 'background' (or 'essence'); cp. notes 10 and 20 to this chapter.
19. It may be mentioned in this connection that the phenomenon in question—misery in a period of rapidly expanding industrialization (or of 'early capitalism'; cp. note 36 below, and text) has recently been explained by a hypothesis which, if it can be upheld, would show that there was a great deal in Marx's theory of exploitation. I have in mind a theory based on Walter Euken's doctrine of the two pure monetary systems (the gold and the credit system), and his method of analysing the various historically given economic systems as 'mixtures' of pure systems. Applying this method, Leonhard Miksch has recently pointed out (in a paper 'Die Geldordnung der Zukunft', *Zeitschrift für das Gesamte Kreditwesen*, 1949) that the credit system leads to *forced investments*, i.e. the consumer is forced to save, to abstain; 'but the capital saved by way of these forced investments', Miksch writes, 'does not belong to those who were forced to abstain from consumption, but to the entrepreneurs'.

    If this theory proves acceptable, then Marx's analysis (but neither his 'laws' nor his prophecies) would be vindicated to a considerable extent. For there is only a small difference between Marx's 'surplus value' which, by rights, belongs to the worker but is 'appropriated' or 'expropriated' by the 'capitalist', and Miksch's 'forced savings' which become the property, not of the consumer who was forced to save, but of the 'entrepreneur'. Miksch himself hints that these results explain much of the economic development of the nineteenth century (and of the rise of socialism).

    It should be noted that Miksch's analysis explains the relevant facts in terms of *imperfections* in the competitive system (he speaks of an 'economic monopoly of money creation which is possessed of stupendous power') while Marx attempted to explain corresponding facts with the help of the assumption of a free market, i.e. of competition. (Furthermore, 'consumers' and 'industrial workers' cannot, of course, be completely identified.) But whatever the explanation, the facts—described by Miksch as 'intolerably anti-social'—remain; and it is to Marx's credit, both that he did not accept these facts, and that he tried hard to explain them.
20. Cp. note 10 to this chapter, especially the passage on the 'natural' price (also note 18 and text); it is interesting that in the third volume of *Capital*, not far from the passages quoted in note 10 to this chapter (see *Das Kapital*, III/2, 352; italics mine), and in a similar context, Marx makes the following methodological remark: '*All science would be superfluous if the forms of appearance of things coincided with their essences.*' This is, of course, pure essentialism. That this essentialism borders on metaphysics is shown in note 24 to this chapter.

    It is clear that when Marx speaks repeatedly, especially in the first volume, of the price-form, he has a 'form of appearance' in mind; the essence is 'value'. (Cp. also note 6 to chapter 17 and text.)

21. In *Capital*, pp. 43 ff.: 'The Mystery of the Fetishistic Character of Commodities.'
22. Cp. *Capital*, 567 (see also 328), with Marx's summary: 'If the productivity of labour is doubled then, if the ratio of necessary labour to surplus labour remains unaltered, ... the only result will be that each of them will represent twice as many use-values' (i.e. commodities) 'as before. These use-values are now twice as cheap as before ... Thus it is possible, when the productivity of labour is increasing, that the price of labour power should keep on falling, and yet that *this fall should be accompanied by a constant growth in the quantity of the worker's means of subsistence*.'
23. If productivity increases more or less generally, then the productivity of the gold companies may also increase; and this would mean that gold, like every other commodity, becomes cheaper if appraised in labour hours. Accordingly, the same would hold for gold as for other commodities; and when Marx says (cp. the foregoing note) that the quantity of the worker's real income increases, this would, in theory, also be true of his income in gold, i.e. in money. (Marx's analysis in *Capital*, p. 567, of which I have quoted only a summary in the foregoing note, is therefore not correct wherever he speaks of 'prices'; for 'prices' are 'values' expressed in gold, and these may remain *constant* if productivity increases equally in all lines of production, including the production of gold.)
24. The strange thing about Marx's value theory (as distinct from the English classical school, according to J. Viner) is that it considers human labour as fundamentally different from all other processes in nature, for example, from the labour of animals. This shows clearly that the theory is based ultimately upon a *moral* theory, the doctrine that human suffering and a human lifetime spent is a thing fundamentally different from all natural processes. We can call this the doctrine of the *holiness of human labour*. Now I do not deny that this theory is right in the moral sense; that is to say, that we should act according to it. But I also think that an economic analysis should not be based upon a moral or metaphysical or religious doctrine of which the holder is unconscious. Marx who, as we shall see in chapter 22, did not consciously believe in a humanitarian morality, or who repressed such beliefs, was building upon a moralistic basis where he did not suspect it—in his abstract theory of value. This is, of course, connected with his essentialism: the essence of all social and economic relations is human labour.
25. For interventionism, cp. notes 22 to chapter 17 and 9 to chapter 18. (See also note 2 to the present chapter.)
26. For the *paradox of freedom* in its application to economic freedom, cp. note 20 to chapter 17, where further references are given.

    The problem of the *free market*, mentioned in the text only in its application to the labour market, is of very considerable importance. Generalizing from what has been said in the text, it is clear that the idea of a free market is paradoxical. If the state does not interfere, then other semi-political organizations such as monopolies, trusts, unions, etc., may interfere, reducing the freedom of the market to a fiction. On the other hand, it is most important to realize that without a carefully protected free market, the whole economic system must cease to serve its only rational purpose, that is, *to satisfy the demands of the consumer*. If the consumer cannot choose; if he must take what the producer offers; if the producer, whether a private producer or the state or a marketing department, is master of the market, instead of the consumer; then the situation must arise that the consumer serves, ultimately, as a kind of money-supply and rubbish-remover for the producer, instead of the producer serving the needs and desires of the consumer.

Here we are clearly faced with an important problem of social engineering: the market must be controlled, but in such a way that the control does not impede the free choice of the consumer and that it does not remove the need for the producers to compete for the favour of the consumer. Economic 'planning' that does not plan for economic freedom in this sense will lead dangerously close to totalitarianism. (Cp. F. A. von Hayek's *Freedom and the Economic System*, Public Policy Pamphlets, 1939/40.)

27. Cp. note 2 to this chapter, and text.
28. This distinction between machinery serving mainly for the *extension* and machinery serving mainly for the *intensification* of production is introduced in the text largely with the aim of making the presentation of the argument more lucid. Apart from that, it is also, I hope, an improvement of the argument.

    I may give here a list of the more important passages of Marx, bearing on the trade cycle (*t-c*), and on its connection with unemployment (*u*): *Manifesto*, 29 f. (*t-c*).—*Capital*, 120 (monetary crisis = general depression), 624 (*t-c* and currency), 694 (*u*), 698 (*t-c*), 699 (*t-c* depending on *u*; automatism of the cycle), 703–705 (*t-c* and *u* in interdependence), 706 f. (*u*). See also the third volume of *Capital*, especially chapter XV, section on *Surplus of Capital and Surplus of Population, H.o.M.*, 516–528 (*t-c* and *u*) and chapters XXV–XXXII (*t-c* and currency; cp. especially *Das Kapital*, III/2, 22 ff.). See also the passage from the second volume of *Capital* from which a sentence is quoted in note 17 to chapter 17.
29. Cp. the *Minutes of Evidence, taken before the Secret Committee of the House of Lords appointed to inquire into the causes of Distress*, etc., 1875, quoted in *Das Kapital*, III/1, pp. 398 ff.
30. Cp. for example the two articles on *Budgetary Reform* by C. G. F. Simkin in the Australian *Economic Record*, 1941 and 1942 (see also note 3 to chapter 9). These articles deal with counter cycle policy, and report briefly on the Swedish measures.
31. Cp. Parkes, *Marxism—A Post Mortem*, especially p. 220, note 6.
32. The quotations are from *Das Kapital*, III/2, 354 f. (I translate 'useful commodities' although 'use-value' would be more literal.)
33. The theory I have in mind (held, or very nearly held, by J. Mill as J. Viner informs me) is frequently alluded to by Marx, who struggled against it without, however, succeeding in making his point quite clear. It can be expressed briefly as the doctrine that all capital reduces ultimately to wages, since the 'immobilized' (or as Marx says, 'constant') capital has been produced, and paid for, in wages. Or in Marx's terminology: There is no constant but only variable capital.

    This doctrine has been very clearly and simply presented by Parkes (*op. cit.*, 97): 'All capital is variable capital. This will be plain if we consider a hypothetical industry which controls the whole of its processes of production from the farm or the mine to the finished product, without buying any machinery or raw material from outside. The entire cost of production in such an industry will consist of its wage bill.' And since an economic system as a whole can be considered as such a hypothetical industry, within which machinery (constant capital) is always paid for in terms of wages (variable capital), the sum total of constant capital must form part of the sum total of variable capital.

I do not think that this argument, in which I once believed myself, can invalidate the Marxian position. (This is perhaps the only major point in which I cannot agree with Parkes's excellent criticism.) The reason is this. If the hypothetical industry decides to *increase* its machinery—not only to replace it, or to make necessary improvements—then we can look upon this process as a typical Marxian process of accumulation of capital *by the investment of profits*. In order to measure the success of this investment, we should have to consider whether the profits in succeeding years had increased in proportion to it. Some of these new profits may be invested again. Now during the year in which they were invested (or profits were accumulated by conversion into constant capital), they were paid for in the form of variable capital. But once they have been invested, they are, in the following periods, considered as part of the constant capital, since they are expected to contribute proportionally to new profits. If they do not, the rate of profit must fall, and we say that it was a mal-investment. The rate of profit is thus a measure of the success of an investment, of the productivity of the newly added constant capital, which, though originally always paid for in the form of variable capital, none the less becomes constant capital in the Marxian sense, and exerts its influence upon the rate of profit.

34. Cp. chapter XIII of the third volume of *Capital*, for example, *H.o.M.*, 499: 'We see then, that in spite of the progressive fall in the rate of profit, there may be ... an absolute increase in the mass of the produced profit. And this increase may be progressive. And it *may* not only be so. On the basis of capitalist production, it *must* be so, aside from temporary fluctuations.'
35. The quotations in this paragraph are from *Capital*, 708 ff.
36. For Parkes's summary, cp. *Marxism—A Post Mortem*, p. 102.

    It may be mentioned here that the Marxian theory that revolutions depend on misery has been to some extent confirmed in the last century by the outbreak of revolutions in countries in which misery actually increased. But contrary to Marx's prediction, these countries were not those of developed capitalism. They were either peasant countries or countries where capitalism was at a primitive stage of development. Parkes has given a list to substantiate this statement. (Cp. *op. cit.*, 48.) It appears that revolutionary tendencies decrease with the advance of industrialization. Accordingly, the Russian revolution should not be interpreted as premature (nor the advanced countries as over-ripe for revolution), but rather as a product of the typical misery of capitalist infancy and of peasant misery, enhanced by the misery of war and the opportunities of defeat. See also note 19, above.
37. Cp. *H.o.M.*, 507.

    In a footnote to this passage (i.e. *Das Kapital*, III/1, 219), Marx contends that Adam Smith is right, against Ricardo.

    The passage from Smith to which Marx probably alludes is quoted further below in the paragraph: it is from the *Wealth of Nations* (vol. II, p. 95 of the Everyman edition).

    Marx quotes a passage from Ricardo (*Works*, ed. MacCulloch, p. 73 = Ricardo, Everyman edition, p. 78). But there is an even more characteristic passage in which

Ricardo holds that the mechanism described by Smith 'cannot ... affect the rate of profit' (*Principles*, 232).

38. For Engels, cp. *H.o.M.*, 708 (= quoted in *Imperialism*, 96).
39. For this change of front, cp. note 31 to chapter 19, and text.
40. Cp. Lenin, *Imperialism: The Highest Stage of Capitalism* (1917); *H.o.M.*, 708 (= *Imperialism*, 97).
41. This may be an excuse, though only a very unsatisfactory excuse, for certain most depressing remarks of Marx, quoted by Parkes, *Marxism—A Post Mortem* (213 f., note 3).—They are most depressing since they raise the question whether Marx and Engels were the genuine lovers of freedom one would like them to be; whether they were not more influenced by Hegel's irresponsibility and by his nationalism than one should, from their general teaching, expect.
42. Cp. *H.o.M.*, 295 (= *GA*, Special Volume, 290–1): 'By more and more transforming the great majority of the population into proletarians, the capitalist mode of production creates the force which ... is compelled to carry out this revolution.' For the passage from the *Manifesto*, cp. *H.o.M.*, 35 (= *GA*, Series I, vol. vi, 536).—For the following passage, cp. *H.o.M.*, 156 f. (= *Der Buergerkrieg in Frankreich*, 84).
43. For this amazingly naïve passage, cp. *H.o.M.*, 147 f. (= *Der Buergerkrieg in Frankreich*, 75 f.).
44. For this policy, cp. Marx's *Address to the Communist League*, quoted in notes 14 and 35–37 to chapter 19. (Cp. also, for example, notes 26 f. to that chapter.) See further the following passage from the *Address* (*H.o.M.*, 70 f.; italics mine = *Labour Monthly*, Sept. 1922, 145–6): 'Thus, for instance, if the petty bourgeoisie purpose to purchase the railways and factories, the workers must demand that such railways and factories shall simply be confiscated by the State without compensation; for they are the property of the reactionaries. If the democrats propose proportional taxation, the workers must demand progressive taxation. If the democrats themselves declare for a moderate progressive tax, the workers must insist on a steeply graduated tax; so steeply graduated as to cause the collapse of large capital. If the democrats propose the regulation of the National Debt, the workers must demand State bankruptcy. *The demands of the workers will depend on the proposals and measures of the democrats.*' These are the tactics of the Communists, of whom Marx says: 'Their battle-cry must be: "Revolution in permanence!"'

NOTES TO CHAPTER TWENTY-ONE

1. Cp. notes 22 to chapter 17 and 9 to chapter 18, and text.
2. Engels says in the *Anti-Dühring* that Fourier long ago discovered the 'vicious circle' of the capitalist mode of production; cp. *H.o.M.*, 287.
3. Cp. *H.o.M.*, 527 (= *Das Kapital*, III/1, 242).
4. Cp., for example, Parkes, *Marxism—A Post Mortem*, pp. 102 ff.
5. This is a question which I wish to leave open.
6. This point has been emphasized by my colleague, Prof. C. G. F. Simkin, in discussions.
7. Cp. text to note 11 to chapter 14, and end of note 17 to chapter 17.
8. Cp. H. A. L. Fisher, *History of Europe* (1935), Preface, vol. I, p. vii. The passage is quoted more fully in note 27 to chapter 25.

NOTES TO CHAPTER TWENTY-TWO

1. For Kierkegaard's fight against 'official Christianity', cp. especially his *Book of the Judge*. (German edn, by H. Gottsched, 1905.)
2. Cp. J. Townsend, *A Dissertation on the Poor Laws, by a Wellwisher of Mankind* (1817); quoted in *Capital*, 715.

   On p. 711 (note 1) Marx quotes 'the spirited and witty Abbé Galiani' as holding similar views: 'Thus it comes to pass', Galiani says, 'that the men who practise occupations of primary utility breed abundantly.' See Galiani, *Della Moneta*, 1803, p. 78.

   The fact that even in Western countries, Christianity is not yet entirely free from the spirit of defending the return to the closed society of reaction and oppression can be seen from the excellent polemic of H. G. Wells against Dean Inge's biased and pro-fascist attitude towards the Spanish civil war. Cp. H. G. Wells, *The Common Sense of War and Peace* (1940), pp. 38–40. (In referring to Wells's book, I do not wish to associate myself with anything he says on federation, whether critical or constructive; and especially not with the idea propounded on pp. 56 ff., regarding fully empowered world commissions. The fascist dangers involved in this idea seem to me enormous.) On the other hand, there is the opposite danger, that of a pro-communist Church; cp. note 12 to chapter 9.
3. Cp. Kierkegaard, *op. cit.*, 172.
4. But Kierkegaard said something of Luther that may be true of Marx also: 'Luther's corrective idea ... produces ... the most sophisticated form of ... paganism.' (*Op. cit.*, 147.)
5. Cp. *H.o.M.*, 231 (= Ludwig Feuerbach, 56); cp. notes 11 and 14 to chapter 13.
6. Cp. note 14 to chapter 13, and text.
7. Cp. my *The Poverty of Historicism*, section 19.
8. Cp. *H.o.M.*, 247 f. (= *GA*, Special Volume, 97).
9. For these quotations, cp. *H.o.M.*, 248, and 279 (the latter passage is shortened = *GA*, Special Volume, 97 and 277).
10. Cp. L. Laurat, *Marxism and Democracy*, p. 16. (Italics mine.)
11. For these two quotations, cp. *The Churches Survey Their Task* (1937), p. 130, and A. Loewe, *The Universities in Transformation* (1940), p. 1. With the concluding remark of this chapter, cp. also the views expressed by Parkes in the last sentences of his criticism of Marxism (*Marxism—A Post Mortem*, 1940, p. 208).

NOTES TO CHAPTER TWENTY-THREE

1. Concerning Mannheim, see especially *Ideology and Utopia* (quoted here from the German edn, 1929). The terms 'social habitat' and 'total ideology' are both due to Mannheim; the terms 'sociologism' and 'historism' have been mentioned in the last chapter. The idea of a 'social habitat' is Platonic.

   For a criticism of Mannheim's *Man and Society in an Age of Reconstruction* (1941), which combines historicist tendencies with a romantic and even mystical holism, see my *The Poverty of Historicism, II* (*Economica*, 1944).
2. Cp. my interpretation in 'What is Dialectic?' (*Mind*, 49, especially p. 414; also *Conjectures and Refutations*, especially p. 325.)

3. This is Mannheim's term (cp. *Ideology and Utopia*, 1929, p. 35). For the 'freely poised intelligence', see *op. cit.*, p. 123, where this term is attributed to Alfred Weber. For the theory of an intelligentsia loosely anchored in tradition, see *op. cit.*, pp. 121–34, and especially p. 122.
4. For the latter theory, or, rather, practice, cp. notes 51 and 52 to chapter 11.
5. Cp. 'What is Dialectic?' (p. 417; *Conjectures and Refutations*, p. 327). Cp. note 33 to chapter 12.
6. The analogy between the psycho-analytic method and that of Wittgenstein is mentioned by Wisdom, 'Other Minds' (*Mind*, vol. 49, p. 370, note): 'A doubt such as "I can never really know what another person is feeling" may arise from more than one of these sources. This over-determination of sceptical symptoms complicates their cure. The treatment is like psycho-analytic treatment (to enlarge Wittgenstein's analogy) in that the treatment is the diagnosis and the diagnosis is the description, the very full description, of the symptoms.' And so on. (I may remark that, using the word 'know' in the ordinary sense, we can, of course, never know what another person is feeling. We can only make hypotheses about it. This solves the so-called problem. It is a mistake to speak here of doubt, and a still worse mistake to attempt to remove the doubt by a semiotico-analytic treatment.)
7. The psycho-analysts seem to hold the same of the individual psychologists, and they are probably right. Cp. Freud's *History of the Psycho-Analytic Movement* (1916), p. 42, where Freud records that Adler made the following remark (which fits well within Adler's individual-psychological scheme, according to which feelings of inferiority are predominantly important): 'Do you believe that it is such a pleasure for me to stand in your shadow my whole life?' This suggests that Adler had not successfully applied his theories to himself, at that time at least. But the same seems to be true of Freud: None of the founders of psycho-analysis were psycho-analysed. To this objection, they usually replied that they had psycho-analysed themselves. But they would never have accepted such an excuse from anybody else; and, indeed, rightly so.
8. For the following analysis of scientific objectivity, cp. my *The Logic of Scientific Discovery*, section 8 (pp. 44 ff.).
9. I wish to apologize to the Kantians for mentioning them in the same breath as the Hegelians.
10. Cp. notes 23 to chapter 8 and 39 (second paragraph) to chapter 11.
11. Cp. notes 34 ff., to chapter 11.
12. Cp. K. Mannheim, *Ideology and Utopia* (German edn, p. 167).
13. For the first of these two quotations, cp. *op. cit.*, 167. (For simplicity's sake, I translate 'conscious' for 'reflexive'.) For the second, cp. *op. cit.*, 166.
14. Cp. *Handbook of Marxism*, 255 (= *GA*, Special Volume, 117–18): 'Hegel was the first to state correctly the relation between freedom and necessity. To him, freedom is the appreciation of necessity.' For Hegel's own formulation of his pet idea, cp. *Hegel Selections*, 213 (= *Werke*, 1832–1887, vi, 310): 'The truth of necessity, therefore, is freedom.' 361 (= *WW*, xi, 46): '... the *Christian* principle of self-consciousness—Freedom.' 362 (= *WW*, xi, 47): 'The essential nature of freedom, which involves in it absolute necessity, is to be displayed as the attainment of a consciousness of itself (for it is in its very nature, self-consciousness) and it thereby realizes its existence.' And so on.

NOTES TO CHAPTER TWENTY-FOUR

1 I am here using the term 'rationalism' in opposition to 'irrationalism' and not to 'empiricism'. Carnap writes in his *Der Logische Aufbau der Welt* (1928), p. 260: 'The word "rationalism" is now often meant ... in a modern sense: *in contradistinction to irrationalism*.'

In using the term 'rationalism' in this way, I do not wish to suggest that the other way of using this term, namely, in opposition to empiricism, is perhaps less important. On the contrary, I believe that this opposition characterizes one of the most interesting problems of philosophy. But I do not intend to deal with it here; and I feel that, in opposition to empiricism, we might do better to use another term—perhaps 'intellectualism' or 'intellectual intuitionism'—in place of 'rationalism' in the Cartesian sense. I may mention in this context that I do not *define* the terms 'reason' or 'rationalism'; I am using them as labels, taking care that nothing depends on the words used. Cp. chapter 11, especially note 50. (For the reference to Kant, see note 56 to chapter 12, and text.)

2. *This is what I tried to do in 'Towards a Rational Theory of Tradition' (*The Rationalist Annual*, 1949, pp. 36 ff., and now in *Conjectures and Refutations*, pp. 120 ff.).

3. Cp. Plato's *Timaeus* 51e. (See also the cross-references in note 33 to chapter 11.)

4. Cp. chapter 10, especially notes 38–41, and text.

In Pythagoras, Heraclitus, Parmenides, Plato, mystical and rationalist elements are mixed. Plato especially, in spite of all his emphasis on 'reason', incorporated into his philosophy such a weighty admixture of irrationalism that it nearly ousted the rationalism he inherited from Socrates. This enabled the Neo-Platonists to base their mysticism on Plato; and most subsequent mysticism goes back to these sources.

It may perhaps be accidental, but it is in any case remarkable that there is still a cultural frontier between Western Europe and the regions of Central Europe which coincide very nearly with those regions that did not come under the administration of Augustus' Roman Empire, and that did not enjoy the blessings of the Roman peace, i.e. of the Roman civilization. The same 'barbarian' regions are particularly prone to be affected by mysticism, even though they did not invent mysticism. Bernard of Clairvaux had his greatest successes in Germany, where later Eckhart and his school flourished, and also Boehme.

Much later Spinoza, who attempted to combine Cartesian intellectualism with mystical tendencies, rediscovered the theory of a mystical intellectual intuition, which, in spite of Kant's strong opposition, led to the post-Kantian rise of 'Idealism', to Fichte, Schelling, and Hegel. Practically all modern irrationalism goes back to the latter, as is briefly indicated in chapter 12. (Cp. also notes 6, 29–32 and 58, below, and notes 32–33 to chapter 11, and the cross-references on mysticism there given.)

5. With the 'mechanical activities', cp. notes 21 and 22 to this chapter.

6. I say 'discarded' in order to cover the views (1) that such an assumption would be false, (2) that it would be unscientific (or impermissible), though it might perhaps be accidentally true, (3) that it would be 'senseless' or 'meaningless', for example in the sense of Wittgenstein's *Tractatus*; cp. note 51 to chapter 12, and note 8 (2) to the present chapter.

In connection with the distinction between 'critical' and 'uncritical' rationalism, it may be mentioned that the teaching of Duns Scotus as well as of Kant could be interpreted as approaching 'critical' rationalism. (I have in mind their doctrines of the 'primacy of will', which may be interpreted as the primacy of an irrational decision.)

7. In this and the following note a few remarks on paradoxes will be made, especially on the *paradox of the liar*. In introducing these remarks, it may be said that the so-called 'logical' and 'semantical' paradoxes are no longer merely playthings for the logicians. Not only have they proved to be important for the development of mathematics, but they are also becoming important in other fields of thought. There is a definite connection between these paradoxes and such problems as the *paradox of freedom* which, as we have seen (cp. note 20 to chapter 17 and notes 4 and 6 to chapter 7), is of considerable significance in political philosophy. In point (4) of this note, it will be briefly shown that the various *paradoxes of sovereignty* (cp. note 6 to chapter 7, and text) are very similar to the paradox of the liar. On the modern methods of solving these paradoxes (or perhaps better: of constructing languages in which they do not occur), I shall not make any comments here, since it would take us beyond the scope of this book.

(1) *The paradox of the liar* can be formulated in many ways. One of them is this. Let us assume that somebody says one day: 'All that I say to-day is a lie'; or more precisely: 'All statements I make to-day are false'; and that he says nothing else the whole day. Now if we ask ourselves whether he spoke the truth, this is what we find. If we start with the assumption that what he said was true, then we arrive, considering *what* he said, at the result that it must have been false. And if we start with the assumption that what he said was false, then we must conclude, considering *what* he said, that it was true.

(2) Paradoxes are sometimes called 'contradictions'. But this is perhaps slightly misleading. An ordinary contradiction (or a self-contradiction) is simply a logically false statement, such as 'Plato was happy yesterday and he was not happy yesterday'. If we assume that such a sentence is false, no further difficulty arises. But of a paradox, we can neither assume that it is true *nor that it is false*, without getting involved in difficulties.

(3) There are, however, statements which are closely related to paradoxes, but which are, more strictly speaking, only self-contradictions. Take for example the statement: 'All statements are false.' If we assume that this statement is true, then we arrive, considering *what* it says, at the result that it is false. But if we assume that it is false, then we are out of the difficulty; for this assumption leads only to the result that not all statements are false, or in other words, that there are some statements—at least one—that are true. And this result is harmless; for it does not imply that our original statement is one of the true ones. (This does not imply that we can, in fact, construct a language *free of paradoxes* in which 'All statements are false' or 'All statements are true' can be formulated.)

In spite of the fact that this statement 'All propositions are false' is not really a paradox, it may be called, by courtesy, 'a form of the paradox of the liar', because of its obvious resemblance to the latter; and indeed, the old Greek formulation of this paradox (Epimenides the Cretan says: 'All Cretans always lie') is, in this terminology, rather 'a form of the paradox of the liar' i.e. a contradiction rather than a paradox. (Cp. also next note, and note 54 to this chapter, and text.)

(4) I shall now show briefly the similarity between the paradox of the liar and the various *paradoxes of sovereignty*, for example, of the principle that the best or the wisest or the majority should rule. (Cp. note 6 to chapter 7 and text.)

C. H. Langford has described various ways of putting the paradox of the liar, among them the following. We consider two statements, made by two people, A and B.

A says: 'What B says is true.'

B says: 'What A says is false.'

By applying the method described above, we easily convince ourselves that each of these sentences is paradoxical. Now we consider the following two sentences, of which the first is the principle that the wisest should rule:

(A) The principle says: What the wisest says under (B) should be law.

(B) The wisest says: What the principle states under (A) should not be law.

8. (1) That the principle of avoiding all presuppositions is 'a form of the paradox of the liar' in the sense of note 7 (3) to this chapter, and therefore self-contradictory, will be easily seen if we describe it like this. A philosopher starts his investigation by assuming without argument the principle: 'All principles assumed without argument are impermissible.' It is clear that if we assume that this principle is true, we must conclude, considering what it says, that it is impermissible. (The opposite assumption does not lead to any difficulty.) The remark 'a counsel of perfection' alludes to the usual criticism of this principle which was laid down, for example, by Husserl. J. Laird (*Recent Philosophy*, 1936, p. 121) writes about this principle that it 'is a cardinal feature of Husserl's philosophy. Its success may be more doubtful, for presuppositions have a way of creeping in.' So far, I fully agree; but not quite with the next remark: '... the avoidance of all presuppositions may well be a counsel of perfection, impracticable in an inadvertent world.' (See also note 5 to chapter 25.)

(2) We may consider at this place a few further 'principles' which are, in the sense of note 7 (3) to this chapter, 'forms of the paradox of the liar', and therefore self-contradictory.

(*a*) From the point of view of social philosophy, the following 'principle of sociologism' (and the analogous 'principle of historism') are of interest. They can be formulated in this way. 'No statement is absolutely true, and all statements are inevitably relative to the social (or historical) habitat of their originators.' It is clear that the considerations of note 7 (3) apply practically without alteration. For if we assume that such a principle is true, then it follows that it is not true but only 'relative to the social or historical habitat of its originator'. See also note 53 to this chapter, and text.

(*b*) Some examples of this kind can be found in Wittgenstein's *Tractatus*. The one is Wittgenstein's proposition (quoted more fully in note 46 to chapter 11): 'The totality of true propositions is ... the totality of natural science.' Since this proposition does not belong to natural science (but, rather, to a meta-science, i.e. a theory that speaks about science) it follows that it asserts its own untruth, and is therefore contradictory.

Furthermore, it is clear that this proposition violates Wittgenstein's own principle (*Tractatus*, p. 57), 'No proposition can say anything about itself ...'

* But even this last quoted principle which I shall call '*W*' turns out to be a form of the paradox of the liar, and to assert its own untruth. (It therefore can hardly be—as Wittgenstein believes it to be—equivalent to, or a summary of, or a substitute for, 'the whole theory of types', i.e. Russell's theory, designed to avoid the paradoxes which he discovered by dividing expressions which look like propositions into three

classes—true propositions, false propositions, and meaningless expressions or pseudo-propositions.) For Wittgenstein's principle *W* may be re-formulated as follows:

(W^+) Every expression (and especially one that looks like a proposition) which contains a reference to itself—either by containing its own name or an individual variable ranging over a class to which it itself belongs—is not a proposition (but a meaningless pseudo-proposition).

Now let us assume that W^+ is true. Then, considering the fact that it is an expression, and that it refers to every expression, it cannot be a proposition, and is therefore *a fortiori* not true.

The assumption that it is true is therefore untenable; W^+ cannot be true. But this does not show that it must be false; for both, the assumption that it is false and the other that it is a meaningless (or senseless) expression, do not involve us in immediate difficulties.

Wittgenstein might perhaps say that he saw this himself when he wrote (p. 189; cp. note 51 (1) to chapter 11): 'My propositions are elucidatory in this way: he who understands me finally recognizes them as senseless ...'; in any case, we may conjecture that he would incline to describing W^+ as meaningless rather than false. I believe, however, that it is not meaningless but simply false. Or more precisely, I believe that in every formalized language (e.g. in one in which Goedel's undecidable statements can be expressed) which contains means for speaking about its own expressions, and in which we have names of classes of expressions such as 'propositions' and 'non-propositions', *the formalization of a statement which, like* W^+, *asserts its own meaninglessness, will be self-contradictory and neither meaningless nor genuinely paradoxical*; it will be a meaningful proposition merely because it asserts of every expression of a certain kind that it is not a proposition (i.e. not a well-formed formula); and such an assertion will be true or false, but not meaningless, simply because to be (or not to be) a well-formed proposition is a property of expressions. For example, 'All expressions are meaningless' will be self-contradictory, but not genuinely paradoxical, and so will be the expression 'The expression x is meaningless', if we substitute for 'x' a name of this expression. Modifying an idea of J. N. Findlay's, we can write:

The expression obtained by substituting for the variable in the following expression, 'The expression obtained by substituting for the variable in the following expression x the quotation name of this expression, is not a statement', the quotation name of this expression, is not a statement.

And what we have just written turns out to be a self-contradictory statement. (If we write twice 'is a false statement' instead of 'is not a statement', we obtain a paradox of the liar; if we write 'is a non-demonstrable statement', we obtain a Goedelian statement in J. N. Findlay's writing.)

To sum up. Contrary to first impressions, we find that a theory which implies its own meaninglessness is not meaningless but false, since the predicate 'meaningless', as opposed to 'false', does not give rise to paradoxes. And Wittgenstein's theory is therefore not meaningless, as he believes, but simply false (or, more specifically, self-contradictory).

(3) It has been claimed by some positivists that a tripartition of the expressions of a language into (i) true statements, (ii) false statements, and (iii) meaningless

expressions (or, better, expressions other than well-formed statements), is more or less 'natural' and that it provides, because of their meaninglessness, for the elimination of the paradoxes and, at the same time, of metaphysical systems. The following may show that this tripartition is not enough.

The General's Chief Counter-Espionage Officer is provided with three boxes, labelled (i) 'General's Box', (ii) 'Enemy's Box' (to be made accessible to the enemy's spies), and (iii) 'Waste Paper', and is instructed to distribute all information arriving before 12 o'clock among these three boxes, according to whether this information is (i) true, (ii) false, or (iii) meaningless.

For a time, he receives information which he can easily distribute (among it true statements of the theory of natural numbers, etc., and perhaps statements of logic such as *L*: 'From a set of true statements, no false statement can be validly derived'). The last message *M*, arriving with the last incoming mail just before 12 o'clock, disturbs him a little, for *M* reads: 'From the set of all statements placed, or to be placed, within the box labelled "General's Box", the statement "0 = 1" cannot validly be derived.' At first, the Chief Counter-Espionage Officer hesitates whether he should not put *M* into box (ii). But since he realizes that, if put into (ii), *M* would supply the enemy with valuable true information, he ultimately decides to put *M* into (i).

But this turns out to be a big mistake. For the symbolic logicians (experts in logistic?) on the General's staff, after formalizing (and 'arithmetizing') the contents of the General's box, discover that they obtain a set of statements which contains an assertion of its own consistency; and this, according to Goedel's second theorem on decidability, leads to a contradiction, so that '0 = 1' can actually be deduced from the presumably true information supplied to the General.

The solution of this difficulty consists in the recognition of the fact that the tripartition-claim is unwarranted, at least for ordinary languages; and we can see from Tarski's theory of truth that no definite number of boxes will suffice. At the same time we find that 'meaninglessness' in the sense of 'not belonging to the well-formed formulæ' is by no means an indication of 'nonsensical talk' in the sense of 'words which just don't mean anything, although they may pretend to be deeply significant'; but to have revealed that metaphysics was just of this character was the chief claim of the positivists.*

9. It appears that it was the difficulty connected with the so-called 'problem of induction' which led Whitehead to the disregard of argument displayed in *Process and Reality*. (Cp. also notes 35–7 to this chapter.)

10. It is a moral decision and not merely 'a matter of taste' since it is not a private affair but affects other men and their lives. (For the opposition between æsthetic matters of taste and moral problems, cp. text to note 6 to chapter 5, and chapter 9 especially text to notes 10–11.) The decision with which we are faced is most important from the point of view that the 'learned', who are faced with it, act as intellectual trustees for those who are not faced with it.

11. It is, I believe, perhaps the greatest strength of Christianity that it appeals fundamentally not to abstract speculation but to the imagination, by describing in a very concrete manner the suffering of man.

12. Kant, the great equalitarian in regard to moral decisions, has emphasized the blessings involved in the fact of human inequality. He saw in the variety and individuality

of human characters and opinions one of the main conditions of moral as well as material progress.

13. The allusion is to A. Huxley's *Brave New World.*
14. For the distinction between facts, and decisions or demands, cp. text to notes 5 ff. to chapter 4. For the 'language of political demands' (or 'proposals' in the sense of L. J. Russell) cp. text to notes 41–43, chapter 6 and note 5(3) to chapter 5.

    I should be inclined to say that the theory of the innate intellectual equality of all men is false; but since such men as Niels Bohr contend that the influence of environment is alone responsible for individual differences, and since there are no sufficient experimental data for deciding this question, 'probably false' is perhaps all that should be said.
15. See, for example, the passage from Plato's *Statesman*, quoted in the text to note 12 to chapter 9. Another such passage is *Republic*, 409e–410a. After having spoken (409b & c) of the '*good judge ... who is good because of the goodness of his soul*', Plato continues (409e, f.), 'And are you not going to establish physicians and judges ... who are to look after those citizens whose physical and mental constitution is healthy and good? Those whose physical health is bad, they will leave to die. And those whose soul is bad-natured and incurable, they will actually kill.'—'Yes,' he said, 'since you have proved that this is the best thing, both for those to whom it happens, and for the state.'
16. Cp. notes 58 to chapter 8 and 28 to chapter 10.
17. An example is H. G. Wells, who gave to the first chapter of his book, *The Common Sense of War and Peace*, the excellent title: 'Grown Men Do Not Need Leaders'. (Cp. also note 2 to chapter 22.)
18. For the problem and the paradox of tolerance, cp. note 4 to chapter 7.
19. The 'world' is not rational, but it is the task of science to rationalize it. 'Society' is not rational, but it is the task of the social engineer to rationalize it. (This does not mean, of course, that he should 'direct' it, or that centralized or collectivist 'planning' is desirable.) Ordinary language is not rational, but it is our task to rationalize it, or at least to keep up its standards of clarity. The attitude here characterized could be described as '*pragmatic rationalism*'. This pragmatic rationalism is related to an uncritical rationalism and to irrationalism in a similar way as critical rationalism is related to these two. For an uncritical rationalism may argue that the world is rational and that the task of science is to discover this rationality, while an irrationalist may insist that the world, being fundamentally irrational, should be experienced and exhausted by our emotions and passions (or by our intellectual intuition) rather than by scientific methods. As opposed to this, pragmatic rationalism may recognize that the world is not rational, but demand *that we submit or subject it to reason*, as far as possible. Using Carnap's words (*Der Logische Aufbau*, etc., 1928, p. vi) one could describe what I call 'pragmatic rationalism' as 'the attitude which strives for clarity everywhere but recognizes the never fully understandable or never fully rational entanglement of the events of life'.
20. For the problem of the standards of clarity of our language, cp. the last note and note 30 to chapter 12.
21. Industrialization and the Division of Labour are attacked, for example, by Toynbee, *A Study of History*, vol. I, pp. 2 ff. Toynbee complains (p. 4) that 'the prestige of the Industrial System imposed itself upon the "intellectual workers" of the Western

World ...; and when they have attempted to "work" these materials "up" into "manufactured" or "semi-manufactured" articles, they have had recourse, once again, to the Division of Labour ...' In another place (p. 2) Toynbee says of physical scientific periodicals: 'Those periodicals were the Industrial System "in book form", with its Division of Labour and its sustained maximum output of articles manufactured from raw materials *mechanically*.' (Italics mine.) Toynbee emphasizes (p. 3, note 2) with the Hegelian Dilthey that the spiritual sciences at least should keep apart from these methods. (He quotes Dilthey, who said: 'The real categories ... are nowhere the same in the sciences of the Spirit as they are in the sciences of Nature.')

Toynbee's interpretation of the division of labour in the field of science seems to me just as mistaken as Dilthey's attempt to open up a gulf between the methods of the natural and the social sciences. What Toynbee calls 'division of labour' could better be described as co-operation and mutual criticism. Cp. text to notes 8 f. to chapter 23, and Macmurray's comments upon scientific co-operation quoted in the present chapter, text to note 26. (For Toynbee's anti-rationalism, cp. also note 61 to chapter 11.)

22. Cp. Adolf Keller, *Church and State on the European Continent* (Beckly Social Service Lecture, 1936). I owe it to Mr. L. Webb that my attention has been drawn to this interesting passage.

23. For moral futurism as a kind of moral positivism, cp. chapter 22 (especially text to notes 9 ff.).

I may draw attention to the fact that in contradistinction to the present fashion (cp. notes 51 f. to chapter 11), I attempt to take Keller's remarks seriously and question their truth, instead of dismissing them, as the positivist fashion would demand, as meaningless.

24. Cp. note 70 to chapter 10 and text, and note 61 to chapter 11.

25. Cp. Matthew 7, 15 f.: 'Beware of false prophets, which come to you in sheep's clothing, but inwardly they are ravening wolves. Ye shall know them by their fruits.'

26. The two passages are from J. Macmurray, *The Clue to History* (1938), pp. 86 and 192. (For my disagreement with Macmurray cp. text to note 16 to chapter 25.)

27. Cp. L. S. Stebbing's book, *Philosophy and the Physicists*, and my own brief remark on the Hegelianism of Jeans in 'What is Dialectic?' (*Mind*, 1940, 49, p. 420; now in *Conjectures and Refutations*, p. 330).

28. Cp., for example, notes 8–12 to chapter 7, and text.

29. Cp. chapter 10, especially the end of that chapter, i.e. notes 59–70, and text (see especially the reference to McTaggart in note 59); the note to the *Introduction*; notes 33 to chapter 11 and 36 to chapter 12; notes 4, 6, and 58 to the present chapter. See also Wittgenstein's insistence (quoted in note 32 to the present chapter) that the contemplation of, or the feeling for, the world as a *limited whole* is the mystical feeling.

A much-discussed recent work on mysticism and its proper rôle in politics is Aldous Huxley's *Grey Eminence*. It is interesting mainly because the author does not seem to realize that his own story of the mystic and politician, Father Joseph, flatly refutes the main thesis of his book. This thesis is that training in mystical practice is the only educational discipline known that is capable of securing to men that absolutely firm moral and religious ground which is so dearly needed by people who influence public policy. But his own story shows that Father Joseph, in spite of his training, fell into temptation—the usual temptation of those who wield power—and that he was unable to resist; absolute power corrupted him absolutely. That is to say, the only historical evidence discussed at any length by the author disproves his thesis completely; which, however, does not seem to worry him.

30. Cp. F. Kafka, *The Great Wall of China* (English transl. by E. Muir, 1933), p. 236.
31. Cp. also note 19 to this chapter.
32. Cp. Wittgenstein's *Tractatus*, p. 187: 'Not *how* the world is, is the mystical, but *that* it is.—The contemplation of the world *sub specie aeterni* is its contemplation as a limited whole.—The feeling of the world as a limited whole is the mystical feeling.' One sees that Wittgenstein's mysticism is typically holistic.—For other passages of Wittgenstein (*loc. cit.*) like: 'There is indeed the inexpressible. This *shows* itself; it is the mystical', cp. Carnap's criticism in his *Logical Syntax of Language* (1937), pp. 314 f. Cp. also note 25 to chapter 25, and text. See also note 29 to the present chapter and the cross-references given there.
33. Cp. chapter 10, for example notes 40, 41. The tribal and esoteric tendency of this kind of philosophy may be exemplified by a quotation from H. Blueher (cp. Kolnai, *The War against the West*, p. 74, italics mine): 'Christianity is emphatically an aristocratic creed, free of morals, unteachable. The Christians know one another by their exterior type; they form a set in human society who never fail in mutual understanding, and *who are understood by none but themselves*. They constitute a secret league. Furthermore, the kind of love that operates in Christianity is that which illuminates the pagan temples; it bears no relation to the Jewish invention of so-called love of mankind or love of one's neighbours.' Another example may be taken from E. von Salomon's book, *The Outlaws* (quoted also in note 90 to chapter 12; the present quotation is from p. 240; italics mine): '*We recognized one another in an instant*, though we came from all parts of the Reich, having got wind of skirmishes and of danger.'
34. This remark is not meant in a historicist sense. I do not mean to prophesy that the conflict will play no part in future developments. I only mean that by now we could have learned that the problem does not exist, or that it is, at any rate, insignificant as compared with the problem of the *evil religions*, such as totalitarianism and racialism, with which we are faced.
35. I am alluding to *Principia Mathematica*, by A. N. Whitehead and B. Russell. (Whitehead says, in *Process and Reality*, p. 10, note 1, that the 'introductory discussions are practically due to Russell, and in the second edition wholly so'.)
36. Cp. the reference to Hegel (and many others, among them Plato and Aristotle) in A. N. Whitehead, *Process and Reality*, p. 14.
37. Cp. Whitehead, *op. cit.*, pp. 18 f.
38. Cp. Kant's Appendix to his *Prolegomena*. (*Works*, ed. by Cassirer, vol. IV, 132 f. For the translation 'crazy quilt', cp. Carus' English edition of Kant's *Prolegomena*, 1902 and 1912, p. iv.)
39. Cp. Whitehead, *Process and Reality*, pp. 20 f.

    Concerning the attitude of *take it or leave it*, described in the next paragraph, cp. note 53 to chapter 11.
40. Cp. Whitehead, *op. cit.*, 492. Two of the other antitheses are: 'It is as true to say that the World is immanent in God, as that God is immanent in the World ... It is as true to say that God creates the World, as that the World creates God.' This is very

reminiscent of the German mystic Scheffler (Angelus Silesius), who wrote: 'I am as great as God, God is as small as me, I cannot without him, nor he without me, be.'

Concerning my remark, later in the paragraph, that I just do not understand what the author wishes to convey, I may say that it was only with great reluctance that I wrote this. The 'I do not understand' criticism is a rather cheap and dangerous kind of sport. I simply wrote these words because, in spite of my efforts, they remained true.

41. Cp. Kant's letter to Mendelssohn of April 8th, 1766. (*Works*, ed. by Cassirer, vol. IX, 56 f.)

42. Cp. Toynbee, *A Study of History*, vol. VI, 536 f.

43. Toynbee says (*op. cit.*, 537) of the 'traditionally orthodox minds' that they 'will see our investigation as an attack upon the historicity of the story of Jesus Christ as it is presented in the Gospels'. And he holds (p. 538) that God reveals himself through poetry as well as through truth; according to his theory, God has 'revealed himself in folk-lore'.

44. Following up this attempt to apply Toynbee's methods to himself, one could ask whether his *Study of History* which he has planned to consist of thirteen volumes is not just as much what he terms a *tour de force* as the 'histories like the several series of volumes now in course of publication by the Cambridge University Press'—undertakings which he brilliantly compares (vol. I, p. 4) to 'stupendous tunnels and bridges and dams and liners and battleships and skyscrapers'. And one could ask whether Toynbee's *tour de force* is not, more particularly, the manufacturing of what he calls a 'time machine', i.e. an escape into the past. (Cp. especially Toynbee's medievalism, briefly discussed in note 61 to chapter 11. Cp. further note 54 to the present chapter.)

45. I have not so far seen more than the first six volumes. Einstein is one of the few scientists mentioned.

46. Toynbee, *op. cit.*, vol. II, 178.

47. Toynbee, *op. cit.*, vol. V, 581 ff. (Italics mine.)

In connection with Toynbee's neglect, mentioned in the text, of the Marxian doctrines and especially of the *Communist Manifesto*, it may be said that on p. 179 (note 5) of this volume, Toynbee writes: 'The Bolshevik or Majoritarian wing of the Russian Social-Democratic Party renamed itself "the Russian Communist Party" (in homage to the Paris Commune of a.d. 1871) in March, 1918 ...' A similar remark can be found in the same volume, p. 582, note 1.

But this is not correct. The change of name (which was submitted by Lenin to the party conference of April, 1917; cp. *Handbook of Marxism*, 783; cp. also p. 787) referred, obviously enough, to the fact that 'Marx and Engels called themselves Communists', as Lenin puts it, and to the *Communist Manifesto*.

48. Cp. Engels, *Socialism: Utopian and Scientific* (see note 9 to chapter 13). For two historical roots of Marx's communism (Plato's and, perhaps, Pythagoras'—archaism, and the *Acts*, which seem to be influenced by it) see especially note 29 to chapter 5; see also notes 30 to chapter 4, 34–36 to chapter 6, and notes 3 and 8 to chapter 13 (and text).

49. Cp. Toynbee, *op. cit.*, vol. V, 587.

50. Cp. chapter 22, especially text to notes 1–4, and the end of that chapter.

51. The passage is not isolated; Toynbee very often expresses his respect for the 'verdict of history'; a fact that is in keeping with his doctrine that it is 'the claim of Christianity ... that God has revealed Himself in history'. This 'Neo-Protestant doctrine' (as

K. Barth calls it) will be discussed in the next chapter. (Cp. especially note 12 to that chapter.)

In connection with Toynbee's treatment of Marx, it may be mentioned that his whole approach is strongly influenced by Marxism. He says (*op. cit.*, vol. I, p. 41, note 3): 'More than one of these Marxian coinages have become current even among people who reject the Marxian dogmas.' This statement refers especially to the use of the word 'proletariat'. But it covers more than the mere use of words.

52. Cp. Toynbee, *op. cit.*, vol. III, 476. The passage refers back to vol. I, part I, A, 'The Relativity of Historical Thought'. (The problem of the 'relativity' of historical thought will be discussed in the next chapter.) For an excellent early criticism of historical relativism (and historicism), see H. Sidgwick's *Philosophy—Its Scope and Relations* (1902), Lecture IX, especially pp. 180 f.
53. For if *all* thought is in such a sense 'inevitably relative' to its historical habitat that it is not 'absolutely true' (i.e. not true), then this must hold for this contention as well. Thus it cannot be true, and therefore not an inevitable 'Law of Human Nature'. Cp. also note 8 (2, *a*) to this chapter.
54. For the contention that Toynbee escapes into the past, cp. note 44 to this chapter and note 61 to chapter 11 (on Toynbee's medievalism). Toynbee himself gives an excellent criticism of archaism, and I fully agree with his attack (vol. VI, 65 f.) upon nationalist attempts to revive ancient languages, especially in Palestine. But Toynbee's own attack upon industrialism (cp. note 21 to the present chapter) seems to be no less archaistic.—For an escape into the future, I have no other evidence than Toynbee's announced prophetic title of part XII of his work: *The Prospects of the Western Civilization*.
55. The 'tragic worldly success of the founder of Islam' is mentioned by Toynbee in *op. cit.*, III, p. 472. For Ignatius Loyola, cp. vol. III, 270; 466 f.
56. Cp. *op. cit.*, vol. V, 590.—The passage quoted next is from the same volume, p. 588.
57. Toynbee, *op. cit.*, vol. VI, 13.
58. Cp. Toynbee, vol. VI, 12 f. (The reference is to Bergson's *Two Sources of Morality and Religion*.)

The following historicist quotation from Toynbee (vol. V, 585; italics mine) is interesting in this context: 'Christians believe—and *a study of History assuredly proves them right*—that the brotherhood of Man is *impossible for Man to achieve in any other way* than by enrolling himself as a citizen of a *Civitas Dei* which transcends the human world and has God himself for its king.' How can a study of history prove such a claim? Is it not a highly responsible matter to assert that it can be proved?

Concerning Bergson's *Two Sources*, I fully agree that there is an irrational or intuitive element in every creative thought; but this element can be found in rational scientific thought also. Rational thought is not non-intuitive; it is, rather, intuition *submitted to tests and checks* (as opposed to intuition run wild). Applying this to the problem of the creation of the open society, I admit that men like Socrates were inspired by intuition; but while I grant this fact, I believe that it is their *rationality* by which the founders of the open society are distinguished from those who tried to arrest its development, and who were also, like Plato, inspired by intuition—only by an intuition unchecked by reasonableness (in the sense in which this term has been used in the present chapter). See also the note to the *Introduction*.

59. Cp. note 4 to chapter 18.

NOTES TO CHAPTER TWENTY-FIVE

1 The so-called conventionalists (H. Poincaré, P. Duhem, and more recently, A. Eddington); cp. note 17 to chapter 5.
2. Cp. my *The Logic of Scientific Discovery*.
3. The 'bucket theory of the mind' has been mentioned in chapter 23. (*For the 'searchlight theory of science', see also my 'Towards a Rational Theory of Tradition,' now in my *Conjectures and Refutations*, especially pp. 127 f.*) The 'searchlight theory' contains, perhaps, just those elements of Kantianism that are tenable. We might say that Kant's mistake was to think the searchlight itself incapable of improvement; and that he did not see that some searchlights (theories) may fail to illuminate facts which others bring out clearly. But this is how we give up using certain searchlights, and make progress.
4. Cp. note 23 to chapter 8.
5. For the attempt to avoid all presuppositions, cp. the criticism (of Husserl) in note 8 (1) to chapter 24, and text. The naïve idea that it is possible to avoid presupposition (or a point of view) has also been attacked on different lines by H. Gomperz. (Cp. *Weltanschauungslehre*, I, 1905, pp. 33 and 35; my translation is perhaps a little free.) Gomperz's attack is directed against radical empiricists. (Not against Husserl.) 'A philosophic or scientific attitude towards facts', Gomperz writes, 'is always an attitude of thought, and not merely an attitude of enjoying the facts in the manner of a cow, or of contemplating facts in the manner of a painter, or of being overwhelmed by the facts in the manner of a visionary. We must therefore assume that the philosopher is not satisfied with the facts as they are, but thinks about them ... Thus it seems clear that behind that philosophical radicalism which pretends ... to go back to immediate facts or data, there is always hidden an uncritical reception of traditional doctrines. For some thoughts about the facts must occur even to these radicals; but since they are unconscious of them to such a degree as to hold that they merely admit the facts, we have no choice but to assume that their thoughts are ... uncritical.' (Cp. also the same author's remarks on *Interpretation* in *Erkenntnis*, vol. 7, pp. 225 ff.)
6. Cp. Schopenhauer's comments on history (*Parerga*, etc., vol. II, ch. XIX, § 238; *Works*, second German edition, vol. VI, p. 480).
7. (1) To my knowledge, the theory of causality sketched here in the text was first presented in my book, *Logik der Forschung* (1935)—now translated as *The Logic of Scientific Discovery* (1959). See pp. 59 f. of the translation. As here translated, the original brackets have been eliminated, and numbers in brackets as well as four brief passages in brackets have been added, partly in order to make a somewhat compressed passage more intelligible, and partly (in the case of the two last brackets) to make allowance for a point of view I had not clearly seen in 1935, the point of view of what A. Tarski has called 'semantics'. (See, e.g., his *Grundlegung der wissenschaftlichen Semantik*, in *Actes du Congrès International Philosophique*, vol. III, Paris, 1937, pp. 1 ff., and R. Carnap, *Introduction to Semantics*, 1942.) Owing to Tarski's development of the foundations of semantics, I no longer hesitate (as I did when writing the book referred to) to make full use of the terms 'cause' and 'effect'. For these can be defined, using Tarski's concept of truth, by a semantic definition such as the following: Event *A* is the cause of event *B*, and event *B* the effect of event

A, if and only if there exists a language in which we can formulate three propositions, *u*, *a*, and *b*, such that *u* is a true universal law, *a* describes *A*, and *b* describes *B*, and *b* is a logical consequence of *u* and *a*. (Here the term 'event' or 'fact' may be defined by a semantic version of my definition of 'event' in my *The Logic of Scientific Discovery*, pp. 88 ff., say, by the following definition: An event *E* is the common designatum of a class of mutually translatable singular statements.)

(2) A few historical remarks concerning the *problem of cause and effect* may be added here. The Aristotelian concept of cause (viz., his formal and material cause, and his efficient cause; the final cause does not interest us here, even though my remark holds good for it too) is typically essentialistic; the problem is to explain change or motion, and it is explained by reference to the hidden structure of things. This essentialism is still to be found in Bacon's, Descartes', Locke's, and even Newton's views on this matter; but Descartes' theory opens the way to a new view. He saw the essence of all physical bodies in their spatial extension or geometrical shape, and concluded from this that the only way in which bodies can act upon one another is by pushing; one moving body *necessarily* pushes another from its place because both are extended, and therefore cannot fill the same space. Thus *the effect follows the cause by necessity, and all truly causal explanation* (*of physical events*) *must be in terms of push*. This view was still assumed by Newton, who accordingly said about his own theory of gravitation—which, of course, employs the idea of pull rather than push—that nobody who knows anything of philosophy could possibly consider it a satisfactory explanation; and it still remains influential in physics in the form of a dislike of any kind of 'action at a distance'.—Berkeley was the first to criticize the explanation by hidden essences, whether these are introduced to 'explain' Newton's attraction, or whether they lead to a Cartesian theory of push; he demanded that science should *describe*, rather than *explain* by essential or necessary connections. This doctrine, which became one of the main characteristics of positivism, loses its point if our theory of causal explanation is adopted; for explanation becomes then a kind of description; it is a description which makes use of universal hypotheses, initial conditions, and logical deduction. To Hume (who was partly anticipated by Sextus Empiricus, Al-Gazzâli, and others) is due what may be called the most important contribution to the theory of causation; he pointed out (as against the Cartesian view) that we cannot know anything about a necessary connection between an event *A* and another event *B*. All we can possibly know is that events of the kind *A* (or events similar to *A*) have so far been followed by events of the kind *B* (or events similar to *B*). We can know that, in point of fact, such events were connected; but since we do not know that this connection is a necessary one, we can say only that it has held good in the past. Our theory fully recognizes this Humean criticism. But it differs from Hume (1) in that it explicitly formulates the *universal hypothesis* that events of the kind *A* are always and everywhere followed by events of the kind *B*; (2) that it asserts the truth of the statement that *A* is the cause of *B*, provided that the universal hypothesis is true.—Hume, in other words, only looked at the events *A* and *B* themselves; and he could not find any trace of a causal link or a necessary connection between these two. But we add a third thing, a universal law; and with respect to this law, we may speak of a causal link, or even of a necessary connection. We could, for example, define: Event *B* is *causally linked* (or *necessarily connected*) with event *A* if and only if *A* is the cause of

B (in the sense of our semantic definition given above).—Concerning the question of the truth of a universal law, we may say that there are countless universal laws whose truth we never question in daily life; and accordingly, there are also countless cases of causation where in daily life we never question the 'necessary causal link'. From the point of scientific method, the position is different. For we can never rationally establish the truth of scientific laws; all we can do is to test them severely, and to eliminate the false ones (this is perhaps the crux of my *The Logic of Scientific Discovery*). Accordingly, all scientific laws retain for ever a hypothetical character; they are assumptions. And consequently, all statements about specific causal connections retain the same hypothetical character. We can never be certain (in a scientific sense) that *A* is the cause of *B*, precisely because we can never be certain whether the universal hypothesis in question is true, however well it may be tested. Yet, we shall be inclined to find the specific hypothesis that *A* is the cause of *B* the more acceptable the better we have tested and confirmed the corresponding universal hypothesis. (For my theory of *confirmation*, see chapter X and also appendix *ix of *The Logic of Scientific Discovery*, especially p. 275, where the temporal coefficients or indices of confirmation sentences are discussed.)

(3) Concerning my theory of historical explanation, developed here in the text (further below), I wish to add some critical comments to an article by Morton G. White, entitled 'Historical Explanation' and published in *Mind* (vol. 52, 1943, pp. 212 ff.). The author accepts my analysis of causal explanation, as originally developed in my *Logik der Forschung* (now translated as *The Logic of Scientific Discovery*). (He mistakenly attributes this theory to an article by C. G. Hempel, published in the *Journal of Philosophy*, 1942; see, however, Hempel's review of my book in *Deutsche Literaturzeitung*, 1937, (8), pp. 310 to 314.) Having found what in general we call an explanation, White proceeds to ask what is *historical* explanation. In order to answer this question, he points out that the characteristic of a biological explanation (as opposed, say, to a physical one) is the occurrence of *specifically biological terms* in the explanatory universal laws; and he concludes that an historical explanation would be one in which *specifically historical terms* would so occur. He further finds that all laws in which anything like specific historical terms occur are better characterized as sociological, since the terms in questions are of a sociological character rather than of an historical one; and he is thus ultimately forced to identify 'historical explanation' with 'sociological explanation'.

It seems to me obvious that this view neglects what has been described here in the text as the *distinction between historical and generalizing sciences*, and their specific problems and methods; and I may say that discussions on the problem of the method of history have long ago brought out the fact that history is interested in specific events rather than in general laws. I have in mind, for example, Lord Acton's essays against Buckle, written in 1858 (to be found in his *Historical Essays and Studies*, 1908), and the debate between Max Weber and E. Meyer (see Weber's *Gesammelte Aufsaetze zur Wissenschaftslehre*, 1922, pp. 215 ff.). Like Meyer, Weber always rightly emphasized that history is interested in *singular events*, not in universal laws, and that, *at the same time*, it is interested in *causal explanation*. Unfortunately, however, these correct views led him to turn repeatedly (e.g. *op. cit.*, p. 8) against the view that causality is bound up with universal laws. It appears to me that our theory of historical explanation, as developed in the text, removes the difficulty and at the same time explains how it could arise.

8. The doctrine that crucial experiments may be made in physics has been attacked by the conventionalists, especially by Duhem (cp. note 1 to this chapter). But Duhem wrote before Einstein, and before Eddington's crucial eclipse observation; he even wrote before the experiments of Lummer and Pringsheim which, by falsifying the formulæ of Rayleigh and Jeans, led to the Quantum theory.

9. The dependence of history upon our interest has been admitted both by E. Meyer and by his critic M. Weber. Meyer writes (*Zur Theorie und Methodik der Geschichte*, 1902, p. 37): 'The selection of facts depends upon the historical interest taken by those living at the present time ...' Weber writes (*Ges. Aufsaetze*, 1922, p. 259): 'Our ... interest ... will determine the range of cultural values which determines ... history.' Weber, following Rickert, repeatedly insists that our interest, in turn, depends upon ideas of value; in this he is certainly not wrong, but he does not add anything to the methodological analysis. None of these authors, however, draw the revolutionary consequence that, since all history depends upon our interest, *there can be only histories, and never a 'history'*, a story of the development of mankind 'as it happened'.

For two interpretations of history which are opposed to one another, cp. note 61 to chapter 11.

10. For this refusal to discuss the problem of the 'meaning of meaning' (Ogden and Richards) or rather of the 'meanings of meaning' (H. Gomperz), cp. chapter 11, especially notes 26, 47, 50, and 51. See also note 25 to the present chapter.

11. For moral futurism, cp. chapter 22.

12. Cp. K. Barth, *Credo* (1936), p. 12. For Barth's remark against 'the Neo-Protestant doctrine of the revelation of God in history', cp. *op. cit.*, 142. See also the Hegelian source of this doctrine, quoted in text to note 49, chapter 12. Cp. also note 51 to chapter 24. For the next quotation cp. Barth, *op. cit.*, 79.

* Concerning my remark that the story of Christ was *not* 'the story of an unsuccessful ... nationalist revolution', I am now inclined to believe that it may have been precisely this; see R. Eisler's book *Jesus Basileus*. But in any case, it is not a story of worldly success.*

13. Cp. Barth, *op. cit.*, 76.

14. Cp. Kierkegaard's Journal of 1854; see the German edition (1905) of his *Book of the Judge*, p. 135.

15. Cp. note 57 to chapter 11, and text.

16. Cp. the concluding sentences of Macmurray's *The Clue to History* (1938; p. 237).

17. Cp. especially note 55 to chapter 24, and text.

18. Kierkegaard was educated at the University of Copenhagen in a period of intense and even somewhat aggressive Hegelianism. The theologian Martensen was especially influential. (For this aggressive attitude, cp. the judgement of the Copenhagen Academy against Schopenhauer's prize essay on the *Foundations of Morals*, of 1840. It is very likely that this affair was instrumental in making Kierkegaard acquainted with Schopenhauer, at a time when the latter was still unknown in Germany.)

19. Cp. Kierkegaard's Journal of 1853; see the German edition of his *Book of the Judge*, p. 129, from which the passage in the text is freely translated.

Kierkegaard is not the only Christian thinker protesting against Hegel's historicism; we have seen (cp. note 12 to this chapter) that Barth also protests against it.

A remarkably interesting criticism of Hegel's teleological interpretation of history was given by the Christian philosopher, M. B. Foster, a great admirer (if not a follower) of Hegel, at the end of his book *The Political Philosophies of Plato and Hegel*. The main point of his criticism, if I understand him rightly, is this. By interpreting history teleologically, Hegel does not see, in its various stages, ends in themselves, but merely means for bringing about the final end. But Hegel is wrong in assuming that historical phenomena or periods are means to an end which can be conceived and stated as something distinguishable from the phenomena themselves, in a way in which a purpose can be distinguished from the action which seeks to realize it, or a moral from a play (if we wrongly assume that the sole purpose of the play was to convey this moral). For this assumption, Foster contends, shows a failure to recognize the difference between the work of a *creator* and that of an instrument maker, a technician or '*Demiurge*'. '... a series of works of creation may be understood as a development', Foster writes (*op. cit.*, pp. 201–3), '... without a distinct conception of the end to which they progress ... the painting, say, of one era may be understood to have developed out of the era preceding it, without being understood as a nearer approximation to a perfection or end ... Political history, similarly, ... may be understood as development, without being interpreted as a teleological process.—But Hegel, here and elsewhere, lacks insight in the significance of creation.' And later, Foster writes (*op. cit.*, p. 204; italics partly mine): 'Hegel regards it as a sign of inadequacy of the religious imagery that those who hold it, while they assert that there is a plan of Providence, deny that the plan is knowable ... To say that the plan of Providence is inscrutable is, no doubt, an inadequate expression, but the truth which it expresses inadequately is not that God's plan is knowable, but that, as Creator and not as a Demiurge, *God does not work according to plan at all*.'

I think that this criticism is excellent, even though the creation of a work of art may, in a very different sense, proceed according to a '*plan*' (although not an end or purpose); for it may be an attempt to realize something like the Platonic idea of that work—that perfect model before his mental eyes or ears which the painter or musician strives to copy. (Cp. note 9 to chapter 9 and notes 25–26 to chapter 8.)

20. For Schopenhauer's attacks upon Hegel, to which Kierkegaard refers, cp. chapter 12, for example, text to note 13, and the concluding sentences. The partly quoted continuation of Kierkegaard's passage is *op. cit.*, 130. (In a note, Kierkegaard later inserted 'pantheist' before 'putridity'.)
21. Cp. chapter 6, especially text to note 26.
22. For the Hegelian ethics of domination and submission, cp. note 25 to chapter 11. For the ethics of hero-worship, cp. chapter 12, especially text to notes 75 ff.
23. Cp. chapter 5 (especially text to note 5).
24. We can 'express ourselves' in many ways without communicating anything. For our task of using language for the purpose of rational communication, and for the need of keeping up the standards of clarity of the language, cp. notes 19 and 20 to chapter 24 and note 30 to chapter 12.
25. This view of the problem of the 'meaning of life' may be contrasted with Wittgenstein's view of the problems of the 'sense of life' in the *Tractatus* (p. 187): 'The solution of the problem of life is seen in the vanishing of this problem.—(Is not this the reason why men to whom after long doubting the sense of life became clear,

could not then say wherein this sense consisted?)' For Wittgenstein's mysticism, see also note 32 to chapter 24. For the interpretation of history here suggested, cp. notes 61 (1) to chapter 11, and 27 to the present chapter.

26. Cp., for example, note 5 to chapter 5 and note 19 to chapter 24.

It may be remarked that the world of facts is in itself complete (since every decision can be interpreted as a fact). It is therefore for ever impossible to *refute* a monism which insists that there are only facts. But irrefutability is not a virtue. Idealism, for example, cannot be refuted either.

27. It appears that one of the motives of historicism is that the historicist does not see that there is a third alternative, besides the two which he allows: either that the world is ruled by superior *powers*, by an 'essential destiny' or Hegelian 'Reason', or that it is a mere wheel of chance, irrational, on the level of a gamble. *But there is a third possibility*: that *we* may introduce reason into it (cp. note 19 to chapter 24); that although the world does not progress, *we* may progress, individually as well as in co-operation.

This third possibility is clearly expressed by H. A. L. Fisher in his *History of Europe* (vol. I, p. vii, italics mine; partly quoted in text to note 8 to chapter 21): 'One intellectual excitement has ... been denied me. Men wiser and more learned than I have discerned in history a plot, a rhythm, a pre-determined pattern. These harmonies are concealed from me. I can see only one emergency following upon another as wave follows wave, only one great fact with respect to which, *since it is unique, there can be no generalizations*, only one safe rule for the historian: that he should recognize ... the play of the contingent and the unforeseen.' And immediately after this excellent attack upon historicism (with the passage in italics, cp. note 13 to chapter 13), Fisher continues: 'This is not a doctrine of cynicism and despair. *The fact of progress is written plain and large on the page of history; but progress is not a law of nature*. The ground gained by one generation may be lost by the next.'

These last three sentences represent very clearly what I have called the 'third possibility', the belief in our responsibility, the belief that everything rests with us. And it is interesting to see that Fisher's statement is interpreted by Toynbee (*A Study of History*, vol. V, 414) as representing 'the modern Western belief in the omnipotence of Chance'. Nothing could show more clearly the attitude of the historicist, his inability to see the third possibility. And it explains perhaps why he tries to escape from this alleged 'omnipotence of chance' into a belief in the omnipotence of the *power* behind the historical scene—that is, into historicism. (Cp. also note 61 to chapter 11.)

I may perhaps quote more fully Toynbee's comments on Fisher's passage (which Toynbee quotes down to the words 'the unforeseen'): 'This brilliantly phrased passage', Toynbee writes, 'cannot be dismissed as a scholar's conceit; for the writer is a Liberal who is formulating a creed which Liberalism has translated from theory into action ... This modern Western belief in the omnipotence of Chance gave birth in the nineteenth century of the Christian Era, when things still seemed to be going well with Western Man, to the policy of *laissez-faire* ...' (Why the belief in a progress for which we ourselves are responsible should imply a belief in the omnipotence of Chance, or why it should produce the policy of *laissez-faire*, Toynbee leaves unexplained.)

28. By the 'realism' of the choice of our ends I mean that we should choose ends which can be realized within a reasonable span of time, and that we should avoid distant

and vague Utopian ideals, unless they determine more immediate aims which are worthy in themselves. Cp. especially the principles of piecemeal social engineering, discussed in chapter 9.

The final manuscript of volume I of the first edition of this book was completed in October, 1942, and that of volume II in February, 1943.

Index